Upgrade and Repair with Jean Andrews

Jean Andrews, Ph.D.

Premier
Press

Premier Press

Upgrade and Repair with Jean Andrews is published by Premier Press, a division of Course Technology.

Senior Product Manager:
Laura Hildebrand

Senior Editor:
William Pitkin III

Senior Marketing Manager:
Jason Sakos

Associate Product Managers:
Tim Gleeson and Nick Lombardi

Editorial Assistant:
Christy Urban

Copyeditor:
Chris Smith

Senior Manufacturing Coordinator:
Laura Burns

Production Editor:
Megan Belanger

Quality Assurance:
Nicole Ashton

Cover Design:
Mike Tamanachi

Compositor:
GEX Publishing Services

BRIEF CONTENTS

TABLE OF CONTENTS

CHAPTER SEVENTEEN
Installing and Using Windows 9x   697

ACKNOWLEDGMENTS

Thank you to the wonderful people at Course Technology who continue to provide support, warm encouragements, patience, and guidance. Laura Hildebrand, Kristen Duerr, Philippa Lehar, and Nick Lombardi of CT. Thank you, Nicole Ashton and John Bosco for your careful attention to the technical accuracy of the book.

Thank you to all the people who took the time to voluntarily send encouragements and suggestions for improvements to the previous edition. Your input and help is very much appreciated. The reviewers all provided invaluable insights and showed a genuine interest in the book's success. Thank you to Thomas Bruckman (Manhattan Energy Services), Allan Brussolo (The Cittone Institute), Russell Davis (Pittsburgh Technical Institute), Berry Smith (Virginia College at Huntsville), Allan Souder (Seneca College, Ontario), and Henry Yoder (Pittsburgh Technical Institute). Thank you to Tony Woodall of Omega Computers for your outstanding research efforts.

This book is dedicated to the covenant of God with man on earth. Part of the proceeds from this book goes to Joy Land, a home for children in Hyderabad, A.P., India.

Jean Andrews, Ph.D.

PHOTO CREDITS

Figure	Credit
3-17 NLX Slimline case	Courtesy of Enlight Corporation USA.
4-10 Golden Orb cooling fan	Courtesy of Thermaltake USA Inc.
7-2 Maxtor 1394 external hard drive	Courtesy of Maxtor Corporation. © 2002 Maxtor Corporation. All Rights Reserved.
9-5 iRock MP3 player	Courtesy of First International Digital Inc.
12-10 IBM Thinkpad dock	Courtesy of IBM Corporation. Unauthorized use not permitted.
12-19 Brother HL-1870N laser printer	Courtesy of Brother International Corporation.
12-24 Epson SC82 inkjet printer	Courtesy of Epson America Inc.

Figures 1-5, 1-9, 1-11, 1-15, 1-16, 1-29, 1-36, 2-16, and 17-25 courtesy of Jennifer Dark.

1

Hardware

The first part of this book was written to be the very best tool on the market today to prepare you to support personal computer hardware. It takes you from the just-a-user level to the I-can-fix-this level for the most common PC hardware concerns. This book achieves its goals with an unusually effective combination of tools that powerfully reinforce both concepts and hands-on, real-world experience.

Part 1 includes:

- ♦ Comprehensive end-of-chapter material, including a chapter summary and key terms.
- ♦ Step-by-step instructions on installation, maintenance, optimizing system performance, and troubleshooting.
- ♦ A wide array of photos and screen shots support the text, displaying in detail the exact hardware features you will need to understand, purchase, install and maintain your hardware.

In addition, the carefully structured, clearly written text is accompanied by graphics that provide the visual input essential to learning. Coverage is balanced—while focusing on new hardware, it also covers the real work of PC repair, where some older technology remains in widespread use and still needs support. For example, the book covers the latest ATX motherboard form factor, but also addresses the capabilities and maintenance of the AT motherboard form factor because many are still in use.

To ensure a successful learning experience, this book includes the following pedagogical features:

◆ Learning Objectives: Every chapter opens with a list of learning objectives that sets the stage for you to absorb the lessons of the text.

◆ Comprehensive Step-by-Step Troubleshooting Guidance: Troubleshooting guidelines are included in almost every chapter.

◆ Step-by-Step Procedures: The book is chock-full of step-by-step procedures, covering subjects from understanding how the latest technologies work to hardware installation and maintenance.

◆ Art Program: Numerous detailed photographs, three-dimensional art, and screenshots support the text, displaying hardware devices exactly as you will see them in your work.

 Tip icons include pointers from the author's experiences that provide additional insight for the topic at hand.

Caution icons highlight critical safety information. Follow these instructions carefully to protect yourself, the PC, and its data

 Note icons highlight additional information about the subject being discussed.

◆ Chapter Summary: This bulleted list of concise statements summarizes all major points of the chapter.

◆ Key Terms: The content of each chapter is further reinforced by an end-of-chapter key-term list. The definitions of all terms are included at the end of the book in a full-length glossary.

1

HOW COMPUTERS WORK

In this chapter, you will learn:

♦ That a computer requires both hardware and software to work

♦ About the many different hardware components inside and connected to a computer

♦ About the instructions and data stored on the motherboard

♦ How a CPU works and how it communicates with other devices

♦ About the binary number system

Like millions of other computer users, you have probably used your micro-computer to play games, explore the Internet, write papers, build spread-sheets, or create a professional-looking proposal or flyer. You can use all these applications without understanding exactly what goes on within your computer case or monitor. But if you are curious to learn more about computers, and if you want to graduate from simply being the end user of your computer to becoming the master of your machine, then this book is for you. The only assumption made here is that you are a computer user—that is, you can turn on your machine, load a software package, and use that software to accomplish a task. No experience in electronics is assumed.

This chapter introduces you to the inside of your computer, a world of electronic and mechanical devices that has evolved over just a few years to become one of the most powerful technical tools of our society.

HARDWARE NEEDS SOFTWARE TO WORK

In the world of computers, the term **hardware** refers to the physical components of the computer, such as the monitor, keyboard, memory chips, and hard drive. The term **software**, on the other hand, refers to the set of instructions that directs the hardware to accomplish a task. In Figure 1-1, a passenger directs a chauffeur who directs a car, just as a computer user directs software, which, in turn, controls hardware to perform a given task.

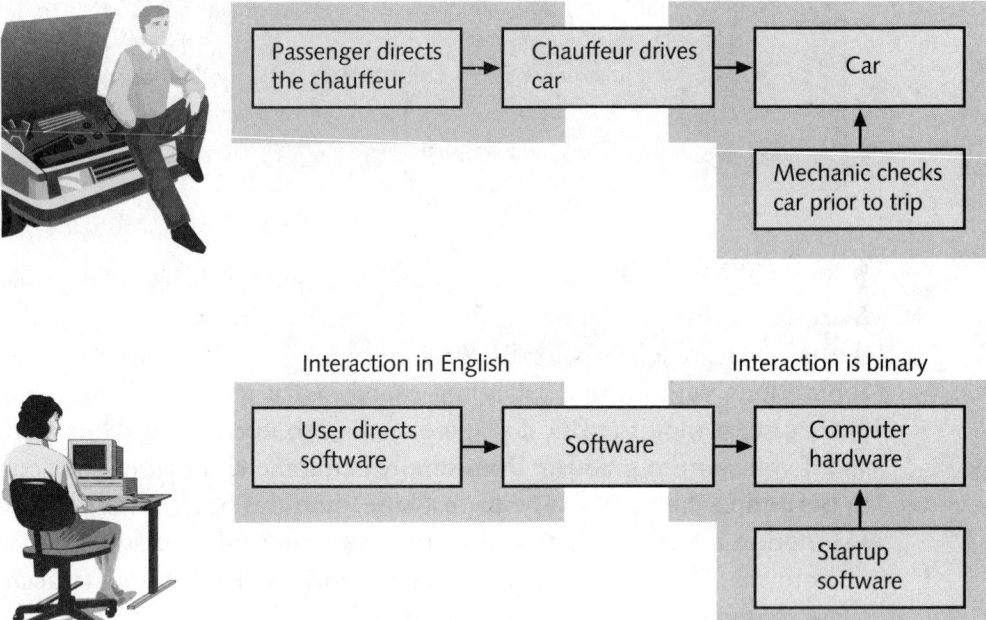

Figure 1-1   A user interacts with a computer much as a passenger interacts with a chauffeured car

In order to perform a computing task, hardware is used by software for four basic functions (see Figure 1-2):

- Input
- Processing
- Output
- Storage

Also, hardware components must communicate both data and instructions among themselves, which requires an electrical system to provide power, because these components are electrical.

Figure 1-2   Computer activity consists of input, processing, storage, and output

Looking again at Figure 1-1, note that the interaction between the passenger and the chauffeur is in English, but that the chauffeur must translate these directions, such as "Go to the airport," into mechanical directions that the car can "understand," such as pressing the gas pedal, braking when necessary, and turning the wheel to control the car until it reaches the airport. In the same fashion, a computer user interacts with a computer in a language that the user and the software understand, but software must convert that instruction into a form that hardware can "understand." As incredible as it might sound, every communication between hardware and software, or between software and other software, is reduced to a simple yes or no, which inside the computer is represented by two simple states: on and off (see Figure 1-3).

Figure 1-3   All communication, storage, and processing of data inside a computer are in binary until presented as output to the user

This technology of storing and reading only two states is called *binary*, and the number system that only uses two digits, 0 and 1, is called the **binary number system**. A 1 or 0 in this system is called a **bit**, or binary digit. Because of the way the number system is organized, grouping is often done in groups of 8 bits, each of which is called a **byte**. (Guess what four bits are called? A nibble!) In a computer, all counting and calculations use the binary number system. Counting in binary goes like this: 0, 1, 10, 11, 100, 101, and so forth. All letters and characters are converted to a binary code before being stored in a computer. For example, the uppercase letter A in binary code is 0100 0001, and the number 25 is 0001 1001 (see Figure 1-4).

The letter A stored as 8 bits:

"A" =   0 1 0 0 0 0 0 1   =

The number 25 stored as 8 bits:

25 =   0 0 0 1 1 0 0 1   =

Figure 1-4   All letters and numbers are stored in a computer as a series of bits, each represented in the computer as on or off

You'll learn more about the binary number system later in this chapter.

PC HARDWARE COMPONENTS

In this section, we cover the major hardware components of a microcomputer system used for input, output, processing, storage, electrical supply, and communication.

Most input and output devices are outside the computer case. Most processing and storage components are contained inside the case, as is the case with the **central processing unit (CPU)**, also called the **microprocessor** or **processor**. The CPU is the most important chip in the computer. As its name implies, this device is central to all processing done by the computer. Data received by input devices is read by the CPU, and output from the CPU is written to output devices. The CPU writes data and instructions in storage devices and performs calculations and other data processing. Whether inside or outside the case, and regardless of the function the device performs, each hardware device requires these elements to operate:

- *A method for the CPU to communicate with the device.* The device must send data to and/or receive data from the CPU. The CPU might need to control the device by passing instructions to it, and/or the device might need to request service from the CPU.

- *Software to instruct and control the device.* A device is useless without software to control it. The software must know how to communicate with the device at the detailed level of that specific device, and the CPU must have access to this software in order to interact with the device. Each device responds to a specific set of instructions based on the device's functions. The software must have an instruction for each possible action you expect the device to accomplish. The specific functions depend on the purpose of the individual device, but every function must have an accompanying instruction in order to control the device.

- *Electricity to power the device.* Electronic devices require electricity to operate. Devices can receive power from the power supply inside the computer case, or they can have their own power supply by way of a power cable to an electrical outlet.

Hardware Used for Input and Output

Most input/output devices reside outside the computer case. These devices communicate with components inside the computer case through a wireless connection or through cables attached to the case at a connection called a **port**, sending data and/or instructions to the computer and receiving them from the computer. Most computer ports are located on the back of the case (Figure 1-5), but some models have ports on the front of the case for easy access. For wireless connections, a wireless device communicates with the system using a radio wave or infrared port. The most popular input devices are a keyboard and a mouse, and the most popular output devices are a monitor and a printer.

On/off switch

Power in

Mouse port

Keyboard port

USB ports

Parallel port

Serial ports

Video port (for monitor)

Network port

Microphone port

Phone line connection
for modem

Speaker port

Figure 1-5   Input/output devices connect to the computer case by ports, usually found on
the back of the case

The **keyboard** is the primary input device of a computer (see Figure 1-6). The keyboards
that are standard today are called enhanced keyboards and hold 102 keys. Ergonomic keyboards are curved to make them more comfortable for the hands and wrists. In addition,
some keyboards come equipped with a mouse port—a plug by means of which a mouse
(another input device) can be attached to the keyboard—although it is more common for
the mouse port to be located directly on the computer case. Electricity to run the keyboard comes from inside the computer case and is provided by wires in the keyboard cable.

A **mouse** is a pointing device used to move a pointer on the screen and to make selections. The bottom of a mouse houses a rotating ball or an optical sensor that tracks movement and controls the location of the pointer. The one, two, or three buttons on the top
of the mouse serve different purposes for different software. For example, Windows 2000
uses the left mouse button to execute a command and the right mouse button to display
information about the command.

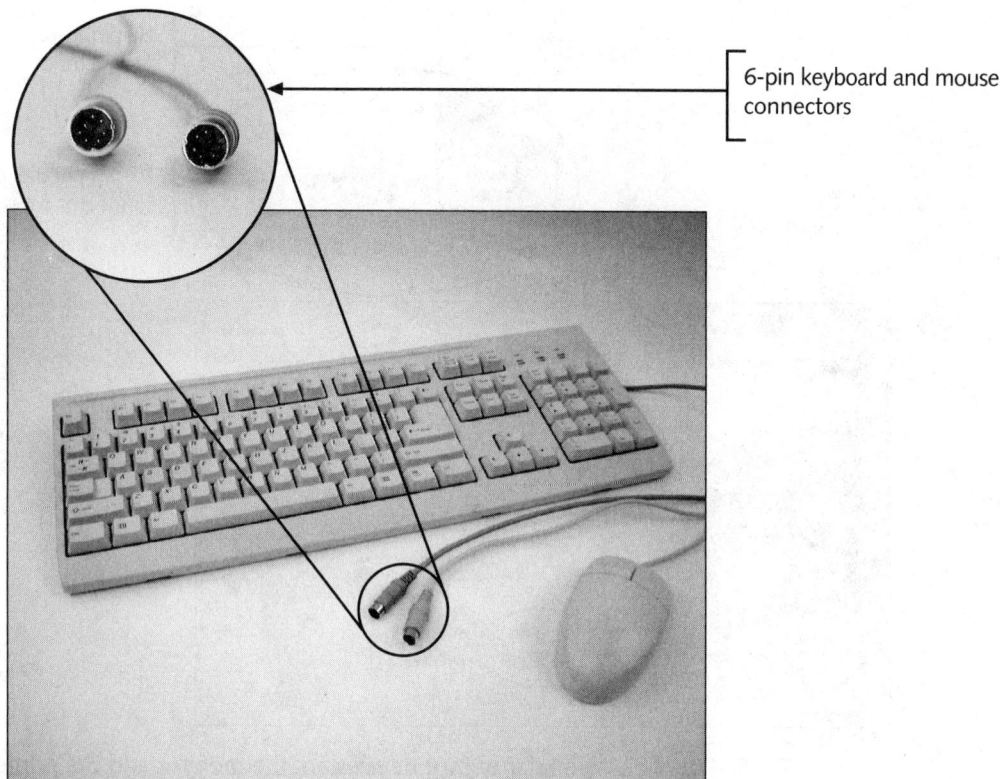

6-pin keyboard and mouse connectors

Figure 1-6   The keyboard and the mouse are the two most popular input devices

The monitor and the printer are the two most popular output devices (see Figure 1-7). The **monitor** is the visual device that displays the primary output of the computer. Hardware manufacturers typically rate a monitor according to the size of its screen (in inches) and by the monitor's resolution, which is the number of dots on the screen used for display.

The **printer** produces output on paper, often called **hard copy**. The most popular printers available today are ink-jet, laser, and dot matrix printers. The monitor and the printer need separate power supplies. Their electrical power cords connect to electrical outlets. Sometimes the computer case provides an electrical outlet for the monitor's power cord, to eliminate the need for one more power outlet.

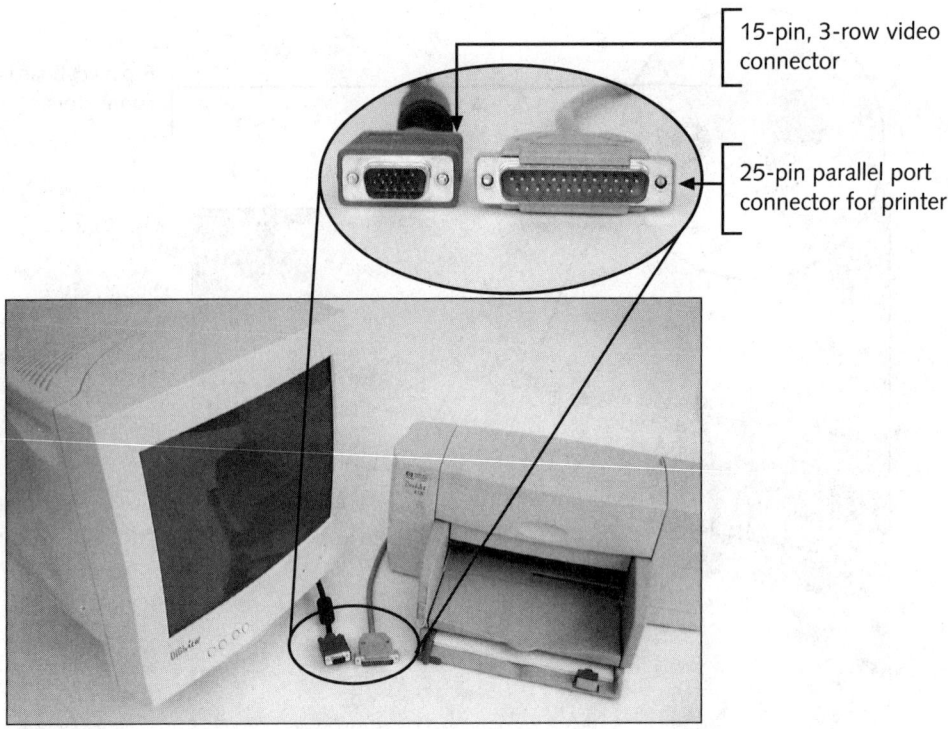

15-pin, 3-row video connector

25-pin parallel port connector for printer

Figure 1-7   The two most popular output devices are the monitor and the printer

Hardware Inside the Computer Case

Most storage and all processing of data and instructions are done inside the computer case, so before we look at components used for storage and processing, let's look at what you see when you first open the computer case. Most computers contain these devices inside the case (see Figure 1-8):

- A motherboard containing the CPU, memory, and other components

- A floppy drive, hard drive, and CD-ROM drive used for permanent storage

- A power supply with power cords supplying electricity to all devices inside the case

- Circuit boards used by the CPU to communicate with devices inside and outside the case

- Cables connecting devices to circuit boards and the motherboard

Pentium II CPU
Power supply
Power cords
CD-ROM drive
Floppy drive is hidden in this bay
Zip drive
Hard drive
Front of case
Data cable
Motherboard
Circuit boards (expansion cards)
Rear of case

Figure 1-8   Inside the computer case

Among the things you first notice when you look inside a computer case are boards that contain electronic components. A **circuit board** is a board that holds microchips, or integrated circuits (ICs), and the circuitry that connects these chips. All circuit boards contain microchips, which are most often manufactured using **CMOS (complementary metal-oxide semiconductor)** technology. CMOS chips require less electricity and produce less heat than do chips manufactured using earlier technologies such as TTL (transistor-transistor logic).

The other major components look like small boxes, including the power supply, hard drive, CD-ROM drive, and floppy drive. Devices that the CPU communicates with that are not located directly on the motherboard are called **peripheral devices**; these are linked to the CPU through a connection to the motherboard. Some peripheral devices are linked to the motherboard by a circuit board designed for that purpose. These circuit boards, called **expansion cards**, are installed in long, narrow slots on the motherboard called **expansion slots**.

There are two types of cables inside the case: data cables, which connect devices to one another, and power cables or power cords, which supply power. Most often, you can distinguish between the two by the shape of the cable. Data cables are flat and wide, and power cords are round and small. There are some exceptions to this rule, so the best way to identify a cable is to trace its source and destination.

The Motherboard

The largest and most important circuit board in the computer is the **motherboard**, also called the **main board** or **system board** (see Figure 1-9), which contains the CPU, the component where most processing takes place. Because all devices must communicate with the CPU on the motherboard, all devices in a computer are either installed directly on the motherboard, linked to it by a cable connected to a port on the motherboard, or indirectly linked to it by expansion cards. Some ports on the motherboard stick outside the case to accommodate external devices such as a keyboard, and some ports provide a connection for a device inside the case, such as a floppy disk drive.

Pentium II motherboard

- BIOS
- Power supply connection
- Pentium CPU
- AGP slot for video card
- Chip set
- Slots for RAM
- Battery
- PCI slots for high speed I/O devices
- ISA slots for slower devices

Figure 1-9   All hardware components are either located on the motherboard or directly or indirectly connected to it, because they must all communicate with the CPU

Figure 1-10 shows the ports provided to the outside of the case by this motherboard: a keyboard port, a mouse port, two serial ports, two USB ports, and a parallel port. A **serial port** is so called because data is transferred serially (one bit follows the next); it is often used for an external modem or serial mouse (a mouse that uses a serial port). A **parallel port** transmits data in parallel and is most often used by a printer. A **USB (universal serial bus) port** is a newer port used by many different input/output devices such as keyboards, printers, scanners, and mice.

Figure 1-10   A motherboard provides ports for common I/O devices

Listed below are the major components found on all motherboards, some of which are labeled in Figure 1-9 and are discussed in detail in the sections that follow.

Components used primarily for processing:

- Central processing unit (CPU), the computer's most important chip
- Chip set that supports the CPU by controlling many motherboard activities

Components used for temporary storage:

- Random access memory (RAM) used to hold data and instructions as they are processed
- Cache memory to speed up memory access (optional, depending on the type of CPU)

Components that allow the CPU to communicate with other devices:

- Traces, or wires on the motherboard used for communication
- Expansion slots to connect expansion cards to the motherboard
- The system clock that keeps communication in sync

Electrical system:

- Power supply connections to provide electricity to the motherboard and expansion cards

Programming and setup data stored on the motherboard:

- Flash ROM, a memory chip used to permanently store instructions that control basic hardware functions (explained in more detail later in the chapter)
- CMOS setup chip that holds configuration data

The CPU and the Chip Set

The CPU, or microprocessor, is the chip inside the computer that performs most of the actual data processing. The CPU, which is installed in a slot or socket on the motherboard, is central to all processing done by a computer. Every command from the computer's operating system (OS) is passed to the CPU, which controls all the hardware components in the computer.

All CPUs today operate in one of two modes: 16-bit or 32-bit, which are sometimes called **real mode** and **protected mode**. There are several differences between these two modes, but fundamentally, 16-bit mode or real mode means that the CPU processes 16 bits of data at one time, and in 32-bit mode or protected mode, it processes 32 bits at a time.

Indeed, the speed of a CPU is partly determined by how much data it can process at one time and how much data it can send or receive at one time. Every CPU has lines coming to it that are embedded on the motherboard collectively called a **bus** (see Figure 1-11). These lines are devoted to different purposes. Some lines on the bus are designated to carry data, and as such are called the **data bus** or **data path**. Early CPUs used a 16-bit data path and processed 16 bits at one time. Today's CPUs, however, can use one size for the data path but another for internal processing. For example, the Pentium III CPU uses a 64-bit data path coming to and from the CPU, but internally it processes 32 bits at a time. Other lines on a bus are used for addresses, control signals, and voltage.

Bus lines

Bottom of the CPU socket

Figure 1-11   On the bottom of the motherboard, you can see bus lines ending at the CPU socket

Note An operating system must be using the same mode the CPU is using. All CPUs for today's PCs, when they are first turned on, begin processing in real mode and must be instructed to change over to protected mode. Only DOS stays in real mode; the other OSes quickly switch to protected mode, which is much faster than real mode.

The CPU could not do its job, without the assistance of the **chip set**, a group of microchips on the motherboard that control the flow of data and instructions to and from the CPU, providing careful timing of activities (see Figure 1-12). While this book will touch on different types of machines, it focuses on the most common personal computers (PCs), referred to as IBM-compatible. These are built around microprocessors and chip sets manufactured by Intel Corporation, AMD, VIA, SiS, Cyrix, and other manufacturers. The Macintosh family of computers, manufactured by Apple Computer, Inc., is built around a family of microprocessors manufactured by Motorola Corporation.

Figure 1-12 This motherboard uses two chips in its chip set (notice the bus lines coming from each chip)

Storage Devices

In Figure 1-2, you saw two kinds of storage: temporary and permanent. The CPU uses temporary storage, called **primary storage** or **memory**, to temporarily hold both data and instructions while it is processing them. Primary storage is much faster to access than permanent storage. However, when they are not being used, the data and instructions must be kept in permanent storage, sometimes called **secondary storage**, such as a floppy disk, CD, or hard drive.

To help you understand the concept of primary and secondary storage, imagine that you must do some research at the library. You go to the stacks and pull out several books, carry them over to a study table, and sit down with your notepad and pencil to take notes and do some calculations. When you're finished, you leave with your notepad full of information and calculations, but you don't take the books with you. In this example, the stacks are permanent storage, and the books (data and instructions) are permanently kept there. The table is temporary storage, a place for you to keep data and instructions as you work with them. The notepad is your output from all that work, and you are the CPU, doing the work of reading the books and writing down information. (See Figure 1-13.) Reading a book that is lying on the table is much faster than running back and forth to the stacks every time you want to refer to it, which is what the CPU would have to do if it were not for primary storage, or memory. Also, you can see that the table (memory) gives fast access and is temporary, while the stacks (secondary storage) give slow access but are permanent.

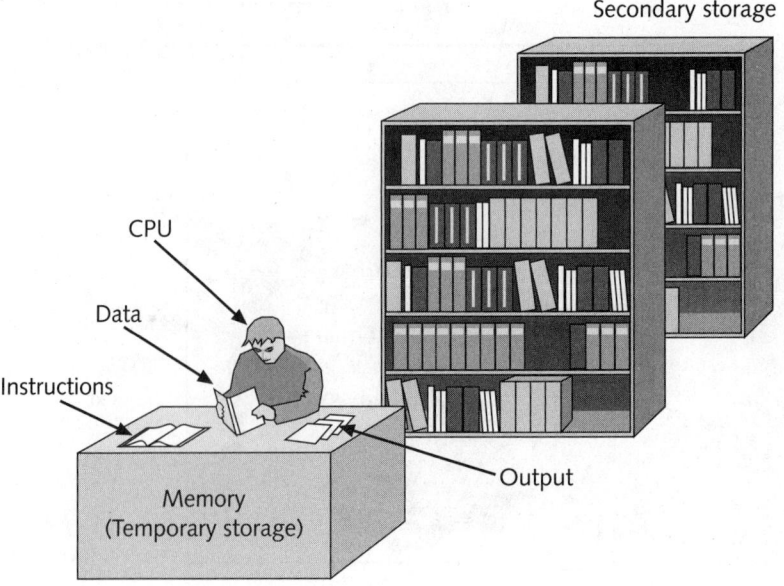

Figure 1-13 Memory is a temporary place to hold instructions and data while the CPU processes both

1

Primary Storage Primary storage is provided by devices called **memory** or **random access memory (RAM)**, located on the motherboard and on other circuit boards. RAM chips can be installed individually directly on the motherboard or in banks of several chips on a small board that plugs into the motherboard (see Figure 1-14). The most common types of boards that hold memory chips are called **SIMMs (single inline memory modules)**, **DIMMs (dual inline memory modules)**, and **RIMMs (memory modules manufactured by Rambus, Inc.)** (See Figure 1-15.) Most motherboards today use DIMMs.

DIMM

Two extra slots for
additional DIMMs

Figure 1-14   A SIMM, DIMM, or RIMM holds RAM and is mounted directly on a
motherboard

Memory is useless to the system until it has been assigned addresses that the operating system, device drivers, and BIOS can use to communicate with it. These memory addresses are numbers that are assigned to each usable cell of memory, and the assignments are normally done when the OS is first loaded. How memory addresses are assigned and used is covered in the next chapter.

184-pin RIMM

168-pin DIMM

72-pin SIMM

30-pin SIMM

Figure 1-15   Types of RAM modules

RAM is used to temporarily hold data and instructions while the CPU processes both. Whatever information is stored in RAM is lost when the computer is turned off, because RAM chips need a continuous supply of electrical power to hold data or software stored in them. This kind of memory is called **volatile** because it is temporary in nature. By contrast, another kind of memory holds its data permanently, even when the power is turned off. This type of memory is **nonvolatile** and is called **ROM (read–only memory).**

TIP   Using Windows 9x, you can see what type of CPU and how much memory you have installed. Right-click the My Computer icon on your desktop, select Properties from the shortcut menu, and click the General tab.

Secondary Storage   As you know, the RAM on the motherboard is called primary storage. Primary storage temporarily holds both data and instructions as the CPU processes them. These data and instructions are also permanently stored on devices such as CDs, hard drives, and floppy disks, in locations that are remote from the CPU. Data and instructions cannot be processed by the CPU from this remote storage (called *secondary storage*), but must first be copied into primary storage (RAM) for processing.

The most important difference between these types of storage is that secondary storage is permanent. When you turn off your computer, the information in secondary storage remains intact. The four most popular secondary storage devices are hard disks, floppy disks, Zip drives, CD-ROMs, and DVDs. Figure 1-16 shows a hard drive subsystem.

IDE connection
on system board

Power cord

IDE 40-pin
data cable

Connection for
a second drive

Hard drive

Figure 1-16 A PC's hard drive subsystem

 Don't forget that primary storage, or RAM, is temporary; as soon as you turn off the computer, any information there is lost. That's why you should always save your work frequently into secondary storage.

A **hard drive** is a sealed case containing platters or disks that rotate at a high speed (see Figure 1-17). As the platters rotate, an arm with a sensitive read/write head reaches across the platters, both writing new data to them and reading existing data from them. Most hard drives today use a technology called **EIDE (Enhanced Integrated Drive Electronics)**, which originated from IDE technology. **IDE (Integrated Drive Electronics)** is a group of standards that governs how a hard drive works, and EIDE is a group of standards that governs how a secondary storage device such as a hard drive, CD-ROM drive, or Zip drive can interface with a system.

 People in the industry often use the term *IDE* for both IDE and EIDE.

Figure 1-17   Hard drive with sealed cover removed

IDE provides two connectors, called the primary and secondary channels, on a mother-board for two data cables (see Figure 1-18). Each IDE cable has a connection at the other end for an IDE device and a connection in the middle of the cable for a second IDE device. Therefore, a motherboard can accommodate up to four IDE devices in one system. Hard drives, Zip drives, CD-ROM drives, and tape drives, among other devices, can use these four IDE connections, which are controlled by the chip set. A typical system has one hard drive connected to one IDE connector and a CD-ROM drive connected to the other; power to the hard drive comes through a power cable from the PC's power supply (see Figure 1-19).

Storing Files on a Hard Drive   The operating system is responsible for storing the files and folders on a secondary storage device such as a hard drive, using organizational meth-ods called a **file system**. Regardless of the file system used, however, every OS manages a hard drive by using directories (Windows calls these folders), subdirectories, and files. By creating different directories on a hard drive, you can organize your program files and data files by placing programs in one directory and files created by those programs in a second directory. This organization is comparable to keeping paper records in separate folders. You can also organize files on other secondary storage media such as floppy disks or Zip drives.

IDE cable going to
CD-ROM drive

Primary IDE connector

Secondary IDE connector

IDE cable going to
hard drive

Figure 1-18   A motherboard usually has two IDE connectors, each of which can
accommodate two devices; a hard drive usually connects to the motherboard
using the primary IDE connector

40-pin IDE cable

CD-ROM drive

Connection for a second
device on this cable

Hard drive

Figure 1-19   Two IDE devices connected to a motherboard using both IDE connections
and two cables

Under DOS, a filename can contain up to eight characters and the file extension can contain up to three characters, which are separated by a period, like so: filename.ext. (Be sure to not use a space, period, asterisk, question mark, or backslash in a filename or file extension.) Under Windows 95 and later Windows OSes, filenames can be as long as 255 characters and may contain spaces. When using long filenames in Windows 9x, remember that the DOS portion of the system can only understand eight-character file names with three-character extensions. When the DOS part of the system is operating, it will truncate long filenames and assign new eight-character ones. (Windows NT/2000/XP has no DOS core and therefore does a better job of managing long filenames.)

A **directory table** is a list of files and subdirectories. When a hard drive is first installed and formatted, there is a single directory table on the drive called the **root directory**. For logical drive C, the root directory is written as C:\. This root directory can hold files or other directories, which can have names such as C:\Tools. These directories—called **subdirectories**, **child directories**, or **folders**—can, in turn, contain other directories, as in the following: C:\wp\data\myfile.txt.

When you write the drive and directories pointing to the location of the file, the drive and directories are called the **path** to the file. In the preceding example, the C: identifies the drive (if the directory had been on a floppy disk, it would have been either A: or B:). The first part of the file before the period (myfile) is called the filename, and the part after the period (txt) is called the file extension—which, for Windows and DOS, always has three or fewer characters. The file extension identifies the file type, such as .doc for Microsoft Word document files or .xls for Microsoft Excel spreadsheet files.

Windows uses several different file systems, the most common of which for hard drives is the FAT (file allocation table) file system. The FAT file system is based on a table that is a very long list of all the entries on a hard drive that can hold data. Two FAT file systems used by Windows for hard drives are FAT16 and FAT32. (The 16 or 32 stands for the size of each number in the table—16 bits or 32 bits, although, for FAT32, only 28 of them are used to hold a number.)

There is one entry in the FAT for each cluster on the hard drive. A **cluster** is the smallest unit of space on the hard drive used to hold data that is addressed by the OS. An OS puts files on the hard drive in increments of whole clusters. All clusters on a hard drive are assigned a single number, beginning with zero. The OS identifies a cluster by this cluster number and knows how many bytes or characters of data a cluster can hold. All clusters on a logical drive hold the same number of bytes. The OS relates to the hard drive by using, among other things, the FAT and the directory table, which tells the OS the name of a file and the first cluster number for that file. A logical drive such as drive C has only one FAT, but can have several directory tables—one for each subdirectory on the drive.

Figure 1-20 shows the inside of a computer case with three IDE devices. The CD-ROM drive and the Zip drive share an IDE cable, and the hard drive uses the other cable. Both cables connect to the motherboard at the two IDE connections. A hard drive receives its power from the power supply by way of a power cord (see Figure 1-21). Looking back at Figure 1-20, you can see the power connections to the right of the cable connections on each drive (the power cords are not connected, in order to make it easier to see the cable configuration).

Figure 1-20   This system has a CD-ROM and Zip drive sharing the secondary IDE cable, and a hard drive using the primary IDE cable

The labels in Figure 1-20 read, from top to bottom: CD-ROM drive; Secondary IDE cable; Zip drive; Two IDE connections on the motherboard; Hard drive; Primary IDE cable; Unused connection for fourth IDE device; Both cables connected to motherboard.

The labels in Figure 1-21 read: Hard drive; Power supply; Power connected.

Figure 1-21   A hard drive receives power from the power supply by way of a power cord connected to the drive

Another secondary storage device almost always found inside the case is a floppy drive. Floppy drives come in two sizes: 3½ inches and 5¼ inches (referring to the size of the disks the drives can hold). The newer 3½-inch disks use more advanced technology and actually hold more data than the older 5¼-inch disks did. Older motherboards did not provide a connector for a floppy drive, but newer ones do (see Figure 1-22). A floppy drive cable can accommodate two drives. The drive at the end of the cable is drive A. If another drive were connected to the middle of the cable, it would be drive B in a computer system (see Figure 1-23). Electricity to a floppy drive is provided by a power cord from the power supply that connects to a power port at the back of the drive.

Floppy drive connector

Secondary IDE connector

Primary IDE connector

Figure 1-22   A motherboard usually provides a connection for a floppy drive cable

Floppy drive data cable

Two possible connections for another floppy drive

Connection for power cord

Figure 1-23   One floppy drive connection on a motherboard can support one or two floppy drives

Floppy drives are not as necessary as they once were, because the industry is moving toward storage media that can hold more data, such as CDs and Zip disks. For years, every PC and notebook computer had a floppy drive, but many newer notebook computers don't include floppy drives, and some manufacturers offer floppy drives on desktop systems as add-on options only.

A CD-ROM (compact disc read–only memory) drive is considered standard equipment on most computer systems today, because software is mainly distributed on CDs. Figure 1-24 shows the rear of a CD-ROM drive with the IDE data cable and power cord connected.

CD-ROM drive

IDE cable
Power cord

Figure 1-24   Most CD-ROM drives are EIDE devices and connect to the motherboard by way of an IDE data cable

Don't let the name of the CD-ROM drive confuse you. It's really not memory, but secondary storage because, when the power is turned off, the data stored on a CD is still intact. The term ROM is somewhat incorrectly used by the industry but implies that the data can only be read from a CD and not written to it.

Motherboard Components Used for Communication Among Devices

When you look carefully at the motherboard, you see many fine lines on both the top and the bottom of the board's surface (refer back to Figure 1-11). These lines, sometimes called **traces**, are circuits, or paths, that enable data, instructions, and power to move from component to component on the board. This system of pathways used for communication and the protocol and methods used for transmission are collectively referred to as the bus. (A **protocol** is a set of rules and standards that any two entities use for communication.) The paths, or lines, of the bus that are used to move data are called the data bus.

Sometimes a bus provides a port on the outside of the computer case for an external device to connect to by way of a cable or cord, or the bus might provide a slot on the motherboard into which a circuit board fits. In any case, a device always connects to a single bus on the motherboard. A motherboard can have several different buses; each type of bus has data lines, address lines, and control lines.

 TIP   An operating system relates to the bus, so the OS must support the bus in order for the bus to be used by the system.

Binary data is put on a line of a bus by placing voltage on that line. You can visualize that bits are "traveling" down the bus in parallel, but in reality, the voltage placed on each line is not "traveling," but is rather all over the line. When one component at one end of the line wants to write data to another component, the two components get in sync for the write operation. Then the first component places voltage on several lines of the bus, and the other component immediately reads the voltage on these lines.

The CPU or other devices interpret the voltage, or lack of voltage, on each line on the bus as binary digits (0s or 1s). Some buses have data paths that are 8, 16, 32, or 64 bits wide. For example, a bus that has eight wires, or lines, to transmit data is called an *8-bit bus*. Figure 1-25 shows an 8-bit bus between the CPU and memory that is transmitting the letter A (binary 01000001). All bits of a byte are placed on their lines of the bus at the same time. Remember there are only two states inside a computer: on and off, which represent zero and one. On a bus, these two states are no voltage for a zero and voltage for a one. So the bus in Figure 1-25 has voltage on two lines and no voltage on the other six lines, in order to pass the letter A on the bus. This bus is only 8 bits wide, but most buses today are much wider: 16, 32, 64, or 128 bits wide. Also, most buses today use a ninth bit for error checking. Adding a check bit for each byte allows the component reading the data to verify that it is the same data written to the bus.

Figure 1-25   A data bus has traces, or lines, that contain voltage interpreted by the CPU and other devices as bits

1

The width of a data bus is called the **data path size**. A motherboard can have more than one bus, each using a different protocol, speed, data path size, and so on. The main bus on the motherboard that communicates with the CPU, memory, and the chip set goes by several names: **system bus**, *memory bus*, *host bus*, *front side bus*, or *external bus*. In our discussions, we'll use the term *system bus*. The data portion of most system buses on today's motherboards is 64 bits wide with or without additional lines for error checking.

One of the most interesting lines, or circuits, on a bus is called the **system clock** or system timer, which is dedicated to timing the activities of the chips on the motherboard. A crystal on the motherboard (Figure 1-26), similar to that found in watches, generates continuous pulses to produce the system clock. These pulses are carried on traces over the motherboard to chips and expansion slots to ensure that all activities are performed in a synchronized fashion. Remember that everything in a computer is binary, and this includes the activities themselves. Instead of continuously working to perform commands or move data, the CPU, bus, and other devices work in a binary fashion. Do something, stop, do something, stop, and so forth. Each device works on a clock cycle or beat of the clock. Some devices, such as the CPU, do two or more operations on one beat of the clock, and others do one operation for each beat. Some devices might even do something on every other beat, but all work according to beats or cycles. You can think of this as similar to children jumping rope. The system clock (child turning the rope) provides the beats or cycles, while devices (children jumping) work in a binary fashion (jump, don't jump). In the analogy, some children jump two or more times for each rope pass.

Motherboard crystal generates the system clock

Figure 1-26   The system clock is a pulsating electrical signal sent out by this component, which works much like a crystal in a wristwatch (one line, or circuit, on the motherboard bus is dedicated to carrying this pulse)

How fast is the clock ticking? The beats, called the **clock speed**, are measured in **hertz (Hz)**, which is one cycle per second, **megahertz (MHz)**, which is one million cycles per second, and **gigahertz (GHz)**, which is one billion cycles per second. Most motherboard buses today operate at 100MHz, 133MHz, 200MHz, or 400MHz. In other words, data or instructions can be put on the system bus at the rate of 400 million every second. A CPU operates from 166MHz to more than 3GHz. In other words, the CPU can put data or instructions on its internal bus at this much higher rate. Although we often refer to the speed of the CPU and the motherboard bus, it is more accurate to talk about the frequency of these devices, because the term "speed" implies a continuous flow, while the term "frequency" implies a digital or binary flow: on and off, on and off.

The lines of a bus, including data, instruction, and power lines, often extend to the expansion slots (see Figure 1-27). The size and shape of an expansion slot are dependent on the kind of bus it is using. Therefore, one way to determine the kind of bus you have is to examine the expansion slots on the motherboard.

Pins on connector edge of expansion card

PCI slot

Bus lines

Figure 1-27   The lines of a bus end at an expansion slot where they connect to pins that connect to lines on the expansion card inserted in the slot

Figure 1-28 shows three types of expansion slots:

- **PCI (Peripheral Component Interconnect) expansion slot.** The PCI bus was invented for devices that are faster than the 16-bit ISA bus but can't run as fast as the system bus between memory and the CPU. The PCI bus runs in sync with the system bus at one-third or one-half the speed. All Windows OSes support PCI.

- **AGP (Accelerated Graphics Port) expansion slot.** The AGP bus was designed to accommodate a fast video card, which is a circuit board that controls the monitor. Windows 98 and Windows 2000/XP support AGP. A motherboard will have only a single AGP slot to accommodate one monitor.

■ **ISA (Industry Standard Architecture) expansion slot.** The first motherboards of the 1980s only had one bus, the system bus, which supported several ISA slots. The first ISA slot had only eight lines for data and was called
the 8-bit ISA slot. It had 20 address lines and ran at 4.77 MHz, which means
that data was transferred on the bus at a rate of 4,770,000 transfers per second. Today's system buses run up to 400 MHz, have a 64-bit wide data path
and a 36-bit or more wide address path. These system buses, sometimes
called memory buses, front-side buses, or local buses, always connect directly
to the CPU and memory, but are much too fast to support the slow ISA slots,
which connect to the system bus by way of slower I/O buses that act as middle
men. Later, the 8-bit ISA slot was improved by adding an additional 8 lines for
data, and this version is known as the 16-bit ISA slot. This slot runs at 8.33 MHz
and has 24 lines for the address bus. All operating systems for personal computers
today support the 16-bit ISA slot although its use is diminishing in favor of
faster I/O buses. You can see three ISA slots in Figure 1-29. An 8-bit expansion
card, as shown in the figure, can use the first part of the 16-bit slot.

AGP slot
PCI slots

16-bit ISA slots

Figure 1-28   PCI bus expansion slots are shorter than ISA slots and offset farther; the one
AGP slot is set farther from the edge of the board

Each of these types of expansion slots communicates with the CPU by way of its own bus.
There is a PCI bus, an AGP bus, and an ISA bus, each running at different speeds and pro-
viding different features to accommodate the expansion cards that use these different slots.
But all these buses connect to the main bus or system bus, which connects to the CPU.

With a little practice, you can identify these slots by their length, by the position of the breaks in the slots, and by the distance from the edge of the motherboard to a slot's position. Look for all three of these expansion slots in Figure 1-28.

Circuit board mounted in slot

16-bit ISA expansion slots

Ports for devices to connect to the card

Motherboard

Figure 1-29   This 8-bit ISA sound card is mounted in the 8-bit part of a 16-bit ISA slot on a motherboard

In addition, the following types of ports also exist:

- The USB is designed to provide ports off the motherboard for slower external devices such as a mouse, keyboard, scanner, video camera, or digital telephone. The USB bus supports up to 127 devices, which can be daisy chained together and connected to a single USB port on a motherboard. Windows 95 with the USB update, Windows 98/Me, and Windows 2000/XP support USB.

- FireWire, sometimes called IEEE 1394 or simply 1394, is a very fast bus designed to connect fast external devices to a port off the motherboard called a FireWire or 1394 port. The bus was designed by the Institute of Electrical and Electronic Engineers (IEEE), led primarily by Apple Computer, which named the bus *FireWire*. Windows 98/Me and Windows NT/2000/XP support FireWire.

 Device Manager under Windows 9x and Windows 2000/XP (Windows NT does not have a Device Manager) is the primary tool used to manage bus resources and the devices that use them. To access Device Manager using Windows 9x, right-click the My Computer icon on the desktop, select Properties from the shortcut menu, and click on the Device Manager tab. (For Windows 2000/XP, from the System Properties window, click on the Hardware tab, and then click Device Manager.)

Interface (Expansion) Cards

Circuit boards other than the motherboard inside the computer are sometimes called circuit cards, adapter boards, expansion cards, interface cards, or simply **cards** and are mounted in expansion slots on the motherboard (see Figure 1-29). Figure 1-30 shows the motherboard and expansion cards installed inside a computer case. By studying this figure carefully, you can see the video card installed in the one AGP slot, a sound card and network card installed in two PCI slots (the other two PCI slots are not used), and a modem card installed in an ISA slot. Two ISA slots are not used. Also notice the ports provided by these cards, showing at the rear of the PC case. You can see a full view of a video card in Figure 1-31. These cards all enable the CPU to connect to an external device or, in the case of the network card, to a network. The video card provides a port for the monitor. The sound card provides ports for speakers and microphones. The network card provides a port for a network cable to connect the PC to a network, and the modem card provides ports for phone lines. The technology to access these devices is embedded on the card itself, and the card also has the technology to communicate with the slot it is in, the motherboard, and the CPU.

Figure 1-30 Four cards installed on a motherboard providing ports for several devices

15-pin, 3-row
video port

Figure 1-31 The easiest way to identify this video card is to look at the port on the end of the card

The easiest way to determine the function of a particular expansion card (short of seeing its name written on the card, which doesn't happen very often) is to look at the end of the card that fits against the back of the computer case. A network card, for example, has a port designed to fit the network cable. An internal modem has one, or usually two, telephone jacks as its ports. However, as you examine the ports on the back of your PC, realize that sometimes the motherboard provides ports of its own.

The Electrical System

The most important component of the computer's electrical system is the *power supply*, usually located near the rear of the case (see Figure 1-32). This power supply does not actually generate electricity but converts it and reduces it to a voltage that the computer can handle. A power supply receives 110–120 volts of AC power from a wall outlet and converts it to a much lower DC voltage. Older power supplies had power cables that provided either 5 or 12 volts DC. Newer power supplies provide 3.3, 5, and 12 volts DC. In addition to providing power for the computer, the power supply runs a fan directly from the electrical output voltage to help cool the inside of the computer case. A temperature level of over 185 degrees Fahrenheit (85 degrees Celsius) can cause components to fail. When a computer is running, this fan and the spinning of the hard drive are the two primary noisemakers.

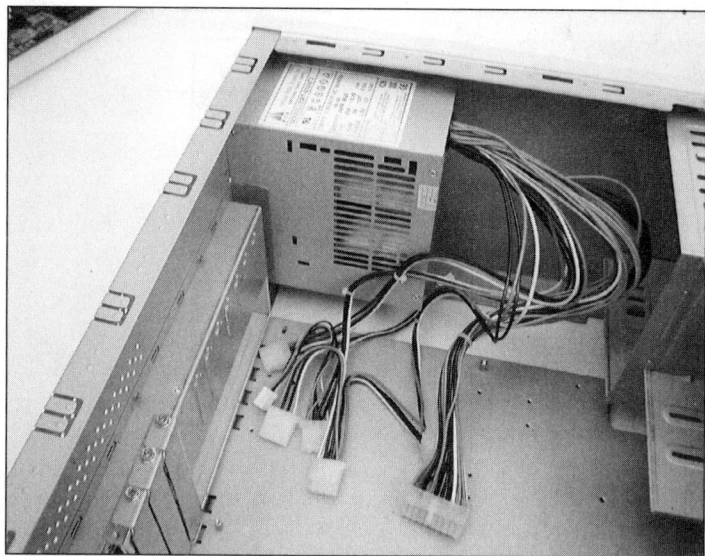

Figure 1-32   Power supply with connections

Every motherboard has one or a pair of connections to provide electrical power from the power supply to the motherboard and to other components that receive their power from ports and expansion slots coming off the motherboard (see Figure 1-33). Each bus has wires, or lines, designated to carry voltage to power expansion cards. Figure 1-34 shows the lines on the motherboard that are part of the bus ending at an expansion slot, some of which are carrying power.

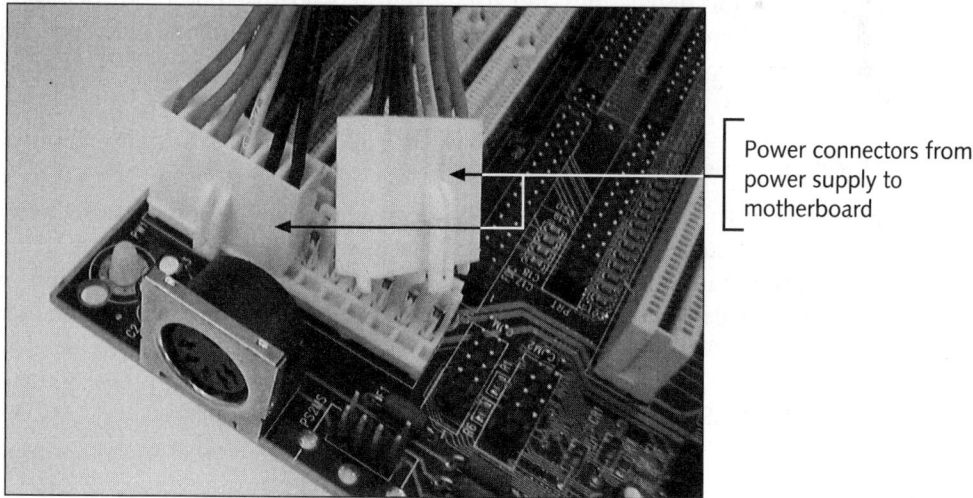

Power connectors from power supply to motherboard

Figure 1-33   The motherboard receives its power from the power supply by way of one or two connections located near the edge of the board

ISA expansion slots

ISA bus lines

Figure 1-34   Bus lines ending at expansion slots, some of which carry electrical power needed by cards

INSTRUCTIONS AND DATA STORED ON THE MOTHERBOARD

Some very basic instructions and data are stored on the motherboard—just enough to provide rudimentary information about the setup of the computer, start the computer, and look for an operating system stored on a secondary storage device such as a hard drive or floppy disk. These data and instructions are stored on special ROM (read-only memory) chips on the motherboard, by setting physical switches on the board, and through using CMOS configuration chips.

In the case of ROM chips, the distinction between hardware and software becomes vague. Most of the time, it's easy to distinguish between hardware and software. For example, a floppy disk is hardware, but a file on the disk containing a set of instructions is software. This software file, sometimes called a **program**, might be stored on the disk today, but you can erase that file tomorrow and write a new one to the disk. In this case, it is clear that a floppy disk is a permanent physical entity, whereas the program is not. Sometimes, however, hardware and software are not so easy to distinguish. For instance, a ROM chip on a circuit board inside your computer has software instructions permanently etched into it during fabrication. This software is actually a part of the hardware and is not easily changed. In this case, hardware and software are closely tied together, and it's difficult to separate the two, either physically or logically. Some even give a new name to such hybrid components, calling them **firmware**.

BIOS

These ROM chips hold programs or software that, among other things, tell the CPU how to perform many fundamental input/output tasks, and they are therefore sometimes called **BIOS (basic input/output system)** chips. See Figure 1-35 for an example of a ROM BIOS chip on a video card. The motherboard contains a vital ROM BIOS chip (Figure 1-36) that contains the programming necessary to start the computer (called **startup BIOS**) and to perform other fundamental functions such as interacting with the floppy disk drive and keyboard (called **system BIOS**). In addition, some complex hardware devices contain BIOS software embedded directly on the card.

You'll learn more about how the BIOS starts, or boots, your computer in the next chapter.

Figure 1-35   A ROM BIOS chip on a video card holds programs that provide instructions to operate the card

ROM BIOS chip

Figure 1-36   The ROM BIOS chip on the motherboard contains the programming to start up the PC as well as perform many other fundamental tasks

Some BIOSes on the motherboard and operating systems support a power-saving feature called the Advanced Configuration and Power Interface (ACPI) standards. Using ACPI, a system can be powered up by an external device such as a keyboard. Windows 9x and Windows 2000 support ACPI, as do most new motherboard BIOSes. Microsoft calls an ACPI-compliant BIOS a "good" BIOS. To see if your BIOS is ACPI compliant, check this Microsoft URL: www.microsoft.com/windows2000/professional/howtobuy/upgrading/compat.

As you add new hardware components to your system, or new BIOS features become available, you might want to upgrade these utility programs. In the past, this meant buying new ROM chips and exchanging them on the motherboard. However, ROM chips on motherboards today can be reprogrammed. Called **flash ROM**, the software stored on these chips can be overwritten by new software that remains on the chip until it is overwritten.

CMOS

Another chip on the motherboard contains a very small amount of memory, or RAM—enough to hold configuration or setup information about the computer. This is called the **CMOS configuration chip** or **CMOS setup chip**, or CMOS RAM. This chip, shown in Figure 1-37, is responsible for remembering system information such as how memory is allocated, which hard drives and floppy drives are present, how the serial and parallel ports are configured, and so forth. When the computer is first turned on, it looks to this CMOS chip to find out what hardware it should expect to find. The CMOS chip is powered by a trickle of electricity from a small battery located on the motherboard or computer case, usually close to the chip itself; thus, even though the CMOS chip is RAM (temporary memory), when the computer is turned off, the chip retains its data.

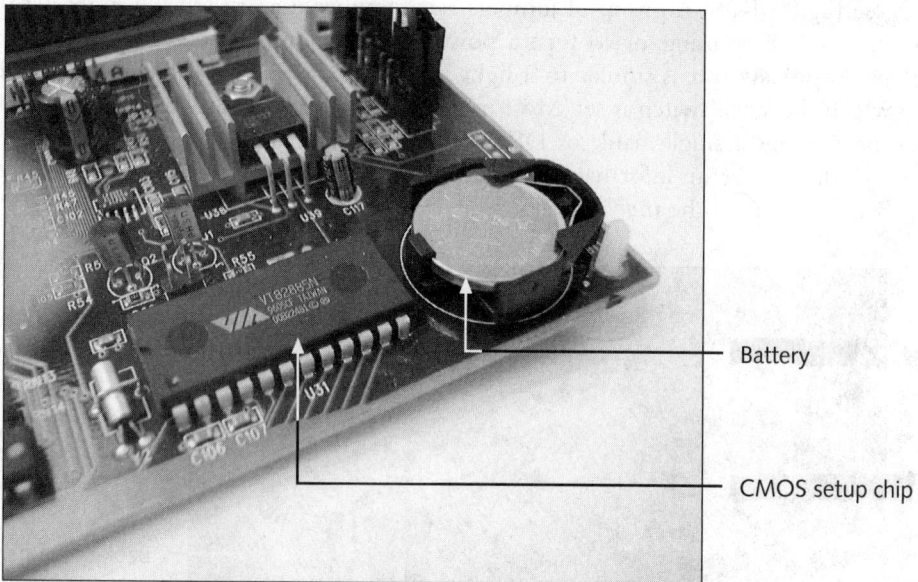

Figure 1-37   The CMOS setup chip, powered by a battery when the PC is turned off, contains data about the system configuration as well as the current time and date

The program to change CMOS setup is stored in the ROM BIOS chip and can be accessed during the startup process. The keystrokes to enter CMOS setup are displayed somewhere on the screen during startup in a statement such as "Press the Del key to enter setup" (different BIOSes use different keystrokes). The CMOS setup does not normally need to be changed except when there is a problem with hardware, a new floppy drive is installed, or a power-saving feature needs to be disabled or enabled. The CMOS setup can also hold a power-on password to help secure a system. Know that this password is not the same password that can be required by a Windows OS at startup.

Even though a computer has many CMOS chips, the term "CMOS chip" has come to mean the one chip on the motherboard that holds the configuration or setup information. If you hear the following: "What does CMOS say?" or "Let's change CMOS," the person is talking about the configuration or setup information stored on this one CMOS chip. The program to change CMOS setup is stored in the ROM BIOS chip and can be accessed during the startup process.

Jumpers

A motherboard can also retain setup or installation information in different settings of jumpers or DIP switches on the board. **Jumpers** are considered open or closed based on whether a jumper cover is present on two small wires that stick up off the motherboard (see Figure 1-38). A group of jumpers is sometimes used to tell the system at what speed the CPU is running, or to turn a power-saving feature on or off. A **DIP (dual inline package) switch** is similar to a light switch and is on or off based on the direction in which the small switch is set. Most motherboards have at least one, often several, jumpers, and perhaps a single bank of DIP switches (see Figure 1-39), although the trend is to include most setup information in CMOS rather than to have a jumper or switch on the board that has to be mechanically set.

Bank of jumpers

Jumper cover

Figure 1-38   Setup information about the motherboard can be stored by setting a jumper on (closed) or off (open). A jumper is closed if the cover is in place, connecting the two wires that make up the jumper; a jumper is open if the cover is not in place.

1

Figure 1-39   A motherboard can use a bank of DIP switches for configuration settings

HOW A CPU WORKS AND COMMUNICATES WITH OTHER DEVICES

Remember that the CPU is responsible for most processing, but the CPU depends on the chip set, system clock, and buses to move data to and from I/O devices, memory, and secondary storage. This section explains from a hardware perspective how the CPU does this, and discusses in general terms how a CPU works. One purpose of this section is to help you understand just how binary a computer is—that is, to emphasize that everything is done using only two states, on and off.

How the CPU Works

The CPU contains three basic components: an input/output (I/O) unit, one or more arithmetic logic units (ALU), and a control unit (see Figure 1-40). The I/O unit manages data and instructions entering and leaving the CPU. The control unit manages all activities inside the CPU itself. The ALU unit does all comparisons and calculations. The CPU also needs places to store data and instructions as it works on them. Registers are small holding areas inside the CPU that work very much as RAM does outside the CPU. There are registers to hold counters, data, instructions, and addresses that the ALU is currently processing.

Figure 1-40   Beginning with the Pentium CPU, a CPU has two arithmetic logic units and can process two instructions at the same time

In addition to the registers, the CPU has its own internal memory cache that holds data and instructions waiting to be processed by the ALU. Also notice in Figure 1-40 that there is an external bus where data, instructions, addresses, and control signals are sent into and out of the CPU. The CPU has its own internal bus for communication to the internal cache. The CPU's internal bus operates at a much higher frequency than the external, or system, bus. (You can now see why the system bus is sometimes called the **external bus**; the industry sometimes calls these internal and external buses the **back side bus** and the **front side bus**.)

Older CPUs had only a single ALU, but beginning with the Pentium CPU, the CPU now contains at least two ALUs so that the CPU can process two instructions at the same time. For the Pentiums, the front side data bus is 64 bits wide, but the back side data bus is only 32 bits wide because of this dual-processing design. This is why the industry calls the Pentium a 32-bit processor; it processes 32 bits at a time internally, even though it uses a 64-bit bus externally. Intel has recently released a 64-bit processor, called the Itanium, that has a 128-bit external data bus.

How the CPU Uses Memory

The CPU accesses memory by way of the data bus. Remember that memory is a temporary holding place for data and instructions to be processed by the CPU. Each byte of memory is assigned an address so that the CPU can keep track of where things are in memory, much as cells in a spreadsheet are each assigned an address. Figure 1-41 shows a segment of memory holding the instructions to add two numbers, and also holding the two numbers to be added. Each memory cell has an address in the figure: A1, A2, A3, and so forth. Each cell can hold an instruction, such as *Add A6*, or data such as the value 75. A **memory address** is a number assigned to each cell in RAM that can hold one byte. (You'll learn more about memory addresses and other system resources in the next chapter.)

Figure 1-41   Memory is identified by a memory address and can hold data or instructions

Whereas cells in a spreadsheet are assigned a letter and a number, for example A2, memory addresses are simple counting numbers such as 1, 2, 3, 4, and so forth. The command in cell A1 of Figure 1-41 that says *Move A5* would actually be *Move 5*. That would not mean move the number 5, but move the value in memory address 5.

How the CPU and Devices Use the System Bus to Communicate

The system bus on a motherboard has three components: a data bus, an address bus, and a control bus (see Figure 1-42). You have already seen how the data bus works. This section explains how the address bus and control bus work and how the chip set is involved in managing both buses.

The Address Bus

In addition to communicating data and instructions, the CPU must also communicate memory addresses. In the last example, the CPU issued the command *Move 5*, meaning to move the contents of memory address 5 to a CPU register. The CPU puts the memory address 5 on the **address bus**. Memory or other devices do not send addresses to the CPU. All memory addressing originates with the CPU, and an address is written to and read from the address bus as bits. In our example, the address bus is read by the memory controller, which is part of the chip set on the motherboard (see Figure 1-43). The memory controller is responsible for using this address to find the correct address in memory (in our example, the location numbered 5) and put the data in that location on the data bus to be read by the CPU.

Data bus

Data bus and address bus lines
carry bits in parallel, all lines
working together

CPU

Address
bus

Lines on the control bus
work independently of
each other

Control
bus

Figure 1-42   A bus consists of a data bus, an address bus, and a control bus

Address bus

Chip
Set

CPU

Data bus

Memory

Figure 1-43   The CPU tells the memory controller from which memory address
to fetch data

On older motherboards, lines on a bus were designated for data, addresses, or
control, and were only used for one purpose. Motherboards today use lines
that are multiplexed, meaning that the same line can be used for more than one
purpose, alternating its use on different cycles of the system clock.

The Control Bus

The CPU also sends control signals to devices, and devices send control signals to the CPU using the **control bus**. Each CPU can have its own unique group of control signals, but there are some controls that are common to all CPUs:

- A system clock control line provides the timing for most components on the motherboard, including the CPU.

- Interrupt request (IRQ) lines, sometimes called **IRQ channels**, are used by devices to get the attention of the CPU. If a device puts voltage on an IRQ line (in technical jargon, you could say the line is *raised*), then the CPU knows to stop whatever it is doing and service the device. An IRQ works much like a pull cord on an old city trolley. A passenger can pull the cord to signal the trolley driver to stop the trolley as a service to the passenger.

  Each device is assigned an IRQ number at startup, and sometimes a component is responsible for managing a single IRQ for several devices. An example of this is the USB controller that uses a single IRQ for all USB devices connected to it (see Figure 1-44). The controller is assigned an IRQ number at startup. In the figure, if either the scanner or the digital camera wants attention, the USB controller puts voltage on the IRQ line. When the CPU responds, the controller knows which device needs attention and will communicate with the device, serving as the middleman between the device and the CPU. (You'll learn more about IRQ numbers and other system resources in the next chapter.)

Figure 1-44   The USB controller has a single IRQ line that it raises when any USB device needs attention

- Read/write control lines are used by the CPU to tell memory and other devices if the address on the address bus is to be used for a read or a write operation. There can be several read/write lines on the control bus.

- I/O control lines are used by the CPU to tell devices and memory how the address lines are about to be used. The address bus is used for two kinds of addresses: memory addresses and I/O addresses. You have already learned about memory addresses; I/O addresses are used to communicate with I/O devices such as a mouse or modem. (You'll learn more about I/O addresses and other system resources in the next chapter.) The I/O control lines are used to tell memory and I/O devices whether the addresses about to be placed on the address bus are to be read as memory addresses or I/O addresses. If the I/O control line has voltage on it, devices know to expect addresses on the address bus to apply to them, and the memory controller ignores what is on the address bus. If the I/O control line does not have voltage, then the memory controller knows to read the addresses, and I/O devices ignore whatever is on the address bus. Figure 1-45 shows memory, a modem, and a video card all "listening" at the I/O control line. Only memory responds, because the I/O control line does not have voltage.

Figure 1-45   If the I/O control line is not raised, only the memory controller will use the addresses on the address bus

UNDERSTANDING BINARY

With computers, *everything* is binary. A computer's world is a binary world, and communication of instructions and data by the devices that process them is always in binary. Every communication, every process (including the storage of data and instructions) in a computer is a series of zeros and ones. When you study how computers work, keeping this binary concept in mind makes everything much clearer.

Let's look at how binary works in a little more detail, comparing it to something we're all familiar with: decimal notation. When you count in decimal, there are 10 digits, or numerals, 0 through 9. Using these 10 numerals, you can count only up to 9. Once you count all the values from 0 to 9, you need a way to indicate that you have already counted these 10 values. To do this, you add a second column, or place, which represents the number of times you have counted to 10, so it is called the "tens" place. In this second place, just as in the first, you have 10 numerals. Each time you have counted to 10, you add one to the value in the tens column, or tens place, up to 9. The next time you count to 10, you need a third column, or place, to record that you have counted 10 groups of 10, or 100. For example, in Figure 1-46, the number 255 says that you have counted to 100 twice, you have counted to 10 five times, and you have also counted to 5. Another way of saying the same thing is to express 255 as follows: (100 × 2) + (10 × 5) + 5=255.

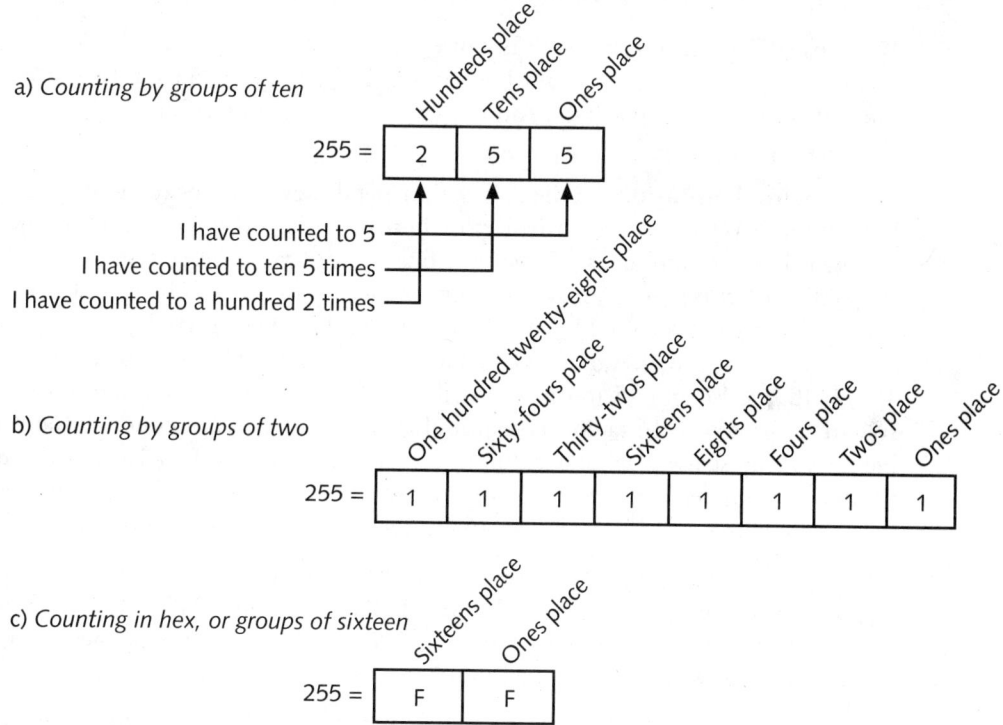

Figure 1-46 Three important number systems in studying computers are decimal, binary, and hex

Binary works in a similar way, except that you only have two numerals, or binary digits, 0 and 1. You can only count up to 1 using the first column, or first place. You then need another place (the twos place) to indicate how many times you have counted to two, so in binary you write two as 10, which is one group of two and no ones. In other words, you have counted to two one time and have not counted any more ones. The next value when counting is 11, which means you have counted to two 1 time and have also counted to one. In binary, 11 is three. To count to four, you run out of values in the first two columns, or places, and must add a new place, the fours place. Four is 100 in binary. Five is 101 (four plus one), six is 110 (four plus two), seven is 111 (four plus two plus one), and with eight, we need a new column, or place. Eight is 1000 in binary. Notice that each place is a multiple of two except for the first place, the "ones" place. The places are eights, fours, twos and ones. As with decimal, the numeral that you put in a place indicates how many of that place you add to get your final value. Remember, though, that with binary, you only have two possible numerals, or bits; either you count 0 or 1 of each group. Therefore, to arrive at the number 255, you must have eight columns, or places:

Group of:	128	64	32	16	8	4	2	1	
How many groups:	1	1	1	1	1	1	1	1	
Total:	128 +	64 +	32 +	16 +	8 +	4 +	2 +	1	= 255

We're using 255 in our example because it's the largest 8-bit number. Values are stored in a computer in groups of eight bits, or one byte, making 255 the largest number that can be stored in a single byte. You'll see this number quite frequently when studying about computers.

Hexadecimal notation, or hex, is a shorthand way that the computer displays long binary numbers, making them easier for human beings to understand. The hex number system is built on multiples of two, just like the binary number system, which makes it simple for the computer to make the conversion from binary to hex just before a number is displayed on the screen. However, the hex number system has 16 numerals, which are 0, 1, 2, 3, 4, 5, 6, 7, 8, 9, A, B, C, D, E, and F. The last six lettered numerals are the same as 10, 11, 12, 13, 14, and 15 in our decimal system. Columns, or places, in the hex number system are groups of 16 (a convenient multiple of two). You can count all the way up to F before you must use a second column, or place. In decimal, F is 15, and the next value written as 16 in decimal is 10 in hex, saying we have one group of 16 and no ones. In hex, the third column, or place, is 16×16, or 256. The hex number 100 is 256 in decimal.

Looking at Figure 1-46, you can see that in hex, the value 255 is written as FF, which is F groups of sixteen (15×16) and F ones (15×1), yielding $240 + 15 = 255$. Sometimes hex numbers are written followed by a lowercase h to indicate that they are hex values, like this: FFh. At other times, a hex number is preceded by 0x, as in 0xFF.

Memory addresses are often displayed in hex. For example, the decimal memory address 819,205 converted to hexadecimal looks like this: C8005. Error messages displaying a hex memory address use a colon somewhere within the hex number, like this C800:5. This format is called a segment/offset form.

Letters and other characters must be assigned a numeric value before they can be stored in a computer, and that value must be converted to binary. The most popular coding scheme for letters and characters is the **ASCII (American Standard Code for Information Interchange)** standard, which has assigned an 8-bit code for letters, symbols, and other characters. Table 1-1 lists the computer terms introduced in this section and their definitions.

Table 1-1   Computer terminology

Term	Definition
Bit	A numeral in the binary number system: a 0 or a 1
Byte	8 bits
Kilobyte	1,024 bytes, which is 2^{10}, often rounded to 1,000 bytes
Megabyte	Either 1,024 kilobytes or 1,000 kilobytes, depending on what has come to be standard practice in different situations. For example, when calculating floppy disk capacities, 1 megabyte = 1,000 kilobytes; when calculating hard drive capacity, traditionally, 1 megabyte = 1,024 bytes.
Gigabyte	1,000 megabytes or 1,024 megabytes, depending on what has come to be standard practice in different situations
ASCII	American Standard Code for Information Interchange coding scheme used for microcomputers, which assigns a 7- 8-bit code to all characters and symbols.
Hex	Short for hexadecimal. A number system based on 16 values (called base 16), which is explained in detail below. Uses the sixteen numerals 0, 1, 2, 3, 4, 5, 6, 7, 8, 9, A, B, C, D, E, and F. Hex numbers are often followed by a lowercase h to indicate they are in hex (example: 78h).

CHAPTER SUMMARY

- A computer requires both hardware and software to work.

- The four basic functions of the microcomputer are input, output, processing, and storage of data.

- Data and instructions are stored in a computer in binary, which uses only two states for data—on and off, or 1 and 0—which are called bits. Eight bits equal one byte.

- The four most popular input/output devices are the printer, monitor, mouse, and keyboard.

- The most important component inside the computer case is the motherboard, also called the main board or system board. It contains the most important microchip inside the case, the central processing unit (CPU), a microprocessor, as well as access to other circuit boards and peripheral devices. All communications between the CPU and other devices must pass through the motherboard.

- Ports on the motherboard include serial, parallel, and USB ports. It is expected that motherboards in the future will also have FireWire ports.

- A ROM BIOS microchip is a hybrid of hardware and software containing programming embedded into the chip. These chips are called firmware.

- All microchips are manufactured using one of two types of technology: CMOS (complementary metal-oxide semiconductor) or TTL (transistor-transistor logic). Most CPUs are CMOS chips.

❑ Each hardware device needs a method to communicate with the CPU, software to control it, and electricity to power it.

❑ Devices outside the computer case are connected to the motherboard by way of ports on the case.

❑ The chip set on a motherboard controls most activities on the motherboard.

❑ Primary storage, called memory or RAM, is temporary storage used by the CPU to hold data and instructions while it is processing both.

❑ RAM is stored on single chips, SIMMs, DIMMs, and RIMMs.

❑ Secondary storage is slower than primary storage, but is permanent storage. The most common examples of secondary storage devices are floppy disks, hard drives, and CD-ROM drives.

❑ Most hard drives use EIDE (Enhanced Integrated Drive Electronics) technology, which can accommodate up to four EIDE devices on one system.

❑ A file system is a method by which the OS organizes the files on a hard drive. The most popular file system for Windows is FAT, which can be either FAT16 or FAT32.

❑ Using FAT, clusters are listed in the FAT and filenames are listed in a directory table.

❑ Directories (folders) can contain files and other child directories or subdirectories (folders).

❑ Under DOS a filename can contain eight characters with a three-character extension. Using Windows, a long filename can contain up to 255 characters, including spaces.

❑ The buses on the motherboard are used to communicate data, instructions, and electrical power to components on the board. A single bus includes a data bus, address bus, and control bus.

❑ A motherboard has several buses, including the system bus, the PCI bus, the AGP bus, and the ISA bus.

❑ The system clock is used to synchronize activity on the motherboard, sending continuous pulses over the bus that are used by different components to control the pace of activity.

❑ The frequency of activity in a computer is measured in MHz, or 1 million cycles per second. The CPU operates at a much higher frequency than other components in the system.

❑ Electricity is supplied to components both inside and outside the computer case by the power supply inside the case. Some components external to the case get their power from their own electrical cable.

❑ ROM BIOS on a motherboard holds basic software needed to start up a PC and begin the process of loading an operating system. Most ROM chips are flash ROM, meaning that these programs can be updated without exchanging the chip.

❐ Setup, or configuration, information in a PC is stored in the CMOS chip on the motherboard and can also be set by means of jumpers and switches. The CMOS chip is powered by a battery on the motherboard when the power is turned off.

❐ The CPU has a control unit, I/O unit, and arithmetic logic unit. It uses registers to hold data and instructions while it processes them, and uses a memory cache to hold data and instructions just before they are processed.

❐ A CPU has an internal bus that runs at a different speed than the external bus. The main bus on the motherboard is sometimes called the system bus, external bus, front side bus, or memory bus. The bus inside the CPU is called the internal bus or the back side bus.

❐ An interrupt request line (IRQ) is used by a device or controller to get the attention of the CPU.

❐ IRQs are assigned at startup. Sometimes a device will have its own IRQ, and sometimes a controller will have a single IRQ assigned to it that it can use to service several devices.

❐ Hexadecimal notation, or hex, is a shorthand way that the computer displays long binary numbers so that they're easier for human beings to understand. The hex number system is built on multiples of sixteen (a convenient multiple of two), making it simple for the computer to make the conversion from binary to hex.

❐ Letters and other characters must be assigned a numeric value before they can be stored in a computer. The most popular coding scheme for letters and characters is the ASCII (American Standard Code for Information Interchange) standard, which has assigned an 8-bit code for letters, symbols, and other characters.

KEY TERMS

address bus
ASCII (American Standard Code for Information Interchange)
back side bus
binary number system
BIOS (basic input/output system)
bit (binary digit)
bus
byte
cards

central processing unit (CPU)
child directory
chip set
circuit board
clock speed
cluster
CMOS (complementary metal-oxide semiconductor)
CMOS configuration chip
CMOS setup chip

control bus
data bus
data path
data path size
DIMM (dual inline memory module)
DIP (dual inline package) switch
directory table
EIDE (Enhanced Integrated Drive Electronics)
expansion card

expansion slot
external bus
file extension
file system
filename
firmware
flash ROM
folder
front side bus
gigahertz (GHz)
hard copy
hard drive
hardware
hertz (Hz)
hexadecimal notation
host bus
I/O addresses
IDE
IRQ (interrupt request number)
internal bus
ISA (Industry Standard Architecture)
jumper
keyboard

local bus
main board
megahertz (MHz)
memory
memory address
memory bus
microprocessor
monitor
motherboard
mouse
nonvolatile
operating system (OS)
parallel port
path
PCI (Peripheral Component Interconnect) bus
peripheral devices
port
power supply
primary storage
printer
processor
program
protected mode

protocol
random access memory (RAM)
real mode
RIMM
ROM (read-only memory)
ROM BIOS
root directory
secondary storage
serial port
SIMM (single inline memory module)
software
subdirectory
system board
system bus
system clock
trace
USB (universal serial bus)
port
video card
volatile

2

HOW AN OS WORKS WITH HARDWARE AND OTHER SOFTWARE

In this chapter, you will learn:

♦ How hardware and software interact.

♦ The steps involved in booting your computer

♦ How an OS relates to other software

♦ How an OS launches applications

HARDWARE AND SOFTWARE INTERACTION: AN OVERVIEW

Just as a chauffeur controls a car at the direction of a passenger, software controls hardware at the direction of a user. Software consists of programs written by programmers that instruct computers to perform specific tasks.

For most people, the word "software" conjures images of application software, such as word-processing or database programs, with which users interact directly. Application software, however, is only one of three categories of PC software; the other two categories are

- BIOS and device drivers

- Operating system (OS)

BIOS and Device Drivers

The **BIOS (basic input/output system)** is *hard-coded* into a computer chip called the ROM BIOS chip. The BIOS programs fall into three categories:

- Programs to control I/O devices (called **system BIOS**)

- Programs to control the startup of a computer (called **startup BIOS**)

- A program to change the setup information stored in CMOS (called **CMOS setup**)

BIOS is sometimes called *firmware* because it is both hardware and software, and consists of a group of programs.

Device drivers are small programs stored on the hard drive that tell the computer how to communicate with input/output devices. They are necessary for communication between the OS and more complex devices, such as digital cameras, CD or DVD drives, and printers. Device drivers can come from a device manufacturer, or an OS can use its own device drivers.

The Operating System

After startup, the OS works with system BIOS and device drivers to provide instructions to the hardware to perform tasks, much as a driver uses controls to operate an automobile. In essence, the OS acts as the middleman between applications and hardware, managing hardware, running applications, providing an interface for users, and storing, retrieving, and manipulating files.

When a computer is turned on, startup BIOS and then the OS are in control of preparing the computer for user interaction.

Figure 2-1 shows the various layers of software between an application and system hardware.

One advantage of using BIOS and device drivers to interface with hardware is that it frees the OS or application software from having to know the specifics of how to communicate with a device. For example, different printers understand data and commands according to different sets of rules and standards called *protocols*. Application software and the OS can pass print requests to the printer driver, which communicates with the printer. With the device drivers doing the interpreting, application software developers do not have to include the specific protocol and standards for every printer that might be used by the applications they write.

System Resources

Notice in Figure 2-1 that an additional layer—beyond the application software, OS, BIOS, and device drivers—exists: system resources. Just as a chauffeur has tools, such as the steering wheel, accelerator, and brake, to control a car, and the car has tools, such as the oil warning light, to alert the chauffeur when it needs attention, software has system resources to control hardware, and hardware has system resources to alert software that it needs attention. Think of a system resource as a tool used by either hardware or software to communicate with the other.

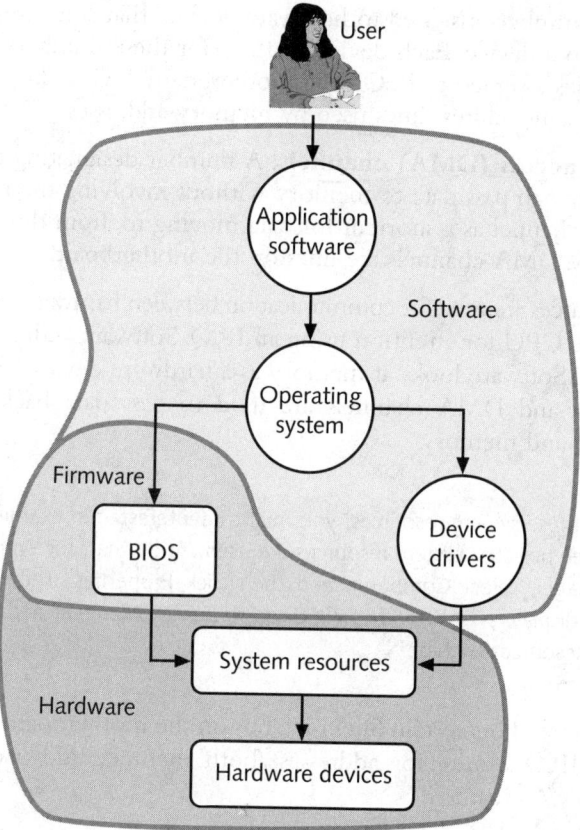

Figure 2-1   There are several layers between applications and hardware

 The OS communicates with hardware by using these resources, but the OS does not relate directly to the system resources; it uses BIOS or device drivers for the interface.

There are four types of system resources:

- **Interrupt request numbers (IRQs).** A control line of a motherboard bus that a hardware device can use to signal the CPU that the device needs attention. Some lines have a higher priority for attention than others. Each IRQ line is assigned a number (0 to 15) to identify it.

- **Memory addresses.** Numbers that are assigned to physical memory located either in RAM or ROM chips. Software can access this memory by using these addresses. On the motherboard, memory addresses are transferred on the address bus.

- **I/O addresses.** Numbers assigned to hardware devices that software uses to send a command to a device. Each device "listens" for these numbers and responds to the ones assigned to it. On the motherboard, I/O addresses are transferred on the same address lines used by memory addresses.

- **Direct memory access (DMA) channels.** A number designating a channel whereby the device can pass data to memory without involving the CPU. Think of a DMA channel as a shortcut for data moving to/from the device and memory. Physically, DMA channels are lines on the motherboard.

All four types of system resources are used for communication between hardware and software. Hardware devices signal the CPU for attention using an IRQ. Software addresses a device by one of its I/O addresses. Software looks at memory as a hardware device and addresses it with memory addresses, and DMA channels are used to pass data back and forth between a hardware device and memory.

 TIP As you read about these system resources, you might be interested in examining your own computer to see how the system resources are used. To do that, for Windows 98, go to Device Manager, select Computer, and then click Properties. The Computer Properties window displays. For Windows 2000, go to Device Manager and, from the menu, click View, Resources by type.

All four system resources depend on certain lines on a bus on the motherboard. Some lines on the bus are used for IRQs, some for addresses (both memory addresses and I/O addresses), and some for DMA channels.

Interrupt Request Number (IRQ)

When a hardware device needs the CPU to do something, such as when the keyboard needs the CPU to process a keystroke after a key has been pressed, the device needs a way to get the CPU's attention, and the CPU must know what to do once its attention is turned to the device. These interruptions to the CPU are called **hardware interrupts**, and the device initiates an interrupt by placing voltage on the designated IRQ (interrupt request) line assigned to it, somewhat like how a passenger on a trolley car pulls a cord to signal the driver to stop. This voltage on the line serves as a signal to the CPU that the device has a request that needs processing. (Often, a hardware device that needs attention from the CPU is referred to as "needing servicing.") Many processes that the CPU carries out are initiated by interrupts, and are said to be interrupt-driven.

 You'll learn more about hardware interrupts, as well as software interrupts, later on in this chapter.

In the old days, only five IRQs were available for devices, and each device had to have its own IRQ. This made it difficult for more than five devices to be connected to a PC at any one time. Now, however, certain IRQs can be shared by several devices. For example, notice in Figure 2-2 that IRQ 11 is being shared by several devices on this Windows 2000 system. You can look to the left of the IRQ number and see that some of these IRQs are being managed by the ISA bus controller, and the others are managed by the PCI bus controller. ISA-managed IRQs cannot be shared, but PCI-managed IRQs can be shared.

Figure 2-2   Windows 2000 Device Manager shows the current assignments for system resources

TIP   To see how the IRQs are assigned on your computer, use MSD for DOS and Device Manager for Windows 9x and Windows 2000/XP. (Windows NT does not have Device Manager.) For Windows 9x, click Start, point to Settings, click Control Panel, and double-click System. Click the Device Manager tab. Select Computer and click Properties. For Windows 2000, a quick way to access Device Manager is to right-click My Computer on the desktop and select Properties from the shortcut menu. Click the Hardware tab and then click the Device Manager button. On the menu, click View, then Resources by Type, if necessary. Click the plus sign next to Interrupt request (IRQ) to open the list of assigned IRQs.

With interrupts, the hardware device or the software initiates communication by sending a signal to the CPU, but a device can be serviced in another way, called **polling**. With polling, software that is constantly running has the CPU periodically check the hardware device to see if service is needed. Not very many devices use polling as the method of communication; most hardware devices use interrupts. A joystick is one example of a device that does use polling, however. Software that is written to manage a joystick has the CPU check the joystick periodically to see if the device has data to communicate, which is why a joystick does not need an IRQ to work.

Memory Addresses

An operating system relates to memory as a long list of cells that it can use to hold data and instructions, somewhat like seats in a theater can hold people (see Figure 2-3). Just as each seat is assigned a number, each memory location or cell is assigned a number beginning with zero. These number assignments are made when the OS is first loaded and are called **memory addresses**, and the numbers are assigned to physical memory located either in RAM or ROM chips. Software can access this memory by using these addresses. These addresses are most often displayed on the screen as hexadecimal (base 16 or hex) numbers in segment/offset form (for example, C800:5, which, in decimal, is 819,205).

Let's first look at how memory addresses are assigned, and then we'll turn our attention to how the CPU makes use of them.

How Memory Addresses Are Assigned The CPU has a fixed number of memory addresses available to it, determined by the CPU and the bus it is using. These memory addresses can be assigned to any type of physical memory in the system that needs to be addressed by the CPU, including ROM and RAM chips on expansion cards and ROM and RAM chips on the motherboard, which can hold either data or instructions. Once addresses have been assigned, the CPU sees this physical memory as a single list that can be accessed by using the memory addresses.

 Memory addresses are, for the most part, assigned during the boot process.

Figure 2-3 Memory addresses are assigned to each location in memory and these locations can store data or instructions

The number of available memory addresses partly depends on the size of the memory bus. Today's CPUs use a 32-bit or wider address bus, which makes it possible for them to address 4 gigabytes (GB) of memory or more, although no desktop PC today actually has that much RAM. Older PCs, however, could address only 1MB of memory, which was allocated by DOS and Windows 9x systems as shown in Table 2-3.

Table 2-1 applies to DOS and Windows 9x only. Windows NT/2000/XP uses an altogether different memory-mapping design, in which there is no conventional, upper, or extended memory; it's all just memory.

Table 2-1   Division of memory under DOS and Windows 9x

Range of Memory Addresses	Range Using Hex Terminology	Type of Memory
0 to 640K	0 to A0000	Conventional or base memory
640K to 1024K	A0000 to FFFFF	Upper memory (A through F ranges)
Above 1024K	100000 and up	Extended memory

Windows offers a calculator that can quickly convert numbers in binary, digital, and hexadecimal. You can use it to follow along with the conversions used here. Enter a number in one number system, and then click another number system to make the conversion. To access the calculator in Windows 9x or Windows NT/2000/XP, click Start, Programs, Accessories, Calculator.

The first 640K of memory was used by DOS and applications, and the addresses from 640K to 1024K were used by the BIOS and device drivers. Later, when the 16-bit ISA bus with 24 address lines was introduced, memory addresses above 1024K became available and were called **extended memory**. Windows 9x still uses these same divisions of memory, although it makes the most use of extended memory.

Memory addresses are expressed using hexadecimal notation. Because the hex numbers in upper memory begin with A through F, the divisions of upper memory are often referred to as the A range, B range, C range, and so on, up to the F range.

Once memory addresses have been assigned to memory, they can be used for communication with all software layers. For example, during output operations, application software must pass information to the OS, which in turn passes that information to a device driver or to the BIOS. The BIOS and device drivers managing input devices must pass information to the OS, which passes it to the application software. These layers of software all identify the data they want to share by referring to the memory address of the data.

Shadowing ROM   Sometimes system BIOS programs are copied from the ROM BIOS memory into RAM because reading from RAM chips is generally faster than reading from

ROM chips. The process of copying programs from ROM to RAM for execution is called **shadowing ROM,** or just **shadow RAM**. If the ROM programs are executed directly from the ROM chips, the memory addresses are assigned to this ROM. If the programs are first copied to RAM and then executed, the same memory addresses are assigned to this area of RAM. The instructions work the same, either way.

In the setup of your computer, you usually have the choice of whether to shadow system BIOS. For DOS and Windows 9*x*, accept the default setting for this option.

I/O Addresses

Another system resource that is made available to hardware devices is input/output addresses, or I/O addresses. I/O addresses, or **port addresses**, sometimes simply called **ports**, are numbers that the CPU can use to access hardware devices in much the same way that it uses memory addresses to access physical memory. The address bus on the motherboard sometimes carries memory addresses and sometimes carries I/O addresses. If the address bus has been set to carry I/O addresses, then each device is "listening" to this bus (see Figure 2-4). If the address belongs to it, then it responds; otherwise, it ignores the request for information. In short, the CPU "knows" a hardware device as a group of I/O addresses. If it wants to know the status of a printer or a floppy drive, for example, it passes a particular I/O address down the address bus on the motherboard.

1. CPU turns up signal on bus that says, "I/O addresses are on the address line"
2. All I/O device controllers listen for their addresses
3. CPU transmits an I/O address
4. The device that "owns" that address responds

Figure 2-4   I/O address lines on a bus work much like an old telephone party line; all devices "hear" the addresses, but only one responds

A few common assignments for I/O addresses are listed in Table 2-2. (Because these addresses are hex numbers, you sometimes see them written with 0x in front, like this: 0x0040, or with the h following, like this: 0040h.)

Table 2-2   IRQs and I/O addresses for devices

IRQ	I/O Address	Device
0	0040-005F	System timer
1	0060-006F	Keyboard controller
2	00A0-00AF	Access to IRQs above 7
3	02F8-02FF	COM2
3	02E8-02EF	COM4
4	03F8-03FF	COM1
4	03E8-03EF	COM3
5	0278-027F	Sound card or parallel port LPT2
6	03F0-03F7	Floppy drive controller
7	0378-037F	Printer parallel port LPT1
8	0070-007F	Real-time clock
9-10		Available
11		SCSI or available (SCSI is a bus system often used for fast hard drives)
12	238-23F	System-board mouse
13	0F8-0FF	Math coprocessor
14	1F0-1F7	IDE hard drive
15	170-170	Secondary IDE hard drive or available

Because IBM made many address assignments when the first PC was manufactured in the late 1970s, common devices such as hard drives, floppy drives, or keyboards have no problem with I/O addresses. Their BIOS can simply be programmed to use these standard addresses. Devices such as scanners or network cards, however, which were not assigned I/O addresses in the original IBM list, can be configured to use more than one group of addresses depending on how they are set up during either the installation or boot process. Figure 2-5 shows how I/O addresses are assigned on a Windows 98 computer.

COM and LPT Assignments

Notice the COM and LPT assignments in Table 2-2. COM1 and COM2 are preconfigured assignments that can be made to serial devices such as modems, and LPT1 and LPT2 are preconfigured assignments that can be made to parallel devices such as printers. For example, rather than assigning an IRQ and some I/O addresses to a modem, the modem is configured to use the assignments previously made to COM2, making it easier to configure the modem and to avoid conflicts with other devices that also need an IRQ and some I/O addresses.

It is common for a system to assign COM1 or COM2 to a serial port and LPT1 or LPT2 to a parallel port. When an external modem connects to a serial port that has been assigned COM1, the modem is using the system resources assigned to COM1. If a printer is connected to the parallel port assigned to LPT1, it is using the system resources assigned to LPT1.

Figure 2-5   Use Device Manager to view I/O address assignments on a Windows 98 computer

Direct Memory Access (DMA) Channels

Another system resource used by hardware and software is a DMA (direct memory access) channel, a shortcut method whereby an I/O device can send data directly to memory, bypassing the CPU. A chip on the motherboard contains the DMA logic and manages the process.

Some devices, such as a hard drive or sound card, are designed to use DMA channels, and others, such as the mouse, are not. Those that use the channels might be able to use only a certain channel, say channel 3, and no other. Alternatively, the BIOS might have the option of changing a DMA channel number to avoid conflicts with other devices. Conflicts occur when more than one device uses the same channel.

 DMA channels are not as popular as they once were because their design makes them slower than newer methods. However, slower devices such as floppy drives, sound cards, and tape drives may still use DMA channels.

Using System Resources

Now let's look at examples of how the system resources help carry out hardware and software interrupts. This will help show you how the resources work together.

Hardware Interrupts Once the CPU is interrupted by an IRQ, the job of the IRQ is over and the CPU must handle the interruption. To do that, the CPU must use a program designed to interface with the device. This program to process an interrupt is called the **request handler** or **interrupt handler**. The program is either a part of the total BIOS in a system or is a device driver that had previously been installed on the hard drive.

To see how the process of handling an interrupt works, we'll use the example of a keyboard that uses an IRQ to request attention from the CPU. Figure 2-6 shows the process it uses, which works like this:

1. A key is pressed on the keyboard. The keyboard controller puts voltage on its assigned IRQ 1 to the CPU, saying "I need attention." The CPU sees the IRQ, acknowledges it, and turns its attention to servicing it. By sending the acknowledgment, it is requesting that the device controller send a number called an *interrupt* (abbreviated *INT*) that tells the CPU what service the device needs.

2. The keyboard controller sends INT 9 to the CPU, saying that it has a pressed key to process. The CPU uses this value to locate the program to handle this interrupt.

3. The CPU looks to a table in RAM called the **interrupt vector table**, or **vector table**, that contains a list of memory address locations of interrupt handlers. The INT value passed to the CPU by the controller points to the correct row in the table where the memory addresses in which the instructions to service the keyboard (a portion of system BIOS) are stored.

4. The CPU looks to the location in memory of the request handler and begins to follow the instructions there.

5. The CPU, following the interrupt handler instructions, processes the keystroke.

Figure 2-6 The story of a hardware interrupt, where the request handler is BIOS

The BIOS and operating system initialize the interrupt vector table during booting, but later another program can modify the vector table to change the interrupt handler location to execute another program instead. This is a common method that a virus uses to propagate itself.

Software Interrupts   When software, rather, than hardware, initiates communication, such as when the user of word-processing software issues the command to save a file to the hard drive, this is known as a **software interrupt**, which is demonstrated in Figure 2-7. Both hardware and software interrupts use the same numeric INT (interrupt) values to communicate their requests to the CPU. The interrupt value for a call to the hard drive for I/O interaction is INT 13.

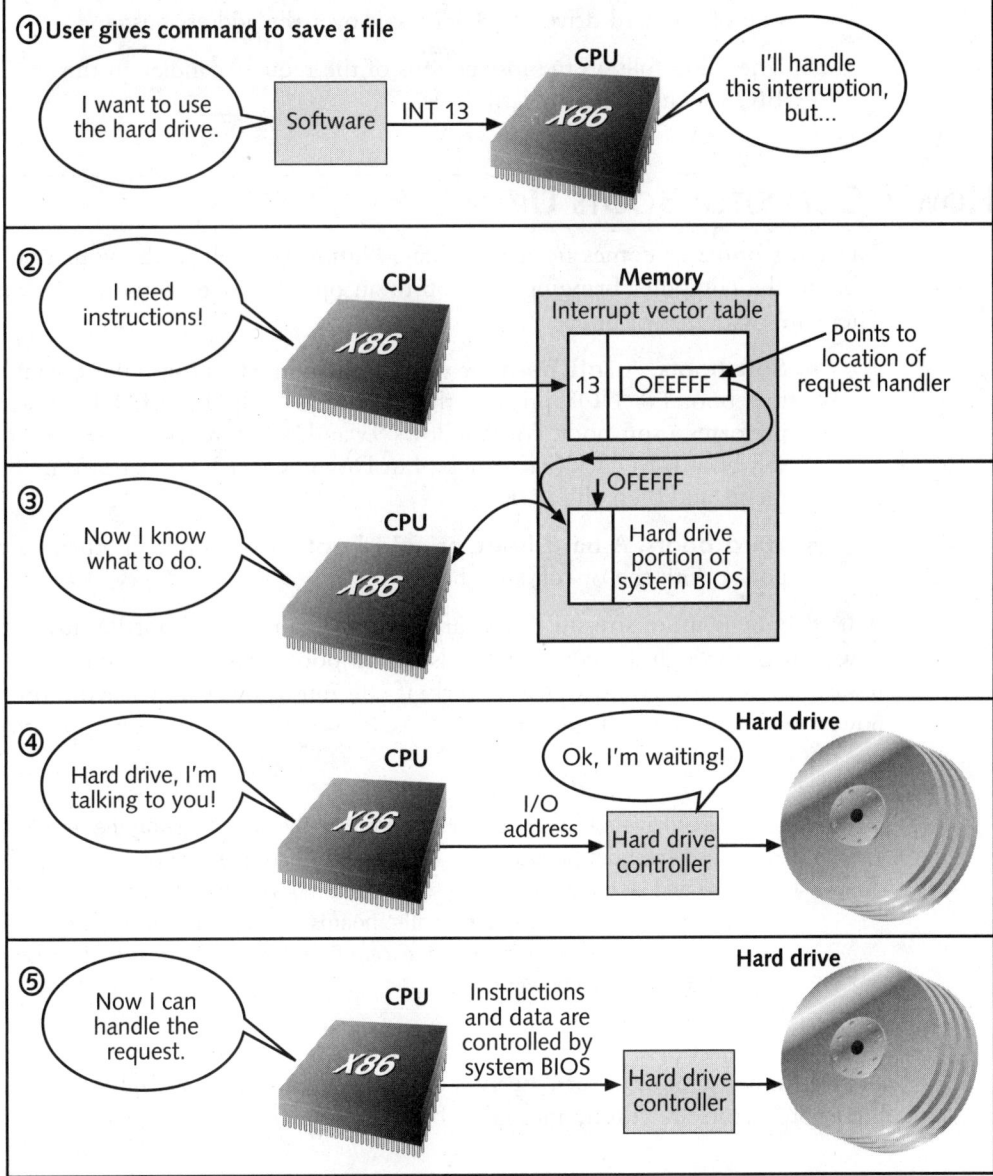

Figure 2-7   The story of a software interrupt

The software interrupt process as shown in Figure 2-7 works like this:

1. The CPU receives the software interrupt, INT 13.

2. The CPU turns to the interrupt vector table, using the INT value to locate the correct request handler.

3. The CPU locates the handler in memory.

4. The CPU alerts the hard drive that instructions are forthcoming by sending one of the hard drive's I/O addresses over the address bus.

5. The CPU follows the instructions of the request handler, in this case, system BIOS, to manage the hard drive.

HOW A COMPUTER BOOTS UP

The term **booting** comes from the phrase "lifting yourself up by your bootstraps" and refers to the computer bringing itself up to an operable state without user intervention. There are two types of boots:

- **Soft boots.** A **soft boot**, or **warm boot**, involves using the operating system to reboot. For DOS, pressing the three keys Ctrl, Alt, and Del at the same time performs a soft boot. For Windows 9x and Windows NT/2000/XP, one way to soft boot is to click Start, click Shut Down, select Restart from the Shut Down menu, and then click OK.

- **Hard boots.** A **hard boot**, or **cold boot**, involves initially turning on the power with the on/off switch.

A hard boot is more stressful on your machine than a soft boot because of the initial power surge through the equipment. Also a soft boot is faster. Always use the soft boot to restart unless that method will not work. If you must power down, avoid turning off the power switch and immediately turning it back on without a pause, because this can damage the machine.

 Some PCs have a reset button on the front of the case. Pressing the reset button starts the boot process at an earlier point than does the operating-system method and is, therefore, a little slower, but might work when the operating-system method fails. (For newer motherboards, pressing the reset button is the same thing as powering off and on, except that there is no stress to the system caused by the initial power surge.)

A successful boot process depends on the hardware, the BIOS, and the operating system all performing without errors; if errors do occur, they might or might not stall or lock up the boot. (Errors are communicated as beeps or as messages on screen.)

2

The functions performed during the boot are listed here. Startup BIOS is in control for the first three steps and the beginning of the fourth step, at which point control is turned over to the OS.

1. Startup BIOS tests essential hardware components. This test is called the power-on self test (POST).

2. Setup information is used to configure both hardware and software.

3. Hardware components are assigned system resources that they will later use for communication.

4. Startup BIOS finds the OS, which is loaded, configured, and executed.

5. Hardware devices are matched up with the BIOS and device drivers that control them.

6. Some application software may be loaded and executed.

This boot process can be divided into four basic parts:

- **POST.** The ROM BIOS startup program surveys hardware resources and needs, and assigns system resources to meet those needs (see Figure 2-8). The ROM BIOS startup program begins the startup process by reading configuration information stored in DIP switches, jumpers, and the CMOS chip, and then comparing that information to the hardware—the CPU, video card, disk drive, hard drive, and so on. Some hardware devices have BIOSes of their own that request resources from the startup BIOS, which attempts to assign these system resources as needed.

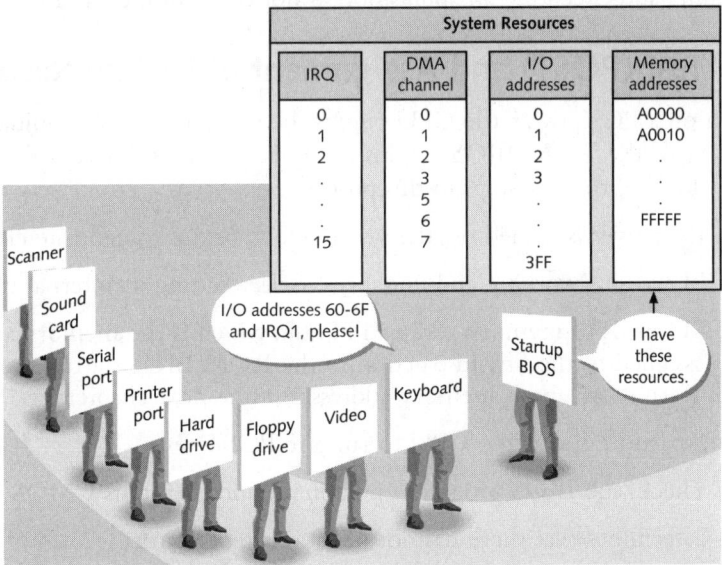

Figure 2-8   The ROM BIOS startup program surveys hardware resources and needs and assigns system resources to satisfy those needs

- **The ROM BIOS startup program searches for and loads an OS.** Most often, the OS is loaded from logical drive C: on the hard drive. Configuration information on the CMOS chip tells the startup BIOS where to look for the OS. Most newer BIOSes support loading the OS from the hard drive, a floppy disk, a CD, or a Zip drive. The BIOS turns to that device, reads the beginning files of the OS, copies them into memory, and then turns control over to the OS. This part of the loading process works the same for any operating system; only the OS files being loaded change.

- **The OS configures the system and completes its own loading.** The OS checks some of the same things that startup BIOS checked, such as available memory and whether that memory is reliable. Additionally, the OS continues beyond that by loading the software to control a mouse, CD-ROM, scanner, and other peripheral devices. These devices generally have device drivers stored on the hard drive.

- **The user executes application software.** When you tell the OS to execute an application, the OS first must find the application software on the hard drive, CD-ROM, or other secondary storage device, copy the software into memory, and then turn control over to it. Finally, you can command the application software, which makes requests to the OS, which, in turn, uses the system resources, system BIOS, and device drivers to interface with and control the hardware. At this point, the user is like the passenger in the back seat of the car with the chauffeur at the wheel. The trip has begun.

Let's look a bit more closely at the first three of these steps, beginning with the POST. (The fourth part, loading and executing an application, is not covered in detail in this book.)

Power-on Self Test (POST) and Assignment of System Resources

When you turn on a PC's power, the CPU begins the startup process by initializing itself and then turning to the ROM BIOS for instructions. The ROM BIOS then performs POST. Listed below are the key steps in this process.

1. When the power is turned on, the system clock begins to generate clock pulses.

2. The CPU begins working and initializes itself, resetting its internal values.

3. The CPU turns to memory address FFFF0h, which is the memory address always assigned to the first instruction in the ROM BIOS startup program. (You'll learn more about memory addresses in the next chapter.)

4. This instruction directs the CPU to run the POST tests.

5. POST checks the BIOS program operating it and then tests CMOS RAM.

6. A test determines that there has not been a battery failure.

7. Hardware interrupts are disabled, which this means that pressing a key on the keyboard or using another input device at this point will not affect anything.

8. Tests are run on the CPU, and it is further initialized.

9. A check determines if this is a cold boot. If so, the first 16K of RAM is tested.

10. Hardware devices installed on the computer are inventoried and compared to configuration information.

11. Video, memory, keyboard, floppy disk drives, hard drives, ports, and other hardware devices are tested and configured (if you press and hold any keys while POST checks the keyboard, an error occurs); the hardware that POST finds is checked against the data stored in the CMOS chip, jumpers, and/or DIP switches to determine if they agree. In addition, IRQ, I/O addresses, and DMA assignments are made. The OS will later complete this process.

 During POST, before the CPU has checked the video system, errors encountered up to this point are communicated by beeps. Short and long beeps indicate an error; the coding for the beeps depends on the BIOS. After POST checks and verifies the video controller card (note that POST does not check to see if a monitor is present or working), POST can use the monitor to display its progress. After checking video, POST checks RAM by writing and reading data. A running count of RAM is displayed on the monitor during this phase.

12. Some devices are set up to go into "sleep mode" to conserve electricity.

13. The DMA controller is checked.

14. Interrupt vectors are moved into the interrupt vector table.

15. The interrupt controller is checked.

16. CMOS setup (a BIOS program to change CMOS configuration data) is run if requested.

17. BIOS begins its search for an OS.

Assigning System Resources

System resources are assigned to devices by more than one method. Jumpers and DIP switches might be set to request a resource (for example, a jumper might be set "on" if IRQ 5 is requested or "off" if IRQ 7 is requested), or the resources needed might simply be hard-coded into the BIOS as part of the ROM programming that cannot be changed.

For earlier computers, system resources were always assigned to the device during the boot process. Think of the process as a dialog: The startup BIOS recognizes that a hardware device is present. The BIOS asks the device, "What resources do you need?" The device says, "I need this IRQ, these I/O addresses, this DMA channel, and these addresses in upper memory for my BIOS." For legacy hardware, a device is the sole owner of these resources, and problems occur when more than one device attempts to use the same resource. (However, remember from our earlier discussion of IRQs that some newer buses allow more than one device to share the same IRQ, and newer protected-mode BIOSes don't require upper memory addresses.) Today, more flexible Plug and Play devices simply say, "I need one IRQ, some I/O addresses, and this many memory addresses for my BIOS. Please tell me the resources I can use."

If a computer takes full advantage of the Windows 9x OS, its BIOS is a Plug and Play BIOS, meaning that BIOS configures the Plug and Play devices before it loads Windows 9x. A Plug and Play device allows BIOS to select the device's computer resources, such as an IRQ, an I/O address, and DMA channels. BIOS first enables the devices that are not Plug and Play, and then tries to make the Plug and Play devices use the leftover resources. The BIOS then turns this information over to Windows when it loads, which completes the assignment of resources.

Plug and Play

Plug and Play (PnP) is a standard designed to make the installation of new hardware devices easier. If a system's BIOS is a Plug and Play BIOS, it will begin the process of configuring hardware devices in the system. It gathers information about the devices and then passes that information to the operating system. If the operating system is also Plug and Play compliant, it will use that information to complete the hardware-configuration process. For a system to be fully Plug and Play, the BIOS, the operating system, and all attached devices must be Plug and Play. (A Plug and Play hardware device will have something like Windows 9x Ready or Windows 9x Compliant written on the box.)

The Plug and Play standard applies to the operating system, to BIOS on the motherboard, and to BIOS on devices. Windows 9x and Windows 2000/XP support Plug and Play, but Windows NT does not. Windows 2000/XP Plug and Play is more advanced than the Windows 9x version and does not use the startup BIOS to help with Plug and Play configurations. Therefore, on a Windows 2000/XP system, it is not important if the motherboard BIOS is Plug and Play.

Plug and Play under Windows or the motherboard BIOS does not assign resources to a device if the device does not allow it. For example, if a legacy sound card requires a certain group of upper memory addresses that are hard-coded into its on-board BIOS, there's nothing that Plug and Play can do about that. (Hard-coded is computer jargon for something being coded so that it cannot be changed.) Plug and Play simply tries to work around the problem as best it can. If two non–Plug and Play hardware devices require the same resource and their BIOS does not provide for accepting a substitute, these two devices cannot coexist on the same PC.

Newer devices that contain a BIOS that is Plug and Play compliant are more cooperative. At startup, they simply send a request and then wait for the OS to assign the resources they need to work. Startup BIOS that is Plug and Play does some of the up-front work for Windows 9x, but Windows 2000 does all its Plug and Play configuration without the help of BIOS. How Windows 9x and BIOS cooperate to use Plug and Play during startup is covered later in the chapter.

ESCD (extended system configuration data) Plug and Play BIOS is an enhanced version of Plug and Play that creates a list of all the things you have done manually to the configuration that Plug and Play does not do on its own. This ESCD list is written to the BIOS chip so that the next time you boot, the startup BIOS can faithfully relay that information to Windows 9x. The BIOS chip for ESCD BIOS is a special RAM chip called *Permanent RAM*, or *PRAM*, that can hold data written to it without the benefit of a battery, which the CMOS setup chip requires.

How the BIOS Finds and Loads the OS

Once POST and the first pass at assignment of resources are complete, the next step is to load an OS. Most often, the OS is loaded from logical drive C: on the hard drive. The minimum information required on the hard drive to load an OS is listed below (you can see some of these items labeled in Figure 2-9).

- A small segment (512 bytes) of information at the very beginning of the hard drive is called the Master Boot Record (MBR). The MBR contains two items:

- The master boot program, which is needed to locate the beginning of the OS on the drive.

- A table that contains a map to the logical drives on the hard drive and indicates which drive is the boot drive. This table is called the *partition table*.

- At the beginning of the boot drive (usually drive C:) is the OS boot record, which loads the first program file of the OS. For Windows 9x, that program is Io.sys, and for Windows NT/2000/XP, that program is Ntldr.

- The boot loader program for the OS (Io.sys or Ntldr) begins the process of loading the OS into memory. The program files needed for each OS are covered later in the chapter.

Figure 2-9   A hard drive might contain more than one logical drive; the Master Boot Record at the beginning of the drive contains information about the location of each logical drive, indicates which drive is the boot drive, and holds the master boot program that begins the boot process for the operating system

Often a hard drive is divided or partitioned into more than one logical drive, for example, drive C: and drive D:, as seen in Figure 2-9. Whether a hard drive has one or several logical drives, it always contains a single partition table, located at the very beginning of the drive, which tells BIOS these things:

- How many partitions the drive has and how each partition is divided into one or more logical drives
- Which partition contains the drive to be used for booting (called the active partition)
- Where each logical drive begins and ends

The master boot program at the beginning of the table is used to start the boot process from the hard drive. One logical drive on the hard drive is designated as the boot drive, and the OS is stored on it. At the beginning of this logical drive is the OS boot record, which knows the names of the files that contain the core programs of the OS.

The process for BIOS to load the OS begins with BIOS looking to CMOS setup to find out which secondary storage device should contain the OS (see Figure 2-10). Setup might instruct the BIOS to first look to drive C:, and, if no OS is found there, then to try drive A:; or the order might be A: and then C:. If BIOS looks first to drive A: and does not find a disk in the drive, it turns to drive C:. If it first looks to drive A: and finds a disk in the drive, but the disk does not contain the OS, then an error message is displayed. You must replace the disk with one that contains the OS or simply remove the disk to force the BIOS to continue on to drive C: to find the OS.

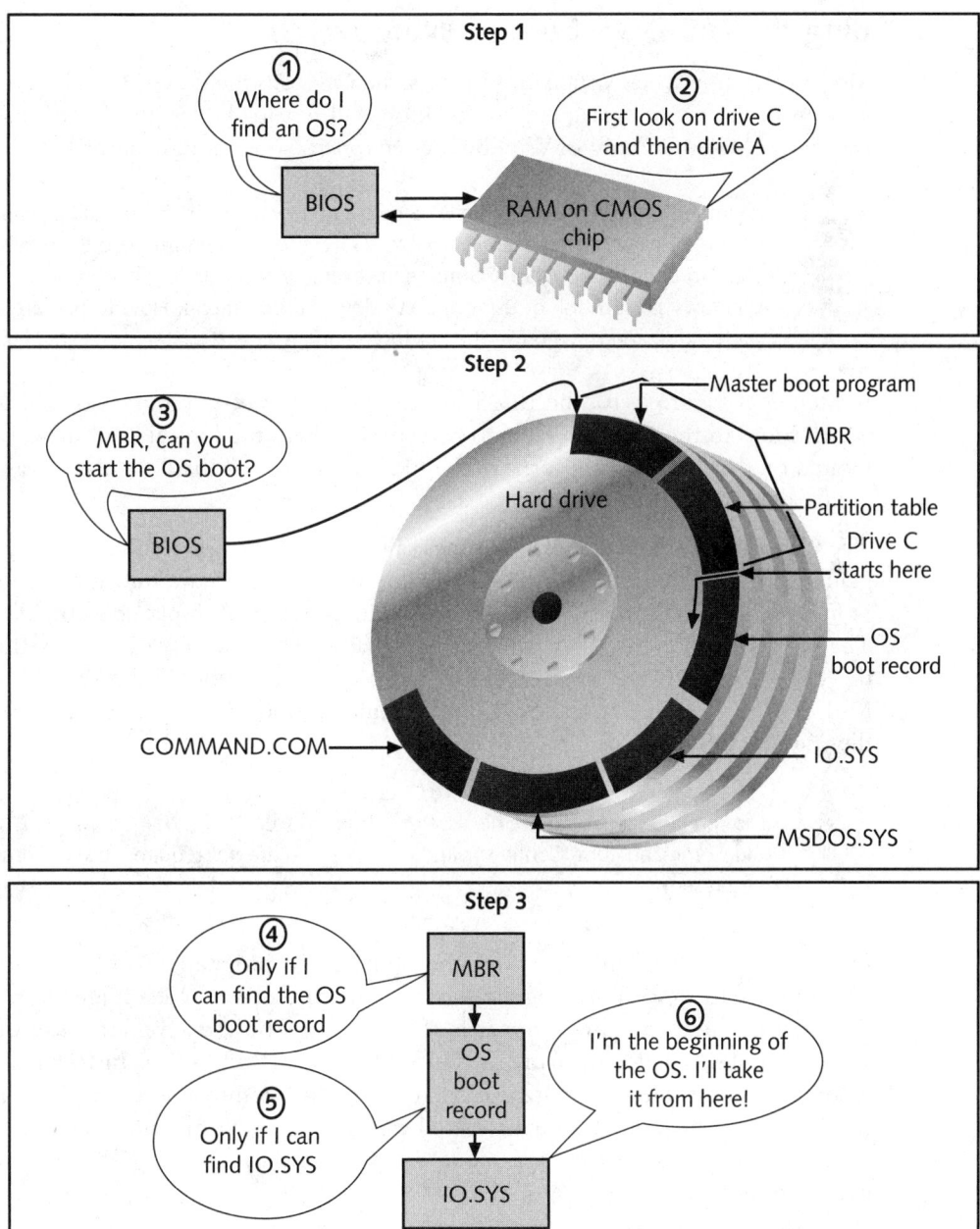

Figure 2-10   BIOS searches for and begins to load an operating system (in this example, Windows is the OS)

Loading the MS-DOS Core of Windows 9x

Most of the time when you load Windows, the OS loads the desktop. If, however, the GUI portion of the OS is corrupted, the desktop will not load. It is possible to load only the real-mode MS-DOS core of Windows, which gives you a command prompt.

 It's important to understand the DOS core and how to use the command prompt because they are often used as troubleshooting tools when the hard drive fails. You can boot to this MS-DOS mode in several ways, including booting from a Windows startup disk or using the Windows Startup menu. How to prepare a startup disk and how to use the Startup menu are covered later in the chapter.

In Step 2 of Figure 2-10, the BIOS locates the master boot program on the hard drive, which looks to the partition table to determine where the logical boot drive is physically located on the drive. It then turns to the OS boot record of that logical drive and executes the program there.

The OS boot record program, sometimes called the **bootstrap loader**, is a very short program; it loads just one hidden file that makes up the DOS core into memory (see step 3 of Figure 2-10, and Figure 2-11). A **hidden file** is a file not displayed in the directory list. The OS boot record program knows the filename, which is Io.sys. The Io.sys file contains the basic I/O software for real mode and requires that the Msdos.sys file be present. Msdos.sys is a text file containing some parameters and switches that can be set to affect the way the OS boots.

 The three OS files that are necessary to boot to MS-DOS mode are Io.sys, Msdos.sys, and Command.com. Config.sys and Autoexec.bat are not required, but are used if they are present.

Once Io.sys is loaded into memory, the boot record program is no longer needed, and control turns to Io.sys. This program looks on the hard drive for a configuration file named Config.sys, which contains commands that tell Io.sys how many files it can open at any one time (Files=) and how many file buffers to create (Buffers=). A **buffer** is a temporary holding area for files. Config.sys also includes the commands to load device drivers (Device=) as well as other information. The following is an example of a typical command in Config.sys, which gives real-mode Io.sys access to memory above 1 MB, called extended memory:

```
Device=himem.sys
```

Several drivers can be loaded into memory from commands in Config.sys. Io.sys puts these programs in memory wherever it chooses. However, a program can request that it be put in a certain memory location.

Figure 2-11   Operating system completes the boot process; MS-DOS core is loaded and command prompt presented to user

Sometimes Config.sys is used to create a RAM drive. A **RAM drive** is an area of memory that looks and acts like a hard drive, except that it is much faster. It is sometimes used to hold data in memory when the hard drive is not accessible. The Windows 9*x* startup disk contains commands to create a RAM drive that it then uses to hold compressed files stored on the startup disk as it uncompresses them. An example of a command in Config.sys to create a RAM drive is

```
Device=ramdrive.sys 2048
```

This command tells the OS to create a RAM drive that is 2048K in size.

After Config.sys is executed, Io.sys looks for another OS file named Command.com. This file has three parts: more code to manage I/O, programs for internal OS commands such as COPY and DIR, and a short program that looks for another file named Autoexec.bat.

Some OS commands are *internal commands*, meaning that they are embedded in the Command.com file; others are *external commands*, meaning that they have their own program files. An example of an external command is Format, stored in the program file Format.com. Windows puts many of these command files in the \Windows\Command folder on the hard drive.

Command-line commands are not case-sensitive; that is, you could enter FORMAT, Format, or format.

Autoexec.bat

The filename Autoexec.bat stands for **automatically executed batch program**. The file lists OS commands that are executed automatically each time the OS is loaded. The following two commands (or similar prompt and path commands) are typically in the Autoexec.bat file:

```
PATH C:\;C:\PCTOOLS;
Restart.com
```

The PATH command lists two paths separated by semicolons. This command directs the OS to look in two different directories for program files. Without the benefit of the PATH command, the OS might not look in these locations. The Restart command causes the system to reboot.

Rather than appending an entry to the existing PATH command line, some software installation programs use the SET command to append a path to the PATH command without editing the existing PATH command line itself. It works like this:

```
SET PATH=%PATH%;C:\VERT
```

The path C:\VERT is appended to the existing PATH command.

The SET command is also used to create and assign a value to an environmental variable that can later be read by an application. A software installation program might add a SET command to your Autoexec.bat file. This command might look something like this:

```
SET MYPATH=C:\VERT
```

Later the software will use the environmental variable MYPATH to find out which folder on the hard drive contains its data.

The boot process into real mode with a command prompt is completed after Autoexec.bat has finished executing. At this point, Command.com is the program in charge, providing you with a command prompt and waiting for your command. On the other hand, if a program or menu was executed from Autoexec.bat, it might ask you for a command.

If you want to finish loading Windows, use the Win command. Enter this command at the C prompt:

```
C:\> Win
```

HOW AN OS RELATES TO OTHER SOFTWARE

Now that you have learned about several of the more important hardware devices and how system resources on the motherboard are used to enable their interaction with software, we turn our attention to the OS and how it interfaces with other software, including BIOS, device drivers, and applications. Because the CPU operates in two modes, real mode and protected mode, the OS must be able to operate in each mode, which also affects the mode that an application uses. Therefore, we begin our discussion of software by looking more carefully at each of these modes.

Real (16-Bit) and Protected (32-Bit) Operating Modes

Remember that the two modes a CPU can operate in are **real mode** (sometimes called 16-bit mode) and **protected mode** (sometimes called 32-bit mode). There are several differences between real mode and protected mode, which are discussed in this section, but the fundamental difference is that in real mode, a CPU processes 16 bits at a time and in protected mode, it processes 32 bits at a time.

In real mode, illustrated in Figure 2-12, a CPU assumes that only one application or program is running at a time, which is called single tasking, so it gives that program direct access to all hardware devices including memory. It uses a 16-bit data path and 1 MB of memory addresses, unless a memory extender is used, which is an OS utility program that provides an OS with memory addresses above 1 MB, called extended memory. The DOS and Windows 9x memory extender is Himem.sys.

 TIP Real mode is limited to 16-bit data processing because originally only 16 lines on the motherboard bus were devoted to transmitting data to and from the CPU.

Figure 2-12   Real mode, or MS-DOS mode, provides single-tasking, 1024K of memory addresses, and direct access to RAM using a 16-bit data path

In protected mode, more than one program can run at the same time, which is a type of *multitasking*. Each program can be safely contained within its own range of resources. Here lies the meaning behind the two terms, real and protected. Real mode means that the software has "real" access to the hardware, and protected mode means that more than one program can be running and each one is "protected" from the other(s).

In protected mode, as shown in Figure 2-13, more than one program can run, and the programs have access to memory addresses of 4096 MB or 4 GB, or sometimes more, depending on the motherboard, CPU, and OS being used. In protected mode, the OS does not allow a program direct access to RAM, but works as the mediator between memory and programs. This allows the OS some latitude in how it uses RAM. If the OS is low on RAM, it can store some data on the hard drive. This method of using the hard drive as though it were RAM is called **virtual memory**, and data stored in virtual memory is stored in a file on the hard drive called a **swap file** or **page file**. The OS manages the entire process, and the applications know nothing about this substitution of hardware resources for RAM. The programs running in protected mode just see memory addresses and have no idea where they are located.

Figure 2-13   Protected mode is multitasking program access to more than 1024K of memory addresses using 32-bit data segments where the OS manages direct memory access

Even after protected mode became available, hardware and software needed to be backward compatible (able to support older technology), so real mode is still supported by today's CPUs and operating systems. In fact, the CPU starts in real mode and must be told to switch to protected mode. For this reason, an OS starts in real mode and commands the CPU to switch to protected mode before allowing user interaction or loading an application. DOS and the MS-DOS mode of Windows 9x operate in real mode. Windows 9x and Windows NT/2000/XP start out in real mode and then switch to protected mode. Table 2-3 summarizes the differences between real mode and protected mode.

Table 2-3 A CPU and an OS operate in either real mode or protected mode

Real mode	Protected mode
16-bit data path	32-bit data path
Only one program runs at a time	Several programs can be loaded and running
The CPU can access up to 1 MB of memory unless a memory extender is used.	The CPU can access 4 GB or more of memory
Programs have direct access to hardware	Programs access hardware by way of the operating system

How Real and Protected Modes Are Used by an OS

The OS must be in sync with the CPU, using the same mode it is using. Not only that, applications must be compiled to run in either real or protected mode. In addition, there is a mode that is a hybrid of real and protected mode that was used by older software written for Windows 3.x, where the mode is real but the intent is to run more than one program in a pseudo-protected environment. This unique situation that occurred with Windows 3.x is important because it helps to make clear the different ways in which an OS can manage applications.

Windows 3.x was not really an OS, but neither did it act like normal application software. It was installed by DOS and used DOS as its operating system and, therefore, is considered to be a DOS application. Windows 3.x provided an *operating environment*, which refers to the overall support that it provided to application software, and applications were installed under Windows 3.x. The two primary things that Windows 3.x provided that DOS did not were a graphical user interface (GUI) and a limited form of multitasking.

16-bit and 32-bit Software

Applications and device drivers written for Windows 3.*x* are called *16-bit Windows software*. Data access is 16 bits at a time, and each program is written so that it should not infringe on the resources of other applications that might be running. Software written for Windows 95 and higher are called *32-bit drivers* or *32-bit applications*. In short, there are three general types of software that run on PCs:

- 16-bit DOS software designed to run in real mode as the only program running and expecting direct access to hardware. Under DOS, an application might attempt to serve as its own device driver. These programs could use only the first 1 MB of memory.

- 16-bit Windows software designed for Windows 3.*x* to run where other programs might also be running. These applications might or might not attempt to directly access hardware resources and could most likely use extended memory.

- 32-bit Windows software designed to run in protected mode with other software and that can be loaded in extended memory. These applications never attempt to access hardware directly.

Nearly all applications and device drivers written today are 32-bit, although 16-bit software still exists.

DOS, with or without Windows 3.*x*, is a real-mode OS. Windows 9*x*, on the other hand, is a hybrid operating system. Some of Windows 9*x* uses 16-bit data access (called 16-bit programs) and some of Windows 9*x* uses 32-bit data access (called 32-bit programs). The Windows 9*x* 16-bit components exist primarily for backward-compatibility with older hardware and software. Because the 32-bit programs access twice as much data at one time as 16-bit programs do, the 32-bit programs are faster. This fact largely explains why Windows 9*x* is faster than DOS. Windows NT/2000/XP are true 32-bit OSes; all OS programs are written using 32-bit coding methods.

A 32-bit OS will allow a 16-bit program to run by providing it with an environment that appears to the program to be a 16-bit environment. This technique is called virtual real mode.

After Windows 9x is loaded, you can switch to real mode by using the Shut Down menu. Click Start, Shut Down, and then select Restart in MS-DOS mode from the menu. You will get a C:\ prompt and a full screen from which you can run DOS commands or applications. Windows Me, Windows 2000, and Windows XP do not support accessing real mode while the OS is loaded, although recovery procedures using these operating systems sometimes are done in real mode, as you will see in later chapters.

How an OS Uses BIOS and Device Drivers

Looking back at Figure 2-1, you can see that an operating system uses programs designed to interact with specific hardware devices. There are two kinds of programs used for this purpose: BIOS and device drivers. In Figure 2-1, you can see that some device drivers belong to the OS and others do not. You can also see that the total BIOS in a system can be located in several places in the system. The OS communicates with simple devices, such as floppy drives or keyboards, through BIOS, and with more complex devices, such as digital cameras or CD-ROM drives, through device drivers. We first look at the BIOS and then turn our attention to device drivers.

How an OS Uses System BIOS

System BIOS contains the programming instructions to run the simple hardware devices that are common to every system, specifically the keyboard and floppy disk drive. In addition, system BIOS can be used to access the hard drive. In the case of the hard drive, an OS has a choice of using system BIOS or device drivers. Most often, it will use device drivers because they are faster. One reason device drivers are faster than system BIOS is that device drivers are executed from RAM, and BIOS is stored in ROM, and RAM access is faster than ROM access. However, sometimes the OS will use system BIOS to access the hard drive when older software requires it.

 There is a good way to determine whether the BIOS or a device driver is controlling a device. If the device is configured using CMOS setup, most likely system BIOS controls it. If the device is configured using the OS, most likely a driver controls it.

For example, in Figure 2-14, the setup main menu for an Award BIOS system shows the ability to configure, or set, the system date and time, the Supervisor Password (power-on password), floppy drive diskettes, the hard drive, and the keyboard. Figure 2-15 shows another setup window for this same BIOS that can configure serial ports, an infrared port, and a parallel port. All these devices can be controlled by system BIOS. On the other hand, there is no setup window in this BIOS to control the DVD drive or Zip drive that are installed on this system. The BIOS is not aware of these devices; this means they are controlled by device drivers.

```
                         AwardBIOS Setup Utility
    Main      Advanced  Power     Boot    Exit

    System Time          [11:42:09]            Item Specific Help
    System Date          [04/04/2000]
    Legacy Diskette A    [1.44M, 3.5 in.]    <Enter> to select field;
    Legacy Diskette B    [None]              <+>, <-> to change value
    Floppy 3 Mode Support [Disabled]

  ▶ Primary Master       [Auto]
  ▶ Primary Slave        [Auto]
  ▶ Secondary Master     [Auto]
  ▶ Secondary Slave      [Auto]
  ▶ Keyboard Features

    Language             [English]
    Supervisor Password  [Disabled]
    User Password        [Disabled]
    Halt On              [All Errors]
    Installed Memory     128MB

    F1   Help  ↑↓ Select Item  -/+   Change Values   F5   Setup Defaults
    ESC  Exit  ⇄  Select Menu   Enter Select Sub Menu  F10  Save and Exit
```

Figure 2-14   Use the BIOS setup main menu for Award BIOS to configure some of the devices controlled by system BIOS

```
                       Award BIOS Setup Utility
         Advanced

┌──────────────────────────────────────────┬──────────────────────────┐
│        I/O Device Configuration           │   Item Specific Help     │
├──────────────────────────────────────────┼──────────────────────────┤
│  Onboard FDC Swap A & B      [No Swap]    │                          │
│  Floppy Disk Access Control  [R/W]        │  <Enter> to select if    │
│                                           │  switch drive letter     │
│  Onboard Serial Port 1:      [3F8H/IRQ4]  │  assignments or not.     │
│  Onboard Serial Port 2:      [2F8H/IRQ3]  │                          │
│  UART2 Use Infrared          [Disabled]   │                          │
│                                           │                          │
│  Onboard Parallel Port:      [378H/IRQ7]  │                          │
│  Parallel Port Mode:         [ECP + EPP]  │                          │
│  ECP DMA Select:             [3]          │                          │
│                                           │                          │
│                                           │                          │
│                                           │                          │
│                                           │                          │
│                                           │                          │
│                                           │                          │
├──────────────────────────────────────────┴──────────────────────────┤
│  F1   Help  ↑↓  Select Item  -/+   Change Values   F5   Setup Defaults│
│  ESC  Exit  ⇄   Select Menu  Enter Select Sub Menu F10  Save and Exit │
└──────────────────────────────────────────────────────────────────────┘
```

Figure 2-15   Use this Award BIOS setup window to configure several I/O devices, including the serial, parallel and infrared ports

 TIP CMOS setup windows are accessed during startup. A system displays a message at the bottom of the screen saying something like "Press Del to enter setup." Pressing the indicated key launches a program stored on the ROM BIOS microchip to change the contents of CMOS RAM. This BIOS setup program provides windows like those in Figures 2-14 and 2-15.

How Device Drivers Control Hardware

Device drivers, which are software designed to interface with specific hardware devices, serve the same functions as BIOS programs, but unlike BIOS, they are stored on the hard drive rather than on ROM chips. Some device drivers are provided by the OS, and some are provided by the manufacturer of the specific hardware device with which they are designed to interface. In either case, unlike BIOS, device drivers are usually written for a particular OS and must be rewritten to be used with another.

When you purchase a printer, DVD drive, Zip drive, digital camera, scanner, or other hardware device, bundled with the device is a set of floppy disks or CDs that contain the device drivers (see Figure 2-16). You must install these device drivers under the operating system so it will have the necessary software to control the device. In most cases, you install the device and then install the device drivers. There are a few exceptions, however, such as a digital camera using a serial port to download pictures. In this case, you install the software to drive the digital camera before you plug in the camera. (See the device documentation to learn what to do first.)

Figure 2-16   A device such as this CD-ROM drive comes packaged with its device drives stored on a floppy disk or CD. Alternately, you can use device drivers built into the OS

You can find device drivers in a number of sources. Some come with and are part of the operating system, some come with hardware devices when they are purchased, and some are provided for download over the Internet from a device manufacturer's Web site.

There are two kinds of device drivers: 16-bit real-mode drivers and 32-bit protected-mode drivers. Windows 9*x* supports both, but Windows NT/2000/XP uses only 32-bit drivers.

Device Drivers Under Windows 9*x*   Windows 9*x* comes with 32-bit drivers for hundreds of hardware devices, and automatically loads these drivers into extended memory (memory above 1024K) at startup or when the device first needs them. That said, not all older devices are supported by Windows drivers, so a system might sometimes need to use an older 16-bit real-mode device driver. These 16-bit drivers are loaded by entries in the Config.sys, Autoexec.bat, and System.ini files, text files used to configure DOS and Windows 3.x that are supported by Windows 9x for backward-compatibility. These drivers use upper-memory addresses. When the driver is installed, the driver-installation program makes appropriate entries in these files.

 Under DOS, when a program such as a device driver stays in memory until it is required by the CPU, it is called a **terminate-and-stay-resident (TSR) program**. The term is seldom used today, except when talking about real-mode programs.

Windows uses Autoexec.bat and Config.sys in order to be backward-compatible with DOS, and uses System.ini in order to be backward-compatible with Windows 3x. However, using 16-bit drivers can slow performance, so to get the most out of Windows 9x, you should use 32-bit protected-mode drivers designed for Windows 9x. When selecting a driver to install, be sure the driver claims to be Windows 9x compatible, which means that it is a 32-bit driver and you can install the driver using the Add New Hardware wizard. If the driver must be installed using a setup program provided by the driver manufacturer and cannot be installed using the Add New Hardware wizard, then it is a 16-bit driver.

Windows 9x keeps information about 32-bit drivers in the *Windows registry*, a database of hardware and software settings, Windows configuration settings, user parameters, and application settings. Windows 32-bit drivers are sometimes called dynamic drivers because they can be loaded into memory when the device is accessed and then unloaded to conserve memory when the device is disconnected or turned off. Drivers that always remain in memory are called static drivers.

Sometimes, to address bugs, make improvements, or add features, manufacturers release device drivers that are more recent than those included with Windows. Whenever possible, it is best to use the latest driver available for a device provided by the device manufacturer. You can usually download these updated drivers from the manufacturer's Web site. For example, suppose you have just borrowed a printer from a friend but you forgot to borrow the CD with the printer drivers on it. You can go to the printer manufacturer's Web site, download the drivers to a folder on your PC, and install the driver under Windows. Figure 2-17 shows you a Web page from the Hewlett-Packard (HP) Web site showing a list of downloadable drivers for ink-jet printers.

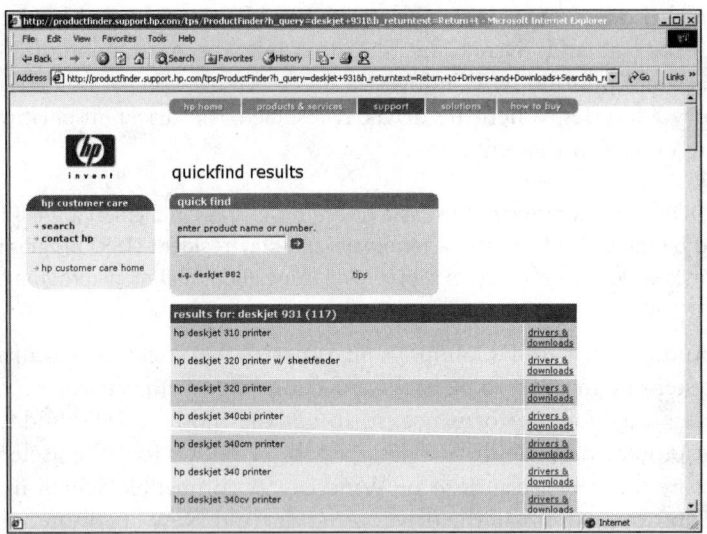

Figure 2-17   Download the latest device drivers from a manufacturer's Web site

Sixteen-bit drivers under Windows 9*x* can cause slow performance, so use 32-bit drivers whenever possible. Sometimes it can be difficult to determine whether a device driver is 16-bit or 32-bit. One way to identify whether Windows 9*x* is using a 16-bit driver is to go into Device Manager and look for an exclamation point beside the device, which indicates that the driver has a problem. This might indicate that the driver is a 16-bit driver. If a driver is loaded from Config.sys or Autoexec.bat, it is a 16-bit driver; if it is loaded from the registry, it is a 32-bit driver. System.ini can contain both types. Table 2-4 summarizes basic information about device drivers under Windows 9*x*.

Device Drivers Under Windows 2000   Windows 2000 installs protected-mode drivers in the same way as Windows 9*x*, but Windows 2000 does not claim to support 16-bit device drivers. For Windows 2000, always check the hardware compatibility list (HCL) to determine if a driver will work under Windows 2000. Go to this Microsoft Web site and search for your device:

www.microsoft.com/windows2000/professional/howtobuy/upgrading/compat

If the device does not install properly or produces errors, check the manufacturer's Web site for a driver that the manufacturer says is compatible with Windows 2000.

Table 2-4 Two types of device drivers and how to use them under Windows 9x

Characteristic	16-bit Device Drivers	32-bit Device Drivers
Operating mode	Real mode	Protected mode
Use of memory	May use upper memory addresses	Stored in extended memory
How loaded	Loaded by a command line in Config.sys, Autoexec.bat, or System.ini	Automatically loaded from the registry by Windows 9x at startup or when the device is used
How changed	Edit the Config.sys or Autoexec.bat files	From Device Manager, select the device and use the Properties, Driver tab
How to identify the type	In Device Manager, look for an exclamation point beside the device name	Look to see how the driver is loaded: from the registry, System.ini, Autoexec.bat or Config.sys. Also, look for no exclamation point beside the device name in Device Manager.
When to use this type	Use a 16-bit driver under Windows only when a 32-bit driver is not available. When operating under DOS, 16-bit drivers are required.	When you can, always use 32-bit drivers because they are faster and give fewer configuration problems.

HOW AN OS LAUNCHES APPLICATIONS   (8) MAIN CATEGORIES

Most application software fits into eight categories: word processing, spreadsheets, database management, graphics, communications, games, mathematical modeling, and software development tools. Each category contains many different products. For example, some popular database-management packages include Access, Paradox, and Filemaker; two popular word-processing packages include Word and WordPerfect. Some application-software manufacturers produce suites of software, which combine a word-processing program and spreadsheet program, and usually include a database-management program, a presentation package, an e-mail package, and a World Wide Web browser package. Suites have many advantages, including providing similar user interfaces. The programs are designed to make it easy to move data from one suite program to another, and files within a suite's programs can be linked, so that updates to data or text are automatically recorded in all linked files.

Application software is designed to work on top of a particular OS—that is, the application depends on the OS, such as Windows 98 or Windows 2000, in order to run. An application depends on an OS to provide access to hardware resources, manage its data in memory and in secondary storage, and perform many other background tasks. For example, consider a situation in which Windows 98 loads an application and executes it. The application cannot run or even load itself without Windows 98, much as a document cannot be edited without a word-processing program. Windows 98 stays available to the application for the entire time the application is running. The application passes certain functions to Windows 98, such as reading from a CD-ROM or printing.

An application written to work with one OS, such as Windows 98, does not necessarily work with another, such as a Macintosh system. There are, however, some exceptions. For instance, OS/2 is written so that any application designed to work with DOS also works with OS/2, an early selling point for OS/2. To take full advantage of an operating system's and an application's power, however, you should buy application software written specifically for your OS.

Application software is downloaded from the Internet, or comes written on floppy disks or on CD-ROMs, and usually must be installed on a hard drive in order to run. During the installation, the install program creates folders on the hard drive and copies files to them. For Windows, it also makes entries in the Windows registry and puts files in the folder and subfolders that it later uses as software components to perform various tasks. It can also place icons on the desktop and add entries to the Start menu. Because the install program does all the work for you, installing a software package usually is very easy.

How Application Software Is Loaded and Initialized

Starting application software seems like a simple task. For example, in Windows 98, you click the shortcut icon on the desktop, and the application window opens, ready for you to use it. But much happens behind the scenes between your click and the appearance of the application awaiting your next command. Software or programs are stored in program files on a secondary storage device, such as a hard drive or CD, until needed. Before they can be executed, they must first be copied or loaded into RAM and assigned memory addresses, as Figure 2-18 shows.

Figure 2-18   RAM is a hardware resource, and memory addresses are a system resource; both are used when loading software into memory for execution

Even the operating system programs must be copied from the hard drive into memory before these programs are executed. The process from a bird's eye view goes like this, and is illustrated in Figure 2-19:

1. The OS program files are copied into memory and assigned memory addresses and then executed.

2. The OS copies a program file into memory, which is executed.

3. The program requests data from the hard drive, which is copied into memory, and then the program uses that data.

In Figure 2-19, you can see that memory is used by the OS, the applications, and data. In addition, BIOS and device drivers are also using memory and are executed from memory as the OS needs them.

Figure 2-19   Both the operating system and application software must be loaded into memory before execution, and existing data must also be copied from secondary storage into memory to be processed. After processing, data must be saved back to secondary storage

Understanding the process of loading and initializing software is important to people responsible for supporting PCs. Listed below are the major steps that must take place. This section describes the process in detail for several OSes.

1. The OS receives the command to execute the application.

2. The OS locates the program file for the application.

3. The OS loads the program file into memory.

4. The OS gives control to the program.

5. The program requests memory addresses from the OS for its data.

6. The program initializes itself and possibly requests that data from secondary storage be loaded into memory.

7. The program turns to the user for its first instruction.

We begin with Windows 98 in MS-DOS mode as our OS. Before we discuss the specific command to load software in real mode, let's first look at the command prompt the user sees and what information it provides. If you booted a Windows 98 PC from a floppy disk into command prompt mode, the MS-DOS prompt would look like this:

```
A:\>
```

This prompt is called the *A: prompt*. The MS-DOS prompt (A:\>) displayed immediately after booting means that the OS was copied from drive A:, which is where the startup disk containing enough of the OS to load in real mode is stored. Drive A: then becomes the default drive and default directory, sometimes called the *current working drive* and *directory*, which the OS automatically uses to save and retrieve files. The colon following the letter identifies the letter as the name of a drive, and the backslash identifies the directory on the drive as the root or main directory. The > symbol is the prompt symbol that the OS uses to say, "Enter your command here."

To make the hard drive (drive C:) the default drive, enter C: at the A: prompt. The prompt now changes to

```
C:\>
```

Recall that when a hard drive is first formatted for use by an OS, the format procedure creates a single directory on the drive, called the **root directory**. This directory is written in the OS command lines as a single backslash (\) (or forward slash in the case of Unix) with no other directory name following. In the preceding OS prompt, the backslash indicates that it is the root directory.

Launching the Program File

At the command prompt, when you type a single group of letters with no spaces, the OS assumes that you want to execute a program with the filename that you just typed, stored in a program file in the current directory. The OS first attempts to find the program file by that name, then copies the file into RAM, and then it executes the program. Let's use the program Mem.exe, a Windows 9x utility, to display how memory is currently allocated, as our example. The program file Mem.exe is stored on the hard drive in C:\Windows\command folder. Note what happens in Figure 2-20 when you type *mem* at the A: prompt, like this:

```
A:\>mem
```

The OS says it cannot find the program to execute. It looked only on the floppy disk (drive A:) for Mem.com, Mem.exe, or Mem.bat, the three file extensions that MS-DOS recognizes for programs. If the OS doesn't find any of these files in the current directory, it stops looking and displays the error message:

```
Bad command or file name
```

2

To help the OS locate the program file, you must first change the default drive to the hard drive by giving the command:

```
A:\> C:
```

Notice in Figure 2-20 that the prompt changes to C:\>, indicating that the logical drive C: on the hard drive is the default drive. Now you change the default directory on the hard drive to \Windows\Command using the CD (change directory) command like this:

```
C:\>CD\windows\command
```

Remember that DOS and Windows commands are not case sensitive, so it makes no difference whether you type CD, Cd, or cd. The prompt now looks like this:

```
C:\WINDOWS\COMMAND>
```

Next, as shown in Figure 2-20, you enter the *mem* command again, and this time the OS locates and executes the program file.

```
A:\>mem
Bad command or file name

A:\>c:

C:\>cd\windows\command

C:\WINDOWS\COMMAND>mem

Memory Type          Total    Used       Free
- - - - - - - - - -  - - - - - - -  - - - -  - - - - - -
Conventional          640K     160K       480K
Upper                  0K       0K         0K
Reserved               0K       0K         0K
Extended (XMS)    130,036K   2,112K   127,924K

Total memory      130,676K   2,272K   128,404K

Total under 1 MB      640K     160K       480K

Largest executable program size       479K (490, 816 bytes)
Largest free upper memory block        0K        (0 bytes)
MS-DOS is resident in the high memory area.

C:\WINDOWS\COMMAND>
```

Figure 2-20 Finding a program file

There is another way to tell the OS where to look to find program files. As part of the boot procedure, you can give the OS a list of paths in which to look for executable program files beyond the default directory by using the PATH command. You can cause the

PATH command to be executed automatically during the boot process by storing the command in the Autoexec.bat file. You can also execute the PATH command at any time after booting. The last PATH command you execute overrides any previous ones. To see the list of paths that are presently active, type PATH at the command prompt, and then press Enter (see Figure 2-21). To enter a new list of paths, type PATH followed by each path name, separating one path from the next by a semicolon, as shown in the second PATH command in Figure 2-21.

```
C:\>path
PATH=F:\;A:\;G:\

C:\>path F:\;A:\G:\C:\;C:\Windows\Command

C:\>path
PATH=F:\;A:\G:\C:\;C\WINDOWS\COMMAND

C:\>
```

Figure 2-21   The PATH command

In Figure 2-21, the first PATH command displays the list of active paths, which are three logical drives, F:, A:, and G:. The second PATH command changes this list, giving the OS the same three logical drives as well as the drive C: root directory and the C:\Windows\Command directory. The last PATH command displays the new list of active paths.

When you tell the OS to execute a program, you can also include the path to that program file as part of the command line. For example, if the Mem.exe file is stored in the directory C:\Windows\Command, you can execute the program by typing the following:

```
A:\> C:\Windows\Command\Mem.exe
```

Here, you are telling the OS that the name of the program file is Mem.exe and that its location is in the directory \Windows\Command on drive C. With this method, the directory and drive that contains the Mem program need not be the defaults, nor do you need to use the PATH command.

In summary, using the MS-DOS mode of Windows 9*x*, the OS searches for executable program files using the following rules:

1. If no path is given before the filename, the OS looks in the current directory.

2. If there is a path given in front of the filename in the command line, the OS looks in that path.

3. If no path is given, and the file is not in the current directory, the OS looks in the paths given to it by the last PATH command executed.

Although the PATH command and Autoexec.bat are not necessary in Windows 9*x*, you can use them. If you have an Autoexec.bat file in your root directory when Windows 9*x* starts, it reads the PATH command stored in that file. You can also store DOS commands in batch files and execute them from Windows 9*x* by double-clicking the filename of the batch file in Explorer.

If you don't have an Autoexec.bat file with a PATH command, Windows 9*x* uses a default path of C:\Windows;C:\Windows\Command. Not all paths to program files must appear in the PATH command, as they must in DOS.

Copying the Program into Memory

Recall that once the OS finds the program file, it copies the file into memory (RAM) in a location that the OS chooses (see Figure 2-22). After it does so, the OS goes to the first address in memory occupied by the program to receive its first instruction. If the program requests some memory for its data (and most will), the OS decides which memory addresses to give the program (usually the memory after the program).

Figure 2-22   Application software is stored in files but executed from memory

If the program wants to write or read data to or from memory, the OS manages these tasks. If the program needs to print, display something on the screen, or read from or write to the hard drive or a floppy disk, the OS does the work and returns to the program when finished. In other words, the OS is the "software behind the software," doing the background tasks for an application or utility program.

Loading Application Software Using the Windows Desktop

In graphical mode, once an application is installed, Windows 9x and Windows NT/ 2000/XP offer four ways to execute software:

- Place a shortcut icon directly on the desktop for the applications you use often and want to get to quickly. These shortcuts contain the command line used to execute the application. To view this command line, right-click an application icon. A drop-down menu then appears; select Properties. The icon's Properties box appears (see Figure 2-23). From this box, you can view the complete command line that the icon represents.

Shortcut icon

Shortcut Properties dialog box

Path to program file

Desktop

Taskbar

Figure 2-23   Windows has icons on the desktop that point to program files on the hard drive

- Click the Start button, select Programs, and select the program from the list of installed software.

- Use the Run command. Click the Start button on the Windows taskbar, and then click Run to display the Run dialog box (see Figure 2-24). In this box, enter a command line or click Browse to search for a program file to execute.

- Execute a program or launch an application file by double-clicking the filename in Windows Explorer or My Computer.

Command line

Use Browse to search for
a program file

2

Figure 2-24 The Windows Run dialog box allows you to enter DOS-like commands

CHAPTER SUMMARY

❏ A computer requires both hardware and software to work.

❏ Three types of software are BIOS (or firmware), operating systems (OSs), and application software.

❏ Application software relates to the OS, which relates to BIOS and device drivers to control hardware.

❏ Operating systems use BIOS, manage secondary storage and primary storage, help diagnose problems with hardware and software, interface between hardware and software, and perform various housekeeping tasks.

❏ When a PC is first turned on, the startup BIOS is in control. It later loads the OS and then turns control over to it.

❏ Four system resources that aid in the communication between hardware and software are I/O addresses, IRQs, DMA channels, and memory addresses.

❏ An IRQ is a line on a bus that a device uses to alert the CPU that it needs servicing.

❏ A DMA channel provides a shortcut for a device to send data directly to memory, bypassing the CPU.

❏ Memory addresses are hexadecimal numbers, often written in segment/offset form, assigned to RAM and ROM so that the CPU can access both.

❏ The CPU sends a device's I/O address over the address bus when it wants to initiate communication with the device.

❏ COM and LPT are preconfigured assignments of system resources that can be used by a device. For example, COM1 is IRQ 4 and I/O addresses 03F8 through 03FF.

❏ A hardware interrupt is initiated by a hardware device sending an IRQ to the CPU. A software interrupt is initiated by the software sending an interrupt number (INT) to the CPU.

❏ For DOS, the three types of logical primary memory are conventional (or base) memory, upper memory, and extended memory.

❑ Software manages memory by means of memory addresses that point to locations in RAM. The number of memory addresses is partly limited by the number of wires on the bus devoted to these addresses.

❑ BIOS and an OS can support two common standards: ACPI to conserve power and Plug and Play to make device installations easier.

❑ RAM and ROM BIOS on the motherboard and other circuit boards need memory addresses assigned to the BIOS so the CPU can access these programs.

❑ The size of the data segment that software can access at one time is determined by the number of wires on the bus assigned for the data path.

❑ Startup BIOS performs a power-on self test (POST) that surveys and tests hardware, examines setup information, and assigns system resources to the hardware. Startup BIOS then begins the process of loading the OS.

❑ When the OS loads from a hard drive, the first program BIOS executes is the Master Boot Record (MBR), which executes the OS boot record, which, for DOS, attempts to find Io.sys and Msdos.sys on the hard drive.

❑ Io.sys and Msdos.sys together with Command.com form the kernel, or core, of MSDOS mode Windows 9x. Other files are needed to load the GUI desktop and run GUI applications.

❑ Autoexec.bat and Config.sys are two files that contain commands used to customize the 16-bit portion of the Windows 9x load process.

❑ Device drivers are written using either 16-bit or 32-bit code. Most drivers today are 32-bit protected-mode drivers loaded from the registry by Windows.

❑ Real mode is used by DOS and is limited to running a single program and using a 16-bit data path and 1024K of memory addresses.

❑ Protected mode allows more than one program to run at a time, can use a 32-bit data path, and has more than 1024K of memory addresses. In protected mode, the OS manages access to RAM and does not allow a program direct access to it.

❑ Virtual memory is "fake" memory, whereby data is stored in a swap file on the hard drive. The OS makes applications think that they are using real memory.

❑ Device drivers are either written using 16-bit or 32-bit code.

❑ Older 16-bit device drivers are loaded from Autoexec.bat, Config.sys, or System.ini by Windows 9x to be backward-compatible with DOS and Windows 3.x.

❑ Using MS-DOS mode of Windows 9x, a program can be executed from a command prompt. A PATH command is required if the program is not in the default directory and the path is not included before the filename in the command line.

❑ From the Windows desktop, programs can be launched from the Start menu, a shortcut icon on the desktop, the Run dialog box, or Windows Explorer or My Computer.

KEY TERMS

AGP (Accelerated
  Graphics Port) bus
Autoexec.bat
BIOS (basic
  input/output system)
booting
bootstrap loader
buffer
CD (change directory)
  command
cold boot
device driver
DMA (direct memory
  access) channel
extended memory
hard boot
hardware interrupt
hidden file
interrupt handler
interrupt vector table

I/O addresses
IRQ (interrupt request
  number) line
ISA (Industry Standard
  Architecture) slot
memory address
operating system (OS)
page file
partition table
PCI (Peripheral
  Component
  Interconnect) bus
Plug and Play (PnP)
polling
port address
power-on self test
  (POST)
protected mode
RAM drive
request handler

ROM (read-only
  memory)
root directory
shadow RAM or
  shadowing ROM
soft boot
software interrupt
startup BIOS
swap file
system BIOS
system resource
System.ini
TSR (terminate-and-
  stay resident)
vector table
virtual memory
virtual real mode
warm boot

2

3

ELECTRICITY AND POWER SUPPLIES

In this chapter, you will learn:

- ♦ How electricity is measured
- ♦ How to protect your computer system from damaging changes in electrical power
- ♦ About the different types of form factors and computer cases
- ♦ How to detect and correct power supply problems
- ♦ About Energy Star specifications

In the first two chapters of this book, you learned about most hardware components of the computer except the power supply, which provides the power to all other components inside the computer case. To troubleshoot problems with the power system of a PC, you need a basic understanding of electricity. This chapter begins by discussing how to measure electricity, and the form in which it comes to you as house current. The chapter then addresses the power supply, backup power sources, how to measure power supply output, and how to change a defective power supply. Finally, you will be introduced to form factors and learn how Energy Star devices save energy.

ELECTRICITY: A BASIC INTRODUCTION

To most people, volts, ohms, watts, and amps are vague words that simply have to do with electricity. If these terms are mysterious to you, they will become clear in this section as electricity is discussed in non-technical language, using simple analogies.

Electricity is energy; water is matter. However, the two have enough in common to make some analogies. Consider Figure 3-1. The water system shown in the top part of the figure is closed—that is, the amount of water in the system remains the same because no water enters and no water leaves the system. The electrical system in the lower part of the figure is similar in several respects. Think of electricity as a stream of tiny charged particles (electrons) that flow like water along the path of least resistance.

Figure 3-1   Two closed systems: (a) water system with pump, wheel, and pool; (b) electrical system with battery and light bulb

Just as water flows down because of the force of gravity, electricity flows from negative to positive because of the force of like charges repelling one another. The water pump produces water pressure in the system by lifting the water, and a battery produces electrical pressure in the system by creating a buildup of negative charges in one location (in the form of electrons) that are driven to move. This difference in charge, which is similar to water pressure in a water system, is called potential difference. Water seeks a place of rest, moving from a high to a low elevation, and electrons seek a place of rest by moving from a negatively charged location (sometimes called "hot") to a positively charged location (sometimes called "ground"). In the figure, as the water flows through the closed system, some of its force is harnessed by the water wheel and is converted to a form of energy, motion. Also in the figure, as the electrons flow in the closed electrical system called a circuit, some of the force of the moving electrons is harnessed by the light bulb and converted to another form of energy, light. Once the water returns to the pool, water pressure decreases, and the water is at rest. Once the electrons arrive at the positive side of the battery, electrical potential difference decreases, and the system is at rest.

 TIP Electron flow goes from the hot point, or negative terminal, to the ground or positive terminal. Because early theories of electricity assumed that electricity flowed from positive to negative, most electronics books show the current flow from positive to negative. This theory is called conventional current flow; if it were used in Figure 3-1, the positive and negative symbols would be reversed in the figure.

Electrical energy has properties that can be measured in various ways. The description above (of an electrical system that includes a battery and a light bulb) illustrates some simple principles that apply to the most complex electrical systems. We next use this simple electrical system to define four properties of electricity, all of which can be measured (see Table 3-1).

Table 3-1   The measures of electricity

Unit	Definition	An Example As Applied to a Computer
Volts (measures potential difference)	Abbreviated as V (for example, 110 V). Volts are measured by finding the potential difference between the electrical charges on either side of an electrical device in an electrical system.	An AT power supply supplies four separate voltages: +12 V, -12 V, +5 V, -5 V. An ATX power supply supplies these and also +3.3 V.
Amps or amperes (measures electrical current)	Abbreviated as A (for example, 1.5 A). Amps are measured by placing an ammeter in the flow of current and measuring that current.	A 17-inch monitor requires less than 2 A to operate. A small laser printer uses about 2 A. A CD-ROM drive uses about 1 A.

Table 3-1   The measures of electricity (continued)

Unit	Definition	An Example As Applied to a Computer
Ohms (measures resistance)	Abbreviated with the symbol Ω (for example, 20 Ω). Devices are rated according to how much resistance they offer to electrical current. The ohm rating of a resistor or other electrical device is often written somewhere on the device. The resistance of a device is measured when the device is not connected to an electrical system.	Current can flow in typical computer cables and wires with a resistance of near zero Ω.
Watts (measures power)	Abbreviated W (for example, 20 W). Watts are calculated by multiplying volts by amps.	A computer power supply is rated at 200 to 600 W.

Voltage

The first measure of electricity listed in Table 3-1 is potential difference. First, consider how to measure the water pressure. If you measure the pressure of the water directly above the water wheel, and then measure the pressure just as the water lands in the pool, you find that the water pressure above the wheel is greater than the water pressure below it.

Now consider the electrical system. If you measure the electrical charge on one side of the light bulb and compare it to the electrical charge on the other side of the bulb, you see a difference in charge. The potential difference in charge creates an electrical force called **voltage**, which drives the electrons through the system between two points. Voltage is measured in units called **volts (V)**.

In Figure 3-2, the leads of a **voltmeter**, a device for measuring electrical voltage, are placed on either side of a light bulb that is consuming some electrical power. The potential difference between the two points on either side of the device is the voltage in the closed system. Voltage is measured when the power is on.

Amps

The volume of electrons (or electricity) flowing through an electrical system is called current. Look back at Figure 3-1. The volume or amount of water flowing through the water system does not change, although the water pressure changes at different points in the system. To measure that volume, you pick one point in the system and measure the volume of water that passes through that point over a period of time. The electrical system is similar. If you measure the number of electrons, or electrical current, at any point in this system, you

12 volts

Figure 3-2　A voltmeter measuring the voltage across a bulb and a battery

find the same value as at any other point, because the current is constant throughout the system. (This assumes that there is only a single pipe or a single wire in the entire closed water or electrical system.) Electrical current is measured in **amperes (A)**, abbreviated **amps**. Figure 3-3 shows the measuring device called an **ammeter**, which measures electrical current in amps. You place the ammeter in the path of the electrical flow so that the electrons must flow through the ammeter. The measurement is taken with the power on and might not be completely accurate because the ammeter can influence the circuit.

> **TIP**　Because the current flows through an ammeter, check the rating of the ammeter before measuring amps to make sure it can handle the flow of electricity. More flow than the ammeter is designed to handle can blow the meter's fuse.

The Relationship Between Voltage and Current

Refer again to the water system in Figure 3-1. To increase the volume of water flowing through the system, you increase the difference in water pressure between the low and high points (which is referred to as the pressure differential). As the pressure differential increases, the water flow (or current) increases, and as the water pressure differential decreases, the water flow (or current) decreases. Another way of saying this is: there is a direct relationship between pressure differential and current. An electrical system works in the same way. As the electrical potential difference (or voltage) increases, the electrical current increases; as the voltage decreases, the current decreases. There is a direct relationship between voltage and current.

12 volts

Figure 3-3   Battery and bulb circuit with ammeter in line

Ohms

Suppose you are working your water pump to full capacity. If you still want to increase the overall power of your water system—so the wheel turns faster to produce more mechanical energy—you can decrease the resistance to water flow, which allows more water to flow to push the wheel faster. You might use a larger pipe or a lighter water wheel, or, if the system has a partially open water valve, you can open the valve more, all of which would lower resistance to water flow. As resistance decreases, current increases. As resistance increases (smaller pipes, heavier wheel, partially closed valve), current decreases.

Similarly, **resistance** in an electrical system is a property that opposes the flow of electricity. As the electrical resistance increases, the flow of electrons decreases. As the resistance decreases, the electricity increases. (A condition of low resistance that allows current to flow in a completed circuit is called **continuity**). When too much electricity flows through a wire, heat energy (similar to friction) is created in the wire. This heat energy can cause the wire to melt or burn, which can result in an electrical fire, just as too much water current in a pipe can cause it to burst. Reducing the size of a wire reduces the amount of electricity that can safely flow through. Electrical resistance is measured in **ohms (Ω)**.

Resistors are devices used in electrical circuits to resist the flow of electricity. These devices control the flow of electricity in a circuit, much as partially closed valves control the flow of water.

Relationships Among Voltage, Current, and Resistance

Voltage and current have a direct relationship. This means that when voltage increases, current increases. Resistance has an inverse relationship with voltage and current. This means that as resistance increases, either current or voltage decreases. As resistance decreases, either current or voltage increases. This last statement is known as Ohm's Law. A similar statement defines the relationship among the units of measure: volts, amps, and ohms. One volt drives a current of one amp through a resistance of one ohm.

Wattage

Wattage is the total amount of power needed to operate an electrical device. When thinking of the water system, you recognize that the amount of water power used to turn the water wheel is not just a measure of the water pressure that forces current through the system. The amount of power is also related to the amount of water available to flow. For a given water pressure, you have more power with more water flow and less power with less water flow. A lot of power results when you have a lot of pressure and a lot of current.

As with the water system, electrical power increases as both voltage and current increase. Wattage, measured in **watts (W)**, is calculated by multiplying volts by amps in a system (W = V × A). For example, 120 volts times 5 amps is 600 watts. Note that while volts and amps are measured to determine their value, watts are calculated from those values.

AC and DC

Electricity can be either AC, alternating current, or DC, direct current. **Alternating current (AC)** is current that cycles or oscillates back and forth rather than traveling in only one direction. House current in the U.S. oscillates 60 times in one second (60 hertz), changing polarity from +110 V to −110 V, and causing current to flow in different directions, depending on whether it's positive or negative in the cycle. AC is the most economical way to transmit electricity to our homes and workplaces. Alternating current can be forced to travel great distances by decreasing current and increasing voltage (high pressure and low volume). When it reaches its destination, the voltage can be decreased and the current increased (low pressure and high volume) to make it more suitable for driving our electrical devices.

Direct current (DC) travels in only one direction and is the type of current required by most electronic devices, including a computer. A **rectifier** is a device that converts alternating current to direct current. A **transformer** is a device that changes the ratio of current to voltage. Large transformers are used to reduce the high voltage on power lines coming to your neighborhood to a lower voltage before the current enters your home. The transformer does not change the amount of power in this closed system; if it decreases voltage, then it increases current. The overall power stays constant, but the ratio of voltage to current changes.

A computer power supply changes and conditions the house electrical current in several ways, functioning as both a transformer and a rectifier (see Figure 3-4). It steps down the voltage from the 110-volt house current to 3.3, 5, and 12 volts, or to 5 and 12 volts, and changes incoming alternating current to direct current, which the computer and its peripherals require. The monitor, however, receives the full 110 volts of AC voltage, converting that current to DC.

Label lists voltages for motherboard connector

Vents for cooling fan

External power source

Connectors for hard drives and other drives

P1 power connector to motherboard

Connector for floppy drive

Figure 3-4   Computer power supply with connections

Recall that direct current flows in only one direction, from hot to ground. For a PC, a line may be either +5 or –5 volts in one circuit, or +12 or –12 volts in another circuit, depending on whether the circuit is on the positive side or negative side of the power output. Several circuits coming from the power supply accommodate different devices with different power requirements.

Hot, Neutral, and Ground

When AC comes from the power source at the power station to your house, it travels on a hot line and completes the circuit from your house back to the power source on a neutral line, as seen in Figure 3-5. When the two lines get to your house and enter an electrical device, such as a lamp or radio, the electricity flows through the device to complete the circuit between the hot line and the neutral line. The device contains resistors and other electrical components that control the flow of electricity between the hot and neutral lines. The hot source is seeking ground, which it finds by returning to the power station on the neutral line.

A short circuit, or a short, occurs when the electricity is allowed to flow uncontrolled from the hot line to the neutral line or from the hot line to ground. Electricity naturally finds the easiest route to ground. Normally that path is through some device that is controlling the current flow and then back through the neutral line. If an easier path (one with less resistance) is available, the electricity follows that path. This can cause a short, a sudden increase in flow that can create a sudden increase in temperature—enough to start a fire and injure both people and equipment. Never put yourself in a position where you are the path of least resistance between the hot line and ground!

A fuse is a component included in a circuit and designed to prevent too much current from flowing through the circuit. A fuse is commonly a wire inside a protective case, which is rated in amps. If too much current begins to flow, the wire gets hot and eventually melts, breaking the circuit, as an open switch would, and stopping the current flow. Many devices have fuses, which can be easily replaced when damaged. You will learn to test a fuse later in the chapter.

Figure 3-5 Normally, hot contacts neutral to make a closed circuit in the controlled environment of an electrical device such as a lamp. An out-of-control contact is called a short, and the flow of electricity is then diverted to the ground.

To prevent the uncontrolled flow of electricity from continuing indefinitely, which can happen because of a short, the neutral line is grounded. Grounding a line means that the line is connected directly to the earth, so that, in the event of a short, the electricity flows into the earth and not back to the power station. The grounding serves as an escape route for out-of-control electricity. The earth is at no particular state of charge, and so is always capable of accepting a flow of current.

The neutral line to your house is grounded many times along the way (in fact at each electrical pole) and is also grounded at the breaker box where the electricity enters your house. You can look at a three-prong plug and see the three lines: hot, neutral, and ground (see Figure 3-6). Generally, electricians use green or bare wire for the ground wire, white for neutral, and black for hot in home wiring for 110-volt circuits. In a 220-volt circuit, black and red are hot, white is neutral, and green or bare is ground. To verify that a wall outlet is wired correctly, use a simple receptacle tester, as shown in Figure 3-7.

Neutral

Hot

Ground

Figure 3-6   A three-prong plug showing hot, neutral, and ground

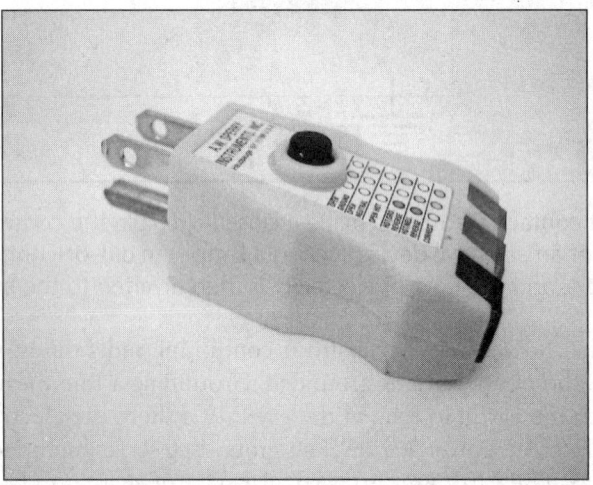

Figure 3-7   Use a receptacle tester to verify that hot, neutral, and ground are wired correctly

 CAUTION

Beware of the different uses of black wire. In PCs, black is used for ground, but in home wiring, black is used for hot!

Even though you might have a three-prong outlet in your home, the ground plug might not be properly grounded. To know for sure, test the outlet with an inexpensive outlet tester.

CAUTION

It's very important that PC components be properly grounded. Never connect a PC to an outlet or use an extension cord that doesn't have the third ground plug. The third line can prevent a short from causing extreme damage. In addition, the bond between the neutral and ground helps eliminate electrical noise (stray electrical signals) within the PC sometimes caused by other electrical equipment sitting very close to the computer.

Some Common Electronic Components

It's important to understand what basic electronic components make up a PC and how they work. Basic electronic components in a PC include transistors, capacitors, diodes, ground, and resistors. Figure 3-8 shows the symbols for these components. Materials used to make these and other electronic components can be:

- *Conductors.* Material that easily conducts electricity, such as gold or copper

- *Insulators.* Material that resists the flow of electricity, such as glass or ceramic

- *Semiconductors.* Material such as silicon whose ability to conduct electricity, when a charge is applied, falls between that of a conductor and an insulator

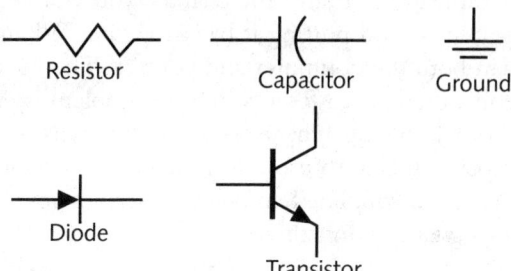

Figure 3-8   Symbols for some electronic components and ground

A **transistor** is an electronic device that can serve as a gate or switch for an electrical signal and can amplify the flow of electricity. Invented in 1947, the transistor is made of three layers of semiconductor material. A charge (either positive or negative, depending on how the transistor was designed) placed on the center layer can cause the two outer layers of the transistor to complete a circuit to create an "on" state. An opposite charge placed on the center layer can cause the reverse to happen, causing the transistor to create an "off" state. Manipulating these charges to the transistor allows it to hold a logic state, either on or off (translated to 0 or 1 in binary). When the transistor is maintaining this state, it requires almost no electrical power. Because the initial charge sent to the transistor is not as great as the resulting current created by the transistor, sometimes a transistor is used as a small amplifier. The transistor is the basic building block of an integrated circuit (IC) that is used to build a microchip.

A **capacitor** is an electronic device that can hold an electrical charge for a period of time and is used to smooth out the uneven flow of electricity through a circuit. Capacitors inside a PC power supply create the even flow of current needed by the PC. Capacitors maintain their charge long after current is no longer present, which is why the inside of a power supply can be dangerous even when it is unplugged.

A **diode** is a semiconductor device that allows electricity to flow in only one direction. (A transistor contains two diodes.) One to four diodes used in various configurations can be used to convert the AC to DC. Singularly or collectively, depending on the configuration, these diodes are called a rectifier.

As explained above, a resistor is an electronic device that limits the amount of current that can flow through it.

PROTECTING YOUR COMPUTER SYSTEM

Now that you have learned some basic information about how electricity works, it will be easier to understand how power is supplied to a computer. But first, let's look at ways to protect your computer system. As you read the rest of the chapter, you will begin to look inside a computer and start taking it apart and putting it back together. When you work on a computer, it is possible to harm both the computer and yourself. The most common accident that happens when someone attempts to fix a computer problem is erasing software or data. Experimenting without knowing what you are doing can cause damage. There are many safety precautions you can take to prevent these sorts of accidents, as well as the ones that are physically dangerous to you. The text below describes potential sources of damage to computers and how to guard against them.

Here are a few general safety precautions to keep in mind:

- Make notes as you work so that you can backtrack later if necessary.
- When unpacking hardware or software, remove the packing tape and cellophane from the work area as soon as possible.
- Keep components away from your hair and clothing. Don't wear loose clothing that will get in your way as you work.
- Keep screws and spacers in an orderly place, such as a cup or tray.

3

- Don't stack boards on top of each other, as you could accidentally dislodge a chip this way.

- When handling motherboards and expansion cards, don't touch the chips on the boards. Hold expansion cards by the edges. Don't touch any of the soldered components on a card, and don't touch chips or edge connectors unless absolutely necessary.

- Don't touch a chip with a magnetized screwdriver.

- Don't use a graphite pencil to change DIP switch settings, because graphite is a conductor of electricity, and the graphite can lodge in the switch.

- In a classroom environment, after you have reassembled everything, have your instructor check your work before you put the cover back on and power up.

- Always turn off a computer before moving it. A computer's hard drive is always spinning while it is on, unless it has a sleep mode. Therefore, it is important not to move, kick, or jar a computer while it is running.

- To protect disks, keep them away from magnetic fields, heat, and extreme cold. Don't open the shuttle window on a floppy disk or touch the surface of the disk.

You will learn about additional safety precautions in the remainder of this section.

Protecting Against Electricity

To protect both yourself and the equipment when working inside a computer, turn off the power, unplug the computer, and always use a ground bracelet (which you will learn more about later). Never touch the inside of a computer while it is turned on. In addition, consider the monitor and the power supply to be "black boxes." Never remove the cover or put your hands inside this equipment unless you know about the hazards of charged capacitors and have been trained to deal with them. Both the power supply and the monitor can hold a dangerous level of electricity even after they are turned off and disconnected from a power source. The power supply and monitor have enough power inside them to kill you, even when they are unplugged.

Static Electricity

Electrostatic discharge (ESD), commonly known as **static electricity**, is an electrical charge at rest. A static charge can build up on the surface of an ungrounded conductor and on nonconductive surfaces such as clothing or plastic. When two objects with dissimilar electrical charges touch, static electricity passes between them until the dissimilar charges are made equal. To see how this works, turn off the lights in a room, scuff your feet on the carpet, and touch another person. Occasionally you'll be able to see and feel the charge in your fingers. If you can feel the charge, then you discharged at least 3,000 volts of static electricity. If you hear the discharge, then you released at least 6,000 volts. If you see the discharge, then you released at least 8,000 volts of ESD. A charge of much, much less than 3,000 volts can damage electronic components. You can touch a chip on an expansion card or motherboard and damage the chip with ESD and never feel, hear, or see the discharge.

There are two types of damage that ESD can cause in an electronic component: catastrophic failure and upset failure. A catastrophic failure destroys the component beyond use. An upset failure damages the component so that it does not perform well, even though it may still function to some degree. Upset failures are the most difficult to detect because they are not so easily observed.

CAUTION

A monitor can also damage components with ESD. Do not place or store expansion cards on top of or next to a monitor, which can discharge as much as 29,000 volts onto the screen.

To protect the computer against ESD, always ground yourself before touching electronic components, including the hard drive, motherboard, expansion cards, processors, and memory modules. Ground yourself and the computer parts, using one or more of the following static control devices or methods:

- *Ground bracelet or static strap.* A **ground bracelet** is a strap you wear around your wrist. The other end is attached to a grounded conductor such as the computer case or a ground mat, or it can plug into a wall outlet (only the ground prong makes a connection!). The bracelet also contains a resistor that prevents electricity from harming you. Figure 3-9 shows a ground bracelet.

3

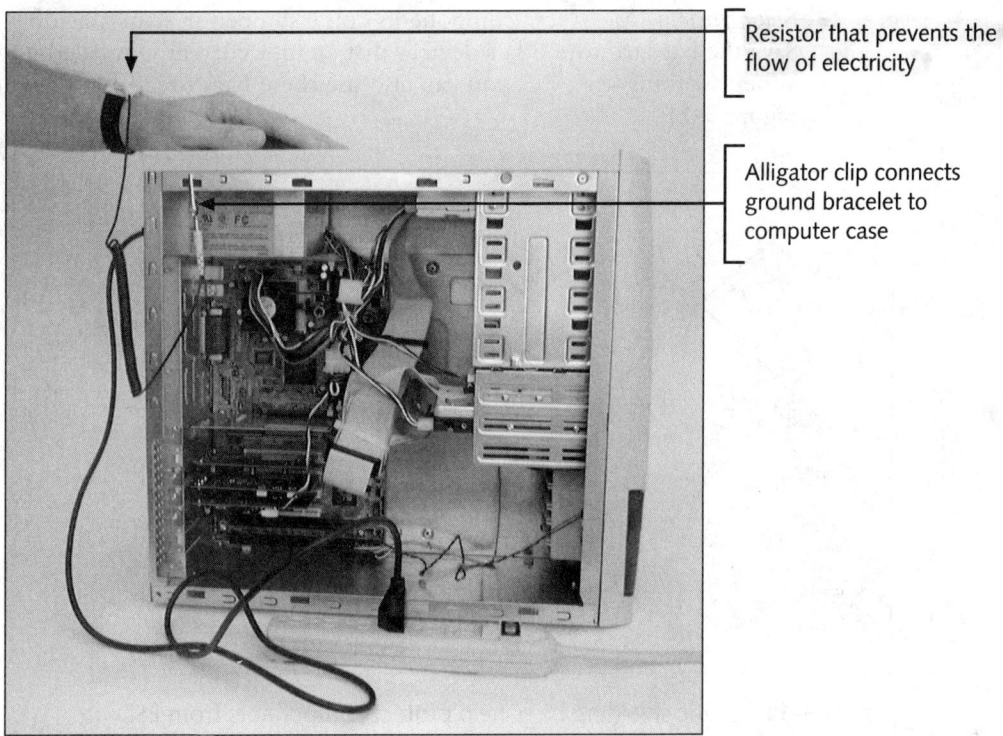

Resistor that prevents the
flow of electricity

Alligator clip connects
ground bracelet to
computer case

Figure 3-9   A ground bracelet, which protects computer components from ESD, can clip
to the side of the computer case and eliminates ESD between you and
the case

■ *Ground mats.* Ground mats can come equipped with a cord to plug into a wall
outlet to provide a grounded surface on which to work. If you lift the component off the mat, it is no longer grounded and is susceptible to ESD. Figure 3-10
shows a ground mat.

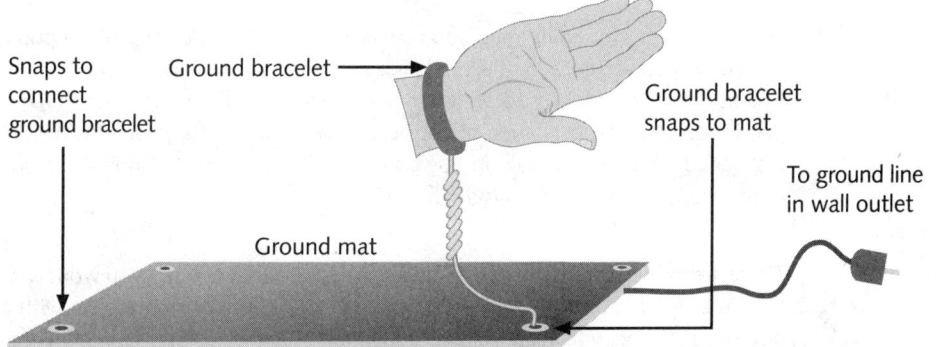

Snaps to
connect
ground bracelet

Ground bracelet

Ground bracelet
snaps to mat

To ground line
in wall outlet

Ground mat

Figure 3-10   A ground bracelet can be connected to a ground mat, which is grounded
by the wall outlet

- *Static shielding bags.* New components come shipped in static shielding bags. Save the bags to store other devices that are not currently installed in a PC. When working on a PC, you can also use these bags to lay components on. See Figure 3-11.

Figure 3-11   Static shielding bags help protect components from ESD

The best way to guard against ESD is to use a ground bracelet together with a ground mat. Consider a ground bracelet to be essential equipment when working on a computer. However, if you find yourself in a situation where you must work without one, touch the computer case or the power supply before you touch a component. When passing a chip to another person, ground yourself and then touch the other person·before you pass the chip. Leave components inside their protective bags until ready to use. Work on hard floors, not carpet, or use antistatic spray on the carpets. Generally, don't work on a computer if you or the computer have just come inside from the cold, as the potential for ESD is higher.

Besides using a grounding mat, you can also create a ground for the computer case by leaving the power cord to the case plugged into the wall outlet. This is safe enough because the power is turned off when you work inside the case. However, if you happen to touch an exposed area of the power switch inside the case, it is possible to get a shock. Because of this risk, in this book, you are directed to unplug the power cord to the PC before you work inside the case.

There are exceptions to the rule of always being grounded when you work with PCs. You *don't* want to be grounded when working inside a monitor or with a power supply or with high-voltage equipment such as a laser printer. These devices maintain high charges of electricity, even when the power is turned off. Inside a monitor case, the electricity stored in capacitors poses substantial danger.

3

When working inside a monitor, you don't want to be grounded, because you would provide a conduit for the voltage to discharge through your body. In this situation, be careful not to ground yourself. The situation is similar when working with a power supply. *Don't* wear a ground bracelet when working inside these devices, because you don't want to be the ground for these charges!

Recall that ESD (electrostatic discharge) is a brief flow of electricity caused by contact between two objects that have a difference in voltage potential. Now that you better understand the concept of grounding, you can see why it is important that you be grounded before you work with most computer components. If both you and the component you are going to work with are grounded, then there will be no potential voltage difference between you and the component, and no electrical discharge will occur when you touch it.

EMI (Electromagnetic Interference)

Another phenomenon that can cause electrical problems with computers is **electromagnetic interference (EMI)**. EMI is caused by the magnetic field that is produced as a side effect when electricity flows. EMI in the radio frequency range, which is called radio frequency interference (RFI), can cause problems with radio and TV reception. Data in data cables that cross an electromagnetic field can become corrupted, causing crosstalk. Crosstalk is partly controlled by using shielded data cables covered with a protective material. Power supplies are also shielded to prevent them from emitting EMI.

 PCs can emit EMI to other nearby PCs, which is one reason a computer needs to be inside a case. To help cut down on EMI between PCs, always install face plates in empty drive bays or slot covers over empty expansion slots.

If a PC persists in giving mysterious, intermittent errors, one thing to suspect is EMI. Try moving the PC to a new location. If the problem persists, try moving it to a location that uses an entirely different electric circuit. One simple way to detect the presence of EMI is to use an inexpensive AM radio. Turn the tuning dial away from a station into a low-frequency range. With the radio on, you can hear the static produced by EMI. Try putting the radio next to several electronic devices to detect the EMI they emit.

If EMI in the electrical circuits coming to the PC is a significant problem, you can use a line conditioner that filters out the electrical noise causing the EMI. Line conditioners are discussed later in this chapter.

Surge Protection and Battery Backup

In addition to protecting your PC against ESD and EMI, you need to consider how power coming into a computer is regulated. A wide range of devices on the market filter the AC input to computers and their peripherals (that is, condition the AC input to eliminate highs and lows) and provide backup power when the AC fails. These devices, installed between the house current and the computer, fall into three general categories: surge suppressors, power conditioners, and uninterruptible power supplies (UPSs). All these devices should have the UL (Underwriters Laboratory) logo, which ensures that the device has been tested by this agency, a provider of product safety certification.

Surge suppressors protect equipment against sudden changes in the level of power, such as spikes that result from lightning strikes. Power conditioners and uninterruptible power supplies both condition the power passing through them (alter it so as to provide continuous voltages). Both provide a degree of protection against **spikes** (temporary surges of voltage) and raise the voltage when it drops during **brownouts** (temporary reductions of voltage). These devices are measured by the load they support in watts, volt-amperes (VA), or kilovolt-amperes (kVA).

To determine how much VA is required to support your system, multiply the amperage of each component by 120 volts and then add up the VA for all components. For example, a 17-inch monitor has 1.9 A written on the back of the monitor, which means 1.9 amps. Multiply that value times 120 volts and you see that 228 VA is required. A Pentium PC with a 17-inch monitor and tape backup system requires about 500 VA of support.

Surge Suppressors

A **surge suppressor**, also called a **surge protector**, provides a row of power outlets and an on/off switch that protects equipment from overvoltages on AC power lines and telephone lines. A surge suppressor might be a shunt type that absorbs the surge, a series type that blocks the surge from flowing, or a combination of the two. The shunt-type suppressor is measured by **clamping voltage**, a term that describes the let-through voltage. Surge suppressors can come as power strips (note that not all power strips have surge protection), wall-mounted units that plug into AC outlets, or consoles designed to sit underneath the monitor on a desk top. Some provide an RJ-11 telephone jack to protect modems and fax machines from spikes.

Whenever there is a power outage, unless you have a reliable power conditioner or UPS installed, unplug all power cords to the PC, printers, monitors, and the like. Sometimes when the power returns, there are sudden spikes accompanied by another brief outage. You don't want to subject your equipment to these surges. When buying a surge suppressor, look for those that guarantee against damage from lightning and that reimburse for equipment destroyed while the surge suppressor is in use.

CAUTION

Surge suppressors are not always reliable, and once the fuse inside the suppressor is blown, a surge suppressor no longer protects equipment from a power surge. It continues to provide power without warning you that the protection is lost.

A **data line protector** serves the same function for your telephone line to your modem that a surge suppressor does for the electrical lines. Telephone lines carry a small current of electricity and need to be protected against spikes, just as electrical lines do. The let–through rating for a data line protector for a phone line should be no more than 260 volts.

Power Conditioners

In addition to providing protection against spikes, **power conditioners** also regulate, or condition, the power, providing continuous voltage during brownouts. These voltage regulators, sometimes called **line conditioners**, can come as small desktop units.

These electricity filters are a good investment if the AC in your community suffers from excessive spikes and brownouts. However, if the device is rated under 1 kVA, it will probably only provide corrections for brownouts, not for spikes. Line conditioners, like surge suppressors, provide no protection against a total blackout (complete loss of power).

Uninterruptible Power Supply

Unlike a power conditioner, the **UPS (uninterruptible power supply)** provides a backup power supply in the event that the AC fails completely. The UPS also offers some filtering of the AC. The power supplies in most computers can operate over a wide range of electrical voltage input, but operating the computer under these conditions for extended periods of time can shorten the life not only of the power supply, but also of the computer. UPSs offer these benefits:

- Condition the line for both brownouts and spikes
- Provide backup power during a blackout
- Protect against very high spikes that could damage the equipment

A UPS device suitably priced for personal computer systems is designed as either a standby device, an inline device, or a line-interactive device (which combines features of the first two). Among these three types of UPS devices, there are several variations on the market, whose prices vary widely.

A common UPS device is a rather heavy box that plugs into an AC outlet and provides one or more outlets for the computer and its peripherals (see Figure 3-12). It has an on/off switch, requires no maintenance, and is very simple to install.

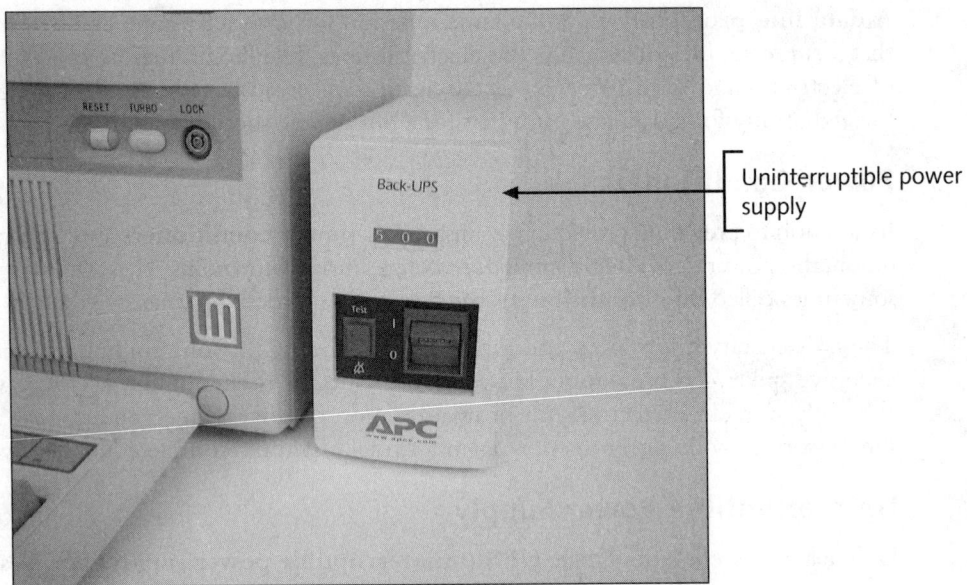

Uninterruptible power supply

Figure 3-12   Uninterruptible power supply (UPS)

The Intelligent UPS Some UPSs can be controlled by software from a computer, to allow for additional functionality. For example, from the front panel of some UPSs you can check for a weak battery. If the UPS is an **intelligent UPS**, you can perform the same function from utility software installed on your computer. In order for a UPS to accommodate this feature, it must have a serial port connection to the PC and a microprocessor on board. Some of the things this utility software and an intelligent UPS can do are:

- Diagnose the UPS
- Check for a weak battery
- Monitor the quality of electricity received
- Monitor the percentage of load the UPS is carrying during a blackout
- Automatically schedule the weak-battery test or UPS diagnostic test
- Send an alarm to workstations on a network to prepare for a shutdown
- Close down all servers protected by the UPS during a blackout
- Provide pager notification to a facilities manager if the power goes out
- After a shutdown, allow for startup from a remote location over phone lines

Windows NT, Windows 2000, and Windows XP offer support for intelligent UPSs. You can monitor and control the devices from the UPS dialog box accessible through Control Panel. The Windows 2000 controls were developed by Microsoft and American Power Conversion (APC), a leading manufacturer of UPSs.

What to Consider When Buying a UPS When you purchase a UPS, cost often drives the decision about how much and what kind of protection you buy. However, do not buy an inline UPS that runs at full capacity. A battery charger operating at full capacity produces heat, which can reduce the life of the battery. The UPS rating should exceed your total VA or wattage output by at least 25 percent. Also be aware of the degree of line conditioning that the UPS provides. Consider the warranty and service policies as well as the guarantee the UPS manufacturer gives for the equipment that the UPS protects. Table 3-2 lists some UPS manufacturers.

3

Table 3-2   UPS manufacturers

Manufacturer	Web site
MGE UPS Systems	www.mgeups.com
American Power Conversion Corp. (APC)	www.apcc.com
Tripp Lite	www.tripplite.com
Belkin Components	www.belkin.com
Invensys	www.bestpower.com
Liebert Corporation	www.liebert.com
Para Systems, Inc.	www.minuteman-ups.com
Toshiba International Corp.	www.tic.toshiba.com

THE COMPUTER CASE AND FORM FACTORS

Because power supplies and computer cases are often sold together and must be compatible with each other, we now turn our attention to the computer case. Also, the power supply and case must be purchased to fit the motherboard. When you put together a new system, or replace components in an existing system, the form factors of the motherboard, power supply, and case must all match. The **form factor** is a description of the size, shape, and general makeup of a hardware component.

When you are deciding which form factor to use, the motherboard drives the decision because it determines the overall power of the system and what it can do. Once you've decided to use a certain form factor for the motherboard, then you must use the same form factor for the case and power supply. Using a matching form factor for the power supply and case assures you of these things:

- The motherboard will fit in the case.
- The power supply cords to the motherboard will provide the correct voltage, and the connectors will match the connections on the board.
- The holes in the motherboard will align with the holes in the case for anchoring the board to the case.
- Holes in the case will align with ports coming off the motherboard.
- For some form factors, wires for switches and lights on the front of the case will match up with connections on the motherboard.

Case, Power Supply, and Motherboard Form Factors

There are several form factors that apply to power supplies, cases, and motherboards: the older and outdated XT, AT, ATX, LPX, NLX, and backplane systems. Each of these form factors has several variations. The four most common form factors used on personal computers today are the AT, Baby AT, ATX, and Mini-ATX. The most popular form factor is the ATX. This form factor and earlier, less common, and up-and-coming form factors are discussed next.

AT Form Factor

The **AT** form factor, sometimes called **full AT**, is used on older motherboards that measured 12" × 13.8". This form factor uses the full-size AT cases used by the original IBM AT (Advanced Technology) personal computer. Later, a smaller, more convenient version of AT was invented called the Baby AT. Full AT motherboards cannot be used with smaller AT cases or with newer ATX cases. Because of their dimensions and configuration, full AT systems are difficult to install, service, and upgrade. One problem with the AT form factor is that the CPU is placed on the motherboard in front of the expansion slots; long cards in these slots might not fit because they will bump into the CPU. You can visualize this problem by looking at the AT motherboard in Figure 3-13. Recall that power supplies for AT systems supply +5, -5, +12 and -12 volts to the motherboard and other components. Full AT boards are no longer being produced by most manufacturers.

Figure 3-13 The CPU on the AT motherboard sits in front of the expansion slots

Baby AT

Baby AT was the industry standard form factor from about 1993 to 1997 because of its improved flexibility over full AT. Power supplies designed for the Baby AT form factor blow air out of the computer case. At 13" × 8.7", Baby AT motherboards are smaller than full AT motherboards and will fit into many types of cases, including newer ATX cases that are designed to provide backward compatibility. The problem with the position of the CPU in relation to expansion slots still was not resolved in the Baby AT motherboards. In addition, because of the configuration of the motherboard and its orientation within the case, drives and other devices are not positioned close to their connections on the motherboard, meaning that cables might reach across the motherboard and not be long enough.

ATX

ATX is the most common form factor in use today. It is an open, nonproprietary industry specification that was originally developed by Intel in 1995. ATX improved upon AT by making it easier to add and remove components, providing greater support for I/O devices and processor technology, and lowering costs. Components on the motherboard are arranged so as not to interfere with each other and for better position inside the case. Also, the position of the power supply and drives inside the case makes it easier to connect them to the motherboard, and makes it possible to reduce cable lengths, which can help reduce the potential for EMI and corrupted data. The number of wires needed to connect the switches and lights on the front of the case to components inside the case is reduced, making the installation simpler and reducing the potential for mistakes.

An ATX motherboard measures 12" × 9.6", making it smaller than a full AT motherboard. On an ATX motherboard, the CPU and memory slots are rotated 90 degrees from the position on the AT motherboard so that instead of sitting in front of the expansion slots, the CPU and memory slots sit beside them, so as not to interfere with full-length expansion cards. See Figure 3-14. The ATX power supply and motherboard use a single power connector called the P1 connector that, in addition to the voltages provided by AT, includes a +3.3-volt circuit for a low-voltage CPU. In addition to the P1 connector, there can be one or more auxiliary connectors used to supply power to the CPU fan. ATX motherboards and power supplies cannot be used in cases designed for Baby AT and LPX, though many ATX cases will accommodate Baby AT motherboards.

An additional difference between AT and ATX systems is that the power supply fan blows air into the case rather than out of it, cooling the processor directly. Using an ATX power supply can help lower noise and cost of cooling, because the power supply has a side vent located in just the right position to blow air on the processor and expansion cards. This can reduce the need to add additional fans and heat sinks.

Another feature of an ATX motherboard that is not found on AT boards is a **soft switch**, sometimes called the **soft power** feature. Using this feature, an OS, such as Windows 98 or Windows 2000, can turn off the power to a system after the shutdown procedure is done. Also, CMOS can be configured to cause a keystroke or network activity to power up the system (wake on LAN). On older AT systems, when the PC is running and a user presses the power switch on the front of the case, the power is abruptly turned off. The operating system does not have the opportunity to close down gracefully and, on the next power up, the system might have errors. With a soft switch controlling an ATX system and an operating system that supports the feature, if the user presses the power switch on the front of the case while the computer is on, the OS will go through a normal shutdown procedure before powering off.

In addition to regular ATX, there are several other types of ATX boards. **Mini-ATX** is a smaller ATX board (11.2" × 8.2") and can be used with ATX cases and power supplies. **MicroATX** addresses some newer technologies that have come along since the original development of ATX. **FlexATX** allows for maximum flexibility in the design of system cases and boards and therefore can be a good choice for custom systems.

P1 power connector

16-bit ISA expansion slot

AGP slot
Five PCI expansion slots

Parallel port
Two serial ports

Two USB ports
Keyboard and mouse port

Slot 1 for Pentium III with supporting braces

Four RAM slots with one DIMM installed

Figure 3-14   The CPU on an ATX motherboard sits beside the expansion slots and does not block the room needed for long expansion cards

LPX and Mini LPX

LPX and **Mini-LPX** were originally developed by Western Digital and are often used in low-cost systems that are sold in large electronics stores. Mini-LPX is a smaller version of the LPX motherboard. In LPX systems, the motherboard has only one expansion slot, in which a **riser card**, or **bus riser**, is mounted (see Figure 3-15). Expansion cards are then mounted on the riser card, ending up parallel to the motherboard instead of perpendicular to it as in AT and ATX. A low-end video controller is included on the motherboard, making a video card unnecessary and reducing the overall price of the system. LPX systems are not easy to upgrade and cannot handle the physical size of recently developed processors. They are also not designed to handle the higher temperature at which faster processors operate. In addition, a manufacturer often makes proprietary changes to the standard LPX motherboard design, thus forcing you to use only the manufacturer's power supply. LPX and Mini-LPX use small cases called low profile cases and slimline cases, which are discussed in the next section.

Figure 3-15   The slimline LPX riser form factor uses a riser card to provide expansion slots, and the video controller is contained on the motherboard

NLX

NLX is a newer form factor for low-end personal computer motherboards. NLX boards look something like LPX boards and are also used with low-profile cases. However, NLX boards provide greater support for current and up-and-coming processor technologies. The NLX form factor is designed to be flexible and to use space efficiently. In Figure 3-16 you can see that the NLX motherboard has a slot to be used by a riser board that contains additional expansion slots and connectors for the floppy drive and hard drives.

Backplane Systems

Backplane systems do not use a true motherboard. The backplane is a board that normally sits against the back of a proprietary case that has slots on it for other cards. **Active backplanes** contain no circuits other than bus connectors and some buffer and driver circuits. **Passive backplanes** contain no circuitry at all; the circuits are all located on a mothercard, a circuit board that is plugged into the backplane and contains a CPU. These systems are generally not used in personal computers. Passive backplanes are sometimes used for industrial rack-mounted systems and high-end file servers. A rack-mounted system is not designed for personal use, and often several of these systems are mounted in cases stacked on a rack for easy access by technicians.

Types of Cases

There are several types and sizes of cases on the market for each form factor. The computer case, sometimes called the chassis, houses the power supply, motherboard, expansion cards, and drives. The case has lights and switches on the front panel that can be used to control and monitor the PC. Generally, the larger the case, the larger the power supply and the more amps it carries. These large cases allow for the extra space and power that are needed for a larger number of devices, such as multiple hard drives needed in a server.

Figure 3-16   The NLX form factor uses a riser card that connects to the motherboard and provides expansion slots for expansion cards

Cases for personal computers and notebooks fall into three major categories: desktop cases, tower cases, and laptop cases. Within each of these categories, there are several variations.

Desktop Cases

The classic case with four drive bays and around six expansion slots that sits on your desktop and does double duty as a monitor stand is called a desktop case. The motherboard sits on the bottom of a desktop case and the power supply is near the back. Because of the space a desktop case takes up, it has fallen out of favor in recent years and is being replaced by smaller and more space-efficient cases.

For low-end desktop systems, **compact cases**, sometimes called **low-profile** or **slimline cases**, follow either the NLX, LPX, or Mini-LPX form factor. They are likely to have fewer drive bays, but they generally still provide for some expansion. You can see the rear of a compact case in Figure 3-17. An LPX motherboard that uses this case has a riser card for expansion cards, which is why the expansion card slots in the figure are running parallel to the motherboard sitting on the bottom of the case.

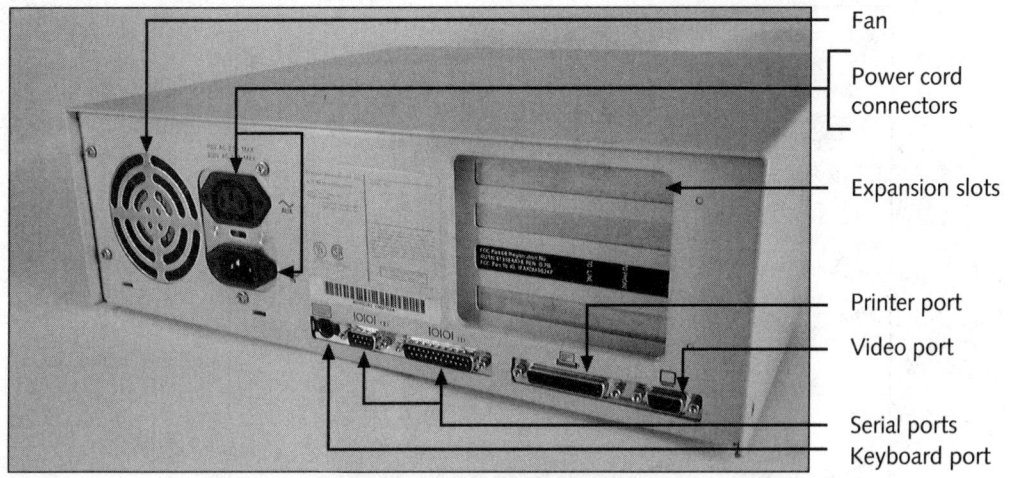

Fan

Power cord connectors

Expansion slots

Printer port

Video port

Serial ports
Keyboard port

Figure 3-17   Because the expansion slots are running parallel to the motherboard on the bottom of this desktop case, you know a riser card is used

Tower Cases

A **tower case** can be as much as two feet high and has room for several drives. This type of case is often used for servers but is also good for PC users who anticipate making upgrades, because tower cases provide maximum space for working inside a computer and moving components around. Variations in tower cases include the minitower, midsize tower, and full-size tower.

Midsize towers, also called miditowers, are the most popular. They are midrange in size and generally have around six expansion slots and four drive bays, providing moderate potential for expansion. The minitower, also called a microtower, is the smallest type of tower case and does not provide room for expansion. These cases, sometimes called slimline tower cases, are built for NLX systems. Other minitowers can accommodate Baby AT and Mini-ATX motherboards. Minitowers are good for PC users who are concerned about space, plan to stick with the system they bought, do not plan to upgrade, and want to buy another system when their current one is outdated. A minitower that accommodates a Baby AT or a full ATX system is shown in Figure 3-18. Full-size towers are used for high-end personal computers and servers. They are usually built to accommodate ATX, Mini-ATX, and Baby AT systems. Figure 3-19 shows examples of each of the three main tower sizes, as well as two desktop cases.

Figure 3-18   Minitower for a Baby AT or full ATX motherboard

Notebook Cases

Notebook cases are used for portable computers that have all the components of a desktop computer. Most notebooks weigh between six and eight pounds. The cost and power of notebook systems can vary widely. As with other small systems, notebooks can present difficulties in expansion. The smallest notebook cases are called subnotebooks. Full subnotebook systems usually only weigh about three or four pounds. Notebook designs are often highly proprietary, but generally, they are designed to conserve space, allow portability, use less power, and produce less heat. The case fan in a notebook is usually attached to a thermometer and runs only when the temperature needs to be lowered. Additionally, the transformer and rectifier functions of the power supply are often moved to an AC adapter located on the power cable.

In summary, when selecting a computer case, remember that the case needs to fit its intended use. For example, if you are building an entry-level server that will have a floppy drive, three hard drives, and a CD-ROM drive, you might also need two case fans to keep all these drives cool. Therefore, you know that you will need a case that has slots and space for everything. In addition, you need to look at the total electrical requirements when everything is running at the same time, and make sure that you get a power supply that can handle them.

Figure 3-19   Tower and desktop cases

There are many different manufacturers of cases and power supplies. Some specialize in high-end custom systems, while others make a variety of cases, from rack-mounted servers to low-profile desktops. A few case and power supply vendors are listed in Table 3-3.

Table 3-3   Manufacturers of cases and power supplies for personal computers

Manufacturer	Web Site
Alien Media	www.alienmedia.com.au/cases
Axxion Group Corporation	www.axxion.com
Sunus Sunteck	www.suntekgroup.com
Enlight Corporation	www.enlightcorp.com
PC Power and Cooling	www.pcpowerandcooling.com
PCI Case Group	www.pcicase.co.uk/menu.htm
Casse Industry Corp.	www.kingspao.com
Colorcase	www.colorcase.com

DETECTING AND CORRECTING POWER SUPPLY PROBLEMS

If you assemble a PC from parts, most often you purchase a computer case with the power supply already installed in it. However, you might need to exchange the power supply of an existing PC because it is damaged, or because you need to upgrade to one with more power. In this section, you will learn how to troubleshoot the power system and power supply in your computer as well as how to upgrade and install power supplies. The first step in this process is to learn how to measure the voltage of a power supply.

Measuring the Voltage of a Power Supply

If you suspect a problem with a power supply, the simplest and preferred solution is to exchange it with a new one. However, in some situations, you might want to measure the voltage output. When a power supply is working properly, voltages all fall within an acceptable range (plus or minus 10 percent). However, be aware that even if measured voltage is within the appropriate range, a power supply can still cause problems. This is because problems with power supplies are intermittent—in other words, they come and go. Therefore, if the voltages are correct, you should still suspect the power supply to be the problem when certain symptoms are present. (You will learn about troubleshooting power supplies later in this chapter.) To learn for certain whether the power supply is the problem, replace it with a unit you know is good.

Using a Multimeter

A voltmeter measures the difference in electrical potential between two points, in volts, and an ammeter measures electrical current in amps. Figure 3-20 shows a **multimeter**, which can be used as either a voltmeter or an ammeter, or can measure resistance or continuity (the presence of a complete circuit with no resistance to current), depending on a dial or function switch setting. Less expensive multimeters commonly measure voltage, resistance, and continuity, but not amps. Measure voltage and amps while the electricity is on. Measure resistance and continuity while the electricity is off. For the specific details of how to use your multimeter, consult the manual, which explains what you can measure with the multimeter and how to use it.

Figure 3-20   A digital multimeter

A multimeter can provide either a digital or an analog display. A digital display shows the readings as digits displayed on an LCD (liquid crystal display) panel. A digital multimeter is sometimes called a DMM (digital multimeter) or a DVM (digital voltage meter). An analog display shows the readings as a needle moving across a scale of values. Multimeters are sometimes small, portable battery-powered units. Larger ones are designed to sit on a countertop and are powered by a wall outlet.

When you use a multimeter, you must tell it three things before you begin: (1) what you want it to measure (voltage, current, or resistance), (2) whether the current is AC or DC, and (3) what range of values it should expect. If you are measuring the voltage output from a wall outlet (110–120 V), the range should be much higher than when measuring the voltage output of a computer power supply (3–12 V). Setting the range high assures you that the meter can handle a large input without pegging the needle (exceeding the highest value that the meter is designed to measure) or damaging the meter. However, if you set the range too high, you might not see the voltage register at all. Set the range low enough to ensure that the measure is as accurate as you need, but not so low as to be less than the expected voltage. When you set the range too low on some digital multimeters, the meter reads OL on the display.

For example, to measure the voltage of house current, if you expect the voltage to be 115 volts, set the voltage range from 0 to somewhere between 120 and 130 volts. You want the high end of the range to be slightly higher than the expected voltage. Most meters do not allow a very large voltage or current into the meter when the range is set low, to protect the meter. Some multimeters are **autorange meters**, which sense the quantity of input and set the range accordingly.

A meter comes with two test probes. One is usually red and the other black. Install the red probe at the positive (+) jack on the meter and the black probe at the negative (−) jack.

How to Measure Voltage   To measure voltage, place the other end of the black probe at the ground point and the other end of the red probe at the hot point, without disconnecting anything in the circuit, and with the power on. For example, to measure voltage using the multimeter in Figure 3-20, turn the function switch dial to DCV for DC voltage measurement. This meter is autoranging, so this is all that needs to be set. With the power on, place the two probes in position and read the voltage from the LCD panel. The DATA-H (data hold) switch allows you to freeze the displayed reading.

CAUTION

When using a multimeter to measure voltage, current, or resistance, be careful not to touch a chip with the probes.

How to Measure Current In most troubleshooting situations, you will measure voltage, not current. However, you should know how to measure current, which is discussed here. To measure current in amps, the multimeter itself must be part of the circuit. Disconnect the circuit at some point so that you can connect the multimeter in line to find a measure in amps. Not all multimeters can measure amps.

How to Measure Continuity You can also use a multimeter to measure continuity. If there is little or no resistance (less than 20 ohms gives continuity in a PC) in a wire or a closed connection between two points, the path for electricity between the two points is unhindered or "continuous." This measurement is taken with no electricity present in the circuit.

For example, if you want to know that pin 2 on one end of a serial cable is connected to pin 3 on the other end of the cable, set the multimeter to measure continuity, and work without the cable being connected to anything. Put one probe on pin 2 at one end of the cable and the other probe on pin 3 at the other end. If the two pins connect, the multimeter indicates this with a reading on the LCD panel, or a buzzer sounds (see the multimeter documentation). In this situation, you might find that the probe is too large to extend into the pinhole of the female connection of the cable. A straightened small paper clip works well here to extend the probe. However, be very careful not to use a paper clip that is too thick and might widen the size of the pinhole, because this can later prevent the pinhole from making a good connection.

One way to determine if a fuse is good is to measure continuity. Set a multimeter to measure continuity, and place its probes on each end of the fuse. If the fuse has continuity, then it is good. If the multimeter does not have a continuity setting, set it to measure resistance. If the reading in ohms is approximately zero, there is no resistance and the fuse is good. If the reading is infinity, there is infinite resistance and the fuse is blown and should not be used.

How to Measure the Voltage of a Power Supply

To determine whether a power supply is working properly, measure the voltage of each circuit supported by the power supply. First, open the computer case and identify all power cords coming from the power supply. Look for the cords from the power supply to the motherboard and other power cords to the drives (see Figure 3-21).

Probes
Multimeter
Power supply
Hard drive connection
Unused miniature power
connector for floppy drive
Motherboard
P8 and P9

PB1   PB2

Figure 3-21   Multimeter measuring voltage on an AT motherboard

The computer must be turned on to test the power supply output. Be very careful not to touch any chips or disturb any circuit boards as you work. The voltage output from the power supply is no more than 14 volts, which is not enough to seriously hurt you if you accidentally touch a hot probe. However, you can damage the computer if you are not careful.

You can hurt yourself if you accidentally create a short circuit from the power supply to ground through the probe. If you touch the probe to the hot circuit and also to ground, the current is diverted from the computer circuit and through the probe to ground. This short might be enough to cause a spark or to melt the probe, which can happen if you allow the two probes to touch each other while one of them is attached to the hot circuit and the other is attached to ground. Make sure the probes only touch one metal object, preferably only a single power pin on a connector, or you could cause a short.

Because of the danger of touching a hot probe to a ground probe, you might prefer not to put the black probe into a ground lead that is too close to the hot probe. Instead, when the directions say to place the black probe on a lead that is very close to the hot probe, you can use a black wire lead on an unused power supply connection meant for a hard drive. The idea is that the black probe should always be placed on a ground or black lead.

All ground leads are considered at ground, no matter what number they are assigned. Therefore, you can consider all black leads to be equal. For an AT motherboard, the ground leads for P8 and P9 are the four black center leads 5, 6, 7, and 8. For an ATX motherboard, the ground leads are seven black leads in center positions on the ATX P1 power connector. The ground leads for a hard drive power connection are the two black center leads, 2 and 3.

We first discuss how to measure the power output for AT and ATX motherboards and then for a secondary storage device.

Measuring Voltage Output to an AT Motherboard

1. Remove the cover of the computer. The voltage range for each connection is often written on the top of the power supply. The two power connections to the motherboard are often labeled P8 and P9. Figure 3–22 shows a closeup of the two connections, P8 and P9, coming from the power supply to the motherboard. Each connection has six leads, for a total of 12 leads. Of these 12, four are ground connections, and lead 1 is a "power good" pin, used to indicate that the motherboard is receiving power. A common arrangement for these 12 leads is listed in Table 3–4.

2. Set the multimeter to measure voltage in a range of 20 volts, and set the AC/DC switch to DC. Insert the black probe into the − jack and the red probe into the + jack of the meter.

3. Turn on the multimeter, and turn on the computer.

4. To measure the +12-volt circuit and all four ground leads:

   a. Place the red probe on lead 3. The probe is shaped like a needle (alligator clips don't work too well here). Insert the needle down into the lead housing as far as you can. Place the black probe on lead 5. The acceptable range is +10.8 to +13.2 volts.

   b. Place the red probe on lead 3, and place the black probe on lead 6. The acceptable range is +10.8 to +13.2 volts.

   c. Place the red probe on lead 3, and place the black probe on lead 7. The acceptable range is +10.8 to +13.2 volts.

   d. Place the red probe on lead 3, and place the black probe on lead 8. The acceptable range is +10.8 to +13.2 volts.

5. To measure the −12-volt circuit, place the red probe on lead 4, and place the black probe on any ground lead or on the computer case, which is also grounded. The acceptable range is −10.8 to 13.2 volts.

Figure 3-22   AT power supply connections

Table 3-4   Twelve leads to the AT motherboard from the AT power supply

Connection	Lead	Description	Acceptable Range
P8	1	"Power Good"	
	2	Not used or +5 volts	+4.4 to +5.2 volts
	3	+12 volts	+10.8 to +13.2 volts
	4	−12 volts	−10.8 to −13.2 volts
	5	Black ground	
	6	Black ground	
P9	7	Black ground	
	8	Black ground	
	9	−5 volts	−4.5 to −5.5 volts
	10	+5 volts	+4.5 to +5.5 volts
	11	+5 volts	+4.5 to +5.5 volts
	12	+5 volts	+4.5 to +5.5 volts

6. To measure the −5-volt circuit, place the red probe on lead 9, and place the black probe on any ground. The acceptable range is −4.5 to −5.5 volts.

7. To measure the three +5-volt circuits:

   a. Place the red probe on lead 10, and place the black probe on any ground. The acceptable range is +4.5 to +5.5 volts.

   b. Place the red probe on lead 11, and place the black probe on any ground. The acceptable range is +4.5 to +5.5 volts.

   c. Place the red probe on lead 12, and place the black probe on any ground. The acceptable range is +4.5 to +5.5 volts.

8. Replace the cover.

Measuring Voltage Output to an ATX Motherboard   To measure the output to the ATX motherboard, follow the same procedure as with the AT motherboard. Recall that the ATX board uses 3.3, 5, and 12 volts coming from the power supply. Figure 3-23 shows the power output of each pin on the connector. Looking at Figure 3-23, you can see the distinguishing shape of each side of the connector. Notice the different hole shapes (square or rounded) on each side of the connector, ensuring that the plug from the power supply is oriented correctly in the connector. Also notice the notch on the connector and also on the pinout diagram on the right side of the figure. Use this notch to help orient you as you read the pinouts. Table 3-5 lists the leads to the motherboard and their acceptable voltage ranges.

Figure 3-23   Power connection on an ATX motherboard

Table 3-5   Twenty leads to the ATX motherboard from the ATX power supply

Unnotched Side			Notched Side		
Lead	Description	Acceptable Range	Lead	Description	Acceptable Range (volts)
1	+12 volts	+10.8 to +13.2V	11	+5 volts	+4.5 to +5.5V
2	+5 volts standby	+4.5 to +5.5V	12	+5 volts	+4.5 to +5.5V
3	Power Good		13	-5 volts	-4.5 to -5.5V
4	Black ground		14	Black ground	
5	+5 volts	+4.5 to +5.5V	15	Black ground	
6	Black ground		16	Black ground	
7	+5 volts	+4.5 to +5.5V	17	Pwr supply on	
8	Black ground		18	Black ground	
9	+3.3 volts	+3.1 to +3.5V	19	-12 volts	-10.8 to -13.2V
10	+3.3 volts	+3.1 to +3.5V	20	+3.3 volts	+3.1 to +3.5V

3

TIP   Dell ATX power supplies and motherboards made after 1998 might not use the standard P1 pinouts for ATX, although the power connectors look the same. For this reason, *never* use a Dell power supply with a non-Dell motherboard, or a Dell motherboard with a non-Dell power supply, without first verifying that the power connector pinouts match; otherwise, you might destroy the power supply, the motherboard, or both. A pinout converter to convert the P1 connector of a Dell power supply or motherboard to standard ATX can be purchased from Centrix International Corp. (*www.centrix-intl.com*). Also, PC Power and Cooling (*www.pcpowerandcooling.com*) makes a power supply modified to work with a Dell motherboard.

Testing the Power Output to a Floppy or Hard Drive   The power cords to the floppy disk drive, hard drive, and CD-ROM drive all supply the same voltage: one +5-volt circuit and one +12-volt circuit. The power connection to any drive uses four leads; the two outside connections are hot, and the two inside connections are ground (see Figure 3-23). The power connection to a 3.5-inch floppy disk drive is usually a miniature connection, as shown in Figure 3-22. Follow these steps to measure the voltage to any drive:

1. With the drive plugged in, turn the computer on.
2. Set the multimeter to measure voltage as described previously.
3. Place the red probe on lead 1, shown in the drive connection callout in Figure 3-23, and place the black probe on lead 2 or 3 (ground). The acceptable range is +10.8 to +13.2 volts.
4. Place the red probe on lead 4, and place the black probe on lead 2 or 3 (ground). The acceptable range is +4.5 to +5.5 volts.

You may choose to alter the method you use to ground the black probe. In Step 4 above, the red probe and black probe are very close to each other. You may choose to keep them farther apart by placing the black probe in a ground lead of an unused hard drive connection.

Upgrading Your Power Supply

Sometimes a power supply upgrade is necessary when you are adding new devices. If you are installing a hard drive or DVD drive and are concerned that the power supply is not adequate, test it after you finish the installation. Make as many of the devices in your system work at the same time as possible. For example, you can make both the new drive and the floppy drive work at the same time by copying files from one to the other. If the new drive and the floppy drive each work independently, but data errors occur when both are working at the same time, suspect a shortage of electrical power.

If you prefer a more technical approach, you can estimate how much total wattage your system needs by calculating the watts for each circuit and adding them together, as discussed earlier. In most cases, the computer's power supply is more than adequate if you add only one or two new devices.

Most often you purchase a computer case with a power supply already installed in it, but power supplies can be purchased separately from cases. Power supplies for microcomputers range from 200 watts for a small desktop computer system to 600 watts for a tower floor model that uses many multimedia or other power-hungry devices. Most case vendors also make power supplies (refer to Table 3-3).

The easiest way to fix a power supply you suspect is faulty is to replace it. You can determine if the power supply really is the problem by turning off the PC, opening the computer case, and setting the new power supply on top of the old one. Disconnect the old power supply's cords and plug the PC devices into the new power supply. Turn on the PC and verify that the new power supply solves your problem before installing it.

Follow this procedure to install a power supply:

1. Turn off the power.

2. Remove all external power cables from the power supply connections.

3. Remove the case cover.

4. Disconnect all power cords from the power supply to other devices.

5. Determine which components must be removed before the power supply can be safely removed from the case. You might need to remove the hard drive, several cards, or the CD-ROM drive. In some cases, you may even need to remove the motherboard.

6. Remove all the components necessary to get to the power supply. Remember to protect the components from static electricity as you work.

7. Unscrew the screws on the back of the computer case that hold the power supply to the case.

8. Look on the bottom or back of the case for slots that are holding the power supply in position. Often the power supply must be shifted in one direction to free it from the slots.

9. Remove the power supply.

10. Place the new power supply into position, sliding it into the slots used by the old power supply.

11. Replace the power supply screws.

12. Replace all other components.

13. Before replacing the case cover, connect the power cords, turn on the PC, and verify that all is working.

14. Turn off the PC and replace the cover.

Introduction to Troubleshooting

Troubleshooting a PC problem begins with isolating it into one of two categories: problems that prevent the PC from booting and problems that occur after a successful boot. Begin by asking the user questions like these to learn as much as you can:

- Please describe the problem. What error messages, unusual displays, or failures did you see?

- When did the problem start?

- What was the situation when the problem occurred?

- What programs or software were you using?

- Did you move your computer system recently?

- Has there been a recent thunderstorm or electrical problem?

- Have you made any hardware, software, or configuration changes?

- Has someone else been using your computer recently?

- Can you show me how to reproduce the problem?

Next, ask yourself, "Does the PC boot properly?" Figure 3-24 shows you the direction to take, depending on the answer. If the screen is blank and the entire system is "dead"—no lights, spinning drive, or fan—then proceed to troubleshooting the power system.

Figure 3-24   Begin PC problem solving by asking the question, "Does the PC boot properly?"

Recall from Chapter 1 that when POST completes successfully, it sounds a single beep indicating that all is well, regardless of whether the monitor is working or even present. If you hear the beep, then the problem is with the video, and the next step is to troubleshoot it. If you don't hear the beep or you hear more than one, then POST encountered an error. In that case, proceed to troubleshooting the motherboard (which you will learn about in the next chapter).

If an error message appears on the screen, then the obvious next step is to respond to the message. An example of such an error is "Keyboard not present." If the error message occurs as the OS loads, and you don't understand the message or know what to do about it, begin by troubleshooting the OS.

If video is working but the boot message is confusing or unreadable, then begin to eliminate the unnecessary. Perform a clean boot. For Windows 9x, the simplest way is to boot to Safe Mode. If that doesn't work, use your bootable rescue disk.

If the PC boots up properly, turn your attention to the system that is not working and begin troubleshooting there. In this chapter, since you are learning about electricity and power supplies, we will look in more detail at how to troubleshoot the power system.

Troubleshooting the Power System

First, let's look at some general guidelines and some questions to ask when you are having power problems:

- Are there any burnt parts or odors? (Definitely not a good sign!)

- Is everything connected and turned on? Any loose cable connections? Is the computer plugged in?

- Are all the switches turned on? Computer? Monitor? Surge protector? Uninterruptible power supply? Separate circuit breaker? Is the wall outlet (or surge protector) good?

- If the fan is not running, turn off the computer, open the case, and check the connections to the power supply. Are they secure? Are all cards securely seated?

For most of the newer ATX power supplies, a wire runs from the power switch on the front of the ATX case to the motherboard. This wire must be connected to the pins on the motherboard and the switch turned on before power comes up. Check that the wire is connected correctly to the motherboard. Figure 3-25 shows the wire, which is labeled "REMOTE SW," connected to pins on the motherboard labeled "PWR.SW." If you are not sure of the correct connection on the motherboard, see the motherboard documentation. Next, check the voltage output from the power supply.

Then, remove all nonessential expansion cards (modem, sound card, mouse) one at a time. This verifies that they are not drawing too much power and pulling the system down. It is possible that the expansion cards are all good but that the power supply cannot provide enough current for all the add-on boards. Perhaps there are too many cards, and the computer is overheating. The temperature inside the case should not exceed 113 degrees F (45 degrees C). You might need to add extra cooling fans, which are discussed in the next chapter.

Vacuum the entire unit, especially the power supply's fan vent, or use compressed air to blow out the dust. Excessive dust insulates components and causes them to overheat. Use an ESD-safe service vac that can be purchased from electronic tools suppliers.

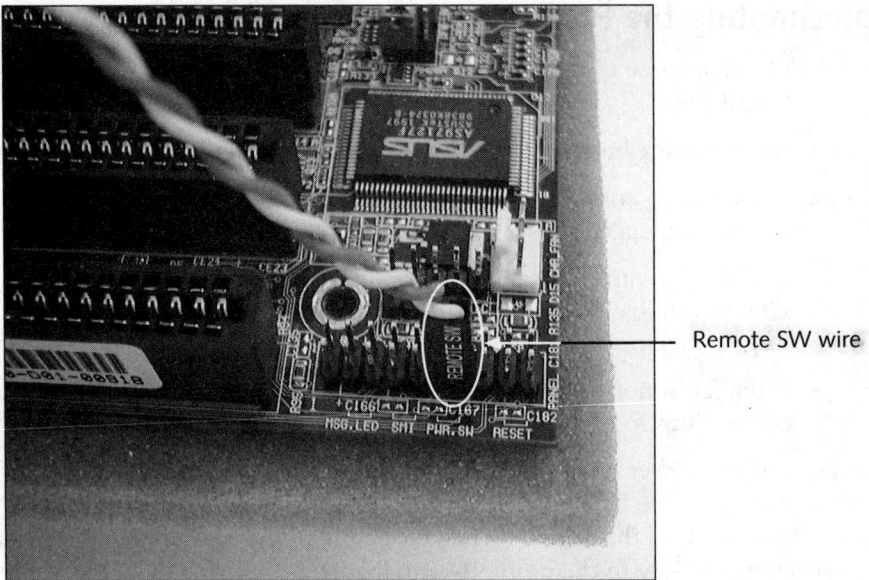

Remote SW wire

Figure 3-25   For an ATX power supply, the remote switch wire must be connected to the motherboard before power will come on

 Remember from earlier in the chapter that strong magnetic or electrical interference can affect how a power system functions. Sometimes an old monitor will emit too much static and EMF (electromagnetic force), and bring a whole system down. When you are troubleshooting power problems, remember to check for sources of electrical or magnetic interference.

Troubleshooting the Power Supply Itself

Problems with the PC's power supply or the house current can express themselves in the following ways:

- The PC sometimes halts during booting. After several tries, it boots successfully.
- Error codes or beep codes occur during booting, but the errors come and go.
- The computer stops or hangs for no reason. Sometimes it might even reboot itself.
- Memory errors appear intermittently.
- Data is written incorrectly to the hard drive.
- The keyboard stops working at odd times.
- The motherboard fails or is damaged.
- The power supply overheats and becomes hot to the touch.

An overheated system can cause intermittent problems. Use compressed air or an antistatic vacuum to remove dust from the power supply and the vents over the entire computer. Check that the power supply fan and the fan over the CPU are both working.

The symptoms of electrical power problems might be caused by a brownout (reduced current) of the house current or by a faulty power supply. If you suspect that the house current could be low, check other devices that are using the same circuit. A copy machine, laser printer, or other heavy equipment might be drawing too much power. Remove the other devices from the same house circuit.

A system with a standard power supply of about 250 watts that has multiple hard drives, multiple CD-ROM drives, and several expansion cards is most likely operating above the rated capacity of the power supply, which can cause the system to perform unexpected reboots or give intermittent, otherwise unexplained errors. Upgrade the power supply as needed to accommodate an overloaded power system.

If these suggestions don't correct the problem, check the power supply by measuring the voltage output or by exchanging it for one you know is good. For an AT motherboard, be certain to follow the black-to-black rule when attaching the power cords to the motherboard. Remember that the power supply might give correct voltages when you measure it, but still be the source of problems.

An electrical conditioner might solve the problem of intermittent errors caused by noise in the power line to the PC. Try installing an electrical conditioner to monitor and condition the voltage to the PC.

Troubleshooting the Power Supply Fan

Power supply problems are sometimes caused by a fan that is not working properly. Usually just before a fan stops working, it hums or whines, especially when the PC is first turned on. If this has just happened, replace the fan if you are trained to service the power supply. If not, then replace the entire power supply, which is considered an **FRU (field replaceable unit)** for a PC support technician. If you replace the power supply or fan and the fan still does not work, the problem might not be the fan. The problem might be caused by a short somewhere else in the system drawing too much power. Don't operate the PC with the fan not working. Computers without cooling fans can quickly overheat and damage chips. To troubleshoot a nonfunctional fan, which might be a symptom of another problem and not a problem with the fan itself, go through the following steps:

- Turn the power off and remove all power cord connections to all components, including the connections to the motherboard, and all power cords to drives. Turn the power back on. If the fan comes on, the problem is with one of the systems you disconnected, not with the power supply or its fan.

- Turn the power off and reconnect the power cords to the drives. If the fan comes on, you can eliminate the drives as the problem. If the fan does not come on, try one drive after another until you identify the drive with the short.

- If the drives are not the problem, suspect the motherboard subsystem. With the power off, reconnect all power cords to the drives.
- Turn the power off and remove the power to the motherboard by disconnecting P8 and P9 or P1. Turn the power back on.
- If the fan comes back on, the problem is probably not the power supply, but a short in one of the components powered by the power cords to the motherboard. The power to the motherboard also powers interface cards.
- Remove all interface cards and reconnect plugs to the motherboard.
- If the fan still works, the problem is with one of the interface cards. If the fan does not work, the problem is with the motherboard or something still connected to it.

Power Problems with the Motherboard

The motherboard, just like all other components inside the computer case, should be grounded to the chassis. Look for a metal screw that grounds the board to the computer case. However, a short might be the problem with the electrical system if some component on the board is making improper contact with the chassis. This short can cause serious damage to the motherboard. Check for missing standoffs (small plastic or metal spacers that hold the motherboard a short distance away from the chassis), the problem that most often causes these improper connections.

Shorts in the circuits on the motherboard might also cause problems. Look for damage on the bottom side of the motherboard. These circuits are coated with plastic, and quite often damage is difficult to spot.

Frayed wires on cable connections can also cause shorts. Disconnect hard drive cables connected directly to the motherboard. Power up with P8 and P9 or P1 connected, but all cables disconnected from the motherboard. If the fan comes on, the problem is with one of the systems you disconnected.

 TIP Never replace a damaged motherboard with a good one without first testing the power supply. You don't want to subject another good board to possible damage.

Overheating

If your computer freezes after it has been running for a while, you may have an overheating problem. First, check whether there is airflow within the case. Open the case and make sure the CPU and power supply fans are turning and that cables will not fall into the fans and prevent them from turning when you close the case. While you have the case open, use an antistatic vacuum designed to be used around electronic equipment or a can of compressed air (both are available at most computer supply stores) to blow dust off the motherboard and the CPU heat sink. Check the vents of the case and clear them of any foreign material that may be blocking airflow.

3

After you close the case back, leave your system off for a few hours. When you power the computer up again, let it run for ten minutes, go into CMOS setup, check the temperature readings, and reboot. Next, let your system run until it shuts down. Power it up again, and check the temperature in setup again. A significant difference in this reading and the first one you took after running the computer for 10 minutes indicates an overheating problem. Try adding an extra case fan or more powerful fans than the ones you already have. When adding extra fans, for every fan that blows air out of the case, use one that blows air into the case. Also, you can monitor the temperature inside the case using a temperature sensor that sounds an alarm when a high temperature is reached or uses software to alert you of the problem.

Be careful when trying to solve an overheating problem. The excessive heat itself may damage the CPU and the motherboard, and the hard reboots that are necessary when your system freezes may damage the hard drive. If you suspect that components have been damaged, try substituting comparable components that you know are good.

ENERGY STAR SYSTEMS (THE GREEN STAR)

As you are building or maintaining a computer, one very important power consideration is energy efficiency and conservation. **Energy Star systems** and peripherals have the U.S. Green Star, which indicates that they satisfy certain energy-conserving standards of the U.S. Environmental Protection Agency (EPA). Devices that can carry the Green Star are computers, monitors, printers, copiers, and fax machines. Such devices are designed to decrease the overall consumption of electricity in the U.S., to protect and preserve natural resources. These standards, sometimes called the **Green Standards**, generally mean that the computer or the device has a standby program that switches the device to sleep mode when it is not being used. During **sleep mode**, the device must use no more than 30 watts of power.

 Office equipment is among the fastest growing source of power consumption in industrialized nations. Much of this electricity is wasted, because computers and other equipment are often left on overnight. Because Energy Star devices go into sleep mode when they are unused, they create overall energy savings of about 50 percent.

Power Management Methods and Features

Computer systems use several different power management methods to conserve energy. Some are listed below:

- Advanced Power Management (APM), championed by Intel and Microsoft
- AT Attachment (ATA) for IDE drives
- Display Power Management Signaling (DPMS) standards for monitors and video cards
- Advanced Configuration and Power Interface (ACPI), used with Windows 98 and Windows 2000/XP and supported by system BIOS

These energy-saving methods are designed to work in incremental steps, depending on how long the PC is idle. Several specific features that can sometimes be enabled and adjusted using CMOS setup or using the OS are discussed in the following sections. In CMOS setup, a feature might not be available, setup might include additional features, or a feature might be labeled differently from those described below. (How to change these settings is covered in the next chapter.)

- *Green timer on the motherboard*. This sets the number of minutes of inactivity that must pass before the CPU goes into sleep mode. You can enable or disable the setting and select the elapse time in number of minutes.

- *Doze time*. **Doze time** is the time that elapses before the system reduces 80 percent of its power consumption. This is accomplished in different ways by different systems. For example, when one system enters doze mode, the system BIOS slows down the bus clock speed.

- *Standby time*. The time before the system reduces 92 percent of its power consumption is **standby time**. For example, a system might accomplish this by changing the system speed from turbo to slow and suspending the video signal.

- *Suspend time*. The time before the system reduces 99 percent of its power consumption is **suspend time**. The way this reduction is accomplished varies. The CPU clock might be stopped and the video signal suspended. After entering suspend mode, the system needs a warmup time so that the CPU, monitor, and other components can reach full activity.

- *Hard drive standby time*. **Hard drive standby time** is the amount of time before a hard drive shuts down.

Figure 3-26 shows the Power Management Setup screen of the CMOS setup for Award BIOS for an ATX Pentium II motherboard. Using the Video options on the left of the screen, you can enable or disable power management of the monitor. When power management is enabled, you can control Energy Star features. The PM Timers feature controls doze, standby, and suspend modes for the hard drive. The Power Up Control determines the way the system can be controlled when it is started or when power to the computer is interrupted. The features on the right side of the screen monitor the power supply fan, CPU fan, optional chassis fan, temperatures of the CPU and the motherboard (MB), and voltage output to the CPU and motherboard.

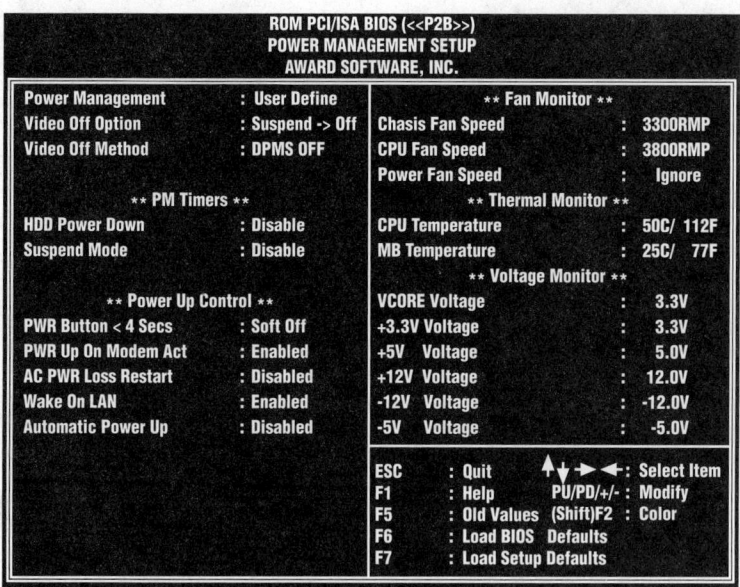

Figure 3-26   A Power Management Setup screen showing power management features

Energy Star Monitors

Most computers and monitors sold today are Energy Star compliant, displaying the green Energy Star logo onscreen when the PC is booting. In order for a monitor's power-saving feature to function, the video card or computer must also support this function. Most monitors that follow the Energy Star standards adhere to the **Display Power Management Signaling (DPMS)** specifications developed by VESA, which allow for the video card and monitor to go into sleep mode simultaneously.

Windows 98 sometimes recognizes that a monitor is an Energy Star monitor by its brand and model. For Windows 98, right-click the desktop, select Properties from the shortcut menu, click the Settings tab, and click Advanced. The monitor Properties dialog box opens. Click the Monitor tab, and the dialog box in Figure 3-27 is displayed, showing the Energy Star check box.

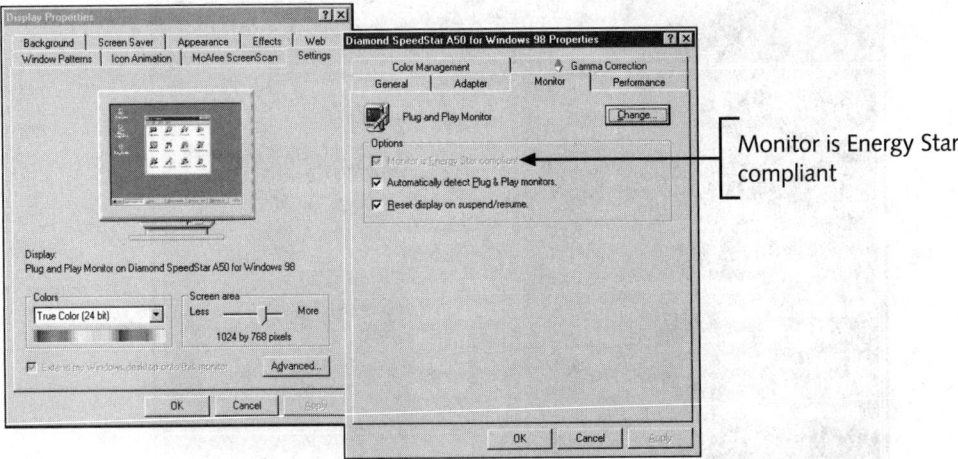

Monitor is Energy Star compliant

Figure 3-27   In Windows 98, the Energy Star check box is grayed for this monitor and cannot be unchecked

To use the Energy Star features of your monitor, click the Screen Saver tab in the Properties dialog box to open the dialog box shown in Figure 3-28. Click the Settings button of the energy savings feature. You can set system standby to activate after a specified number of minutes. Select the minutes under Turn off monitor. This feature causes your Energy Star monitor to go into sleep mode. Some monitors have an additional feature that allows the PC to shut off the monitor after a selected number of minutes of inactivity. Read the documentation that comes with the monitor to learn what features a monitor has and how to use them.

Figure 3-28   Using the monitor's Energy Star features

3

For Windows 2000, right-click on the desktop, and select Properties. The Desktop Properties window opens. Click the Screen Saver tab. If your monitor is Energy Star compliant, you will see the Energy Star logo at the bottom. When you click Power..., the Power Options Properties window opens, and you can change your power options. See Figure 3-29. Your power options might be different depending upon the power management features your BIOS supports.

Figure 3-29   Changing power options in Windows 2000

 TIP   Problems might occur if system BIOS is turning off the monitor because of power management settings, and Windows 9x is also turning off the monitor. If the system hangs when you try to get the monitor going again, try disabling one or the other setting.

CHAPTER SUMMARY

- An electrical circuit is created by a combination of voltage, current, and resistance.
- Electrical voltage is a measure of the potential difference in an electrical system.
- Electrical current is measured in amps, and electrical resistance is measured in ohms. One volt drives a current of one amp through a resistance of one ohm, which is one watt of power.
- Wattage is a measure of electrical power. Wattage is calculated by multiplying volts by amps in a system.
- Microcomputers require direct current (DC), which is converted from alternating current (AC) by the PC's power supply inside the computer case.
- A PC power supply is actually a transformer and rectifier, rather than a supplier, of power.

- Materials used to make electrical components include conductors, insulators, and semiconductors.
- A transistor is a gate or switch for an electrical signal, a capacitor holds an electrical charge, a diode allows electricity to flow in one direction, and a resistor limits electrical current.
- To protect a computer system against ESD, use a ground bracelet, ground mat, and static shielding bags.
- Protect a computer system against EMI by covering expansion slots (which also reduces dust inside the case), by not placing the system close to or on the same circuit as high-power electrical equipment, and by using line conditioners.
- Devices that control the electricity to a computer include surge suppressors, line conditioners, and UPSs.
- A surge suppressor protects a computer against damaging spikes in the electrical voltage.
- Line conditioners level out the AC to reduce brownouts and spikes.
- A UPS provides enough power to perform an orderly shutdown during a blackout.
- There are two kinds of UPSs: the true UPS, called the inline UPS, and the standby UPS.
- The inline UPS is the more expensive, because it provides continuous power. The standby UPS must switch from one circuit to another when a blackout begins.
- An intelligent UPS can be controlled and managed from utility software at a remote computer, or from a computer connected to the UPS through a serial cable.
- Data line protectors are small surge suppressors designed to protect modems from spikes on telephone lines.
- A form factor is a set of specifications for the size and configuration of hardware components such as cases, power supplies, and motherboards.
- The most common form factor in use today is ATX. There is a variation called Mini-ATX. ATX superseded the earlier AT and Baby AT form factors.
- Other form factors include LPX and NLX, in which expansion cards are mounted on a riser card that plugs into the motherboard.
- Case types include desktop, low-profile or slimline desktops, mini-tower, midi-tower, full tower, and notebook. The most popular case type in use today is the midi-tower.
- A multimeter is a device that can measure volts, amps, ohms, and continuity in an electrical system.
- Before replacing a damaged motherboard in a PC, first measure the output of the power supply to make sure that it did not cause the damage.
- A faulty power supply can cause memory errors, data errors, system hangs, or reboots, and it can damage a motherboard or other components.
- The U.S. Environmental Protection Agency has established Energy Star standards for electronic devices, to reduce energy consumption.
- Devices that are Energy Star compliant go into a sleep mode in which they use less than 30 watts of power.
- PCs that are Energy Star compliant often have CMOS settings that affect the Energy Star options available on the PC.

KEY TERMS

active backplane
alternating current (AC)
ammeter
ampere or amp (A)
AT
ATX
autorange meter
Baby AT
backplane system
brownouts
bus riser
capacitor
clamping voltage
compact case
continuity
data line protector
diode
direct current (DC)
Display Power Management Signaling (DPMS)
doze time
EMI (electromagnetic interference)

Energy Star systems
ESD (electrostatic discharge)
field replaceable unit (FRU)
FlexATX
form factor
full AT
Green Standards
ground bracelet
hard drive standby time
intelligent UPS
line conditioner
line-interactive UPS
low-profile case
LPX
microATX
Mini-ATX
Mini-LPX
multimeter
NLX
ohms (Ω)
passive backplane
power conditioner

rectifier
resistance
resistor
riser card
sleep mode
slimline case
soft power
soft switch
spikes
standby time
static electricity
surge suppressor or surge protector
suspend time
tower case
transformer
transistor
UPS (uninterruptible power supply)
volt (V)
voltage
voltmeter
watt (W)
wattage

3

4

THE MOTHERBOARD

In this chapter, you will learn:

♦ About the types of motherboards

♦ About components on the motherboard

♦ A basic procedure for building a computer

♦ How to install a motherboard

♦ How to troubleshoot a motherboard

Chapters 1 and 2 surveyed the hardware and software that make up a personal computer and described how they work together to create a functioning computer system. Chapter 3 discussed how electricity powers a computer and introduced various PC form factors. In this chapter, we begin to examine in detail how the components of a computer work in harmony and with accuracy. Our starting point is the motherboard, the central site of computer logic circuitry and the location of the most important microchip in the computer, the CPU.

To understand the ideas in this chapter, you should (1) know the definitions of bit, byte, kilobyte, and hexadecimal (hex), and (2) be able to read memory addresses written in hex.

149

TYPES OF MOTHERBOARDS

A motherboard's primary purpose is to house the CPU and allow all devices to communicate with it and with each other. In Chapter 3 you were introduced to the two most popular motherboards, the older AT and the newer ATX. The AT motherboard has a power connection for 5- and 12-volt lines coming from the power supply. To accommodate newer CPUs that use less voltage, the ATX has lines for 5, 12, and 3.3 volts from the power supply. Figure 4-1 shows that the ATX motherboard uses a single 20-pin power connection called the **P1 connector**, but the AT board uses two power connections, the **P8 connector** and the **P9 connector**.

Each board is available in two sizes. ATX boards include more power-management features, support faster systems, and are easier to install. Table 4-1 summarizes AT and ATX boards and their form factors.

Table 4-1   Types of motherboards

Type of Motherboard	Description
AT	• Oldest type of motherboard still used in some systems • Uses P8 and P9 power connections (see Figure 4-1) • Measures 30.5 cm × 33 cm (12 inches × 13 inches)
Baby AT	• Smaller version of AT. Small size is possible because motherboard logic is stored on a smaller chip set. • Uses P8 and P9 power connections • Measures 33 cm × 22 cm (12 inches × 8.7 inches)
ATX	• Developed by Intel for Pentium systems • Has a more conveniently accessible layout than AT boards • Includes a power-on switch that can be software-enabled and extra power connections for extra fans • Uses a P1 connector (see Figure 4-1) • Measures 30.5 cm × 24.4 cm (12 inches × 9.6 inches)
Mini ATX	• An ATX board with a more compact design • Measures 28.4 cm × 20.8 cm (11.2 inches × 8.2 inches)

P1 on an ATX motherboard

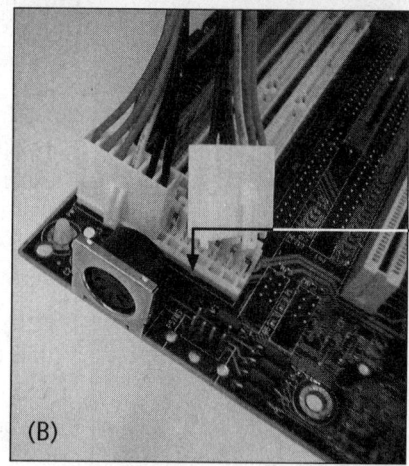

P8 and P9 on an AT motherboard

Figure 4-1 ATX uses a single P1 power connection (A), but AT type motherboards use P8 and P9 power connections (B)

The main components on a motherboard are the following:

- CPU and its accompanying chip set (recall that the chip set is a group of chips on the motherboard that controls the timing and flow of data and instructions to and from the CPU)
- System clock
- ROM BIOS
- CMOS configuration chip and its battery
- RAM
- RAM cache (optional)
- System bus with expansion slots

- Jumpers and DIP switches
- Ports that are directly on the board
- Power supply connections

Of the components listed above, you can replace or upgrade the following five: CPU, ROM BIOS chip, CMOS battery, RAM, and RAM cache. Because you can exchange these items without returning the motherboard to the manufacturer, they are called field replaceable units (FRUs).

Before examining the most important motherboard components, let's look at the motherboard itself as a component (see Figures 4-2 and 4-3).

Figure 4-2 A typical AT motherboard with memory cache and socket 7 for the Intel Classic Pentium CPU; the CPU with a fan on top is installed as well as two SIMM memory modules

4

P1 Power connector

Two IDE connectors

Floppy drive connector

DIP switches

16-bit ISA expansion slot

AGP slot

Five PCI expansion slots

Flash ROM
Parallel port

Two serial ports

Two USB ports

Keyboard and mouse port

Slot 1 for Pentium III with
supporting braces

Four RAM slots with one
DIMM installed

Figure 4-3   An ATX motherboard with a Pentium III and one DIMM module installed

When you buy a motherboard, your selection determines the following components:

- Types and speeds of the CPU you can use

- Chip set on the board (already installed)

- Memory cache type and size

- Types and number of expansion slots: ISA, PCI, and AGP

- Type of memory, including what kind and how much of SRAM (on board or inside CPU housing) and DRAM (SIMMs, DIMMs, or RIMMs)

- Maximum amount of memory you can install on the board and the incremental amounts by which you can upgrade memory

- Type of case you can use

- ROM BIOS (already installed)

- Type of keyboard connector

- Presence or absence of different types of proprietary video and/or proprietary local bus slots

- Presence or absence of IDE adapters and SCSI controller

- Presence or absence of COM ports, LPT ports, and mouse port

Because the motherboard determines so many of your computer's features, selecting the motherboard is a very important decision when you purchase a computer or assemble one from parts. Depending on which applications and peripheral devices you plan to use with the computer, you can take one of three different approaches to selecting a motherboard. The first option is to select the board that provides the most room for expansion, so you can upgrade and exchange components and add devices easily. A second approach is to select the board that best suits the needs of the computer's current configuration, knowing that when you need to upgrade, you will likely switch to new technology and a new motherboard. The third approach is to select a motherboard that meets your present needs with moderate room for expansion.

Ask the following questions when selecting a motherboard:

- Is the motherboard designed so that long expansion cards don't get in the way of the CPU or other important devices you might want to access?

- Does the motherboard support the CPU you plan to use?

- What type of BIOS does the motherboard use?

- What bus speeds and type of memory does the board support, and how much memory can the board hold?

- Does the board use many embedded devices?

- Does the board fit the case you plan to use?

- Does the board support your legacy cards?

- What is the warranty on the board?

- How extensive and user-friendly is the documentation?

- How much support does the manufacturer supply for the board?

Sometimes a motherboard contains a component that is more commonly offered as a separate device. A component on the board is called an embedded component or an on-board component. One example is support for video. The video port might be on the motherboard or might require a video card. The cost of a motherboard with an embedded component is usually less than the combined cost of a motherboard with no embedded component and an expansion card. If you plan to expand, be cautious about choosing a proprietary board that has many embedded components. Such boards often do not easily accept add-on devices from other manufacturers. For example, if you plan to add a more powerful video card, you might not want to choose a motherboard that contains an embedded video controller. Even though you can often set a switch on the motherboard to disable the proprietary video controller, there is little advantage to paying the extra money for it.

If you have an embedded component, make sure you can disable the component so that you can use another external component if needed. You disable a component on the motherboard through jumpers on the board or through CMOS setup.

Table 4-2 lists some manufacturers of motherboards with their Web addresses.

Table 4-2 Major manufacturers of motherboards

Manufacturer	Web Address
Motherboards.com	www.motherboards.com
Abit	www.abit.com.tw
American Megatrends, Inc. (AMI)	www.megatrends.com or www.ami.com
ASUS	www.asus.com
Dell	www.dell.com
First International Computer of America, Inc.	www.fica.com
Gateway	www.gateway.com
Gigabyte Technology Co., Ltd.	us.giga-byte.com
IBM	www.ibm.com
Intel Corporation	www.intel.com
Iwill Corporation	www.iwill.net
Supermicro Computer, Inc.	www.supermicro.com
Tyan Computer Corporation	www.tyan.com

COMPONENTS ON THE MOTHERBOARD

Now that you have learned about types of motherboards, let's take a look at some components on the motherboard: the system clock, the CPU and chip set, ROM BIOS, RAM, buses and expansion slots, and components used to change hardware configuration settings (jumpers, DIP switches, and CMOS). You will learn where these components are located on the motherboard and how they function.

The System Clock

Remember from Chapter 1 that the motherboard contains a system clock that keeps the beat for many motherboard activities. We use units called megahertz (MHz) to measure clock frequency. One megahertz (MHz) is equal to 1,000,000 beats, or cycles, of the clock per second. A single clock beat or cycle was once the smallest unit of processing the CPU or another device could execute, meaning that it could only do one thing for each beat of the clock. Some CPUs today can perform two activities per clock cycle.

Even though the speed at which a CPU can operate is often referred to as the CPU speed, it is more accurate—but less common—to speak of the CPU frequency. Speed implies continuous motion, and there is nothing continuous about the way a CPU works. It works by doing something, waiting for the clock beat, doing something, waiting for the clock beat, and so forth. Activities are binary: doing and waiting, and are measured in frequency of activity. For example, you might say that a CPU can operate at a frequency of 550 MHz, but we inaccurately call this the speed of the CPU.

A **wait state** occurs when the CPU must wait for another component, for example when slower dynamic RAM reads or writes data. To allow time for the slow operation, CMOS setup information specifies that the CPU maintain a wait state. If the CPU normally can do something in two clock beats, for example, it is told to wait an extra clock beat, meaning that its cycle takes a total of three clock beats. It works for two beats and then waits one beat, which makes for a 50 percent slowdown. Wait states might be incorporated to slow the CPU so that the rest of the motherboard activity can keep up. Wait states are set as part of the motherboard's default settings and are only changed in rare circumstances, such as when the board becomes unstable.

The CPU and the Chip Set

IBM and IBM-compatible computers manufactured today use a microprocessor chip made by Intel (*www.intel.com*) or AMD (*www.amd.com*), and to a lesser degree by Cyrix, which is currently owned by VIA Technologies (*www.via.com.tw*), and other manufacturers. Early CPUs by Intel were identified by model numbers: 8088, 8086, 80286, 386, and 486. The next CPU introduced after the 486 was named the Pentium, and several Intel CPUs after that include Pentium in their name. The model numbers can be written with or without the 80 prefix and are sometimes preceded with an i, as in 80486, 486, or i486.

You need to know how to identify a CPU installed in a system and what performance to expect from that CPU. The following attributes are used to rate CPUs:

1. *CPU speed measured in gigahertz.* The first CPU used in an IBM PC was the 8088, which worked at about 4.77 MHz, or 4,770,000 clock beats per second. An average speed for a new CPU today is about 2 GHz, or 2,000,000,000 beats per second. In less than a minute, this processor beats more times than your heart beats in a lifetime!

2. *Efficiency of the programming code.* Permanently built into the CPU chip are programs that accomplish fundamental operations, such as comparing or adding two numbers. Less efficient CPUs require more steps to perform these simple operations than more efficient CPUs. These groups of instructions are collectively called the **instruction set**.

3. *Number of transistors.* The number of electronic switches, or transistors, in the processor circuitry is a measure of its overall computing power.

4. *Number of registers.* A register is a place for the CPU to hold data and instructions as it is processing them. These registers are on the CPU chip. The more registers, the less often the CPU has to access memory.

5. *Word size.* Word size, sometimes called the internal data path size, is the largest number of bits the CPU can process in one operation. Word size ranges from 16 bits (2 bytes) to 64 bits (8 bytes).

6. *Data path.* The data path, sometimes called the external data path size, is the largest number of bits that can be transported into the CPU. The size of the data path is the same as the system bus size, or the number of bits that can be transported along the bus at one time. (The data path ranges from 8 bits to 64 bits.) The word size need not be as large as the data path size; some CPUs can receive more bits than they can process at one time.

7. *Maximum number of memory addresses.* A computer case has room for a lot of memory physically housed within the case, but a CPU has only a fixed range of addresses that it can assign to this physical memory. How many memory addresses the CPU can assign limits the number of physical memory chips that the computer can effectively use. The minimum number of memory addresses a CPU can use is one megabyte (where each byte of memory is assigned a single address). Recall that one megabyte (MB) is equal to 1,024 kilobytes (K), which is equal to 1,024 × 1,024 bytes, or 1,048,576 memory addresses. The maximum number of memory addresses for Pentium CPUs is 4,096 megabytes, which is equal to 4 gigabytes (GB).

8. *The amount of memory included with the CPU.* Most present-day CPUs have memory cache on the processor chip, and also inside the processor housing on a small circuit board. In documentation, the chip is sometimes called a die. Memory on the die is called internal cache, primary cache, level 1, or L1 cache. Memory not on the die is called secondary cache, level 2, or L2. In addition, some processors have L3 cache, which is farther away from the CPU than L2 cache.

9. *Multiprocessing ability.* Some microchips are really two processors in one, and can do more than one thing at a time. Others are designed to work in cooperation with other CPUs installed on the same motherboard.

10. *Special functionality.* There are also special-purpose CPUs, such as the Pentium MMX, which is designed to manage multimedia devices efficiently.

Until Intel manufactured the Pentium series of chips, the three most popular ways of measuring CPU power were speed measured in megahertz, word size in bits, and data path size in bits. The criteria for measuring the power of a CPU have changed since the introduction of the Pentium. The word size and path size have remained the same for the last few years, so we have been more interested in clock speed, bus speed, internal cache, and especially, the intended functionality of the chip, such as its ability to handle graphics well (MMX technology). Now, with the more recent introduction of the Itanium CPU by Intel, the word size and path size have increased and, once more, these attributes are used to compare processors.

The Pentium and Its Competitors

The most popular CPU microchips by Intel for personal computers are the Pentium series of chips. A Pentium processor has two arithmetic logic units (ALUs), meaning that it can perform two calculations at the same time; it is therefore a true multiprocessor. Pentiums have a 64-bit external path size and two 32-bit internal paths, one for each ALU. To compare the Pentium family of chips with its competitors, you need to understand bus speed, processor speed, the multiplier, and memory cache. Each of these is introduced here and then discussed in more detail later in the chapter.

Recall that **bus speed** is the frequency or speed at which data moves on a bus. Remember also that a motherboard has several buses; later in the chapter you will learn the details of each. Each bus runs at a certain speed, some faster than others. Only the fastest bus connects directly to the CPU. This bus goes by many names. It's called the **motherboard bus**, or the **system bus**, because it's the main bus on the motherboard connecting directly to the CPU, or the Pentium bus because it connects directly to the Pentium. It's called the host bus because other buses connect to it to get to the CPU, and it's also called the **memory bus** because it connects the CPU to RAM. It's called the external bus or the **front side bus** because it connects to the front side of the CPU that faces the outside world. Although the name memory bus is the most descriptive of the four, this book uses the more popular term, system bus. The common speeds for the system bus are 100 MHz, 133 MHz, 200 MHz, 400 MHz, and 533 MHz, although the bus can operate at several other speeds, depending on how the motherboard is configured.

 When you read that Intel supports a motherboard speed of 100 MHz or 133 MHz, the speed is referencing the system bus speed. In documentation you sometimes see the system bus speed called the bus clock because the pulses generated on the clock line of the bus determine its speed. Other slower buses connect to the system bus, which serves as the go-between for other buses and the CPU.

Processor speed is the speed at which the CPU operates internally. If the CPU operates at 400 MHz internally, but 100 MHz externally, the processor speed is 400 MHz, and the system bus speed is 100 MHz. In this case, the CPU is operating at four times the speed of the bus. This factor is called the **multiplier**. If you multiply the system bus speed by the multiplier, you get the processor speed, or the speed of the CPU:

System bus speed $\times$ multiplier = processor speed

You can use jumpers on the motherboard to set the system bus speed, or bus clock. The jumpers set the multiplier, which then determines the CPU speed, or processor speed. Common multipliers are 1.5, 2, 2.5, 3, 3.5, and 4. Running a motherboard or CPU at a higher speed than that suggested by the manufacturer is called overclocking and is not recommended because the speed is not guaranteed to be stable. Also, the actual speed of the CPU might be slightly higher or lower than the advertised speed.

A **memory cache** is a small amount of RAM (referred to as static RAM, or SRAM) that is much faster than the rest of RAM, which is called dynamic RAM (DRAM). DRAM loses its data rapidly and must be refreshed often. SRAM is faster than DRAM because SRAM does not need refreshing and can hold its data as long as power is available. The

CPU processing of programming code and data can be speeded up by temporarily storing them in SRAM cache. The size of the cache a CPU can support is a measure of its performance, especially during memory-intensive calculations.

Recall that a memory cache can exist on the CPU die or inside the CPU housing on another die. A memory cache on the CPU die is called **internal cache**, **primary cache**, or **Level 1 (L1)** cache. A cache outside the CPU microchip is called **external cache**, secondary cache, or **Level 2 (L2)** cache. L2 caches are usually 128K, 256K, 512K, or 1 MB in size. In the past, all L2 cache was contained on the motherboard, but beginning with the Pentium Pro, some L2 cache has been included, not on the CPU microchip like the L1 cache, but on a small circuit board with the CPU chip, within the same physical Pentium housing. If there is L2 cache in the processor housing and additional cache on the motherboard, then the cache on the motherboard is called **Level 3 (L3) cache**. Some advanced processors by AMD have L1, L2, and L3 cache inside the processor housing. In this case, the L3 cache is farther removed from the CPU than the L2 cache, even though both are inside the CPU housing.

Also remember that the bus between the processor and the L2 cache is called the **back side bus**, or cache bus, and is not visible, because it is completely contained inside the CPU housing (see Figure 4-4). On the Pentium Pro and Pentium II, this cache bus runs at half the speed of the processor.

Figure 4-4   Some Pentiums contain L2 cache on separate dies (discrete L2 cache), and some contain L2 cache on the same die (Advanced Transfer Cache)

Some Pentium III CPUs contain L2 cache directly on the same die as the processor core making it difficult to distinguish between L1 and L2 cache; this is called **Advanced Transfer Cache (ATC)**. ATC makes it possible for the Pentium III to fit on a smaller and less expensive form factor. The ATC bus is 256 bits wide and runs at the same speed as the processor. Pentium III L2 cache stored on a separate microchip within the CPU housing is called **discrete L2 cache** (see Figure 4-4). With discrete L2 cache, the Pentium III cache bus is 64 bits wide and runs at half the speed of the processor. All Pentium III processors have either 512K of discrete cache or 256K of ATC. The Pentium 4 uses 256K of ATC.

Some CPUs use a type of Level 1 cache called **Execution Trace Cache**. For example, the Pentium 4 has 8K of Level 1 cache used for data, and an additional 12K of Execution Trace Cache that contains a list of decoded operations that are waiting to be executed. Many times a CPU decides to follow one branch of operations in a program of instructions instead of another branch. Only branches of operations that the CPU has determined will be executed are stored in the Execution Trace Cache, making for a faster execution process.

Table 4-3 lists the six types of Pentium CPUs: Classic Pentium, Pentium MMX, Pentium Pro, Pentium II, Pentium III, and Pentium 4. Earlier variations of the Pentium II processor included the Celeron and Xeon. Recently, however, Intel stopped calling the Xeon the Pentium Xeon and simply refers to it as the Xeon, making it another group of CPUs that are different, yet similar to the Pentiums. Several significant Intel CPUs are discussed in the following sections.

Table 4-3 The Intel Pentium and Xeon family of CPUs

Processor	Latest Processor Speeds (MHz or GHz)	Primary L1 Cache	Secondary L2 Cache	System Bus Speeds (MHz)
Classic Pentium	60 to 200 MHz	16K	None	66
Pentium MMX	133 to 266 MHz	32K	None	66
Pentium Pro	150 to 200 MHz	16K	256K, 512K, or 1 MB	60, 66
Pentium II	233 to 450 MHz	32K	256K, 512K	66, 100
Celeron	850 MHz to 1.8 GHz	32K or Execution Trace Cache	128K Advanced Transfer Cache or 256K Advanced Transfer Cache	Up to 400
Pentium II Xeon	400 or 500 MHz	32K	512K, 1 MB, or 2 MB	100
Pentium III	450 MHz to 1.33 GHz	32K	512K unified, non-blocking cache or 256K Advanced Transfer Cache	100, 133
Pentium III Xeon	600 MHz or 1 GHz	32K	256K, 1 MB, or 2 MB Advanced Transfer Cache	100 or 133
Xeon MP	1.4 GHz to 1.6 GHz	Execution Trace Cache	256K L2 Cache with 512K or 1 MB L3 Cache	400
Xeon DP	1.8 GHz to 2.4 GHz	Execution Trace Cache	256K or 512K Advanced Transfer Cache	400
Pentium 4	1.4 GHz to 2.8 GHz	Execution Trace Cache	256K or 512K Advanced Transfer Cache	400 or 533

Classic Pentium   The first Pentium chip was introduced in March 1993, and has now become affectionately known as the "Classic Pentium." Early problems with this first Pentium (which Intel later resolved) could cause errors such as incorrect calculations on spreadsheets. The Classic Pentium is no longer manufactured.

Pentium MMX   The Pentium MMX (Multimedia Extension) targets the home market. It speeds up graphical applications and performs well with games and multimedia software.

4

Pentium Pro   When the Pentium Pro was first released, Intel recommended it for 32-bit applications that rely heavily on fast access to large amounts of cache memory. It was the first Pentium to offer Level 2 cache inside the CPU housing, as well as other features not available on the Classic Pentium. The Pentium Pro was popular for computing-intensive workstations and servers, but, because it does not perform well in real mode, it does not perform well with older 16-bit application software written for DOS or Windows 3.x.

Pentium II   The Pentium II was designed for graphics-intensive workstations and servers, and works well with 3-D graphic manipulation, CAD (computer-aided design), and multimedia presentations. The Pentium II is the first Pentium to use a slot (slot 1) instead of a socket to connect to the motherboard. (CPU sockets and slots are covered later in the chapter.) Intel chose to patent slot 1, and, in doing so, forced its competitors to stay with the slower socket technology as they developed equivalent processors. The Pentium II can use the 100-MHz system bus with processor speeds up to 500 MHz.

The Celeron processor is a low-end Pentium II processor that targets the low-end multimedia PC market segment. It uses Level 2 cache within the processor housing and works well with Windows 9x and the most common applications.

The Pentium II Xeon processor is a fast, high-end Pentium II processor designed exclusively for servers and powerful workstations. It can support up to eight processors in one computer and is recommended for use with Windows NT, Windows 2000, and Unix operating systems.

Pentium III   The Pentium III (see Figure 4-5) uses either a slot or a socket and runs with the 100-MHz or 133-MHz memory bus with a processor speed up to 1 GHz. The Pentium III introduced Intel's performance enhancement called SSE, for Streaming SIMD Extensions. (SIMD stands for single instruction, multiple data, and is a method used by MMX to speed up multimedia processing.) SSE is an instruction set designed to improve multimedia processing even further over MMX.

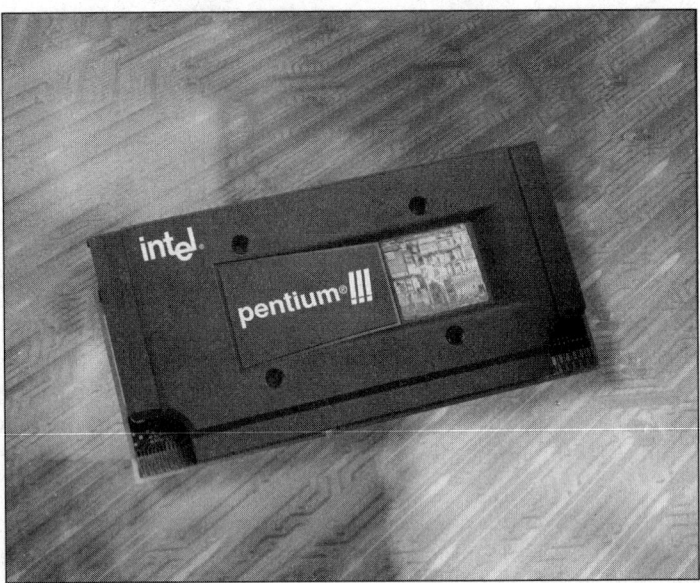

Figure 4-5   This Pentium III is contained in a SECC cartridge that stands on its end in slot 1 on a motherboard

The Pentium III Xeon is a high-end Pentium III processor that runs on the 133 MHz system bus and is designed for mid-range servers and high-end workstations. It uses a 330-pin slot called the SC330 (slot connector 330), sometimes called slot 2, and is contained within a cartridge called a Single Edge Contact Cartridge (SECC).

Pentium 4   The Pentium 4 processor (see Figure 4-6) can currently run at up to 2.8 GHz. It provides increased performance for multimedia applications such as digital video, as well as for new Web technologies. It currently uses a 400 or 533 MHz system bus.

Some of the improvements that the Pentium 4 is designed to provide are increased efficiency in creating digital files, faster ways to work with pictures, new ways for the user to interface with the computer (such as through natural speech), and greater responsiveness with Internet applications. It uses a processor architecture that Intel calls NetBurst and is supported by the Intel 845 and 850 chip sets.

Mobile Pentiums   There are mobile versions of several Intel Pentium processors. The Pentium II, Pentium III, Celeron, and Pentium 4 processors all have versions designed for use in notebook computers. The mobile Pentium 4 M (for Mobile) provides the highest performance for notebooks used for multimedia, video, and other data-intensive operations, and is designed to support many low-power features which extend battery life. It is currently available from 1.4 GHz to 2 GHz on a 400 MHz system bus and uses the 845MP Intel chip set.

4

CPU
Frame to hold cooler

Socket 478

Figure 4-6   The Pentium 4

Competitors of the Advanced Pentiums   Table 4-4 shows the performance ratings of five competitors of the Pentium advanced processors. When VIA (*www.viatech.com*) purchased Cyrix, it came out with a new processor, the VIA C3 (see Figure 4-7), which is similar to, but faster than, the earlier Cyrix III processor. The Cyrix and VIA processors use the same sockets as those used by earlier Pentium processors.

Table 4-4   VIA and AMD competitors of the Intel processors

Processor	Latest Clock Speeds (MHz)	Compares to	System Bus Speed (MHz)	Socket of Slot
Cyrix M II	300, 333, 350	Pentium II, Celeron	66, 75, 83, 95, 100	Socket 7
Cyrix III	433 to 533	Celeron, Pentium III	66, 100, 133	Socket 370
VIA C3	Up to 1 GHz	Celeron	100 or 133	Socket 370
AMD-K6-2	166 to 475	Pentium II, Celeron	66, 95, 100	Socket 7 or Super Socket 7
AMD-K6-III	350 to 450	Pentium II	100	Super Socket 7
AMD Athlon	Up to 1.9 GHz	Pentium III	200	Slot A or Socket A
AMD Duron	1 GHz to 1.3 GHz	Celeron	200	Socket A
AMD Athlon MP	1.4 GHz to 1.8 GHz	Pentium III	200 to 400+	OPGA

Figure 4-7   The Cyrix III competes with the Intel Celeron and the Pentium III

Earlier AMD (*www.amd.com*) processors used a special type of socket called Super Socket 7, which supports an AGP video slot and 100 MHz system bus. The AMD Athlon can use a proprietary 242-pin slot called Slot A that looks like the Intel slot 1, which also has 242 pins. Also, the AMD Athlon and the AMD Duron use a socket called Socket A that has 462 pins. The latest AMD processor is the Athlon MP, shown in Figure 4-8.

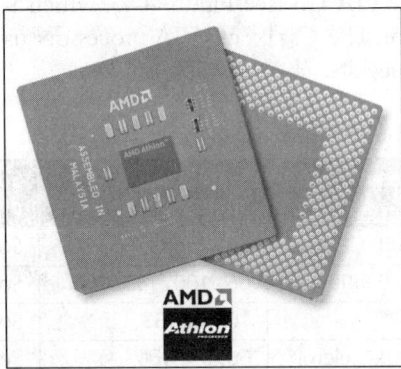

Figure 4-8   The AMD Athlon competes with the Intel Pentium III

Intel Itanium: The Next-Generation Processor

Intel's newest processor is called the Itanium, Intel's first 64-bit processor for microcomputers. Recall from Chapter 2 that earlier processors always operated in real mode, which used a 16-bit data path. Later, protected mode was introduced, which uses a 32-bit data path. Almost all applications written today use 32-bit protected mode, because all CPUs manufactured today for microcomputers use a 32-bit data path. Beginning with the Itanium, this will change, but slowly. Even though the Itanium is designed for high-end

4

enterprise servers, the industry fully expects 64-bit processors to eventually reach the personal computer market. To take full advantage of a 64-bit processor, such as the Itanium, software developers must recompile their applications to use 64-bit processing, and operating systems must be written to use 64-bit data transfers. Microsoft provides a 64-bit version of Windows XP that will work with the Itanium processor. Intel has promised that the Itanium will provide backward compatibility with older 32-bit applications, although the older applications will not be able to take full advantage of the Itanium's capabilities.

Earlier CPUs use one of two types of instruction sets: **RISC (reduced instruction set computing)** or **CISC (complex instruction set computing)**. CISC CPUs have a larger amount of instructions that programmers can use, but are generally slower than RISC CPUs. The Itanium uses a new instruction set, the **EPIC (explicitly parallel instruction computing)** architecture. With EPIC, the CPU receives a bundle of instructions that contains programming instructions as well as instructions that tell the CPU how to execute two instructions at a time in parallel, using the multiprocessing abilities of the CPU.

Table 4-5 shows the specifications for the two Itanium processors. Note the inclusion of an L3 cache. The Itanium uses an L1 cache on the processor die and an L2 and L3 cache on the processor board. The L2 cache is closer to the CPU than the L3 cache.

Table 4-5   The Intel Itanium processors

Processor	Current Processor Speeds	L1 Cache	L2 Cache	L3 Cache	System Bus Speeds
Itanium	733 and 800 MHz	32K	96K	2 MB or 4 MB	266 MHz
Itanium 2	900 MHz to 1 GHz	32K	256K	1.5 MB or 3 MB	400 MHz

CPU Heat Sinks and Cooling Fans

Because a CPU generates so much heat, computer systems use a cooling fan to keep the temperature below the Intel maximum allowed limit of 185 degrees F/85 degrees C (see Figure 4-9). Good CPU cooling fans can maintain the temperature at 90–110 degrees F (32 to 43 degrees C). At one time, CPU cooling fans were optional equipment used to prevent system errors and to prolong the life of the CPU. Today's power-intensive CPUs require one or more cooling fans in order to maintain a temperature that will not damage the CPU. High-end systems can have as many as seven or eight fans mounted inside the computer case. Ball-bearing cooling fans last longer than other kinds.

Cooling fan
Processor
Slot braces
Heat sink
Cooling fan power connection

Figure 4-9   A CPU cooling fan mounts on the top or side of the CPU housing and is powered by an electrical connection to the motherboard

The cooling fan usually fits on top of the CPU with a wire or plastic clip. Sometimes a cream-like thermal compound is placed between the fan and the CPU. This compound draws heat from the CPU and passes it to the fan. The thermal compound transmits heat better than air and makes the connection between the fan and the CPU airtight. The fan is equipped with a power connector that connects to one of the power cables coming from the power supply.

Older CPUs used a heat sink instead of a cooling fan. A **heat sink** is a clip-on device that mounts on top of the CPU; it has fingers or fins at its base that pull the heat away from the CPU. Most cooling fans today that are designed to mount on the CPU housing also have a heat sink attached, as shown in Figure 4-9. The combination heat sink and cooling fan is sometimes called a cooler. Heat sinks are sometimes mounted on top of other chips to keep them cool. For example, in Figure 4-6 you can see a heat sink mounted on the top of a chip sitting behind the Pentium 4 CPU in the figure. Also notice in Figure 4-6 the frame to hold the cooler for the Pentium 4.

Some motherboards feature a power connection for the cooling fan that sounds an alarm if the fan stops working. Because the fan is a mechanical device, it is more likely to fail than the electronic devices inside the case. To protect the expensive CPU, you can purchase a temperature sensor for a few dollars. The sensor plugs into a power connection coming from the power supply and is mounted on the side of the case. It sounds an alarm when the inside of the case gets too hot.

4

Before installing a cooling fan, read the directions carefully. Clips that hold the fan and heat sink to the CPU frame or housing are sometimes difficult to install, and you must be very careful to use just the right amount of thermal compound. Too much compound can slide off the housing and damage circuits on the motherboard.

A good example of a CPU cooling fan is the Golden Orb fan by Thermaltake, Inc. (*www.thermaltake.com*) shown in Figure 4-10. Unlike some older fans, the Golden Orb can provide sufficient cooling for newer and hotter processors. A unique feature of the Golden Orb is that the heat sink is constructed around the fan, rather than beneath it. This helps the heat dissipate at a faster rate.

Figure 4-10   The Golden Orb cooling fan

Besides using fans and heat sinks to keep a CPU cool, there are some more exotic options such as refrigeration, peltiers, and water coolers. These solutions, for the most part, are used by hobbyists attempting to overclock a CPU to the max. A peltier is a heat sink carrying an electrical charge causing it to act as an electrical thermal transfer device. The peltier's top surface can be as hot as 500 degrees while the bottom surface next to the CPU can be as cool as 45 degrees. The major disadvantage of a peltier is that this drastic difference in temperature can cause condensation inside the case when the PC is turned off. Refrigeration can also be used. These units contain a small refrigerator compressor that sits inside the case and can reduce temperatures to below zero. The most popular method of cooling overclocked CPUs is a water cooler unit. A small water pump sits inside the computer case, and tubes move distilled water up and over the CPU to keep it cool. Some manufacturers of these types of cooling systems are AquaStealth (*www.aquastealth.com*), asetek (*www.vapochill.com*), and FrozenCPU (*www.frozencpu.com*). Remember, overclocking is not a recommended best practice.

CPU Packages

There are nine package types used to house Intel processors in desktop PCs and high-end workstations:

- *SECC (Single Edge Contact Cartridge)*. The processor is completely covered with a black plastic housing, and a heat sink and fan are attached to the housing. You can't see the circuit board or edge connector in a SECC package. The Pentium II and Pentium III use a SECC package in slot 1 with 242 contacts. The Pentium II Xeon and Pentium III Xeon use a SECC with 330 contacts. You can see the SECC in Figure 4-5.

- *SECC2 (Single Edge Contact Cartridge, version 2).* The SECC2 is similar to the SECC, but it does not have a heat sink thermal plate, and the edge connector on the processor circuit board is visible at the bottom of the housing. Pentium II and Pentium III use the SECC2 package with 242 contacts.

- *SEP (Single Edge Processor).* This package is similar to the SECC package, but because the processor is not completely covered by the black plastic housing, the circuit board is visible at the bottom of the housing. The first Celeron processors used the SEP package in slot 1. It has 242 contacts.

- *PPGA (Plastic Pin Grid Array).* The processor is housed in a square box designed to fit flat into Socket 370 (see Figure 4-11). Pins are on the underside of the flat housing, and heat sinks or fans can be attached to the top of the housing by using a thermal plate or heat spreader. The early Celeron processors used this package with 370 pins.

- *PGA (Pin Grid Array).* Pins on the bottom of this package are staggered and can be inserted only one way into the socket. The Xeon processors use this package with 603 pins.

- *OOI/OLGA (Organic Land Grid Array).* Used by some Pentium 4s, this package has 423 pins and is similar to the PGA package, but is designed to dissipate heat faster.

- *FC-PGA (Flip Chip Pin Grid Array).* This package looks like the PPGA package and uses Socket 370. Coolers can be attached directly to the top of the package. Some Pentium III and Celeron processors use this package.

- *FC-PGA2 (Flip Chip Pin Grid Array 2).* This package is similar to the FC-PGA package, but has a heat sink attached directly to the die of the processor. When used by a Pentium III or Celeron processor, it has 370 pins. When used by the Pentium 4, it has 478 pins.

- *PAC (Pin Array Cartridge).* The Itaniums use this flat cartridge, which is about the size of an index card. It uses either the PAC418 socket, which has 418 pins, or the PAC611 socket, which has 611 pins.

4

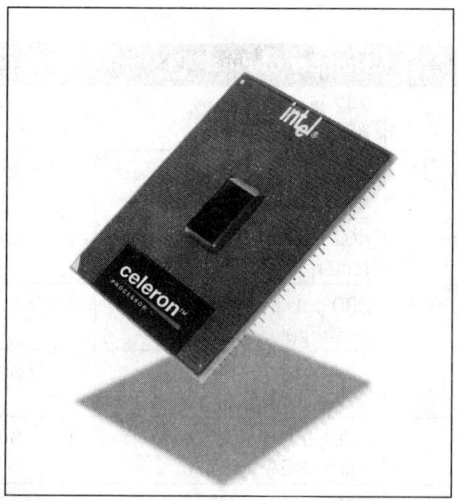

Figure 4-11   The Intel Celeron processor is housed in the PPGA form factor, which has pins on the underside that insert into Socket 370

CPU Slots and Sockets

Recall from Chapter 2 that a slot or socket is the physical connection used to connect a device (the CPU) to the motherboard. The type of socket or slot supplied by the motherboard for the processor must match that required by the processor. Table 4-6 lists several of the types of sockets and slots used by CPUs. Slots 1 and 2 are proprietary Intel slots, and Slot A and Socket A are proprietary AMD connectors.

Table 4-6   CPU sockets and slots

Connector Name	Used by CPU	Number of Pins	Voltage
Socket 4	Classic Pentium 60/66	273 pins 21 × 21 PGA grid	5 V
Socket 5	Classic Pentium 75/90/100/120/133	320 pins 37 × 37 SPGA grid	3.3 V
Socket 6	Not used	235 pins 19 × 19 PGA grid	3.3 V
Socket 7	Pentium MMX, Fast Classic Pentium, AMD KS, AMD KS, Cyrix M	321 pins 37 × 37 SPGA grid	2.5 V to 3.3 V
Super Socket 7	AMD KS-2, AMD KS-III	321 pins 37 × 37 SPGA grid	2.5 V to 3.3 V
Socket 8	Pentium Pro	387 pins 24 × 26 SPGA grid	3.3 V
Socket 370 or PGA370 Socket	Pentium III FC-PGA, Celeron PPGA, Cyrix III	370 pins in a 37 × 37 SPGA grid	1.5 V or 2 V

Table 4-6   CPU sockets and slots (continued)

Connector Name	Used by CPU	Number of Pins	Voltage
Slot 1 or SC242	Pentium II, Pentium III	242 pins in 2 rows, rectangular shape	2.8 V and 3.3 V
Slot A	AMD Athlon	242 pins in 2 rows, rectangular shape	1.3 V to 2.05 V
Socket A or Socket 462	AMD Athlon and Duron	462 pins, SPGA grid, rectangular shape	1.1 V to 1.85 V
Slot 2 or SC330	Pentium II Xeon, Pentium III Xeon	330 pins in 2 rows, rectangular shape	1.5 V to 3.5 V
Socket 423	Pentium 4	423 pins 39 × 39 SPGA grid	1.7 V and 1.75 V
Socket 478	Pentium 4	478 pins in a dense micro PGA (mPGA)	1.7 V and 1.75 V
Socket PAC418	Intel Itanium	418 pins	3.3 V
PAC611	Itanium 2	611 pins	3.3 V
Socket 603	Xeon DP and MP	603 pins	1.5 and 1.7 V

The earlier Pentiums used a **pin grid array (PGA)** socket, where the pins were aligned in uniform rows around the socket. Later sockets use a **staggered pin grid array (SPGA)**, where pins are staggered over the socket to squeeze more pins into a small space.

PGA and SPGA sockets are all square or close to it. Earlier CPU sockets, called dual inline pin package (DIPP) sockets, were rectangular with two rows of pins down each side. DIPP and some PGA sockets, called **low insertion force (LIF) sockets**, were somewhat troublesome to install because it was difficult to apply even force when inserting them. Current CPU sockets are called **zero insertion force (ZIF) sockets** and have a small lever on the side of the socket that lifts the CPU up and out of the socket. Push the lever down, and the CPU moves into its pin connectors with equal force over the entire housing. The heat sink or fan clips to the top of the CPU. With this method, you can more easily remove the CPU and replace it with another if necessary.

Most processors today come in more than one package, so it is important to match the processor package to the motherboard with the correct socket or slot. Slot 1, Slot A, and slot 2 are all designed to accommodate processors using SEP or SECC housings that stand on end much like an expansion card. The CPU is secured in the slot with clips on each side of the slot. You can attach a heat sink or cooling fan to the side of the CPU case. Some motherboards that have a slot 1 can accommodate processors that are using flat packages, for example, the Celeron using a PPGA package by using a riser CPU card (see Figure 4-12). The riser card inserts into slot 1, and the Celeron processor inserts into Socket 370 on the riser card. This feature, sometimes called a "slocket," allows you to upgrade an older Pentium II system to the faster Celeron. Always consult the motherboard documentation so you know which processors the board can support.

370-pin socket

CPU riser card

Clip to hold SECC
processor or riser
card in place

Slot 1

4

Figure 4-12   A riser card can be used to install a Celeron processor into a motherboard
with slot 1

Be aware of the processor's voltage requirements. For example, the Pentium 4 receives its voltage from the +12-volt power line to the motherboard, rather than the lower-voltage lines used by previous Pentiums. For this reason, some motherboards have a new power connector, the ATX12V, on the board. In some setups, a power cord designed to power a drive connects to this small connector. Other variations are the Celeron processor that uses 2.00 volts and the Pentium III FC-PGA that uses either 1.60 or 1.65 volts. A motherboard built to support only the Celeron may not step down the voltage for a Pentium III FC-PGA processor. This excess voltage can damage the Pentium III. Again, it is always important to use only a processor and processor package that the motherboard documentation claims the board can support.

CPU Voltage Regulator

As you can see from Table 4-5, different CPUs require different levels of voltage on the motherboard. Some CPUs require one voltage for external operations and another for internal operations. Those that require two different voltages are called **dual-voltage CPUs**. The others are called **single-voltage CPUs**. A CPU voltage regulator controls the amount of voltage to the CPU. Some CPUs require that you set the jumpers on the motherboard to control the voltage, and other CPUs automatically control the voltage without your involvement.

Figure 4-13 shows sample documentation of the jumper settings to use for various CPU voltage selections on a particular motherboard that requires jumpers to be set. Notice that the two jumpers called JP16, located near Socket 7 on the board, accomplish the voltage selection. For single voltage, for the Pentium, Cyrix 6x86, or AMD K5, both jumpers are open. Dual voltage, used by the Pentium MMX, Cyrix M2, and AMD K6, is selected by opening or closing the two jumpers according to the diagram. Follow the recommendations for your CPU when selecting the voltages from documentation.

A voltage regulator module (VRM) can be installed on some motherboards that can sense what CPU is present and insure that the correct voltage is used. When you upgrade the CPU, sometimes it is necessary to install a VRM to regulate the voltage.

The Chip Set

Recall from Chapter 1 that a chip set is a set of chips on the motherboard that collectively controls the memory cache, external buses, and some peripherals. Intel makes the most popular chip sets, which are listed in Table 4-7. The Intel 440BX chip set is the first PC chip set to offer a system bus that runs at 100 MHz, allowing a Pentium II running at 350 MHz or 400 MHz to reach its full potential for performance in desktop PCs. Before this, the system bus slowed the CPU speed. The 440BX chip set is also the first chip set to use the mobile version of the Pentium II processor for notebooks. Often you see this chip set advertised with "AGP" in the name, as in the Intel 440BX AGP chip set. The 440GX chip set is an evolution of the 440BX.

CPU TYPE	JP16	CPU Voltage	
		Core	I/O
Single Voltage Intel P54C/CQS/CT Cyrix 6x86 AMD K5	2 ◯◯ 4 1 ◯◯ 3 open	3.5 V	3.5 V
Dual Voltage Intel P55C/MMX Cyrix 6x86L/M2 AMD K6	2 ◯◯ 4 1 ◯◯ 3 open	2.8 V	3.4 V
	2 ●◯ 4 1 ●◯ 3 1-2 closed, 3-4 open	2.9 V	3.4 V
	2 ◯● 4 1 ◯● 3 1-2 open, 3-4 closed	3.2 V	3.4 V

Figure 4-13   A CPU voltage regulator can be configured using jumpers on the motherboard to apply the correct voltage to the CPU

Table 4-7 Intel chip sets

Common Name	Model Number	Comments
"E" chipset family	E8870	Supports up to four Itanium 2 processors using a 400 MHz system bus
	E7500	Supports dual Xeon processors using a 400 MHz system bus and up to 128 GB of memory
Intel i800 Series	860	Supports dual Xeon processors using a 400 MHz system bus and up to eight RIMMs
	850 and 850E	Designed for the Pentium 4 or Celeron and supports the 400 MHz or 533 MHz system bus using up to eight RIMMs. Supports ECC memory.
	845E	Designed for the Pentium 4 or Celeron supporting 400 MHz or 533 MHz system bus using two DIMM DDR modules. Supports ECC memory.
	845G or 845 GL	Designed for the Pentium 4 or Celeron and supports the 400 MHz or 533 MHz (845G-only) system bus using two DIMM DDR or DIMM SDR modules.
	845	Designed for the Pentium 4 or Celeron and supports the 400 MHz system bus using two DIMM DDR or three DIMM SDR modules. Supports ECC memory.
	840	Designed for dual processor systems using Pentium II Xeon or Pentium III Xeon processors
	820	Designed for Pentium II and Pentium III systems
	815, 815E, or 815EP	Designed for the Celeron or Pentium III and uses a 66/100/133 MHz system bus
	810	First Intel chip set to eliminate the PCI bus as the main device interconnection
Orion	460GX	Designed for up to four Itanium processors and four DIMMs
	450GX, KX	Supports Pentium Pro (includes support for multiprocessors)
	450NX	Designed for servers with multiple Pentium II or Pentium II Xeon processors
Natoma	440FX	Supports Pentium Pro and Pentium II (discontinued in January, 1999)
	440BX	Designed for servers and workstations (Pentium II and III)
	440GX	Designed for servers and workstations using the Pentium II Xeon and Pentium III Xeon
	440ZX	Designed for entry-level PCs using Pentium II
	440LX	Designed for Celeron processors
	440MX	Designed for notebook computers (M = mobile)
	440EX	Designed for smaller system boards such as the Mini-ATX

Table 4-7 Intel chip sets (continued)

Common Name	Model Number	Comments
Triton III	430VX	Value chip set, supports SDRAM
	430MX	Used for notebooks (M = mobile)
	430TX	Supports SDRAM, ultra DMA; replaced the VX and MX
Triton II	430HX	High performance, supports dual processors
Triton I	430FX	The oldest chip set, no longer produced

The 400 series of Intel chip sets uses the PCI bus as the interconnection between slower buses and the system bus. How the PCI bus does this is covered later in the chapter. The Intel i800 series of chip sets introduced a new way for I/O buses to interface with the faster system bus and ultimately to the CPU. With the i800 series, the interconnection between buses is done using a hub interface architecture, whereby all I/O buses connect to a hub, which connects to the system bus. This hub is called the hub interface, and the architecture is called Accelerated Hub Architecture (see Figure 4-14). The fast end of the hub, which contains the graphics and memory controller (GMCH), connects to the system bus and is called the hub's **North Bridge**. The slower end of the hub, called the **South Bridge**, contains the I/O Controller Hub (ICH). All I/O devices except display and memory connect to the hub by using the slower South Bridge.

Figure 4-14 Using Intel 800 series Accelerated Hub Architecture, a hub Interface is used to connect slower I/O buses to the system bus

Currently, Intel dominates the chip set market for several reasons. The major advantage that Intel has over other chip set manufacturers is that Intel knows more about its own

Intel CPUs than other manufacturers do, and the chip sets are therefore most compatible with the Pentium family of CPUs. Intel's investment in research and development also led to the development of the PCI bus, the universal serial bus, the AGP, and more recently, the Accelerated Hub Architecture. Manufacturers of chip sets are listed in Table 4-8.

Table 4-8   Chip set manufacturers

Company	URL
ALI, Inc.	www.aliusa.com
AMD	www.amd.com
Intel Corporation	www.intel.com
Philips Semiconductors	www.semiconductors.phillips.com
Silicon Integrated Systems Corp. (known as SiS)	www.sis.com
Standard Microsystems Corp.	www.smsc.com
United Microelectronics Corp. (UMC)	www.umc.com
VIA Technologies, Inc. combined with AMD, Inc.	www.viatech.com

ROM BIOS

Recall from earlier chapters that there is one ROM chip on the motherboard that contains BIOS. BIOS manages the startup process (startup BIOS) and many basic I/O functions of the system (system BIOS). To identify your motherboard and BIOS, do the following:

1. Turn the system power off and unplug the keyboard.

2. Turn the power on. You will get a keyboard error, which stops the startup process.

3. Look for the long string of numbers in the lower-left corner of your screen, which identifies the motherboard.

4. Look for the BIOS manufacturer and version number somewhere near the top of the screen.

Many years ago, when a new device became available, such as the 3½-inch floppy disk drive, your PC sometimes could not use the new device until you upgraded the BIOS. You did that by replacing the old BIOS chip with a new chip that supported the new device. Now, however, it's much easier. Most of today's new devices are not supported by the system BIOS at all, but by device drivers, which are software programs installed on the hard drive as an add-on part of the OS. But, if some new feature does require an upgrade to BIOS, you can do that with flash ROM. Installing a larger hard drive is an example of a hardware upgrade that might require a BIOS upgrade because the existing BIOS does not support large drives. Older BIOS supports hard drives with capacities up to only 504 MB. If you have this problem (large drive, old BIOS), you can solve it in one of two ways. Either upgrade BIOS or use special software designed to get around the problem. Often the device manufacturer supplies such software. Table 4-9 lists BIOS manufacturers.

Table 4-9 BIOS manufacturers

Company	URL
American Megatrends (AMI)	*www.ami.com* or *www.megatrends.com*
Phoenix Technologies (First BIOS, Phoenix, and Award)	*www.phoenix.com*
Compaq and Hewlett-Packard	*thenew.hp.com*
Dell	*www.dell.com*
IBM	*www.ibm.com*
Micro Firmware (BIOS upgrades)	*www.firmware.com*
Unicore (BIOS upgrades)	*www.unicore.com*

Technically speaking, flash ROM is called EEPROM (electrically erasable programmable read-only memory), which means that you can change the programming on the chip through software on your PC. The updated programming will be retained until you change it again, even when you turn off your PC for long periods of time. Flash ROM allows you to upgrade system BIOS without having to replace the ROM chip.

Makers of BIOS code are likely to change BIOS frequently, because it is so easy for them to provide the upgrade on the Internet. You can get upgraded BIOS code from manufacturers' Web sites or disks or from third-party BIOS resellers' Web sites or disks.

Figure 4-15 shows a sample Web site for flash ROM BIOS upgrades. See the Web site of the manufacturer of your BIOS or of the motherboard manufacturer for more information.

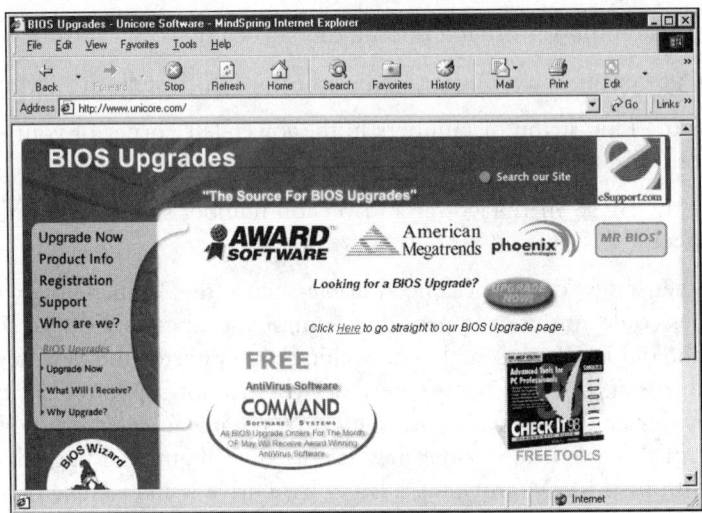

Figure 4-15 Flash ROM BIOS upgrades for most BIOS manufacturers can be downloaded from *www.unicore.com*

To upgrade flash ROM, follow the directions that came with your motherboard and the upgrade software itself. Generally, you perform these tasks:

- Set a jumper on the motherboard or change a setting in CMOS setup to tell the BIOS to expect an upgrade.

- Copy the upgrade BIOS software to a bootable disk.

- Boot from the disk and follow the menu options to upgrade the BIOS. If the menu gives you the option to save the old BIOS to disk, do so in case you need to revert to the old BIOS.

- Set the jumper back to its original setting, reboot the system, and verify that all is working.

CAUTION

Be *very careful* that you upgrade the BIOS with the correct upgrade and that you follow the manufacturer's instructions correctly. Upgrading with the wrong file could make your system BIOS totally useless. If you're not sure that you're using the correct upgrade, *don't guess*. Check with the technical support for your BIOS before moving forward. Before you call technical support, have the information that identifies your BIOS available.

Buses and Expansion Slots

As cities grow, so do their transportation systems. Small villages have only simple, two-lane roads, but large cities have two-lane and four-lane roads, and major freeways, each with its own set of traffic laws, including minimum and maximum speeds, access methods, and protocols. As microcomputer systems have evolved, so too have their "transportation" systems. The earliest PC had only a single simple bus. Today's PCs have four or five buses, each with different speeds, access methods, and protocols. As you have seen, backward compatibility dictates that older buses be supported on a motherboard, even when faster, better buses exist. All this makes for a maze of buses on a motherboard.

Bus Evolution

Just as a city's road system improves to increase the speed and number of lanes of traffic, buses have evolved around these similar issues, data path and speed. Cars on a freeway travel at a continuous or constant speed, but traffic on a computer's CPU or bus travels in a digital (on and off) manner, rather than in an analog (continuous) manner. The system clock keeps the beat for components. If a component on the motherboard works by the beat, or clock cycle, then it is said to be synchronized, or in sync, with the CPU. For example, earlier in the chapter, it was said that the back side bus of the Pentium II worked at half the speed of the CPU. This means that the CPU is doing something on each clock cycle, but the back side bus is doing something on every other clock cycle.

Some components don't attempt to keep in sync with the CPU, even to work at a half or a third of clock cycles. These components are said to be working asynchronously with the

CPU. They might be working at a rate determined by the system clock or by another crystal on or off the motherboard. Either way, the frequency will be much slower than the CPU's and not in sync with it. If the CPU requests something from one of these devices, and the device is not ready, the device will issue wait states to the CPU until it can catch up.

Devices attached to the 8-bit or 16-bit ISA bus are examples of these slower devices. The 16-bit **ISA bus** works at a rate of 8.33 MHz, compared to system bus speeds of 66 MHz to 400 MHz for faster buses. Buses that work in sync with the CPU and the system clock are called **local buses**. Buses that work asynchronously with the CPU at a much slower rate are called **expansion buses**. The system bus is a local bus, and the ISA bus is an expansion bus. Table 4-10 lists the various buses, in order of throughput speed from fastest to slowest.

Table 4-10   Buses listed by throughput

Bus	Bus Type	Data Path in Bits	Address Lines	Bus Speed in MHz	Throughput in gigabytes/sec, megabytes/sec, or megabits/sec
System bus	Local	64	32	66, 75, 100 . . .	Up to 3.2 GB/sec
AGP	Local video	32	NA	66, 75, 100 . . .	Up to 528 MB/sec
PCI	Local I/O	32	32	33, 66	Up to 264 MB/sec
VESA or VL Bus	Local video or expansion	32	32	Up to 33	Up to 250 MB/sec
FireWire	Local I/O or expansion	1	Addresses are sent serially	NA	Up to 1.2 GB/sec
MCA	Expansion	32	32	12	Up to 40 MB/sec
EISA	Expansion	32	32	12	Up to 32 MB/sec
16-bit ISA	Expansion	16	24	8.33	8 MB/sec
8-bit ISA	Expansion	8	20	4.77	1 MB/sec
USB	Expansion	1	Addresses are sent serially	3	Up to 480 Mbps

Some of the motherboard buses in Table 4-10 are outdated, and some are in use today. (You will learn more about these buses in the next chapter.) Historically, the 8-bit ISA (Industry Standard Architecture) bus came first, and was later revised to the 16-bit ISA bus to keep up with the demand for wider data path sizes. Then, in 1987, IBM introduced the first 32-bit bus, the MCA (Micro channel Architecture) bus, and competitors followed with the 32-bit EISA (Extended Industry Standard Architecture) bus. Because these buses are not synchronized with the CPU, they are all expansion buses. Of these buses, the only one still in use today is the 16-bit ISA. A relatively new expansion bus is the universal serial bus (USB), which targets slow I/O devices such as the mouse, digital camera, and scanner. Its advantage is that USB devices are easily installed and configured.

A local bus is synchronized with the CPU. In the sense that a local bus is a bus that is close to, or "local to," the CPU, there is only one "true" local bus, the system bus, or memory bus, which connects directly to the CPU. All other buses must connect to it to get to the

CPU. A **local I/O bus** is a bus designed to support fast I/O devices such as video and hard drives; it runs synchronized with the system clock, which means that it is also synchronized with the CPU. One type of local I/O bus is the PCI bus, which is standard with Pentium systems. Local I/O buses did not always exist on a PC, but were created as the need arose for a bus that was synchronized with the system clock, and was not as fast as the system bus, but was faster than an expansion bus. The evolution of local I/O buses includes earlier proprietary designs, the VESA bus, the PCI bus, and the newer AGP bus. Of these, only the PCI and AGP buses are still sold. The FireWire, or IEEE 1394, bus is the latest local I/O bus and is becoming more popular. It can work either synchronously or asynchronously, and so is classified as either a local or expansion bus. The VESA bus could also be set to work either way.

Why So Many Buses?

When the first PCs were introduced in the early 1980s, there was only one bus on the motherboard, called the system bus, which ran at the same speed as the CPU (4.77 MHz). Everything on the motherboard working with the CPU or the bus kept the same beat, following the pulses of the one system clock. (This first bus is now called the 8-bit ISA bus.) Things today are not so simple. With the speeds of different hardware components evolving at different rates, a single speed for all components is no longer practical. The CPU works at one speed, the bus connecting the CPU to memory is working at a slower speed, and the bus communicating with I/O devices must work at an even slower speed. As manufacturers attempt to improve performance, new buses are invented to accommodate the characteristics of particular devices. In fact, there might be as many as five or six different buses working at different speeds on the same motherboard. Each bus will have a set speed that all components connected to it will work at. There are components that convert data moving from bus to bus to the speed of the new bus.

What a Bus Does

Look on the bottom of the motherboard, and you will see a maze of circuits that make up a bus. These embedded wires are carrying four kinds of cargo:

- *Electrical power*. Chips on the motherboard require power to function. These chips tap into a bus's power lines and draw what they need.

- *Control signals*. Some of the wires on a bus carry control signals that coordinate all the activity.

- *Memory addresses*. Memory addresses are passed from one component to another, as these components tell each other where to access data or instructions. The number of wires that make up the memory address lines of the bus determines how many bits can be used for a memory address. The number of wires thus limits the amount of memory the bus can address.

- *Data*. Data is passed over a bus in a group of wires, just as the memory addresses are. The number of lines in the bus used to pass data determines how much data can be passed in parallel at one time. The number of lines depends on the type of CPU and determines the number of bits in the data path. (Remember that a data path is that part of the bus on which the data travels; it can be 8, 16, 32, 64 or more bits wide.)

When comparing buses, users most often focus on the width of the data path and the overall bus speed. But you should also consider the type of expansion slot the bus allows. The number of fingers on the edge connector of the expansion card and the length of the edge connector are determined by the bus that controls that expansion slot. Various bus connections are shown in Figure 4-16.

On-Board Ports

Many motherboards contain **on-board ports** such as a keyboard port and a mouse port. In addition, a parallel printer port and one or two serial ports might be located directly on the motherboard. Few older motherboards contain more ports than these. Some systems also have a video or network port, and newer motherboards contain one or two USB ports.

 You don't have to replace an entire motherboard if one port fails. Most ports on a motherboard can be disabled through CMOS setup. On older motherboards, look for jumpers or DIP switches to disable ports. Then use an expansion card for the port instead.

4

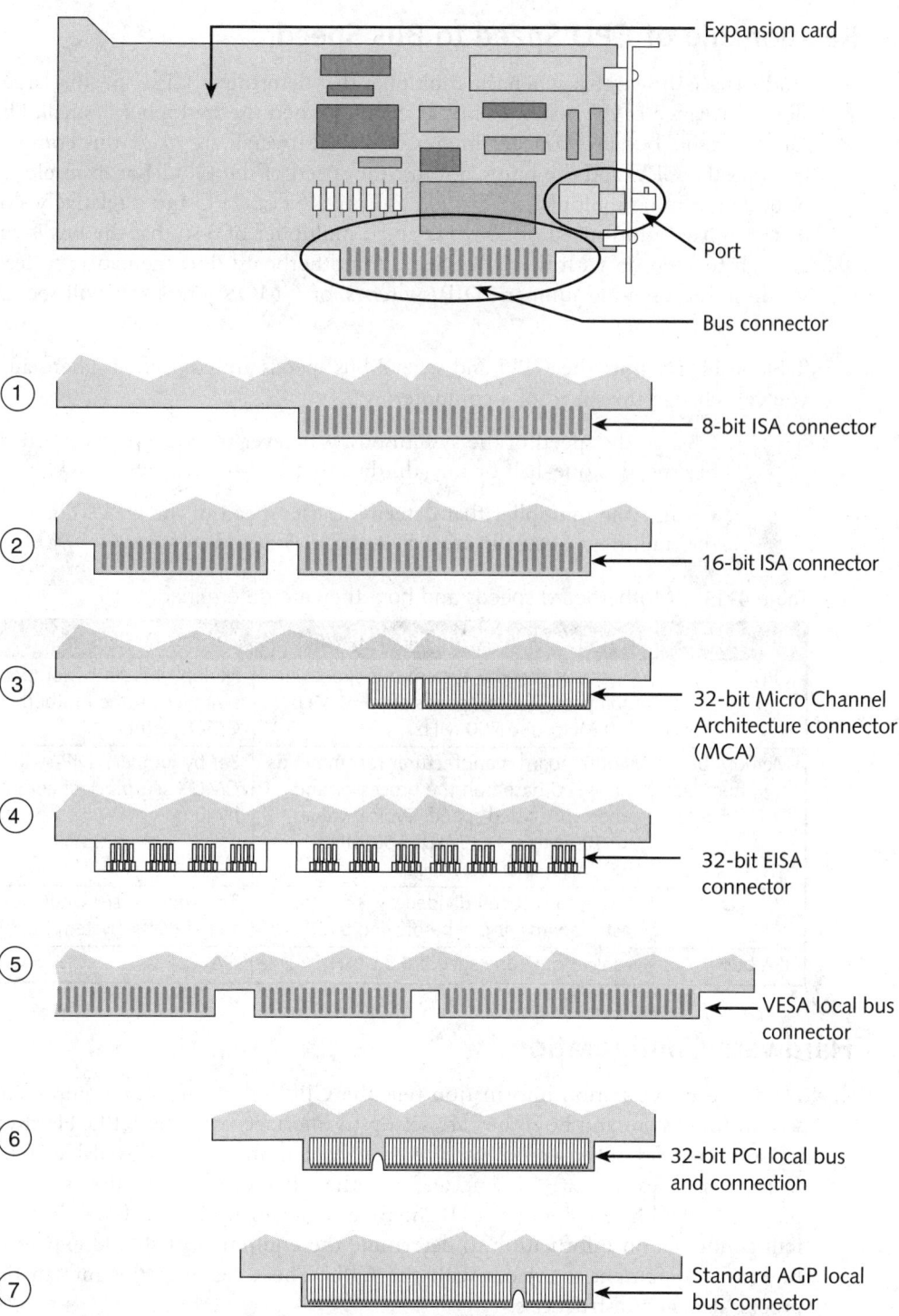

Figure 4-16 Seven bus connections on expansion cards

Relationship of CPU Speed to Bus Speed

Studies have shown that when the multiplier that determines CPU speed is large, the overall performance of the system is not as good as when the multiplier is small. This is a reasonable result because you are interested in the overall speed of the computer, which includes the CPU and the buses, not just the speed of the CPU. For example, a bus speed of 60 MHz and a multiplier of 5 yield a relatively fast CPU but a relatively slow bus. It's better to have a bus speed of 80 MHz and a multiplier of 3 so that the bus is running fast enough to keep up with the CPU. See the motherboard documentation to learn how to set these speeds using jumpers, DIP switches, or CMOS setup. You will see an example later in this chapter.

Table 4-11 lists how the CPU and several bus speeds are controlled. There are two ways you can change the speed of a computer:

1. Change the speed of the system bus. Whatever the system bus speed is, the PCI bus speed is one-half or one-third of that.

2. Change the multiplier that determines the speed of the CPU. The choices for the multiplier normally are 1.5, 2, 2.5, 3, 3.5, and so forth.

Table 4-11   Motherboard speeds and how they are determined

Bus or Device	How Speed Is Determined	How Controlled
CPU	Processor speed = system bus speed × multiplier. Typical speeds are 450 MHz, 500 MHz, and 750 MHz.	Multiplier is set by jumpers or DIP switches on the motherboard or in CMOS setup.
Memory bus or system bus	Motherboard manufacturer recommends the speed based on the processor and processor's rated speed. Typical values are 100 MHz, 133 MHz, 200 MHz, 400 MHz, and 533 MHz.	Set by jumpers, DIP switches, or in CMOS setup. Most commonly set by jumpers.
PCI bus	System bus speed divided by 2 (or for faster boards, it can be divided by 3).	The speed is set when you set the speed of the system bus.
ISA bus	Runs at only one speed: 8.33 MHz.	NA

Hardware Configuration

Hardware configuration information tells the CPU what hardware components are present in the system and how they are set up to interface with the CPU. Hardware configuration includes information such as how much memory is available, which power management features are present, and whether disk drives, hard drives, modems, serial ports, and the like are connected. Remember that during POST, BIOS looks to the system configuration information to determine the equipment it should expect to find and how that equipment interfaces with the CPU. The CPU uses this information later to process data and instructions.

Configuration information is provided on the motherboard in three different ways, as discussed in Chapter 2: DIP switches, jumpers, and CMOS. Storing configuration information by physically setting DIP switches or jumpers on the motherboard or peripheral devices is inconvenient, because it often requires you to open the computer case to make a change. A more convenient method is to use the CMOS chip to hold the information in the small amount of RAM on the chip. A program in BIOS can then be used to easily make changes to setup. In this section, you will learn more about each method of storing configuration information. You will also see examples of CMOS setup screens.

Setup Data Stored by DIP Switches

Many older computers and a few newer ones store setup data using DIP switches on the motherboard, as shown in Figure 4-17. A DIP (dual inline package) switch is a switch that has an ON position and an OFF position. ON represents binary 1, and OFF represents binary 0. If you add or remove equipment, you can communicate that to the computer by changing a DIP switch setting. When you change a DIP switch setting, use a pointed instrument, such as a ballpoint pen, to push the switch. Don't use a graphite pencil, because graphite conducts electricity. Pieces of graphite dropped into the switch can damage it.

Figure 4-17   DIP switches are sometimes used to store setup data on motherboards

Setup Data Stored by Jumpers

Most computers hold additional configuration information by using jumpers on the motherboard. A jumper consists of two pins sticking up side by side, with a cover over the two pins making a connection. The two pins and the connection together serve as electrical connectors on the motherboard. If the pins are not connected with a cover, the setting is considered OFF. If the cover is present, the setting is ON. If the cover is hanging on one pin, it is "parked" so you won't lose it. You can see all three situations in Figure 4-18.

Figure 4-18   A 6-pin jumper group on a circuit board has (a) no pins covered, (b) a cover parked on one pin, and (c) two jumpers capped or covered

For older motherboards, the presence of cache memory is a typical setting that was communicated to the computer by jumpers. Jumpers are also used to communicate the type and speed of the CPU to the system, or to disable a feature on the motherboard, such as keyboard power-up. (With this feature enabled, you can press a key to power up the system.) You change the jumper setting by removing the computer case, finding the correct jumper, and then either placing a metal cover over the jumper or removing the cover already there. Figure 4-19 shows a diagram of a motherboard with the keyboard power-up jumper shown.

Figure 4-19   The keyboard power-up jumper allows you to use your keyboard to power up the computer

Setup Data Stored on a CMOS Chip

Computers today store most configuration information on one CMOS chip, also called the real-time clock/nonvolatile RAM (RTC/NVRAM) chip, that retains the data even when the computer is turned off. (There are actually many CMOS chips on a motherboard, used for various purposes.) On older computers (mostly IBM 286 PCs built in the 1980s), changes are made to the CMOS setup data using a setup program stored on a floppy disk. One major disadvantage of this method (besides the chance that you might lose or misplace the disk) is that the disk drive must be working before you can change the setup. An advantage of this method is that you can't change the setup unintentionally. If you have an older computer and you are missing the floppy disk that has the setup program, check the Web site of the motherboard manufacturer or the BIOS manufacturer for a replacement disk.

Changing CMOS Using the Setup Program   On newer computers, you usually change the data stored in the CMOS chip by accessing the setup program stored in ROM BIOS. You access the program by pressing a key or combination of keys during the boot process. The exact way to enter setup varies from one motherboard manufacturer to another. Table 4-12 lists the keystrokes needed to access CMOS setup for some common BIOS types.

Table 4-12   How to access CMOS setup

BIOS	Key to Press During POST to Access Setup
AMI BIOS	Del
Award BIOS	Del
Older Phoenix BIOS	Ctrl+Alt+Esc or Ctl+Alt+s
Newer Phoenix BIOS	F2 or F1
Dell computers using Phoenix BIOS	Ctrl+Alt+Enter
Older Compaq computers such as the Deskpro 286 or 386	Place the diagnostics disk in the disk drive, reboot your system, and choose Computer Setup from the menu.
Newer Compaq computers such as the ProLinea, Deskpro, Deskpro XL, Deskpro XE, or Presario	Press the F10 key while the cursor is in the upper-right corner of the screen, which happens just after the 2 beeps during booting.*
All other older computers	Setup is accessed by using a setup program on the disk that came with the PC.
*For Compaq computers, the CMOS setup program is stored on the hard drive in a small, non-DOS partition of about 3 MB. If this partition becomes corrupted, you must run setup from a floppy disk. If you cannot run setup by pressing F10 at startup, suspect a damaged partition or a virus taking up space in conventional memory.	

For the exact method you need to use to enter setup, see the documentation for your motherboard. A message such as the following usually appears on the screen:

```
Press DEL to change Setup
```

or

```
Press F8 for Setup
```

When you press the appropriate key or keys, a setup screen appears with menus and Help features that are often very user-friendly. Although the exact menus will depend on the maker and version of components you are working with, the sample screens that follow will help you become familiar with the general contents of CMOS Setup screens. Figure 4-20 shows a main menu for setup. On this menu, you can change the system date and time, the keyboard language, and other system features.

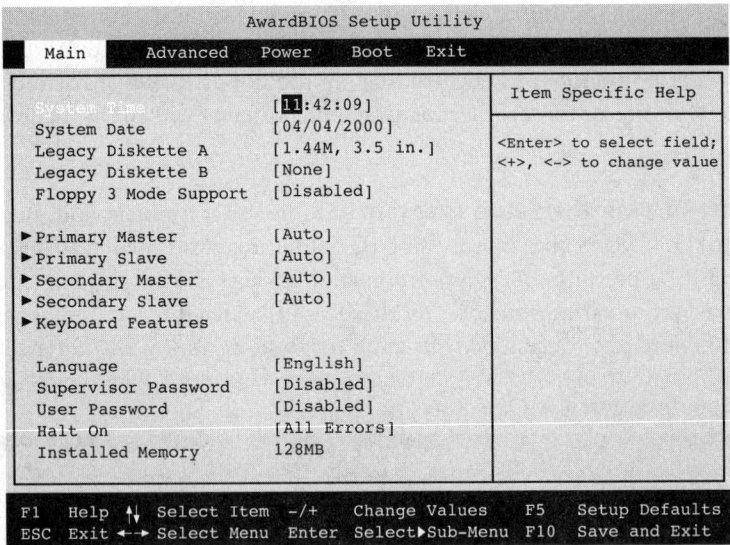

```
                    AwardBIOS Setup Utility
   Main     Advanced   Power    Boot    Exit

                                         ┌─────────────────────────┐
   System Time          [11:42:09]       │  Item Specific Help     │
   System Date          [04/04/2000]     │                         │
   Legacy Diskette A    [1.44M, 3.5 in.] │ <Enter> to select field;│
   Legacy Diskette B    [None]           │ <+>, <-> to change value│
   Floppy 3 Mode Support [Disabled]      │                         │
                                         │                         │
 ▶ Primary Master       [Auto]           │                         │
 ▶ Primary Slave        [Auto]           │                         │
 ▶ Secondary Master     [Auto]           │                         │
 ▶ Secondary Slave      [Auto]           │                         │
 ▶ Keyboard Features                     │                         │
                                         │                         │
   Language             [English]        │                         │
   Supervisor Password  [Disabled]       │                         │
   User Password        [Disabled]       │                         │
   Halt On              [All Errors]     │                         │
   Installed Memory     128MB            │                         │
                                         └─────────────────────────┘

  F1   Help  ↑↓ Select Item  -/+   Change Values   F5   Setup Defaults
  ESC  Exit  ←→ Select Menu   Enter Select▶Sub-Menu F10  Save and Exit
```

Figure 4-20   CMOS Setup Main menu

Recall the discussion of power management from Chapter 3. The power menu in CMOS Setup allows you to configure automatic power-saving features for your system, such as suspend mode. A sample power menu is shown in Figure 4-21.

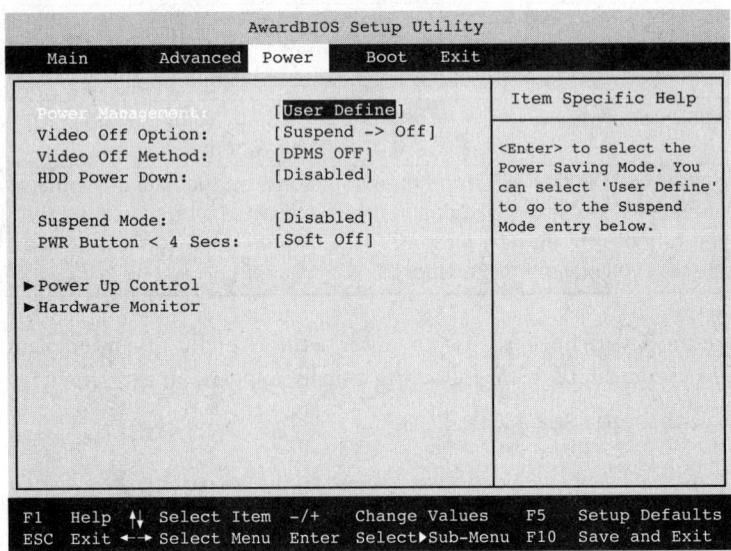

```
                    AwardBIOS Setup Utility
   Main     Advanced   Power    Boot    Exit

                                         ┌─────────────────────────┐
   Power Management:    [User Define]     │  Item Specific Help     │
   Video Off Option:    [Suspend -> Off]  │                         │
   Video Off Method:    [DPMS OFF]        │ <Enter> to select the   │
   HDD Power Down:      [Disabled]        │ Power Saving Mode. You   │
                                          │ can select 'User Define'│
   Suspend Mode:        [Disabled]        │ to go to the Suspend    │
   PWR Button < 4 Secs: [Soft Off]        │ Mode entry below.       │
                                          │                         │
 ▶ Power Up Control                       │                         │
 ▶ Hardware Monitor                       │                         │
                                          │                         │
                                          │                         │
                                          │                         │
                                          │                         │
                                          └─────────────────────────┘

  F1   Help  ↑↓ Select Item  -/+   Change Values   F5   Setup Defaults
  ESC  Exit  ←→ Select Menu   Enter Select▶Sub-Menu F10  Save and Exit
```

Figure 4-21   CMOS Setup Power menu

Figure 4-22 shows a sample Boot menu in CMOS Setup. Here, you can set the order in which the system tries to boot from certain devices. Most likely you will want to have the BIOS attempt to boot from the floppy drive first, and if no disk is present, turn to the hard drive. You will learn more about this in the installation procedures at the end of this chapter, as well as in later chapters.

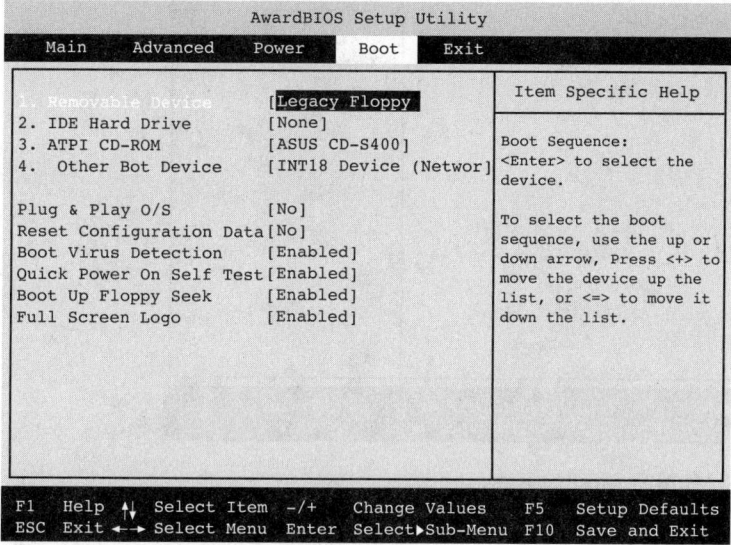

Figure 4-22   CMOS Setup Boot menu

Other configuration options may be contained on an Advanced menu in the setup program or on other menus, depending on which specific CMOS chip you are working with. When you exit the setup program, you can exit without saving your changes or exit and save your changes to the CMOS RAM chip. An exit screen such as the one shown in Figure 4-23 gives you various options, such as saving or discarding changes and exiting the program, restoring default settings, or saving changes and remaining in the program.

Battery Power to the CMOS Chip   Most configuration data in newer computers is stored in a CMOS chip that is battery-powered when the system power is off (see Figure 4-24). The advantage of a CMOS chip over other types of chips is that a CMOS chip requires very little electricity to hold data. A small trickle of electricity from a nearby battery enables the CMOS chip to hold the data even while the main power to the computer is off. If the battery is disconnected or fails, setup information is lost. An indication that the battery is getting weak is that the system date and time are incorrect after the PC has been turned off.

There are several types of CMOS batteries:

- A 3.6 V lithium battery with a four-pin connector; connects with a Velcro strip

- A 4.5 V alkaline battery with a four-pin connector; connects with a Velcro strip

- A 3.6 V barrel-style battery with a two-pin connector; soldered on

- A 3 V lithium coin-cell battery

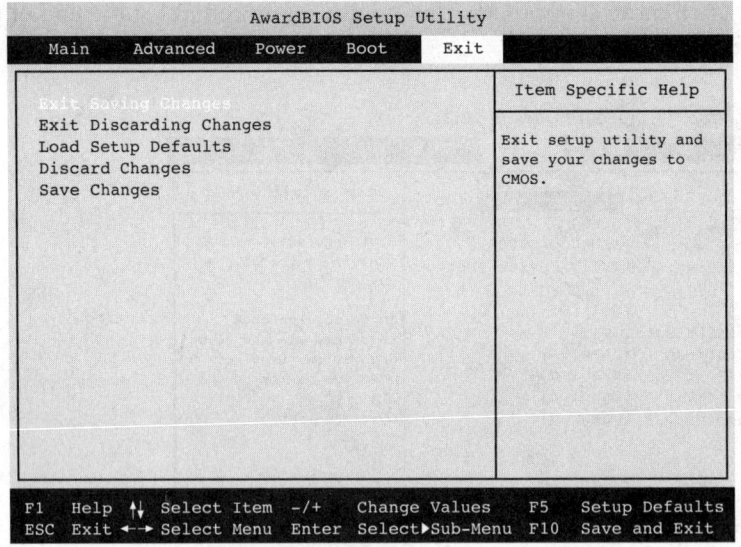

Figure 4-23   CMOS Setup Exit menu

Figure 4-24   The battery that powers the CMOS chip may be on the motherboard
                   or attached nearby

The coin cell is the most common type of CMOS battery. It is shown in Figure 4–25.

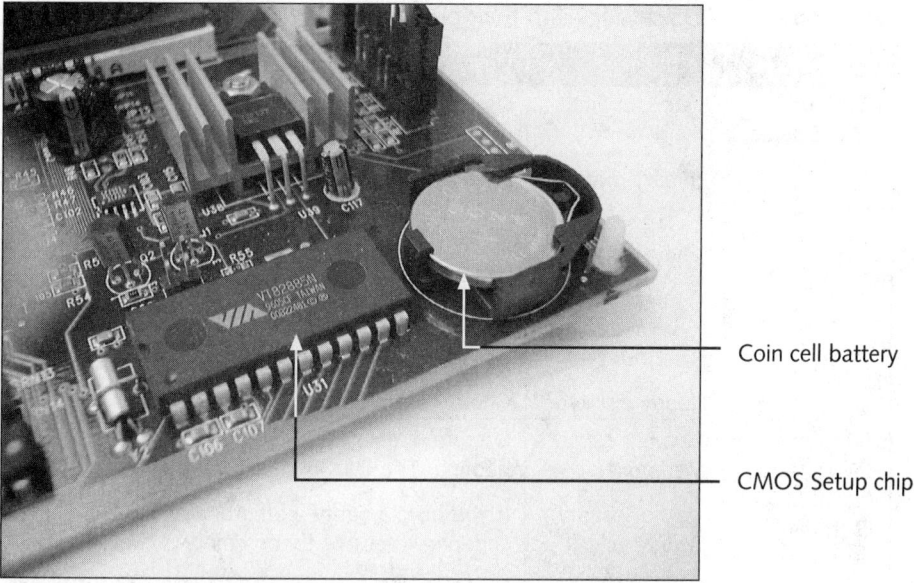

Coin cell battery

CMOS Setup chip

4

Figure 4-25   The coin cell is the most common type of CMOS battery

Setting Startup Passwords in CMOS   Access to a computer can be controlled using a **startup password**, sometimes called a **power-on password**. During booting, or startup, the computer asks for a password. If you do not enter the password correctly, the boot process is terminated. The password is stored on the CMOS chip and is changed by accessing the setup screen. (This password is not the same as the OS password.) Many computers also provide a jumper near the CMOS chip that, when set to "on," causes the computer to "forget" any changes that have been made to default settings stored in CMOS. By jumping these pins, you can disable a password.

Lists of CMOS Settings   Motherboard manuals should contain a list of all CMOS settings, an explanation of their meanings, and their recommended values. When you purchase a motherboard or a computer, be sure the manual is included. If you don't have the manual, you can sometimes go to the motherboard manufacturer's Web site and download the information you need to understand the specific CMOS settings of your computer. Some CMOS settings are listed in Table 4-13.

Table 4-13   CMOS settings and their purpose

Category	Setting	Description
Standard CMOS setup	Date and time	Used to set system date and time (called the real-time clock).
	Primary display	Used to tell POST and DOS (but not Windows) the type of video being used.
	Keyboard	Used to tell system if keyboard is installed or not installed. Useful if the computer is used as a print or file server and you don't want someone changing settings.
	Hard disk type	Used to record size and mapping of the drive.
	Floppy disk type	Choices are usually 3½ inch and 5¼ inch.
Advanced CMOS setup (a.k.a. BIOS Features setup)	Above 1 MB Memory test	Used to disable POST check of this memory to speed up booting. The OS will check this memory anyway.
	Memory parity Error check	If you have a parity motherboard, used to enable parity checking to ensure that memory is correct.
	Numeric Processor test	Enabled unless you have an old 386 or 486SX computer.
	System boot Sequence	Used to establish the drive the system turns to first to look for an OS. Normally drive A, then C.
	External cache Memory	Enable L2 cache. A frequent error in setup is to have cache but not use it because it's disabled here.
	Internal cache Memory	Normally enabled; disable only for old 386 computers.
	Password Checking option	Used to establish a startup password. Use this only if you need to prevent someone untrustworthy from using your PC.
	Video ROM Shadow C000, 16K	For DOS and Windows 9x, shadowing video ROM is recommended because ROM runs slower than RAM.
	System ROM Shadow F000, 64K	Enabling shadow system ROM is recommended.
	IDE multi-block mode	Enables a hard drive to read or write several sectors at a time. Dependent on the kind of hard drive you have.
	Boot sector virus protection	Gives a warning when something is being written to the boot sector of the hard drive. Can be a nuisance if your software is designed to write to the boot sector regularly. When installing or upgrading an operating system, disable this protection so the OS install process can alter the boot sector without interruption.

Table 4-13   CMOS settings and their purpose (continued)

Category	Setting	Description
Advanced Chip Set Setup	AT bus clock selection	Gives the number by which the CPU speed is divided to get the ISA or EISA bus speed.
	ISA bus speed	Gives the number by which the PCI bus speed is divided to get the ISA bus speed.
	Bus mode	Can be set to synchronous or asynchronous modes. In synchronous mode, the bus uses the CPU clock. In asynchronous mode, its own AT bus clock is used.
	AT cycle wait state	The number of wait states the CPU must endure while it interfaces with a device on the ISA or EISA bus. Increase this if an old and slow ISA card is not working well.
	Memory read wait state	Number of wait states the CPU must endure while reading from RAM.
	Memory write wait state	Number of wait states the CPU must endure while writing to RAM.
	Cache read option	Sometimes called "cache read hit burst." The number of clock beats needed to load four 32-bit words into the CPU's internal cache (4-1-1-1 is the usual choice).
	Fast cache read/write	Refers to external cache. Enable it if you have two banks of cache, 64K or 256K.
	Cache wait state	Refers to external cache. The number of wait states the CPU must use while accessing cache.
	AGP capability	Switches between AGP 1x, AGP 2x, and AGP 4x versions.
	AGP aperture size	Adjusts the amount of system memory AGP can address.
	VGA BIOS sequence	Determines order in which PCI/AGP is initialized; important mainly with dual monitors.
	Processor serial number	Allows processor ID# to be switched off for privacy (Pentium III only).
Power Menu (a.k.a. Power Management)	Power management	Disable or enable all power management features. These features are designed to conserve electricity.
	Video off method	Sets which way video to the monitor will be suspended.
	HDD power down	Disable or enable the feature to shut down the hard drive after a period of inactivity.

Table 4-13   CMOS settings and their purpose (continued)

Category	Setting	Description
	Wake on LAN	Wake on LAN allows your PC to be booted from another computer on the same network. It requires an ATX power supply that supports the feature.
	Wake on keyboard	Allows you to power up your PC by pressing a certain key combination.
IDE HDD Auto-detect	Automated query	Detects HDDs installed on either IDE channel; allows you to specify whether Normal, Large, or LBA mode.
Hardware Device Settings (only found on "jumper-less " MB's)	CPU operating speed	Sets the appropriate speed for your CPU.
	External clock	Sets the system bus speed.
	I/O voltage	Sets the appropriate I/O voltage.
	Core voltage	Sets the appropriate core voltage.
Note: The titles, locations, and inclusion or exclusion of BIOS categories and settings depend on the manufacturer and/or BIOS version. For instance, Plug and Play may be a group of settings sharing a category with other settings in one version of BIOS, while Plug and Play may be its own category in another BIOS version.		

TIP In documentation, a.k.a. stands for "also known as."

Protecting Documentation and Configuration Settings

If the battery goes bad or is disconnected, you can lose the settings saved in CMOS RAM. If you are using default settings, reboot with a good battery and instruct setup to restore the default settings. Setup would have to autodetect the hard drive present, and you would need to set the date and time, but you could easily recover from the problem. However, if you have customized some of the CMOS settings, you will need to restore those settings. The most reliable way to do that is to keep a written record of all the changes you have made to CMOS.

If you are permanently responsible for a computer, you should consider a written record of what you have done to this PC an essential tool for maintaining the PC. Use a small notebook or similar document and keep CMOS settings, records of hardware and software installed, network settings, and the like in the notebook. Suppose someone decides to tinker with a PC for which you are responsible and changes a jumper on the motherboard, but no longer remembers which jumper he or she changed. The computer no longer works, and the documentation for the board is now invaluable. If documentation is lost or misplaced, what should be a simple job of reading the settings for each jumper and checking them on the board can become a long and tedious research task. Keep the documentation well labeled in a safe place. If you have several computers to maintain, you might consider a filing system for each computer. Another method is to tape a cardboard folder to the inside top of the computer case and safely tuck the hardware documentation here. This works well if you are responsible for several computers spread over a wide area.

Regardless of the method you use, it's important that you keep your written record up to date and keep it and the hardware documentation in a safe place. It's probably not a good idea to leave it in the care of users who might not realize its value. The notebook and documentation will be invaluable to you as you solve future problems with this PC.

Saving and Restoring CMOS Settings Using a Third-Party Utility Software

If you lose CMOS settings, another way to restore them is to use a backup of the settings that you have previously saved to a floppy disk. One third-party utility that allows you to save CMOS settings is Norton Utilities by Symantec (*www.symantec.com*).

You can also download a shareware utility to record CMOS settings. The files might change with new releases of the software.

1. Access the Internet and use a search engine to search for a site offering Cmos.zip. At the time of this writing, two locations are *www.ibiblio.org/pub/micro/pcstuff/ freedos/files/util/system/cmos.zip* and *www.computerhope.com/download/hardware.htm*. Then go to the address.

2. Select and download CMOS.ZIP. You can then exit the Internet.

3. Unzip the compressed file and print the CMOS.DOC documentation.

4. Double-click the CMOS.EXE file you unzipped. The program shows the current content of CMOS memory in a DOS box.

5. Enter **S** (for Save) at the command line. Enter the drive letter of your floppy drive and a filename to save the current CMOS settings to floppy disk, such as **A:MYCMOS**.

6. Enter **Q** to quit the program.

When you want to retrieve the contents of the file from the floppy disk, run the CMOS.EXE program again, and enter **L** (for Load) at the command line, specifying the name of the file you saved on the floppy disk.

BUILDING A COMPUTER: AN INTRODUCTION

Now that you have learned about how motherboards work and what components they include, you can begin learning how to build your own computer. The final section in this chapter will discuss in detail how a motherboard is installed. First, though, let's look at the overall process for building your own computer. In Chapter 3, you took your first look inside a computer and learned your way around by taking it apart. In this section, you will begin to learn how to put a new one together from separately purchased parts. You will need this information as you learn to install specific components in this chapter and the rest of the book. This is a general overview of the process and is not meant to include the details of all possible installation scenarios, which can vary according to the components and OS you are installing.

Whenever you install or uninstall software or hardware, keep a notebook with details about the components you are working on, configuration settings, manufacturer's specifications, and other relevant information. This will help you if you need to back-track later, and can also help in documenting and troubleshooting your computer system. Keep all hardware documentation for this system together with the notebook in an envelope in a safe place.

The general process for putting together a computer is as follows:

1. *Verify that you have all parts you plan to install.* Check device manufacturers' Web sites for updated BIOS and device drivers for your system.

2. *Prepare the computer case* by installing the case fan, removing the plates that cover the drive bays, and installing the spacers that keep the motherboard from touching the case. Because today's CPUs run at high temperatures, it is a good idea to have at least one case fan in addition to the power supply fan, to ensure good case ventilation. Also, preparing the case before actually installing components lessens the risk of damaging components as you are installing them.

3. *Install drives,* such as CD-ROM or DVD drive, hard drive, and floppy drive. Have a plan as to which drives to install in which locations, to avoid getting cables tangled or having them interfere with airflow or with access to other components. As you are installing drives, verify jumper settings for Master/Slave or SCSI ID. (You will learn more about this in Chapter 7.)

4. *Determine proper configuration settings for the motherboard.* Especially important are any jumpers, DIP switches, or CMOS settings specifically for the CPU, and RAM speeds and timing. Gather as much information as possible from manufacturer documentation. Read the motherboard manual from cover to cover. You can also check manufacturer Web sites for suggestions for optimizing system settings.

5. *Set any jumpers or switches on the motherboard.* This is much easier to do before you put the board in the case.

6. *Install the CPU and CPU cooler.* With some motherboards, the CPU comes already installed on the board, in which case you just need to install the cooler. You might need to add thermal grease, discussed below.

7. *Install RAM* into the appropriate slots on the motherboard.

8. *Install the motherboard and attach cabling* that goes from the case switches to the motherboard and from the power supply to the drives. Pay attention to how cables are labeled and to any information in the documentation on where they are to be attached. (The next section covers details on how to install a motherboard.) Position and tie cables neatly together to make sure they don't obstruct the fans.

9. *Install the video card* (which can also be called the display adapter, video adapter, or graphics accelerator) onto the motherboard. Usually this card goes into the AGP slot, as you saw in Chapter 1.

10. *Plug the computer into a power source and attach the monitor and keyboard.* Note that you are not attaching the mouse at this point. You will not need it for the initial

setup. Though the mouse generally does not cause problems during setup, it is a good idea not to initially install anything you don't absolutely need.

11. *Boot the system and enter CMOS setup.* As you learned earlier in the chapter, there are several ways to do this, depending on what type of system you have.

12. *Make sure settings are set to the default.* If components come new from the manufacturer, they are probably already at default settings. If you are salvaging a component from another system, you may need to reset settings to the default. There is generally a jumper or switch that will set all CMOS settings to default settings. You will need to do the following while you are in CMOS:

    - Check the time and date.
    - Check the floppy drive type.
    - Make sure abbreviated POST is disabled. While you are setting up a system, you generally want the system to do as many tests as possible. Once you know the system is working, you can choose to abbreviate POST.
    - Set the boot order to drive A, then drive C, if you will be booting the OS from a floppy disk. Set the boot order to CD-ROM, then drive C, if you will be booting the OS from a CD. This determines which drive the system looks to for the OS. You may need to change the boot order later, as explained in Step 19.
    - Make sure autodetect hard disk is set so that the system will automatically look for drives.
    - Leave everything else as default unless you know that the setting should be otherwise.
    - Save and exit.

13. *If you are booting from a floppy disk, insert a bootable setup disk* that contains the files that allow you to format the hard drive. (Refer to Chapter 3 for a list of files that should be on this disk.)

14. *Observe POST* and verify that no errors occur.

15. *Prepare the hard drive for the OS.* You will learn how to do this in Chapter 7.

16. *Reboot the system and run ScanDisk on drive C.* ScanDisk is an OS utility that checks the hard drive for errors and repairs them. Chapter 7 covers this in detail.

17. *Connect the mouse.*

18. *Install the OS from CD or floppy.* Generally, it is best to install the OS before any expansion cards, such as a sound card or a modem card. Installing multiple cards at once can confuse Plug and Play, especially during OS installation. Unless you are very familiar with all components' resource requirements, it is almost always less trouble to install one device at a time on a new system. If you are setting up multiple systems with the exact same configuration, build the first system one card at a time. If no major errors occur, then, on a second system, try installing all cards at once, after the OS has been loaded. If this

approach is successful, then you can save a little time by installing all hardware devices before you install the OS. However, you should still reboot whenever you are given the option, as the OS detects each device.

19. *Change the boot order in CMOS* so that it is not booting from a CD first. If you set the order as drive A, then drive C, you can boot from a floppy disk later as needed. This is the most common boot order.

20. *Check for conflicts with system resources.* For Windows, use Device Manager to verify that the OS recognizes all devices and that there are no reported conflicts. If your motherboard comes with a CD that contains some motherboard drivers, install them now. Remember that the drivers that Windows installed for the devices it sensed might not be the latest drivers. Windows makes its best guess at what drivers to use, but if your version of Windows is older than some of your components, it might not have the correct or newest drivers for those devices. Using Device Manager, you can see what drivers are installed for a device. If Windows is not using the newest drivers, update the drivers using the latest drivers from the CD that comes with the device.

21. *Install any other expansion cards and/or drives* and install appropriate drivers, one device at a time, rebooting and checking for conflicts after each installation.

22. *Verify that all is operating properly, and make any final OS and/or CMOS adjustments,* such as power management settings.

INSTALLING THE MOTHERBOARD

Now that you have learned about the general process of putting together a computer, you will learn how to install a motherboard. The following section provides you with information on how to install and configure a motherboard and how to test the installation. You will learn even more about this in the chapter on purchasing or building your own PC (Chapter 14).

CAUTION

As with any installation, remember from Chapter 3 the importance of using a ground strap to ground yourself when working inside a computer case, to protect components against ESD.

Preparing the Motherboard to Go into the Case

Before you begin preparing the motherboard, read the manual that comes with it from beginning to end. The steps in this procedure are general, and you will need to know information specific to your motherboard. Visually familiarize yourself with the configuration of the case and the motherboard.

Setting the Jumpers

The first step in preparing the motherboard to go in the case is to set the jumpers or DIP switches. When doing an installation, read the motherboard documentation carefully, looking for explanations of how jumpers and DIP switches on the board are used, which will differ from one motherboard to another. For example, there might be a jumper group that controls the system bus frequency and another group that controls the CPU frequency multiple. Then set the jumpers and DIP switches according to the hardware you will be installing.

4

Adding the CPU, Fan, and Heat Sink

Now that you have set the jumpers on the motherboard, you are ready to add the CPU itself. The motherboard we are using in this example has a slot 1 for the Pentium II, which comes packaged either in a single edge contact cartridge (SECC) or a single edge processor package (SEPP) for the Celeron processor. For either processor, the motherboard uses a universal retention mechanism (URM), which is preinstalled on the board. Follow these steps to install the fan on the side of the processor first, and then install the processor on the motherboard:

1. Unfold the URM arms. Flip both arms up until they lock into position (Figure 4-26).

2. Examine the fan and processor to see how the fan brace lines up with holes in the side of the SECC (see Figure 4-27).

URM supporting arms

Figure 4-26   Preparing URM arms to receive the CPU (the arms are in the upright position)

Figure 4-27   The braces on the fan align with holes in the side of the SECC

3. Place the fan directly on the side of the SECC. The two should fit tightly together, with absolutely no space between them.

4. After the fan and SECC are fitted together, place the SECC on a table and push the clamp on the fan down and into place, to secure the fan to the SECC (see Figure 4-28).

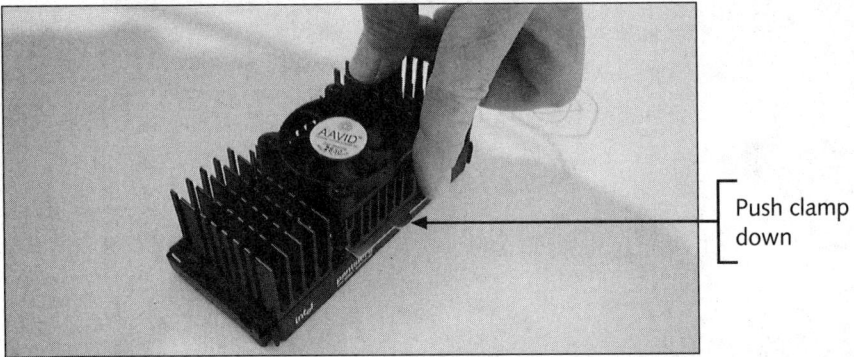

Figure 4-28   Push the clamp on the fan down until it locks in place, locking the fan to the SECC

5. Insert the fan and SECC into the supporting arms (Figure 4-29). The SECC should fit snugly into slot 1, similar to the way an expansion card settles down into an expansion slot. The arms should snap into position when the SECC is fully seated. Be certain you have a good fit here.

4

Fan and
SECC

Supporting
arms

Slot 1

Figure 4-29   Insert the fan and SECC into the supporting arms and slot 1

6. Lock the SECC into position by pulling the SECC locks outward until they lock into the supporting arm lock holes.

7. Connect the power cord coming from the fan to the power connection on the motherboard (Figure 4-30). Look for the power connection near slot 1. If you have trouble locating it, see the motherboard documentation.

Power for CPU fan

Figure 4-30   Connect the fan power cord to the motherboard

The next step is to install RAM in the memory slots. How to buy and install memory for a specific motherboard are covered in Chapter 6.

Installing the Motherboard in the Case

Here are the steps for installing the motherboard in the case:

1. Install the faceplate. The **faceplate** or I/O shield is a metal plate that comes with the motherboard and fits over the ports to create a well-fitted enclosure around them. A case might have several faceplates designed for several brands of motherboards. Select the correct one and discard the others (see Figure 4-31). Insert the faceplate in the hole at the back of the case (see Figure 4-32).

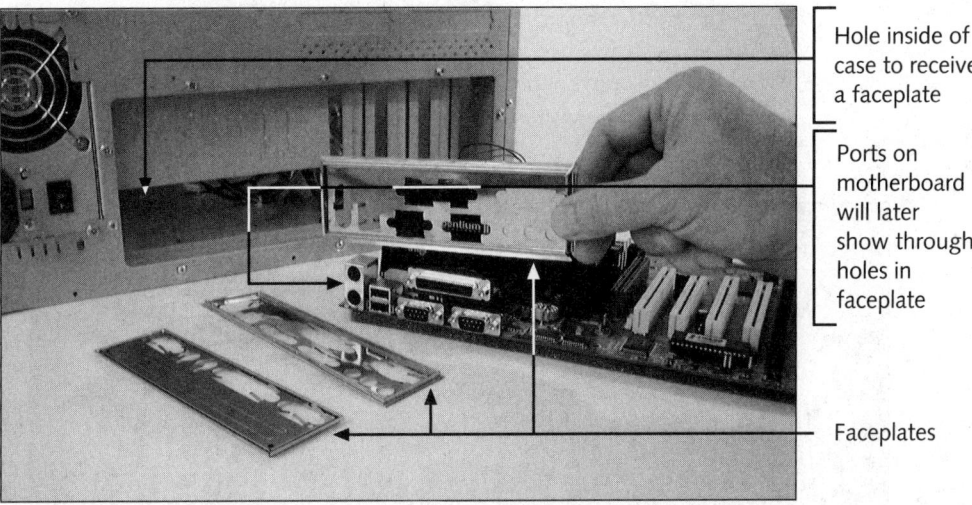

Hole inside of case to receive a faceplate

Ports on motherboard will later show through holes in faceplate

4

Faceplates

Figure 4-31   The computer case comes with several faceplates. Select the faceplate that fits over the ports that come off the motherboard. The other plates can be discarded.

Faceplate

Figure 4-32   Install the faceplate in the hole at the rear of the computer case

2. Install the standoffs. **Standoffs**, also called **spacers**, are round plastic or metal pegs that separate the motherboard from the case, so that components on the back of the motherboard do not touch the case. Make sure the locations of the standoffs match the screw holes on the motherboard. If you need to remove a standoff to move it to a new slot, needle-nose pliers work well to unscrew the standoff. The case will have more holes than you need, in order to support several brands of motherboards.

3. Place the motherboard inside the case and use screws to attach it to the case. Figure 4-33 shows how you must align the standoffs to the holes on the motherboard. The screws will fit into the standoffs you installed earlier. There should be at least four standoff/screw sets, and there may be as many as six. Use as many as there are holes for in the motherboard.

Holes for screws

Standoffs

Figure 4-33   Three standoffs and four screw holes are visible

4. Connect the power cord from the power supply to the P1 power connection on the motherboard. (If you are using an AT motherboard, you will have two power connections, P8 and P9, which are connected using the black-to-black rule.)

5. Connect the wire leads from the front panel of the case to the motherboard. These are the wires for the switches and lights on the front of the computer. Because your case and your motherboard may not have been made by the same manufacturer, you will need to pay close attention to the source of the wires to determine where they connect on the motherboard. For example, Figure 4-34 shows a computer case that has five wires from the front panel that connect to the motherboard.

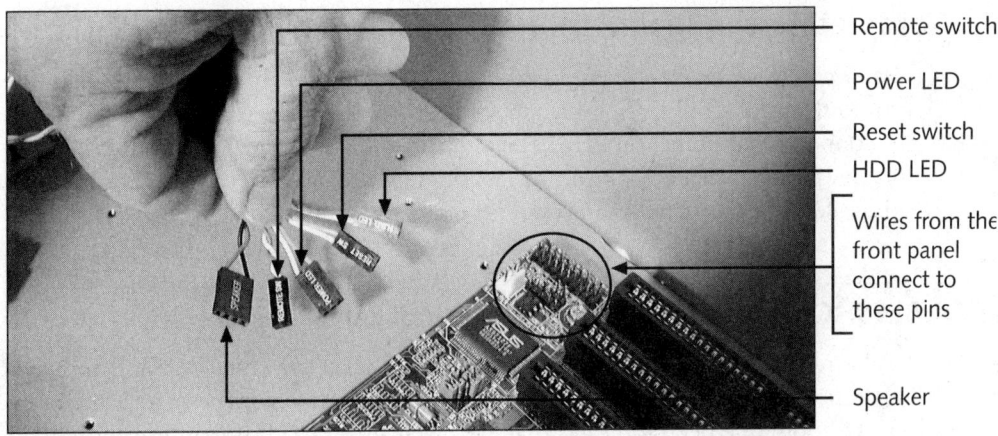

Figure 4-34   Five wires from the front panel connect to the motherboard

The five connectors are:

- *Reset switch.* Used to reboot the computer
- *HDD LED.* Controls a light on the front panel that lights up when any IDE device is in use. (LED stands for light-emitting diode; an LED is a light on the front panel.)
- *Speaker.* Controls the speaker
- *Power LED.* Light indicating that power is on
- *Remote switch.* Controls power to the motherboard; must be connected for the PC to power up

To know which wire connects to which pins, see the motherboard documentation. Sometimes the documentation is not clear, but it's okay to guess when connecting a wire to a connection. If it doesn't work, no harm is done.

 To help orient the connector on the motherboard pins, look for a small triangle embedded on the connector that marks one of the outside wires as pin 1 (see Figure 4-36). Look for pin 1 to be labeled on the motherboard as a small 1 embedded on the board to either the right or the left of the group of pins. Also, sometimes the documentation will mark pin 1 as a square pin in the diagram, rather than round like the other pins.

Figure 4-35   Look for the small triangle embedded on the wire lead connectors to correctly orient the connector to the motherboard connector pins

Completing the Installation

After you have installed the motherboard, you will install drives and other components. How to do this is covered in later chapters. Finally, turn on the system and make sure everything is connected properly. You may need to change the hardware configuration settings discussed in the previous section. As you set configuration data, remember to create a rescue disk of these settings so that you can restore them if something goes wrong.

TROUBLESHOOTING THE MOTHERBOARD AND CPU

When troubleshooting the motherboard, use whatever clues POST can give you. Recall that, before video is checked out, POST reports any error messages as beep codes. When a PC boots, one beep indicates that all is well after POST. If you hear more than one beep, look up the beep code in Appendix A. Error messages on the screen indicate that video is working. If the beep code or error message is not in Appendix A, try the Web site of the ROM BIOS manufacturer for information. Figure 4-36 shows the Web site for AMI with explanations of beep codes produced by its startup BIOS.

Remember that you can try substituting good hardware components for suspected bad ones. Be cautious here. A friend once had a computer that would not boot. He replaced the hard drive, with no change. He replaced the motherboard next. The computer booted up with no problem; he was delighted, until it failed again. Later he discovered that a faulty power supply had damaged his original motherboard. When he traded the bad one for a good one, the new motherboard also got zapped! Check the voltage coming from the power supply before putting in a new motherboard! (Instructions on troubleshooting the power supply are in Chapter 3.)

A power-saving feature might be the source of the problem. Ask yourself, "Is the system in a doze or sleep Mode?" Many "green" systems can be programmed through CMOS to suspend the monitor or even the drive if the keyboard or CPU has been inactive for a few minutes. Pressing any key will usually resume operations exactly where the user left off.

If you have just upgraded the CPU and the system will not boot, reinstall the old CPU, flash BIOS, and then try the new CPU again. Verify that you have installed thermal paste between the CPU and the heat sink.

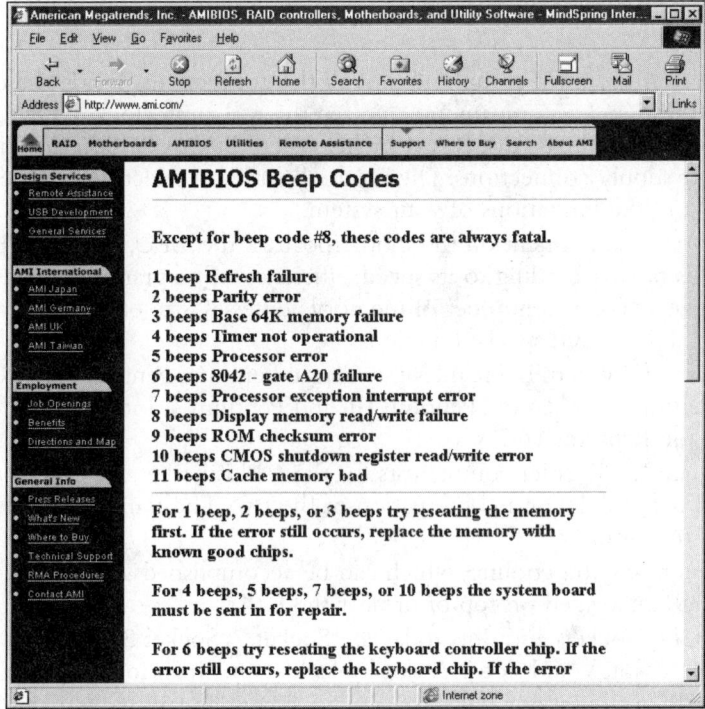

Figure 4-36   The ROM BIOS manufacturer's Web site is a good source of information about beep codes

If this doesn't resolve the problem, try these things:

- If the fan is running, reseat or replace the CPU, BIOS, or RAM. Try installing a DIMM in a different slot. A POST code diagnostic card is a great help at this point. These cards used for troubleshooting are covered in Chapter 13.

- Sometimes a dead computer can be fixed by simply disassembling it and reseating cables, adapter cards, socketed chips, and SIMMs, DIMMs, or RIMMs. Bad connections and corrosion are common problems.

- Check jumpers, DIP switches, and CMOS settings.

- Look for physical damage on the motherboard.

- If the battery is dead, or dying, it may cause problems. Sometimes, after a long holiday, a weak battery will cause the CMOS to forget its configuration.

- Reduce the system to essentials. Remove any unnecessary hardware, such as expansion cards, and then try to boot again.

- Exchange the CPU.

- Exchange the motherboard, but before you do, measure the voltage output of the power supply, in case it is producing too much power and has damaged the board.

CHAPTER SUMMARY

❏ The motherboard is the most complicated of all the components inside the computer. It contains the CPU and accompanying chip set, the real-time clock, ROM BIOS, CMOS configuration chip, RAM, RAM cache, system bus, expansion slots, jumpers, ports, and power supply connections. The motherboard you select determines both the capabilities and the limitations of your system.

❏ The most important component on the motherboard is the CPU, or central processing unit. The CPU is rated according to its speed, efficiency of programming code, word size, data path size, maximum number of memory addresses, size of internal cache, multiprocessing abilities, and special functions.

❏ The Intel Pentium CPU family includes the Classic Pentium, Pentium MMX, Pentium Pro, Pentium II, Celeron, Pentium III, and Pentium 4. Intel's newest processor family is called the Itanium.

❏ AMD and VIA are Intel's chief competitors for the CPU market. CPUs can use either RISC or CISC technology or a combination of the two. The Itanium uses EPIC, an altogether new technology.

❏ Newer CPUs require extra cooling, which can be accomplished with a CPU heat sink and cooling fan, located on top of or near the CPU.

❏ The common CPU sockets and slots today are Socket 7, Socket 370, Socket 423, Socket 603, slot 1, Slot A, and slot 2. A slot looks like an expansion slot.

❏ Because some CPUs require one voltage for internal core operations and another voltage for external I/O operations, motherboards might have a voltage regulator on board.

❏ Some components can be built into the motherboard, in which case they are called on-board components, or they can be attached to the system in some other way, such as on an expansion card.

❏ ROM chips contain the programming code to manage POST and system BIOS and to change the CMOS settings. The setup or CMOS chip holds configuration information.

❏ A chip set is a group of chips on the motherboard that supports the CPU. Intel is the most popular manufacturer of chip sets.

❏ The total BIOS of a system includes the ROM BIOS on the motherboard as well as BIOS on expansion cards. Plug and Play BIOS is designed to work in harmony with Windows 9x to resolve resource conflicts from expansion cards and other devices. Flash ROM allows the ROM BIOS to be upgraded without having to change the ROM chip.

❏ Dynamic RAM (DRAM) is slower than static RAM (SRAM) because dynamic RAM must be refreshed. RAM usually comes packaged as a SIMM, DIMM, or RIMM memory module.

❏ Two kinds of static RAM cache for the slower DRAM are internal and external cache, sometimes called Level 1 and Level 2 or Level 3 cache, also called L1 and L2 or L3 cache.

❏ L1 cache is contained on the CPU microchip, and L2 and L3 cache are external to this microchip. L2 and L3 can be on the motherboard or in the CPU housing. If a processor has L2 cache, then cache on the motherboard is called L3 cache.

❏ The Itanium has L1, L2, and L3 cache.

❏ A bus is a path on the motherboard that carries electrical power, control signals, memory addresses, and data to different components on the board.

❏ A bus can be 16, 32, 64, or more bits wide. The first ISA bus had an 8-bit data path. The second ISA bus had a 16-bit data path.

❏ Some well-known buses are the 16-bit ISA bus, 32-bit MCA, and EISA buses, and the two local buses, the VESA bus and the PCI bus. A local bus is designed to allow fast devices quicker and more direct access to the CPU than that allowed by other buses.

❏ Expansion slots can be located on the motherboard, but they are sometimes stacked vertically in the computer case on a second board devoted to that purpose.

❏ Jumpers on the motherboard can be used to set the motherboard speed and the CPU multiplier that determines the CPU speed.

❏ Sometimes the CPU must be slowed down to accommodate slower devices, by means of wait states that cause it to wait one clock beat. Wait states often mean a significant reduction in performance.

❏ When building a new system, install the drives, motherboard, and expansion cards. Only install essential components before you install the OS. Then add other components one at a time, verifying that each component is working before adding another.

❏ When installing the motherboard, install the CPU and memory and set jumpers and DIP switches on the board before installing it in the case.

KEY TERMS

Advanced Transfer Cache (ATC)
back side bus
bus speed
CISC (complex instruction set computing)
clock speed
discrete L2 cache
dual-voltage CPU
EPIC (explicitly parallel instruction computing)
Execution Trace Cache
expansion bus
external cache
faceplate
front side bus
heat sink
Host bus

instruction set
internal bus
internal cache
ISA bus
Level 1 (L1) cache
Level 2 (L2) cache
Level 3 (L3) cache
local bus
local I/O bus
low insertion force (LIF) socket
memory bus
memory cache
motherboard bus
multiplier
North Bridge
on-board ports
P1 connector
P8 connector
P9 connector

pin array cartridge (PAC)
pin grid array (PGA)
power on password
primary cache
processor speed
RISC (Reduced Instruction Set Computing) chips
single-voltage CPU
South Bridge
spacers
staggered pin grid array (SPGA)
standoffs
startup password
system bus
wait state
zero insertion force (ZIF) socket

5

SUPPORTING I/O DEVICES

In this chapter, you will learn:

♦ How to install peripheral I/O devices

♦ How to use ports and expansion slots for add-on devices

♦ About keyboards and how to troubleshoot them

♦ About different types of pointing devices

♦ How monitors and video cards relate to the system, and how to troubleshoot them

This chapter focuses on how to install and support I/O devices. You will first learn about procedures and guidelines that are common to most installations, including how to use serial, parallel, USB, and IEEE 1394 ports, as well as expansion slots. Then you will learn about the essential I/O devices for a PC: keyboard, mouse, and video. This chapter builds the foundation for later chapters in which you will learn about hard drives, SCSI devices, and multimedia devices.

BASIC PRINCIPLES OF PERIPHERAL INSTALLATIONS

When you add a new peripheral to a computer, the device needs a device driver or BIOS, system resources (which might include an IRQ, DMA channel, I/O addresses, and upper memory addresses), and application software. Consider these fundamental principles:

- The peripheral is a hardware device that is controlled by software. You must install both the hardware and the software.

- The software might be of different types. For example, a device could require driver software that interfaces directly with the hardware device and an application software package that interfaces with the driver. You must install all levels of software.

- Remember from Chapter 2 that more than one peripheral device might attempt to use the same computer resources. This conflict could disable one or both devices. Possible conflicts arise when more than one device attempts to use the same IRQ, DMA channel, I/O addresses, or (for 16-bit drivers) upper memory addresses.

A Review of System Resources

Before discussing principles of installation, let's review the concepts of the four system resources that were first explained in Chapter 2.

- An IRQ is a line on a bus that serves as an interrupt request line and is assigned to a device. The device raises the IRQ when it needs the attention of the CPU.

- Each device needs a group of I/O addresses that the CPU will use to get the attention of the device and communicate with it.

- Older device drivers and BIOS written in real mode require some upper memory addresses between 640K and 1024K. These programs sometimes will not work unless given the specific memory addresses they are requesting.

- Some devices require a DMA channel to speed up data transfer across the bus. The DMA channel and upper memory addresses are also assigned at startup.

- System resources are assigned at startup.

- Plug and Play devices do not request specific I/O addresses, DMA channels, or IRQs, but use those assigned to them by the BIOS and OS. Drivers for PnP devices are 32-bit drivers loaded in extended memory, so upper memory addresses are not needed.

- Legacy devices are not PnP and require specific system resources. Legacy drivers are 16-bit drivers loaded into base or upper memory. A legacy device or driver can sometimes be forced to use alternate resources by setting jumpers on the device or switches in the command line to load the driver.

- Sometimes a bus controller is assigned a single set of resources for all the devices using the bus.

One example of a bus controller managing resources for devices on the bus is the PCI bus. The system resources needed by PCI devices are assigned to the PCI controller, which then manages these resources. Other types of subsystems that have a controller to manage system resources for the devices connected to the controller include SCSI, USB, and IEEE 1394. In all these cases, the controller can be embedded on the motherboard as part of the chip set or can be on a host adapter in an expansion slot. Whether on the motherboard or host adapter, the controller is assigned system resources, which are used to manage the devices connected to it. With SCSI, USB, and IEEE 1394, only one IRQ and I/O address assignment is needed for the controller, and the devices managed by the controller don't need individual resources assigned to them; they all share the resources assigned to the controller.

5

Installation Overview

You follow three basic steps to install an add-on device:

1. Install the device.
2. Install the device driver.
3. Install the application software.

The device can be either internal (installed inside the computer case) or external (installed outside the case). Devices installed inside the case are drives (hard drives, floppy drives, CD-ROM drives, DVD drives, Zip drives, etc.) or devices that are inserted in expansion slots on the motherboard (a modem card, video capture card, etc.). You can install an external device using an existing port (serial, parallel, USB, IEEE 1394 port, and so forth), or a port provided by an interface card installed in an expansion slot. Figure 5-1 shows the back of a PC case with several ports labeled. Only one of these ports, the video port, does not come directly off the motherboard.

An example of an external device that might use an expansion card is a scanner. When you buy a scanner, the package might include an expansion card that provides a port for the scanner. You are buying:

- Scanner
- Expansion card that interfaces with the computer (for example, a SCSI host adapter to provide a SCSI port for the scanner)
- Cable to connect the scanner to its expansion card
- Device driver on disk
- Application software for using the scanner
- Documentation

PS/2 keyboard port
PS/2 mouse port
Two USB ports

Two serial ports

Parallel port

Two USB ports
Ethernet LAN port

Three audio ports

Video port

Figure 5-1   Rear of computer case showing ports; only one port (the video port) is not
coming directly off the motherboard

Installing the hardware includes installing the expansion card in an expansion slot on the
motherboard and then plugging in the scanner itself. After physically installing the device,
you will need to install the device driver. The driver and the scanner expansion card are
specific for each brand and model of scanner; however, the application software might
work with most scanners. In fact, you might have several applications that use the same
hardware device.

The rest of this section discusses hardware devices and application software in detail, and
reviews some of what you have learned about device drivers, before turning to standard ports
on a computer system for installing devices.

Purchasing and Installing a Hardware Device

Internal devices are usually less expensive than external devices, because external devices have the additional expense of their own power supply and case. Internal devices also offer the advantage of not taking up desk space, and their cables and cords are neatly tucked away. An advantage of external devices is that they can be moved easily from one computer to another.

If you've ever shopped for a peripheral device, such as a printer or a sound card, you know what a large variety of features and prices today's market offers. Research pays. When selecting a device, you should know the following about your computer system:

- Which CPU, system bus, and local bus you have

- How much memory you have

- What size hard drive your system has

- Which OS you are using and what version it is (for example, Windows 98 Second Edition, or Windows 2000 Professional)

- How much space is available on your hard drive

- For internal devices, how many drives, bays, or expansion slots and what kinds of slots are free in your computer

In addition to a basic knowledge of your system, you might need some technical information. For example, most computers have a power supply that well exceeds the requirements of the standard system, making it possible to add internal devices without exceeding the total available wattage. However, if your computer is old (for computers, that's over five years), and you're adding more than one internal device, the power supply could limit your choices. If you install more internal devices than the power supply can handle, you might need to upgrade the power supply.

When selecting a hardware device, consider these things:

- Is the device Plug and Play? Accept nothing less.

- Does the device offer all the features you are looking for, without too many features that you will not use?

- Is the documentation easy to read and comprehensive?

- Does the manufacturer's Web site offer lots of help, including technical support and the latest drivers?

- What is the warranty on the device?

- Is the device compatible with your current hardware and software?

 When buying a device and other components that the device will use, such as an expansion card or cable, if you buy everything from the same source, they are more likely to be compatible.

When installing an external device, turn off the PC and plug in the device and reboot. If the device is PnP, the Add New Hardware Wizard launches, prompting you to install the device drivers. You'll see examples of installing external devices later in this chapter. To install a PnP expansion card such as a video card, modem card, network card, IEEE 1394 controller, USB controller, wireless NIC, or sound card, follow these general directions:

- Protect the PC from ESD by using an antistatic bracelet and ground mat.

- Unplug the PC, move things out of the way, and remove the case cover. Figure 5-2 shows a computer case with panels on the side. Remove the screws on the rear of the case holding the panel in place, and slide the panel to the rear.

Slide to rear

Figure 5-2   Some cases have panels on each side; slide the panel to the rear to remove it

- Locate the slot you plan to use, and remove the faceplate from the slot. In Figure 5-3, you can see two PCI slots that have their faceplates removed, and two more PCI slots with faceplates in place. Sometimes a faceplate will punch out, and sometimes you remove a faceplate screw to remove the faceplate.

- Insert the expansion card in the expansion slot. Be careful to push the card directly into the slot, without rocking it from side to side. Rocking it from side to side can widen the expansion slot, making it more difficult to keep a good contact. If you have a problem getting the card into the slot, you can put the end away from the side of the case in the slot first and gently rock the card from front to rear into the slot. The card should feel snug in the slot. You can almost feel it drop into place. Later, if the card does not work, most likely it is not seated securely in the slot. Check that first and then, if possible, try a different slot.

- Insert the screw that connects the card to the case (see Figure 5-3). Be sure to use this screw, because if it's not present, the card can creep out of the slot over time.

Figure 5-3   Secure an expansion card in the slot with a screw

- Replace the case cover, power cord, and other peripherals. (If you like, you can leave the case cover off until you've tested the device, in case it doesn't work and you need to reseat it.)

- Plug in whatever device is intended to use the port on the rear of the card. For example, for a video card, plug in the monitor; for a sound card, plug in the speakers; or for a modem card, plug in the phone line.

- Reboot the PC. The Add New Hardware Wizard will launch, prompting you to install the device drivers. Install the drivers and finish the wizard.

- Test the device.

It is not likely that you will be purchasing devices today that are not Plug and Play, but many legacy devices are still around, and you, as a PC support technician, must know how to support them. Special concerns when dealing with legacy devices are covered later in the chapter.

When installing specialized devices such as CAD/CAM devices, security card readers, or temperature sensors, always read the documentation carefully before you begin. Installation goes much like other more common devices and generally follows the same procedures outlined above.

USING PORTS AND EXPANSION SLOTS FOR ADD-ON DEVICES

Devices can be plugged directly into a port (serial, parallel, USB, or IEEE 1394), or they can use an expansion card plugged into an expansion slot. This section addresses the details of both kinds of installations.

All computers come with one or two serial ports, one parallel port, and, on newer computers, one or more USB ports or an IEEE 1394 port. Newer motherboards have several on-board ports, but, on older motherboards, an **I/O controller card** in an expansion slot supplied the serial and parallel ports.

In comparing speeds, the ports are rated in this order: IEEE 1394 has a data transmission rate of 1.2 Gbps (Gigabits per second); Hi-Speed USB is rated at 480 Mbps (Megabits per second); Original USB is rated at 12 Mbps; parallel ports are rated at 1.5 Mbps and serial ports are rated at 115.2 Kbps (Kilobits per second).

Using Serial Ports

In Chapter 1, you were introduced to serial ports, which transmit data in single bits, or serially. You can identify these ports on the back of a PC case by (1) counting the pins and (2) determining whether the port is male or female. Figure 5-4 shows serial ports, a parallel port, and a game port, for comparison. On the top is one 25-pin female parallel port and one 9-pin male serial port. On the bottom is one 25-pin male serial port and a 15-pin game port. Serial ports are sometimes called DB-9 and DB-25 connectors. DB stands for data bus and refers to the number of pins on the connector. Serial ports are almost always male ports, and parallel ports are almost always female ports.

25-pin female parallel port

9-pin male serial port

15-pin female game port

25-pin male serial port

Figure 5-4   Serial, parallel, and game ports

To simplify the allocation of system resources, two configurations for serial ports were designated as COM1 and COM2, and then later two more configurations were designated as COM3 and COM4. These COM assignments each represent a designated IRQ and I/O address, as seen in Table 5-1. Think of the serial ports as physical ports, and of COM1 and COM2 as logical assignments to these physical ports, much as a phone number is a logical assignment to a physical telephone. In reality, COM1 is just a convenient way of saying IRQ 4 and I/O address 03F8h. Also notice in Table 5-1 that the two parallel port configurations are named LPT1 and LPT2 and each is assigned an IRQ and I/O address. DOS, all the Windows operating systems, and most applications that use serial devices know about and comply with these assignments. For example, you can tell your communications software to use COM1 to communicate with a modem, and it then knows that the modem is using IRQ 4 to signal the CPU and "listening" for instructions by way of I/O address 03F8h.

Table 5-1 Default port assignments on many computers

Port	IRQ	I/O Address (in Hex)	Type
COM1	IRQ 4	03F8 – 3FF	Serial
COM2	IRQ 3	02F8 – 2FF	Serial
COM3	IRQ 4	03E8 – 3EF	Serial
COM4	IRQ 3	02E8 – 2EF	Serial
LPT1	IRQ 7	0378 – 37F	Parallel
LPT2	IRQ 5	0278 – 27F	Parallel

Serial ports were originally intended for input and output devices, and parallel ports were intended for printers. Serial ports can be configured for COM1, COM2, COM3, or COM4. Parallel ports can be configured as LPT1, LPT2, or LPT3.

Most serial and parallel ports today are connected directly to the motherboard, and the COM and LPT assignments are made in CMOS setup. The ports can also be enabled and disabled in setup. Sometimes the setup screen shows the COM assignments, and sometimes you see the actual IRQ and I/O address assignments (see Figure 5-5). Older I/O controller cards used jumpers and DIP switches to configure the serial and parallel ports on the card.

A serial port conforms to the standard interface called RS-232c (stands for Reference Standard 232 revision c) and is sometimes called the RS-232 port. This interface standard originally called for 25 pins, but since microcomputers only use nine of those pins, manufacturers often installed a modified 9-pin port. Today some computers have a 9-pin serial port, and some have a 25-pin serial port, or both. Both ports work the same way. The 25-pin port uses only nine pins; the other pins are unused. Serial 25-pin ports are often found on modems. You can buy adapters that convert 9-pin ports to 25-pin ports, and vice versa, to accommodate a cable you already have.

5

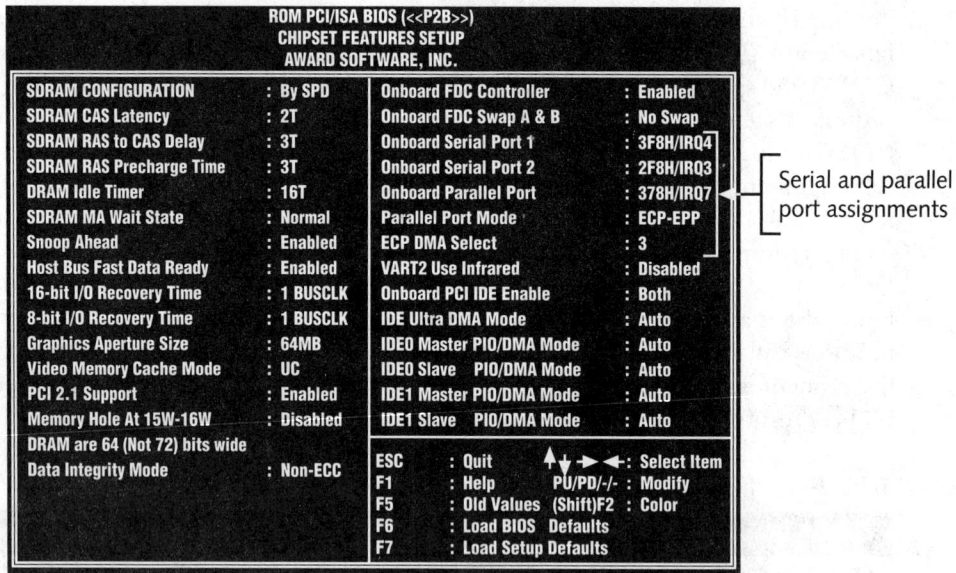

```
                    ROM PCI/ISA BIOS (<<P2B>>)
                     CHIPSET FEATURES SETUP
                     AWARD SOFTWARE, INC.

 SDRAM CONFIGURATION      : By SPD    Onboard FDC Controller    : Enabled
 SDRAM CAS Latency        : 2T        Onboard FDC Swap A & B     : No Swap
 SDRAM RAS to CAS Delay   : 3T        Onboard Serial Port 1      : 3F8H/IRQ4
 SDRAM RAS Precharge Time : 3T        Onboard Serial Port 2      : 2F8H/IRQ3
 DRAM Idle Timer          : 16T       Onboard Parallel Port      : 378H/IRQ7
 SDRAM MA Wait State      : Normal    Parallel Port Mode         : ECP-EPP
 Snoop Ahead              : Enabled   ECP DMA Select             : 3
 Host Bus Fast Data Ready : Enabled   VART2 Use Infrared         : Disabled
 16-bit I/O Recovery Time : 1 BUSCLK  Onboard PCI IDE Enable     : Both
 8-bit I/O Recovery Time  : 1 BUSCLK  IDE Ultra DMA Mode         : Auto
 Graphics Aperture Size   : 64MB      IDEO Master PIO/DMA Mode   : Auto
 Video Memory Cache Mode  : UC        IDEO Slave  PIO/DMA Mode   : Auto
 PCI 2.1 Support          : Enabled   IDE1 Master PIO/DMA Mode   : Auto
 Memory Hole At 15W-16W   : Disabled  IDE1 Slave  PIO/DMA Mode   : Auto
 DRAM are 64 (Not 72) bits wide
 Data Integrity Mode      : Non-ECC   ESC  : Quit        ↑↓→←: Select Item
                                      F1   : Help     PU/PD/-/-: Modify
                                      F5   : Old Values (Shift)F2 : Color
                                      F6   : Load BIOS  Defaults
                                      F7   : Load Setup Defaults
```

Serial and parallel port assignments

Figure 5-5   CMOS setup screen for chipset features

One of the nine pins on a serial port transmits data in a sequence of bits, and a second pin receives data sequentially. The other seven pins are used to establish the communications protocol. Recall from Chapter 1 that a protocol is a set of agreed-upon rules for communication that is established before data is actually passed from one device to another. Table 5-2 describes the functions of the pins of a serial port connection to a modem connected to another remote modem and computer. External modems sometimes use lights on the front panel to indicate the state of these pins. The labels on these modem lights are listed in the last column.

The table is included not so much to explain the use of each pin as to show that more than just data is included in a serial communication session. Also, when the system is using serial ports, one of the devices is called the **DTE (Data Terminal Equipment)**, and the other device is called the **DCE (Data Communications Equipment)**. For example, a modem is called the DCE, and the computer on which it is installed is called the DTE.

Table 5-2   9-pin and 25-pin serial port specifications

Pin Number for 9-Pin	Pin Number for 25-pin	Pin Use	Description	LED Light
1	8	Carrier detect	Connection with remote is made	CD or DCD
2	3	Receive data	Receiving data	RD or TXD
3	2	Transmit data	Sending data	SD or TXD

Table 5-2   9-pin and 25-pin serial port specifications (continued)

Pin Number for 9-Pin	Pin Number for 25-pin	Pin Use	Description	LED Light
4	20	Data terminal ready	Modem hears its computer	TR or DTR
5	7	Signal ground	Not used with PCs	
6	6	Data set ready	Modem is able to talk	MR or DSR
7	4	Request to send	Computer wants to talk	RTS
8	5	Clear to send	Modem is ready to talk	CTS
9	22	Ring indicator	Someone is calling	RI

Null Modem Connection

When two DTE devices, such as two computers, are connected, software can transmit data between the devices over a special cable called a **null modem cable**, or a **modem eliminator**, without the need for modems. The cable is not a standard serial cable but has several wires cross-connected in order to simulate modem communication. For example, two computers can be connected by a null modem cable using their serial ports. Based on the 9-pin specifications in Table 5-2, each computer expects to send data on pin 2 and receive data on pin 3. A 9-pin null modem cable would connect pin 2 on one end of the cable to pin 3 on the other end of the cable with a single wire. Similarly, pin 3 would be connected to pin 2 on the other end of the cable, so that the received data on one end is the sent data on the other end. Crossing pins 2 and 3 allows data to be sent from one computer and received by the other on the serial port pins that each computer expects to use. Standard modem software can often be used to transmit data, but because there are no actual modems in the connection, very fast, accurate transfer is possible.

Table 5-3 describes the pins connected and crossed for a 25-pin null modem cable. Figure 5-6 shows the same information as a graphic.

Infrared Transceivers

An infrared transceiver that supports infrared devices, such as wireless keyboards, mice, and printers, often connects to a serial port. In addition, a PC might use an infrared device to connect to a network. If the transceiver is Plug and Play, connect the device and turn on the PC. Windows automatically detects and installs the infrared driver, using the Add New Hardware Wizard. For legacy transceivers, install the transceiver using the Add New Hardware icon in Control Panel, or run the device driver setup program. The transceiver uses the resources of the serial port for communication and also creates a virtual infrared serial port and virtual infrared parallel port for infrared devices. During the installation, you are told what these virtual ports are and given the opportunity to change them. For example, if you physically connect the transceiver to COM2, the virtual ports will be COM4 for infrared serial devices and LPT3 for an infrared printer. The IRQ and I/O addresses for the infrared system are those assigned to COM2. To activate the transceiver, double-click the Infrared icon in Control Panel. If the icon is not displayed, press F5 to refresh Control Panel.

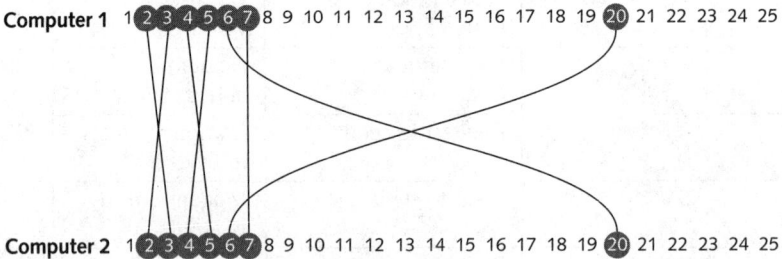

Figure 5-6   Wire connections on a 25-pin null modem cable used to transmit data

Table 5-3   Pin connections for a 25-pin null modem cable

Pin on one end is	Connected to the pin on the other end	So that
2	3	Data sent by one computer is received by the other.
3	2	Data received by one computer is sent by the other.
6	20	One end says to the other end, "I'm able to talk."
20	6	One end hears the other end say, "I'm able to talk."
4	5	One end says to the other, "I'm ready to talk."
5	4	One end hears the other say, "I'm ready to talk."
7	7	Both ends are grounded.

In addition, sometimes a motherboard provides a 5-pin connection for its own proprietary IrDA-compliant infrared transceiver. In this case, the transceiver mounts on the outside of the case, and a wire goes through a small hole in the case to connect to the 5-pin connection. The motherboard manual instructs you to use CMOS setup to enable "UART2 Use Infrared." When you do that, the COM2 serial port is disabled because the transceiver is using the resources for that port. The transceiver drivers are then installed and used the same way as described above.

A common problem with infrared devices is the line-of-sight issue; there must be an unobstructed "view" between the infrared device and the receiver. This is the main reason the industry is moving away from infrared and toward other wireless technologies. In

Chapter 12 you will see an example of a wireless keyboard and mouse that use radio signals for communication.

The UART Chip

Serial ports are controlled by a chip called the **UART (universal asynchronous receiver-transmitter) chip**. This chip controls all nine pins of a serial port, establishes the communications protocol, and converts parallel data bits coming from the system bus into serial bits for transmission. It also converts incoming serial data bits it receives into the parallel form needed by the system bus. The first UART chip was the 8250, and the next version was called the 16450 chip. The 16550 version of the UART chip contains a FIFO buffer (first in, first out buffer) that solves the problem of lost data that sometimes occurs with the 16450 UART. Also, look for improved versions of the chip labeled 16550A, 16550AF, and 16550AFN, each improving on the one before it; there are now 16750 and 16950 versions offered as well. Some computers don't actually have the physical chip on the board, but the UART logic is contained in another chip. However, in all cases, utility software can tell you what is present.

The UART 16550 driver is built into all Windows operating systems. For any Windows OS, to verify that the port is configured correctly, use Device Manager. Click the + sign beside Ports to reveal the list of ports. Click a communications port, such as COM1, and then click Properties. Click the Port Settings tab. You see the Properties dialog box in Figure 5-7, for Windows 9x, but other Windows OSs look the same. Note that the drop-down list shows the bits per second, or baud rate, of the port, which is currently set at 115,200 bps.

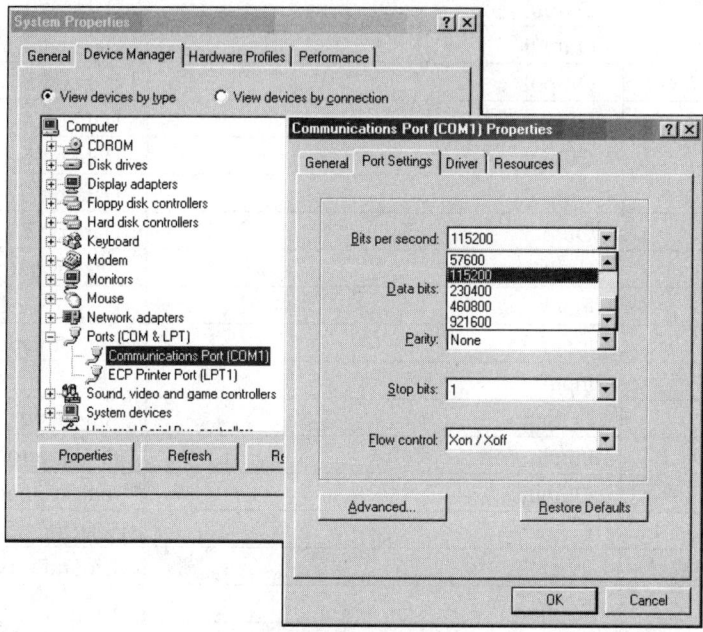

Figure 5-7   Properties of the COM1 serial port in Windows 9x

Using Parallel Ports

Parallel ports, commonly used by printers, transmit data in parallel, eight bits at a time. If the data is transmitted in parallel over a very long cable, the integrity of the data is sometimes lost because bits may separate from the byte they belong to. Most parallel cables are only six feet (1.8 meters) long, though no established standard sets maximum cable length. However, avoid using a parallel cable longer than 15 feet (4.5 meters) to ensure data integrity. Hewlett-Packard recommends that cables be no longer than 10 feet (3 meters).

Parallel ports were originally intended to be used only for printers. However, some parallel ports are now used for input devices. These bidirectional parallel ports are often used for fast transmission of data over short distances. One common use is to download and upload data from a PC to a laptop. Some external CD-ROM drives use a bidirectional parallel port to transmit and receive data. If you use an existing parallel port to install a peripheral device, installation is very simple. Just plug the device into the port and load the software. To accommodate a second parallel port, configure the port as LPT2. An example of this is described in the next section.

The uses of the pin connections for a 25-pin parallel port are listed in Table 5-4.

Table 5-4   25-pin parallel port pin connections

Pin	Input or Output from PC	Description
1	Output	Strobe
2	Output	Data bit 0
3	Output	Data bit 1
4	Output	Data bit 2
5	Output	Data bit 3
6	Output	Data bit 4
7	Output	Data bit 5
8	Output	Data bit 6
9	Output	Data bit 7
10	Input	Acknowledge
11	Input	Busy
12	Input	Out of paper
13	Input	Select
14	Output	Auto feed
15	Input	Printer error
16	Output	Initialize paper
17	Output	Select input
18	Input	Ground for bit 0
19	Input	Ground for bit 1
20	Input	Ground for bit 2

Table 5-4   25-pin parallel port pin connections (continued)

Pin	Input or Output from PC	Description
21	Input	Ground for bit 3
22	Input	Ground for bit 4
23	Input	Ground for bit 5
24	Input	Ground for bit 6
25	Input	Ground for bit 7

5

Types of Parallel Ports

Parallel ports fall into three categories: standard parallel port (SPP), **Enhanced Parallel Port (EPP)**, and **Extended Capabilities Port (ECP)**. The standard parallel port is sometimes called a normal parallel port or a Centronics port, named after the 36-pin Centronics connection used by printers (see Figure 5-8). A standard port allows data to flow in only one direction and is the slowest of the three types of parallel ports. EPP and ECP are both bidirectional. ECP was designed to increase speed over EPP by using a DMA channel; therefore, when using ECP mode you are using a DMA channel. Over the years both hardware and software manufacturers have implemented several parallel port designs, all attempting to increase speed and performance. To help establish industry standards, a committee was formed in the early 1990s, supported by the Institute of Electrical and Electronics Engineers (IEEE), which created the **IEEE 1284** standards for parallel ports. These standards require backward compatibility with previous parallel port technology. Both EPP and ECP are covered under the IEEE 1284 specifications.

When using EPP or ECP printers and parallel ports, be sure to use a printer cable that is IEEE 1284 compliant. Look for the label somewhere on the cable. Older cables that are not compliant will not work properly with these printers.

Configuring Parallel Ports

When configuring a parallel port, if the port is on an I/O card, look to the documentation for the card to learn how to assign system resources to the port. If the parallel port is coming directly off the motherboard, then look to CMOS setup to configure the port (refer back to Figure 5-5). Setup can have up to three different settings for parallel ports. For the BIOS in this figure, choices for parallel port mode are Normal, EPP, ECP, and EPP + ECP. If you select ECP or EPP + ECP, you must also make an ECP DMA selection. Choices are DMA Channel 1 or 3.

If you are having trouble using a serial or parallel port, check CMOS setup to make sure the port is enabled. If you are having problems with resource conflicts, try disabling ECP mode for the parallel port. EPP mode gives good results and does not tie up a DMA channel.

DB 25-pin connection
(PC end)

36-pin Centronics
connection (printer end)

Figure 5-8 A parallel cable has a DB-25 connection at the PC end of the cable and a
36-pin Centronics connection at the printer end of the cable. Printers can use
this 36-pin Centronics connector or the smaller and less common mini-Centronis
connector that also has 36 pins.

Using USB Ports

A relatively new I/O bus is the USB, originally created by a seven-member consortium
including Compaq, Digital Equipment, IBM, Intel, Microsoft, NEC, and Northern Telecom.
It is designed to make the installation of slow peripheral devices as effortless as possible. USB
is much faster than regular serial ports and uses higher-quality cabling. USB is also much easier to manage, since it eliminates the need to manually resolve resource conflicts. It is expected
that USB will ultimately replace both serial and parallel ports as the technology matures and
more devices are built to use USB.

USB allows for **hot-swapping** and is **hot-pluggable**, meaning that a device can be
plugged into a USB port while the computer is running, and the host controller will sense
the device and configure it without your having to reboot the computer. Some I/O devices
that are now available with a USB connection are the mouse, joystick, keyboard, printer,
scanner, monitor, modem, digital camera, fax machine, and digital telephone.

One to four USB ports are found on most new motherboards today (see Figure 5-9), and
older motherboards that don't have USB ports can be upgraded by adding a PCI-to-USB
controller card in a PCI slot to provide a USB port. USB Version 1 (sometimes called Basic
Speed USB or Original USB) allowed for two speeds, 1.5 Mb (megabits) per second and
12 Mb per second, and works well for slow I/O devices. USB Version 2 (sometimes called
Hi-Speed USB) allows for up to 480 Mb per second, which is 40 times faster than
Original USB. Hi-Speed USB is backward-compatible with slower USB devices. For
more information on USB, see the USB Implementers Forum, Inc, (*www.usb.org*) the organization responsible for developing USB.

Figure 5-9   A motherboard with two USB ports and a USB cable; note the rectangular shape of the connection as compared to the nearby serial and parallel D-shaped ports

A **USB host controller**, which for most motherboards is included in the chipset, manages the USB bus. Sometimes a motherboard will have two USB controllers; each is enabled and disabled in CMOS setup. As many as 127 USB devices can be daisy chained together using USB cables, whereby one device provides a USB port for the next device. Figure 5-10 shows a keyboard and a mouse daisy chained together connecting to a single USB port on an iMac computer. There can also be a standalone **hub** into which several devices can be plugged.

Figure 5-10   A keyboard and a mouse using a USB port daisy-chained together

For full-speed devices, use Hi-Speed USB cables, which can be up to five meters long, to connect devices or a device and a hub. The USB cable has four wires, two for power and two for communication. The two power wires (one carries voltage and the other is ground) allow the host controller to provide power to a device. The connector on the host computer or hub end is called the A-Male connector, and the connector on the device end of the cable is called the B-Male connector. The A-Male connector is flat and wide, and the B-Male connector is square.

In USB technology, the host controller polls each device, asking if data is ready to be sent or requesting to send data to the device. The host controller manages communication to the CPU for all devices, using only a single IRQ, I/O address range, and DMA channel. The OS and the USB host controller automatically assign system resources at startup. See Figure 5-11.

Figure 5-11   Only one IRQ, I/O address, and DMA channel are needed for a USB host controller to manage multiple devices

Windows 95 OSR 2.1 was the first Microsoft OS to support USB, although Windows 98 offers much improved USB support. Windows 95 with the USB update, Windows 98, Windows 2000, and Windows XP support original USB, but Windows NT does not. Using Windows XP, you can download a patch for the OS that supports Hi-Speed USB.

You can read more about USB on the forum Web site at *www.usb.org*.

5

Preparing to Install a USB Device

To install a USB device, you need:

- A motherboard or expansion card that provides a USB port
- An OS that supports USB
- A USB device
- A USB device driver

Windows 98 provides many USB device drivers. If you are installing a USB device, don't use a device driver from the manufacturer that claims to work only for Windows 95. Windows 98 and later OSs made several improvements in USB support that you should take advantage of.

Installing a USB Device

Follow these steps to install a USB device:

1. Using Device Manager, verify that the USB host controller driver is installed under Windows. See Figure 5-12 for an example of Device Manager under Windows 98. Note in the figure the symbol for USB. If the controller is not installed, install it from the Control Panel by double-clicking the **Add New Hardware** icon. If you have a problem installing the controller, verify that support for USB is enabled in setup.

2. Turn off the PC and plug in the USB device. When you reboot, Windows should launch the Add New Hardware Wizard to install the device drivers. If the wizard does not launch, go to the Control Panel and use the Add New Hardware icon. If that fails to install the drivers, look for and run the setup program on the CD or floppy disk that came with the device. After the drivers are installed, you should see the device listed in Device Manager. Verify that Windows sees the device with no conflicts and without errors.

3. Install the application software to use the device. For example, most scanners come with some software to scan and edit images. After you have installed the software, use it to scan an image.

 If USB devices do not work, use CMOS setup to make sure USB support is enabled on the motherboard.

Figure 5-12   Using Device Manager, verify that the USB host controller is installed

Using IEEE 1394 Ports

FireWire and **i.Link** are the common names for another peripheral bus officially named **IEEE 1394** (or sometimes simply called 1394) after the group that designed the bus. The Institute of Electrical and Electronics Engineers was primarily led by Apple Computer and Texas Instruments in the initial design. FireWire is similar in design to USB, using serial transmission of data, but faster. FireWire supports data speeds as high as 1.2 Gbps (Gigabits per second), much faster than USB. Whereas USB is targeted to replace slow serial and parallel ports, FireWire is likely to replace SCSI as a solution for high-volume, multimedia external devices such as digital camcorders, DVDs, and hard drives. SCSI is a very fast, but difficult to configure, peripheral bus that will be discussed in Chapter 8.

FireWire devices can be daisy chained together and managed by a host controller using a single set of system resources (an IRQ, an I/O address range, and a DMA channel). The one host controller can support up to 63 FireWire devices. Just as with USB, FireWire must be supported by the operating system. Windows XP, Windows 2000, and Windows 98 all support FireWire. (Windows 95 and Windows NT do not.) The 1394 Trade Association has developed a new standard, IEEE **1394.3**, designed for peer-to-peer data transmission. Using this new standard, imaging devices such as scanners and digital cameras can send images and photos directly to printers without involving a computer.

IEEE 1394 ports are sometimes found on newer high-end motherboards and are expected to become standard ports on all new motherboards, as commonplace as USB ports are now. These ports have two types of connectors: a 4-pin port that does not provide voltage to a device and a 6-pin port that does. See Figure 5-13. The two extra pins in the 6-pin port are used for voltage and ground. The cable for a 6-pin port is fatter than the 4-pin cable.

(Device requires AC adapter)

4-pin Cable

(Two pins are used for voltage and ground)

6-pin Cable

5

Figure 5-13   Two types of IEEE 1394 cable connectors; the 6-pin cable provides voltage to the device from the PC

The four wires used for data in a 1394 cable are two pairs of shielded twisted-pair cable wrapped in a common cord. Shielding refers to enclosing wires in a protective covering to reduce interference, and twisted-pair refers to the fact that two wires are twisted to reduce interference. Some network cabling is also shielded and uses twisted-pair wires. In fact, IEEE 1394 uses a design similar to Ethernet, the most popular network design. Just as with Ethernet, data is broken into small packets before it is sent over 1394 cable. Each device on the IEEE 1394 network can communicate with any other device on the network without involving the computer's CPU.

IEEE 1394 uses **isochronous data transfer**, meaning that data is transferred continuously without breaks. This works well when transferring real-time data such as that received by television transmission. Because of the real-time data transfer and the fact that data can be transferred from one device to another without involving the CPU, IEEE 1394 is an ideal medium for data transfers between consumer electronics products such as camcorders, VCRs, TVs, and digital cameras.

Figure 5-14 shows an example of how this might work. A person can record a home movie using a digital camcorder and download the data through a digital VCR to a 1394-compliant external hard drive. The 1394-compliant digital VCR can connect to and send data to the hard drive without involving the PC. The PC can later read the data off the hard drive and use it as input to video-editing application software. A user can edit the data and design a professional video presentation complete with captioning and special effects. Furthermore, if the digital camcorder is also 1394-compliant, it can download the data directly to the PC by way of a 1394 port on the PC. The PC can then save the data to a regular internal hard drive.

The current standard for IEEE 1394 is IEEE 1394.A, which supports speeds of 100, 200, or 400 Mbps, and allows for cable lengths up to 4.5 meters (15 feet). Just as with USB, devices using this standard are hot-pluggable. A new standard under development, IEEE 1394B, will support speeds up to 3.2 Gbps (gigabits per second) and extend the maximum cable length to 100 meters (328 feet).

Figure 5-14   IEEE 1394 can be used as the interface technology to connect consumer audio/visual equipment to a PC

Windows 98, Windows 2000, and Windows XP support IEEE 1394. Windows 98 Second Edition supports IEEE 1394 storage devices, but IEEE 1394 printers and scanners are not supported. Windows 2000/XP supports all these devices. For Windows 98 Second Edition, you can download an update from the Microsoft Web site (*windowsupdate.microsoft.com*). The update solves previous problems that occurred when devices were removed while the PC was still running.

To use a 1394 port with Windows 98, follow these steps:

1. Verify that Windows 98 recognizes that an IEEE 1394 controller is present on the motherboard. Using Device Manager, look for the 1394 Bus Controller listed as an installed device. Click the + sign beside the controller in Device Manager to see the specific brand of 1394 controller that the board contains. If the controller is not installed or is not working, reinstall the driver. In Control Panel, double-click the **Add New Hardware** icon. If you have problems installing the driver, verify that 1394 support is enabled in setup.

2. Plug the device into the 1394 port. Install the device drivers for the 1394-compliant device. Without rebooting, you should be able to use the Add New Hardware icon in Control Panel. For example, after you have installed the drivers for a camcorder, you should see the device listed in Device Manager under Sound, video and game controllers. If you don't see the device listed, turn the device off and back on.

3. Install the application software to use the device. A 1394-compliant camcorder is likely to come bundled with video-editing software, for example. Run the software to use the device.

   For motherboards that don't support IEEE 1394, you can install an IEEE 1394 host adapter to provide the support. For example, FireBoard Red by Unibrain, Inc. uses a PCI expansion slot and follows the IEEE 1394A standard. See *www.unibrain.com*.

Using PCI Expansion Slots

The **PCI (Peripheral Component Interconnect) bus** is now the standard local I/O bus, not only with Pentium CPUs but also with RISC CPUs. A standard PCI bus has a 32-bit data path and runs at 33 MHz when the motherboard runs at 66 MHz. However, the PCI specifications can also use a 64-bit data path and can run at a speed of 66 MHz when the system bus runs at 133 MHz. Also, an addendum to the PCI specifications, called PCI-X, released in September 1999, enables PCI to run at 133 MHz.

One advantage of the PCI local bus is that devices connected to it can run at one speed while the CPU runs at a different speed. The PCI bus expansion slots are shorter than ISA slots (see Figure 5-15) and set a little farther away from the edge of the motherboard. Also, PCI slots are usually white. Figure 5-16 shows the pinouts (position and meaning of each pin) for the standard PCI slot.

PCI slots

16-bit ISA slots

Figure 5-15   PCI bus expansion slots are shorter than ISA slots and offset farther

Figure 5-16   Standard PCI slot pinouts

In addition to supporting I/O devices connected to it, the PCI bus also serves another function for the Intel 400 series chip set. The PCI bus interfaces with the expansion bus and the system bus or memory bus, serving as the go-between for the two, controlling the input and output to the expansion bus. As you can see in Figure 5-17, the system bus is isolated from the ISA bus by the PCI bus. The connection between the two is the PCI bridge. The bridge allows the PCI bus to control the traffic not only from its own local devices but also from the ISA bus.

Figure 5-17   In some systems, the PCI bus serves as the middleman between the memory bus and the expansion bus

In Figure 5-17, the SCSI host adapter (discussed at length in Chapter 8) and a network interface card (NIC) are connected to the PCI bus. (Physically, each card is inserted in a PCI expansion slot.) The PCI bridge/controller accesses the local bus where the CPU and memory are allowed to run at top speed without interference or wait states. If the CPU wants to send data to the network card, for example, it dumps it on the PCI bridge/controller at top speed. The controller puts the data in its own buffer, or temporary memory storage, and then writes it to the network card at a pace slower than the system bus. The bridge/controller eliminates interference with the system bus.

Figure 5-17 also shows the interface from the PCI bus to the ISA bus. This interface is a significant feature that distinguishes the PCI bus from other buses. The PCI bus was not designed to replace the traditional expansion bus, but to support it. The ISA bus in the diagram passes data through the interface to the PCI bus, which in turn passes the data on to the system bus, to the CPU, and to memory.

The PCI bus also supports **bus mastering**. A bus mastering device is an intelligent device (i.e., it has a microprocessor installed that manages the device) that, when attached to the PCI bus, can gain access to memory and other devices on the bus without interrupting the action of the CPU. The CPU and the bus mastering devices can run concurrently and independently.

Because of the effective design of the PCI bus, the throughput performance, or the data transfer rate per second, is 132 MB when the bus is running at 33 MHz with a 32-bit data path. **Throughput performance**, or **data throughput**, is a measure of the actual data transmitted by the bus, not including error-checking bits or redundant data.

Recall that the PCI bus is a local bus, meaning that it runs in sync with the system clock and the CPU. Because the PCI bus is faster than the ISA bus, PCI slots are often used for fast I/O devices such as network cards or SCSI host adapters. The PCI bus master, which is part of the motherboard chip set, manages the PCI bus and the expansion slots. The PCI bus master assigns IRQ and I/O addresses to PCI expansion cards, which is why you don't see jumpers or DIP switches on these cards. To be more accurate, the PCI bus assigns resources to a PCI slot; move the card to a different slot to assign a new set of resources to it.

> When installing a PCI card, most likely you do not need to configure the IRQ or I/O address for the card, because the startup BIOS and PCI bus controller do this for you.

The PCI bus uses an interim interrupt between the PCI card and the IRQ line to the CPU. PCI documentation calls these interrupts A, B, C, and D, and so forth. One interrupt is assigned to each PCI expansion slot. The PCI bus master then maps each of these internal PCI bus interrupts to IRQs, using IRQs that are available after legacy ISA bus devices have claimed their IRQs. The startup BIOS records which IRQs have been used by ISA devices and then assigns the unused ones to the PCI bus master during the boot process.

> Newer motherboards sometimes have an audio modem riser (AMR) slot that can accommodate a small modem card or sound card. These small cards are inexpensive, since most of the logic to support audio or the modem is contained within the motherboard chip set. The AMR slot makes it possible to add the card at a low cost, without using up a PCI or ISA slot.

Use Device Manager to see which IRQ has been assigned to a PCI device. For example, for Windows 95, Release 1, Figure 5-18 displays the resources assigned to a PCI video card. Notice that the IRQ assigned to the card is IRQ 9.

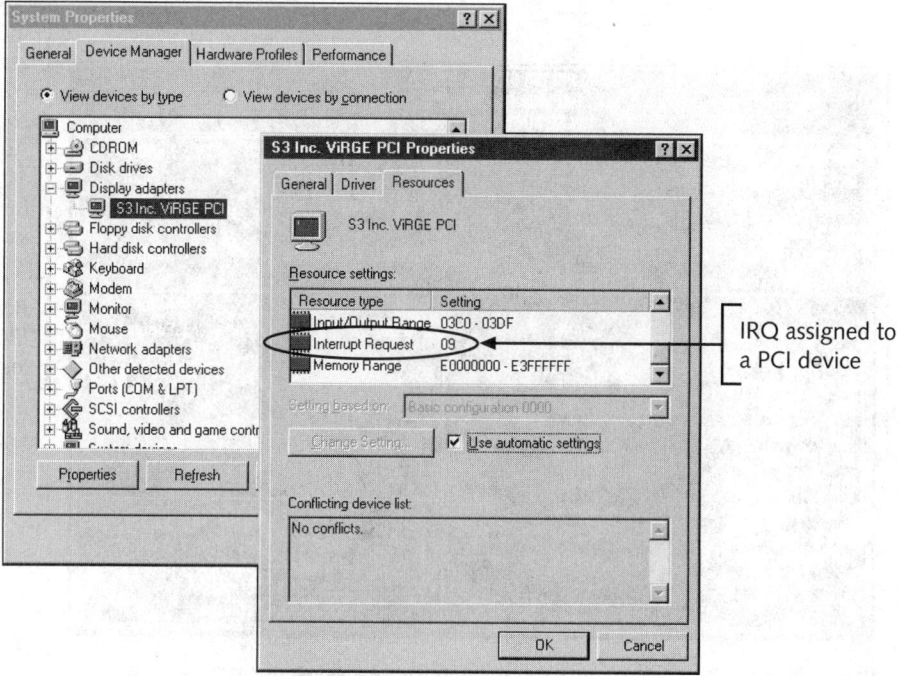

Figure 5-18   Use Device Manager to determine which IRQ has been assigned to a PCI device

Sometimes BIOS gives the PCI bus master an IRQ that a legacy ISA device needs, which can prevent either device from working. In CMOS setup, you can specify which IRQ to assign to a PCI slot, or you can tell setup that a particular IRQ is reserved for a legacy device, and thereby prevent the PCI bus from using it. See Figure 5-19.

If two heavy-demand PCI devices end up sharing an IRQ, they might not work properly. If you suspect this to be the case, try moving one of the devices to a different PCI slot, so that a device with a heavy demand (such as a 1394 adapter) is matched with a low-demand device (such as a modem).

PCI Bus IRQ Steering

PCI 2.1 specifications support **PCI bus IRQ steering**, which can help solve the problem of not having enough IRQs to support all devices in a system. In order for the system to use the feature, both the motherboard BIOS and Windows must support it. Windows 95 Release 2 (OSR2) and Windows 98 support PCI bus IRQ steering.

During booting, startup BIOS records the IRQs used by ISA devices and the PCI bus in a table that Windows can read later when reassigning IRQs. Sometimes an IRQ conflict can happen when startup BIOS is not aware that a legacy (not Plug and Play) ISA device is using a certain IRQ and assigns that IRQ to the PCI bus, which assigns it to a PCI device. With PCI bus IRQ steering, Windows can sometimes resolve the problem by reassigning another IRQ to the PCI bus, allowing the legacy device to be the sole owner of its IRQ.

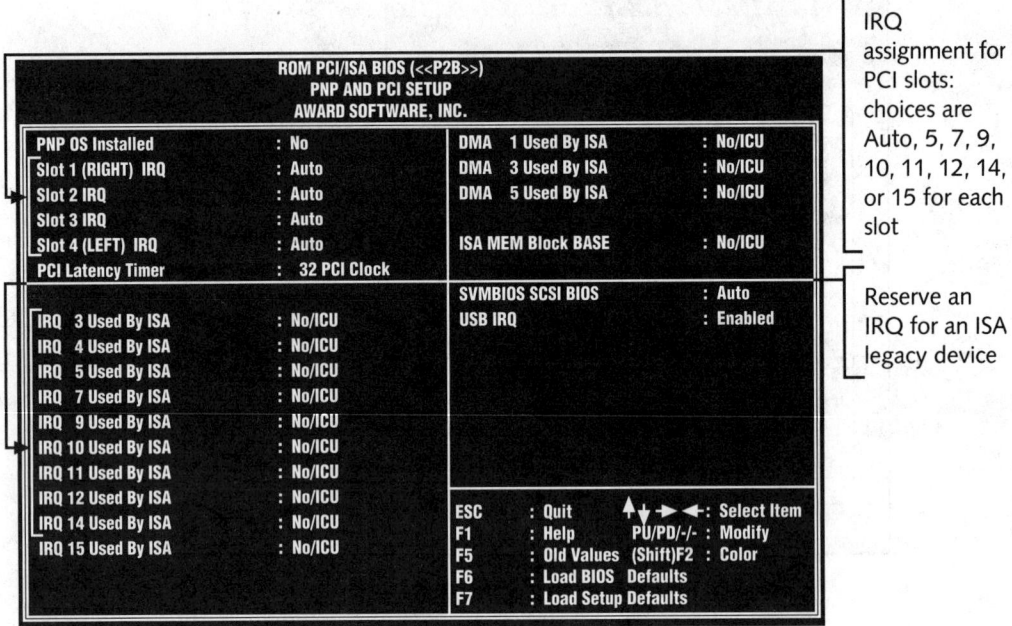

IRQ assignment for PCI slots: choices are Auto, 5, 7, 9, 10, 11, 12, 14, or 15 for each slot

Reserve an IRQ for an ISA legacy device

Figure 5-19   CMOS setup screen for Plug and Play and PCI options

In order to make this happen, Windows must detect an unused IRQ that it can use for the substitution. It then puts a holder on the IRQ, meaning that it reserves this IRQ for PCI only. The IRQ is no longer available for an ISA device as long as Windows has the holder on it. See Figure 5-20 for one example.

PCI bus IRQ steering can cause a particular problem. If Windows 9x puts a holder on an IRQ, it might cause the PCI device using it to have problems. Also, if two PCI devices are having conflicts, sometimes PCI bus IRQ steering can mask the problem, making it difficult to diagnose. Finally, PCI bus IRQ steering can erroneously put a hold on an IRQ that is being used by an ISA device. Figure 5-21 shows an example of this, where IRQ 10 is needed by an Adaptec SCSI host adapter, but PCI steering has put a hold on the IRQ. In this case, you can either claim IRQ 10 for the SCSI host adapter in CMOS setup, or you can disable PCI bus IRQ steering.

TIP   Sometimes problems with resource conflicts can be solved by enabling PCI bus IRQ steering, and sometimes they can be resolved by disabling the feature!

Figure 5-20   PCI bus IRQ steering has placed a holder on IRQ 10, making it unavailable to ISA devices

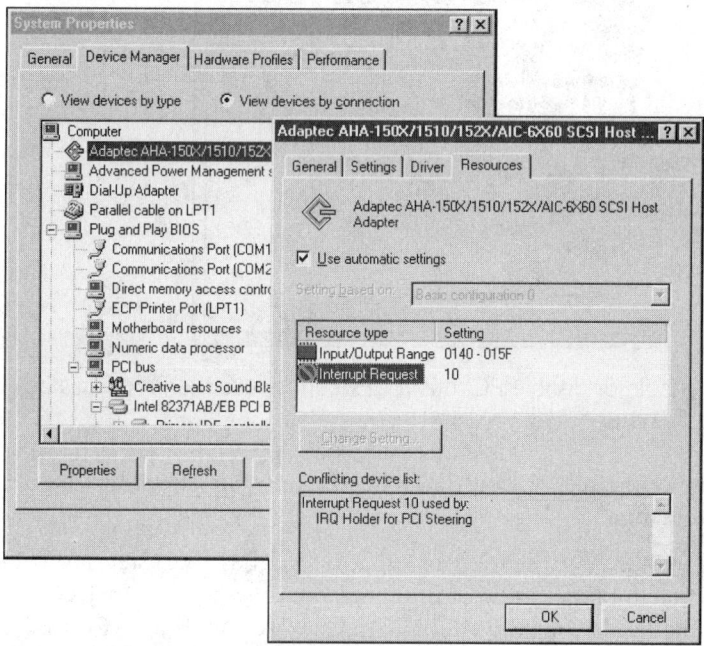

Figure 5-21   A conflict with IRQ 10 is caused by PCI steering putting a hold on the IRQ

For Windows 9x, to either enable or disable PCI bus IRQ steering, use Device Manager. Do the following:

1. Click **Start**, **Settings**, **Control Panel**. Double-click the **System** icon. Select the **Device Manager** tab.

2. Select **View device by connection**. Select **PCI bus**, and click **Properties**. The PCI bus Properties dialog box is displayed.

3. Select the **IRQ Steering** tab, as shown in Figure 5-22 for Windows 98.

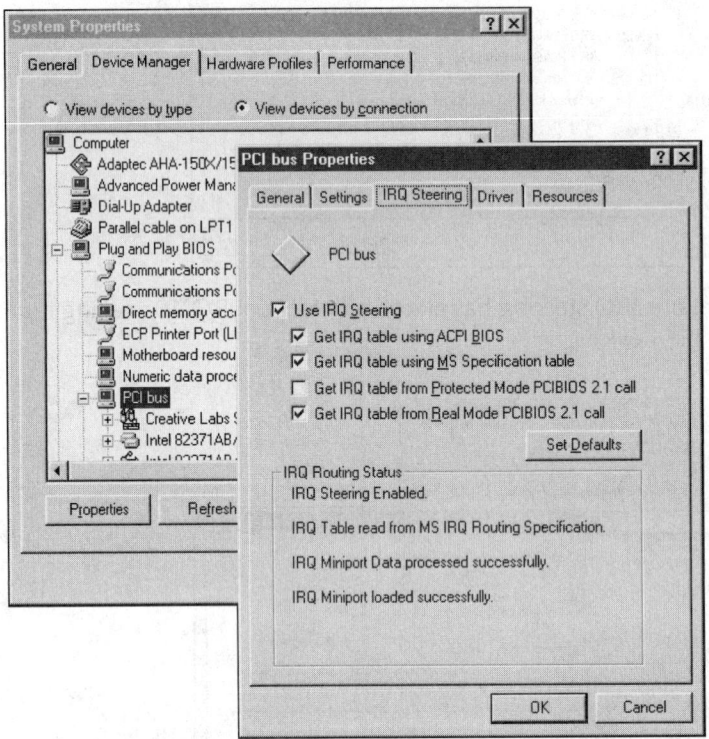

Figure 5-22 To enable or disable PCI bus IRQ steering, use the Properties box of the PCI bus

4. To enable or disable PCI bus IRQ steering, use the check box beside **Use IRQ Steering**.

Windows 2000 and Windows XP do not support PCI bus IRQ steering because of the more complicated technologies they can support, but they do support IRQ sharing if the system BIOS on the motherboard is ACPI-compliant. IRQ 9 is used for this purpose and can be shared by several PCI devices. Windows 2000 and Windows XP do not use the Plug and Play information presented to them by the Plug and Play BIOS at startup. If you have used CMOS setup to manually assign IRQs to slots on the motherboard, this information might be used by Windows 2000/XP on a motherboard that is not ACPI-compliant, but it will be ignored when the motherboard is ACPI-compliant.

Microchannel Architecture (MCA) Bus

With the introduction of the line of PS/2 computers in 1987, IBM introduced the first 32-bit bus for personal computers, the **Micro Channel Architecture (MCA) bus**. IBM did not intend the MCA bus to be compatible with ISA buses. Circuit boards used in older IBM computers could not be used in the PS/2 line. (The PS/2 Models 25 and 30 still included the older ISA bus in order to support legacy cards.)

IBM chose to patent the bus so that other companies could not economically manufacture and market it. IBM intended to control a subset of the bus market with MCA. In response, Compaq and eight other companies (called the "Gang of Nine") joined forces to design and build a competing 32-bit bus, the EISA bus.

The EISA Bus

Designed to compete with the MCA bus, the **EISA (Extended ISA) bus** (pronounced "ease-sa") has a 32-bit data path. The bus is compatible with older ISA buses so that expansion boards having 8-bit or 16-bit data paths work on the EISA bus. The speed of the EISA bus is about 20 MHz. To accommodate a 16-bit or 8-bit ISA circuit board, the 32-bit EISA has two slots that have the same width as 16-bit ISA slots. However, the EISA bus slots are deeper than 16-bit slots. All 32-bit circuit boards have longer fingers on the edge connectors that go deep into the EISA slot, connecting to the 32-bit pins. A 16-bit circuit board reaches only partway down the slot, connecting at a shallower level only to the 16-bit pins.

Using ISA Expansion Slots

Used on the first IBM 8088 PCs in the early 1980s, the ISA bus had an 8-bit data path. Later, IBM revised the ISA bus to have a 16-bit path. The IBM AT personal computer used this bus and the 80286 chip, which is why the 16-bit bus is sometimes called the AT bus. IBM wanted this bus to be backward-compatible with the older 8-bit ISA bus, so that the older 8-bit circuit boards would fit into the newer AT computers. To maintain compatibility, IBM kept the old 62-line slot connector and added another slot connector beside it to provide the extra 8 bits. Slots with both connectors are called 16-bit slots. Many new motherboards today have at least one 16-bit slot, which can be used by either an 8-bit or 16-bit ISA card. The trend for newer motherboards is not to have any ISA slots, as few new ISA devices are being manufactured. You saw the pinout descriptions of the 8-bit and 16-bit ISA slots in Chapter 2.

Using legacy ISA bus devices is a little more difficult than using either USB or PCI, because the configuration is not as automated. The ISA bus itself does not manage the system resources, as do the USB and PCI bus masters. It is up to the ISA device to request system resources at startup. If the ISA device does not support Plug and Play, then you select the I/O address, DMA channel, and IRQ by setting jumpers or DIP switches on the card. If the ISA device is Plug and Play compliant, then at startup Plug and Play allocates the required resources to the device. To discover if a device is Plug and Play compliant, look for "Ready for Windows 95" or "Ready for Windows 98" on the box, or read the documentation.

Because a PC support technician must know how to deal with older technology such as a legacy ISA expansion card, we next turn our attention to solving problems when installing legacy hardware and device drivers.

Installing Legacy Hardware

When adding new devices to a system, the most difficult problems you are likely to encounter are resource conflicts between legacy devices or problems using legacy device drivers.

Solving Problems with Legacy Hardware

Suppose you install a legacy network card in a system, and the card does not work and the modem card has stopped working. Most likely you have a resource conflict. The tool to use to help in resolving hardware conflicts in Windows is Device Manager. This tool is not infallible, because it depends on what the OS knows about resources being used, and sometimes a device does not tell the OS what it is using. Follow this general approach when installing a legacy device:

1. Know the system resources already in use. See the documentation for devices already installed and/or use Device Manager. As you learned in earlier chapters, you should keep a notebook dedicated to your PC, in which you keep records of each device and the present settings of the device, as well as any changes you make to your system.

2. Know what resources the device will need (see the documentation). Install the device using resources that are not already used by your system. If the device is set to use a resource already in use, read the documentation to see if you can set a jumper or DIP switch to use an alternate resource. For example, Figure 5-23 shows a modem that has a bank of DIP switches on the back of the card and a bank of jumpers on the card itself (see Figure 5-24). By using combinations of these DIP switches and jumpers, you can configure this modem to use a specific set of IRQ and I/O addresses.

Figure 5-23   Diagram of a modem card

Microphone port

Speaker port

Two RJ-11 phone connections

Bank of DIP switches

Figure 5-24   Ports and DIP switches on the back of an internal modem

CAUTION

Don't change a DIP switch or jumper on a device without (1) writing down the original settings so you can backtrack, and (2) carefully reading the documentation.

3. After you install a card, if it does not work, try reseating the card in the slot or using a different slot.

4. If the device still does not work or another device stops working, suspect a resource conflict. If you do have a conflict, use Device Manager, CMOS setup, and documentation for the motherboard and devices to first identify and then resolve the conflict. To find out what resources your system is using, for Windows 9x, follow Step 5 below.

5. Click **Start**, point to **Settings**, click **Control Panel**, **System**, and then **Device Manager**. Click **Computer** and then **Properties**. Select the **View Resources** tab. The window in Figure 5-25 is displayed. From it, you can view current assignments for IRQs, I/O addresses, DMA channels, and upper memory addresses.

6. Once you have found the conflicting resource, try these things to resolve the conflict:

   - If the device is a legacy ISA device, physically set the device's jumpers or DIP switches to use a different resource.

   - If a legacy device can only use one IRQ, then use CMOS setup to reserve that IRQ for the device.

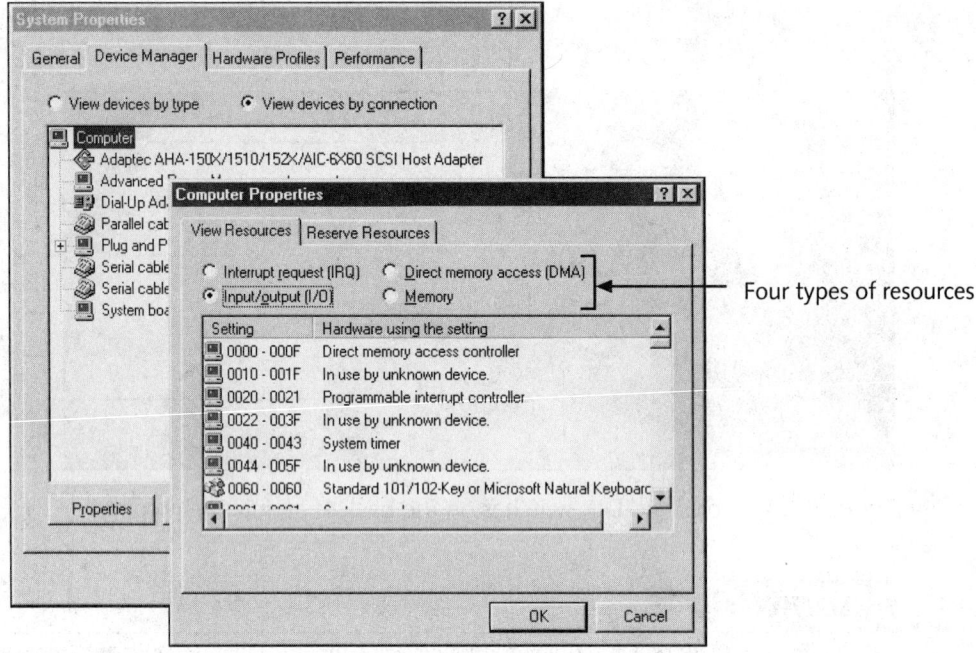

Figure 5-25   Use Device Manager to see I/O addresses currently in use

- If your PC supports PCI bus IRQ steering, enable the feature. That alone might solve the problem.

- Using PCI bus IRQ steering, tell Windows 98 to use a different IRQ for a PCI device. To do that, use the Properties box for the device in Device Manager.

- Move the device to a different slot. Use the slot closest to the CPU, if you can.

- Disable PCI bus IRQ steering.

- Suspect that the documentation for the device is wrong, that the device is faulty, or that there is a problem with the motherboard or the OS. Try a new device in this system, or try this device in another working system.

Solving Problems with Legacy Drivers

Windows 9x contains 32-bit drivers for hundreds of hardware devices, and even more are provided by the device manufacturers. However, there are some older legacy devices that do not have 32-bit drivers, so you are forced to use a 16-bit real-mode device driver. These 16-bit drivers are loaded by entries in the Config.sys, Autoexec.bat, or System.ini file and probably use upper memory addresses. Back up these files before you begin the installation. Then run a setup program on the floppy disk or CD provided with the device. Use the Run dialog box or double-click the program file name in Explorer. The setup program copies the driver files to the hard drive and adds the DEVICE= command to Config.sys. In addition, it might make entries in Autoexec.bat or, for drivers written for

Windows 3.x, it might make entries in System.ini. After you have verified that the device is working, note the changes made to Autoexec.bat, Config.sys, and System.ini. You might want to keep a record of the commands the setup program put in these files, in case you need it for future troubleshooting.

If you have problems with installing or running a legacy driver, do these things:

- Make every effort to locate a 32-bit driver for the device. Check the Microsoft Web site at *support.microsoft.com*, and check the device manufacturer's Web site. Use a search engine to search the Web for shareware drivers.

- Create an empty copy of Autoexec.bat and Config.sys on your hard drive. Boot up into MS-DOS mode and run the setup program from the command prompt. Look at the entries it puts into Autoexec.bat and Config.sys and copy these command lines into your original versions of Autoexec.bat and Config.sys.

In the rest of the chapter, we will look at the essential I/O devices for a PC: the keyboard, pointing devices, and video display.

KEYBOARDS

Keyboards have either a traditional straight design or a newer ergonomic design, as shown in Figure 5-26. The word "ergonomic" means "designed for safe and comfortable interaction between human beings and machines." The ergonomically safer keyboard is designed to keep your wrists high and straight. Some users find it comfortable, and others do not. Figure 5-27 demonstrates the correct position of hands and arms at the keyboard. Keyboards also differ in the feel of the keys as you type. Some people prefer more resistance than others, and some like more sound as the keys make contact. A keyboard might have a raised bar or circle on the F and J keys to help your fingers find the home keys as you type. Another feature is the depth of the ledge at the top of the keyboard that holds pencils, etc. Some keyboards have a mouse port on the back of the keyboard, and specialized keyboards have trackballs or magnetic scanners for scanning credit cards in retail stores.

Figure 5-26   An ergonomic keyboard

Figure 5-27   Keep wrists level, straight, and supported while at the keyboard

Computer keyboards have been criticized by users who work with them for hours at a time because they can cause a type of repetitive stress injury (RSI) known as carpal tunnel syndrome (CTS). CTS is caused by keeping the wrists in an unnatural position and having to execute the same motions (such as pressing keys on a keyboard) over prolonged periods.

You can help prevent carpal tunnel syndrome by keeping your elbows at the same level as the keyboard and keeping your wrists straight and higher than your fingers. I've found that a keyboard drawer that slides out from under a desk surface is much more comfortable, because the keyboard is low enough for me to keep a correct position. If I'm working at a desk with no keyboard drawer, I sometimes type with the keyboard in my lap to relieve the pressure on my arms and shoulders.

Keyboards use one of two common technologies in the way the keys make contact: foil contact or metal contact. With a foil-contact keyboard, when you press a key, two layers of foil make contact and close a circuit. A small spring just under the keycap raises the key again after it is released.

Metal-contact keyboards are more expensive and heavier, and generally provide a different touch to the fingers than foil-contact keyboards. Made by IBM and AT&T, as well as other companies, the metal-contact keyboards add an extra feel of solid construction that is noticeable to most users, giving the keystroke a clear, definitive contact. When a key is pressed, two metal plates make contact, and a spring is again used to raise the key when it is released.

Keyboard Connectors

Keyboards connect to a PC by one of four methods: a PS/2 connector (sometimes called a mini-DIN), a DIN connector, a USB port, or, more recently, a wireless connection. The DIN connector (DIN is an acronym of the German words meaning "German industry standard") is round and has five pins. The smaller round PS/2 connector has six pins. See

Figure 5-28. Table 5-5 shows the pinouts for both connector types. If the keyboard you are using has a different connector from the keyboard port of your computer, use a keyboard connector adapter, like the one shown in Figure 5-29, to convert DIN to PS/2 or PS/2 to DIN. Also, some keyboards are cordless, using radio transmission (or, for older cordless devices, infrared) to communicate with a sensor connected to the keyboard port. For example, a cordless keyboard made by Logitech (*www.logitech.com*) uses a receiver that plugs into a normal keyboard port.

6-pin PS/2 connector (mini-DIN)

5-pin DIN connector

Figure 5-28   Two common keyboard connectors are a PS/2 connector and a DIN connector

DIN connection

PS/2 connection

Figure 5-29   A keyboard adapter

Table 5-5   Pinouts for keyboard connectors

Description	6-Pin Connector (PS/2)	5-Pin Connector (DIN)
Keyboard data	1	2
Not used	2	3
Ground	3	4
Current (+5 volts)	4	5
Keyboard clock	5	1
Not used	6	-

Regardless of the type of connection or the construction of the keyboard, when a key is pressed, the same logical progression occurs. First, pressing a key produces a **make code**. Releasing the key produces a **break code**. A chip in the keyboard processes these codes to produce a scan code that is sent to the CPU. The chip determines the location of the pressed key and sends that location, together with the IRQ, to the CPU. The scan code is temporarily stored in memory. The keyboard driver, which is most often stored in the system BIOS, converts the scan code to the character assigned to that code, according to the keyboard driver selected. The drivers available to interpret scan codes vary by language.

Installing Keyboards

Most often, installing a keyboard simply means plugging it in and turning on the PC, because the system BIOS manages the keyboard, and no keyboard drivers are necessary. The exception to this is a wireless keyboard that needs a driver to work. In this case, you must use a regular keyboard to install the software to use the wireless keyboard. Plug in the receiver, insert the CD or floppy drive, and run the setup program on the disk. You can then use the wireless keyboard.

Troubleshooting Keyboards

Often dirt, food, or drink in the keyboard causes one or more keys to stick or not work properly. Because of their low cost, the solution for a keyboard that doesn't work is most often to replace it. However, you can try a few simple things to repair one that is not working.

A Few Keys Don't Work

If a few keys don't work, remove the caps on the bad keys with a chip extractor. Spray contact cleaner into the key well. Repeatedly depress the contact in order to clear it out. Don't use rubbing alcohol to clean the key well, because it can leave a residue on the contact. If this method of cleaning solves the problem, then clean the adjacent keys as well.

Turning the keyboard upside down and lightly bumping multiple keys with your flat palm will help loosen and remove debris.

The Keyboard Does Not Work At All

If the keyboard does not work at all, first determine that the cable is plugged in. PC keyboard cables may become loose or disconnected. If the cable connection is good and the keyboard still does not work, swap it with another keyboard of the same type that you know is in good condition, to verify that the problem is in the keyboard and not in the computer.

If the problem is in the keyboard, check the cable. If possible, swap the cable with a known good one, perhaps from an old discarded keyboard. Sometimes a wire in a PC keyboard cable becomes pinched or broken. Most cables can be easily detached from the keyboard by removing the few screws that hold the keyboard case together, then simply unplugging the cable. Be careful as you work; don't allow the keycaps to fall out! In Chapter 3 you learned how to use a multimeter to test a cable for continuity. You can use this method to verify that the cable is good.

On the motherboard, the chip set and the ROM BIOS chip both affect keyboard functions. You might choose to flash BIOS to verify that system BIOS is not the source of the problem. Otherwise the entire motherboard might have to be replaced.

Key Continues to Repeat After Being Released

This problem can be caused by a dirty contact. Some debris may have conductive properties, short the gap between the contacts, and therefore cause the key to repeat. Try cleaning the key switch with contact cleaner.

Very high humidity and excess moisture will sometimes short key switch contacts and cause keys to repeat, because water is an electrical conductor. The problem will usually resolve itself once the humidity level returns to normal. You can hasten the drying process by using a fan (not a hot hair dryer) to blow air at the keyboard.

Keys Produce the Wrong Characters

This problem is usually caused by a bad chip. PC keyboards actually have a processor mounted on the logic board inside the keyboard. Try swapping the keyboard for one you know is good. If the problem goes away, replace the keyboard.

Major Spills on the Keyboard

When coffee or drinks with sugar in them spill on the keyboard, they create a sticky mess. The best solution to stay up and running is to simply replace the keyboard. You can try to save the keyboard by thoroughly rinsing it in running water, such as a bathroom shower. Make sure the keyboard dries thoroughly before you use it. Let it dry for two days on its own, or less if you set it out in the sun or in front of a fan.

 For a list of keyboard manufacturers, see Table 5-6 at the end of the "Pointing Devices" section.

POINTING DEVICES

A pointing device allows you to move a pointer on the screen and perform tasks such as executing (clicking) a command button. Common pointing devices are the mouse, the trackball, and touch pads (see Figure 5-30).

Figure 5-30   The most common pointing devices: a mouse, a trackball, and a touchpad

Mouse technologies include the wheel mouse and the optical mouse. Inside a wheel mouse is a ball that moves freely as you drag the mouse on a surface. As shown in Figure 5-31, two or more rollers on the sides of the ball housing turn as the ball rolls against them. Each roller turns a wheel. The turning of the wheel is sensed by a small light beam as the wheel "chops" the light beam when it turns. The chops in the light beams are interpreted as mouse movement and are sent to the CPU. One of two rollers tracks the x-axis (horizontal) movement of the mouse, and a second roller tracks the y-axis (vertical) movement.

An optical mouse replaces the ball in a standard mouse with a microchip, miniature red light, and camera. The light illuminates the work surface, the camera takes 1,500 snapshots every second, and the microchip reports the tiniest changes to the PC. An optical mouse works on most surfaces and doesn't require a mouse pad. The bottom of an optical mouse has a tiny hole for the camera rather than a ball, and the light glows as you work. An example of an optical mouse is IntelliEye by Microsoft.

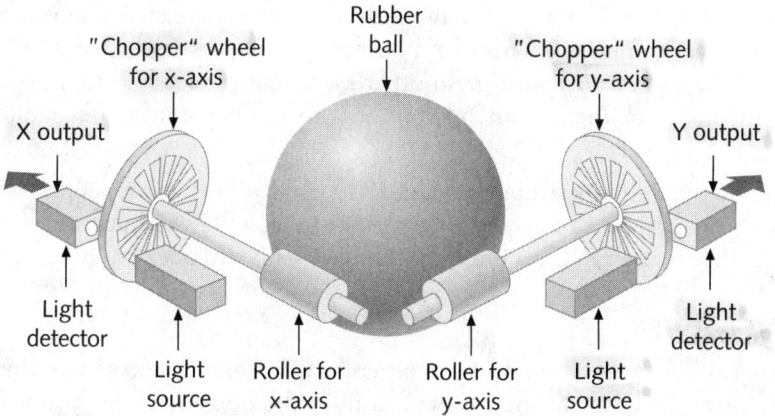

Figure 5-31   How a wheel mouse works

A mouse can have two or three buttons. Software must be programmed to use these buttons. Almost all applications use the left button. Windows 9x has made great use of the right button. The center button has recently been converted into a scroll wheel that you can use to move through large documents on screen. Many applications allow you to customize button functions on the mouse.

A mouse can connect to the computer by several methods:

- By using the serial port (the mouse is then called a **serial mouse**)

- By using a dedicated round mouse port coming directly from the motherboard (**motherboard mouse** or **PS/2–compatible mouse**)

- By using a mouse bus card that provides the same round mouse port (**bus mouse**) as discussed above

- By using a USB port

- By using a Y-connection with the keyboard so that both the keyboard and the mouse can share the same port

- By using a cordless technology whereby the mouse sends signals to a sensor on the PC or to an access point connected to the PC

Except for the cordless mouse, all of the above produce the same results (that is, the mouse port type is "transparent to the user"). Therefore, the advantages and disadvantages of each connection type are based mainly on the resources they require. The motherboard mouse is the first choice for most users because the port on the motherboard does not take up any resources that other devices might need. If you are buying a new mouse that you plan to plug into the motherboard port, don't buy a bus mouse unless the motherboard documentation states that you can use a bus mouse. The motherboard port and the bus port are identical, but a bus mouse might not work on the motherboard port.

If you have a motherboard mouse port, use it. If it becomes damaged, you can switch to a serial port or bus port. The motherboard mouse port will most likely use IRQ 12. If you are not using a mouse on this port, the motherboard might release IRQ 12 so that other devices can use it. Check the documentation for your motherboard to determine how the unused IRQ is managed.

The serial mouse requires a serial port and an IRQ for that port. Most people prefer a USB or bus mouse to a serial port mouse because they can assign the serial ports to other peripheral devices. A bus mouse can use a bus card if the motherboard does not have a mouse port.

Cleaning the Mouse

The rollers inside the wheel mouse housing collect dirt and dust and occasionally need cleaning. Remove the cover to the mouse ball from the bottom of the mouse. The cover usually comes off with a simple press and shift or turn motion. Clean the rollers with a cotton swab dipped in a very small amount of liquid soap.

Other Pointing Devices

Other pointing devices are trackballs, touch pads, and touch screens. A trackball is really an upside-down wheel mouse. You move the ball on top to turn rollers that turn a wheel sensed by a light beam. A touch pad allows you to duplicate the mouse function, moving the pointer by applying light pressure with one finger somewhere on a pad that senses the x, y movement. Some touch pads let you double-click by tapping their surface. Buttons on the touch pad serve the same function as mouse buttons. Use touch pads or trackballs where surface space is limited, because they remain stationary when you use them. Touch pads are popular on notebook computers.

A touch screen is an input device that can be embedded inside a monitor for a desktop system or an LCD panel in a notebook, or the touch screen can be installed on top of the monitor screen or LCD panel as an add-on device. As an add-on device, the touch screen has its own AC adapter to power it. The touch screen is a grid that senses clicks and drags similar to those created by a mouse and sends these events to the computer by way of a serial or USB connection. When installing a touch screen add-on device, follow the manufacturer's directions to attach the touch screen to the monitor or LCD panel, connect the USB or serial cable and the power cable, and then install the touch screen device drivers and management software. Reboot the PC. The touch screen must then be calibrated to account for the monitor's resolution using the management software. If the resolution is later changed, the touch screen must be recalibrated. The screen can be cleaned with a damp cloth using a solution of alcohol and water.

Table 5-6 gives sources for more information about keyboards and pointing devices.

Table 5-6   Manufacturers of keyboards and pointing devices

Manufacturer	Web site
Mitsumi	www.mitsumi.com
Logitech	www.logitech.com
Microsoft	www.microsoft.com

Table 5-6   Manufacturers of keyboards and pointing devices (continued)

Manufacturer	Web site
Intel	*www.intel.com*
Belkin	*www.belkin.com*
Keytec, Inc	*www.magictouch.com*

Troubleshooting a Mouse

If the mouse does not work or the pointer moves like crazy over the screen, do the following to troubleshoot the mouse:

- Check the mouse port connection. Check for dust or dirt inside the mouse. Reboot the PC.
- Try a new mouse.
- Using Device Manager and the Add New Hardware icon in Control Panel, first uninstall and then reinstall the mouse driver. Reboot the PC.
- Reboot the PC and select the logged option from the startup menu to create the Bootlog.txt file. Continue to boot and check the log for errors.

COMPUTER VIDEO

The primary output device of a computer is the monitor. The two necessary components for video output are the video controller and the monitor itself.

Monitors

The common types of monitors today are rated by screen size, resolution, refresh rate, and interlace features. Many older VGA (Video Graphics Adapter) monitors are still in use, but most sold today meet the standards for Super VGA. Monitors use either the older CRT (cathode-ray tube) technology used in television sets or the newer LCD (liquid crystal display) technology used in notebook PCs and also available for desktop use. LCD monitors for desktops are called **flat panel monitors** or flat panel displays.

How a CRT Monitor Works

Most monitors use CRT technology, in which the filaments at the back of the cathode tube shoot a beam of electrons to the screen at the front of the tube, as illustrated in Figure 5-32. Plates on the top, bottom, and sides of the tube control the direction of the beam. The beam is directed by these plates to start at the top of the screen, move from left to right to make one line, and then move down to the next line, again moving from left to right. As the beam moves vertically down the screen, it builds the displayed image. By turning the beam on and off and selecting the correct combination of colors, the grid in front of the filaments controls what goes on the screen when the beam hits that portion of the line or a single dot on the screen. Special phosphors placed on the back of the monitor screen light up when hit and produce colors. The grid controls which one of three electron guns is fired, each gun targeting a different color (red, green, or blue) positioned on the back of the screen.

Figure 5-32   How a CRT monitor works

Choosing the Right Monitor

How a monitor works and what features are available on monitors are summarized in Table 5-7 and discussed next.

Table 5-7   Some features of a monitor

Monitor Characteristic	Description
Screen size	Diagonal length of the screen surface
Refresh rate	The number of times an electronic beam fills a video screen with lines from top to bottom in one second
Interlaced	The electronic beam draws every other line with each pass, which lessens the overall effect of a lower refresh rate.
Dot pitch	The distance between adjacent dots on the screen
Resolution	The number of spots, or pixels, on a screen that can be addressed by software
Multiscan	Monitors that offer a variety of refresh rates so they can support several video cards
Green monitor	A monitor that saves electricity and supports the EPA Energy Star program

Screen Size

The screen size of a monitor is the one feature that most affects price. The larger the screen size, the more expensive the monitor. Common sizes of monitor screens are 14 inches, 15 inches, 17 inches, and 21 inches. Macintosh computers can use special monitors designed for page layouts on legal-sized paper. The 15-inch monitor is the most popular, and the small 14-inch monitor is losing popularity.

When you match a monitor to a video card, a good rule of thumb is to match a low-end video card to a small, 14-inch monitor, a midrange video card to a 15-inch monitor, and a high-end video card to a 17-inch or larger monitor, to get the best performance from both devices. However, you can compare the different features of the video card to those of the monitor, such as the resolutions supported, the refresh rate, and the bandwidth. **Bandwidth** as it applies to analog communication is the difference between the highest and lowest frequencies that an analog communications device such as a video cable can carry.

Monitor sizes are measured on the diagonal. The monitor I'm now using is advertised as having a 17-inch screen. The actual dimensions of the lighted screen are 9½ inches by 11½ inches. The diagonal measurement of the lighted area is 15 inches, and the diagonal measurement of the screen surface is 17 inches.

5

Refresh Rate

The **refresh rate**, or vertical scan rate, is the number of times in one second an electronic beam can fill the screen with lines from top to bottom. Refresh rates differ among monitors. The Video Electronics Standards Association (VESA) has set a minimum refresh rate standard of 70 Hz, or 70 complete vertical refreshes per second, as one requirement of Super VGA monitors. Slow refresh rates make the image appear to flicker, while faster refresh rates make the image appear solid and stable. The refresh rate is set by using the Display icon in the Control Panel.

Interlaced or Noninterlaced

Interlaced monitors draw a screen by making two passes. On the first pass, the electronic beam strikes only the even lines, and on the second pass the beam strikes only the odd lines. The result is that a monitor can have a slow refresh rate with a less noticeable overall effect than there would be if the beam hit all lines for each pass. Interlaced monitors generally have slightly more flicker than **noninterlaced** monitors, which always draw the entire screen on each pass. Buy a noninterlaced monitor if you plan to spend long hours staring at the monitor. Your eyes will benefit.

Dot Pitch

The **dot pitch** is the distance between the spots, or dots, on the screen that the electronic beam hits. Remember that three beams build the screen, one for each of three colors (red, green, and blue). Each composite location on the screen is really made up of three dots and is called a triad. The distance between a color dot in one triad and the same color dot in the next triad is the dot pitch. The smaller the pitch, the sharper the image. A dot pitch of .28 mm or .25 mm gives the best results and costs more. Although less expensive monitors can have a dot pitch of .35 mm or .38 mm, they can still create a fuzzy image, even with the best video cards.

Resolution

Resolution is a measure of how many spots on the screen are addressable by software. Each addressable location is called a **pixel** (for picture element) which is composed of several triads. Because resolution depends on software, the resolution must be supported by the video controller card, and the software you are using must make use of the resolution capabilities of the monitor. The standard for most software packages is 800 × 600 pixels, although many monitors offer a resolution of 1024 × 768 pixels or higher. The resolution is set in Windows from the Display icon in Control Panel, and requires a driver specific for that resolution. Higher resolution usually requires more video RAM.

Multiscan Monitors

Multiscan monitors offer a variety of vertical and horizontal refresh rates so they can support a variety of video cards. They cost more but are much more versatile than other monitors.

Green Monitors

A "Green" monitor is a monitor that saves electricity, thus making its contribution to conserving natural resources. A Green monitor meets the requirements of the EPA Energy Star program and uses 100 to 150 watts of electricity. When the screen saver is on, the monitor should use no more than 30 watts of electricity.

Monitors and ELF Emissions

There is some debate about the danger of monitors giving off ELF (extremely low frequency) emissions of electromagnetic fields. Standards to control ELF emissions are Sweden's MPR II standard and the TCO '95 standards. The TCO '95 standards also include guidelines for energy consumption, screen flicker, and luminance. Most monitors manufactured today comply with the MPR II standard, and very few comply with the more stringent TCO '95 standards.

Flat Panel Monitors

Flat panel monitors are increasing in popularity, though their cost is still much higher than that of comparable CRT monitors. Flat panel monitors take up much less desk space than CRT monitors, are lighter, and require less electricity to operate. An LCD panel produces an image using a liquid crystal material made of large, easily polarized molecules. Figure 5-33 shows the layers of the LCD panel that together create the image. At the center of the layers is the liquid crystal material. Next to it is the layer responsible for providing the color to the image. These two layers are sandwiched between two grids of electrodes. One grid of electrodes is aligned in columns, and the other electrodes are aligned in rows. The two layers of electrodes make up the electrode matrix. Each intersection of a row electrode and a column electrode forms one pixel on the LCD panel. Software can manipulate each pixel by activating the electrodes that form it. The image is formed by scanning the column and row electrodes, much as the electronic beam scans a CRT monitor screen.

The polarizer layers outside the glass layers in Figure 5-33 are responsible for preventing light from passing through the pixels when the electrodes are not activated. When the electrodes are activated, light on the back side of the LCD panel can pass through one pixel on the screen, picking up color from the color layer as it passes through.

There are two kinds of LCD panels on the market today: **active-matrix** and **dual-scan passive matrix** displays. A dual-scan display is less expensive than an active-matrix display and provides an image of lower quality. With dual-scan display, two columns of electrodes are activated at the same time. With active-matrix display, a transistor that amplifies the signal is placed at every intersection in the grid, which further enhances the pixel quality.

Flat panel monitors are built to receive either an analog signal or a digital signal from the video card and have two ports on the monitor to accommodate either signal. If the signal is analog, it must be converted to digital before the monitor can process it. Flat panel monitors are designed to receive an analog signal so that you can use a regular video card that works with a CRT monitor, thus reducing the price of upgrading from a CRT to an LCD monitor. As you will see in the upcoming discussion of video cards, video cards convert digital data from the CPU to analog before sending it to the monitor. Therefore, with analog flat panel monitors, the data is converted from digital to analog and back to digital before being used by the flat panel monitor. These conversions reduce the quality of the resulting image. To get the best output, use a digital flat panel monitor along with a digital video card designed to support the monitor.

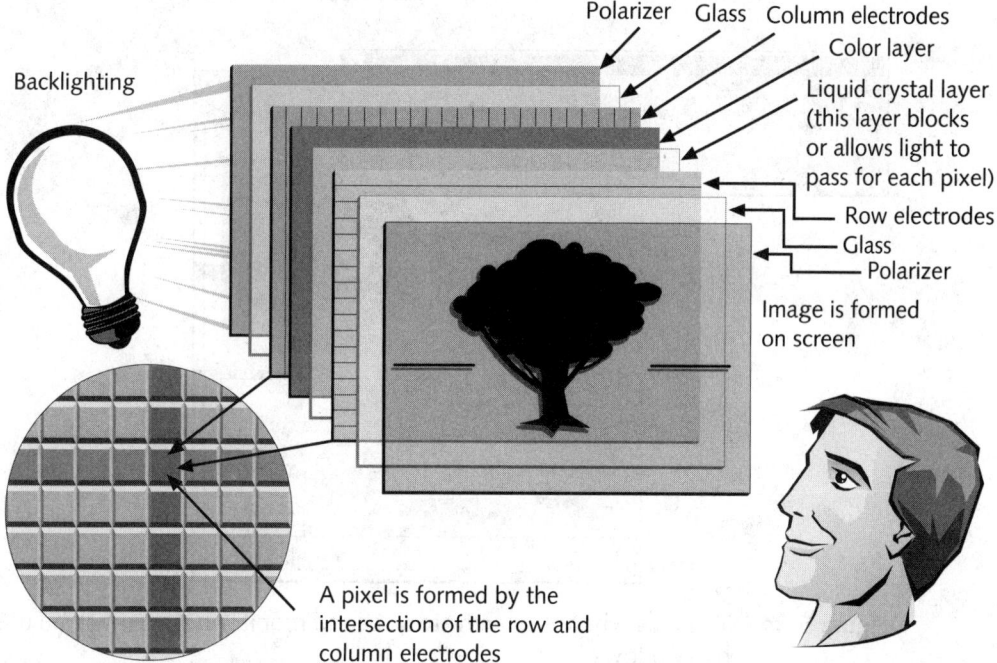

Figure 5-33   Layers of an LCD panel

Installing Dual Monitors

To increase the size of your Windows desktop, you can install more than one monitor for a single computer. This dual-monitor installation procedure assumes that you are using Windows 9x and that you already have a monitor installed. Setting up dual monitors gives you more space for your Windows desktop as well as some redundancy if one goes down. To install a second monitor and a dual-monitor setup:

1. Verify that the original video card is working properly, determine whether it is PCI or AGP, and decide whether it is to be the primary monitor.

2. Install a second adapter card to the PCI slot nearest to the AGP slot if the original monitor has an AGP adapter, or to the PCI slot immediately next to the original PCI adapter if the original monitor has a PCI adapter, and attach the second monitor.

3. If CMOS has the setting, adjust CMOS to initialize the primary adapter first, if necessary.

4. Boot the system. Windows will recognize the new hardware and may prompt you for the location of the drivers. At this time, a message will appear saying that if you can see the message, the installation was successful, and telling you to adjust the display properties.

5. Open **Display Properties** from Control Panel. The Display Properties window shown in Figure 5-34 appears. Select the **Settings** tab.

Figure 5-34   You must choose to activate a second monitor before it will be used by Windows

6. Notice that the two monitors in the figure are labeled 1 and 2. (If the two monitors are not present, try rebooting your PC.) Click on the image of the new monitor (number 2), or select the correct adapter from the drop-down menu under Display. Click **Yes** to enable the monitor.

7. Adjust the settings to your preferences and check the **Extend my Windows desktop onto this monitor** box. To save the settings, click **Apply**.

 Settings for each video adapter that you add to your system must be saved/applied individually. Up to nine separate adapters can be added to a single system.

8. The dialog box also shown in Figure 5-34 is displayed. Click **OK** to apply the settings.

5

Once you have added a second monitor to your system, you move from one monitor to another simply by moving your mouse. Switching from one monitor to the other does not require any special keystroke or menu option.

Video Cards

Recall that the video controller card is the interface between the monitor and the computer. These cards are sometimes called graphic adapters, video boards, graphics cards, or display cards. Sometimes the video controller is integrated into the motherboard. If you are buying a motherboard with an integrated video controller, check that you can disable the controller on the motherboard if it needs replacement or gives you trouble. You can then install a video card and bypass the controller on the motherboard.

The quality of a video subsystem is rated according to how it affects overall system performance, video quality (including resolution and color), power-saving features, and ease of use and installation. Because the video controller on the video card is separated from the core system functions, manufacturers can use a variety of techniques to improve performance without being overly concerned with compatibility with functions on the motherboard. An example of this flexibility is seen in the many ways memory is managed on a video controller. This section discusses the buses used by video cards, how a video card works, and the features available on video cards, especially video memory. The two main features to look for in a video card are the bus it uses and the amount of video RAM it has or can support. Also know that a motherboard might have its own on-board video controller and video port, but that this video subsystem will probably be very basic and lack many of the features you'll read about in this section.

The Buses Used by Video Cards

There are three buses that have been used for video cards in the last ten years or so, the VESA bus, the PCI bus, and the AGP bus. The VESA and AGP buses were developed specifically for video cards, and the PCI bus is used for many types of cards, including a video card.

Several years ago, in an attempt to create a standard for local 32-bit buses, many manufacturers endorsed the **VESA (Video Electronics Standards Association) VL bus**. Many motherboards offered the VESA local bus for video and memory circuit boards. The expansion slot for a VESA local bus included the 16 bits for the ISA slot plus an added extension with another 116 pins (see Figure 5-35). About 1995, the VESA bus was replaced with the faster PCI bus. Nowadays you seldom see a PC that uses a VESA video card.

Figure 5-35 VESA local bus expansion slot

More recently, an even faster bus, the APG bus, has replaced the PCI bus for video cards, although a PCI bus is used for a second video card if a system has two monitors (dual monitors). The AGP is designed to provide fast access to video. Motherboards have a single AGP slot to support one AGP video card (see Figure 5-36). AGP is more like a port than a bus, since it does not allow for expandability and can only support a single card. The faster AGP bus has a direct connection to the CPU without having to use the slower PCI bus.

The AGP bus runs at the same speed as the system bus, connects directly to it, and has a 32-bit-wide data path. AGP runs faster than PCI, which runs at half the system bus speed. AGP also offers additional features that give it an overall better performance for video than PCI. It offers an improved rendering of 3-D images when software is designed to use it.

AGP can share system memory with the CPU to do its calculations and, therefore, it does not always have to first copy data from system memory to video memory on the graphics card. This feature, known as direct memory execute (DIME), is probably the most powerful feature of AGP. The first AGP specification defined AGP 2X, which allowed AGP to transfer two cycles of data during a single AGP clock beat. The AGP 2.0 specification defined AGP 4X, whereby four cycles of data can be transferred during a single AGP clock beat, yielding an overall data throughput of more than 1 GB/sec (gigabytes per second). Compare that to the throughput of the PCI bus, which is either 132 or 264 MB/sec.

AGP Slot

5

Figure 5-36   A motherboard will have only one AGP slot, which is used to support a video/graphics card

Figure 5-36 shows a 132-pin AGP slot on a motherboard. Another AGP standard, called the AGP Pro, has provision for a longer slot. This 180-pin slot has extensions on both ends that contain an additional 20 pins on one end and 28 pins on the other end that are used to provide extra voltage to the AGP video card in the slot. AGP Pro is used for high-end video cards that consume more than 25 watts of power. The first AGP Pro standard ran at the same speed as AGP 4X. The latest AGP standard is AGP 8X that runs at eight cycles of data per clock cycle (2.1 Gbps).

When matching video cards to AGP slots, be aware of the several variations in AGP slots. All AGP speeds support a 3.3 V slot identified by a notch or key near the right end of the slot and a 1.5 V slot identified by a notch or key near the left end of the slot. In addition, there is an AGP universal slot that has no notch and can accommodate either 1.5 V or 3.3 V cards. The AGP Pro slot might be a 1.5 V, 3.3 V, or universal slot. AGP slots on a motherboard are backward compatible with older AGP standards, but you should not use a faster AGP video card in a slower AGP slot. Also, when using an AGP Pro video card, leave the PCI slot next to it empty in order to improve ventilation and prevent overheating.

In order for AGP to work at its full potential, the motherboard must be running at a minimum of 100 MHz, and the operating system must support AGP. Windows 98, Windows 2000, and Windows XP support AGP. See *www.agpforum.org* and *developer.intel.com/technology/agp/* for more information.

How a Video Card Works

A video card performs four basic tasks, as seen in Figure 5-37. The RAM DAC (digital-to-analog converter) technology may be housed on a single RAM DAC chip on the video card or may be embedded in the video chip set. RAM DAC actually includes three digital-to-analog converters, one for each of the monitor's three color guns: red, green, and blue (RGB).

The bus external to the video card is the PCI bus or the AGP bus, but the card itself also has an internal video bus. Bandwidth in relation to a bus is the volume of data that can travel on the bus. Current video buses use a data path that may be 32 bits, 64 bits, 128 bits, or even 256 bits wide. The effective bandwidth of the bus is partly determined by the width of the data path and the amount of memory on the card.

Four Basic Functions of a Video Card
① The digital data goes from the system bus to the video chip set on the video card.
② The video chip set writes the digital data to video memory on the card.
③ The data stored in video memory is passed to the digital analog converter (RAM DAC), where it is converted from digital data to analog data.
④ RAM DAC passes the analog data to the monitor.

Figure 5-37   Four basic functions of a video card

On the video card, performance is affected by the chip set, memory, and the RAM DAC, as well as by the bus speed and size. One method to improve performance is to allow both the video chip set and the RAM DAC (both the input and the output processes) to access video memory at the same time. This method, called **dual porting**, requires a special kind of video RAM discussed later in this section. Another method of increasing performance is to place a processor on the video card, making the card a graphics accelerator.

Graphics Accelerators

One of the more important advances made in video cards in recent years has been the introduction of graphics accelerators. A **graphics accelerator** is a type of video card that has its own processor to boost performance. With the demands that graphics applications make in the multimedia environment, graphics accelerators have become not just an enhancement, but a common necessity.

The processor on a graphics accelerator card is similar to a CPU, but is specifically designed to manage video and graphics. Some features included on a graphics accelerator are MPEG decoding, 3-D graphics, dual porting, color space conversion, interpolated scaling, EPA Green PC support, digital output to flat panel display monitors, and application support for popular high-intensity graphics software such as AutoCAD, Quark, and Windows 9x/NT/2000/XP. All these features are designed to reduce the burden on the motherboard CPU and perform the video and graphics functions much faster than the motherboard CPU.

Video Memory

Older video cards did not have memory, but today they need memory to handle the large volume of data generated by increased resolution and color. Video memory is stored on video cards as memory chips. The first video cards to have memory all used DRAM chips, but now video memory chips can use several technologies. This section discusses how much video memory is needed and what kinds of video memory chips can be used on a card for the best possible performance.

How Much Video Memory Is Needed?

The amount of data received by a video card from the CPU for each frame (or screen) of data is determined by the screen resolution (measured in pixels), the number of colors, which is called the **color depth** (measured in bits), and enhancements to color information called alpha blending. The more data required to generate a single screen of data, the more memory is required to hold that data. Memory on the video card that holds one frame of data before it is sent to the monitor is called a frame buffer. The video card has other needs for memory besides the frame buffer, including the memory used by some cards to store font or other graphical information. Table 5-8 shows the amount of memory needed to hold the frame buffer, which is determined by the screen resolution and number of colors.

Table 5-8   Video RAM required for different video resolutions and color depths

Video Resolution	4-bit Color Depth (16 colors)	8-bit Color Depth (256 colors)	16-bit Color Depth (65,000 colors)	24-bit True Color (16.7 million colors)	32-bit (24-bit True Color with 8-bit Alpha Channel)
640 x 480	256K	512K	1 MB	1 MB	2 MB
800 x 600	512K	512K	1 MB	2 MB	2 MB
1,024 x 768	1 MB	1 MB	2 MB	4 MB	4 MB
1,152 x 1,024	1 MB	2 MB	2 MB	4 MB	4 MB
1,280 x 1,024	1 MB	2 MB	4 MB	4 MB	6 MB
1,600 x 1,200	2 MB	2 MB	4 MB	6 MB	8 MB

Color depth is directly related to the number of bits used to compose one pixel and can be 4, 8, 16, or 24 bits per pixel. The larger the number of bits allocated to storing each piece of data, the more accurate the value can be; in like manner, the greater the number of bits allocated to store the value of pixel color, the greater the number of color shades you can use and color depth you can have.

When pixels are built on screen, each one uses three channels for color: red, green, and blue. However, for building 3-D graphics, a fourth channel, called the alpha channel, is sometimes added. The alpha channel controls the way the three colors are displayed and can add transparency or opacity to the image. Adding these effects is called alpha blending, which can create the effect of shading or making one color partly visible behind another color, as when you are looking through colored glass at a different color. The alpha channel adds another 8 bits to the information kept for each pixel. When 24-bit true color is used with an 8-bit alpha channel, 32 bits per pixel is needed, resulting in 32-bit graphics used by high-end video cards. The memory required for these cards is listed in the last column of Table 5-8.

Another factor that determines how much video memory is required is the bus width on the card. Just as with motherboards, the RAM configuration on the card must conform to the bus width so that data can move from the bus to the card. A normal 1-MB memory chip on a video card has a bus width of 32 bits. In Figure 5-38, because each 1-MB video RAM chip is 32 bits wide, you can see why 2 MB of memory are needed if the video bus is 64 bits wide. In fact, this bit width of the video chip is the reason that a video card that has a 64-bit bus width and only 1 MB of installed memory is so slow. If your video card uses a 64-bit bus, be sure to install at least 2 MB of RAM.

Figure 5-38   Video bus with 64-bit width addressing two 1-MB memory chips with 32-bit widths

In Figure 5-39, 4 MB of RAM are required to make the most efficient use of the 128-bit video bus width. Some manufacturers of video chip sets have developed a method to use a 128-bit bus with less than 4 MB of memory. For example, the Tseng Labs ET6000 chip set uses a special kind of video RAM called **MDRAM (multibank DRAM)** that is able to use the full 128-bit bus path without requiring the full 4 MB of RAM.

Figure 5-39   128-bit video bus addressing 4 MB of video memory

All these factors affect how much memory is required to build a single frame buffer. In Table 5-8, you can see that the most memory needed to build a single frame buffer is 8 MB. However, in addition to needing memory to hold each frame buffer, a graphics accelerator card might also need memory for other purposes. Software that builds 3-D graphics on screen often uses textures, and sometimes a graphics card holds these textures in memory to build future screens. Large amounts of video RAM keep the card from having to retrieve these textures from the hard drive or system RAM multiple times. In addition, to improve performance, the graphics card might use double or triple buffering, in which the card holds not just the frame being built, but the next one or two frames. Because of texturing and triple buffering, a card might need as much as 32 MB of RAM. See the graphics card documentation for information about memory recommendations for maximum performance.

Types of Video Memory

You have already been introduced to several different versions of video memory. Dual-ported memory, one type of which is sometimes called **video RAM**, or **VRAM**, is designed so that video memory can be accessed by both the input and output processes at the same time. MDRAM memory chips are designed so that the full width of the video bus can be used with fewer memory chips than needed to provide the full bus width access to RAM. Three other types of memory chips designed to improve performance of video cards are: WRAM, SGRAM, and 3-D RAM.

SGRAM (synchronous graphics RAM) is similar to SDRAM, discussed in Chapter 6, but designed specifically for video card processing. SGRAM, like SDRAM, can synchronize itself with the CPU bus clock, which makes the memory faster. SGRAM also uses other methods to increase overall performance for graphics-intensive processing, but is not dual-ported memory. It is used on moderate to high-end cards where the very highest resolutions are not required.

WRAM (window RAM) is a type of dual-ported RAM, but is faster and less expensive than VRAM. WRAM was named more for its ability to manage full-motion video than for its ability to speed up Microsoft Windows video processing. WRAM's increase in speed is primarily due to its own internal bus on the chip, which has a data path that is 256 bits wide. WRAM is used on high-end graphics cards with very high resolutions and true color.

Some video processing involves simulating 3-D graphics; **3-D RAM** was designed specifically to improve this performance. Much of the logic of 3-D processing is embedded on the chip itself. A graphics card chip set normally calculates which pixel of a 3-D graphic is to be displayed, depending on whether or not the pixel is behind other pixels and, therefore, out of sight in a 3-D graphic. After the pixel is drawn and a calculation is made as to whether or not the pixel is seen, if the pixel is not to be displayed, the chip set writes it back to memory to be used later. With 3-D RAM, the chip set simply passes the data to the 3-D RAM chip that draws the pixel and decides whether or not to display it without involving the chip set.

For more information about video cards, including graphics accelerators, see the Web sites of the manufacturers listed in Table 5-9.

Table 5-9   Video card manufacturers

Manufacturer	Web Site
ASUSTeK Computer, Inc.	www.asus.com
ATI Technologies, Inc.	www.ati.com
Creative Technology, Ltd.	www.creative.com
Gainward Co., Ltd.	www.gainward.com
Hercules Computer Technology	www.hercules.com
Matrox Graphics, Inc.	www.matrox.com
MSI Computer Corporation	www.msicomputer.com
Number Nine Visual Technology	www.nine.com
nVidia	www.nvidia.com
VisionTek	www.visiontek.com

Troubleshooting Video Problems

For monitors, as well as other devices, do the easy things first. Make simple hardware and software adjustments. Also, remember the "trade good for suspected bad" method. Many monitor problems are caused by poor cable connections or bad contrast/brightness adjustments. Also check if the monitor is still under warranty. Remember that many warranties are voided if an unauthorized individual works inside the monitor. When servicing a monitor, take the time to clean the screen with a soft dry cloth.

When you first turn on your PC, the first thing you see on the screen is the firmware on the video card identifying itself. You can use this information to search the Web, especially the manufacturer's Web site, for troubleshooting information about this card.

Typical monitor problems and how to troubleshoot them are described next.

Power Light (LED) Does Not Go On; No Picture

- Is the monitor plugged in? Verify that the wall outlet works by plugging in a lamp, radio, etc.

- If the monitor power cord is plugged into a power strip or surge protector, verify that the power strip is turned on and working and that the monitor is also turned on. Look for an on/off switch on the front and back of the monitor. Some monitors have both.

- If the monitor power cord is plugged into the back of the computer, verify that the connection is tight and the computer is turned on.

- A blown fuse could be the problem. Some monitors have a fuse that is visible from the back of the monitor. It looks like a black knob that you can remove (no need to go inside the monitor cover). Remove the fuse and look for the broken wire indicating a bad fuse.

- The monitor may have a switch on the back for choosing between 110 volts and 220 volts. Check that the switch is in the right position.

If none of these solutions solves the problem, the next step is to take the monitor to a service center.

Power LED Light Is On, No Picture on Power-Up

- Check the contrast adjustment. If there's no change, then leave it at a middle setting.

- Check the brightness adjustment. If there's no change, then leave it at a middle setting.

- Is the cable connected securely to the computer?

- If the monitor-to-computer cable detaches from the monitor, exchange it for a cable you know is good, or check the cable for continuity.

- If this solves the problem, reattach the old cable to verify that the problem was not simply a bad connection.

- Confirm that the proper system configuration has been set up. Some older motherboards have a jumper or DIP switch you can use to select the monitor type.

- Test a monitor you know is good on the computer you suspect to be bad. Do this and the previous step to identify the problem. If you think the monitor is bad, make sure that it also fails to work on a good computer.

- Check the CMOS settings or software configuration on the computer. When using Windows 9x, boot into safe mode (press F5 during the boot) to allow the OS to select a generic display driver and low resolution. If this works, change the driver and resolution.

- Reseat the video card. For a PCI card, move the card to a different expansion slot. Clean the card's edge connectors, using a contact cleaner or a white eraser. Do not let crumbs from the eraser fall into the expansion slot.

- If there are socketed chips on the video card, remove the card from the expansion slot and, using a screwdriver, press down firmly on each corner of each socketed chip on the card. Chips sometimes loosen because of thermal changes; this condition is called **chip creep**.

- Trade a good video card for the video card you suspect is bad. Test the video card you think is bad on a computer that works. Test a video card you know is good on the computer that you suspect may be bad. Whenever possible, do both.

- If the video card has socketed chips that appear dirty or corroded, consider removing them and trying to clean the pins. You can use a clean pencil eraser to do this. Normally, however, if the problem is a bad video card, the most cost-effective measure is to replace the card.

- Go into CMOS setup and disable the shadowing of video ROM.

- Test the RAM on the motherboard with diagnostic software.

- For an older motherboard that supports both VESA and PCI, if you are using a VESA video card, try using a PCI card. For a motherboard that is using an AGP video card, try using a PCI video card in a PCI slot.

- Trade the motherboard for one you know is good. Sometimes, though rarely, a peripheral chip on the motherboard of the computer can cause the problem.

Power On, But Monitor Displays the Wrong Characters

- Wrong characters are usually not the result of a bad monitor but of a problem with the video card. Trade the video card for one you know is good.

- Exchange the motherboard. Sometimes a bad ROM or RAM chip on the motherboard displays the wrong characters on the monitor.

Monitor Flickers and/or Has Wavy Lines

- Monitor flicker can be caused by poor cable connections. Check that the cable connections are snug.

- Does the monitor have a degauss button to eliminate accumulated or stray magnetic fields? If so, press it.

- Check if something in the office is causing a high amount of electrical noise. For example, you might be able to stop a flicker by moving the office fan to a different outlet. Bad fluorescent lights or large speakers can also produce interference. Two monitors placed very close together can also cause problems.

- If the vertical scan frequency (the refresh rate at which the screen is drawn) is below 60 Hz, a screen flicker may appear. Use Control Panel, Display icon to make the adjustment. Use the highest refresh rate offered.

- For older monitors that do not support a high enough refresh rate, your only cure may be to purchase a new monitor.

- Before making a purchase, verify that the new monitor will solve the problem.

- Check Control Panel, Display, Settings to see if a high resolution (greater than 800 × 600 with more than 256 colors) is selected. Consider these issues:

  1. The video card might not support this resolution/color setting.
  2. There might not be enough video RAM; 2 MB or more may be required.
  3. The added (socketed) video RAM might be of a different speed than the soldered memory.

No Graphics Display or the Screen Goes Blank When Loading Certain Programs

This problem may be caused by the following:

- A special graphics or video accelerator card is not present, or is defective.
- Software is not configured to do graphics, or the software does not recognize the installed graphics card.
- The video card does not support the resolution and/or color setting.
- There might not be enough video RAM; 2 MB or more might be required.
- The added (socketed) video RAM might be of a different speed than the soldered memory.
- The wrong adapter/display type is selected. Start Windows 9x from safe mode to reset the display.

Screen Goes Blank 30 Seconds or One Minute After the Keyboard Is Left Untouched

A "Green" motherboard (one that follows energy-saving standards) used with an Energy Saver monitor can be configured to go into a standby or doze mode after a period of inactivity. This might be the case if the monitor resumes after you press a key or move the mouse. Doze times can be set for periods from as short as 20 seconds to as long as one hour.

The power LED light normally changes from green to orange to indicate Doze Mode. Monitors and video cards using these energy-saving features are addressed in Chapter 3.

You might be able to change the doze features by entering the CMOS menu and looking for an option such as Power Management, or in Windows 9x by opening Control Panel and selecting Display, Screen Saver.

Some monitors have a Power Save switch on the back of the monitor. Make sure this is set as you want.

 Problems might occur if the motherboard power-saving features are turning off the monitor, and Windows 9x screen saver is also turning off the monitor. If the system hangs when you try to get the monitor going again, try disabling one or the other. If this doesn't work, then disable both.

Poor Quality Color Display

For this problem, try the following:

- Read the documentation for the monitor to learn how to use the color-adjusting buttons to fine-tune the color.
- Exchange video cards.
- Add more video RAM; 2 MB or 4 MB might be required for higher resolutions.
- Check if a fan or large speaker (speakers have large magnets) or another monitor nearby could be causing interference.

Picture Out of Focus or Out of Adjustment

For this problem, try the following:

- Check the adjustment knobs on the control panel on the outside of the monitor.
- Change the refresh rate. Sometimes this can make the picture appear more focused.
- You can also make adjustments inside the monitor that might solve the problem. If you have not been trained to work inside the monitor, take the monitor to a service center.

Crackling Sound

An accumulation of dirt or dust inside the unit might be the cause. Someone trained to work on the inside of the monitor can vacuum the inside.

To Configure or Change Monitor Settings and Drivers in Windows

If the video card is supported by Windows, you can change the driver and settings by double-clicking the Display icon in Control Panel. For drivers not supported by Windows, you can reinstall the drivers by using the CD or floppy disks that come with the video card. The settings for this type of driver can most likely be changed through Control Panel's Display icon.

To Change the Video Driver Configuration

Double-click the Display icon in Control Panel. Select the Settings tab to change the color palette, the resolution (for example, from 800×600 to 1024×768), or the driver for the video card or monitor type. Click Advanced on the Settings tab to show the Change Display Type window (see Figure 5-40 for Windows 98). From this window, you can change the video card or the monitor type.

5

Figure 5-40   Changing the video card type in Windows 98

If you increase the resolution, the Windows icons and desktop text become smaller. Select Large Fonts on the Settings tab and increase the Desktop Icon size on the Appearance tab.

Returning to Standard VGA Settings

When the display settings don't work, return to standard VGA settings as follows:

- For Windows 9x, reboot the system and press the F8 key after the first beep.

- When the Microsoft Windows 9x Startup menu appears, select safe mode to boot up with minimal configurations and standard VGA display mode.

- Double-click the Display icon in Control Panel and reset to the correct video configuration.

CHAPTER SUMMARY

- ❑ Adding new devices to a computer requires installing hardware and software and resolving possible resource conflicts.
- ❑ All hardware devices require some resources from a computer, which might include an IRQ, DMA channel, I/O addresses, and, for legacy devices, some upper memory addresses to contain their device drivers.
- ❑ Use Device Manager under Windows to determine what resources currently installed devices are using.
- ❑ Most computers provide two serial ports and one parallel port to be used for a variety of devices. Newer motherboards also provide one or more USB ports and an IEEE 1394 port.
- ❑ The PCI bus is presently the most popular local bus. The VESA local bus is a standard designed by the Video Electronics Standards Association for video cards. For video cards, the VESA bus was replaced by PCI, which has been replaced by the AGP bus.
- ❑ Generally, expansion cards use the PCI slots or the older and slower ISA slots. The EISA and MCA buses are no longer used.
- ❑ A null modem connection is used to connect two computers using their serial ports and a cable, but no modems.
- ❑ The UART chip controls serial ports.
- ❑ Because data might get corrupted, parallel cables should not exceed 15 feet (4.5 meters) in length. HP recommends that the cables not exceed 10 feet (3 meters).
- ❑ Three types of parallel ports are: standard, EPP, and ECP. The ECP type uses a DMA channel.
- ❑ Serial ports are sometimes configured as COM1, COM2, COM3, or COM4, and parallel ports can be configured as LPT1, LPT2, or LPT3.
- ❑ The USB bus only uses one set of system resources for all USB devices connected to it, and USB devices are hot-pluggable.
- ❑ The IEEE 1394 bus provides either a 4-pin or 6-pin connector, uses only one set of system resources, and is hot-pluggable.
- ❑ The PCI bus runs in sync with the CPU, and the PCI controller manages system resources for all PCI cards. Resources are assigned to PCI slots during startup.
- ❑ If the motherboard and the OS both support PCI bus IRQ steering, IRQs can be reassigned by the OS after booting, in order to resolve a conflict. Windows 9x supports IRQ steering, but Windows 2000 and Windows XP only support IRQ sharing.
- ❑ A keyboard can use a DIN, PS/2, USB, or wireless connection.
- ❑ Two types of monitors are CRT and LCD. CRT costs less, but LCD takes up less desktop space.
- ❑ Features to consider when purchasing a monitor are screen size, refresh rate, interlaced, dot pitch, resolution, multiscan ability, and Green Standards used by the monitor.

❐ A video card is rated by the bus that it uses and the amount of video RAM on the card. Both features affect the overall speed and performance of the card.

❐ Some types of video memory are SGRAM, WRAM, and 3-D RAM.

KEY TERMS

5

1394.3
3-D RAM
active matrix
bandwidth
break code
bus mastering
bus mouse
chip creep
color depth
data throughput
DCE (Data Communications Equipment)
dot pitch
DTE (Data Terminal Equipment)
dual porting
dual-scan passive matrix
ECP (Extended Capabilities Port)
EISA (Extended ISA) bus
EPP (Enhanced Parallel Port)

FireWire
flat panel monitor
graphics accelerator
hot-pluggable
hot-swapping
hub
IEEE 1284
IEEE 1394
i.Link
interlaced
I/O controller card
isochronous data transfer
make code
MDRAM (multibank DRAM)
Micro Channel Architecture (MCA) bus
modem eliminator
motherboard mouse
multiscan monitor
noninterlaced
null modem cable

PCI (Peripheral Component Interconnect) bus
PCI bus IRQ steering
pixel
PS/2-compatible mouse
refresh rate
resolution
serial mouse
SGRAM (synchronous graphics RAM)
throughput performance
UART (universal asynchronous receiver-transmitter) chip
USB host controller
VESA (Video Electronics Standards Association) VL bus
VRAM (video RAM)
WRAM (window RAM)

6

MEMORY AND FLOPPY DRIVES

In this chapter, you will learn:

♦ About the different kinds of physical memory and how they work

♦ How to upgrade and troubleshoot memory

♦ How floppy drives work and how to support them

In earlier chapters, you learned how several important hardware components work and how to support them. This chapter looks at two more components: memory and floppy drives. Memory is required in order for a system to work. Memory is stored on microchips, which are often stored on memory modules called SIMMs, DIMMs, or RIMMs. Adding more memory to a system can sometimes drastically improve performance. Floppy drives were once considered essential devices for file storage and installing software on a computer, but are now mainly used for troubleshooting a failed boot. Much of what you learn about floppy drives in this chapter will also apply to your study of hard drives in the next chapter.

PHYSICAL MEMORY

Recall that memory temporarily holds data and instructions as the CPU processes them and that computer memory is divided into two categories: ROM and RAM. ROM retains its data when the PC is turned off, but all data stored in RAM is lost (except for data stored on the CMOS chip). RAM is further divided into two categories: **static RAM (SRAM)** and **dynamic RAM (DRAM)**. Most DRAM today is stored on DIMMs (see Figure 6-1) and, to a lesser degree, on RIMMs. ROM, on the other hand, stores its data on chips socketed or soldered to the circuit boards. One or two ROM chips on a motherboard hold system BIOS and startup BIOS programs, and many devices and circuit boards such as a video card have ROM chips on them. This section examines the different technologies of RAM and ROM, focusing on RAM technologies.

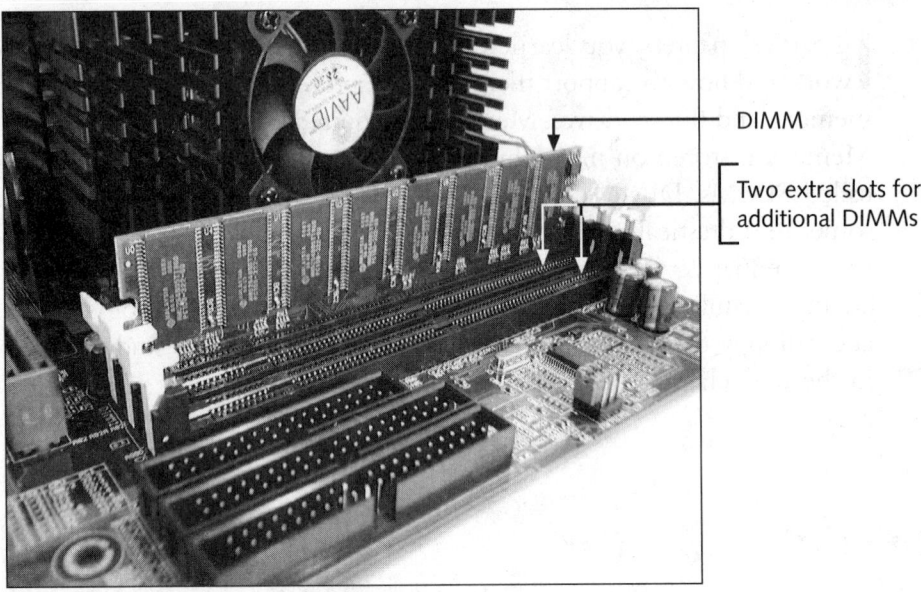

DIMM

Two extra slots for additional DIMMs

Figure 6-1   DRAM on most motherboards today is stored on DIMMs

ROM on the Motherboard

Recall that ROM, or read-only memory, consists of memory chips that contain programs (called ROM BIOS) that are acid-etched into the chips at the factory (see Figure 6-2). The programs on a ROM chip (sometimes called firmware) are permanent; they cannot be changed. **EPROM (erasable programmable ROM)** chips can have their programs changed. They have a special window that allows the current memory contents to be erased with an ultraviolet light, so that the chip can be reprogrammed. **EEPROM (electrically erasable programmable ROM)** chips (also known as flash ROM chips), also allow their programs to be changed. On EEPROM chips, a higher voltage is applied to a pin to erase its previous memory before a new instruction set or data is electronically written. However, for the discussions in this chapter, consider the EPROM, EEPROM, and ROM chips as providing firmware that is not erasable during normal PC operations. In addition, when the text refers to ROM chips, they may be EPROM, EEPROM, or ROM chips that are not erasable.

ROM BIOS chip

Figure 6-2   The ROM BIOS on newer motherboards can be upgraded using software provided by the BIOS manufacturer

When you purchased your computer, it contained several ROM chips on the motherboard and some on the expansion boards. These ROM chips contain the programming that the computer uses to boot up and to do routine utility operations, such as reading from and writing to hardware devices and performing basic data manipulation. As discussed in earlier chapters, the ROM chips on the motherboard contain much of the BIOS for your computer.

Newer ROM chips are usually soldered onto the motherboard and are updated by flashing. Older ROM chips were socketed onto the motherboard and manually replaced by removing the chip and inserting a new one in the socket.

Flash Memory

Flash memory makes it possible to replace the programming on a chip rather than replace the physical chip itself. **Flash memory** acts more like secondary storage than like other types of memory, because it does not lose its data when the power is turned off. However, flash memory is different from a hard drive that holds its data as a magnetized area on a platter, because flash memory holds its data electronically. Also, flash memory is an electronic device and provides much faster data access than a mechanical device, such as a hard drive, though flash memory is more expensive.

Flash memory uses EEPROM chips and is sometimes found on PC Cards (PCMCIA cards), which look like thick credit cards, used to add additional storage to a notebook computer. Flash ROM is one example of this kind of memory on a motherboard. (You learned how to flash ROM on the motherboard in Chapter 4.) Flash memory is also used to hold picture data in digital cameras.

RAM on the Motherboard

Recall that, besides ROM, the other kind of computer memory is RAM, random access memory. In the 1980s, RAM chips were either socketed or soldered directly on motherboards, but today all RAM used as main memory is housed on SIMMs, DIMMs, or RIMMs. Memory chips on these modules can only hold their data for a few milliseconds and must be refreshed every few milliseconds. Also recall that memory that needs refreshing is called dynamic RAM (DRAM), pronounced "DEE-RAM." To **refresh** RAM means that the computer must rewrite the data to the chip. Refreshing RAM is done by the memory controller, which is part of the chip set on the motherboard.

Besides serving as main memory, RAM also provides a memory cache. These memory chips hold their data for as long as the power is on, and are therefore called static RAM (SRAM), pronounced "ESS-RAM." A motherboard can have a lot of main memory to hold data and instructions as they are processed, and a little memory cache to help speed up the access time to main memory. Recall from Chapter 4 that cache memory is contained on the motherboard or inside the CPU housing. On the motherboard, it is either on individual chips or on a memory module called a **COAST (cache on a stick)**. Figure 6-3 shows a motherboard that contains 256K of SRAM installed on the board in two single chips. A COAST slot is available to hold an additional 256K. At first, all cache memory was put on the motherboard, then cache was stored inside the CPU housing, and more recently, we have seen cache for some systems put in both places.

DRAM and SRAM use several technologies, summarized in Table 6-1. Of all the memory technologies listed, the two current DRAM technologies are Direct Rambus DRAM and Double Data Rate SDRAM (SDRAM II). SRAM is stored inside the processor housing on most current desktop motherboards. Other technologies are considered obsolete, although you still need to be aware of them in case you see them on older motherboards you support. You will read more about these technologies in the sections that follow.

Table 6-1   Types of memory (SRAM and DRAM)

Main Memory (DRAM)	Cache Memory (SRAM)
DRAM, needs constant refreshing	SRAM, does not need refreshing
Slower than SRAM because of refreshing time	Faster, but more expensive
Physically housed on DIMMs, SIMMs, and RIMMs	Physically housed on the motherboard on COAST modules or single chips or included inside the processor case

Table 6-1   Types of memory (SRAM and DRAM) (continued)

Main Memory (DRAM)	Cache Memory (SRAM)
Technologies include: • FPM • EDO • BEDO • Synchronous DRAM (SDRAM) • SyncLink SDRAM (SLDRAM) • Double Data Rate SDRAM (DDR SDRAM or SDRAM II) • Direct Rambus DRAM	Technologies include: • Synchronous SRAM • Burst SRAM • Pipelined burst • Asynchronous SRAM • Housed within the processor case (new trend)
Memory addresses assigned	No memory addresses assigned

6

SRAM chip manages cache

Jumpers for cache size selection

2 SRAM chips (128K each)

Memory cache slot (COAST)

Figure 6-3   SRAM on this motherboard is stored in individual chips, and the board also has a COAST slot

Static RAM Technologies

SRAM provides faster access than DRAM because data does not need to be constantly rewritten to SRAM, saving the CPU time used to refresh data in DRAM. Memory chips are made up of transistors, which are switches. An SRAM transistor switch can stay in place as long as it has voltage available, but DRAM transistor switches are charged by capacitors, which must be recharged. SRAM chips are more expensive than DRAM chips. Therefore, most computers have a little SRAM and a lot of DRAM. Table 6-2 summarizes how SRAM is used in different memory caches on and off the motherboard. This table summarizes the information about memory caches in Chapter 4.

Table 6-2 Where memory caches are found in a system

Memory Cache	Where Located
L1 cache	On the CPU die. All CPUs today have L1 cache.
L2 cache	Inside the CPU housing. The first CPU to contain L2 was the Intel Pentium Pro.
L2 cache	On the motherboard of older systems
L3 cache	Inside the CPU housing, further away from the CPU than the L2 cache. The Intel Itanium housing contains L3 cache.
L3 cache	On the motherboard when there is L2 cache in the CPU housing. Used with some newer AMD processors.

How Memory Caching Works Memory caching (see Figure 6-4) is a method used to store data or programs in SRAM for quick retrieval. Memory caching requires some SRAM chips and a cache controller. When memory caching is used, the cache controller anticipates what data or programming code the CPU will request next, and copies that data or programming code to the SRAM chips. Then, if the cache guessed correctly, it can satisfy the CPU request from SRAM without having to access the slower DRAM. Under normal conditions, memory caching guesses right more than 90 percent of the time and is an effective way of speeding up memory access.

The memory controller sends data and control signals over the system bus. The methods used to coordinate how and when data and control signals are sent and read differ with various kinds of memory. SRAM uses a synchronous or asynchronous method (explained below). Synchronous SRAM is more expensive and about 30 percent faster than asynchronous SRAM. Here is a summary of the different types of SRAM:

- **Synchronous SRAM** requires a clock signal to manage or synchronize its control signals; the cache memory can then run in step with the CPU. Synchronous SRAM can be either burst or pipelined burst SRAM.

- With **burst SRAM**, data is sent in a two-step process: first the data address, and then a series of data transmissions.

- **Pipelined burst SRAM** uses more clock cycles per transfer than does burst SRAM without pipelining, but is less expensive.

- **Asynchronous SRAM** does not work in step with the CPU clock, which makes it unable to process as much data in one request and results in overall slower memory access.

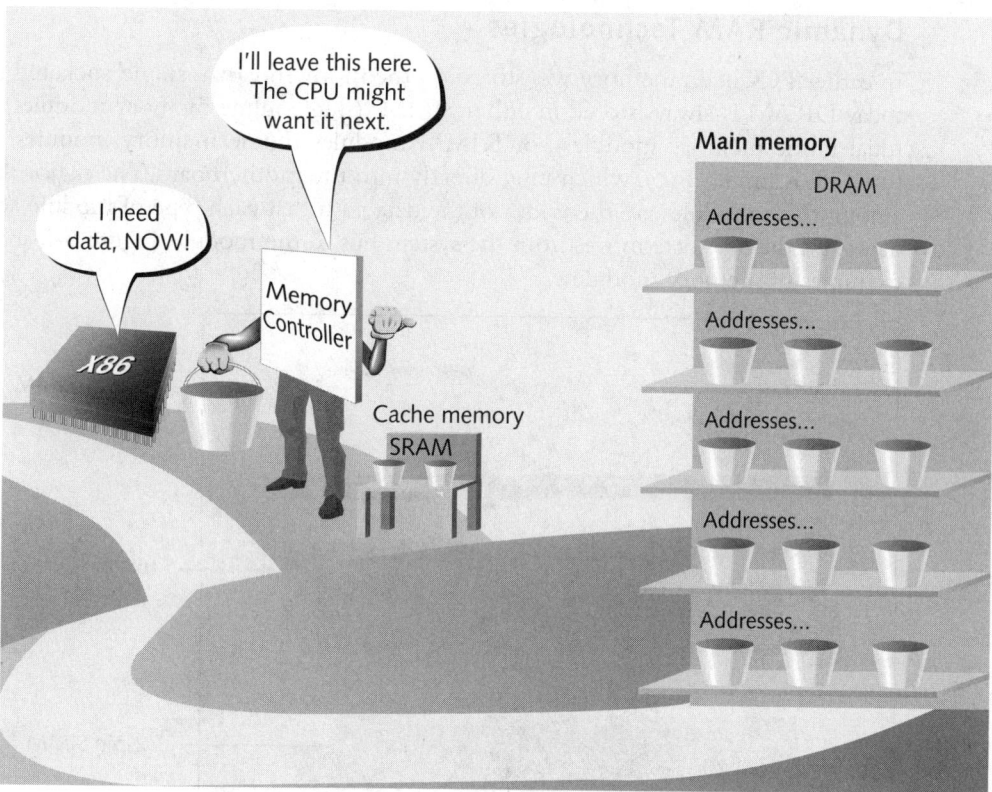

Figure 6-4   A memory cache (SRAM) temporarily holds data in expectation of what the CPU will request next

To understand the difference between asynchronous and synchronous memory, think of this analogy. Children are jumping rope with a long rope, and one child on each end turns the rope. A child who cannot keep in step with the turning rope can only run through on a single pass, and must come back around to make another pass. A child who can keep in step with the rope can run into the center and jump a while, until he or she is tired and runs out. Which child can perform the most rope-jumping cycles in a given amount of time? The one who can keep in step with the rope. Similarly, synchronous memory can retrieve data faster than asynchronous memory can, because it keeps time with the system clock.

SRAM on the Motherboard   Systems today are generally built to include all the SRAM needed for optimum performance. If the cache memory is inside the CPU housing, you have no control over how much is present; it is dependent on the type of CPU you are using, so upgrading cache memory is not a concern.

Older cache memory modules are expensive because they are not used much anymore, so it might be less expensive to replace the motherboard than to upgrade the cache. Before you buy new SRAM, check the documentation for the motherboard to determine which kinds of SRAM the board can support, and then see what kind of SRAM the board already has. You might need to replace the existing SRAM on the board to upgrade to a larger or faster cache.

Dynamic RAM Technologies

In earlier PCs, main memory was stored on the motherboard as single, socketed chips, but today DRAM is always stored in either SIMMs (single inline memory modules), DIMMs (dual inline memory modules), or RIMM modules (inline memory modules manufactured by Rambus, Inc.), which plug directly into the motherboard. The major differences among these modules are the width of the data path that each type of module accommodates and the way data moves from the system bus to the module. Figure 6-5 shows some examples of memory modules.

184-pin RIMM

168-pin DIMM

72-pin SIMM

30-pin SIMM

Figure 6-5 Types of RAM modules

Table 6-3 shows a summary of DRAM technologies, which you will read about in more detail in this section.

Table 6-3 DRAM memory technologies

Technology	Description	Used With
Conventional	Used with earlier PCs but currently not available.	• 30-pin SIMM
Fast page (FPM)	Improved access time over conventional memory. FPM may still be seen today.	• 30-pin or 72-pin SIMM • 168-pin DIMM
Extended data out (EDO)	Refined version of FPM that speeds up access time. Still seen on older motherboards.	• 72-pin SIMM • 168-pin DIMM
Burst EDO (BEDO)	Refined version of EDO that significantly improved access time over EDO. BEDO is seldom used today because Intel chose not to support it.	• 72-pin SIMM • 168-pin DIMM
Synchronous DRAM (SDRAM)	SDRAM runs in sync with the system clock and is rated by clock speed, whereas other types of memory run independently of (and slower than) the system clock.	• 66/100/133/150 MHz, 168-pin DIMM • 66/100/133 MHz, 144-pin SO-DIMM
DDR (Double-data rate) SDRAM	A faster version of SDRAM that can run up to 400 MHz.	• 400/370/333/300/266/200 MHz, 184-pin DIMM • 266 MHz, 200-pin SO-DIMM
Rambus DRAM (RDRAM)	RDRAM uses a faster system bus (800 MHz or 1066 MHz). Currently, a RIMM can use a 16-or 32-bit data path.	• 1066 MHz, 232-pin RIMM using a 32-bit data path • 800 MHz, 232-pin RIMM using a 32-bit data path • 1066 MHz, 184-pin RIMM using a 16-bit data path • 800 MHz, 184-pin RIMM using a 16-bit data path

6

The goal with each new technology is to increase overall throughput while retaining accuracy. FPM was used on motherboards that ranged in speed from 16 to 66 MHz. EDO was used on motherboards rated at about 33 to 75 MHz, and SDRAM and Direct Rambus are used on motherboards rated 66 MHz and higher. The older the motherboard, the older the memory technology it can use, so, as a PC technician, you must be familiar with all these technologies even though the boards sold today only use the latest.

TIP Smaller versions of DIMMs and RIMMs, called SO-DIMMs and SO-RIMMs, exist for use in notebook computers. (SO stands for "small outline.") You will learn more about these in Chapter 12.

SIMM Technologies SIMMs first used FPM and then EDO technologies. **FPM (fast page mode)** memory improved on the earlier memory types by sending the row address just once for many accesses to memory near that row. Earlier memory types required a complete row and column address for each memory access. SIMMs using FPM technology had 30 pins on the edge connector, and came in sizes of 256K to 4 MB. Later FPM SIMMs had 72 pins on the edge connector, came in sizes up to 16 MB, and were slightly longer. **EDO (extended data out)** memory improved on FPM memory. EDO memory is used on 72-pin SIMMs, some earlier DIMMs, and video memory and is often used to provide on-board RAM on various expansion boards. SIMMs are rated by speed, measured in nanoseconds. Common SIMM speeds are 60, 70, or 80 ns. This speed is a measure of access time, the time it takes for the CPU to receive a value in response to a request. Access time includes the time it takes to refresh the chips. An access time of 60 ns is faster than an access time of 70 ns. Therefore, the smaller the speed rating, the faster the chip.

DIMM Technologies DIMMs are also rated by speed and the amount of memory they hold. DIMMs have 168 or 184 pins on the edge connector of the board and hold from 8 MB to 1 GB of RAM. (There is also a 144-pin SDRAM DIMM that is not used with newer motherboards but that you still might see on older systems.) The first DIMMs used EDO or **burst EDO (BEDO)** and then used **synchronous DRAM (SDRAM)** technology. BEDO is a refined version of EDO with improved access time over EDO. BEDO is not widely used today because Intel chose to not support it. BEDO and EDO DIMMs have two notches on the edge connector.

Either 3.3 volts or 5.0 volts can power SDRAM modules. Purchase DIMMs that use the voltage supported by your motherboard. Your motherboard also determines if you can use buffered, unbuffered, or registered DIMMs. Buffers are used by EDO DIMMs, and registers are used by SDRAM DIMMs. Registers and buffers hold data and amplify a signal just before the data is written to the module. To determine which feature a DIMM has, check the position of the two notches on the DIMM module. In Figure 6-6, the position of the notch on the left identifies the module as registered (RFU), buffered, or unbuffered memory. The notch on the right identifies the voltage used by the module. The position of the notches not only helps identify the type of module but also prevents the wrong kind of module from being used on a motherboard.

Synchronous DRAM is currently the most popular memory type. SDRAM is rated by the system bus speed and operates in sync and at the same speed as does the system clock, whereas older types of memory (FPM, EDO, and BEDO) all run at a constant speed. SDRAM currently comes in three variations: regular SDRAM, DDR SDRAM (SDRAM II), and SyncLink (SLDRAM). Of these technologies, DDR SDRAM is the most popular.

Figure 6-6   The positions of two notches on a DIMM identify the type of DIMM and the voltage requirement, and also prevent the wrong type from being installed on the motherboard

Double Data Rate SDRAM (DDR SDRAM), sometimes called **SDRAM II**, runs twice as fast as regular SDRAM and can hold up to 2 GB of RAM. Instead of processing data for each beat of the system clock, as regular SDRAM does, it processes data when the beat rises and again when it falls, doubling the data rate of memory. If a motherboard is running at 100 MHz, then SDRAM II is running at 200 MHz with a data path of 64 bits. DDR SDRAM is supported by a consortium of 20 major computer manufacturers. It is an open standard, meaning that no royalties need to be paid to use it. DDR SDRAM modules have only one notch on the edge connector, whereas regular SDRAM modules have two notches.

SyncLink DRAM (SLDRAM) was developed by a consortium of twelve DRAM manufacturers. It improved on regular SDRAM by increasing the number of memory banks that can be accessed simultaneously from four to sixteen. A **bank** is a location on the motherboard that contains slots for memory modules. Banks are discussed in more detail later in this chapter. SLDRAM did not have enough support in the industry and is now considered obsolete.

RIMM Technologies   **Direct Rambus DRAM** (sometimes called **RDRAM** or **Direct RDRAM** or simply Rambus) is named after Rambus, Inc., the company that developed it. RDRAM data can travel on a 16- or 32-bit data path, and a new RDRAM technology using a 64-bit data path is soon to be released. RDRAM works like a packeted network, not a traditional system bus, and can run at internal speeds of 400 MHz to 1066 MHz, using a 200 to 533-MHz system bus. Current speeds are 800 and 1066 MHz.

RDRAM uses RIMM memory modules. With RIMMs, each socket must be filled so that continuity throughout all sockets is maintained. If the socket does not hold a RIMM, then it must hold a placeholder module called a **C-RIMM (Continuity RIMM)** to ensure continuity throughout all slots. The C-RIMM does not contain any memory chips. (See Figure 6-7.) An earlier version of Rambus memory is Concurrent RDRAM, which is not as fast as Direct RDRAM. Rambus designed the RDRAM technology but does not actually manufacture RIMMs. It licenses the technology to memory manufacturers. Because these manufacturers must pay licensing fees to use RDRAM, the industry might turn more to SDRAM memory advancements than to Rambus, even though Intel is promoting RDRAM. Currently, the industry is still on the fence between the two. A good example of this is the Intel motherboard that supports the Pentium 4 processor, which can be bought to support either DIMMs or RIMMs.

Figure 6-7 A C-RIMM or RIMM must be installed in every RIMM slot on a motherboard

Parity and Error Checking

In older machines, RAM existed as individual chips socketed to the motherboard in banks or rows of nine chips each. Each bank held one byte by storing one bit in each chip, with the ninth chip holding a parity bit (see Figure 6-8). On older PCs the parity chip was separated a little from the other eight chips. **Parity** refers to an error-checking procedure whereby either every byte has an even number of ones or every byte has an odd number of ones. The use of a parity bit means that every byte occupies nine rather than eight bits.

Figure 6-8 Eight chips and a parity chip represent the letter A in ASCII with even parity

Parity is a method of testing the integrity of the bits stored in RAM or some secondary medium, or testing the integrity of bits sent over a communications device. When data is written to RAM, the computer calculates how many ON bits (binary 1) there are in the eight bits of a byte. If the computer uses odd parity, it makes the ninth or parity bit either a 1 or a 0, to make the number of ones in the nine bits odd. Using even parity, the computer makes the parity bit a 1 or 0 to make the number of ones in the nine bits even.

Later, when the byte is read back, the computer checks the odd or even state. If the number of bits is not an odd number for odd parity or an even number for even parity, a **parity error** occurs. A parity error always causes the system to halt. On the screen you see the error message "Parity Error 1" or "Parity Error 2" or a similar error message about parity. Parity Error 1 is a parity error on the motherboard; Parity Error 2 is a parity error on an expansion board. Parity errors can be caused by RAM chips that have become undependable and are unable to hold data reliably. Sometimes this happens when the chips overheat or power falters.

Older DRAM memory used parity checking, but today's memory uses an altogether new method of error checking called **ECC (error-correcting code)** that not only can detect an error in a single bit but also can correct it. Memory modules today are either ECC or non-ECC, and there are some improvements in ECC that might be used by ECC memory. The first ECC method could detect and correct an error in one bit of the byte. Newer ECC methods can detect an error in two bits but cannot correct these double-bit errors.

Some older motherboards support **parity memory**, and some only use **nonparity memory**. If a SIMM has an odd number of chips, most likely it is parity memory; an even number of chips usually indicates nonparity memory. Most manufacturers use nonparity memory to save processing time, and therefore money.

Some SDRAM memory modules support ECC. DIMMs that support ECC have a ninth chip on the module (the ECC chip), whereas it normally has only eight chips. The module is identified as a 71- or 72-bit DIMM instead of a 64-bit DIMM. ECC uses an extra 7 or 8 bits to verify the integrity of every 64 bits stored on the module, and to correct any error, when possible. ECC memory costs more than regular memory but is more reliable.

When buying memory to add to a motherboard, know that in most cases, you must match the type of memory to the type the board supports. Older boards supported either parity or nonparity memory, and newer boards support either ECC or non-ECC memory. In some cases, you can install parity memory on a nonparity board or ECC memory on a non-ECC board, but error checking will not be enabled. To see if your motherboard supports parity or ECC memory, look for the ability to enable or disable the feature in CMOS setup, or check the motherboard documentation.

UPGRADING MEMORY

To upgrade memory means to add more RAM to a computer. Many computers, when first purchased, have empty slots on the motherboard, allowing you to add SIMMs, DIMMs, or RIMMs to increase the amount of RAM. This section describes issues you should consider when purchasing and upgrading memory.

6

What to Look for When Buying Memory Chips and Modules

Memory chips and memory modules are sold at different speeds and sizes and use different technologies and features. This section looks at several of the criteria you should use when buying memory.

Generally, use the fastest memory that your motherboard can support. The documentation for a motherboard states what speed of memory to use on the board, usually written as something like "Use 70 ns or faster." In this example, 60 ns will work on this board, but 80-ns memory will cause problems. (Remember that the smaller the number, the faster the memory.) It is possible, but not recommended, to mix the speed of memory modules on a motherboard, but don't mix the speeds within a single memory bank.

When a computer first boots up, the system must detect what type of memory is installed. To do so, the system can use two methods: Parallel Presence Detect (PPD), which uses resistors to communicate the type of memory present, or Serial Presence Detect (SPD), which stores information about the memory type in EPROM. When purchasing memory for a system, you must match the method used by the module to what the motherboard expects. See the motherboard documentation to know which type to buy. If the board does not specify the method used, assume PPD.

Another feature of memory is called **CAS Latency (CL)**, which reflects the number of clock cycles that passes while data is written to memory. Values are two or three clock cycles. CL2 (CAS Latency 2) is a little faster than CL3 (CAS Latency 3). Again, use the memory type recommended by the motherboard manufacturer.

Chips can be high-grade, low-grade, remanufactured, or used. Poor-quality memory chips can cause frequent **General Protection Fault (GPF)** errors in Windows, application errors, and errors that cause the system to hang, so it pays to know the quality and type of memory you are buying. The following guidelines will help ensure that you are purchasing high-quality memory chips.

Tin or Gold Leads

Memory modules and the banks that hold them can be either tin or gold. On a motherboard, the connectors inside the memory slots are made of tin or gold, as are the edge connectors on the memory modules. Once, all memory sockets were made of gold, but now most are made of tin to reduce cost. You should match tin leads to tin connectors and gold leads to gold connectors to prevent a chemical reaction between the two different metals, which can cause corrosion. Corrosion can create intermittent memory errors and even make the PC unable to boot.

Remanufactured and Used Modules

Stamped on each chip of a RAM module is a chip ID that identifies the date the chip was manufactured. Look for the date in the YYWW format, where YY is the year the chip was made, and WW is the week of that year. For example, 9910 indicates a chip made in the 10th week of 1999. If you see date stamps on a chip that are older than one year, these chips are probably used memory. If some chips are old, but some are new, the module is probably remanufactured. When buying memory modules, look for ones on which all chips have dates that are relatively close together and less than a year old.

Re-Marked Chips

New chips have a protective coating, which gives them a polished, reflective surface. If the surface of the chip is dull or matted, or you can scratch the markings off with a fingernail or knife, suspect that the chip has been re-marked. **Re-marked chips** have been used and returned to the factory, marked again, and then resold.

How Much and What Kind of Memory to Buy

When you add more memory to your computer, ask yourself these questions:

- How much memory do I have, and how much memory do I need?
- How many memory slots are on my motherboard, and what type and size of memory do these slots support?
- How much additional memory is cost-effective?
- What size and type modules should I buy to be compatible with the memory I already have installed?

This section discusses these questions in detail. To find out how much memory is already installed, right-click the My Computer icon and select the General tab. How much memory do you need? With the demands today's software places on memory, the answer is probably, "All I can get." Both Windows 95 and Windows 98 need from 24 MB to 32 MB of memory. Windows 2000 and Windows XP require 64 MB of RAM. But for best performance, install 128 MB into a Windows 9x system and 256 MB into a Windows 2000/XP system.

To know how much memory your system has, for Windows, right click My Computer and select Properties from the drop-down menu. In the System Properties window, click the General tab. To find out what type and size of memory modules your board supports, consult your motherboard documentation. Open the case and look at the memory sockets to determine how many sockets you have and what size and type of modules are already installed. If all the slots are full, sometimes you can take out small-capacity modules and replace them with larger-capacity modules, but you can only use the size of modules that the board is designed to support.

Next decide how many and what size and type of modules to buy. To do that you need to understand how some modules are installed in banks and how a motherboard supports only a certain combination of modules.

How Much Memory Can Fit on the Motherboard?

To determine how much memory your computer can physically hold, read the documentation that comes with your computer. Not all sizes of memory modules fit on any one computer. Use the right number of SIMMs, DIMMs, or RIMMs with the right amount of memory on each module to fit the memory banks on your motherboard. We next look at several examples.

30-Pin SIMMs On older motherboards, 30-pin SIMMs are installed in groups of four. SIMMs in each group or bank must be of the same type and size. See the motherboard documention for the exact combination of SIMMs in each bank that the board can support.

72-Pin SIMMs 72-pin SIMMs have a 32-bit data path and are installed in groups or banks of two to accomodate a 64-bit system bus data path. Most older motherboards that use these SIMMs have one to three banks that can be filled with two, four, or six SIMMs. The two SIMMs in each bank must match in size and speed. See the motherboard documentation for the sizes and type of SIMMs the board supports.

DIMMs Most DIMMs have a 64-bit data path and can thus be installed as a single module rather than in pairs. There are DIMMs with a 128-bit data path that are not presently widely used. Pentium motherboards that use DIMM modules use only one socket to a bank, since a DIMM module accommodates a data path of 64 bits. DIMMs come as either single-sided modules (chips on only one side of the module) or double-sided modules (chips on both sides). Single-sided DIMMs come in 8, 16, 32, 64, and 128 MB sizes, and double-sided DIMMs come in 32, 64, 128, 256, and 512 MB, 1 GB, and 2 GB sizes.

For example, a Pentium motherboard might use 168-pin DIMM modules, and the documentation says to use unbuffered, 3.3V, PC100 DIMM SDRAM modules. The PC100 refers to the speed of the modules, meaning that the modules should be rated to work with a motherboard that runs at 100 MHz. You have the choice of using ECC modules. If you choose not to use them, then CMOS setup should show the feature disabled. There are three DIMM sockets on the board, and each socket represents one bank. Figure 6-9 shows the possible combinations of DIMMs that can be installed in these sockets.

DIMM Location	168-pin DIMM		Total Memory
Socket 1 (Rows 0&1)	SDRAM 8, 16, 32, 64, 128, 256MB	x1	
Socket 2 (Rows 2&3)	SDRAM 8, 16, 32, 64, 128, 256MB	x1	
Socket 3 (Rows 4&5)	SDRAM 8, 16, 32, 64, 128, 256MB	x1	
	Total System Memory (Max 768MB)	=	

Figure 6-9 This table is part of the motherboard documentation and is used to show possible DIMM sizes and calculate total memory on the motherboard

RIMM Modules

When you purchase a system using RIMMs, all RIMM slots will be filled with either RIMMs or C-RIMMs. When you upgrade, you replace one or more C-RIMMs with RIMMs. Match the new RIMMs with those already on the motherboard, following the recommendations of the motherboard documentation.

Table 6-4 gives one example of the RDRAM memory configuration for a motherboard. In the table, an RDRAM device is one chip on a RIMM module that has a 16- or 18-bit data path (with or without ECC). The board uses two RDRAM channels and has two RIMM banks with two slots in each bank. Memory on a RIMM can be stored in one to four channels. Each bank serves one channel, which is why the motherboard is called a dual channel board. It uses PC600 or PC800 RDRAM, which refers to the speeds of 600 MHz or 800 MHz.

The board also supports two densities of RIMMs, either 128/144 Mb or 256/288 Mb, which refers to the amount of data each chip (device) on the RIMM can hold. A RIMM that has four chips, each of which holds 128 Mb or 16 MB of data, yields a RIMM that is 64 MB in size. A chip that is rated 144 Mb is the ECC version of a non-ECC 128-Mb chip. A 256-Mb RIMM has chips that each hold 32 MB of RAM. Multiply that by the number of devices on the RIMM for the RIMM size. The 288-Mb RIMM is the ECC version of the 256-Mb RIMM.

Table 6-4   One motherboard's memory configurations using RIMMs

Rambus Technology	4 RDRAM Devices per RIMM	6 RDRAM Devices per RIMM	8 RDRAM Devices per RIMM	12 RD RAM Devices per RIMM	16 RDRAM Devices per RIMM
128/144 Mb	64 MB	96 MB	128 MB	192 MB	256 MB
256/288 Mb	128 MB	192 MB	256 MB	384 MB	512 MB

The motherboard can hold up to four RIMMS. The first bank on this motherboard must contain two RIMMs, and the second bank can contain two RIMMs or two C-RIMMs. The RIMMs in each bank must have the same size and density, meaning that they must hold the same amount of memory and have the same number of DRAM devices or chips. The RIMMs in one bank must run at the same speed as the RIMMs in the other bank, although the RIMMs in one bank can have a different size and density than the RIMMs in the other bank.

Match Memory Modules to the Motherboard

When you are placing memory on the motherboard, match the type of memory to the motherboard requirements. For example, if the motherboard supports RIMMs and the documentation says that you must use 600 or 800 speed RIMMs, then 700 speed RIMMs will not work. Also, avoid mixing speeds on the same motherboard. For example, if you use a SIMM having one speed in one bank and a SIMM having another speed in the other bank, your computer will only work as fast as the slower bank. Always put the slower SIMMs in the first bank. However, to ensure the most reliable results, use the same speed of SIMMs in all banks and also buy the same brand of SIMMs.

Reading Ads About Memory Modules

Figure 6-10 shows a typical memory module ad listing various types of SIMMs, DIMMs, and RIMMs. When you are selecting memory, the number of pins, the speed, the size, and the type of module are all important. We will now examine the ad to see how all this information is given to us.

MEMORY

72-PIN EDO

16MB	4x32 EDO	6ONS	$8
32MB	8X32 EDO	6ONS	$14
64MB	16X32 EDO	6ONS	$23
128MB	16X32 EDO7	6ONS	$107

168-PIN LONG DIMMS EDO

64MB	8x64	6ONS 3.3VOLT	$77
64MB	8X72 (unbuffered)	6ONS 3.3VOLT ECC	$89
64MB	8X72 (buffered)	6ONS 3.3VOLT ECC	$51
128MB	16X64	6ONS 3.3VOLT	$157
128MB	16X72 (unbuffered)	6ONS 3.3VOLT ECC	$177
128MB	16X72 (buffered)	6ONS 3.3VOLT ECC	$157
256MB	32X72 (buffered)	6ONS 3.3VOLT ECC	$252

168-PIN LONG DIMMS SDRAM (66MHz)

32MB	4X64	$8
64MB	8X64	$11
128MB	16X64	$21

168-PIN SDRAM PC100/133/150

32MB	4X64	8NS	$7
64MB	8X64	8NS	$9
64MB PC133	8X64	7.5NS	$9
64MB	8X72	8NS	$11
128MB	16X64	8NS	$15
128MB PC133	16X64	7.5NS	$15
128MB PC150	16X64	7NS	$18
128MB	16X72	8NS	$17
128MB PC133	16X72	7.5NS	$19
256MB	32X64	8NS	$25
256MB PC133	32X72	7.5NS	$25
256MB PC150	32X64	7NS	$34
256MB	32X72	8NS	$31
256MB PC133	32X72	7.5NS	$31
512MB	64X72	8NS	$72
512 PC133	64X64	7.5NS	$52
512MB PC133	64X72	7.5NS	$77
1024MB PC133	128X72	7.5NS	$244

DDR RAM PC1600/2100

128MB	16X64	200MHZ	$21
128MB	16X64	266MHZ	$21
128MB	16X72	200MHZ	$24
128MB	16X72	266MHZ	$24
256MB	32X64	200MHZ	$36
256MB	32X64	266MHZ	$36
256MB	32X72	200MHZ	$41
256MB	32X72	266MHZ	$41
512MB	64X72	266MHZ	$159

www.corsairmicro.com

CORSAIR

PC100/133/150

CM654S128A-BX2	128MB	16X64	8NS	$29
CM654S128A-133C2	128MB PC133	16X64 CAS2	7.5NS	$31
CM654S128A-150C2	128MB PC150	16X64 CAS2	7NS	$32
CM734S128A-BX2	128MB	16X72	8NS	$32
CM734S128-133	128MB PC133	16X72	7.5NS	$38
CM654S256-BX2	256MB	32X64	8NS	$49
CM654S256-133C2	256 PC133	32X64 CAS2	7.5NS	$51
CM654S256-150C2	256 PC150	32X64 CAS2	7NS	$52
CM724S256-133	256 PC133	32X72	7.5NS	$58
CM724S256-BX2	256MB	32X72	8NS	$58
CM744S512-133	512MB PC133	64X72	7.5NS	$279
CM744S1024-133	1024MB PC133	128X72	7.5NS	$349

GX CHIPSETS

CM734S128A-GX	128MB	16X72	8NS	$31
CM724S256-GX2	256MB	32X72	8NS	$56

RAMBUS

CM616DR128-800	128MB	RDRAM	800MHZ	$52
CM618DR128-800	128MB	RDRAM	800MHZ	$59
CM616DR256-800	256MB	RDRAM	800MHZ	$119
CM618DR256-800	256MB	RDRAM	800MHZ	$127

VALUE SELECT MEMORY PC100/133

VS64MB100	64MB	8X64	8NS	$16
VS64MB133	64MB PC133	8X64	7.5NS	$16
VS128MB100	128MB	16X64	8NS	$20
VS128MB133	128MB PC133	16X64	7.5NS	$20
VS256MB100	256MB PC100	32X64	8NS	$37
VS256MB133	256MB PC133	32X64	7.5NS	$37
VS256REG133	256MB PC133	32X72	7.5NS	$54
VS512MB133	512MB PC133	64X64	7.5NS	$71

DDR RAM PC2100/2400

CM64SD128-2100	128MB	16X64 DDR	266MHZ	$36
CM64SD128-2400C2	128MB (CAS 2)	16X64 DDR	300MHZ	$38
CM64SD128-2100C2	128MB (CAS 2)	16X64 DDR	266MHZ	$41
CM72SD128-2100	128MB	16X72 DDR	266MHZ	$44
CM64SD256-2100	256MB	32X64 DDR	266MHZ	$52
CM64SD256-2400C2	256 MB (CAS 2)	16X64 DDR	300MHZ	$67
CM72SD256-2100	256MB	32X72 DDR	266MHZ	$76
CM72SD256R-2100	256MB (REG)	32X72 DDR	266MHZ	$66
CM72SD512R-2100	512MB (REG)	64X72 DDR	266MHZ	$339

Figure 6-10 Typical memory module ad

The total amount of memory on each module is listed in the first column for some modules and in the second column for others. SIMMs are listed in the ad as 72-pin EDO memory, and the information includes the density of the module, which tells us (1) the width of the data bus, (2) if the module supports error checking, and (3) the size of the module. Here's how it works. The density is written as two numbers separated by a ×, such as 8 × 32, and is read "8 by 32." Let's start with the second number. If the second number is 32 or 64, then it's the width of the data bus in bits, grouped as eight bits to a byte. If the number is 36 or 72, then it's the width of the data bus plus an extra bit for each byte, used for either parity (for parity memory) or error checking and correction (for ECC memory). Look down the second column and note that this company is only offering 32, which means that the memory is not error checking and works on a 32-bit bus. When calculating the size of the module, ignore the ninth bit and use only the values 32 or 64 to calculate size. Convert this number to bytes by dividing the number by 8, and then multiply that value (number of bytes) by the number on the left in the density listing, to get the size of the module. For example, if the density is 8 × 32, then the size of the module is 8 × (32/8) = 8 × 4 = 32 MB.

There are several choices for DIMMs in the ad. For SDRAM, match the speed of the DIMM to the motherboard speed, and match other features to those specified by your motherboard. If the right-hand number in the density is 72, the DIMM is error-checking, and if the number is 64, the DIMM is not error-checking. For Rambus memory, an 18 in the product code indicates error checking, and a 16 does not.

Installing Memory

When installing RAM modules, remember to protect the chips against static electricity, as you learned in Chapter 3. Always use a ground bracelet as you work. Turn the power off and remove the cover to the case. Handle memory modules with care. Don't stack cards, because you can loosen a chip. Usually modules pop easily into place and are secured by spring catches on both ends. Look for the notches on one side or in the middle of the module that orient the module in the slot. For most SIMMs, the module slides into the slot at an angle, as shown in Figure 6-11. (Check your documentation for any instructions specific to your modules.) Place each module securely in its slot. Turn on the PC and watch the amount of memory being counted by POST during the boot process. If all the memory you expect does not count up correctly, power off the system, then remove and reseat each module carefully. To remove a module, release the latches on both sides of the module and gently rotate the module out of the socket at a 45-degree angle.

Figure 6-11 Installing a SIMM module

For DIMM modules, as shown in Figure 6-12, small latches on each side of the slot hold the module in place. Pull the supporting arms on the sides of the slot outward. Look on the DIMM edge connector for the notches, which will help orient the DIMM correctly over the slot, and insert the DIMM straight down into the slot. When the DIMM is fully inserted, the supporting arms should pop back into place. Figure 6-13 shows a DIMM being inserted into a slot on a motherboard.

Figure 6-12   Installing a DIMM module

Figure 6-13   Insert the DIMM into the slot by pressing straight down until the supporting
arms lock into position

For RIMM modules, if a C-RIMM is already in the slot, remove the C-RIMM and then
insert the RIMM. Most often, placing memory on the motherboard is all that is necessary
for installation. When the computer powers up, it counts the memory present without any
further instruction and senses the features that the modules support, such as parity or
ECC. For some computers, you must tell the setup how much memory is present. Read
the motherboard documentation to determine what yours requires.

You will see an example of installing RIMMs when you build a PC in Chapter 14.

6

Troubleshooting Memory

When upgrading memory, if the computer does not recognize new SIMMs, DIMMs, or RIMMs, or if memory error messages appear, do the following:

- Check that you have the right memory modules supported by your motherboard.

- Check that you have installed the right size modules as stated in the motherboard documentation. Verify each module that was already installed or newly installed.

- Remove and reinstall the module. Make sure it is seated in the socket at the same height as other modules.

- Remove the newly installed memory and check if the error message disappears. Try the memory in different sockets. Try installing the new memory without the old installed. If the new memory works without the old, then the problem is that the modules are not compatible.

- Clean the module edge connectors with a soft cloth or contact cleaner. Blow or vacuum dust from the memory sockets.

- Try flashing your BIOS. Perhaps BIOS is having problems with the new memory which can be solved by a BIOS upgrade.

If memory errors such as repeated General Protection Faults occur during normal operation, and you have not just upgraded memory, do the following:

- Run a current version of anti-virus software to check for viruses.

- Run diagnostic software such as PC-Technician to test memory. You will learn more about diagnostic software and hardware in Chapter 13.

- Are the memory modules properly seated? Remove and reinstall each one. For a DIMM module, try a different memory slot.

- Look for bent pins or chips installed the wrong way on cache memory.

- Replace memory modules one at a time. For example, if the system only recognizes six out of eight megabytes of RAM, swap the last two SIMM modules. Did the amount of recognized RAM change? You might be able to solve the problem just by reseating the modules.

- Sometimes a problem can result from a bad socket or a broken trace (a fine printed wire or circuit) on the motherboard. If so, you might have to replace the entire motherboard.

- The problem might be with the OS or applications. Download the latest patch for the software from the manufacturer's Web site.

- If you have just installed new hardware, the hardware device might be giving an error, which is interpreted by the OS as a memory error. Try uninstalling the new hardware.

- A Windows error that occurs randomly and contains this or similar text, "exception fault 0E at >>0137:BFF9z5d0," probably indicates a memory error. Test, reseat, or replace RAM.

> The utility Memtest86 is a good way to test for errors in your installed memory modules. Check the site *www.memtest86.com* to download this program.

FLOPPY DRIVES

In the first part of this chapter, you learned about different types of memory and how memory works, as well as how to install memory on a motherboard. In this section, you will learn how data is stored on a floppy disk, how to manage that data, and how to install a floppy disk drive on a PC. Although many have predicted that floppy drives will become obsolete, their convenience and availability, the low cost of disks, and their proven usefulness and dependability have solidly rooted them in the marketplace and on almost every personal computer system.

Recall that memory is organized in two ways: physically (pertaining to hardware) and logically (pertaining to software). Similarly, data is stored on a secondary storage device physically and logically. Physical storage involves how data is written to and organized on the storage media, while logical storage involves how the OS and BIOS organize and view the stored data. This section explains first how data is physically stored on a floppy disk and then how the OS logically views the data.

How Data Is Physically Stored on a Floppy Disk

Years ago, floppy drives came in two sizes: 5¼ inches and 3½ inches. Today, new computers are equipped with only 3½-inch drives. However, because some older computers still have 5¼-inch floppy disk drives, this section covers 5¼-inch disks as well. Although they are physically larger, 5¼-inch disks do not hold as much data as 3½-inch disks, because they do not store data as densely. Table 6-5 summarizes the capacity of the four common types of floppy disks. The 5¼-inch double-density disks and the 3½-inch extra-high-density disks are hardly ever seen; most disks today are 3½-inch high-density and hold 1.44 MB of data.

Table 6-5   Floppy disk types

Type	Storage Capacity	Number of Tracks per Side	Number of Sectors per Track	Cluster Type
3½-inch extra-high-density	2.88 MB	80	36	2 sectors
3½-inch high-density	1.44 MB	80	18	1 sector
3½-inch double-density	720K	80	9	2 sectors
5¼-inch high-density	1.2 MB	80	15	1 sector
5¼-inch double-density	360K	40	9	2 sectors

6

Regardless of disk size and density, the physical hardware used to access a disk looks and works much the same way. Figure 6-14 shows the floppy drive subsystem, which consists of the floppy disk drive, its cable, and its connections. The data cable leaving the floppy drive leads to a controller for the drive on the motherboard. In older computers, the controller board was plugged into the expansion bus in an expansion slot. The board communicated with the CPU, passing data to and from the floppy disk. These controller boards were called I/O cards and often served multiple functions, having connections for a hard drive, floppy drive, and serial and parallel ports. Today, the controller is built into the motherboard so that the data cable goes directly from the drive to the motherboard.

A floppy drive is connected to either the controller card or motherboard by a 34-pin data cable. The cable has the controller connection at one end and a drive connection at the other. A second drive connection is placed in the middle of the cable to accommodate a second floppy drive. Having two drives share the same cable is a common practice for floppy drives as well as hard drives and other drives.

Floppy drives receive power from the power supply by way of a power cord. The power cord plugs into the back of the drive and has a smaller connection than the power cord for other drives in the system.

Figure 6-14   Floppy drive subsystem: floppy drive, data cable, and power connection

Floppy disks, no matter what density or size, store data in much the same way. When first manufactured, disks have nothing written on them; they are blank sheets of magnetically coated plastic. Before data can be written on the disk, it must first be mapped in concentric circles called **tracks**, which are divided into segments called **sectors** (see Figure 6-15).

Figure 6-15   3½-inch double-density floppy disk showing tracks and sectors

The process of marking tracks and sectors to prepare the disk to receive data is called **formatting** the disk. Figure 6-15 shows a formatted 3½-inch double-density floppy disk. According to Table 6-5, there are 80 tracks, or circles, on the top side of the disk and 80 more tracks on the bottom. The tracks are numbered 0 through 79. Each side of the disk has 9 sectors, numbered 1 through 9. Although the circles, or tracks, on the outside of the disk are larger than the circles closer to the center, all tracks store the same amount of data. Data is written to the tracks as bits, either a 0 or 1. Each bit is a magnetized, rectangular spot on the disk. Between the tracks and spots are spaces that are not magnetized. This spacing prevents one spot from affecting the magnetism of a nearby spot. The difference between a 0 spot and a 1 spot is the orientation of the magnetization of the spot on the disk surface.

Data is written to and read from the disk via a magnetic **read/write head** mechanism in the floppy drive (see Figure 6-16). Two heads are attached at the end of an actuator arm that freely moves over the surface of the disk. The arm has one read/write head above the disk and another below the disk. Moving in unison back and forth across the disk, the two heads lightly touch the surface of the disk, which is spinning at either 300 rpm (revolutions per minute) or 360 rpm, depending on the type of disk. (Note that the read/write heads of a hard drive never touch the surface. You will learn more about hard drives in the next chapter.) Data is written first to the bottom and then to the top of the disk, beginning at the outermost circle and moving in. Tunnel-erase heads on either side of the read/write head, as shown in Figure 6-17, ensure that the widths of the data tracks do not vary. As the data is written, the erase heads immediately behind and to the sides of the write head clean up both sides of the magnetized spot, making a clean track of data with no "bleeding" from the track. The magnetized area does not spread far from the track. All tracks are then the same width, and the distance between tracks is uniform.

Actuator arm

Top read-write head

Disk turns on spindle

Figure 6-16 Inside a floppy disk drive

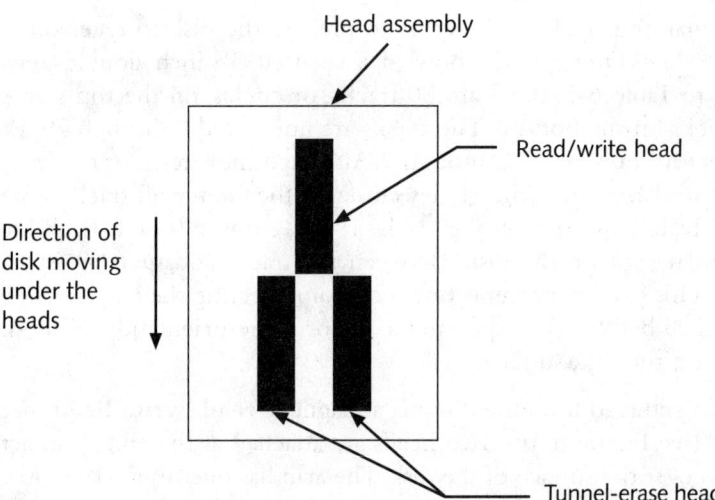

Figure 6-17   Uniform track widths are created by floppy drive read/write heads as the center head writes data while the two tunnel-erase heads clean up from behind

The disk is actually a piece of Mylar similar to that used for overhead transparencies. The surface of the Mylar is covered with a layer of either cobalt oxide or iron oxide (rust) that can hold a magnetic charge. Some floppy disks use another layer of Teflon to protect the oxide layer and to allow the read/write heads to move more smoothly over the surface. During formatting, the tracks are created by laying down a repeating character, the ÷ (division) symbol in ASCII code, which is hex F6 or 1111 0110 in binary. The tracks are divided into sectors, and the sector that starts a new track is marked with a designated code. For 3½-inch floppy disks, the sector address mark written on the disk during formatting marks the beginning sector. After formatting, actual data is written on the disk by overwriting the F6h patterns on the tracks.

Different disk types use varying degrees of magnetic strength when data is written to a disk or when a disk is formatted. For example, a 3½-inch high-density disk can hold more data than a double-density disk because the data is written closer together. Data on the high-density disk is recorded at about twice the magnetic strength as data on the double-density disk. The high-density disk surface is not as sensitive to a magnetic field as the double-density is and therefore can handle data written to it with double the magnetic strength.

When data is read from the disk surface, the read/write head changes roles. It passes over a track, waiting for the right position on the disk to appear. When the correct sector arrives, the controller board opens a gateway, and the magnetic charge on the disk passes voltage to the read/write head. The voltage is immediately amplified and passed to the controller board, which in turn passes the data to the expansion bus.

How Data Is Logically Stored on a Floppy Disk

A **cluster**, sometimes called a **file allocation unit**, is a group of sectors that is the smallest unit on a disk used to hold a file or a portion of a file. "Sector" refers to the way data is physically stored on a disk, while "cluster" describes how data is logically organized. The BIOS manages the disk as physical sectors, but the OS considers the disk only as a long list of clusters that can each hold a fixed amount of data (see Figure 6-18). The OS keeps that list of clusters in the **file allocation table (FAT)**.

Figure 6-18   Clusters, or file allocation units, are managed by the OS in the file allocation table (FAT), but BIOS manages these clusters as one or two physical sectors on the disk

The 3½-inch high-density floppy disk has 80 tracks and 18 sectors per track on each side. Each side has 80 tracks × 18 sectors, or 1,440 sectors. This type of disk has only one sector per cluster, making 1,440 × 2 sides, or 2,880 clusters. Because each cluster holds 512 bytes (one sector) of data, a 3½-inch high-density floppy disk has 2,880 × 512 = 1,474,560 bytes of data. Divide this number by 1,024 to convert bytes to kilobytes. The storage capacity of this disk is 1,440 kilobytes. Divide by 1,000 to convert kilobytes to megabytes, and the storage is 1.44 MB.

 There is a discrepancy in the computer industry regarding the definition of a megabyte. Sometimes 1 megabyte = 1,000 kilobytes; at other times, we use the relationship of 1 megabyte = 1,024 kilobytes.

The Formatting Process for a Floppy Disk

The formatting of all floppy disks is similar, regardless of size or density. During formatting, the Format command without added options performs the following steps:

- Creates the tracks and sectors by writing tracks as a series of F6s in hex and, as necessary, writing the sector address mark to identify the beginning sector on a track
- Creates the boot record (discussed below)
- Creates two copies of the file allocation table (FAT) (discussed in detail on the following page)
- Creates the root directory

These basic steps are described in detail next. Later in this chapter, you will learn how to add options to the Format command.

Creating the Tracks and Sectors

The Format command prepares a disk for use by dividing it into tracks and sectors. The first step in the formatting process erases any data on the disk. In its simplest form, without adding any parameters, the Format command always overwrites existing data with the F6h character.

The Boot Record

At the beginning of each floppy disk, the first sector contains basic information about how the disk is organized. This information includes the number of sectors, the number of sectors per cluster, the number of bits in each FAT entry, and other basic information that an OS or BIOS needs to read the data on the disk. This information is stored in the first sector on the disk, called the **boot sector**, or **boot record**. At the end of the boot record is a small program, called the **bootstrap loader**, that can be used to boot from the disk. Table 6-7 shows the layout of the boot record and its contents. The boot record indicates which version of DOS or Windows was used to format the disk and is always located at the beginning of the disk at track 0, sector 1 (bottom of the disk, outermost track). This uniformity of layout and content allows any version of DOS or Windows to read any floppy disk. (You will learn about hard drive boot records in Chapter 7.)

Table 6-6   Contents of the floppy disk boot record

Bytes per sector
Sectors per cluster
Number of FATs
Size of the root directory
Number of sectors
Medium descriptor byte
Size of the FAT
Sectors per track

Table 6-6 Contents of the floppy disk boot record (continued)

Number of heads (always 2)
Number of hidden sectors
Program to load the OS

The ninth item in Table 6-6 is the number of heads. A head refers to the read/write head that is a part of the physical components of the drive. Because the disk always has only one top and one bottom with a read/write head assigned to each, the number of heads is always two. The last item in Table 6-6 is the program that searches for and loads Io.sys if it is present on the disk. Recall from Chapter 2 that if Io.sys, Msdos.sys, and Command.com are on the disk, the disk is said to be bootable.

All boot records, however, are the same whether or not the disk is bootable. When the PC is looking for a bootable disk during POST, if a disk is in the drive, the program stored in the boot record is executed. If this program does not find Io.sys, the disk is not bootable and a message appears, such as the following:

```
Non-system disk or disk error...Replace and strike any key
when ready...Disk boot failure
```

POST terminates until the user intervenes. Only the program in the boot record can determine if the disk is bootable.

The File Allocation Table (FAT)

When formatting a floppy disk, after the boot record is created, the next step is to write two copies of the FAT to the disk. The FAT lists the location of files on the disk in a one-column table. Because the width of each entry in the column on a floppy disk is 12 bits, the FAT is called a 12-bit FAT, or **FAT12**. The FAT lists how each cluster (or file allocation unit) on the disk is currently used. A file is stored in one or more clusters that do not have to be contiguous on the disk. In the FAT, some clusters might be marked as bad (the 12 bits to mark a bad cluster are FF7h). These bits can be entered in the FAT when the disk is formatted or added later with the Recover command. An extra copy of the FAT is kept immediately following the first. If the first is damaged, sometimes you can recover your data and files by using the second copy. All the clusters that belong to a single file are called a **cluster chain**. If these clusters are not stored consecutively on the disk, the file is called a **fragmented file**.

The Root Directory Table

After creating the file allocation tables, the formatting process sets up the root directory table. Recall that the root directory, or main directory, is a table listing all the files assigned to this table. The root directory contains a fixed number of rows to accommodate a predetermined number of files and subdirectories; the number of available rows is dependent upon the disk type. A 3½-inch high-density floppy disk has 224 entries in the root directory.

The root directory will later contain information about each file and subdirectory stored in it. Each directory entry is 32 bytes long, although only 22 bytes are used. Table 6-7 lists how the 22 bytes are used.

Table 6-7   Root directory information for each file

Root Directory Bytes	Usage
8	Name of file
3	File extension
1	Attribute byte (special meaning for each bit)
10	Not used
2	Time of creation or last update
2	Date of creation or last update
2	Starting cluster number in binary
4	Size of file in binary

Notice that the root directory contains only the starting cluster number. To find out what other clusters store the file, look in the file allocation table. By dividing the size of the file by the number of bytes per cluster and rounding up to the nearest whole number, you can determine how many clusters the file occupies.

Also note that there is no place for the period (often referred to as "dot") that we normally see between the filename and the file extension in OS command lines. The period is not stored in directories but is only used in OS command lines to indicate where the filename ends and the file extension begins. For the long filenames in Windows 9x and Windows NT/2000/XP, more room in the directory is required. This is provided by using more than one entry in the directory for a single file, enough to accommodate the length of the filename. Both the long filename and the DOS version short filename are stored in the directory.

Time and date of creation or last update are stored in a coded form that is converted to a recognizable form when displayed on the screen. The date and time come from the system date and time, which the OS gets from the real-time clock during the boot. At the command prompt, you can change these with the Date and Time commands. Using the Windows desktop, you can change the date and time in the Control Panel. The earliest possible date allowed is 1/1/1980.

The file attributes are used for various purposes. One file attribute byte is broken into bits, and each bit has a specific meaning. The first two bits are not used. The meanings of the other six bits are listed in Table 6-8, beginning with the leftmost bit in the byte and moving to the right. Several of these bits can be changed using the Attrib command.

Table 6-8   Meaning of each bit in the directory attribute byte for each file (reading from left to right across the byte)

Bit	Description	Bit = 0	Bit = 1
1, 2	Not used		
3	Archive bit	Not to be archived	To be archived
4	Directory status	File	Subdirectory

Table 6-8 Meaning of each bit in the directory attribute byte for each file (reading from left to right across the byte) (continued)

Bit	Description	Bit = 0	Bit = 1
5	Volume label	Not volume label	Is volume label
6	System file	Not system file	Is system file
7	Hidden file	Not hidden	Hidden
8	Read-only file	Read/write	Read-only

The root directory and all subdirectories contain the same information about each file. Only the root directory has a limitation on the number of entries. Subdirectories can have as many entries as disk space allows. Because long filenames require more room in a directory than short filenames, assigning long filenames reduces the number of files that can be stored in the root directory.

Using Commands to Manage a Floppy Disk

Two commands to manage a floppy disk are described in this section. Both commands can also be used on hard drives.

Format Drive: /S /V:Volumename /Q /U /Autotest

Recall that the Format command is used to format a disk or a hard drive. Table 6-9 shows options for this command.

Table 6-9 Options for the Format command

Format Command Option	Description
/V	Allows you to enter a volume label only once when formatting several disks. The same volume label is used for all disks. A volume label is displayed at the top of the directory list to help you identify the disk.
/S	Stores the system files on the disk after formatting. Writes the two hidden files and Command.com to the disk, making the disk bootable.
/Q	Recreates the root directory and FATs if you want to quickly format a previously formatted disk that is in good condition. /Q does not read or write to any other part of the disk.
/F:size	Specifies the size of a floppy disk. If the size is not specified, the default for that drive is used. The common values for size are: /F:360 is 360K, double-density 5¼-inch disk /F:1.2 is 1.2 MB, high-density 5¼-inch disk /F:720 is 720K, double-density 3½-inch disk /F:1.44 is 1.44 MB, high-density 3½-inch disk

Table 6-9   Options for the Format command (continued)

Format Command Option	Description
/U	Allows for an unconditional format of the disk, which does a more thorough job of formatting the disk by erasing all data. Use this option when you have been getting read/write errors on the disk. Using the /U option makes it impossible to unformat a disk.
/Autotest	Does not prompt the user before and during the format

Chkdsk [drive:] /F /V

The Chkdsk command reports information about a disk. Use the /F option to have Chkdsk fix errors it finds. These might include errors in the FAT caused by clusters that are marked as being used but that do not belong to a particular file (called **lost clusters**), and by clusters that are marked in the FAT as belonging to more than one file (called **cross-linked clusters**). To check the disk for errors and repair them, use this command:

```
CHKDSK A: /F
```

To redirect the output from the Chkdsk command to a file that you can later print, use this command:

```
CHKDSK A: >Myfile.txt
```

 For hard drives, Chkdsk is mostly outdated by ScanDisk. You will learn more about hard drives in the next chapter.

Using Windows to Manage a Floppy Disk

In Windows, you use Windows Explorer to manage floppy disks. Open Explorer in Windows 9x (click Start, Programs, Windows Explorer, or right-click My Computer and select Explore from the menu) and follow the directions below to manage files and folders on your floppy disk and hard drive.

Shortcut Menu Options

The easiest way to manage drives, disks, folders, and files in Windows Explorer is to use the shortcut menus. To access a shortcut menu, right-click the item or icon representing the item you want to work with. For example, when you right-click the floppy drive item or icon in Explorer, the shortcut menu in Figure 6-19 appears. To format the floppy disk, select Format from the menu.

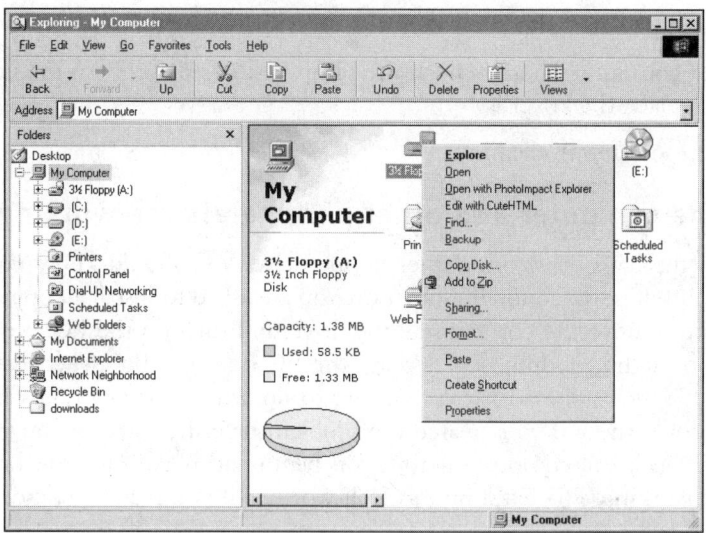

Figure 6-19   Use the shortcut menu to manage items in Explorer

Exchanging and Supporting Floppy Drives

When a floppy drive cannot read a disk or malfunctions in some other way, the problem can have many causes. This section describes problems that can occur with a floppy drive and its support system, how to replace the drive, and how to add an additional floppy drive to a computer system.

Many computers today come with one 3½-inch floppy drive, a hard drive, and a CD-ROM drive. The machine might have one or two empty bays for a second floppy drive or for a Zip drive. If you don't have an extra bay and want to add another drive, you can attach an external drive that comes in its own case and has its own power supply.

Floppy drives are now so inexpensive that it is impractical to repair one. Once you've determined that the drive itself has a problem, open the case, remove the drive, and replace it with a new one. This procedure takes no more than 30 minutes, assuming that you don't damage or loosen something else in the process and create a new troubleshooting opportunity.

Replacing a Floppy Drive

Following is a five-step summary of how to replace a floppy drive. Each step is described in more detail in the sections that follow.

1. Check that the computer and other peripherals are working. Can you boot to the hard drive or another floppy drive? You should know your starting point.

2. Turn off the computer and remove the cover.

3. Unplug the data cable and power cable from the old drive. Unscrew and dismount the drive.

4. Slide the new drive into the bay. Reconnect the data cable and power cable.

5. Turn the computer on and check the setup. Test the drive. Turn the computer off and replace the cover.

Now let's look at each step in detail.

Check that the computer and other peripherals are working.

Can you boot to the hard drive or another floppy drive? You should know your starting point. Imagine yourself in the following situation. You are asked to install a floppy disk drive in a computer. You remove the cover, install the drive, and turn on the PC. Nothing happens. No power, no lights, nothing. Or perhaps the PC does not boot successfully, giving errors during POST that appear to have nothing to do with your newly installed floppy drive. Now you don't know if you created the problem or if it existed before you started. That is why you check the computer before you begin and make sure you know what's working and not working. The extra time is well worth it if you face a situation like this.

Here is a suggestion for a quick system check of a PC that you should do before you start to work:

- Turn on the computer and verify that it boots to the OS with no errors.

- Using Windows, open a program and perform a task from the program.

- Get a directory listing of files on a floppy disk and a CD-ROM.

- If the computer is connected to a printer, print a test page.

Turn off the computer and remove the cover.

As you learned in Chapter 3, guard the computer against static electricity by using a ground bracelet, working on a hard floor (not on carpet), and grounding yourself before you touch any components inside the case. Never touch anything inside the case while the power is on. Remove the cover and set its screws aside in a safe place.

Next, prepare to remove the power cable. The power supply cable is a four-pronged cable that attaches to the back of the drive, as in Figure 6-20. The cable can be difficult to detach because the connection is very secure. Be careful not to apply so much pressure that you break off the corner of the logic board. Steady the board with one hand while you dislodge the power cable with the other.

Floppy drive

Power cord

6

Figure 6-20   Power supply connection on the back of the drive (note how well this drive manufacturer has labeled Pin 1 on the data connection)

Unplug the data cable and power cable from the old drive, and unscrew and dismount the drive.

Before removing the cables and the drive, note carefully how they are assembled, to help you reassemble them later. The data cable might go to an adapter card or directly to the motherboard. Before removing the cable, note that the cable has a color or stripe down one side. This edge color marks this side of the cable as pin 1. Look on the board to which the cable is attached. Verify that pin 1 or pin 2 is clearly marked, either by a number embossed on the board or by a square solder pad on the bottom of the circuit board, and that the colored edge is aligned with pin 1 on both the board and the drive. Sometimes pin 1 on the floppy drive is marked, and sometimes the drive housing is constructed so that the cable built for the drive inserts in only one direction. Note the position of pin 1 on the drive.

Look at the cable connecting drive A to the floppy drive controller card or to the motherboard. There is a twist in the cable. This twist reverses these leads in the cable, causing the addresses for this cable to be different from the addresses for the connection that doesn't have the twist. The position of the twist in the cable determines which drive will be drive A (see Figure 6-21). This drive is always the one that the startup BIOS looks to first for a bootable disk, unless a change has been made in CMOS setup, instructing startup BIOS to look to a different drive. By switching the drive to before or after the twist, you exchange drives A and B. Some computers have two drives attached to the same cable. In this case, the drive attached behind the twist is drive A, and the one attached before the twist is drive B. After you are familiar with the cable orientation and connection, remove the cable from the floppy drive.

Connects to motherboard or older controller card

Edge color on cable indicates the pin 1 side of cable

Drive B connections (2 styles)

Twist in cable

Drive A connector

Figure 6-21   Twist in cable determines which drive will be drive A

Now that the cable is detached, you can remove the floppy drive. Some drives have one or two screws on each side of the drive, attaching the drive to the drive bay. After you remove the screws, the drive usually slides to the front and out of the case. Sometimes you must lift a catch underneath the drive as you slide the drive forward. Be careful not to remove any screws that hold a circuit card on top of the drive to the drive housing; all this should stay intact.

Slide the new drive into the bay. Reconnect the data cable and power cable.

If the new drive is too narrow to fit snugly into the bay, you can buy an adapter kit with extensions for narrow drives that allow them to reach the sides of the bay. Screw the drive down with the same screws used on the old drive. You might have difficulty reaching the screw hole on the back of the drive if it is against the side of the case. Make sure the drive is anchored so that it cannot slide forward or backward or up or down, even if a user turns the case on its side.

Next, you reconnect the data cable, making sure that the colored edge of the cable is connected to the pin 1 side of the connection, as shown in Figure 6-22. Most connections on floppy drives are oriented the same way, so this one probably has the same orientation as the old drive. The power cable goes into the power connection in only one direction. Be careful not to offset the connection by one pin.

Figure 6-22 Connect colored edge of cable to pin 1

Turn the computer on, check the setup, and test the drive.

Double-check all connections and turn on the computer. If you changed disk types, you must inform CMOS setup by accessing setup and changing the drive type. Test the drive by formatting a disk or doing a Diskcopy. If you determine that all is well, replace the cover and you're done.

Note that you can run the computer while the cover is off. If the drive doesn't work, having the cover off makes it easier to turn off the computer, check connections, and try again. Just make certain that you don't touch anything while the computer is on. Leaving the computer on while you disconnect a cable and connect it again is very dangerous for the PC and will probably damage something.

Adding a New Drive

Adding a new drive is no problem if you have an empty bay, an extra power cable, and an extra connection on the floppy drive data cable. Slide the drive into the bay, screw it down, connect the cable and power cable, change setup, and you're done. If you don't have an extra power cable, you can use a "Y" splitter on the power cable for the existing floppy drive, to provide the power connection.

You can test a floppy drive for accuracy and alignment using a digital diagnostic disk designed for that purpose and utility software such as TestDrive by MicroSystems Development Technologies, Inc. (*www.msd.com/diags*).

When a Floppy Disk Drive Doesn't Work

Sometimes a problem with the floppy drive arises during POST, and BIOS displays an error message. Error messages in the 600 range occur when the floppy drive did not pass the POST test. These problems can be caused by the power supply, the drive, the controller board (if one is present), or the motherboard.

Even if POST finds no errors, you might still have a problem. If you put a disk in a faulty drive and issue a command to access the disk, an error message such as the following might appear on the screen:

```
General failure reading drive A, Abort, Retry, Fail?
```

If nothing happens and the computer simply stops working, the problem might have several causes, including the following:

- The application you are running is pointing to a different drive.
- Windows just encountered an unrelated error that has locked up the system.
- The System BIOS or CMOS setup is not correctly configured.
- The disk in the drive is not formatted.
- The floppy drive is bad.
- The shutter window on the floppy disk cannot open fully.
- The cable from the motherboard to the drive is damaged or poorly connected.
- The edge color on the cable is not aligned with pin 1.
- The power supply is bad.
- The power supply cable to the drive is loose or disconnected.
- The command just issued has a mistake or is the wrong command.
- The disk is inserted incorrectly.

You might discover more items to add to this list. I once helped someone with a drive error. We took the 3½-inch floppy disk out of the drive and opened the shuttle window (the spring-loaded metal cover that opens to reveal the disk inside the plastic housing) to find a blade of grass on the disk surface. We removed the grass, and the disk worked perfectly. This person then remembered that she had dropped the disk in the grass. When you have any computer trouble, check the simple things first. Here are a few suggestions for solving drive problems:

- Remove the disk. Does the shuttle window move freely? Do you see any dirt, hair, or other foreign material on the disk's Mylar surface? Does the disk spin freely inside the housing cover? Some new disks simply need a little loosening up. Put the disk back in the drive and try to access it again.

- Does the light on the correct drive go on? Maybe you are trying to access drive B, but the disk is in drive A.

- Does another disk work in the drive? If so, the problem is probably caused by the disk, not the drive. The exception is when the drive is out of alignment. When it is, the drive cannot read a disk that it did not format, although it might read a disk that it formatted with its own alignment. To test this possibility, try several disks, and note whether the drive reads only those disks that it has recently formatted. If so, then you might have identified the problem, and you can replace the drive.

- Does the drive light come on? If not, the problem might be with the software or the hardware. Try to access the disk with other software. Can the OS access the drive with a simple Dir A: command? Can File Manager or Windows Explorer access the disk? How about using the Chkdsk A: command? If the light doesn't come on even then, the problem might involve the power to the drive or the hardware connections inside the case. Does the other drive work? If neither light comes on, consider the power supply or the motherboard as the source of your problem.

- Does the light come on at boot and then stay on? This is most likely caused by the cable not being attached correctly to pin 1. Check the edge color to see that it is aligned with pin 1.

- Has this drive been used recently? Perhaps the system setup has lost CMOS data. The system might think it has a 720K drive when it really has a 1.44-MB drive. Access setup and check the drive specifications. Also check CMOS that drives A and B are not switched. Some setups have this option.

- Reboot the machine and try again. Many problems with computers disappear with a simple reboot. If a soft boot doesn't do it, try a hard boot.

- Try cleaning the drive's read/write heads. Use a head-cleaning kit that includes a paper disk and a cleaning solution. Follow the directions that come with the kit. You can purchase a kit at any store that sells computer supplies.

- If the drive still does not work with any disk and any software, then you must dig deeper. Inside the case, the hardware that can cause this problem is the drive itself, the data cable from the motherboard to the drive, the power supply, the power cable, or the motherboard. To find the culprit, replace each hardware component with a known good component, one component at a time, until the problem goes away. It is helpful to have access to another working computer from which you can borrow parts.

 TIP When you are trying to discover which device is causing a problem during a troubleshooting session, you can trade a suspected device for one you know is good (called a known good device). You can also install the device you suspect is bad in a computer system you know is working. If the problem follows the device, then you know the device is bad.

■ Turn off the computer and open the computer case. Check every connection from the motherboard to the drive. Check the power cable connection.

■ Take the power cable from the second working floppy drive and put it on the nonworking one, to eliminate the power cable as the problem.

■ Replace the data cable and try the drive again. Make sure to align the cable correctly with pin 1. If that does not work, exchange the drive itself and try again.

■ If the drive still does not work, suspect the motherboard or the ROM BIOS on the motherboard. Try flashing ROM.

Some Common Error Messages and Their Meanings

Here are some common error messages that might be caused by problems with a floppy drive, together with what they mean.

```
Non-system disk or disk error. Replace and strike any key
when ready.
No operating system found.
```

These messages say that you are trying to boot from a disk that is not bootable. Remove the disk from the drive and press any key. The computer bypasses the floppy drive and loads the OS from the hard drive. If you intended to boot from the floppy drive, the disk should have been formatted and made bootable as described in Chapter 2.

If you had no disk in the floppy drive, you can assume that some of your critical OS files are missing from the hard drive. In this case, boot from a bootable floppy disk or rescue disk, and check whether the files have been erased accidentally from your hard drive.

```
Bad or missing COMMAND.COM
Error in Config.sys line xx
Himem.sys not loaded
Missing or corrupt Himem.sys
```

These errors appear when the OS is loading and the two hidden files are present, but system files such as Command.com, Config.sys, and Himem.sys, are not present, are corrupt, or, in the case of Config.sys, have an incorrect entry. Replace the missing or corrupt file. To test for errors in Autoexec.bat and Config.sys, you can hold down the F8 key while

DOS is loading; this causes lines in these files to execute one at a time as you watch the screen. Also, press F5 to bypass these two files during the boot.

Incorrect DOS version

This message appears when you try to use a DOS command such as Format or Backup. Remember that these are external commands in DOS because they require a program that is not part of Command.com to execute. DOS contains a number of programs that reside on the hard drive in a directory named \DOS or, in the case of Windows 9x, in a directory named \Windows\Command. When you type the Format or Backup command, you are executing these programs. DOS knows which version of DOS these programs belong to, and the error message indicates that the Format or Backup program you are using does not belong to the same version of DOS that you have loaded. To determine the version of DOS currently loaded, use the VER command. If you get the error when trying to run a DOS application, try using the SETVER command in config.sys.

Invalid Drive Specification

You are trying to access a drive that the OS does not know is available. For example, the error might appear in this situation: During booting, an error message indicates that BIOS cannot access the hard drive. You boot from a floppy disk in drive A and see an A prompt. You then try to access drive C from the A prompt, and you see the above message. DOS or Windows is telling you that it can't find drive C because it failed the test during POST. As far as the OS is concerned, the hard drive does not exist.

Not ready reading drive A:, Abort, Retry, Fail?

This message means the floppy disk in drive A is not readable. Perhaps the disk is missing or is inserted incorrectly. The disk might have a bad boot record, errors in the FAT, or bad sectors.

General failure reading drive A:, Abort, Retry, Fail?

This message means the floppy disk is badly corrupted or not yet formatted. Sometimes this error means that the floppy drive is bad. Try another disk. If you determine that the problem is the disk and not the drive, the disk is probably unusable. A bad boot record sometimes gives this message.

Track 0 bad, disk not usable

This message typically occurs when you are trying to format a disk using the wrong disk type. Check your Format command. Most manufacturers write the disk type on the disk. If you have a 3½-inch floppy disk, you can tell if you are using a high-density or double-density disk by the see-through holes at the corners of the disk. The high-density disk has holes on two corners; the double-density has a hole on only one corner. Don't try to format a disk using the wrong density.

Write-protect error writing drive A:

The disk is write-protected and the application is trying to write to it. To write to a 3½-inch floppy disk, the write-protect window must be closed, meaning that the switch must be toward the center of the disk so that you cannot see through the write-protect hole. To write to a 5¼-inch floppy disk, the write-protect notch must be uncovered.

6

CHAPTER SUMMARY

- SRAM is fast, static RAM and is used as a memory cache, which speeds up the overall computer performance by temporarily holding data and programming that may possibly be used by the CPU in the near future. SRAM does not require constant refreshing.

- DRAM (dynamic RAM) is slower than SRAM because it needs constant refreshing.

- DRAM is stored on three kinds of modules: SIMM, DIMM, and RIMM modules.

- SIMM memory modules can use either EDO or FPM technology. EDO is faster and only slightly more expensive than FPM, but the motherboard must support this type of memory to make use of its increased speed.

- DIMM memory modules can use either BEDO (burst EDO) or synchronous DRAM (SDRAM).

- Direct Rambus DRAM and Double Data Rate SDRAM (DDR SDRAM) are two technologies that are contending to be the next DRAM technology standard.

- Flash memory holds data permanently until it is overwritten, and is commonly used on flash ROM chips and memory cards for notebook computers.

- Synchronous DRAM (which moves in sync with the system bus) is a faster kind of memory than the less expensive asynchronous DRAM (which does not move in sync with the system bus) found on SIMMs.

- When buying memory, use only gold edge connectors on memory modules that will be inserted in slots containing gold connections, and use only tin connectors in tin slots.

- When buying memory, beware of remanufactured and re-marked memory chips, because they have been either refurbished or re-marked before resale.

- RIMMs use a narrower data path than SIMMs or DIMMs in order to provide faster transmission of data. Unlike with SIMMs and DIMMs, data moves from the system bus sequentially through each RIMM module.

- Older motherboards sometimes provided an extra COAST slot to upgrade SRAM, but most systems today come with an optimum amount of SRAM inside the CPU housing and/or on the motherboard.

- When upgrading memory, use the type, size, density and speed of memory that the motherboard supports, and match the memory modules already installed.

- Floppy disks are popular because they are cheap and convenient, and are considered a standard device.

- Data is stored on floppy disks in concentric circles called tracks or cylinders. Each track is divided into sectors. Each sector holds 512 bytes of data.

- Different types of floppy disks vary according to the organization of tracks and sectors, the density at which data can be stored, and the intensity of the magnetic spots on the magnetized plastic surface of the disk.

- The smallest unit of space allocated to a file is called a cluster. On 3½-inch high-density floppy disks, one cluster is the same as one sector, which is 512 bytes.

- When a disk is formatted for use, the formatting process creates tracks and sectors and places a boot record, file allocation table (FAT), and root directory on the disk.

❏ Basic information about how a floppy disk is organized is stored in the first sector of the disk, called the boot sector or the boot record. At the end of a boot record is a small program, called the bootstrap loader, that can be used to boot from the disk.

❏ The file allocation table (FAT) lists the location of files on a disk in a one-column table.

❏ The Format command is used to format floppy disks and logical drives. The /S option with the Format command makes a drive bootable.

❏ Chkdsk checks drives for errors and repairs them.

❏ Windows Explorer can be used to format a floppy disk.

❏ Before beginning to install hardware such as a floppy drive, check the other peripherals so that if you encounter any problems, you will know whether they were preexisting or were caused during the installation.

❏ Error messages in the 600 range occur when a floppy drive does not pass the POST test.

❏ When troubleshooting a floppy drive, check the physical condition of the disk as well as error messages, CMOS settings, and cables connected to the drive.

KEY TERMS

asynchronous SRAM
bank
boot record
boot sector
bootstrap loader
burst EDO (BEDO)
burst SRAM
CAS Latency (CL)
cluster
cluster chain
COAST (cache on a stick)
C-RIMM (Continuity RIMM)
cross-linked clusters
Direct Rambus DRAM
Direct RDRAM
Double Data Rate SDRAM (DDR SDRAM)

dynamic RAM (DRAM)
ECC (error-correcting code)
EDO (extended data out)
EEPROM (electrically erasable programmable ROM)
EPROM (erasable programmable ROM)
FAT12
file allocation table (FAT)
file allocation unit
flash memory
formatting
FPM (fast page mode)
fragmented file
General Protection Fault (GPF)
lost clusters

nonparity memory
parity
parity error
parity memory
pipelined burst SRAM
RDRAM
read/write head
refresh
re-marked chips
SDRAM II
sectors
static RAM (SRAM)
synchronous DRAM (SDRAM)
synchronous SRAM
SyncLink DRAM (SLDRAM)
tracks

7

UNDERSTANDING AND INSTALLING HARD DRIVES

In this chapter, you will learn:

♦ About hard drive technologies
♦ How communication with hard drive BIOS is accomplished
♦ How a hard drive is logically organized to hold data
♦ How to install a hard drive

This chapter introduces hard drive technology and explains how a hard drive is logically organized, how to install one, and what to do when a hard drive fails or produces errors. You will learn how important it is to keep good backups of the file system and data. No amount of experience replacing a defective hard drive can substitute for good backups. The data itself is often the most valuable thing in your computer case.

HARD DRIVE TECHNOLOGY

Two technologies are important to understanding how hard drives work: the technology used within the hard drive to read and write data to the drive, and the technology of how the hard drive interfaces with the system. You will first learn about the different hard drive interfaces and then about the way the drive itself works.

Types of Hard Drive Interfaces

The majority of hard drives interface with the motherboard by means of **Enhanced IDE (EIDE)**, which is an interface standard that applies to other drives besides hard drives, including CD-ROM drives, Zip drives, tape drives, and so forth. EIDE is an extension of **IDE (Integrated Device Electronics**, formerly **Integrated Drive Electronics)** technology.

The EIDE Interface Standards

The Enhanced IDE (EIDE) standards define how hard drives and other drives such as CD-ROM drives, tape drives, and Zip drives relate to the system. The first standard that EIDE drives used was ATA-2. This standard allowed for up to four IDE devices on the same PC. These IDE devices could be hard drives, CD-ROM drives, or tape drives as well as other IDE devices. Drives other than hard drives can use the EIDE interface if they follow the **ATAPI (Advanced Technology Attachment Packet Interface)** standards. As standards were developed, different drive manufacturers adopted different names for them, which can be confusing. Standards today specify data transfer speed more than any other single factor. When selecting a drive standard, select the fastest standard you can, but keep in mind that the operating system, BIOS on the motherboard, and the drive must all support this standard. If one of these three does not support the standard, the other two will probably revert to using a slower standard that all three can use.

Table 7-1 lists the different **ANSI (American National Standards Institute)** standards for IDE drives. The most popular standard today is Ultra ATA/100, which also supports older standards. If you install an ATA/100 hard drive on a single IDE cable with a slower drive, such as an ATA/66 CD-ROM drive, both drives will work, but at the slower speed, 66 MB/per second. Also, ATA/66, ATA/100, and ATA/133 all use a special 40-pin IDE cable that has 40 additional wires used to reduce crosstalk on the cable. These 40 ground wires are in between the signal wires and are all connected to ground. This special IDE cable is called an ATA/100 cable or an **80 conductor IDE cable**.

Using ATA/100 and earlier standards, BIOS and the OS address data on a hard drive using 28 bits for the address, making the largest addressable space on a hard drive 137 GB. A new ATA standard called ATA/ATAPI-6 was incorporated within the ATA/133 standard that allows 48 bits for the address, increasing the addressable space on a hard drive up to 144 petabytes (144,000,000,000,000,000 bytes). For your system to support drives larger than 137 GB, the OS, the system BIOS, the IDE controller, and the hard drive must all support the standard. Windows 98 and higher supports drives larger than 137 GB when a driver provided by the hard drive manufacturer is installed. Before investing in a drive larger than 137 GB, verify that your system BIOS and the IDE controller support it. If your motherboard does not support these drives, first check with the BIOS manufacturer for a possible update and flash BIOS. If an updated BIOS is not available, you can purchase an IDE controller that has compliant BIOS on the card.

There are two cabling methods used by drives larger than 137 GB: the drive can use an 80 conductor IDE cable used by ATA/100 and above (called parallel ATA or PATA), or the drive can use serial ATA (SATA). A serial IDE cable is much narrower and has fewer pins than a parallel IDE cable. The IDE controller must use the same type connector and cabling method as the drive, although you can purchase an adapter to convert an 80 conductor IDE connection on a hard drive to a serial ATA connection. Also, if you want to install an IDE hard drive that uses a newer standard than your motherboard supports, you can install an IDE controller card to support the drive and disable the IDE controller on your motherboard.

 For more information on ATA/ATAPI-6, see the Technical Committee T13 Web site at *www.t13.org*. The T13 committee is responsible for the ATA standards.

Table 7-1   Summary of ANSI interface standards for IDE drives

Standard (may have more than one name)	Speed	Description
IDE/ATA ATA	Speeds range from 2.1 MB/sec to 8.3 MB/sec	The first ANSI hard drive standard for IDE hard drives. Limited to no more than 528 MB. Supports PIO and DMA transfer modes.*
ATA-2 Fast ATA	Speeds up to 16.6 MB/sec	Breaks the 528-MB barrier. Allows up to four IDE devices. Supports PIO and DMA transfer modes.
ATA-3	Little speed increase	Improved version of ATA-2.
Ultra ATA Fast ATA-2 Ultra DMA DMA/33	Speeds up to 33.3 MB/sec	Defined a new DMA mode but only supports slower PIO modes.
Ultra ATA/66 Ultra DMA/66	Speeds up to 66.6 MB/sec	Uses a special 40-pin cable that provides additional ground lines on the cable to improve signal integrity.
Ultra ATA/100	Speeds up to 100 MB/sec	Uses the special 40-pin cable with additional grounding.
Ultra ATA/133	Speeds up to 133 MB/sec	Uses the special 40-pin cable with additional grounding.

*PIO (Programmed I/O) transfer mode uses the CPU to transfer data and is slower than DMA transfer mode that transfers data directly from the drive to memory without involving the CPU.

In most cases, a PC technician does not need to know which IDE standard a hard drive supports, because BIOS autodetection selects the best possible standard supported by both hard drive and BIOS. There are two exceptions. If two hard drives share the same IDE cable and the drives use different standards, both drives will run at the slower speed.

For example, if you connect an ATA/66 drive and an ATA/100 drive on the same cable, both drives will run at 66 MB/per second. Another exception is when you install a new drive and BIOS does not recognize the drive or detects the drive and reports in CMOS setup that the drive has a smaller capacity than it actually does. In this situation, your older BIOS or IDE controller card does not support the newer IDE standard the drive is using. The solution is to either flash BIOS, replace the controller card, or replace the motherboard.

Following the EIDE standard, a motherboard can support up to four EIDE devices. The motherboard offers two IDE connectors, or channels: a primary and secondary channel (see Figure 7-1). Each channel can accommodate an IDE data cable. The cable has two connectors on it: one connector in the middle of the cable and one at the far end for two EIDE devices. An EIDE device can be a hard drive, DVD drive, CD-ROM drive, Zip drive, or other type of drive. One device is configured to act as the master controlling the channel, and the other device on the channel is the slave. There are, therefore, four possible configurations for four IDE devices in a system:

- Primary IDE channel, master device
- Primary IDE channel, slave device
- Secondary IDE channel, master device
- Secondary IDE channel, slave device

These designations are made either by setting jumpers or DIP switches on the devices or by using a special cable-select data cable. You will see an example of an IDE installation later in the chapter.

 When installing a hard drive on the same channel with an ATAPI drive such as a CD-ROM drive, always make the hard drive the master and the ATAPI drive the slave.

Other Interface Standards

Other than EIDE, the second most popular interface for hard drives as well as other drives is SCSI, which is discussed in the next chapter. Some other technologies used to interface between the hard drive and the system bus are IEEE 1394 and Fibre Channel. IEEE 1394, also known as FireWire and i.Link (named by Sony Corporation), was discussed in Chapter 5. It uses serial transmission of data and is popular with multimedia and home entertainment applications. For example, Maxtor, Inc. (*www.maxtor.com*), a large hard drive manufacturer, makes a hard drive designed for home entertainment electronics that uses 1394 for the external hard drive interface (see Figure 7-2).

Hard Drive Technology   321

Figure 7-1   A motherboard has two IDE channels; each can support a master and slave drive using a single IDE 40-pin cable

Figure 7-2   Maxtor 1394 external hard drive

Another example of 1394 providing the interface for a hard drive is fireLINE External HotDrive by Evergreen Technologies. This external hard drive is intended for general-purpose storage and connects to a PC through a 1394 port provided either directly on the motherboard or by way of a 1394 expansion card. Motherboard manufacturers have been slow to provide 1394 support, mostly favoring support for USB instead. Generally, IDE is the slowest, SCSI is midrange, and 1394 is the fastest, with some overlaps in these speeds. For a system to use 1394, the operating system must support it. Windows 98, Windows 2000, and Windows XP support 1394, but Windows 95 and Windows NT do not.

Fibre Channel is another type of interface that can support hard drives. Fibre Channel is designed for use in high-end systems that have multiple hard drives. It competes with SCSI for these high-end solutions. As many as 126 devices can be connected to a single Fibre Channel bus, as compared to 16 SCSI devices, including the host adapter. Fibre

Channel is faster than SCSI when more than five hard drives are strung together to provide massive secondary storage, but it is too expensive and has too much overhead to be a good solution for the desktop PC or workstation.

How Hard Drives Work

Hard drives have one, two, or more platters that are stacked together and spin in unison. Read/write heads are controlled by an actuator and move in unison across the disk surfaces as the disks rotate on a spindle (see Figure 7-3). PCs can use several types of hard drives, all using a magnetic medium on the platters.

Spindle

Platters or disks

Read/write head

Actuator

Figure 7-3   Inside a hard drive case

Figure 7-4 shows a hard drive with four platters. All eight sides of these four platters are used to store data, although on some hard drives the top side of the first platter just holds information used to track the data and manage the disk. Each side, or surface, of one hard drive platter is called a **head**. (Don't confuse this with the read/write mechanism that moves across a platter, which is called a **read/write head**.) The drive in Figure 7-4 has eight heads. Each head is divided into tracks and sectors. The eight tracks shown in Figure 7-4, all of which are the same distance from the center of the platters, together make up one cylinder. If a disk has 300 tracks per head, it also has that same number of cylinders. Just as with floppy disks, data is written to a hard drive beginning at the outermost track. The entire first cylinder is filled before the read/write heads move inward and begin filling the second cylinder.

The drive fits into a bay inside the computer case and is securely attached with supports or braces and screws. This helps prevent the drive from being jarred while the disk is spinning and the heads are very close to the disk surfaces.

Figure 7-4 labels:
Eight tracks (one on each head) make one cylinder
Actuator shaft
Voice coil
Magnet
Magnet housing

Figure 7-4   A hard drive with four platters

A hard drive requires a controller board filled with ROM programming to instruct the read/write heads how, where, and when to move across the platters and write and read data. For today's hard drives, the **hard drive controller** is mounted on a circuit board on or inside the drive housing and is an integral part of it. The controller and the drive are permanently attached to one another. Older drives such as MFM, RLL, ESDI, ST-506, and ST-412 had the controller board as a separate, large expansion card connected to the drive with two cables. Today, the controller of an IDE drive usually connects to the motherboard by way of a data cable from the drive to an IDE connection directly on the motherboard. Older motherboards did not have an IDE connection, so a small **adapter card** served as a simple pass-through from the drive to the motherboard. The data cable attached to the drive and the adapter card, which was inserted in an ISA slot on the motherboard. Sometimes an adapter card connects a hard drive to a motherboard to compensate for a motherboard BIOS that does not support a large-capacity drive. The adapter card contains the necessary BIOS to support the drive in the place of the system BIOS.

IDE Technology

Almost all hard drives on the market today use IDE standards, which use a varying number of sectors for each cylinder, depending on how close to the outer edge the cylinder is. Figure 7-5 shows a hardware subsystem including an IDE hard drive and its connection to a motherboard. In addition to the connection for the 40-pin data cable, the hard drive has a connection for the power cord from the power supply.

Figure 7-5   A PC's hard drive subsystem

Tracks and Sectors on an IDE Drive

Before learning how data is written to a hard drive, let's look at how the track and sector markings are written to the drive. The older MFM and RLL technologies use a straight-forward method of writing the tracks and sectors on the drive. They have either 17 or 26 sectors per track over the entire drive platter (see Figure 7-6). The larger tracks near the outside of the platter contain the same number of bytes as the smaller tracks near the center of the platter. This arrangement makes formatting a drive and later accessing data simpler, but it wastes drive space. The number of bytes that a track can hold is determined by the centermost track, and all other tracks are forced to follow this restriction.

Figure 7-6   Floppy drives and older hard drives use a constant number of sectors per track

Today's IDE drives eliminate this restriction. The number of sectors per track on an IDE drive is not the same throughout the platter. In this new formatting system, called **zone bit recording** (Figure 7-7), tracks near the center have the smallest number of sectors per track, and the number of sectors increases as the tracks get larger. In other words, each track on an IDE drive is designed to have the optimum number of sectors appropriate to the size of the track. What makes this arrangement possible, however, is one fact that has not changed: every sector on the drive still has 512 bytes. If it weren't for this consistency, the OS would have a difficult time indeed communicating with the drive!

36 sectors per track

18 sectors per track

Figure 7-7   Zone bit recording can have more sectors per track as the tracks get larger

Because each track can have a different number of sectors, the OS cannot communicate with an IDE drive by contacting the hard drive controller BIOS and using sector and track coordinates, as it does with floppy disks and older hard drives. Newer, more sophisticated methods must be used that are discussed later in the chapter.

Low-Level Formatting

Recall from Chapter 6 that when the OS formats a floppy disk, it writes sector and track markings on the disk. With IDE drives, since the track and sector markings no longer follow a simple pattern, they are written on the hard drive at the factory. This process is called **low-level formatting**. The OS still executes the remainder of the format process (creating a boot sector, FAT, and root directory), which is called **high-level formatting** or **operating system formatting**.

With older RLL and MFM technology, the system BIOS, OS, or utility software such as Norton Utilities or SpinRite could perform the low-level format; even now a low-level format routine is still part of standard system BIOS. For an IDE drive, however, using system BIOS or standard utility software to low-level format would be a catastrophe. Formatting an IDE drive in this way could permanently destroy the drive, unless the drive controller BIOS were smart enough to ignore the command.

Because IDE drives are low-level formatted by the manufacturer, they cannot be low-level formatted as part of preventive maintenance, as older drives can be. The track and sector markings on the drive created at the factory are normally expected to last for the life of the drive. For this reason IDE drives are often referred to as disposable drives. When the track and sector markings fade, as they eventually do, and the drive gives many "Bad Sector or Sector Not Found" errors or becomes unusable, you just throw the drive away and buy a new one!

However, options for formatting the IDE drive are becoming more commonplace. Some better-known IDE drive manufacturers offer a low-level format program specific to their drives. If an IDE drive continues to give errors or even totally fails, ask the manufacturer for a program to perform a low-level format of the drive. Sometimes these programs are only distributed by the manufacturer to dealers, resellers, or certified service centers.

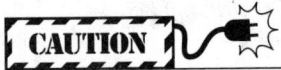

CAUTION

It's risky to low-level format an IDE drive using a format program other than one provided by the manufacturer, although some have tried and succeeded. Probably more drives have been permanently destroyed than saved by taking this risk, however. IDE drives last several years without a refresher low-level format. By that time, you're probably ready to upgrade to a larger drive anyway.

Table 7-2 lists hard drive manufacturers. The same manufacturers usually produce IDE drives (covered in this chapter) and SCSI drives (covered in the next chapter).

Table 7-2   Hard drive manufacturers

Company	URL
Conner Peripherals	www.seagate.com
Fujitsu America, Inc.	www.fujitsu.com
IBM PC Company	www.ibm.com
Maxell Corporation	www.maxell.com
Maxtor Corporation	www.maxtor.com
Seagate Technology LLC	www.seagate.com
Sony Corporation of America	www.sony.com
Western Digital Corporation	www.wdc.com

COMMUNICATING WITH THE HARD DRIVE BIOS

Now that you have learned about physical characteristics of a hard drive, let's look at how the OS and system BIOS communicate with the hard drive BIOS software, before moving on to logical organization of hard drives. Recall from earlier in the chapter that, beginning with IDE hard drives, the number of sectors per track varies from one track to another. Therefore, with IDE drives, the OS and system BIOS could not count on using actual hard drive cylinder, head, and sector coordinates when making requests for data through the hard drive BIOS (which is how requests were made with early hard drives; see Figure 7-8). Instead, sophisticated methods were developed so that system BIOS and the OS could communicate with the hard drive controller BIOS, but only the hard drive controller BIOS dealt with physically locating the data on the drive.

Figure 7-8   With older hard drives, cylinder, track, and sector information was communicated at each level

Calculating Drive Capacity on Older Drives

Back when hard drives were smaller and used a constant number of sectors per track, measuring drive capacity was straightforward. All sectors in a track held 512 bytes regardless of the radius of the track. If you knew the number of tracks, heads, and sectors per track, you could calculate the storage capacity of a drive, because all tracks had the same number of sectors. Software and operating systems were written to interface with BIOS, which managed a hard drive by this method of assuming that for each hard drive there was a fixed relationship among the number of sectors, tracks, heads, and cylinders.

Most system BIOS programs permit a user-defined hard drive type. When you choose a user-defined drive type, you must tell the BIOS setup the number of heads, tracks, and sectors that the drive has, as well as some other information, so that system BIOS knows how to address the drive. This information is usually written on the top of the drive housing.

Using this information, you can calculate the capacity of the drive. For example, the drive capacity for an older drive that has 855 cylinders, 7 heads, and 17 sectors/track is calculated as 855 cylinders $\times$ 7 heads $\times$ 17 sectors/track $\times$ 512 bytes/sector, which gives 52,093,440 bytes. Divide this value by 1,024 to convert to KB and then divide by 1,024 again to convert to MB, yielding a drive capacity of 49.68 MB.

When installing a hard drive, it was once necessary to tell CMOS setup the drive capacity. Today, most system BIOS offers **autodetection**, a method whereby the BIOS detects the new drive and automatically selects the correct drive capacity and configuration.

Adjusting for More Complex Hard Drive Organization

As hard drive size and technology improved, the OS and other software required new methods to relate to hard drive BIOS because of two situations:

- Beginning with IDE technology, the number of sectors per track varied depending on the location of the track, which made it impossible for the OS and software to address the data on the hard drive using actual cylinder, head, and sector parameters.

- When hard drives were small, the maximum size of the parameters that the OS and software sent to hard drive BIOS was established. These maximum values placed limitations on the size hard drive that software can address using actual cylinder, head, and sector parameters. These parameters and values are discussed later in this chapter.

Although new technology was needed to address these issues, it was important for the industry to retain backward-compatibility so that legacy operating systems and other software could work with newer hard drives. As is common in the evolution of computers, clever methods were devised to "trick" older technology so that it could work in newer environments. The older, legacy technology (in this case, software) still sees its world unchanged because the newer technology (in this case, BIOS) shelters it from the new methodology. These "deceptions" can happen at several stages of communication, in the following ways:

- *CHS mode or normal mode used for drives less than 528 MB.* The hard drive can use a complex cylinder, head, and sector organization that only the controller BIOS knows. However, the controller BIOS communicates to system BIOS in terms of the older methodology. When this method is used, the actual organization of the hard drive is called the **physical geometry** of the drive, and the organization communicated to system BIOS is called the **logical geometry** of the drive. This method is called the **CHS (cylinder, head, sector) mode**, or **normal mode**. Using CHS mode, a drive can have no more than 1,024 cylinders, 16 heads, 63 sectors per track, and 512 bytes per sector. Therefore, the maximum amount of storage on a hard drive using CHS mode is 528 MB or 504 MB, depending on how the calculations are done (1K = 1,000 or 1K = 1,024).

- *Large mode or ECHS mode used for drives between 504 MB and 8.4 GB.* The hard drive controller BIOS sends the logical geometry to system BIOS, but system BIOS communicates a different set of parameters to the OS and other software. This method is called **translation**, and system BIOS is said to be in **large mode**, or **ECHS (extended CHS) mode**. Large mode is not as popular as LBA mode.

- *LBA mode used for drives larger than 504 MB.* The hard drive controller BIOS and system BIOS communicate using a method entirely different from cylinder, head, and sector information. System BIOS sends cylinder, head, and sector information to the software, which uses neither logical nor physical geometry. This method of translation is referred to as **LBA (logical block addressing) mode**. System BIOS simply views the drive as a long list of sequential numbers (0, 1, 2, 3, ...) called LBAs or addressable sectors. LBA mode is the most popular way to deal with drives larger than 504 MB and is the only way to deal with drives larger than 8.4 GB.

- The OS and software can bypass the system BIOS altogether and communicate directly with the controller BIOS by using device drivers. This is the method used by Windows NT, Windows 2000, and Windows XP. True to its compromising nature, Windows 9x has its own 32-bit protected mode device drivers to access hard drives, bypassing system BIOS. However, in order to support DOS and other older software, Windows 9x also supports using system BIOS to access drives.

Don't confuse the hard drive capacity with a logical drive capacity. Using large mode, a hard drive can be up to 8.4 GB, but each logical drive (for example, drive C) on the hard drive using the FAT16 file system cannot be that big. For DOS and Windows 9x, FAT16 logical drives can be no larger than 2048 MB, or 2GB. For Windows NT/2000/XP, FAT16 logical drives can be no larger than 4GB.

To use the operating system to report the capacity of a hard drive, at a command prompt, enter the command Chkdsk. For Windows, using Windows Explorer, right-click the drive letter and select Properties from the shortcut menu. Report the capacity of each logical drive on the hard drive and then add them together to get the entire hard drive capacity, assuming all space on the hard drive is partitioned and formatted. For Windows 9x, use Fdisk, and for Windows 2000/XP, use Disk management to report the capacity of an entire hard drive regardless of whether or not the drive is fully partitioned and formatted.

Installations Using Legacy BIOS

The preceding information about how hard drives communicate with system BIOS becomes useful when you are installing a hard drive into a system that has older BIOS. If you want to install a large-capacity drive on a PC whose BIOS does not support it, you have the following choices:

- Let the BIOS see the drive as a smaller drive.

- Upgrade the BIOS.

- Upgrade the entire motherboard.

- Use software that interfaces between the older BIOS and the large-capacity drive.

- Use an adapter card that provides the BIOS to substitute for system BIOS.

This first option may or may not work, depending on your BIOS. Some BIOSs that do not support large-capacity drives do not recognize a large drive, but simply see the larger hard drive as a smaller drive they can support. In this case, the BIOS assigns a drive capacity smaller than the actual capacity. You can use this method, although it wastes drive space.

Most large-capacity drives come with software that performs the translation between an older BIOS and the large-capacity drive. Examples of such translation or disk overlay software are Disk Manager by Ontrack Data International, Inc. (*www.ontrack.com*), SpeedStor by Storage Dimensions, and EZ-Drive by StorageSoft (*www.storagesoft.com*). You can find the software on a floppy disk with the drive or download it from the drive manufacturer's Web site. Boot from a floppy disk with the software installed and follow directions on the screen. A small partition or logical drive is created on the hard drive to manage the drive for the older BIOS. It's important to keep this disk in a safe place, in case you need it to access the hard drive because the software on the drive has become corrupted. A disadvantage of using this method is that if you boot from a regular bootable floppy disk, you might not be able to access the hard drive.

Some hard drives come with disk manager software already installed on the drive. For a drive manufactured by Maxtor, the disk manager software is found in a directory called \MAX in a 112-MB partition that BIOS recognizes as drive C. The rest of the drive is assigned to other partitions or logical drives, such as drive D or drive E.

Adapter cards are available to provide the BIOS that substitutes for system BIOS. This is the recommended method if your motherboard does not have an upgrade for system BIOS. One manufacturer of these cards is Promise Technology, Inc.

The best solution is to upgrade BIOS. However, remember that the new BIOS must also relate correctly to the chip set on the motherboard. Follow the recommendations of the motherboard manufacturer when selecting a BIOS upgrade.

 Some BIOSs support a method of data transfer that allows multiple transfers of data on a single software interrupt. This method is called **block mode** and should be used if your hard drive and BIOS support it. However, if you are having problems with hard drive errors, one thing you can try is disabling block mode. Use CMOS setup to make the change.

HOW A HARD DRIVE IS LOGICALLY ORGANIZED TO HOLD DATA

This section covers how a file system works and how to install one on a hard drive. The goal of this section is to help you understand what must be written on a hard drive so that you can boot from the hard drive and get to a command prompt such as C:\> using the hard drive. For this to happen, the drive must have track and sector markings written on the drive, a file system must be installed, and files needed to boot the PC must be copied to the root directory of the drive.

Recall that today's hard drives come from the factory already low-level formatted (that is, with track and sector markings already in place). When you install one of these hard drives, after the drive is physically installed and system BIOS has recognized the drive and determined the drive capacity, the next step is to install a file system on the drive. For current Windows operating systems, there are three choices of file systems, FAT16, FAT32, and NTFS. All Windows operating systems support FAT16. Windows 95 Second Edition, Windows 98, Windows 2000, and Windows XP support FAT32. Windows NT, Windows 2000, and Windows XP support NTFS. The NTFS file system is best installed during the Windows setup process or after Windows is installed, so it is not covered in this chapter. You can install the FAT16 or FAT32 file system from a command prompt after booting from a startup disk.

For either file system, the high-level divisions are called **partitions**, and within the partitions, the drive is further divided into **logical drives** or **volumes**. Logical drives have letters assigned to them, such as drive C or drive D, and each logical drive has its own file system, such as FAT32 or NTFS, to manage files on the logical drive. This section discusses how partitions and logical drives are organized and used by the OS, and how to use OS commands to partition and format a hard drive for first use.

After the physical installation, preparing a hard drive to hold files requires the following three steps:

1. *Low-level format.* This physically formats the hard drive and creates the tracks and sectors. For hard drives today, this has already been done by the time you buy the drive and does not involve an OS.

2. *Partitioning the hard drive.* Even if only one partition is used, this step is still required. The DOS and Windows Fdisk program sets up a **partition table** at the beginning of the hard drive. This table lists how many partitions are on the drive, their locations, and which partition is the boot partition. Within each partition, Fdisk also creates logical drives, assigning letters to these drives. Using Windows 2000/XP, the Diskpart command can be used at a command prompt or the Disk Management tool can be used within Windows to partition a drive.

3. *High-level format.* This process builds a file system for each logical drive. The OS must do this for each logical drive on the hard drive. As each logical drive is formatted, the OS creates an OS boot record, a root directory, and two copies of FAT for the logical drive, just as it does for a floppy disk. High-level formatting is done using the Format command.

Hard Drive Partitions and Logical Drives

Although you might have a 10-GB hard drive that is only a single physical drive, an OS can divide this single physical drive into more than one logical drive. Using Fdisk, Diskpart, or Disk Management to partition a drive, two kinds of divisions are made. First, the physical drive is divided into one or more partitions, and then each partition is further divided into logical drives or volumes. (A logical drive is sometimes called a logical partition; don't

7

let the two uses of the term "partition" confuse you; partitions and logical partitions are divisions at different levels.) Figure 7-9 shows a typical example in which the hard drive is divided into two partitions. The first partition contains one logical drive (drive C), and the second partition is divided into two logical drives (D and E). The partition table at the very beginning of the drive records all these divisions. The partition table is located in the first sector of the hard drive on head 0, track 0, sector 1. This sector is called the master boot sector or the **Master Boot Record (MBR)**. Table 7-3 lists the contents of a partition table. Don't confuse this first physical sector of the hard drive with sector 1 as Windows knows it. The OS's sector 1 comes after the physical sector 1 and is the first sector in the logical drive C.

Figure 7-9   A hard drive is divided into one or more partitions that contain logical drives

Table 7-3   Hard drive partition table in the MBR

Item	Bytes Used	Description
1	446 bytes	Program that calls the boot program on the OS boot record
2	16-byte total 1 byte 3 bytes 1 byte 3 bytes 4 bytes 4 bytes	Description of the first partition Is this the bootable partition? (Yes = 90h, No = 00h) Beginning location of the partition System indicator; possible values are: 0 = Not a DOS partition 1 = DOS with a 12-bit FAT 4 = DOS with a 16-bit FAT 5 = Not the first partition 6 = Partition larger than 32 MB Ending location of partition First sector of the partition table relative to the beginning of the disk Number of sectors in the partition
3	16 bytes	Describes second partition, using same format as first partition
4	16 bytes	Describes third partition, using same format as first partition
5	16 bytes	Describes fourth partition, using same format as first partition
6	2 bytes	Signature of the partition table, always AA55

The partition table is exactly 512 bytes long, occupying one sector. During POST, the partition table program, which is stored at the beginning of the Master Boot Record, executes and checks the integrity of the partition table itself. If the partition table program finds any corruption, it refuses to continue execution, and the disk is unusable. If the table entries are valid, the partition table program looks in the table to determine which partition is the active partition, and it executes the bootstrap loader program in the boot record of that partition.

 TIP Sometimes the Master Boot Record is the target of a **boot sector virus**, which can cause problems with the boot process and data retrieval. The Windows 9x Fdisk /MBR command or the Windows 2000/XP Fixmbr command is used to repair damage to the program in the MBR.

The **active partition** is the partition on the hard drive that is used to boot the OS. It contains only a single logical drive (drive C), and is always the first partition on the drive. Windows 2000/XP call the active partition the **system partition**.

Using DOS or Windows 9x, a hard drive can have one or two partitions. Using Windows NT/2000/XP, a drive can have up to four partitions. A partition can be a **primary partition** (having only one logical drive in the partition, such as drive C) or an **extended partition** (having more than one logical drive, such as drive D and drive E).

There can be only one extended partition on a drive. Therefore, with DOS and Windows 9x, the drive can have one primary and one extended partition. Under Windows NT/2000/XP, the drive can have four partitions, but only one of them can be an extended partition. The active partition is always a primary partition.

Choice of File Systems

After the hard drive is formatted and ready for use, you are not usually aware that the several logical drives on the hard drive all belong to the same hard drive. For example, Figure 7-10 shows three drives, C, D, and E, that are logical drives on one physical hard drive. If you right-click on one drive, such as drive D in the figure, and select Properties from the shortcut menu, you can see the amount of space allotted to this logical drive and how much of it is currently used. Also note in the figure that drive D is formatted using the FAT32 file system. It is possible for one logical drive to be formatted with one file system and other logical drives on the same hard drive to be formatted with a different file system such as FAT16 or NTFS.

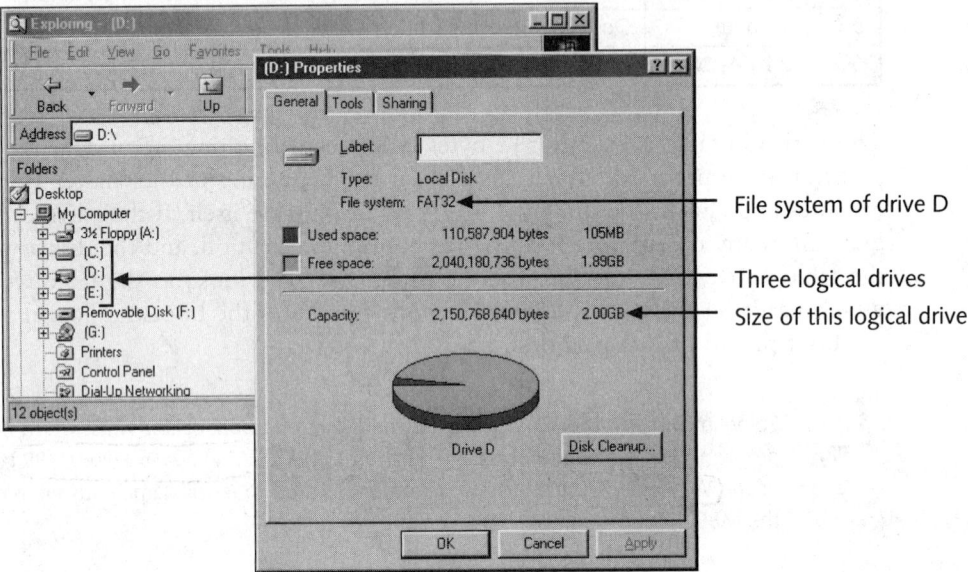

Figure 7-10   This hard drive contains three logical drives

 When partitioning a hard drive using the Windows 9x Fdisk utility, you have two choices for a file system, FAT16 or FAT32. Use FAT32 unless the same PC will also be running Windows NT, which does not support FAT32.

FAT16   DOS and all versions of Windows support the FAT16 file system that uses 16 bits for each cluster entry in the FAT. Using FAT16, the smallest cluster size is four sectors. Each cluster is 512 bytes/sector (4 sectors/cluster, or 2,048 bytes). A one-character file takes up 2,048 bytes of space on a hard drive. For larger drives, the number of sectors in one cluster is even more. When the drive contains many small files, with cluster size so large, these files can create a lot of wasted space called **slack**.

Virtual File Allocation (VFAT)   Windows 95 and Windows for Workgroups offered an improved method of hard drive access, called **VFAT**, or **virtual file allocation table**. VFAT used 32-bit protected-mode device drivers for hard drive access. In Windows for Workgroups, VFAT is called 32-bit file access. The Windows 95 version of VFAT supported long filenames up to 255 characters. Using VFAT, the FAT still used 16 bits per cluster entry. VFAT has been rendered outdated by FAT32.

FAT32   Beginning with Windows 95 OSR2, Microsoft offered a FAT that contains 32 bits per FAT entry instead of the older 12-bit or 16-bit FAT entries. Only 28 of the bits are used to hold a cluster number; the remaining four bits are not presently used.

FAT32 is efficient for logical drives up to 16 GB. In this range, the cluster size is 8K. After that, the cluster size increases to about 16K for drives in the 16-GB to 32-GB range. You are then reaching a drive size that warrants a more powerful file management system than FAT32, such as NTFS. Windows 2000/XP only supports FAT32 for drives up to 32 GB.

If you are currently using FAT16 and are considering switching to FAT32, you can use a third-party utility such as PartitionMagic by PowerQuest Corporation (*www.powerquest.com*) to scan your hard drive and tell you how much of the drive is used for slack space. Knowing this can help you decide if the change will yield you more usable drive space.

How Many Logical Drives?

In addition to creating partitions on a hard drive and deciding which type of file system to use, the Fdisk, Diskpart, or Disk Management is used to create logical drives within these partitions. The active or primary partition has only one logical drive, C. You decide how large this logical drive is when you set the size of the active partition. The extended partition can use all or some of the remaining free space on the drive (some space can go unused). You also decide how large the extended partition is, up to the amount of available free space on the drive. Within the extended partition, you can put several logical drives. You determine how many logical drives and what portion of the extended partition is allotted to each.

Some people prefer to use more than one logical drive to organize their hard drives, especially if they plan to have more than one OS on the same drive. However, the main reason you need multiple logical drives is to optimize space and access time to the drive. The larger the logical drive, the larger the cluster size, and the more slack or wasted space. When deciding how to allocate space to logical drives, the goal is to use as few logical drives as possible and still keep cluster size to a minimum. You can also use FAT32 for very large drives, which results in an even smaller cluster size for the logical drive size.

Table 7-4 gives the information you need to decide how to slice your drive. Notice that the largest logical drive possible using FAT16 is 2 GB (this limitation is rooted in the largest cluster number that can be stored in a 16-bit FAT entry). However, you can see from the table that, to make a drive that big, the cluster size must be huge. Also, the largest hard drive that FAT16 can support is 8.4 GB; if the drive is larger than that, you must use FAT32. The sizes for logical drives using the NTFS file system are included to make the table complete.

Table 7-4 Size of some logical drives compared to cluster size for FAT16, FAT32, and NTFS

File System	Size of Logical Drive	Size of Cluster
FAT16	Up to 128 MB	4 sectors per cluster
	128 to 256 MB	8 sectors per cluster
	256 to 512 MB	16 sectors per cluster
	512 MB to 1 GB	32 sectors per cluster
	1 GB to 2 GB*	64 sectors per cluster
FAT32	512 MB to 8 GB	8 sectors per cluster
	8 GB to 16 GB	16 sectors per cluster
	16 GB to 32 GB	32 sectors per cluster
	More than 32 GB**	64 sectors per cluster
NTFS	Up to 512 MB	1 sector per cluster
	512 MB to 1 GB	2 sectors per cluster
	More than 1 GB	4 sectors per cluster

*For DOS and Windows 9X, the largest FAT16 is 2 GB, for Windows NT/2000/XP, the largest FAT16 is 4GB.
**Windows 2000/XP does not support FAT32 for drives larger than 32 GB.

Fdisk, Diskpart, or Disk Management assigns a drive letter to each logical drive. For a primary partition, drive C is assigned to the one volume, and drives D, E, and so forth are assigned to volumes in the extended partition. However, if a second hard drive is installed in a system, the program takes this into account when assigning drive letters. If the second hard drive has a primary partition, the program assigns it as drive D, leaving drive letters E, F, G, H, and so forth for the volumes in the extended partitions of both hard drives. For example, in a two-hard-drive system where each hard drive has a primary partition, an extended partition, and three logical drives, the drive letters for the first hard drive will be C, E, and F, and the drive letters for the second hard drive will be D, G, and H.

If the second hard drive is not going to be the boot device, it does not have to have a primary partition. If you put only a single extended partition on that drive, then the program assigns the drive letters C, D, and E to the first drive and F, G, H, and so forth to the second drive.

When to Partition a Drive

There are several reasons to partition a drive:

- When you first install a new hard drive, you must partition it to prepare it for use.

- If an existing hard drive is giving errors, you can repartition the drive and reformat each logical drive to begin fresh. You will destroy all data on the drive, so back up important data first.

- If you suspect a virus has attacked the drive, you can back up critical data and repartition it to begin with a clean drive.

- If you want to wipe a hard drive clean and install a new OS, you can repartition a drive in preparation for formatting it with a new file system. If you do not want to change the size of the partitions or the number of partitions, you do not have to repartition the drive.

When installing Windows 9x, before you use the Windows 9x CD for Windows 9x upgrades, you can boot from a bootable disk that has the Fdisk.exe program file on it. Then use Fdisk to partition the hard drive, installing enough of a previous version of Windows to boot from it. During a Windows 9x installation, if the drive is not partitioned, the install procedure automatically executes Fdisk to partition the drive.

You can use Fdisk to partition a drive or you can use some third-party software such as PartitionMagic. Fdisk is simple and easy to use, but PartitionMagic has some advantages over Fdisk. A major one is that when Fdisk partitions a drive, it erases all data on the existing partitions that it changes or overwrites, but PartitionMagic protects data when it changes the partitions on the drive. Also, PartitionMagic has a more user-friendly GUI interface.

There are times when you should not use Fdisk to partition a drive, such as when the drive has been partitioned by third-party software such as Disk Manager or SpeedStor. Recall that these products implement drive translation to enable a large hard drive to exist in a system whose system BIOS does not support large drives. To know if a large hard drive has been partitioned to do disk translation, look for entries in the Config.sys file that point to third-party software to manage the drive. Examples of these command lines are Dmdrvr.bin, Sstor.sys, Harddrive.sys, and Evdisk.sys. If you find lines with these filenames mentioned, use this third-party software to repartition the drive. Know that if you boot from a floppy disk, you cannot access a hard drive that is using drive translation, unless the floppy disk contains the right drivers provided by the drive translation software. Most drive translation software provides a way to create a floppy disk to be used in emergencies when the hard drive does not boot.

TIP Windows 2000 and Windows XP have a command prompt mode called the Recovery Console. By loading the Recovery Console, you get to a C prompt from which you can enter DOS-like commands. One command used at the command prompt is Diskpart, which is similar to the Fdisk program. Using Diskpart, you can create and delete partitions and view information about existing partitions. From within Windows 2000/XP, use Disk Management instead of Diskpart.

Volume Types and Fault Tolerance

Some methods of hard drive partitioning are more fault tolerant than others. **Fault tolerance** is the ability of a computer to respond to a fault or catastrophic event, such as a hardware failure or power outage, in such a way that data is not lost. One data duplication method is **RAID (redundant array of inexpensive disks)**, which involves writing data to multiple hard drives to provide better performance and data recovery. The different types of volumes and types of RAID are listed and described in Table 7-5.

Table 7-5 Types of volumes and RAID levels

Volume Type or RAID Level	Intended Purpose	Description
Simple	Uses only a single hard drive	Simple volumes on dynamic disks are equivalent to the basic drive.
Spanned	Increases system performance and volume capacity	Data fills up one drive before moving on to the next. The set of drives is treated as a single volume (a single virtual drive). Reading from more than one disk can improve performance.
RAID 0: Disk striping without parity	Increases system performance and volume capacity	With disk striping, data is alternately written to two or more hard drives, creating a single logical drive on one or more physical drives. Because more than one drive is doing the work, performance improves.
RAID 1: Disk mirroring or disk duplexing	Provides fault tolerance	Data is written twice, once to each of two drives. Disk mirroring uses only a single HDD controller. Disk duplexing uses two controllers, one for each drive.
RAID 5: Disk striping with parity	Increases performance and volume capacity and provides fault tolerance	Data is written to three or more drives, and parity information is distributed across these drives, so that if one drive fails, the other drives can re-create the data stored on the failed drive.

Windows 9x does not support fault-tolerant methods. Windows NT uses a slightly different terminology to describe fault-tolerant volumes than does Windows 2000/XP.

Table 7-6 summarizes which methods are used by the various OSs. The table uses the prevalent terms that are used in each OS documentation to describe the methods supported.

Table 7-6   Types of volumes and RAID used in different versions of Windows

Windows Version	Volume Types Supported
Windows 9x	---
Windows NT	RAID-0 (striped), RAID-1 (mirrored), RAID-5
Windows 2000	Simple, spanned, striped (RAID-0), mirrored (RAID-1), RAID-5
Windows XP	Simple, spanned, striped (RAID-0), mirrored (RAID-1), RAID-5

Windows 2000 Professional and Windows XP support RAID 0 and call it a **striped volume**. In addition to spanned volumes and striped volumes, Windows 2000 Server and Windows XP support RAID 1, which they call a **mirrored volume**, and RAID 5, which they call a **RAID-5 volume**.

To create any type of RAID volume under Windows 2000 or Windows XP, you must use dynamic drives. However, if you are upgrading from Windows NT and already have a RAID system set up, Windows 2000 and Windows XP support the setup using basic drives. The primary advantage of using dynamic drives over basic drives is that the 1-MB database not only contains information about the volumes on its hard drive, but also contains information about all volumes on all hard drives in the system. This database is automatically replicated on all drives. If one database fails, it is quickly and automatically restored using a copy of the database on another drive. Dynamic drives have little advantage for a system with only a single hard drive, especially considering that only Windows 2000 and Windows XP can read dynamic drives.

What Happens During Formatting

Once you have partitioned a drive and create logical drives within each partition, you use the Format command to format each logical drive. (You will learn more about using these commands later in this chapter, when you learn how to install a drive.) The OS format for each logical drive creates these file system items at the beginning of each logical drive:

- OS boot record

- FAT

- Root directory

An OS boot record at the beginning of a logical drive is used during the boot process to inform the OS how the logical drive is organized. If the logical drive is the boot device, the boot program at the end of the boot record will load the first Windows hidden file, Io.sys, which requires that Msdos.sys and Command.com be present. Table 7-7 shows the complete record layout for the boot record. The medium descriptor byte tells the OS what type of disk this is. The values of this descriptor byte are given in Table 7-8.

Table 7-7 Layout of the boot record on each logical drive

Description	Number of Bytes
Machine code	11
Bytes per sector	2
Sectors per cluster	1
Reserved	2
Number of FATs	1
Number of root directory entries	2
Number of logical sectors	2
Medium descriptor byte	1
Sectors per FAT	2
Sectors per track	2
Heads	2
Number of hidden sectors	2
Total sectors in logical volume	4
Physical drive number	1
Reserved	1
Extended boot signature record	1
32-bit binary volume ID	4
Volume label	11
Type of file system (FAT12, FAT16, or FAT32)	8
Program to load operating system (bootstrap loader)	Remainder of the sector

Table 7-8 Disk type and descriptor byte

Disk Type	Descriptor Byte
3½-inch double-density floppy disk, 720K	F9
3½-inch high-density floppy disk, 1.44 MB	F0
Hard disk	F8

Recall that the total number of bytes for each file entry in a floppy drive directory is 32. The layout of the root directory is the same for hard drives as for floppy disks. Although earlier versions of Windows did limit the number of entries in the root directory, Windows 98 and later Windows OSs do not. Note, however, that Microsoft recommends that you keep only about 150 entries in any one directory. Having any more entries slows access to the directory.

INSTALLING A HARD DRIVE

Now that you have learned about hard drives, we turn our attention to the step-by-step process of installing an IDE hard drive. To install an IDE hard drive, do the following:

1. Set jumpers or DIP switches on the drive, physically install the drive inside the computer case, and attach the power cord and data cable.

2. Inform CMOS setup of the new drive, or verify that autodetect correctly detected the drive.

3. Use the Fdisk utility to create one or more partitions on the drive and divide the extended partition (if there is one) into logical drives.

4. Use the Format command to high-level format each logical drive.

5. Install the OS and other software (not covered in this book).

To install an IDE drive, you need the drive, a 40-pin data cable, and perhaps a kit to make the drive fit into a much larger bay. If the motherboard does not provide an IDE connection, you also need an adapter card.

Prepare for Installation

Remember from earlier chapters that it is a good idea to keep notes whenever you install new hardware or software or make any other changes to your PC system. As with installing any other devices, before you begin installing your hard drive, make sure you know where your starting point is, and take notes so that you can backtrack later if necessary. How is your system configured? Is everything working properly? Verify which of your system's devices are working before installing a new one. Later, if a resource conflict occurs and causes a device to malfunction, the information will help you isolate the problem.

 TIP When installing hardware and software, don't install too many things at once. If something goes wrong, you won't know what's causing the problem. Install one device, bring up the system, and confirm that the new device is working before installing another.

Make sure that you have a good bootable disk or Windows 9x rescue disk; test it to make sure it works. As always, just in case you lose setup information in the process, make sure you have a record of your CMOS setup on a disk or, at the least, write down any variations in setup from the default settings. Two good places to record CMOS settings are the notebook you keep about this computer and the manual for the motherboard.

Read Documentation

Before you take anything apart, carefully read all the documentation for the drive and adapter card, and the part of your PC documentation that covers hard drive installation. Look for problems you have not considered, such as IRQ or DMA conflicts if this is a second hard drive for your system, or if you have an older, limited version of system BIOS. Also check the setup of your computer to be sure it accommodates the size and type of hard drive you want to install. If you plan to choose a user-defined drive type in the setup (where you must enter the drive specifications), make sure your PC accepts the values you want. Check your motherboard documentation or CMOS setup screen.

Plan Drive Configuration

Remember, there can be up to two IDE controllers on a motherboard, the primary and secondary IDE controller. Each controller can support up to two drives, a master and a slave, for a total of up to four IDE drives in a system. When possible, leave the hard drive as the single drive on one controller, so that it does not compete with another drive for access to the controller and possibly slow down performance. Use the primary channel before you use the secondary channel. Put slow devices together on the same controller. For example, suppose you have a Zip drive, CD-ROM drive, and two hard drives. Since the two hard drives are faster than the Zip drive and CD-ROM drive, put the two hard drives on one controller and the Zip drive and CD-ROM drive on the other. Place the fastest devices on the primary channel and the slower devices on the secondary channel. If you have three or fewer devices, allow the fastest hard drive to be your boot device and the only device on the primary channel.

Make sure that you can visualize the entire installation. If you have any questions, find answers to them before you begin. Either keep reading until you locate the answer, call technical support, or ask a knowledgeable friend. You may discover that what you are installing will not work on your computer, but that is better than coping with hours of frustration and a disabled computer. You can't always anticipate every problem, but at least you can know that you made your best effort to understand everything in advance. What you learn in thorough preparation pays off every time!

Prepare Your Work Area and Take Precautions

The next step is to prepare a large, well-lit place to work. Set out your tools, documentation, new hardware, and notebook. Remember the basic rules concerning static electricity, which you learned in Chapter 3. Ground yourself and the computer; wear a ground bracelet during the installation. Avoid working on carpet in the winter, when there's a lot of static electricity.

Some added precautions for working with hard drives are:

- Handle the drive carefully.

- Do not touch any exposed circuitry or chips.

- Prevent other people from touching exposed microchips on the drive.

- When you first take the drive out of the static-protective package, touch the package containing the drive to a screw holding an expansion card or cover, or to a metal part of the computer case, for at least two seconds. This will drain the static electricity from the package and from your body.

- If you must set down the drive outside the static-protective package, place it component-side up on top of the static-protective package on a flat surface.

- Do not place the drive on the computer case cover or on a metal table.

Turn off the computer and unplug it. Unplug the monitor and move it to one side. Remove the computer case cover. Check that you have an available power cord from the power supply.

 TIP If there are not enough power cords from a power supply, you can purchase a Y connector that can add an additional power cord.

Examine the locations of the drive bays and the length of the data cables. Decide which bay will hold which drive. Bays designed for hard drives will not have access to the outside of the case, unlike bays for Zip drives and other drives in which disks are inserted. Also, some bays are wider than others, to accommodate wide drives such as CD-ROM drives and DVD drives (see Figure 7-11). Will the data cable reach to the drives and the motherboard connector? If not, rearrange your plan for locating the drives in the bays, or purchase a custom-length data cable.

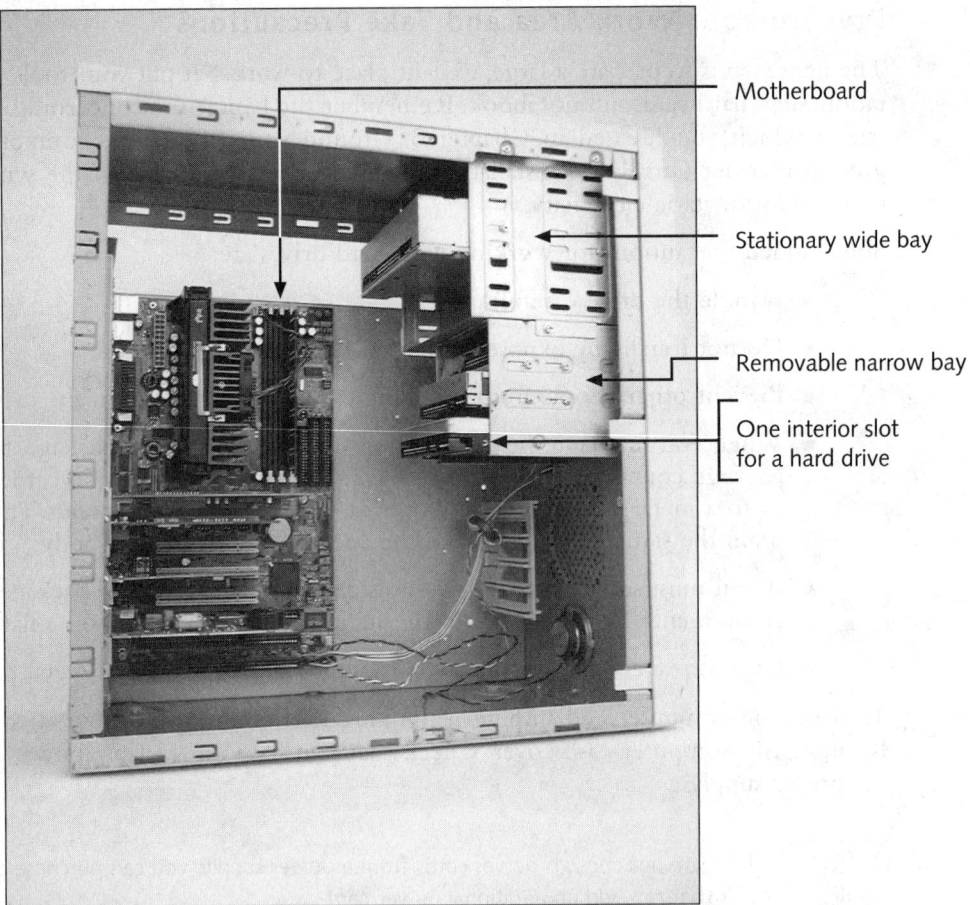

Figure 7-11   Plan for the location of drives within bays

Set Jumpers and DIP Switches

Configuration is normally done by setting jumpers on the drive housing. Often, diagrams of the jumper settings are printed on the top of the hard drive housing (see Figure 7-12). If they are not, see the documentation or visit the Web site of the drive manufacturer. A typical jumper arrangement is shown in Figure 7-13. The four choices for jumper settings for this drive are listed in Table 7-9. Note that your hard drive might not have the first configuration as an option, but it should have a way of indicating if the drive will be the master device. The factory default setting is usually correct for the drive to be the single drive on a system. Before you change any settings, write down the original ones. If things go wrong, you can revert to the original settings and begin again. If a drive is the only drive on a controller, set it to single. For two drives on a controller, set one to master and the other to slave.

Diagrams of jumper settings

Figure 7-12   An IDE drive most likely will have diagrams of jumper settings for master and slave options printed on the drive housing

Some hard drives have a cable select configuration option. If you choose this configuration, you must use a cable-select data cable. When you use one of these cables, the drive nearest the motherboard is the master, and the drive farthest from the motherboard is the slave. You can recognize a cable-select cable by a small hole somewhere in the data cable.

JB

5 3 1
6 4 2
Single drive configuration

5 3 1
6 4 2
Master drive configuration (dual drives)

5 3 1
6 4 2
Slave drive configuration (dual drives)

Key: ■ Jumper added
        ▪ Jumper pins

Figure 7-13   Jumper settings on a hard drive and their meanings

Table 7-9   Jumper settings on an IDE hard drive

Configuration	Description
Single-drive configuration	This is the only hard drive on this IDE channel. (This is the standard setting.)
Master-drive configuration	This is the first of two drives; it most likely is the boot device.
Slave-drive configuration	This is the second drive using this channel or data cable.
Cable-select configuration	The cable-select data cable determines which of the two drives is the master and which is the slave.

Mount the Drive in the Bay

Next, look at the drive bay that you will use for the drive. The bay might be stationary, or it might be removable. With a removable bay, you first remove the bay from the computer case and mount the drive in the bay. Then the bay is put back into the computer case. In Figure 7-14, you can see a stationary bay for large drives and a removable bay for small drives, including the hard drive. In this example, you will see how the hard drive is installed in a computer case that has three other drives: a CD-ROM drive, a Zip drive, and a floppy drive. Do the following to install the hard drive in the bay:

1. Remove the bay for the hard drive and insert the hard drive in the bay. You can line up the drive in the bay with the front of the computer case (see Figure 7-14) to see how drives will line up in the bay. Put the hard drive in the bay flush with the front of the bay so it will butt up against the computer case once the bay is in position (see Figure 7-15). Line up other drives in the bay so they are flush with the front of the computer case. In our example, a floppy drive and Zip drive are already in the bay.

2. You must be able to securely mount the drive in the bay; the drive should not move when it is screwed down. Line up the drive and bay screw holes, and make sure everything will fit. After checking the position of the drive and determining how screws are placed, install four screws (two on each side) to mount the drive in the bay.

CAUTION

Be sure the screws are not too long. If they are, you can screw too far into the drive housing and damage the drive itself.

Stationary bay
for large drives

Floppy drive

Removable bay
for small drives

7

Figure 7-14   Line up the floppy drive in the removable bay, flush with the front
of the case

Floppy drive

Zip drive

Hard drive

Figure 7-15   Position the hard drive flush with the end of the bay

Do not allow torque to stress the drive. For example, don't force a drive into a space that is too small for it. Also, placing two screws in diagonal positions across the drive can place pressure diagonally on the drive.

3. Decide whether to connect the data cable to the drive before or after you insert the bay inside the computer case, depending on how accessible the connections are. In this example, the data cables are connected to the drives first and then the bay is installed inside the computer case. In the photograph in Figure 7-16, the data cables for all the drives in the bay are connected to the drives.

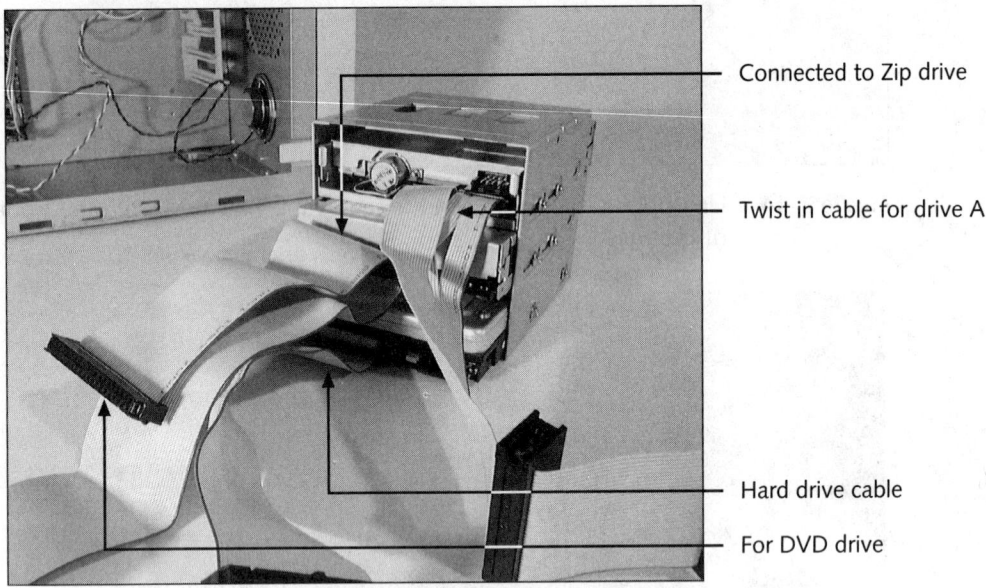

Connected to Zip drive

Twist in cable for drive A

Hard drive cable

For DVD drive

Figure 7-16   Connect the cables to all three drives

4. The next step is to place the bay back into position and secure the bay with the bay screw or screws (see Figure 7-17).

Figure 7-17 Secure the bay with the bay screw

5. Install a power connection to each drive (Figure 7-18). In Figure 7-18, the floppy drive uses the small power connection, and the other drives use the large ones. It doesn't matter which of the power cords you use, because they all produce the same voltage. Also, the cord only goes into the connection one way.

Figure 7-18 Connect a power cord to each drive

6. Next, connect the data cable to the IDE connector on the motherboard. See Figure 7-19. Make certain pin 1 and the edge color on the cable are aligned correctly at both ends of the cable. Normally, pin 1 is closest to the power connection.

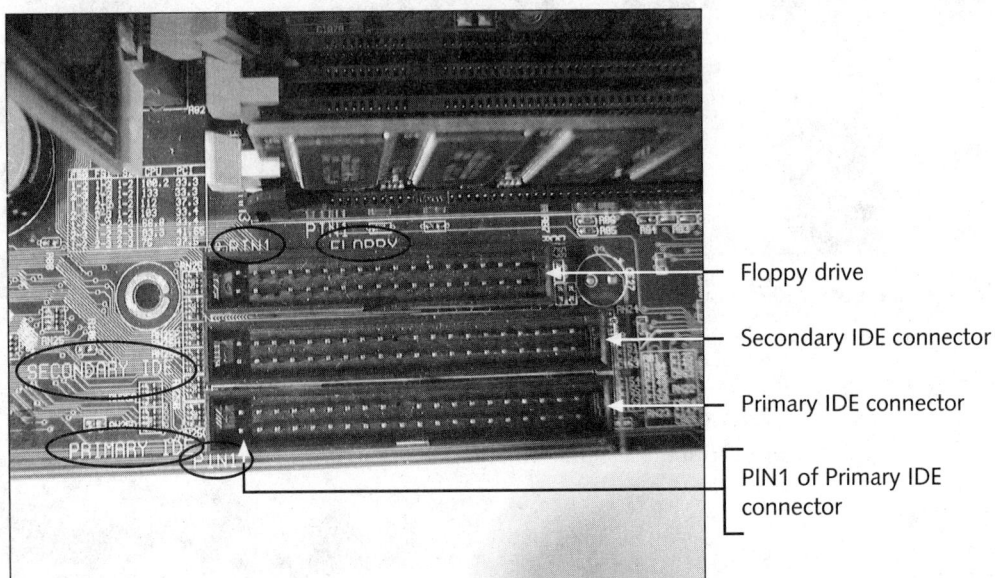

Figure 7-19 Floppy drive and two IDE connectors on the motherboard

7. If you are mounting a hard drive in an external bay, install a bay cover in the front of the case. Internal bays do not need this cover (see Figure 7-20).

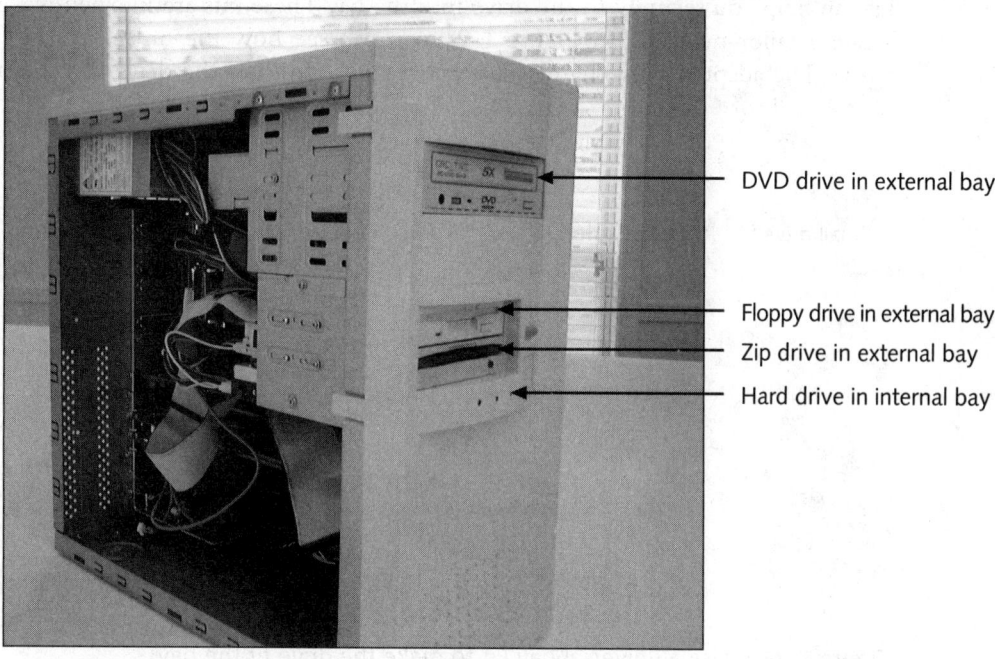

— DVD drive in external bay

— Floppy drive in external bay
— Zip drive in external bay
— Hard drive in internal bay

Figure 7-20   A tower case may have internal or external bays

8. When using a motherboard connection, if the wire connecting the motherboard to the hard drive light on the front of the case was not connected when the motherboard was installed, connect it now. If you reverse the polarity of the LED wire, the light will not work. Your motherboard manual should tell you the location of the LED wires on the motherboard.

TIP If the drive light does not work after you install a new drive, try reversing the LED wire on the motherboard pins.

9. Before you replace the computer case, plug in the monitor and turn on the computer. Verify zthat your system BIOS can find the drive before you replace the cover and that it recognizes the correct size of the drive. If you encounter problems, refer to the troubleshooting section later in this chapter.

If the Bay Is Too Large

If you are mounting a hard drive into a bay that is too large for the drive, a universal bay kit can help you securely fit the drive into the bay. These kits are inexpensive and should create a tailor-made fit. In Figure 7-21 you can see how the universal bay kit adapter works. The adapter spans the distance between the sides of the drive and the bay.

Figure 7-21   Use a universal bay kit to make the drive fit the bay

Use CMOS Setup to Change Hard Drive Settings

When you first boot up after installing a hard drive, go to CMOS setup and verify that the drive has been recognized and that the settings are correct. Figure 7-22 (a,b,c,d) shows the four screens that are typical in setup programs, which allow you to change hard drive parameters. In Figure 7-22a, you can see the choice for IDE HDD Auto Detection in the third item in the second column. For most hard drive installations, if Auto Detection is not enabled, enable it, save, and exit setup. Later, after you have rebooted with the new drive detected, you can return to setup, view the selections that it made, and make changes where appropriate.

Setup for Large-Capacity Hard Drives

Recall that the two ways BIOS relates to large-capacity drives are LBA and large mode. Notice in Figure 7-22b the column labeled mode, referring to how BIOS relates to the drive. Choices are normal, large, LBA, and auto. Most likely, when auto is the choice, setup will automatically select LBA.

```
                    ROM PCI/ISA BIOS (<<P2B>>)
                        CMOS SETUP UTILITY
                       AWARD SOFTWARE, INC.

   STANDARD CMOS SETUP              SUPERVISOR PASSWORD
   BIOS FEATURES SETUP              USER PASSWORD
   CHIPSET FEATURES SETUP           IDE HDD AUTO DETECTION
   POWER MANAGEMENT SETUP           SAVE & EXIT SETUP
   PNP, AND PCI SETUP               EXIT WITHOUT SAVING
   LOAD BIOS DEFAULTS
   LOAD SETUP DEFAULTS

   Esc : Quit                       ↑↓→← : Select Item
   F10 : Save & Exit Setup          (Shift)F2 : Change Color
```

Figure 7-22a CMOS setup utility opening menu

```
                    ROM PCI/ISA BIOS (<<P2B>>)
                       STANDARD CMOS SETUP
                       AWARD SOFTWARE, INC.

  Date (mm:dd:yy) : Wed, Mar 25 1998
  Time (hh:mm:ss) :  9 :  5 :  2

  HARD DISKS     TYPE    SIZE   CYLS   HEAD   PRECOMP   LANDZ   SECTOR   MODE
  Primary Master  : Auto    0      0      0        0       0        0    NORMAL
  Primary Slave   : None    0      0      0        0       0        0    ----------
  Secondary Master: Auto    0      0      0        0       0        0    NORMAL
  Secondary Slave : None    0      0      0        0       0        0    ----------

  Drive A : 2.88M, 3.5 in.
  Drive B : 1.44M, 3.5 in.
  Floppy 3 Mode Support : Disabled      Base Memory    :   ØK
                                        Extended Memory :  ØK
  Video  : EGA/VGA                      Other Memory   :   512K
  Halt On : All Errors                  Total Memory   :   512K

  Esc : Quit        ↑↓→← : Select Item        PU/PD/+/- : Modify
  F1  : Help        (Shift)F2 : Change Color
```

Figure 7-22b Standard CMOS setup

In Figure 7-22c (starting with the 10th item in the second column), you can see the hard drive features that the chip set on this motherboard supports. They are Ultra DMA, PIO, and DMA modes. Leave all these settings at Auto and let BIOS make the choice according to its detection of the features your hard drive supports.

In Figure 7-22d, you can see in the 12th item of the first column that BIOS on this motherboard supports block mode. From this screen you can also select the boot sequence (see the ninth item in the first column). Choices for this BIOS are A, C; A, CD Rom, C; CD Rom, C, A; D, A; F, A; C only; Zip, C; and C, A. Also notice on this screen (eighth item in the first column) that this BIOS supports booting from a SCSI drive even when there is an IDE drive present. Booting from the IDE drive is the default setting.

```
                    ROM PCI/ISA BIOS (<<P2B>>)
                       CHIPSET FEATURES
                      AWARD SOFTWARE, INC.

SDRAM Configuration      : By SPD   Onboard FDC Controller       : Enabled
SDRAM CAS Latency        : 2T       Onboard FDC Swap A & B        : No Swap
SDRAM RAS to CAS Delay   : 3T       Onboard Serial Port 1        : 3F8H/IRQ4
SDRAM RAS Precharge Time : 3T       Onboard Serial Port 2        : 2F8H/IRQ3
DRAM Idle Timer          : 16T      Onboard Parallel Port        : 378H/IRQ7
SDRAM MA Wait State      : Normal   Parallel Port Mode           : ECP+EPP
Snoop Ahead              : Enabled  ECP DMA Select               : 3
Host Bus Fast Data Ready : Enabled  VART2 Use Infrared           : Disabled
16-bit I/O Recovery Time : 1BUSCLK  Onboard PCI IDE Enable       : Both
8-bit I/O Recovery Time  : 1BUSCLK  IDE Ultra DMA Mode           : Auto
Graphics Aperture Size   : 64MB     IDE0 Master PIO/DMA Mode     : Auto
Video.Memory Cache Mode  : UC       IDE0 Slave  PIO/DMA Mode     : Auto
PCI 2.1 Support          : Enabled  IDE1 Master PIO/DMA Mode     : Auto
Memory Hole At 15M-16M   : Disabled IDE1 Slave  PIO/DMA Mode     : Auto

DRAM are 64 (Not 72), bits wide
Data Integrity Mode      : Non-ECC  Esc : Quit           ↑↓→←  : Select Item
                                    F1  : Help     PU/PD/+/-    : Modify
                                    F5  : Old Values (Shift)F2 : Color
                                    F6  : Load BIOS  Defaults
                                    F7  : Load Setup Defaults
```

Figure 7-22c   CMOS setup for chip set features

```
                    ROM PCI/ISA BIOS (<<P2B>>)
                       BIOS FEATURES SETUP
                      AWARD SOFTWARE, INC.

CPU Internal Core Speed   : 350Mhz  Video  ROM BIOS  Shadow  : Enabled
                                    C8000  - CBFFF   Shadow  : Disabled
Boot Virus Detection      : Enabled CC000  - CFFFF   Shadow  : Disabled
CPU Level 1 Cache         : Enabled D0000  - D3FFF   Shadow  : Disabled
CPU Level 2 Cache         : Enabled D4000  - D7FFF   Shadow  : Disabled
CPU Level 2 Cache ECC Check : Disabled D8000 - DBFFF  Shadow  : Disabled
BIOS Update               : Enabled DC000  - DFFFF   Shadow  : Disabled
Quick Power On Self Test  : Enabled
HDD Sequence SCSI/IDE First : IDE   Boot Up NumLock Status     : On
Boot Sequence             : A,C     Typematic Rate Setting     : Disabled
Boot Up Floppy Seek       : Disabled Typematic Rate (Chars/Sec) : 6
Floppy Disk Access Control : R/W    Typematic Delay (Msec)     : 250
IDE HDD Block Mode Sectors : HDD MAX
Security Option           : System
PS/2 Mouse Function Control : Auto  Esc : Quit          ↑↓→←  : Select Item
PCI/VGA Palette Snoop     : Disabled F1 : Help     PU/PD/+/-    : Modify
OS/2 Onboard Memory > 64M : Disabled F5 : Old Values (Shift)F2 : Color
                                    F6  : Load BIOS  Defaults
                                    F7  : Load Setup Defaults
```

Figure 7-22d   CMOS setup for BIOS features

After you have confirmed that your drive is recognized and that all its settings are correct, you will use the Fdisk and Format commands to set the logical organization of the drive.

Use Fdisk to Partition a Drive

To use Fdisk, boot from a startup disk that has the Fdisk.exe utility on it and enter Fdisk at the command prompt. The Fdisk opening menu shown in Figure 7-23 appears. Select option 1 to create the first partition. The menu in Figure 7-24 appears. Use option 1 to create the primary DOS partition. If you plan to install Windows 9x later, be sure this partition is at least 150 MB, preferably more. Make this first partition the active partition, which is the partition that is used to boot the OS. Fdisk automatically makes this partition drive C.

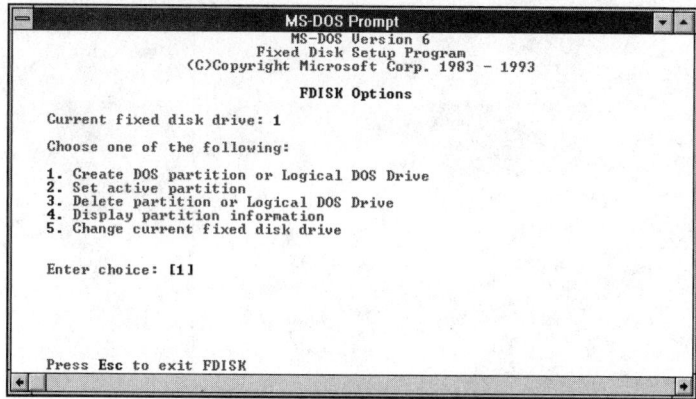

Figure 7-23   Fixed disk setup program (FDISK) menu

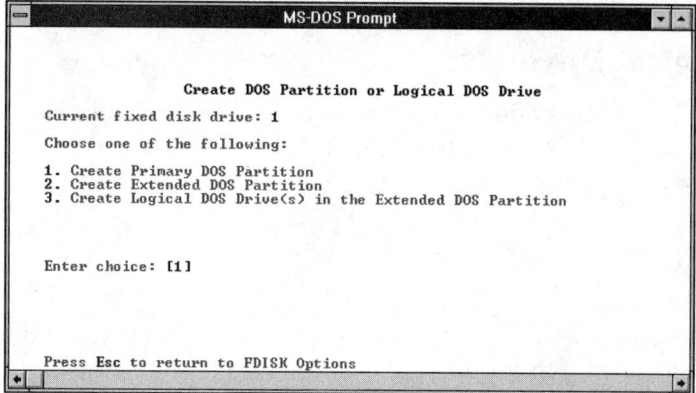

Figure 7-24   FDISK menu to create partitions and logical drives

Next, use option 2, shown in Figure 7-24, to create an extended DOS partition using the remainder of the hard drive. Then use option 3 to create logical drives in the extended partition.

When you are creating logical drives using Fdisk, you decide how large you want each drive to be. If you have at least 512 MB available for the drive, a message appears asking, "Do you wish to enable large disk support (Y/N)?" If you respond Y, then Fdisk assigns the FAT32 file system to the drive. Otherwise, it uses FAT16.

When Fdisk is completed, the hard drive has a partition table, an active and extended partition, and logical drives within these partitions. As seen in Figure 7-23, you can choose option 4 to display partition information (see Figure 7-25). After you exit the FDISK window, reboot the PC before you format the logical drives.

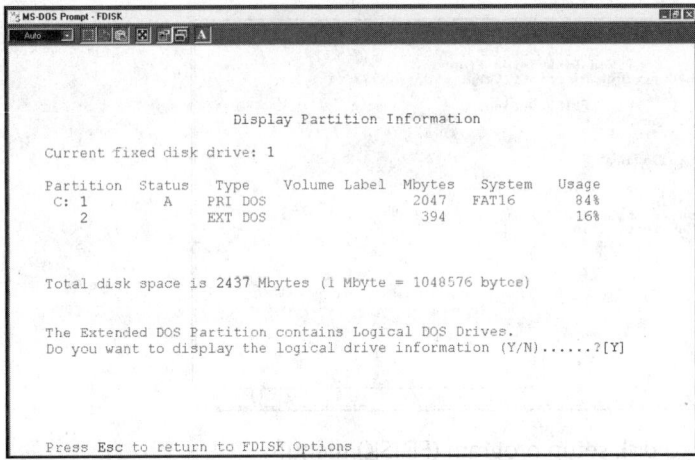

Figure 7-25   FDISK displays partition information

Format Each Logical Drive

Now that the hard drive is partitioned and logical drives have been created and assigned drive letters, the next step is to format each logical drive. The three commands used to format logical drives C, D, and E are:

```
Format C:/S
Format D:
Format E:
```

In the Format command line, the /S option makes the drive bootable, and the drive letter tells the OS which drive to format.

Using Windows to Partition and Format a New Drive

If you are installing a new hard drive in a system that is to be used for a new Windows installation, it is not necessary to boot from a bootable startup disk. After you have physically installed the drive, boot from the Windows setup CD and follow the directions on the screen to install Windows on the new drive. The setup process will partition and format the new drive before it begins the Windows installation. Also, if you are installing a second hard drive in a system that already has Windows 2000/XP installed on the first hard drive, use Windows to partition and format the drive. After physically installing the second hard drive, boot into Windows as usual. Then use Disk Management to partition and format the new drive. The details of using Disk Management are not covered in this chapter.

 Fdisk under Windows 98 can incorrectly display the size of hard drives larger than 64 GB. The capacity will be reported as the true capacity, less 64 GB. For example, Fdisk will show a 120 GB drive to be 56 GB (120 GB – 64 GB). For drives larger than 64 GB, check with the hard drive manufacturer for freeware that you can use to partition and format the drive. For instance, Western Digital has Data Lifeguard Tools and Maxtor has MaxBlast software. When using Windows 9X, for drives larger than 64GB, check with the hard drive.

A Note on Moving a Hard Drive or Changing BIOS

When you move a large-capacity hard drive from one computer to another, you can lose data. If you use large mode on the first computer and LBA mode on the other, you might not be able to access the drive's data. Also, the translation methods for LBA mode might not be the same from one BIOS to another. For this reason, back up the data on the drive before you move it. If the BIOS on the new computer does not let you access the data on the drive, you can partition and format the drive again, and then move the backed-up data onto the newly formatted drive.

Don't change options in setup unless you are sure of what you are doing. You might also lose access to the data on the drive if you have formatted and stored data on a hard drive using one mode and then change to a different mode in setup. Returning to the correct mode might not solve the problem, because changing modes can destroy data. To recover access to the hard drive (although data may be lost), repartition and reformat the drive using the correct mode.

CHAPTER SUMMARY

- Most hard drives today use IDE technology, which has a complex method of organizing tracks and sectors on the disks.

- There are several ANSI standards that pertain to hard drives, including IDE, ATA, Fast ATA, Ultra ATA, Ultra ATA/66, Ultra ATA/100, and Ultra ATA/133.

- Hard drive capacity for drives less than 8.4 GB is determined by the number of heads, tracks, and sectors on the disk, each sector holding 512 bytes of data.

❑ For the FAT file system, the DOS or Windows operating system views a hard drive through a FAT (file allocation table), which lists clusters, and a directory, which lists files.

❑ A hard drive is divided into partitions, which might also be divided into logical drives, or volumes. A Master Boot Record (MBR) at the beginning of the hard drive contains a table of partition information. Each logical drive contains a boot record, FAT, and root directory for the FAT file system.

❑ To create a RAID volume using Windows 2000 or Windows XP, you must use a dynamic drive.

❑ Physical geometry is the actual organization of heads, tracks, and sectors on the drive, whereas logical geometry is head, track, and sector information that the hard drive controller BIOS presents to system BIOS and the OS. The logical geometry may not be the same as the physical geometry, but, for drives less than 8.4 GB, should yield the same capacity when calculations are made.

❑ Drives larger than 8.4 GB use LBA mode, whereas the BIOS and OS view the drive as addressable sectors. The capacity of the drive is calculated as the number of addressable sectors multiplied by the number of bytes per sector, which is almost always 512 bytes.

❑ System BIOS and software can use CHS, large mode, or LBA mode to manage a hard drive. The size of the drive and the drive manufacturer determine which mode is used.

❑ The FAT, or file allocation table, lists all clusters on the hard drive and describes how each is allocated. FAT16 uses 16-bit entries, VFAT enabled Windows to use 32-bit protected-mode device drivers for hard drive access, and FAT32 uses 32-bit entries to hold the cluster numbers.

❑ DOS and the first release of Windows 95 support the FAT16 file system for hard drives. Windows 95 Release 2 and Windows 98 support FAT16 and FAT32 file systems. Windows NT supports FAT16 and the NTFS file systems. Windows 2000 and XP support FAT16, FAT32, and the NTFS file systems.

❑ The FAT16 file system can be used for drives less than 8.4 GB. Larger drives use the FAT32 or the NTFS file system.

❑ Commands to manage a hard drive include Fdisk, Diskpart, Format, Defrag, and ScanDisk.

❑ Some ways to optimize drive space and access speed are to reduce fragmentation and to scan the disk for errors.

❑ Installing a hard drive includes setting jumpers or DIP switches on the drive; physically installing the adapter card, cable, and drive; changing CMOS setup; and partitioning, formatting, and installing software on the drive.

❑ An IDE device such as a hard drive can be installed as a master drive, slave drive, or single drive on a system.

❑ The EIDE standards support two IDE connections, a primary and a secondary. Each connection can support up to two IDE devices for a total of four devices on a system.

❑ IDE devices under the EIDE standard can be hard drives, CD-ROM drives, tape drives, Zip drives, and others.

❑ Large-capacity hard drives must have either LBA mode or large mode set in CMOS in order for system BIOS to support the drive. Without this support, other options can be used, including device driver software or a special EIDE adapter card specific to the drive.

❑ Protect the drive and the PC against static electricity during installation.

❑ Most BIOSs today can autodetect the presence of a hard drive if the drive is designed to give this information to BIOS.

❑ For DOS or Windows 9x, a drive must have one primary partition and can have one extended partition. The drive boots from the primary partition. The extended partition can be subdivided into several logical drive partitions. Windows NT, Windows 2000, and Windows XP support four partitions, one of which can be an extended partition.

❑ Use more than one partition to optimize the cluster size, to handle drives greater than 2 GB when using FAT16, or to improve the organization of the software and data on the drive.

❑ With FAT32, the hard drive can be partitioned using a single partition with a single logical drive.

❑ The OS, or high-level format for the FAT file system, creates the FATs, root directory, and boot record on the drive and marks any bad clusters in the FAT that the low-level format has previously identified.

❑ Low-level formats should be used as a last resort to restore an unreliable IDE hard drive. Use only the low-level format program recommended by the drive manufacturer.

Key Terms

80 conductor IDE cable

active partition

adapter card

ANSI (American National Standards Institute)

ATAPI (Advanced Technology Attachment Packet Interface)

autodetection

backup

block mode

boot sector virus

chain

CHS (cylinder, head, sector) mode

ECHS (extended CHS) mode

enhanced BIOS

Enhanced IDE (EIDE)

extended partition

fault tolerance

hard drive controller

head

high-level formatting

Integrated Device Electronics or Integrated Drive Electronics (IDE)

large-capacity drive

large mode

LBA (logical block addressing) mode

logical drive

logical geometry

lost allocation units

low-level formatting

Master Boot Record (MBR)

normal mode

operating system formatting

partition

partition table

physical geometry

primary partition

slack

translation

virtual file allocation table (VFAT)

volume

zone bit recording

8

ALL ABOUT SCSI

In this chapter, you will learn:
♦ About basics of SCSI technology and components
♦ How SCSI hard drives compare to IDE drives
♦ How to install a SCSI device
♦ Some troubleshooting tips for SCSI

In the last chapter, you learned about installing and supporting IDE hard drives. This chapter covers another technology, SCSI, which is used to provide better performance and greater expansion capabilities for many internal and external devices, including hard drives, CD-ROM drives, DVD drives, and scanners. SCSI devices tend to be faster, more expensive, and more difficult to install than similar IDE devices. This chapter discusses how SCSI technology works, as well as advantages and disadvantages of SCSI.

SCSI BASICS

SCSI (pronounced "scuzzy") stands for **Small Computer System Interface** and is a standard for communication between a subsystem of peripheral devices and the system bus. The SCSI bus is a system that can contain, and be used by, up to seven or fifteen devices, depending on the SCSI standard. The SCSI bus controller can be an expansion card called a host adapter or can be embedded on the motherboard. In this section, you will learn how a SCSI subsystem is structured, how it works, and what variations of SCSI there are.

The SCSI Subsystem

If a motherboard does not have an embedded SCSI controller, the gateway from the SCSI bus to the system bus is the host adapter, which is a card inserted into an expansion slot on the motherboard. The adapter card, called the **host adapter**, is responsible for managing all the devices on the SCSI bus. A host adapter can support both internal and external SCSI devices, using one connector on the card for a ribbon cable to connect to internal devices, and an external port that supports external devices (see Figure 8-1). All the devices and the host adapter form a single daisy chain. In Figure 8-1 this daisy chain has two internal devices and two external devices, with the SCSI host adapter in the middle of the chain.

Figure 8-1   Using a SCSI bus, a SCSI host adapter can support internal and external SCSI devices

When a device on the SCSI bus must communicate with the system bus, the data passes through the host adapter. The host adapter keeps up with the interchange between the devices on the SCSI bus and the system bus. SCSI technology has the added advantage of letting two devices on the SCSI bus pass data between them without going through the CPU. This method of data transmission provides a convenient way to back up a SCSI hard drive to a tape drive on the same SCSI subsystem, without involving the CPU.

Figure 8-2 compares IDE and SCSI bus communication. With an IDE drive (on the left in Figure 8-2), the CPU communicates with the hard drive controller, which is contained in the hard drive case, through the system bus. Recall from Chapter 7 that the hard drive controller communicates directly with the system bus. With a SCSI hard drive (on the right in the figure), the CPU communicates over the system bus to the SCSI host adapter, which communicates over the SCSI bus to the SCSI interface controller in the hard drive case. This SCSI interface controller communicates with the hard drive controller, which, in turn, communicates with the hard drive.

8

Figure 8-2   SCSI hard drives communicate with the CPU through the SCSI host adapter, but IDE drives communicate directly on the system bus

There are many SCSI standards that have evolved over several years. The maximum number of devices the SCSI bus can support depends on the type of SCSI being used. Some SCSI buses can link up to seven, others up to fifteen devices. Each device on the bus is assigned a number from 0 to 15 called the **SCSI ID**, by means of DIP switches, dials on the device, or software settings. The host adapter is generally assigned a number larger than all other devices, either 7 or 15; some come factory-set to the highest SCSI ID. Cables connect the devices physically in a daisy chain, sometimes called a straight chain. The devices can be either internal or external, and the host adapter can be at either end of the chain or somewhere in the middle. The SCSI ID identifies the physical device, which can have several logical devices embedded in it. For example, a CD-ROM jukebox—a CD-ROM changer with trays for multiple CDs—might have seven trays. Each tray is considered a logical device and is assigned a **Logical Unit Number (LUN)** to identify it, such as 1 through 7 or 0 through 6. The ID and LUN are written as two numbers separated by a colon. For instance, if the SCSI ID is 5, the fourth tray in the jukebox is device 5:4.

SCSI devices such as hard drives, tape drives, or CD-ROM drives interface with the host adapter rather than directly with the CPU. The technology of a SCSI device can be the same as the technology of a similar device that is not SCSI, with the added ability to use the SCSI bus and communicate with the host adapter. A device is a SCSI device not because of its technology, but because of the bus it uses.

Just like an IDE drive, a SCSI drive has its controller mounted inside the drive housing and can have a variable number of sectors per track. Low-level formatting a SCSI drive is sometimes possible, and even recommended by the manufacturer, because the SCSI controller is likely to contain the firmware to do the job. See the drive's documentation. In theory, a SCSI drive can simply be an IDE drive with one more chip on the controller card in the drive housing and a different kind of data connection designed to fit the SCSI standard. In practice, however, SCSI drives are of higher quality, having higher rotational speeds and lower seek times than IDE drives. The SCSI chip within the drive housing that controls data transfer over the SCSI bus is called the **SBAC (SCSI bus adapter chip)**.

To reduce the amount of electrical "noise," or interference, on a SCSI cable, each end of the SCSI chain has a **terminating resistor**. The terminating resistor can be a hardware device plugged into the last device on each end of the chain, or the chain can have software-controlled termination resistance, which makes installation simpler.

Now that you've learned the basic structure and function of a SCSI subsystem, let's look at two important components of it in detail: host adapters and device drivers.

Host Adapters

An important issue when you install a SCSI bus system for the first time is the sophistication of the host adapter. More expensive host adapters are often easier to install because the installation software does more of the work for the installer and offers more help than does less expensive adapter software. This section discusses issues to consider when selecting a host adapter.

BIOS

A SCSI host adapter controller has BIOS that uses memory addresses on the PC and controls the operation of the SCSI bus. This SCSI controller uses a DMA channel, IRQ, and I/O addresses. You must install a SCSI device carefully to avoid resource conflicts with devices that are not on the SCSI subsystem. When you are looking for a host adapter, look for one that is Plug and Play compatible and has a configuration utility built into its ROM, to make the setup process easier. Check also for software that will configure termination and assign system resources. It is easier to work with this software than to set jumpers or DIP switches on the card, because it allows you to make a change without opening up the case. Also, look for a host adapter whose BIOS can configure SCSI devices using the bus controlled by the adapter. Finally, see how many devices the BIOS supports; for today's systems and SCSI devices, it is best to use a host adapter that supports up to 15 peripherals.

Expansion Slot

The host adapter must fit the expansion slot you plan to use. SCSI host adapters are made for 8-bit ISA, 16-bit ISA, 16-bit MCA, 32-bit MCA, 32-bit EISA, VL-Bus, and PCI buses. For a Pentium motherboard, you probably can choose either a 16-bit ISA host adapter or a PCI host adapter. Choose the 32-bit PCI bus for faster data transfer rate, instead of the 16-bit ISA bus.

Bus Mastering

Choose a host adapter that uses bus mastering, discussed in Chapter 5, if your system bus supports it. Remember that a bus master attached to the PCI bus can access memory and other devices without accessing the CPU. For PCI buses that do support bus mastering, you have the added advantage that, when bus mastering is used, the SCSI host adapter does not require a DMA channel.

Table 8-1 lists vendors for host adapters.

Table 8-1   Vendors for SCSI host adapters

Vendor	Web Site
Adaptec (now owned by DPT)	www.adaptec.com or www.dpt.com
Diamond Multimedia	www.diamondmm.com
Promise Technology	www.promise.com

SCSI Device Drivers

SCSI device drivers are needed to enable an operating system to communicate with a host adapter. Many computers have some SCSI interface software in their system BIOS—enough, in fact, to allow a SCSI hard drive to be the boot device of the system. The system BIOS can access the SCSI drive, execute the load program in the drive's Master Boot Record, and load the SCSI device drivers stored on the hard drive into memory. If a system has two hard drives, one IDE and one SCSI, the IDE drive must be the boot device, unless system BIOS can support booting from a SCSI drive even when an IDE drive is present. This is because the motherboard BIOS takes precedence over the BIOS on the SCSI host adapter, which generally includes driver support for hard drives.

For most SCSI devices, support is not built into the host adapter BIOS or the system BIOS, and separate drivers are required. Although many drivers are available, it is best to use the drivers recommended by or provided by the device vendor. Two popular driver types are **Advanced SCSI Programming Interface (ASPI)** and **Common Access Method (CAM)**. Both of these device driver standards describe the way the host adapter communicates with the SCSI device driver. ASPI, which is the more popular of the two, was originally developed by Adaptec and then licensed to other makers of SCSI devices. With CAM, a single driver can control several host adapters.

The manufacturer of the host adapter usually provides the SCSI driver on floppy disk or CD-ROM. Windows 9x, Windows NT, Windows 2000, and Windows XP all have built-in support for many SCSI devices. These OSs also provide SCSI drivers for a SCSI CD-ROM drive on their rescue disks, such as the Windows 9x startup disk, so that you can have access to the SCSI CD-ROM drive when troubleshooting a failed boot.

Variations in SCSI

Just as with IDE/ATA standards, SCSI standards have improved over the years and use different names. SCSI standards are developed by the SCSI T10 Technical Committee (*www.t10.org*) and sent to ANSI, which publishes and maintains the official versions of the standards. The SCSI Trade Association, which promotes SCSI devices and standards, can also be accessed at *www.t10.org*. In addition to varying standards, SCSI also uses different types of cabling and different bus widths. This section covers variations within SCSI technology.

Bus Width

The two general categories of all SCSI standards used on PCs have to do with the width in bits of the SCSI data bus, either 8 bits **(narrow SCSI)** or 16 bits **(wide SCSI)**. In almost every case, if the SCSI standard is 16 bits, then the word "wide" is in the name for the standard. In most cases, the word "narrow" is not mentioned in names for 8-bit standards. Narrow SCSI uses a cable with a 50-pin connector (also called an A cable), and wide SCSI uses a cable with a 68-pin connector (also called a P cable).

The wide SCSI specification allows for a data path of 32 bits, although this is not widely implemented in PCs. When you see a SCSI device referred to as wide, you can generally assume 16 bits.

Signaling Methods Used on SCSI Cables

A SCSI cable can be built in two different ways, depending on the method by which the electrical signal is placed on the cable: single-ended and differential. Both types of cables send a signal on a pair of twisted wires. In **single-ended (SE)** cables, one of the wires carries voltage and the other is a ground, and in **differential** cables, both wires carry voltage, and the signal is calculated to be the difference between the two voltages (see Figure 8-3). A single-ended cable is less expensive than a differential cable, but the maximum cable length cannot be as long because data integrity is not as great. With differential cabling, the signal accuracy is better; noise on the line and electromagnetic interference are less likely to affect the signaling because the reading is the difference between the two signals rather than the amplitude of the one signal. Differential signaling also sends an extra verifying signal for each bit, which provides greater reliability and reduces the chance of data errors.

8

(a) Single-ended signaling

(b) Differential signaling

Figure 8-3   A SCSI pair of wires can carry a signal using (a) ground and a signal, or (b) a positive and negative signal, but differential signaling is less likely to be affected by noise on the line

When differential signaling was first introduced, the difference in voltage between the two wires was high (called **HVD**, or **High Voltage Differential**). This required a large amount of power and circuitry, and made it impossible to mix differential and single-ended devices on a system without burning out the hardware. HVD became obsolete with the introduction of the SCSI-3 standard. The introduction of **Low Voltage Differential (LVD)** signaling and termination made it possible to develop less expensive, low-voltage interfaces on the device, host adapter, cables, and terminators. As its name implies, LVD signaling uses lower voltages on the two-wire pair. It provides for cable lengths up to 12 meters (about 39.4 feet) and is required with Ultra SCSI standards. There is a type of LVD signaling that can work with SE devices and cables, called LVD/SE multimode. If an LVD/SE device is used on a bus with SE devices, it will use the SE method of signaling, which is slower and cannot accommodate longer cable lengths. Table 8-2 lists the four types of cables and gives descriptions of each.

Table 8-2   SCSI cables

SCSI Cable	Maximum Length (Meters and Feet)	Maximum Speed	Transfer Rate	Description
Single-ended (SE)	3 M (10 ft) for wide or 6 M (20 ft) for narrow SCSI	20 MHz	40 Mbps	One wire in the pair is ground.
High voltage differential (HVD)	25 M (82 ft)	20 or 40 MHz	40 Mbps	Both wires in the pair have high voltage.
Low voltage differential (LVD)	12 M (40 ft) for 15 devices or 25 M (80 ft) for 7 devices	320 MHz	80 Mbps	Both wires in the pair have low voltage.
LVD/SE multimode				If one SE device is on the bus, the smaller length and speed apply.

CAUTION

Never use an HVD device on a bus with SE or LVD devices, because the high voltage put on the cable by the HVD device can destroy the low-voltage devices.

Cables for both narrow SCSI and wide SCSI can be either single-ended or differential. Single-ended HVD and LVD cables look the same, so you must make sure that you are using the correct cable. It's important to know that you cannot look at a cable, the cable connector, or the connector on a device and know what type of signaling it is using. It is possible that connecting an HVD device to a SCSI bus that is using SE or LVD devices will burn them up with the high voltage from the HVD device. Look at the device documentation to know what type of signaling a device is using, or you can look for a symbol on the device to indicate the signaling method used. Figure 8-4 shows the different symbols that are used on devices and cables to show what kind of signaling they use.

Figure 8-4   These symbols tell what type of signaling a device or cable uses

Adapters are available for mixing single-ended and differential devices and cables, but it is not recommended. It is not a good idea to mix single-ended and differential signaling types because of the different ways they transmit data. Even with adapters, incompatible connections between single-ended and differential signals can damage both the host adapter and the devices connected to it. An exception to this principle is LVD/SE devices that are designed to work with either LVD or SE and revert to SE mode whenever the two are connected. Even then, however, know that you are running the device at a slower speed than it could be running if connected to an all-LVD signaling system, and that all cables in the system must meet the SE standard lengths.

Connectors Used with SCSI Cables

The connector type or the number of pins on a SCSI cable connector is not affected by the signaling method used. Within each signaling method, the number of pins can vary. Figure 8-5 shows just a few of the many types of SCSI connectors. Although there are two main types of SCSI connectors, 50-pin (A cable) and 68-pin (P cable), there are other, less common types as well, such as the 80-pin SCA (Single Connector Attachment) connector used with some hot-swapping drives. Only 80-pin connectors supply power to the device in the connector; other devices require separate power connections. A SCSI bus can support more than one type of connector, and you can use connector adapters in order to plug a cable with one type of connector into a port using another type of connector.

(a) DB-25 SCSI connector

(b) 50-pin (A-cable), low-density SCSI connector

(c) 50-pin (A-cable), high-density SCSI connector

(d) 68-pin (P-cable), high-density SCSI connector

(e) 80-pin SCA SCSI connector (used by hot-swappable devices)

Figure 8-5   The most popular SCSI connectors are 50-pin A cable connectors for narrow SCSI and 68-pin P cable connectors for wide SCSI

 TIP   If you select a host adapter that supports both 50-pin connections and 68-pin connections, you can add a variety of devices to your system without having to purchase a second host adapter.

For each type of connector, there can be variations in shape and pin density. Different companies and device manufacturers can make different connector types. For example, in an attempt to trim the size of the connector, a 25-pin SCSI connector was designed for narrow SCSI. The problem was that this connector looked like a parallel port connector. Never plug a SCSI connector into a parallel port or vice versa; you can damage equipment that way, because the signals work completely differently.

The good news in all this variety is that adapters are generally available to connect one type of connector to another, meaning that you can mix wide and narrow SCSI devices that use different connector variations. If you have any wide devices on your system at all, the cable from the host adapter must have a 68-pin connector, and you will need to use converters to attach 50-pin narrow devices.

TIP When constructing an external SCSI chain, attach wide devices first (closest to the host adapter), and finish the chain with your narrow devices.

Most recent SCSI devices and buses use 50-pin or 68-pin connectors that are formed in a D shape so that they cannot be plugged in wrong. Older 50-pin connectors did not have this shape and could be oriented incorrectly. To line up a 50-pin connector to an internal SCSI device, look for a red or blue stripe on one side of the cable; this stripe lines up with pin 1 on the connector. Look also for a tab on one edge of the connector and a corresponding notch where you are to insert it.

The SCSI bus inside a computer is a ribbon cable, and the device connectors for internal devices are plugs at different positions on the cable. Having multiple connectors on the SCSI bus (see Figure 8-6) enables you to easily connect multiple internal devices. One end of the bus attaches to the host adapter, and for best results, you should always plug a device into the last connector on the bus.

8

Connects to host adapter

Connects to SCSI device

Connects to SCSI device

Figure 8-6 This 50-pin SCSI ribbon cable can accommodate two narrow SCSI devices

For external SCSI chains, there are two connectors on each device, both of which can send or receive information, meaning that it doesn't matter which connector on one device is linked to which connector on the next. A cable goes from the host adapter to a connector on the first device, then another cable goes from the second connector on the first device to a connector on the second device, and so on. The last connector on the last device must be filled with a terminator, unless that device provides software termination. External SCSI chains work like some Christmas lights: if one goes out, they all go out. Therefore, when connecting devices in an external SCSI chain, you should make sure to snap in the retaining clips or wires to complete the connection.

Termination

Termination prevents an echo effect from electrical noise and reflected data at the end of the SCSI daisy chain, which can cause interference with the data transmission. Each end of a SCSI chain must be terminated, and there are several ways to terminate the chain:

- The host adapter can have a switch setting that activates or deactivates a terminating resistor on the card, depending on whether or not the adapter is at one end of the chain. Sometimes a host adapter uses auto termination to adjust for problems with termination.

- A device can have either a single SCSI connection requiring that the device be placed at the end of the chain, or the device can have two connections. When a device has two connections, the second connection can be used to connect another device or to terminate the chain by placing an external terminator on the connection. This external terminator serves as the terminating resistor (see Figure 8-7).

Figure 8-7   External SCSI terminator

- The device at the end of the chain can also be terminated by a resistor that is physically mounted on the device in a specially designated socket.

- Some devices have built-in terminators (internal terminators) that you can turn on or off with a jumper setting on the device.

- Termination can be controlled by software.

Figure 8-1 showed the terminators that are needed at the end of both internal and external SCSI chains. In the figure, there is no terminator on the host adapter, which has both internal and external devices attached to it. Only when you have both types of devices attached to a host adapter do you remove termination from the host adapter.

There are several types of terminators:

- **Passive terminators**, the least reliable type, are used with SCSI-1 devices that operate at low speed and at short distances. It uses simple resistors only and is rarely used today, as it is not sufficient for today's faster SCSI devices and longer cabling distances. Passive termination should only be used with narrow SCSI.

- **Active terminators** include voltage regulators in addition to the simple resistors used with passive termination. Most of today's single-ended SCSI cables use active termination, which was recommended with SCSI-2. Active termination is used with wide SCSI and is required with fast SCSI. It also works better over longer distances than passive termination.

- **Forced perfect terminators (FPTs)** are a more advanced version of active terminators and include a mechanism to force signal termination to the correct voltage, eliminating most signal echoes and interference. FPTs are more expensive and more reliable than passive and active terminators.

Passive terminators, active terminators, and FPTs are all used with single-ended SCSI cables. Differential cables use either HVD or LVD terminators.

SCSI-1, SCSI-2, and SCSI-3

The three major versions of SCSI are SCSI-1, SCSI-2, and SCSI-3, commonly known as Regular SCSI, Fast SCSI, and Ultra SCSI. SCSI-1 was the original version of the SCSI standard. It covered the design of wiring on the SCSI bus, but it did not include a common command set. Therefore, there were still a lot of incompatibilities between SCSI-1 devices. With SCSI-1, only an 8-bit data bus was used, and there could be only seven devices besides the host adapter.

SCSI-2 improved the standard by developing a common command set so that devices could communicate with each other more easily. It also introduced wide SCSI, which expanded the width of the data bus to 16 bits and the number of possible devices to 15. SCSI-2 also made parity checking of the data bus mandatory.

SCSI-3, which has grown to the point where it is a set of standards rather than a single standard, supports both parallel and serial data transmission, supports FireWire connections, and increases the possible rate of data transfer to 320 MB/sec and higher. The **SPI (SCSI Parallel Interface)** standard is part of SCSI-3 and specifies how SCSI devices are connected. SPI has been through three versions; the latest is Ultra 320 SCSI. Beginning with Ultra SCSI (SCSI-3), the SCSI standard supports SCAM, which you learned about earlier in the chapter. SCSI-3 uses an 8-, 16-, or 32-bit data bus and supports up to 32 devices on a system.

 Because SCSI can be so difficult to configure, there is a growing trend in the industry to replace SCSI with FireWire, especially since some newer high-end motherboards are beginning to provide FireWire support. Another contender to replace SCSI is FCAL (Fiber Channel Arbitrated Loop), which uses fiber optic cabling. Both FireWire and FCAL use serial data transmission. FCAL is used on higher-end systems than FireWire.

Because there are several variations of SCSI standards, when you buy a new SCSI device, you must be sure that it is compatible with the SCSI bus you already have, taking into consideration that some SCSI standards are backward-compatible. If the new SCSI device is not compatible, you cannot use the same SCSI bus, and you must buy a new host adapter to build a second SCSI bus system, increasing the overall cost of adding the new device.

Table 8-3 summarizes characteristics of the different SCSI standards. Other names used in the industry for these standards are also listed in the table. Note that both Fast SCSI (SCSI-2) and Ultra SCSI (SCSI-3) have narrow and wide versions.

Table 8-3   Summary of SCSI standards

Standard Name	Standard Number	Bus Width (Narrow = 8 bits, Wide = 16 bits)	Transfer Rate (MB/sec)	Maximum Number of Devices
Regular SCSI	SCSI-1	Narrow	5	8
Fast SCSI or Fast Narrow	SCSI-2	Narrow	10	8
Fast Wide SCSI or Wide SCSI	SCSI-2	Wide	20	16
Ultra SCSI, Ultra Narrow, or Fast-20 SCSI	SCSI-3	Narrow	20	8
Wide Ultra SCSI or Fast Wide 20	SCSI-3	Wide	40	16
Ultra2 SCSI or SPI-2	SCSI-3	Narrow	40	8
Wide Ultra2 SCSI	SCSI-3	Wide	80	16
Ultra3 SCSI or SPI-3	SCSI-3	Narrow	80	8
Wide Ultra3 SCSI or Ultra 160 SCSI	SCSI-3	Wide	160	16
Ultra 320 SCSI (Ultra 4 SCSI or SPI-4)	SCSI-3	Wide	320*	16

* SPI-4 is expected to soon be rated at 640 MBps and then 1,280 MBps

Table 8-4 summarizes cable specifications for these SCSI standards.

Table 8-4   SCSI standard cable specifications

SCSI Standard Name	Maximum Length of Single-Ended Cable (Meters)	Maximum Length of Differential Cable (Meters)	Cable Type
Regular SCSI	6	25	50-pin
Fast SCSI or Fast Narrow	3	25	50-pin
Fast Wide SCSI or Wide SCSI	3	25	68-pin
Ultra SCSI, Ultra Narrow, or Fast-20 SCSI	1.5	25	50-pin
Wide Ultra SCSI or Fast Wide 20	1.5	25	68-pin
Ultra2 SCSI or SPI-2		12 LVD	50-pin
Wide Ultra2 SCSI			68-pin
Ultra3 SCSI or SPI-3		12 LVD	50-pin
Wide Ultra3 SCSI or Ultra 160 SCSI		12 LVD	68-pin
Ultra 320 SCSI (Ultra 4 SCSI or SPI-4)		12 LVD	68-pin

COMPARING IDE AND SCSI

Before we move on to how to install SCSI devices, let's compare SCSI to IDE technology you already know about from the last chapter. When selecting hard drives and other devices, you will need to know which technology they use and the advantages and disadvantages of each. When you are using a single disk drive with an operating system such as Windows 98 or Windows Me, you may actually find that an IDE drive provides better performance than a comparable SCSI drive. The features of SCSI drives that are improvements over IDE increase performance mainly in systems where a heavy load is placed on the system and on its components—for example, when there are multiple hard drives installed on a high-end server. Also, some operating systems, such as Windows 2000 and XP, include increased support for SCSI features and are better able to take advantage of them.

Consider the following issues when choosing between an IDE hard drive and a SCSI hard drive:

- IDE supports only four internal devices; SCSI supports both internal and external devices and allows you to add more devices to a system. If you don't have enough expansion drive bays with IDE, this can solve the problem.

- SCSI devices are generally of higher quality than IDE devices, and more expensive.

- IDE devices require a separate IRQ for each device; SCSI requires only one for the entire chain.

- Both IDE and SCSI are generally backward-compatible, in that most faster hardware can work with slower devices.

- A SCSI hard drive with its supporting host adapter and cable costs more than an IDE hard drive.

- A SCSI subsystem provides faster data transfer than an IDE drive, although the SCSI bus is the source of the performance rather than the hard drive technology.

- SCSI generally provides better performance than IDE and is often used on high-demand servers.

- A good SCSI host adapter allows you to connect other SCSI devices to it, such as a printer, scanner, or tape drive.

- Without SCSI technology, if you have two IDE drives on the same IDE channel, only one of them can be busy at any one time. For instance, without SCSI, if one of your IDE devices is a CD-ROM, the hard drive must wait for the CD-ROM to complete a task before it can work again. With SCSI, two or more devices can operate simultaneously. If you plan to transfer a lot of data from CD-ROM to hard drive, this is a good reason to choose SCSI.

In summary, SCSI is more expensive than IDE, but gives you better performance.

 It is possible, but not recommended, to mix SCSI and IDE devices on a system. Both types of devices will try to monopolize the PCI bus, and you may experience resource conflicts as a result.

SCSI INSTALLATION

As you have learned, there are many different types of SCSI and many variations within the components of a SCSI subsystem. Although the installation of a SCSI system may sound complicated and requires many decisions about what components to buy, the installation instructions for SCSI devices and host adapters are usually very thorough and well written. If you carefully follow all instructions, SCSI installations can be smooth and problem-free. This section covers how to install SCSI devices, beginning with a host adapter and then moving on to a scanner and a hard drive as examples. First, let's look at some basic steps for SCSI installation:

1. Set any jumpers or switches on the host adapter and install it in the correct expansion slot on your motherboard.

2. For each device that has them, use jumpers or switches to assign the SCSI ID.

3. Attach cabling to the host adapter and then to each device.

4. Verify that both ends of the SCSI chain are terminated.

5. Power up one device. After you verify that it is working, power up the next device. Continue until you have verified that all devices are working.

6. Install drivers and software required to interface between the SCSI subsystem and the operating system.

Installing a Host Adapter Card

For a Plug and Play system using Windows 9x or Windows 2000/XP, follow these general steps to install a host adapter:

1. Install the card in an expansion slot.

2. In most cases, the default settings for the host adapter are the correct ones, but you can change or verify these settings using the setup program. For example, to use a setup program that comes on a floppy disk bundled with the adapter, boot the PC from the floppy disk. The disk boots the system (using DOS) and automatically executes the SCSI setup program. In this example of one setup program, the two options on the opening menu are SCSI Disk Utilities (for installing a SCSI hard drive) and Configure the Host Adapter. Select **Configure the Host Adapter**. You see the host adapter configuration screen. See Figure 8-8.

3. Verify the settings. Under the Advanced Configuration Options in Figure 8-8, you see two settings: enable or disable Plug and Play, and enable or disable SCAM support. Both are normally set to enable. Note in Figure 8-8 that the SCSI ID for the host adapter is 7 and that parity checking is enabled. After verifying settings, exit the setup program, remove the floppy disk, and reboot.

4. When Windows 9x loads, it senses a new hardware device and automatically launches the Add New Hardware Wizard. Because Windows supports the host adapter, it loads the device drivers automatically and installs the host adapter.

Figure 8-8 Setup software included with a SCSI host adapter is used to change SCSI BIOS settings on the card

8

5. To verify that the host adapter is correctly installed, open **Device Manager**. Double-click **SCSI controllers for Windows 98**. The Adaptec host adapter should be displayed, as shown in Figure 8-9 (For Windows 2000/XP Device Manager, to view a device's properties, right click on the device and select **Properties** from the shortcut menu). Select the host adapter and click **Properties** to display the host adapter Properties dialog box also shown in Figure 8-9. Click the **Resources** tab to note the resources assigned to the card by Plug and Play.

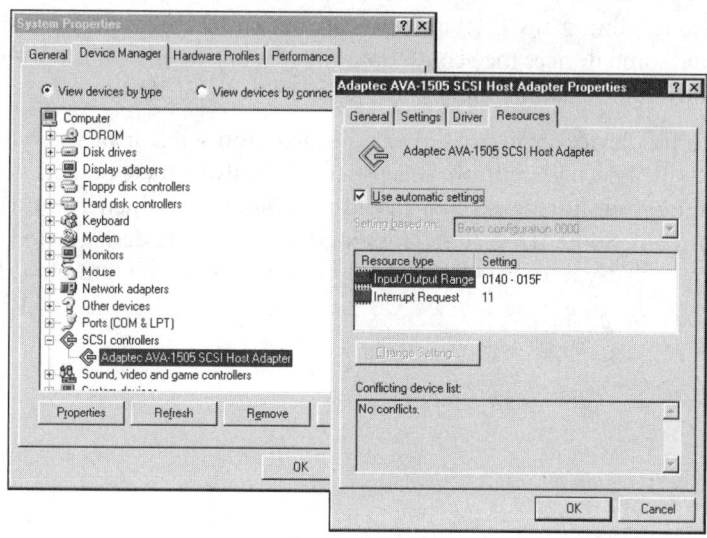

Figure 8-9 Device Manager displays the newly installed host adapter

Notice the broken diamond symbol in Figure 8-9, which you saw earlier in the chapter in Figure 8-4. The symbol for single-ended SCSI devices is sometimes used to symbolize SCSI in general.

After you have installed the host adapter, you are ready to install the external SCSI device. For example, if the device is a SCSI scanner, follow these directions:

1. Install the software to run the scanner, which will include the scanner driver.

2. Plug the SCSI cable into the host adapter port.

3. Plug the other end of the cable into the scanner.

4. Set the SCSI ID on the scanner.

5. Connect the scanner's power cord to a wall outlet, and turn the scanner on.

6. Restart your PC and test the scanner.

Setting Device IDs During Installation

If your SCSI subsystem is SCAM-compliant, SCSI IDs will be assigned automatically. However, SCAM will not work unless your OS, devices, and host adapter all support the SCAM standard. Without SCAM compliance, you must set device SCSI IDs manually. Remember that each ID must be unique; no two devices on the same SCSI channel can have the same ID number. (If you have more than one SCSI adapter on a system, you can reuse IDs.) For narrow SCSI, there are the IDs 0–7, and for wide SCSI, there are the IDs 0–15. Generally, you can assign almost any ID number to any device. However, the host adapter usually has the ID 7, and some devices may come from the manufacturer with the ID already set. Many SCSI hard drives, for example, are automatically set to SCSI ID 6.

To set IDs for external devices, you use either a push-button selector or rotary selector, as shown in Figure 8-10. The push-button selector has buttons to increase and decrease the number, and the rotary selector works like an old television dial, which you turn to point to the number you want. Some ID selectors for external devices are designed to be adjusted with a screwdriver, so that you cannot accidentally change the ID by bumping the device.

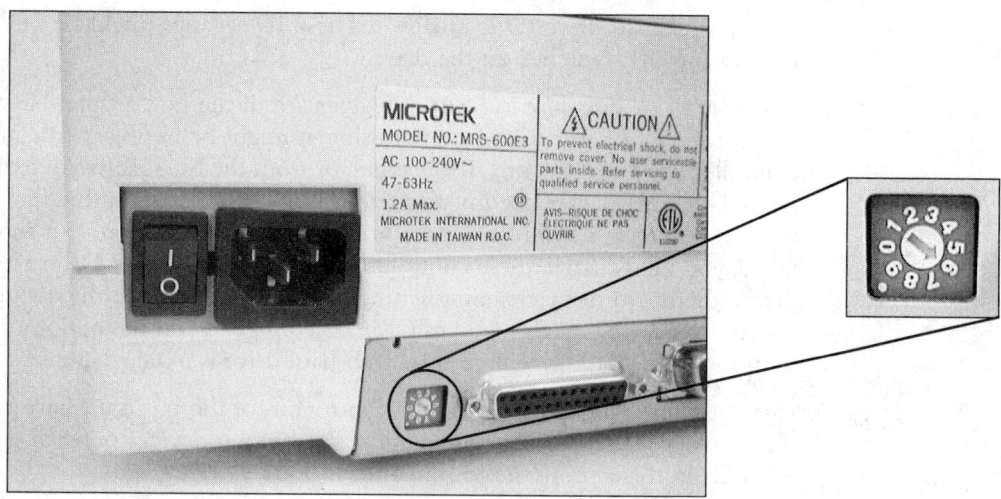

Figure 8-10   This rotary dial on the rear of a SCSI scanner is used to set the SCSI ID, which is now set to 6

8

To set IDs for internal devices, you use a set of jumpers on the device. Most newer devices use a binary code to set IDs, with three pin pairs for narrow SCSI and four pin pairs for wide SCSI. Figure 8-11 shows the jumper settings for wide SCSI IDs.

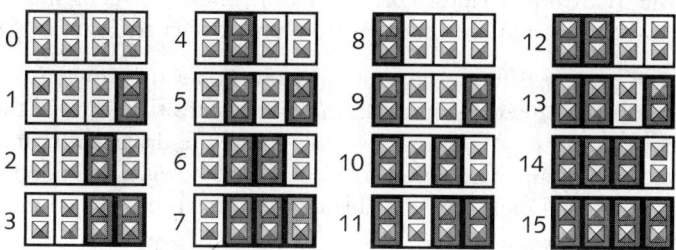

Figure 8-11   Wide SCSI ID binary jumper settings for internal devices

Installing a SCSI Hard Drive

When you install a SCSI hard drive, make sure that your host adapter and the cables you are using are compatible with the SCSI drive. The vendor can help you here. Read the documentation for both the SCSI host adapter and the hard drive before beginning; most SCSI documentation is well written and thorough. In addition to the procedure already discussed in Chapter 7 for IDE hard drives, a SCSI installation requires that you configure the SCSI host adapter and the SCSI hard drive so that they can communicate with each other. This is done as follows:

  1. *Set SCSI IDs.* Set the ID for each device on the SCSI bus. The host adapter documentation will probably explain that the host adapter must be set to ID 7. If the hard drive will be the boot device for the system, its ID is likely to be 0.

The second hard drive ID is usually 1. These ID settings might be set by jumpers or DIP switches on the drive.

2. *Disable or enable disk drive and hard drive controllers.* If the host adapter has a built-in disk drive controller that you are not using, it might be necessary to disable the controller with jumpers or DIP switches, or from the SCSI software setup program. The host adapter documentation will explain how to do this. Incidentally, if you are not using a SCSI hard drive or disk drive controller on your motherboard, you must disable these controllers by setting jumpers or DIP switches on the motherboard or by changing settings in CMOS setup. See the documentation for your motherboard. Sometimes CMOS setup gives you the option of booting from the SCSI hard drive even if an IDE hard drive is installed.

3. *Check terminating resistors.* Devices on both ends of the bus must have terminating resistors. Check the documentation for the two devices on each end of the SCSI chain to see how the termination is done.

4. *Run CMOS setup for a SCSI system.* After you have physically installed the SCSI host and drive, tell setup that the SCSI system is present. Remember that for SCSI devices, the computer does not communicate with the hard drive directly, but interfaces with the SCSI host adapter. To use a SCSI hard drive, some computers require that you tell setup that no hard drive is present. The SCSI host provides that information to the computer during startup. Sometimes, the computer setup lets you choose a SCSI hard drive type. That's all it needs to know, and the SCSI host adapter takes over from there. To recognize a SCSI drive, some computers require that the drive type be set to 1 in CMOS setup.

5. *Load SCSI device drivers.* Windows operating systems offer their own SCSI drivers, although if the host adapter documentation recommends that you use the adapter's driver instead, then do so. After you physically install the drive and change CMOS setup, the next step in any hard drive installation is to boot from a floppy disk. The hard drive package will include a bootable disk that loads the device driver to access the SCSI system.

TROUBLESHOOTING SCSI DEVICES

When you are using a variety of SCSI devices, installation and configuration can get complicated. To make this process as easy as possible, keep these general tips in mind:

- As always, keep detailed notes on device installation and configuration for use in troubleshooting and backtracking, and always read all the documentation for devices you are trying to add to and use with your system. Record all switch and jumper settings for your SCSI devices. Record all system resources and addresses used by the host adapter.

- If you are adding several SCSI devices to your system, add them one at a time rather than all at once. First install the host adapter and, if you are using one, the SCSI hard drive, and make sure they are working before you try to install additional peripherals.

- Use components of good quality. Do not sacrifice quality just to pay a little less. For example, higher-quality cables usually experience less degradation of data and less interference, and higher-quality active terminators generally do a better job than cheaper passive ones, even if you have some devices that are not Fast SCSI.

- Limiting cable length whenever possible helps to improve performance and reduce the chance that data will become corrupted.

Here are some things to check if you have problems with installing SCSI devices:

- SCSI drivers will look for their devices when the computer boots, so make sure that all external SCSI devices are turned on before you turn on the computer.

- Check the connections of all SCSI cables, power connections, and adapters. Sometimes moving and reattaching them can clear up connection problems.

- Many problems with SCSI devices are caused by incorrect termination. Remember that both ends of a SCSI chain must be terminated and that termination should be disabled at all other points in the chain. If the host adapter is at one end of the chain, it must have termination enabled; if it is in the middle of the chain, it must have termination disabled.

- Check with the manufacturer of your motherboard to make sure you have the most updated BIOS, so that PCI slots will operate correctly. Also check to make sure you have up-to-date drivers for your SCSI devices.

- For a PCI host adapter, install it in a PCI bus that supports bus mastering—which not all PCI slots on older motherboards do. Try removing the host adapter and reseating it in another PCI slot.

Once you have installed SCSI devices, if you have IDE devices also, your system will attempt to boot from the IDE drive first. To cause it to boot from a SCSI drive, you must either change the boot order or remove the non-SCSI drives to cause it to boot from a SCSI drive. If your system has only SCSI drives installed and still will not boot, check these things:

- The BIOS setup drive configuration for your computer should be set to "No Drives Installed." Most BIOSs only support IDE drives. If you tell the system that no drives are installed, it will attempt to boot from another device, such as a SCSI drive.

- Verify that the SCSI drive that you want to boot from is partitioned, that it has a primary partition, and that the boot partition is set as active.

- If nothing else works, back up the SCSI hard drive and then do a low-level format on it. There is a Format utility included with the host adapter for this purpose.

CHAPTER SUMMARY

- The SCSI bus requires a controller embedded on the motherboard or on a host adapter inserted into an expansion slot. If the motherboard has a SCSI controller, a

SCSI port or connector will be found somewhere on the board. The host adapter is the more common way of supporting SCSI.

❑ The term "SCSI hard drive" refers more to the bus used by the drive than to the technology of the drive. Internally, SCSI and IDE drives work in basically the same way.

❑ There are several variations of SCSI buses and devices, including SCSI-1, SCSI-2, SCSI-3, Wide SCSI, Ultra SCSI, and Ultra Wide SCSI.

❑ Every SCSI bus subsystem requires a SCSI controller and unique SCSI IDs assigned to each device, including the host adapter.

❑ The SCSI host adapter should generally be set to ID 7 or 15, since these IDs have the highest priority.

❑ The narrow SCSI bus has an 8-bit data path, and the wide SCSI bus has a 16-bit data path.

❑ Each end of the SCSI bus must have a terminating resistor, which can be controlled by hardware or software.

❑ Narrow SCSI uses a 25-pin or 50-pin connector (also called an A cable), and wide SCSI uses a 68-pin connector (also called a P cable).

❑ The two types of SCSI cabling are single-ended and differential.

❑ There are three types of termination for single-ended cabling: passive, active, and forced perfect.

❑ There are two types of termination for differential SCSI cabling: HVD and LVD. HVD was made obsolete with the introduction of SCSI-3. HVD uses a higher voltage than does LVD signaling.

❑ When selecting a SCSI host adapter, consider the SCSI standards the adapter supports, the bus slot the adapter will use, the device driver standard used by the host adapter, the issue of single-ended versus differential SCSI, SCAM compliance, and whether or not the host offers bus mastering.

❑ Each device on a SCSI bus is assigned a number from 0 to 15, called the SCSI ID. Logical devices within a physical device, such as trays within a CD changer, are assigned a separate number called a LUN.

❑ The two main types of SCSI device drivers are ASPI and CAM. When selecting a host adapter, you should pick one that supports either ASPI or CAM.

❑ You can limit the chance of data becoming corrupted by buying high-quality cables, limiting cable length, and using high-end terminators.

❑ If you have an IDE hard drive and a SCSI hard drive installed on the same system, the system will attempt to boot from the IDE hard drive first. If you want to boot from a SCSI drive, you must change the boot order in Setup or remove the non-SCSI drives.

❑ One of the most common causes for problems with the SCSI subsystem is incorrect termination.

KEY TERMS

active terminator

ASPI (Advanced SCSI Programming Interface)

CAM (Common Access Method)

differential

forced perfect terminator (FPT)

host adapter

HVD (High Voltage Differential)

LUN (Logical Unit Number)

LVD (Low Voltage Differential)

narrow SCSI

passive terminator

SBAC (SCSI bus adapter chip)

SCSI (Small Computer System Interface)

SCSI ID

single-ended (SE)

SPI (SCSI Parallel Interface)

terminating resistor

termination

wide SCSI

8

9

MULTIMEDIA DEVICES AND MASS STORAGE

In this chapter, you will learn:

♦ How multimedia works on a PC

♦ About multimedia devices such as sound cards, digital cameras, and MP3 players

♦ About optical storage technologies such as CD and DVD

♦ How certain hardware devices are used for backups and fault tolerance

♦ How to install multimedia and mass storage components

♦ How to troubleshoot multimedia and mass storage components

The ability of PCs to create output in a vast array of media—audio, video, and animation, as well as text and graphics—has turned PCs into multimedia machines. The multimedia computer has much to offer, from video conferencing for executives to tools for teaching the alphabet to four year olds. This chapter examines multimedia devices, what they can do, how they work, and how to support them. You will also learn about storage devices such as CD, DVD, removable drives, and tape drives, including installation and troubleshooting. These mass storage devices are used to hold multimedia data and, in some cases, are used to hold backups.

MULTIMEDIA ON A PC

The goal of **multimedia** technology is to create or reproduce lifelike representations for audio, video, and animation. Remember that computers store data digitally, and ultimately as a stream of only two numbers: 0 and 1. In contrast, sights and sounds have an infinite number of variations and are analog in nature. The challenge of multimedia technology is to bridge these two worlds.

CPU Technologies for Multimedia

Two enhancements by Intel to CPU technology designed with multimedia applications in mind are **MMX (Multimedia Extensions)**, used by the Pentium MMX, Pentium Pro, and Pentium II, and **SSE (Streaming SIMD Extension)**, used by the Pentium III. (**SIMD**, which stands for **single instruction, multiple data**, is a process that allows the CPU to receive a single instruction and then execute it on multiple pieces of data rather than having to receive the same instruction each time the data is received.) The Pentium 4 uses both MMX and SSE. Multimedia software tends to use input/output operations more than it performs complex computations. Both MMX and SSE were designed to speed up the repetitive looping of multimedia software and manage the high-volume input/output of graphics, motion video, animation, and sound. MMX technology added new instructions designed for repetitive processing, more efficient ways to pass those instructions to the CPU, and increased CPU cache. SSE added improvements to 3-D graphics and speech recognition. To compete with SSE, AMD introduced 3DNow!, a CPU instruction set that helps AMD processors perform better in 3D graphics and other multimedia data processing.

 TIP To know if software or hardware is taking advantage of a CPU enhancement for multimedia, look on the product package for the Intel MMX, Intel SSE, or AMD 3DNow! symbols.

Multimedia Devices

Now let's look at some specific devices that are used for multimedia support. Many multimedia capabilities are added to a system using sound cards and other adapter cards. There are also externally attached devices such as digital cameras or MP3 players. In this section, you will learn about these and other devices.

Sound Cards

A sound card is an expansion card that records sound, saves it to a file on your hard drive, and plays it back. Some cards give you the ability to mix and edit sound, and even to edit the sound using standard music score notation. Sound cards have ports for external stereo speakers and microphone input. Also, sound cards may be Sound Blaster compatible, which means that they can understand the commands sent to them that have been written for a

Sound Blaster card, which is generally considered the standard for PC sound cards. Some play CD audio by way of a cable connecting the CD to the sound card. For good quality sound you definitely need external speakers and perhaps an amplifier.

Sound passes through three stages when it is computerized: (1) digitize or input the sound, that is, convert it from analog to digital, (2) store the digital data in a compressed data file, and later (3) reproduce or synthesize the sound (digital to analog). Each of these stages is discussed next, followed by a discussion of sound card installation. Table 9-1 lists some manufacturers of sound cards.

Table 9-1   Sound card manufacturers

Abit	www.abit.com.tw
Aopen	www.aopen.com
Elements	www.elements-pc.com
Guillemot Corporation	us.guillemot.com
SIIG	www.siig.com
Syba	www.syba.com
Turtle Beach	www.tbeach.com

9

A good source for information about hardware devices (and software also) is a site that compares product prices, features, and technical specifications, such as *www.cnet.com* and *www.pricewatch.com*. On the CNET Networks and Price Watch sites, you can also find company information and product reviews.

Sampling and Digitizing the Sound

Converting sound from analog to digital storage is done by first sampling the sound and then digitizing it. When you record sound, the analog sound is converted to analog voltage by a microphone and is passed to the sound card, where it is digitized. The critical factor in the performance of a sound card is the accuracy of the samples (determined by the sample size, which can be either 8 or 16 bits). The **sampling rate** of a sound card (the number of samples taken of the analog signal over a period of time) is usually expressed as samples (cycles) per second, or **hertz (Hz)**. One thousand hertz (one kilohertz) is written as kHz. A low sampling rate provides a less accurate representation of the sound than does a high sampling rate. Our ears detect up to about 22,000 samples per second, or hertz. The sampling rate of music CDs is 44,100 Hz, or 44.1 kHz. When you record sound on a PC, the sampling rate is controlled by the recording software.

The larger the sample size, the more accurate the sampling. If 8 bits are used to hold one number, then the sample range can be from -128 to +127. This is because 1111 1111 in binary equals 255 in decimal, which, together with zero, equals 256 values. Samples of sound are considered to be both positive and negative numbers, so the range is -128 to +127 rather than 0 to 255. However, if 16 bits are used to hold the range of numbers, then the sample range increases dramatically, because 1111 1111 1111 1111 in binary is 65,535 in decimal, meaning that the sample size can be -32,768 to +32,767, or a total of 65,536 values. Music CDs use this 16-bit sample size.

Thus, an 8-bit sound card uses a sample size of 256. A 16-bit sound card has a sample size of 65,536. Sound cards typically use 8- or 16-bit sample sizes, with a sampling rate from 4,000 to 44,000 samples per second. For high-quality sound, use a 16-bit sound card. Samples may also be recorded on a single channel (mono) or on two channels (stereo).

 Don't confuse the sample size of 8 bits or 16 bits with the ISA bus size that the sound card might use to attach to the motherboard. A sound card may use an 8-bit sample size but a 16-bit ISA bus. When you hear people talk about an 8-bit sound card, they are speaking of the sample size, not the bus size.

Installing a Sound Card

Most sound cards come with a device driver as well as all the software needed for normal use, such as application software to play music CDs. The installation of a sample sound card is described on the next page. The card used is a PNP Creative Labs Sound Blaster card that uses a PCI slot and supports a 128-voice wave table (a table of stored sample sounds that is used to reconstruct and reproduce recorded sound). It will work under DOS 6+, Windows 9x, and Windows NT/2000/XP. The card comes with drivers and software on a CD-ROM and a user's guide.

The three main steps in this example of a sound card installation are to install the card itself in an empty PCI slot on the motherboard, install the driver, and then install the applications stored on the CD that comes with the sound card.

The Sound Blaster card shown in Figure 9-1 has three internal connections (connections to something inside the case) and one jumper group that enables or disables a speaker amplifier. If you are using a speaker system with an external amplifier, disable the amplifier on the card by setting the jumper on the sound card to "disable amplifier."

Figure 9-1   The Sound Blaster sound card has three internal connections and one jumper group that controls amplifier support

Follow these steps to install a sound card:

1. Make sure that you are properly grounded. Wear a grounding bracelet and follow other procedures to guard against ESD, as described in Chapter 3.

2. Turn the PC off, remove the cover, and locate an empty expansion slot for the card. Since this installation uses the connecting wire from the sound card to the CD-ROM drive (the wire comes with the sound card), place the sound card near enough to the CD-ROM drive so that the wire can reach between them.

3. Attach the wire to the sound card (see Figure 9-2) and to the CD-ROM drive.

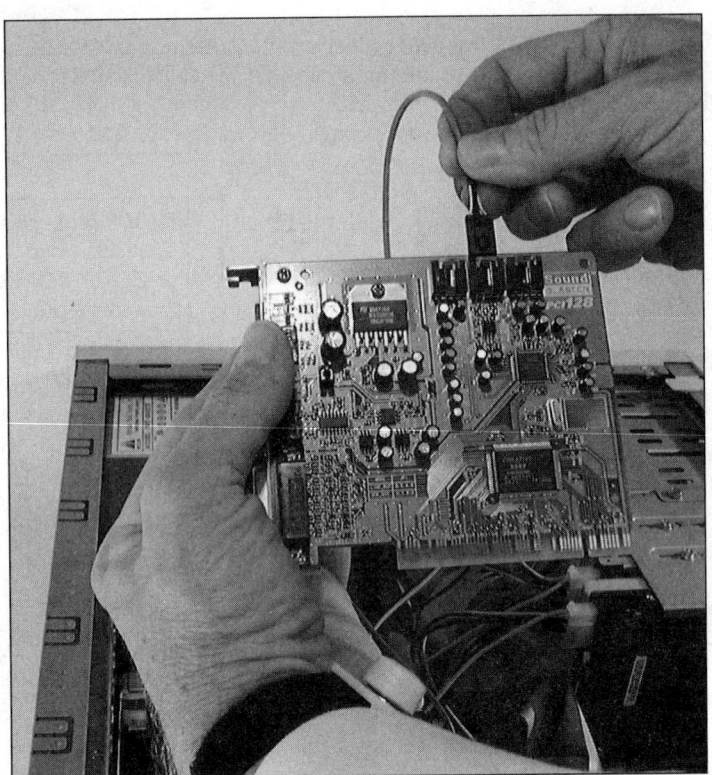

Figure 9-2   Connect the wire to the sound card that will make the direct audio
connection from the CD

4. Remove the cover from the slot opening at the rear of the PC case and place the card into the PCI slot, making sure that the card is seated firmly. Use the screw taken from the slot cover to secure the card to the back of the PC case.

5. Check again that both ends of the wire are still securely connected and that the wire is not hampering the CPU fan, then replace the case cover.

6. Plug in the speakers to the ports at the back of the sound card, and turn on the PC. The speakers may or may not require their own power source. Check the product documentation or manufacturer's Web site for more information.

 There can be several ports, on a sound card. Most likely the speaker ports are the green center ports on the card.

Notice that the installation in the preceeding example was in a system using a CD-ROM drive. Later in the chapter, you'll see an example of a sound card installed in a system with a DVD drive. If you are using a speaker system with an amplifier, disable the amplifier on the card. To do so, set the jumper on the sound card to disable amplifier support (see Figure 9-1).

Installing the Sound Card Driver

Once the card is installed, the device drivers must be installed. The example below uses a driver installation under Windows 98 as an example. When Windows 98 starts, it detects that new hardware is present. The New Hardware Found dialog box opens, indicating that it has discovered the Sound Blaster PCI128. Follow these steps to install the sound card driver:

1. The New Hardware Wizard gives you this option: **Search for the Best Driver for Your Device (Recommended)**. Select this option and click the **Next** button.

2. Clear all check boxes and check only the **Specify a Location** check box.

3. Click the **Browse** button and point to the driver path, such as **D:\Audio\English\Win98drv**.

   In this example, the CD-ROM drive is drive D, and the sound card's user guide listed the location of the driver on the CD. Substitute your CD-ROM drive letter and, for other sound card installations, see the documentation for the location of the driver on the CD-ROM.

4. Click **Next** to continue the driver installation.

5. Click **Finish** when the installation is complete, and reboot your PC.

With most sound cards, on the CD containing the sound card driver, you can find some application software for the special features offered by the card. Sometimes, as is the case with this Sound Blaster card, this software is installed at the same time as the drivers, so you can use the software at this point in the installation. With other sound cards, you can install the additional software after the driver installation is complete and the sound card is working. See the documentation that comes with the sound card to learn if application software is present, and how and when to install it.

After you have installed the driver, rebooted, and entered Windows, verify that the card and the driver are correctly installed in Windows 98 by using Device Manager.

1. Click **Start**, point to **Settings**, click **Control Panel**, and then double-click **System**.

2. Select the **Device Manager** tab. Figure 9-3 shows the sound card installed.

9

Figure 9-3   Device Manager shows the sound card installed and the resources it is using

3. To see the resources used by the card, select the card and click **Properties**. The Properties box is displayed. Click the **Resources** tab.

Troubleshooting problems with sound cards is covered later in the chapter.

Digital Cameras

Digital cameras are becoming more popular as quality improves and prices decrease. Digital camera technology works much like scanner technology, except that it is much faster. It essentially scans the field of image set by the picture taker, and translates the light signals into digital values, which can be stored as a file and viewed, manipulated, and printed with software that interprets the stored values appropriately.

TWAIN is a standard format used by digital cameras and scanners for transferring images. To transfer images to your PC, first install the software bundled with your camera or other device that contains the images. Transfer the image to your computer's hard drive using a cable supplied with the camera (a serial cable, a parallel cable, a USB cable, or a FireWire cable), a wireless or infrared connection, or an external storage medium such as a flash RAM card. CompactFlash, SmartMedia, SanDisk, and Sony Memory Sticks are different types of flash RAM cards. Figure 9-4 shows a SmartMedia card from a digital camera inserted into a FlashPath card that can then be inserted into a floppy disk drive to upload images to the PC. Some printers are also capable of uploading images directly from flash RAM cards. You can use a site such as *www.cdnet.com* or *www.compusa.com* to find and compare other digital cameras and flash card readers.

TIP   It has been said that TWAIN stands for "technology without an interesting name," although the TWAIN organization's Web site (*www.twain.org*) says the term is not an acronym.

FlashPath

SmartMedia

9

Figure 9-4   The small SmartMedia card holds the digital images from a digital camera, and FlashPath allows a PC to read SmartMedia by way of a floppy disk drive

Once the images are on the PC, use the camera's image-editing software, or another program such as Adobe PhotoShop, to view, touch up, and print the picture. The picture file, which is usually in **JPEG (Joint Photographic Experts Group)** format, can then be imported into documents. JPEG is a common compression standard for storing photos. Most JPEG files have a .jpg file extension.

Most digital cameras also have a video-out port that allows you to attach the camera to any TV, using a cable provided with the camera. You can then display pictures on TV or copy them to videotape. Table 9-2 lists manufacturers of digital cameras.

Table 9-2   Digital camera manufacturers

Canon	www.usa.canon.com
Casio	www.casio.com
Epson	www.epson.com
Fujifilm	www.fujifilm.com
Hewlett-Packard	www.photosmart.com
Kodak	www.kodak.com
Minolta	www.minolta.com
Nikon	www.nikonusa.com
Olympus	www.olympusamerica.com
Sony	www.sony.com/di
Toshiba	www.toshiba.com

MP3 Players

A popular audio compression method is **MP3**, a method that can reduce the size of a sound file as much as 1:24 without much loss in quality. An MP3 player is a device or software that plays these MP3 files. MP3 players are small but can store a lot of information. Figure 9-5 shows a typical MP3 player.

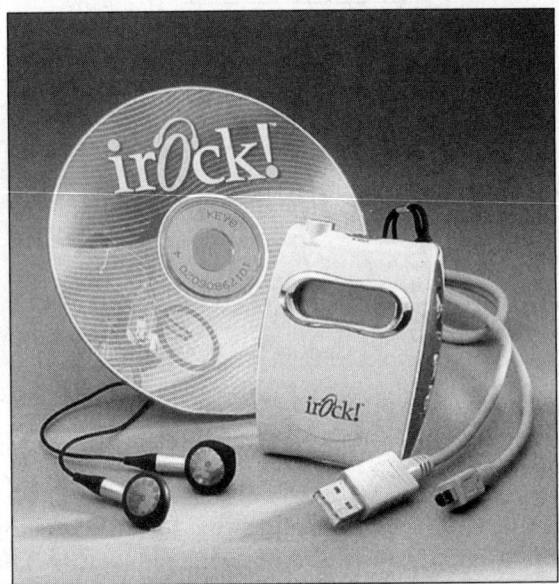

Figure 9-5   An MP3 player with player software, headphones, and cable used to download MP3 files from a PC

Compression Methods Used with MP3 Players

One of the better-known multimedia data compression standards is MPEG, an international standard for data compression for motion pictures, video, and audio. Developed by the **Moving Pictures Experts Group (MPEG)**, it tracks movement from one frame to the next, and only stores what changes, rather than compressing individual frames. MPEG compression can yield a compression ratio of 100:1 for full-motion video (30 frames per second, or 30 fps).

There are currently several MPEG standards, MPEG-1, MPEG-2, MPEG-3, and MPEG-4. MPEG-1 is used in business and home applications to compress images. MPEG-2 is used to compress video films on DVD-ROM. MPEG-3 is used for audio compression, and MP3 is a type of MPEG-3 compression. MPEG-4 is used for video transmissions over the Internet.

MPEG compression is possible because it cuts out or drastically reduces sound that is not normally heard or noticed by the human ear. In the regular audio CD format (uncompressed), one minute of music takes up about 10 MB of storage. The same minute of music in MP3 format takes only about 1 MB of memory. This makes it possible to download music in minutes rather than hours. Sound files downloaded from the Internet are most often MP3 files. MP3 files have an .mp3 file extension. For more information about MPEG and MP3, see *www.mpeg.org*.

How MP3 Players Work

Most portable MP3 players today store MP3 files in onboard memory or hard drives, which can be expanded using an add-on flash RAM card such as SmartMedia, CompactFlash, or Memory Stick. MP3 files are downloaded from the PC to the MP3 player, in contrast to using a digital camera, which transfers or uploads data to the PC.

You can download and purchase MP3 music files from Web sites such as EMusic (*www.emusic.com*) and MP3.com (*www.mp3.com*). Once the files are downloaded to your PC, you can play them on your PC using MP3 player software such as Windows Media Player or MusicMatch Jukebox (see *www.musicmatch.com*), transfer them to a portable MP3 player, or convert them into an audio CD if your computer has a rewritable CD (CD-RW) drive. There are also CD/MP3 players that can play CDs in either standard audio format or MP3 format. A CD can store 10 hours or more of music in MP3 format. You can also play the MP3 files directly from the Internet without first downloading them, which is called **streaming audio**. MP3 files are generally transferred to portable devices using a USB or serial cable.

Also, you can convert files from your regular music CDs into MP3 files (a process called ripping), and play them on your computer or download them to an MP3 player. "Ripper" software copies the music file from the CD, and encoder software compresses the file into MP3 format. CD rippers, MP3 encoders, and MP3 player software can be downloaded from the Internet. For example, see the MusicMatch site at *www.musicmatch.com*.

Table 9-3 lists some manufacturers of MP3 players.

Table 9-3   MP3 player manufacturers

Creative Labs	www.creative.com
I-Jam	www.ijamworld.com
Imation	www.imation.com
Intel	www.intel.com
Panasonic	www.panasonic.com
Pine Technology	www.pineusa.com
Samsung	www.samsungusa.com
Sensory Science owned by SONICblue	www.sensoryscience.com
SONICblue	www.sonicblue.com
Sony	www.sel.sony.com

Video Capture Card

An NTSC (National Television Standards Committee) video capture card is another multimedia option. With this card, you can capture input from a camcorder or directly from TV. Video can be saved as motion clips or stills, edited, and, with the right card, copied back to video tape for viewing with a VCR and television. Look for these features on a video capture card:

- An IEEE 1394 (FireWire) port to interface with a digital camcorder
- Data transfer rates, which affect the price of the card
- Capture resolution and color-depth capabilities of the card
- Ability to transfer data back to the digital camcorder or VCR
- Stereo audio jacks
- Video-editing software bundled with the card

Other options include a TV tuner that makes it possible to turn your PC into a television, complete with instant replay and program scheduling. Ports on a video capture card might include an antenna or cable TV port for input and a TV or VCR port for output. Other ports are a PC monitor video port and possibly an IEEE 1394 port for a camcorder. Expect the card to fit into an AGP slot and take the place of your regular video card. For an excellent example of a video capture card, see the All-in-Wonder RADEON card from ATI Technologies at *www.ati.com*.

Table 9-4 lists some manufacturers of video capture cards.

Table 9-4   Video capture card manufacturers

ASUS	*www.asus.com*
ATI	*www.ati.com*
Creative Labs	*www.creative.com*
Diamond	*www.diamondmm.com*
Matrox	*www.matrox.com*
Pinnacle Systems	*www.pinnaclesys.com*

OPTICAL STORAGE TECHNOLOGY

CDs and DVDs are popular storage media for multimedia data, and CDs are the most popular way of distributing software. Both DVD and CD-ROM technologies use patterns of tiny pits on the surface of a disc to represent bits, which are then readable by a laser beam. This is why they are called optical storage technologies. CD-ROM drives use the **CDFS (Compact Disc File System)** or the **UDF (Universal Disk Format)** file system, and DVD-drives only use the newer UDF. Windows supports both file systems, which include several standards used for audio, photographs, video and other data.

Most CD-ROM drives support several CDFS formats, and most DVD drives support CDFS and several UDF formats. In this section, you will learn about the major optical storage technologies, including their similarities and differences, their storage capacities, and variations within each type.

CD-ROM

Of the multimedia components discussed in this chapter, the most popular is the CD-ROM drive. CD-ROMs are used to distribute software and sound files. CD-ROM drives are read-only devices. Read/writable CD drives are discussed later in this chapter.

During the manufacturing process, data can be written to a CD-ROM disc only once, because the surface of the disc is actually embedded with the data. Figure 9-6 shows a CD-ROM surface that is laid out as one continuous spiral of sectors of equal length that hold equal amounts of data. If laid out in a straight line, this spiral would be 3.5 miles long. The surface of a CD-ROM stores data as pits and lands. **Lands** are raised areas, and **pits** are recessed areas on the surface, each representing either a 1 or a 0, respectively. The bits are read by the drive with a laser beam that distinguishes between a pit and a land by the amount of deflection or scattering that occurs when the light beam hits the surface.

9

Figure 9-6   The spiral layout of sectors on a CD-ROM surface

A small motor with an actuator arm moves the laser beam to the sector on the track it needs to read. If the disc were spinning at a constant speed, the speed near the center of the disc would be greater than the speed at the outer edge. To create the effect of **constant linear velocity (CLV)**, the CD-ROM drive uses a mechanism that speeds up the disc when the laser beam is near the center of the disc, and slows down the disc when the laser beam is near the outer edge. Thus, the beam is over a sector for the same amount of time no matter where the sector is. (Since the outer edge has more sectors than the inner edge, the light beam needs more time to read near the outer edge than it does near the inner edge.) The transfer rate of the first CD-ROM drives was about 150K per second of data (150 KBps), with the rpm (revolutions per minute) set to 200 when the laser was near the center of the disc. This transfer rate was about right for audio CDs. To show video and motion without a choppy effect, the speed of the drives was increased to double speed (150K per second × 2), quad speed (150K per second × 4), and so on. It is not uncommon now to see CD-ROM drives with speeds at 72 times the audio speed. Audio CDs must still drop the speed to the original speed of 200 rpm and a transfer rate of 150KBps.

Because of the problems of changing speeds using CLV, newer, faster CD-ROM drives use a combination of CLV and **constant angular velocity (CAV)**, the same technology used by hard drives, whereby the disc rotates at a constant speed.

When you choose a CD-ROM drive, look for the multisession feature, which means that the drive can read a disc that has been created in multiple sessions. To say a disc was created in **multisessions** means that data was written to the disc at different times rather than in a single long, continuous session.

Some CD-ROM drives have power-saving features controlled by the device driver. For example, when the drive waits for a command for more than five minutes, it enters Power Save Mode, causing the spindle motor to stop. The restart is automatic when the drive receives a command.

Table 9-5 lists manufacturers of CD-ROM drives.

Table 9-5   CD-ROM drive manufacturers

Acer Peripherals	www.global.acer.com
ASUS	www.asus.com
Addonics Technologies	www.addonics.com
Axonix	www.axonix.com
Benq	www.benq.com
Circo Technology	www.circotech.com
Creative Labs	www.creativelabs.com www.creative.com
Hewlett-Packard	www.hpcdwriter.com
Panasonic	www.panasonic.com
Samsung	www.samsung.com
Sanyo	www.sanyo.com
Sony	www.sony.com
TDK	www.tdk.com/multimedia

Caring for CD-ROM Drives and Discs

Most problems with CD-ROMs are caused by dust, fingerprints, scratches, defects on the surface of the CD, or random electrical noise. Don't use a CD-ROM drive if it is standing vertically, such as when someone turns a desktop PC case on its side to save desktop space. Use these precautions when handling CDs or DVDs:

- Hold the CD by the edge; do not touch the bright side of the disc where data is stored.

- To remove dust or fingerprints, use a clean, soft, dry cloth.

- Do not write on, or paste paper to, the surface of the CD. Don't paste any labels to the top of the CD, because this can imbalance the CD and cause the drive to vibrate.

- Do not subject the CD to heat or leave it in direct sunlight.

- Do not use cleaners, alcohol, and the like on the CD.

- Do not make the center hole larger.

- Do not bend the CD.

- Do not drop the CD or subject it to shock.

- If a CD gets stuck in the drive, use the emergency eject hole to remove it. Turn off the power to the PC first. Then insert an instrument such as a straightened paper clip into the hole to manually eject the tray.

How a CD-ROM Drive Can Interface with the Motherboard

CD-ROM drives can interface with the motherboard in several ways. The drive can:

- Use an IDE interface; it can share an IDE connection and/or cable with a hard drive. IDE is the most popular interface method for CD-ROM drives. These drives follow the **ATAPI (Advanced Technology Attachment Packet Interface)** standard, an extension of the IDE/ATA standard that allows tape drives and CD-ROM drives to be treated just like another hard drive on the system.

- Use a SCSI interface with a SCSI host adapter

- Use a proprietary expansion card that works only with CD-ROMs from a particular manufacturer

- Use a proprietary connection on a sound card

- Be a portable drive and plug into an external port on your PC, such as a USB port or SCSI port

Most CD-ROM drives are Plug and Play compliant. These drives allow a system to avoid resource conflicts. Boxes marked "Designed for Windows" indicate Plug and Play CD-ROM drives.

Installing a CD-ROM Drive

Once installed, the CD-ROM or CD-RW drive becomes another drive on your system, such as drive D or E. After it is installed, you access it just like any other drive by typing D: or E: at the command prompt, or by accessing the drive through Windows Explorer. The major differences are (1) the CD-ROM drive is read-only (you cannot write to it) and (2) a CD-ROM drive is slower to access than a hard drive.

The most popular interface for a CD-ROM drive is IDE, although you will occasionally see a SCSI CD-ROM drive. SCSI installations are covered in Chapter 8. Figure 9-7 shows the rear of an IDE CD-ROM drive. Note the jumper bank that can be set to cable select, slave, or master. Recall from Chapter 7 that, for enhanced IDE (EIDE), there are four choices for drive installations: primary master, primary slave, secondary master, and secondary slave. If the drive will be the second drive installed on the cable, then set the drive to slave. If the drive is the only drive on the cable, choose master, since single is not a choice. The cable select setting is used if a special IDE cable-select cable determines which drive is master or slave. If the CD-ROM drive is sharing an IDE channel with a hard drive, make the hard drive the master and the CD-ROM drive the slave.

Figure 9-7   Rear view of an IDE CD-ROM drive

When given the choice of putting the CD-ROM drive on the same cable with a hard drive or on its own cable, choose to use its own cable. If the CD-ROM drive shares a cable with a hard drive, it can slow down the hard drive's performance. Most systems today have two IDE connections on the motherboard, so most likely you will be able to use IDE2 for the CD-ROM drive.

Follow these general steps to install a CD-ROM drive, using safety precautions to protect the system against ESD:

1. Open the case and slide the drive into an empty bay. If the bay uses rails, screw the rails in place. If you have no rails, then put two screws on each side of the drive, tightening the screws so the drive can't shift, but avoiding over-tightening them. Use the screws that come with the drive; screws too long can damage the drive. If necessary, buy a mounting kit to extend the sides of the drive so that it will fit into the bay and be securely attached.

2. Connect a power cord to the drive.

3. For IDE drives, connect the 40-pin cable to the IDE adapter and the drive, being careful to follow the pin 1 rule: match the edge color on the cable to pin 1 on both the adapter card and the drive. Generally, the colored edge will be closest to the power connector.

4. Attach the audio cord if you have a sound card. Don't make the mistake of attaching a miniature power cord designed for a 3½-inch disk drive coming from the power supply to the audio input connector on the sound card. The connections appear to fit, but you'll probably destroy the drive by doing so.

5. Some drives have a ground connection, with one end of the ground cable attaching to the computer case. Follow the directions included with the drive.

6. Check all connections, and turn on the power. Press the eject button on the front of the drive. If it works, then you know power is getting to the drive. Put the case cover back on.

7. Turn on the PC. If the drive is Plug and Play, Windows will automatically launch the Found New Hardware Wizard. Windows supports IDE CD-ROM drives using its own internal 32-bit drivers without add-on drivers, so the installation of drivers requires little intervention on your part. If the Found New Hardware Wizard does not launch, click **Start**, **Settings**, **Control Panel**, and double-click **Add New Hardware**. Click **Next** when you are prompted to begin installing the software for the new device. Complete the installation by following the directions on the Add New Hardware Wizard.

8. Windows assigns the next available drive letter to the drive. To dictate what the drive letter should be, use Device Manager. Access Device Manager, select the CD-ROM drive, and click **Properties**, then click the **Settings** tab (see Figure 9-8), where the drive is designated E:. Select a range of letters to be used by the drive and click **OK**.

Figure 9-8   You can specify the drive letter assigned to the CD-ROM drive from the Properties box for the drive

When you update or install additional features on applications software, some software expects the same drive letter for the CD-ROM drive that was used when it was first installed. Permanently setting the CD-ROM drive letter satisfies the requirements of this software.

9. The drive is now ready to use. Press the eject button to open the drive shelf, and place a CD in the drive. Since data on CDs is written only on the bottom, be careful to protect it. Now access the CD using Explorer (use the assigned drive letter).

If you have a problem reading the CD, verify that the CD is placed in the tray label-side-up, and that the format is compatible with your drive. If one CD doesn't work, try another—the first CD may be defective or scratched.

A CD-ROM drive can be set so that when you insert a CD, software on the CD automatically executes, a feature called Autorun or Autoplay. To turn the feature on, from Device Manager, right-click on the CD-ROM drive and select Properties. From the Properties window, select the Settings tab and select Auto insert notification. To prevent a CD from automatically playing when the feature is enabled, hold down the Shift key when inserting the CD.

CD-R and CD-RW

A CD-ROM is a read-only medium, meaning that CD-ROM drives can only read, not write. In the past, writing to a CD required expensive equipment and was not practical for personal computer use. Now, **CD-R (CD-recordable)** drives and disks are much more affordable, making "burning" your own CD a viable option. These CD-R discs can be read by regular CD-ROM drives and are excellent ways to distribute software or large amounts of data. Besides allowing for a lot of data storage space on a relatively inexpensive medium, another advantage of distributing software and/or data on a CD-R disc is that you can be assured that no one will edit or overwrite what's written on the disc.

A regular CD-ROM is created by pressing pits into the surface of the disc, but a CD-R disc is created differently. Heat is applied to special chemicals on the disc, which causes these chemicals to reflect less light than the areas that are not burned, thus creating the same effect as a pit does on a regular CD. You can tell the difference between a CD and a CD-R disc by the color of the bottom of the disk. CD-R discs have a blue, black, or some other color tint, and CDs are silver. Referring to writing data to a CD-R as "burning" the CD-R is actually fairly accurate. When you purchase and install a CD-R drive, good software to manage the writing process is an important part of the purchase, because some less robust software can make burning a disc a difficult process. Also, some CD-R drives are multisession drives and some are not.

Also available, at a higher cost, is a **CD-RW (CD-rewritable)** drive, which allows you to overwrite old data with new data. The process of creating a CD-RW disc is similar to that used for CD-R discs. The chemicals on the surface of the CD-RW disc are different, allowing the process of writing a less-reflective spot to the surface of the disc to be reversed so that data can be erased. One drawback to CD-RW discs is that the medium cannot always be read successfully by older CD-ROM drives or by some audio CD players.

CD-RW discs are useful in the process of developing CDs for distribution. A developer can create a disc, test for errors, and rewrite to the disc without having to waste many discs during the development process. Once the disc is fully tested, then CD-R discs can be burned for distribution. The advantages of distributing on CD-R discs rather than CD-RW discs are that CD-R discs are less expensive and can be read by all CD-ROM drives.

 TIP A CD-R or CD-RW is expected to hold its data for many years; however, you can prolong the life of a CD-R or CD-RW by protecting it from exposure to light.

DVD

With multimedia, the ability to store massive amounts of data is paramount to the technology's success. The goal of storing a full-length movie on a single unit of a computerized, inexpensive storage medium has been met by more than one technology, but the technology that has clearly taken the lead in popularity is **DVD (digital video disc or digital versatile disc)** technology (see Figure 9-9). It takes up to seven CDs to store a full-length movie, and only one DVD disc. A DVD disc can hold 8.5 GB of data, and, if both the top and bottom surfaces are used, can hold 17 GB of data, which is enough for more than eight hours of video storage. DVD uses the Universal Disk Format (UDF) file system.

Figure 9-9   A DVD device

When you look at the surface of a CD and a DVD, it is difficult to distinguish between the two. They both have the same 5-inch diameter and 1.2-mm thickness, and the same shiny surface. However, a DVD disc can use both the top and bottom surface for data. If the top of the disc has no label, data is probably written on it, and it is most likely a DVD. Because DVD uses a shorter wavelength laser, it can read smaller, more densely packed pits, which increases the disc's capacity. In addition, there is a second layer added to DVD discs, an opaque layer that also holds data, which almost doubles the capacity of the disc.

DVD uses MPEG-2 video compression and requires an MPEG-2 controller to decode the compressed data. This decoder can be (1) firmware on a controller card that comes bundled with the DVD drive, (2) software that comes bundled with the DVD drive and installed at the time the DVD drive is installed, or (3) the decoder is contained on a video capture card. Audio is stored on DVD in Dolby AC-3 compression. This audio compression method is also the standard used by HDTV (high-definition TV). Dolby AC-3 compression is also known as Dolby Digital Surround or Dolby Surround Sound, and it supports six separate sound channels of sound information for six different speakers, each producing a different sound. These speakers are known as Front Left and Right, Front Center, Rear Left and Right, and Subwoofer. Because each channel is digital, there is no background noise on the channel, and a sound engineer can place sound on any one of these speakers. The sound effects can be awesome!

Besides DVD-ROM, new DVD devices have recently come on the market that are read-writable. Table 9-6 describes these devices.

Table 9-6   DVD devices

DVD Device	Description
DVD-ROM	Read-only device. A DVD-ROM drive can also read CD-ROMs.
DVD-R	DVD recordable. Uses a similar technology to that used by CD-R drives. Holds about 4.7 GB of data. Can read DVD-ROM discs.
DVD-RAM	Recordable and erasable. Multifunctional DVD device that can read DVD-RAM, DVD-R, DVD-ROM, and CD-R discs.
DVD-R/RW or DVD-ER	Rewritable DVD device, also known as erasable, recordable device. Media can be read by most DVD-ROM drives.
DVD+R/RW	A technology similar to and currently competing with DVD-RW. Can read DVD-ROM and CD-ROM discs, but will not be compatible with DVD-RAM discs.

The last three items in Table 9-6 are competing with one another. All have similar, but not identical, features, and compatibility and standards are issues. It's yet to be seen which of these three media will prevail in the marketplace although DVD-RAM appears to be moving ahead. When purchasing one, pay close attention to compatibility with other media, such as CD-ROM, and to the availability and price of discs.

Table 9-7 lists manufacturers of DVD drives.

Table 9-7   DVD drive manufacturers

Acer Communications and Multimedia	*www.acercm.com*
Addonics	*www.addonics.com*

Table 9-7 DVD drive manufacturers (continued)

Creative Labs	www.creative.com
Hewlett-Packard	www.hp.com
IBM	www.ibm.com
Intel	www.intel.com
Pioneer	www.pioneerelectronics.com
Sony Electronics	www.sel.sony.com
Toshiba	www.toshiba.com

Installing a DVD Drive

For our example of installing a DVD drive we are using the Creative PC-DVD Encore by Creative Labs, Inc. (*www.americas.creative.com*) because it uses a hardware decoder, making it a more complicated installation than when using a software decoder. Besides the documentation and a sample DVD game disc, the parts that are included in the DVD drive kit are shown in Figure 9-10. The data coming from the DVD drive is split into video data and sound data. Recall that video data must be decoded before being sent to the monitor, and sound data must be decoded before being sent to a regular sound card (one that does not process Dolby sound). In both cases, this is accomplished by the DVD decoder card. Figure 9-11 shows the flow of data in the completed system.

 A good example of a DVD drive that uses a software decoder is the Creative Lab's Ovation 16x. This IDE drive comes with an audio cable, IDE cable, and CD that contains the drivers and decoder software. Installation is much simpler than the example here because there is no decoder card to install.

Figure 9-10 Parts that are included in the DVD drive kit

Figure 9-11 Data flow in the DVD subsystem

To help make the final installation of parts easier to visualize, we set up the installation outside the case and took the photo shown in Figure 9-12. This photo was taken simply to help you understand the final installation. No power was turned on while the components were in this position!

Video data "loops back" to DVD decoder

Decoded audio data to sound card

Video card

Sound card

DVD decoder card

IDE data cable carries video data

9

DVD drive

Audio data to decoder

VGA output to monitor

Audio output to speakers

Figure 9-12   The complete DVD subsystem, including the drive (right) and various components installed on the motherboard (left)

The DVD decoder card (Figure 9-13) has connections for audio in, audio out, video in, and video out. In addition, there are two other external ports, one for TV out and one for Dolby digital sound out. Use the TV out port to play DVD movies from your PC, and the Dolby port if you have a Dolby speaker system.

Output to a Dolby digital sound device

Audio out (to sound card)

Audio in (from DVD drive)

PCI connection

VGA in (from video card using loopback cable)

VGA out (to monitor)

TV out (using TV cable provided)

Figure 9-13   DVD decoder card

The rear of the DVD drive is shown in Figure 9-14, and a diagram of the rear panel is shown in Figure 9-15. Looking closely at Figure 9-14, note that the jumper is set so that the drive will be a slave on the IDE connection.

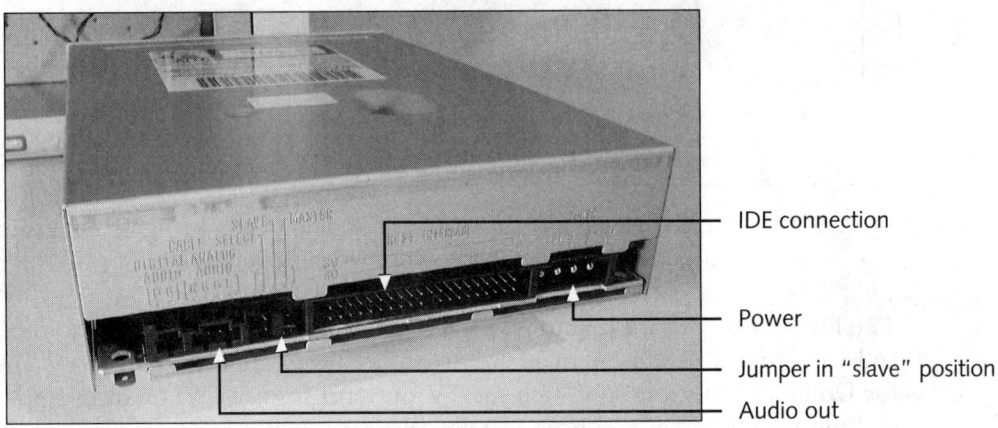

IDE connection

Power

Jumper in "slave" position

Audio out

Figure 9-14   Rear of DVD drive (see Figure 9-15 for an explanation of each connection)

Figure 9-15   Rear panel of the DVD drive

Looking at the location of the bay for the DVD drive, we decide to connect the audio cable first, slide the drive into the bay, and then connect the remaining cable and cord. Survey your own situation for the best approach. Follow these steps to install the DVD components:

1. Turn off the PC and remove the case cover. Confirm that the jumper on the DVD drive is set to slave (the default setting).

2. Connect the DVD drive audio cord to the analog audio connection on the rear of the drive.

3. Remove the faceplate covering the bay opening on the front of the computer case.

4. Slide the drive into the bay from the front of the bay.

5. Secure the drive in the bay with two screws on each side of the drive.

6. Attach the IDE data cable to the drive, being careful to align the edge color of the cable with pin 1 on the drive (Figure 9-16).

7. Connect a power cord to the power connection on the drive.

8. Connect the audio cord coming from the DVD drive to the audio in connection on the DVD decoder card.

9. Connect the second audio cord first to the audio out connection on the DVD decoder card and then to the audio in connection on the sound card (refer back to Figure 9-12). The cord has two plugs at the sound-card end. Select the plug that fits the sound-card connection.

10. Insert the DVD decoder card in a PCI expansion slot and secure it with a screw.

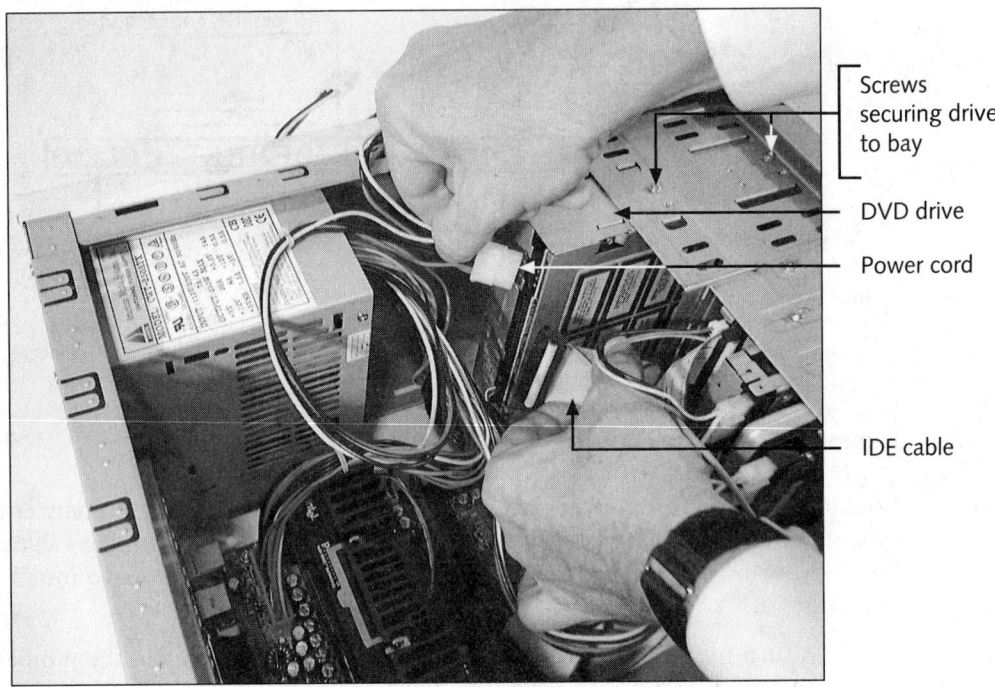

Screws securing drive to bay

DVD drive

Power cord

IDE cable

Figure 9-16 After the DVD drive is secured in its bay, attach the IDE data cable and power cord

11. Replace the case cover. Install the video loopback cable (see Figure 9-17), which presents video data to the DVD decoder for decoding before the decoder sends the video data on to the monitor.

Video out—
from DVD decoder
to monitor

Video out—
from video card

Video in—to
DVD decoder

9

Figure 9-17   The video loopback cable installed in the DVD subsystem

12. Turn on the PC. Windows will recognize and use the drive as a CD-ROM drive without additional device drivers. To use the drive as a DVD drive, you must install the device drivers that come bundled with the drive. Insert the installation disk in the floppy disk drive and enter **A:Setup** in the Run dialog box to start the installation.

HARDWARE USED FOR BACKUPS AND FAULT TOLERANCE

How valuable is your data? How valuable is your software? In many cases, the most valuable component on the desktop is not the hardware or the software, but the data. Think about each computer you support. What would happen if the hard drive failed? You should create backups to prepare for just that situation. Whether your hard drive contains a large database or just a few word-processing files, make backups. Never keep an important file on only one medium. Make a duplicate copy to a disk, to a file server, or to tape backup. Consider keeping some of your backups in an off-site location.

Your backup policy depends on what you are backing up. If you use your PC to interface with a server, for example, and all data is stored on the server and not on the PC, then you will only back up software. (The person responsible for the server usually backs up the data. You may want to check with the responsible party in your organization to make sure this is being done.) If you keep original application software disks and CDs in a safe place, and if you have multiple copies of them, you might decide not to back up the applications. In this case, if a hard drive fails, your chore is to reload several software packages.

However, if you maintain a large database on the hard drive of your PC, you need to seriously consider a sophisticated backup method. Suppose this database is quite large and is edited daily, several times a day. If this database is lost, so are thousands of labor hours. Plan for the worst case! A good tape backup system is probably in order. Maintain 5 or 10 tapes, on which a complete backup of the database is made each night.

Popular hardware devices used for making hard drive backups on standalone personal computers or small servers include tape, Zip, and Jaz drives, and read-write CDs. However, in a business environment, if a PC is connected to a file server, the most practical backup approach is to back up data from the PC's hard drive to the file server. Data on both the PC and the file server can become corrupted. However, the file server most likely uses its own automated backup utility to back up to either tape or a larger mainframe computer. This section first discusses using tape drives and then using removable drives for backups.

Tape Drives

Tape drives (Figure 9-18) are an inexpensive way of backing up an entire hard drive or portions of it. Tape drives are more convenient for backups than floppy disks or other types of removable disks. Tapes have capacities of anywhere from several hundred kilobytes to several gigabytes and come in several types and formats. Although tape drives don't require that you use special backup software to manage them, you might want to invest in specialized backup software to make backups as efficient and effortless as possible. Many tape drives come with bundled software, and Windows offers a Backup utility that can use tape drives. Several of the more common standards and types of tape drives and tapes are described in this section.

The biggest disadvantage of using tape drives is that data is stored on tape by **sequential access**, meaning that, in order to read data from anywhere on the tape, you must start at the beginning of the tape and read until you come to the sought-after data. Sequential access makes recovering files slow and inconvenient, which is why tapes are not used for general-purpose data storage.

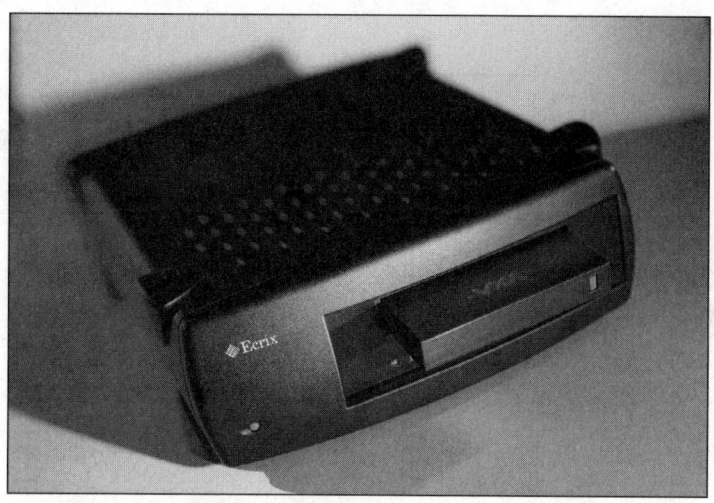

Figure 9-18   An external tape drive

Table 9-8 lists some manufacturers of tape drives.

Table 9-8   Tape drive manufacturers

DLT	www.dlttape.com
Exabyte	www.exabyte.com
Hewlett Packard	www.hp.com
Iomega	www.iomega.com
Quantum Corporation	www.quantum.com
Seagate	www.seagate.com
Sony	www.sony.com

How a Tape Drive Interfaces with a Computer

A tape drive can be external or internal. An external tape drive costs more but can be used by more than one computer. A tape drive can interface with a computer in these ways:

- An external tape drive can use the parallel port (see Figure 9-19) with an optional pass-through to the printer (so that the drive and the printer can use the same parallel port).

- An external or internal drive can use a SCSI bus. This method works well if the tape drive and the hard drive are on the same SCSI bus, which contains a data pass-through just to the SCSI system.

- An external or internal drive can use its own proprietary controller card or the floppy drive interface.

- An internal drive can use the IDE ATAPI interface.

Figure 9-19   An external tape drive can use the parallel port for input/output, with an optional pass-through to the printer

Currently, the most popular tape drive interfaces are SCSI and IDE ATAPI. Figure 9-20 shows the rear of an ATAPI tape drive. You can see the connections for a power supply and a 40-pin IDE cable as well as jumpers to set the drive to master, slave, or cable select. This setup is similar to any IDE device. When installing an ATAPI tape drive, avoid putting the drive on the same IDE data cable as the hard drive, or it might hinder the hard drive's performance. A typical configuration is to install the hard drive as the sole device on the primary IDE channel and let a CD-ROM drive and tape drive share the second channel. Set the CD-ROM drive to master and the tape drive to slave on that channel.

Figure 9-20   The rear of an ATAPI IDE tape drive

The Tapes Used by a Tape Drive

Tape drives accommodate one of two kinds of tapes: full-sized **data cartridges** are 4 × 6 × ⅝ inches, and the smaller **minicartridges**, like the one in Figure 9-21, are 3¼ × 2½ × ⅗ inches. Minicartridges are more popular because their drives can fit into a standard 5½-inch drive bay of a PC case.

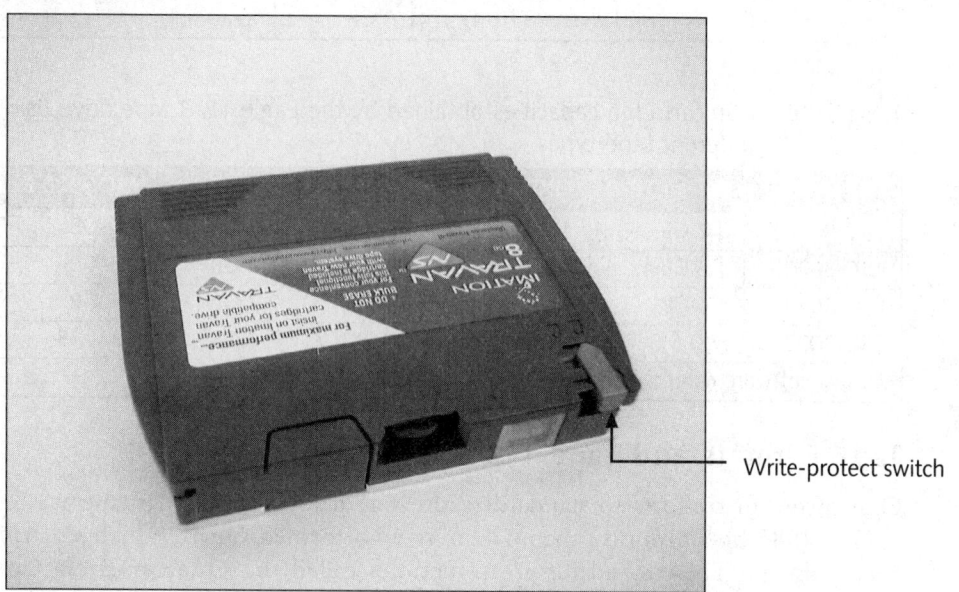

Write-protect switch

Figure 9-21 Minicartridge for a tape drive has a write-protect switch

The technology used by tape drives to write to tapes is similar to that used by floppy drives (see Chapter 6). A FAT at the beginning of the tape tracks the location of data and bad sectors on the tape. The tape must be formatted before data can be written to it. Buy factory-formatted tapes to save time.

Standards for writing data to tapes have not developed as well as consumers would like, making it necessary to carefully match tapes to tape drives when purchasing and using them. Several standards exist, which have been promoted by different organizations as well as by individual manufacturers. Below are tables about two different tapes, each from a different tape drive manufacturer, showing the tape formats and tape types that are supported by their tape drives. Table 9-9 shows that the Seagate Travan 8- or 20-GB drives can support QIC-3080 and TR-5 tapes. Table 9-10 shows that the Eagle TR-3 tape minicartridge tape drive can use either the QIC-3010 or QIC-3020 format and five tape types. Note that these drives are also likely to be able to read other formats that are compatible with these formats.

Table 9-9   Tape formats for the Seagate Travan 8-GB and 20-GB tape drives

Tape Drive	Tape Format	Capacity	Tape Function
Travan NS 8-GB drive	Travan 8 (TR-4) QIC-3080 QIC-Wide (3080)	8 GB 3.2 GB 4 GB	Read and write Read and write Read and write
Travan 20-GB drive	Travan 20 (TR-5) Travan 8 (TR-4)	20 GB 8 GB	Read and write Read only

Table 9-10   Minicartridge capacities obtained by the Eagle TR-3 tape drive using five different tape types

Tape Format	Travan TR-3	QIC Wide	MC 3000XL	TR-3 Extra	MC 3020 Extra
QIC-3020*	3.2 GB	1.7 GB	1.4 GB	4.4 GB	3.2 GB
QIC-3020	1.6 GB	850 MB	680 MB	2.2 GB	1.6 GB
QIC-3020*	1.6 GB	840 MB	680 MB	2.2 GB	1.6 GB
QIC-3020	800 MB	420 MB	340 MB	1.1 GB	800 MB
*Using software compression with an assumed 2:1 compression ratio					

Tape Formats and Tape Types

One of the first efforts to standardize the way data is written to tape was established around 1983 by a group of manufacturers who formed Quarter-Inch Cartridge Drive Standards, Inc. These standards are sometimes called the **Quarter-Inch Committee (QIC)**, or **quarter-inch cartridge** standards. Many QIC standards have been developed, but only a few are used today. 3M developed a standard, called Travan, based on the QIC format. Travan has been backed by many leaders in the tape drive industry. There are different levels of Travan standards, called TR-1 through TR-5, each based on a different QIC standard.

Removable Drives

A removable drive can be either an external or internal drive. Using a removable drive provides several advantages:

- Increases the overall storage capacity of a system

- Makes it easy to move large files from one computer to another

- Serves as a convenient medium for making backups of hard drive data

- Makes it easy to secure important files (To keep important files secure, keep the removable drive in a safe when it is not being used.)

When purchasing a removable drive, consider how susceptible the drive is when dropped. The **drop height** is the height from which the manufacturer says you can drop the drive without making the drive unusable. Also consider how long the data will last on the drive. The **half-life** (sometimes called life expectancy or shelf life) of the disk is the time it takes for the magnetic strength of the medium to weaken by half. Magnetic media, including traditional hard drives and floppy disks, have a half-life of five to seven years, but writable optical media such as CD-Rs have a half-life of 30 years.

An internal removable drive should also be Plug and Play compliant, meaning that the drive can interface with Plug and Play BIOS and with Windows 9x and Windows 2000 installations without manual setting of switches and jumpers.

Types of Removable Drives

One type of removable drive is the Iomega 3½-inch Zip drive, which stores 100 MB or 250 MB of data on each of its disks and has a drop height of 8 feet (see Figure 9-22). An internal 100-MB Zip drive costs less than $100 and uses an IDE interface. The external Zip drive plugs into the parallel port, a USB port, or a SCSI port. The drive and disk look like a traditional 3½-inch floppy disk drive and disk, but the disk is slightly larger. If you include a Zip drive on a new PC, consider it an add-on, not a replacement for the standard 3½-inch floppy disk drive. Zip drives can't read standard 3½-inch floppy disks.

Two other removable drive technologies are SuperDisk, developed by Imation, which stores 120 MB of data and SuperDisk, manufactured by Maxell that stores 240 MB of data. SuperDisk 120 MB drives are backward-compatible with double-density (720K) and high-density (1.44 MB) floppy disks, and SuperDisk 240 MB drives are back-compatible with SuperDisk 120 MB drives and both size floppy disks. The SuperDisk is really two disk drives in one. It can use the old technology to read from and write to regular floppy disks, and it can use laser technology to read/write 120 MB or 240 MB disks. SuperDisk is up to 27 times faster than regular floppy drives. One advantage SuperDisk has over Zip drives is its backward compatibility with regular floppy disks. A disadvantage of SuperDisk is that the medium is not as popular as Zip drives, so if you plan to exchange the disks with other users, most likely you will want to use a Zip drive. SuperDisk drives can be purchased as external (parallel port and USB) or internal drives.

9

Figure 9-22   An internal Zip drive kit includes the IDE Zip drive, documentation, drivers on floppy disk, and one Zip disk

The Iomega Jaz drive is one example of a removable hard drive that stores 1 GB or 2 GB of data on each removable disk. Both the internal and external models use a SCSI connection although you can purchase an adapter to enable the external SCSI Jaz drive to use a USB port. Iomega advertises that you can back up 1 GB of data from your fixed hard drive to the Jaz drive in as little as five minutes. The drop height is three feet.

Installing a Removable Drive

Installing an internal removable drive is similar to installing a hard drive. For an IDE drive, set the drive to master or slave on an IDE channel. If the external or internal drive is a SCSI drive, the SCSI host adapter must already be installed and configured. How to install a SCSI host adapter is covered in Chapter 8. Do the following to install an external drive:

1. Identify the connectors. Many removable drives use either the parallel port, a USB port, or a SCSI port for connection. A parallel drive has a 25-pin connector for the cable to the 25-pin parallel port on the back of the PC, and another 25-pin connector for the printer cable. A SCSI drive has a 25-pin, 50-pin, or 68-pin connector on the drive for the cable to the PC, and another connector for the next SCSI device on the external SCSI bus. For USB, there might be a second USB connection on the device for pass-through to another USB device.

2. For a parallel device, turn off your PC and connect the parallel cable from the drive to the parallel port on the PC. If you have a printer, connect the printer cable to the printer port on the drive. Go to Step 6.

3. For a USB device, connect the USB cable to the USB port. Go to Step 6.

4. For a SCSI device, with the SCSI host adapter installed, connect the SCSI cable to the drive and to the SCSI port on the host adapter.

5. For a SCSI drive, set the drive's SCSI ID. You might also need to set the host adapter to recognize an external device. See the documentation for the host adapter. (SCSI is covered in Chapter 8.)

6. Check all your connections and plug the AC power cord for the drive into a wall socket.

7. Turn on your PC and install the software. See the installation procedures in the documentation that came with the removable drive. Most often, the software is on an accompanying disk.

8. If you have problems, turn everything off and check all connections. Power up and try again.

RAID

Besides maintaining good backups, you can also protect data by continuously writing two copies of the data, each to a different hard drive. This method is most often used on high-end, high-cost file servers, but it is occasionally appropriate for a single-user workstation.

Collectively, these several methods, used to improve performance and/or automatically recover from a failure, are called **RAID (redundant array of independent disks)**. There are several levels of RAID, but this section discusses only the three most commonly used (Table 9-11). If the RAID method can help recover data when one hard drive fails, it is a way to implement **fault tolerance**, which is the ability of a computer to respond to a fault or catastrophic event, such as a hardware failure or power outage, in such a way that data is not lost. Only the first level, RAID 0, is financially practical for a standalone workstation and does not help with fault tolerance.

Table 9-11   The three most common RAID levels

RAID Level and Common Name	Intended Purpose	Description
RAID 0: Disk striping without parity	Increases system performance and volume capacity	Data is written to two or more hard drives. The set of drives is treated as a single volume (a single virtual drive). Because more than one drive is doing the work, performance improves.
RAID 1: Disk mirroring or disk duplexing	Provides fault tolerance and increases performance	Data is written twice, once to each of two drives. Disk mirroring uses only a single HDD controller. Disk duplexing uses two controllers, one for each drive.
RAID 5: Disk striping with parity	Increases performance and volume capacity and provides fault tolerance	Data is written to three or more drives, and parity information is distributed across these drives, so that if one drive fails, the other drives can re-create the data stored on the failed drive.

RAID 0

RAID Level 0 increases the logical drive capacity by treating two or more drives as a single logical drive, but it includes only one copy of data. Therefore, it does not let you recover from a failure. RAID 0 is one method of **disk striping**, in which more than one hard drive is treated as a single volume and data is written across more than one physical drive. For an array of two hard drives, some data is written to one hard drive and some to the other; both drives make up one logical drive, or volume, and data is only written once. If one drive fails, data on the entire logical drive can be lost. RAID 0 is supported by Windows NT, Windows 2000, and Windows XP, but not by Windows 9x. However, you should know that RAID can be implemented by a hard drive controller without the involvement or knowledge of the operating system. This method is called hardware RAID; the method by which the operating system manages the RAID array is called software RAID.

RAID 1

RAID Level 1 is designed to protect data from a hard drive failure by writing the data twice, once to each of two drives. One type of RAID Level 1 is called **disk mirroring**, in which the two hard drives both use the same controller.

The advantages of RAID 1 disk mirroring are:

- If either drive fails, the data is still safe on the other drive.
- Disk reads are speeded up because the system has two places to read from.

The disadvantages of this type of RAID 1 are:

- Having two hard drives in the same computer is more expensive.
- Because the data is written twice, hard drive capacity is, in effect, cut in half.
- Disk writes are slowed down because the data must be written twice.

One weakness in drive mirroring is that both hard drives are using the same controller. If the controller fails, neither hard drive is accessible. An improvement of disk mirroring, also considered RAID 1, is **duplexing**, in which each hard drive has its own controller on its own adapter card. The initial cost is higher, but if one adapter fails, you are protected from losing the data on both drives. If a workstation cannot back up to a server on a network, disk mirroring or duplexing might be appropriate (if the data is considered valuable enough to merit the added expense).

RAID 5

RAID 5, disk striping with distributed parity, is currently the most popular RAID implementation and provides optimum fault tolerance. RAID 5 is an interesting variation of RAID 0 combined with RAID 1 and RAID 4, and improves fault tolerance and drive capacity. RAID 5 requires at least three hard drives. RAID 4, disk striping with parity, is not often used today, but to understand RAID 5, we must first examine how RAID 4 works. In Figure 9-23, RAID 4 uses four hard drives grouped as one virtual hard drive. When any data is written to this one drive, the data is divided into three segments. Each segment is written to one of the first three drives, and parity information about the three segments is written to the fourth drive.

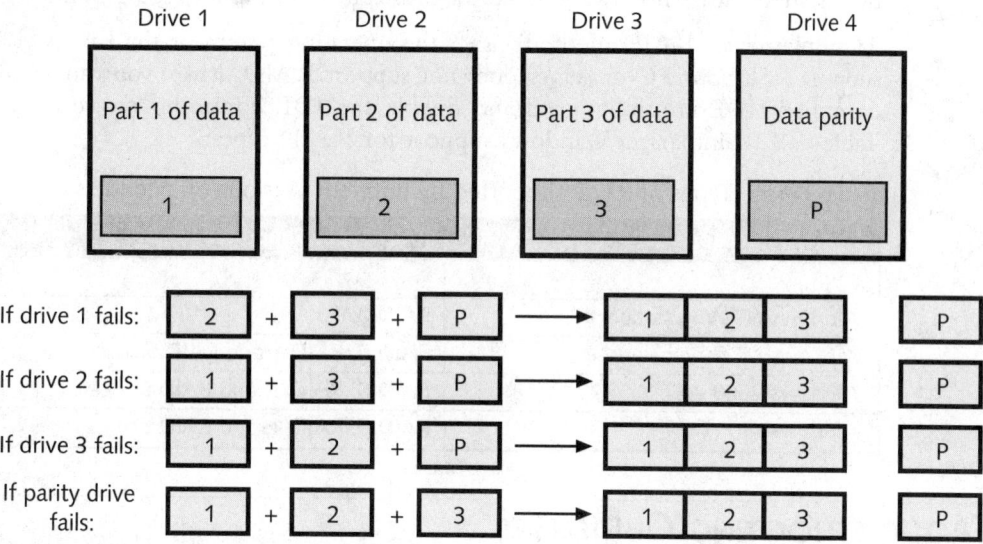

Figure 9-23   RAID 4, disk striping with parity, allows for increased drive capacity as well as fault tolerance: any one drive can fail and data can still be re-created

If any of the four drives fails, the data can be recovered from the other three drives, using the method illustrated in the lower half of Figure 9-23. Using any two segments and the parity information, the three segments can be recreated, or, if the parity drive fails, the three segments are still safely stored on the first three drives. RAID 5, rather than storing all parity information on a single, dedicated parity drive, distributes parity information over all the drives, thus removing the performance bottleneck created by having a single parity drive.

To understand how data is recovered using parity information, consider this simple example. Suppose three numbers are stored on three different drives. If you store the sum of the three numbers on the fourth, or parity, drive, you can use the information you have to calculate a missing number. For example, let's say the three numbers are 1, 2, and 6, you store their sum (9) on the parity drive. If the first number is lost, you can calculate it from the sum and the other two numbers. Actual RAID parity is much more complicated that this, but you get the idea.

When a drive fails, the data can be regenerated on the replacement drive, using information from the other drives. First replace the failed drive with a new drive. For example, to generate the data on the new drive when using Windows NT Server, go to the Disk Administrator of the Administrator Tools and execute a Regenerate command.

Windows NT does the rest. The action is automatic, and you can still use the computer for other operations while regenerating is taking place.

For file servers using RAID 5 that must work continuously, it might be practical to use hardware that allows for hard drive hot-swapping, which means that you can remove one hard drive and insert another without powering down the computer. However, hard drives that can be hot-swapped cost significantly more than regular hard drives.

To implement a RAID method, either the operating system or third-party software must support it. If your PC or server does not support RAID drives, you can install a RAID-compliant IDE controller card and disable the IDE controller on your motherboard. Table 9-12 summarizes Windows support for RAID types.

Table 9-12   Types of RAID supported by different versions of Windows

Windows Version	RAID Types Supported
Windows 9x	---
Windows NT Workstation	RAID 0
Windows NT Server	RAID 0, RAID 1 and RAID 5
Windows 2000	RAID 0, RAID 1, and RAID 5
Windows XP	RAID 0, RAID 1, and RAID 5

TROUBLESHOOTING GUIDELINES

This section covers some troubleshooting guidelines for CD-ROM, CD-RW, DVD, DVD-RW, and tape drives as well as sound cards. Remember, with these components, as with others you have learned about, not to touch chips on circuit boards or disk surfaces where data is stored, stack components on top of one another, or subject them to magnetic fields or ESD.

Problems with CD-ROM, CD-RW, DVD, or DVD-RW Installation

The following are general guidelines to use when a CD-ROM, CD-RW, DVD, or DVD-RW drive installation gives problems:

Computer does not recognize the drive (no drive D listed in Windows 9x Explorer)

- Check the data cable and power cord connections to the drive. Is the stripe on the data cable correctly aligned to pin 1? (Look for an arrow or small 1 printed on the drive. For a best guess, pin 1 is usually next to the power connector.)
- For an IDE drive, is the correct master/slave jumper set? For example, if both the hard drive and the CD-ROM or DVD drive are hooked up to the same ribbon cable, one must be set to master and the other to slave. If the CD-ROM or DVD drive is the only drive connected to the cable, then it should be set to single or master.
- For an IDE drive, is the IDE connection on the motherboard disabled in CMOS setup?

- If you are using a SCSI drive, are the proper IDs set, and is the device terminated if it is the last item in the SCSI chain? Are the correct SCSI drivers installed?

- If you are booting from a startup disk, check drivers, including entries in Config.sys and Autoexec.bat, and verify that Mscdex.exe is in the correct directory.

- Is another device using the same port settings? Check system resources listed in Device Manager. Is there an IRQ conflict with the IDE primary or secondary channel or the SCSI host the drive is using?

- Suspect a boot virus. This is a common problem. Run a virus scan program.

Troubleshooting Sound Problems

Problems with sound can be caused by a problem with the sound card itself, but they can also be a result of system settings, bad connections, or a number of other issues. Below are some questions you can use to try to diagnose the problem.

- Is the sound cable attached between the drive and the analog audio connector on the sound card?

- Are the speakers turned on?

- Is the speaker volume turned down?

- Are the speakers plugged into the line "Out" or the "Spkr" port of the sound card (the middle port)?

- Is the transformer for the speaker plugged into an electrical outlet on one end and into the speakers on the other end?

- Is the volume control for Windows turned down? (To check, click Start, Programs, Accessories, Multimedia, Volume Control.)

- Does the sound card have a "diagnose" file on the install disk?

- Does Device Manager report a problem with the card? Is another device using the same I/O addresses or IRQ number?

- Using Device Manager, uninstall the sound card and then reinstall it using the Add New Hardware applet in Control Panel.

- To check for a bad connection, turn off the computer and remove and reinstall the sound card.

- Replace the sound card with one you know is good.

Troubleshooting Tape Drives

The following is a list of tape drive problems you might encounter and suggestions for dealing with them.

A minicartridge does not work

- If you are trying to write data, verify that the minicartridge is write-enabled.

- Are you inserting the minicartridge correctly? Check the user guide.

- Check that you are using the correct type of minicartridge. See the user guide.

- Is the minicartridge formatted? The software performs the format and can take an hour or more.

- Retension the tape. Use the backup software to do this. Some tape drives require this, and others do not. Retensioning fast-forwards and rewinds the tape to eliminate loose spots.

- Take the minicartridge out and reboot. Try the minicartridge again.

- Try using a new minicartridge. The old one may have worn out.

- As with floppy disks, if the tape was removed from the drive while the drive light was on, the data being written at that time may not be readable.

Data transfer is slow

- Does the tape software have an option for optimizing speed and/or data compression? Try turning one, and then the other, off and on.

- Some tape drives can use an optional accelerator card to speed up data transfer. See the tape drive user guide.

- Try a new minicartridge.

- If the tape drive can do so, completely erase the tape and reformat it. Be sure that the tape drive can perform this procedure before you tell the software to do it.

- If you have installed an accelerator card, verify that the card is connected to the tape drive.

- Check that there is enough memory for the software to run.

The drive does not work after the installation

- Check that pin 1 is oriented correctly to the data cable at both ends.

- Check for a resource conflict. The tape drive normally requires an IRQ, DMA channel, and I/O address.

The drive fails intermittently or gives errors

- The tape might be worn out. Try a new tape.

- Clean the read/write head of the tape drive. See the tape drive user guide for directions.

- For an external tape drive, move the drive as far as you can from the monitor and computer case.

- Reformat the tape.

- Retension the tape.

- Verify that you are using the correct tape type and tape format.

CHAPTER SUMMARY

- Multimedia PCs and devices are designed to create and reproduce lifelike presentations of sight and sound.

- All computer communication is digital. To be converted to digital from analog, sound and images are sampled, which means their data is measured at a series of representative points. More accurate sampling requires more space for data storage.

- MMX and SSE by Intel and 3DNow! by AMD improve the speed of processing graphics, video, and sound, using improved methods of handling high-volume repetition during I/O operations.

- In order to take full advantage of MMX, SSE, or 3DNow! technology, software must be written to use its specific capabilities.

- Installing a sound card includes physically installing the card, then installing the sound card driver and sound applications software.

- The middle plug on the sound card is used for the speaker out, or sound out, function.

- Digital cameras use light sensors to detect light and convert it to a digital signal stored in an image file using JPEG format.

- MP3 is a version of MPEG compression used for audio files. Portable MP3 players store and play MP3 files downloaded from a PC, using internal memory and flash storage devices.

- A video capture card allows you to capture input from a camcorder or directly from TV.

- CD-ROMs are optical read-only devices with data physically embedded into the surface of the disc.

- The speed of some CD-ROM drives slows down as the laser beam moves from the inside to the outside of the disc.

- CD-ROM drives can have an IDE or SCSI interface, or they can connect to the system bus through a proprietary expansion card or through a connection on a sound card.

- The most common interface for CD-ROM drives is IDE, which uses the ATAPI standard, an extension of the IDE/ATA standard developed for tape drives and CD-ROM drives, so that they can be treated just like another drive on the system.

- Data is only written to the shiny underside of a CD-ROM, which should be protected from damage.

- A DVD can store a full-length movie and uses an accompanying decoder card to decode the MPEG-compressed video data and Dolby AC-3 compressed audio.

9

- Tape drives are an inexpensive way of backing up an entire hard drive or portions of it. Tape drives are more convenient for backups than floppy disks or other types of removable disks.
- The three most popular removable drives are Zip, SuperDisk, and Jaz drives.
- Use RAID to mirror data stored on a hard disk and to increase hard drive capacity by making more than one hard drive work as a single virtual drive.

KEY TERMS

ATAPI (Advanced Technology Attachment Packet Interface)

CDFS (Compact Disc File System)

CD-R (CD-recordable)

CD-RW (CD-rewritable)

constant angular velocity (CAV)

constant linear velocity (CLV)

data cartridge

disk mirroring

disk striping

drop height

duplexing

DVD (digital video disc or digital versatile disk)

fault tolerance

half-life

hertz (Hz)

JPEG (Joint Photographic Experts Group)

lands

minicartridge

MMX (Multimedia Extensions)

MP3

MPEG (Moving Pictures Experts Group)

multimedia

multisession

pits

Quarter-Inch Committee or quarter-inch cartridge (QIC)

RAID (redundant array of independent disks)

sampling rate

sequential access

SIMD (single instruction, multiple data)

SSE (Streaming SIMD Extension)

streaming audio

UDF (Universal Disk Format)

10

SUPPORTING MODEMS

In this chapter, you will learn:

♦ How modems work and how to install them

♦ About communications software that modems use to communicate with the OS

♦ Guidelines for troubleshooting modems

Almost all home computers and many corporate desktop computers have modems. This chapter focuses on how modems work as well as how to install and troubleshoot them. In the next chapter, you will learn how to connect a PC to a network and to the Internet, using a modem, cable modem, DSL, or other hardware for the connection.

ALL ABOUT MODEMS

A **modem** is a device used by a PC to communicate over a phone line. A modem can be an external device (see Figure 10-1) connected to a USB or serial port or it can be a modem card (see Figure 10-2), which can use either an ISA or PCI slot.

Figure 10-1   SupraSonic external modem

Flash ROM microchip

Figure 10-2   3Com U.S. Robotics 56K Winmodem modem card

Table 10-1 lists some modem manufacturers.

Table 10-1   Modem manufacturers

Manufacturer	Web Site
U.S. Robotics	*www.usr.com*
Creative Labs	*www.americas.creative.com*
Zoom	*www.zoom.com*

To reduce the total cost of a computer system, some motherboards have a small expansion slot, less than half the length of a PCI slot, called an **audio/modem riser (AMR)** (see Figure 10-3) slot or a **communication and networking riser (CNR)** slot. The small slot accommodates a small, inexpensive type of modem card called a **modem riser card**. In addition, the AMR slot can support an audio riser card, and the CNR slot can support an audio riser card or a networking riser card. Part of a riser card's audio, modem, or networking logic is on the card and part on a controller on the motherboard.

Figure 10-3   An audio/modem riser slot can accommodate an inexpensive modem riser card

Regardless of the type of modem card or external device, a modem is both hardware and firmware. Firmware on ROM chips on the device contains the protocol and instructions needed to format and convert data so that it can be transported over phone lines to a receiving modem on the other end. In general, modems are considered to be hardware, but it is fundamental to an understanding of communications that you also consider them to be firmware.

Computers are digital; regular phone lines are analog. Earlier chapters discussed the difference between digital data and analog data, and Figure 10-4 shows how this concept applies to phone lines. Data is stored inside a PC and communicated to a modem as binary, or digital, data (0s and 1s). A modem converts this data into an analog signal (the process is called **modulation**) that can travel over a phone line, and then the modem at the receiving end converts it back to digital (this process is called **demodulation**) before passing it on to the receiving PC. The two processes of MOdulation/DEModulation lead to the name of the device: modem.

Figure 10-4   Modems convert a digital signal to analog and then back to digital

Sound traveling over regular phone lines is transmitted as analog signals, meaning that there are an infinite number of sound values, just as there are an infinite number of sound values in the human voice. Even though the data from a PC is inherently digital, it too must be converted to an analog signal in order to be transmitted over phone lines. PC data must be converted from two simple states or measurements (0 and 1, or off and on) to waves (like sound waves) that have a potentially infinite number of states or measurements. Modems use different characteristics of waves to correspond with the 0s and 1s of digital communication.

On a PC, the modem provides a connection for a regular phone line called an **RJ-11** connection, which is the same type of connection that you see for a regular phone wall outlet (Figure 10-5). In addition to a line-in connection from the wall outlet, a modem also has an extra RJ-11 connection for a telephone.

Figure 10-5   An RJ-11 connection on a modem is the same as that used for a regular phone connection

A modem must be able to both receive and transmit data. Communication in which there can be transmission in only one direction at a time is called **half-duplex**; an example of this type of communication is a CB radio. A modem that can only communicate in one direction at a time is called a half-duplex modem. Communication that allows transmission in both directions at the same time is called **full-duplex**; regular voice phone conversations are an example of full-duplex communication. If a modem can communicate in both directions at the same time, it is called a full-duplex modem.

How Modems Are Rated

Using Windows 9x, you can view the properties of an installed modem on a PC. Many people install their modems by simply choosing settings supplied by others, or by allowing the installation program to use default selections. This section explains what each modem property means and how it affects the modem's performance and compatibility with other modems.

Getting Started

When you first use a modem to make a dial-up call to another PC, you hear the modem making noises as the dial-up is completed. What you hear are the sounds of the two modems establishing the rules of communication between them. The process is called **handshaking**, or **training**. In this handshaking phase, the calling modem and the receiving modem are communicating the protocols and determining speeds they can support, deciding how to handle data compression and error checking, and what methods of data transfer will be used. The protocols agreed on must be supported by both modems, and they attempt to use the faster and more reliable protocols first.

Modem Speeds

The speed at which a modem passes data over phone lines is partly determined by the transmission standard the modem is using. Modem speed is usually measured in **bits per second (bps)**. On older, slower modems, you might find the speed expressed as **baud rate**, which is the number of times a signal changes in one second. On older modems, the baud rate is equal to the bps rate, because one signal represents one bit. On more modern modems, one signal can represent more than one bit, so faster modems are measured in bps (and baud rates may differ from bps rates). When modem speed is measured using baud rate, the number of bps will always be equal to or a multiple of the baud rate. The most commonly rated modem speed in use today is 56.6 Kbps, although there are still a few modems around that are rated at 28.8 Kbps or 33.6 Kbps.

The maximum speed of a modem is often written into the manufacturer's name for the modem. To see what your modem rating is when using Windows 9x, click Start, point to Settings, click Control Panel, and double-click Modems. You see the Modems Properties dialog box in Figure 10-6. In this figure, the installed modem is labeled as a U.S. Robotics 56K Fax Internal PnP modem. The 56K portion of the name indicates the maximum speed of the modem: 56 Kbps.

10

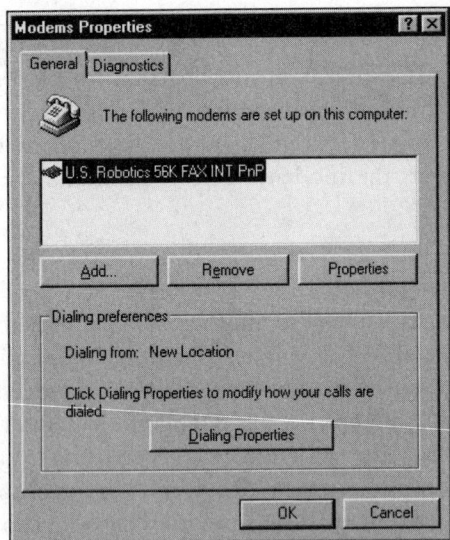

Figure 10-6   The maximum modem speed is often included in the modem name (in this case, 56 Kbps)

The Ceiling on Modem Speeds

Many factors contribute to limitations on modem speeds. Analog phone lines were designed to provide only sufficient audio signal quality to support the transmission of the human voice, affecting the ability to attain high transmission speeds for data. Newer digital phone lines have limitations as well. Older phone lines (before 1940) were analog from beginning to end, with no digital components. This is not true today. Regular (analog) telephone lines are always analog as they leave a house or office building; however, the analog signals are almost always converted to a digital signal at some point in the transmission. These digital signals are then transmitted and converted back to analog signals at some point before traveling the last step between a local central telephone company office and the phone of the person receiving the call.

One limitation on modem speeds over regular phone lines results from the method used when an analog signal is converted to a digital signal. The phone company takes a sampling of the analog signal (8,000 samples every second) and converts each sample to an 8-bit byte. So, modem transmission is limited to this 8,000 bytes/second (64,000 bits/second) transmission of the digital signal.

 TIP Because of the sampling rate used by phone companies when converting an analog signal to digital, taking into account the overhead of data transmission (bits and bytes sent with the data that are used to control and define transmissions), the maximum transmission rate that a modem can attain over a regular phone line is about 56,000 bps or 56 Kbps.

Other factors further limit modem speed. The line also often has some disturbance, called **noise**, which can be caused by lines bumping against one another in the wind, bad wiring, lightning, or interference from nearby fluorescent lighting, radios, or TVs. This reduction in line quality is called a dirty or noisy line. A line that consistently produces high-quality results is called a clean line.

Modem Standards

The telecommunications industry sets standards to determine modem speed and protocols. The industry-approved standards for international communication were written by the **CCITT (Comité Consultatif International Télégraphique et Téléphonique)**. In 1992, the CCITT was incorporated into the **ITU (International Telecommunication Union)**, an intergovernmental organization approved by the United Nations to be responsible for adopting standards governing telecommunications. You might see the standards used by modems referred to as the CCITT standards (more common) or as the ITU standards. The CCITT standards are listed in Table 10-2.

Look for a modem that supports the most standards including the latest standard, V.92. The more standards a modem supports, the better it can communicate with a variety of other modems.

 TIP   Avoid purchasing a modem using a proprietary standard, because it may only be able to communicate with another modem by the same manufacturer.

10

Table 10-2   Modem transmission standards

Standard	Applies Mainly to	Description
Bell 212A	Speed (up to 1,200 bps)	This older standard supports 1,200 bps.
CCITT V.32	Speed (up to 9,600 bps)	This standard runs at 9,600 bps, includes error checking, and can negotiate standards with other modems. This standard was used for quite some time.
HST	Speed (up to 14.4 Kbps)	This older proprietary standard, created by U.S. Robotics, supports 9,600 or 14,400 bps. (U.S. Robotics also supports the CCITT standards.)
CCITT V.32bis	Speed (up to 14.4 Kbps)	This standard is an improvement over V.32 (up to 14.4 Kbps) (bis means "second" in Latin), and has a speed of 14,400 bps.
CCITT V.34	Speed (up to 33.6 Kbps)	This standard transmits at 28,800 bps, or 28.8 Kbps. Optional higher speeds are 31.2 Kbps and 33.6 Kbps.

Table 10-2   Modem transmission standards (continued)

Standard	Applies Mainly to	Description
MNP Class 4	Error correction	Developed by Microcom, Inc. and called the Microcom Networking Protocol (MNP), this standard provides error detection and correction, and also automatically adjusts the speed of transmission according to the quality of the phone line. Earlier classes of MNP standards for error correction are Class 2 and Class 3.
CCITT V.42	Error correction	This is an error-correcting standard that adopted the methods used by MNP Class 4. Data that is corrupted during transmission is automatically retransmitted using this standard. A modem can use this standard for error correction and one of the standards listed above for speed.
MNP Class 5	Data compression	The MNP Class 5 standard provides data compression, which can double normal transmission speeds between modems. It is common to see both MNP Class 4 and MNP Class 5 supported by a modem. They are sometimes called MNP-4 and MNP-5.
CCITT V.42bis	Data compression	An improved version of V.42 that also uses data compression. Many modems use the V.42bis standard for data compression and error checking and, at the same time, use the V.34 standard for data transmission protocols.
V.44	Data compression	An improved version of V.42bis.
K56flex	Speed (up to 56 Kbps)	One of two earlier standards used to attain a speed of up to 56 Kbps. This standard was backed by Lucent Technologies and Rockwell International Corp.
x2	Speed (up to 56 Kbps)	One of two earlier standards that support a speed of 56 Kbps. This standard was supported by U.S. Robotics.
V.90	Speed (up to 56 Kbps)	The current standard used to attain speeds of 56 Kbps. It replaces both K56flex and x2.
V.92	Speed (up to 56 Kbps)	Improves on V.90 adding three new features: quick connect (reduces handshake time), modem on hold (allows call waiting without breaking the connection to the ISP), and improves upload speeds for large files.

Although most modems today are rated and advertised to transmit at 56 Kbps, this speed is seldom accomplished. When one PC is communicating with another, even if both PCs are equipped with 56K modems and using clean phones lines, the actual attained speed will most likely not exceed 34 Kbps. When you connect to your ISP (Internet service provider) using a 56 Kbps modem, if the ISP is using a digital connection to the phone company, you can achieve slightly higher transmission speeds.

Data Compression

A modem includes firmware housed on the modem that can perform error correction and data compression. These and other functions of data communication can be performed by either hardware (firmware on the modem) or software (programs on the PC).

When data compression is performed by a modem, it applies to all data that is transmitted by the modem. If data compression is performed by the software on the PC, it applies to single-file transfer operations.

Data compression done by the modem follows either the MNP-5, CCITT V.42, or V.42bis protocol. All three of these protocols also perform error correction.

Error Correction

As seen in Table 10-2, there are several standards that include error correction; one modem often supports more than one standard. During the handshaking process, the answering modem tries to establish an error-correction protocol with the other modem by first suggesting the fastest, best standard. If the calling modem responds by accepting that standard, then it is used by both. If the calling modem does not support the suggested protocol, then the two modems negotiate to find the best protocol they both can use, or simply decide not to use error correction.

Error correction works by breaking data up into small packets called **frames**. The sending modem performs some calculations on a frame of data and sums these calculations into a checksum. A **checksum** is a summary calculation of data and will later be used to check or verify the accuracy of the data when received. A checksum works somewhat like a parity bit, except that it is a little more complicated and applies to more data. The checksum is attached to the data frame, and they are transmitted together. The receiving modem performs the same calculations and compares its answer to the checksum value received. If they do not agree, then the receiving modem requests a new transmission of the packet. This process does slow down the transmission of data, especially on dirty or noisy phone lines, but accuracy is almost 100 percent guaranteed.

More About Handshaking

Now that you understand several of the different protocols that must be established between two modems before they can communicate data, you can better understand what happens when two modems perform a handshake. Here are some key points about the process:

- When a modem answers an incoming call, this answering modem sends a modem tone, sometimes called a **guard tone**, which the calling modem recognizes as another modem and not a human voice, and so it does not break the connection.

- The answering modem sends a signal called the **carrier**. This is an unmodulated (unchanging) or continuous tone at a set frequency (also called pitch), that depends on the speed of communication the answering modem is attempting to establish with the calling modem. This process, called "establishing carrier," sounds like static, which you hear during handshaking.

10

- After the carrier is established, the two modems enter the equalization stage, which sounds like hissing or buzzing on the line. The modems are both testing the line quality and compensating for poor quality by changing the way they transmit.

- When this process completes, the speed of transmission, called the **modem speed** or the **line speed**, is set between them.

- The speakers on the modems are now turned off. Next the modems begin to talk about how they will transmit data. The answering modem asks if the other modem can support MNP-4, MNP-5, V.42, V.42bis, and so on. After some interchange, the methods of data transmission are agreed upon, and the hand-shaking is complete. The two modems can now communicate.

External modems show you the status of what is happening by turning lights on and off on the front of the modem and displaying messages on an LCD panel (called a display readout). Internal modems, of course, don't have these lights available for you to see, so communications software sometimes displays a pseudo-modem panel on your computer screen.

When a modem is first activated (turned on), it initializes itself and then raises (turns on) its Clear to Send (CTS) signal and, for an external modem, the CTS light also goes on. When the PC receives the CTS signal from its modem, it will raise its Request to Send (RTS) signal in order to begin a call. For external modems, the RTS or RS light goes on.

 Communications technicians use the terms "raising" and "dropping" signals to mean that the signal is either started or stopped, respectively.

Serial Port Settings

Besides communication between modems, the serial ports that the modems are using are being controlled by the UART logic. UART-to-UART communication is controlled by the **port settings**. Five protocols that control these port settings are described in Table 10-3.

Table 10-3   Port settings control how serial ports communicate

Port Setting	Description	Common Values
Bits per second (port speed)	What will be the speed of the transmission in bps? The **port speed** should usually be about four times the modem speed.	2400; 4800; 9600; 19,200; 38,400; 57,600; 115,200; 230,400; 460,800; 921,600 bps
Data bits	How many bits are to be used to send a single character of data? Only 7 bits are required for standard ASCII characters, but in most cases, you should use 8 bits.	7 or 8 bits

Table 10-3 Port settings control how serial ports communicate (continued)

Port Setting	Description	Common Values
Parity	Will there be error checking, and if so, what will be its format? In most cases, let the modem do error checking and use no parity checking on the serial port.	Odd, even, or none
Stop bits	What will be the code to indicate that a character (its string of bits) is starting or ending? In most cases, use 1 bit.	1, 1.5, or 2 bits
Flow control	How will the flow of data be controlled? **Flow control** stops the flow of data if the receiving port is being overloaded. Flow control is controlled by software (Xon/Xoff) or hardware (RTS/CTS). Always use RTS/CTS.	Software (Xon/Xoff) or hardware (RTS/CTS)

To understand how port settings and modem settings both affect communication, look at Figure 10-7. Communication between the DTE and the DCE (computer and modem) is controlled by the port settings and communication between two DCE devices (two modems) is controlled by the modem settings.

10

Figure 10-7 A computer communicates with a modem differently from the way a modem communicates with another modem

To see the modem and port settings using Windows 98, open Device Manager and select the modem. Then click Properties. The modem Properties dialog box opens. Click the Connection tab (see Figure 10-8). On this window, if you click the Advanced button, the Advanced Connection Settings window opens, also shown in Figure 10-8. From these two windows you can see all the port settings listed in Table 10-3, except the port speed which is on the Modem tab of the modem's Properties box.

Figure 10-8   Port and modem settings under Windows 98

For Windows 2000/XP, open Device Manager and right click on the modem. Select Properties from the shortcut menu. The modem's Properties box opens. Click the Modem tab to view the port speed. If the modem is an internal modem, you cannot view or change the other port settings. If the modem is an external modem using a serial port, to view the port setting for that serial port, in Device Manager, right click on the serial port and select Properties. The serial port's Properties box opens as showing in Figure 10-9.

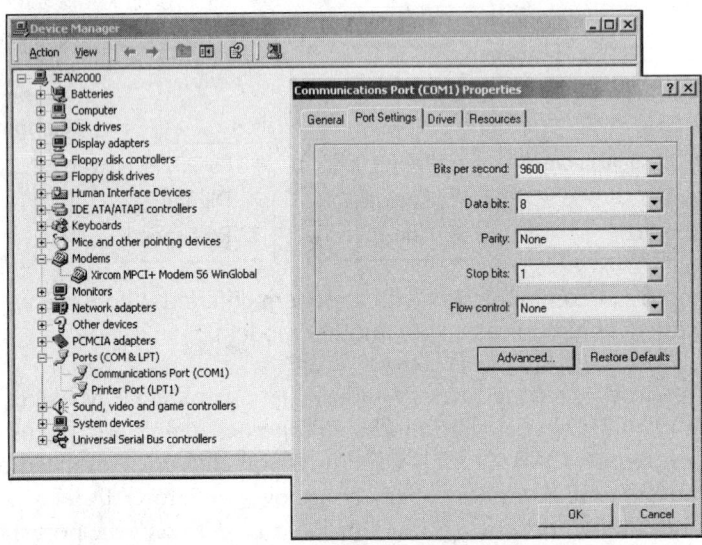

Figure 10-9   Port settings for a Windows 2000 serial port

Modem Features

In addition to the speed, protocols, data compression, and error correction that are used to rate a modem, there are other features. Some additional abilities you might want to look for in a modem are:

- *Caller ID* (provided that you subscribe to that service from the phone company) is supported.

- *Display readout* on external modems provides information about the status of the modem. (See Chapter 5, Table 5-2, for a list of modem lights and their meanings. The modem can also have an LCD panel for messages such as Training or Idle.)

- *Flash ROM* allows you to upgrade your modem to support future standards.

- *Plug and Play for Windows* makes modem installation more automatic.

- *Voice/data capability* allows the modem to also serve as a telephone, complete with built-in speaker and microphone.

- *Auto-answer* makes it possible for the modem to receive incoming calls while you are away from the PC.

Regardless of the expansion slot an internal modem uses, it has its own UART on the modem card and provides its own serial port logic to the computer system. This is why an internal modem must be configured to have its own COM port assigned to it for its UART to control. A typical configuration for a PC is to have COM1 assigned to the serial mouse and COM2 assigned to the internal modem. (An external modem does not need a COM port assigned to it, because it uses the existing port assignments already configured on the system.) The UART on the motherboard is not used by the internal modem, because the modem is not using the COM ports on the motherboard.

10

> **TIP** Sometimes a COM port on a motherboard can compete for resources with the COM port on an internal modem, causing a conflict. In this case, use CMOS setup to disable the conflicting COM port on the motherboard.

Installing and Configuring a Modem

Follow these general steps to install an internal modem:

1. Read the modem documentation.

2. Determine which serial port is available on your system.

3. Set any jumpers or DIP switches on the modem card. (See your documentation for details about your card. An example is shown in Figure 10-10. Common jumper and DIP switch settings are for COM ports, IRQ, and I/O addresses, and to indicate whether or not the card will use Plug and Play.)

Jumper bank for
IRQ setting

Jumper bank for COM
port selection

Figure 10-10   A modem might have jumpers to set IRQ and COM values; the default
jumper settings should be set to use Plug and Play rather than dictate
these values

4. Turn off your computer and remove the case. Find an empty slot, remove the faceplate, and save the screw. Mount the card firmly into the slot, and replace the screw to anchor the card.

5. Replace the cover. (You can test the modem before replacing the cover.)

6. Plug the telephone line from the house into the line jack on the modem. The second RJ-11 jack on the modem is for an optional telephone. It connects a phone so that you can more easily use this same phone jack for voice communication.

For an external modem, follow these general steps:

1. If the modem does not come with a cable, don't skimp on price here; buy a high-quality cable. Connect the cable to the modem and to the serial or USB port.

2. Plug the electrical cord from the modem into an 110V AC outlet.

3. Plug the telephone line from the house into the line jack on the modem. The second jack on the modem is for an optional telephone.

Turn on your computer and follow these steps to configure the modem using Windows 98:

1. Turn on the PC. Windows 9x Plug and Play detects a new hardware device. Allow the OS to identify the modem and install the drivers, or provide your own disk. You might have to boot twice: once to allow Plug and Play to detect the UART and again to detect the modem. Also, if your modem has add-on features such as a Fax service, you might have to reboot again as this feature is installed. Follow directions onscreen until you reach the Windows 98 desktop.

Sometimes an installation disk has several directories, one for each operating system it supports. For example, for Windows 98, look for a directory named \WIN98.

2. After the modem drivers are installed, configure the modem. Click **Start**, point to **Settings**, click **Control Panel**, and then double-click **Modem**. The Modem Properties box opens. Click the installed modem and then click **Properties**.

3. Use the properties listed below unless you have a specific reason to do otherwise (such as to compensate for a noisy phone line).

   ■ Set the modem speed at the highest value in the drop-down list, which is the highest value supported by this modem.

   ■ Set the port protocol at "8, No, and 1," which is computer jargon for 8 bits, no parity, and 1 stop bit.

   ■ Use hardware flow control.

   The type of expansion slot (ISA or PCI) an internal modem uses or the port (serial or USB) an external modem uses affects ease of installation and the performance of the modem.

4. If you want to use Windows 98 to make calls without using other software, create a Dial-Up Networking connection. Double-click the **My Computer** icon, and then double-click **Dial-Up Networking**. The Dial-Up Networking window opens. The Make New Connection wizard opens, as in Figure 10-11.

5. Follow the connection wizard to specify the name of the connection and the phone number to call. When the wizard is done, the connection icon appears in the Dial-Up Networking window. Double-click the icon to make the call.

For Windows 2000/XP, installation is performed as it is for Windows 9x. However, some options in the modem Properties dialog box are slightly different. To configure the modem, click Start, point to Settings, click Control Panel, and double-click the Phone and Modem Options icon. When the Phone and Modem Options dialog box opens, click the Modems tab. Select the modem and click Properties. The modem Properties dialog box opens. Configure the modem using this dialog box.

Problems during modem installation and ways to detect and resolve conflicts are covered under the Troubleshooting section later in the chapter. The last step after the modem installation is complete is to test the modem using communications software.

10

Figure 10-11   Create a Dial-Up Networking connection

An excellent software utility you can use to test a modem is HyperTerminal, a quick and easy way to make a phone call from a Windows PC. Later in the chapter, you will learn how to use commands in HyperTerminal to troubleshoot a modem; the following procedure is designed to verify that your modem is working. Follow these steps to test your modem:

1. For Windows 2000/XP and Windows 98, click **Start**, point to **Programs**, **Accessories**, **Communications**, and click **HyperTerminal**. For Windows 95, click **Start**, point to **Programs**, **Accessories**, and click **HyperTerminal**.

2. Double-click the **Hypertrm.exe** icon in the HyperTerminal window.

3. When you see the Connection Description dialog box, enter a descriptive name for your connection (such as **test modem**) and select an icon for the shortcut. Click **OK**.

4. Enter the phone number to dial, and select the modem from the list of dial-up devices (most likely it's the only entry). Click **OK**.

5. Click **Dial** to make the call. Even if you dial an out-of-service number, you can still hear your modem make the call. This confirms that your modem is installed and configured to make an outgoing call.

 If you don't see HyperTerminal under the Accessories group of Windows, it might not be installed. To install a Windows utility, use the Add/Remove Programs icon in Control Panel.

THE AT COMMAND SET

One of the pioneers in modem communications, Hayes Microcomputer Products, developed a language for PCs to use to control modems. Hayes did not patent or copyright the language, so most modems today are built to understand this language. Any modem that contains the logic to understand this language is said to be Hayes-compatible, and the language has become a de facto standard. (A **de facto standard** is a standard that does not have official backing, but is considered a standard because of widespread use and acceptance by the industry.)

The Hayes language for modem control is called the **AT command set** because, when the modem is receiving commands, each command line is prefaced with AT for ATtention. A modem that uses this language stays in command mode at any time that it is not connected to another modem. When a modem is in command mode and bits and bytes are sent to it from a PC, the modem interprets the bytes as commands to be followed, rather than as data to be sent over a phone line. It leaves command mode when it either receives an incoming call or dials out, and returns to command mode when a call is completed or a special escape sequence is sent to it by its computer.

Other manufacturers of modems have added to the Hayes AT command set, but Table 10-4 lists a few of the core AT commands that most modems understand. The commands that begin with the ampersand character (&) are part of the extended command set; the others are part of the basic command set. When a modem is in command mode, it responds to each command with OK or gives the results after performing the command. You can type a command from a communications software window to be executed immediately or enter a command from a dialog box for the modem configuration to be executed later, when the modem makes a call.

> All communication between software and a modem, including AT commands, use the **TAPI (Telephony Application Programming Interface)**, a standard jointly developed by Intel and Microsoft, to connect a PC to telephone services. **Telephony** is the technology of telephones, and TAPI is a type of API (application programming interface) that Windows can use when it needs to command the modem.

Table 10-4   AT commands for Hayes-compatible modems

Command	Description	Some Values and Their Meanings
AT	Gets the modem's attention	AT (modem should respond with OK)
*70	Disable call waiting	ATDT*70,4045551212
+++	Escape sequence: tells the modem to return to command mode. You should pause at least 1 second before you begin the sequence. After you end it, wait another second before you send another command. Don't begin this command with AT.	+++ (follow each + with a short pause; use this when trying to unlock a hung modem; don't begin the command with AT)

Table 10-4   AT commands for Hayes-compatible modems (continued)

Command	Description	Some Values and Their Meanings
On	Go Online: tells the modem to return to online data mode. This is the reverse command for the escape sequence above.	ATO0 Return online O1 Return online and retrain (perform training or handshaking again with the remote system)
A/	Repeat last command: repeat last command performed by the modem. Don't begin the command with AT, but do follow it with Enter. Useful when redialing a busy number.	
In	Identification: instructs the modem to return to product identification information	I0 Return the product code I3 Return the modem ROM version
Zn	Reset: instructs the modem to reset and restore the configuration to that defined at power on	ATZ0 Reset and return to user profile 0 Z1 Reset and return to user profile 1
&F	Factory default: instructs the modem to reload the factory default profile. In most cases, use this command to reset the modem rather than using the Z command.	AT&F (this method is preferred to ATZ when trying to solve a modem problem)
A	Answer the phone: instructs the modem to answer the phone, transmit the answer tone and wait for a carrier from the remote modem	
Dn	Dial: tells the modem to dial a number. There are several parameters that can be added to this command. A few are listed on the right.	ATD5551212 Dial the given number D Causes the dialing to pause DP Use pulse dialing DT Use tone dialing DW Wait for dial tone D& Wait for the credit card dialing tone before continuing with the remaining dial string
Hn	Hang up: tells the modem to hang up	ATH0 Hang up H1 Hang up and enter command mode
Mn	Speaker control: instructs the modem as to how it is to use the speaker	ATM0 Speaker always off M1 Speaker on until carrier detect M2 Speaker always on
Ln	Loudness: sets the loudness of the modem's speaker	ATL1 Low L2 Medium L3 High
Xn	Response: tells the modem how it is to respond to a dial tone and busy signal	ATX0 Blind dialing; the modem does not need to hear the dial tone and will not hear a busy signal X4 Modem must first hear the dial tone and responds to a busy signal (this is the default value)

These commands, which you can use to control a modem from HyperTerminal, are the same commands that software uses to communicate with modems. Knowing these commands can be useful when you are troubleshooting a problem connecting a modem with an ISP. To use HyperTerminal to control a modem using the AT command set, follow these steps:

1. For Windows 2000/XP and Windows 98, click **Start**, point to **Programs**, **Accessories**, **Communications**, and click **HyperTerminal**. For Windows XP, click **All Programs**. For Windows 95, click **Start**, point to **Programs**, **Accessories**, and click **HyperTerminal**.

2. For Windows 9x, double-click the **Hypertrm.exe** icon in the HyperTerminal window.

3. When the Connection Description dialog box opens, click **Cancel**. You see an empty HyperTerminal window. Type **AT** and press **Enter**. The modem responds with OK to acknowledge the command session. See Figure 10-12.

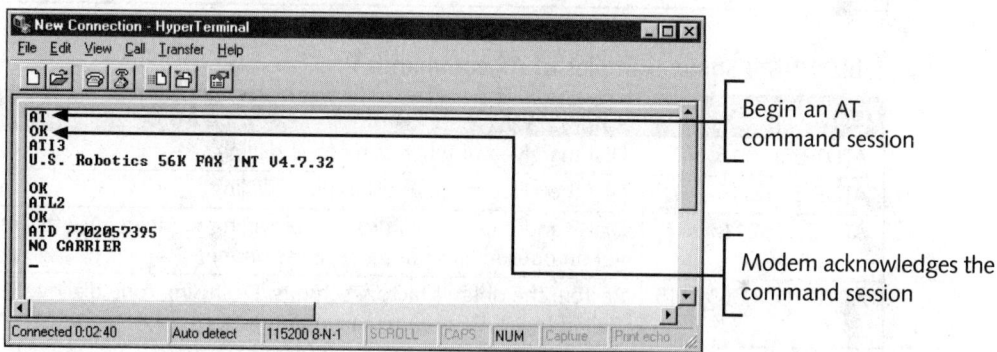

Figure 10-12 HyperTerminal can be used to control a modem using the AT command set

4. Enter any AT command. For example, in Figure 10-12, the ATI3 command causes the modem to report its ROM version, the ATL2 command sets the loudness to medium, and the ATD command followed by a phone number causes the modem to dial a number. Notice in the figure that the modem responds that no modem was connected on the other end (NO CARRIER).

Table 10-5 shows an example of an interchange between a modem and a user. Other examples of AT commands and their meanings are listed in Table 10-6.

Table 10-5   An example of a dialog between a user and a modem

Source	Command or Response	Description
From user	ATD 5551221 [Enter]	Dial the specified phone number.
From modem	CONNECT 19200	Modem responds with the agreed-on bps. At this point, you can transfer data using a utility provided by the communications software. Then wait at least 1 second before the next command.
From user	+++	Escape sequence telling the modem to return to command mode (then pause 1 second).
From modem	OK	Modem responds by giving you the OK response.
From user	ATH0 [Enter]	Disconnect the line.
From modem	OK	Modem responds by giving you the OK response.

Table 10-6   Some examples of AT commands

Command	Description
ATDT 5552115	Dial the given number using tone dialing.
ATDP 5552115	Dial the given number using pulse dialing.
ATD 9,5552115	Dial 9 and pause, then dial the remaining numbers (use this method to get an outside line from a business phone).
AT &F1DT9,5552115	Restore the default factory settings. Dial using tone dialing. Pause after dialing the 9. Dial the remaining numbers.
ATM2L2	Always have the speaker on. Set loudness of speaker at medium.
ATI3	Report the modem ROM version.

Windows uses AT commands to help in diagnosing problems with modems. Using Windows 98, to have the OS perform a diagnostic test of a modem, in the Control Panel, click the Modems icon. A Modems Properties box displays (see Figure 10-13). Select the COM port the modem is installed on and click More Info... Wait a moment as the OS communicates with the modem and then displays a list of AT commands and their responses in the More Info... dialog box also showing in Figure 10-13.

For Windows 2000/XP, you can get a similar diagnostic test. Open Device Manager, right-click on the modem, and select Properties from the shortcut menu. The modem's Properties box opens. Click the Diagnostics tab and then click the Query Modem button.

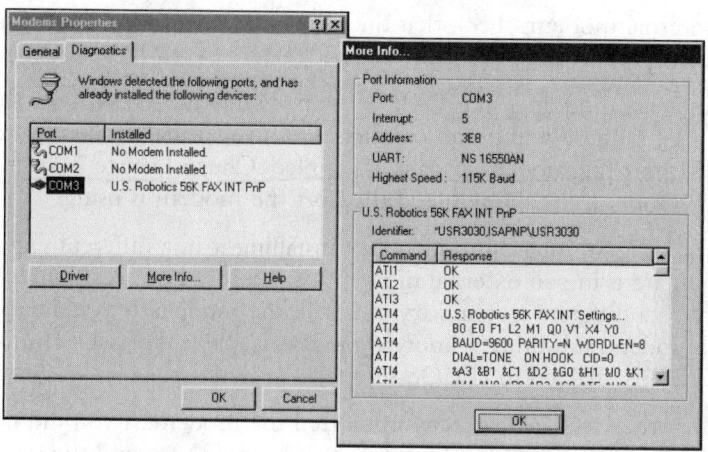

Figure 10-13   Windows 98 uses AT commands to perform a diagnostic test of a modem

TROUBLESHOOTING GUIDELINES FOR MODEMS

This section provides a guide to solving problems with modems and communicating over phone lines. Some keys to troubleshooting are: determine what works and what doesn't work, find out what has worked in the past that doesn't work now, and establish what has changed since things last worked. Much of this can be determined by asking the user and yourself questions and by trying the simple things first. Below is a list of problems you may encounter with your modem and suggestions on how you can proceed.

The modem does not respond

- Make sure the modem is plugged into the phone jack.

- If you are using an external modem, make sure it is plugged into the computer and that the connection is solid.

- There are two RJ-11 ports on a modem. Check that the phone line from the wall outlet is connected to the line-in port.

- Plug a phone directly into the wall jack you are using, and make sure that there is a dial tone.

- If necessary, make sure to instruct the modem to dial an extra character to get an outside line, such as 9 or 8.

If this is a new installation that has never been used before, check these things:

- Make sure the modem is set to the same COM port and IRQ that the software is set to.

- Make sure that no other device is configured to the same COM port or IRQ as the modem.

10

- For an internal modem, check that the DIP switches and jumpers agree with the modem properties in the OS.

- For an internal modem, using CMOS setup, disable the COM port the modem is set to use, so there will be no conflicts. For an external modem, verify that the COM port the modem is using is enabled. Check Device Manager for reported errors on the modem and the port the modem is using.

- If you are using an internal modem, try installing it in a different expansion slot. If you are using an external modem using a serial port card, move the serial port card to a different slot and try to install the modem. If you are using an external modem, substitute a known-good serial cable. For a USB modem, verify that USB is enabled in CMOS setup.

- Check that the software correctly initialized the modem. If you did not give the correct modem type to the software, it may be trying to send the wrong initialization command. Try AT&F. (Under Windows 9x, click Start, point to Settings, and click Control Panel. Double-click Modems. Select the modem and click Modem Properties, Connection, Advanced. The dialog box in Figure 10-14 opens. Enter the AT&F command under Extra settings.) Retry the modem. (For Windows 2000/XP, from Control Panel, double-click Phone and Modem Options. Click the Modems tab and then click Properties. On the modem properties dialog box, click the Advanced tab, and enter the command under Extra initialization commands.)

- Make sure you have enough RAM and hard drive space. Then close all other applications currently running, reboot the PC, and try the modem again.

The modem says there is no dial tone, even though you can hear it

- Make sure the phone cord from the wall outlet is plugged into the line jack on the modem.

Figure 10-14   The Extra settings box allows you to send extra AT commands to the modem on any call

- The modem might not be able to detect the dial tone, even if you can hear it. Try unplugging any other equipment plugged into this same phone line, such as a fax machine.

- Try giving the ATX0 command before you dial. Enter the command under Extra Settings, as in Figure 10-14. If that doesn't help, then remove the ATX0 command.

- Straighten your phone lines! Don't let them get all twisted and crossed up with other heavy electrical lines.

- If there has been a recent lightning storm, the modem may be damaged. Replace the modem with one you know works.

The modem dials and then says that the other end is busy, even when you know that it is not

- This can happen with international calls if the modem does not recognize the signal as a ring. Try giving the ATX0 command first.

- Straighten the phone lines and remove extra equipment, as described above.

The sending modem and the receiving modem take a very long time to negotiate the connection

10

- This is probably because of a noisy phone line. Try calling again or using a different number.

- Remove other equipment from your line. A likely suspect is a credit card machine.

- Turn off data compression and try again.

- Turn off error correction and try again.

- Try forcing your modem to use a slower speed.

During a connection, it sounds as if the handshaking starts all over again

Modems normally do this if the phone line is noisy and would cause a lot of data to become corrupted; it's called retraining, and it sometimes can solve the problem as the modems renegotiate, compensating for the noisy line. Do the things listed above to clear your line of equipment and twisted phone lines.

File transfers are too slow

Make sure your modem is configured to use data compression, if possible.

The modem loses connection at odd times or is slow

- Check the communications software for the speed assigned to it. Many times people set the communications software speed for the modem speed instead of the port speed, which is what the software is asking for, and which should be about four times the modem speed.

- You may have a noisy phone line. Try the connection using the same brand and model of modem on both lines. If performance is better, the problem is most likely the phone line.

- Is the phone line from the modem to the jack too long? About four feet is the limit; otherwise, electromagnetic interference may be the problem.

- Straighten the phone lines and clear the line of any extra equipment.

- Reinstall the modem. Allow Windows to detect the modem for you and install its own drivers.

The modem drops the connection and gives the NO CARRIER message

- Most likely the connection was first dropped by the remote modem. Is someone trying to use a phone extension on this line?

- Disable call waiting. To do this, put *70 before the dialing number. Some communications software has a setting to disable call waiting. If not, you can put these three characters in the Extra settings box of Advanced Connections Settings (see Figure 10-14).

- Remove extra equipment from the line and straighten the phone lines.

- Check the modem settings and make sure "Error control required to connect" is not checked.

- Try using a different modulation type under Advanced Connection Settings of your modem properties.

- The remote modem may not support the high speeds used. Try reducing the port speed to 9600 or lower.

Whenever the weather is bad, the connection disconnects often

This is caused by a dirty phone line. Remove any extra equipment and straighten the lines. (This can help your connection regardless of weather conditions.)

Whenever large files are downloaded, some of the data is lost

Make sure that hardware flow control is on, and that software flow control is off, for the software, the COM port, and the modem. (Use software settings options, the COM port Properties box, and the modem Properties box.)

The connection fails whenever large files are uploaded or downloaded

There may be a buffer overflow. Try these things to gain better control of data flow:

- Make sure that hardware flow control is on, and that software flow control is off, for the software, the COM port, and the modem.

- Is the serial port speed set too high for the UART chip you have? Lower the port speed.

- For an external modem, try a different cable.

You get nothing but garbage across the connection

- Check the port settings. Try 8 data bits, no parity, and one stop bit (8, No, and 1).

- Slow down the port speed.

- Slow down the modem speed.

- Try a different modulation type.

CHAPTER SUMMARY

- Modem cards use either an ISA slot or a PCI slot, though on some systems, the motherboard has a shortened CNR or AMR slot that supports a modem riser card.
- External modems use a serial or USB port.
- Modems are both hardware and firmware.
- Modems convert digital computer signals to analog signals (through modulation) for transmission over phone lines, then back into digital signals on the receiving end (through demodulation).
- A modem can be either half-duplex (like a CB radio, with which communication can travel in only one direction at a time) or full duplex (like a regular voice phone conversation, in which communication can travel in two directions at once).
- Modems are classified according to how they set rules for communication (handshaking), and how fast they pass data over phone lines (measured in bits per second).
- The most commonly used modem speed rating today is 56.6 Kbps. The current standard for 56 Kbps transmission is the V.92 standard.
- Modem standards were written by the CCITT, now called the ITU. The more standards a modem supports, the more easily it will be able to communicate with other modems.
- The firmware housed on a modem can perform error correction and data compression. These data communication functions can also be performed by software on the PC.
- Features to look for in a modem include caller ID, display readout, Flash ROM, Plug and Play, the ability to serve as a telephone, and auto-answer.
- Computers are classified as DTE, and modems are classified as DCE. Communication between DTEs through DCEs is affected by the port speed on either end and by the communication speed between the two DCEs.
- HyperTerminal is a utility used to test modem connection and troubleshoot a modem. From HyperTerminal, you can control the modem using the AT command set, which contains the same commands that are used in communication between the modem and the PC.

10

❑ As with other devices, when troubleshooting a modem, determine what does and does not work, what worked in the past that doesn't work now, and what has been changed since things last worked.

❑ Common causes of modem problems include line noise, bad connections, interference from other devices, and speed mismatches.

KEY TERMS

AT command set

audio/modem riser (AMR)

baud rate

bits per second (bps)

carrier

CCITT (Comité Consultatif International Télégraphique et Téléphonique)

checksum

communication and networking riser (CNR)

de facto standard

demodulation

error correction

flow control

frame

full-duplex

guard tone

half-duplex

handshaking

ITU (International Telecommunications Union)

line speed

modem

modem riser card

modem speed

modulation

noise

port settings

port speed

RJ-11

TAPI (Telephony Application Programming Interface)

telephony

training

V.90

11

PCs ON A NETWORK

In this chapter, you will learn:

♦ About the basics of networking

♦ About different types of addresses used on networks

♦ How local networks are structured

♦ How to connect a PC to a LAN and divide a network into segments

♦ How to connect networks to each other

♦ How to troubleshoot a network connection

In the last chapter, you learned about modems, which are used for dial-up connections to the Internet. This chapter discusses how to connect PCs to each other in networks and how to connect those networks to each other and to the Internet. The development of networks enabled computers to share resources and data. This chapter introduces basic networking concepts, outlines the different levels of network communication, and explains how computers are identified on a network. In addition, you'll learn how local networks are built, how bridges and switches can segment large local networks, and how routers connect networks.

NETWORKING BASICS

As a system of interlinked computers, a network needs both software and hardware to work. Hardware on a network includes a **NIC (network interface card)**, designed for the physical network technology used, as well as external devices such as **hubs**, which are used to join or connect the nodes of a local network.

Software includes an operating system installed on each computer on the network and perhaps a **NOS (network operating system)** to control the entire network and its resources. If the network is small (fewer than 20 computers), it can be a **peer-to-peer network**, in which each computer on the network has the same authority as the other computers. Recall from Chapter 6 that a Windows peer-to-peer network is called a **workgroup**. Larger networks use the **client/server** model, in which access to a network is controlled by a NOS using a centralized database. A **client** computer provides a user ID and password to a **server** that validates the data against the security database. In a Windows network, this server is called the **domain controller**, and the network model is called a **domain**. Popular network operating systems are Windows NT/2000, Windows.NET, Novell NetWare, Unix, and Linux. Windows has client software built in for Windows and Novell NetWare servers. Alternately, for Novell NetWare, you can install Novell client software.

A network can have more than one workgroup or domain in operation, and some computers might not belong to any workgroup or domain. A computer joins a workgroup or domain in order to share resources with other computers and devices in the group or domain. Company policy controls how many workgroups or domains can exist within the company network based on user needs, security concerns, and administrative overhead required to manage the groups.

How Network Communication Works

When you mail a letter using the U. S. Postal Service, you most likely are not aware of the many different systems involved in its successful delivery. Figure 11-1 shows a simple view of those systems. A sender drops a letter in the mail and therefore is communicating indirectly (virtually) with the recipient by way of the letter. The systems that take the letter from the mailbox to the hand of the receiver are the direct (physical) means of communication.

On any network (including the Internet), you will see many similarities with this analogy. Communication between two computers can be broken down into separate systems or **layers**. There are **protocols** for communication between the layers of the system. Each layer must communicate directly with the layers above it and below it through these established protocols. Virtual communication also takes place as one layer on the originating side communicates with its counterpart layer on the destination side.

Figure 11-1   Communication is virtual between sender and receiver, but direct between adjacent systems in the Postal Service

Understanding Network Layers

When networks first began to be developed in the 1970s, there was little or no standardization in how communication between computers and other devices was to be accomplished. In an effort to identify and standardize all the levels of communication needed in networks, the **ISO (International Organization for Standardization)** developed a networking model called the **OSI (Open Systems Interconnect) reference model**, which is illustrated in Figure 11-2. The OSI reference model provides a universally accepted conceptual model of how data is transmitted on a network or between two or more networked devices. This model separates communication into seven layers that describe what happens within the operating system (top five layers) and the network card (lower two layers) so that two applications (such as a browser and a Web server) can communicate over a network. Each layer communicates directly with the layer just above it and the layer just below it. As with the postal system analogy of Figure 11-1, communication between adjacent layers is considered direct, but communication between matching layers is considered virtual because the matching layers are not directly connected (they have to communicate via the adjacent layers below them).

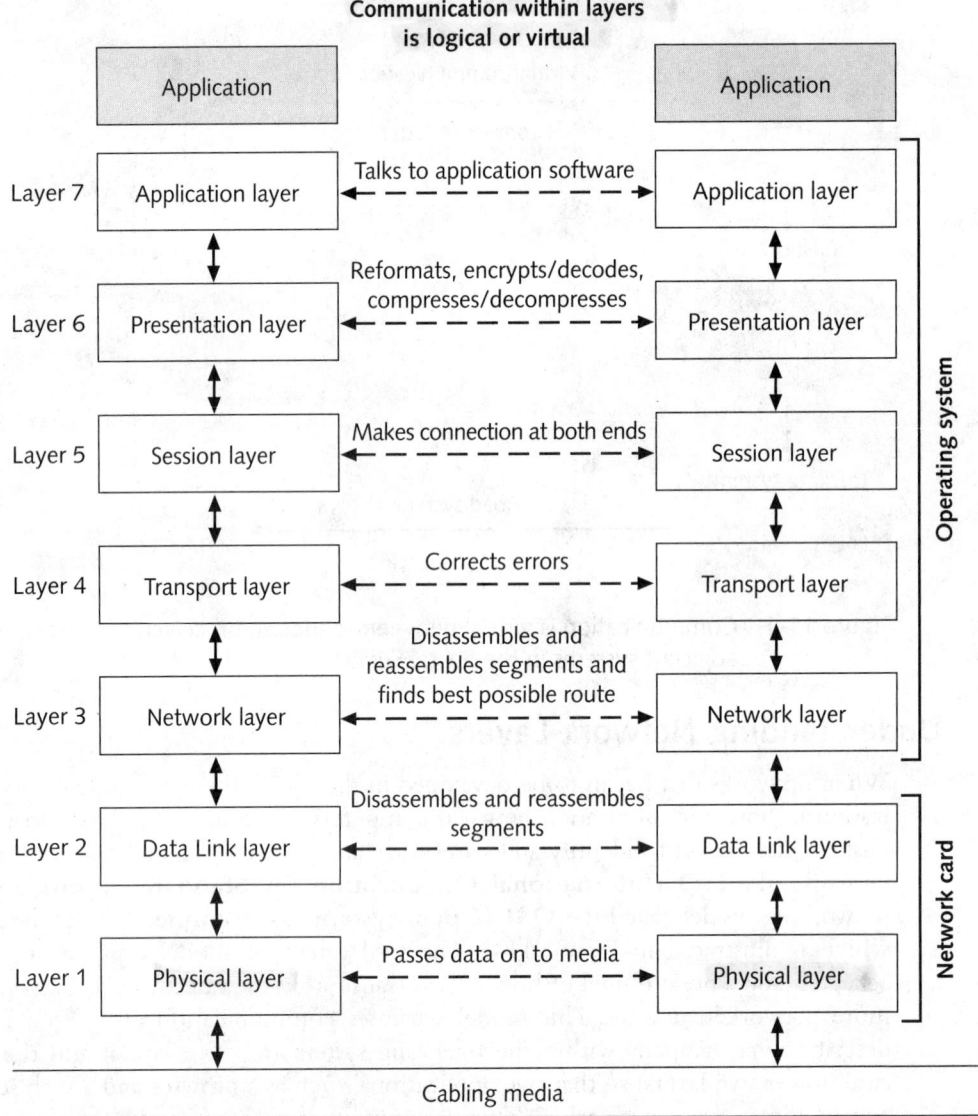

Figure 11-2   The OSI reference model identifies seven layers of network communication

Here is a short description of each layer in the OSI model:

- Application layer (Layer 7). The **Application layer** is responsible for interfacing with applications software such as word-processing programs or Web browsers.

- Presentation layer (Layer 6). The **Presentation layer** receives requests for files from the Application layer and presents the requests to the Session layer. The Presentation layer reformats, compresses, or encrypts data as necessary.

- Session layer (Layer 5). The **Session layer** is responsible for establishing and maintaining a session between two networked stations or hosts (covered in more detail later in the chapter).

- Transport layer (Layer 4). The **Transport layer** is responsible for error checking and for requesting retransmission of data if it detects errors. The Transport layer might or might not guarantee successful transmission or delivery of data, depending on how sensitive the transmission is to some loss of data.

- Network layer (Layer 3). The **Network layer** divides a block of data into segments that are small enough to travel over a network and finds the best possible route by which to send them. These segments of data are called **packets**, **data packets**, or **datagrams** and contain data, along with special identifying information in headers and trailers at the beginning and end of the packet called **frames**. Packets have a maximum size depending on the type of network. It is the responsibility of the networking protocols to break the data into segments small enough for the network and to add identifying information to each packet.

- Data Link layer (Layer 2). The **Data Link layer** is responsible for receiving packets of data from the Network layer and presenting them to the Physical layer for transport. If the packets are too large, the Data Link layer breaks them up into even smaller packets.

- Physical layer (Layer 1). The **Physical layer** passes data packets on to the cabling or the wireless media involved in data transmission. At this point, the data is just bits to be passed on; the Physical layer does not distinguish the frames from the data that constitutes the body of the transmission.

As you study the OSI model and network communication, remember that not all networks have a separate layer that matches each of the seven OSI model layers. In fact, no network today perfectly follows this model, but it does serve the networking industry as a reference point for discussing different levels or layers within a network.

The OSI Model Applied to a Local Network

When setting up a network, you have a lot of choices to make. Suppose you are setting up a small peer-to-peer network. Let's look at networking decisions in the context of the OSI model, as illustrated in Figure 11-3. The Data Link and Physical layers of the OSI model are determined by the physical network structure you use. For example, if you decide to use Ethernet, the most popular physical network technology for a LAN, then you will buy Ethernet NICs, cables, and hubs. A **LAN (local area network)** is a network that covers a fairly small geographical area, usually confined to one building or to a small group of buildings that are physically close to each other. (You'll learn much more about Ethernet later in this chapter.)

Figure 11-3 The applications, the operating system, and the network technology all determine how the OSI model is applied to a network

The top five layers are affected by choices about operating system, applications you need to support, and user needs. Which OS do you use? This decision is most likely driven by user needs and by what applications the network must support. Because so many applications are written for Windows, it is common to use Windows on computers connected to the network, and there is often a mix of several versions of Windows and other OSs on the same network. For example, a network might have a mix of computers using Windows 98, Windows NT, Windows 2000, Windows XP, Linux, and the Mac OS. As long as these operating systems can communicate using the same protocols, they can all coexist on the same network.

Windows supports three suites of protocols to be used at the top five layers of the OSI model, which are shown in Figure 11-3 and listed below. AppleTalk, which is shown in the figure but not listed here, is the default networking protocol for Macintosh computers.

- *TCP/IP (Transmission Control Protocol/Internet Protocol)* is the protocol suite used on the Internet and so should be your choice if you want to connect your network to the Internet, with each workstation having Internet access. Novell NetWare, Linux, Unix, and Mac OS also support TCP/IP.

- *IPX/SPX (Internetwork Packet Exchange/Sequenced Packet Exchange)* is a NW Link protocol suite designed for use with Novell NetWare NOS. It is somewhat similar to TCP/IP but is not supported on the Internet.

- *NetBEUI (Network BIOS Extended User Interface)* is a proprietary Windows protocol suite and is a good choice if your network is isolated from the Internet. NetBEUI is faster than TCP/IP but does not support routing to other networks and therefore is not supported on the Internet.

To use one of these protocols on a network, the first step is to physically connect the computer to the network by installing the NIC in the computer and connecting the network cable to the hub or other network device. The next step is to install the protocol in the operating system. (You'll learn how to connect a computer to a network and to install the protocol later in this chapter.)

Once the protocol is installed, it will automatically associate itself with any NICs it finds, which is called binding. **Binding** occurs when a higher-level protocol or OSI layer is associated with a lower-level protocol or layer. When the two protocols or layers are bound, communication continues between then until they are unbound, or released.

ADDRESSING ON A NETWORK

Every device on a network has a unique address. Part of learning about a network is learning how a device (such as a computer or a printer) or a program (such as a Web server) is identified on the network. On a network, there are four methods used to identify devices and programs:

11

- A **MAC address (Media Access Control address)**, also known as a **physical address**, **adapter address**, or **hardware address**, is a unique address that is permanently embedded in a NIC and identifies a device on a LAN. A MAC address is a value that is expressed as six pairs of hexadecimal numbers and letters, often separated by hyphens. The MAC address is used only by hosts inside the local network and is not used outside the LAN. (A **host** is any computer or other device on a network that can be addressed on a network.)

- An **IP address** is a series of four numbers separated by dots that identifies a computer, printer, or other device on a TCP/IP network such as the Internet or an intranet. (An **intranet** is a company network that uses TCP/IP.) Each of the four numbers can be no larger than 255. An example of an IP address is 109.168.0.104. Consider a MAC address a local address and an IP address a long distance address.

- Character-based names, including domain names, host names, and **NetBIOS (Network Basic Input/Output System)** names, are used to identify a PC on a network with easy-to-remember letters rather than numbers. (**Host names** are used to identify hosts on a network.) In general, these character-based names are often called computer names.

- A **port address** is a number between 0 and 65,535 that identifies a program running on a computer. These port addresses are not the same as the I/O addresses discussed in previous chapters.

Figure 11-4 shows how each of these addresses relates to the OSI model. The sections that follow explain the different address types in more detail.

OSI model	Managing component	Identifying address
Application Presentation Session Transport Network	Operating system	Host name (joesmith.mycompany.com) NetBIOS name (joesmith) IP address (98.16.200.10)
Data Link Physical	Network card	MAC address (87-AA-17-D3-00-01)

Figure 11-4 How devices on a network are identified at different layers of the OSI model

MAC Addresses

A computer, network printer, or other device on a network connects to the network by way of a NIC. When a NIC is manufactured, it is assigned a MAC address at the factory that is unique to and most likely will never change for that card. No two MAC addresses are the same because of standards set by the **IEEE (Institute of Electrical and Electronics Engineers)**, which is a nonprofit organization that develops standards for the computer and electronics industries. The standard for MAC addresses was specified in RFC 802. An **RFC (Request for Comments)** begins as a suggestion for network specifications and may be developed into an accepted standard, as RFC 802 was for MAC addresses.

MAC addresses are used at the Data Link layer for computers on the same network to communicate. If a host does not know the MAC address of another host on the same network, it uses the higher-layer protocols to discover the MAC address. Because the Data Link layer protocols control traffic only on their own networks, computers on different networks cannot use their MAC addresses for communication. In order for the host to communicate with a host on another LAN across the corporate intranet or Internet, it must know the address of the host that is used by the TCP/IP protocols. These addresses are IP addresses (see Figure 11-5).

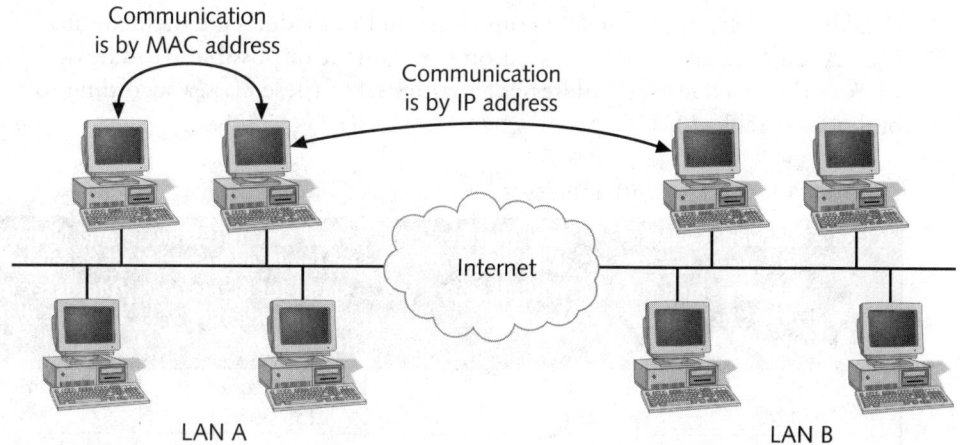

Figure 11-5   Computers on the same LAN use MAC addresses to communicate, but computers on different LANs use IP addresses to communicate over the Internet

IP Addresses

All the protocols of the TCP/IP suite identify a device on the Internet or an intranet by its IP address. An IP address is 32 bits long, made up of 4 bytes separated by periods, as in this address: 190.180.40.120. The largest possible 8-bit number is 11111111, which is equal to 255 in decimal, so the largest possible IP address in decimal is 255.255.255.255, which in binary is 11111111.11111111.11111111.11111111. Each of the four numbers separated by periods is called an **octet** (for 8 bits) and can be any number from 0 to 255, making a total of 4.3 billion potential IP addresses (256 × 256 × 256 × 256). Because of the allocation scheme used to assign these addresses, not all of them are available for use.

The first part of an IP address identifies the network, and the last part identifies the host. It's important to understand how the bits of an IP address are used in order to understand how routing happens over interconnected networks such as the Internet and how the IP protocol is used to locate an IP address anywhere on the globe. When data is routed over interconnected networks, the network portion of the IP address is used to locate the right network. Once the data has arrived at the local network, the host portion of the IP address is used to identify one computer on the network that is to receive the data. Finally, the IP address of the host must be used to identify its MAC address so the data can travel on the host's LAN to that host. The next section explains this in detail.

Classes of IP Addresses

When a business, college, or some other organization applies for IP addresses, a range of addresses appropriate to the number of hosts on the organization's networks is assigned.

11

IP addresses that can be used by companies and individuals are divided into three classes: Class A, Class B, and Class C, based on the number of possible IP addresses in each network within each class. IP addresses are assigned to these classes according to the scheme outlined in Table 11-1.

Table 11-1   Classes of IP addresses

Class	Network Octets (Blanks in the IP address stand for octets used to identify hosts.)	Total Number of Possible Networks or Licenses	Host Octets (Blanks in the IP address stand for octets used to identify networks.)	Total Number of Possible IP Addresses in Each Network
A	0.__.__.__ to 126.__.__.__	127	__.0.0.1 to __.255.255.254	16 million
B	128.0.__.__ to 191.155.__.__	16,000	__.__.0.1 to __.__.255.254	65,000
C	192.0.0.__ to 223.255.255.__	2,000,000	__.__.__.1 to __.__.__.254	254

You can determine the class of an IP address and the size or type of company to which an address is licensed by looking at the address. More importantly, you also can determine what portion of an IP address is dedicated to identifying the network and what portion is used to identify the host on that network.

Figure 11-6 shows how each class of IP address is divided into the network and host portions. A Class A address uses the first octet (leftmost) for the network address and the remaining octets for host addresses. A Class A license assigns a single number that is used in the first octet of the address, which is the network address. The remaining three octets of the IP address can be used for host addresses that uniquely identify each host on this network. The first octet of a Class A license is a number between 0 and 126. For example, if a company is assigned 87 as its Class A network address, then 87 is used as the first octet for every host on this one network. Examples of IP addresses for hosts on this network are 87.0.0.1, 87.0.0.2, and 87.0.0.3. (The last octet does not use 0 or 255 as a value, so 87.0.0.0 would not be valid). In the example's address 87.0.0.1, the 87 is the network portion of the IP address, and 0.0.1 is the host portion of the address. Because three octets can be used for Class A host addresses, one Class A license can have approximately $256 \times 256 \times 254$ host addresses, or about 16 million IP addresses. Only very large corporations with heavy communication needs can get a Class A license.

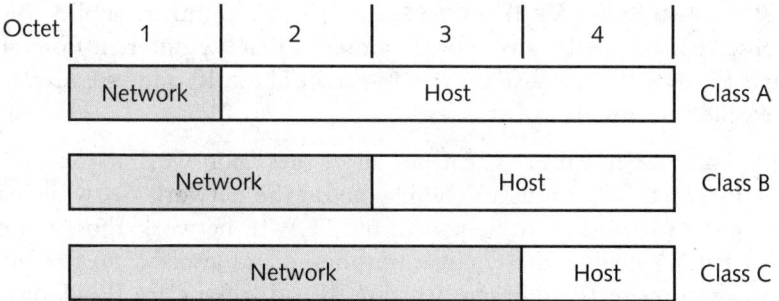

Figure 11-6 The network portion and host portion for each class of IP addresses

A Class B address uses the first two octets for the network portion and the last two for the host portion. A Class B license assigns a number for each of the first two leftmost octets, leaving the third and fourth octets for host addresses. How many host addresses are there in one Class B license? The number of possible values for two octets is about 256 × 254 (some IP addresses are reserved, so these numbers are approximations), or about 65,000, host addresses in a single Class B license. The first octet of a Class B license is a number between 128 and 191, which gives about 63 different values for a Class B first octet. The second number can be between 0 and 255, so there are approximately 63 × 256, or about 16,000, Class B networks. For example, suppose a company is assigned 135.18 as the network address for its Class B license. The first two octets for all hosts on this network are 135.18, and the company uses the last two octets for host addresses. Examples of IP addresses on this company's Class B network are 135.18.0.1, 135.18.0.2, and 135.18.0.3. In the first example listed, 135.18 is the network portion of the IP address, and 0.1 is the host portion.

A Class C license assigns three octets as the network address. With only one octet used for the host addresses, there can be only 254 host addresses on a Class C network. The first number of a Class C license is between 192 and 223. For example, if a company is assigned a Class C license for its network with a network address of 200.80.15, some IP addresses on the network would be 200.80.15.1, 200.80.15.2, and 200.80.15.3.

Class D and Class E IP addresses are not available for general use. Class D addresses begin with the octet 224 through 239 and are used for **multicasting**, in which one host sends messages to multiple hosts, such as when it is transmitting a video conference over the Internet. Class E addresses begin with 240 through 254 and are reserved for research.

Different Ways of Assigning IP Addresses

When a small company is assigned a Class C license, it obtains 254 IP addresses for its use. If it has only a few hosts (say, less than 25 on a network), many IP addresses go unused, which is one of the reasons that there is a shortage of IP addresses. But suppose that the company grows and now has 300 workstations on the network and is running out of IP addresses. There are two approaches to solving this problem: (1) use private IP addresses, and (2) use dynamic IP addressing. Many companies use a combination of both methods. Following is an explanation of each of these solutions.

Public, Private, and Reserved IP Addresses When a company applies for a Class A, B, or C license, it is assigned a group of IP addresses that are different from all other IP addresses and are available for use on the Internet. These IP addresses available to the Internet are called **public IP addresses**.

One thing to consider, however, is that not all of these 300 workstations need to have access to the Internet, even though they may be on the network. So, while each workstation may need an IP address to be part of the TCP/IP network, those not connected to the Internet don't need addresses that are unique and available to the Internet and therefore can use private IP addresses. **Private IP addresses** are IP addresses that are used on private intranets that are isolated from the Internet. Because the hosts are isolated from the Internet, no conflicts arise.

In fact, a small company most likely will not apply for a license of public IP addresses at all but instead solely rely on private IP addresses for its internal network. A company using TCP/IP can make up its own private IP addresses to use on its intranet. RFC 1918 recommends that the following IP addresses be used for private networks:

- 10.0.0.0 through 10.255.255.255

- 172.16.0.0 through 172.31.255.255

- 192.168.0.0 through 192.168.255.255

When assigning these isolated IP addresses, also keep in mind that a few IP addresses are reserved for special use by TCP/IP and should not be used. They are listed in Table 11-2.

Table 11-2   Reserved IP addresses

IP address	How it is used
255.255.255.255	Broadcast messages
0.0.0.0	A currently unassigned IP address
127.0.0.1	Indicates your own workstation

All IP addresses on a network must be unique for that network. A network administrator may assign an IP address to a standalone computer (for example, if someone is testing networking software on a PC that is not connected to the network). As long as the network is a private network, the administrator can assign any IP address he or she desires. On an isolated private network, the administrator is free to make up his or her own private IP addresses, although a good administrator avoids using the reserved addresses.

Dynamically Assigned IP Addresses

If an administrator must configure each host on a network manually, assigning it a unique IP address, the task of going from PC to PC to make these assignments and keeping up with which address is assigned to which PC can be an administrative nightmare. The solution is to have a server automatically assign an IP address to a workstation each time it comes onto the network. Instead of IP addresses being permanently assigned to workstations (called static IP addresses), an IP address is assigned for the current session only (called **dynamic IP addresses**). When the session is terminated, the IP address is returned to the list of available addresses. Because not all workstations are online at all times, fewer IP addresses than the total number of workstations can satisfy the needs of the network. Also, you can use private IP addresses for the range of IP addresses that can be assigned to workstations. When a workstation has an IP address assigned to it, it is said that the workstation is leasing the IP address. **Internet service providers (ISPs)**, organizations through which individuals and businesses connect to the Internet, use dynamic IP addressing for their subscribers.

The server that manages these dynamically assigned IP addresses is called a DHCP **(Dynamic Host Configuration Protocol)** server. In this arrangement, workstations are called **DHCP clients**. DHCP software resides on both the client and the server to manage the dynamic assignments of IP addresses. DHCP client software is built into Windows 9x and Windows NT/2000/XP.

When you configure a DHCP server, you specify the range of IP addresses that can be assigned to clients on the network. Figure 11-7 shows the configuration window for a DHCP server that is embedded as firmware on a router. The configuration window is accessed by using a Web browser on the network and entering the IP address of the router into the Web browser address box. In the figure, you can see that the router's IP address is 192.168.1.1, and the starting IP address to be assigned to clients is 192.168.1.100. Because the administration has specified that there can be up to 50 clients, the range of IP addresses is therefore 192.168.1.100 to 192.158.1.149. Also shown in the figure is a list of currently assigned IP addresses and the MAC address of the computer that currently leases that IP address.

Beginning IP address

IP addresses currently assigned to MAC addresses

Number of addresses that can be assigned

Figure 11-7   A DHCP server has a range of IP addresses it can assign to clients on the network

Network Address Translation

If the hosts on a network using private IP addresses need to access the Internet, a problem arises because the private IP addresses are not allowed on the Internet. The solution is to use **NAT (Network Address Translation)**, which uses a single public IP address to access the Internet on behalf of all hosts on the network using other IP addresses. When a computer on the network tries to access the Internet, it must go through a server, router, or other device that substitutes its own IP address for that of the computer requesting the information. Because the device is standing in proxy for the other hosts that want Internet access, it is called a **proxy server**. Figure 11-8 shows how a proxy server stands between the network and the Internet. This proxy server has two network cards installed. One card connects to the LAN, and the other card connects to a cable modem and on to the ISP and the Internet.

Because a proxy server stands between a LAN and the Internet, it often does double duty as a firewall. A **firewall** is software or hardware that protects a network from illegal entry. Because networks are so often attacked by worms and hackers from the Internet, even a small LAN will often have a device that stands between the LAN and the Internet serving as a proxy server, DHCP server, and firewall. As a firewall, it filters out any unsolicited traffic coming from the Internet.

Figure 11-8   A proxy server stands between a private network and the Internet

Windows 98 SE, Windows Me, Windows 2000, and Windows XP offer a NAT service called Microsoft Internet Connection Sharing (ICS). With it, two or more PCs on a home network can share the same IP address when accessing the Internet. Under ICS, one PC acts as the proxy server for other PCs on the home network.

Host Names and NetBIOS Names

Each computer on a TCP/IP network is assigned an IP address, but these numbers are hard to remember. Host names and NetBIOS names use characters rather than numbers to identify computers on a network and are easier to remember and use than IP addresses. (You'll learn how to assign host and NetBIOS names to the computers on your network later in this chapter.) In addition, a company might have a **domain name** that can be used to identify the network. An example of a domain name is amazon.com.

How Host Names and NetBIOS Names Are Related

Recall that NetBEUI is a proprietary Windows network protocol used for Windows LANs not connected to the Internet. NetBEUI supports NetBIOS, which is a protocol used by applications to communicate. Before TCP/IP became such a popular protocol, Windows assumed that the protocol of choice would be NetBEUI and assumed that all computers on a network would be assigned a NetBIOS name such as *joesmith* or *Workstation12*. These names usually are assigned when the operating system is installed. In contrast, TCP/IP identifies computers by IP addresses, but TCP/IP also allows a computer to be assigned a character-based host name such as *joesmith*. The host name can also have a domain name that identifies the network attached like this: *joesmith.mycompany.com*. On a TCP/IP network, the NetBIOS name or host name must be associated with an IP address before one computer can find another on the network. This process of associating a character-based name to an IP address is called **name resolution**.

There are two name resolution services that track relationships between character-based names and IP addresses: **DNS** (**Domain Name System**, also called **Domain Name Service**) and **Microsoft WINS** (**Windows Internet Naming Service**). DNS tracks host names, and WINS tracks NetBIOS names. Windows networks sometimes use a combination of DNS and WINS.

Windows 98 assumes that a computer name is a NetBIOS name, which can have only 15 characters, but Windows 2000 and Windows XP assume that the computer name is a host name, which uses the TCP/IP convention for host names. If the name is 15 characters or fewer, it will work as a NetBIOS name or a TCP/IP name on either a NetBEUI network or a TCP/IP network. If a host name is used, it can be up to 63 characters including letters, numbers and hyphens, as long as the computer is not part of a workgroup. If the computer is part of a workgroup, the host name should not exceed 15 characters. Microsoft is slowly abandoning NetBIOS as the default naming convention in favor of TCP/IP host names.

11

Remember that applications that use NetBEUI use NetBIOS API calls to communicate with other applications on the network. Applications that are using TCP/IP to communicate over the network use a type of API call known as **WinSock (Windows Sockets)**. WinSock is a part of the TCP/IP utility software installed with TCP/IP.

An application can make a NetBIOS API call to another computer on a network and identify the remote computer by its NetBIOS name even though the network is using TCP/IP. When dealing with these hybrid networks, you should know that the NetBIOS name of the remote computer must be related to an IP address before TCP/IP can make the connection.

PHYSICAL NETWORK ARCHITECTURES

There are several LAN architectures, or ways of structuring a network. The architecture of a network describes the overall design of the network, including physical components, network technologies, interfacing software, and the protocols needed to establish reliable communication among nodes on the network. (A **node**, or **host**, is one device on the network such as a workstation, server, or printer.) The four most popular physical network architectures (sometimes called **hardware protocols**) for local networks are Ethernet, token ring, FDDI, and wireless LAN technology. An older type of network technology is Attached Resource Computer network (ARCnet), which is seldom seen today. This section discusses the most popular architectures, including the network problems they were designed to solve as well as their advantages and disadvantages.

The **Institute of Electrical and Electronics Engineers (IEEE)** creates standards for computer and electronics industries. The networking standard, IEEE 802, was named for the year (1980) and the month (February) that the committee devising the standards first met. The IEEE 802 standard consists of a series of specifications for networking. For example, IEEE 802.2 describes the standard for Logical Link Control, which defines how networks that use different protocols communicate with each other. For more information on the IEEE 802 standards, see the IEEE Web site, *www.ieee.org*.

Ethernet

Ethernet is the most popular network architecture used today. There are three variations of Ethernet, primarily distinguished from one another by speed: 10-Mbps Ethernet, 100-Mbps or Fast Ethernet, and Gigabit Ethernet. These three types are described below. Figure 11-9 shows several types of cables used with Ethernet, and Table 11-3 compares cable types and Ethernet versions.

- *10-Mbps Ethernet.* The first Ethernet specification was invented by Xerox Corporation in the 1970s, and in 1980 was enhanced and became known as Ethernet IEEE 802.3. This type of Ethernet operates at 10 Mbps (megabits per second) and uses either **shielded twisted-pair (STP) cable**, **unshielded twisted-pair (UTP) cable**, or **coaxial cable**. STP uses a covering around the pairs of wires inside the cable that protects it from electromagnetic interference caused by electrical motors, transmitters, or high-tension lines. It costs more than unshielded cable, so it's only used when the situation demands it. Twisted-pair cable uses a connector that looks like a large phone jack and is called an **RJ-45 connector**, and thin coaxial cable uses a **BNC connector**. There are several variations of this speed of Ethernet. 10BaseT Ethernet uses UTP cable that is rated by category. CAT-3 (category 3) is less expensive than the more popular CAT-5 cable. **10Base5** Ethernet (sometimes called **ThickNet**) uses thick coaxial cable such as RG8. **10Base2** Ethernet (sometimes called **ThinNet**) uses a less expensive, smaller coaxial cable such as RG58.

- *100-Mbps Ethernet or Fast Ethernet.* This improved version of Ethernet (sometimes called **100BaseT** or **Fast Ethernet**) operates at 100 Mbps and uses UTP or STP cable. 100BaseT networks can support slower speeds of 10 Mbps so that devices that run at either 10 Mbps or 100 Mbps can coexist on the same LAN. Two variations of 100BaseT are 100BaseTX and 100BaseFX. The most popular variation is 100BaseTX, which uses CAT-5 twisted-pair cable, Enhanced CAT-5 (CAT-5e), or CAT-6 that has less cross talk than CAT-5 or CAT-5e. 100BaseFX uses fiber-optic cable, shown in Figure 11-9. Fiber cable comes in three types: single-mode (thin, difficult to connect, expensive, and best performing), multi-mode (most popular), and plastic fiber (thick, easy to connect, short cable lengths required).

- *1000-Mbps Ethernet or Gigabit Ethernet.* This latest version of Ethernet operates at 1,000 Mbps and uses twisted-pair cable and fiber-optic cable. While not yet widely used, **Gigabit Ethernet** is expected to be used for high-speed LAN backbones and for server-to-server connections.

11

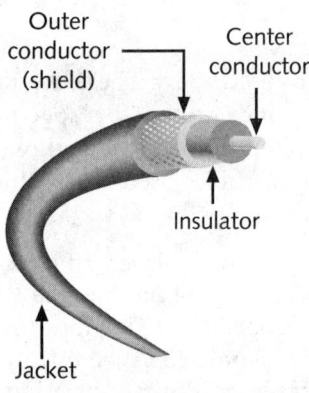

Outer conductor (shield)

Center conductor

Insulator

Jacket

a) Coaxial cable

b) Unshielded twisted-pair (UTP)

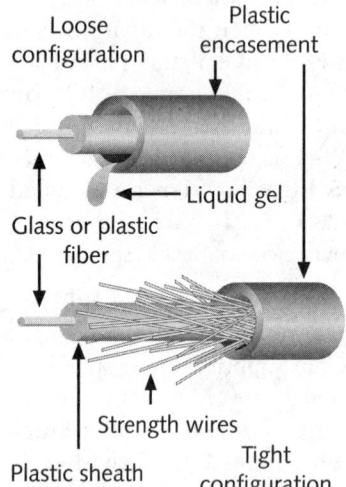

Loose configuration

Plastic encasement

Liquid gel

Glass or plastic fiber

Strength wires

Plastic sheath

Tight configuration

c) Fiber-optic cables with tight and loose sheaths

Copper conductor

Shielding

Color-coded insulation

Plastic encasement

d) Shielded twisted-pair (STP)

Figure 11-9   Networking cables

Table 11-3   Variations of Ethernet and Ethernet cabling

Cable System	Speed	Cables and Connectors	Maximum Cable Length
10Base2 (ThinNet)	10 Mbps	Coaxial uses a BNC connector.	185 meters or 607 feet
10Base5 (ThickNet)	10 Mbps	Coaxial uses an AUI 15-pin D-shaped connector.	500 meters or 1,640 feet

Table 11-3   Variations of Ethernet and Ethernet cabling (continued)

Cable System	Speed	Cables and Connectors	Maximum Cable Length
10BaseT and 100BaseT (Twisted-pair)	10 to 100 Mbps	UTP or STP uses an RJ-45 connector.	100 meters or 328 feet
10BaseF, 10BaseFL, 100BaseFL, 100BaseFX or 1000BaseFX (fiber-optic)	10 Mbps up to 1 Gbps	Fiber-optic cable uses an0 ST or SC fiber-optic connector.	500 meters up to 2 kilometers (6,562 feet)

Important coaxial cables you should be aware of are RG59 used for cable TV and VCR transmission, RG6 which has greater shielding than RG59 and is used for Satellite Dish signals and video applications requiring greater shielding, RG8 used by ThickNet Ethernet, and RG58 used by ThinNet Ethernet. Also, the outside jacket of coaxial cable is normally made of extruded PVC (poly vinyl cloride) which is not safe when used inside plenums (areas between the floors of buildings). More expensive plenum cable covered with Teflon is used in these situations.

Ethernet Topology

Ethernet networks can be configured as either a bus topology or a star topology. **Topology** is the arrangement or shape used to physically connect devices on a network to one another. Figure 11-10 shows examples of bus and star topologies. A **bus topology** connects each node in a line and does not have a centralized point of connection. Cables just go from one computer to the next one, and the next. A **star topology** connects all nodes to a centralized hub. PCs on the LAN are like the points of a star around the hub in the middle, which connects the nodes on the LAN.

11

Terminator

Bus design

Terminator

a) Ethernet can be constructed with a bus design

Hub

Star design

b) Ethernet can be constructed with a star design using a hub

Figure 11-10   Ethernet is a simple and popular network technology

The star arrangement is more popular because it is easier to maintain than the bus arrangement. In a star topology, a hub works by passing all data that flows to it to every device that is connected to the hub. An Ethernet hub **broadcasts** the data packet to every device, as shown in Figure 11-11. Think of a hub as just a pass-through and distribution point for every device that is connected to it, without regard for what kind of data is passing through and where the data might be going. See Figure 11-12.

In Figure 11-11, when computer A sends data to the hub, the hub replicates the data and sends it on to every device connected to it. Computers B, C, and D all get a copy of the data. It's up to these computers to decide if the data is intended for them. For this reason, a hub can generate a lot of unnecessary traffic on a LAN, which can result in slow performance when several nodes are connected to the hub.

Figure 11-11   Any data that is received by a hub is replicated and passed on to every device connected to it

As networks grow, more hubs can be added. Figure 11-13 shows an example of a network that uses three hubs in sequence. The hubs themselves form a bus network, but the computers connected to each hub form a star. This combination network configuration, which uses a logical bus for data delivery but is wired as a physical star, is an example of a **star bus topology**.

RJ-45 port

Twisted-pair cable

RJ-45 connector

BNC terminator

BNC port

Figure 11-12   A hub is a pass-through device to connect nodes on a network

11

Figure 11-13   A star bus network uses more than one hub

How Ethernet Controls Data Traffic

An Ethernet network is a passive network, meaning that the network just sits there and waits for a PC to use it. Ethernet works much like an old telephone party line, where each computer is like a party-line caller. When you wanted to make a call on a party line, you had to pick up the telephone and listen. If there was a dial tone (carrier), then you could make a call. If someone else was talking, you had to hang up and try again later. If two people attempted to make a call at the same time, both calls would fail. Both callers would have to hang up and begin again. The first one back on the line would be able to make a call.

Similarly, a computer that wants to send packets over Ethernet first listens on the network for silence. If it hears nothing, it begins to transmit after a small delay. As it transmits, it is also listening. If it hears something other than its own data being transmitted, it stops transmitting and sends out a signal that there has been a **collision**, which occurs when two computers attempt to send data at the same time. A collision can cause packets that were just sent to be corrupted. Each computer waits for a random amount of time and then tries to transmit again, first listening for silence. This type of network technology is called a **contention-based** system because each computer must contend for an opportunity to transmit on the network.

Computers using Ethernet gain access to the network using the **CSMA/CD (Carrier Sense Multiple Access with Collision Detection)** method. The name of the method describes the three characteristics of the way computers communicate on Ethernet:

1. A computer must sense that the network is free to handle its transmission before initiating a signal (*carrier sense*).

2. Many computers use the same network (*multiple access*).

3. Each computer must detect and manage collisions (*collision detection*).

Another method that can be used by a network technology to control collisions is **CSMA/CA (Carrier Sense Multiple Access with Collision Avoidance)**, whereby each computer signals its intent to send data before it is sent. This method is not as popular as CSMA/CD because it adds extra traffic to the network. A third method of managing traffic on a network is by passing a **token**, which is a small packet used on token ring networks to send data from one station to the next. Whoever has the token has the right to pass data. Token ring and FDDI both use this token method.

Repeaters

Because signals transmitted over long distances on a network can weaken (a process called **attenuation**), devices are added to amplify signals in large LANs (see Figure 11-14). For example, for a 10Base2 (ThinNet) Ethernet cable, if the cable exceeds 185 meters (607 feet), amplification is required. A **repeater** is a device that amplifies signals on a network. There are two kinds of repeaters. An **amplifier repeater** simply amplifies the incoming signal, noise and all. A **signal-regenerating repeater** reads the signal and then creates an exact duplicate of the original signal before sending it on. Ethernet uses a signal-regenerating repeater.

Signal weakens

Signal regenerated

Repeater

Figure 11-14   A repeater on a network restores the clarity of the signal, which degrades over a distance because of attenuation

Repeaters help overcome the limitations on the length of cables that can be used, because with a repeater, signals can travel further. But there are still limitations, because Ethernet networks have a limit on the maximum amount of time a signal can take to reach the network, and since repeaters can slow down travel time, too many repeaters can cause problems on a network. A hub acts as a signal-regenerating repeater.

Token Ring

Token ring is a less popular LAN technology developed by IBM that transmits data at 4 Mbps or 16 Mbps. Physically, a token ring network is arranged in a star topology, because each node is connected to a centralized device and not to the other nodes in the network. However, a token actually travels in a ring on the network. The token is either free or busy, and a node must have the token to communicate. If a node receives the token and finds it free (no data attached), if it wants to communicate, it attaches data to the token and passes it on. If it finds the token is busy (data is already attached), it cannot attach new data. If a node reads data addressed to it, it puts a code on the token so that, when the token reaches the sending node, this node will read the code, know the data has been successfully received, and remove the data from the token.

There are two wires in each connection that runs from a node to the hub, and a token moves up one to the node, down the other back to the hub, up to the next node and so on, until it ends up back at its starting point. In other words, the token is traveling in a ring. Because it is physically a star and logically a ring, it is sometimes called a **star ring topology**. The centralized device to which the network nodes are connected is called a **Controlled-Access Unit (CAU)**, a **Multistation Access Unit (MSAU** or sometimes just **MAU)**, or a **Smart Multistation Access Unit (SMAU)**. Figure 11-15 shows a sample token ring configuration with three workstations connected to an MSAU, although the MSAU in the figure can support up to eight workstations. One end of the MSAU has a Ring In connection where data flows into the MSAU, and the other end has a Ring Out connection where data flows out.

11

Figure 11-15   A Token ring network uses a centralized device called a MAU
(Multistation Access Unit)

Each workstation contains a token ring LAN card with a 9-pin connector for the token ring cable, which connects each workstation to an MSAU. Token ring cables can be either UTP or STP cables that have two twisted pairs, for a total of four wires in the cable. STP cables for token ring use either an IDC (IBM Data Connector) or UDC (Universal Data Connector).

FDDI

The **Fiber Distributed Data Interface** (**FDDI**, pronounced "fiddy") uses a token that travels in a ring like a token ring. But with FDDI, data frames travel on the ring without the token, and multiple nodes can have data on the ring at the same time. Nodes on a FDDI network can be connected in a ring using a **ring topology**, meaning that each node is connected to two other nodes, although most FDDI networks use hubs in a physical star topology. FDDI provides data transfer at 100 Mbps, which is much faster than token ring or regular Ethernet, and a little faster than Fast Ethernet, which also runs at about 100 Mbps. At one time, FDDI used only fiber-optic cabling, but now it can also run on UTP. FDDI is often used as the network technology for a large LAN in a large company or ISP. FDDI is also used as a backbone network to connect several LANs in a large building.

Wireless LANs

Wireless LAN (WLAN) technology, as the name implies, does not use cables or wires to connect the computers on the network. Connections are made using a wireless NIC (network interface card), which includes an antenna to send and receive signals. Wireless LANs can also make connections using infrared transmission. Wireless LANs are popular in places where networking cables are difficult to install, such as outdoors or in a historic building with wiring restrictions. Wireless networks are often used in combination with a wired LAN, as shown in Figure 11-16. Two devices can communicate using wireless, or a wireless device can connect to a LAN by way of an access point.

Figure 11-16   Nodes on a wireless LAN connect to a cabled network by way of an access point

 A LAN using a bus formation is often depicted in a logic diagram as a straight line with devices connecting to it, and a LAN using a ring formation is sometimes depicted as a circle. This method merely shows that devices are connected and is a nondescript way of drawing a LAN that might use a bus, ring, or star topology. Since most LANs are Ethernet, the most common way of drawing a LAN is to use a straight line.

Access points are strategically placed so that nodes can access at least one access point from anywhere in the covered area, using radio waves. When two computers communicate, each using a wireless connection, they communicate through the access point instead of communicating directly with each other.

The first IEEE standard that outlined wireless LAN specifications was IEEE 802.11, published in 1990. Most current wireless LAN devices operate under the 1999 IEEE **802.11b** standard also called **Wi-Fi**, and called AirPort by Apple Computers, although there are other wireless technologies available, such as Bluetooth. 802.11b uses a frequency range of 2.4 GHz and has a distance range of about 100 meters. Bluetooth is a standard for short-range wireless communication and data synchronization between devices. This standard was developed by a group of electronics manufacturers, including Ericsson, IBM, Intel, Nokia, and Toshiba, and it is overseen by the Bluetooth Special Interest Group. Bluetooth, which has a range of only 10 meters, also works in the 2.4 GHz frequency range, is easy to configure, and is considered a viable option for short-range connections such as connecting a PDA to a cell phone so that the PDA can connect to a remote network.

For more information on Wi-Fi, see *www.wi-fi.org*, and for more information on AirPort, see *www.apple.com*. For information on Bluetooth, see *www.bluetooth.com*.

IEEE has two more up-and-coming wireless standards, 802.11a and 802.11g. 802.11a works in the 5.0 GHz frequency range and is, therefore, not compatible with 802.11b. It has a shorter range from wireless device to an access point (50 meters compared to 100 meters for 802.11b), but is much faster than 802.11b and does not have to deal with interference from cordless phones, microwave ovens, and Bluetooth devices, as does 802.11b. It is expected that 802.11b and 802.11a devices will coexist for some time. 802.11g is another IEEE wireless standard that is not yet widely available; it will be compatible with 802.11b, but faster.

Although wireless LANs have some obvious advantages in places where running cables would be difficult or overly expensive, wireless LANs tend to be slower than wired networks, especially when they are busy. Another problem with wireless LANs is security. Companies are reluctant to use them when it is possible for an unauthorized person with a receiving device to intercept wireless LAN transmissions. Security on a wireless LAN is accomplished by filtering the MAC address of wireless NICs allowed to use the access point and by encrypting data sent over the wireless LAN.

Segmenting a Network

As you have learned, when two or more computers are connected, they form a network and are sometimes connected by hubs. For small networks, hubs are sufficient, but in larger networks, more intelligent devices are needed that can help reduce the traffic on the network. **Bridges** and **switches** are used to divide networks into **segments**, which decreases the amount of traffic on the overall network. This section describes how bridges and switches work and explains how they are different from each other.

Before we discuss these devices, you need to understand the following terms and concepts:

- All communication on a local network uses the MAC address to identify the destination computer. Other computers on the network receive the packet, but, because it is not addressed to them, they discard it.

- Bridges and switches are more intelligent than hubs and make decisions about whether or not to allow traffic to pass, or where to forward that traffic, reducing traffic on each segment and improving network performance.

A network engineer will add a bridge or switch at a strategic place on the network, such as between two floors or between two buildings, to contain heavy traffic within each of two segments created by the bridge. Bridges and switches use MAC addresses, which they store in routing tables, to determine where to send packets.

To help you understand how bridges work, suppose you have a town that has a river going through it, as shown in Figure 11-17. Traffic on the West Side must pass over the bridge to reach the East Side. At the bridge stands a bridge attendant who looks at the source and destination addresses of each traveler (packet). Suppose that a traveler from the West Side approaches the bridge attendant. The attendant looks at the address where the traveler wants to go (the destination address). The attendant then searches for the destination address in his routing table. If he finds the address in the table, the table gives the side the address is on. He then grants or refuses the traveler permission to pass, based on that knowledge. If the attendant does not find the destination address in the routing table, he allows the traveler to cross. Also, the attendant will update his routing table by adding information he has just learned. By knowing that the traveler came from the West Side and knowing the source address of the traveler, he can enter this source address into his routing table as one address on the West Side. At first, the attendant doesn't know much about addresses on each side, but as many travelers come from both sides of the bridge, his table will become more complete, and the attendant can be more efficient at his job.

Figure 11-17   A bridge is an intelligent device making decisions concerning network traffic

A bridge on a network works in a similar way to our hypothetical bridge separating two sides of town with an attendant. A network bridge keeps a routing table for each network segment it connects to. The tables start out empty, and all data packets that reach the bridge from one segment are passed on to the other segment connected to the bridge. As packets appear at the bridge, the bridge records the source MAC address in its routing table for that segment. The next time a packet appears at the bridge, the bridge will look at its destination and will route it across the bridge only if the destination is on a different network segment or it does not recognize the destination. Figure 11-18 shows a bridge device.

Figure 11-18   A bridge

To understand the difference between a bridge and a switch, we must look at a more complicated situation where three or more network segments are involved, as shown in Figure 11-19. When a packet arrives at a bridge, the bridge searches the routing table of only that segment. The bridge only makes a single decision: "Is this packet destined for a node on its own network segment?" If the answer is "Yes," then the packet is refused. It will reach its destination without the use of the bridge. If the answer is "No," then the bridge simply broadcasts the packet to all other network segments connected to it, except the network segment that the packet came from. In Figure 11-19, if a packet arrives from network segment A, the bridge searches its routing table for network segment A. If it doesn't find the MAC address of the packet in that table, it broadcasts the packet to network segments B and C.

You can now clearly see why bridging does not work well with large networks (such as the Internet). Broadcasting messages over several large networks would produce much unnecessary traffic on these networks. Bridging is effective at separating high-volume areas on a LAN and works best when it is used to connect LANs that usually do not communicate outside of their immediate network.

Figure 11-19 A bridge or switch connects two or more segments and decides whether or not to allow the packet to pass through, depending on its destination MAC address

A switch, on the other hand, does not work by sending broadcast messages. Just like a bridge, a switch keeps a table of the MAC addresses of all the devices connected to it. It uses this table to determine which path to use when sending packets. Recall the discussion of Figure 11-19 for a moment. Like a bridge, a switch will not let a packet pass to other networks if it is addressed to a location on its own network segment. However, unlike a bridge, a switch passes a packet only to its destination network segment, instead of to all segments other than the one it came from (the source). Figure 11-20 compares how a bridge works with how a switch works.

For example, in Figure 11-19, if Computer 10 on Network segment C sends a packet to Computer 7 on Network segment B, the switch receives the packet because the hub on Computer 10's network segment is broadcasting. Using the destination address in the header of the packet, the switch searches all the tables for all the network segments connected to it to determine the segment to which the packet is addressed. The switch then forwards the packet to Network segment B, rather than broadcasting the packet to all the network segments connected to it.

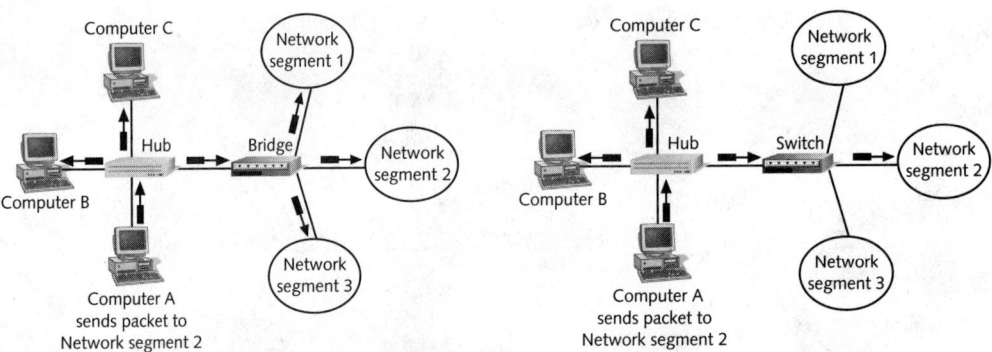

Figure 11-20   A switch is more intelligent than a bridge and can determine which network segment a packet needs to be sent to

CONNECTING A PC TO A NETWORK

Connecting a PC to a network requires a NIC, network cable (called a **patch cable**), and a device for the PC to connect to, such as a hub. (Wireless PCs may require only a wireless NIC.) This section shows how NICs work, how to install them, and how to set up a network protocol. You will also learn about ways to divide a network into segments for improved performance, using bridges and switches.

Access to and resources on a network are controlled by individual computers (called a **peer-to-peer network**) or by a centralized server database (called a **client/server network**). For Windows, a peer-to-peer network is called a **workgroup** and a client/server network is called a **domain**.

 The simplest network of all does not use hubs, bridges, or switches and consists of two PCs connected by a **crossover cable**, which is a network cable in which the read wire and the write wire on one PC exchange functions when they are connected to the second PC.

How NICs Work

A NIC plugs into a motherboard expansion slot, provides a port or ports on the back of the card for connection to a network, and manages the communication and hardware network protocol for the PC. An individual NIC can be designed to support Ethernet, token ring, or FDDI network architectures, but not all three. However, it might be designed to handle more than one cabling system. See Figure 11-21 for some examples of network cards. The network card and the device drivers controlling the network card are the only components in the PC that are aware of the type of physical network being used. In other words, the type of network in use is transparent to the applications software using it.

a. FDDI

b. Token ring

c. Ethernet

Figure 11-21   Three different types of network cards: (a) FDDI, (b) token ring, and (c) Ethernet

A network card sends and receives data to and from the system bus in parallel, and sends and receives data to and from the network in series. In addition, the network card is responsible for converting the data it is transmitting into a signal that is in a form appropriate to the network. For example, a fiber-optic FDDI card contains a laser diode that converts data to light pulses before transmission, and a twisted-pair Ethernet card converts data from the 5-volt signal used on the motherboard to the voltage used by twisted-pair cables. The component on the card that is responsible for this signal conversion is called the **transceiver** (transmitter-receiver). It is common for an Ethernet card to contain more than one transceiver, each with a different port on the back of the card, in order to accommodate different cabling media. This type of Ethernet card is called a **combo card** (see Figure 11-22).

Combo card

BNC port

RJ-45 port

RJ-45 connector

Twisted-pair (UTP) cable

ThinNet coaxial cable
attaches here

Terminator

BNC T-connector

Figure 11-22   This Ethernet combo card can use either a BNC or RJ-45 connection,
depending on the cabling system used

Different networks have different ways of identifying network nodes. Ethernet and
Token Ring cards have MAC addresses hard-coded on the card by the manufacturer.
These addresses are 6-byte (48-bit) hex addresses unique to each card. Part of the MAC
address contains the manufacturer, and part of the address is unique to each card; therefore, no two adapters should have the same MAC address.

Network cards require an IRQ, an I/O address, and, for DOS and Windows 9x real
mode, upper memory addresses. If the network card is on the PCI bus, then the PCI bus
controller manages the IRQ and I/O address requirements. Network cards may be Plug
and Play, or they can use jumpers or DIP switches on the card to determine which
resources to request. When selecting a network card, three things are important:

- Except for wireless connections, the speed and type of network to which you
  are attaching (for example, 100BaseT Ethernet, token ring, FDDI, or a proprietary network standard)

- The type of cable you are using (for example, shielded twisted-pair, coaxial,
  or fiber-optic cable)

- The type of slot you are using (PCI or ISA). PCI is faster than ISA and is the
  preferred choice.

We next discuss how to install a NIC and a network protocol under Windows 9x and
Windows 2000.

Installing a Network Card Under Windows 9x

Windows 95 supports Ethernet, token ring, and ARCnet networking cards. Windows 98 supports ATM, Ethernet, token ring, FDDI, IrDA (Infrared Data Association standards for infrared communications), and ARCnet networking cards. In most situations, Windows 9x detects a network card when the PC is first turned on and automatically configures the card for you, although some settings can be changed using the Properties window of the NIC. After the device drivers are installed, go to Device Manager and verify that the card is recognized with no errors.

For legacy NICs (not Plug and Play), you must use DIP switches, jumpers, or a firmware setup utility to change the IRQ and I/O address range assigned to the card. To install a legacy NIC using Windows 9x, do the following:

1. Set DIP switches or jumpers and physically install the network card in the PC. (If the card is Plug and Play, it most likely will not have jumpers or DIP switches to set.)

2. Turn on the PC. Windows 9x detects the new device and configures it for you. You can check the settings by using the Device Manager: click **Start**, point to **Settings**, click **Control Panel**, and then double-click **System**. The System Properties window appears.

3. Select the **Device Manager** tab (see Figure 11-23). The network card should be in the list under Network Adapters.

4. Select the card from the list and click **Properties**. The card's Properties window appears. Look for any conflicts or other errors reported by Device Manager.

5. The IRQ and the I/O address of the card can be found on the Resources tab. If this is not a Plug and Play card, and you know what the card DIP switches and jumpers are set to, you can compare those values to the values shown here. Click **OK** when done.

6. Click **OK** again to save your changes.

If Windows does not recognize a legacy card at startup, after the boot, run a setup program that you should find on the floppy disk that came with the card. This floppy disk also should contain drivers for the NIC. If the drivers do not load correctly, try downloading updated drivers from the Web site of the network card's manufacturer. You'll find other troubleshooting tips for installing NICs later in this chapter.

11

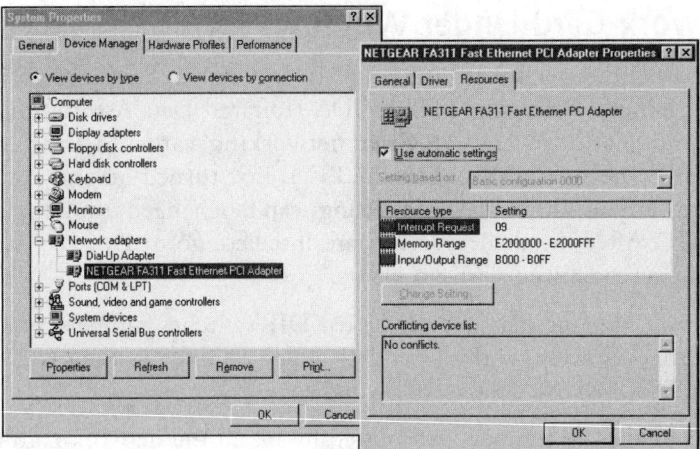

Figure 11-23 A network adapter's resources show in the properties option of the Device Manager window

Installing a NIC Under Windows 2000/XP

After a NIC is physically installed and the PC is turned on, Windows 2000 automatically detects the card and guides you through the process of installing drivers. After the installation, verify that the card is installed with no errors by using Device Manager. In Device Manager, the network card should be listed under Network adapters. Right-click the card and select Properties to view the card's properties.

Another way to access the NIC Properties window in Windows 2000/XP is to use the Network and Dial-up Connections applet in the Control Panel:

1. For Windows 2000, open the **Control Panel** and double-click the **Network and Dial-up Connections** icon. For Windows XP, in Control Panel, double-click **Network Connections**.

2. When the dialog box opens, right-click the **Local Area Connection** icon.

3. From the shortcut menu, select **Properties** to view the Local Area Connection Properties window (see Figure 11-24). Click **Configure**. The Properties window for the card appears. (Another way to access the Network and Dial-up Connections applet is to right-click on My Network Places on the desktop and select Properties from the shortcut menu.)

Figure 11-24   NIC Properties window under Windows 2000

Installing a Wireless NIC

Installing a wireless NIC works the same way as installing a regular NIC except you must use the NIC's configuration software to specify wireless network parameters. A wireless connection requires the computer to be within an acceptable range of an access point or another wireless device that it will communicate with directly. This distance is determined by the type of wireless technology used, which most likely will be 802.11b. This wireless standard supports ranges from 100 meters to more than 500 meters depending on the speed the access point or other computer is configured to run. Generally, the higher the speed the shorter the range between devices.

Do the following to install and configure a wireless NIC in a PC or notebook:

1. Install the wireless NIC and turn on the computer. The computer will immediately detect the device and launch the Found New Hardware Wizard. Follow the wizard to load the device drivers using the CD that came bundled with the NIC. If Windows prompts you to restart the computer, do so.

2. Configure the NIC to use the same wireless parameters as the access point or other computer. Run a setup program on the CD that came with the NIC to install the NIC configuration software, and then launch the software.

3. Consult the documentation to find out how to use the software. Figure 11-25 shows an example of the configuration window for a wireless NIC, but yours might look different. Using the configuration software, you can view the status of the wireless connection and change the wireless parameters. Look at

Figure 11-27 for an example of the wireless configuration software reporting the following information about the connection:

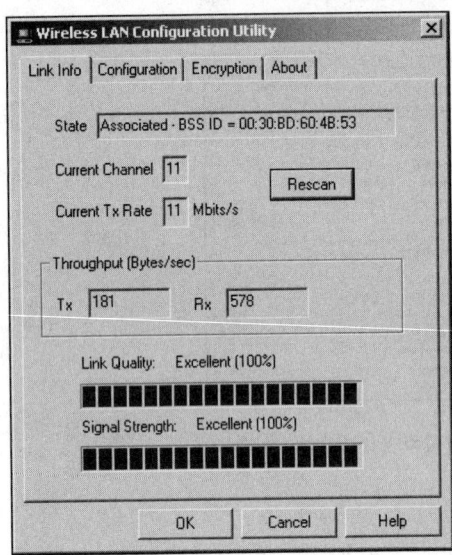

Figure 11-25   Wireless NIC configuration software reports the status of the current connection

- *State*. The state is the status of the current connection and reports the BSS ID (basic service set identifier) which is the MAC address of the access point device that the NIC is currently using.

- *Current Channel*. 802.11b uses 14 different channels. The United States can use channels 1 through 11. The access point device is configured to use one of these eleven channels, which is reported by the NIC software.

- *Current Tx Rate*. Current transmission rate, which is 11 Mbits/sec in the figure.

- *Throughput, Link Quality, and Signal Strength*. These values indicate throughput rate and how strong the signal is.

Figure 11-25 also shows a Rescan button. You can click this button to tell the NIC to scan for a new access point.

4. Click the Configuration tab to change how the NIC functions (see Figure 11-26). Changes you can make on this screen include:

- *Mode*. The mode indicates if the computer is to communicate through an access point (Infrastructure mode) or if the computer is to communicate directly with another wireless device (Ad Hoc mode).

- *SSID.* The SSID (service set identifier) is currently set to ANY which says the NIC is free to connect to any access point it finds. You can enter the name of an access point in order to specify this NIC should connect only to this one access point. To know the name assigned to a particular access point, ask the network administrator responsible for managing the wireless network.

- *Tx Rate.* You can specify the transmission rate or leave it at fully automatic so that it is free to use the best transmission rate possible.

- *PS Mode.* When disabled, the PC will not be allowed to enter sleep mode so that network communication continues uninterrupted. Enable PS Mode to allow the PC to go into sleep mode.

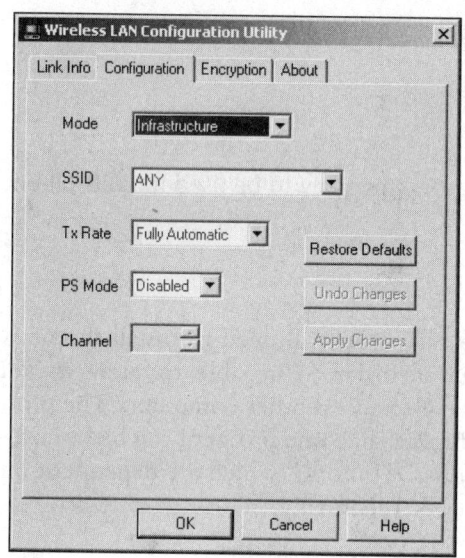

Figure 11-26   Configure how a wireless NIC will connect to a wireless LAN

5. This NIC supports encrypted wireless transmission. To enable encryption, click the Encryption tab (see Figure 11-27). Select 64-bit or 128-bit encryption and enter a secret passphrase. This passphrase is a word, such as "ourpassphrase", which generates a digital key used for encryption. Every computer user must enter the same passphrase, which can be changed at any time. Click OK to close the configuration software.

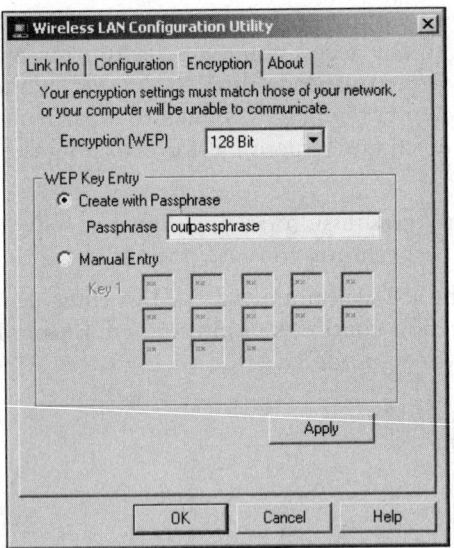

Figure 11-27   Enter a passphrase that generates a key to be used for 128-bit encryption to secure a wireless LAN

Installing the Network Protocol

Once you have physically installed the NIC, you will need to install the network protocol and give the computer a name in order to be able to view it in Network Neighborhood or My Network Places and to access other computers. The protocol used on a network is bound to the NIC, and more than one protocol can be bound to a NIC. The NIC uses the two lower layers of the OSI model, which are dependent on the network technology used, such as Ethernet or token ring.

 If Network Neighborhood is not displayed on the desktop, then OS networking protocols (for example, NetBEUI or TCP/IP) have not yet been installed or are giving problems.

Here, you will learn how to install two network protocols, **NetBEUI (NetBIOS Extended User Interface)** and **TCP/IP (Transmission Control Protocol/Internet Protocol)**, and how to configure both. Note that even after you've installed a protocol, you will not be able to access resources on the other computers on the network until at least one of those computers has been configured to share its resources. How to share resources is covered in Chapter 25.

Connecting to a NetBEUI Network

To use NetBEUI (a proprietary Microsoft protocol suite used only by Windows computers) to connect to a network using Windows 98, do the following:

NetBEUI is not routable and therefore cannot be used to communicate over the Internet.

1. Access the Control Panel and double-click the **Network** applet. The Network window opens. (You can also access the applet by right-clicking on the Network Neighborhood icon on the desktop and selecting Properties from the shortcut window.)

For Windows 9x, if you don't see the Network Neighborhood icon on the desktop, then a network protocol has not been installed or is giving errors.

2. Click **Add** to display the Select Network Component Type window, as shown in Figure 11-29.

3. Select **Protocol**, click **Add**, and the Select Network Protocol window opens. Select **Microsoft** on the left and **NetBEUI** on the right. See Figure 11-28. Click **OK**.

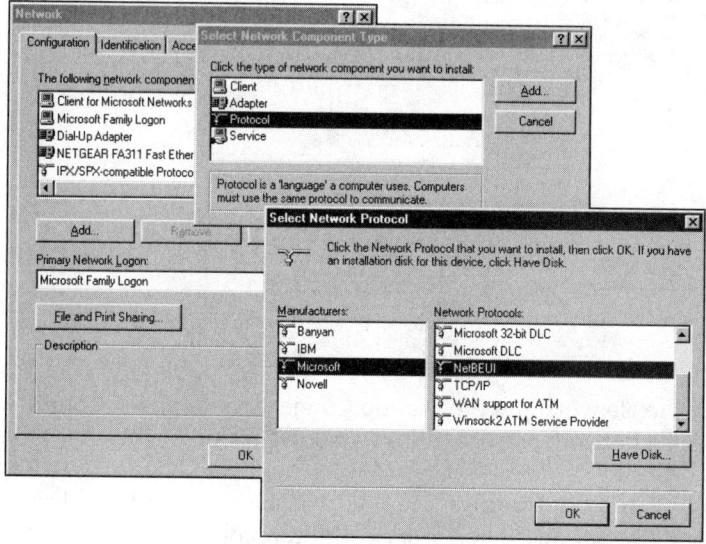

Figure 11-28   Using Windows 98, install a network protocol using the Network applet in Control Panel

To connect to a network using NetBEUI on a Windows 2000/XP computer, do the following:

1. Access the Control Panel and open the **Network and Dial-up Connections** applet.

2. Right-click the **Local Area Connection** icon and select **Properties** from the shortcut menu. The Local Area Connection Properties window opens (see Figure 11-29).

3. From this window, you can uninstall and install network components. Click **Install**. The Select Network Component Type windows opens, which is also shown in Figure 11-29. Select **Protocol**, and then click **Add**.

4. The Select Network Protocol window appears. Select **NetBEUI Protocol** from the list of uninstalled protocols, and then click **OK**.

5. When you return to the Local Area Connection Properties window, you should see NetBEUI Protocol checked as an installed component. Click **Close**. Windows 2000 does not automatically bind NetBEUI to an installed dial-up adapter, but will bind it to the network adapter providing this local network connection.

6. On the Windows desktop, double-click the **My Network Places** icon and view this and other computers on the network.

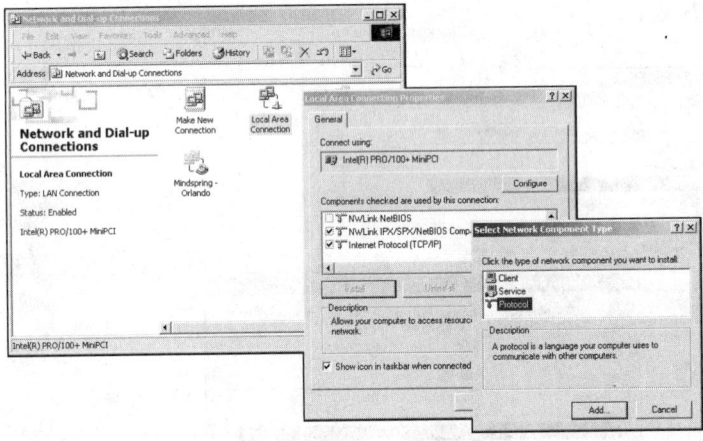

Figure 11-29   Use the Network and the Dial-up Connections applet in Control Panel to install a network protocol using Windows 2000

Notice that NetBEUI is automatically bound to any network cards or dial-up adapters that it finds installed. (Recall that when a network protocol is associated with a network card or modem, the process is called *binding*.) For example, in Figure 11-30 the two adapters already installed are a network card (NetGear FA311 Fast Ethernet PCI Adapter) and dial-up adapter. The dial-up adapter is a modem card that has been configured to use

Dial–up Networking so that it can dial up and connect to a network such as that provided by an ISP to connect to the Internet.

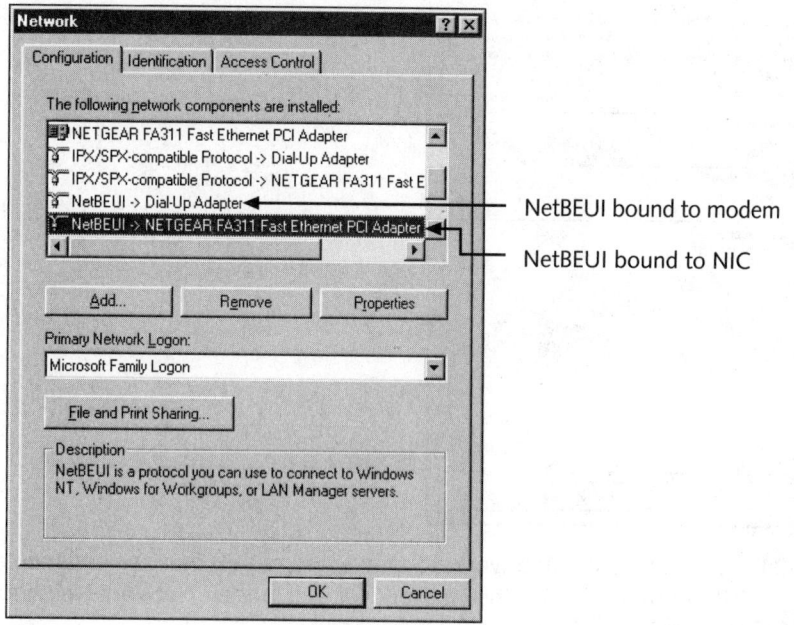

NetBEUI bound to modem

NetBEUI bound to NIC

Figure 11-30   A network protocol automatically binds itself to any network adapter or dial-up adapter it finds installed

Configuring the NetBEUI Connection

The only configuration that NetBEUI requires is that the computer be given a name. Windows 9x assumes that a computer name is a NetBIOS name. (NetBIOS is a protocol that applications use to communicate, and a NetBIOS name for a computer can consist of up to 15 characters.) To assign a NetBIOS name to a Windows 9x computer, follow these directions:

1. Access the Control Panel and double-click the **Network** icon.

2. Click the **Identification** tab. See Figure 11-31.

3. Enter the name of the workgroup (Golden in this example). (A **workgroup** is a group of computers on a network that share files, folders, and printers.) All users in the workgroup must have the same workgroup name entered on this window.

4. Enter the NetBIOS name of the computer (Patricia in this example). Each computer name must be unique within the workgroup.

5. Click **OK** to exit the window.

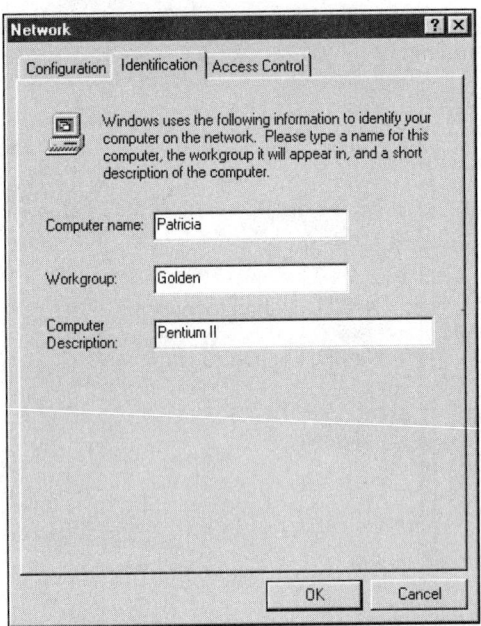

Figure 11-31   Each computer in a workgroup in Windows 98 must be assigned a name that other users on the network will see in their Network Neighborhood window

Windows 2000/XP uses host names, which are also character-based but can be up to 63 characters. However, as long as a computer's name is 15 characters or fewer, it can be both a NetBIOS name and a host name.

For Windows 2000, follow these directions to give a host name to a computer:

1. On the Windows 2000 desktop, right-click on **My Computer**, and select **Properties** from the shortcut menu. The System Properties window appears.

2. Click the **Network Identification** tab and then click the **Properties** button. The Identification Changes window appears (see Figure 11-32).

3. Enter the Computer name (Jean2000 in this example).

4. For a workgroup, select Workgroup and enter the workgroup name (Golden in this example). If the PC is to join a domain (a network where logging on is controlled by a server), enter the name of the domain here, such as mycompany.com. When configuring a PC on a network, always follow the specific directions of the network administrator responsible for the network.

5. Click **OK** to exit the Identification Changes window and **OK** to exit the System Properties window. Restart your computer.

6. On the Windows 2000 desktop, open the **My Network Places** icon and double-click **Computers Near Me** to view this and other computers on the network.

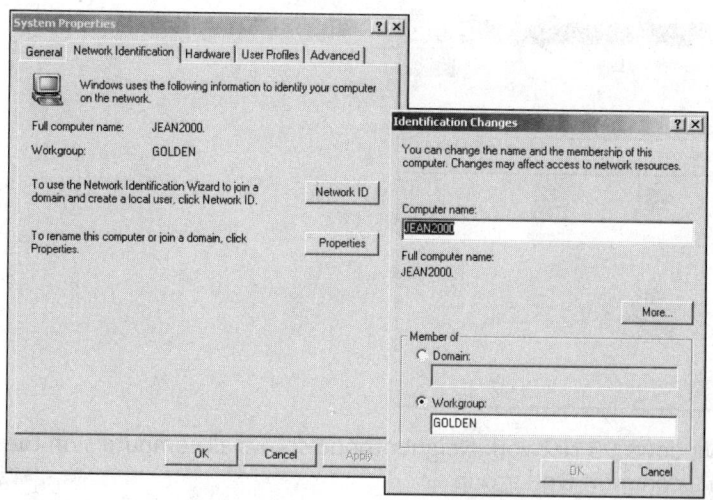

Figure 11-32   Windows 2000 uses the Identification Changes dialog box to assign a host name to a computer on a network

For Windows XP, follow these directions to give a host name to a computer:

1. Click **Start** and right click **My Computer**. Select **Properties** from the shortcut menu. The System Properties window appears.

2. Click the **Computer Name** tab and then click **Change**. The Computer Name Changes dialog box appears. Enter the computer name and the workgroup or domain name. Click **OK** to exit the Computer Name Changes window and **OK** to exit the System Properties window. Restart your PC.

3. To view others on the network, click **Start**, **My Network Places** and then, for a workgroup, click **View workgroup computers**.

On the desktop, open Network Neighborhood, and you should be able to see this and other computers on the network. Figure 11-33 shows an example of Network Neighborhood.

Network Neighborhood for Windows 9x and My Network Places for Windows 2000/XP can be viewed on the desktop and in Windows Explorer. By default, Windows 98 puts Network Neighborhood in both places, Windows 2000 puts My Network Places in both places, and Windows XP only puts My Network Places in Windows Explorer.

11

Figure 11-33   Windows 98 Network Neighborhood shows all computers on the LAN in a common workgroup

Connecting to a TCP/IP Network

NetBEUI works as long as you don't need to connect to the Internet or route requests to other networks. (For these reasons, NetBEUI is known as a nonroutable protocol.) For these situations, TCP/IP is needed. This section describes how to install and configure TCP/IP using Windows 98 and Windows 2000.

To install and configure TCP/IP, you will need to know the answers to these questions, which are supplied by your network administrator:

1. Will the PC use dynamic or static IP addressing?

2. If static IP addressing is used, what are the IP address, subnet mask, and gateway for this computer?

3. How is DNS to work? Do you enable or disable it? If enabled, what are the IP addresses of your DNS servers?

4. Is a proxy server used to connect to other networks (including the Internet)? If so, what is the IP address of the proxy server?

Here is a quick explanation of what all these questions mean. Recall from earlier in the chapter that in dynamic addressing the computer asks a DHCP server for its IP address each time it connects to the network. The server will also give the PC its subnet mask and gateway so that the computer will know how to communicate with other hosts that are not on its own network. A **gateway** is a computer or other device that allows a computer on one network to communicate with a computer on another network. A **default gateway** is the gateway a computer uses to access another network if it does not have a better option. A **subnet mask** is a group of four numbers (dotted decimal numbers) that tells TCP/IP if a remote computer is on the same or a different network. A **DNS server** is a computer that can find an IP address for another computer when only the domain name is known.

Install and Configure TCP/IP Using Windows 98

If TCP/IP is not already installed, you must install it. For Windows 98, do the following:

1. Access the Control Panel and double-click the **Network** icon. The Network window opens.

2. Click **Add** to display the Select Network Component Type window, as shown in Figure 11-36.

3. Select **Protocol**, click **Add**, and the Select Network Protocol window opens. Select **Microsoft** on the left and **TCP/IP** on the right. See Figure 11-34. Click **OK**. The system asks for the Microsoft Windows 98 CD and requests that you reboot the system.

4. When you return to the Network window, notice that TCP/IP is automatically bound to any network cards or modems that it finds installed.

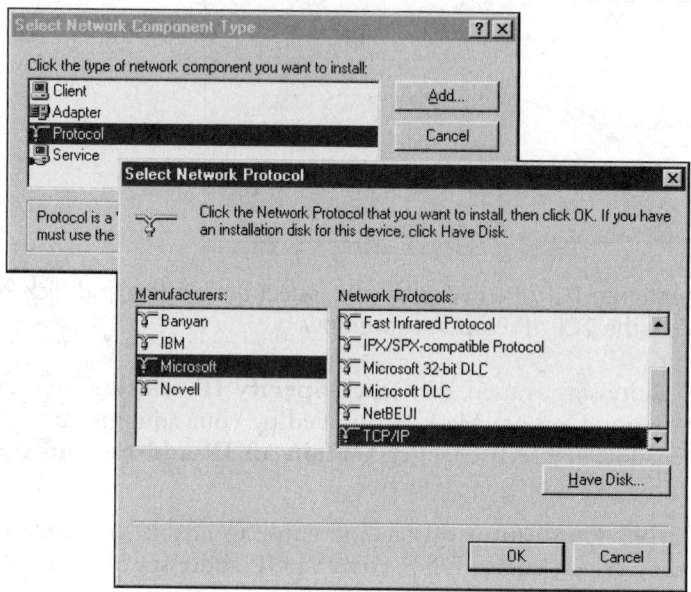

11

Figure 11-34   To install TCP/IP in Windows 98, use the Select Network Protocol dialog box

The next step is to configure TCP/IP for each of the bindings listed that you will use. Most likely, you will be using dynamic IP addressing and the DNS service is initially disabled (later the DHCP server will tell the PC to enable it). The DHCP server might also act as the proxy server so that computers inside the network can make connections to computers outside the network using the proxy server's public IP address. In

Windows 98, to configure TCP/IP bound to a NIC to communicate over a local network, do the following:

1. In the Network window, select the item where TCP/IP is bound to the NIC. (In Figure 11–35, that item is TCP/IP->NETGEAR FA311 Fast Ethernet PCI Adapter.) Then, click **Properties**. The TCP/IP Properties window appears.

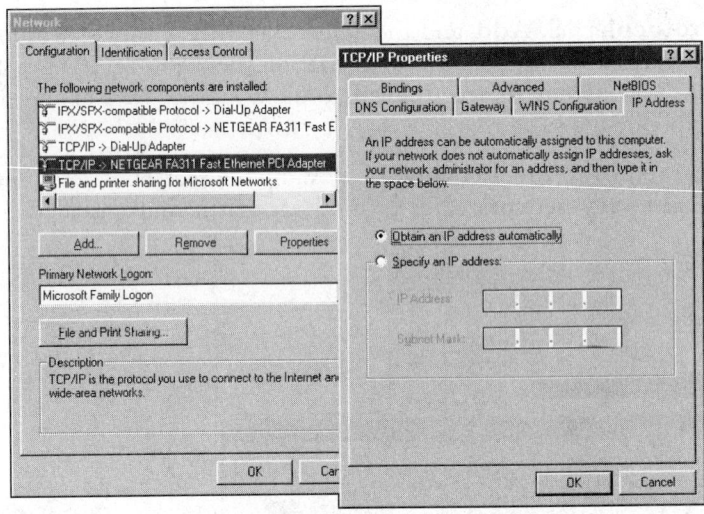

Figure 11-35   To configure TCP/IP in Windows 98, select the binding and click Properties to view the TCP/IP Properties window

2. If static IP addressing is used, then click **Specify IP address**, and then enter the IP Address and Subnet Mask as supplied by your administrator. If dynamic IP addressing is used, click **Obtain an IP address automatically**. This will most likely be your selection.

3. Click the **DNS Configuration** tab and chose to enable or disable DNS (see Figure 11–36). If you enable DNS, enter the IP addresses of your DNS servers. If your network administrator has given you other specific values for the TCP/IP configuration, you will find the tabs for these settings on this window. But, in most cases, this is all that is needed to configure TCP/IP.

4. When finished, click **OK** to exit the Properties window, and then **OK** to exit the Network window.

5. On the desktop, verify that you can see your and other computers on the network in Network Neighborhood on the desktop. If you don't see others on the network, reboot the PC.

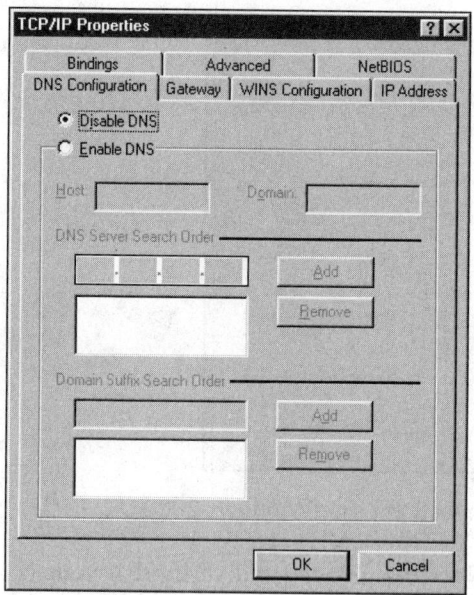

Figure 11-36   Configure DNS service under TCP/IP for Windows 98

Install and Configure TCP/IP using Windows 2000

For Windows 2000/XP, when a network card is installed, TCP/IP is installed by default. However, if TCP/IP has been uninstalled or is giving you problems, you can install it again. Use the same procedure given earlier to install NetBEUI under Windows 2000, this time selecting TCP/IP as the network protocol to install.

To set the TCP/IP properties for the connection follow the steps below.

1. Using Control Panel, open the **Network and Dial-up Connection** applet. Right-click the **Local Area Connection** icon, and then select **Properties** from the shortcut menu. See Figure 11-37.

2. Select **(Internet Protocol) TCP/IP** from the list of installed components, and then click the **Properties** button. The TCP/IP Properties dialog box opens, which is also shown in Figure 11-37.

3. For dynamic IP addressing, select **Obtain an IP address automatically**. For static IP addressing, select **Use the following IP address** and enter the IP address, Subnet mask, and Default gateway.

4. To disable DNS until the DHCP server gives the computer the DNS server address, select **Obtain DNS server address automatically**. If you have the IP addresses of the DNS servers, click **Use the following DNS server addresses** and enter the IP addresses. Click **OK** twice to close both windows.

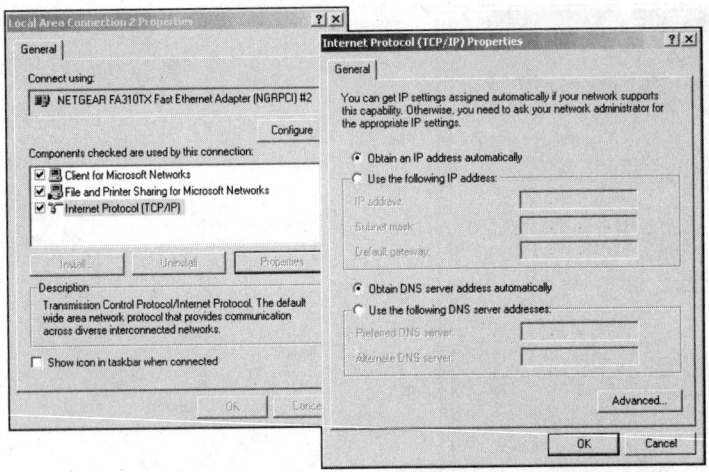

Figure 11-37   Configure a TCP/IP connection using Windows 2000

5. On the desktop, click **My Network Places** and verify that your computer and other computers on the network are visible. If you don't see other computers on the network, reboot the PC.

When a network is configured to use the TCP/IP networking protocol, a useful tool is the **Ping** utility to test for connectivity to another computer. At a command prompt, enter the Ping command followed by the IP address of another computer, such as: *ping 207.46.196.102.*

CONNECTING MULTIPLE NETWORKS

So far you have learned how LANs can be structured and how to set them up, including how to divide large ones into segments using bridges and switches. Other devices and technologies are used to connect networks, allowing them to communicate with each other within a building or around the world. This section discusses routers, which are used to connect networks, as well as bandwidth technologies that networks use to communicate with each other.

Routers

Routers (see Figure 11-38) are responsible for data traveling across interconnected networks. A router can route data to the correct network in a way that is similar to a switch's method. However, a router can also forward a message to its correct destination over the most efficient available route, to destinations far removed from the LANs it is connected to. Switches and bridges use MAC addresses to make decisions, but, for TCP/IP, routers use IP addresses to determine the path by which to send a packet.

Figure 11-38   A typical router

Figure 11-39 shows a simplified view of the way networks work together to send data over the maze of many networks called the Internet. A user in California must pass through many networks to gain access to a server in New York. Each network operates independently of all other networks but can receive a packet from another network and send it on to a third network—while it also manages its own internal traffic. A router is a **stateless** device, meaning that it is unconcerned about the data that it is routing, but is concerned about the destination address of that data.

Routers that connect networks belong to more than one network. In Figure 11-39, Network B contains four routers: Routers 1, 2, 3, and 4. But Routers 3 and 4 also belong to Network C. Network C contains Router 8, which also belongs to the same network as the server in New York that the user wants to access.

How many paths are there on the Internet by which the user in California can access the server in New York? One path is through Router 1, then 3, then 8, and finally to the server. Data going from the server to the user may travel a different path than data traveling from the user to the server. In fact, if there is a lot of data divided into several packets, each packet may take a different route. The packets may not arrive at the user's PC in the same order in which they were sent, and may have to be reassembled before they are presented to the application that will use them.

In Figure 11-39, a router that belongs to a network has an IP address for that network. However, if a router belongs to more than one network, it will have a unique IP address for each network. Physically, this is accomplished by having one NIC for each network a router belongs to, with each NIC having a unique IP address. Router 4 in the diagram belongs to four networks (B, C, D, and E), and would, therefore, have four network cards and four IP addresses, one for each network.

11

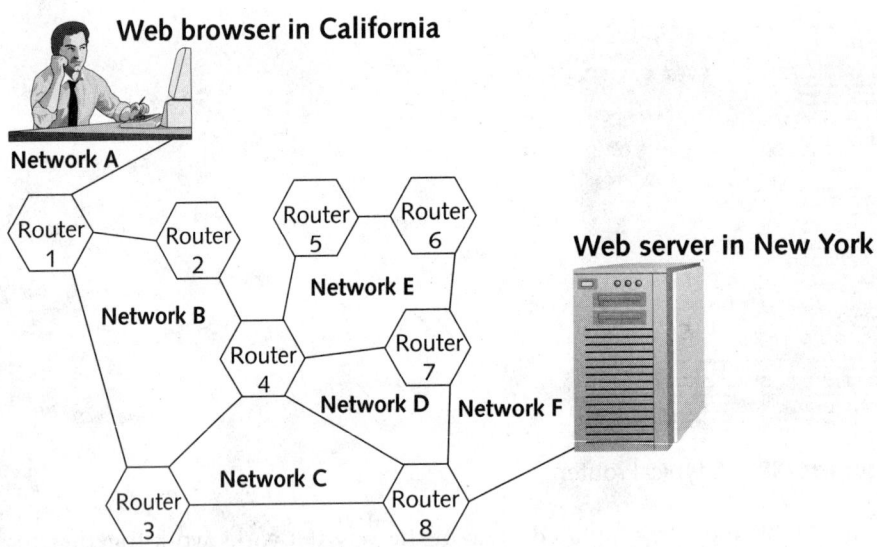

Figure 11-39   The Internet is a web of interconnecting, yet independent, networks

A router can transmit a data packet to a remote network (a network it is not directly connected to) only if the protocol that was used to produce the data packet is a **routable protocol** and can be routed to a remote network. Windows supports several networking protocols: TCP/IP, IPX/SPX, NetBEUI, and AppleTalk. TCP/IP is routable, as is **IPX/SPX (Internetwork Packet Exchange/Sequenced Packet Exchange),** a NWLink networking protocol first introduced by Novell NetWare networks. AppleTalk is used by the Mac OS. NetBEUI is not routable.

If NetBEUI is also being used on a TCP/IP network, then the router will not be able to route these NetBEUI packets. However, a hub replicates and distributes everything that it receives to all devices connected to it. If it receives a NetBEUI packet from one Windows PC on a LAN, intended for another Windows PC on the same LAN, and if a router is also connected to the hub, then the router receives the packet even though the packet was not intended for it. Because the packet is not routable, the router just kills it. No harm is done, because the packet doesn't need to be routed to another network.

A **brouter,** short for bridge and router, functions as both a bridge and a router. The device can route routable protocols including TCP/IP and IPX/SPX packets, and, in these cases, is working as a router. It forwards packets that are not routable, such as NetBEUI packets, to other local networks in the manner that a bridge would forward packets.

Like switches, routers use tables to determine the best route by which to send the data to its destination. When the router receives a packet, it first looks at the packet's destination IP address. Once it has the address, the router can use the tables and the current conditions of the network to decide which would be the best path for the packet. If there is not a good route directly to the destination, the router may forward the packet to another router. When a packet is being sent across a network, it may go through several routers.

A router "learns" about new routes and best routes as it attempts to send packets. You can see the effects of what routers have learned when you first attempt to access a new Web site with your browser. If the browser is slow to respond, click Stop and Refresh to cause the browser to resend the request. The new attempt often receives a quicker response because the routers along the way have learned about routes that did or did not work.

Bandwidth Technologies

When you study the infrastructure of networks and how they connect to each other, much attention is given to how much data can travel over a given communication system in a given amount of time. This measure of data capacity is called **bandwidth**, also called **data throughput** or **line speed**. The greater the bandwidth, the faster the communication. In analog systems, bandwidth is the difference between the highest and lowest frequency that a device can transmit. Frequencies are measured in cycles per second, or hertz (Hz). In digital systems such as computers and computer networks, bandwidth is a measure of data transmission in bits per second (bps), one thousand bits per second (Kbps) or one million bits per second (Mbps). The Internet is dependent on technologies that provide varying degrees of bandwidth, each serving a different purpose and following a different set of standards. A list of bandwidth technologies, their speeds, and their uses is shown in Table 11-4. Different bandwidth technologies are used for LANs and larger networks, since the larger the network, the more bandwidth it requires. In this section, you will learn about some common bandwidth technologies.

11

Table 11-4 Bandwidth technologies

Technology	Maximum Throughput Speeds	Common Uses
GSM mobile telephone service	9.6 to 14.4 Kbps	Wireless technology used for personal and business mobile telephones
Regular telephone (POTS, for Plain Old Telephone Service)	Up to 56 Kbps	Home and small business access to an ISP using a modem
X.25	56 Kbps	Provides communication between mainframes and terminals
ISDN	64 Kbps to 128 Kbps	Small to medium size business access to an ISP
IDSL	128 Kbps	(ISDN Digital Subscriber Line) Home and small business access to an ISP
DSL Lite or G.Lite	Up to 384 Kbps upstream and up to 6 Mbps downstream	Less expensive version of DSL
ADSL (Asymmetric Digital Subscriber Line)	640 Kbps upstream and up to 6.1 Mbps downstream	Most bandwidth is from ISP to user

Table 11-4   Bandwidth technologies (continued)

Technology	Maximum Throughput Speeds	Common Uses
SDSL (Symmetric DSL)	1.544 Mbps	Equal bandwidths in both directions
HDSL (High-bit-rate DSL)	Up to 3 Mbps	Equal bandwidths in both directions
Cable modem	512 Kbps to 5 Mbps	Home or small business to ISP
VDSL (Very-high-rate DSL)	Up to 55 Mbps over short distances	Future technology of DSL under development
802.11b wireless	5.5 Mbps or 11 Mbps	Most popular wireless
802.11a wireless	Up to 54 Mbps	Not readily available
Frame Relay	56 Kbps to 45 Mbps	Businesses that need to communicate internationally or across the country
Fractional T1	N times 64 Kbps (where n = number of channels or portions of a T1 leased)	Companies expecting to grow into a T1 line, but not yet ready for a T1
T1	1.544 Mbps	To connect large companies to branch offices or an ISP
Token Ring	4 or 16 Mbps	Used for local network
Ethernet	10 or 100 Mbps	Most popular technology for a local network
T3	45 Mbps	Large companies that require a lot of bandwidth and transmit extensive amounts of data
OC-1	52 Mbps	ISP to regional ISP
FDDI	100 Mbps	Supports network backbones from the 1980s and early 1990s. Also used to connect LANs across multiple buildings
ATM	25, 45, 155, or 622 Mbps	Large business networks and LAN backbones
OC-3	155 Mbps	Internet or large corporation backbone
Gigabit Ethernet	1 Gbps	New under-development technology
OC-24	1.23 Gbps	Internet backbone, uses optical fiber
OC-256	13 Gbps	Major Internet backbone, uses optical fiber
SONET (Synchronous Optical Network)	51, 155, 622, 1244, or 2480 Mbps	Major backbones

Here is a summary of some of the more common bandwidth technologies:

- *Regular telephone lines.* Regular telephone lines, the most common way to connect to an ISP, require an internal or external modem. As you learned in the last chapter, a modem converts a PC's digital data (data made up of zeros and ones) to analog data (continuous variations of frequencies) that can be communicated over telephone lines.

- *Cable modem.* **Cable modem** communication uses cable lines that already exist in millions of households. Just as with cable TV, cable modems are always connected. Cable modem is an example of broadband media. **Broadband** refers to any type of networking medium that carries more than one type of transmission. With a cable modem, the TV signal to your television and the data signals to your PC share the same cable. Just like a regular modem, a cable modem converts a PC's digital signals to analog when sending them out and converts incoming analog data into digital.

- *ISDN.* **ISDN (Integrated Services Digital Network)** is a technology developed in the 1980s that uses regular phone lines, and is accessed by a dial-up connection. ISDN is actually an early implementation of DSL. For home use, an ISDN line is fully digital and consists of two channels, or phone circuits, on a single pair of wires, called B channels, and a slower channel used for control signals, called a D channel. Each B channel can support speeds up to 64,000 bps. The two lines can be combined so that, effectively, data travels at 128,000 bps, which is about three to five times the speed of regular phone lines.

- *DSL.* **DSL (Digital Subscriber Line)** is a broadband technology that uses ordinary copper phone lines and uses a range of frequencies on the copper wire that are not used by voice, thus making it possible for you to use the same phone line for voice and DSL at the same time. (ISDN is an early example of DSL.) The voice portion of the phone line requires a dial-up as normal, but the DSL part of the line is always connected.

- *Satellite access.* People who live in remote areas and want high-speed Internet connections often are limited in their choices. DSL and cable modems may not work where they live, but satellite access is available from pretty much anywhere. Technology is even being developed to use satellites to offer Internet access on commercial airlines. Customers can use their own laptops to connect to the Internet through a connection at their seats to a satellite dish in the airplane. A satellite dish mounted on top of your house or office building communicates with a satellite that is used for communication by an ISP offering the satellite service.

- *Wireless access.* Wireless refers to several technologies and systems that don't use cables for communication, including public radio, cellular phones, one-way paging, satellite, infrared, and private, proprietary radio. Because of the expense and the concern that increasing use of wireless might affect our

11

health, as well as airplane control systems, pacemakers, and other sensitive electronic devices, wireless is not as popular as wired data transmission. Wireless is an important technology for mobile devices and for Internet access in remote locations where other methods are not an option.

When configuring a PC to connect to the Internet using cable modem, ISDN, or DSL, the most common method is to use a NIC in the PC that connects to the cable modem, DSL transceiver, or ISDN transceiver by way of a network cable. The NIC is then configured to use the TCP/IP protocol. When the PC is rebooted, it should connect to the ISP providing the cable modem, DSL, or ISDN service and receive an assigned IP address from the service.

TROUBLESHOOTING A NETWORK CONNECTION

If you are having problems with connecting to the network, follow the guidelines below. First, here are some symptoms of NIC problems:

- You cannot make a connection to the network.

- Network Neighborhood or My Network Places does not show any other computers on the network.

- You receive an error message during installation.

- Device Manager shows a yellow exclamation point or a red X beside the name of the NIC.

- There are two lights on a NIC: one that stays on steadily to let you know there is a physical connection, and another that blinks to let you know there is activity. If you see no lights, you know there is no physical connection between the NIC and the network. This means there is a problem with the network cable, the card, or the hub.

Here are some ways you can try to address these and other networking problems:

- Determine whether other computers on the network are having trouble with their connections. If the entire network is down, the problem is not isolated to the PC and the NIC you are working on.

- Try rebooting the PC to reset the network connections. For a network controlled by a domain server, be sure you log off the current session before you turn off the PC, so that the server will not still think you are logged on and be unable to log you back on until it times out. When you power the PC back up, configure the network protocols.

- Make sure the NIC and its drivers are installed, by checking for the NIC in Device Manager. Try uninstalling and reinstalling the NIC drivers.

- If a network card cannot make a successful connection to the network, the problem might be an IRQ conflict. Try disabling PCI bus IRQ steering (using Device Manager), which you learned about in Chapter 5.

- Check the network cable to make sure it is not damaged and that it does not exceed the recommended length for the type of network you are using.

- Connect the network cable to a different port on the hub. If that doesn't help, you may have a problem with the cable or the NIC itself. Uninstall the NIC drivers, replace the NIC, and then install new drivers.

- Check to see whether you have the most current version of your motherboard BIOS. The motherboard manufacturer should have information on whether an upgrade is available.

- It is possible the access point device has been configured for MAC address filtering in order to control which wireless NICs can use the access point. Check with the network administrator to determine if this is the case and, if necessary, give the administrator the NIC's MAC address to be entered into a table of acceptable MAC addresses.

In addition, Windows TCP/IP includes several diagnostic tools useful in troubleshooting problems with TCP/IP. The most useful is **Ping (Packet Internet Groper)**, which tests connectivity and is discussed here. Ping sends a signal to a remote computer. If the remote computer is online and hears the signal, it will respond. Ipconfig under Windows NT/ 2000/XP and Winipcfg under Windows 9x test the TCP/IP configuration. Try these things to test TCP/IP configuration and connectivity:

- For Windows NT/2000/XP, at the command prompt, enter *Ipconfig /all*, or, for Windows 9x, click Start, Run, enter *Winipcfg* in the Run dialog box, and then click OK. If the TCP/IP configuration is correct and an IP address is assigned, the IP address, subnet mask, and default gateway appear along with the adapter address. For dynamic IP addressing, if the PC could not reach the DHCP server, then it will assign itself an IP address. This is called IP auto-configuration. The Winipcfg window and the results of the Ipconfig command both show the IP address as the IP Autoconfiguration Address, and the address will begin with 169. In this case, suspect that the PC is not able to reach the network or the DHCP server is down. Try to release the current IP address and lease a new address. To do this with Winipcfg, with the network card selected, click the Release button, and then click the Renew button. For Ipconfig, first use the *Ipconfig /release* command, and then use the *Ipconfig /renew* command.

- Next, try the loopback address test. At a command prompt, enter the command *Ping 127.0.0.1* (with no period after the final 1). This IP address always refers to your local computer. It should respond with a reply message from your computer. If this works, TCP/IP is likely to be configured correctly. If you get any errors up to this point, then assume that the problem is on your PC. Check the installation and configuration of each component such as the network card and the TCP/IP protocol suite. Remove and reinstall each component and watch for error messages, writing them down so that you can recognize or research them later as necessary. Compare the configuration to that of a PC that is working on the same network.

- Next, Ping the IP address of your default gateway. If it does not respond, then the problem may be with the gateway or with the network to the gateway.

- Now try to Ping the host computer you are trying to reach. If it does not respond, then the problem may be with the host computer or with the network to the computer.

- If you have Internet access and substitute a domain name for the IP address in the Ping command, and the Ping works, then you can conclude that DNS works. If an IP address works, but the domain name does not work, the problem lies with DNS. Try this command: *ping microsoft.com*.

CHAPTER SUMMARY

- ❑ The OSI model describes network communication as consisting of seven layers: Application, Presentation, Session, Transport, Network, Data Link, and Physical. The top five, Application through Network, describe what happens within the operating system. The bottom two, Data Link and Physical, describe what happens on the network card.

- ❑ When you are setting up a network, decisions that you make about the operating system, applications you need to support, and user needs affect the top five layers of the OSI model, and decisions about the physical structure of the network affect the bottom two layers.

- ❑ The three protocols that Windows supports for use in the top five OSI layers are TCP/IP (which is the protocol suite for the Internet), IPX/SPX (which is designed for use with Novell NetWare), and NetBEUI (which is a proprietary Windows protocol for use on networks isolated from the Internet). Only TCP/IP is supported on the Internet.

- ❑ When a protocol is installed on a computer, it automatically binds itself to any NICs it finds. More than one protocol can be associated with a single NIC.

- ❑ The four types of addresses on a Windows network are MAC addresses, IP addresses, character-based names such as NetBIOS names, host names, domain names, and port addresses.

- ❑ MAC addresses are physical addresses for NICs that are assigned at the factory and generally do not change. They are used at the Data Link layer and can only be used for communication within a network.

❑ IP addresses identify devices on the Internet and other TCP/IP networks. They consist of four numbers separated by periods. The first part of an IP address identifies the network, and the last identifies the host. The class of an IP address determines how much of the address is used as the network identifier and how much is used for the host identifier.

❑ IP addresses can either be public or private. For private IP addresses to be able to access the Internet, they must go through NAT (network address translation) so that their requests all appear to be coming from a single public IP address for that network.

❑ Character-based names, such as fully qualified domain names, are used as an easy way to remember IP addresses.

❑ The IP address associated with a host name can change. DNS (Domain Name Service) and WINS (Windows Internet Naming Service) track the relationship between host names and IP addresses. DNS is more popular because it works on all platforms.

❑ The four most popular physical network architectures for LANs are Ethernet, token ring, FDDI, and wireless LAN.

❑ A PC connects to a network using a NIC (network interface card), which communicates with the NIC on the other PC using a set of hardware protocols (such as Ethernet or Token Ring). The OSs on the two computers use a different set of protocols (such as NetBEUI or TCP/IP) to communicate.

11

❑ Network protocols must break data into packets small enough for the network on which they will be traveling. Before they are transmitted on the network, headers and trailers that tell where data came from and where it is going are added to the packets.

❑ The most widely used LAN architecture today is Ethernet, which is less expensive and easier to maintain that some other technologies. Variations include ThickNet, ThinNet and twisted-pair.

❑ Ethernet uses a logical bus and can be configured as a star topology, in which all nodes are connected to a centralized hub, or a bus topology, which connects nodes in a line and does not have a centralized point of connection.

❑ An Ethernet hub broadcasts all data that flows through it on to every node that is connected to it. It does not make decisions about where to send packets.

❑ Only one computer can transmit on an Ethernet network at a time. If two attempt to transmit simultaneously, a collision occurs. Computers on an Ethernet network use CSMA/CD to detect and manage collisions.

❑ Token Ring networks are physically configured in a star topology but are logically rings because of how data packets travel on them. A data packet is preceded by a token, which travels in one direction around the ring, up and down the connection from the PC to the hub.

❏ A FDDI network uses tokens and is structured as a ring but does not require a centralized hub as a token ring network does. It is faster than token ring.

❏ Wireless LANs make connections using wireless NICs, which include antennas or infrared transmission to send and receive signals in places where networking cables are difficult to install. A wireless LAN can be used in combination with a wired LAN.

❏ Bridges and switches are used to segment large networks, decreasing the overall amount of traffic on the network and making it easier to manage.

❏ A bridge that connects several network segments only decides whether a packet is destined for a computer on its own segment and, if it is not, sends the packet to all other network segments. A switch sends a packet only to the network segment for which it is destined. Both keep source and destination MAC addresses in routing tables and learn new addresses as packets are sent.

❏ NICs and the device drivers that control them are designed to work with a particular network architecture and are the only components in the PC that are aware of the type of physical network being used. A NIC can be designed to use more than one type of cabling and can use a PCI or ISA slot.

❏ A NIC is identified by a MAC address, which is set by the manufacturer and is unique to the device.

❏ When installing a NIC, first physically install the card, then install the networking protocol you intend to use, then give the computer a name.

❏ Windows 98 assumes that a computer name is a NetBIOS name, which can have up to 15 characters. Windows 2000 and Windows XP assume that a computer name is a host name, which follows the TCP/IP convention and can have up to 63 characters.

❏ NetBIOS names are limited to 15 characters. Windows 9x assumes that a computer name is a NetBIOS name, but later versions of Windows assume that a computer name is a host name, which can be up to 63 characters.

❏ A computer will not appear in Network Neighborhood or My Network Places until it has a networking protocol installed.

❏ NetBEUI is a fast network protocol that can be used on an isolated network. For Internet access, use TCP/IP. TCP/IP requires that the PC be assigned an IP address.

❏ Applications that use TCP/IP for network communication use WinSock to make API calls to the OS.

❏ Communication between TCP/IP networks uses an IP address rather than a MAC address to locate the destination computer.

❏ When configuring TCP/IP, you must know if IP addresses are statically or dynamically assigned.

❏ When troubleshooting a NIC on a PC, check connections in the rest of the network, cabling and ports for the PC, the NIC itself (substituting one known to be working), BIOS, and device drivers.

❐ Ping is a useful TCP/IP utility to check network connectivity.

❐ Two other useful troubleshooting tools are Ipconfig (Windows NT, Windows 2000, and Windows XP) and Winipcfg (Windows 9x), which test TCP/IP configuration.

❐ Routers are used to connect networks. If a router belongs to more than one TCP/IP network, it has a unique IP address for each network and routes packets according to IP addresses.

❐ Routers are more efficient than switches in choosing routes for packets over long distances.

❐ TCP/IP and IPX/SPX are routable networking protocols. NetBEUI, a Microsoft proprietary protocol, is not.

❐ Bandwidth measures how much data can travel over a given communication system in a given amount of time. Common bandwidth technologies include regular telephone lines, cable modem, ISDN, DSL, satellite access, and wireless access.

KEY TERMS

100BaseFX
100BaseT
10Base2
10Base5
10BaseT
adapter address
amplifier repeater
Application layer
attenuation
bandwidth
binding
BNC connector
bridge
broadband
broadcast
brouter
bus topology
cable modem
CAU (Controlled-Access Unit)
client
client/server
coaxial cable

collision
combo card
contention-based
CRC (cyclical redundancy check)
crossover cable
CSMA/CA (Carrier Sense Multiple Access with Collision Avoidance)
CSMA/CD (Carrier Sense Multiple Access with Collision Detection)
Data Link layer
data packets
data throughput
datagram
DHCP (Dynamic Host Configuration Protocol) server
DNS (domain name) service or domain name system)
DNS server
domain name

DSL (Digital Subscriber Line)
dynamic IP address
Ethernet
Fast Ethernet
FDDI (Fiber Distributed Data Interface)
frame
Gigabit Ethernet
hardware address
host
host name
hub
IEEE (Institute of Electrical and Electronics Engineers)
Internet service provider (ISP)
Intranet
IP address (Internet Protocol address)
IPX/SPX (Internetwork Packet Exchange/Sequenced Packet Exchange)

11

ISDN (Integrated Services Digital Network)

ISO (International Organization for Standardization)

ISP (Internet service provider)

LAN (local area network)

line speed

MAC (Media Access Control) address

MAU (Multistation Access Unit)

MSAU

multicasting

name resolution

NAT (Network Address Translation)

NetBEUI (NetBIOS Extended User Interface)

NetBIOS (Network Basic Input/Output System)

network adapter

network interface card (NIC)

Network layer

NIC (network interface card)

node

NOS (network operating system)

octet

OSI (Open Systems Interconnect) reference model

packet

patch cable

peer-to-peer network

physical address

Physical layer

Ping

Presentation layer

private IP address

proxy server

public IP address

repeater

RFC (Request for Comments)

ring topology

RJ-45 connector

routable protocol

router

server

Session layer

shielded twisted-pair (STP) cable

signal-regenerating repeater

SMAU (Smart Multistation Access Unit)

star bus topology

star ring topology

star topology

stateless

static IP address

subnet mask

switch

TCP/IP (Transmission Control Protocol/Internet Protocol)

ThickNet

ThinNet

token

transceiver

Transport layer

unshielded twisted-pair (UTP) cable

wireless LAN (WLAN)

WINS (Windows Internet Naming Service)

WinSock (Windows Sockets)

12

NOTEBOOKS, PDAs, AND PRINTERS

> **In this chapter, you will learn:**
> - How to support, upgrade, and add peripheral devices to notebooks
> - About technologies relating to personal digital assistants (PDAs)
> - How printers work and how to troubleshoot them

So far in this book, you've learned about how computers work, some of the devices used to work with them, and how to connect a PC to a network. Most of the devices you've learned about have related to desktop computers, which are stationary and cannot be moved around easily. This chapter covers two types of devices that provide for greater portability: notebook computers and personal digital assistants (PDAs). As a PC technician, you must be familiar with these devices and be aware of specific concerns when supporting them. In addition, this chapter also covers printers and how to support them.

NOTEBOOK COMPUTERS

A **notebook** or **laptop computer** is a computer designed to be portable (see Figure 12-1). Notebooks use the same technology as do PCs, but with modifications to use less power, take up less space, and work when on the move. This section discusses the special needs of supporting notebooks, and shows how to add memory to a notebook, add peripheral devices, and find online resources for notebook support.

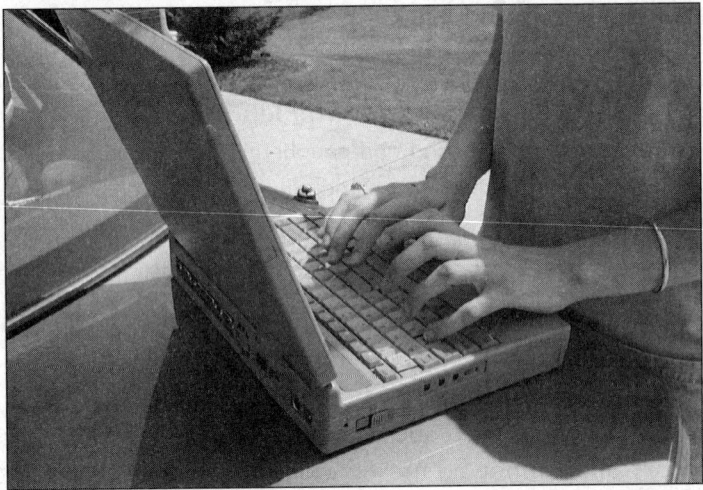

Figure 12-1   A notebook is a computer designed for portability

Notebooks and their replacement parts cost more than desktop PCs with similar features because components are designed to be more compact and to endure movement when in use. They use thin LCD panels instead of CRT monitors for display, compact hard drives that can withstand movement even during operation, and small memory modules and CPUs that require less power than regular components. Recall that LCD monitors, including notebook LCD panels, use several different technologies and that active matrix (sometimes called thin film transistor or TFT) technology generally gives better quality than does passive matrix (sometimes called dual-scan twisted nematic or DSTN) technology.

A notebook can be powered in several ways including an AC adapter (to use regular house current to power the notebook), a DC adapter (to use DC power such as that provided by automobile cigarette lighters), and a battery pack. Types of batteries are the older and mostly outdated Ni-Cad (nickel-cadmium) battery, the longer-life NiMH (nickel-metal-hydride) battery, and the current Lithium Ion battery that is more efficient than earlier batteries. A future battery solution is the fuel cell battery that is supposed to provide a continuous operating time of up to 10 hours. A notebook user might need one or more batteries and a DC adapter for travel and an AC adapter at home and for recharging the batteries. Always power down the notebook before switching power sources.

 LCD panels on notebooks are fragile and can be damaged fairly easily. Take precautions against damaging a notebook's LCD panel with rough use.

The types and features of notebooks vary widely, as they do for PCs. However, notebooks are generally purchased as a whole unit, including both hardware and software, and you

are not as likely to upgrade the hardware and OS on a notebook as you might be for a desktop PC. In fact, some notebook manufacturers refuse to support a notebook that has had the OS upgraded or new hardware components added. When supporting any notebook, pay careful attention to the stipulations on the warranty that accompanies it. Some warranties are voided if you open the notebook case or install memory, batteries, or a hard drive that was not made by, or at least authorized by, the notebook manufacturer.

In contrast, recall that most desktop PCs are designed to be highly modular, letting you easily interchange, upgrade, and enhance components. In fact, PCs are often assembled from components purchased from various vendors and manufacturers. Notebook computers, on the other hand, can be very proprietary in design, which means that many of the skills needed to support them are brand-specific. In this section, we'll look at a few universal support issues, but remember that procedures can vary from one notebook brand to another.

Upgrading Memory

Notebooks use four types of memory (see Figure 12-2) that are all smaller than regular SIMMs, DIMMs, or RIMMs. **SO-DIMMs** (**small outline DIMMs** and pronounced "sew-dims") come in two types. 72-pin SO-DIMMs, which support 32-bit data transfers, use FPM or EDO (which you learned about in Chapter 6) and could be used as single modules in 386 or 486 machines but must be used in pairs in Pentium machines. 144-pin SO-DIMMs, which support 64-bit data transfers, use EDO and SDRAM and can be used as single modules in Pentium machines. Another type of memory for notebooks is the 160-pin **SO-RIMM (small outline RIMM)**, which uses a 64-bit data path and Rambus technology discussed in Chapter 6. Also, before notebooks used memory modules, some notebooks provided memory slots to accommodate memory stored on a small card the size of a credit card. This **credit card memory** was installed by inserting it in this special memory slot, which looks like the PC Card slots for different add-on devices discussed later in the chapter, but could only be used for memory. Sub-notebook computers sometimes use 144-pin MicroDIMMs that are smaller than 50-DIMMs and have a 64-bit data path.

2.35" 72–pin SO–DIMM   2.66" 144–pin SO–DIMM

160–pin SO–RIMM   Credit card memory

Figure 12-2   Four types of memory used on notebook computers

CAUTION

Before upgrading memory, make sure you are not voiding your warranty. Search for the best buy, but make sure you use memory modules made by or authorized by the notebook manufacturer and designed for the exact model of your notebook. Installing generic memory might save you money but might also void the warranty of the notebook.

To install memory, see the notebook user guide for directions. The following is an example of how to install memory on one notebook. Directions vary from one notebook computer to another.

1. Turn off the notebook and remove all cables.

2. Lift the keyboard brace, as shown in Figure 12-3. (Your notebook might have a different way to enter the system—for example, from the bottom of the case.)

Figure 12-3   Lift the keyboard brace

3. Turn the keyboard over and toward the front of the notebook. See Figure 12-4. The keyboard is still connected to the notebook by the ribbon cable.

4. Lift up the plastic sheet covering the memory module socket.

5. Insert the SO-DIMM module into the socket. See Figure 12-5. The socket braces should snap into place on each side of the module when the module is in position.

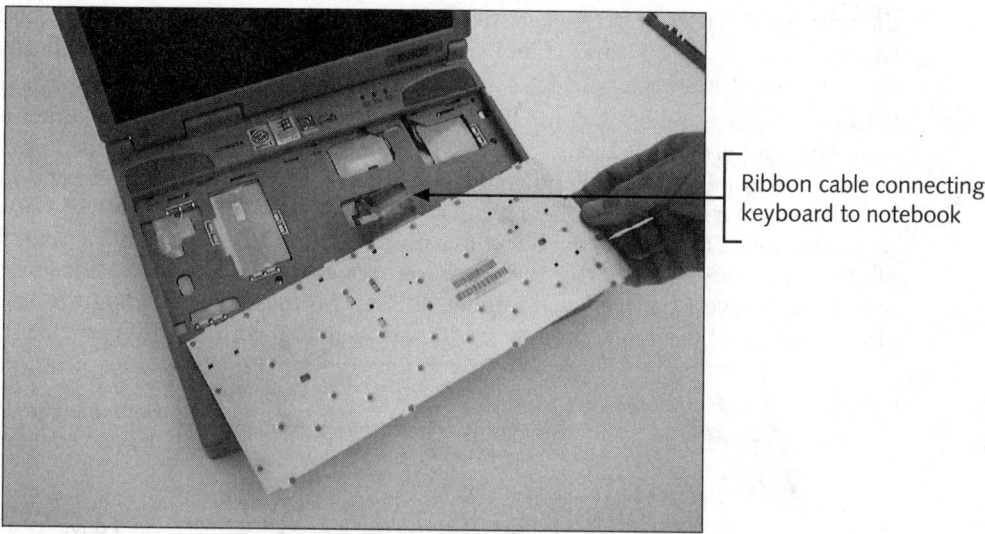

Ribbon cable connecting keyboard to notebook

Figure 12-4   Turn the keyboard over toward the front of the notebook to expose memory module sockets

12

Figure 12-5   Install the SO-DIMM into the memory socket

6. Replace the keyboard and keyboard brace. (If you entered from the bottom, you might be replacing a cover on the bottom of the case in this step.)

7. Power up the notebook so that it can detect the new memory.

Other Field Replaceable Units for Notebooks

Besides memory, other field replaceable units (FRUs) for notebooks might be the hard drive, the LCD panel, the motherboard, the CPU, the keyboard, the PC Card socket assembly, the CD-ROM drive, the floppy drive, a sound card, a pointing device, the AC adapter, the battery pack, and the DC controller. Parts either made or approved by the notebook manufacturer must be used to replace all these parts. The **DC controller** is a card inside the notebook that converts voltage to CPU core voltage. The DC controller can support battery mode, AC adapter mode, and various sleep modes and must be specifically rated for the notebook's processor.

A hard drive for a notebook computer can be an external or internal drive. External devices, including hard drives, connect to ports on the notebook or to a port provided by a PC Card. Internal drives are much smaller than normal drives; for a comparison, see Figure 12-6. When installing an internal hard drive, floppy drive, CD/CD-RW drive, DVD/DVD-RW drive, or removable drive, follow specific directions given by the notebook manufacturer. For example, to replace the hard drive for the notebook shown in Figure 12-7, first remove the floppy disk drive to reveal the hard drive under it. Remove the screws holding the hard drive in place, remove the drive, and replace it with a drive designed to fit this particular cavity.

Hard drive for a desktop computer

Hard drive for a notebook

Figure 12-6 Hard drives for notebooks are smaller than hard drives for desktop computers

Bottom of notebook

Floppy drive

Hard drive

Figure 12-7 First remove the floppy drive to reveal the hard drive cavity

A notebook does not contain the normal PCI and ISA expansion slots found in desktop systems. Most internal cards such as modems, SCSI host adapters, IEEE 1394 controllers, USB controllers, and network adapters use proprietary slots designed and supported by the notebook manufacturer. It is expected that the notebook industry will soon embrace a more generic method of connecting an internal card to a notebook using the Mini PCI Card specifications. The standards include three types of cards, Type I, II and III, that specify how the internal card provides a port on the notebook. Type I and II cards connect to the motherboard using a 100-pin stacking connector, and Type III cards use a 124-pin stacking connector, are smaller than the Type I and II cards, and are expected to be the most popular.

Connecting Peripheral Devices to Notebooks

A notebook provides ports on its back or sides (see Figure 12-8), which are used for connecting peripherals. Some notebooks have fewer ports than the one in Figure 12-8 and are designed to be used with a port replicator, such as the one shown in Figure 12-9. A **port replicator** provides additional ports to allow a notebook to easily connect to a full-sized monitor, keyboard, and other peripheral devices. A notebook can also be designed to work with a **docking station**, which provides extra ports as well as additional storage media, such as a Zip drive or floppy disk drive (see Figure 12-10).

Figure 12-8   Ports on the back of a notebook

Figure 12-9   A port replicator makes it convenient to connect a notebook computer to resources and peripherals at your office

Figure 12-10 An IBM ThinkPad dock, an example of a docking station

A popular way to add peripheral devices to a notebook is by using **PC Cards**, also called **PCMCIA (Personal Computer Memory Card International Association) Cards** in **PC Card slots** (see Figure 12-11), formally called **PCMCIA slots**. A PC Card is about the size of a credit card, but thicker, and inserts into a PC Card slot. Once intended only for memory cards, PC Card slots can now be used by many devices, including modems, network cards for wired or wireless networks, CD-ROMs, sound cards, SCSI host adapters, IEEE 1394 controllers, USB controllers, and hard disks. Unlike PCs, notebooks don't have the traditional expansion slots that connect to an I/O bus to add peripheral devices to a system. In notebooks, PC Card slots connect to the 16-bit PCMCIA I/O bus on the notebook motherboard. Some docking station PCs also have a PC Card slot, so that the device you use with your notebook can also be attached to the docking station.

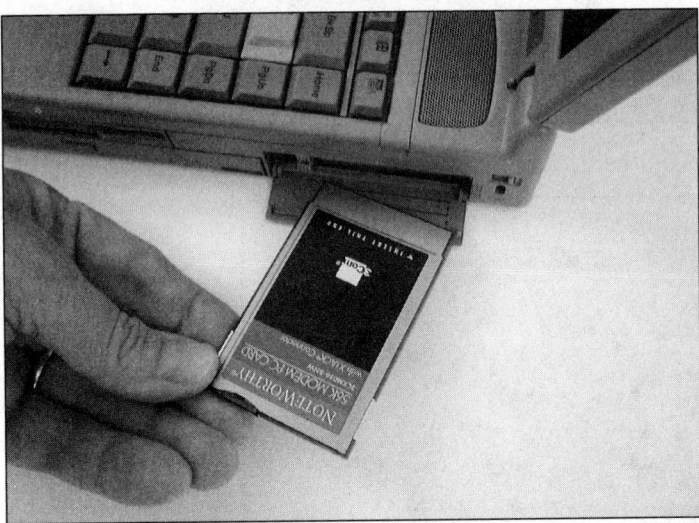

Figure 12-11 Many peripheral devices are added to a notebook using a PC Card slot; here, a modem PC Card is inserted in a PC Card slot

The PCMCIA organization has developed four standards for these slots. The latest PCMCIA specification is called **CardBus** and improves I/O speed, increases the bus width to 32 bits, and supports lower-voltage PC Cards while maintaining backward compatibility with earlier standards. Three standards for PCMCIA slots pertain to size, and are named Type I, Type II, and Type III. Generally, the thicker the PC Card, the higher the standard. A thick hard drive card might need a Type III slot, but a thin modem card might only need a Type II slot. Type I cards can be up to 3.3-mm thick and are primarily used for adding RAM to a notebook PC. Type II cards can be up to 5.5-mm thick and are often used as modem cards. Type III cards can be up to 10.5-mm thick, which is large enough to accommodate a portable disk drive. When buying a notebook PC, look for both Type II and Type III PC Card slots. Often, one of each is included. For improved performance, look for 32-bit CardBus slots.

The operating system must provide two services for the PC Card, a socket service and a card service. The socket service establishes communication between the PC Card and the notebook when the card is first inserted, and then disconnects communication when the card is removed. The card service provides the device driver to interface with the card once the socket is created.

The PC Card might contain a data cable to an external device, or it might be self-contained. For example, in Figure 12-12, the PC Card on the left is the interface between the notebook PC and an external CD-ROM drive. The card is inserted in the PC Card slot, and the data cable from the PC Card connects to the external CD-ROM drive, which requires its own power supply that must be connected into a wall outlet. The PC Card on the right in Figure 12-12 is a modem card; when inserted in the PC Card slot, it provides a direct connection for the telephone line to the modem (Figure 12-13).

Figure 12-12   Two examples of PC Cards, one self-contained (the modem), the other connected to an external device (the CD-ROM drive)

PC Cards can be hot-swapped, but you must stop one card before inserting another. Hot-swapping allows you to remove one card and insert another without powering down the PC. For example, if you are currently using a wireless network card in the PC Card slot of a Windows 2000 notebook and want to switch to the CD-ROM, first turn off the network card, remove it and insert the CD-ROM card with the attached external CD-ROM drive. For Windows 2000, to stop the card, use the Add/Remove Hardware icon in Control Panel.

The Add/Remove Hardware Wizard starts; click Next, and on the next screen select Uninstall/Unplug a device and click Next again. On the next screen, select Unplug/Eject a device. A list of devices appears (see Figure 12-14). Select the device and click Next. On the final screen you are told you can safely unplug the device, and you are given the option to display an Unplug/Eject icon in the taskbar when the device is used again. In Windows 9x, to stop a card, use the PC Card icon in the Control Panel, and for Windows XP, use the Safely Remove Hardware icon in the system tray.

Figure 12-13   Connect the phone line to the modem PC Card

Figure 12-14   Before removing a PC card from the notebook, stop the Card
(open the socket)

There is a bug in Windows XP that causes the system to hang if you remove a PC Card while the system is in sleep mode or is hibernating. To solve the problem, download the latest service pack for Windows XP.

The first time you insert a PC Card into a notebook, the Found New Hardware Wizard launches and steps you through the installation process where you can use the drivers provided by the hardware manufacturer or use Windows drivers. The next time you insert the card in the notebook, the card is detected and starts up without help.

Other smaller slots used on notebooks include a slot for a Secure Digital (SD) Card and a slot for a Compact Flash Card. Both cards are about the size of a postage stamp. These slots are used primarily for flash memory, but can also be used for other devices. For example, IBM uses a Compact Flash Type II slot for its Microdrive, a miniature 1 GB hard drive that is useful for storing multimedia files.

There are several flash memory products on the market including CompactFlash Type I and II, SmartMedia (introduced in Chapter 9), Microdrive, Secure Digital (SD), Memory Stick and MagicGate. These flash cards can be used in sockets designed specifically for them or you can purchase adapter sleeves that enable the cards to use a PC Card slot. In order to use a PC Card slot, the smaller flash card must be inserted in an adapter sleeve that fits the slot and the card must be PCMCIA compliant.

Flash cards and PC Cards can also be read by desktop computers when the card is inserted in a card reader that can handle the specific format. For example, one card reader is the SwapBox PC Card Reader by SCM Microsystems (*www.scmmicro.com*). The card reader interfaces with a desktop computer by way of an ISA or PCI slot. PC Cards, such as a modem card or Ethernet card, can be inserted in the reader which can handle Type I, II and III PC Cards. In addition, when used with adapter sleeves, the SwapBox can accept other PCMCIA compliant cards such as Smart Media and CompactFlash cards.

Another popular use of a PC Card is to interface with a network. Figure 12-15 shows a PC Card that serves as the NIC to an Ethernet 100BaseT network. The RJ-45 connection is at the end of a small cord connected to the PC Card. This small cord is called a dongle or pigtail and is used so that the thick RJ-45 connection does not have to fit flat against the PC Card.

12

Dongle or pigtail

RJ-45 connection

PC Card

Figure 12-15   This PC Card serves as a NIC for an Ethernet 100BaseT network

USB ports have become a popular way of adding devices to notebooks. For example, if the notebook does not have a RJ-45 port for an Ethernet connection, you can buy a device to plug into the USB port that provides the Ethernet port. Another example shown in Figure 12-16 is a wireless keyboard and mouse that use a receiver connected to a USB port. Installing this keyboard and mouse on a Windows 2000 notebook is very simple. You simply plug in the receiver to the USB port. Windows displays a message that it has located the device and the mouse and keyboard are ready to use. This ease of installation is fast making USB the preferred method of connecting peripheral devices.

Keyboard PS/2 connector

USB connector

Figure 12-16 This wireless keyboard and mouse by Logitech use a receiver that connects to either a USB or keyboard port

Supporting Notebooks

Except for the differences discussed in this section, notebooks work identically to desktop PCs, and the troubleshooting guidelines in previous chapters also apply to notebooks. When troubleshooting notebooks, be especially conscious of warranty issues; know what you can do within the guidelines of the warranty. The documentation that comes with a notebook is much more comprehensive than what comes with a PC and most often contains troubleshooting guidelines for the notebook. Remember that the loaded OS and the hardware configuration are specific to the notebook, so you can rely on the notebook manufacturer for support more than you can for a desktop PC. Sometimes a notebook is designed so that the hard drive can be replaced or upgraded without violating warranties. See the notebook documentation for details. For questions about supporting a notebook that are not answered in the documentation, see the Web site of the notebook manufacturer. Some popular manufacturers of notebooks and their Web sites are listed in Table 12-1.

Table 12-1   Notebook manufacturers

Manufacturer	Web site
Acer America	global.acer.com
ARM Computer	www.armcomputer.com
Compaq Computer	www.hp.com
Dell Computer	www.dell.com
Gateway	www.gateway.com
Hewlett-Packard	www.hp.com
IBM	www.ibm.com
MicronPC	www.micronpc.com
PC Notebook	www.pcnotebook.com
Sony	www.sonystyle.com
Toshiba America	www.csd.toshiba.com
WinBook	www.winbook.com

PDAs

Notebooks provide portability or flexibility, but even the smallest ones have to be carried in a case the size of a briefcase and can be cumbersome in some situations, especially for simple tasks such as checking addresses, viewing stock prices, or recording and receiving short messages. **PDAs (Personal Digital Assistants)**, sometimes called a personal PC or a handheld PC, provide greater ease of use with such applications. A PDA, such as a Palm Pilot or a Pocket PC, is a small, handheld computer that has its own operating system and applications. Figure 12-17 shows the Compaq iPAQ H3800 PDA with its universal cradle and cable, which are used to connect to a PC.

Like a notebook, a PDA is battery-powered, uses either a grayscale or color active matrix or dual-scan passive matrix display, and can sometimes benefit from additional memory. Other PDA hardware includes a stylus used to operate the PDA by touching the screen. You tap the screen with the stylus to open applications or make selections on menus. You can also hold down the stylus to scroll through menu options. For quick access to commonly used applications such as a calendar or an address book, most PDAs provide application buttons below the screen that you can press to bring up the application. A PDA might use an AC/DC adapter that can plug into the PDA itself or into the universal cradle. Some PDAs have optional accessories such as the fold-out keyboard shown in Figure 12-18.

USB port   Serial port

Universal cradle

Figure 12-17 The Compaq iPAQ H3800 PDA comes with a cradle and a cable to attach to a USB or serial port on another computer

PDA snaps in here

Figure 12-18 This fold-out keyboard attaches to a PDA

When purchasing a PDA, first decide how you will be using it, and then match the features of the PDA to its intended purpose. Here are the main things to consider in purchasing a PDA. The next sections cover several of these items.

- What applications come with the PDA, and what can be added later?
- How easy is the PDA to use, and how thorough is the documentation?

- How easy is it to keep the PDA synchronized with your desktop computer or notebook, and will your organization approve the type of PDA synchronization?

- What support is available on the manufacturer's Web site? What software can be downloaded for the PDA from this site, and what is the cost of that software?

- What type of batteries does the PDA use, and what is the battery life?

- Can the PDA use e-mail and the Web, and what extra hardware and software is required to do that?

- What additional devices can be purchased to make the PDA more versatile and easier to use?

- What operating system does the PDA use? How easy is the OS to use?

- What is the warranty? (Does the warranty cover such things as dropping the PDA or damaging the LCD panel by pressing too hard on it?)

- What is the price of the PDA, and what is the price of additional years of warranty?

Battery Life on a PDA

Battery life on a PDA varies by model, and short battery life is the one largest complaint against PDAs. Some PDAs use batteries that can be recharged, and others do not. If your PDA's battery runs down all the way and discharges, you will lose all the data and applications on it! Many manufacturers suggest that you get in the habit of setting your PDA in its cradle whenever you are not carrying it, and never trust it with data or downloaded software for more than a few hours. It is a good idea to have a cradle and adapter wherever you use your PDA; you may want to keep one at your home, another at your office, and another in your briefcase.

Applications on a PDA

You can use a PDA to store addresses and phone numbers, manage a calendar, run word processing, send e-mail, access Web sites, play music, and exchange information with a desktop computer. Some PDAs come with all application software preinstalled, and others require the user to download applications at additional cost. Other PDAs support the applications that come preinstalled and cannot download others. Some PDAs allow you to download e-mail or Web site content from a desktop computer or a notebook, and others can access the Internet directly by way of a modem or wireless connection. Not all Web sites are designed to be accessed by a PDA, and the Web content readable by a PDA is more limited than that readable by a desktop or notebook computer.

Connecting a PDA to a PC

Typically, a PDA comes with a universal cradle that has an attached cable to connect to a desktop computer or notebook by way of a serial or USB port, or a PDA might use an infrared connection. The process by which the PDA and the PC "talk" to each other through the universal cradle, cable, and USB or serial connection is called **synchronization**. This

12

process enables you to back up information on your PDA to the PC, work with PDA files on the PC, and download applications to the PDA that you have downloaded off the Web using the PC. Special software, such as ActiveSync by Microsoft, might be needed to perform synchronization between the PDA and the other computer attached via the cable. You will need to install this software before connecting the PDA to the PC. Follow the instructions in the PDA documentation and on the CD included with it to install the software.

Some PDAs can also synchronize with a desktop or notebook computer through wireless technology. The Compaq PDA shown in Figure 12-17 supports the **Bluetooth** standard. For wireless synchronization to occur, both the PDA and the PC must be set up to use the same wireless standard. The PC and the PDA must each have a wireless transmitter/receiver (transceiver) and software installed to use it. Some PDAs have an embedded transceiver, and others require an add-on device. Again, study the PDA documentation to know if a PDA supports wireless technology.

To set up a PDA and a PC to communicate, do the following:

1. Read the PDA documentation about how to synchronize it with the PC and install on the PC the synchronization software that came bundled with the PDA. If the synchronization software must first be launched, launch it.

2. Connect the PDA to the PC by way of a USB cable or serial cable that most likely also came bundled with the PDA.

3. The PDA and PC should immediately synchronize. Data entered on one device should be reflected on the other.

4. If you have problems, check these things:

   - Is the USB or serial cable plugged in at both ends?
   - For a USB connection, verify the USB controller is working in Device Manager with no conflicts.
   - Is the USB or serial port enabled in CMOS setup?
   - Is the PDA turned on?
   - Check the PDA documentation for other things to do and try.
   - Uninstall and reinstall the PDA software on the PC.
   - Check the Web site of the PDA manufacturer for problems and solutions.

PDA Manufacturers and Operating Systems

There are two main OSs for PDAs: Pocket PC and Palm OS. You may also see Pocket PC referred to as Windows CE 3.0; Windows CE was an earlier Microsoft handheld OS. Given the prominence of Microsoft Windows in most markets it has entered, it is interesting to note that Palm OS and Pocket PC have basically equal shares of the market for PDA OSs. The principal difference between the two OSs is in the applications they support. Pocket PC is considered to be a more versatile OS that can better be used to download and run applications similar to those supported by Windows, such as Microsoft Word or Excel. Palm OS is less complex, easier to use, and is considered the best choice if the PDA is only to be used for simple tasks such as using e-mail, an address book, or a calendar. Table 12-2 lists some manufacturers of PDAs running Palm OS, and Table 12-3 lists some manufacturers of PDAs running Pocket PC.

Table 12-2   Manufacturers of Palm OS PDAs

Manufacturer	Web site
HandEra	www.handera.com
Handspring	www.handspring.com
IBM	www.ibm.com
Palm	www.palm.com
Samsung	www.samsungelectronics.com/pda

Table 12-3   Manufacturers of Pocket PC PDAs

Manufacturer	Web site
Casio	www.casio.com/personalpcs
Compaq	www.hp.com
Hewlett-Packard	www.hp.com
Toshiba	www.toshiba.com

PRINTERS

This section discusses how printers work, what types of printers there are, and how to support them. Local printers connect directly to a computer by way of a parallel port, serial port, USB port, infrared connection, wireless connection, IEEE 1394 port, SCSI port, or PC Card connection, or a computer can access a network printer by way of the network. Printers can have a variety of options including extra paper trays to hold different sizes of paper, special paper feeders, staplers, collators, and sorters. Printers can also be combined with fax machines, copiers, and scanners in the same machine. Most often, printers are powered by AC power, but some printers use batteries. Let's begin by looking at several types of printers for desktop computing.

Laser Printers

Laser printers are a type of electrophotographic printer and range from small, personal desktop models to large network printers capable of handling and printing large volumes continuously. Figure 12-19 shows an example of a typical laser printer for a desktop computer system, the Brother HL-1870N.

Laser printers require the interaction of mechanical, electrical, and optical technologies to work. Understanding how they work will help you support and service them. This section also explains why the safety precautions stated in laser printer user manuals are necessary.

How a Laser Printer Works

Laser printers work by placing toner on an electrically charged rotating drum and then depositing the toner on paper as the paper moves through the system at the same speed the

12

drum is turning. Figure 12-20 shows the six steps of laser printing. The first four use the printer components that undergo the most wear. They are contained within the removable cartridge to increase the life of the printer. The last two steps are performed outside the cartridge. Follow the steps of laser printing below while you refer to Figure 12-20.

Figure 12-19   The Brother HL-1870N network-ready desktop laser printer

Figure 12-20   The six progressive steps of laser printing

1. *Cleaning.* The drum is cleaned of any residual toner and electrical charge.

2. *Conditioning.* The drum is conditioned to contain a high electrical charge.

3. *Writing.* A laser beam discharges a lower charge to only those places where toner is to go.

4. *Developing.* Toner is placed onto the drum where the charge has been reduced.

5. *Transferring.* A strong electrical charge draws the toner off the drum onto the paper. This is the first step that takes place outside the cartridge.

6. *Fusing.* Heat and pressure fuse the toner to the paper.

Note that Figure 12-20 shows only a cross-section of the drum, mechanisms, and paper. Remember that the drum is as wide as a sheet of paper. The mirror, blades, and rollers in the drawing are also as wide as paper. Also know that toner responds to a charge and will move from one surface to another if the second surface has a more positive charge than the first. As you visualize the process, first note the location of the removable cartridge in the drawing, the photosensitive drum inside the cartridge turning in a clockwise direction, and the path of the paper, which moves from right to left.

Step 1: Cleaning. Figure 12-21 shows a clear view of the cleaning step. First a sweeper strip cleans the drum of any residual toner, which is swept away from the drum by a sweeping blade. A cleaning blade completes the physical cleaning of the drum. Next the drum is cleaned of any electrical charge by erase lamps (located in the hinged top cover of the printer), which light the surface of the drum to neutralize any electrical charge left on the drum.

Sweeping blade

Cleaning blade

Drum

Sweeper strip

Figure 12-21   The cleaning step cleans the drum of toner and electrical charge

Step 2: Conditioning. The conditioning step puts a uniform electrical charge of −600V on the surface of the drum. The charge is put there by a primary charging roller or primary corona, which is charged by a high-voltage power supply assembly. The primary charging roller in Figure 12-20 is inside the toner cartridge, and regulates the charge on the drum, ensuring that it is a uniform −600 V.

Step 3: Writing. In the writing step, the uniform charge that was applied in Step 2 is discharged only where you want the printer to print. This is done by controlling mirrors to reflect laser beams onto the drum in a pattern that recreates the image desired. This is the first step in which data from the computer must be transmitted to the printer. Figure 12-22 shows the process. Data from the PC is received by the formatter (1) and passed on to the DC controller (2), which controls the laser unit (3). The laser beam is initiated and directed toward the octagonal mirror called the **scanning mirror**. The scanning mirror (4) is turned by the scanning motor in a clockwise direction. There are eight mirrors on the eight sides of the scanning mirror. As the mirror turns, the laser beam is directed in a sweeping motion that can cover the entire length of the drum. The laser beam is reflected off the scanning mirror, focused by the focusing lens (5), and sent on to the mirror (6), which is also shown in Figure 12-20. The mirror deflects the laser beam to a slit in the removable cartridge and on to the drum (7).

Figure 12-22   The writing step, done by an invisible laser beam, mirrors, and motors, causes a discharge on the drum where the image will be

The speed of the motor turning the drum and the speed of the scanning motor turning the scanning mirror are synchronized so that the laser beam completes one pass, or scanline, across the drum and returns to the beginning of the drum (right side of the drum in Figure 12-22) to begin a new pass, until it completes the correct number of passes for each inch of the drum circumference. For example, for a 300 dots per inch (dpi) printer, the beam makes 300 passes for every one inch of the drum circumference. The laser beam is turned on and off continually as it makes a single pass down the length of the drum, so that dots are written along the drum on every pass. For a 300-dpi printer, 300 dots are written along the drum for every inch of linear pass. The 300 dots per inch down this single pass, along with 300 passes per inch of drum circumference, together accomplish the resolution of 300 × 300 dots per square inch of many desktop laser printers.

TIP A laser printer can produce better quality printouts than a dot matrix printer, even when printing at the same dpi, because it can vary the size of the dots it prints, creating a sharp, clear image. HP calls this technology of varying the size of dots **REt (Resolution Enhancement technology)**.

In a laser printer, where the laser beam strikes the surface of the drum, the drum discharges from its conditioned charge of −600 V down to −100 V where toner will be placed on the drum. Toner does not stick to the highly charged areas of the drum.

Just as the scanning laser beam is synchronized to the rotating drum, the data output is synchronized to the scanning beam. Before the beam begins moving across the scanline of the drum, the **beam detect mirror** detects the laser beam by reflecting it to an optical fiber. The light travels along the optical fiber to the DC controller, where it is converted to an electrical signal that synchronizes the data output. The signal is also used to diagnose problems with the laser or scanning motor.

The laser beam has written an image to the drum surface as a −100 V charge. The −100 V charge on this image area will be used in the developing stage to transmit toner to the drum surface.

Step 4: Developing. Figure 12-23 shows the developing step, in which toner is applied by the developing cylinder to the discharged (−100 V) areas of the drum. Toner transfers from the cylinder to the drum as the two rotate very close together. The cylinder is coated with a layer of toner, made of black resin bonded to iron, which is similar to the toner used in photocopy machines. The toner is held on the cylinder surface by its attraction to a magnet inside the cylinder. (A toner cavity keeps the cylinder supplied with toner.) A **control blade** prevents too much toner from sticking to the cylinder surface. The toner on the cylinder surface takes on a negative charge (between −200 V and −500 V) because the surface is connected to a DC power supply called the DC bias.

The negatively charged toner is more negative than the −100 V on the drum surface, but less negative than the −600 V surface. This means that the toner is attracted to the −100 V area of the drum surface (the −100 V area is positive relative to the toner). The toner is repelled from the −600 V part of the drum surface, which is negative relative to the toner. The result is that toner sticks to the drum where the laser beam has hit and is repelled from the area where the laser beam has not hit.

You can adjust printer density manually at the printer or through software controlling the printer. With laser printers, when you adjust print density, you are adjusting the DC bias charge on the developing cylinder, which controls the amount of toner attracted to the cylinder, which, in turn, results in a change in print density.

Step 5: Transferring. In the transferring step, the transfer charging roller, or transfer corona (shown in Figure 12-20), produces a positive charge on the paper that pulls the toner from the drum onto the paper when the paper is passed between the transfer charging roller and the drum. The static charge eliminator (refer again to Figure 12-20) weakens the positive charge on the paper and the negative charge on the drum so that the paper does not

12

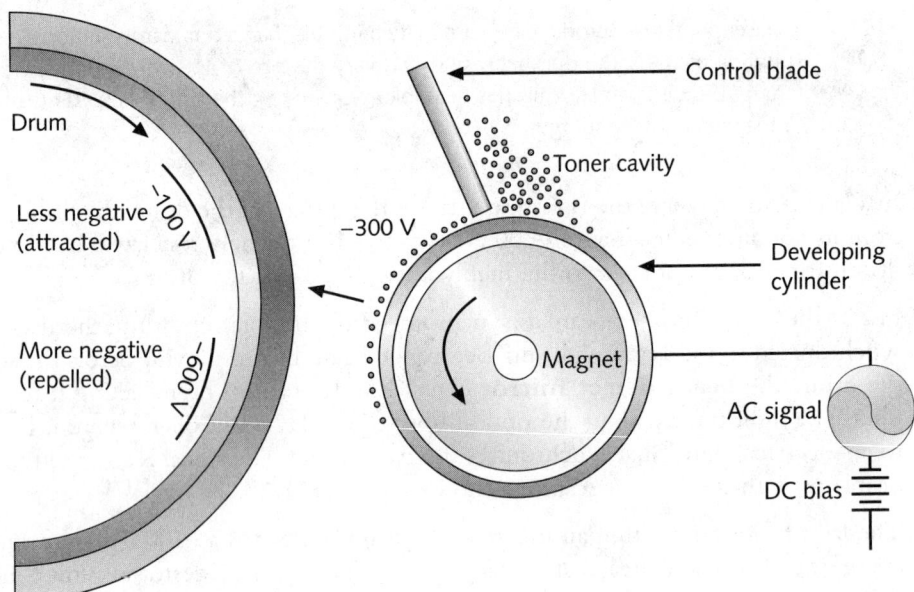

Figure 12-23   In the developing step, charged toner is deposited onto the drum surface

adhere to the drum, which it would otherwise do because of the difference in charge between the two. The stiffness of the paper and the small radius of the drum also help the paper move away from the drum and toward the fusing assembly. Very thin paper can wrap around the drum, which is why printer manuals usually instruct you to use only paper designated for laser printers.

Step 6: Fusing. The fusing step causes the toner to bond with the paper. Up to this point, the toner is merely sitting on the paper. The fusing rollers apply both pressure and heat to the paper. The toner melts, and the rollers press the toner into the paper. The temperature of the rollers is monitored by the printer. If the temperature exceeds an allowed maximum value (410 degrees F for some printers), the printer shuts down.

The previous steps describe how a black and white printer works. Color laser printers work in a similar way, but the writing process repeats four times, one for each toner color of cyan, magenta, yellow, and black. Then the paper passes to the fusing stage, where the fuser bonds all toner to the paper and aids in blending the four tones to form specific colors.

Ink-Jet Printers

Ink-jet printers don't normally provide the high-quality resolution of laser printers, but are popular because they are small and can print color inexpensively. Ink-jet printers tend to smudge on inexpensive paper as there is too much ink dispersion, and they are slower than laser printers. The quality of the paper used with ink-jet printers significantly affects the quality of printed output. Only use paper designed for an ink-jet printer, and to get the best results, use a high-grade paper. Figure 12-24 shows one example of an ink-jet printer.

Figure 12-24   An example of an ink-jet printer

How an Ink-Jet Printer Works

An ink-jet printer resembles a dot-matrix printer in several ways. Both printers use a print head that moves across the paper, creating one line of text with each pass. Also, both types of printer put ink on the paper using a matrix of small dots, although ink-jet printers use much smaller dots than do dot-matrix printers. (You will learn more about dot-matrix printers later in the chapter.)

Different types of ink-jet printers form their droplets of ink in different ways. Printer manufacturers use several technologies, but the most popular is the bubble-jet. Bubble-jet printers use tubes of ink that have tiny resistors near the end of each tube. These resistors heat up and cause the ink to boil. Then, a tiny air bubble of ionized ink (which means that it has an electrical charge) is ejected onto the paper. A typical bubble-jet print head has 64 or 128 tiny nozzles, all of which can fire a droplet simultaneously. Plates carrying a magnetic charge direct the path of ink onto the paper to form shapes.

Ink-jet printers include one or more cartridges of ink. When purchasing an ink-jet printer, look for the kind that uses two separate cartridges, one for black ink and one for three-color printing. If an ink-jet printer does not have a black ink cartridge, then it produces black by combining all colors of ink to produce a dull black. Having a separate cartridge for black ink means that it prints a true black and, more importantly, does not use the more expensive colored ink. You can replace the black cartridge without also replacing the colored ink cartridge.

Figure 12-25 shows the two ink cartridges for the Hewlett-Packard DeskJet 712C. The cartridge on the left contains red, blue, and yellow ink (official names are magenta, cyan, and yellow), and the cartridge on the right contains black ink. The print head assemblage in the figure is located in the center position because the top cover has been lifted. Normally when the printer is not in use, the head assemblage sits to the far right of the printing area. This is called the home position and helps protect the ink in the cartridges from drying out.

12

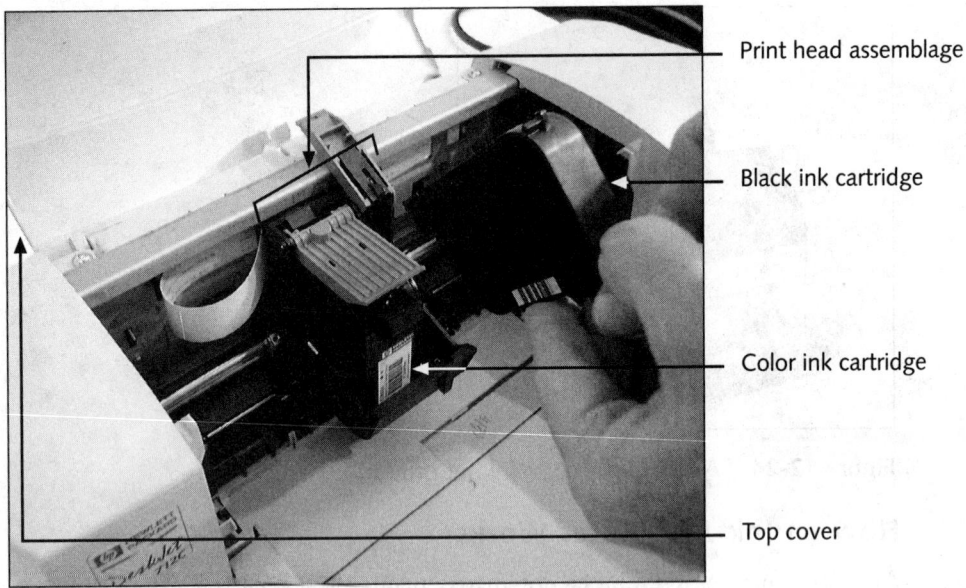

Print head assemblage

Black ink cartridge

Color ink cartridge

Top cover

Figure 12-25   The ink-jet cartridges of an ink-jet printer

Photo-Quality Ink-Jet Printers

A new generation of ink-jet printers has emerged that can give photo-quality results, especially when used with photo-quality paper. Until this new technology was developed, increasing the quality of an ink-jet printer meant increasing the dpi (dots per inch). Earlier ink-jet printers used 300 dpi, but ink-jet printers today can use as many as 1,400 dpi. Increasing the dpi has its drawbacks. Doing so increases the amount of data sent to the printer for a single page, and all those dots of ink on the page can produce a wet page. An improved technology that gives photo-quality results mixes different colors of ink to produce a new color that then makes a single dot. Hewlett-Packard calls this PhotoREt II color technology. HP mixes as many as 16 drops of ink to produce a single dot of color on the page, producing up to 30 times as many shades of color as conventional ink-jet printing does. The results are dramatic, and the cost of an ink-jet printer using photo-quality technology is not significantly different from that of a standard ink-jet printer.

Dot-Matrix Printers

Dot-matrix printers are less expensive than other types of printers, but they don't give nearly the print quality. For many desktop PC users, they have been replaced with ink-jet or laser printers. The one reason you still see so many around is that they are impact printers and can print multicopy documents, which some businesses still find useful. A dot-matrix printer has a print head that moves across the width of the paper, using pins to print a matrix of dots on the page. The pins shoot against a cloth ribbon, which hits the paper, depositing the ink. The ribbon provides both the ink for printing and the lubrication for the pinheads.

Occasionally, you should replace the ribbon of a dot matrix printer. Although the print head can wear out, replacing it is probably not cost-effective because it costs almost as much as the printer itself. If the print head fails, buy a new printer. Overheating can damage a print head (see Figure 12-26). Keep the print head as cool as possible so that it will last longer. Keep the printer in a cool, well-ventilated area, and don't use it to print more than 50 to 75 pages without allowing the head to cool down.

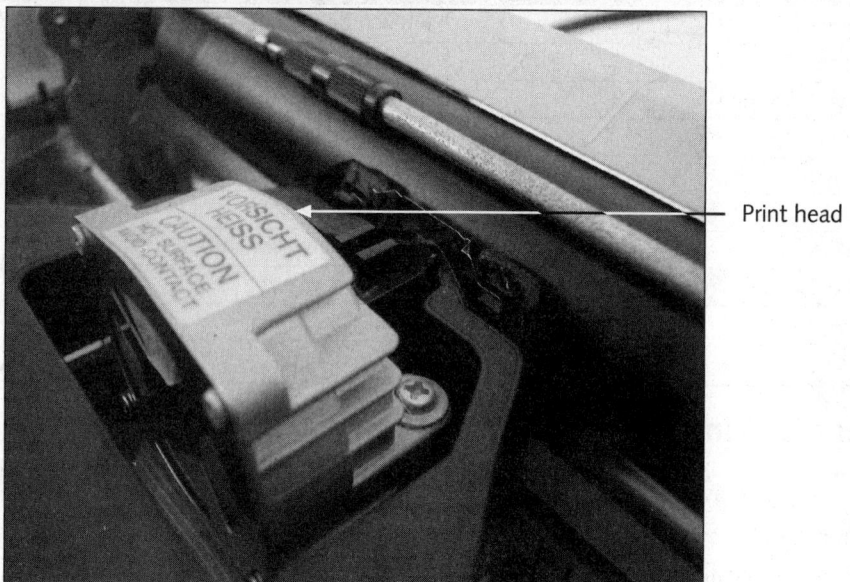

Print head

Figure 12-26   Keep the print head of a dot-matrix printer as cool as possible so that it will last longer

Thermal Printers and Solid Ink Printers

Two relatively new printer technologies that are similar to each other are thermal printers and solid ink printers. Both are non-impact printers that use heat to produce printed output. Thermal printers use wax-based ink that is heated by heat pins that melt the ink onto paper. The printer's print head containing these heat pins is as wide as the paper. The internal logic of the printer determines which pins get heated in order to produce the printed image. Thermal printers are popular in retail applications for printing bar codes and price tags. A thermal printer can burn dots onto special paper as done by older fax machines (called direct thermal printing) or the printer can use a ribbon that contains the wax-based ink (called thermal wax transfer printing). One variation of thermal printing uses thermal dye sublimation technology to print identification cards and access cards.

Solid ink printers such as the Xerox Phaser 8200 store ink in solid blocks, which Xerox calls ColourStixs. The sticks or blocks are easy to handle and several can be inserted in the printer to be used as needed, avoiding the problem of running out of ink in the middle of a large print job. The solid ink is melted into the print head which spans the width of the paper. The head jets the liquid ink onto the paper as it passes by on a drum. The design is simple, print quality is excellent, and solid ink printers are easy to set up and maintain. The greatest disadvantage to solid ink printing is the time it takes for the print head to heat up to begin

12

a print job, which is about 15 minutes. For this reason, some solid ink printers anticipate a print job might be coming based on previous use of the printer and automatically heat up. Table 12-4 lists manufacturers of printers.

Table 12-4   Printer manufacturers

Printer Manufacturer	Web Site
Brother	www.brother.com
Canon	usa.canon.com
Hewlett Packard	www.hp.com
IBM	www.ibm.com
Lexmark	www.lexmark.com
Okidata	www.okidata.com
SATO	www.satoamerica.com
Seiko Epson	www.epson.com
Tally	www.tally.com
Xerox	www.xerox.com

Installing a Printer

In this section, you will learn how to install a local printer. A computer can have several printers installed. Windows designates one printer to be the **default printer**, which is the printer Windows prints to unless another is selected. Follow these steps to install a printer:

- Physically attach the printer to the computer by way of a parallel port, serial port, USB port, SCSI port, IEEE 1394 port, PC Card connection, Infrared connection, or wireless access point. Recall from Chapter 5 that, for a parallel port connection, use an IEEE 1284-compliant printer cable.

- Install the printer drivers. There are two approaches to do this. You can have Windows install the driver or you can use the printer manufacturer's installation program. In most cases, it is best to use the printer manufacturer's method. The exception to this is if you have several printers installed that are similar, Windows does a better job of preventing files used by one printer installation to be overwritten by files from another installation. To use the manufacturer's installation process, insert the printer driver CD that comes bundled with the printer in the CD-ROM drive and follow directions on screen to install the printer.

- Alternately, you can use the Windows Printer window to install the printer. For Windows 98 and Windows 2000 click **Start**, **Settings**, and **Printer** to open the Printer window. For Windows XP, to open the Printer window, click **Start**, **Printers** and **Faxes**. From the Printer window, click **Add Printer** and follow the Add Printer wizard to install the printer.

- Once the printer drivers are installed, test the printer. To do this, open the Printer window and right click the printer. Select **Properties** from the shortcut menu. Click the **General** tab and then click the **Print Test Page** button.

From the Printer window you can also delete printers, change the Windows default printer, purge print jobs in order to troubleshoot failed printing, and perform other printer maintenance tasks. If a printer is giving problems or you want to upgrade the printer drivers in order to add new functionality, search the printer manufacturer's Web site for the latest drivers for your printer and operating system. Download the drivers to a folder on the hard drive such as C:\Downloads\Printer, and then double click on the driver file to extract files and launch the installation program to update the printer drivers.

A local printer connects directly to the PC, but a network printer is accessed over the network. A network printer contains a NIC and connects directly to the network or is shared on the network by another PC. One way to install a network printer on a remote PC is to locate the printer in Network Neighborhood or My Network Places and right click on the printer. From the shortcut menu select Install or Connect and follow directions on screen.

Troubleshooting Guidelines for Printers

This section first discusses general printer troubleshooting and then how to troubleshoot problems specific to each of the three major types of printers. The first thing to do to prevent problems with printers is to follow manufacturer's directions when using the printer and to perform routine maintenance on the printer.

Printer Maintenance

Routine printer maintenance procedures vary widely from manufacturer to manufacturer and printer to printer. First, make sure consumables for the printer are on hand such as paper, ink ribbons, ColourStixs, toner cartridges, and ink cartridges. For each printer you support, research the printer documentation or the manufacturer's Web site for specific things you should do to maintain the printer and how often you should do them. For example, the HP Color LaserJet 4600 printer has a printer maintenance plan that says to replace the transfer roller assembly after 120,000 pages have printed and replace the fusing assembly after 150,000 pages. The plan also says the black ink cartridge should last for about 9,000 pages and the color ink cartridge for about 8,000 pages. HP offers for purchase the image transfer kit, the image fuser kit and the ink cartridges designed for this printer. The kits, called **printer maintenance kits**, include the specific printer components, step-by-step instructions for performing the maintenance, and any special tools or equipment you will need to do the maintenance. The Web site and printer documentation includes instructions to command the printer to report how many pages have printed since each maintenance task was performed.

When you perform routine maintenance on a printer, clean inside and outside the printer. Clean the outside of the printer with a damp cloth. Don't use ammonia-based cleaners. Clean the inside of the printer with a dry cloth and remove dust, bits of paper and stray toner. Don't use an anti-static vacuum cleaner. For a laser printer, wipe the rollers with a dry cloth from side to side to remove loose dirt. Don't touch the soft black roller (the transfer roller) as doing so can cause poor print quality. If you get toner on your clothes, dust it off and clean your clothes with cold water. Hot water will set the toner.

Search the printer manufacturer's Web site for lists of common problems and what to do about them. Some Web sites also offer a newsgroup service where you can communicate with others responsible for supporting a particular printer. Following is a guide for general and specific printer troubleshooting. If you have exhausted this list and still have a problem, turn to the manufacturer's Web site for additional information and support.

General Printer Troubleshooting

Printing problems can be caused by the printer, the PC hardware or OS, the application using the printer, the printer cable, or, in the case of a printer installed on a network, the network. Follow the steps in Figure 12-27 to isolate the problem to one of the following areas:

- The application attempting to use the printer

- The OS and printer drivers
- Connectivity between the PC and the printer
- The printer

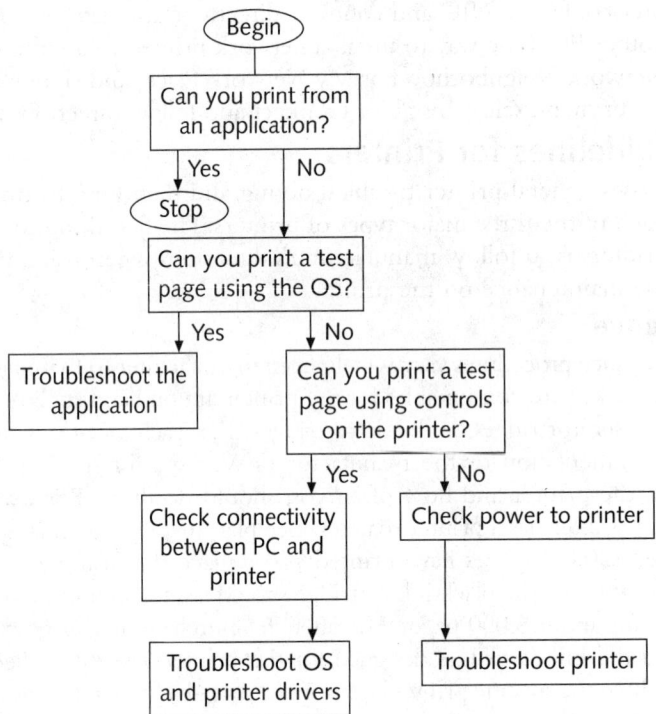

Figure 12-27   How to isolate a printer problem

The sections that follow address printer problems caused by the hardware, including the printer and the printer cable.

Verify a Printer Self-Test Page Can Print   To eliminate the printer as the problem, print a test page at the printer. For directions to print a self-test page, see the user guide for the printer. For example, you might have to hold down a button or buttons on the front panel of the printer. If this test page prints correctly, it confirms that the printer is working correctly. A printer test page generally prints some text and some graphics and prints information about the printer, such as the printer resolution and how much memory is installed. Verify that the information on the test page is correct. For example, if you know that the printer should have 2 MB of on-board printer memory, but it only reports 1 MB, then there is a problem with memory.

If the self-test page does not print or prints incorrectly (for example, it has missing dots or smudged streaks through the page), then troubleshoot the printer until it prints correctly. Does the printer have paper? Is the paper installed correctly? Is there a paper jam? Try resetting the printer. For a laser printer, check that a toner cartridge is installed. For an inkjet printer, check that ink cartridges are installed. Check that power is getting to the printer. Check the user guide for the printer and the printer Web site for troubleshooting suggestions. Also, some printers allow you to flash BIOS on the printer.

If none of these steps works, you may need to take the printer to a certified repair shop. Before you do, though, try contacting the manufacturer. The printer documentation can be very helpful and most often contains a phone number to technical support for the printer manufacturer.

Problem with the Printer Cable   If the printer self-test worked, but the OS printer test did not work, the problem might be with the printer cable.

- Check that the cable is firmly connected at both ends.

- Many businesses use an older switch box (sometimes called a T-switch) to share one printer between two computers. A printer cable connects to the printer port of each computer. The two cables connect to the switch box. A third cable connects from the switch box to the printer. A switch on the front of the box controls which computer has access to the printer. Switch boxes were built with older dot-matrix printers in mind. Some switch boxes are not recommended for ink-jet or laser printers that use a bidirectional parallel cable, and can even damage a printer. For these printers, remove the switch box.

- Try a different cable. Use a shorter cable (cables longer than 10 feet can sometimes cause problems). Verify that the cable is IEEE 1284 compliant.

- Try printing using the same printer and printer cable, but a different PC.

- Enter CMOS setup of the PC and check how the parallel port is configured. Is it disabled? Set to ECP or bidirectional? Recall from Chapter 5 that an ECP parallel port requires the use of a DMA channel. Try setting the port to bidirectional.

Problems with Laser Printers

This section covers some problems that can occur with laser printers. For more specific guidelines for your model of printer, refer to the printer documentation or the manufacturer's Web site.

Poor print quality due to low toner   Poor print quality, including faded, smeared, wavy, speckled, or streaked printouts, often indicates that the toner is low. All of the major mechanical printer components that normally create problems are conveniently contained within the replaceable toner cartridge. In most cases, the solution to poor quality printing is to replace this cartridge. Follow these general guidelines:

- If you suspect the printer is overheated, unplug the printer and allow it to cool.

- Remove the toner cartridge and gently rock it from side to side to redistribute the toner. Replace the cartridge. If this solves the problem, plan to replace the toner cartridge soon. Don't shake the cartridge too hard, to avoid flying toner.

- If this doesn't solve the problem, try replacing the toner cartridge immediately.

- EconoMode (a mode that uses less toner) may be on; turn it off.

- On some laser printers, you can clean the mirror. Check the user guide for directions.

- A single sheet of paper may be defective. Try new paper.

- The paper may not be of high enough quality. Try a different brand of paper. Only use paper recommended for use in a laser printer.

- Clean the inside of the printer with a dry, lint-free cloth. Don't touch the transfer roller.

- If the transfer roller is dirty, the problem will probably correct itself after printing several sheets. If not, then take the printer to an authorized service center.

 TIP Extreme humidity may cause the toner to clump in the cartridge and give a low toner message. If this is a consistent problem in your location, you might want to invest in a dehumidifier for the room where your printer is located.

Printer stays in warm-up mode   The warming up message on the front panel of the printer should go off as soon as the printer establishes communication with the PC. If this doesn't happen, try the following:

- Turn the printer off and disconnect the cable to the computer.

- Turn on the printer. If it now displays a Ready message, the problem is communication.

- Verify that the cable is connected to the correct printer port, not to a serial port.

- Verify that data to the installed printer is being sent to the parallel port. For example, open the Properties dialog box of the installed printer, as described above. Verify that the print job is being sent to LPT1, as shown in Figure 12-28.

- Check that the parallel port is enabled in CMOS setup and is set to the correct mode.

- Replace the cable.

A Paper Jam or Paper Out message is displayed

- If paper is jammed inside the printer, follow the directions in the printer documentation to remove the paper. Don't jerk the paper from the printer mechanism, but pull evenly on the paper, with care.

- If there is no jammed paper, then remove the tray and check the metal plate at the bottom of the tray. Can it move up and down freely? If not, replace the tray.

- When you insert the tray in the printer, does the printer lift the plate as the tray is inserted? If not, the lift mechanism might need repairing.

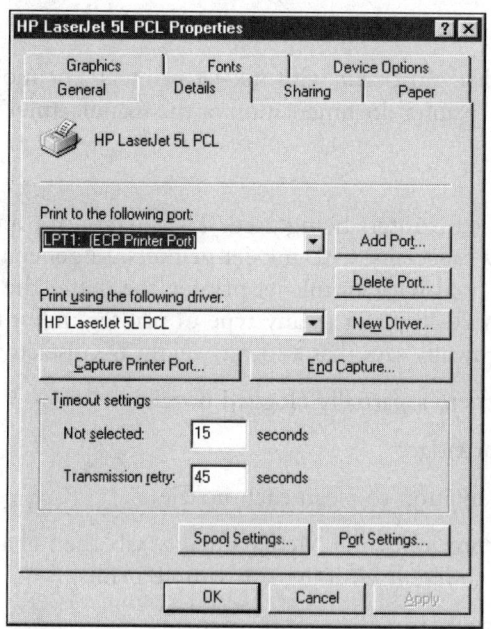

Figure 12-28   Verify that print data is being sent to the correct parallel port

Printed images are distorted   If print images are distorted and there is no paper jam, there might be foreign material inside the printer that is interfering with the mechanical components. Check for debris that might be interfering with the printer operation.

Printing is slow   Laser printers are rated by two speed properties: the time it takes to print the first page (measured in seconds) and the print speed (measured in pages per minute). Try the following if the printer is slow:

- Space is needed on the hard drive to manage print jobs. Clean up the drive. Install a larger drive if necessary.

- Add more memory to the printer. See the printer manual for directions.

- Lower the printer resolution and the print quality (which lowers the RET settings).

- Upgrade the computer's memory or the CPU.

A portion of the page does not print   For some laser printers, if the printer does not have enough memory to hold the entire page, an error occurs. For others, only a part of the page prints. Some may signal this problem by flashing a light or displaying an error message on the display. (For some HP LaserJet printers that have a control panel, the error message for low memory is "20 Mem Overflow.") The solution is to install more memory or to print only simple pages with few graphics. Print a self-test page to verify how much memory is installed. Check the printer guide to determine how much memory the printer can support and what kind of memory to buy.

Problems with Ink-Jet Printers

This section covers some problems that can occur with ink-jet printers. For more specific guidelines for your printer, refer to the printer documentation or the manufacturer's Web site.

Print quality is poor

- Is the correct paper for ink-jet printers being used? The quality of paper determines the final print quality, especially with ink-jet printers. In general, the better the quality of the paper used with an ink-jet printer, the better the print quality. Do not use less than 20-lb paper in any type of printer, unless the printer documentation specifically says that a lower weight is satisfactory.

- Is the ink supply low, or is there a partially clogged nozzle?

- Remove and reinstall the cartridge.

- Follow the printer's documentation to clean each nozzle.

- In the Printer Setup dialog box, click the Media/Quality tab, then change the Print Quality selection. Try different settings with sample prints.

- Is the print head too close to or too far from the paper?

- If you are printing on transparencies, try changing the fill pattern in your application.

Printing is intermittent or absent

- Is the ink supply low?

- Are nozzles clogged?

- Replace the ink cartridges or replenish the ink supply.

Lines or dots are missing from the printed page   The ink nozzles on an ink-jet cartridge occasionally dry out, especially when the printer sits unused for a long time. Symptoms of this are missing lines or dots on the printed page. With older ink-jet printers, you had to clean the ink-jet nozzles manually, but now newer printers often let you clean the nozzles automatically, using software or buttons on the front panel of the printer. This section uses the HP 710C series of printers to describe how to use supporting software to clean the nozzles.

When the printer software is installed, it places a printer toolbox icon on the desktop and adds several tabs to the printer Properties dialog box. Use a tab on the printer Properties dialog box to clean the ink-jet nozzles. Here is what you do:

1. Click **Start**, point to **Settings**, and click **Printers**. The Printers window opens. Right-click the ink-jet printer icon and select **Properties** from the shortcut menu.

2. Click the **Services** tab. Figure 12-29 shows the list of services available for this printer.

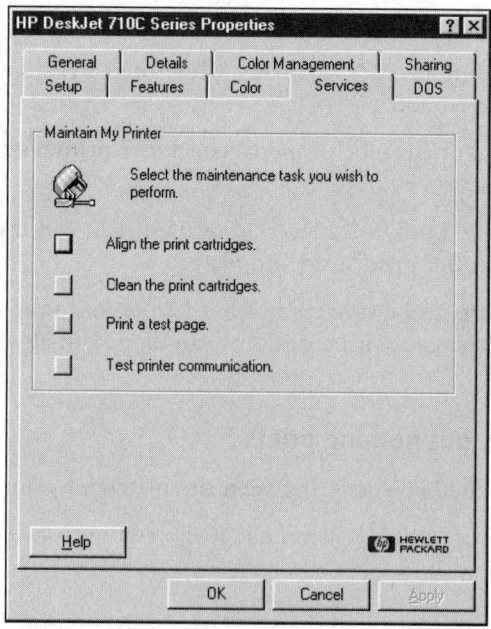

Figure 12-29   Use the Services tab under the printer Properties box to auto-clean the ink-jet nozzles

3. Click **Clean the print cartridges** to clean the ink-jet nozzles automatically.

4. A test page prints. If the page prints sharply with no missing dots or lines, then you are finished. If the page does not print correctly, perform the auto-clean again.

5. You might need to perform the auto-clean procedure six or seven times to completely clean the nozzles. If the problem persists, don't attempt to manually clean the nozzles; contact the manufacturer or vendor for service.

Ink streaks appear on the printed page   Sometimes dust or dirt gets down into the print head assemblage, which can cause streaks or lines on the printed page. Follow the manufacturer's directions to clean the print cartridge assemblage. Use clean distilled water and cotton swabs to clean the cartridge cradle and the face and edges of the print cartridge, being careful not to touch the nozzle plate. To prevent the ink-jet nozzles from drying out, don't leave the print cartridges out of their cradle for longer than 30 minutes.

Problems with Dot-Matrix Printers

This section covers some problems that can occur with dot-matrix printers. Again, for more specific guidelines for your printer, see the printer documentation or the manufacturer's Web site.

Print quality is poor

- Begin with the ribbon. Does it advance normally while the carriage moves back and forth? Replace the ribbon.

- If the new ribbon still does not advance properly, check the printer's advance mechanism.

- Adjust the print head spacing. Look for a lever adjustment you can use to change the distance between the print head and plate.

- Check the print head for dirt. Make sure it's not hot before you touch it. If debris has built up, wipe each wire with a cotton swab dipped in alcohol or contact cleaner.

Print head moves back and forth, but nothing prints

- Check the ribbon. Is it installed correctly between the plate and print head?

- Does the ribbon advance properly? Is it jammed? If the ribbon is dried out, it needs to be replaced.

CHAPTER SUMMARY

- A notebook is a computer designed for portability. Notebooks cost more than comparable PCs because they are more compact and can withstand movement and jars, even when in use. Notebooks don't contain expansion slots for I/O devices, but rather use PC Card slots.

- Notebooks use credit card memory, SO-DIMMs, and SO-RIMMs for upgrading memory.

- Upgrading memory on a notebook varies from one notebook to another; see the notebook's user guide for specific instructions.

- When upgrading components on a notebook, including memory, use components that are the same brand as the notebook, or use only components recommended by the notebook manufacturer.

- PC Cards are a popular way to add peripheral devices to notebooks. The latest PC Card specification is CardBus. There are three types of PC Cards, which vary in thickness: Types I, II, and III.

- A PDA provides even more portability than a notebook computer, for applications such as address books and calendars. PDAs are designed to provide handheld computing power and can interface with a desktop or notebook computer to transfer files and applications.

- PDAs synchronize with PCs through a USB, serial, or wireless port. Two standards for wireless communication are Bluetooth and IEEE 802.11b.

- The three most popular printers are laser, ink-jet, and dot-matrix. Laser printers produce the highest quality, followed by ink-jet printers. Dot-matrix printers have the advantage of being able to print multicopy documents.

❐ The six steps that a laser printer performs to print are cleaning, conditioning, writing, developing, transferring, and fusing. The first four steps take place inside the removable toner cartridge.

❐ Ink-jet printers print by shooting ionized ink at a sheet of paper.

❐ The nozzles of an ink-jet printer tend to clog, especially when the printer remains unused. The nozzles can be cleaned automatically by means of printer software or buttons on the front panel of the printer.

❐ Dot-matrix printers print by projecting pins from the print head against an inked ribbon that deposits ink on the paper.

❐ When troubleshooting printers, first isolate the problem. Narrow the source to the printer, cable, PC hardware, operating system including the device driver, application software, or network.

KEY TERMS

beam detect mirror
Bluetooth
CardBus
control blade
credit card memory
DC controller
default printer
docking station
IEEE 802.11b
laptop computer
notebook

PC Card
PC Card slot
PCMCIA (Personal Computer Memory Card International Association) Card
PCMCIA slot
PDA (Personal Digital Assistant)
port replicator

printer maintenance kit
REt (Resolution Enhancement technology)
scanning mirror
SO-DIMM (small outline DIMM)
SO-RIMM (small outline RIMM)
synchronization

12

13

TROUBLESHOOTING AND MAINTENANCE FUNDAMENTALS

In this chapter, you will learn:

♦ About your role as a PC technician in troubleshooting and maintenance, and tools available to help you in those roles

♦ How to approach a troubleshooting problem

♦ How to develop a preventive maintenance plan and what to include in it

This chapter gives you some common-sense guidelines to solving computer problems. In trying to solve a computer problem, you want to avoid making the situation worse by damaging the equipment, software, or data, or by placing undue stress on the user. When approaching a computer problem, follow the important safety precautions that you have learned in other chapters as well as the ones you will learn in this chapter.

TROUBLESHOOTING PERSPECTIVES AND TOOLS

As a PC troubleshooter, you might have to solve a problem on your own PC or for someone else. As a PC technician, you might fulfill four different job functions:

- *PC support technician.* A PC support technician works on-site, closely interacting with users, and is responsible for ongoing PC maintenance. Of the four technicians listed here, a PC support technician is the only one responsible for the PC before trouble occurs, and therefore able to prepare for a problem by keeping good records and maintaining backups (or teaching the user how to do so).

- *PC service technician.* A PC service technician goes to a customer site in response to a service call and, if possible, repairs a PC on-site. PC service technicians are usually not responsible for ongoing PC maintenance but do usually interact with the user.

- *Bench technician.* A bench technician works in a lab environment, might not interact with users of the PCs being repaired, and is not permanently responsible for them. Bench technicians probably don't work at the site where the PC is kept. They may be able to interview the user to get information about the problem, or may simply receive a PC to repair without being able to talk to the user.

- *Help-desk technician.* A help-desk technician provides telephone support. Help-desk technicians, who do not have physical access to the PC, are at the greatest disadvantage of the four. They can only interact with users over the phone and must obviously use different tools and approaches than the technician at the PC.

This chapter emphasizes the job of the on-site PC support technician. However, the special needs and perspectives of the service technician, bench technician, and help-desk technician are also addressed.

Troubleshooting Tools

There are several hardware and software tools that can help you diagnose and repair computer problems. The tools you choose depend on the amount of money you can spend and the level of PC support you are providing.

Tools that are essential for PC troubleshooting are listed below. All but the bootable rescue disk can easily be purchased in one handy PC tool kit:

- Bootable rescue disk for any OS you might work on (you may need several different ones)

- Ground bracelet and/or ground mat

- Flat-head screwdriver

- Phillips-head or cross-head screwdriver

- Torx screwdriver set, particularly size T15

- Tweezers, preferably insulated ones, for picking pieces of paper out of printers or dropped screws from tight places

- Chip extractor to remove chips (to pry up the chip; a simple screwdriver is usually more effective, however)

- Extractor, a spring-loaded device that looks like a hypodermic needle (when you push down on the top, three wire prongs come out that can be used to pick up a fallen screw, where hands and fingers can't reach)

The following tools might not be essential, but they are very convenient:

- Multimeter to check the power supply output (this is discussed in Chapter 3)

- Needle-nose pliers for holding objects in place while you screw them in (especially those pesky nuts on cable connectors)

- Flashlight to see inside the PC case

- AC outlet ground tester

- Small cups or bags to help keep screws organized as you work

- Antistatic bags to store unused parts

- Pen and paper for taking notes

- Diagnostic cards and diagnostic software

- Utility software

- Virus detection software on disks

Keep your tools in a toolbox designated for PC troubleshooting. If you put disks and hardware tools in the same box, don't include a magnetized screwdriver, and be sure to keep the disks inside a plastic case. Make sure the diagnostic and utility software you use is recommended for the hardware and software you are troubleshooting.

Bootable Rescue Disk

Recall from Chapter 2 that an essential tool for PC troubleshooting is a bootable rescue disk. Not only can it boot the PC even when the hard drive fails, but you are ensured of the cleanest boot possible. By "clean boot" we mean that the boot does not load any extraneous software, drivers, or other memory-resident programs (TSRs), which might be loaded from startup routines on the hard drive.

Diagnostic Cards and Software

Although not essential, many hardware and software tools can help you diagnose a PC problem. Before purchasing these tools, read the documentation about what they can and cannot do, and, if possible, read some reviews about the product. The Internet is a good source of information. One hardware diagnostic tool is a diagnostic card, which is discussed next. Then we will look at several diagnostic software applications.

POST Diagnostic Cards   **Diagnostic cards** are designed to discover and report computer errors and conflicts at POST. If you have a problem that prevents the PC from booting, you can install the diagnostic card in an expansion slot on the motherboard and then attempt to boot. The card monitors the boot process and reports errors, usually as coded numbers on a small LED panel on the card. You then look up the number in the documentation that accompanies the card to get more information about the error and its source.

Examples of these cards are:

- POSTcard V3 by Unicore Software, Inc. (*www.unicore.com*)
- Post Code Master by MSD, Inc. (*www.msd.com*)
- POSTmortem Diagnostics Card by System Optimization, Inc. (*www.sysopt.com*)

Diagnostic Software   Diagnostic software is generally used to identify hardware problems. Although many diagnostic software programs are available, here we look at only a few. If the software rates itself as being at the professional level, it generally assumes greater technical expertise and also provides more features than end-user or novice-level software. The most effective diagnostic software does not run from the OS, because the OS may sometimes mask a hardware problem. Here are a few examples of diagnostic software.

- *PC-Technician by Windsor Technologies, Inc.*—This professional-level PC diagnostic software loads and operates without using the PC's installed operating system, because it has its own proprietary OS built in. Results are thus unaltered by any errors in the PC's OS. PC-Technician can relocate itself during testing and successfully test all of main memory. The ability to relocate is important, since software that tests memory cannot test the portion where it is currently loaded. PC-Technician bypasses standard ROM BIOS when translation mode is used by the system, so that the diagnostic software communicates directly with the hard drive controller. PC-Technician comes with test plugs (called loop-back plugs) that test parallel and serial ports by looping data out of and back to the port. These loop-back tests (also called wrap tests) determine that hardware ports are working. There is a downloadable version of this software called TuffTEST-Pro. For more information, see the company Web site at *www.windsortech.com*.

- *PC-Diagnosys by Windsor Technologies, Inc.*—This software is designed for less experienced PC technicians and end users; it is smaller, easier to use, and less expensive than PC-Technician. See *www.windsortech.com*.

General-Purpose Utility Software

Utility software can be designed to diagnose problems, repair and maintain the software on a PC, recover corrupted or deleted data on the hard drive or floppy disks, provide security, monitor system performance, and download software updates from the Internet. The utility software might use the installed operating system or might provide its own. Three utilities that are useful when solving hardware problems are outlined in Table 13-1.

Table 13-1   Utility software used to solve hardware problems

Software	Manufacturer Web Site	Description
Norton Utilities by Symantec	www.symantec.com	Norton Utilities by Symantec is general-purpose, user-friendly utility software that provides a variety of functions, including the ability to recover lost or damaged data from a hard drive.
CheckIt Suite by Smith Micro Software	www.checkit.com	CheckIt by Smith Micro is a general-purpose software and hardware utility product that includes hard drive testing, performance testing, port testing (loop-back plugs are included), and setup for resource conflicts.
PartitionMagic by PowerQuest	www.powerquest.com/ partitionmagic	PartitionMagic lets you create, resize, and merge partitions on a hard drive without losing data. You can use the software to easily run multiple operating systems, convert file system types, and fix partition table errors.
SANDRA Pro by 3B Software	www.3bsoftware.com	SANDRA Pro is benchmarking, diagnostic and tune-up software that can be used to solve hardware and software problems.

 In addition to general-purpose utility software, you should have anti-virus software available to scan for viruses when you are diagnosing a PC problem and also use the software regularly to prevent viruses from attacking your system.

13

YOUR APPROACH TO TROUBLESHOOTING

When a computer doesn't work and you're responsible for fixing it, you should generally approach the problem first as an investigator and discoverer, always being careful not to compound the problem through your own actions. If the problem seems difficult, see it as an opportunity to learn something new. Ask questions until you understand the source of the problem. Once you understand it, you're almost done, because most likely the solution will be evident. Take the attitude that you can understand the problem and solve it, no matter how deeply you have to dig, and you probably will. In this section we look at how to approach a troubleshooting problem, including how to interact with the user and how to handle an emergency.

Fundamental Rules

Here are a few fundamental rules for PC troubleshooting that I've found work for me.

Make backups before making changes   Whether you are working on hardware or software, always back up essential programs and data before working on a computer.

Approach the problem systematically   Start at the beginning and walk through the situation in a thorough, careful way. This one rule is invaluable. Remember it and apply it every time. If you don't find the explanation to the problem after one systematic walk-through, then repeat the entire process. Check and double-check to find the step you overlooked the first time. Most problems with computers are simple, such as a loose cable or circuit board. Computers are logical through and through. Whatever the problem, it's also very logical.

Divide and conquer   This rule is the most powerful. Isolate the problem. In the overall system, remove one hardware or software component after another, until the problem is isolated to a small part of the whole system..Here are a few examples of applying this rule:

- Remove any memory-resident programs (TSRs) to eliminate them as the problem.
- Boot from a disk to eliminate the OS and startup files on the hard drive as the problem.
- Remove any unnecessary hardware devices, such as a scanner card, internal modem, and even the hard drive.

Once down to the essentials, start exchanging components you know are good for those you suspect are bad, until the problem goes away.

Don't overlook the obvious   Ask simple questions. Is the computer plugged in? Is it turned on? Is the monitor plugged in? Most problems are so simple that we overlook them because we expect the problem to be difficult. Don't let the complexity of computers fool you. Most problems are easy to fix. Really, they are!

Check the simple things first   It is more effective to first check the components that are easiest to replace. For example, if the video does not work, the problem may be with the monitor or the video card. When faced with the decision of which one to exchange first, choose the easy route: exchange the monitor before the video card.

Make no assumptions   This rule is the hardest one to follow, because there is a tendency to trust anything in writing and assume that people are telling you exactly what happened. But documentation is sometimes wrong, and people don't always describe events as they occurred, so do your own investigating. For example, if the user tells you that the system boots up with no error messages, but that the software still doesn't work, boot for yourself. You never know what the user might have overlooked.

Become a researcher   Following this rule is the most fun. When a computer problem arises that you can't easily solve, be as tenacious as a bulldog. Read, make phone calls, ask questions, then read more, make more calls, and ask more questions. Take advantage of every available resource, including online help, the Internet, documentation, technical support, and books such as this one. What you learn will be yours to take to the next problem. This is the real joy of computer troubleshooting. If you're good at it, you're always learning something new.

Write things down   Keep good notes as you're working. They'll help you think more clearly. Draw diagrams. Make lists. Write down what you're learning clearly and precisely. Later, when the entire problem gets "cold," these notes will be invaluable.

Reboot and start over   This is an important rule. Fresh starts are good for us and uncover events or steps that might have been overlooked. Take a break; get away from the problem. Begin again.

Establish your priorities   This rule can help make for a satisfied customer. Decide what your first priority is. For example, it might be to recover lost data, or to get the PC back up and running as soon as possible. Consult the user or customer for advice when practical.

Keep your cool and don't rush   In an emergency, protect the data and software by carefully considering your options before acting and by taking practical precautions to protect software and OS files. When a computer stops working, if unsaved data is still in memory or if data or software on the hard drive has not been backed up, look and think carefully before you leap! A wrong move can be costly. The best advice is not to hurry. Carefully plan your moves. Read the documentation if you're not sure what to do, and don't hesitate to ask for help. Don't simply try something, hoping it will work, unless you've run out of more intelligent alternatives!

Don't assume the worst   When it's an emergency and your only copy of data is on a hard drive that is not working, don't assume that the data is lost. Much can be done to recover data. Recall from Chapter 7 that if you want to recover lost data on a hard drive, don't write anything to the drive; you might write on top of lost data, eliminating all chances of recovery.

13

Know your starting point   Before trying to solve a computer problem, know for certain that the problem is what the user says it is. If the computer does not boot, carefully note where in the boot process it fails. If the computer does boot to an OS, before changing anything or taking anything apart, verify what does and what doesn't work, preferably in the presence of the user.

Gathering Information

When you are trying to solve a computer problem, the rules above will prepare you to apply a successful course of action. Before you take corrective action, however, you need to gather as much information about the situation as possible. This section covers ways to gather information on a computer problem you are troubleshooting.

Interacting with the User

Ask the user to explain exactly what happened when the computer stopped working. What procedure was taking place at the time? What had just happened? What recent changes did the user make? When did the computer last work? What has happened in the meantime? What error messages did the user see? Re-create the circumstances that existed when the computer stopped, and in as much detail as you can. Make no assumptions. All users make simple mistakes and then overlook them. If you realize that the problem was caused by the user's mistake, take the time to explain the proper procedures, so that the user understands what went wrong and what to do next time.

Use diplomacy and good manners when you work with a user to solve a problem. For example, if you suspect that the user dropped the PC, don't ask, "Did you drop the PC?" but rather put the question in a less accusatory manner: "Could the PC have been dropped?" If the user is sitting in front of the PC, don't assume you can take over the keyboard or mouse without permission. Also, if the user is present, ask permission before you make a software or hardware change, even if the user has just given you permission to interact with the PC.

When working at the user's desk, consider yourself a "guest" and follow these general guidelines:

- Don't "talk down" to or patronize the user.
- Don't take over the mouse or keyboard from the user without permission.
- Don't use the phone without permission.
- Don't pile your belongings and tools on top of the user's papers, books, etc.
- Accept personal inconvenience to accommodate the user's urgent business needs. For example, if the user gets an important call while you are working, delay your work until the call is over.

Whether or not you are at the user's desk, you should follow these guidelines when working with the user:

- Don't take drastic action such as formatting the hard drive before you ask the user about important data that may not be backed up.
- Provide users with alternatives where appropriate before making decisions for them.
- Protect the confidentiality of data on the PC such as business financial information.
- Don't disparage the user's choice of computer hardware or software.
- If you have made a mistake or must pass the problem on to someone with more expertise, be honest.

In some PC support situations, it is appropriate to consider yourself as a support to the user as well as to the PC. Your goals may include educating the user as well as repairing the computer. If you want users to learn something from a problem they caused, explain how to fix the problem and walk them through the process, if necessary. Don't fix the problem yourself unless they ask you to. It takes a little longer to train the user, but is more productive in the end because the user learns more and is less likely to repeat the mistake.

Ask the user questions to learn as much as you can about the problem. Refer to Chapter 3 for several sample questions, the most important being, "Can you show me how to reproduce the problem?"

Investigating the Problem on the Computer

After you have interviewed the user, the next step in troubleshooting is to gather as much information as you can about the problem by examining the computer. Find out these things:

- What operating system is installed?

- What physical components are installed? What processor, expansion cards, drives, and peripheral devices are installed? Is the PC connected to a network?

- What is the nature of the problem? Does the problem occur before or after the boot? Does an error message appear? Does the system hang at certain times? Start from a cold boot and do whatever you must do to cause the problem to occur. What are the specific steps you took to duplicate the problem?

- Can you duplicate the problem? Does the problem occur every time you do the above steps, or is the problem intermittent? Intermittent problems are generally more difficult to solve than problems that occur consistently.

Isolating the Problem

The next step in problem solving is to isolate the source of the problem by doing the following:

Consider the possibilities   Given what you've learned by interviewing the user, examining the computer, and duplicating the problem, consider what might be the source of the problem, which might or might not be obvious at this point. For example, if a user complains that his Word documents are getting corrupted, possible sources of the problem might be that the user does not know how to save documents properly, the software or the OS might be corrupted, the PC might have a virus, or the hard drive might be intermittently failing.

Eliminate the simple things first   In our example of the problem with corrupted Word documents, the most obvious or simplest source of the problem is that the user is not saving documents properly. Eliminate that possibility before you look at the software or the hard drive as the source of the problem. Another example is a CD-ROM drive that does not work. The problem might be that the CD is scratched or bent. Check that first.

Eliminate the unnecessary   This rule can be applied in many ways—for example, when the PC will not boot successfully. In this case, it is often unclear if the problem is with the hardware or software. When using Windows 9x, you can boot into safe mode (press F5 at startup) and eliminate much of the OS customized configuration. But if you still have problems, you may be able to boot from your bootable rescue disk.

13

Boot from a disk that you know is good and that has a minimal OS configuration (i.e., no Config.sys or Autoexec.bat files). By doing so, you eliminate all the application software loaded at startup on the PC and much of the OS. If the problem goes away, you can deduce that the problem is with (1) the software on the PC or (2) the hard drive and/or its subsystem that is used as the boot device.

If you suspect the problem is caused by faulty hardware, eliminate any unnecessary hardware devices. If the PC still boots with errors, disconnect the network card, the CD-ROM drive, the mouse, and maybe even the hard drive. You don't need to remove the CD-ROM or hard drive from the bays inside the case. Simply disconnect the data cable and the power cable. Remove the network card from its expansion slot. Remember to place it on an antistatic bag or grounded mat, not on top of the power supply or case. If the problem goes away, you know that one or more of these devices is causing the problem. Replace one at a time until the problem returns. Remember that the problem might be a resource conflict. If the network card worked well until the CD-ROM drive was reconnected, and now neither works, try the CD-ROM drive without the network card. If the CD-ROM drive now works, you most likely have a resource conflict.

Trade good for suspected bad   When diagnosing hardware problems, this method works well if you can draw from a group of parts that you know work correctly. Suppose the monitor does not work; it appears dead. The parts of the video subsystem are the video card, the power cord to the monitor, the cord from the monitor to the PC case, and the monitor itself. Also, don't forget that the video card is inserted into an expansion slot on the motherboard, and the monitor depends on electrical power. Suspect each of these five components to be bad; try them one at a time. Trade the monitor for one that you know works. Trade the power cord, trade the cord to the PC video port, move the video card to a new slot, and trade the video card. When you're trading a good component for a suspected bad one, work methodically by eliminating one component at a time. Don't trade the video card and the monitor and then turn on the PC to determine if they work. It's possible that both the card and the monitor are bad, but first assume that only one component is bad before you consider whether multiple components need trading.

In this situation, suppose you keep trading components in the video subsystem until you have no more variations. Next, take the entire subsystem—video card, cords, and monitor—to a PC that you know works, and plug each of them in. If they work, you have isolated the problem to the PC, not the video. Now turn your attention back to the PC: the motherboard, the software settings within the OS, the video driver, etc. Knowing that the video subsystem works on the good PC gives you a valuable tool. Compare the video driver on the good PC to the one on the bad PC. Make certain the CMOS settings, software settings, etc., are the same.

Trade suspected bad for good   An alternate approach works well in certain situations. If you have a working PC that is configured similarly to the one you are troubleshooting (a common situation in many corporate or educational environments), rather than trading good for suspected bad, you can trade suspected bad for good. Take each component that you suspect is bad and install it in the working PC. If the component works on the good PC, then you have eliminated it as a suspect. If the working PC breaks down, then you have probably identified the bad component.

Intermittent Problems

Intermittent problems can make troubleshooting challenging. The trick in diagnosing problems that come and go is to look for patterns or clues as to when the problems appear. If you or the user can't reproduce the problem at will, ask the user to keep a log of when the problems occur and exactly what messages appear. Show the user how to get a printed screen of the error messages when they appear. Here's the method:

- For simple DOS systems, the Print Screen key directs the displayed screen to the printer.

- In Windows, the Print Screen key copies the displayed screen to the Clipboard.

- Launch the Paint software accessory program and paste the contents of the Clipboard into the document. You might need to use the Zoom Out command on the document first. You can then print the document with the displayed screen, using Paint. You can also paste the contents of the Clipboard into a document created by a word-processing application such as Word.

PREVENTIVE MAINTENANCE

So far we have mainly discussed how to troubleshoot problems that have already occurred. In this section, we will discuss some steps you can take to prevent certain computer problems from occurring in the first place. The more preventive maintenance work you do to begin with, the fewer problems you are likely to have later, and the less troubleshooting and repair you will have to do.

13

If you are responsible for the PCs in an organization, make and implement a preventive maintenance plan to help prevent failures and reduce repair costs and downtime. In addition, you need a disaster recovery plan to manage failures when they occur. PC failures are caused by many different environmental and human factors, including heat, dust, magnetism, power supply problems, static electricity, human error (such as spilled liquids or an accidental change of setup and software configurations), and viruses. The goals of preventive maintenance are to reduce the likelihood that the events that cause PC failures will occur and to lessen the damage if they do occur.

When designing a preventive maintenance plan, consider what you can do to help prevent each cause of PC failure, and write into the plan the preventive actions you can take. Think through the situation caused by each problem. What would happen to the PC, the software, the data, the user's productivity, and so on, if a failure occurred? What would you do and what materials would you like to have in that situation? What can you do ahead of time to help make the situation less disastrous? Your answers to those questions will lead you to create effective preventive maintenance and disaster recovery plans. This section focuses on the preventive maintenance plan.

For example, consider the problem caused by a user accidentally changing the CMOS setup. What can you do to prevent that from occurring? If it does occur, how can you solve the problem? What can you do now to prepare for that event? By answering these three questions, you might arrive at these preventive maintenance and recovery procedures: (1) make a backup copy of setup to floppy disk, (2) label the disk and keep it in a safe place, (3) educate the user about the importance of not changing setup, and (4) keep a maintenance record of this PC, including the last time setup was backed up.

When a PC Is Your Permanent Responsibility

When you are the person responsible for a PC, either as the user or as the ongoing support person for the PC and the user, prepare for future troubleshooting situations. This section describes tasks and procedures for doing this.

Organize the Hard Drive Root Directory

In the root directory, keep only startup files for your system and necessary initialization files for the software. Software applications or files containing data don't belong in the root directory, although these applications will sometimes put initialization files in the root directory to be used when they first load. Keep application software files and their data in separate directories.

Filenames and extensions can help identify files that application software puts in the root directory to initialize itself. For example, Prodigy.bat is a DOS batch file that the Prodigy software uses to execute. Other software packages often use .bat files for this same purpose. Other file extensions to look for as initialization files are .ini, .bin, and .dat. If you are not sure of the purpose of one of these files, leave it in the root directory. Some software packages might not work if their file isn't in the root directory.

Create Rescue Disks

After you have cleaned up the root directory, make a set of rescue disks for the OS, and test your disks to make sure that they work; label them with the computer model, date, and OS version, and keep them available at the PC. If you have problems with the hard drive, you can use these disks to boot the PC.

Document All Setup Changes, Problems, and Solutions

When you first set up a new computer, start a record book about this computer, using either a file on disk or a notebook dedicated to this machine. In this notebook or file, record any changes in setup data as well as any problems you experience or maintenance that you do on this computer. Be diligent in keeping this notebook up to date, because it will be invaluable in diagnosing problems and upgrading the equipment. Keep a printed or handwritten record of all setup data for this machine, and store this with the hardware and software documentation.

You can also keep a record of all troubleshooting you do on a computer, in a word-processing document that lists all the problems you have encountered and the solutions you used. This will help you save time in troubleshooting problems you have encountered before. Store the document file on a floppy disk that you keep with the computer's documentation.

If you are not the primary user of the computer, you might want to keep the hardware documentation separate from the computer itself. Label the documentation so that you can easily identify that it belongs to this computer. Some support people tape a large envelope inside the computer case, containing important documentation and records specific to that computer. Keep the software reference manuals in a location that is convenient for users.

Record Setup Data

Keep a record of CMOS, showing hard drive type, drive configuration, and so on. Use a CMOS save program, or use Norton Utilities or similar third-party utility software to save the setup data to a floppy disk. This information should be stored on a floppy disk along with the software necessary to use it. Label the disk with the PC type, date, and any information needed to use the disk. Put the disk in a safe place.

If you don't have access to software to save setup data, use the Print Screen key to print the setup screens. If the Print Screen key does not work while you view setup on the PC, carefully copy down on paper all default settings and settings that you have changed. CMOS can lose these settings, and you will want to be able to reconstruct them when necessary. To do that, you would restore default settings and then use your written record to change the ones that you have manually set. Also keep a record of DIP switch settings and jumper settings on the motherboard. You can record these settings the first time you remove the cover of the machine. At the very least, record the settings before you change them! Keep all this information in your notebook.

When installing an expansion card, write down in your notebook information about the card, and keep the documentation that came with it in your notebook. If you must change jumper settings or DIP switches on the card, be certain to write down the original settings before you change anything. When the card is configured correctly, write down the correct settings in your notebook or on the documentation for the card. It is unlikely that a user will accidentally change these settings and then ask you to fix them, but you never know!

Take Practical Precautions to Protect Software and Data

If software files become corrupted, the most thorough approach is to restore the software from backups or to reinstall the software. To simplify both of these time-consuming tasks, here are a few suggestions:

- Before you install a new software package, back up the Windows 2000/XP system state.

- For Windows 9x, because many software packages overwrite files in the \Windows\System directory during installation, if you have the hard drive space, back up this entire directory before you begin an installation.

- Don't compress your hard drive, because compressed drives are more likely to become corrupted than those that are not compressed.
- Don't store data files in the same directory as the software, so that there will be less chance of accidentally deleting or overwriting a software file.

Back up original software   According to copyright laws, you have the right to make a backup of the installation CD or floppy disks in case the CD or disks fail. The copyright most likely does not allow you to distribute these backup copies to friends, but you can keep your copy in a safe place in the event that something happens to the originals.

Back up data on the hard drive   Don't expect the worst, but prepare for it! If important data is kept on the hard drive, back up that data on a regular basis to tape (using utility software designed for that purpose), to removable hard drives, to floppy disks, or to a company file server. The procedures and methods for keeping good backups are beyond the scope of this book, but the principle needs stating: don't keep important data on only one medium.

A Preventive Maintenance Plan

In addition to the guidelines given above, it is important to develop an overall preventive maintenance plan. If your company has established written guidelines for PC preventive maintenance, read them and follow the necessary procedures to make them work. If your company does not have an established plan, make your own. A preventive maintenance plan tends to evolve from a history or pattern of malfunctions within the organization. For example, dusty environments can mean more maintenance, whereas a clean environment can mean less maintenance. Table 13-2 lists some guidelines for developing a preventive maintenance plan that may work for you.

 Dust is not good for a PC because it acts like a blanket, insulating PC parts, which can cause them to overheat; therefore, ridding the PC of dust is an important part of preventive maintenance. Some PC technicians don't like to use a vacuum inside a PC because they're concerned about ESD that the vacuum might produce. Use compressed air to blow the dust out of the chassis, power supply, and fan, or use a special antistatic vacuum designed to be used around sensitive equipment.

Table 13-2   Guidelines for developing a PC preventive maintenance plan

Component	Maintenance	How Often
Inside the case	• Make sure air vents are clear. • Use compressed air to blow the dust out of the case, or use a vacuum to clean vents, power supply, and fan. • Ensure that chips and expansion cards are firmly seated.	Yearly
CMOS setup	• Keep a backup record of setup (for example, using Norton Utilities or CMOS Save).	Whenever changes are made

Table 13-2 Guidelines for developing a PC preventive maintenance plan (continued)

Component	Maintenance	How Often
Floppy drive	• Only clean the floppy drive when the drive does not work.	When the drive fails
Hard drive	• Perform regular backups. • Automatically execute a virus scan program at startup. • Defragment the drive and recover lost clusters regularly. • Don't allow smoking around the PC. • Place the PC where it will not be jarred, kicked, or bumped.	At least weekly At least daily Monthly Always Always
Keyboard	• Keep the keyboard clean. • Keep the keyboard away from liquids.	Monthly Always
Mouse	• Clean the mouse rollers and ball.	Monthly
Monitor	• Clean the screen with a soft cloth. • Make sure air vents are clear.	At least monthly Always
Printers	• Clean out the dust and bits of paper, using compressed air and a vacuum. Small pieces of paper can be removed with tweezers, preferably insulated ones. • Clean the paper and ribbon paths with a soft, lint-free cloth. • Don't re-ink ribbons or use recharged toner cartridges. • If the printer uses an ozone filter, replace it as recommended by the manufacturer.	At least monthly or as recommended by the manufacturer
UPS/Suppressors	• Run weak battery test • Run diagnostic test	As recommended by manufacturer
Software	• If directed by your employer, check that only authorized software is present. • Regularly delete files from the Recycle Bin and \Temp directories.	At least monthly
Written record	• Keep a record of all software, including version numbers and the OS installed on the PC. • Keep a record of all hardware components installed, including hardware settings. • Record when and what preventive maintenance is performed. • Record any repairs done to the PC.	Whenever changes are made

13

The general idea of preventive maintenance is to do what you can to make a PC last longer and give as little trouble as possible. You may also be responsible for ensuring that data is secure and backed up, that software copyrights are not violated, and that users are supported. As with any plan, when designing your preventive maintenance plan, first define your overall goals, and then design the plan accordingly. The guidelines listed in Table 13-2 address primarily the problems that prevent a PC from lasting long and from performing well.

When Moving Equipment

When shipping a PC, remember that rough handling can cause damage, as can exposure to water, heat, and cold. The PC can also be misplaced, lost, or stolen. When you are preparing a PC for shipping, take extra precautions to protect it and its data. Also, remember to not lift heavy objects without using a back brace. Follow these general guidelines when preparing to ship a PC:

- Back up the hard drive onto a tape cartridge or other backup medium separate from your computer. If you don't have access to a medium that can back up the entire drive, back up important system and configuration files to a floppy disk. Whatever you do, don't ship a PC that has the only copy of important data on the hard drive, or data that should be secured from unauthorized access.

- Remove any removable disks, tape cartridges, or CDs from the drives. Make sure that the tapes or disks holding the backup data are secured and protected during transit. Consider shipping them separately.

- Turn off power to the PC and all other devices.

- Disconnect power cords from the electrical outlet and the devices. Disconnect all external devices from the computer.

- If you think someone might have trouble later identifying which cord or cable belongs to which device or connection, label the cable connections with white tape or white labels.

- Coil all cords and secure them with plastic ties or rubber bands.

- Pack the computer, monitor, and all devices in their original shipping cartons or similar boxes with enough packing material to protect them.

- Purchase insurance on the shipment. Postal insurance is not expensive and can save you a lot of money if materials are damaged in transit.

Disposing of Used Equipment

As a PC technician, it will often be your responsibility to dispose of used equipment and consumables, including batteries, printer toner cartridges, and monitors. Table 13-3 lists such items and how to dispose of them. Manufacturer documentation and local environmental regulators can also provide disposal instructions or guidance. Monitors and power supplies can contain a charge even after the devices are unplugged. To discharge the capacitors in either device, place a screwdriver across a hot prong and the ground prong of the electrical connections, as shown in Figure 13-1. To discharge the actual CRT in a monitor, the monitor must be opened. Ask a technician trained to fix monitors to do this for you.

A **material safety data sheet (MSDS)** explains how to properly handle substances such as chemical solvents. An MSDS includes information such as physical data, toxicity, health effects, first aid, storage, disposal, and spill procedures. It comes packaged with the chemical, or you can order one from the manufacturer, or find one on the Internet (see *www.ilpi.com/msds*).

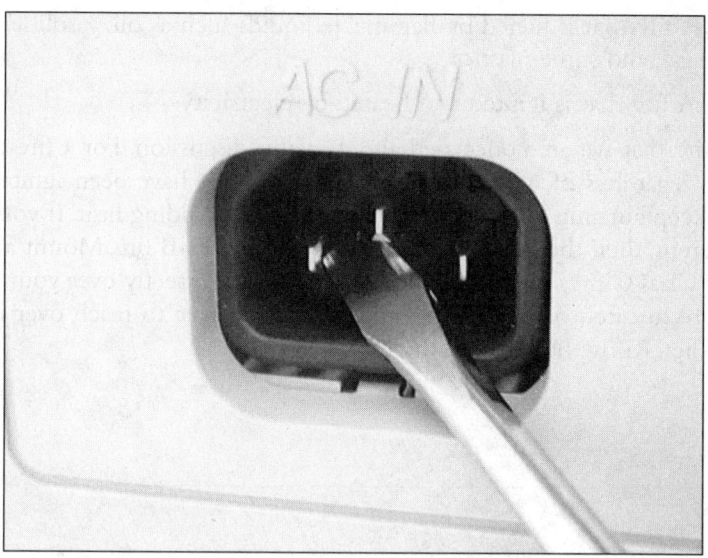

Figure 13-1 Discharge the capacitors in a monitor before disposal

Table 13-3 Computer parts and how to dispose of them

Part	How to Dispose
Alkaline batteries including AAA, AA, A, C, D, and 9 volt	Dispose of these batteries in the regular trash, but first check to see if there are recycling facilities for them available in your area.
Button batteries used in digital cameras, Flash Path, and other small equipment Battery packs used in notebooks	These batteries can contain silver oxide, mercury, lithium, or cadmium and are considered hazardous waste. Dispose of these by returning them to the original dealer or by taking them to a recycling center. To recycle them, pack them separately from other items. If you don't have a recycling center nearby, contact your county for local regulations for disposal.
Laser printer toner cartridges	Return these to the manufacturer or dealer to be recycled.
Ink-jet printer cartridges Computers Monitors Chemical solvents and cans	Check with local county or environmental officials for laws and regulations in your area for proper disposal of these items. The county might provide a recycling center that will receive them. Before disposing of a monitor, first discharge the monitor.

Fire Extinguishers

No discussion of preventive maintenance would be complete without mentioning the importance of having a fire extinguisher handy that is rated to handle fires that are ignited by electricity. The National Fire Protection Association (NFPA), an organization that creates standards for fire safety, says a fire has one of three ratings:

- *Class A.* A fire that is fueled by ordinary combustible materials such as wood, trash, or clothes

- *Class B.* A fire that is fueled by flammable liquids such as oil, gasoline, kerosene, propane gas, and some plastics
- *Class C.* A fire that is ignited and heated by electricity

It's the Class C fire that we are concerned about in this discussion. For a fire to be rated as a Class C fire, regardless of what is burning, the fire must have been ignited by electricity and must keep burning because electrical energy is providing heat. If you take away the electrical current, then the fire becomes a Class A or Class B fire. Mount a fire extinguisher rated for Class C fires near your workbench but not directly over your work area. If equipment were to catch on fire, you wouldn't want to have to reach over it to get to the fire extinguisher. Know how to use the extinguisher.

CHAPTER SUMMARY

- ❏ Tools for solving computer problems include a repair kit, bootable disk, and diagnostic hardware and software.
- ❏ Two important rules when troubleshooting are to eliminate unnecessary hardware and software and to trade components you know are good for those you suspect may be bad.
- ❏ Learn to ask the user good questions (using good manners and diplomacy) that help you understand the history behind the problem.
- ❏ One good method of solving intermittent problems is to keep a log of when they occur.
- ❏ Problems with computers can be divided into two general groups: those that prevent the computer from booting successfully and those that occur after the computer boots.
- ❏ Diagnostic cards give error codes based on POST errors.
- ❏ Diagnostic software performs many tests on a PC. Some of these software programs use their own proprietary operating systems.
- ❏ Utility software can update and repair device drivers and applications. Some utility software downloads these updates from the Internet.
- ❏ Keep a bootable disk containing the root directory files of your system.
- ❏ Keep backups of hard drive data and software.
- ❏ Keep a written record of the CMOS setup, or save it on disk.
- ❏ PC failures are caused by many environmental and human factors, including heat, dust, magnetism, power supply problems, static electricity, spilled liquids, viruses, and human error.
- ❏ The goals of preventive maintenance are to make PCs last longer and work better, protect data and software, and reduce the cost of repairs.

❏ A PC preventive maintenance plan includes blowing dust from the inside of the computer case, keeping a record of setup data, backing up the hard drive, and cleaning the mouse, monitor, and keyboard.

❏ Protecting software and hardware documentation is an important preventive maintenance chore.

❏ Never ship a PC when the only copy of important data is on its hard drive.

❏ A Class C fire extinguisher is rated to put out a fire ignited and kept burning by electricity.

KEY TERMS

diagnostic cards	**diagnostic software**	**material safety data sheet (MSDS)**

13

14

PURCHASING A PC OR BUILDING YOUR OWN

In this chapter, you will learn:

◆ Some guidelines to use when purchasing a PC

◆ How to prepare for assembling a PC yourself

◆ How to assemble a PC from separately purchased parts

This chapter presents guidelines for purchasing a new PC and detailed, step-by-step procedures for building a PC from parts. If you need a computer for your own personal use, consider assembling it yourself, not necessarily to save money, but to benefit in other ways. If you don't want to build a PC, you must choose between purchasing a brand-name PC or a clone.

After-sales service and support are probably the most important criteria to consider when purchasing a PC. In general, a brand-name PC (such as IBM or Compaq) might cost more but generally will provide better service and support than a PC built with parts manufactured by companies whose names you don't recognize. Important reasons for choosing to build your own PC are the knowledge to be gained and the complete control over every part purchased, which will allow you to make your own customized integrated system.

SELECTING A PERSONAL COMPUTER TO MEET YOUR NEEDS

So far, this book has been full of information concerning which computers, peripheral devices, operating systems, and software to buy and how to manage and maintain them once they are yours. However, hardware and software are changing daily, and it's important to stay informed if you make buying decisions or give purchasing advice on an ongoing basis.

Sometimes it is appropriate to upgrade an existing PC rather than purchase a new one. Consider adding more memory, upgrading the CPU or adding a second CPU, adding a second hard drive, upgrading the video card, upgrading the motherboard, and adding additional fans for cooling. Generally, if the cost of the upgrade does not exceed half the value of the current system, an upgrade is appropriate if the resulting system does not contain legacy components that prevent the upgraded system from performing well. Don't upgrade a computer system that is older than five years as the cost of upgrade will probably exceed the value of the current system. In this case, a new PC is your best option.

You can choose one of three alternatives when selecting a PC: buy a brand-name PC, buy a clone, or buy parts and assemble a PC yourself—which, in effect, results in your own personally designed clone. A brand-name PC, sometimes called an **IBM-compatible PC**, is a PC manufactured by a company with a widely recognized name such as Compaq, Packard Bell, Dell, Gateway, or IBM. A **clone** is generally understood to mean a PC that has been assembled by a local company with parts manufactured by several companies. There are advantages and disadvantages to purchasing both brand-name and clone PCs, in the areas of warranties, service contracts, and ease of obtaining replacement and additional parts. For instance, while it may seem advantageous that brand-name PCs and most clones come with some software already installed, the software is not necessarily standard, brand-name software. The preinstalled software can be any variety of shareware, unknown software, and so forth, and the documentation and original installation disks for the software may not be included in the total package.

When selecting a computer system that will include both hardware and software, begin by taking an overall view of the decisions you must make. Start by answering these questions:

- How will the computer be used now and in the future?

- What functionality do you want the computer to have (within its intended use)?

- What hardware and software do you need, to meet this functionality?

- What is your budget?

- If you determine that a clone meets your needs, do you want to assemble it yourself?

In order to make the best possible decision, consider the first question to be the most important, the second question the next most important, and so on. For example, if you intend to use the computer for multimedia presentations and accessing the Internet, the functionality required is considerably different from that of a computer used for software development.

After you have identified the intended purpose of the computer, list the functionality required to meet the needs of the intended purpose. For example, if the computer is to be used for playing games, some required functionality might be:

- Ability of the hardware to support game software

- Excellent video and sound

- Sophisticated input methods, such as a joystick or controller

If the computer is to be used for software development, required functionality might include:

- The ability to support the standard hardware and software environment that most customers using the developed software might have

- The ability to run software development tools and hardware to support the software

- A high-quality monitor and a comfortable keyboard and mouse for long work hours

- A removable, high-capacity storage device for easy transfer and storage of developed software

- Reliable warranty and service to guarantee minimal "downtime"

Once the required functionality is defined, the next step, defining what hardware and software are needed, is much easier. For example, if a comfortable keyboard designed for long work hours is required, begin by researching the different types of keyboards available, and try out a few in the stores if necessary. It would be a mistake to purchase the cheapest keyboard in the store for this intended purpose. However, for game playing, an expensive, comfortable keyboard is probably not needed because most games use other input devices. Spending your resources on a sophisticated joystick probably makes more sense.

As noted above, the least possible amount of downtime is a required functionality for software development. This is also true for many business-use computers, and it is the most important reason a business chooses a brand-name computer over a clone.

Purchasing a Brand-Name PC vs. a Clone

As you have most likely noticed, brand-name PCs generally cost more than clone PCs with similar features. One reason for this is that you are paying extra money for after-sales service. For example, some PCs come with a three-year warranty, a 24-hour-service help line with a toll-free number, and delivery of parts to your place of business. A clone manufacturer might also give good service, but this may be due to the personalities of a few employees, rather than to company policies. Most likely, clone company policies are not as liberal and all-encompassing as those of a brand-name manufacturer. Most brand-name manufacturers provide additional support generally not provided by clone manufacturers, such as functional Web sites, updated drivers and utilities, and online troubleshooting or user manuals.

14

On the other hand, many brand-name manufacturers use nonstandard parts with their hardware and nonstandard approaches to setting up their systems, making their computers more proprietary than clones. One of the most common ways for a brand-name manufacturer to make its computer more proprietary is to put components, such as support for video, directly on the motherboard rather than use more generic expansion cards.

Additionally, rather than being updated by a setup program in BIOS, the CMOS setup program might be stored on the hard drive. The shape and size of the computer case might be such that a standard motherboard does not fit; only the brand-name board will do. These practices can make upgrading and repairing brand-name PCs more difficult, because you are forced to use the brand-name parts and brand-name service. Also, in some areas of the country, it may be difficult to find authorized dealers and service centers for brand-name PCs.

Selecting Software

When selecting software, review the required functionality you identified, which drives your decisions about software selection. Choose the operating system first. When choosing application software, consider these questions:

- What do you want the software to do? (This will be defined by your answer to the functionality question above.)

- Is compatibility with other software or data required? Consider compatibility with your own existing system as well as with office systems if you telecommute.

- Is training available, if you do not already have the skills needed to use the software?

- How good is the software's documentation?

- What are the company's upgrade policies?

- How well known or popular is the software? (The more popular, the more likely you'll find good training materials, trained people, technical support, and other compatible software and hardware.)

Caution is in order if you are buying a brand-name or clone computer that has preinstalled software that you are not familiar with. The software may not provide the functionality that you need, and may not have good documentation or reliable upgrades or support. Unless you feel that you have the skill to manage this software, you're probably better off staying with mainstream-market software. One way to identify which brand of software is the most prevalent in the industry is to browse the computer books section of a local bookstore, looking for the software that has the most "how to" books written about it. Also see trade magazines, the Internet, and your local retailer.

 A good resource for reviews of hardware and software components, plus free trial downloads of many software programs, is *www.cnet.com* by CNET Networks, Inc.

Selecting Hardware

The two most important criteria to consider when selecting hardware are compatibility and functionality. Begin by considering the motherboard. (See Chapter 4 for more information about how to select one.) Here are other topics you should consider:

- Use only 100% Plug and Play components and be certain the BIOS is ACPI compliant.

- If you intend to use the PC for multimedia applications, including games, you will want a high-speed CPU, a high-quality video card, and plenty of memory.

- If you plan to use the PC for heavy network use, buy a PC with plenty of processing power.

- If you connect to the Internet using a modem, buy a high-quality one.

- When selecting a computer case, keep in mind that tower cases generally offer more room than desktop units and are easier to work with when adding new devices. Make sure the case has a reset button and, if security is an issue, a key lock in order to limit access to the inside of the case. Some cases even have a lock on the floppy drive to prevent unauthorized booting from a floppy disk.

- Select a power supply that will supply enough power for your components. (Refer to Chapter 3 for help on calculating the total power needs of your system.)

- In addition to the power supply fan and CPU fan, consider buying an auxiliary fan for additional cooling. Fans are not expensive and can help keep a lower temperature inside the case.

Selecting a Total Package

When selecting a complete computer package, including hardware and software, consider these points:

14

- What hardware and software are included? Are the hardware and software compatible with those found on the general market? (For example, if you wanted to upgrade your video card or word processor, how difficult would that be?)

- What is the warranty and return or exchange policy?

- What on-site or local service is available? Do you know of anyone who has used this service, and was it satisfactory?

- Is the system ACPI and Energy Star compliant? (For information about ACPI and Energy Star, see Chapter 3.)

- What software comes preinstalled?

- What documentation or manuals come with the system?

- Does the manufacturer maintain a Web site with useful support features, utilities, and updates?

- Does the motherboard allow for expansion of RAM?

- What expansion slots are not being used? (Always allow for some room to grow.)

- Can features such as video on the motherboard be disabled if necessary? (Refer back to Chapter 4 for other guidelines on selecting motherboards.)

- How much does the system cost?

When considering price, keep in mind that high-priced to middle-range-priced PCs are most likely to be network-compatible and easily expandable; they offer a broader range of support, and have had extensive testing of vendor products for reliability and compatibility. Low-priced PCs may not have been tested for network compatibility; they offer a limited range of support, and the quality of components may not be as high.

> **CAUTION**
>
> Beware of pirated software installed on preassembled PCs. Vendors sometimes sell counterfeit software by installing unauthorized software on computers. This practice is called **hard-disk loading**. Vendors have even been known to counterfeit disk labels and Certificates of Authenticity. Look for these warning signs that software purchased from vendors is pirated: it has no end-user license, mail-in product registration card, documentation, or original CDs; documentation is photocopied, or disks have handwritten labels. Accept nothing less than the original installation CDs for all installed software.

When considering preinstalled software, remember that sometimes unneeded software is more of a hindrance than a help, needlessly taking up space. For example, it is not uncommon for a brand-name computer to come with three or four applications for Internet access (for example, America Online, CompuServe, and Microsoft Network) because of licensing agreements distributors have with online providers. Typically, only one is needed. Sometimes having more than one on your computer can cause problems.

PREPARING TO BUILD YOUR OWN PC

Assembling your own PC takes time, skill, and research, but it can be a great learning experience. You might even want to consider it your "rite of passage" toward being a PC technician. All the skills needed to be a PC technician are tested: research, knowledge of user needs and the computer market, planning, organization, patience, confidence, problem solving, and extensive knowledge of both hardware and software. If you intend to become a corporate-level technician, you most certainly should put together at least one whole PC before starting your first job.

However, don't build your PC in order to save money, because you probably won't. The total price of all parts usually about equals the price of a comparable clone PC that is pre-built. Here are a few good reasons to assemble your own PC:

- The whole process can be quite fun.

- Knowledge is power. The knowledge and experience gained in researching the parts to buy, studying the documentation, and finally assembling the PC can't be overemphasized.

- When you buy all the parts and software for a PC individually, you are also getting the documentation for each hardware component. This is most likely not the case when you buy a PC already assembled. If you plan to upgrade your PC later, having this documentation can be very valuable.

- Many prebuilt PCs come with software preloaded. You may not receive the original CDs or disks or the documentation for these programs, which can be a problem when you try to maintain your system, and most likely indicates that the software is illegally distributed. (Don't accept software preinstalled unless it also includes the installation disks and documentation.) When you buy each software package individually, you are assured that the distribution is legal, and you have the installation disks, CDs, and documentation.

- When you purchase each computer part individually, you are more likely to understand exactly what you are buying, and you can be more particular about the selection of each component. You have control over the brand and features of each component in the PC.

Here are a few reasons why you might not want to build your own PC:

- If you are in a rush to get a PC up and running, assembling your own is probably not a good idea, especially if you are a first-time builder. The process takes time and requires patience, and the first time you do it, you most likely will make a few mistakes that will need to be resolved.

- Individual parts may be warrantied, but if you build your own PC, there is no overall warranty on the PC. If a warranty or a service agreement is important, then look for a ready-built PC with these services included.

- Clone PCs have been tested to ensure that individual components are compatible. When building your own PC, it is possible you might select components that are incompatible. For this reason, buy high-quality mainstream components to best ensure compatibility.

- Don't plan to assemble a PC for the first time unless you have access to an experienced technician or a technical service center you can consult if you encounter a problem you cannot resolve. For example, you might buy all the parts from a store that has a service center. The store might offer to assemble the PC for you for a charge ($50 to $75 is about right). If you find you cannot resolve a problem, you can always go back to the store for this service.

- Remember, don't assemble the PC to save money, because you probably won't.

14

Getting Ready for Assembly: Selecting Parts

If you have decided to buy parts and assemble a PC, expect the process to take some time. The motherboard and expansion cards are full of connections, ports, and perhaps jumpers, and you must read the documentation carefully to determine just how to configure the motherboard and all components to work together. Technicians in service centers can assemble a PC in less than an hour, but they have already assembled the same group of parts many times!

Planning the assembly of a PC is like packing for a camping trip to a remote location. You must plan for everything you will need before you begin. As you select and purchase each part, two things are important: functionality and compatibility with other parts.

Almost every computer needs these essentials: motherboard, CPU, RAM, hard drive, CD-ROM drive (or you can substitute a DVD drive or CD-RW drive for added functionality), floppy drive, case, power supply, video card, monitor, keyboard, and mouse. And, most likely, you will also want a sound card and modem. Make careful and informed decisions about every part you buy. Selecting each component requires reviewing your functionality, compatibility, and budget needs and determining what parts meet your criteria. Select the motherboard first, and then select the rest of the parts around this one most important component.

When selecting parts, including the motherboard, carefully examine the documentation. Look for good documentation that you can understand without struggling. When buying parts for your first assembly, you should probably not use mail order. Buy from a reputable local dealer who will allow you to examine a part and look at the documentation, and who is willing and able to answer any technical questions you may have. Know the return policy of the store and the manufacturer's warranty for the part.

If you can buy the motherboard, CPU, and memory from the same dealer, who can help you determine that all three are compatible, do so to avoid later problems with compatibility. The documentation for the motherboard is quite valuable. Make sure it's readable and complete. If it's not, look on the manufacturer's Web site for additional documentation before making the purchase. Does the motherboard support USB, FireWire, or SCSI? The CPU will need at least one fan or cooler. Does the entire system need additional fans? Ask the dealer for recommendations, and read the documentation for the CPU. Often a dealer will sell a motherboard with the CPU and fan already installed and jumpers on the motherboard set correctly.

After you have selected the motherboard, RAM, and CPU, select the case and accompanying power supply. Remember the two rules: the case must meet your predetermined functionality, and it must be compatible with other parts (especially the motherboard). Check the motherboard documentation for extra power cords the CPU might require, and make sure the power supply provides these. Next, select the hard drive and other drives.

If the video logic is not included on the motherboard (for clone motherboards it probably will not be), select the video card next, and make sure that you have an AGP slot to accommodate it. There are several types of AGP slots. Match your AGP video card to the type your motherboard provides. Last, select other peripherals, including a mouse, keyboard, and monitor.

Getting Ready for Assembly: Final Preparations

When all parts are purchased, prepare for the assembly well. Prepare a work area that is well lit and uncluttered. Read all the documentation and plan the assembly through, from beginning to end, before you start. If you have questions or are unsure how to proceed, find the answers to your concerns before you begin. For example, if you're not sure how to set the jumpers on the motherboard, even after you have read the documentation, take the documentation to your technical support (dealer, service center, a knowledgeable friend) and ask for help in interpreting the settings in the documentation before you start the work. Often you can find a detailed diagram of the motherboard on the manufacturer's Web site, complete with proper settings for specific CPUs.

CAUTION

While working, don't get careless about protecting yourself and your equipment against static electricity (review the safety precautions in Chapter 3). Always use the ground strap on your wrist.

BUILDING A PERSONAL COMPUTER, STEP BY STEP

This section is a step-by-step, detailed description of building a simple Pentium 4 PC that includes a hard drive, a floppy drive, and a CD-ROM drive. Depending on what you have decided you want your computer for, and what functionality and budget you are operating with, you may choose to build a different PC, with a different CPU and different parts. Documentation and manufacturer Web sites are, as always, good resources for installation procedures and general information on specific parts. While we do not have the space to provide instructions on the assembly of many different PCs, the following examples will provide you with background and guidance, and demonstrate how to approach the task at hand.

The text describes some of the problems actually encountered during an assembly. I wish I could invite you to work beside me, reading the documentation for that jumper setting, deciding just which card should go in which slot for the best overall fit, and enjoying the pleasure of turning on the PC and seeing it boot up for the first time. However, the best I can do is introduce you to the experience through this book. My hope is that you will one day have the opportunity to experience it for yourself.

Overview of the Assembly Process

Once the research is done and the parts purchased, organize everything you'll need to assemble the PC. Have the parts with the accompanying documentation and software available, together with your PC tools. You'll need a safe place to work, with a ground mat and ground strap. Be careful to follow all the safety rules and precautions discussed in this chapter and in previous chapters. Work methodically and keep things organized. If you find yourself getting frustrated, take a break. Remember, you want the entire experience to be fun!

14

The general process for putting together a computer is as follows:

1. Verify that you have all parts that you plan to install.

2. Prepare the computer case by installing the case fans and I/O shield, removing the plates that cover the drive bays, and installing the spacers.

3. Install the drives.

4. Determine proper configuration settings for the motherboard, and set any jumpers or switches on the motherboard.

5. Install the CPU and CPU fan.

6. Install RAM into the appropriate slots on the motherboard.

7. Install the motherboard and attach cabling.

8. Install the video card.

9. Plug the computer into a power source, and attach the monitor, keyboard, and mouse.

10. Boot the computer, check the CMOS settings, and make sure that everything is configured and working properly before replacing the computer case. At this point you are ready to install the OS and any other software you want to have on your system.

Step 1: Verify You Have All the Parts

For the PC we are building in this chapter, the parts purchased before beginning the assembly are listed below. The parts to be installed inside the case and some tools are shown in Figure 14-1.

- ATX case with power supply (ATX12V-compliant power supply required for this motherboard, because the Pentium 4 requires a supplemental power connector)

- Motherboard (Intel Desktop Board D850MV)

- Pentium 4 CPU that runs at 1.5 GHz

- Two 128-bit RIMMs

- AGP video card

- Hard drive (20 GB 5400 RPM ATA100)

- Floppy drive

- CD-ROM drive

- Monitor, mouse, and keyboard

- Cables, cords, drivers, and documentation

Motherboard with
CPU installed

CPU fan
Video card
Drive cables
Auxiliary fan

Ground bracelet

RIMMs

C-RIMMs

Drives and documentation

CD-ROM drive
Hard drive
Floppy drive

Figure 14-1   Components needed to assemble a PC

Before you begin installation, make sure you have everything you need to complete it, including tools, documentation, and all the components. As we discussed in earlier chapters, it is a good idea to have a notebook for all product documentation, lists of the components and settings for your PC, and detailed installation and troubleshooting notes.

Step 2: Prepare the Computer Case

Before you can install components in a computer case, you must prepare the case. Figure 14-2 shows the empty computer case before any components are installed in it. The first step to prepare the case is to install an auxiliary case fan, as shown in Figure 14-3. In addition to the power supply fan and the CPU fan, an auxiliary case fan over the vent underneath the power supply will help keep the temperature inside the case at a level that will not damage the CPU. Position the fan in place over the vent and secure it with four screws.

14

Figure 14-2   The empty computer case

Figure 14-3   Install at least one case fan to provide additional cooling

Next, install the spacers (Figure 14-4) in the holes on the bottom of the case, to keep the motherboard from touching the case and possibly shorting out. When you install the motherboard, the holes on the motherboard will line up with the spacers, as shown in Figure 14-4. Hold the motherboard over the case so you can see where the holes in the motherboard line up with holes in the case, and install spacers in these holes in the case.

Install a spacer in every hole in the case that lines up with a hole in the motherboard, so that all the holes in the motherboard can have screws. You should use at least four spacers and will probably use six. However many you use, you will end up with some holes in the case that you don't use. The other holes are there so that the case can accommodate more than one motherboard form factor.

Spacer

Hole in motherboard

Figure 14-4   The spacers line up with the holes on the motherboard and keep it from touching the case

The next step to prepare the case is to install an I/O shield. Recall that in Chapter 4 you learned how to install an I/O shield in a computer case to help protect ports coming off the motherboard. If the case comes with several shields, as it probably will, remember to select the one that correctly fits the ports on your motherboard.

14

Step 3: Install Drives

The next step is to install drives in the case. Some technicians prefer to install the motherboard first, but we are installing the drives before the motherboard because, if the motherboard is already in the case before the drives are installed, there is the risk of dropping one of the drives on the motherboard and damaging it. Also, once the drives are installed, we will not attach power cords until after the motherboard is in place so that the cords will not be in the way when we install the motherboard.

Looking back at Figure 14-2, you can see that this case has a group of wide bays in which we will install the CD-ROM drive and a narrow removable bay in which we will install the floppy drive and hard drive. In Chapter 7 you saw how you can remove a narrow removable bay and install the drives in the bay outside the case, then put the bay with the drives installed back in the case. This case is better designed than the one in Chapter 7 and has a cutout on the back side of the removable bay so that you can install screws on both sides of the drives without removing the bay. The cutout is labeled in Figure 14-2.

When installing drives, be sure to use short screws that will not protrude too deeply into the drive and damage it. Follow these steps to install the drives:

Set IDE Jumpers on Each IDE Drive in the System

Before we get into the details of installing the drives, let's quickly review IDE installations, previously covered in Chapter 7. Recall that there can be up to two IDE controllers on a motherboard, the primary and secondary IDE controller. Each controller can support up to two drives, a master and a slave, for a total of up to four IDE drives in a system. When possible, leave the hard drive as the single drive on one controller so that performance is not affected. Recall that each IDE drive must be configured as single, master, slave, or cable select. Configuration is normally done by setting jumpers on the drive housing, and the explanation of the jumper settings is most often printed somewhere on the housing. You saw how to set jumpers on an IDE drive in Chapter 7. In our installation, we set the IDE hard drive as the single drive on the primary controller and the IDE CD-ROM drive as a single drive on the secondary controller. Following the settings label on each drive, set the jumpers on each drive to master.

Install the CD-ROM Drive

We decided to install the CD-ROM drive in the top wide bay to keep it up out of the way. Follow these steps and be sure you are wearing your ground bracelet as you work:

- Remove the faceplates from the front of the upper bay.
- Install the CD-ROM drive in the bay, aligning it with the front of the case and securing it with screws, as shown in Figure 14-5. (After the motherboard is installed, we'll also install the CD-ROM data cable, power cord, and audio cord.)

Install the Hard Drive

This case has only a single bay (the lowest bay) that does not have an opening to the front of the case. Install the hard drive in this last position. Position the hard drive flush with the front of the bay so that it will butt up against the computer case. Secure it with four screws, two on each side of the drive. Note that for this computer case, because there is a cutout on the back side of the removable bay, you do not have to remove the bay to install the drive.

Install the Floppy Drive

Follow these steps to install the floppy drive:

- Place the floppy drive in the bay, noting where the screw holes in the drive align with the side of the bay. On this case, the floppy drive is recessed in the case, and it will fit snugly against the front of the drive bay. On many cases, however, you

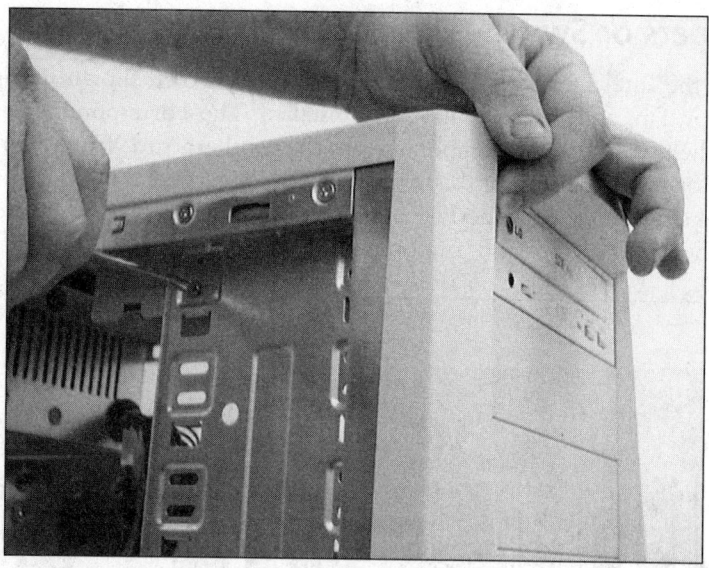

Figure 14-5   Align the CD-ROM drive with the front of the case and secure it with screws

will have to align the floppy drive with the bay and the front of the case so the drive fits flush with the front of the case. How this front cover alignment is done depends on the case design.

- Secure the floppy drive to the bay with four screws, two on each side of the bay (see Figure 14-6).

Figure 14-6   After aligning the drives, secure them with screws

Step 4: Set Jumpers or Switches on the Motherboard

We are installing the Intel Desktop Board D850MV motherboard shown in Figure 14-7 with the processor, fan, and memory modules installed. The corresponding diagram in Figure 14-8 will help you identify components on the motherboard. When working with the motherboard or other circuit boards, be particularly concerned about the possibility of ESD damage. Make sure you are properly grounded at all times. Also, try not to touch edge connectors or other sensitive portions of components.

Figure 14-7   The Intel D850MV motherboard

A   ADI AD1885 audio codec
B   ATAPI auxiliary line-in connector
C   AGP connector
D   ATAPI CD-ROM connector
E   Front panel audio connector
F   Chassis intrusion connector
G   12 V processor core voltage connector
H   Processor fan connector (CPU fan)
    (tachometer input)
I   Intel 82850 Memory Controller Hub (MCH)
J   Processor socket
K   RIMM sockets
L   RIMM fan connector (fan 1)
M   Power connector
N   Disk drive connector

O   Primary IDE connector
P   Secondary IDE connector
Q   Front panel USB connector
R   Alternate power/sleep LED connector
S   Chassis fan connector (fan 2)
    (tachometer input)
T   Battery
U   Speaker
V   BIOS configuration jumper
W   SCSI hard drive activity LED connector
X   Intel 82801BA I/O Controller Hub (ICH2)
Y   PCI bus add-in card connectors
Z   Communication and Networking Riser
    (CNR) (optional)
AA Chassis fan (fan 3)

Figure 14-8   Diagram of the Intel D850MV motherboard

14

Figure 14-9 shows the ports on the back of this motherboard. There are ports for the mouse and the keyboard, four USB ports, a 25-pin parallel port, two 9-pin serial ports, audio and network ports. Note that this motherboard has embedded support for sound and Ethernet, eliminating the need for separate expansion cards to add these features.

Parallel port

RJ-45 Ethernet port

Sound ports

Two USB ports
Two serial ports
Two USB ports
Keyboard and mouse ports

Figure 14-9 The ports on the D850MV motherboard include network and sound ports

The first thing to do when preparing a motherboard to go into the case is to study the motherboard's documentation and determine what jumpers or DIP switches are on the board and how to set them. Many motherboards support more than one processor or system bus speed, and jumper or DIP switch settings depend on which processor you are installing at what speed. The motherboard we are using in this chapter supports only the Pentium 4 processor, which can run at 1.4, 1.5, 1.6, 1.7, or 1.8 GHz, and the system bus runs at 400 MHz. There are no jumpers or DIP switches to set to configure the processor or bus speed. There is one set of three jumpers that is used to configure the BIOS. The position of this group is shown in Figure 14-8, and the options for the jumpers are shown in Figure 14-10. Set the jumper group to the normal setting so that BIOS uses the current configuration for booting. Once set, the jumpers should only be changed if you are trying to recover when the power-up password is lost or flashing BIOS has failed. Figure 14-11 shows the jumper cap in the normal position.

Jumper Position	Mode	Description
1 ▢ ⬤ ◯ 3	Normal (default)	The current BIOS configuration is used for booting.
1 ▢ ⬤ ⬤ 3	Configure	After POST, the BIOS displays a menu in CMOS setup that can be used to clear the user and supervisor power-on passwords.
1 ▢ ◯ ◯ 3	Recovery	Used to recover from a failed BIOS update. Details can be found on the motherboard CD.

Figure 14-10   BIOS configuration jumper settings

Jumpers set for normal boot

Figure 14-11   BIOS setup configuration jumpers

Step 5: Install the CPU and CPU Fan

Next, we will install the CPU and the CPU fan on the motherboard. If you look back in Chapter 4 at Figure 4-6, you can see this Pentium 4 installed on the motherboard. Notice in that figure the frame or retention mechanism that is used to hold the cooler in place. This frame might come separately from the board or be preinstalled. If necessary, follow the directions that came with the motherboard to install the frame.

The next step is to install the processor. (Again, don't forget to wear your ground strap as you work.) Lift the ZIF socket lever as shown in Figure 14-12. Place the processor on the socket so that the corner marked with a triangle is aligned with the connection of the lever to the socket. Once the processor is in place, lower the lever to insert the processor firmly into the socket. As you work, be very careful not to force the processor in at an offset or disoriented position.

14

Figure 14-12   Install the processor in the mPGA478B socket

Before installing the CPU fan over the CPU, place a small amount of thermal compound on top of the processor. This grease-like substance will help in transferring heat from the processor to the heat sink. Do not use too much; if you do, it may squish out the sides and interfere with other components.

The fan and heat sink are surrounded by a clip assembly; these components together are sometimes called the CPU cooling assembly. Line the clip assembly up with the retention mechanism, already installed on the motherboard, and press lightly on all four corners to attach it. Once the fan is in place, push down the two clip levers on top of the CPU fan (Figure 14-13). Different coolers use different types of clipping mechanisms, so follow the directions that come with the cooler. This one was a little difficult to clip onto the processor, and the plastic levers and housing seemed a little flimsy, so proceed with caution.

Figure 14-13   The clip levers attach the cooling assembly to the retention mechanism around the processor

Step 6: Install RAM on the Motherboard

From discussions in Chapter 6, you know how to select the right kind of RAM and the right amount for your motherboard, and you know that you should be careful to match size, manufacturer, production batch, and mode. Our motherboard has four RIMM slots that can support from 128 MB to 2 GB of RAM with ECC or non-ECC support. We will be installing two RIMMs, each with 128 MB of memory. Recall from Chapter 4 that when you are installing RIMMs, every memory socket must be filled; sockets in which you do not have actual memory modules must contain the placeholder C-RIMMs (continuity RIMMs), which do not contain any memory chips but provide continuity throughout the sockets.

The four memory sockets on this motherboard are divided into two banks, bank 0 and bank 1. Install the pair of RIMMs into bank 0, which is the one closest to the processor, as shown in Figure 14-14. These two RIMMs have to be of the same size and type, 128 MB RDRAM in this case. If you were installing memory into bank 1 as well, that pair of RIMMs would only have to match each other, not the RIMMs in bank 0.

RIMM supporting arms
in outward position

Figure 14-14   Install RIMMs in bank 0

Before inserting each module in its socket, pull the supporting arms on the sides of the socket outward. Notches on the edge of each module will help you orient it correctly in the socket. Insert the module straight down in the socket; when it is fully inserted, the supporting arms should pop back into place.

Step 7: Install the Motherboard and Attach Cabling

Let's review what we've done so far. We've prepared the case by installing the auxiliary fan and the spacers, installed drives, and attached the processor, cooling assembly, and memory modules to the motherboard. The next step is to install the motherboard itself into the case and attach the cabling and power connections.

- Place the motherboard into the case so that the holes on the motherboard align with the holes on the spacers. Attach the motherboard to the case, using the spacers to receive the screws (see Figure 14-15). Be careful not to use excessive force when moving the motherboard into place and attaching it to the case, as this could warp the board and damage the circuits on it.

Figure 14-15   Use screws to attach the motherboard to the case via the spacers

- Connect a power cord from the power supply to the case fan. (We did not do this earlier so that the connection between this fan and the power supply would not be in the way when we installed the motherboard.)

- Connect the power cords to the drives, as shown in Figure 14-16. You will connect one to each of the three drives.

Power cord to
CD-ROM drive

Hard drive power cord

Figure 14-16   Attach power cords to the CD-ROM drive, the hard drive, and the floppy drive

- Connect the 4-pin auxiliary power cord, as shown in Figure 14-17. This cord supplies the supplemental power required for a Pentium 4 processor. Most processors get all their power from the motherboard and do not require a separate connection to the power supply, so this is an exception to the rule. You are likely to have exceptions in your installation as well, which is why it's so important to read your documentation thoroughly, preferably before you begin installation.

14

Figure 14-17   The auxiliary 4-pin power cord provides power to the Pentium 4 processor

■ Connect the 20-pin ATX P1 power cord from the power supply to the motherboard, as shown in Figure 14-18.

Figure 14-18   The 20-pin connector supplies power to the motherboard

■ Once the power cords are connected, locate and connect the front leads to the switches, speaker, and lights on the front of the case (see Figure 14-19). Note that each front lead is labeled. Sometimes there will be corresponding labels screen-printed on the board to tell you which lead goes on which pins. If the pins are not labeled on the board, as with this motherboard, check your documentation. The motherboard might come with a sticker that goes on the inside of the case, showing a diagram of the motherboard with labels for the front leads. If the motherboard documentation is not clear, you can also check the motherboard manufacturer's Web site for additional documentation. Figure 14-20 shows the documentation for this motherboard, which describes the connectors for each of the leads. The power switch lead is already connected to the bank of connectors. Note that there is not a connector for a speaker, since the motherboard has its own speaker, and that the ground and +5V connectors are not used.

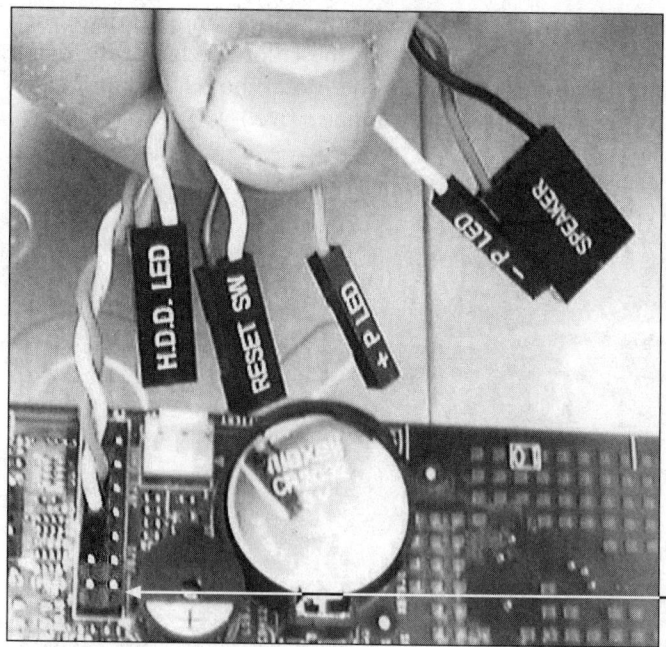

Bank of pins for front leads

Figure 14-19 The front leads provide power to the switches, lights, and speaker on the front of the case

Figure 14-20 Connector group for front panel leads

14

- Next, install the data cables to each drive (Figure 14-21). Install the floppy drive cable with the twist between the motherboard and the drive, making this drive A in the final configuration. Connect one IDE cable to the hard drive and the primary IDE connector on the motherboard, and connect a second IDE cable to the CD-ROM drive and the secondary IDE connector on the motherboard. To orient the cable connectors, look on each drive for a small 1 that indicates pin 1, and align that with the colored edge of the data cable for that drive. Look for pin 1 labeled on the motherboard. (In most cases, pin 1 is next to the power connection on a floppy drive.)

Figure 14-21   Attach data cables from the motherboard to all three drives

- Normally the CD audio cord connects from the CD-ROM drive to the sound card, in order to play music CDs. Since sound support is embedded on the motherboard, look at the motherboard documentation to determine where to connect the CD audio cord to the board. Connect the CD audio cord to the CD-ROM drive and the other end to the connector on the motherboard, as shown in Figure 14-22.

Figure 14-22   The CD audio cord connects near the sound ports

Step 8: Install the Video Card

The next step is to install the video card, which is the only expansion card we are including in this installation, since the sound card and network logic are built into this motherboard. In general, when installing an expansion card, first read the documentation for the card and set any jumper switches or DIP switches on the card. Like most cards today, the video card we are installing is Plug and Play compatible and has no jumpers.

Next, select the expansion slot you plan to use on the motherboard, remove the faceplate for the selected slot from the computer case, and insert the card in the slot. We will be inserting this video card into the single AGP slot on this motherboard. There are several different types of AGP slots. The video card we are installing, shown in Figure 14-23, fits into an AGP 4x slot and includes a registration tab that allows the card to fit into an AGP Pro slot.

Registration tab

Figure 14-23   The video card, with a tab that allows it to be used in an AGP Pro slot

Before you install the video card in the AGP slot, install the AGP retention mechanism over the AGP slot. This piece, shown in Figure 14-24, helps stabilize the card. Your motherboard might or might not include this extender.

14

Figure 14-24   The AGP extender helps to stabilize the video card

When inserting a card in an expansion slot, press the card straight down into the slot. As you insert the card, don't allow the card to wobble in the slot, because that could widen the slot and prevent a tight fit. Make sure the card is inserted solidly in the slot, and then, using the same screw that held the faceplate in position, screw the card to the computer case (Figure 14-25).

Figure 14-25   Secure the video card using the same screw that held the faceplate in place

Step 9: Plug the Computer In and Attach External Devices

The installation of devices inside the case is now complete. Before you plug the computer in, make sure that no cords are obstructing the fans. Figure 14-26 shows the case with all the internal components installed. Notice that some cables are coiled and tied with plastic ties (you could also use rubber bands). This way, they will not be in the way of other components, and the inside of the case will be less cluttered, making it easier to work inside the case when making changes to components. You would not do this, however, until you had tested the system to make sure everything works.

Figure 14-26   The case with all the internal components installed

Attach the monitor, keyboard and mouse, and plug the computer in. You can attach the mouse at this point, or you can leave it off and attach it after you have tested the system. It is unlikely that the mouse will cause problems during the initial startup process, but you won't really need it, and it is a good idea not to start off with anything that you don't absolutely need, especially when first constructing a system.

Step 10: Boot the Computer, Check Settings, and Verify Operation

It is a good idea to test the system before replacing the case cover, to make it easier to make changes if something goes wrong. However, since some systems require the cover to be on to achieve proper airflow, do not run the system for any length of time without the cover on. Also, some server cases have cover switch latches that do not allow you to power up the system unless the case cover is in place. The boot process and CMOS settings were covered in Chapter 2 and were reviewed in the general installation process in Chapter 4, which we have followed in this chapter. Boot the system and enter CMOS setup by pressing F2. The method to enter setup is different for some motherboards; check the documentation for the motherboard you are using. Refer back to Chapter 4 for the list of CMOS settings you need to check. If you are booting from a floppy disk, insert a bootable setup disk that contains the files that allow you to format the hard drive (see Chapter 3 for a list of those files).

When you exit CMOS, the computer will reboot. Observe POST and verify that no errors occur. If there are no errors, congratulations! You have put your system together correctly. (If there are errors, see your motherboard documentation or Appendix A in this book for explanations.) Turn the computer off and slide the case cover back in place, as shown in Figure 14-27. Now you are ready to prepare the hard drive for the OS (Chapter 7) and install the operating system and any other software you need on your system. Figure 14-28 shows the complete system.

Figure 14-27   Slide the case cover back on once you know the system is working

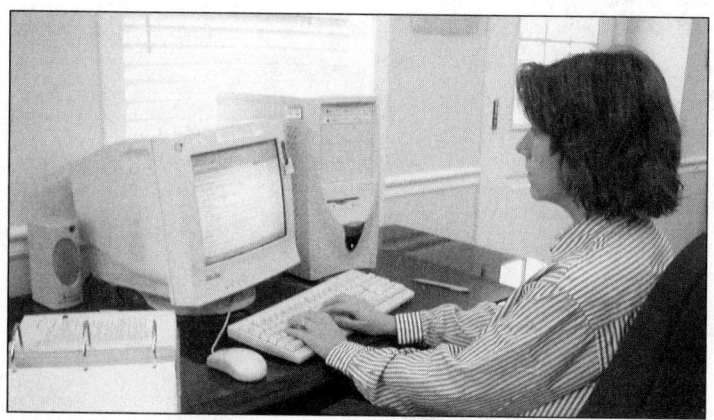

Figure 14-28   The complete system

CHAPTER SUMMARY

❏ The most important reason to buy a brand-name PC rather than a clone is after-sales service.

❏ Many brand-name PCs use proprietary designs that force you to use only that particular brand name's parts and service when upgrading or maintaining the PC.

❏ Middle-range PCs offer more network capability, more expandability, more support, and more prior testing than do low-end PCs.

❏ Some reasons to build your own PC are the knowledge you will gain, the control you will have over the choice of individual parts, the availability of documentation and original software disks, and the satisfaction of having built the PC yourself.

❏ When choosing to build your own PC, be aware that the process will take time, that you will likely encounter problems along the way, that there will be no warranty on the assembled product, and that you probably will not save money.

❏ Plan the project of assembling a PC well. Get answers to any questions you may have on the details before you begin. Keep things organized as you work. Expect the project to be fun.

❏ When assembling a PC, follow this general plan: (1) Verify that you have all parts you plan to install, (2) Prepare the computer case, (3) Install drives, (4) Determine and set jumpers and DIP switches for the motherboard, (5) Install the CPU, CPU fan, and RAM on the motherboard, and then install the motherboard in the case, (6) Attach all cables and power cords, (7) Install the video card and any other expansion cards, (8) Connect the peripherals (mouse, keyboard, and monitor), (9) Plug the computer in, verify that settings are correct and that no errors occur, and replace the computer case, and (10) Install the OS and any other software you need on your system.

KEY TERMS

clone   hard-disk loading   IBM-compatible PC

2

Software

The second part of this book was written to be the very best tool on the market today to prepare you to support operating systems used on personal computers. It takes you from the just-a-user level to the I-can-fix-this level for the most common PC operating system concerns. This book achieves its goals with an unusually effective combination of tools that powerfully reinforce both concepts and hands-on, real-world experience.

Part 2 includes:

- ◆ Comprehensive review and practice end-of-chapter material, including a chapter summary and key terms.

- ◆ Step-by-step instruction on installation, maintenance, optimizing system performance, and troubleshooting.

- ◆ A wide array of photos and screen shots support the text, displaying in detail exactly how to best understand, purchase, install, and maintain your software.

In addition, the carefully structured, clearly written text is accompanied by graphics that provide the visual input essential to learning. Part 2 begins with a survey and comparison of all major operating systems. Then you learn to work from the command prompt using MS-DOS commands needed for drastic troubleshooting situations. Next you will install and learn to use each major Microsoft operating system. The chapters are organized so that you can install and learn to use and support Windows 98, then proceed to Windows NT, then to Windows 2000, and finally, to Windows XP. You will learn about the special concerns of Windows on a network, on the Internet, and on notebook computers. You will also be introduced to Linux and the Mac OS.

To ensure a successful learning experience, this book includes the following pedagogical features:

♦ Learning Objectives: Every chapter opens with a list of learning objectives that sets the stage for you to absorb the lessons of the text.

♦ Comprehensive Step-by-Step Troubleshooting Guidance: Troubleshooting guidelines are included in almost every chapter.

♦ Step-by-Step Procedures: The book is chock-full of step-by-step procedures, covering subjects from understanding how the latest operating system technologies work to installation and maintenance.

♦ Art Program: Numerous detailed photographs, three-dimensional art, and screenshots support the text, displaying operating system screens exactly as you will see them in your work.

 Tip icons include pointers from the author's experiences that provide additional insight for the topic at hand.

Caution icons highlight critical safety information. Follow these instructions carefully to protect yourself, the PC, and its data.

 Note icons highlight additional information about the subject being discussed.

♦ Chapter Summary: This bulleted list of concise statements summarizes all major points of the chapter.

♦ Key Terms: The content of each chapter is further reinforced by an end-of-chapter key-term list. The definitions of all terms are included at the end of the book in a full-length glossary.

15

INTRODUCING AND COMPARING OPERATING SYSTEMS

In this chapter, you will learn:

♦ What an operating system does

♦ How DOS began and how it is used today

♦ About the various Windows operating systems and the differences between them

♦ Advantages and disadvantages of common non-Windows operating systems

Personal computers have changed the way we work, play, and do business. Everyone, no matter how young or old they are or how they make their living, encounters a personal computer in some way almost daily. So, in a very real sense, we are all computer users. You might use a personal computer to write documents, build spreadsheets, make a purchase using the Web, or e-mail your friends. No matter how experienced a computer user you are, this book can take you from the just-a-user stage to understanding what happens behind the scenes when you click on that Web site link or install that new screen saver. Not only will you understand what happened, but you'll also be able to customize your operating system (OS) and applications, troubleshoot and solve problems with the OS, and optimize your system for best performance. The goals of this book are to enable you to compare different operating systems and make wise buying decisions about them and to empower you to understand, troubleshoot, customize, and optimize a Windows operating system. To begin using this book, nothing more is expected of you than to be a knowledgeable computer user.

In this chapter, you will learn what an operating system does and how it relates to the user. Operating systems continue to evolve as hardware and software technologies improve. As you read about various OSs in this chapter, you will see the evolution from DOS to Windows 9x and to Windows NT/2000/XP. You will also be introduced to alternate OSs (Unix, Linux, OS/2, and Mac OS).

WHAT AN OPERATING SYSTEM DOES

An **operating system** is a computer program that controls a computer. A computer is like an automobile; it doesn't work unless a driver controls it. In Figure 15-1, the passenger and chauffeur make the automobile a functioning tool that can be used to accomplish a task. Without their intelligence, skill, and direction, the car is nothing more than an interconnected assemblage of electronic and mechanical devices. Software performs a similar function for hardware. Software is the intelligence of the computer; it senses what hardware is present, decides how it is configured and used, and then uses that hardware to perform tasks.

The operating system is the most important and primary software used to control a computer, much like a chauffeur driving a car. Applications such as Microsoft Word or Lotus Notes depend on the operating system to be the middleman between them and the hardware. You can think of an application as a passenger in a car who depends on a chauffeur to drive the car. However, sometimes a user drives an application such as when you are using Microsoft Excel to build a spreadsheet. In this case, you're the passenger depending on the chauffeur (two layers of software—application and operating system) to drive your car (hardware).

Figure 15-1   A user interacts with a computer much as a passenger interacts with a chauffeured car

A computer might have several applications installed to meet various needs of the users, but it only needs one operating system. There are many operating systems on the market, each designed to support different types of hardware systems and user needs:

- *DOS*. The first OS among IBM computers and IBM-compatible computers was DOS, the disk OS. Because DOS was written for early PCs, it has significant limitations today. DOS was the OS used by early versions of Windows. Two of them were Windows 3.1 and Windows 3.11 (collectively referred to as 3.x). Windows 3.x did not perform OS functions but simply served as a user-friendly intermediate program between DOS and applications and the user.

- *Windows 9x*. The more recent Windows 95, Windows 98, and Windows Me, which we collectively call Windows 9x, are true operating systems with a DOS core and provide a user-friendly interface. Windows 98 is the most popular OS for desktop computers for home use. (Many people chose to not upgrade from Windows 98 to Windows Me because they did not consider it a significant enough upgrade.)

- *Windows NT, Windows 2000, and Windows XP*. Windows NT comes in two versions: Windows NT Workstation for workstations, and Windows NT Server to control a network. Windows 2000 is an upgrade of Windows NT, and Windows XP is an upgrade of Windows 2000. Windows 2000 also comes in several versions, some designed for the desktop and others designed for high-end servers. Windows 2000 Professional is popular as an OS for the corporate desktop. Windows 2000 Server, Advanced Server, and Datacenter Server are network server OSs. Windows XP currently comes in two main versions: Windows XP Home, and Windows XP Professional. Windows XP is expected to first replace Windows 9x and then replace Windows 2000.

- *Unix*. Unix is a popular OS used to control networks and to support applications used on the Internet.

- *Linux*. Linux is a scaled-down version of Unix that is provided, in basic form, free of charge and includes open access to the programming code of the OS. It is often used for server applications.

- *OS/2*. OS/2, developed by IBM and Microsoft, is used less commonly for home desktop PC use but is used in certain types of networks. Windows NT was developed using some of the core components of OS/2 and was intended by Microsoft to replace OS/2.

- *Mac OS*. Mac OS is available only for Apple Macintosh computers and is often used for graphics applications and in educational settings.

You will learn more about each of these OSs later in this chapter. Although there are important differences between them, OSs share four main functions including:

- *Managing hardware*
  - Managing the BIOS (programs permanently stored on hardware devices)
  - Managing memory, which is a temporary place to store data and instructions as they are being processed

15

- Diagnosing problems with software and hardware
- Interfacing between hardware and software (that is, interpreting application software needs to the hardware and interpreting hardware needs to application software)

■ *Managing files*
- Managing files on hard drives, floppy drives, CD-ROM drives, and other drives
- Creating, storing, retrieving, deleting, and moving files

■ *Providing a user interface*
- Performing housekeeping procedures requested by the user, often concerning secondary storage devices, such as formatting new disks, deleting files, copying files, and changing the system date
- Providing a way for the user to manage the desktop, hardware, applications, and data

■ *Managing applications*
- Installing and uninstalling applications
- Running applications and managing the interface to the hardware on behalf of an application

In short, an operating system controls the hardware components that make up a computer and also provides an interface that a user or an application can use. Figure 15-2 illustrates that an OS must relate to the user, to applications, and to various hardware components. You can also see that the OS must relate to these hardware devices by way of the **CPU (central processing unit)**, also called a **microprocessor**, the most important microchip in the system that is responsible for processing all data and instructions.

Figure 15-2   Users and applications depend on the OS to relate to all hardware components

Operating System Components

An operating system is made up of several internal components, which you will learn about throughout this book. Every operating system has two main components: the shell and the kernel (see Figure 15-3). A **shell** is that portion of the OS that relates to the user and to applications. The shell provides a command, menu, or icon interface to the user using various interface tools such as Windows Explorer, the Control Panel, or My Computer.

Figure 15-3   Inside an operating system, different components perform various functions

The core, or **kernel**, of the OS is responsible for interacting with hardware. It has more power to communicate with hardware devices than the shell so that applications operating under the OS cannot get to hardware devices without the shell passing those requests to the kernel. This structure provides for a more stable system.

An operating system needs a place to keep hardware and software configuration information, user preferences, and application settings that are used when the OS is first loaded and are accessed as needed by hardware, applications, and users. This information can be kept in a database or text files. Windows uses a database for most of this information called the **registry**. In addition, some data is kept in text files called **initialization files**, which often have an .ini or .inf file extension.

How an OS Relates to Users

When a PC is first turned on, the operating system is executed. After the OS is in control, it either automatically executes an application software program or turns to the user for its next instruction. If you are working with the OS, you will see an interface on the monitor screen. This interface can be command-driven, menu-driven, or icon-driven.

Command-Driven Interfaces

With a command-driven interface, you key in command lines to tell the OS to perform operations. For example, in Figure 15-4, the VER command reports the operating system version. DOS and Unix use command-driven interfaces, and other OSs may provide access to a command-driven interface. For instance, the command-driven interface of a command window under Windows 9x provides the C prompt, which can look like this:

```
C:\Windows>  or  C:\>
```

To access this window, sometimes called a DOS box, click Start, Programs, MS-DOS Prompt. Computer technicians who are good typists and are very familiar with DOS-like commands often prefer this kind of OS interface. What shows in the prompt depends on the current drive and directory.

15

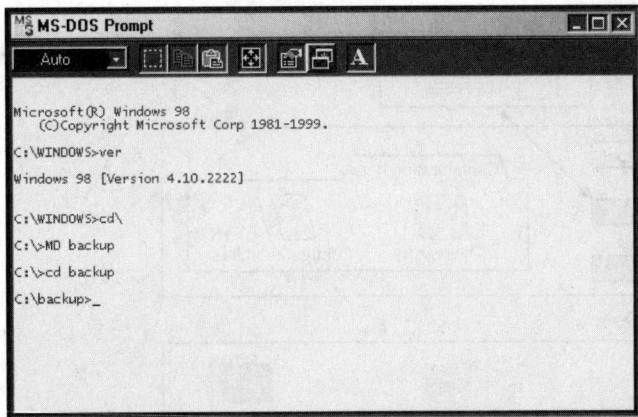

Figure 15-4   An operating system command-driven interface: a DOS box

Menu-Driven Interfaces

Some OSs allow you to choose from a list of options displayed on the screen. An example of such a menu-driven interface is Explorer in Windows 98. From the drop-down menus, you can format disks, rename files, copy and delete files, and perform many other operations to manage files and storage devices (see Figure 15-5). Note that Explorer uses icons as well as menus.

Icon-Driven Interfaces

Today's OSs are more likely to use an icon-driven interface than a command-driven one. With an icon-driven interface, sometimes called a **GUI (graphical user interface)**, you perform operations by selecting icons (or pictures) on the screen. When an OS is first executed, the initial screen that appears, together with its menus, commands, and icons, is called the **desktop**. Figure 15-6 shows the Windows 2000 default desktop, which has an icon-driven interface. You double-click an icon with the mouse to execute an applications software program or right-click an icon to see its shortcut menu. Just about all OSs today offer a combination of menu and icon-driven interfaces such as the Control Panel window in Figure 15-6, which includes both menus and icons.

Figure 15-5   A menu-driven interface: Explorer in Windows 98

Figure 15-6   An icon-driven interface: Windows 2000 desktop

Comparing Operating Systems

The goal of this section is to help you understand what each OS does best and how to compare features of each in order to make wise buying decisions and technical comparisons. It's impossible to adequately do that without including in our discussions some technical terms. Most of these terms are covered in detail in the next chapter, but, for now, we offer some basic definitions. To understand the differences between OSs, you need to understand the following terms:

- Each process that a CPU is aware of is called a **thread**.

■ **Single-tasking** occurs when the CPU or an OS can run only one program at a time. The CPU is aware of and is actively running only one thread. In Figure 15-7, DOS is a single-tasking OS, which can manage only one application at a time, passing a single thread to the CPU. All older CPUs used when DOS was written could only handle a single thread.

a) Single tasking

Application → DOS → CPU

Single threading

b) Cooperative multitasking

Application
Application → Windows 3.x → DOS → CPU

c) Preemptive multitasking

Multithreading

Application
Application → Windows 95 → CPU

Figure 15-7   Windows 3.x used cooperative multitasking with a single thread to the CPU. Windows 95 and later Windows OSs use preemptive multitasking with multithreading to the CPU.

■ **Multitasking** is doing more than one thing at the same time. In Figure 15-8 you can see two applications open on the Windows 98 desktop, and you can move from one to the other by clicking your mouse on each window. In one sense, the OS is multitasking because it is supporting two applications at the same time. However, both applications can't use the CPU at the same time. For example, if you command Microsoft Excel to print a large spreadsheet and, before the printing is done, command Microsoft Word to save a large document, both applications will be requesting resources from the OS at the same time. The OS manages this multitasking by sharing its resources between the two applications, doing part of one task and part of the other, switching back and forth until both tasks are done. The OS and the CPU that the OS is using are not multitasking in the true sense of the word because they are only doing one thing at a time. All OSs today support some form of multitasking so that two or more applications can be open at a time. The type of multitasking they use partly depends on the CPU. Some CPUs can actually multitask (perform two commands at the same time, each from a different thread), but, in order to get a true multitasking system, you need two CPUs, each processing a thread at the same time. Having two or more CPUs in the same system is called **multiprocessing**.

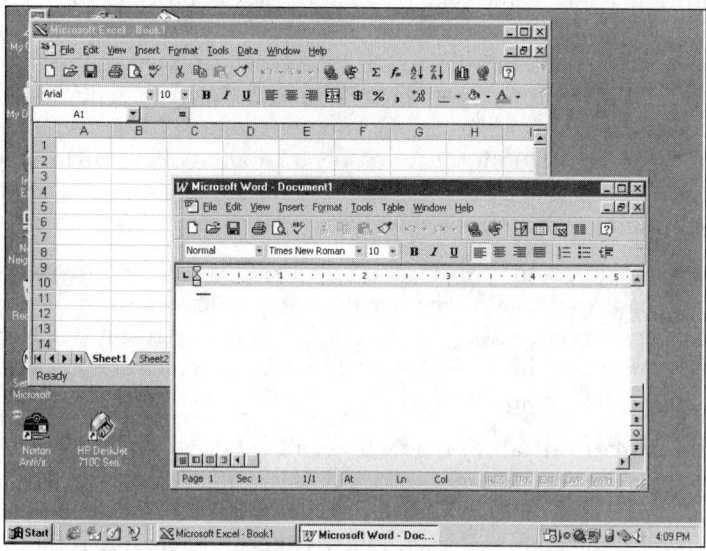

Figure 15-8   A multitasking environment allows two or more applications to run simultaneously

- **Cooperative multitasking** (see Figure 15-7) was used by Windows 3.x, which was designed for the older i386 and i486 CPUs by Intel that could only handle a single thread. Cooperative multitasking is sometimes called **task switching** because it is not true multitasking, in that the CPU is only aware of one program running at a time. But Windows 3.x is switching back and forth between applications so that more than one application can be loaded at the same time. Also, Windows 3.x used DOS as the underlying OS. Windows 3.x passed one thread to DOS, which passed it to the CPU. DOS and the CPU were not aware that more than one application was open. Using Windows 3.x, you could observe cooperative multitasking when you had two applications open, each in its own window. You didn't need to close one application before opening another. However, with cooperative multitasking, if one program was doing something (for example, when you saw the hourglass on the screen while the software was attempting to print or save a file) you could not click on another application and immediately switch to it.

- **Preemptive multitasking**, also shown in Figure 15-7, is another type of pseudo-multitasking whereby the OS allots CPU time to an application for a specified period, and then preempts the processing to give the CPU to another application. The end result is that the computer appears to be doing true multitasking. If two threads are running, the CPU can be aware of both, but still only one is active. Windows 95 was the first version of Windows to provide preemptive multitasking, and it requires the cooperation of the CPU. The OS and the CPU are managing two programs at once using multithreading.

- **Environment** refers to the type of support the OS provides to the applications software. For example, in order for applications software to offer you a window with mouse movement, buttons to click, and icons to view, it must be supported by a GUI environment, such as Windows. Such an application is said to need a "GUI environment" to work. Another example is the DOS environment that offers to its applications software only a "single-tasking environment" in which a software package does not expect another applications software package to be running concurrently with it.

- **16-bit mode** and **32-bit mode**, also called **real mode** and **protected mode**, respectively, have to do with whether the CPU processes 16 or 32 bits at a time. OSs, applications, and CPUs all operate in either 16-bit (real) or 32-bit (protected) modes. 16-bit OSs support cooperative multitasking, and 32-bit OSs support preemptive multitasking.

- **FAT (file allocation table)** is a table on a hard drive or floppy disk that tracks the locations of files on a disk. A disk is composed of **tracks**, which are concentric circles on the disk surface, shown in Figure 15-9. Each track is divided into several segments, each called a **sector**. A **cluster** is the smallest unit of space on a disk for storing data and is made up of one or more sectors. The FAT contains a list of clusters, and which clusters are used for each file stored on the disk. The most recent version of FAT, FAT32, is a more efficient method of organization for large drives than FAT16 (the earlier version).

One sector

One track

Figure 15-9   A hard drive or floppy disk is divided into tracks and sectors. Several sectors make one cluster.

- A computer provides several ports on the back of the computer case to connect different devices, such as a keyboard, mouse, or printer.

- **RAM (random access memory)** is temporary memory stored on chips inside the computer. These chips are stored on memory modules, some of which are shown in Figure 15-10. Memory is a place for the CPU to store programs and data while it is processing both, and the information stored in

RAM disappears when the computer is turned off. Because of hardware limitations at the time, DOS divided memory into categories called base memory, upper memory, and extended memory. Windows 9x still uses this same arrangement, although it makes better use of these categories, and is not as limited by them. Windows NT/2000/XP uses an altogether new and more efficient arrangement called memory paging. The goal of each OS is the same: provide as much memory as possible for software to use so as not to hinder software performance.

184-pin RIMM

168-pin DIMM

72-pin SIMM

30-pin SIMM

Figure 15-10   Types of RAM modules

15

Now that you've learned some basic terms relating to OSs, let's compare several OSs keeping in mind several criteria:

- What kind of interface does the OS provide for the user?
- Can the OS support some form of multitasking?
- How many and what kinds of applications are written to work with the OS?
- What are the hardware requirements to make efficient use of the OS?
- What computer ports and other hardware devices and features does the OS support?
- How does the OS perform in a network?

The following sections compare the most well-known OSs used in PCs and the OS used in Macintoshes, including their advantages and disadvantages. When choosing an OS, consider all the criteria discussed in these sections. Your choice will be determined by the size and type of your microcomputer system, your familiarity with the various OSs, and the applications software you plan to use. As you read these sections, keep in mind the four main functions of an operating system (managing hardware, providing a user interface, working with files, and running applications), and notice how each OS performs these functions differently.

DOS (Disk Operating System)

DOS was the first OS used by IBM microcomputers. For years DOS remained the unchallenged standard for OSs used by IBM and IBM-compatible machines. It is a simple operating system, and simple often means reliable. PC technicians should be familiar with DOS because it can be very effective in troubleshooting situations when a more complex OS fails.

 To see what the DOS command-driven interface looks like, refer back to Figure 15-4.

With Windows 3.x, DOS ran in the background as the true OS and used Windows 3.x as a middle layer, or "go-between" program, between the application and DOS, providing the operating environment for application software packages. In this environment, users could interact with applications directly through Windows or directly through DOS. Windows 3.x supported cooperative multitasking because it managed more than one open application by passing segments to DOS, which then, in turn, interfaced with hardware. However, DOS and Windows applications tended to conflict with each other when sharing hardware devices.

 A point of historical interest: Windows 3.11, called Windows for Workgroups, was the first Windows environment designed to interface with a network without depending on separate application software to do the job. Windows 3.x (3.1 and 3.11) is no longer in general use and has been replaced by Windows 9x.

DOS is still used in some proprietary systems where older hardware and software (sometimes called **legacy** hardware or software) are still doing the job and there is little reason to upgrade either. However, the primary use of DOS today is as a troubleshooting tool. Windows 9x has a DOS core, and when the Windows 9x GUI interface fails to load, the only recourse is to fall back to the tried-and-true DOS portion of the OS stored on floppy disks or the hard drive. Also, Windows NT, 2000, and XP all offer some form of a recovery tool that includes a command prompt where you issue DOS-like commands. You'll learn about these in future chapters.

Table 15-1 summarizes the advantages and disadvantages of DOS.

Table 15-1   Advantages and disadvantages of DOS

Advantages	Disadvantages
• DOS runs on small, inexpensive micro-computers with a minimum amount of memory and hard drive space. • Text-based DOS programs are faster and more compact than comparable graphics-intensive GUI programs. • Some older applications are still in use today that were written for DOS and older hardware because of the low overhead of DOS compared to more modern OSs. • DOS is still a viable option for some specialized applications using a dedicated computer that does not involve heavy user interaction—for example, a micro-computer dedicated to controlling an in-house phone system. • DOS can be used to boot up and troubleshoot a computer when a more sophisticated OS is too cumbersome and has too much overhead.	• Memory management is awkward and sometimes slow. • DOS has no icon-driven interface. • DOS does only single-tasking; that is, it supports only one application running at a time. • DOS was not designed for use on networks. A separate applications software program is necessary for a DOS machine to access a network. • The last standalone version is DOS 6.22, which does not take advantage of the many new CPU features now available. (However, Windows 9x has a newer DOS core.) • Hardly any new software is being written for DOS.

WINDOWS OPERATING SYSTEMS

In this section, you will learn about Windows 9x, NT, 2000, and XP. The previous section on DOS introduced DOS's relationship to Windows, specifically to Windows 3.x, which is not discussed in detail in this section because it is not commonly used any-more. As you read this section, you will learn about the evolution of Windows OSs and some of the corresponding changes in technology.

Windows 9x

Windows 95, Windows 98, and Windows Me (referred to collectively as Windows 9x) take us two steps closer to a new OS but do not completely eliminate DOS. Windows 95 is the marriage of Windows for Workgroups (Windows 3.11) with an updated version of DOS sometimes known as DOS 7.0, together with some completely new additions and improvements to the OS. Windows 95 also introduced an improved and more auto-mated method of installing new hardware devices, called Plug and Play. Windows 98 added several new features to the OS and Windows Me added even more, but both retain the fundamental DOS core and are a blend of low-end and high-end technologies. These operating systems fulfill the Microsoft commitment to be **backward-compatible** with older software and hardware while still taking advantage of newer technology.

15

As an example of a Windows 9x interface, Figure 15-11 shows a desktop for Windows 98 Second Edition. A window is open, showing the Control Panel, which provides a centralized location from which to administer hardware, software, and system settings, and the Start and Programs menus are open. These features will appear much the same on other Windows 9x desktops.

Figure 15-11   The Windows 98 SE desktop

Table 15-2 lists the hardware requirements of Windows 9x. Note that Table 15-2 gives the *recommended* minimum to run each version of Windows 9x. You may find different values in other documentation, because these OSs may run under lower specifications than the recommended minimums. System requirements can also change depending on whether you are installing on a new system or upgrading an older system, as well as which features you choose to install. Also, sometimes Microsoft lists the minimum requirements to *install* an OS, which might be different than the requirements to *run* an OS. (Requirements in Table 15-2 are for running the OS.) Keep these differences in mind when reviewing the lists of minimum hardware requirements for OSs throughout this chapter.

Table 15-2   Recommended minimum hardware requirements for Windows 9x

Description	Windows 95	Windows 98	Windows Me
Processor	486 or higher	Pentium	Pentium 150 MHz
RAM	8 MB	24 MB	32 MB
Free hard drive space	50 MB	195 MB	320 MB

Table 15-3 summarizes the advantages and disadvantages of Windows 9x.

Table 15-3   Advantages and disadvantages of Windows 9x

Advantages	Disadvantages
• Windows 9x offers a very user-friendly and intuitive GUI interface. • Windows 9x offers almost complete backward-compatibility for applications written for DOS and earlier versions of Windows. • Windows 9x is a mix of older and newer OS technology and allows both older and newer software and hardware to run. • Windows 9x offers the ability for one PC to talk with another over phone lines without additional software. It works well for low-end network use, such as when two users want to exchange files. • Disk access time under Windows 9x is improved over DOS and Windows 3.x. • Plug and Play features make installing some new hardware devices easier than with earlier OSs. • Windows 9x supports preemptive multi-tasking. While the hourglass is showing on the window of an application, you can make another application active by clicking on its window. • Because it is the most popular OS today, many users are comfortable with it and are reluctant to change.	• Because of its hardware requirements, Windows 9x cannot be used on some older PCs. • Because of the attempt to bridge older and newer technology, there are some problems with failures and errors created in this hybrid environment.

15

How Windows 9x Differs from Windows 3.x and DOS

Windows 9x is an OS that bridges two worlds. In Figure 15-12, you see that Windows 3.x and DOS constitute a 16-bit world, with memory management centered around base, upper, and extended memory limitations. Windows 9x still has a DOS-based core, uses many 16-bit programs, and must manage memory in fundamentally the same way as DOS does. However, Windows 95 introduced 32-bit programming, an early form of memory paging, networking, and many other features available in Windows NT/2000/XP. Windows 9x includes hundreds of device drivers, some of which can be loaded and unloaded as needed. (**Device drivers** are software programs stored on the hard drive that are designed to run an input/output hardware device, such as a monitor or a mouse.)

Windows 9x claims to be completely backward-compatible with older software and with hardware designed to work in a DOS and Windows 3.x environment. Windows 9x uses cooperative multitasking when supporting 16-bit applications and preemptive multitasking when supporting 32-bit applications.

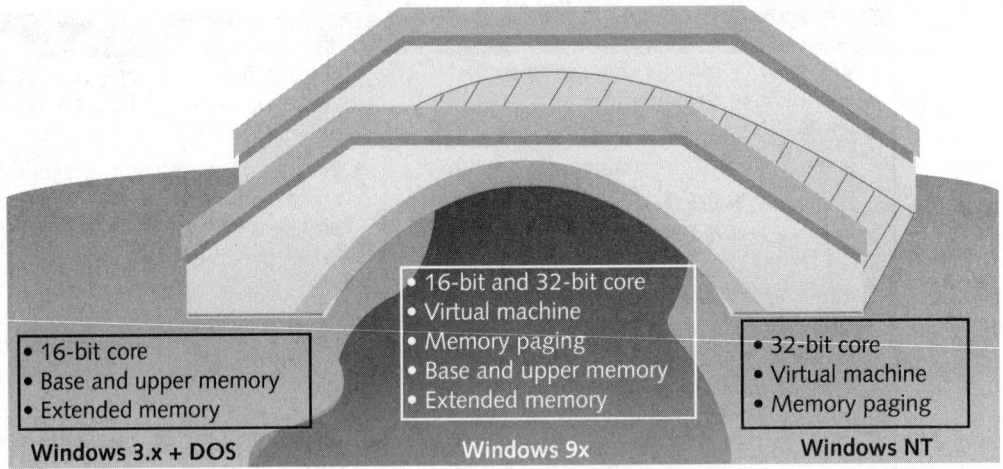

Figure 15-12   Windows 9x is the bridge from DOS to Windows NT

Windows 98 Upgrades

Microsoft has produced two upgrades for Windows 98: Windows 98 Second Edition (Windows 98 SE) and Windows Millennium Edition (Windows Me). Each upgrade has significant enhancements over its predecessor.

Windows 98 SE includes several patches, or fixes, for the first edition of Windows 98, updates of existing components, and some new components. Most new features involve improved networking and Internet access. Improved support for ATM networks includes the addition of Point-to-Point Protocol (PPP) over ATM, which allows a dial-up connection over an ATM network. Security for a dial-up connection over regular phone lines was also upgraded. ATM is a high-speed network technology used by wide area networks.

A new feature is Internet Connection Sharing (ICS), which makes it possible for a Windows 98 PC to access the Internet through another computer on a local network so that only one computer requires a direct connection to an ISP. This feature means that several PCs on a small home network can share the same access to an ISP without incurring additional charges and without installing third-party software. Support for modems that use a USB port and support for a wake-on-LAN connection are also included. (A **LAN**, or **local area network**, is a small computer network that is usually confined to one building or other geographically small area.) Wake-on-LAN means that a PC can go into a low-power state and then return to standard power when the network card detects activity from another computer on the network.

Windows Me takes us one step closer to the merging of Windows 9x and Windows 2000 because it contains features from each OS, although, at its core, it is still a Windows 9x upgrade. It's designed for home users and not for businesses. It focuses on enhancements to multimedia features such as support for video cameras, digital cameras, scanners, and a jukebox recorder. It includes a compression utility for video files and a video editor. True to its goal as a home PC operating system, the OS is very user-friendly, including more informative error messages and troubleshooting utilities. The more technical differences among Windows 95, Windows 98 and Windows Me are covered in Chapter 17.

 To learn which version of Windows is installed, right-click the My Computer icon and select Properties from the shortcut menu. The System Properties windows opens. Click the General tab.

When deciding to upgrade from one version of Windows 9x to another, if you have the hardware power to support it, you are better off upgrading from Windows 95 to Windows 98 because of the many tools and features that add to the stability of Windows 98. The upgrade from Windows 98 to Windows Me is not as important unless you need the added support for multimedia devices.

Windows NT

Windows NT (New Technology) breaks with previous versions of Windows. Although older applications written for DOS and DOS with Windows might work under Windows NT, Windows NT developers do not guarantee compatibility between the OSs. Windows NT takes an aggressive and altogether new approach toward managing hardware resources and interfacing with applications software. It completely eliminates the underlying relationship with DOS.

Windows NT supports preemptive multitasking and multiprocessing (two or more CPUs). Windows NT is designed to work within a powerful networked environment. Computers called servers are configured to store programs and data used remotely by other computers called clients. With client/server arrangements, an organization's resources can be used more effectively, since computers are networked together to share these resources. Windows NT Workstation is designed to run on clients, and Windows NT Server to run servers. Table 15-4 summarizes the advantages and disadvantages of Windows NT.

Goals of Windows NT

Windows NT was conceived when IBM and Microsoft collaborated in building OS/2. While IBM took over OS/2, Microsoft redesigned and added to the original code, calling the new OS Windows NT. The next two evolutions of the OS were called Windows 2000 and Windows XP. Windows NT/2000/XP have many of the same objectives as Unix and are considered the primary competitors to Unix in the client/server industry. Because Windows NT/2000/XP also function on a LAN, they are considered competitors of NetWare software by Novell, which is popular for managing LANs. Finally, Windows NT/2000/XP compete for some of the standalone PC market, contending with Windows 9x. In this discussion about the goals of Windows NT, the

15

information given also applies to Windows 2000/XP. For an OS to contend for so many markets, it needs to meet many goals, including those discussed below.

Table 15-4   Advantages and disadvantages of Windows NT

Advantages	Disadvantages
• Windows NT is designed to run in powerful client-server environments and targets both the client and the server market.	• The hardware requirements of Windows NT eliminate it as a plausible option for older, low-end PCs.
• Windows NT offers a completely new file management system, different from earlier Windows OSs.	• Windows NT is not compatible with some older hardware and software.
• Windows NT Workstation offers both networking over a LAN and dial-up connections over phone lines.	• Windows NT does not use some of the technologies or have the newer features used by Windows 2000 and XP, including Safe Mode, Plug and Play, USB support, Device Manager, and FAT32.
• Windows NT Server offers powerful security both as a file server and for network administration.	• Windows NT is largely outdated and replaced by Windows 2000.
• Windows NT supports preemptive multitasking and multiprocessing.	

Room to Grow   Windows NT is designed for expandability, so it can more easily accommodate new hardware and software. The main way that NT does this is by using a modular approach to performing tasks. For example, DOS and Windows 9x allow applications to have direct access to memory, but Windows NT/2000/XP do not allow an application direct access to memory or other hardware devices. Applications are required to pass their requests to NT, which processes them and gives to the application as much memory as it requests if that memory is currently not used by other applications. Because of this layer of protection between software and hardware, when hardware requirements change, Windows NT manages the change; the application is insulated from the change. (However, a disadvantage to this approach is that Windows NT must have an interface to all new device drivers before any application operating under Windows NT can use a new device.)

Portability to Different Platforms   Because of Windows NT's modular approach, it easily ports to different platforms or hardware configurations, including different CPU technologies. The Windows NT installation CD-ROM comes with three directories ready to accommodate three different CPU technologies. (For Intel-based CPUs, the directory on the CD is \i386.) Windows NT can accommodate several CPU technologies because it isolates parts of the OS from other parts in a modular fashion. The part of the OS that interacts with the hardware is the **HAL (hardware abstraction layer)**, which is the layer between the OS and the hardware. The HAL is available in different versions, each designed to address the specifics of a particular CPU technology. The HAL is the only part of the OS that has to change when platforms change. The other components of the OS need not be changed when the platform changes.

Compatibility with Other OSs and Legacy Software   Because Windows NT had its beginnings in OS/2, Microsoft is committed to Windows NT being compatible with software written for OS/2. Generally, Windows NT does not support legacy devices (older computer devices that do not use current technology). As long as DOS applications don't attempt to access resources directly, they too can run under Windows NT.

Security   Windows NT provides security similar to that on Unix systems, which is greater than that found in Windows 9x. Windows NT security features include the following:

- The requirement that a user have a logon ID and password to gain access to the PC
- Security between users on the same PC, so that one user can block another user from data or software
- Auditing trails to identify security breaches
- Memory protection between different applications loaded at the same time

Performance and Reliability   Although no OS is fault proof, Windows NT/2000/XP provides a much more stable environment than do many OSs, including Windows 9x. Windows NT/2000/XP are less likely to hang, or "lock up," than are other PC OSs. If an application stalls, other applications also loaded are less likely to be affected. When using powerful workstations, Windows NT/2000/XP outperform Windows 9x.

Windows NT vs. Windows 9x

When comparing Windows NT and Windows 9x, remember the following two important points. First, if Windows NT is installed on a PC that is not as powerful as the type of computer it is designed to run on, Windows NT does not perform as well as Windows 9x would on that PC. However, on a powerful workstation PC with a configuration recommended for Windows NT, Windows NT usually performs faster and better than Windows 9x. The second important point is that Windows NT is not another evolution of DOS, Windows 3.x, and Windows 9x. In fact, the opposite is true. Windows NT was developed before Windows 95. Windows 95 and its upgrade, Windows 98, were built as a bridge between the old (DOS with Windows 3.x) and the new (Windows NT).

While Windows 9x and Windows NT Workstation differ dramatically in underlying architecture and structure, they share many features, including a similar user interface, some of the same utilities (such as Internet Explorer and Microsoft Messaging), and other features such as system policies, user profiles, and hardware profiles. Windows NT Workstation offers higher performance, reliability, and security than does Windows 9x. On the other hand, Windows 9x has less demanding hardware requirements, offers broad application and device compatibility, and works well on notebook PCs because of better power management features and Plug and Play capability.

The key to appreciating the advantage that Windows NT has over Windows 9x is in the platforms and settings that Windows NT targets. Windows NT is designed to satisfy the needs of powerful workstations networked in a corporate environment. Windows 9x,

15

however, is used on low-end PCs dominating the home market, where multimedia application software and ease of installation are more of an issue than network security and high-end performance.

One major difference between Windows 9x and Windows NT is that Windows NT is a full 32-bit operating system, operating in protected mode as soon as it receives control from BIOS. Windows 9x begins the boot process in real mode and loads some real-mode components before shifting to protected mode. Windows 9x supports real-mode device drivers; Windows NT does not allow them. Table 15-5 lists the major differences between Windows NT and Windows 9x.

Table 15-5   Comparing Windows NT to Windows 9x

Feature	Windows 9x	Windows NT
Hardware requirements	Low, requiring a 486 PC with 8–16 MB of RAM	High, requiring a Pentium with 16–32 MB of RAM
Hardware compatibility	Supports most legacy devices	Supports most current devices, but does not claim backward-compatibility with legacy devices
Software compatibility	Fully backward-compatible with older DOS and Windows 3.x applications	No support for any application that attempts to access hardware directly
Installation	Offers Plug and Play capability	Does not offer Plug and Play and offers less device driver support
Power management	Built-in power management for laptops	None
Performance	Offers multitasking for 32-bit and 16-bit applications	Also offers preemptive multitasking for 32-bit applications and cooperative multitasking for 16-bit applications. Has significantly better performance on systems with at least 32 MB of RAM
Reliability and stability	Much better than Windows 3.x	Very high reliability and stability; all applications run in protected memory space
Security	Allows violation of the logon process controlled from a server	Very high security down to the file level

Windows NT Workstation includes the following features:

- *Desktop performance.* Supports a powerful multitasking environment and multiple microprocessors for true multitasking

- *Hardware profiles.* Can maintain separate hardware profiles for different hardware configurations on the same PC.

- *Internet Explorer.* Provides a built-in Web browser (Internet Explorer).

- *Peer Web services.* Provides a personal Web server.

- *Security.* Provides security for individual files, folders, and other resources. User access to a PC's resources can be controlled by user IDs and passwords on the standalone PC or managed from a network controller.

- *Stability.* Uses protective processing, which prevents applications from causing errors in other applications or in Windows NT itself.

Many of these same features, including Internet Explorer, hardware profiles, and user access, are available from Windows 9x as well. The minimum hardware requirements for Windows NT on an IBM-compatible PC are listed below. However, even though Windows NT does run on this minimum hardware configuration, remember that you need a powerful high-end PC to experience the full benefits of Windows NT.

- Pentium-compatible processor or higher

- 16 MB of RAM (32 MB is recommended)

- 125 MB of hard disk space

While the minimum requirements listed above refer to IBM-compatible machines, Windows NT can run on other computers as well, providing the same interface and functionality. The main difference between Windows NT running on an IBM-compatible CPU and Windows NT on other computers is in the HAL. The hardware platforms supported by Windows NT are listed below. This book focuses only on the Intel-based CPUs of IBM-compatible machines.

- Intel x86-based (486 or higher) processor

- MIPS R4x00-based processor

- Alpha AXP-based processor

- PReP-compliant PowerPC-based processor

15

Hardware Supported by Windows NT   Many hardware devices are not supported by Windows NT. For this reason, before you decide to install Windows NT, determine if all components on your PC will work under Windows NT. For instance, you might have to replace a network card, modem, video card, and so on, before Windows NT works. To determine if a hardware component is supported by Windows NT, see the **hardware compatibility list (HCL)** for Windows NT that comes with the software. The most recent copy is available on the Microsoft Web site at *www.microsoft.com/hcl*. On the list, which you can search by hardware category and/or company name, are all hardware devices supported by Windows 98, Windows NT, Windows 2000, and Windows XP. For instance, Figure 15-13 shows the partial results of a search for video cards compatible with

Windows NT 4.0. If a device is not on the list, ask the manufacturer if there is a driver specifically for Windows NT (not just Windows 9x). If no driver exists, this device will not work under Windows NT.

The Windows NT Desktop   Beginning with Windows NT 4.0, the Windows NT desktop took on a similar look and feel to Windows 9x. Figure 15-14 shows the Windows NT desktop with the Start menu and Control Panel, both of which work just as they do in Windows 9x, although some Control Panel icons are different.

Figure 15-13   Some video capture cards compatible with Windows NT from the HCL

The Windows NT Command Prompt   Another similarity between Windows NT and Windows 9x is the command prompt that allows the user to enter DOS-like commands. To access the command prompt, click Start, point to Programs, and then click Command Prompt (as in Figure 15-14). The Command Prompt window opens, as in Figure 15-15. From the command prompt, you can enter DOS-like commands. In Windows 9x, the DOS prompt is actually accessing a version of DOS. In Windows NT, however, the Command Prompt interface is provided as a convenience for those wanting to use familiar DOS-like commands. There are no actual DOS programs underlying and running under Windows NT.

Figure 15-14   The Windows NT desktop is similar to that of Windows 9x

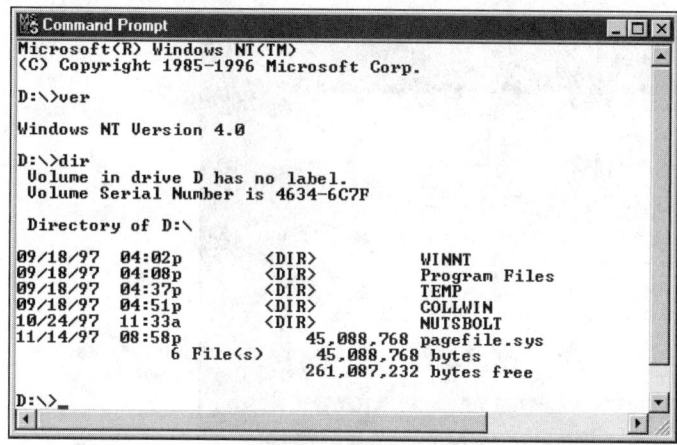

Figure 15-15   The Windows NT command prompt uses DOS-like commands

Choosing Between Windows 9x and Windows NT   Although there is still a large installed base of Windows NT, it is now outdated, having been superseded by Windows 2000 and Windows XP. In most situations, you would not choose to install it on a new system or upgrade from Windows 9x to Windows NT. Rather, you would be making the decision to choose between Windows 9x and Windows 2000 or Windows 9x and Windows XP. However, if you happen to be in a situation where you are forced to decide between Windows 9x and Windows NT as your PC OS, consider the following:

- Does Windows NT support all the hardware devices on your PC? (Check the hardware compatibility list.)

- Is the PC powerful and big enough to support Windows NT? (See the hardware requirements listed earlier in this chapter, and then allow extra resources for your applications.)

- Will the software you intend to use on the PC work better under Windows 98 or Windows NT? Running older DOS and Windows 16-bit applications might be a problem in a Windows NT environment. Verify that your current, older software works under Windows NT, or plan to replace the current software with 32-bit versions. Be aware, however, that some 32-bit programs written for Windows 9x might not work under Windows NT because of differences in the API calls to the operating system. An **API (application program interface)** is a method by which one program calls another program to perform a task.

Windows 2000

Windows 2000 is actually a suite of operating systems, each designed for a different sized computer system. The Windows 2000 desktop (see Figure 15-16) looks much the same as that of Windows 9x and NT. Windows 2000 is built on the Windows NT architecture and was designed to ultimately replace both Windows 9x for low-end systems and Windows NT for midrange and high-end systems. For the most part, Windows 2000 has already replaced Windows NT, and Windows XP is slowly replacing Windows 2000.

Figure 15-16   The Windows 2000 Professional desktop

Windows 2000 includes four operating systems:

- *Windows 2000 Professional* was designed to replace both Windows 9x and Windows NT Workstation as a personal computer desktop or notebook OS. It is an improved version of Windows NT Workstation, using the same new technological approach to hardware and software, and includes all the popular features of Windows 9x, including Plug and Play.

- *Windows 2000 Server* is the improved version of Windows NT Server and is designed as a network operating system for low-end servers.

- *Windows 2000 Advanced Server* is a network operating system that has the same features as Windows 2000 Server but is designed to run on more powerful servers.

- *Windows 2000 Datacenter Server* is a network operating system that is another step up from Windows 2000 Advanced Server. It is intended to be used in large enterprise operations centers.

Hardware and software must qualify for all the Windows 2000 products just as they must qualify for Windows NT. For hardware, check the Hardware Compatibility List at *www.microsoft.com/hcl*. For software applications, search the list of compatible software applications list at *www.microsoft.com/windows2000/professional/howtobuy/upgrading/compat/default.asp*.

Table 15-6 compares the hardware specifications for Windows 2000 products.

Table 15-6   Comparing Windows 2000 products

Description	Windows 2000 Professional	Windows 2000 Server	Windows 2000 Advanced Server	Windows 2000 Datacenter Server
Minimum processor required (CPU)	133 MHz Pentium-compatible	133 MHz Pentium-compatible	133 MHz Pentium-compatible	133 MHz or higher
Minimum hard drive size	2 GB	2 GB	2 GB	2 GB
Minimum hard drive free space	650 MB	1 GB	1 GB	1 GB
Minimum RAM	64 MB	128 MB minimum supported; 256 MB minimum recommended	128 MB minimum supported; 256 MB minimum recommended	256 MB
Maximum RAM supported	4 GB	4 GB	8 GB	64 GB
Maximum CPUs in one system	2	4	8	32

15

Windows 2000 and Windows 98

Windows 2000 was built on Windows NT and is basically the next evolution of Windows NT with the added user-friendly features of Windows 98. For the corporate desktop or home market, in most cases you would choose to use Windows XP rather than Windows 2000. However, if you must select between Windows 2000 and Windows 98, Windows 2000 is a better choice for the corporate desktop and Windows 98 is the better choice for the home PC. Because of the power management improvements that Windows 2000 has over Windows 98, Windows 2000 is the best choice for notebook computers. For the business environment, Windows 2000 offers better support for very large hard drives, more security, and better reliability. For home users, Windows 98 works best with games, music, and video, and offers the best support for the most hardware and software products.

Table 15-7 summarizes the advantages and disadvantages of Windows 2000.

Table 15-7   Advantages and disadvantages of Windows 2000

Advantages	Disadvantages
• Windows 2000 provides powerful support to a network, including advanced security for the network and the ability to organize access to network resources in a centralized location on the network called an Active Directory.	• Just as with Windows NT, Windows 2000 hardware requirements disqualify it as an option for an older, low-end PC operating system.
• Windows 2000 is backward-compatible with all Windows NT and Windows 9x applications and most Windows 3.x and DOS applications.	• Windows 2000 is not scalable. Rather than having one OS that can easily handle a major computer system upgrade, the user must purchase one version of Windows 2000 for a small system and another to handle the upgraded system.
• Windows 2000 is really four operating systems, each targeting a different sized computer and different computing needs, thus making the OS suite extremely versatile.	• Although the perception of Windows as a high-end network operating system is changing, traditionally Windows has not been as stable as the Unix operating system for large enterprise use.

Reliability   Windows 2000 is more reliable than Windows 98. The Windows File Protection feature of Windows 2000 prevents Windows system files and device drivers from being overwritten by faulty application installation programs or deleted by users, which prevents corruption and improves system reliability. By contrast, Windows 98 does not always ask for your permission before allowing an application to alter or overwrite a critical system file. Also, Windows 2000 has some new tools to help application developers build installation disks for their products and troubleshoot application problems.

Security   Windows 2000 offers better security than previous operating systems. The **NTFS (NT file system)** developed for Windows NT and used by Windows 2000 and Windows XP gives better security. Windows 2000 has its own data encryption system and uses Kerberos (a security standard) to encrypt a user ID and password as the user logs on to the network from a Windows 2000 workstation. None of these features are available under Windows 98.

Personalized Start Menu Windows 2000 includes a personalized Start menu that shows only the applications used most often so that the menus are not cluttered with applications seldom used. See Figure 15-17. The down arrows indicate that there are more applications in the list but they are hidden from view. To see these applications, hold your cursor over the menu for a brief moment.

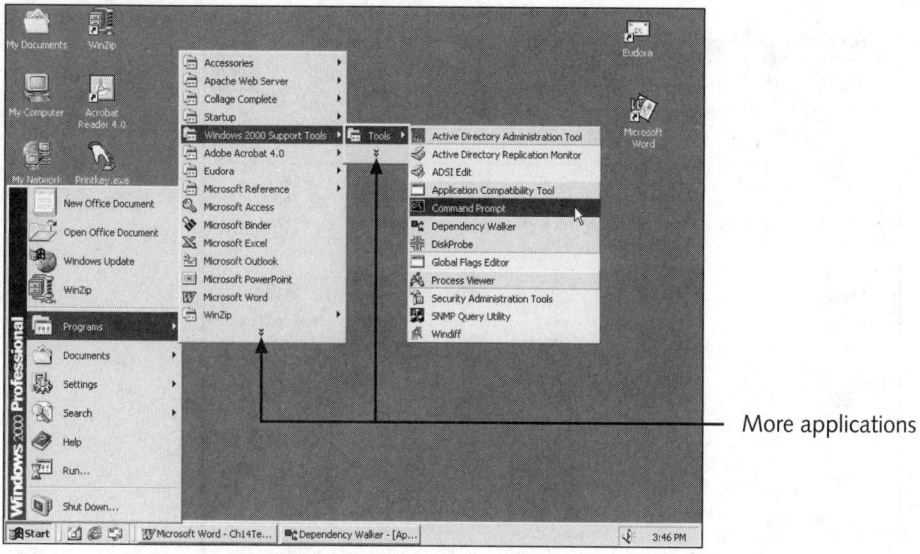

More applications

Figure 15-17 The Windows 2000 personalized Start menu does not initially show applications that are not often used

Power Use Windows 2000 and Windows 98 use the **Advanced Configuration and Power Interface (ACPI)**, which enables a computer to power down unused devices to conserve power, and gives the user much more control over power to the system. The Windows 2000 ACPI features are improved over those of Windows 98. Both require the cooperation of an ACPI-compliant motherboard. For example, on a PC with an ACPI motherboard, to set the Power Options of Windows 2000, open the Control Panel shown in Figure 15-18. Double-click the Power Options icon. The Power Options Properties dialog box opens. Click the Advanced tab (see Figure 15-19). From the list of power options, select what will happen when you press the power button on your computer case. For example, you can set the computer to change to Standby mode when you press the power button. On the Hibernate tab, you can also control when and how the system goes into hibernation, a state whereby little power is used but open applications are restored the next time you power up.

ACPI specifications were developed by Compaq, Intel, Microsoft, Phoenix, and Toshiba to allow for reliable power management through hardware and software cooperation. For more information about ACPI, see *www.acpi.info/index.html*. You'll also learn more about ACPI later in this book.

15

Because Windows 2000 uses NT technology, it does not support older device drivers written for DOS or Windows 9x, nor does it support all legacy devices or software. If you have a legacy application or device, you might have to use Windows 98. To determine if your hardware is supported under Windows 2000, see the Microsoft Web site *www.microsoft.com/hcl*. For software applications, search the list of compatible software applications list at *www.microsoft.com/windows2000/professional/howtobuy/upgrading/compat/default.asp*.

Figure 15-18   Windows 2000 Control Panel

Added Notebook Computer Features   The following features are available for notebook computers using Windows 2000, but are not a part of Windows 98:

- A feature called Offline Files and Folders allows you to download files and folders from a network to the PC so you can work on them offline. When the PC is later connected to the network, the files and folders can be uploaded to the network so that any changes are kept current on the network.

- The technology is included in Windows 2000 to allow a notebook user to work from home and connect to the corporate network over the Internet in a secure connection. To do this, Windows 2000 encrypts data before it is transmitted over the Internet.

- The power management features of Windows 2000 are enhanced and improved over those of Windows 98.

In summary, Windows 2000 Professional is designed as a desktop client computer operating system for a large network in a corporate or educational environment. Windows 98 is best used on a PC in a home or on a small network. Finally, for a notebook computer, Windows 2000 is the best choice.

Figure 15-19 Windows 2000 offers several features to control power available from the Power Options icon of Control Panel

Windows 2000 and Windows NT

Windows 2000 is the upgrade of Windows NT. It contains the same core technology and provides a number of new capabilities. Windows 2000 supports the FAT16, FAT32, and NTFS file systems. The Windows 2000 registry is organized and edited the same way as the Windows NT registry. Utilities, such as Event Viewer and Dr. Watson, also work the same way with minor changes. Windows 2000 provides an encrypted file system for added security and support for virtual private networks (secure connections over the Internet between a person and a business or between two businesses). Windows 2000 Help and Troubleshooter utilities are much more comprehensive than the Windows NT or Windows 98 utilities. Windows 2000 supports multiple monitors, IEEE 1394 (FireWire), USB, and ACPI.

Added Features Recall that Windows NT does not support Plug and Play. Windows 2000 uses an advanced version of Plug and Play that does all the work for configuring a system and does not use the Plug and Play features of a motherboard.

Many of the specific differences between Windows NT and Windows 2000 are beyond the scope of this chapter and are covered in detail later in this book in the chapters on each operating system.

Windows XP

Windows XP attempts to accomplish integration of 9x and 2000, while providing added support for digital and networking technologies. The two main versions are Windows XP Home and Windows XP Professional, though editions for the advanced server market will

15

likely be available by the time this book is published. Both editions have these features, among others:

- A new user interface, which is shown in Figure 15-20. Notice how different it looks from the desktops for earlier Windows versions such as Windows 9x and Windows 2000.

- The ability for two users to log on simultaneously, both with their own applications open

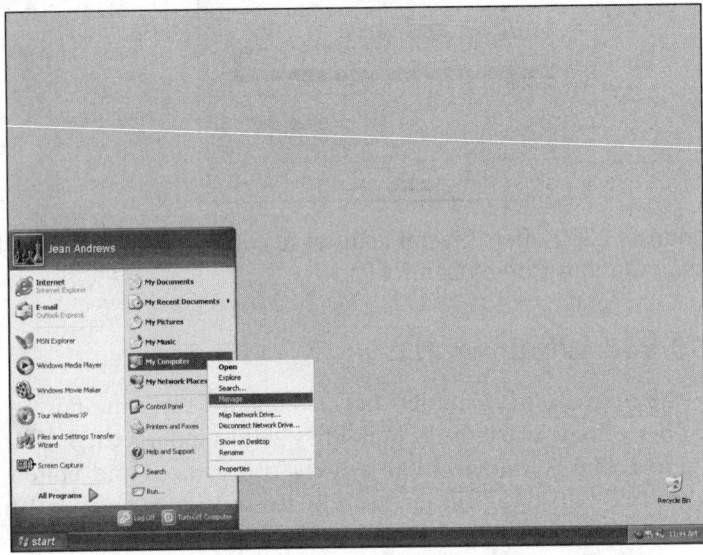

Figure 15-20   The Windows XP desktop and Start menu

- Windows Media Player for Windows XP, which provides a centralized application for working with digital media

- Windows Messenger for instant messaging, conferencing, and application sharing

- An expanded Help feature

- Advanced security features

Here are some of the features that Windows XP Professional adds to the home edition:

- Features for remote access, including remote desktop and roaming user profiles

- Additional security features

- Multilingual capabilities

- Support for new higher performance processors

There is also Windows XP 64-bit Edition designed to be used with a high-end CPU such as the Intel Itanium. This version of Windows XP is designed mostly for servers or heavily technical workstation users who need greater amounts of memory and higher performance than standard desktop users, for example, for scientific and engineering applications. For instance, an aircraft designer who needs to simulate how various conditions affect aircraft materials might use Windows XP on a system supporting resource-intensive simulation and animation applications.

Windows Internet Explorer, Windows Media Player, a firewall, and other Microsoft products are tightly integrated with the Windows XP operating system. Some users see this as a disadvantage and others see it as an advantage. Full evaluation of the integration of Microsoft software with the Windows XP operating system is beyond the scope of this overview.

The minimum requirements for Windows XP Professional are:

- A minimum of 64 MB of RAM, with 128 MB recommended

- At least 1.5 GB of free hard drive space, with 2 GB recommended

- A CPU that runs at least 233 MHz, with a 300 MHz CPU recommended. Remember that Windows XP can support two CPUs.

 TIP Remember that the requirements of an OS will vary depending on which version you have installed and what applications and hardware you have installed with it.

Windows XP provides several enhancements over Windows 2000 and other earlier versions. Table 15-8 summarizes the advantages and disadvantages of Windows XP.

Table 15-8 Advantages and disadvantages of Windows XP

Advantages	Disadvantages
• Provides better integration of Windows 9x and NT than did Windows 2000.	• Requires nearly a gigabyte of hard drive space for the operating system itself, and at least a 233 MHz processor with 64 MB of RAM.
• Offers significant GUI enhancements over earlier versions of Windows.	
• Adds features but uses only slightly more total memory for the OS than does Windows 2000.	• Programs used with Windows XP may require more than the minimum system specifications for the operating system.
• Adds advanced file sorting options, such as sorting pictures by resolution or sound files by artist.	• Nearly eliminates support for device drivers not approved by Microsoft.
• Includes built-in support for compressed files.	• Security concerns with centralized storage of online information in Microsoft Passport, a repository of the user IDs and passwords you use on the Internet.
• Has improved troubleshooting tools and is generally more stable than previous Windows OSs.	

15

Windows XP and Previous Windows OSs

Windows XP is replacing all previous versions of Windows in the home market and for the corporate desktop. If your hardware and applications qualify, select Windows XP Home Edition for a home PC over Windows 98/Me. For a corporate environment, use Windows XP Professional over Windows NT/2000. The only exception to this is compatibility issues with older hardware and software.

OTHER OPERATING SYSTEMS

As a PC technician you are likely to see a variety of operating systems on all kinds of personal computers. Windows and non-Windows operating systems share many of the same functions and goals. In this section, you will learn about Unix, Linux, OS/2, and Mac OS. Pay close attention to the advantages and disadvantages of each as well as comparisons between the technologies.

Unix

Unix originally was written for mainframe computers in the early 1970s; only in the past few years has it become available for many different kinds of computers, including PCs, and it is also a popular OS for networking. Unix computers are often used for Internet support. Problems with Unix stem mostly from the lack of consistency from one vendor's version to another. Hardware requirements for Unix vary widely depending on the version installed.

Table 15-9 summarizes the advantages and disadvantages of the Unix OS, including comparisons of Unix and Windows.

Table 15-9   Advantages and disadvantages of Unix

Advantages	Disadvantages
• Unix was written for powerful microcomputer systems and has strong multitasking capability, including preemptive multitasking. • Unix manages large quantities of memory well. • Unix performs very well in a networking environment. • Unix does not require as much memory or processor time as Windows does. • Unix systems generally do not crash as frequently as Windows systems. • Design and implementation of Unix include support for remote management.	• Unix industry standards are not uniform, making it difficult for Unix developers, administrators, and users to move from one Unix vendor to another. • Unix requires a powerful, large microcomputer system. • Few business applications software packages have been written for Unix for PCs, although there are several very powerful database packages available under Unix, such as Informix and Oracle. • Unix does not provide the user-friendly GUI that Windows OSs include. • Unix does not include some of the customized applications development and Web publishing features that Windows has.

Linux

A variation of Unix that has recently gained in popularity is Linux (pronounced "Lih-nucks"), an OS originally created by Linus Torvalds when he was a student at the University of Helsinki in Finland. Basic versions of this OS are available for free, and all the underlying programming instructions (called source code) are also freely distributed. Like Unix, Linux is distributed by several different companies, whose versions of Linux are sometimes called **distributions**. Popular distributions of Linux include SuSE (*www.suse.com*), RedHat (*www.redhat.com*), Caldera (*www.caldera.com*), Mandrake (*www.linux-mandrake.com*), and TurboLinux (*www.turbolinux.com*). Linux can be used both as a server platform and a desktop platform, but its greatest popularity has come in the server market. Hardware requirements for Linux vary widely, depending on the distribution and version installed.

 For more information on Linux, see *www.linux.org* as well as the Web sites of the different distributors of Linux.

Table 15-10 summarizes the advantages and disadvantages of Linux.

Table 15-10   Advantages and disadvantages of Linux

Advantages	Disadvantages
• Linux rarely crashes. • Basic versions can be downloaded and installed free. • Linux distributions that include technical support and software packages are available at a lower cost than other operating systems. • Linux generally handles network connections better than Windows. • Source code is available to users, enabling customization of the development environment. • Linux on an inexpensive PC is an excellent training tool toward learning Unix.	• Linux can be difficult to install, particularly for users who are not familiar with Unix commands. • Linux does not provide a GUI, though a Windows-like office suite can be installed. • Documentation can be spotty. • Linux can be difficult for casual users to operate. • Optimizing a Linux system can take a significant investment of time and research. • Not many applications are available for Linux on the desktop.

15

Network services such as a Web server or e-mail server often are provided by a computer running the Linux operating system. Linux is well suited to support various types of servers. Because Linux is very reliable and does not require a lot of computing power, it is sometimes used as a desktop OS, although it is not as popular for this purpose because it is not easy to use. As a PC support technician, you should know a little about Linux, including a few basic commands, which are covered in a later chapter.

Because many users prefer a Windows-style desktop, several applications have been written to provide a GUI shell for Unix and Linux. These shells are called X Windows. A typical X Windows screen is shown in Figure 15-21.

Figure 15-21   X Windows software provides a GUI shell for Linux and Unix users

OS/2

OS/2, written by IBM in cooperation with Microsoft Corporation, was designed as a replacement for DOS. OS/2 requires at least a 486 processor, 12–16 MB of RAM, and 100–300 MB of free hard drive space (depending on which features are installed). Many airline ticketing systems, worldwide and local banks, prisons, railroad systems, and U.S. government branches use OS/2. OS/2 never gained popularity for individual PC users. Although some people have predicted the downfall of OS/2 for years, its use continues, and applications are still being written for it. Recently, IBM adapted OS/2 for use with Web business solutions, including support for Web server software, Web protocols, and database interaction. Table 15-11 summarizes the advantages and disadvantages of OS/2.

Macintosh Operating System (Mac OS)

The Mac OS is available only on Macintosh computers. Both were first introduced in 1984. Several versions of the Macintosh OS have been written since, the latest being Mac OS X (ten), which offers easy access to the Internet and allows any Macintosh computer to become a Web server for a small network. Because it is easy to use, the Mac OS has been popular in educational environments from elementary school through the university level. It also provides excellent support for graphics and multimedia applications. Mac OS X requires at least 128 MB of RAM and 1.5 GB of hard drive space.

The Mac OS X interface is significantly different from that of the Mac OS 9, including two new features called the dock and the toolbar, as shown in Figure 15-22. When a Mac is turned on, a program called the Finder is automatically launched. This is the program that provides the desktop, which functions as the GUI for the Mac OS. Generally, under normal Mac OS operation, you cannot quit the Finder program.

Table 15-11   Advantages and disadvantages of OS/2

Advantages	Disadvantages
• OS/2 supports preemptive multitasking.	• Relatively few application software packages are written for OS/2.
• OS/2 can handle large quantities of memory directly and quickly.	• Many microcomputer users are not familiar with OS/2 and avoid it for that reason.
• OS/2 runs many DOS applications better than Windows and Unix.	• OS/2 requires a powerful computer system and large amounts of RAM and hard drive space to run efficiently.
• OS/2 has an icon-driven interface.	
• OS/2 works well in a networking environment.	
• Software designed for OS/2 sometimes runs more efficiently than comparable Windows programs.	

Figure 15-22   The Mac OS desktop is intuitive and easy to use

Windows are used to navigate among files and applications in the Mac. The Mac windows function similarly to windows in Microsoft operating systems, in that they can be minimized or maximized, icons can be moved around within them, and the window on top is active when several are open. You can work within one window, using buttons and menu options to navigate between applications and views, or you can open each application or view in a new Finder window.

Before Apple introduced the iMac, most of the Mac OS was permanently stored in Apple ROM, and only Apple had access to that code. This prevented other companies from manufacturing computers that ran Macintosh software. With the iMac, Apple moved most of the OS code into an upgradeable file called Mac OS ROM, stored on the hard drive, but still stores some startup code in a smaller ROM chip. The Mac OS X ROM file contains programs called managers that perform specific system functions like keeping track of windows, organizing menus, allocating system resources, and many others. Another important difference between Mac OS X and earlier versions is that the Mac OS X provides support for preemptive multitasking and is thus less likely to freeze than were earlier versions when several applications are running simultaneously.

The Mac OS X tries to make user interaction with the OS as smooth and as minimal as possible by providing superior Plug and Play capabilities, so that new hardware devices can be added easily and are automatically recognized by the OS. Additionally, the Mac OS does not allow users to interact directly with the OS code as some other OSs do. This can be an advantage because the Mac OS automatically performs certain functions that the user has to perform with other OSs.

 Although the initial cost of setting up a Macintosh system is generally higher than for a comparable IBM-compatible system, the cost of support and maintenance is generally lower for the Mac.

Table 15-12 summarizes the advantages and disadvantages of the Macintosh OS.

Table 15-12   Advantages and disadvantages of the Macintosh operating system

Advantages	Disadvantages
• The Mac OS has an excellent icon-driven interface, and it is easy to learn and use. • The Mac OS has supported a GUI interface and Plug and Play devices since it was first developed. • The Mac OS manages large quantities of memory. • Many applications exist for the Mac OS to create and edit graphics, build Web sites, and manage multimedia. • Mac OS systems are generally less prone to crashing than Windows systems.	• Historically, the Macintosh was not viewed as a professional computer but rather was relegated to education and game playing. Then the Mac gained a significant place in the professional desktop publishing and graphics markets. Most recently, the availability of more powerful IBM-compatible PCs and OSs to handle the high demands of graphics has reduced the demand for the Mac. • Because IBM-compatible PCs have a larger share of the market than Macintosh computers, software compatible with the Mac OS is not always as readily available.

CHAPTER SUMMARY

- An operating system controls the different hardware components that make up a computer and also provides an interface that a user or an application can use.
- Operating system functions include managing BIOS (programs permanently stored on hardware devices) and memory, interfacing between hardware and software, and performing tasks requested by the user (such as formatting disks and copying or deleting files).
- The two main components of an operating system are the shell and the kernel.
- The Windows registry and initialization files are used to store system information such as configuration settings, application settings, and user preferences.
- Users interact with an OS by a command-driven, menu-driven, or icon-driven interface.
- A thread is a process that the CPU is aware of.
- Multitasking is the ability of a CPU to run more than one program at a time. In cooperative multitasking, the CPU switches back and forth between applications. In preemptive multitasking, the CPU allots a specific period of time to an application and then preempts that application to provide CPU time to another application.
- OSs, applications, and CPUs all operate in either 16-bit (real) mode or 32-bit (protected) mode, depending on how many bits the CPU can process at once.
- The most well-known OSs for microcomputers are DOS, Windows, Unix, Linux, Mac OS, and OS/2.
- DOS was replaced by Windows as the most popular OS, but decisions made when DOS was designed still affect Windows 9x today.
- Windows 95, Windows 98, and Windows Me are collectively referred to as Windows 9x.
- Windows 9x is a bridge between older and newer OS technologies. It can support both 16-bit and 32-bit applications.
- The two upgrades Microsoft released for Windows 98 are Windows 98 SE and Windows Me.
- Windows NT breaks with previous versions of Windows by severing the connection between Windows and DOS and not allowing applications to have direct access to system resources.
- Windows NT is the first fully 32-bit Windows OS. Windows 2000 and XP are also 32-bit.
- Windows 2000 is actually a suite of operating systems: Windows 2000 Professional, Windows 2000 Server, Windows 2000 Advanced Server, and Windows 2000 Datacenter Server.
- Windows NT does not support Plug and Play, does not have a Safe Mode, and does not have a Device Manager. Windows 9x, Windows 2000, and Windows XP support all these.
- Windows XP attempts to accomplish integration of 9x and 2000, while providing added support for digital and networking technologies. The two main versions are Windows XP Home and Windows XP Professional.

15

- Unix was originally written for mainframe computers in the early 1970s. Today, it is available for other types of computers, such as servers and PCs. It is often used for Internet support.

- Linux is a variation of Unix that was created by Linus Torvalds. Basic versions of the OS are available for free download, and the underlying source code is openly distributed.

- OS/2 was written by IBM in cooperation with Microsoft and is now distributed and maintained by IBM. Systems that use OS/2 include airline ticketing systems, worldwide and local banks, and railroads. OS/2 is generally not very popular with PC users.

- Mac OS is only available on Macintosh computers. It has been widely used in educational markets and with graphics-intensive applications.

KEY TERMS

16-bit mode	environment	NTFS (NT file system)
32-bit mode	FAT (file allocation table)	operating system
ACPI (Advanced Configuration and Power Interface)	GUI (graphical user interface)	preemptive multitasking
		protected mode
API (Application Program Interface)	HAL (hardware abstraction layer)	RAM (random access memory)
backward-compatible	HCL (hardware compatibility list)	real mode
cluster	initialization files	registry
cooperative multitasking	kernel	sector
CPU (central processing unit)	LAN (local area network)	shell
	legacy	single-tasking
desktop	microprocessor	task switching
device driver	multiprocessing	thread
distributions	multitasking	track

16

UNDERSTANDING THE BOOT PROCESS AND COMMAND LINE

In this chapter, you will learn:

♦ To understand the process of booting to a command prompt

♦ How to create and use Windows 9x rescue disks to troubleshoot and solve problems when booting Windows

♦ How DOS and Windows 9x view and manage memory

♦ How DOS and Windows 9x use and manage floppy disks and hard drives

An OS relates to hardware and other software by using system resources on the motherboard and operating modes that apply to the CPU and other software. Recall that an OS and a CPU can operate in either real mode or protected mode and that a 32-bit OS such as Windows 9x can provide an environment for 16-bit software as well as 32-bit software. This chapter focuses on using the command line in real mode under Windows 9x, which is called MS-DOS mode. Real mode can be used to boot the computer and troubleshoot problems with Windows when it cannot boot to the Windows desktop. It is important to learn to use the command line because it is the tried-and-true tool for the worst of operating system problems. Also, Windows 9x uses DOS-like core components and, therefore, understanding and learning to use MS-DOS mode commands helps you to understand this foundation of Windows. In addition, when troubleshooting problems with booting Windows 2000/XP, a command prompt provided by the Recovery Console is sometimes the only tool that is available in the worst-case situations. Many of the commands in this chapter also work at the command prompt provided by the Recovery Console. In short, knowing how to use the command prompt is essential to PC troubleshooting.

We begin the chapter by learning how a PC first boots up and loads the operating system. Then, you will learn how to create floppy disks that can be used to boot to a command prompt. Next we will turn our attention to how memory, floppy disks, and hard drives are managed in MS-DOS mode. Finally, we will look at some essential steps to use when troubleshooting a failed boot.

 TIP There are three ways to access a command prompt on a computer running Windows: by booting to it from a bootable disk, by accessing a command prompt window from within Windows, or through the Recovery Console in Windows 2000 or Windows XP. You will learn about the Recovery Console in Chapter 21.

BOOTING UP YOUR COMPUTER

Understanding what happens when you first turn on your PC and boot up to an operating system command prompt or desktop is essential to learning to troubleshoot problems with the operating system. This section looks at the details of that process.

The term "booting" comes from the phrase "lifting yourself up by your bootstraps" and refers to the computer bringing itself up to an operable state without user intervention. Booting can refer to either a soft boot or hard boot. A **hard boot**, or **cold boot**, involves initially turning on the power with the on/off switch. A **soft boot**, or **warm boot**, involves using the operating system to reboot. For DOS, pressing the three keys Ctrl, Alt, and Del at the same time performs a soft boot. For Windows 9x and Windows NT/2000/XP, one way to soft boot is to click Start, click Shut Down, select Restart from the Shut Down menu, and then click OK. You can also press Ctrl + Alt + Del and then select Shut Down from the Close Program dialog box that appears.

A hard boot is more stressful on your machine than a soft boot because of the initial power surge through the equipment. Also, a soft boot is faster. Always use the soft boot method to restart unless the soft boot method doesn't work. If you must power down, avoid turning off the power switch and immediately turning it back on without a pause, because this can damage the machine. Some PCs have a reset button on the front of the case. Pressing the reset button starts the booting process at an earlier point than does the operating-system soft boot and is, therefore, a little slower but might work when the OS soft boot fails. For newer motherboards, pressing the reset button restarts the system without actually powering off and thus avoids the stress to the system caused by the initial power surge when the power first comes on.

Startup BIOS Controls the Beginning of the Boot

A successful boot process depends on the hardware, the BIOS, and the operating system all performing without errors. If errors occur, they might or might not stall or lock up the boot process. The boot process can be divided into four main steps: BIOS checking hardware, loading the OS, the OS initializing itself, and finally loading and executing an application. We will look at a brief overview of all four before we examine the first three parts in detail. Startup BIOS is in control for the first step; control is turned over to the OS in the second step.

Step 1: POST. Startup BIOS tests essential hardware components. This test is called the **power–on self test (POST).** The ROM BIOS startup program surveys hardware resources and needs, and assigns system resources to meet those needs (see Figure 16-1). The ROM BIOS startup program begins the startup process by reading configuration information stored in DIP switches, jumpers, and the CMOS chip, and then comparing that information to the hardware—the CPU, video card, floppy disk drive, hard drive, and so on. Some hardware devices have BIOSs of their own that request resources from startup BIOS, which attempts to assign these system resources as needed.

Figure 16-1   Boot Step 1: ROM BIOS startup program surveys hardware resources and needs and assigns system resources to satisfy those needs

16

Step 2: The ROM BIOS startup program searches for and loads an OS. Most often the OS is loaded from logical drive C on the hard drive. Configuration information on the CMOS chip tells startup BIOS where to look for the OS. Most newer BIOSs support loading the OS from the hard drive, a floppy disk, a CD, or a Zip drive. The BIOS turns to that device, reads the beginning files of the OS, copies them into memory, and then turns control over to the OS. This part of the loading process works the same for any operating system; only the OS files being loaded change.

Step 3: The OS configures the system and completes its own loading. The OS checks some of the same things that startup BIOS checked, such as available memory and whether that memory is reliable. Additionally, the OS continues beyond that by loading the software to control a mouse, CD-ROM, scanner, and other peripheral devices. These devices generally have device drivers stored on the hard drive.

Step 4: The user executes application software. When you tell the OS to execute an application, the OS first must find the application software on the hard drive, CD-ROM, or other secondary storage device, copy the software into memory, and then turn control over to it. Finally, you can command the application software, which makes requests to the OS, which, in turn, uses the system resources, system BIOS, and device drivers to interface with and control the hardware. At this point, the user is like the passenger in the back seat of the car with the chauffeur at the wheel. The trip has begun!

We now look at the first three steps in detail, beginning with the POST.

Power-on Self Test (POST) and Assignment of System Resources

When you turn on the power to a PC, the CPU begins the boot process by initializing itself and then turning to the ROM BIOS for instructions. The ROM BIOS then performs POST. Listed below are the key steps in this process.

- When the power is first turned on, the system clock begins to generate clock pulses.

- The CPU begins working and initializes itself (resetting its internal values).

- The CPU turns to memory address FFFF0h, which is the memory address always assigned to the first instruction in the ROM BIOS startup program.

- This instruction directs the CPU to run POST.

- POST first checks the BIOS program operating it and then tests CMOS RAM.

- A test determines that there has not been a battery failure.

- Hardware interrupts are disabled (this means that pressing a key on the keyboard or using another input device at this point will not affect anything).

- Tests are run on the CPU, and it is initialized further.

- A check determines if this is a cold boot. If so, the first 16 KB of RAM is tested.

- Hardware devices installed on the computer are inventoried and compared to configuration information.

- Video cards, memory, keyboard, floppy disk drives, hard drives, ports, and other hardware devices are tested and configured, and IRQ, I/O addresses, and DMA are assignments made. The OS will later complete this process.

- Some devices are set up to go into "sleep mode" to conserve electricity.

- The DMA controller is checked.

- Interrupt vectors are moved into the interrupt vector table.

- The interrupt controller is checked.

- CMOS setup (a BIOS program to change CMOS configuration data) is run if requested.

- BIOS begins its search for an OS.

During POST, before the CPU has checked the video system, errors are communicated by beeps. Short and long beeps indicate an error; the coding for the beeps depends on the BIOS. After POST checks and verifies the video controller card (note that POST does not check to see if a monitor is present or working), POST can use the monitor to display its progress. After checking video, POST checks RAM by writing and reading data. A running count of RAM is displayed on the monitor during this phase.

Next, the keyboard is checked, and if you press and hold any keys at this point, with some BIOSs an error occurs. Secondary storage, including floppy disk drives and hard drives, is also checked. The hardware that POST finds is checked against the data stored in the CMOS chip, jumpers, and/or DIP switches to determine if they agree.

System resources are assigned to devices by more than one method. Jumpers and DIP switches might be set to request a resource (for example, a jumper might be set "on" if IRQ 5 is requested or "off" if IRQ 7 is requested), or the resources needed might simply be hard-coded into the BIOS as part of the ROM programming that cannot be changed.

On earlier computers, system resources were always assigned to the device during the boot process (see Figure 16-1). Think of the process as a dialog. First, the startup BIOS recognizes that a hardware device is present. The BIOS asks the device, "What resources do you need?" The device says, "I need this IRQ, these I/O addresses, this DMA channel, and these addresses in upper memory for my BIOS." For legacy hardware, a device is the sole owner of these resources, and problems occur when more than one device attempts to use the same resource. (However, remember from our earlier discussion of IRQs that some newer buses allow more than one device to share the same IRQ and newer protected-mode BIOSs don't require upper memory addresses.) Today, more flexible Plug and Play devices simply say, "I need one IRQ, some I/O addresses, and this many memory addresses for my BIOS. Please tell me the resources I can use."

If a computer takes full advantage of the Windows 9x OS, its BIOS is Plug and Play BIOS, meaning that BIOS configures the Plug and Play devices before it loads Windows 9x. A Plug and Play device allows BIOS to select the device's computer resources, such as an IRQ, an I/O address, and DMA channels. BIOS first enables the devices that are not Plug and Play, and then tries to make the Plug and Play devices use the leftover resources. BIOS then turns this information over to Windows 9x when it loads, which completes the assignment of resources. Also recall that Windows 2000 and Windows XP use an advanced version of Plug and Play that does not use the BIOS Plug and Play, and that Windows NT does not support Plug and Play.

16

How the BIOS Finds and Loads the OS

Once POST and the first pass at assignment of resources is complete, the next step is to load an OS. Most often the OS is loaded from logical drive C on the hard drive. The minimum information required on the hard drive to load an OS is listed below. You can see some of these items labeled in Figure 16-2.

- A sector at the very beginning of the hard drive, called the **Master Boot Record (MBR)**, which contains a program needed to locate the beginning of the OS on the drive

- A **partition table**, which contains a map to the logical drives on the hard drive, including how many partitions and logical drives there are, which drive is the boot drive (the active partition), and where each logical drive begins and ends

- At the beginning of the boot drive (usually drive C) the OS boot record that loads the first program file of the OS; for Windows 9x, that program is **Io.sys**

- For Windows 9x, **Msdos.sys** is needed next, followed by **Command.com**. These two files, plus Io.sys, are the core components of the real-mode portion of Windows 9x; Windows NT/2000/XP have a different set of startup files.

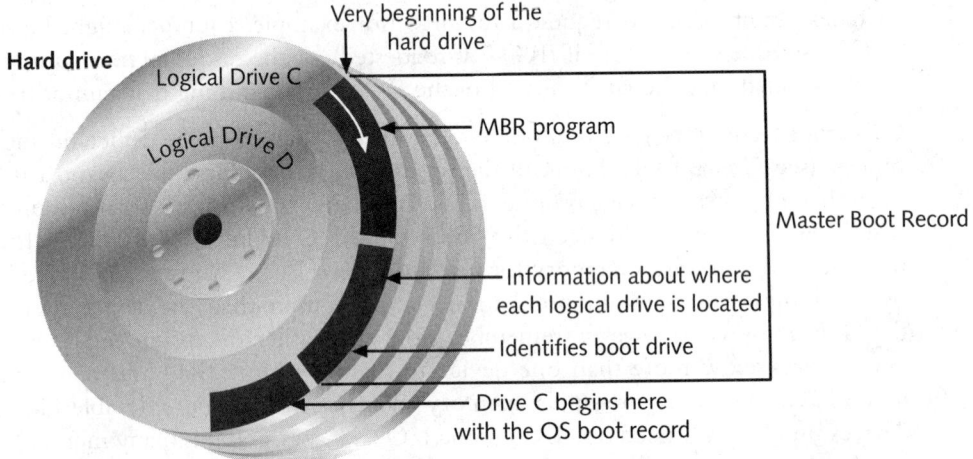

Figure 16-2 A hard drive might contain more than one logical drive; the partition table at the beginning of the drive contains information about the location of each logical drive, indicates which drive is the boot drive, and holds the Master Boot Record that begins the boot process for the operating system

One logical drive on the hard drive, usually drive C, is designated as the boot drive, and the OS is stored on it. At the beginning of this logical drive is the OS boot record, which contains the bootstrap loader, a program that knows the names of the files that contain the core programs of the OS.

The process by which the BIOS loads the OS begins with BIOS looking to CMOS setup to find out which secondary storage device should have the OS (see Figure 16-3). Setup might instruct the BIOS to first look on drive C, and, if no OS is found there, then try drive A; or the order might be A then C. If BIOS looks first to drive A and does not find a disk in the drive, it turns to drive C. If it first looks to drive A and finds a disk in the drive, but the disk does not contain the OS (for Windows 9x, that means the OS boot record, Io.sys, Msdos.sys, and Command.com), then this or a similar error message appears:

```
Non-system disk or disk error, press any key to continue
```

Figure 16-3 Boot Step 2: BIOS searches for and begins to load an operating system (in this example, Windows is the OS)

You must replace the disk with one that contains the OS or simply remove the disk to force the BIOS to continue on to drive C to find the OS.

Loading the MS-DOS Core of Windows 9x

This section describes what first happens during booting when only the MS-DOS core of Windows 9x is loaded, which brings the OS to a real-mode command prompt similar to a DOS command prompt. It's important for a PC technician to understand this real-mode DOS core because it is often used as a troubleshooting tool when the hard drive fails. You can boot to a command prompt in several ways, including booting from a Windows startup disk or using the Windows startup menu. How to prepare a startup disk is covered later in the chapter. How to use the Windows startup menu is covered in Chapter 18.

In Step 2 of Figure 16-3, the BIOS locates the MBR on the hard drive, which looks to the partition table to determine where the logical boot drive is physically located on the drive. It then turns to the OS boot record of that logical drive.

The OS boot record is a very short program; it loads just one hidden file, which makes up the DOS core, into memory (see Figure 16-3, Step 3 and Figure 16-4). (A **hidden file** is a file that is not displayed in the directory list.) The OS boot record program knows the file-name, which is Io.sys. The Io.sys file contains the basic I/O software for real mode and requires that the Msdos.sys file be present. Msdos.sys is a text file that contains some parameters and switches that can be set to affect the way the OS boots. You will learn about the contents of Msdos.sys and how to change it to affect the boot process in Chapter 18.

> The three OS files that are necessary in Windows 9x to boot to a command prompt are Io.sys, Msdos.sys, and Command.com. Config.sys and Autoexec.bat are not required but are used if they are present.

Once Io.sys is loaded into memory, the boot record program is no longer needed, and control is turned over to Io.sys. This program looks for Msdos.sys, reads it, and uses the settings in it. Io.sys then looks on the hard drive for a file named Config.sys. This configuration file contains commands that tell Io.sys how many files it can open at any one time (Files=) and how many file buffers to create (Buffers=). (A buffer is a temporary holding area for files.) Config.sys also includes the commands to load device drivers (Device=) as well as other information. An example of a typical command in Config.sys is the following command, which gives real-mode Io.sys access to memory above 1 MB, called extended memory:

```
Device=himem.sys
```

Several drivers can be loaded into memory from commands in Config.sys. Io.sys puts these programs in memory wherever it chooses. However, a program can request that it be put in a certain memory location.

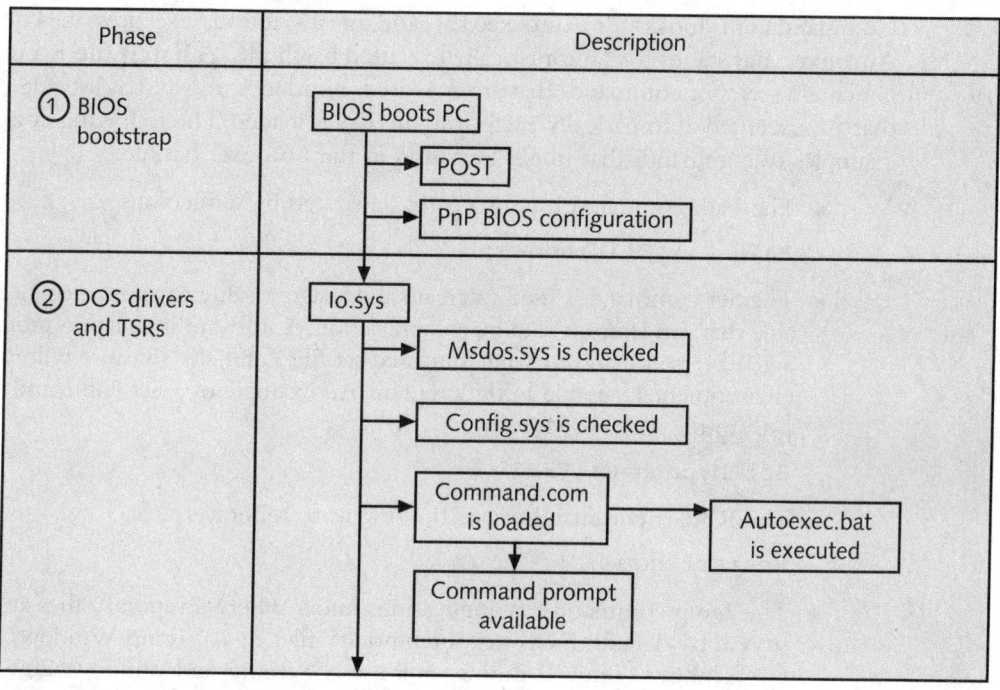

Phase	Description
① BIOS bootstrap	BIOS boots PC → POST → PnP BIOS configuration
② DOS drivers and TSRs	Io.sys → Msdos.sys is checked → Config.sys is checked → Command.com is loaded → Autoexec.bat is executed → Command prompt available

Figure 16-4   Boot Step 3: Operating system completes the boot process; MS-DOS core is loaded and command prompt presented to user

Sometimes Config.sys is used to create a RAM drive. A **RAM drive** is an area of memory that looks and acts like a hard drive, but because it is memory, it is much faster. It is sometimes used to speed up access to often-used software. Windows creates a RAM drive when booting from the startup disk, to hold files after they have been uncompressed, because this eliminates the need to have access to the hard drive and there is not room for them on the floppy disk. An example of a command in Config.sys to create a RAM drive is:

```
device=ramdrive.sys 2048
```

The command tells the OS to create a RAM drive that is 2048K in size.

After Config.sys is executed, Io.sys looks for another OS file, named Command.com. This file has three parts: more code to manage I/O, programs for internal OS commands such as Copy and Dir, and a short program that looks for the Autoexec.bat file.

 Some OS commands are **internal commands**, meaning they are embedded in the Command.com file, and others are **external commands**, meaning they have their own program files. An example of an external command is Format, stored in the file Format.com.

16

Command.com looks for Autoexec.bat and, if it's found, executes it. The filename **Autoexec.bat** stands for "automatically executed batch file." A **batch file** is a text file that contains a series of commands that are executed in order. Autoexec.bat lists OS commands that are executed automatically each time the OS is loaded. The following commands are examples of commands that might be found in the Autoexec.bat file:

- The Path command lists two paths, separated by semicolons.

   `PATH C:\;C:\Windows;`

- The Set command is used to create and assign a value to an environmental variable that can later be read by an application. A software installation program might add a Set command to your Autoexec.bat file. Later, the software will use the environmental variable in the program. An example of a Set command assigning a path to the variable Mypath is:

   `Set Mypath=C:\VERT`

- The Restart command causes the system to reboot.

   `Restart.com`

- The Temp command lets applications know where temporary files are to be stored. By default, DOS stores temporary files in C:\Temp, Windows 9x uses C:\Windows\Temp, Windows NT uses C:\Temp, and Windows 2000/XP uses C:\Winnt\Temp. Add the Temp command to Autoexec.bat if applications are putting temporary files in strange locations.

   `Temp=C:\Temp`

- The Echo command turns on and off the displaying of commands and messages. Use it in a batch file to control output to screen.

   `Echo off`

The boot process into real mode with a command prompt is completed after Autoexec.bat has finished executing. At this point, Command.com is the program in charge, providing you with a command prompt and waiting for your command. On the other hand, if a program or menu was executed from Autoexec.bat, it might ask you for a command.

The command prompt will indicate the drive that loaded the OS. If the OS files were loaded from a floppy disk, the command prompt will be A:\>, and if the OS was loaded from the hard drive, the command prompt will be C:\>. This drive and root directory are now the default drive and default directory, sometimes called the current working drive or directory.

If you want to complete loading Windows, use the Win command. Enter this command at the C prompt:

   `C:\> WIN`

Note that commands used at a command prompt are not case sensitive, that is, you can enter *WIN, Win,* or *win.*

Emergency Startup Disks

Although you normally boot from a hard drive, problems with the hard drive sometimes make it necessary to boot from a floppy disk. A floppy disk that has enough software on it to load an operating system is called a **bootable disk**, or **system disk**. A bootable disk that has some utility programs on it to troubleshoot a failed hard drive is called a **rescue disk**, **emergency startup disk (ESD)**, or **startup disk**. Having a rescue disk available for an emergency is very important, and a PC technician should always have one or more on hand. For DOS, you have to create your own rescue disk, making sure it includes the necessary system files and any utilities that you might need in an emergency.

Beginning with Windows 95, the OS provided an automated method to create a rescue disk. This rescue disk is created under the Control Panel, Add/Remove Programs group. The files on the rescue disk vary with the version of Windows 9x. You can also create your own bootable disk or add your own utilities to the rescue disk created by Windows. In addition, in some situations, you will need a startup disk, which you can use to boot up a PC for the first time after a new hard drive has been installed when the hard drive has nothing written on it.

In this section, you will learn several ways to create these startup disks and then, in the remainder of the chapter, you will learn to use many of the utilities that Windows puts on these disks.

Windows 9x Startup Disks

Windows 9x can create a startup disk for you, complete with everything you need to troubleshoot a failed hard drive or prepare a new hard drive for use. The disk does not need to be created on the same computer that will use it, although in most cases you should use the same version of Windows as used by the computer that will be using the disk. Follow these directions to create a startup disk for Windows 9x.

1. Click **Start** on the Taskbar, point to **Settings**, and then click **Control Panel**.

2. In the Control Panel window, double-click the **Add/Remove Programs** icon.

3. Click the **Startup Disk** tab, and then click the **Create Disk** button (see Figure 16-5).

4. Windows might need the Windows CD to create the disk. Insert the CD if it is requested. The startup disk will then be created.

16

Figure 16-5 Windows might use the Windows CD to create a startup disk

Table 16-1 lists the files included on the startup disk for Windows 98, Second Edition (Windows 98 SE). Other versions of Windows 9x contain some, but not all, of these files.

Table 16-1 Files on the Windows 98 startup disk

File	Description
Aspi2dos.sys	Real-mode Adaptec CD-ROM driver
Aspi4dos.sys	Real-mode Adaptec CD-ROM driver
Aspi8dos.sys	Real-mode Adaptec CD-ROM driver
Aspi8u2.sys	Real-mode Adaptec CD-ROM driver
Aspicd.sys	Real-mode Adaptec CD-ROM driver
Autoexec.bat	Batch file that contains commands executed at startup
Btcdrom.sys	Mylex/BusLogic CD-ROM driver
Btdosm.sys	Mylex/BusLogic CD-ROM driver
Command.com	Command interpreter
Config.sys	Loads device drivers
Drvspace.bin	Used to access compressed hard drive
Ebd.cab	Cabinet file containing other utility program files
Ebd.sys	Identifies the startup disk
Extract.exe	Used to uncompress the Ebd.cab file
Fdisk.exe	Partitions the hard drive
Findramd.exe	Locates the RAM drive during startup
Flashpt.sys	Mylex/BusLogic CD-ROM driver
Himem.sys	Extended Memory Manager
Io.sys	System boot file

Table 16-1   Files on the Windows 98 startup disk (continued)

File	Description
Msdos.sys	Contains boot parameters.
Oakcdrom.sys	Generic device driver for CD-ROM drives.
Ramdrive.sys	Creates a RAM drive at startup.
Readme.txt	Information about the startup disk.
Setramd.bat	Searches for a drive letter to assign the RAM drive.

The file Ebd.cab is a compressed file, called a **cabinet file**, that contains several compressed files that are listed in Table 16-2. You will learn to use many of these commands later in the chapter. During startup, the contents of the cabinet file are uncompressed and copied to the RAM drive because there is not enough space for them on the floppy disk and the startup disk assumes the hard drive might not be accessible. You can also use the Extract command to extract specific files when the RAM drive is not active.

Table 16-2   Files contained in the cabinet file, Ebd.cab

File	Description
Attrib.exe	Changes file attributes.
Chkdsk.exe	Determines the status of a disk and repairs it.
Debug.exe	Debugging utility used to view contents of memory.
Edit.com	Text editor used from a command prompt.
Extract.exe	Extracts files from a cabinet file.
Format.com	Formats a hard drive.
Mscdex.exe	Microsoft utility to interface with a CD-ROM driver.
Scandisk.exe	Checks and repairs hard drives.
Scandisk.ini	Contains parameters for Scandisk.exe.
Sys.com	Copies system files to a disk making it bootable.

Creating Your Own Bootable Rescue Disk for Windows 9x

16

Using Windows Explorer, you can create a system disk (Windows terminology for a bootable disk) and then copy program files to the disk that you might need in an emergency. The first step is to format the disk, which writes tracks on the disk and puts a file system on the disk. More details of what happens during the format operation are covered later in this chapter. To format a floppy disk in Windows 9x, follow these steps:

1. Click the **Start** button on the Taskbar, point to **Programs**, and then click **Windows Explorer**. Right-click either drive A or drive B. The shortcut menu in Figure 16-6 appears.

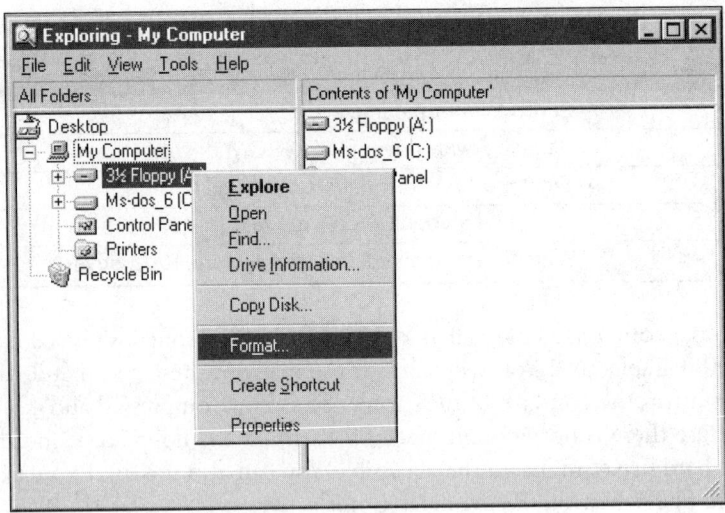

Figure 16-6   Menu for managing a floppy disk

2. Click **Format** on the menu. The dialog box shown in Figure 16-7 opens. Notice that you have three format options: Quick format (does not overwrite existing tracks), Full format (writes new tracks and sector markings), and an option to copy just the system files to the disk; these are the files needed to make the disk bootable (Io.sys, Msdos.sys, and Command.com are copied to the disk).

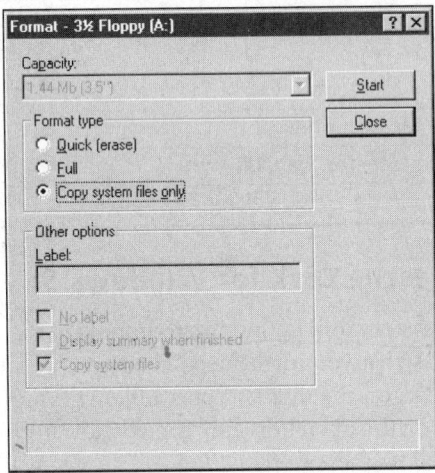

Figure 16-7   Format a disk in Microsoft Windows 9x

3. If the disk has been preformatted at the factory, you can select the third option to copy system files only, but if the disk has never been formatted, select **Full**. Then click **Start**.

From a command prompt, you can create your own bootable rescue disk and manually copy OS utility files to it. To make a bootable rescue disk for Windows 9x, from the command prompt, type:

```
Format A:/S
```

The command erases any files currently on the disk in drive A, and the /S switch copies the two hidden files, Io.sys and Msdos.sys, and Command.com to the disk in drive A, making the disk bootable.

You might also want to put some utility programs on the disk to help in troubleshooting. In addition to the files listed in Tables 16-1 and 16-2, other files you might need are xcopy.exe, MSD.exe, Mem.exe, and More.com. You will learn about these files later in this chapter.

Editing Autoexec.bat and Config.sys

You can change Config.sys and Autoexec.bat to configure your OS environment or troubleshoot boot problems. Use any text editor to edit the files. For example, from a command prompt, use EDIT, a full-screen text editor, and from Windows, use Notepad, WordPad, or Sysedit. From Windows, Sysedit is the preferred method and is covered in Chapter 18.

 TIP If you make a mistake when editing Autoexec.bat or Config.sys, you can cause a boot problem. Before editing these files on your hard drive, always make a rescue disk. If you are editing one of these files on a rescue disk, you can make a backup copy of the file before you edit it or have a second rescue disk ready just in case.

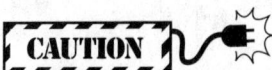 **CAUTION**

Do not use word-processing software, such as Word or WordPerfect, to edit Autoexec.bat or Config.sys, unless you use the ASCII text mode, because word-processing applications place control characters in their document files that prevent the OS from interpreting the file correctly.

You need to know how to edit the Autoexec.bat and Config.sys files at the command prompt. Follow these directions to use Edit.com to edit the Autoexec.bat file on a rescue disk:

1. Boot to the command prompt and make drive A the default drive, as follows:

```
C:\> A:
```

2. If the default directory is not the root directory, make it so, using the CD (Change Directory) command, as follows:

```
A:\DOS> CD\
```

The prompt at the root directory of drive A should look like this:

```
A:\>
```

No matter what the default directory was (in this example, it was \DOS), the backslash (\) in the prompt indicates that the root is now the default.

16

3. If Autoexec.bat exists on the floppy disk, back it up, as follows:

   A:\> `Copy Autoexec.bat Autoexec.bk`

4. Edit the file, as follows:

   A:\> `Edit Autoexec.bat`

Your screen should be similar to the one shown in Figure 16-8. After you have made your changes, to exit from the editor, press the **Alt** key to activate the menus, and choose **Exit** from the File menu. When asked if you want to save your changes, respond **Yes** to exit the editor and save any changes.

5. You can reboot your computer (**Crtl+Alt+Del**) to execute the new Autoexec.bat file, or you can type Autoexec.bat at the command prompt. If the computer stalls during the boot, use another startup disk to reboot. You can also press the **F5** key to bypass the startup files during the boot.

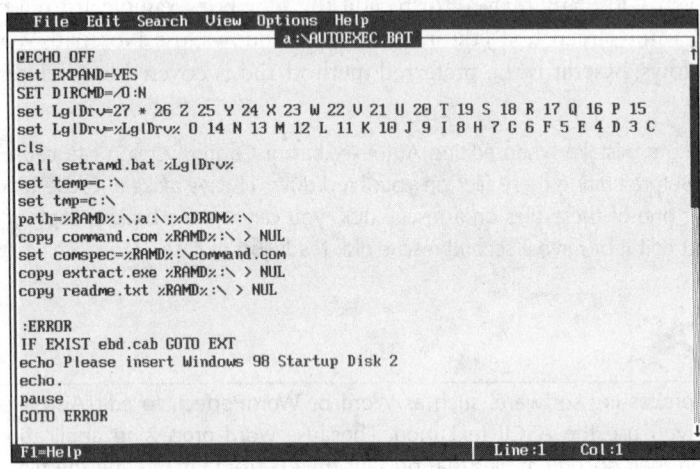

Figure 16-8   Edit Autoexec.bat

Accessing a Command Prompt

There are several ways to get to the command prompt. From the Windows desktop, you can access a command prompt by clicking Start, Programs, MS-DOS Prompt. A command prompt window, sometimes called a **DOS box**, appears, as shown in Figure 16-9. In it you can enter DOS-like commands discussed in this chapter. To exit the window, type Exit at the command prompt. This DOS box is not actually operating in real mode, but is operating in the virtual real mode provided by Windows. In fact, Windows sees this DOS box as the window provided for the 16-bit program Command.com. Every Windows OS offers this command window.

You can also get a DOS box by this alternate method: click Start, Run, and enter Command.com in the Run dialog box. Because you are not using true real mode and Windows is still running in the background, some commands entered from a DOS box might not work correctly or might even produce errors. There is a way to force Windows 9x to create a real-mode environment for a 16-bit program, and it is covered in Chapter 17.

You can use other means to get a true real-mode environment. The easiest way is to click Start, click Shutdown, and select Restart in MS-DOS mode from the Shutdown dialog box. This method only works for Windows 95 and Windows 98. Windows Me, Windows NT, Windows 2000, and Windows XP do not support accessing real mode in this way. For Windows Me and Windows XP, create a MS-DOS startup disk, insert it in the floppy disk drive, and boot from that disk. Recall that the startup BIOS boot sequence must be drive A first and then drive C for you be able to do this. Windows NT and Windows 2000 do not offer the option to create a MS-DOS startup disk, but, in a pinch, you can use one created on another PC to boot a Windows NT/2000 computer to a DOS prompt.

For Windows 9x, you can also boot to a command prompt by holding down the Ctrl key or the F8 key while booting, which causes the OS to display a startup menu. From the menu, select Command prompt only.

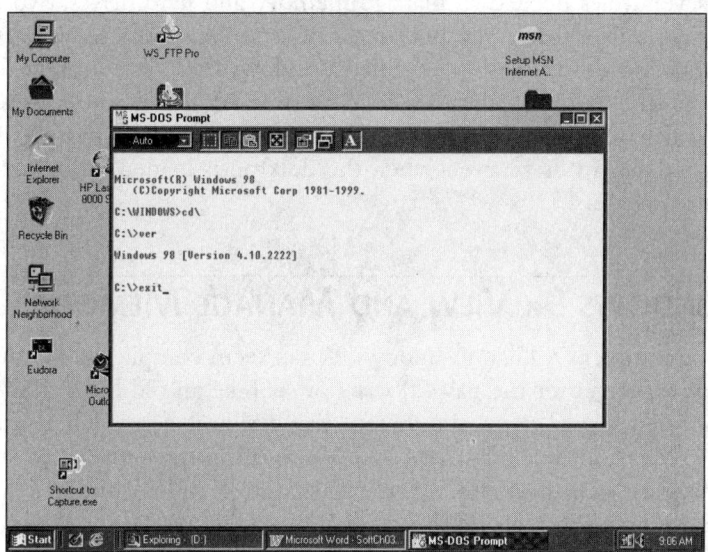

Figure 16-9   A MS-DOS Prompt window operates in the virtual real mode provided by Windows 9x

In some situations, it is appropriate to use a startup disk created by one OS to boot a failed system that has a different OS installed. For example, suppose Windows NT/2000/XP refuses to boot. Using a different PC, you can create a startup disk under Windows 98 and then use it to boot the Windows NT/2000/XP PC. If you can successfully boot to an A prompt, you have demonstrated that the hard drive or files stored on it is the source of the problem. However, it is best to use recovery procedures and disks native to the OS installed.

Suppose there is an important data file on the Windows NT/2000/XP computer and you don't have the proper recovery disks for the OS. You might be able to use the Windows 98 startup disk to recover the file. There are special considerations for Windows NT/2000/XP. These OSs support more than one file system, and a Windows 9x startup disk supports only FAT16 or FAT32. If a Windows NT/2000/XP hard drive has a different file system installed, such as NTFS (New Technology File System), then the Windows 9x startup disk will not be able to read that file system. In this situation, you can work from an A prompt (A:\>), but you will not be able to access the hard drive. The solution is to create rescue disks under these operating systems that can read the file system.

> When Windows 9x (including Windows Me) creates a startup disk, it copies files to the disk from the \Windows\Command\EBD folder. You can also copy these files to a formatted disk to manually create a startup disk.

Looking at the list of files in Tables 16-1 and 16-2 that are stored on a Windows 98 startup disk, you can see several files needed to manage memory and hard drives, two hardware devices that are essential to successfully booting a PC into Windows. Before we discuss how to use a startup disk to troubleshoot a failed Windows boot, let's look at these programs on the startup disk and how the MS-DOS portion of Windows 9x uses them to manage memory and hard drives. These same methods also affect the way Windows 9x manages memory and a hard drive, even when the desktop is loaded, so this knowledge also applies to future chapters.

How DOS and Windows 9x View and Manage Memory

Memory management under DOS and Windows 9x can seem complicated because of the way the process has evolved over the past 20 years or so. Like an old house that has been added to and remodeled several times, the present-day design is not as efficient as that of a brand new house. Decisions made by IBM and Microsoft in the early 1980s still significantly affect, and in some cases limit, the way memory is used under Windows 9x. Because Windows NT, followed by Windows 2000 and Windows XP, have had the luxury of being designed from the ground up, they are free of those limitations.

Earlier versions of DOS operated completely in real mode, which initially allowed access to only the first 1 MB of memory addresses. Later, DOS added a memory extender, **Himem.sys**, that allowed access to memory addresses above 1 MB. Early versions of Windows 3.x working with DOS could keep more than one program loaded at the same time by swapping them in and out of memory; this was called standard mode but was actually real mode with some fancy maneuvering. Later versions of Windows 3.x let 16-bit programs share memory (more than one program could access the same memory and share its data) in a "virtual DOS machine" in 386 enhanced mode. Windows 3.x could also perform virtual memory management by creating a swap file stored on the hard drive and using it as if it were memory.

Windows 95 was the first OS in the evolution of Windows operating systems to support 32-bit protected-mode applications software. Most of the OS code is written in 32-bit protected mode. It still allows 16-bit real-mode device drivers, and 16-bit software can run in a **virtual DOS machine (VDM)**, just as with Windows 3.x, or can run in real mode. A VDM is an environment that a 32-bit protected-mode OS provides for a real-mode program to operate in.

Windows NT made a break with the past. All its code is written in protected mode, and it does not allow other software to operate in real mode, but only in a virtual real mode, which it tightly controls. This makes Windows NT a much more stable OS than Windows 9x.

Table 16-3 summarizes the evolution of operating systems and software as it applies to memory. Notice that Windows NT is the first Microsoft OS to resolve many issues involving real mode, particularly the 1024K limitation imposed by real mode. With DOS and Windows 3.x, this limitation directly affected managing memory resources and, in some cases, can still be significant with Windows 9x.

Table 16-3   Summary of how operating systems have evolved in managing memory

Operating System	Real Mode	Protected Mode
DOS	Operates totally in real mode, but later offered Himem.sys, a device driver that allows programs access to extended memory.	NA
DOS with Windows 2.x	Operated totally in real mode but managed the process of switching programs in and out of memory.	NA
DOS with Windows 3.x	Real mode was called standard mode. Allows only one 16-bit application at a time in memory.	Protected mode is called 386 enhanced mode. Multiple applications can share memory.
Windows 9x	Allows real-mode drivers to be loaded during startup; 16-bit DOS applications are allowed a real-mode session.	Switches back and forth between real mode and protected mode as necessary; supports both 16-bit and 32-bit applications in a virtual machine.
Windows NT/2000/XP	NA	All work is done in protected mode. Supports 32-bit applications. 16-bit applications can operate in a virtual machine only.

16

Physical Memory and Memory Addresses

To understand how memory use evolved, beginning with DOS and moving to Windows NT, you must understand basic memory concepts. A memory address is a number the CPU assigns to ROM or RAM to track the memory it can use. A CPU has a limited number of memory addresses that it can assign to physical memory, determined by the number of memory address lines available on the memory bus.

Some older 16-bit programs work only when they can use certain memory addresses, such as a hexadecimal number like C80000. This address is part of the physical memory's ROM programming; no other address works for it. An example of this kind of memory is a ROM chip on an older video card. Some memory, usually ROM chips on expansion boards, must be assigned one of two, or sometimes three, sets of addresses. You make the choice by setting jumpers or DIP switches on the board or, in more recent cases, when you run an installation program for the board. New Plug and Play boards don't have this restriction. Their ROM code can be assigned any values chosen by the OS or system BIOS. Plug and Play cards are required to use whatever memory addresses are assigned to them. The system is free to assign any address it chooses to this physical memory.

Both RAM and ROM must be assigned memory addresses so the CPU can access this memory. System BIOS stored on motherboard ROM chips must be assigned addresses by the CPU so that the CPU can access that programming. The assigning of addresses to both RAM and ROM occurs during booting, and is sometimes called memory mapping. In Figure 16-10, the memory addresses available to the CPU are listed on the left, and the physical RAM and ROM that need these addresses are on the right. These RAM modules are located on the motherboard, and ROM chips are found on a sound card, network card, and video card in this example. RAM is holding several device drivers, applications, and the OS.

Programming stored on ROM chips is not usually copied into RAM, despite what many people believe. It is simply assigned memory addresses by the CPU. These ROM programs become part of the total memory available to the CPU, and do not use up part of total RAM. The resources they use are memory addresses. The RAM memory is still available to be assigned other addresses. There is an exception, called shadowing ROM, when programs stored on ROM are copied to RAM to improve performance.

Finally, memory management in DOS and Windows 9x presents limitations not so much because of the operating systems themselves, but because applications, device drivers, and BIOS used the standards presented to the industry when DOS was first introduced and these standards are still in effect today. Compared to that of other operating systems, memory management in DOS and Windows 9x is handicapped because DOS has existed longer than most other operating systems. Therefore, DOS must maintain compatibility with software and devices that have been around for a long time. Also, Microsoft made the commitment with Windows 9x that it, too, would be compatible with older software and BIOS written for DOS and Windows 3.x using DOS. Probably the greatest limitation of Windows 9x today is this commitment to maintain backward-compatibility with older software and hardware.

Memory Addresses	Physical Location of Memory	Contents
8 MB		
	RAM	32-bit application's data
		32-bit application
		32-bit BIOS and device drivers
		portion of OS
1024K		
	ROM	system BIOS and startup BIOS
	RAM	16-bit sound card device driver
	ROM	16-bit network card BIOS
	ROM	16-bit video ROM
640K	RAM	16-bit video RAM
	RAM	16-bit application's data
		16-bit application
		16-bit mouse device driver
		operating system
0		data used by BIOS and OS

Extended memory (8 MB to 1024K), *Upper memory* (1024K to 640K), *Conventional or base memory* (640K to 0)

Figure 16-10 Memory map showing how ROM and RAM, on and off the motherboard, might be mapped to memory addresses

16

Areas of the Memory Map

There are several types of memory that the OS manages: conventional, upper, and extended memory. These memory types are logical divisions or categories rather than physical ones, and the divisions are determined by their memory addresses rather than by their physical location. The following sections cover this logical memory management. A segment of

RAM can be assigned memory addresses in the upper memory range today but be assigned a range of addresses in extended memory tomorrow. It's still just RAM, no matter what address it's assigned. The difference is the way the CPU can use this memory because of the addresses assigned to it.

To get a clear picture of this memory-addressing schema, consider the memory map shown in Figure 16-11. The first 640K of memory addresses is called **conventional memory**, or base memory. The memory addresses from 640K up to 1024K are called **upper memory**. Memory above 1024K is called extended memory. The first 64K of extended memory is called the **high memory area (HMA)**.

Conventional Memory

In the early 1980s, when IBM and Microsoft were designing the original PCs, they decided to make 640K of memory addresses available to the user, thinking that this was plenty for anything the user would ever want to do. This 640K of addresses was intended to hold the OS, the applications software, and the data being processed. At that time, 640K of memory addresses was more than enough to handle all the applications available. Today, 640K of memory addresses is inadequate, for the following reasons:

- Many applications are very large programs, requiring a considerable number of memory addresses to hold the programs as well as the data.

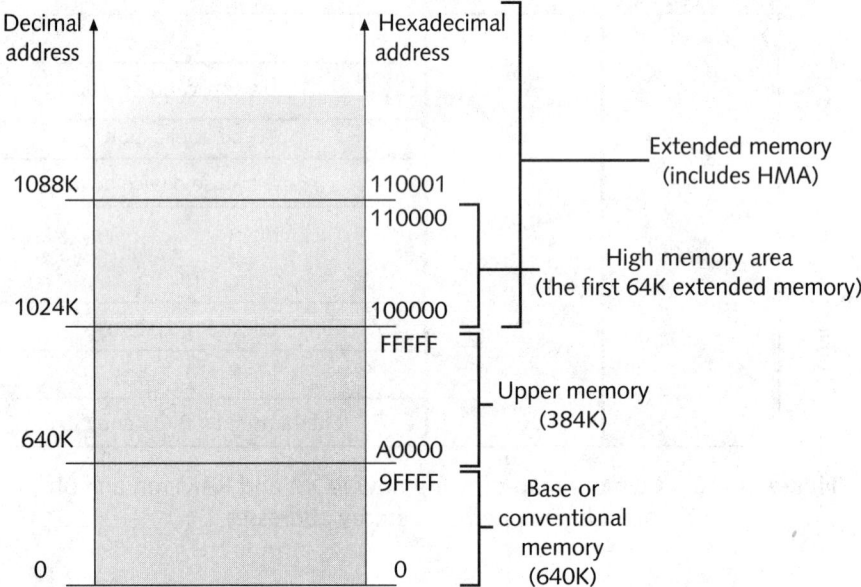

Figure 16-11   Memory address map showing the starting and ending addresses of conventional, upper, and extended memory, including the high memory area

- Often more than one application runs at the same time, each of which requires its own memory area for the program and data. Also, sometimes computers in a network serve more than one user at a time. In the early 1980s, a PC was expected to be used by a single user, operating one application at a time.

- Users expect software to provide a friendly graphical user interface, or GUI. Graphical user interfaces provide icons, graphics, and windows on a screen, all requiring large amounts of memory.

The problem caused by restricting the number of memory addresses available to the user to only 640K could have been easily solved by simply providing more addresses to the user in future versions of DOS. However, another original design decision ruled this out. The next group of memory addresses, the 384K above conventional memory, called upper memory, were assigned to utility operations for the system. The system requires memory addresses to communicate with peripherals. The programs (such as BIOS on a video card or on the motherboard) and data are assigned memory addresses in this upper memory area. For example, the video BIOS and its data are placed in the very first part of upper memory, the area from 640K to 768K. All video ROM written for DOS-based computers assumes that these programs and data are stored in this area. Also, many DOS and Windows applications interact directly with video ROM and RAM in this address range.

Programs almost always expect data to be written into memory directly above the addresses for the program itself, an important fact for understanding memory management. Thus, if a program begins storing its data above its location in conventional memory, eventually it will "hit the ceiling," the beginning of upper memory assigned to video ROM. The major reason that applications have 640K memory limit is that video ROM begins at 640K. If DOS and Windows 9x allowed applications into these upper memory addresses, all DOS-compatible video ROM would need to be rewritten, and many DOS applications that access these video addresses would not work. Know that 32-bit device drivers and applications under Windows 9x don't have this problem because they can run from extended memory and turn to the OS to access video.

Windows NT/2000/XP are not backward-compatible with older hardware and software because they do not manage memory in the same way. You will learn more about how these operating systems manage memory later in this book.

Upper Memory

The memory map in Figure 16-11 shows that the memory addresses from 640K up to (but not including) 1024K are called upper memory. In the hexadecimal number system (see Appendix E for an explanation of this system), upper memory begins at A0000 and goes through FFFFF. Video ROM and RAM are stored in the first part of upper memory, hex A0000 through CFFFF (the A, B, and C areas of memory). Sixteen-bit BIOS programs for other legacy expansion boards are assigned memory addresses in the remaining portions of upper memory. BIOS on the motherboard (system BIOS) is assigned the top part of upper memory, from F0000 through FFFFF (the F area of upper memory). Upper memory often has unassigned addresses, depending on which boards are present in the system. Managing

16

memory effectively involves gaining access to these unused addresses in upper memory and using them to store device drivers and TSR (terminate-and-stay-resident) programs.

Figure 16-12 shows that video memory addresses fall between A0000 and CFFFF. For VGA and Super VGA video, the A and B areas hold data sent to the video card, and the C area contains the video BIOS.

Extended Memory and the High Memory Area

Memory above 1 MB is called extended memory. The first 64K of extended memory is called the high memory area, which exists because a bug in the programming for the older 286 CPU (the first CPU to use extended memory) produced this small pocket of unused memory addresses. Beginning with DOS 5, the OS capitalized on this bug by storing portions of itself in the high memory area, thus freeing some conventional memory where DOS had been stored. This method of storing part of DOS in the high memory area is called "loading DOS high." You will see how to do this later in this chapter.

Extended memory is actually managed by the OS as a device (the device is memory) that is controlled by a device driver. To access extended memory, you need the device driver (called a memory extender) that controls it, and you must use applications that have been written to use the extended memory. The amount of extended memory you can have on your computer is limited by the amount of RAM that can be installed on your motherboard and the number of memory addresses the CPU and the memory bus can support.

Figure 16-12   Memory map of upper memory showing starting and finishing addresses and video ROM and RAM assignments

Utilities that Manage Memory

The two utilities used by Windows 9x to manage memory above 640K are Himem.sys and Emm386.exe. Himem.sys is the device driver for all memory above 640K. The program file **Emm386.exe** contains the software that loads device drivers and other programs into upper memory. Himem.sys is automatically loaded by Windows 9x during the boot process but can also be loaded by an entry in Config.sys. Emm386.exe is not loaded automatically by Windows 9x, but you can load it by an entry in Config.sys.

Using Himem.sys

Himem.sys is considered a device driver because it manages memory as a device. It can be executed by the Device= command in Config.sys. Figure 16-13 shows an example of a very simple Config.sys file on a floppy disk that loads Himem.sys. The Config.sys file is being edited by the Edit.com text editor utility.

To create the file on a floppy disk, you can use either of these two methods:

- Make drive A the default drive and enter this command:

  `A:\> Edit Config.sys`

- Make drive C the default drive and enter this command:

  `C:\> Edit A:Config.sys`

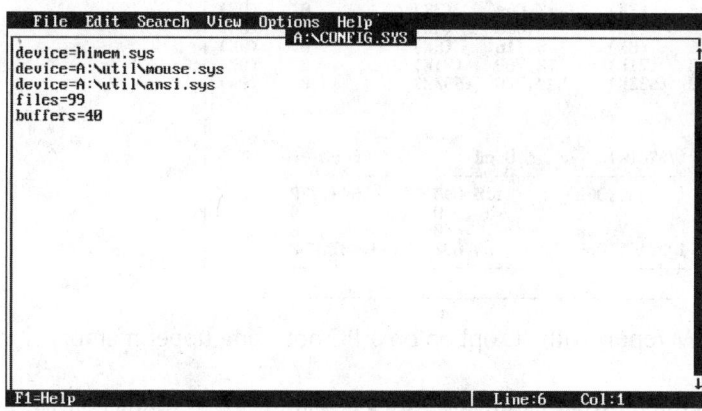

Figure 16-13   Config.sys set to use memory above 640K

The second line in the Config.sys file, device=A:\util\mouse.sys, tells DOS to load into memory a device driver that is found on the floppy disk in the \Util directory, which allows you to use the mouse while in MS-DOS mode.

The third line in the Config.sys file, device=A:\util\ansi.sys, tells DOS to load the device driver Ansi.sys into memory. Ansi.sys helps control the keyboard and monitor, providing color on the monitor and an additional set of characters to the ASCII character set. For more information about ASCII and ANSI, see Appendix D.

16

Using Emm386.exe

In DOS and Windows 9x, Emm386.exe manages the memory addresses in upper memory. Before we see how to use it, let's begin by examining memory when upper memory addresses are not available. To do that, we use the MEM command, which lets us view how memory is currently allocated. Use the /C option to get a complete list and include the |MORE option to page the results on your screen. Figure 16-14 was produced using this command:

```
MEM /C |MORE
```

In Figure 16-14, the first column shows the programs currently loaded in memory. The second column shows the total amount of memory used by each program. The columns labeled Conventional and Upper Memory show the amount of memory being used by each program in each of these categories. This PC is not making use of upper memory for any of its programs. At the bottom of the screen is the total amount of free conventional memory (544,720 bytes) that is available to new programs to be loaded. Making this value as high as possible is the subject of this section.

```
Modules using memory below 1 MB:

Name        Total              Conventional         Upper Memory
--------    ----------------   -----------------    ----------------
MSDOS        18,672   (18K)     18,672   (18K)              0   (0K)
HIMEM         1,168    (1K)      1,168    (1K)              0   (0K)
DBLBUFF       2,976    (3K)      2,976    (3K)              0   (0K)
IFSHLP        2,864    (3K)      2,864    (3K)              0   (0K)
WIN           3,616    (4K)      3,616    (4K)              0   (0K)
COMMAND       8,416    (8K)      8,416    (8K)              0   (0K)
SAVE         72,768   (71K)     72,768   (71K)              0   (0K)
Free        544,720  (532K)    544,720  (532K)              0   (0K)

Memory Summary:

Type of Memory     Total           Used            Free
----------------   -----------     -----------     -----------
Conventional         655,360         110,640         544,720
Upper                      0               0               0
Reserved                   0               0               0
Extended (XMS)   133,156,864          69,632     133,087,232
                   -----------     -----------     -----------
-- More --
```

Figure 16-14   MEM report with /C option on a PC not using upper memory

Creating and Using Upper Memory Blocks   Figure 16-15 shows an example of a Config.sys file that is set to use upper memory addresses. The first line loads the Himem.sys driver. The second line loads the Emm386.exe file. Emm386.exe assigns addresses in upper memory to memory made available by the Himem.sys driver. The NOEMS switch at the end of the command line says to Windows, "Do not create any simulated expanded memory." Expanded memory is an older type of memory above 1 MB that is no longer used by software. The command to load Emm386.exe must appear after the command to load Himem.sys in the Config.sys file.

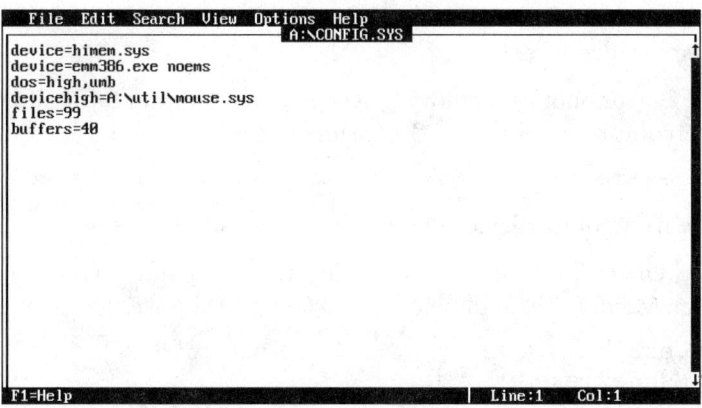

Figure 16-15   Config.sys set to use upper memory

The command DOS=HIGH,UMB serves two purposes. The one command line can be broken into two commands like this:

```
DOS=HIGH
DOS=UMB
```

The DOS=HIGH portion tells the OS to load part of the DOS core into the high memory area ("loading DOS high"). Remember that the high memory area is the first 64K of extended memory. This memory is usually unused unless we choose to store part of DOS in it with this command line. Including this command in Config.sys frees some conventional memory that would have been used by the OS.

The second part of the command, DOS=UMB, creates upper memory blocks. An **upper memory block (UMB)** is a group of consecutive memory addresses in the upper memory area that has had physical memory assigned to it. The OS identifies blocks that are currently not being used by system ROM or expansion boards, and the memory manager makes these blocks available for use. This command, DOS=UMB, enables the OS to access these upper memory blocks. After the UMBs are created, they can be used in these ways:

- `Devicehigh=` command in Config.sys
- `Loadhigh` command in Autoexec.bat
- `Loadhigh` command at the command prompt (explained below)

The next line in the Config.sys file in Figure 16-15 uses a UMB. The command Devicehigh=A:\Util\Mouse.sys tells the OS to load the mouse device driver into one of the upper memory blocks created and made available by the previous three lines. This process of loading a program into upper memory addresses is called loading high.

Loading Device Drivers High   Using the Devicehigh= command in Config.sys, rather than the Device= command, causes the driver to load high. With the Devicehigh= command, the OS stores these drivers in UMBs using the largest UMB first, then the next largest, and so on until all are loaded. Therefore, to make sure there is enough room to hold

16

them all in upper memory, order the Devicehigh= command lines in Config.sys so that the largest drivers are loaded first.

You can determine the amount of memory a device driver allocates for itself and its data by using the MEM command with the /M filename option:

```
MEM /M filename
```

The filename is the name of the device driver without the file extension.

You can also use a UMB from Autoexec.bat using the Loadhigh (LH) command. For example, to load high Mscdex.exe, a utility to access a CD-ROM drive, use either command:

```
LH Mscdex.exe
Loadhigh Mscdex.exe
```

In either case, the program is loaded into the largest UMB available and does not use up more precious conventional memory. Note that before the Loadhigh command will work, the program files Himem.sys and Emm386.exe must be available to the OS and these three lines must be added to Config.sys and executed by booting the computer:

```
Device=HIMEM.SYS
Device=EMM386.EXE NOEMS
DOS=UMB
```

If the Himem.sys and Emm386.exe files are not in the root directory of the boot device, you must include the path to the file name in the Device= line, like this:

```
Device=C:\DOS\HIMEM.SYS
```

> **TIP** When a program is loaded high, two things can go wrong. Either the program might not work from upper memory, causing problems during execution, or there might not be enough room in upper memory for the program and its data. If the program causes the computer to hang when you attempt to run it, or if it simply refuses to work correctly, remove it from upper memory.

Some Default Settings Used by Windows

You have just seen how Windows MS-DOS mode uses Config.sys and Autoexec.bat. Most of the settings that once were put into Config.sys under DOS are now embedded into the Windows 9x Io.sys file. If Config.sys or Autoexec.bat are present, the entries in those files override the default entries in Io.sys. The entries in Io.sys cannot be changed and are listed in Table 16-4.

Table 16-4   Entries in Io.sys that once were in Config.sys

Entry	Description
Buffers=30	The number of file buffers to create.
DOS=HIGH	The DOS core of Windows 9x is loaded into the high memory area (HMA).
Files=60	The number of files that can be open at one time under 16-bit applications.
Himem.sys	Himem.sys is loaded to manage extended memory in Windows 9x.
Lastdrive=Z	The last letter that can be assigned to a logical drive.
Setver.exe	A program that tells DOS applications that the version of DOS they are looking for is the version they are using. The program allows some older DOS applications to run that might otherwise hang.
Shell=Command.com /P	Loads Command.com and executes Autoexec.bat.
Stacks=9,256	The number of frames of instructions that can be held in memory in a queue at one time. Used for backward compatibility with older applications.

MANAGING FLOPPY DISKS AND HARD DRIVES

When a hard drive (sometimes called the HDD) is first installed, it has nothing written on it except empty track markings put there at the factory. A floppy disk is completely blank and does not even have these track markings. The OS must prepare both these media for use by putting track markings on a floppy disk and putting a file system on both floppy disk and hard drive. In addition, the OS is responsible for managing the file system, including creating, deleting, copying and moving directories and files. This section looks at the commands to do all this from a command prompt under Windows 9x. Except for writing a new file system to a hard drive, these same functions can also be done from within Windows using Windows Explorer.

Before we get into how to use specific commands, you will learn about how data is organized on floppy disks and hard drives.

16

How Data is Logically Stored on a Floppy Disk

When a floppy disk is first formatted, sector and track markings are written to the disk. Recall from Chapter 15 that tracks are concentric circles on the disk and a segment of a track, called a sector, always holds 512 bytes of data. All floppy disks, no matter what size or density, and hard drives are divided into tracks and sectors, and each sector holds 512 bytes of data.

A cluster, sometimes called a file allocation unit, is a group of sectors that is the smallest unit on a disk used to hold a file or a portion of a file. "Sector" refers to how data is physically stored on a disk, while "cluster" describes how data is logically organized. The BIOS manages the disk as physical sectors, but the OS considers the disk only as a long list of clusters that can each hold a fixed amount of data (see Figure 16-16). The OS keeps that list of clusters in the file allocation table (FAT).

There are several variations of floppy disks including the older 5¼ inch floppy disk, the 3½inch double-density floppy disk, and the most current floppy disk, the 3½ inch high-density disk, which holds 1.44 MB of data. Let's see how this disk holds that data.

The 3½ inch high-density floppy disk has 80 tracks and 18 sectors per track on each side. Each side has 80 tracks × 18 sectors, or 1,440 sectors. This type of disk has only one sector per cluster, making 1,440 × 2 sides, or 2,880 clusters. Because each cluster holds 512 bytes (one sector) of data, a 3½ -inch high-density floppy disk has 2,880 × 512 = 1,474,560 bytes of data. Divide this number by 1,024 to convert bytes to kilobytes. The storage capacity of this disk is 1,440 kilobytes. Divide by 1,000 to convert kilobytes to megabytes, and the storage is 1.44 MB.

 Note There is a discrepancy in the computer industry regarding the definition of a megabyte. Sometimes 1 megabyte = 1,000 kilobytes; at other times, we use the relationship of 1 megabyte = 1,024 kilobytes.

Figure 16-16   Clusters or file allocation units are managed by the OS in the file allocation table (FAT), but BIOS manages these clusters as one or two physical sectors on the disk

The Formatting Process for a Floppy Disk

The formatting of all floppy disks is similar, no matter what their size or density. During formatting, the Format command without added options performs the following steps:

■ Creates the tracks and sectors by writing tracks as necessary and marks the place on each track where the first sector begins

- Creates the boot record (discussed below)
- Creates two copies of the file allocation table (FAT) (discussed in detail on the following page)
- Creates the root directory

These basic steps are described in detail next. Later in this chapter you will learn how to add options to the formatting process.

Creating the Tracks and Sectors

The Format command prepares a disk for use. The first step in the formatting process erases any data on the disk. In its simplest form, without adding any parameters, the Format command always overwrites all data on the disk.

The Boot Record

At the beginning of each floppy disk, the first sector contains basic information about how the disk is organized, including the number of sectors, the number of sectors per cluster, the number of bits in each FAT entry, and other basic information that an OS or BIOS needs in order to read the data on the disk. This information is stored in the first sector on the disk called the **boot sector,** or **boot record**. At the end of the boot record is a small program, called the **bootstrap loader,** that can be used to boot from the disk. Table 16-5 shows the layout of the boot record and its contents. The boot record indicates which version of DOS or Windows was used to format the disk, and is always located at the beginning of the disk at track 0, sector 1 (bottom of the disk, outermost track). This uniformity of layout and content allows any version of DOS or Windows to read any DOS or Windows disk. You will learn more about hard drive boot records later in this chapter.

Table 16-5   Contents of the floppy disk boot record

1. Bytes per sector
2. Sectors per cluster
3. Number of FATs
4. Size of the root directory
5. Number of sectors
6. Medium descriptor byte
7. Size of the FAT
8. Sectors per track
9. Number of heads (always 2)
10. Number of hidden sectors
11. Program to load the OS

16

The ninth item in Table 16-5 is the number of heads. A head refers to the read/write head that is a part of the physical components of the drive. Because the disk always has only one top and one bottom with a read/write head assigned to each, the number of heads is always two. The last item in Table 16-5 is the program that searches for and loads Io.sys if it is present on the disk. If Io.sys, Msdos.sys, and Command.com are on the disk, the disk is said to be bootable.

All boot records, however, are the same, whether or not the disk is bootable. When the PC is looking for a bootable disk during POST, if a disk is in the drive, the program stored in the boot record is executed. If this program does not find Io.sys, the disk is not bootable and a message appears, such as the following:

```
Non-system disk or disk error...Replace and strike any key
when ready...Disk boot failure
```

POST stops until the user intervenes. Only the program in the boot record can determine if the disk is bootable.

The File Allocation Table (FAT)

When formatting a floppy disk, after the boot record is created, the next step is to write two copies of the FAT to the disk. The FAT lists the location of files on the disk in a one-column table. Because the width of each entry in the column is 12 bits, the FAT is called a 12-bit FAT or **FAT12**. The FAT lists how each cluster or file allocation unit on the disk is currently used. A file is stored in one or more clusters that do not have to be contiguous on the disk. If a file is not stored in consecutive clusters, it is called a **fragmented file**. In the FAT, some clusters might be marked as bad (the 12 bits to mark a bad cluster are FF7h). These bits can be entered in the FAT when the disk is formatted or added later with the Recover command. An extra copy of the FAT is kept immediately following the first. If the first is damaged, sometimes you can recover your data and files by using the second copy.

The Root Directory

After creating the file allocation tables, the formatting process sets up the root directory. Recall that the root directory, or main directory, is a table listing all the files assigned to this table. The root directory contains a fixed number of rows to accommodate a predetermined number of files and subdirectories; the number of available rows is dependent upon the disk type. A 3½-inch high-density floppy disk has 224 entries in the root directory.

The root directory will later contain information about each file and subdirectory stored in it. Each directory entry is 32 bytes long, although only 22 bytes are used. Table 16-6 lists how the 22 bytes are used.

Notice that the root directory contains only the starting cluster number. To find out what other clusters store the file, look in the file allocation table. By dividing the size of the file by the number of bytes per cluster and rounding up to the nearest whole number, you can determine how many clusters the file occupies.

Table 16-6 Root directory information for each file

Root Directory Bytes	Usage
8	Name of file
3	File extension
1	Attribute byte (special meaning for each bit)
10	Not used
2	Time of creation or last update
2	Date of creation or last update
2	Starting cluster number in binary
4	Size of file in binary

Also note that there is no place for the period (often referred to as "dot") that we normally see between the filename and the file extension in OS command lines. The period is not stored in directories but is only used in OS command lines to indicate where the filename ends and the file extension begins. For the long filenames in Windows 9x and Windows NT/2000/XP, more room in the directory is required. This is provided by using more than one entry in the directory for a single file, enough to accommodate the length of the filename. Both the long filename and the DOS version short filename are stored in the directory.

Time and date of creation or last update are stored in a coded form that is converted to a recognizable form when displayed on the screen. The date and time come from the system date and time, which the OS gets from the real-time clock during the boot. At the command prompt, you can change these with the Date and Time commands. Using the Windows desktop, change the date and time in the Control Panel. The earliest possible date allowed for both is 1/1/1980.

The file attributes are used for various purposes. One file attribute byte is broken into bits; each bit has a specific meaning. The first two bits are not used. The meanings of the other six bits are listed in Table 16-7, beginning with the leftmost bit in the byte and moving to the right. You can use several OS commands to change the file attributes; you'll learn about many of them later in this chapter.

16

Table 16-7 Meaning of each bit in the directory attribute byte for each file (reading from left to right across the byte)

Bit	Description	Bit=0	Bit=1
1, 2	Not used		
3	Archive bit	Not to be archived	To be archived
4	Directory status	File	Subdirectory
5	Volume label	Not volume label	Is volume label
6	System file	Not system file	Is system file
7	Hidden file	Not hidden	Hidden
8	Read-only file	Read/write	Read-only

TIP

Bit 3, the archive bit, is a switch used to indicate whether the file has been changed since the last backup and should be backed up next time a backup is made.

The root directory and all subdirectories contain the same information about each file. Only the root directory has a limitation on the number of entries. Subdirectories can have as many entries as disk space allows. Because long filenames require more room in a directory than short filenames, assigning long filenames reduces the number of files that can be stored in the root directory.

In summary, the Format command writes tracks and sectors on the disk, and creates a boot record, an empty file allocation table, and an empty root directory. If you include the /S option in the Format line, you add Io.sys, Msdos.sys, and Command.com, which together make a disk bootable. The three files are referenced in the FAT and in the root directory. The two hidden files have their file attribute bit 7, the hidden bit, set to 1 (hidden). When you make a Windows 9x rescue disk or use Windows Explorer to format a disk making the disk a system disk, these three files are copied to the disk to make the disk bootable.

How a Hard Drive Is Logically Organized to Hold Data

Recall that today's hard drives come from the factory already low-level formatted (that is, with track and sector markings already in place). During installation, after the hard drive is physically installed, the next step is to partition the drive into manageable areas. The high-level divisions are called partitions, and within the partitions, the drive is further divided into logical drives or volumes. This section discusses the different types of divisions, how they are organized and used by the OS, and how to use OS commands to partition and format a hard drive for first use.

Preparing a hard drive to hold data requires the following three steps:

1. *Low-level format.* This physically formats the hard drive and creates the tracks and sectors. For hard drives today, this has already been done by the time you buy the drive, and does not involve an OS.

2. *Partitioning the hard drive.* Even if only one partition is used, this step is still required. The DOS and Windows 9x Fdisk program sets up a partition table at the beginning of the hard drive. Within each partition, Fdisk also creates logical drives, assigning letters to these drives. Windows NT/2000/XP uses the Diskpart program at the command prompt or the Disk Management utility from within Windows to create and delete partitions and logical drives.

3. *High-level format.* This must be done by the OS for each logical drive on the hard drive. As each logical drive is formatted, the OS creates an OS boot record, a root directory, and two copies of VFAT for the logical drive, just as it does for a floppy disk. DOS and Windows 9x uses the Format.com program to do the job, and Windows NT/2000/XP uses Diskpart or Disk Management.

Although you might have a 10 GB hard drive that is only a single physical drive, an OS can divide this single physical drive into more than one logical drive. Figure 16-17 shows the several divisions of a hard drive.

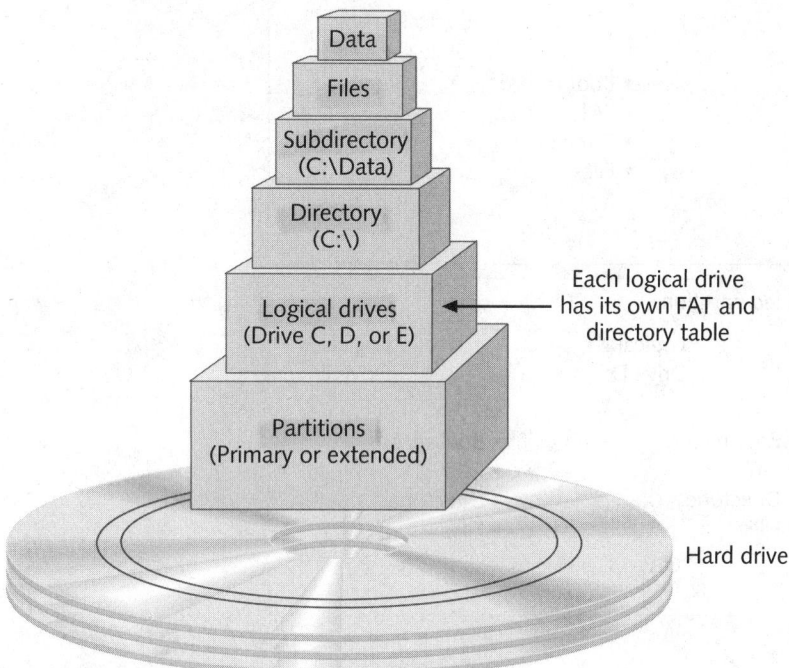

Figure 16-17   A hard drive is divided and organized at several levels

When partitioning the drive using Fdisk, Diskpart, or Disk Management, two kinds of divisions take place. First, the physical drive is divided into one or more partitions, and then each partition is further divided into logical drives or volumes. (A logical drive is sometimes called a logical partition; don't let the two uses of the term "partition" confuse you; partitions and logical partitions are divisions at different levels.) Figure 16-18 shows a typical example; the hard drive is divided into two partitions. The first partition contains one logical drive (drive C), and the second partition is divided into two logical drives (D and E). The partition table at the very beginning of the drive records all these divisions. The partition table is located in the first sector of the hard drive on head 0, track 0, sector 1, which is the MBR that was introduced earlier. Table 16-8 lists the contents of a partition table. Don't confuse this first physical sector of the hard drive with sector 1 as Windows knows it. The OS's sector 1 comes after the physical sector 1 and is the first sector in the logical drive C.

16

Figure 16-18 A hard drive is divided into one or more partitions that contain logical drives

The partition table is exactly 512 bytes long. During POST, the partition table program, which is stored at the beginning of the Master Boot Record, executes and checks the integrity of the partition table itself. If it finds any corruption, it refuses to continue execution, and the disk is unusable. Sometimes the MBR is the target of a **boot sector virus**, which can cause problems with the boot process and data retrieval. The DOS and Windows 9x Fdisk /MBR command or the Windows 2000/XP Fixmbr command is used to repair damage to the MBR.

If the table entries are valid, the partition table program looks in the table to determine which partition is the active partition, and it executes the bootstrap loader program in the boot record of that partition.

Using DOS or Windows 9x, a hard drive can have only one primary partition and one extended partition, although the partition table can contain four partitions. Also, the **primary partition** can only have a single logical drive. In that case, the one logical drive in the primary partition is the only logical drive on the hard drive that can boot the operating system and is the active partition. The **extended partition** can have several logical drives. Using Windows NT/2000/XP, the drive can have up to four partitions, but only one of them can be an extended partition.

Table 16-8   Hard drive partition table in the MBR

Item	Bytes Used	Description
1	446 bytes	Program that calls the boot program on the OS boot record.
2	16-byte total 1 byte 3 bytes 1 byte 3 bytes 4 bytes 4 bytes	Description of first partition. Is this the bootable partition? (Yes = 90h, No = 00h) Beginning location of the partition. System indicator; possible values are: 0 = Not a DOS partition 1 = DOS with a 12-bit FAT 4 = DOS with a 16-bit FAT 5 = Not the first partition 6 = Partition larger than 32 MB Ending location of partition. First sector of the partition table relative to the beginning of the disk. Number of sectors in the partition.
3	16 bytes	Describes second partition, using same format as first partition.
4	16 bytes	Describes third partition, using same format as first partition.
5	16 bytes	Describes fourth partition, using same format as first partition.
6	2 bytes	Signature of the partition table, always AA55.

How Many and What Kind of Logical Drives?

After the hard drive is formatted and ready for use, you are not usually aware that the several logical drives on the hard drive all belong to the same hard drive. For example, Figure 16-19 shows three drives, C, D, and E, that are logical drives on one hard drive. If you right-click the icon for one drive, such as drive D in the figure, and select Properties from the shortcut menu, you can see the amount of space allotted to this logical drive and how much of it is currently used. Also note that in the figure drive D is formatted using the FAT32 file system. It is possible for one logical drive to be formatted with one file system and other logical drives on the same hard drive be formatted using a different file system such as FAT16 or NTFS. You'll see examples of this in future chapters.

16

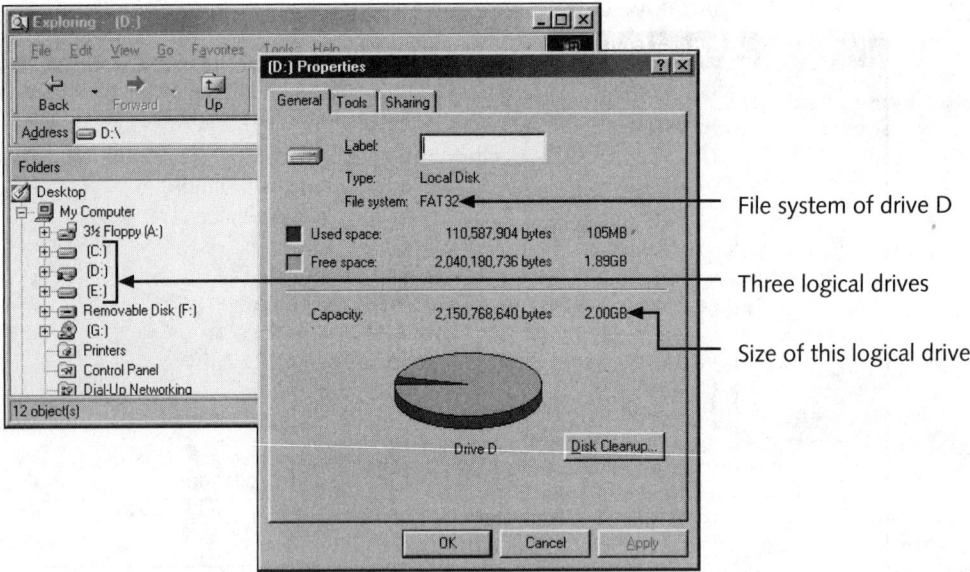

Figure 16-19 This hard drive contains three logical drives

DOS and all versions of Windows support the FAT16 file system. Windows 95 offers a slightly improved file system called VFAT that supports long filenames, and Windows 95, Service Release 2 (sometimes called Windows 95b or Windows 95 OSR2), introduced the FAT32 file system. FAT32 is supported by this and all later versions of Windows 9x, Windows 2000, and Windows XP. Windows NT introduced the NTFS file system, which is also supported by Windows 2000 and Windows XP. You'll learn about the different versions of NTFS in later chapters. The next sections discuss FAT16, VFAT, and FAT32. With these file systems, the primary goal is to reduce the size of one cluster so as to not waste space on the hard drive for short files that don't need large clusters.

FAT16

DOS and all versions of Windows support the FAT16 file system, which uses 16 bits for each cluster entry in the FAT. Using FAT16, the smallest cluster size is four sectors. Each cluster is 512 bytes/sector × 4 sectors/cluster, or 2,048 bytes. A one-character file takes up 2,048 bytes of space on a hard drive. For larger drives, the number of sectors in one cluster is even larger.

Virtual File Allocation (VFAT)

Windows 95 and Windows for Workgroups feature some improved methods of hard drive access, called **VFAT**, or **virtual file allocation table**. These enable Windows to use 32-bit protected-mode device drivers for hard drive access. In Windows for Workgroups, VFAT is called 32-bit file access. Windows 95 supports filenames up to 255 characters. Recall that the filename and extension are stored in the root directory or in a subdirectory list. Each entry in the directory is 32 bytes long, and each 32-byte entry is called a block. Long filenames require more than one block in the directory. The FAT is not affected, but still uses 16 bits per cluster entry. VFAT has been rendered outdated by FAT32.

> Some DOS-based disk utility programs can damage the entries in a directory in these additional blocks because they are not programmed to manage the extra blocks used to hold long filenames. Even a simple DEL command under DOS can leave the extra blocks in the directory used to hold the long filename unavailable for later use. The Windows 9x ScanDisk utility can recover these unreleased blocks.

FAT32

Beginning with Windows 95 OSR2, Microsoft offered a FAT that contains 32 bits per FAT entry instead of the older 12-bit or 16-bit FAT entries. Actually, only 28 of the bits are used to hold a cluster number; the remaining 4 bits are reserved.

FAT32 is recommended for hard drives larger than 512 MB and is efficient for drives up to 16 GB. In this range, the cluster size is 8K. After that, the cluster size increases to about 16K for drives in the 16 GB to 32 GB range. You are then reaching a hard drive size that warrants a more powerful file management system than FAT32, such as NTFS, supported by Windows NT/2000/XP, discussed in later chapters.

> If you are currently using FAT16 and are considering switching to FAT32, you can use PartitionMagic by PowerQuest Corporation (*www.powerquest.com*), to scan your hard drive and tell you how much of the drive is used for slack space. Knowing this can help you decide if the change will yield you more usable drive space. In Chapter 18 you will learn how use a Windows utility to convert a FAT16 drive to FAT32.

How Many Logical Drives?

When you partition a hard drive and create logical drives, you decide how many logical drives you want and how large each drive will be. Some people prefer to use more than one logical drive to organize their hard drives, especially if they plan to have more than one OS on the same drive. However, the main reason you need multiple logical drives is to optimize space and access time to the drive. The larger the logical drive, the larger the cluster size, and the more slack or wasted space. When deciding how to allocate space to logical drives, the goal is to use as few logical drives as possible and still keep cluster size to a minimum. For Windows 9x, use FAT32 in order to get the smaller cluster size.

Table 16-9 gives the information you need to decide how to divide your drive. Notice that the largest logical drive possible using FAT16 is 2 GB (this limitation is rooted in the largest cluster number that can be stored in a 16-bit FAT entry). However, you can see from the table that, to make a drive that big, the cluster size must be huge. Also, the largest hard drive that FAT16 can support is 8.4 GB; if the drive is larger than that, you must use FAT32.

16

Table 16-9   Size of some logical drives compared to cluster size for FAT16, FAT32, and NTFS

File System	Size of Logical Drive	Size of Cluster
FAT16	Up to 128 MB	4 sectors per cluster
	128 to 256 MB	8 sectors per cluster
	256 to 512 MB	16 sectors per cluster
	512 MB to 1 GB	32 sectors per cluster
	1 GB to 2 GB	64 sectors per cluster
FAT32	512 MB to 8 GB	4 sectors per cluster
	8 GB to 16 GB	8 sectors per cluster
	16 GB to 32 GB	16 sectors per cluster
	More than 32 GB	32 sectors per cluster
NTFS	Up to 512 MB	1 sector per cluster
	512 MB to 1 GB	2 sectors per cluster
	More than 1 GB	4 sectors per cluster

When to Partition a Drive

There are several reasons to partition a drive. When you first install a new hard drive, you must partition it to prepare it for use. Also, if an existing hard drive is giving errors, you can repartition the drive and reformat each logical drive to begin fresh. If you suspect that a virus has attacked the drive, you can repartition it to begin with a clean drive. Also, if you want to wipe a hard drive clean and install a new OS, you can repartition a drive in preparation for formatting it with a new file system.

When installing Windows 9x, before you can use the Windows 9x CD for Windows 9x upgrades, you can boot from a bootable disk and use Fdisk to partition the hard drive and install enough of a previous version of Windows on it to boot from it. (When using the Windows 98 Upgrade CD, you will also need the first Window 3.x setup disk or Windows 95 setup CD because Windows 98 upgrade setup asks for it during the Windows 9x installation.) During a Windows 9x installation, if the drive is not partitioned, the install procedure automatically executes Fdisk to partition the drive.

You can use Fdisk to partition a drive or use third-party software such as PartitionMagic. Fdisk is simply and easy to use, but PartitionMagic has some advantages over Fdisk. A major one is that when Fdisk partitions a drive, it erases all data on the existing partitions that it changes or overwrites, but PartitionMagic protects data when it changes the partitions on the drive. Also, PartitionMagic has a more user-friendly GUI interface.

There are times that you should not use Fdisk to partition a drive. If the drive has already been partitioned by third-party software such as Disk Manager or Storage Dimensions' SpeedStor, you should use the same third-party product to repartition the drive. This is because these products implement a type of drive translation that is used to enable a large hard drive to exist in a system whose system BIOS does not support such large drives. To know if a large hard drive has been partitioned to do disk translation, look for entries in the

Config.sys file that point to third-party software to manage the drive. Examples of these command lines are Dmdrvr.bin, Sstor.sys, Harddrive.sys, and Evdisk.sys. If you find lines with these filenames mentioned, use the same third-party software to repartition the drive.

Using Fdisk to Partition a Drive

Windows 9x and DOS use Fdisk to partition a drive. To use Fdisk, boot from a startup disk that has the Fdisk.exe utility on it and enter Fdisk at the command prompt. The Fdisk opening menu, shown in Figure 16-20 appears. Select option 1 to create the first partition. The menu in Figure 16-21 appears. Use option 1 to create the primary DOS partition. If you plan to install Windows 9x later, be sure this partition is at least 150 MB, preferably more. Make this first partition the **active partition**, which is the partition that is used to boot the OS. Fdisk automatically makes this partition drive C.

 In order for a hard drive to be bootable, it must have an active primary partition, which Fdisk will designate as drive C.

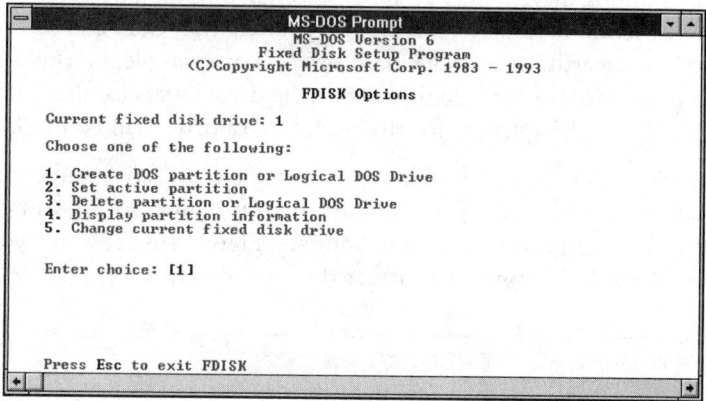

```
┌──────────────────── MS-DOS Prompt ──────────────────────┬─▲─┬─▲─┐
│                         MS-DOS Version 6                 │   │   │
│                      Fixed Disk Setup Program            │
│              (C)Copyright Microsoft Corp. 1983 - 1993    │
│                                                          │
│                         FDISK Options                    │
│                                                          │
│   Current fixed disk drive: 1                            │
│                                                          │
│   Choose one of the following:                           │
│                                                          │
│   1. Create DOS partition or Logical DOS Drive           │
│   2. Set active partition                                │
│   3. Delete partition or Logical DOS Drive               │
│   4. Display partition information                        │
│   5. Change current fixed disk drive                     │
│                                                          │
│                                                          │
│   Enter choice: [1]                                      │
│                                                          │
│                                                          │
│                                                          │
│                                                          │
│   Press Esc to exit FDISK                                │
├─◄─┬──────────────────────────────────────────────────┬──┴─►─┘
```

Figure 16-20   Fixed disk setup program (FDISK) menu

Next, use option 2 shown in Figure 16-21 to create an extended DOS partition using the remainder of the hard drive, then use option 3 to create logical drives in the extended partition.

When you are creating logical drives, you decide how large you want each drive to be. If you have at least 512 MB available for the drive, a message appears asking Do you wish to enable large disk support (Y/N)? If you respond Y, then Fdisk assigns the FAT32 file system to the drive, otherwise it uses FAT16.

16

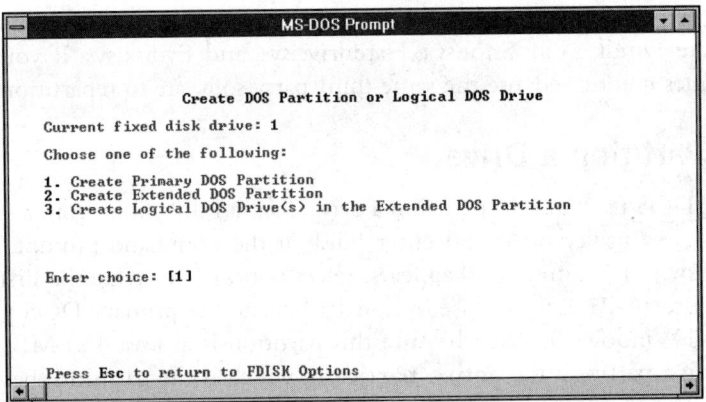

Figure 16-21   FDISK menu to create partitions and logical drives

Fdisk also assigns a drive letter to the logical drive. For a primary partition, drive C is assigned to the one volume and drives D, E, and so forth are assigned to volumes in the extended partition. However, if a second hard drive is installed in a system, Fdisk takes this into account when assigning drive letters. Drive D is assigned to the one volume in the primary partition of the second hard drive, leaving drive letters E, F, G, H and so forth for the volumes in the extended partitions of both hard drives. For example, in a two-hard drive system where each hard drive has three logical drives, the drive letters for the first hard drive will be C, E, and F and the drive letters for the second hard drive will be D, G, and H.

When Fdisk is completed, the hard drive has a partition table, an active and extended partition, and logical drives within these partitions. As seen in Figure 16-20, you can choose option 4 of Fdisk to display partition information (see Figure 16-22). After you exit the Fdisk window, reboot the PC before you format the logical drives.

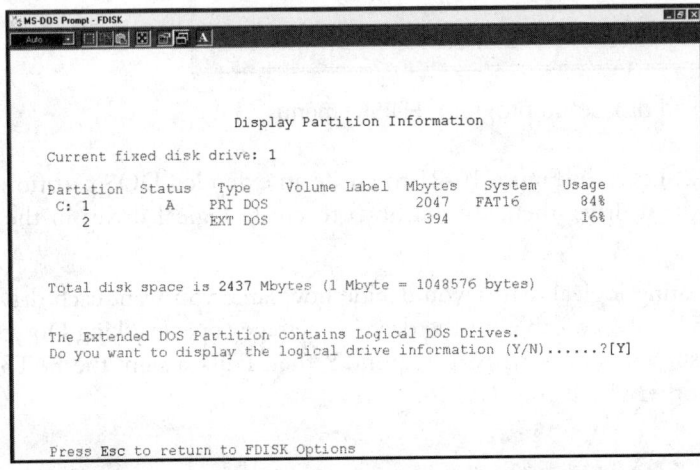

Figure 16-22   FDISK displays partition information

Formatting Each Logical Drive

Now that the hard drive is partitioned and logical drives are created and assigned drive letters, the next step is to format each logical drive. For the configuration in Figure 16-25, the three commands used to format these three logical drives are:

```
Format C:/S
Format D:
Format E:
```

In the Format command line, the /S option makes the drive bootable, and the drive letter tells the OS which drive to format. Other options for the Format command are covered in the next section.

The OS format for each logical drive creates these file system items at the beginning of each logical drive, which are similar to the file system items used on floppy disks:

- Boot record
- FAT
- Root directory

The Boot Record

A boot record is used during the boot process to inform the OS how a logical drive is organized. If the logical drive is the boot device, the boot program at the end of the boot record will load the first Windows hidden file, Io.sys which requires that Msdos.sys and Command.com be present. Table 16-10 shows the complete record layout for the boot record. The medium descriptor byte tells the OS what type of disk this is. The values of this descriptor byte are given in Table 16-11.

Table 16-10 Layout of the boot record on each logical drive

Description	Number of Bytes
Machine code	11
Bytes per sector	2
Sectors per cluster	1
Reserved	2
Number of FATs	1
Number of root directory entries	2
Number of logical sectors	2
Medium descriptor byte	1
Sectors per FAT	2
Sectors per track	2
Heads	2
Number of hidden sectors	2
Total sectors in logical volume	4

16

Table 16-10   Layout of the boot record on each logical drive (continued)

Description	Number of Bytes
Physical drive number	1
Reserved	1
Extended boot signature record	1
32-bit binary volume ID	4
Volume label	11
Type of file system (FAT12, FAT16, or FAT32)	8
Program to load operating system (boot strap loader)	Remainder of the sector

Table 16-11   Disk type and descriptor byte

Disk Type	Descriptor Byte
3½-inch double-density floppy disk, 720K	F9
3½-inch high-density floppy disk, 1.44 MB	F0
Hard disk	F8

The FAT and the Root Directory

The purpose of the FAT and how it is used have already been discussed in detail and will not be repeated here. The layout of the root directory is the same for hard drives as for floppy disks, which were discussed earlier in the chapter. Recall that the total number of bytes for each file entry in a directory is 32. Refer back to Table 16-6 for a list of entries in the root directory.

> Although earlier versions of Windows did limit the number of entries in the root directory, Windows 98 does not. Note, however, that the OS manuals recommend that you keep only about 150 entries in any one directory. Having any more entries slows access to the directory.

Using Commands to Manage a Floppy Disk or Hard Drive

You can use several OS commands to manage a floppy disk and hard drive. A number of commands are described in this section with some of their more common options. For more information about these and other OS commands, type the command name at a command prompt followed by /? (slash and a question mark).

There are two wildcards you can use with filenames to execute a command on a group of files or a file for which you do not know the entire name. The question mark (?) is a wildcard for one character, and the asterisk (*) is a wildcard for more than one character. For example, if you wanted to find all files in a directory that start with A and have a three-letter file extension, you would use the following command:

```
dir a*.???
```

One other thing you need to be aware of when using commands at the command line is how DOS restricts the length of filenames. DOS allows only eight characters for a filename and three for the extension; this is often called the 8.3 format. For filenames that do not meet this format, such as the filename Mydocument.doc, DOS will display the filename with the first few letters and a tilde (~) character:

```
Mydocum~.doc
```

If you have two documents that would have the same name if truncated in this manner, DOS will also add an identifying number. For example, if you have a document named Mydocument.doc and one named Mydocumentnew.doc, in a list of files, DOS will truncate these as follows:

```
Mydocu~1.doc
Mydocu~2.doc
```

If you are entering a long file or folder name in a command line, you can enclose the file name in double quotes, like this: "My long file name.doc".

Fdisk /Status /MBR

As you learned earlier, the Fdisk command creates partitions and logical drives on a hard drive, displays partition information, and restores a damaged Master Boot Record. Table 16-12 shows options for this command.

Table 16-12   Options for the Fdisk command

Fdisk Command Option	Description
/MBR	Repairs a damaged MBR program stored at the beginning of the partition table
/Status	Displays partition information for all hard drives in the system.

Many real-mode commands, such as Fdisk/MBR, have equivalent commands in the Windows 2000 Recovery Console, which you will learn about in Chapter 21. The Recovery Console is also available with Windows XP.

Format Drive: /S /V:Volumename /Q /U /Autotest

16

Recall that the Format command is used to format a disk or a hard drive. For a hard drive, first run Fdisk to partition the drive and create each logical drive. Then use Format to format each logical drive. Table 16-13 shows options for this command.

Table 16-13   Options for the Format command

Format Command Option	Description
/V	Allows you to enter a volume label only once when formatting several disks. The same volume label is used for all disks. A volume label is displayed at the top of the directory list to help you identify the disk.

Table 16-13 Options for the Format command (continued)

Format Command Option	Description
/S	Stores the system files on the disk after formatting. Writes the two hidden files and Command.com to the disk, making the disk bootable.
/Q	Recreates the root directory and FATs if you want to quickly format a previously formatted disk that is in good condition. /Q does not read or write to any other part of the disk.
/F:size	Specifies the size of a floppy disk. If the size is not specified, the default for that drive is used. The common values for size are: /F:360 is 360K, double-density 5¼-inch disk /F:1.2 is 1.2 MB, high-density 5¼-inch disk /F:720 is 720 K, double-density 3½-inch disk /F:1.44 is 1.44 MB, high-density 3½-inch disk
/U	Allows for an unconditional format of the disk, which does a more thorough job of formatting the disk by erasing all data. Use this option when you have been getting read/write errors on the disk.
/Autotest	Does not prompt the user before and during the format.

Dir

Use this command to list files and directories. Some examples are:

DIR /P	List one screen at a time.
DIR /W	Use wide format, where details are omitted and files and folders are listed in columns on the screen.
DIR *.txt	Use wildcard character.
DIR Myfile.txt	Check that a single file is present.

Type

The Type command displays on screen the contents of text file. Some examples are:

`Type Myfile.txt`	Displays file contents
`Type Myfile.txt >PRN`	Redirects output to printer
`Type Myfile.txt |More`	Displays output one screen at a time

Del or Erase

The Del or Erase command erases files or groups of files. Where the command does not include drive and directory information, like the following examples, the OS uses the default drive and directory when executing the command.

For example, to erase all the files in the A:\DOCS directory, use the following command:

```
C:\> ERASE A:\DOCS\*.*
```

To erase all the files in the current default directory, use the following command:

```
A:\DOCS> DEL *.*
```

To erase all files in the current directory that have no file extension, use the following command:

```
A:\DOCS> DEL *.
```

To erase the file named Myfile.txt, use the following command:

```
A:\> DEL MYFILE.TXT
```

Undelete

The Undelete command attempts to recover files that have been deleted. Following are some variations of the Undelete command. The Undelete command is not included in Windows 9x.

To list the files that can be undeleted, without actually undeleting them, use the following command:

```
A:\>UNDELETE /list
```

To recover deleted files without prompting for confirmation on each file, use the following command:

```
A:\>UNDELETE /all
```

Recover

The Recover command attempts to recover a file from damaged sectors on a disk. Always specify the drive, path, and filename of the file you want to recover with the Recover command. If you want to recover several files, use the command on one file at a time. The Recover command is not available in Windows 9x.

To recover the file named Myfile.txt on a floppy disk, use the following command:

```
RECOVER A:\DOCS\MYFILE.TXT
```

Whatever portion of the file that the Recover command can read is stored in the root directory and named A:FILE0000.REC (or the next available number). Copy this file to another disk before trying to recover the second file.

Because the Recover command might mark clusters as bad in the FAT, first use the Diskcopy or Copy command (described below) before using Recover. Data that might have been saved by other methods can sometimes be destroyed by the Recover command.

Diskcopy

The Diskcopy command makes an exact duplicate (sector by sector) of one floppy disk (called the source disk) to another disk of the same size and type (called the target disk).

To duplicate a floppy disk using only a single drive, use the following command:

```
C:\>DISKCOPY A: A:
```

The OS prompts you as many times as necessary to insert the source disk and then insert the target disk to make the exact copy. Data is copied from one disk to the other, byte by

16

byte, including any hidden files, bad sectors, fragmented files, or other contents; everything is copied as is. For this reason, the copy can be faulty if the target disk has bad sectors. Diskcopy ignores the fact that a sector is marked as bad in the FAT and copies to it anyway. The Diskcopy command copies formatting information, so the target disk does not need to be formatted before executing the copy.

Copy

The Copy command copies a single file or group of files. The original files are not altered.

To copy a file from one drive to another, use the following command:

```
A:\>COPY drive:\path\filename.ext drive:\path\filename.ext
```

The drive, path, and filename of the original source file immediately follow the Copy command, and the drive, path, and filename of the destination file follow the source filename. If you do not specify the filename of the copy, the OS assigns the original name of the file. If you omit the drive or path of the source or the destination, then the OS uses the current default drive and path.

To copy the file Myfile.txt from the root directory of drive C to drive A, use the following command:

```
C:\>COPY MYFILE.TXT A:
```

Because a drive or path is not indicated before the filename Myfile.txt, the OS assumes that the file is in the default drive and path.

To copy all files in the C:\DOCS directory to the floppy disk in drive A, use the following command:

```
C:\>COPY C:\DOCS\*.* A:
```

To make a backup file named System.bak of the System.ini file in the \Windows directory of the hard drive, use the following command:

```
C:\WINDOWS> COPY SYSTEM.INI SYSTEM.BAK
```

If you use the Copy command to duplicate multiple files, the files are assigned the names of the original files. When duplicating multiple files, no filename can be listed in the destination portion of the command line.

Xcopy /C /S /Y /D:

The Xcopy command is more powerful than the Copy command. It follows the same general command-source-destination format as the Copy command, but it offers several more options, as outlined next, with a couple of useful examples.

Use the /S option with the Xcopy command to copy all files in the directory \DOCS, as well as all subdirectories under \DOCS and their files, to the disk in drive A. Use the following command:

```
C:\>XCOPY C:\DOCS\*.* A: /S
```

To copy all files from the directory C:\DOCS created or modified on March 14, 2002, use the /D switch, as in the following command:

```
XCOPY C:\DOCS\*.* A: /D:03/14/02
```

Use the /Y option to overwrite existing files without prompting and use the /C option to keep copying even when there is an error.

Deltree

The Deltree command deletes the directory tree beginning with the subdirectory you specify, including all subdirectories and all files in all subdirectories in that tree. Use it with caution!

```
C:\>DELTREE [drive:]path
```

Mkdir [drive:]path or MD [drive:]path

The Mkdir (abbreviated MD, for make directory) command creates a subdirectory entry in a directory. To create a directory named \GAME on drive C, use this command:

```
MKDIR C:\GAME
```

The backslash indicates that the directory is under the root directory. To create a directory named CHESS under the \GAME directory, use this command:

```
MKDIR C:\GAME\CHESS
```

The OS requires that the parent directory GAME already exist before it creates the child directory CHESS.

Figure 16-23 shows the result of the Dir command on the directory \GAME. Note the two initial entries in the directory table, the . (dot) and the .. (dot, dot) entries. These two entries are created by the Mkdir command when the OS initially sets up the directory. You cannot edit these entries with normal OS commands, and they must remain in the directory for the directory's lifetime. The . entry points to the subdirectory itself, and the .. entry points to the parent directory, in this case, the root directory.

16

```
C:\>DIR \GAME /P

  Volume in drive C has no label
  Volume Serial Number is 0F52-09FC
  Directory of C:\GAME

.              <DIR>     02-18-93    4:50a
..             <DIR>     02-18-93    4:50a
CHESS          <DIR>     02-18-93    4:50a
NUKE           <DIR>     02-18-93    4:51a
PENTE          <DIR>     02-18-93    4:52a
NETRIS         <DIR>     02-18-93    4:54a
BEYOND         <DIR>     02-18-93    4:54a
       7 file(s)              0 bytes
                       9273344 bytes free

C:\>
```

Figure 16-23   Dir of the \GAME directory

Chdir [drive:]path or CD [drive:]path or CD..

The Chdir (abbreviated CD, for change directory) command changes the current default directory. In its easiest-to-follow form, you simply state the drive and the entire path that you want to be current:

```
CD C:\GAME\CHESS
```

The command prompt now looks like this:

```
C:\GAME\CHESS>
```

To move from a child directory to its parent directory, use the .. variation of the command:

```
C:\GAME\CHESS> CD..
C:\GAME>
```

Remember that .. always means the parent directory. You can move from a parent directory to one of its child directories simply by stating the name of the child directory:

```
C:\GAME> CD CHESS
C:\GAME\CHESS>
```

Do not put a backslash in front of the child directory name; doing so tells DOS to go to a directory named CHESS that is directly under the root directory.

Rmdir [drive:]path or RD [drive:]path

The Rmdir command (abbreviated RD, for remove directory) removes a subdirectory. Before you can use the Rmdir command, three things must be true:

- The directory must contain no files.

- The directory must contain no subdirectories.

- The directory must not be the current directory.

The . and .. entries are present when a directory is ready for removal. For example, to remove the \GAME directory in the above example, the CHESS directory must first be removed:

```
C:\> RMDIR C:\GAME\CHESS
```

Or, if the \GAME directory is the current directory, use this command:

```
C:\GAME> RD CHESS
```

Once you remove the CHESS directory, you can remove the \GAME directory. You must first leave the \GAME directory like this:

```
C:\GAME>CD..
C:\> RD \GAME
```

Attrib

The Attrib command displays or changes the read-only, archive, system, and hidden attributes assigned to files. To display the attributes of the file MYFILE.TXT, use this command:

```
ATTRIB MYFILE.TXT
```

To hide the file, use this command: `ATTRIB +H MYFILE.TXT`

To remove the hide status of the file, use this command: `ATTRIB -H MYFILE.TXT`

To make the file a read-only file, use this command: `ATTRIB +R MYFILE.TXT`

To remove the read-only status of the file, use this command: `ATTRIB -R MYFILE.TXT`

To turn the archive bit on, use this command: `ATTRIB +A MYFILE.TXT`

To turn the archive bit off, use this command: `ATTRIB -A MYFILE.TXT`

Unformat

The Unformat command might be able to reverse the effect of an accidental format. To unformat a disk, use this command:

```
UNFORMAT C:
```

Path

The Path command lists where the OS should look to find executable program files. This command is discussed here again to make the list of commands more complete. A sample Path command is

```
PATH C:\;C:\DOS;C:\WINDOWS;C:\UTILITY
```

Each path is separated from the next with a semicolon. You should put the most-used paths at the beginning of the line, because the OS searches the paths listed in the Path command line from left to right. The Path command goes in the Autoexec.bat file and can be executed from the OS prompt.

Sys Drive:

The Sys command copies the system files needed to boot to a disk or hard drive. Use the command if the system files on a drive are corrupted. You can access the drive, but you cannot boot from it. The command to copy system files to the hard drive is:

```
SYS C:
```

Chkdsk [drive:] /F /V

The Chkdsk command reports information about a disk. Use the /F option to have Chkdsk fix errors it finds, including errors in the FAT caused by clusters marked as being used but that do not belong to a particular file (called lost allocation units) and clusters that are marked in the FAT as belonging to more than one file (called cross-linked clusters). To check the hard drive for errors and repair them, use this command:

```
CHKDSK C: /F
```

To redirect the output from the Chkdsk command to a file that you can later print, use this command:

```
CHKDSK C: >Myfile.txt
```

The /V option of the Chkdsk command displays all path and filename information for all files on a disk:

```
CHKDSK C: /V
```

Chkdsk is useful when using a startup disk; otherwise, use Scandisk or disk error-checking from the Windows desktop.

16

Scandisk Drive: /A /N /P

The Scandisk command scans a hard drive for errors and repairs them if possible. Scandisk checks the FAT, long filenames, lost and cross-linked clusters, directory tree structure, bad sectors, and compressed structure if the drive has been compressed using Windows DriveSpace or DoubleSpace. The /A parameter is used to scan all nonremovable local drives. Use this command only to display information without fixing the drive:

```
SCANDISK C: /P
```

Use this command to display information and fix errors:

```
SCANDISK C:
```

Use this command to start and stop Scandisk automatically:

```
SCANDISK C: /N
```

If you use the above command, Scandisk will still stop to report errors.

Defrag Drive: /S

The Defrag command examines a hard drive or disk for fragmented files (files written to a disk in noncontiguous clusters) and rewrites these files to the disk or drive in contiguous clusters. Use this command to optimize a hard drive, improving the hard drive performance.

Use the /S:N option to sort the files on the disk in alphabetical order by filename.

```
DEFRAG C: /S:N
```

Use the /S:D option to sort the files on the disk by date and time.

```
DEFRAG C: /S:D
```

Ver

Use the Ver command to display the version of the operating system in use.

Scanreg /Restore /Fix /Backup

The Scanreg command restores or repairs the Windows 98 registry. It uses backups of the registry that Windows 98 Registry Checker automatically makes each day. To restore the registry from a previous backup, use this command:

```
SCANREG /RESTORE
```

A menu appears asking you which backup to use.

To repair a corrupted registry, use this command:

```
SCANREG /FIX
```

To create a new backup of the registry, use this command:

```
SCANREG /BACKUP
```

Don't use this last command if you are having problems with the registry.

Extract filename.cab file1.ext /D

The Extract command extracts files from a cabinet file such as the Ebd.cab file on the Windows 98 startup disk. To list the files that are contained in the cabinet file, use this command:

```
EXTRACT EBD.CAB /D
```

To extract the file Debug.exe from the Ebd.cab file, use this command:

```
EXTRACT EBD.CAB DEBUG.EXE
```

To extract all files from the Ebd.cab cabinet file, use this command:

```
EXTRACT EBD.CAB *.*
```

Debug

The Debug program is an editor that can view and manipulate the components of a file system on floppy disks and hard drives, including the FAT, directories, and boot records. It can also be used to view the contents of memory and hexadecimal memory addresses. To access Debug, enter the command Debug at the command prompt.

Edit [path][filename]

The Edit program (Edit.com) is a text editor that was used earlier in the chapter to edit Autoexec.bat and Config.sys files. It is a handy quick and dirty way to edit text files while working at a command prompt. To edit the file Autoexec.bat on a floppy disk, use this command:

```
EDIT A:\AUTOEXEC.BAT
```

If the file does not already exist, Edit creates the file.

 With older versions of DOS, Qbasic.exe was required for Edit.com to work correctly.

Using Batch Files

16

Suppose you have a list of OS commands that you want to execute several times. Perhaps you have some data files to distribute to several PCs in your office, and, having no LAN, you must walk from one PC to another, doing the same job repeatedly. A solution is to store the list of commands in a batch file on disk and then execute the batch file at each PC. Windows requires that the batch file have a .bat file extension. For example, store these five OS commands on a disk in a file named MYLOAD.BAT:

```
C:
MD\UTILITY
MD\UTILITY\TOOLS
CD\UTILITY\TOOLS
COPY A:\TOOLS\*.*
```

From the command prompt, you execute the batch file, just as you do other program files, by entering the name of the file, with or without the file extension:

        A:\>MYLOAD

All the commands listed in the file will execute, beginning at the top of the list. The batch file above will create a subdirectory under the C drive called Utility\Tools; change to that directory as the default directory, and copy all files from the \Tools directory in drive A into that new subdirectory. Look at any good book on DOS to find examples of the very useful ways you can elaborate on batch files, including adding user menus.

CHAPTER SUMMARY

- For DOS, the three types of memory are conventional (or base) memory, upper memory, and extended memory. These assignments are rooted in how the 20-line memory address bus of early PCs limited memory to 1024K.

- When the OS loads from a hard drive, the BIOS first executes the Master Boot Record (MBR), which executes the OS boot record, which, for Windows 9x, attempts to find Io.sys on the hard drive.

- Io.sys, which uses Msdos.sys, and Command.com, form the core of real-mode Windows 9x. These three files are necessary to boot to a command prompt. Config.sys and Autoexec.bat are not required, but are used if they are present. Other files are needed to load the GUI desktop and run GUI applications.

- Autoexec.bat and Config.sys are two files that contain commands used to customize the 16-bit portion of the Windows 9x load process.

- A floppy disk that has enough software on it to load an operating system is called a bootable disk, or system disk. A bootable disk that has some utility programs on it to troubleshoot a failed hard drive is called a rescue disk, emergency startup disk (ESD), or startup disk.

- Create a startup disk in Windows 9x using the Control Panel, Add/Remove Programs icon.

- The boot process can be divided into four parts: POST, loading the OS, the OS's initializing itself, and loading and executing an application.

- Startup BIOS is in control of the beginning of the boot process, after which it turns control over to the OS.

- The MBR is a small program at the very beginning of the hard drive that is needed to locate the beginning of the OS on the drive.

- A hard drive can be partitioned into one or more logical drives. The partition table contains a map to the logical drives on the hard drive, including an indication of which drive is the boot drive.

- A hidden file is a file not displayed in the directory list. One example is Io.sys, which contains the basic I/O software for real mode.

❑ A RAM drive is an area of memory that looks and acts like a hard drive, only it performs much faster. It is sometimes used to speed up access to often-used software or to hold program files when the hard drive is not accessible.

❑ The file Command.com has three parts: code to manage I/O, programs for internal OS commands such as Copy and Dir, and a short program that looks for the Autoexec.bat file.

❑ You can access a command prompt window, sometimes called a DOS box, in Windows 9x by clicking Start, Programs, and MS-DOS Prompt. You can also access it by clicking Start, Run and typing Command.com in the Run dialog box.

❑ The Himem.sys memory extender was added by DOS to allow access to memory addresses above 1 MB. Himem.sys, along with Emm386.exe, is used by Windows 9x to manage memory above 640K. Emm386.exe contains the software that loads 16-bit device drivers and other programs into upper memory.

❑ Windows 95 was the first version of Windows to support 32-bit protected mode application software. Windows NT was the first version of Windows in which all of the OS code was written in 32-bit protected mode and 16-bit applications could only operate in virtual real mode.

❑ You can use a UMB (upper memory block) from Autoexec.bat with the Loadhigh (LH) command.

❑ The MEM command with the appropriate parameters shows exactly where in upper memory the UMBs are located and what software has been assigned addresses in upper memory.

❑ When a hard drive is first installed, it has nothing written on it except the track and sector markings put there at the factory. A floppy disk is completely blank and does not even have the track and sector markings. The OS is responsible for formatting and managing both hard drives and floppy disks.

❑ Tracks are concentric circles on a disk. A segment of a track is called a sector and always holds 512 bytes of data.

❑ On a floppy disk, the Format command creates tracks and sectors, the boot record, two copies of the file allocation table (FAT), and the root directory.

❑ Basic information about how a floppy disk is organized is stored in the first sector of the disk, called the boot sector or the boot record. At the end of a boot record is a small program, called the bootstrap loader that can be used to boot from the disk.

16

❑ The FAT lists the location of files on a disk in a one-column table. For the file systems FAT12, FAT16, and FAT32, the number after FAT indicates how many bits wide each entry in the column is. FAT12 is a file system for floppy disks.

❑ VFAT is an improvement over FAT16 that was introduced in Windows 95; it supports long filenames. FAT32, which made VFAT obsolete, was introduced in Windows 95 Second Edition. NTFS was introduced with Windows NT.

❑ After a drive is physically installed, the next step is to partition the drive into manageable areas. The high-level divisions are called partitions, and within the partitions, the drive is further divided into logical drives or volumes.

❑ The Fdisk command is used to partition a hard drive. If a drive has been partitioned using third-party software such as Disk Manager or Speed Stor, you may not be able to use Fdisk. You must use the third-party software to change the partitions on the drive.

❑ The largest drive that FAT16 can support is 8.4 GB. FAT32 is recommended for hard drives larger than 512 MB and is efficient for drives up to 16 GB.

❑ The Format command is used to format floppy disks and logical drives. The /S option with the Format command makes a drive bootable. The Unformat command attempts to reverse the effect of an accidental format.

❑ The Del or Erase command deletes files or groups of files. The Undelete command attempts to recover files that have been erased. The Recover command attempts to recover a file from damaged sectors on a disk.

❑ The Diskcopy command makes an exact duplicate of one floppy disk on another disk of the same size and type. The Copy command copies a single file or group of files. The Xcopy command is more powerful that the Copy command and supports copying subdirectories.

❑ The Sys command copies the system files needed to boot to a disk or drive.

❑ Mkdir creates a subdirectory, Chdir changes the current directory, and Rmdir removes a subdirectory.

❑ The Attrib command displays or changes the read-only, archive, system, and hidden attributes assigned to files.

❑ The Path command specifies where the OS should look to find executable program files.

❑ Chkdsk and Scandisk both check drives for errors and repair them. Scandisk does a more thorough scan and basically replaces Chkdsk.

❑ The Scanreg command restores or repairs the Windows 98 registry.

KEY TERMS

active partition
Autoexec.bat
batch file
boot record
boot sector
boot sector virus
bootable disk
bootstrap loader
cabinet file
cache
cold boot
Command.com
conventional memory
DOS box
emergency startup disk (ESD)

Emm386.exe
extended partition
external command
FAT12
fragmented file
hard boot
hidden file
Himem.sys
HMA (high memory area)
internal command
Io.sys
MBR (Master Boot Record)
Msdos.sys
partition table

POST (power-on self test)
primary partition
RAM drive
rescue disk
soft boot
startup disk
system disk
UMB (upper memory block)
upper memory
VDM (virtual DOS machine)
VFAT (virtual file allocation table)
warm boot

17

INSTALLING AND USING WINDOWS 9x

In this chapter, you will learn:

♦ About the different versions and architecture of Windows 9x

♦ How to install and use Windows 9x

♦ How to install hardware and applications with Windows 9x

♦ How to manage hard drives, floppy disks, and memory with Windows 9x

♦ How to get help from Microsoft

As a PC support technician, you need to know how to install, use, and troubleshoot the Windows OSs in common use today. You need to have a general knowledge of how hardware works and a detailed knowledge of how Windows and other types of software work. In Chapter 2, you learned how hardware and software work together, and in Chapter 16 you were introduced to the DOS portion of Windows 9x. This chapter covers how Windows 9x is structured, how it is used, and how it works with various software programs and hardware devices. This information lays the foundation for the next chapter, in which you will learn how to troubleshoot Windows 9x, as well as later chapters on using and troubleshooting other Windows OSs.

WINDOWS 9X VERSIONS AND ARCHITECTURE

Windows 9x has had several releases, including Windows 95, Windows 95 Service Release 2 (SR2), Windows 98, Windows 98 Second Edition (SE), and Windows Me (Millennium Edition). Each of these OSs uses the same basic architectural structure, and each release has improvements over previous versions plus new features. We next discuss the major differences between these releases and then look at the Windows 9x architecture.

How Windows 98 Differs from Windows 95

Windows 98 is basically the same operating system as Windows 95, with the same core components and the same fundamental services to software, hardware, and the user. However, it does offer some added features and improved performance over Windows 95. Some of the added features, including FAT32 and support for USB and DVD, became available with Windows 95 Release 2. Windows 98 also includes some new system tools to monitor and improve system performance, new hardware support, and additional Web tools.

 FAT32 is not compatible with Windows NT or disk compression, including the use of DoubleSpace under Windows 98. To use disk compression or to have a file system compatible with Windows NT, use FAT16. Windows 2000/XP supports FAT32.

Windows 95 and Windows 98 load, run, and install very much the same way. As we continue through this chapter and the next, any significant differences between the two versions will be noted. Table 17-1 summarizes the changes that took place from Windows 95 to Windows 98. Some of the terms in the table may be unfamiliar to you but are covered later in the book.

Table 17-1   Features new to Windows 98

Feature	Description
Troubleshooting utilities	Windows 95 had a few troubleshooting utilities, but the 15 utilities that come with Windows 98 are more interactive.
Update Wizard	The Update Wizard connects to the Microsoft Web site and automatically downloads any new drivers or fixes.
Maintenance Wizard	The Maintenance Wizard can be used to regularly schedule several maintenance tasks, which include running Disk Defragmenter and ScanDisk.
DriveSpace 3	An improved version of DriveSpace for Windows 95, it includes a third level of data compression, called UltraPack, which takes up less space per file than does the regular compression utility, called HiPack.
Power management	Windows 98 supports some power management features, if both hardware and software are present to use them.
Registry Checker	Backs up and restores the registry.

Table 17-1   Features new to Windows 98 (continued)

Feature	Description
Web tools and features	Several Windows 98 features take on an Internet look and feel. Windows 98 also supports viewing TV and interactive programs. You'll need a special TV interface card to do it.
FAT32	FAT32 is a file system that allows for a smaller cluster size on large drives than does the earlier FAT16.
New hardware support	With 1,200 device drivers, Windows 98 supports many more hardware devices than did Windows 95. Also, Windows 98 supports USB, DVD drives, multiple video cards supporting multiple monitors, and faster data throughput for CD-ROM drives.
Win32 Driver Model (WDM)	A new device driver model, also used by Windows NT, makes it possible for the same device driver to be used by both operating systems, making it easier for device manufactures to supply drivers for their devices.

Windows Me

Windows Me, the last Windows 9x upgrade, has a desktop that looks more like Windows 2000 than Windows 98 SE, and, just like Windows 2000, it does not include the option to boot to the DOS command prompt in the Start menu. That means that you cannot boot Windows Me from the hard drive in true real mode, although you do have a MS-DOS Command Prompt window. If you want to get a true real-mode command prompt using Windows Me, create a blank formatted floppy disk and copy Io.sys and Command.com from the \Windows\Command\EBD folder to the disk, and then boot from this disk.

Windows Me does not allow real-mode device drivers and TSRs to be loaded from Config.sys and Autoexec.bat as do earlier versions of Windows 9x. If you want to run these 16-bit programs, your only option is to load them after Windows Me loads. One way to do this is to include them in a batch file that is listed in the Properties tab of the MS-DOS Command Prompt shortcut.

Troubleshooting tools new to Windows Me include:

- System Restore, which automatically backs up the registry and other system files when the system is idle, after about every 10 hours of operating time. When needed, the System Restore Wizard can be used to choose between earlier versions of the saved system.

- System File Protection, which is similar to Windows 2000 System File Protection, prevents system files from being deleted. For example, if you attempt to delete files in the Program Files folder where applications are normally stored, the utility will work in the background to compress and save these files in case you need them later. The utility also prevents an application installation from overwriting newer DLL files with older or nonstandard versions.

17

Windows 9x Architecture

Like other OSs, Windows 9x has a shell and a kernel. The two most important parts of the shell are the **user component** and the GDI. The user component manages input from the keyboard and other user devices, output from the user interface, and the **GDI (Graphics Device Interface)**. The GDI is a component of the OS responsible for presenting the graphical interface to the user and providing graphics support to output devices. The purposes of each component are listed in Table 17-2.

Table 17-2   Core components of Windows 9x

Component Name	Main Files Holding the Component	Functions
Kernel	Kernel32.dll, Krnl386.exe	Handles the basic OS functions such as managing memory, file I/O, and loading and executing programs.
User	User32.dll, User.exe	Controls the mouse, keyboard, ports, and desktop, including the position of windows, icons, and dialog boxes.
GDI	GDI32.dll, GDI.exe	Draws screens, graphics, and lines, and prints them.

Figure 17-1 shows the three core portions of the Windows 9x OS. In Figure 17-1, you can see that the basic Windows 9x core component, the kernel, uses mostly 32-bit code. The 16-bit code is only retained to provide entry points into the kernel from 16-bit application programs. The user portion uses mostly 16-bit code, primarily because it uses less memory than the 32-bit equivalent and does not have a need for significant speed. The GDI core uses a mix of 16-bit and 32-bit code in order to maintain compatibility with 16-bit application programs.

Figure 17-1   Windows 9x uses some 32-bit and some 16-bit code in its three core components

The Windows 9x core relates to users, software, and hardware by way of several modules, as seen in Figure 17-2. Just as DOS and Windows 3.x each provided a shell for the user to interface with the OS, Windows 9x provides a group of user interface tools and a shell for applications. Configuration data that was stored in Windows 3.x ini files is stored in the Windows 9x registry, a database that also contains the initialization information for applications, a database of hardware and software settings, Windows configuration settings, user parameters, and application settings. (You will read about the registry in several places in this chapter and will learn about it in more detail in the next chapter.)

Figure 17-2 The Windows 9x architecture as it relates to the user, application software, and hardware

Virtual Machines

Before we look at the different components in Figure 17-2, you need to understand how these components relate to applications and hardware. Recall from earlier chapters that DOS allows applications direct access to hardware, but, beginning with Windows 95, the Windows operating system manages hardware for applications. Applications call on the OS to access hardware or other software by using an **application programming interface (API) call**. When applications are first loaded by Windows 9x, the methods to access hardware and software are made available to the software through an interface called a **virtual machine**. An application sees a virtual machine as a set of resources made available to it through these predefined APIs. An OS can provide a virtual machine to a single application that commands all the resources of that virtual machine, or the OS can assign a virtual machine to be shared by two or more applications. Think of virtual machines as multiple logical machines within one physical machine, similar in concept to several logical drives within one physical drive.

17

Figure 17-3 shows several virtual machines that Windows 9x can provide. In the figure, the system virtual machine (system VM) is the most important VM under Windows 9x and is where all the OS processes run. It can also support 32-bit and 16-bit Windows application programs, but DOS programs run in their own virtual machines.

A DOS program expects to directly control the hardware of the entire PC, memory included. If a DOS program begins to use memory addresses not assigned to it, errors occur in a multitasking environment. Windows 9x solves this problem by providing the DOS program with its own virtual machine. In effect, the application program says, "I want all of memory and all of this and all of that." Windows 9x says, "OK, here they are," and gives the program its own PC, including all the virtual memory addresses it wants from 0 to 4 GB as well as its own virtual hardware! As far as the DOS program is concerned, it can go anywhere and do anything within its own PC. The DOS application program does not try to communicate with any other application program or to access the data of another program, because it thinks there are no other programs; it controls its entire world, and it's the only program in it. That's a virtual machine.

Figure 17-3   Windows 9x uses the virtual machine concept

One important result of running DOS programs in individual virtual machines is that when a DOS program makes an error, the virtual machine it is using hangs, but other programs and the OS are isolated from the problem and thus are not affected by it.

Windows 16-bit application programs offer a slightly different challenge to Windows 9x. These programs make some of the same mistakes that DOS programs do and can cause the system to hang. However, they also sometimes expect to access other programs and their data. The 16-bit Windows programs don't expect to control the hardware directly and are content to route their requests to Windows. Windows 9x places these programs within the system virtual machine because they communicate with hardware through the OS, but Windows 9x puts these programs together in their own memory space so they can share memory addresses.

The result of this arrangement is that, when a 16-bit Windows program causes an error called a Windows Protection Error or a General Protection Fault, it can disturb other 16-bit programs, causing them to fail. However, it does not disturb DOS programs in their own virtual machine or 32-bit programs that don't share their virtual memory addresses. (You will learn more about virtual memory addresses later in this chapter.)

Components of Windows 9x

We now turn our attention back to the OS components that create, configure, and manage the virtual machines used by software and the OS. Figure 17-2 serves as a simple but complete reference point for all the components of Windows 9x, illustrating how they relate to the user, hardware, and software, and to each other. As you can see, Windows 9x architecture uses a modular approach that divides functions into separate program groups, making each component easier to update and to implement.

One component in Figure 17-2 is the **Virtual Machine Manager (VMM)**, the component responsible for managing virtual machines and all the resources needed by each application running in them. One hardware device that all applications require is memory, and the VMM manages memory and virtual memory for applications. **Virtual memory** uses hard drive space so that it acts like memory. Windows stores virtual memory in a file called a swap file, discussed later in this chapter. The purpose of virtual memory is to increase the amount of memory available. Of course, because a hard drive is much slower than RAM, virtual memory works at a considerably slower speed than real memory. For example, a hard drive may have a data access time of 10 ms (10/1,000 second or 10 milliseconds), whereas RAM speed may be 60 ns (60/1,000,000,000 second or 60 nanoseconds).

Another component, called the **Installable File System (IFS)** manager, is responsible for all disk access. The **Configuration Manager** is responsible for the Plug and Play features of Windows 9x and other hardware configuration tasks such as providing system resources to hardware devices. In Figure 17-2, the only component that is found in Windows 98 but not Windows 95 is the **Win32 Driver Model (WDM)** driver manager, the component responsible for managing device drivers. The WDM makes it possible for device drivers written for Windows 98 to also work with Windows NT.

17

Keep in mind that Windows 9x is a compromise OS, attempting to bridge the 16-bit world and the 32-bit world. It makes many compromises between these two worlds.

Although Windows 9x supports 16-bit device drivers and applications, it's preferable to use 32-bit drivers and 32-bit applications for four main reasons:

- 32-bit drivers and applications are generally much faster than 16-bit software.

- 32-bit drivers and applications can be stored in extended memory, releasing more of the first megabyte of memory.

- 32-bit drivers can be dynamically loaded, meaning that they are loaded into memory when they are needed and then removed when not needed, thus conserving memory. In contrast, 16-bit drivers must be stored in conventional or upper memory and remain there as long as the OS is running.

- 32-bit applications can share data with other 32-bit applications and are generally better designed, making better use of OS resources.

 When Windows 9x is installed over DOS, it searches for 16-bit drivers and replaces them with 32-bit drivers if it can.

INSTALLING WINDOWS 9x

In the previous chapter, you learned how to boot a computer to a C prompt on a working hard drive. In this chapter, you will learn how to install Windows 9x from that point. Remember as you proceed that there are separate installation CDs for installing Windows 9x on a PC without Windows (Microsoft labels the OS as Windows 9x for a New PC) and for installing Windows 9x on a PC with an earlier version of Windows (Microsoft labels the OS as Windows 9x Upgrade). The CDs for installing Windows 9x on a new PC are significantly more expensive than the upgrade CDs. To use the upgrade CDs, you must have a previous version of Windows installed on your hard drive.

A problem arises if you have just replaced a failed hard drive with a new hard drive and you want to do a fresh installation using a Windows 9x Upgrade CD. During the OS installation, the upgrade CD will ask you to provide a Microsoft floppy disk or CD from an earlier version of Windows. If you cannot provide the CD or floppy, the upgrade installation will terminate and you must use the more expensive version, Windows 9x for a New PC.

First, let's look at what's on the Windows 9x installation CD and how to prepare your hard drive for installation.

What's on the Windows 9x CD

The Windows 9x installation CD contains all the files you will need to complete installation of the OS, as well as some system administration tools, instructions and tutorials, and other utilities. The CD includes a setup wizard that guides you through the process of installation and does not require you to work with the OS files themselves.

The Windows 9x installation CD includes files you can use for the following tasks:

- Installing the OS
- Customizing configuration of the operating system
- Configuring and optimizing your desktop
- Network administration
- Diagnosing and troubleshooting system errors
- File management

Figure 17-4 shows the opening screen of the Windows 98 CD. It provides links to find information on software available with Windows 98, play video clips showing the multimedia features of Windows 98, browse the CD for a particular file or program, and add or remove software.

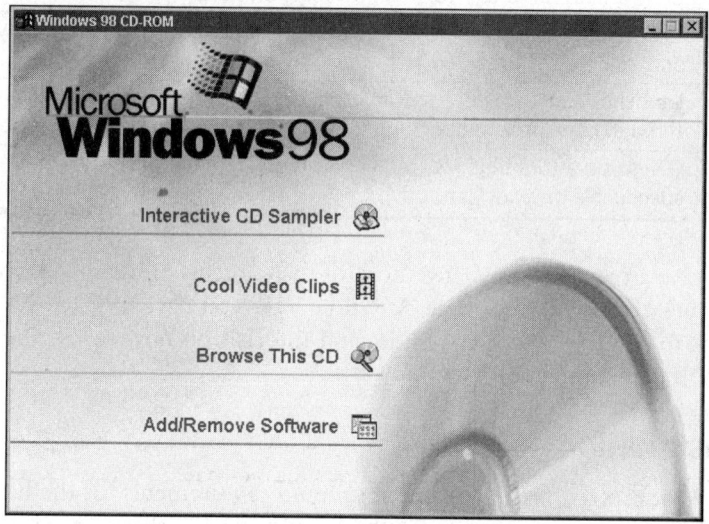

Figure 17-4   The opening screen of the Windows 98 CD provides links you can use to navigate the CD

17

Important folders on the CD and their contents include the following:

- *CD sample* contains subfolders that provide a catalog of and demos of Microsoft products.
- *Drivers* lists hardware drivers by category.
- *Oldmsdos* contains old DOS tools that can be useful in setup and troubleshooting.
- *Sysrec* contains system recovery tools.

Table 17-3 lists some important files on the Windows 9x CD.

Table 17-3   Important files on the Windows 9x CD

File	Function
Autorun.inf	Launches the interactive interface for the CD. (This is the interface shown in Figure 17-4.)
Readme.txt	Explains the layout of the CD and gives the locations of other readme files.
Setup.exe	Begins installation of the OS.
Batch.exe	Creates files that can be used for automated Windows 9x installations.
Checklinks.exe	Contains the Link Check Wizard, which can help you find and fix broken links and program shortcuts.
Netmon.386	Contains the Network Monitor, which enables you to monitor network performance remotely for Windows 9x computers.
Regserv.exe	The Microsoft Remote Registry, which provides a means to remotely view and edit the Windows 9x registry.
Textview.exe	Launches a text viewer that can quickly display text files without having to go through opening and operating a more complex word processing application.
Where.exe	Gives you a tool that you can use from the command line to locate a specific file on your hard drive.

This list does not give a comprehensive inventory of the contents of the installation CD but is an overview of what you will find there. Any time after you have installed Windows 9x, you can refer back to the CD to access utilities and tutorials on how to use the operating system and the tools that are included with it.

Preparing for Installation

Before installing Windows 9x, verify that the minimum requirements for the hardware are met. In order for Windows 9x to perform satisfactorily, the PC should meet the recommended requirements. Minimum and recommended requirements for Windows 95 and Windows 98 are listed below:

Minimum and recommended requirements for Windows 95:

- 486DX, 25 MHz or higher processor
- 4 MB of RAM (8 MB is recommended)
- 40 to 45 MB of hard disk storage, depending on the installation

Minimum and recommended requirements for Windows 98:

- 486DX, 66 MHz or higher processor
- 24 MB of RAM (32 MB is recommended)
- From 140 to 315 MB of hard disk storage, depending on the installation

Windows 9x is most likely to be installed as an upgrade from DOS with Windows 3.x, as an upgrade from Windows 95 to Windows 98, or on a clean hard drive. If you have been having problems with your current operating system and applications, consider doing a clean install rather than an upgrade. A **clean install** ignores any settings in the currently installed OS, including information about installed hardware or software. Therefore, after the clean install, you must reinstall all hardware and application. Therefore, before deciding to do a clean install, verify that you have all the application software installation CDs or floppy disks and then back up all data on the drive. Also take the time to verify that the backup of data is good, and verify that you have all device driver software.

You do not need to format the hard drive, although you should delete all folders on the hard drive used for the OS or applications, including the \Windows folder, files, and sub-folders before you begin the installation. This will force Setup to perform a clean install and make certain no corrupted system files or applications remain. If you like, you can also format the hard drive. Do this if you suspect that a virus is present. If you suspect a boot sector virus is present, use the Fdisk/MBR command (discussed in Chapter 16) to rewrite the master boot sector program. Then do the clean install.

After Windows 9x is installed, reinstall all the application software and then, if you formatted the hard drive, restore the data from backups. This method takes longer than an upgrade, but you get the advantage of a fresh start, and any problems with corrupted applications or system settings will not follow you into the new installation.

An **upgrade install** carries forward as much information as it can about what the current OS knows concerning installed hardware and software, user preferences, and other settings. An upgrade is faster than a clean install because you don't need to reinstall software and hardware. However, problems with an old installation sometimes carry forward into the upgrade.

You can perform either an upgrade or a clean install with either the Windows 9x for a New PC or the Windows 9x Upgrade CD. If you are doing an upgrade, the old operating system must be in good enough shape to boot up because you must begin an upgrade from within the currently installed OS.

17

Installing Windows 9x as a Clean Installation

You can change CMOS settings to specify the order in which system BIOS looks for an OS on the drives on your PC. You might need to change the boot order in CMOS, depending on how you plan to load the OS. Older PCs could only boot from a hard drive or floppy disk. This meant that to use a CD-ROM drive, you had to first boot these PCs from floppy disks and then install the CD-ROM drivers. There are more choices with newer

PCs, some of which can boot from a hard drive, floppy drive, Zip drive, CD-ROM drive, or other type of drive. These newer PCs have drivers for drive types other than hard drives and floppy drives written into their BIOS, allowing you to boot from a different medium.

 If the PC is on a network, it is possible to install the OS from another computer on the network. However, if you want to do an upgrade, you must begin the upgrade from within the current OS. Therefore, if you are performing an installation across a network, you are forced to do a clean install.

Windows 9x comes on a set of floppy disks or on a CD. If you are installing the OS from floppy disks, you can boot from the hard drive or floppy disk. To boot from the floppy disk, insert the Windows 9x Disk 1, which is bootable, and boot the PC. At the A prompt, enter the command *Setup.exe*. You can also boot from a hard drive, go to a C prompt, and insert the Windows 9x Disk 1 in the floppy disk drive. Enter the command *A:\Setup* to execute the Setup program on the floppy disk. Either way, the Windows 9x setup screen appears. Follow the directions on the screen.

 Your CD-ROM drive might be configured to automatically run a CD when it is first inserted. This Autoplay feature will cause the Setup opening menu to appear without your entering the Setup command. To disable the feature, hold down the Shift key while inserting the CD.

If you are installing the OS from a CD (if your PC can boot from a CD-ROM drive) insert the CD in the drive and reboot. If your PC cannot boot from a CD, boot from a floppy disk or hard drive, then insert the CD in the CD-ROM drive and enter the command *D:\Setup.exe*, substituting the drive letter of your CD-ROM drive for *D* if necessary.

 To speed up the installation, you can copy the files and folders on the Windows 98 CD to a folder on your hard drive and run the Setup program from that folder. Also, having the Windows 98 CD files on your hard drive makes it easier to access the files later when adding Windows components or updating drivers.

Installing 9x as an Upgrade

If you are doing an upgrade, before you begin the installation, prepare your hard drive by doing these things:

- Verify that you have enough space on the hard drive. Delete files in the Recycle Bin and temporary directories.

- Run ScanDisk to check and repair errors on the hard drive. From Windows 95, click Start, Programs, Accessories, System Tools, ScanDisk and scan each logical drive in the system. From a Windows startup disk or from DOS, enter the command *Scandisk* at the command prompt. You will learn more about ScanDisk in the next chapter.

- Run a current version of antivirus software to check for viruses.

- If you are upgrading from Windows 3.x, save configuration files so that you can backtrack to it if necessary. Save Autoexec.bat and Config.sys, found in the root directory, and all files with .ini or .grp file extensions in the \Windows directory to a disk. In Windows 3.x, files with the .grp file extension are **group files**, which contain information about a program group displayed in Program Manager.

- Check Config.sys and Autoexec.bat for potential problems. Verify that any hardware devices using device drivers loaded from these files are working under the old OS so you know your starting point when troubleshooting problems under the new OS.

> The Windows 9x upgrade process will move commands in Autoexec.bat used to load TSRs required for 16-bit Windows programs to Winstart.bat. Look for the Winstart.bat file in the root directory after the installation is done. If setup did not find any TSRs to put in the file, it will not be created.

- If there are TSRs such as QEMM386 (a memory manager by Quarterdeck) loaded from Config.sys or Autoexec.bat, and problems arise because they are running during the installation, disable them by converting these lines to remarks or comments by typing *REM* at the beginning of the command lines. Later, after the installation, you can activate them again by removing the REMs at the beginning of lines.

- If you are connected to a network, verify that the connection is working. If it is, Windows setup should be able to reestablish the connection correctly at the end of the installation.

- If you are upgrading from Windows 95 to Windows 98, create a Windows 95 rescue disk for use in the event that the installation fails.

- Decide if you want to use FAT16 or FAT32 for your file system. If you choose FAT16, you can later convert to FAT32 using the Windows Drive Converter. After Windows 98 is installed, to access the Converter, click Start, Programs, Accessories, System Tools, Drive Converter (FAT32). As an alternative, you can use the Run dialog box: For the 16-bit version, enter *cvt.exe*, and for the 32-bit version, enter *cvt1.exe*, and then click OK. The Drive Converter Wizard steps you through the process. Figure 17-5 shows you the first screen of the Drive Converter Wizard.

17

Figure 17-5   Use the Drive Converter Wizard to convert your hard drive to the FAT 32 file system

■ If you are installing Windows on a compressed drive, be aware that the registry can reside on any compressed drive, but the swap file can reside on a compressed drive only if it is compressed using protected-mode software such as DriveSpace. (Compressed drives are hard drives that have a portion of their data compressed in order to save space on the drive.) DriveSpace marks the area for the swap file as uncompressible. If your drive is compressed with real-mode compression software, such as DoubleSpace, then know that you cannot put the swap file on this compressed drive. Best practice is to back up the data and then uncompress the drive. You can later compress it using Windows 98 DriveSpace.

TIP | If you used DOS DoubleSpace (available with DOS 6 and 6.2) to compress the drive, type DBLSPACE at the DOS prompt. If you used DriveSpace (available with DOS 6.22), type DRVSPACE. These utilities will give you statistics about the compressed drive and also allow you to change the size of the uncompressed part of the drive, called the host drive.

Once you have prepared your hard drive for an upgrade installation, do the following to get to the setup screen:

1. Start the PC, loading the current operating system.

2. Close all open applications, including any antivirus software that is running.

3. Insert the CD in the CD-ROM drive or the floppy disk in the floppy drive. When upgrading from Windows 95 to Windows 98, open the Run dialog box and enter the command **D:\Setup.exe**, substituting the drive letter for the CD-ROM drive or floppy drive in the command line. Click **OK**.

4. Follow the instructions on the setup screen. When you are given the opportunity to select the folder to install Windows, select the folder that the current OS is installed in; most likely that is \Windows. If you use the same folder, Setup will use whatever settings it finds there.

Installation Process from the Setup Screen

Once you get to the setup screen, the installation process is the same, no matter whether you are doing an upgrade or a clean install. When installing Windows 9x, you are given the option of creating the Startup disk as discussed in the previous chapter. Be sure to do that to help prepare for emergencies. During the installation, you will also be asked to choose from four setup options:

- *Typical.* This option installs all of the components that are usually installed with Windows 9x. Most often, this is the option to choose.

- *Portable.* Use this option when installing Windows 9x on a notebook computer.

- *Compact.* Use this option if you are short on hard drive space and want the smallest possible installation. No optional components are installed during the installation. After the installation, if you need a component, you can install it by double-clicking the Add/Remove Programs applet in the Control Panel.

- *Custom.* Use this option if you know you will need components that are not normally installed under the Typical installation. You are given the opportunity to select any group of components to be included in the installation.

Windows 9x Setup begins installation in real mode and then switches to protected mode. During real mode, it runs ScanDisk, checks for existing Windows software, performs several system checks, loads the extended memory driver, looks for existing TSRs, and starts Windows, if it is not already started. The Windows logo screen is the first thing the user normally sees during the installation. Setup then switches to protected mode.

Setup creates the registry, getting it ready to contain the hardware information, and then searches for hardware. It loads its own drivers for the detected hardware, or, if it cannot detect the hardware, requests the drivers from the user. Setup then copies the drivers to the hard drive from the installation source or from a floppy disk, CD or other source provided by the user.

Up to this point, if Setup fails and you reboot the PC, you boot into the old OS. At this point, Setup alters the boot records on the hard drive to point to the Windows 9x file, Io.sys, rather than to the old OS system files. After this point, if Setup fails and you reboot, you reboot into Windows 9x.

During a normal installation, the PC reboots and Windows 9x is loaded. Some initial startup programs are run to set the time zone and to change existing application programs to Windows 9x. Depending on the hardware present, the PC may reboot again to load new drivers.

17

During the installation, Setup records information in log files. The primary log file is Setuplog.txt, a text file that is used by Windows to determine how far it got into the installation when it is recovering from a crash. Figure 17-6 shows a portion of Setuplog.txt in which the system ran a virus check on CMOS and began checking drives. The Detection Log (Detlog.txt) keeps a record of hardware detected, as shown in Figure 17-7.

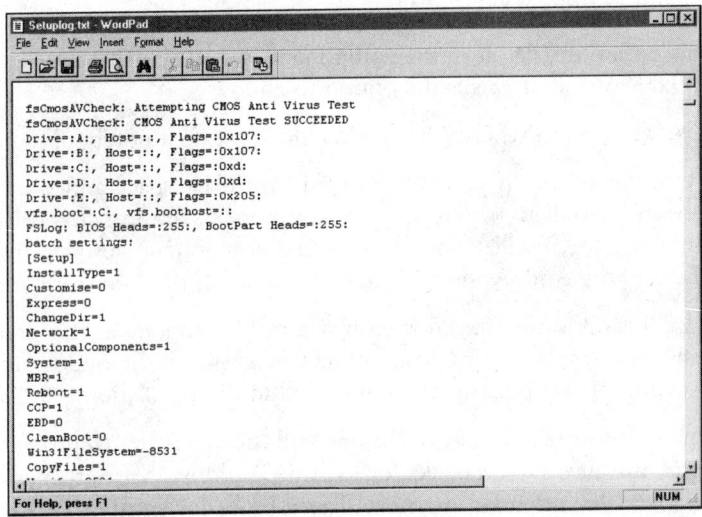

Figure 17-6   Windows records information about the setup process in Setuplog.txt

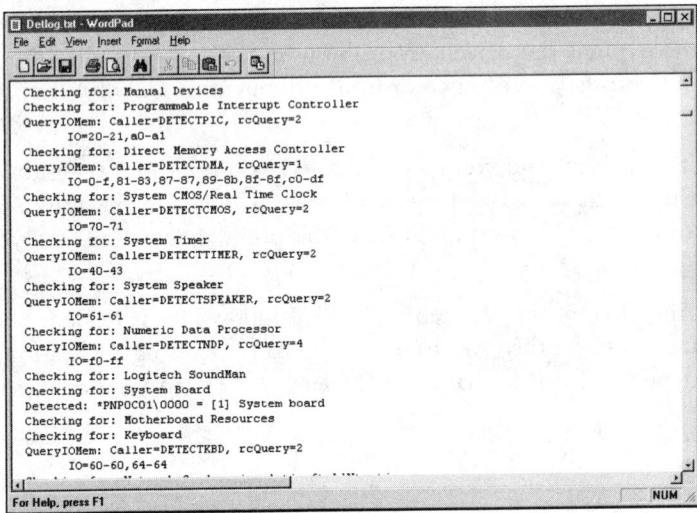

Figure 17-7   The Detlog.txt file shows what hardware has been detected

If the system fails to respond during the hardware detection phase, an entry is recorded in Detcrash.log, a binary file used by Windows to help recover from a crash caused by a problem with hardware. Windows does not use the contents of Detlog.txt; it is created only for the benefit of the user.

For example, if Setup suspects that a network card is present, because it sees a network driver installed in Config.sys, it records in Setuplog.txt and Detlog.txt that it is about to look for the card. If it successfully finds the card, it records the success in Detlog.txt. However, if an error occurs while Setup is searching for the card, an entry is made in the Detcrash.log file.

If the system crashes while trying to detect the network card and Setup is then restarted, it looks at Detcrash.log and Setuplog.txt to determine what it was trying to do at the time of the crash. It skips that step and goes on to the next step, so that it doesn't make the same mistake twice.

Even though Setup might crash several times during the installation process, progress is still being made. By reading the content of the log files, Setup is able to skip steps that cause a problem and move forward.

 TIP Be careful not to delete the log files during the installation process, especially if you've just experienced a crash. Also, restart by using the power on/power off method so that the ISA bus is fully initialized, which does not always happen during a warm boot.

In certain situations you might want to force Setup to begin installation at the beginning instead of looking to Setuplog.txt for the entry point, for example when you think you might have resolved a problem with hardware and want Setup to attempt to find the hardware again. To do that, delete Setuplog.txt to force a full restart.

Customizing Setup

Windows and other software store information about an installation on the setup CD or floppy disks in information files. These **information (.inf) files** are text files with an .inf file extension. One .inf file is Msbatch.inf. Information about your installation can be stored in this file, which can then be used to do an automatic, hands-free installation. All the questions that a user must answer during an installation can be answered by entries in this file so that a user has little to do but begin the installation. For more information about hands-free installations, see the *Microsoft Windows 95 Resource Kit* or the *Windows 98 Resource Kit* by Microsoft Press.

You can add several switches to the Setup.exe command that starts the setup process. Some of these switches and what they do are listed in Table 17-4.

17

Table 17-4 Switches for the Setup command

Switch	Description
Setup /?	Display help for each command-line switch.
Setup /D	Don't use the existing version of Windows to begin Setup. Use this option if you suspect corrupted Windows system files when upgrading Windows.
Setup /IC	Perform a clean boot. Use this option if you suspect drivers loaded from Autoexec.bat or Config.sys are causing a problem with the installation.
Setup /IH	Run ScanDisk in the foreground so that you can view results. Use this option if setup failed earlier and you want to check for hard drive corruption.
Setup /IL	Load the driver for a Logitech mouse. Use this option if you are using a Logitech Series C mouse.
Setup /IN	Do not set up the network.
Setup /IS	Do not run ScanDisk.
Setup /PI	Keep hardware settings that are not default settings. Use this option if a previous try of the installation caused a legacy hardware device to fail.

Table 17-5 lists some problems that might occur while installing Windows 9x and what to do about them.

Table 17-5 Some problems and solutions when installing Windows 9x

Symptom	Description and Solution
An error message about BIOS appears during installation.	This is most likely caused by BIOS not allowing changes to the boot sector to protect it from viruses. Disable the feature in CMOS setup.
Windows 9x stalls during the first restart after installation.	This is probably caused by legacy hardware not configured correctly. Try the following: ■ Remark (REM) out all entries in Config.sys and Autoexec.bat. ■ Disable the ISA enumerator by commenting out this line in System.ini: Device=ISAPNP.386.
During the first restart after installation, an error message appears with information about a bad or missing file.	Probably caused by an error in Config.sys or Autoexec.bat. Try renaming both files so they are not executed. If this solves the problem, then comment out each line in the file, one at a time, until you know which line caused the problem.
During the first restart after the installation, you get an error message about a missing or damaged VxD file.	Run Windows setup again and select the option to Verify or replace the missing VxD (virtual device driver).
After upgrading from Windows 95 to Windows 98, the startup screen still says Windows 95.	This can be caused by one of two problems. The Io.sys file might not have been updated. Use the Sys C: command to replace it. The file Logo.sys is in the root directory, which overrides the logo screen embedded in Io.sys. Delete or rename the file.

Table 17-5   Some problems and solutions when installing Windows 9x (continued)

Symptom	Description and Solution
"Invalid system disk" error appears during setup.	■ Suspect a boot sector virus. Run a current version of antivirus software. ■ If this error occurs while installing Windows when disk management software such as DiskPro is running, Windows might have damaged the hard drive MBR. To recover from this problem, see the documentation for the disk management software.

 For specific error messages that occur during installation and what to do about them, go to the Microsoft Web site *support.microsoft.com* and search on the error message.

Configuring the Windows 9x Startup with Msdos.sys

In Windows 9x, the file Msdos.sys is a text file containing several parameters that affect how the OS boots. You can change some of the entries in this file to customize the boot process. The file is a hidden, read-only, system file, so before you can edit it, you must first use the Attrib command at the command prompt or menus from Explorer to make the file available for editing. Also, make a backup copy of the file in case you want to revert to the form it was in before the changes were made.

From a command prompt, follow these steps to change the options in Msdos.sys:

1. Go to an OS command prompt.

2. Go to the root directory of your hard drive by entering:

   `CD\`

3. Make the file available for editing by entering:

   `ATTRIB -R -H -S MSDOS.SYS`

4. Make a backup copy of the file by entering:

   `COPY MSDOS.SYS MSDOS.BK`

5. Use Edit.com to edit the file by entering:

   `EDIT MSDOS.SYS`

6. Save the file and return it to a hidden, read-only, system file by entering:

   `ATTRIB +R +H +S MSDOS.SYS`

Table 17-6 lists each entry in the Msdos.sys file and its purpose. You can refer to this table as you read about the different options available when installing and configuring Windows 9x.

17

Table 17-6 Contents of the Msdos.sys file options section

Command Line Variable Name	Purpose of the Values Assigned to the Variable
AutoScan	0 = Computer does not scan hard drive. 1 = (Default) Prompts the user before running ScanDisk on the hard drive when booting up after the computer is not shut down properly. 2 = Automatically scans without prompting the user.
BootMulti	0 = (Default) Boot only to Windows 9x. 1= Allows for a dual boot.
BootWin	1 = (Default) Boot to Windows 9x. 0 = Boot to previous version of DOS.
BootGUI	1 = (Default) Boot to Windows 9x with the graphic user interface. 0 = Boot only to the command prompt for DOS 7.0 (the DOS core of Windows 95) or 7.1 (the DOS core of Windows 98). Autoexec.bat and Config.sys will be executed, and you will be in real-mode DOS.
BootMenu	0 = (Default) Don't display the Startup Menu. 1= Display the Startup Menu.
BootMenuDefault	1 through 8 = The value selected from the Startup Menu by Default (Normally this value should be 1).
BootMenuDelay	n = Number of seconds delay before the default value in the Startup Menu is automatically selected.
BootKeys	1= (Default) The function keys work during the boot process (F4, F5, F6, F8, Shift+F5, Ctrl+F5, Shift+F8). 0 = Disable the function keys during the boot process. (This option can be used to help secure a workstation.)
BootDelay	n = Number of seconds the boot process waits (when it displays the message "Starting Windows 95" or "Starting Windows 98") for the user to press F8 to get the Startup Menu (default is 2 seconds).
Logo	1= (Default) Display the Windows 9x logo screen. 0 = Leave the screen in text mode.
Drvspace	1= (Default) Load Drvspace.bin, used for disk compression, if it is present. 0 = Don't load Drvspace.bin.
DoubleBuffer	1= (Default) When you have a SCSI drive, enables double buffering for the drive (see the drive documentation). 0 = Don't use double buffering for the SCSI drive.
Network	1= If network components are installed, include the option, "Safe mode with network support" in the Startup Menu. 0 = Don't include the option on the Startup Menu. (This will normally be set to 0 if the PC has no network components installed. The Startup Menu will be renumbered from this point forward in the menu.)

Table 17-6   Contents of the Msdos.sys file options section (continued)

Command Line Variable Name	Purpose of the Values Assigned to the Variable
BootFailSafe	1= (Default) Include Safe mode in the Startup Menu. 0 = Don't include Safe mode in the Startup Menu.
BootWarn	1= (Default) Display the warning message when Windows 9x boots into Safe mode. 0 = Don't display the warning message.
LoadTop	1= (Default) Load Command.com at the top of conventional memory. 0 = Don't load Command.com at the top of conventional memory. (Use this option when there is a memory conflict with this area of memory.)

Figure 17-8 shows a sample Msdos.sys file. The lines containing x's at the bottom of the file are used to ensure that the file size is compatible with other programs.

```
[Paths]
WinDir=C:\WIN95
WinBootDir=C:\WIN95
HostWinBootDrv=C

[Options]
BootMulti=1
BootGUI=1
BootMenu=1
Network=0
;
;The following lines are required for compatibility with other programs.
;Do not remove them (MSDOS.SYS needs to be >1024 bytes).
;xxxxxxxxxxxxxxxxxxxxxxxxxxxxxxxxxxxxxxxxxxxxxxxxxxxxxxxxxxxxxa
;xxxxxxxxxxxxxxxxxxxxxxxxxxxxxxxxxxxxxxxxxxxxxxxxxxxxxxxxxxxxxb
;xxxxxxxxxxxxxxxxxxxxxxxxxxxxxxxxxxxxxxxxxxxxxxxxxxxxxxxxxxxxxc
;xxxxxxxxxxxxxxxxxxxxxxxxxxxxxxxxxxxxxxxxxxxxxxxxxxxxxxxxxxxxxd
;xxxxxxxxxxxxxxxxxxxxxxxxxxxxxxxxxxxxxxxxxxxxxxxxxxxxxxxxxxxxxe
;xxxxxxxxxxxxxxxxxxxxxxxxxxxxxxxxxxxxxxxxxxxxxxxxxxxxxxxxxxxxf
;xxxxxxxxxxxxxxxxxxxxxxxxxxxxxxxxxxxxxxxxxxxxxxxxxxxxxxxxxxxg
;xxxxxxxxxxxxxxxxxxxxxxxxxxxxxxxxxxxxxxxxxxxxxxxxxxxxxxxxxxh
;xxxxxxxxxxxxxxxxxxxxxxxxxxxxxxxxxxxxxxxxxxxxxxxxxxxxxxxxxi
;xxxxxxxxxxxxxxxxxxxxxxxxxxxxxxxxxxxxxxxxxxxxxxxxxxxxxxxxj
;xxxxxxxxxxxxxxxxxxxxxxxxxxxxxxxxxxxxxxxxxxxxxxxxxxxxxxxk
;xxxxxxxxxxxxxxxxxxxxxxxxxxxxxxxxxxxxxxxxxxxxxxxxxxxxxxl
;xxxxxxxxxxxxxxxxxxxxxxxxxxxxxxxxxxxxxxxxxxxxxxxxxxxxxm
;xxxxxxxxxxxxxxxxxxxxxxxxxxxxxxxxxxxxxxxxxxxxxxxxxxxxn
;xxxxxxxxxxxxxxxxxxxxxxxxxxxxxxxxxxxxxxxxxxxxxxxxxxxo
;xxxxxxxxxxxxxxxxxxxxxxxxxxxxxxxxxxxxxxxxxxxxxxxxxxp
;xxxxxxxxxxxxxxxxxxxxxxxxxxxxxxxxxxxxxxxxxxxxxxxxxq
;xxxxxxxxxxxxxxxxxxxxxxxxxxxxxxxxxxxxxxxxxxxxxxxxr
;xxxxxxxxxxxxxxxxxxxxxxxxxxxxxxxxxxxxxxxxxxxxxxxs
```

Figure 17-8   A sample Msdos.sys file

17

Instructions for Specific Upgrades

You have just learned the basic installation process for Windows 9x. Although most actual installations will follow this general outline, depending on exactly what version and features you are installing, each type of upgrade has its own issues. This section discusses things to consider when upgrading to Windows 95, 98, and Me from earlier operating system versions.

Installing Windows 9x over DOS and Windows 3.x

If DOS and Windows 3.x reside on the PC prior to installing Windows 9x, you can perform an upgrade or a clean install. If you choose an upgrade, this is what happens:

- Windows 9x Setup copies information about existing application programs from the .ini files of Windows 3.x into the Windows 9x registry, eliminating the need for you to install the existing programs into Windows 9x.

- These programs are added to the Start menu of Windows 9x.

- Existing programs can find their .dlls in the same Windows\System folder as they did with Windows 3.x. (DLLs, or dynamic link libraries, contain programming routines for common tasks and will be covered in detail in the next chapter.)

It is possible to install Windows 9x on the same hard drive as another operating system. This is called a dual boot and is covered in Chapter 19. However, there is usually little need to leave DOS or Windows 3.x on the drive. When upgrading from Windows 3.x to Windows 9x, first start Windows 3.x and enter the Setup command using File Manager.

Upgrading from Windows 95 to Windows 98

Upgrading from Windows 95 to Windows 98 is relatively easy, because the two OSs are similar. This upgrade is not as complex as upgrading from DOS with Windows 3.x. Follow these guidelines when upgrading from Windows 95 to Windows 98:

- As with any OS installation, you need to check whether your hardware is compatible with the OS you are planning to install. In this case, most hardware that will work with Windows 95 will work with Windows 98.

- Use up-to-date virus software and virus definitions to scan for viruses on your hard drive.

- You also need to check software packages and programs for compatibility. You can do this by checking the documentation or the manufacturer's Web site for each program. If you are planning an OS upgrade, a software manufacturer will often provide a downloadable **patch**, also called a **service pack**, to make the software compatible with the new OS. The search utility at *www.microsoft.com/windows/compatible/* provides a quick way to determine whether a particular product has been tested for compatibility with Windows.

- Make sure you have at least one full backup of your system as it was under Windows 95. If the upgrade to Windows 98 fails for any reason, you can use your Windows 95 backup to restore the system to the point where you were before you attempted the upgrade.

Once you have backed up your system and made sure its hardware and software are compatible with Windows 98, use the following procedure to perform the upgrade:

1. If your system BIOS runs a program to protect the boot sector of your hard drive from viruses, enter CMOS setup and disable the program because it might interfere with the installation. After the installation you can turn the program back on.

2. Start Windows 95 and close any open applications. If you have antivirus software running in the background, close the software. Close any icons open in the System Tray.

3. Insert the upgrade CD in the CD-ROM drive. Click **Start**, **Run** and enter **D:\Setup** in the Run dialog box (where D is the drive letter of the CD-ROM drive), then click **OK**.

4. When the Setup program opens, it will provide a series of windows to guide you through the setup process. All you have to do is follow the prompts and provide any requested information. Always create the emergency startup disk when you are prompted to do so.

5. After Setup is complete, open and test some of the applications you already had installed under Windows 95. Any problem you have with a particular application may be solved by uninstalling and then reinstalling it, or installing any necessary patches to make it work with Windows 98.

6. Once the upgrade from Windows 95 to Windows 98 is complete and you have verified that your system is working, it is a good idea to back up your system again.

Upgrading from Windows 98 to Windows Me

If you are upgrading from Windows 98 to Windows Me, use the same pre-upgrade checklist that is given for the Windows 95 to Windows 98 upgrade in the previous section. Remember to check the compatibility of hardware and software and to back up your system before you begin. To check whether a particular hardware product has been tested for use with Windows Me, go to *www.microsoft.com/windowsme/upgrade/compat/default.asp*.

In addition to the guidelines in the previous section, do the following before upgrading to Windows Me:

- Uncompress any portions of your hard drive that are compressed. If you are not sure whether your hard drive is compressed, run ScanDisk, which will tell you. Windows Me will not install on a compressed hard drive.

- Uninstall power management tools and disk management tools.

- Read the readme.txt file and any other setup information provided on the Windows Me disk.

The steps to upgrade Windows Me are the same as for Windows 98.

17

Downloading and Installing Updates for Windows 9x

Between releases of OS versions, manufacturers often produce OS updates in the form of patches or service packs that add features, fix bugs, or address security issues. The Microsoft Web site *windowsupdate.microsoft.com/*, provides you with a list of updates available for your OS. In Windows 98 and Windows Me, you can access this page by clicking Windows Update on the Start menu. The update process will examine your system and recommend available updates for you to select, download, and install following directions on the screen.

USING WINDOWS 9X

Now that you have learned how to install and upgrade Windows 9x, let's look at some things you need to know about using it. As a PC technician, you will need to be familiar with keyboard shortcuts for Windows as well as how to manage the desktop and use Windows Explorer.

Keystroke Shortcuts in Windows

Table 17-7 lists a few handy keystrokes to use when working with Windows, including the function keys you can use during startup. You can also use the mouse to accomplish some of these tasks, but keystrokes are faster for experienced typists. Also, sometimes in troubleshooting situations, the mouse is not usable. At those times, knowing the keystrokes is very valuable.

Table 17-7   Keystrokes to help make it easier to work with Windows

General Action	Keystrokes	Description
While loading Windows	F4	Load previous version of DOS.
	F5	Start in safe mode.
	F8 or Ctrl	Display Startup menu.
	Shift + F8	Step-by-step confirmation.
Working with text anywhere in Windows	Ctrl + C Ctrl + Ins	Shortcut for Copy.
	Ctrl + A	Shortcut for selecting all text.
	Ctrl + X	Shortcut for Cut.
	Ctrl + V Shift + Ins	Shortcut for Paste.
	Shift + arrow keys	Hold down the Shift key and use the arrow keys to select text, character by character.
Managing programs	Alt + Tab	While holding down the Alt key, press Tab to move from one loaded application to another.
	Ctrl + Esc	Display the Start menu.

Table 17-7   Keystrokes to help make it easier to work with Windows (continued)

General Action	Keystrokes	Description
	Alt + F4	Close a program window, or, if no window is open, shut down Windows.
	Double-click	Double-click an icon or program name to execute the program.
	Ctrl + Alt + Del	Display the Task List, which you can use to switch to another application, end a task, or shut down Windows.
Managing files, folders, icons and shortcuts	Ctrl + Shift while dragging a file	Create a shortcut.
	Ctrl while dragging a file	Copy a file.
	Shift + Delete	Delete a file without placing it in the Recycle Bin.
	F2	Rename an item.
	Alt + Enter	Display an item's Properties window.
Selecting items	Shift + click	To select multiple entries in a list (such as filenames in Explorer), click the first item and then hold down the Shift key and click the last item you want to select in the list. All items between the first and last are selected.
	Ctrl + click	To select several items in a list that are not listed sequentially, click the first item to select it. Hold down the Ctrl key as you click other items anywhere in the list. All items you have clicked on are selected.
Using menus	Alt	Press the Alt key to activate the menu bar.
	Alt, letter	After the menu bar is activated, press a letter to select a menu option. The letter must be underlined in the menu.
	Alt, arrow keys	After the menu bar is activated, use the arrow keys to move over the menu tree.
	Alt, arrow keys, Enter	After the menu bar is activated and the correct option is highlighted, press Enter to select the option.
	Esc	Press Escape to exit a menu without making a selection.
Managing the desktop	Print Screen	Copy the desktop into the Clipboard.
	Ctrl + Esc	Display the Start menu and move the focus to the menu. (Use the arrow keys to move over the menu.)
	Alt + M	After the focus is on the Start menu, minimizes all windows and moves the focus to the desktop

17

Table 17-7   Keystrokes to help make it easier to work with Windows (continued)

General Action	Keystrokes	Description
Working with windows	Ctrl + Tab and Ctrl + Shift + Tab	Move through tabbed pages in a dialog box.
	Shift + Close (X) button on a window	Close current folder and its parent folders.
	F5	Refresh the contents of a window.
Using the Windows key (Key is labeled with the Windows flag icon)	Win	Display the Start menu.
	Win + E	Start Windows Explorer.
	Win + M	Minimize all windows.
	Win + Tab	Move through items on task bar.
	Win + R	Display the Run dialog box.
	Win + Break	Display the System Properties window.
Using the Applications key (key is labeled with a box and arrow icon)	Application key	When an item is selected, display its shortcut menu.

Managing the Windows 9x Desktop

From the Windows 9x desktop you can make applications automatically load at startup, create shortcuts to files and applications, and make the environment more user-friendly. In this section, you will learn some ways to manage the Windows 9x desktop.

To control display settings, right-click anywhere on the desktop and select Properties from the shortcut menu. The Display Properties window appears as shown in Figure 17-9. Some of the more common things you can do from each tab on the window are:

- *Background*. Select desktop wallpaper or pattern.
- *Screensaver*. Select screensaver and change its settings; change power settings for monitor.
- *Appearance*. Pick and customize a color scheme for the desktop.
- *Effects*. Specify icon settings.
- *Web*. Set Active Desktop properties.
- *Settings*. Change color range and display size.

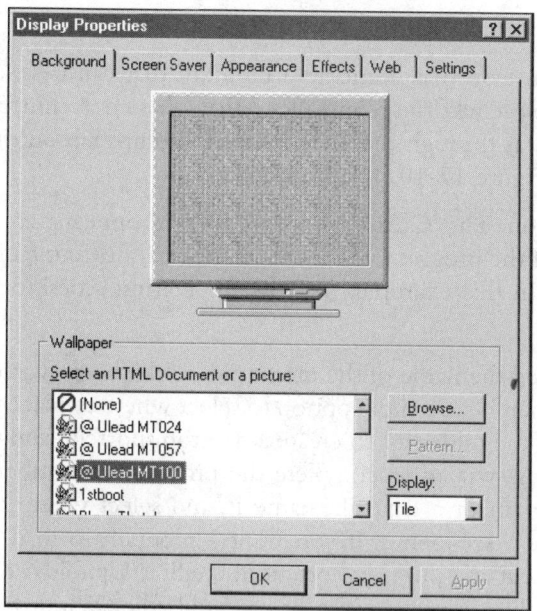

Figure 17-9   The Display Properties window lets you change settings for your desktop

You can also hide and unhide the taskbar at the bottom of the desktop. To do that, click Start, Settings, Taskbar and Start Menu. The Taskbar Properties window appears. (You can also reach this window by right-clicking on the Taskbar and selecting Properties from the shortcut menu.) Then click the Taskbar Options tab and select Auto hide (see Figure 17-10).

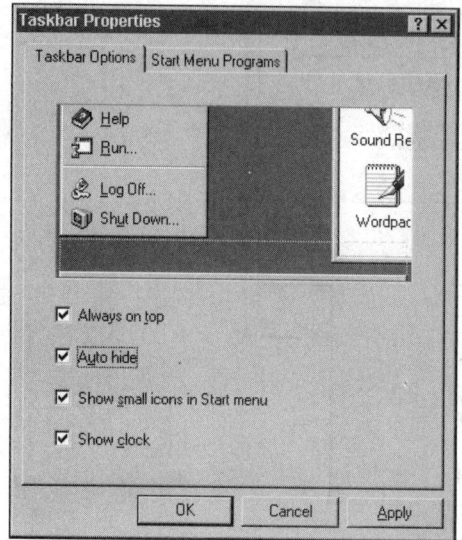

Figure 17-10   Use the Taskbar Properties window to change taskbar settings

17

Working with Shortcuts

A **shortcut** on the desktop is an icon that points to a program that can be executed, or to a file or folder. The user double-clicks the icon to load the software. A shortcut can be created in several ways. One way is through the Start Menu Programs tab on the Taskbar Properties window you saw in Figure 17-10.

From here, click the Add button. The Create Shortcut Wizard appears, as shown in Figure 17-11. Enter the name of the program you want to create a shortcut to, or browse for the file on your computer. In this example, we will be creating a desktop shortcut to the Notepad application.

Once you have entered or selected the name of the program for which you want to create a shortcut, click Next. You will then be given the option to select where to place the short-cut. Select Desktop at the top of the folder list to create a desktop shortcut, and then click Next. Follow the directions in the wizard to complete the process. Remember that you can create a shortcut for a program or a data file, name it, and select where to place it (either on the desktop or in the Start menu). If you want a program to load whenever Windows 9x starts, create a shortcut and put the shortcut in the StartUp folder of the Start menu. All items in the StartUp folder are automatically executed when Windows 9x starts.

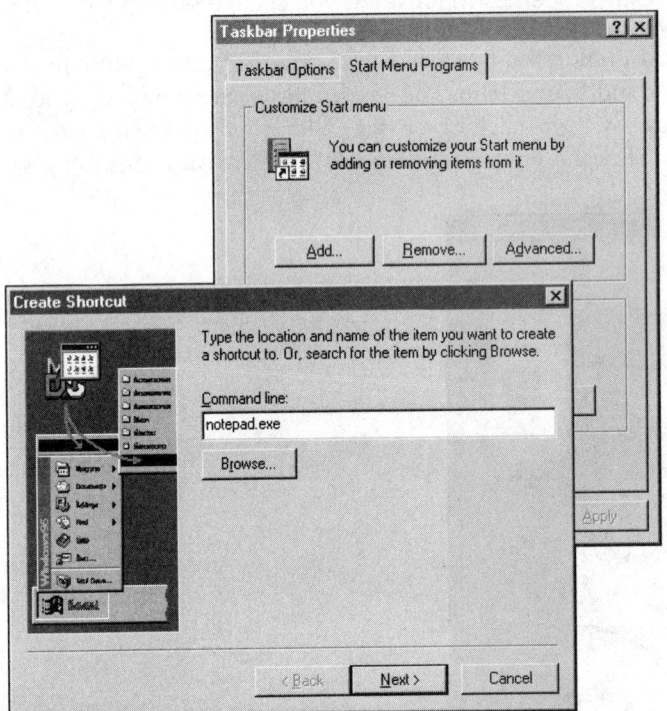

Figure 17-11   Select the item you want to point the shortcut to

> 💡 **TIP** To edit a shortcut, right-click the shortcut and select *Properties* from the menu. To delete a shortcut, select *Delete* from this same menu.

Managing Icons

An icon on the desktop can be a shortcut to an application or it can represent a file that belongs to an application. The telltale sign of the difference is the small bent-arrow short-cut symbol on the icon, as seen in Figure 17-12. The icon on the right represents the document file MyLetter1.doc, stored in the \Windows\Desktop folder, and the icon on the left is a shortcut to the file MyLetter2.doc, which can be stored anywhere on the drive. Also shown in Figure 17-12 are the contents of the \Windows\Desktop folder as seen by Explorer. You can add an icon to the desktop by putting a file in this folder. One way to delete an icon on the desktop is to delete the corresponding file in this folder; however, as you will see, this method can cause problems for the user.

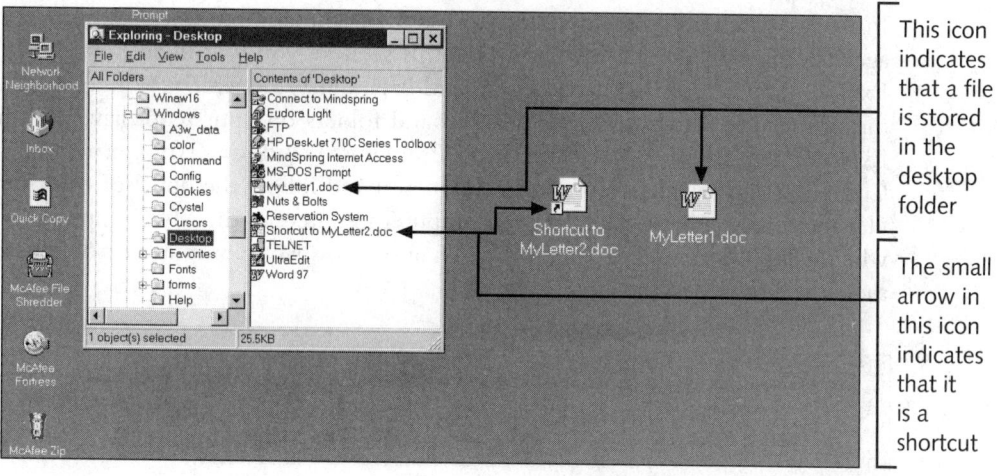

Figure 17-12   One icon is a shortcut, and the other icon represents a file stored in the Desktop folder

If you delete a shortcut icon from the desktop or the \Windows\Desktop folder, such as Shortcut to MyLetter2.doc, the shortcut is gone, but the actual file that the shortcut points to is not deleted. If you delete a document icon, such as MyLetter1.doc, the document itself will be deleted.

An error can occur if the actual document file, MyLetter2.doc, is deleted, but the short-cut to the deleted document remains on the desktop. Figure 17-13 shows a sample error message that occurs when this shortcut is used.

17

File has been deleted

Figure 17-13   The file that the shortcut points to has been deleted, which causes an error when the shortcut is used

Using Windows Explorer to Manage Floppy Disks and Hard Drives

In the last chapter you learned how to use the command prompt of Windows 9x to manage a floppy drive and a hard drive. In this section, you will learn how to use Windows Explorer to manage floppy disks and hard drives in Windows 9x. Windows 9x Explorer is the primary tool for managing the files and folders on your hard drive and disks. Open Explorer in Windows 9x (click Start, Programs, Windows Explorer, or right-click My Computer and select Explore from the menu) and follow the directions below to manage files and folders. Figure 17-14 shows computer resources in the My Computer folder as seen when using Windows Explorer. (You can also access My Computer by double-clicking on the icon on the desktop.)

Figure 17-14   The My Computer view in Windows Explorer

Shortcut Menu Options

The easiest way to manage drives, disks, folders, and files in Windows Explorer is to use the shortcut menus. To access the shortcut menu, right-click the icon representing the item you want to work with. The shortcut menu for the floppy drive is shown in Figure 17-15 as an example.

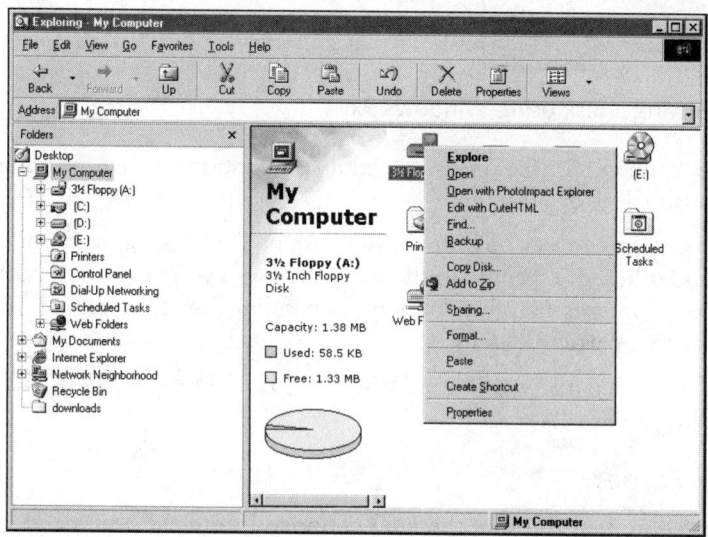

Figure 17-15   Use the shortcut menu to manage items in Explorer

Some of the tasks you can perform from a shortcut menu are listed below.

- If you select Explore, the contents of the selected disk or folder in the floppy drive will be shown in the current Explorer window. If you select Open, the contents of the disk or folder will be shown in a separate window.

- The Create Shortcut option will create a shortcut icon for the selected item. (You learned about creating shortcuts earlier in this chapter.)

- Selecting the Properties option brings up a dialog box showing information about the selected item and allows you to change settings for the item.

- If you have selected a disk or drive, the shortcut menu will contain a Format option. Recall that you can use Explorer to format a floppy disk, as you learned in the previous chapter, by selecting Format from the shortcut menu.

- The Backup option enables you to make a backup of a disk, and the Sharing option enables you to share a drive, folders, or files with other users on your network. Backup and Sharing are covered in later chapters.

- For floppy drives, if you select Copy Disk, a dialog box opens as shown in Figure 17-16, where the disk listed under "Copy from" is the source disk, and the disk listed under "Copy to" is the target disk. Click Start to copy the disk.

- The shortcut menu of a folder allows you to create a new file. The menu lists applications you can use to create the file.

17

Figure 17-16   Copying a disk using Windows 9x

- The shortcut menu for files gives you additional options such as printing and e-mailing the file.

As you can see, some of the options on shortcut menus are the same for files, folders, drives, and disks, and others are specific to the particular item you are looking at. The additional shortcut menu options may be different, depending on what programs you have installed to work with a particular item.

Now let's look in more detail at ways to use Windows 9x Explorer to work with files and folders on your hard drive.

Create a New Folder

To create a folder (equivalent to using the MD command from the command line, which you learned in the last chapter), do the following. Select the folder you want to be the parent folder by clicking the folder name. For example, to create a folder named Chess under the folder named Games, first click the Games folder. Then click the File menu. Select New from the menu. Then select Folder from the submenu that is displayed. The new folder will be created under Games, but its name will be New Folder. Click the folder name once to open the text box and highlight the current folder name, New Folder. Type Chess to change the folder name to Chess, as in Figure 17-17. The maximum depth of folders under folders depends on the length of the folder names.

Figure 17-17   Edit the new folder's name

Delete a Folder

To delete a folder (similiar to using the RD command from the command line) from Explorer, right-click the folder and select Delete from the shortcut menu. A confirmation dialog box asks you if you are sure you want to delete the folder. If you click Yes, the folder and all of its contents, including subfolders, will be sent to the Recycle Bin. Empty the Recycle Bin to free your disk space. Files and folders sent to the Recycle Bin are not deleted until you empty it.

File Attributes

Using Explorer, you can view and change the file attributes (similar to using the command-line Attrib command). From Explorer, right-click a file and select Properties from the shortcut menu. The Properties window appears, as shown in Figure 17-18. From the Properties window, you can change the read-only, hidden, and archive attributes of the file.

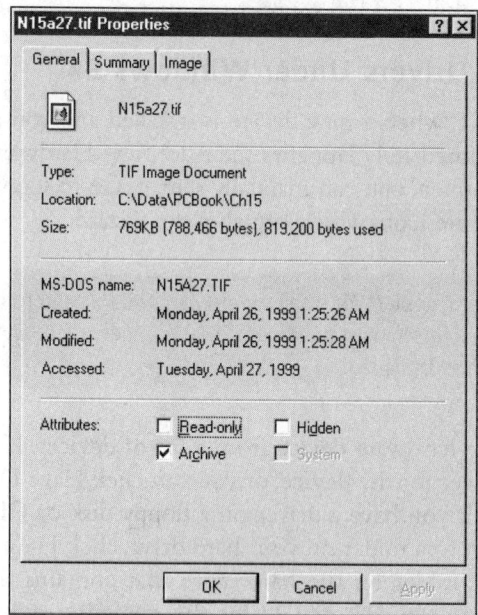

Figure 17-18   Properties of a file in Windows 98

Folder Properties

You can also view and change the properties assigned to folders. Select the folder and from the Explorer menu, click View, Folder Options, and then click the View tab. From this window you can change how and when files are displayed in the folder.

Windows 98 identifies file type primarily by the file extension. In Windows Explorer, by default, Windows 9x hides the file extensions of those files for which it knows which application to use to open or execute the file. For example, just after installation, it hides .exe, .com, .sys, and .txt file extensions but will not hide .doc, .ppt, or .xls files until the software to open these files has been installed. To display all file extensions, in the Folder Options windows, uncheck Hide file extensions for known file types.

17

INSTALLING HARDWARE WITH WINDOWS 9x

In this section, you will learn how to add new hardware to Windows 9x systems and install 16-bit and 32-bit device drivers, using a CD-ROM drive as an example. You will also learn about Plug and Play support in Windows 9x.

Adding New Hardware

After a device is physically installed in a system, the next step is to install the software necessary to interface with it. This software, called a device driver, is written to interface with the specific device and the specific operating system. Knowing how to install and troubleshoot device drivers is an essential skill of a PC support technician.

Installing and Using Device Drivers Under Windows 9x

For Windows 9x or Windows 2000/XP, when a new device is installed and you power up the PC, Windows recognizes it and immediately launches the Add New Hardware Wizard. If the wizard does not automatically launch, you can manually start it. Go to Control Panel and double-click the Add New Hardware icon, which launches the wizard.

 The Control Panel contains several applets, or small programs, that are used to manage Windows. You can view these applets in a list or as icons. Use the View menu in Control Panel to change the way they are displayed.

One step in the wizard is to select the hardware device from a list of devices. If you click OK, Windows will use a Windows driver for the device, or you can click Have Disk to use your own drivers (see Figure 17-19). If you have a driver on a floppy disk or CD or have downloaded a driver from the Internet to a folder on your hard drive, click Have Disk and point the wizard to the disk, CD, or folder on the hard drive that contains the driver. Sometimes you must select a folder on the disk or CD for the operating system to use such as \Win98 to locate the drivers to install under Windows 98 (or \Win2k for Windows 2000, which you will learn more about in later chapters).

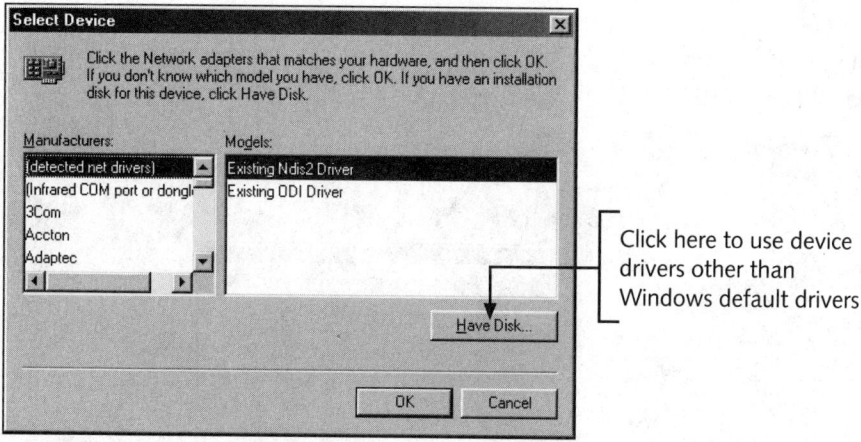

Figure 17-19   To use device drivers supplied by the device manufacturer, click Have Disk

Viewing and Changing Current Device Drivers

You can view and change current device drivers from the Control Panel. For example, in Windows 98, to view the current video driver, click Start, Settings, Control Panel, and then double-click Display. Click the Settings tab to view the currently installed display driver, as shown in Figure 17-20.

Figure 17-20   Use the Settings tab of Display Properties to view the currently installed display driver

To change the video card driver, click Advanced, click the Adapter tab, and then click the Change button. You see the Windows 98 Update Device Driver Wizard. Click Next to see the dialog box in Figure 17-21, which includes options to let Windows 98 search for a new driver from its list of Windows drivers or to display a list of all the drivers in a specific

17

location, so you can select the driver you want. To provide your own driver, click the second option and then click Next. Then, click Have Disk to provide the new driver from a floppy disk, a CD, or a file downloaded from the Internet.

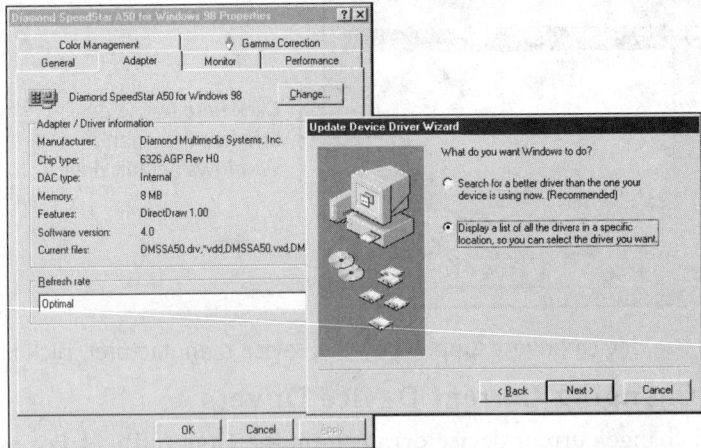

Figure 17-21   The Windows 98 Update Device Driver Wizard enables you to install a new device driver for a previously installed device

If the new driver fails, try uninstalling the device and then reinstalling it. To uninstall a device, access Device Manager (click Start, Settings, Control Panel, double-click System, then click Device Manager), select the device and then click Remove (see Figure 17-22). Then reboot the PC and allow the Found New Hardware Wizard to launch.

Figure 17-22   Use Device Manager to uninstall a device

Installing a CD-ROM Drive with Windows 9x

Now that you have an overview of the process of adding new hardware and device drivers in Windows 9x, let's look at installing a CD-ROM drive as an example and consider how and when you would use 16-bit and 32-bit drivers.

To use the 32-bit Windows driver for your CD-ROM drive, click Start, Settings, Control Panel, and then double-click Add New Hardware. Click Next when you are prompted to begin installing the software for the new device. Complete the installation by following the directions on the Add New Hardware window.

When Windows 9x starts up after you've installed the CD-ROM drive, it assigns the next available drive letter to the drive. To dictate what the drive letter should be, use Device Manager. Click Start, Settings, Control Panel, and then double-click System. Click the Device Manager tab. Select the CD-ROM drive and click Properties, then click the Settings tab (see Figure 17-23), where the drive is designated E:. Select a range of letters to be used by the drive and click OK.

 TIP When you update or install additional features on application software, some software expects the same drive letter for the CD-ROM drive that was used when it was first installed. Permanently setting the CD-ROM drive letter satisfies the requirements of this software.

Figure 17-23   You can specify the drive letter to be assigned to the CD-ROM drive from the Properties box for the drive

Windows 9x supports a wide variety of CD-ROM drives, so most manufacturers assume that Windows will provide 32-bit drivers, and ship the accompanying floppy disk only with 16-bit drivers. You would use these drivers in a situation where your hard drive has failed and you are booting from the rescue disk. Windows 98 automatically puts its own 16-bit drivers on that rescue disk; later in this section, you will learn how to add them to a Windows 95 startup disk that does not include support for CD-ROM drives. These 16-bit drivers supplied by Windows 9x may not work with your CD-ROM drive. If they do not, you would use the 16-bit drivers provided by the manufacturer.

Testing the Drive

The drive is now ready to use. Press the eject button to open the drive shelf, and place a CD in the drive. Since data on CDs is written only on the bottom, be careful to protect it. Damage to either side of the disk can make it unreadable, but the bottom of the disk is the more sensitive side. Now access the CD using Explorer (use the assigned drive letter). If you have a problem reading the CD, verify that the CD is placed in the tray label-side-up and that the format is compatible with your drive. If one CD doesn't work, try another; the first CD may be defective or scratched.

 A CD-ROM drive can be set so that when you insert a CD, software on the CD automatically executes through, a feature called Autorun or Autoplay. To turn the feature on, from Device Manager, right-click on the CD-ROM drive and select Properties. From the Properties window, select the Settings tab and then select Auto insert notification. To prevent a CD from automatically playing when the feature is enabled, hold down the Shift key when inserting the CD.

Update Your Windows 95 Rescue Disk to Include Access to the CD-ROM Drive   In Chapter 16 you created a Windows emergency startup disk to start a system in the event of a hard drive failure. This rescue disk needs to include tools to access the CD-ROM drive, because Windows 9x is normally loaded from a CD-ROM. When you are recovering from a failed hard drive, you will not have access to the 32-bit Windows drivers on the hard drive. Windows 98 automatically adds the real-mode CD-ROM device drivers to the rescue disk, but Windows 95 does not. This section explains how to add this functionality to a Windows 95 rescue disk.

The CD-ROM drive you learned how to install previously came with a disk that includes the following files:

- *Install.exe*. The CD-ROM installation program
- *Cdtech.sys*. CD-ROM device driver
- Instruction files and documentation

Two files are required to access a CD-ROM drive while in real mode: the 16-bit device driver provided by the manufacturer of the CD-ROM drive (or a generic real-mode driver that works with the drive), which in this case is Cdtech.sys, and the 16-bit real-mode OS interface to the driver, Mscdex.exe. The device driver is loaded from Config.sys, and Mscdex.exe is loaded from Autoexec.bat.

If you have run the installation program that came with the CD-ROM drive (Install.exe), then your Autoexec.bat and Config.sys files on your hard drive should already have the correct entries in them. You can add these lines to these same files on your rescue disk, correcting paths to the two files as needed. Copy the two files to your rescue disk so you can access the CD-ROM drive when you boot from this disk, even when the hard drive is not accessible. For example, on a rescue or boot disk designed to access the CD-ROM drive without depending on any files or commands on the hard drive, the Config.sys file might contain this command (the parameters in the command lines are explained below):

```
DEVICE = A:\CDTECH.SYS /D:MSCD001
```

The Autoexec.bat file might contain this command line:

```
MSCDEX.EXE /D:MSCD001 /L:E /M:10
```

The explanations of these command lines are as follows:

- Two files needed to manage the drive are Mscdex.exe and Cdtech.sys, which must be copied to this disk into the root directory.

- When the program Mscdex.exe executes, it uses the MSCD001 entry as a tag back to the Config.sys file to learn which device driver is being used to interface with the drive, which in this case is Cdtech.sys.

- To Mscdex.exe, the drive is named MSCD001 and is being managed by the driver Cdtech.sys.

- Mscdex.exe will use Cdtech.sys as its "go-between" to access the drive.

- Mscdex.exe also assigns a drive letter to the drive. If you want to specify a certain drive letter, use the /L: option in the command line. In our example, the CD-ROM drive will be drive E. If you don't use the /L: option, then the next available drive letter is used.

- The /M: option controls the number of memory buffers.

- If the files referenced in these two commands are stored on the floppy disk in a different directory from the root directory, then include the path to the file in front of the filename.

If your hard drive fails and you start up from your rescue disk, once the CD-ROM drivers are loaded and the CD-ROM drive is recognized, you can copy files needed to troubleshoot the system from the Windows 9x CD, which will be in drive E. If you decide to reinstall Windows, you can type E:\Setup at the command prompt.

If you have installed 16-bit device drivers from your Config.sys and Autoexec.bat files, when Windows 9x is installed, it will often ignore existing Config.sys and Autoexec.bat lines. It turns these lines into comment lines by adding REM to the beginning of the line and handles the CD-ROM drive through its own protected-mode drivers.

17

Optimizing CD-ROM Cache

Recall from Chapter 16 that a cache is a location in memory or the hard drive used to store frequently used data. For CD-ROM drives, a memory cache contains data that was recently read from the CD. Recall that Mscdex.exe is the 16-bit OS utility that manages a CD-ROM drive. The 32-bit CD-ROM utility is CDFS (CD file system), which is automatically loaded by Windows 9x if it detects a CD-ROM drive. CDFS has a caching function similar to hard drive caching done by Vcache. It uses a memory cache to speed up reading from a CD. CDFS decides how much memory to use when caching data, based on the speed of the CD-ROM drive and how much memory is installed in the system. You can affect this decision by using the Performance tab in System Properties. Click Start, Settings, Control Panel, and then double-click System. In the Properties dialog box, click the Performance tab and then click File System. Click CD-ROM on the File System Properties box, as seen in Figure 17-24. By changing the CD-ROM speed in this box, you are changing the amount of memory allotted to the cache. The amount is displayed in the last sentence on this box.

Figure 17-24   By changing the CD-ROM speed in the File System Properties box, you can change the amount of memory VCACHE uses

Plug and Play and Hardware Installations

Plug and Play (PnP) is a set of design specifications for both hardware and software that works toward effortless hardware installations. For a system to be truly Plug and Play, it must meet these criteria:

- The system BIOS must be PnP.

- All hardware devices and expansion cards must be PnP-compliant.

- The OS must be Windows 9x or another OS that supports PnP.

- A 32-bit device driver (VxD) must be available (provided by the device manufacturer or Windows). VxDs are covered later in this chapter.

If all these things are true, hardware installation should be just a matter of installing the new hardware device, turning on the PC, and perhaps providing the 32-bit driver, if it is not included with Windows 9x. During the boot process, Windows 9x surveys the devices and their needs for resources and allocates resources to each device. Windows 9x is free to assign these resources to the devices and avoids assigning the same resource to two devices. For PnP to work, each device in the system must be able to use whatever resources the OS assigns to it.

Components of Plug and Play

A Plug and Play OS such as Windows 9x provides two main services: resource management and run-time configuration. **Resource management** occurs at startup as system resources are allocated to devices. **Run-time configuration** is an ongoing process that monitors any changes in system devices, such as the removal of a PC Card on a notebook computer or docking and undocking a notebook computer to and from a docking station. The BIOS must be able to recognize these changes during OS run time (any time the OS is running) and communicate them to the OS.

Windows 9x uses four components in implementing PnP architecture:

- The Configuration Manager controls the configuration process of all devices and communicates these configurations to the devices.

- The **hardware tree** is a database built each time Windows 9x starts up that contains a list of installed components and the resources they use.

- The **bus enumerator** locates all devices on a particular bus and inventories the resource requirements for these devices.

- The **resource arbitrator** decides which resources are assigned to which devices.

Plug and Play BIOS

As discussed in Chapter 16, BIOS that is PnP-compliant gathers resource configuration information prior to loading Windows 9x, presenting to Windows 9x details it can use to complete the process. Motherboards manufactured after 1994 most likely contain PnP BIOS. PnP BIOS can also be ESCD (extended system configuration data) BIOS. ESCD BIOS creates a list of configuration changes that you have made manually when installing legacy devices and stores that list on the BIOS chip. Even if the hard drive crashes or you must reload Windows 9x, the configuration changes are still available from the BIOS when it goes through the boot process, and it presents the information to Windows 9x at startup.

To discover if your BIOS is PnP, look for a message about the BIOS type on the startup screen. Information about the BIOS might also be displayed on the CMOS setup screen or written on the BIOS chip (see Figure 17-25). You can also use MSD, a 16-bit command-line

17

diagnostic utility, and choose Computer from the menu to get information about your BIOS. The documentation for the motherboard should also say whether the BIOS is PnP.

If the BIOS is not Plug and Play, you can still use Plug and Play Windows 9x software for hardware devices that are Plug and Play. However, you might need to manually configure the hardware, or, in some cases, disable the Plug and Play features of the interface card.

Figure 17-25   Plug and Play BIOS is found on most motherboards built after 1994

INSTALLING APPLICATIONS IN WINDOWS 9X

As the bridge between earlier and later versions of Windows, Windows 9x can use both 16-bit and 32-bit software. This section shows you how to install both. Troubleshooting and uninstalling Windows 9x applications are covered in the next chapter.

Preparing for Software Installation

As with installing hardware, there are several things you can do before installing software on Windows 9x to prepare your system and to increase the likelihood that the installation will be successful:

- *Check available resources.* Check your computer resources to make sure you have (1) enough space on your hard drive, (2) the minimum requirements for memory, and (3) the proper CPU and video monitor. Read the documentation for the software you are installing and make sure you can fulfill any other requirements of the particular software program. The minimum requirements for the software should be listed in the installation manual. Remember that you should not completely fill your hard drive with software and data, because the operating system needs extra space for temporary files and for the swap file, which changes in size depending on how much space is needed. Additionally, recall what you learned about fragmented files in Chapter 16. If your hard drive is too full and you add a new file, the file cannot be written all in one place and will be split up into pieces (fragmented) and stored wherever there is available space on the hard drive. The system will then have to look in several different places on the hard drive to find the whole file, slowing down performance. You will learn more about these performance issues in Windows 9x in the next chapter.

For best performance with Windows 9x, allow a minimum of 100 MB of unused hard drive space for working temporary files used by applications.

- *Protect the original software.* For floppy disks, write-protect the original disks before you begin the installation (set the notch on the disk to open). After the installation is complete, put the original disks or CD-ROM from which you installed the software in a safe place. If you have the original software handy, it will be easier for you to reinstall should something go wrong with the installed software.

- *Back up the registry and system configuration files.* Many older software packages will want to edit Config.sys, Autoexec.bat, Win.ini, and/or System.ini files during the installation. Newer software might add its own entries to the Windows registry. Before you begin the installation, make backup copies of all of these files so that you can backtrack if you want to. (You will learn more about backing up the registry in the next chapter.)

Performing Software Installations

To install software designed for Windows 9x, access the Control Panel and double-click the Add/Remove Programs icon. Insert the software CD in the CD-ROM drive or the floppy disk in the floppy disk drive and then click the Install button. Follow directions on the setup screen. If the CD-ROM drive is set to Autorun, a setup screen might automatically appear as soon as you insert the software installation CD in the drive. For older software, click Start and Run, which displays the Run dialog box. Enter the drive and name of the installation program, for example, *A:Install* or *D:Setup*. Either way, the installation program loads and begins executing. If the installation program asks you a question you cannot answer, you can always abandon the installation and try again later.

Most software will ask you for a serial number unique to your copy of the software, which will probably be written on the CD-ROM or on the first floppy disk, or it might be stamped on the documentation. Write the serial number on the floppy disk or on the CD case, so that you will have it if you lose the documentation later. Copyright agreements often allow you to install the software on only one computer at a time. This serial number identifies the copy of the software that you have installed on this machine.

After the installation is complete and the software is working, update your backup copies of Autoexec.bat, Config.sys, System.ini, Win.ini, and the registry so that they, too, reflect the changes that the application software made to these configuration files.

Troubleshooting Software Installations

If you are having difficulty with the installation of software in Windows 9x, try the following:

- If an application locks up when you first open it, try deleting all files and folders under \Windows\Temp. A software installation sometimes leaves files and folders

17

in the Windows temporary directories. To conserve space on the hard drive, delete all files and folders under \Windows\Temp.

- Look at the Readme.htm hypertext file in the \Windows directory, which will point you to the Programs.txt file, also in the \Windows directory. If there is a problem with the software that was known when Windows was shipped, information about the problem and what to do about it might be in these text files. You can also check the Web site of the software manufacturer or the Microsoft Web site for additional insight.

 A **hypertext** file is a text file that contains hypertext tags to format the file and create hyperlinks to different points in the file or to other files. Hypertext files are used on the World Wide Web and are read and displayed using a Web browser such as Microsoft Internet Explorer or Netscape Navigator. To read a hypertext file using Windows Explorer, double-click the filename, and your default browser will open the file.

Supporting DOS Applications Under Windows 9x

Windows 3.x used **PIF (program information file)** files to manage the virtual machine environment for DOS applications and provided a PIF editor to alter these files. Each application had its own PIF file that was used to specify the DOS environment that Windows 3.x created for it. If an application had no PIF file, Windows 3.x used the settings in the _Default.pif file in the \Windows\System folder.

Windows 9x manages the environment for DOS applications in a similar, but slightly different, fashion. The Apps.inf file contains a section named [PIF95] that contains a master list of settings to be used for all DOS applications listed in the file.

If you want to customize the settings for a DOS application, use the Properties feature of the DOS program file, which will create an individual PIF for the program file and serves as the PIF editor. Right-click the program filename and select Properties from the menu that is displayed. Windows searches for the program's PIF file and, if none is found, creates one using default values. If Windows 9x was installed over Windows 3.x, then _Default.pif still exists in the \Windows\System directory and default values are read from it. Regardless of where the default values come from, any changes made are stored in the PIF for the application. To make the changes, using Explorer, right-click the program filename and select Properties from the shortcut menu. Click the Program tab. (*Note:* the Program tab will not be present for Windows applications.) See Figure 17-26.

If you select Use current MS-DOS configuration, Windows executes the contents of Dosstart.bat, stored in the Windows folder. **Dosstart.bat** is a type of Autoexec.bat file that is executed in two situations: when you select Restart the computer in MS-DOS mode from the shutdown menu, or when you run a program in MS-DOS mode. This file can be used to load real-mode device drivers, but Set commands are not executed.

If you select Specify a new MS-DOS configuration, you can make changes to Autoexec.bat and Config.sys files used for this MS-DOS mode only. For example, if the application runs slowly in DOS mode and does a lot of disk accessing, you can add entries to run real-mode SmartDrive here. SmartDrive normally is not run under Windows 9x, having been replaced by the faster 32-bit Vcache. In this situation, since Windows 9x does not manage disk access in MS-DOS mode, loading SmartDrive from this window is appropriate, since Vcache will not be running.

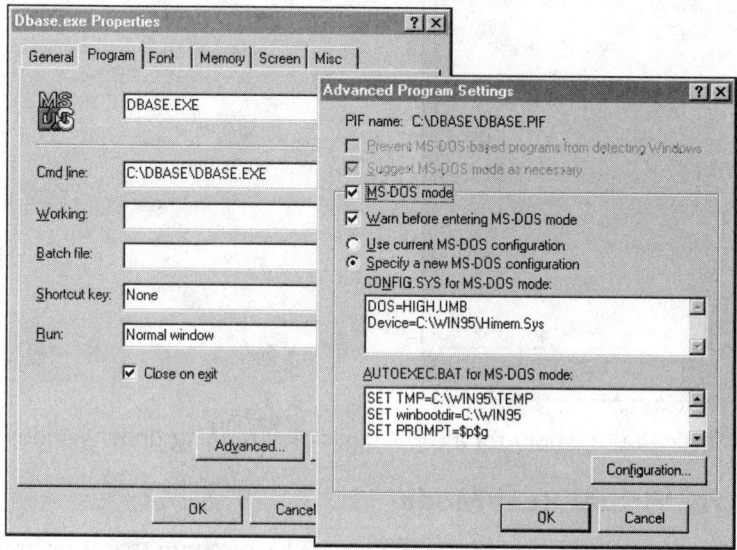

Figure 17-26   Properties sheets for a DOS application affect the way Windows 9x provides an environment for the application

Memory Management with DOS Applications in Windows 9x

When running DOS applications under Windows 9x, a DOS-like environment must be provided to the application. For example, to provide a DOS environment for the DOS program Edit.com on a PC running Windows 9x, go to Explorer and find the file Edit.com in the \Windows\Command directory. Right-click on the filename and select Properties from the drop-down menu that appears. The entries on this Properties Window make up the PIF for this application, which describes the environment that the DOS program uses.

Click the Memory tab, and the screen shown in Figure 17-27 appears, listing the memory options available. From the Memory tab, you can specify how much conventional and extended memory will be made available to the application, or leave the settings at Auto, which allows the application to use whatever is available. The last entry on the tab is MS-DOS protected-mode (DPMI) memory. This entry assigns the amount of protected-mode memory allowed the application. If you check Protected in the Conventional memory frame, the OS will protect memory used by the OS from the application.

Many DOS applications run with no problems using the default Auto settings. However, sometimes a DOS application has a problem with being given too much memory. Limit the amount of memory given the application by using the Properties sheet shown in Figure 17-27.

17

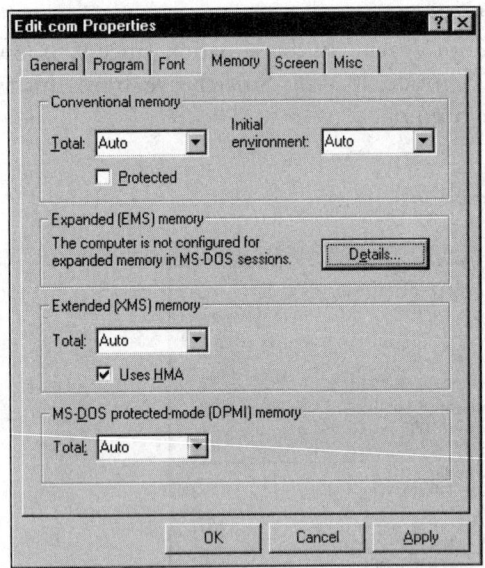

Figure 17-27 Setting up memory for a DOS application running under Windows 9x

Real Mode vs. Virtual Real Mode

An OS that supports protected mode can allow a 16-bit program that is written to work in real mode to run in virtual real mode (sometimes referred to as virtual DOS mode). Figure 17-28 shows the difference between real mode and virtual real mode. In virtual real mode, the program "thinks" it is really working in a real-mode environment. It "thinks" that:

- It is the only program running.

- It has all memory available to it, all 1024K of memory addresses that directly point to RAM.

- It accesses data using a 16-bit data path.

Underneath this environment, the OS is managing memory for the application. It receives the data in a 16-bit path, but is free to use a 32-bit data path to access memory and is also free to use virtual memory for the data.

Figure 17-28   Virtual real mode provides "DOS in a box" to a 16-bit application that was written to run in real mode

Recall that there are two types of 16-bit applications: those written for DOS and those written for Windows 3.x. DOS 16-bit applications expect to run in real mode with no other applications running with them. A Windows 3.x 16-bit application expects to allow Windows to manage memory for it and expects that other applications might also be running in a cooperative multitasking environment.

When Windows 9x runs a 16-bit DOS application, ordinarily it is run in virtual DOS mode in a **virtual DOS machine (VDM)**, sometimes called a **DOS box**, rather than in real mode. In a VDM, the application "thinks" it is running in real mode, but the OS is managing hardware resources using 32-bit drivers and providing virtual memory to the application. If you want a DOS application to have a "real" real mode rather than a virtual real mode, access the Properties box for the application. For example, once again using Edit.com as our example of a 16-bit application, right-click the program filename in Explorer (or you can right-click on the shortcut icon to the program) and select Properties. Click the Program tab and click Advanced. The Advanced Program Settings box is displayed

17

as in Figure 17-29. Click MS-DOS mode to run the application in real mode. You can then choose to give the program its own private set of Config.sys and Autoexec.bat settings to be executed before the program runs. This information is stored in the PIF created for the shortcut. When you execute the shortcut or program, Windows 9x will shut down and reboot in real mode before executing the program.

Figure 17-29   Use the Advanced Program Settings dialog box to run a 16-bit application in a real-mode environment in Windows 9x

 TIP   To access real mode in Windows 9x, select Start and Shutdown. When the Shut Down Windows dialog box appears, select Restart in MS-DOS mode.

MANAGING MEMORY WITH WINDOWS 9x

Memory management did not change fundamentally from DOS to Windows 9x; with Windows 9x memory is still organized as conventional, upper, and extended as it was under DOS. However, Windows 9x has made some improvements in the allocation of this memory and in the automation of the process that make it easier to manage memory. In effect, Windows 9x, which is mostly a 32-bit OS, "lives" in extended memory together with its device drivers and applications and only uses base and upper memory for 16-bit components. This section covers some of the other ways memory is managed in Windows 9x.

Memory Management with Device Drivers in Windows 9x

One of the major improvements in memory management in Windows 9x is the new level of 32-bit protected mode drivers. These 32-bit drivers are automatically loaded into extended memory (not conventional or upper memory) when Windows 9x loads, thus eliminating the need to use the older and slower 16-bit drivers loaded from DEVICE= entries in Config.sys.

Windows 9x offers many 32-bit drivers that can replace older 16-bit drivers written for DOS in real mode. These 32-bit drivers are sometimes called **virtual device drivers** or **VxD drivers**; they have .vxd or .386 file extensions and operate in protected mode.

Another memory management improvement in Windows 9x is that it frees up more of conventional and upper memory, because it no longer uses Smartdrv.exe or Share.exe, two TSRs that required a lot of memory below 1 MB. Smartdrv.exe, a 16-bit driver used to manage disk caching, was replaced by Vcache, 32-bit disk caching that is built into Windows 9x. The 16-bit Share.exe was replaced by the 32-bit Vshare.386, a part of Vmm32.exe that is automatically loaded when Windows 9x starts.

 If you are using all 32-bit drivers and applications in a Windows 9x environment, memory management requires no work on your part. Just let Windows 9x automate the process for you.

Managing Memory for 16-bit Drivers

If you are using older 16-bit drivers under Windows 9x, search for 32-bit drivers to replace them. Look on the device manufacturer's Web site or the Microsoft Web site. If you can't find replacements, you might need to provide some of the same memory management aids needed by DOS.

In Chapter 16, you learned about Himem.sys and Emm386.exe, the two files that Windows uses to manage memory above 640K. Windows 9x uses Himem.sys to manage extended memory just as DOS does, but, instead of being loaded from Config.sys, it's automatically loaded by Io.sys without requiring an entry in Config.sys. When using this automatic method, Io.sys does not load Himem.sys until after the commands in Config.sys have been executed. If you are using Config.sys to load Emm386.exe, then you must include Himem.sys in Config.sys along with Emm386.exe because Emm386.exe must find Himem.sys already loaded before it can load.

If you need to load a 16-bit device driver into a UMB (upper memory block), then you must have a Config.sys file with these lines in it:

```
DEVICE=Himem.sys
DEVICE=Emm386.exe NOEMS
DOS=HIGH,UMB
```

The DEVICEHIGH command to load the driver into a UMB must appear after these three lines in the Config.sys file. However, if you are using all 32-bit drivers, you don't even need the Config.sys file.

17

 To know whether a driver is 16-bit or 32-bit, look at how Windows loads it. If the driver is a 32-bit driver written for Windows 9x, it is loaded from the registry. System.ini can contain both 16-bit and 32-bit drivers. If the driver is loaded from Autoexec.bat or Config.sys, it is a 16-bit driver written for DOS.

During the Windows 9x installation, Windows 9x setup tries to substitute 32-bit drivers for all 16-bit drivers it finds in use, and, if it can, to eliminate the Autoexec.bat and Config.sys files altogether. However, if it can't substitute a 32-bit driver for an older 16-bit driver, it puts (or keeps) the proper lines in the Config.sys file and sets itself up to use the older driver.

Windows 9x Swap File

Windows 9x automates the managing of virtual memory for you, and Microsoft recommends you allow that. To see what virtual memory options Windows 9x offers, click Start, point to Settings, click Control Panel, then select System and select the Performance tab. Click Virtual Memory, and the dialog box in Figure 17-30 is displayed. These settings are used to tell Windows how to manage the swap file. Unless you have a good reason to do otherwise, check Let Windows manage my virtual memory settings.

One reason you might want to manage virtual memory yourself is to make the size of the file permanent in order to prevent Windows from resizing the file, which can slow down performance. To improve performance, first defragment the hard drive so there is plenty of unfragmented space for the file. Then set the maximum and minimum size of the file to the same value, which forces the size to not change. If you have the available hard drive space, set the size to about 2.5 times the amount of RAM.

Figure 17-30   Options for managing virtual memory in Windows 9x

Notice in Figure 17-30 that you can specify the location of the swap file. The name of the swap file in Windows 9x is **Win386.swp**, and its default location is C:\Windows. You can choose to put the swap file on a compressed drive, but Windows does not compress the swap file itself, in order to better ensure the safety of the file.

Virtual Machine Manager

How does Windows 9x provide virtual memory addresses to DOS and 16-bit Windows application programs? By **memory paging**, which involves swapping blocks of memory stored in RAM to the hard drive. Memory paging is managed by the Virtual Machine Manager (VMM).

Figure 17-31   How Windows 9x manages memory

As you can see in Figure 17-31, Windows 9x has virtual memory stored in a swap file and provides virtual memory addresses to application programs. In Figure 17-31, you see three sets of virtual memory addresses. Each set can contain up to 4 GB of addresses, depending on the amount of virtual memory available. The top set is being used by two 16-bit applications. The second set of virtual addresses is being used by a single DOS application, and a third set of addresses is being used by a 32-bit application. Each virtual machine for DOS has a set of virtual memory addresses. The 16-bit Windows programs share a single set of virtual memory addresses, and each 32-bit program has its own individual set of addresses.

In Figure 17-31, all these virtual addresses map onto the page table, which in turn maps onto either physical memory (RAM) or virtual memory on the hard drive (the swap file). Not all virtual memory addresses in Windows 9x have physical or virtual memory assigned to them. These virtual addresses remain unassigned until an application program uses them.

In Windows 9x, the VMM controls the page table, moving 4K pages in and out of physical RAM. If a program requests memory that the memory manager knows is stored in the swap file, the manager generates a **page fault**, which causes the manager to go to the drive to return the data from the swap file to RAM. This action is called a **page-in**. If RAM is full, the manager takes a page and moves it to the swap file, which is called a **page-out**.

17

If RAM is full much of the time, the VMM might spend excessive time moving pages in and out of RAM, which can cause excessive hard drive use and a decrease in overall system performance and can even cause the system to lock up or applications to fail. This situation is sometimes called **disk thrashing** and can cause premature hard drive failure. Symptoms of excessive memory paging are:

- Very high CPU use

- Very slow system response

- Constant hard drive use

To avoid excessive memory paging, leave fewer application programs open at the same time or install more RAM.

GETTING HELP FROM MICROSOFT

Microsoft offers some excellent support for its products. For those serious about learning to provide professional support for Windows 95 or Windows 98, two good books are *Microsoft Windows 95 Resource Kit* and *Microsoft Windows 98 Resource Kit*, both by Microsoft Press. These books expand on many of the concepts you have learned in this chapter about installing and using Windows 9x.

Another valuable source of information, including software utilities, enhancements, and troubleshooting guidelines for Windows 3.x and Windows 9x is the Microsoft Web site. For Microsoft Technical Support Knowledge Base, access *support.microsoft.com/search*.

Figure 17-32 shows the beginning query screen for this Web site. Follow the steps given there to research specific or general topics for Microsoft products. For example, if you want to learn more about how to optimize Windows 95, under My Search is about:, choose *Windows 95*, and enter *optimize* as the key word to search for. Click *GO*. A list of related articles is displayed. Click the article to display it.

Figure 17-32 Microsoft Technical Support Web site

The Microsoft Web site (*www.microsoft.com*) contains many links on hardware and software compatibility, such as the ones you saw earlier in this chapter in the sections on installing hardware and software. These and other Microsoft support links will be useful when you troubleshoot Windows 9x, which you will learn how to do in the next chapter.

CHAPTER SUMMARY

- ❏ The Windows 9x core consists of the kernel, the user, and the GDI and relates to users, software, and hardware by way of the following modules: the VMM, the IFS manager, the Configuration Manager, and the WDM driver manager.

- ❏ Virtual memory uses hard drive space as memory in order to increase the total amount of memory available. In Windows, virtual memory is stored in the swap file.

- ❏ The Windows 9x swap file is Win386.exe, and its default location is C:\Windows.

- ❏ Although Windows 9x supports 16-bit drivers, it is best to use 32-bit drivers whenever possible because they are faster, can be stored in extended memory, and can be dynamically loaded.

- ❏ Virtual machines are multiple logical machines within one physical machine. If an application crashes or produces another type of error within a virtual machine, only that virtual machine is affected, instead of the entire system.

- ❏ Since DOS applications do not account for sharing of resources, Windows can give each DOS application its own virtual machine and therefore its own resources.

- ❏ Windows 95 requires a 486DX, 25 MHz or higher processor; 4 MB of RAM, with 8 MB recommended; and 40 to 45 MB of hard disk storage. Windows 98 requires a 486 DX, 66 MHz or higher processor; 24 MB of RAM, with 32 MB recommended; and 140 to 315 MB of hard disk storage, depending on the installation.

17

❏ When you are installing Windows 9x as a clean install, you may need to change the boot order in CMOS, depending on what type of drive you plan to load the OS from.

❏ Before installing 9x as an upgrade, verify that you have enough hard drive space, run ScanDisk or Chkdsk, run antivirus software, back up critical system files, disable TSRs that might cause problems if they are running during installation, verify that any network connections are working, make sure that the swap file is put on a drive compressed with protected-mode software, and decide whether you want to use FAT16 or FAT32.

❏ Once you reach the setup screen, if Windows is already installed and you want to do a clean install, install the new OS in a different folder than the one used by the currently installed OS, which is probably \Windows.

❏ During setup, you can choose from Typical, Portable, Compact, or Custom installations.

❏ Windows 9x setup begins installation in real mode and later switches to protected mode.

❏ Setuplog.txt and Detlog.tst are two files in which Windows records information about the setup process. Windows uses Setuplog.txt to determine how far it got into an installation when recovering from a crash. Detlog.txt keeps a record of hardware detected. Detcrash.log is a binary file used by Windows to help recover from a crash caused by a problem with hardware.

❏ Information about your Windows installation can be stored in information files, which are text files with an .inf extension, and then used to do a hands-free installation.

❏ Msdos.sys contains several parameters that affect how the OS boots. To edit Msdos.sys, you must first change the file attributes.

❏ If you are installing Windows 9x as an upgrade to DOS and Windows 3.x, you will generally overwrite DOS and Windows 3.x.

❏ Upgrading from Windows 95 to Windows 98 is relatively easy because of the similarity of the two OSs. Before performing the upgrade, check hardware and software compatibility, run antivirus software, and back up your system. The Setup Wizard on the Windows 98 CD will guide you through the setup process. Once setup is complete, test installed applications and back up your system again.

❏ To upgrade to Windows Me, make the same preparations as for other upgrades. In addition, uncompress your hard drive, uninstall power and disk management tools, close open applications, and read the readme.txt file and other setup information before performing the upgrade.

❏ On the Microsoft Web site, you can find a list of available updates for whatever version of Windows you have installed.

❏ Keystroke shortcuts in Windows are useful for experienced typists who may find them faster than the mouse; they are also useful in troubleshooting situations when the mouse does not work.

❏ From the Windows 9x desktop, you can make applications automatically load at startup, create shortcuts to files and applications, and make the environment more user-friendly.

❏ In the Display Properties window, you can change the background, screensaver, appearance, icon effects, Active Desktop settings, color range, and display size for the desktop.

❏ You can create a desktop shortcut, which is an icon pointing to a program, file, or folder, using the Start Menu Programs tab on the Taskbar Properties window. An icon that represents a file itself rather than a shortcut will not have the small arrow that is a part of shortcut icons.

- When adding new hardware to Windows 9x, use the Add New Hardware Wizard. Select the hardware from a list of devices to use a Windows driver, or click Have Disk to use your own drivers (from a manufacturer's disk or from the Internet, downloaded to a folder on your hard drive).

- You can view and change current device drivers from the Control Panel. Windows provides an Update Device Driver Wizard to help you with this process.

- If you have problems with a hardware device or a software program, uninstalling and then reinstalling it might solve the problem.

- Some manufacturers of hardware devices include a disk with 16-bit drivers to be used when Windows 32-bit drivers cannot be accessed, such as when you are booting from a rescue disk.

- When you create a rescue disk in Windows 98, it automatically includes 16-bit CD-ROM drivers on the disk. Windows 95 does not automatically include 16-bit drivers when you create a rescue disk, but you can add them to the disk.

- A cache is a location in memory used to store frequently used data. A CD-ROM cache contains data that was recently read from the disk. CDFS is the disk-caching software for Windows 9x.

- For a Windows 9x system to be truly Plug and Play, the system BIOS must be PnP, all hardware devices and expansion cards must be PnP compliant, and a 32-bit device driver must be available for any installed hardware device.

- For Plug and Play systems, system resources are allocated to devices at startup in the resource management process, and the ongoing run-time configuration process monitors changes in system devices and the corresponding need for resources, and communicates this information to the OS.

- The four components that Windows uses in implementing PnP architecture are the configuration manager, the hardware tree, the bus enumerator, and the resource arbitrator.

- To learn if your BIOS is PnP, look for a message about the BIOS type on the startup screen.

- Windows Explorer is the primary tool for managing the files and folders on your hard drive and disks. Use the shortcut menus within Explorer by right-clicking the item you want to work with and choosing from the options on the menu that appears.

- Create a new folder by selecting the parent folder and then clicking File, New, and Folder. Change the name from New Folder to the desired folder name. To delete a folder, right-click the folder and select Delete from the shortcut menu. All folder contents and subfolders will be deleted.

- By default, Windows 9x Explorer hides file extensions of the files for which it knows which application to use to open or execute the file. By clicking View, Folder Options and the View tab and unselecting Hide file extensions for known file types, you can make Explorer display all file extensions.

- Windows 9x can run both 16-bit and 32-bit software. Use the Add/Remove Programs icon in the Control Panel to install 32-bit software designed for Windows 9x. For older 16-bit software, use the Run dialog box.

- Before installing software with Windows 9x, verify that you have the required system resources, read the documentation, make sure you have a copy of the original software that you keep in a safe place, and back up the registry and system configuration files.

17

❐ If you have a problem with a software installation, check the Readme.htm file and the Programs.txt file in the \Windows directory. These files will contain information about software issues known when Windows was shipped. You can also check the Microsoft Web site for information.

❐ If you are having a problem with a software installation, try deleting the files and folders in the \Windows\Temp folder.

❐ Windows 9x manages DOS applications differently than Windows 3.x. To customize the settings for a DOS application, use the Properties feature of the DOS program file, which will create an individual PIF for the program file and serve as the PIF editor.

❐ Dosstart.bat is a type of Autoexec.bat file that is executed when you select Restart the computer in MS-DOS mode or when you run a program in MS-DOS mode.

❐ An OS that supports protected mode can create a virtual real mode for a 16-bit application so that the application thinks it is the only program running, has all memory available to it, and accesses data using a 16-bit data path. When Windows 9x runs a 16-bit DOS application, it is ordinarily run in a virtual DOS machine.

❐ Windows 9x still organizes memory as conventional, upper, and extended but has made improvements in memory allocation and automation, such as automatically loading 32-bit drivers into extended memory, and freeing up conventional and upper memory by discontinuing use of the TSRs Smartdrv.exe and Share.exe.

❐ Windows 9x automates the management of virtual memory through the Virtual Machine Manger and memory paging.

❐ For detailed information on and support for Windows 9x and other Microsoft products, consult the Microsoft Resource Kits and the Microsoft Web site.

KEY TERMS

application program
     interface (API) call
bus enumerator
clean install
Configuration Manager
disk thrashing
DOS box
Dosstart.bat
GDI (Graphics Device
     Interface)
group files
hardware tree
hypertext
information (.inf) file

Installable File System
     (IFS)
memory paging
page fault
page-in
page-out
patch
PIF (program informa-
     tion file)
resource arbitrator
resource management
run-time configuration
service pack
shortcut
System File Protection

System Restore
upgrade install
user component
virtual device driver
     (VxD)
virtual DOS machine
     (VDM)
virtual machine
Virtual Machine
     Manager (VMM)
virtual memory
VxD driver
WDM (Win32 Driver
     Model)
Win386.swp

18

SUPPORTING AND TROUBLESHOOTING WINDOWS 9X

In this chapter, you will learn:

- ♦ How the boot process works in Windows 9x, and how to troubleshoot it
- ♦ About the Windows 9x registry
- ♦ About tools used to monitor, control, and troubleshoot Windows 9x
- ♦ How to troubleshoot hardware and applications in Windows 9x
- ♦ How to troubleshoot Windows 9x performance

In the previous chapter, you learned how to install and use Windows 9x. You learned about some important configuration files and utilities that are a part of Windows 9x, as well as about some problems that may occur in the process of installing or using it. In this chapter, you will learn more about the boot process for Windows 9x, how to troubleshoot software and hardware, and how to use important utilities and system files in the troubleshooting process. This chapter also covers Windows 9x security, Windows 9x performance, and the Windows 9x registry.

BOOTING WINDOWS 9X

In Chapter 16, you learned how to boot to a command prompt. In this section, you will learn about the startup process in Windows 9x, including the differences between booting Windows 95 and booting Windows 98/Me. Finally, you will learn how to cause an application to load at startup. First, though, you'll learn more about important files that Windows 9x uses when booting up.

Files Used to Customize the Startup Process

There are several files that Windows 9x uses to control the startup process. Recall that DOS requires Io.sys, Msdos.sys, and Command.com in the root directory of the boot device in order to load. In addition, Autoexec.bat and Config.sys are text files that can contain settings for environmental variables and commands to load drivers and TSRs. Windows 9x supports Autoexec.bat and Config.sys for backward compatibility with DOS.

If Autoexec.bat or Config.sys files are present in the root directory, the command lines in them are executed during the boot. They are used to customize the loading process. Just as DOS uses text files to contain information about what is loaded, Windows 3.x also uses text files to hold custom settings that help control the loading process. These files are called initialization files, and some of the entries in these files are read and used by Windows 9x. However, most of Windows 9x settings are stored in the Windows registry rather than in text files.

These text files can be edited with the Edit.com program from the command prompt or any text editor from within Windows. The Windows System Configuration Editor **(Sysedit)** is a handy Windows text editor designed to be used with these files. To use Sysedit, type *sysedit* in the Run dialog box. These files are automatically displayed for editing: Autoexec.bat, Config.sys, **Win.ini**, **System.ini**, and **Protocol.ini** (see Figure 18-1).

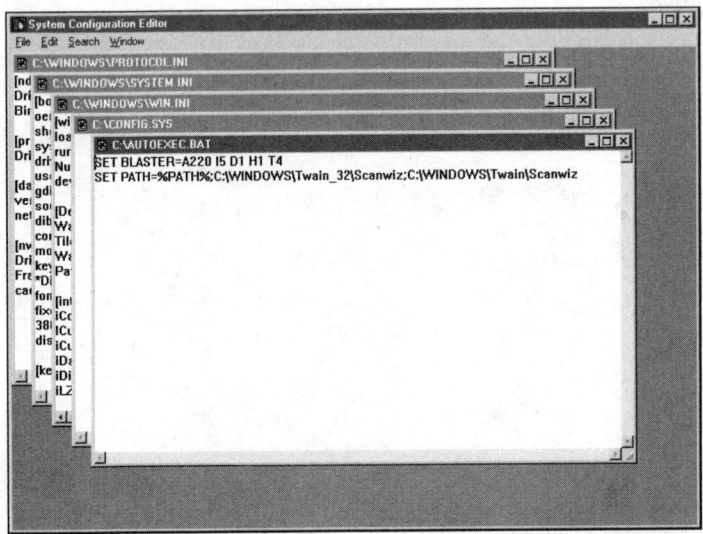

Figure 18-1   Sysedit can be used to edit Windows system files

Recall that an initialization file, which has an .ini file extension, is a file used by Windows or application software to store configuration information needed when Windows or an application is first loaded. An application can have its own .ini files and registry and can also store its information in the Windows .ini files and the Windows registry. Table 18-1 shows Windows .ini files, which Windows 9x supports for backward-compatibility with Windows 3.x.

Table 18-1 Windows .ini files

Windows Initialization File	General Purpose of the File
System.ini	Contains hardware settings and multitasking options for Windows. The [386Enh] section loads protected mode (32-bit) drivers for older applications, which may cause problems in more recent operating systems.
Progman.ini	Contains information about Program Manager groups.
Win.ini	Contains information about user settings, including printer, fonts, file associations, and settings made by applications.
Control.ini	Contains information about the user's desktop, including color selections, wallpaper, and screen saver options.
Mouse.ini	Contains settings for the mouse.
Protocol.ini	Contains information about the configuration of the network.

The contents of files with an .ini extension are organized into sections, which are each given a name. Within a section, values are assigned to variables using this format:

```
[SECTION NAME]

KEY NAME=value
```

Any value to the right of the key name becomes available to Windows or an application software program reading the file; in other words, the key name acts much like the Set command in Autoexec.bat, which assigns a value to a system variable.

System.ini and Win.ini are used by both Windows 3.x and Windows 9x. A sample Windows 9x System.ini file is shown in Figure 18-2. The two sections required for the boot process are [boot] and [386Enh]. Windows 3.x kept many more entries in these sections than does Windows 9x, which really only uses these files for backward compatibility with older applications.

Initialization files are only read when Windows or an application using .ini files starts up. If you change the .ini file for an application, you must restart the software for the change to take effect. If you want the application to ignore a line in the .ini file, you can turn the line into a **comment** line by putting a semicolon or the letters REM at the beginning of the line.

The maximum file size of .ini files is 64K, although files greater than 32K can cause some application software problems. Most applications have a setup program in their program group that is used to make changes to their .ini files.

18

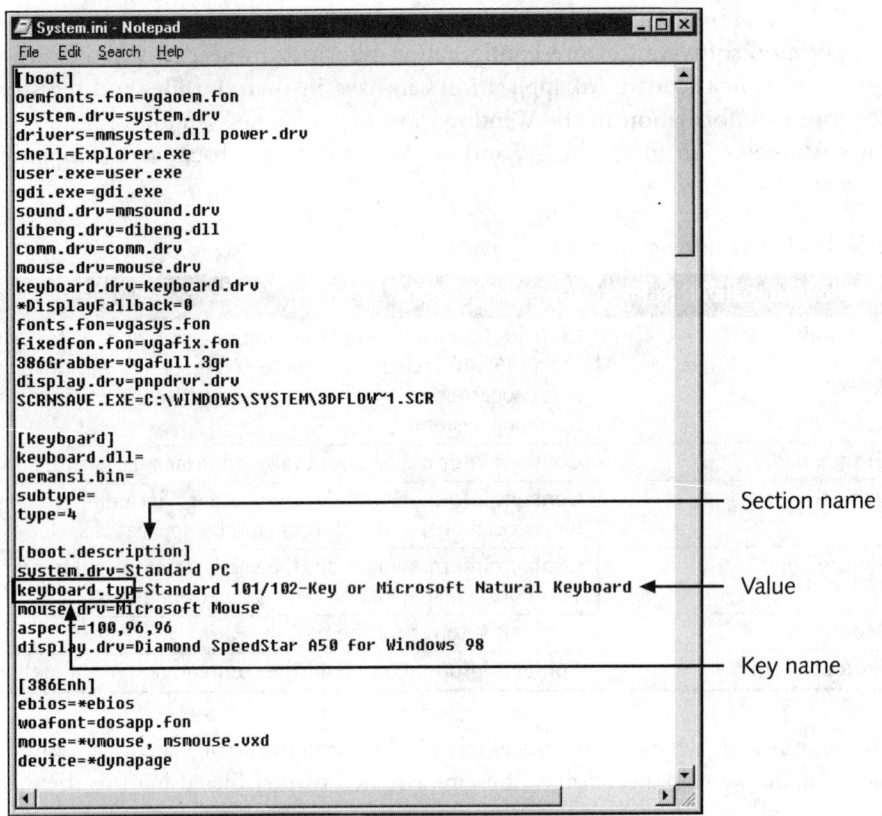

Figure 18-2   A sample Windows 98 System.ini file

> **TIP**   Sometimes it is necessary to manually edit an .ini file that belongs to an application, but you should normally not edit System.ini or other Windows 9x initialization files. Incorrect changes to these files might result in Windows not running correctly, and Windows sometimes overwrites these files when changes are made to Windows through the Control Panel.

We now turn our attention to studying the Windows 9x startup process, in which these and other files are used.

The Windows 9x Startup Process

Windows 9x first loads in real mode and then switches to protected mode. With DOS, the two core real-mode system files responsible for starting up the OS, Io.sys and Msdos.sys, remain in memory, running even after the OS is loaded. With Windows 9x, Io.sys is responsible for only the initial startup process performed in real mode. Then, control is turned over to Vmm32.vxd, which works in protected mode, and Io.sys is terminated.

Windows 9x includes a file named Msdos.sys, but it is only a text file that contains some parameters and switches that can be set to affect the way the OS boots.

Startup in Windows 9x is a five-phase process, as shown in Figure 18-3. We will look at each phase in turn.

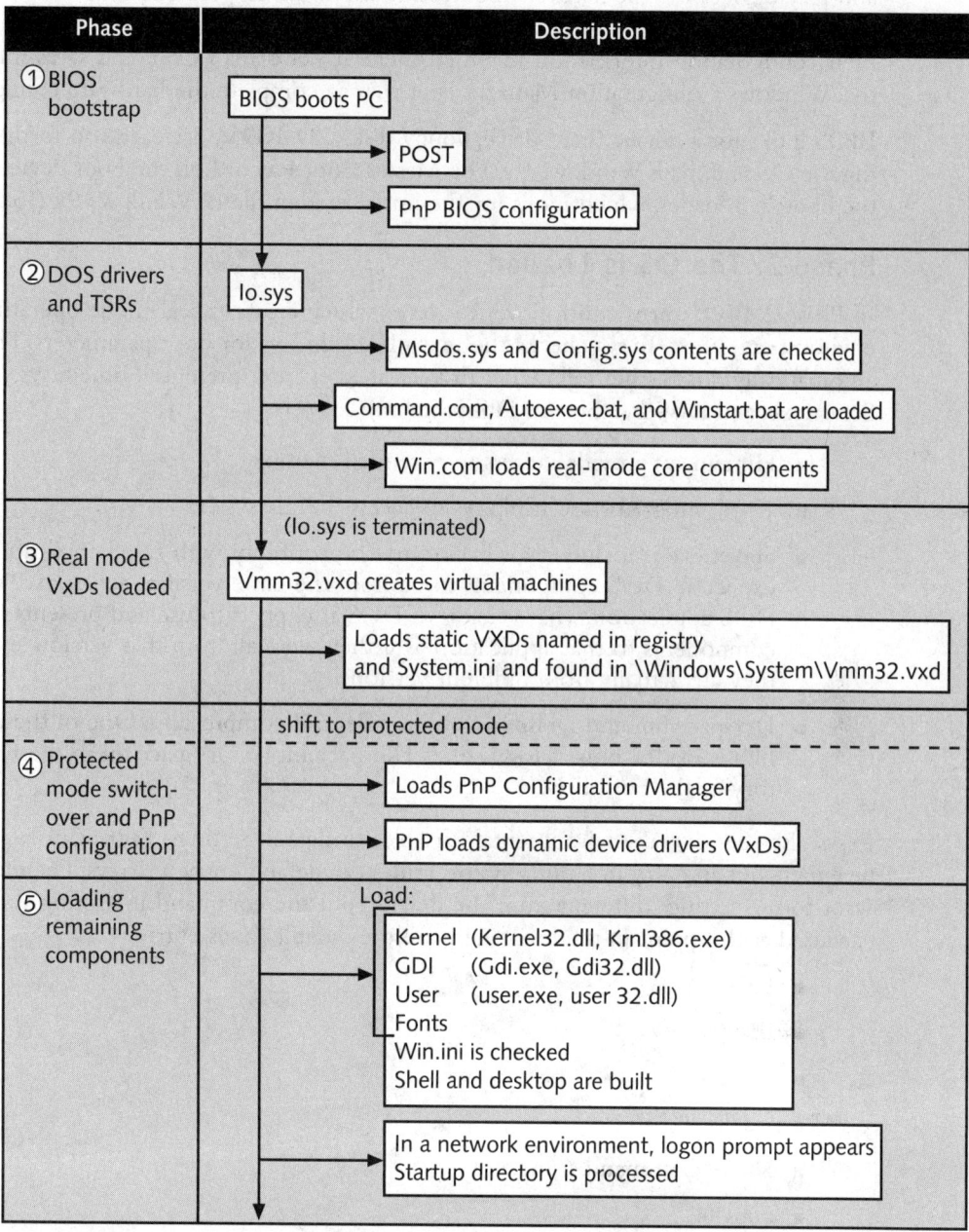

Figure 18-3 Windows 9x core components and the loading process

18

Phase 1: BIOS POST and Bootstrap

Startup BIOS begins the process. If the BIOS is a **Plug and Play (PnP) BIOS**, it examines the devices on the system and determines which ones are Plug and Play compliant. BIOS first enables the devices that are not Plug and Play and then tries to make the Plug and Play devices use the leftover resources. It also looks to permanent RAM for information about hardware and uses that information to help in configuring PnP devices that have their configuration information recorded there. It performs POST and saves information that Windows Configuration Manager later uses to complete the hardware configuration.

BIOS looks for a device (hard drive, floppy disk, CD-ROM drive, and so forth) containing the OS and loads Windows 9x. The Master Boot Record on the boot device executes the bootstrap loader, which looks for the initial hidden file of Windows 9x (Io.sys).

Phase 2: The OS is Loaded

In Phase 2, BIOS turns control over to Io.sys, which creates a real-mode operating system environment. Next, Io.sys checks the text file Msdos.sys for boot parameters. Then Io.sys automatically loads the following drivers if they are present: Himem.sys, Ifshlp.sys, Setver.exe, and Drvspace.bin (or Dblspace.bin).

- Himem.sys provides access to extended memory.

- 16-bit programs use Ifshlp.sys to access the file system.

- Setver.exe is included for backward-compatibility with DOS applications that expect all DOS components to be from the same version. Setver.exe "asks" the DOS application what version of DOS it expects to use and presents DOS components to that application as if they were all from that version, even if they are actually from different versions.

- Drvspace.bin and Dblspace.bin provide disk compression. One of these two files is loaded only if Io.sys finds Dlbspace.ini or Drvspace.ini in the root directory of the boot drive.

Io.sys also sets several environmental variables to default settings. Entries in Io.sys cannot be edited, but an entry in Config.sys overrides the default entry in Io.sys. Therefore, if you want to use settings different from the default, put the command in Config.sys, which is executed at this point in the load. Here are the default Io.sys entries:

- Files=60

- Lastdrive=z

- Buffers=30

- Stacks=9,256

- Shell=Command.com

- Fcbs=4

Next, Io.sys loads Command.com and follows instructions stored in Autoexec.bat and Winstart.bat. The default assignments made to environmental variables that were stored in Autoexec.bat in DOS are listed below:

- Tmp=c:\windows\temp
- Temp=c:\windows\temp
- Prompt=pg
- Path=c:\windows;c:\windows\command

The Tmp and Temp variables are used by some software to locate where to put their temporary files. You can change any of these by making an entry in Autoexec.bat. Next, Io.sys loads Win.com. Then Win.com loads other real-mode core components.

Phase 3: Static VxDs

In Phase 3, Io.sys relinquishes control to the virtual machine manager (VMM) component housed in Vmm32.vxd along with some VxDs. Recall that a VxD is a virtual device driver that works with a virtual machine to provide access to hardware for software running in the VM. Under Windows 3.x, these VxDs were loaded from System.ini and had a .386 file extension. Under Windows 9x, if stored in individual files, they have a .vxd file extension. They are called **static VxDs** because once they are loaded into memory, they remain there. (Conversely, **dynamic VxDs** are loaded into and unloaded from memory as needed.)

Vmm32.vxd is built specifically for a particular computer when Windows 9x is installed and contains some VxDs critical for a successful boot; each installation of Windows will have a different build of this file. (The VxD drivers that are now included in Vmm32.vxd were listed in the [386enh] section of System.ini under Windows 3.x.) Vmm32.vxd terminates Io.sys and, while still in real mode, loads static VxD device drivers as identified in four different locations. They can be embedded in Vmm32.vxd, named in the registry or System.ini, or stored in the .vxd files in the \Windows\System\Vmm32 directory.

If you suspect a problem with a VxD that is part of the Vmm32.vxd file, then store a new version of the .vxd file in the \Windows\System\Vmm32 directory. If Windows finds a VxD driver there, it uses that driver instead of the one embedded in Vmm32.vxd. Also, VxD drivers are listed in the registry and in System.ini. Normally, the entries are the same, and entries in System.ini are only listed there for backward-compatibility. However, if an entry in System.ini differs from an entry in the registry, the value in System.ini is used.

Phase 4: Protected-Mode Switchover and PnP Configuration

At the beginning of Phase 4, Vmm32.vxd switches to protected mode and loads Configuration Manager. Configuration Manager is responsible for configuring legacy and PnP devices. It will use any information that PnP BIOS might have left for it and loads the 32-bit VxDs for the PnP devices.

18

Phase 5: Loading-Remaining Components

In Phase 5, with Vmm32.vxd still in control, the three core components are loaded, and fonts and other associated resources are loaded. Win.ini is checked, and commands stored there are executed to allow for backward-compatibility. The shell and user desktop are loaded. If the computer is working in a networked environment, a logon dialog box is displayed, and the user can log on to Windows 9x and the network. Finally, any processes stored in the Startup directory are performed.

Differences Between the Windows 95 and Windows 98/Me Boot Process

Windows 98 made some minor changes in what happens during startup to speed up the boot process. For instance, Windows 95 waits two seconds while "Starting Windows 95" is displayed so that you can press a key to alter the boot process. Windows 98 eliminated this two-second wait and, in its place, allows you to press and hold the Ctrl key as it loads. If you do that, you see the startup menu that is also available with Windows 95.

Loading an Application at Startup

If you want an application to automatically load at startup, you can:

- Place a shortcut in the C:\\Windows\All Users\Startup Menu\Programs\StartUp folder. (You learned how to create shortcuts in Chapter 17.)
- Put the name of the program file in the Load= or Run= line in Win.ini.
- Manually edit the registry key HKEY_LOCAL_MACHINE\SOFTWARE\ Microsoft\Windows\CurrentVersion\Run (modifying the registry is covered later in this chapter).

TROUBLESHOOTING THE WINDOWS 9X BOOT PROCESS

In the previous section, you learned about the steps in the Windows 9x boot process and the files used in the process. When the boot process does not complete correctly, here are the basic steps you go through to troubleshoot it:

1. Check and address any error messages that occur during a normal boot.

2. If you cannot boot to a normal desktop, boot in safe mode and begin troubleshooting there.

3. If you cannot boot using safe mode, the GUI portion of the OS is not functioning. Boot to the command prompt using the startup menu. Use commands at the C prompt for troubleshooting.

4. If the startup menu is not accessible, the MS-DOS core of the OS is not functioning. Boot from an emergency startup disk and try to access drive C.

5. If you cannot access drive C, then the hard drive is not accessible.

Error Messages Received While Loading Windows 9x

Error messages are your first indications that something is going wrong with the Windows 9x boot process. You can use these messages to figure out how to solve some Windows 9x boot problems. Table 18-2 shows error messages that Windows 9x might produce, along with what to do when you see them. Specific errors are covered later in this section.

Table 18-2   Error messages received while loading Windows 9x

Error Message or Problem	What to Do
"MS-DOS compatibility mode"	■ Windows is using real-mode drivers to access the hard drive rather than the preferred 32-bit drivers. After backing up the Config.sys and System.ini files, remove any references to real-mode drivers for the hard drive in these files. ■ The problem might be due to an outdated motherboard BIOS. Consider updating the BIOS.
"Bad or missing file" "Real mode driver missing or damaged" "Error in config.sys line xx"	■ Verify that Config.sys, Autoexec.bat, (root directory of the hard drive) and System.ini (Windows folder) are present and in the right location. ■ Check Config.sys and Autoexec.bat for errors using the step-by-step confirmation option from the Windows 9x startup menu. To check System.ini, rename the file so that it will not be used and boot with a bare bones version of the file. ■ Look in the Win.ini file for applications that are attempting to load at startup but that have been deleted or uninstalled. Check the Load= or Run= lines.
Cannot open file *.inf	■ This error is caused by insufficient memory. Disable any TSRs running in Autoexec.bat. ■ Close any applications that are running or remove them from the Start folder.
Insufficient disk space	Run ScanDisk and Defragmenter. Check free space on the hard drive.
"Invalid system disk" "Bad or missing command.com"	■ Suspect a boot sector virus. Run a current version of antivirus software. ■ Io.sys could be missing or corrupted. Restore the file from a backup or an emergency startup disk. To restore all real-mode files needed to begin loading Windows 9x, do the following: (1) boot from a Windows 9x emergency startup disk, (2) to restore Io.sys, Msdos.sys, Drvspace.bin, and Command.com, execute the command SYS C:, (3) remove the floppy disk and reboot.
Invalid VxD dynamic link call from IFSMGR	This error is caused by a missing or corrupted Msdos.sys file. Restore the file from a backup or from an emergency startup disk.
Missing system files	Run the SYS C: command.
System Registry file missing	Either System.dat or User.dat is corrupted or missing. For Windows 95, restore them by using either System.da0 or User.da0. For Windows 98/Me, run ScanReg.

18

Table 18-2   Error messages received while loading Windows 9x (continued)

Error Message or Problem	What to Do
VxD error returns to command prompt	A VxD file is missing or corrupted. Run Windows Setup from the Windows 9x CD and choose Verify installed components.
Error containing the text "Kernel32.dll"	An error that contains this text probably indicates a corrupted kernel. Try restoring system files. If that doesn't work, reinstall Windows. *Note*: this error may appear at other times, not just during the boot process.

Windows has several tools you can use to help troubleshoot problems with booting. These utilities listed below are discussed later in this chapter.

- Use System Configuration Utility (Msconfig) to limit what loads during the boot in order to attain the cleanest possible boot.

- Use Device Manager to disable a device that you think is causing a problem.

- Use Automatic Skip Driver Agent (ASDA) to keep Windows from installing a driver that might be corrupted, including built-in Windows drivers.

- The Windows 9x startup menu includes safe mode, the command prompt, and other troubleshooting options.

Microsoft Windows 9x Startup Menu

Normally, when you load Windows, the message *Starting Windows* displays and then the OS loads. However, you can force the menu to appear rather than the *Starting Windows* message by tapping the F8 key or holding down the Ctrl key during the boot.

Startup Menu Options

The Microsoft Windows 9x startup menu options are:

1. Normal

2. Logged (\BOOTLOG.TXT)

3. Safe Mode

4. Safe Mode with network support

5. Step-by-step confirmation

6. Command prompt only

7. Safe Mode command prompt only

8. Previous version of MS-DOS

What to expect when you select each option on the menu is described next. Option 4 is displayed if the OS is configured for a network, and Option 8 is displayed if a previous version of DOS was retained during the Windows 9x installation.

Normal   In Msdos.sys, if BootGUI=1, then this option starts Windows 9x. If BootGUI=0, then this option will boot to the DOS 7.0 or DOS 7.1 prompt (the DOS core of Windows 9x). Either way, the commands in Autoexec.bat and Config.sys will be executed.

If a problem appears when you boot in normal mode, but does not appear when you boot in safe mode, then suspect that Config.sys, Autoexec.bat, System.ini, and Win.ini are the source of your problem. To eliminate Config.sys or Autoexec.bat as the source of the problem, boot using the step-by-step confirmation option on the startup menu. To eliminate Win.ini or System.ini as the source of the problem, use the following procedure:

1. Change the name of the System.ini file in the Windows folder to System.sav.

2. Find the System.cb file in the Windows folder and make a copy of it. Rename the copy System.ini. Do not rename the original System.cb file because you may need it at another time.

3. In the [boot] section of the System.ini file, add this line and then save the file:

   ```
   drivers=mmsystem.dll
   ```

4. Change the name of the Win.ini file in the Windows folder to Win.sav.

5. Restart your computer.

If this works, the problem was in the Win.ini or System.ini files, and you can reexamine these files in detail to determine the exact source of the problem.

> **TIP**   If your mouse stops working when you copy the System.cb file and rename it to System.ini, add the following lines in the specified sections of the new System.ini file:
>
> ```
> [boot]
> mouse.drv=mouse.drv
> [386Enh]
> mouse=*vmouse, msmouse.vxd
> ```

Logged (\BOOTLOG.TXT)   This option is the same as Normal, except that Windows 9x tracks the load and startup activities and logs them to the Bootlog.txt file. A portion of a sample Bootlog.txt file is shown in Figure 18-4. Notice that this file contains information about which components were loaded successfully and which ones were not. This file can be a helpful tool when troubleshooting.

18

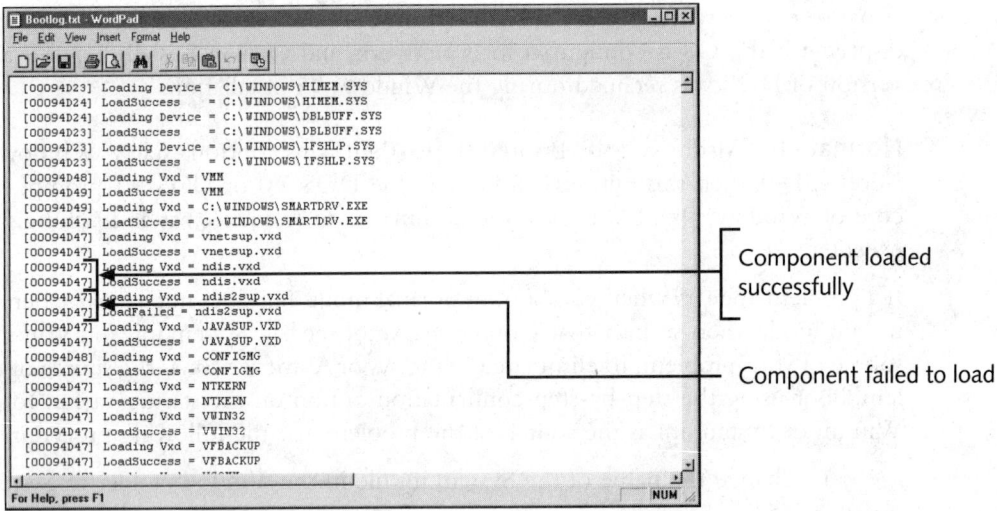

Figure 18-4 The Bootlog.txt file contains information about successful and unsuccessful boot activities

Safe Mode When you are having problems with the Windows 9x boot process but no error message appears during the boot, you can use safe mode to troubleshoot the problems. You can reach safe mode either from the startup menu or by pressing F5 while Windows is loading. Figure 18-5 shows Windows 98 booted into safe mode. Safe mode does not execute entries in the registry, Config.sys, Autoexec.bat, and the [Boot] and [386Enh] sections of System.ini. Also, when you enter safe mode, Windows 98/Me includes support for networks, but Windows 95 does not.

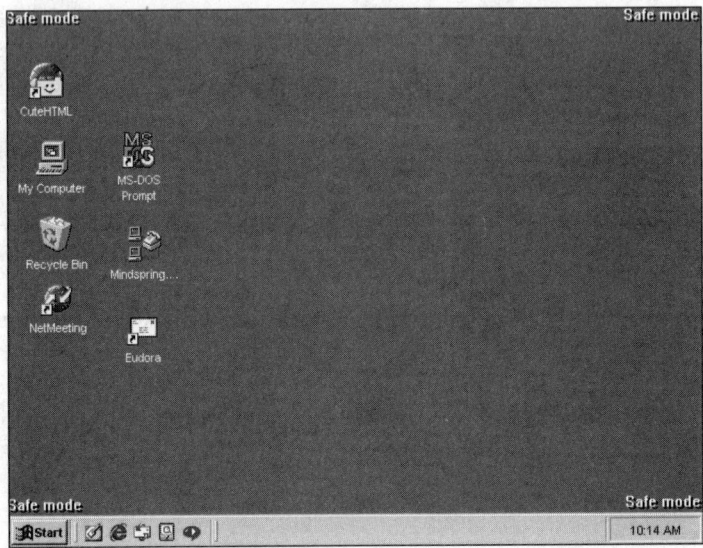

Figure 18-5 Windows 98 safe mode

Safe mode starts Windows 9x with a minimum default configuration to give you an opportunity to correct an error in the configuration. For example, if you selected a video driver that is incompatible with your system, when Windows 9x starts, it detects the problem and enters safe mode with a standard VGA driver selected. You can then go to Device Manager, select the correct driver, and restart Windows.

From the startup menu, you can choose to enter safe mode yourself if you know of a problem you want to correct. For example, if you have previously selected a group of background and foreground colors that makes it impossible to read the screens, you can reboot and choose safe mode. Safe mode gives you the standard color scheme along with the VGA mode. Go to Display Properties, make the necessary corrections, and reboot.

Sometimes you will use safe mode for troubleshooting when you don't know exactly what the problem is. In that situation, once you are in safe mode, use the following checklist:

- Use a current version of antivirus software to scan for a virus.

- Sometimes loading in safe mode is all that is needed. Try to reboot the PC in normal mode.

- If the Safe Recovery dialog box appears, select the option of Use Safe Recovery. Windows 9x will then attempt to recover from previous boot problems. Try to boot again.

- If you were having problems with a device installation before the Windows failure, disable or remove the device in Device Manager. Reboot after disabling each device that you suspect to be a problem.

- If you have just made configuration changes, undo the changes and reboot.

- Look for real-mode drivers or TSRs (programs loaded in Config.sys, Autoexec.bat, or System.ini) that might be causing a problem and disable them by inserting a semicolon or a REM at the beginning of the command line.

- Try to boot again. If the problem is still not solved, restore the registry. For Windows 95, overwrite System.dat with System.da0 and User.dat with User.da0 after making backups of these files. For Windows 98/Me, use ScanReg to restore the registry from backups. (How to do this is covered later in this chapter.)

- Run ScanDisk to repair errors on the hard drive and optimize the drive. While in safe mode, select Start, Programs, Accessories, System Tools, ScanDisk. Under Type of Test, select Thorough. (See Figure 18-6.)

- Run the Defragmenter utility to optimize the drive. (You will learn more about this later in this chapter.)

- For Windows 98/Me, run System File Checker to verify system files.

- For Windows 98/Me, run Automatic Skip Driver Agent (covered later in this chapter) to skip loading any driver that is causing a problem. Reboot and examine the Asd.log file for recorded errors.

18

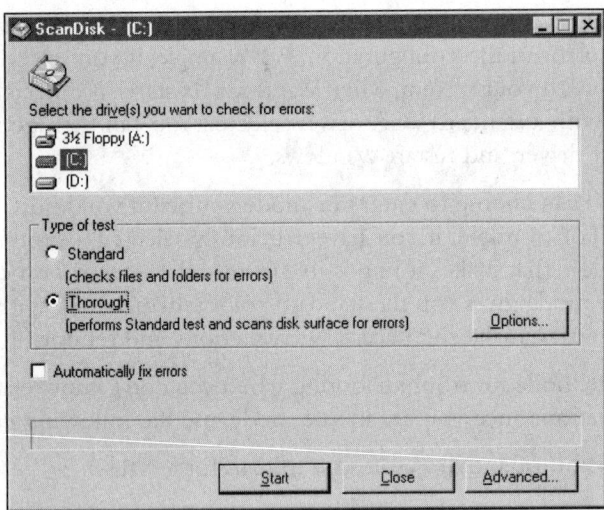

Figure 18-6   Use ScanDisk to check the hard drive for errors

- For Windows 98/Me, use the System Configuration Utility to further reduce the system to essentials and reboot. If the problem goes away, restore one item at a time until the problem returns so as to identify the item that is the source of the problem.

- Using Explorer, search for files in system folders that have changed recently. To sort file and folder names by date last modified using Explorer, click Modified. To reverse the sort order, hold down the Ctrl key while clicking Modified. If software or drivers have been installed recently, suspect that they might be the source of the problem.

Safe Mode with Network Support   This option allows you access to the network when booting into safe mode. It is useful if Windows 95 is stored on a network server and you need to download changes to your PC in safe mode. This option is not available on the startup menu in Windows 98/Me, which automatically includes network support.

To eliminate the network connection as a source of a boot problem you are troubleshooting, first boot in safe mode without network support and then boot in safe mode with network support. If the boot without network support is successful but the boot with network support gives errors, then suspect that the network drivers might be the source of the problem. For Windows 98/Me, disable the network card in Device Manager to eliminate the network drivers as the source of the problem.

Step-by-Step Confirmation   This option asks for confirmation before executing each command in Io.sys, Config.sys, and Autoexec.bat. You can accomplish the same thing by pressing Shift+F8 when the message *Starting Windows 95/98* appears.

Command Prompt Only This option executes the contents of Autoexec.bat and Config.sys but doesn't start Windows 9x. You will be given a DOS prompt. Type WIN to load Windows 9x. This command executes the file Win.com. There are several switches you can use with the WIN command when troubleshooting the OS. Table 18–3 shows these switches.

Table 18-3   Switches Used with the WIN command

Command/Switch	Purpose
WIN /D:M	Starts Windows in safe mode
WIN /D:F	Turns off 32-bit disk access; use this option if there appears to be a problem with hard drive access
WIN /D:S	Instructs Windows not to use memory address F000:0, which is used by BIOS
WIN /D:V	Instructs Windows that the system BIOS should be used to access the hard drive rather than the OS
WIN /D:X	Excludes all upper memory addresses from real mode drivers

In a troubleshooting situation, try each switch until you get one that works. You can then identify the source of the problem and can sometimes put entries in the System.ini file to make the switch a permanent part of the load.

Safe Mode Command Prompt Only This option does not execute the commands in Autoexec.bat or Config.sys. You will be given a DOS prompt.

Previous Version of MS-DOS This option loads a previous version of DOS if one is present. You can get the same results by pressing F4 when the message *Starting Windows 95/98* appears. This option is not available in Windows 98 SE or Windows Me.

Troubleshooting with the Startup Menu

If you are have tried using the previous tools, but have not yet identified the source of the problem, use the following checklist to troubleshoot using the startup menu:

- Try a hard boot. A soft boot might not do the trick, because TSRs are not always "kicked out" of RAM with a soft boot.

- If you have not already done so, try safe mode next.

- Try the option Step-by-step confirmation next. Look for error messages caused by a missing or corrupted driver file. Try not allowing real-mode drivers to load. Once the problem command within Autoexec.bat or Config.sys is identified, you can eliminate the command or troubleshoot it. Specific commands in these files and their purposes were covered in Chapter 16.

- Use the Logged option next and examine the Bootlog.txt file that is created to see if it identifies the problem.

18

- Try booting using the Command prompt only option. From the command prompt, run the real-mode version of ScanDisk, which you will find in the \Windows\Command folder, to scan the hard drive for errors. From a command prompt, enter this command: C:\Windows\Command\Scandisk. If the Scandisk.exe program on the hard drive is corrupted, use the one on the emergency startup disk.

- For Windows 98/Me, from the command prompt, type Scanreg/Fix and try to reboot.

- For Windows 98/Me, from the command prompt, next type Scanreg/Restore and select the latest known good backup of the Windows 9x registry. Try to reboot.

- From the command prompt, you can use the WIN command with the switches that you saw in Table 18-3. If one of these commands solves the problem, look for real-mode drivers that might be in conflict, eliminating those that you can. Examine Bootlog.txt for errors and try booting from safe mode again.

- Try booting with Safe Mode command prompt only. Remember that when you are in safe mode, the registry is not executed. If you suspect a corrupted registry, restore it to its last saved version as you learned to do earlier. Then try the WIN command, with or without the switches as necessary.

Using the Startup Disk for Troubleshooting

If you cannot solve the boot problems you are experiencing by using the troubleshooting utilities within Windows or on the startup menu, use an emergency startup disk to recover from the failed boot. If you do not have an emergency startup disk, create one on another computer and use it to work with the computer that is having the problem. Before using the startup disk, it is a good idea to check it for viruses on a working computer by scanning it with antivirus software. If you find a virus on the emergency startup disk, destroy the disk and use a working computer to create a new one.

To use the emergency startup disk, place it in the floppy disk drive and turn on the PC. It will boot to a startup menu or to an A prompt, depending on the version of Windows 9x you are using. Figure 18-7 shows the Startup Menu.

If you are using a version for which the startup disk boots to a menu, select the first option, which is to start the PC with CD-ROM support. The OS will then examine the system for problems and then provide an A prompt where you can enter commands.

If the system has failed to boot from the hard drive, the first step in troubleshooting at this point is to see if you can access the hard drive. To do that, enter DIR C: at the A prompt. If this step works, then the problem lies in the software that is used on the hard drive to boot, including the OS boot record, OS hidden files, and command interface files. If you cannot access the hard drive, the problem is with the partition table, the Master Boot Record, hard drive, its cabling, or its power source. In this case, you need to examine the hard drive for errors.

```
Microsoft Windows 98 Startup Menu

1. Start Computer With CD-ROM Support.
2. Start Computer Without CD-ROM Support.
3. View the Help File.

   Enter A Choice:              Time Remaining: 30

F5=Safe Mode Shift+F5=Command Prompt Shift+F8=Step Configuration[N]
```

Figure 18-7   Windows 98 rescue disk startup menu

Use Fdisk to examine the partition table. If the table is corrupted, most likely you have lost everything on your hard drive. Try using the Fdisk /MBR command to restore the Master Boot Record on the drive. If this does not work, try creating new partitions on the drive and formatting the drive. All data and software on the drive will be lost. If you cannot use Fdisk on the drive, treat the problem as a hardware problem.

After you have completed troubleshooting the hard drive, eliminating physical problems with the hard drive subsystem, CMOS, and the partition table, the next step is to run the Windows 9x Setup program. When given the opportunity, select Verify installed components. Setup will then restore damaged or missing system files.

THE WINDOWS 9X REGISTRY

In supporting and troubleshooting Windows 9x, you need to understand the role of the registry and .ini files. The registry is a database of configuration information and settings for users, hardware, applications and the OS. Starting with Windows 9x, the registry takes over the essential functions of .ini files. However, Windows 9x still supports .ini files for compatibility with Windows 3.x and legacy software and hardware devices. Entries that 16-bit Windows applications make in Win.ini and System.ini are not added to the registry because these applications cannot access the registry. Entries made in .ini files by applications that can access the registry are copied into the registry. In this section, you will examine how the registry is organized, what kinds of information are in the registry, how and why you might edit the registry, and how to recover from a corrupted registry.

18

How the Registry Is Organized

The registry organizes information in a hierarchical database with a treelike, top-to-bottom design. The Windows 9x System.ini file contains setup parameters. Refer back to Figure 18-2, which shows a portion of the System.ini file. Notice that section names appear in square brackets, key names to the left of the equal signs, and values assigned to these key names to the right of the equal signs. The Windows 9x registry takes on a similar design but enhances it by allowing for keys to cascade to several levels on the tree. Figure 18-8 shows a portion of a Windows 9x registry. Consider names on the left of the window as similar to section names in System.ini; these names are called **keys** by Windows 9x. On the right of the window are value names, such as ScreenSaveTime, and to the right of each name is the **value data** assigned to that name, such as "60." The value names, called values by Windows 9x, are similar to the key names in System.ini, and the value data are similar to the values assigned to key names in System.ini.

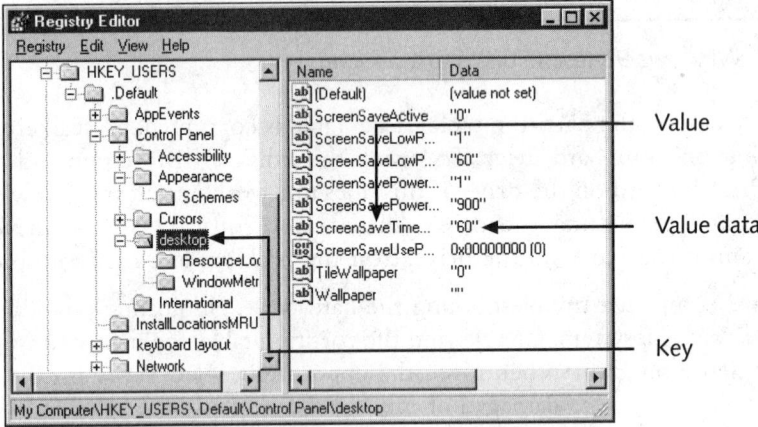

Figure 18-8   Structure of the Windows 9x registry

The registry is organized into six major keys, or branches, which are listed in Table 18-4. The registry is contained in two files, System.dat and User.dat, located in the Windows directory as hidden, read-only, system files, although the information forms only a single database.

Table 18-4   Six major branches, or keys, of the Windows 9x registry

Key	Description
HKEY_CLASSES_ROOT	Contains information about file associations and OLE data (this branch of the tree is a mirror of HKEY_LOCAL_MACHINE\Software\Classes).
HKEY_USERS	Includes user preferences, including desktop configuration and network connections.

Table 18-4   Six major branches, or keys, of the Windows 9x registry (continued)

Key	Description
HKEY_CURRENT_USER	If there is only one user of the system, this is a duplicate of HKEY_USERS, but for a multiuser system, this key contains information about the current user preferences.
HKEY_LOCAL_MACHINE	Contains information about hardware and installed software.
HKEY_CURRENT_CONFIG	Contains the same information in HKEY_LOCAL_MACHINE\Config and has information about printers and display fonts.
HKEY_DYN_DATA	Keeps information about Windows performance and Plug-and-Play information.

Recovering from a Corrupted Registry

Windows 95 has a way to recover from a corrupted registry that is different from the method used by Windows 98/Me. These methods are discussed next.

Windows 95 Backup of the Registry

Windows 95 maintains a backup copy of the two registry files called System.da0 and User.da0. Each time Windows 95 boots successfully, it makes a backup copy of these two files. If Windows 95 has trouble loading and must start in safe mode, it does not back up the registry.

If Windows 95 does not find a System.dat file when it starts, it automatically replaces it with the backup System.da0. If both System.dat and User.dat are missing, or if the WinDir= command is missing in Msdos.sys, Windows 9x tells you that the registry files are missing and starts in safe mode. It then displays the Registry Problem dialog box. Click the Restore From Backup and Restart buttons. The registry files are restored from System.da0 and User.da0. If these files are also missing, the registry cannot easily be restored. You can either restore the files from your own backups or run Windows 9x Setup. There is another option. Look for the file System.1st in the root directory of the hard drive. This is the System.dat file created when Windows 9x was first installed. In an emergency, you can revert to this file.

Windows 98/Me Registry Checker

Windows 98/Me offers a utility called the Registry Checker, which is not available with Windows 95. It automatically backs up the registry each day, and by default, it keeps the last five days of backups. In an emergency, you can recover the registry from one of these backups. You can also tell Registry Checker to make an additional backup on demand, such as when you have just made changes to the registry and want to back up these changes before you make new changes.

To access Registry Checker, select Start, point to Programs, Accessories, System Tools, and then click System Information. The Microsoft System Information window opens (see Figure 18-9). From the menu bar, select Tools and then Registry Checker. Registry

18

Checker tells you if the registry is corrupted and will fix it, if allowed. You can also create a new backup at this time.

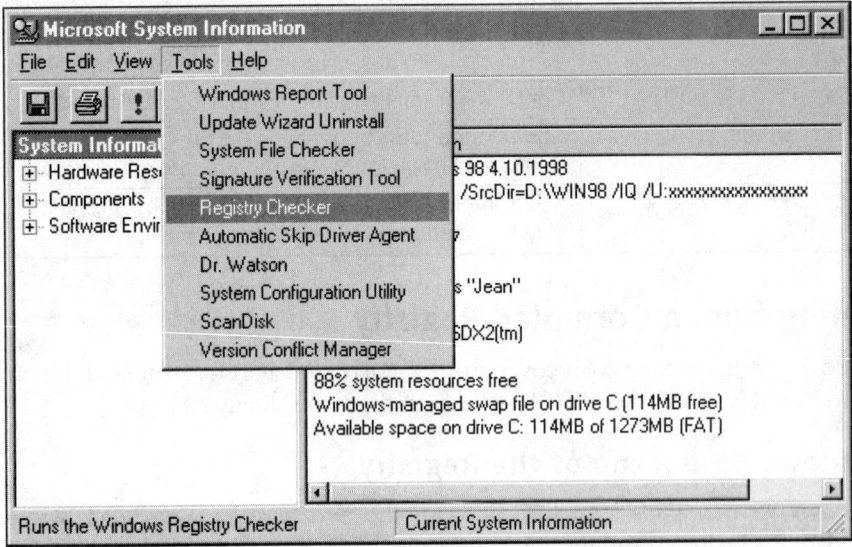

Figure 18-9   The Registry Checker is available under Programs, Accessories, System Tools, System Information Tool; it is used to back up, restore, and repair the Windows 98 registry

Backups are kept in cabinet files in the \Windows\Sysbckup folder as rb001.cab, rb002.cab, and so on. To revert to one of these backups, you must first be in MS-DOS mode. For Windows Me, boot from a bootable disk. For Windows 98, boot from a bootable disk or boot to a MS-DOS prompt from the Windows 98 startup menu (Windows Me does not have this option on the startup menu). From the MS-DOS prompt (not a DOS box within a Windows session), use the commands in Table 18-5 to repair or recover the registry.

Table 18-5   Commands used to repair or recover the registry

Command	Purpose
Scanreg /Restore	Restores the registry from a previous backup. A screen is displayed asking you which backup to use.
Scanreg /Fix	Repairs the corrupted registry. If the problem is inherent to the registry itself, this might work. If the problem is that you want to undo a successful change to the registry, then use the Restore option instead.
Scanreg /Backup	Creates a new backup of the registry at the DOS prompt. Don't do this if the registry is giving you problems.
Scanreg /Opt	Optimizes the registry. ScanReg will look for and delete information in the registry that is no longer used. This reduces the size of the registry, which might speed up booting.
Scanreg /?	Help feature of ScanReg.

Modifying the Registry

When you make a change in Control Panel or Device Manager or many other places in Windows 9x, such as when you install software, the registry is modified automatically. For most users, this is the only way they will ever change the registry. However, there are rare occasions when you might need to edit the registry manually. One example would be if you accidentally deleted the device driver for a hardware device but Device Manager says that the device is still installed. Another example would be if the wrong software starts when Windows 9x is loaded and you cannot correct the problem by changing the Startup folder. Both these problems can be corrected by manually editing the registry.

The first step in editing the registry is to back up the two files System.dat and User.dat. Sometimes the files are small enough to fit on floppy disks and can be copied using Explorer. If the files are too large to copy to floppy disk, copy them to a different folder on the hard drive or use compression software such as PKZIP to copy them to floppy disks. For Windows 98/Me, use Registry Checker to back up the registry. Third-party utility software such as Norton Utilities (*www.symantec.com*) has a registry editor that allows for backing up the registry before entering the editor. The following directions use the Windows 9x Regedit utility to edit the registry.

After backing up the registry files, the next step is to use Regedit.exe, located in the Windows folder. You can use Explorer to locate the file, then double-click it, or you can click Start, and then Run, and type Regedit in the Run dialog box. When you do, the window in Figure 18-10 opens. Open one branch of the tree by clicking on the + sign to the left of the key, and close the branch by clicking on the – sign.

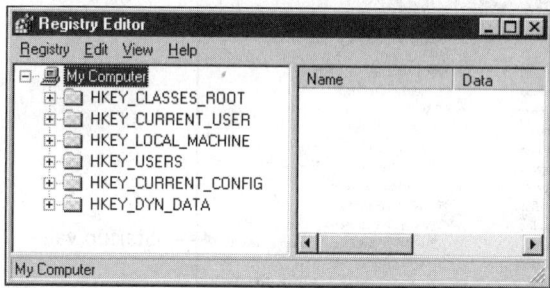

Figure 18-10   The six major keys, or branches, of the registry seen in the Registry Editor

To search for an entry in the registry, click Edit, and then click Find. The Find dialog box is displayed, as in the screen in Figure 18-11, which is ready to find the text "software" in the registry. Enter the key, the value, or the value data, and then click Find Next. You can choose to search keys, values, and/or value data by clicking on the check boxes in the dialog box.

For example, suppose that the wrong programs start when you load Windows 9x. First try to correct the problem without editing the registry. Using Explorer, open the C:\\Windows\All Users\Start Menu\Programs\StartUp folder. Delete any items that you don't want to start when you load Windows. If this does not correct the problem, the problem might be caused by a wrong entry recorded in the registry. Try editing the registry.

18

Figure 18-11   Searching for entries in the registry

First locate Shell Folders, which will be in the following branch: HKEY_CURRENT_
USER\Software\Microsoft\Windows\CurrentVersion\Explorer\Shell Folders. Search
for these keys and subkeys one at a time. (Search for HKEY_CURRENT_USER. After
you have located it, search for Software, and continue through the list until you come to
Shell Folders.)

The value name Startup= in the Shell Folders subkey should be "C:\Windows\Start
Menu\Programs\Startup." If the data is incorrect, right-click Startup and select Modify
from the shortcut menu. Figure 18-12 shows the Edit String dialog box that is displayed.
Change the value data and then click OK.

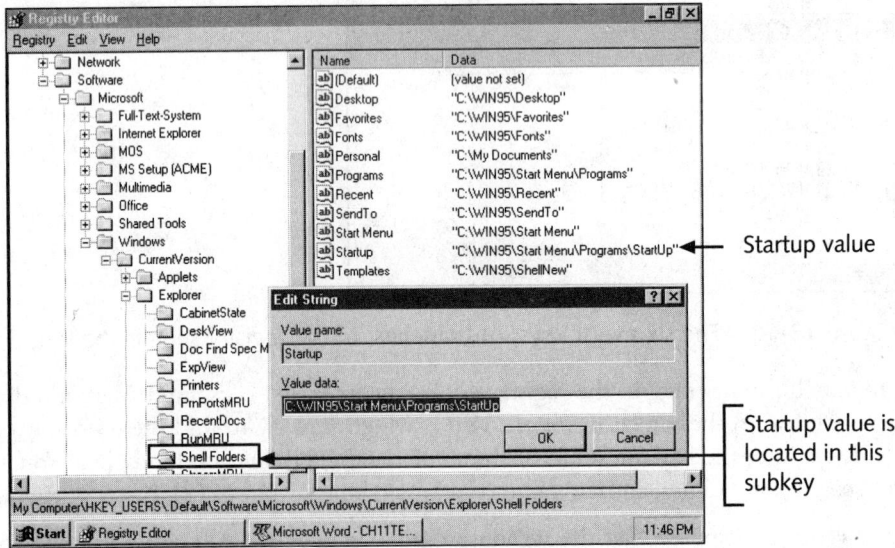

Figure 18-12   Editing an entry in the registry using Regedit.exe

TOOLS USED TO MONITOR, CONTROL, AND TROUBLESHOOT WINDOWS 9X

Windows 9x offers several tools, some of which are listed in Table 18-6, to monitor and improve system performance, control the OS, and to help with troubleshooting. Several of the major tools are covered in this section.

Table 18-6   Windows 9x system performance and troubleshooting tools

Tool	Win 95	Win 98/Me	Description
Automatic Skip Driver Agent File name: Asd.exe Location: \Windows		X	Automatically skips drivers that prevent Windows from loading and records problems encountered in the log file Asd.log. To run, select Automatic Skip Driver Agent from the Tools menu of the System Information window.
Microsoft System Information File name: MSInfo32.exe Location: \Program Files\ Common files\Microsoft shared\Msinfo	X	X	Displays system information, including installed hardware and device drivers. To run, click Start, Programs, Accessories, System Tools, System Information or type Msinfo32.exe in the Run dialog box.
Hardware Diagnostic tool (Hwinfo.exe)		X	Displays the same information as System Information, but in text form. Enter hwinfo /ui in the Run dialog box.
Registry Checker File name: Scanreg.exe Location: \Windows\Command		X	Backs up, verifies, and recovers the Registry. To run, select Registry Checker from the Tools menu of the System Information window.
Windows Update File name: Iexplore.exe Location: www.microsoft. com/windowsupdate	X	X	Download service packs (fixes) for Windows from the Microsoft Web site.
System options in Control Panel	X	X	Several applets in Control Panel can be used in monitoring and tweaking system performance.
System Configuration Utility Filename: MsConfig Location: \Windows\System		X	Allows you to temporarily modify the system configuration to help with troubleshooting. To run, select System Configuration Utility from the menu Tools of the System Information window or type Msconfig in the Run dialog box.
System File Checker File name: Sfc.exe Location: \Windows\System		X	Verifies system files. This tool scans for changed, deleted, or corrupted system files and restores them from the originals on the Windows CD-ROM. To run, select System File Checker from the Tools menu of the System Information window.

18

Table 18-6   Windows 9x system performance and troubleshooting tools (continued)

Tool	Win 95	Win 98/Me	Description
System Monitor File name: Sysmon.exe Location: \Windows		X	System Monitor tracks the performance of some important system components. To run, click Start, Programs, Accessories, System Tools, System Monitor.
Microsoft Backup (\Program Files\Accessories\ Backup\Msbackup.exe)	X	X	Backs up files and folders to prevent loss when your hard drive fails. To run, click Start, Programs, Accessories, System Tools, Backup. The utility is covered in Chapter 24.
System Recovery File name: pcrestor.bat Location: On the Windows 98/ Me CD in \Tools\Sysrec		X	Uses a full system backup created by Microsoft Backup to reinstall Windows and restore the system to its state as of the last backup.
Dr. Watson File name: Drwatson.exe Location: \Windows		X	Traps errors in log files created by applications and takes a snapshot of the system to use for troubleshooting.
Scheduled Task Wizard File name: Mstask.exe Location: \Windows\System	X	X	Schedule tasks such as MS Backup to run at predetermined times.
Version Conflict Manager File name: Vcmui.exe Location: \Windows		X	Installs Windows files over a newer file that might be in the \Windows folder and subfolders.
System Configuration Editor File name: Sysedit.exe Location: \Windows\System	X	X	Text editor to edit files that configure how Windows loads. To run it, enter Sysedit.exe in the Run dialog box. Sysedit automatically opens Protocol.ini, System.ini, Win.ini, Config.sys and Autoexec.bat for editing.
Task Manager File name: Taskman.exe Location: \Windows	X	X	Run, switch and end applications, and access the Shutdown menu. To run it, type Taskman in the Run dialog box.
Signature Verification Tool File name: sigverif.exe Location: \Windows		X	Checks system drivers for digital signatures given them by Microsoft, which ensures they have been tested by Microsoft. To run it, use the System Information window.
Digital Signature Check		X	Identifies drivers that have been digitally signed by Microsoft to verify their integrity. To use it, enabled this key in the registry: HKEY_LOCAL_ MACHINE\Software\Microsoft\Driver Signing.

As Table 18-6 shows, some tools are only available with Windows 98/Me. Many of these tools are accessed from the Microsoft System Information window. To access this window, click Start, point to Programs, Accessories, System Tools, and then click System Information. The dialog box illustrated in Figure 18-13 opens. The System Information utility is available under Windows 95 but does not include the tools listed in Table 18-6.

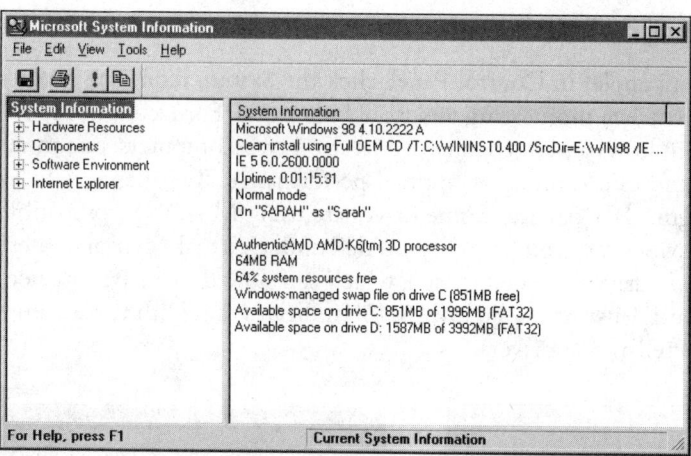

Figure 18-13   Some performance and troubleshooting tools can be accessed through the System Information window

One tool that is available from the System Information window is the System File Checker, which is illustrated in Figure 18-14. To use the utility to restore damaged Windows system files, click Tools on the System Information window and then select System File Checker.

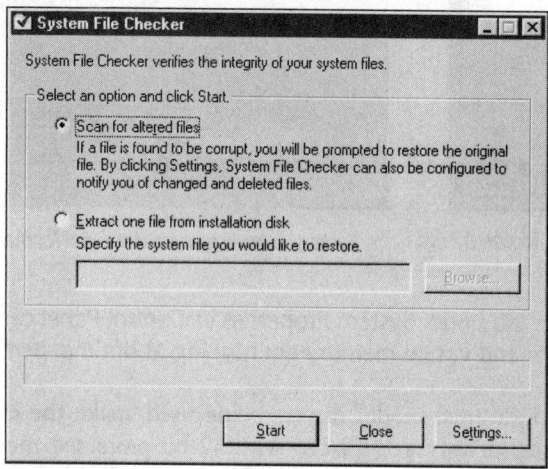

Figure 18-14   The Windows 98 File Checker verifies system files

The same information displayed by the System Information tool can be displayed in text format using the Hardware Diagnostic tool (Hwinfo.exe). To use the tool, type *hwinfo /ui* in the Windows Run dialog box. The Hardware Info window reports information about hardware devices, including drivers used, keys from the registry and how they are used, configuration information, and error and warning information. You can sort and filter the report so that only information about devices with problems is listed.

18

System Applet in Control Panel

To access the System applet in Control Panel, click the System icon. The applet offers several tools for performance monitoring and troubleshooting. For example, the Performance tab in Figure 18-15 shows a performance report from two computers, one in need of performance tuning and one running at optimal performance. Key messages to look for on this screen (see Figure 18-15a) are "Some drives are using MS-DOS compatibility" under File System, and "MS-DOS compatibility mode" under Virtual Memory. These messages mean that real-mode drivers are being used, which can slow down performance, especially when used with hard drive access. Figure 18-15b indicates that both these components are using 32-bit protected-mode drivers.

 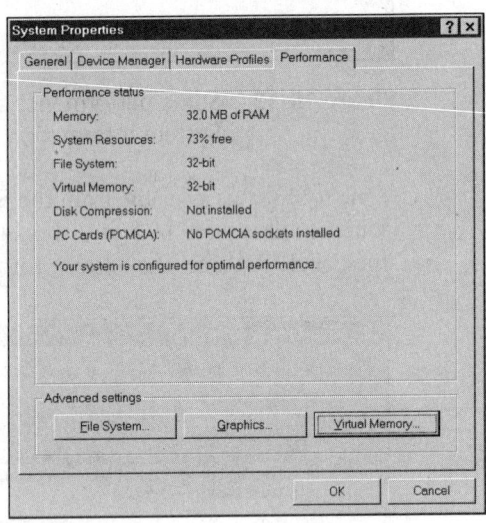

a. Adjustments are needed in order to use 32-bit   b. System running at optimal performance
   protected-mode resource

Figure 18-15   The Performance tab under System Properties in Control Panel can tell you
if your file system and virtual memory are running at optimal performance

Whenever you see MS-DOS mode (real mode) drivers being used, make the effort to do whatever you can to see that these drivers are replaced with 32-bit protected-mode drivers. One important tool to use for this process is the file Ios.ini, a text file that contains the Windows 9x Safe Driver List. Windows 9x uses this list to determine if it can safely substitute a protected-mode driver for a real-mode one. Also, if it attempts to make the substitution but fails, it often records the problem in another file, Ios.log. Check this file for information about the problem.

If a real-mode driver is being used, and you believe that a protected-mode driver should be used in its place, first check Ios.log for any error messages. If you don't find an error message, add the real-mode driver name to the safe driver list in the Ios.ini file. Anything following the semicolon on the line is a comment. You can also use REM to comment out a line.

Sample lines in the Ios.ini file are:

```
[SafeList]
386max.sys   ;   Qualitas
extrados.pro;    Qualitas Memory Manager
extrados.max;    Qualitas Memory Manager
4dos.com     ;   4DOS shell program
ad-dos.com   ;   Afterdark
ad-wrap.com  ;   Afterdark
adi2.com     ;   Afterdark
aspi3x70.sys;    DTC SCSI driver
```

If you are using third-party disk compression software, such as Stacker, make sure to use a 32-bit version of the software. When converting from Windows 3.x to Windows 9x, also upgrade Stacker. If you are still using a 16-bit version of the software, most often an error message about the problem can be found in Ios.log.

System Monitor

System Monitor allows you to monitor how system resources are being used by applications. It can monitor the file system, memory, the kernel, printer sharing services, and network performance data. System Monitor is not automatically installed in a typical installation. To install it, go to Control Panel, Add/Remove Programs. Click Windows Setup, and then select Accessories. To run System Monitor, click Start, point to Programs, Accessories, System Tools, and then click System Monitor.

Figure 18-16 shows System Monitor tracking the kernel and disk cache hits and misses. Under the File menu, you can add and delete items the monitor is tracking. Use System Monitor to help determine if an application is using an inordinate amount of resources or has a memory leak. A memory leak occurs when you exit software and it unloads from memory, but it does not release the memory addresses that it was using for its data back to the OS. Memory leaks can occur when software is corrupted, poorly written, or plagued with a virus. You notice memory leaks when your system gets sluggish after you have launched and exited an application several times before rebooting the system. A reboot releases all memory addresses.

System Configuration Utility

Like loading Windows in safe mode, the System Configuration Utility (mswnconfig.exe) reduces the startup process to its essentials. If starting Windows in this condition eliminates the problem you are troubleshooting, you can use this utility to add items back one at a time until the problem occurs; the source of the problem is related to the last item you added. To use the utility, do the following:

1. To access the utility, click **Start**, point to **Programs**, **Accessories**, **System Tools**, and then click **System Information**. The Microsoft System Information window opens (refer back to Figure 18-9).

18

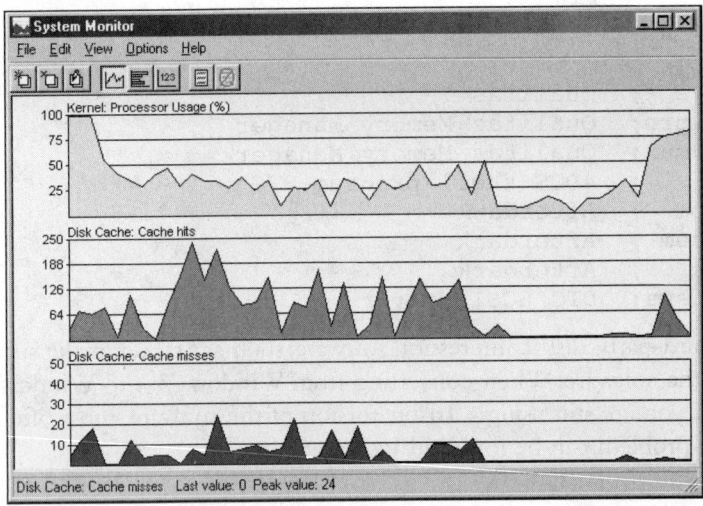

Figure 18-16   System Monitor can track the performance of several system resources

2. From the **Tools** menu, select **System Configuration Utility**. The System Configuration Utility dialog box opens, as in Figure 18-17. Another way to access the window is to type Msconfig in the Run dialog box.

3. To diagnose a problem, select **Diagnostic startup – interactively load device drivers and software**, and then click **OK** to restart your computer.

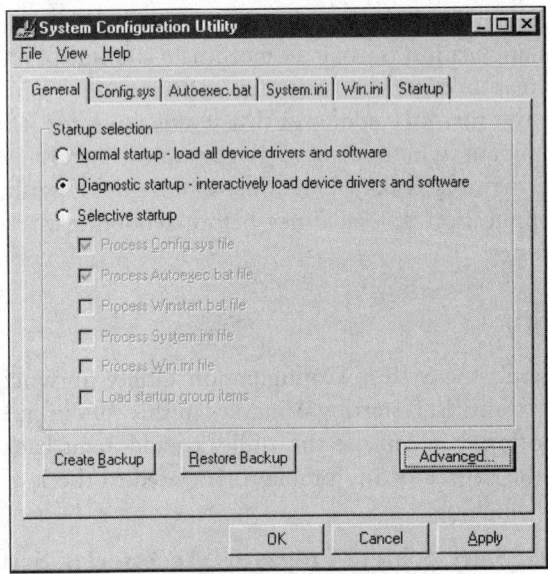

Figure 18-17   The Windows 98 System Configuration Utility helps troubleshoot Windows configuration problems

4. If this solves the problem, then the clean start was successful. Next, select **Selective startup** from the screen shown in Figure 18-17 and methodically select first one item and then another to restore, until the problem reappears. Begin by restoring all entries in Autoexec.bat and Config.sys, to determine if real-mode drivers and programs loaded from these files are the source of the problem.

5. If the problem still occurs, even with the clean boot, then try these things:

- If you have not already done so, scan for a virus, using a current version of antivirus software.
- Use Registry Checker to check for corrupted system files.
- Use System File Checker to check for corrupted system files.
- Check the CMOS setup screen for wrong settings.

Tools to Manage Security

There are several tools and methods in Windows 9x to create, update, and use passwords and user profiles. These tools can be used to avoid or address problems caused by unauthorized access to certain machines or computer features.

User Profiles

Windows 9x (as well as Windows NT/2000/XP) offers **user profiles** that allow the system to restore user preferences each time a user logs on to the system. A user profile can include software and hardware settings such as how the desktop is displayed, what shortcuts are on the desktop, and what printers or other hardware devices are available for a user. When several users use the same computer, user profiles can be a handy way for each user to keep individual settings. Also, on a network, a roaming profile follows the user from computer to computer on the network. User profiles can be collected into a **group profile** so that changes to the group profile affect all users assigned to that group.

There are many security advantages to having a different profile for each user. When you set a user profile, you also set a logon password that a user must type in when booting up the computer. Each user profile has a different logon password, and the settings of the profile can limit what files, folders, applications, and hardware devices the user has access to. In this way, you can limit what users can do on the PC and on the network. To create user profiles, open the Users applet in the Control Panel. The Multi-user Wizard will step you through the process.

18

 In a network environment, Windows 9x can use policy files to define user, network, and computer settings. A policy file has a .pol file extension; examples are Policy.pol and Config.pol. Using the System Policy Editor, a network administrator can create a policy file that affects the entire network, a group of users, or a single user on the network. The policy file can reside on the network server and is read when Windows 9x first boots. Entries in the policy file override entries in the Windows 9x registry, including those placed there by the User applet.

Screen Saver Passwords

Sometimes a user will leave his or her computer idle for a period of time, allowing the screen saver to activate. Setting a screen saver password prevents unauthorized users from accessing the computer logged in under an authorized user's profile while the authorized user is away. Once the screen saver password is set and the screen saver activates, you must enter the correct password to close the screensaver and return to the desktop and any open files and applications. A screen saver password does not protect files on the system. Any user can reboot and access the hard drive without knowing a screen saver password.

To create a screen saver password, click the Screen Saver tab in the Display Properties window. Select a screen saver and check Password protected. To set the password, click the Change button and then enter and confirm a password (see Figure 18-18). Click OK to save your password and then click OK to exit the Display Properties window.

Figure 18-18   You must confirm a screen saver password to set it

Managing a Hard Drive

Earlier in the chapter, you saw the tools ScanDisk and Defrag, both of which check and repair problems with a hard drive, listed as tools to use when troubleshooting the boot process. In the last chapter, you saw how they are used to prepare a hard drive before upgrading Windows. You can also use these utilities when troubleshooting hard drive problems or even software problems that could be caused by an improperly running hard drive. Even when you are not having problems with your hard drive, it is a good idea to run these utilities occasionally to check the health of the drive and possibly avert future problems.

Defrag

Fragmentation is the undesirable placement of a single file in several cluster locations that are not right next to each other, so that data access time is increased. When a hard drive is new and freshly formatted, the OS writes files to the drive beginning with cluster 2, placing the data in consecutive clusters. Each new file begins with the next available cluster. Later, after a file has been deleted, the OS writes a new file to the drive, beginning with the first available cluster in the FAT. If the OS encounters used clusters as it is writing the file, it simply skips these clusters and uses the next available one. In this way, after many files have been deleted and added to the drive, files become fragmented. Fragmentation occurs when files are written to a drive in more than one group of contiguous clusters. The clusters that make up a file are together called a **chain**. For a well-used hard drive, it is possible to have a file stored in clusters at 20, 30, 40, or more locations. Fragmentation is undesirable because (1) when the OS has to access many different locations on the drive to read a file, access time slows down, and (2) if the file should become corrupted, recovering a fragmented file is more complicated than recovering a file in one continuous chain.

For these reasons, one routine maintenance task is to periodically **defragment** the hard drive. Windows 9x includes a real-mode version of the utility called the Defrag command, and there is a defragmentation utility available from the Windows desktop that has a graphical interface. You can also use third-party software such as Norton Utilities. Regardless of the method used, you should defragment your hard drive every six months or so as part of a good maintenance plan.

 TIP To graphically see how badly a drive is fragmented, use Norton Utilities, Windows Disk Defragmenter, or another disk utility to view your FAT. Norton highlights the clusters for each file in a different color so you can easily identify all the clusters that belong to a single file. By moving your cursor over the FAT, you can easily see whether your hard drive is badly fragmented.

To use Windows 9x Disk Defragmenter, choose Start, then Programs, then Accessories, and then System Tools. The menu in Figure 18-19 is displayed. (Two of the other menu items, ScanDisk and DriveSpace, will be discussed next.) Click Disk Defragmenter and select the drive from the dialog box that is displayed. Click OK. When the operation is complete, the message in Figure 18-20 appears; click Yes to exit.

18

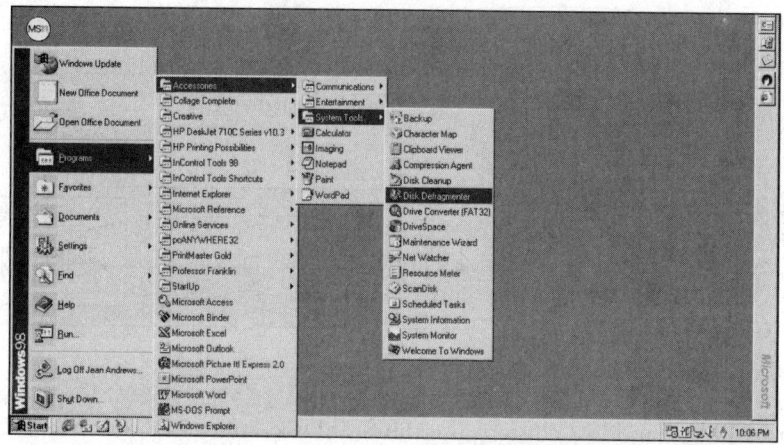

Figure 18-19   Windows 98 utilities

Figure 18-20 Disk Defragmenter results

> **TIP** Defragmenting a large hard drive may take a long time, so plan for this before you begin. If you want to watch the progress as it moves through the FAT, click Show Details on the Disk Defragmenter dialog box.

ScanDisk

As you learned in Chapter 16, a directory on either a floppy disk or hard drive is a table holding information about files in that directory or folder. The directory contains the number of the first cluster in the file. The FAT holds the map to all the other clusters in the file. Occasionally, the mapping in the FAT becomes corrupted, resulting either in lost clusters or in cross-linked clusters, as shown in Figure 18-21. Here File 3 has lost direction and is pointing to a cluster chain that belongs to File 4. Clusters 29–31 are called **cross-linked clusters** because more than one file points to them, and clusters 15–17 and 28 are called **lost clusters**, or **lost allocation units**, because no file in the FAT points to them.

Figure 18-21 Lost and cross-linked clusters

To repair cross-linked and lost clusters, use the ScanDisk utility in either MS-DOS mode or from the Windows 9x desktop. For example, in real mode, at the command prompt, enter the command *Scandisk*. The screen in Figure 18-22 is displayed. When the program finishes scanning the disk, it returns you to a command prompt.

From the Windows desktop, click Start, then Programs, then Accessories, then System Tools, and then ScanDisk, as shown in Figure 18-19. The ScanDisk utility first asks which drive you want to scan and gives you the choice between a standard and thorough scan. The standard scan checks files and folders for errors. The thorough scan does all that the standard scan does plus checks the disk surface. Click Start to begin the scan. Errors are reported as they occur, and final results are displayed as in Figure 18-23.

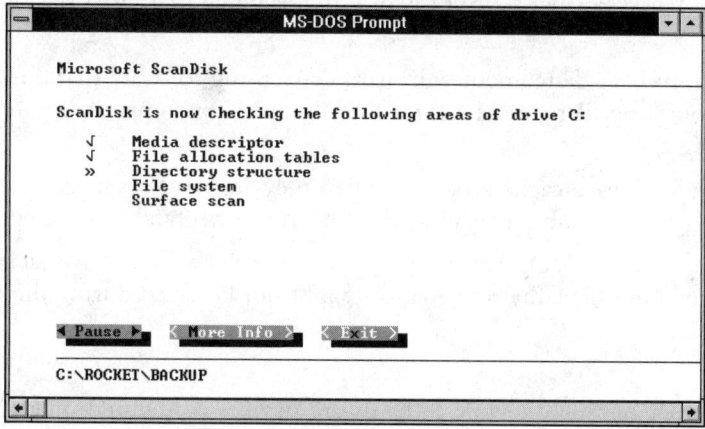

Figure 18-22   ScanDisk in MS-DOS mode

Figure 18-23   ScanDisk results

18

Using DOS Commands Under Windows 9x

A word of caution: using some DOS commands on a hard drive that uses Windows 9x as the OS may cause damage to a hard drive's file structure. With a Windows 9x upgrade, some of these dangerous commands are erased from the \DOS directory on the hard drive. However, you will find DOS commands that come with Windows 9x stored in the \Windows\ Command directory, and some of these should not be used. Here are the ones to avoid:

- Don't use disk utility software that does not know about VFAT, long filenames or FAT32, including older versions of Norton Utilities and Central Point PC Tools.

- Don't use Fdisk, Format C:, Sys C:, or Chkdsk while in a DOS session within Windows 9x.

- Don't optimize or defragment your hard drive using software that does not know about long filenames; look for the Windows 9x compatibility message on the package.

- Don't run hard drive cache programs unless they are written especially for Windows 9x. Remember that Windows 9x has its own built-in caching software.

- Don't use the older DOS backup programs such as Backup or Msbackup, because the long filename information might not be saved during the backup.

Device Manager

Device Manager gives a graphical view of hardware devices configured under Windows and the resources and drivers they use. Using Device Manager, you can make changes, update drivers, and uninstall device drivers. You can also use Device Manager to print a report of system configuration. When a device driver is being installed, Windows 9x might inform you that there is a resource conflict, or the device might simply not work. Use Device Manager as a useful fact-finding tool for the resolution of the problem.

Device Manager is one tab on the System Properties window. To access System Properties, right-click the My Computer icon on the desktop and select Properties from the shortcut menu, or double-click the System icon in Control Panel. From the System Properties window, click the Device Manager tab. The list of devices is displayed, as seen in Figure 18-24. A "+" beside the device name indicates that you can click the device for a list of manufacturers and models installed. The open diamond symbol indicates a SCSI device, and the three-forked symbol is used for USB. Symbols that indicate a device's status are:

- A red X through the device name indicates a disabled device.

- An exclamation point on a yellow background indicates a problem with the device (the device might still be functioning).

- A blue I on a white field indicates that automatic settings were not used and resources have been manually assigned. It does not indicate a problem with the device.

- For Windows Me, a green question mark indicates a compatible driver is installed, (not the driver designed for the device), which means the device might not be fully functioning.

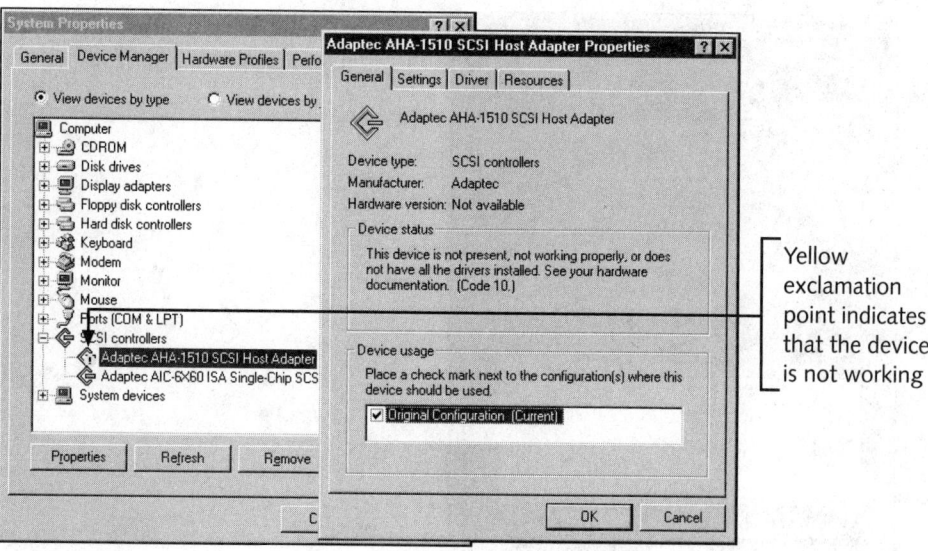

Yellow exclamation point indicates that the device is not working

Figure 18-24   The Properties box of an installed device that is not working

To see a better explanation of a problem, click the device and select Properties. The Device Properties dialog box opens, which can give you helpful information about solving problems including I/O addresses, DMA channels, and IRQs used by the device as well as the names of devices that are also attempting to use the same resources.

In fact, before you start hardware installation, you might want to use Device Manager to print a summary of all hardware installed on the PC and resources being used. This printout can be a record of your starting point before the installation as well as a tool to help resolve conflicts during the installation. To print this summary, access Device Manager and click Print. From the Print dialog box, select All Devices and System Summary for a complete listing.

 If you have a problem with an installed device, use Device Manager to uninstall the device. Select the device and click the Uninstall button. Then reboot and reinstall the device looking for problems during the installation that point to the source of the problem. Sometimes reinstalling a device is all that is needed to solve the problem.

Dr. Watson

A troubleshooting tool you can use when you are having problems running an application is Dr. Watson. **Dr. Watson** is a Windows utility that can record detailed information about the system, errors that occur, and the programs that caused them in a log file named \Windows\Drwatson\WatsonXX.wlg, where XX is an incrementing number. Start Dr. Watson (see Figure 18-25) and then reproduce the application error.

18

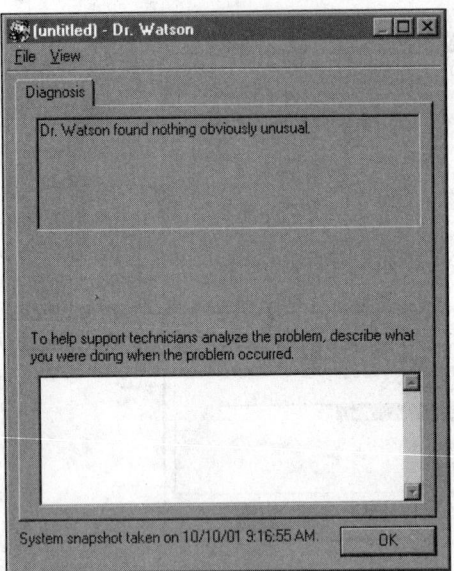

Figure 18-25   The Dr. Watson opening window

Then look at the events logged in the Dr. Watson window under the Diagnosis tab. Use this information to check the Microsoft Web site, *support.microsoft.com*, for the problem and solution. For errors that you cannot reproduce at will, you can load Dr. Watson each time Windows starts by creating a shortcut to Drwatson.exe in the Startup folder.

Windows Help and the Microsoft Web Site

Windows Help might provide useful information when trying to resolve a problem. To access the Troubleshooting tool of Windows Help, click Start, click Help, and then click Troubleshooting. The Help information includes suggestions that can lead you to a solution. For example, in Figure 18-26, the Hardware Troubleshooter suggests that you check to see that the device is not listed twice in Device Manager. If this were the case, you should remove the second occurrence of the device.

Also, the Microsoft Web site, *support.microsoft.com*, has lots of information on troubleshooting. Search on the device, an error message, a Windows utility, a symptom, a software application, an update version number, or key words that lead you to articles about the problem and solutions.

Figure 18-26 Troubleshooter making a suggestion to resolve a hardware conflict

TROUBLESHOOTING HARDWARE IN WINDOWS 9x

Now that you know about some of the tools used for troubleshooting, you will now learn about the general approaches you should take to troubleshooting problems.

Troubleshooting a PC problem begins with isolating it into one of two categories: problems that prevent the PC from booting and problems that occur after a successful boot. Begin by asking the user questions like these to learn as much as you can:

- When did the problem start?

- Were there any error messages or unusual displays on the screen?

- What programs or software were you using?

- Did you move your computer system recently?

- Has there been a recent thunderstorm or electrical problem?

- Have you made any hardware, software, or configuration changes?

- Has someone else been using your computer recently?

- Can you show me exactly what you did when this problem occurred? (Have the user reproduce the problem and watch each step.)

- Next, ask yourself, "Does the PC boot properly?" If not, then begin troubleshooting the failed boot.

18

Here are some general tips for troubleshooting hardware devices:

- Try rebooting your computer. The problem with the device may disappear when Windows redetects it.

- Frequent system lockups might indicate corrupted memory modules. Try using memory testing software to check for intermittent memory errors, which indicate the module needs replacing. An example of memory testing software is DocMemory by CST, Inc. (*www.docmemory.com*).

- For external devices such as monitors, printers, and scanners, try turning on the device before turning on the computer. If you have your computer on and you are rebooting, leave the device on and online.

- If a device doesn't work with one application, try it with another. If the problem only occurs with one application, the problem is probably not with the hardware device but with that application.

- Check Device Manager for errors it reports about the device. If it reports errors, use the Hardware Troubleshooter in Device Manager to help resolve the problem or go to the Microsoft Web site and search on the error message.

- The driver might be corrupted or need updating. Look on the Web for updated device drivers. Search the device manufacturer's Web site or the Microsoft Web site for information about problems with the device and solutions.

- Use Device Manager to uninstall the device and then reinstall it. If you uninstall the device and then reboot, Windows should recognize an uninstalled device and automatically launch the Found New Hardware Wizard. If it doesn't launch, then chances are the device is not working or is not PnP. Special considerations for legacy devices are covered in the next section.

- For PnP devices on expansion cards such as sound cards, modems, and network cards, if you uninstall the device in Device Manager and Windows does not recognize the device when you reboot, the device might not be working. The expansion card needs to be reseated or moved to a different expansion slot. If that doesn't work, the card needs replacing.

- If none of these things work, ask yourself what has changed since the device last worked. For example, maybe you have added another hardware device that is conflicting with the one you are using, or maybe you have added software that conflicts with the software that the problem device is using. Try disabling other devices or try uninstalling software that you suspect is causing the problem. Use Automatic Skip Driver Agent to eliminate other devices that might prevent this one from working.

- The problem might be caused by a lack of resources. If your system is running low on memory or has too many applications open, it might not be able to support a device. A corrupted Windows system file or registry can also cause problems with hardware devices. Try verifying system files or restoring the registry from backup.

- If you still have not resolved the problem, consider it a hardware problem.

Troubleshooting Legacy Devices and Drivers

A device or expansion card that is not PnP is a legacy device. Legacy devices are not able to have their resources assigned to them by PnP, and legacy drivers are older 16-bit drivers that cannot be loaded into extended memory.

Legacy 16-bit drivers are loaded from entries in Autoexec.bat, Config.sys, or System.ini files. These entries are created by an install or setup program that comes with the device drivers and is executed when you install the device. If you are having a problem with a legacy device, do the following:

- Make every effort to find a protected-mode driver for the device. Check the Microsoft Web site and the Web site of the device manufacturer.

- If you cannot find a protected-mode driver, check the entries in Autoexec.bat, Config.sys, and System.ini for errors. Try running the install program again.

- If you are attempting to load the drive high and the MEM report says it's not loaded high, check for errors in these command lines: Device=HIMEM.SYS, Device=EMM386.EXE, and DOS=UMB in the Config.sys file. Then look for either the Devicehigh= command in Config.sys or the Loadhigh command in Autoexec.bat. See Chapter 16 for more information about using upper memory.

- Two legacy devices might be in conflict. Use the System Configuration Utility to disable one device or the other to verify the conflict. Also, Device Manager sometimes is aware of a legacy conflict and suggests a substitution for system resources. A hardware technician uses DIP switches or jumpers on a legacy device to configure it to use a different set of system resources.

Conflicts with Upper Memory Addresses

A device might be attempting to use upper memory addresses that the OS is using for a UMB. When the OS creates a UMB, it assigns memory addresses that it "thinks" are not being used by devices. However, some devices don't tell the OS what memory addresses they are using until the device is activated after booting. This delay causes the OS to think that the memory addresses assigned to a device are available, and the OS creates and loads a TSR into the UMB. If this conflict happens, the system might hang, the TSR might not work properly, and/or the device might not work properly. Try the following approach:

1. Read the documentation that came with the device to find out which memory addresses it is using. Also, try using MSD to display how memory is being used. Once you know the memory addresses being used, you can change the Emm386.exe command line so that this range of addresses is not used.

18

2. Use the Exclude option for the Emm386.exe command line to exclude certain memory addresses. Do not use the last numeral in the hex address in the command line. For example, suppose you read from the documentation that came with the device that it uses addresses CC000 to CFFFF. To exclude these addresses from the addresses used by UMBs, use this command line:

```
DEVICE=EMM386.EXE NOEMS X = CC00 - CFFF
```

Notice in the command line that the last digit of an upper memory address is omitted in the exclude entry. Reboot your computer to activate the change. The memory conflict problem should then be solved.

> **TIP** When reading the documentation, you will find that most addresses are given in hex rather than decimal form. (See Appendix E for an explanation of the hex number system.) Sometimes the memory addresses are written without the last hexadecimal numeral. For example, if the documentation says that the device uses C800 through CFFF, interpret this to mean that the upper memory address range is C8000 through CFFFF. Once you have discovered that the two devices use the same memory addresses, find out if one can use alternate addresses. If so, your problem is solved.

TROUBLESHOOTING APPLICATIONS IN WINDOWS 9x

Remember that Windows 9x supports 16-bit DOS applications, 16-bit Windows 3.x applications, and newer 32-bit applications. This section looks at problems that can occur with all three types of applications and what to do about them. Problems can be caused by viruses, the application itself, by other applications, by the OS, or by hardware.

Here is the general process to use when troubleshooting problems with applications:

- Address any error messages that appear when using the software.

- If you don't understand the error message, write it down or print it and look it up on the Microsoft support Web site or the Web site of the product manufacturer. Follow the directions given on the Web sites to resolve the problem.

- Read the documentation that came with the application and documents on the manufacturer Web site. Perhaps you are using a function incorrectly.

- A virus might be the source of the problem. Run current antivirus software.

- Consider that data files might be corrupted. Try creating new data files used by the software.

- Consider that the hardware the software is using might have a problem. For the hard drive, run ScanDisk and Defrag and check for free disk space. Delete files in the \Windows\Temp folder. For a device other than the hard drive, try using another application to access the device.

- Try uninstalling and reinstalling the software. Back up the data first.

- Perhaps the problem is caused by a conflict with other software. Software conflicts are addressed later in this section.

- Launch Dr. Watson and then try to reproduce the error with the application. Look in the Dr. Watson log files for clues and search the Microsoft Web site.

- Perhaps OS files are corrupted that the application depends on. Try restoring Windows system files. Check the Microsoft Web site for Windows 9x service packs that might resolve the problem. Install all Windows service packs. You might have to reinstall Windows.

Problems with a Software Program Itself

Suppose the computer boots with no errors, and all but one software package on this computer works correctly. When you try to load the problem software package, however, you get an error message and the software terminates. In this situation, you can probably conclude that the software caused the error. Here are some questions you can ask to troubleshoot the problem:

- *Has this software ever worked?* If it has not, then try installing it again. Maybe wrong information was given during the installation. Be sure you check the requirements for the software. Maybe you don't have enough memory or space on your hard drive to create the necessary working files.

- *When was the last time the software worked?* What happened differently then? Did you get an error message that seemed insignificant at the time? What has happened to your computer since the software last worked? Have you added more software or changed the hardware configuration?

- *Could a virus be causing the problem?* Run a current version of antivirus software.

Consider reinstalling the software even if it has worked in the past. Maybe a program file has become corrupted. Before you reinstall it, however, consider whether reinstallation will erase any data that this software has placed on your hard drive. If you're not sure, back up the data. Maybe you can just copy the data to another directory while you reinstall the program. If the installation does erase the data in the original directory, you can copy one file and then another back to the original directory. If you load the program without the data and it works, but the problem recurs when you put the data back in the original directory, then you've found the corrupted data file that caused the problem.

Software often uses configuration files and scripting files that are specific to a particular PC or user. If you reinstall the software, most likely you will lose the configuration information. Either save the configuration files before you begin or print the contents of the files. See the software documentation for the names and location of the configuration files (file extensions of .ini, .inf, and .cfg are common). Consider that the problem with the software might be a corrupted configuration file.

18

TIP   If an application locks up, press Ctrl+Alt+Del and select the program in the Close Program dialog box. Click End Task.

Uninstalling Software

Uninstalling software is clean and easy if the software comes with a well-written uninstall program. Use the Add/Remove Program utility in Control Panel to uninstall it. However, some uninstall programs are not all that great, and sometimes a user will simply delete the folders that contain the software, leaving behind DLL files in the \Windows\System directory, entries in the registry, shortcuts on the desktop, and so on for you, the PC technician, to clean up. Even worse, the user or an uninstall program might delete a DLL file needed by another application or make a wrong deletion in the registry. A **DLL (dynamic-link library)** file is a file with a .dll extension that contains a library of programming routines (or mini programs) to perform common tasks.

When software is installed, it can do these things:

- Create new folders that belong to the application only and store files there
- Store files used only by the application in folders also used by other software. An example is an application's .ini file stored in the \Windows folder.
- Create or overwrite files used by other software. An example is \Windows\ system\CTL3D.DLL, a file used by several applications that might be updated by a software installation.
- Make changes to the Windows registry
- Make changes to .ini files that belong to Windows

When software is uninstalled, deleting folders and their contents that belong only to the application is safe. Deleting entire sections in Windows .ini files that are named after the software or a branch in the registry tree that contains the application's name is also safe. But problems might occur when a change is made to a registry entry that other software depends on or when files are deleted that are used by other software.

Figure 18-27 shows the results of such an error. The problem, in this case, can be resolved by reinstalling the OCR software.

Cannot find CTL3D.DLL. Windows needs this file to run C:\OPLIMIT\OCRAWARE.EXE.

OK

Figure 18-27   The results of an uninstall program deleting a file needed by another application

Sometimes an application is set to automatically launch at startup. After the program is uninstalled, if errors occur when Windows is loaded, look for entries in these places that were not removed by the uninstall program:

- Check the Win.ini file for entries in the Load= and Run= command lines.
- Check the Windows Startup folder for shortcuts.
- Check the registry key HKEY_LOCAL_MACHINE\SOFTWARE\ Microsoft\Windows\CurrentVersion\Run.

TROUBLESHOOTING PROBLEMS WITH WINDOWS PERFORMANCE

If you have just installed Windows and it is performing slowly, check that the minimum hardware requirements have been met. Perhaps you need to upgrade memory or install an additional hard drive. If Windows was once working fine, but is now generally sluggish, applications are slow to load and run, or the system locks up at unexplained times, do the following:

- Check the hard drive. Run ScanDisk and Defrag. Delete unneeded files and empty the Recycle Bin. Generally clean up the hard drive making plenty of room for the swap file and temporary files used by applications.
- Suspect a virus. Run a current version of antivirus software. Clean or delete all files that contain viruses. Restore system files.
- Check for applications loaded at startup that are using up system resources. Close applications not currently in use.
- Look for icons in the **System Tray**, the small area on the right side of the taskbar at the bottom of the screen. These icons represent small applets that are loaded at startup and take up system resources. Keep these icons to a minimum.
- Clean up the registry using the Scanreg /opt command.
- Monitor the system using System Monitor, looking for applications that use an unusual percentage of system resources. Update these applications with the latest versions.
- Remove extraneous software such as fancy screen savers and desktop wallpaper and photos.

18

CHAPTER SUMMARY

- Windows 9x does not need Autoexec.bat or Config.sys to boot but includes them for backward-compatibility with DOS. If they are present in the root directory, their commands are executed during the boot process, overriding the corresponding settings stored in Io.sys and the registry.
- Initialization files, which have the .ini file extension, are used by Windows or application software to store configuration information needed when Windows or an application is first loaded.

❑ The five phases of the Windows 9x boot process are BIOS POST and bootstrap, the loading of the OS, the loading of real mode VxDs, protected-mode switchover and PnP configuration, and loading remaining components.

❑ Applications are loaded at startup by a shortcut in the Startup folder, the name of the program file in the Load= or Run= line in Win.ini, or an entry in the registry.

❑ When troubleshooting Windows 9x boot problems, first check error messages, then boot in safe mode, then boot to the command prompt using the startup menu, and finally try booting from an emergency startup disk.

❑ Using some DOS commands on a hard drive that uses Windows 9x as the OS may cause damage to a hard drive's file structure.

❑ To force Windows 9x startup menu to appear, hold down either the Ctrl key or the F8 key during the boot.

❑ To eliminate Win.ini as the cause of a boot problem, rename it Win.sav and reboot. To eliminate System.ini as the cause of a boot problem, rename it System.sav, make a copy of the System.cb file, and rename that copy System.ini.

❑ In Logged mode, Windows tracks startup activities and logs them to the Bootlog.txt file.

❑ You can reach safe mode either from the Windows startup menu or by pressing F5 while Windows is loading.

❑ When you enter safe mode, Windows 98/Me automatically includes support for networks, but Windows 95 does not.

❑ Safe mode starts Windows 9x with a minimum default configuration to give you an opportunity to correct an error in the configuration.

❑ Choosing Command Prompt Only from the startup menu executes the contents of Autoexec.bat and Config.sys but does not start Windows and instead brings you to a DOS prompt. Use the WIN command to load Windows 9x.

❑ Use the startup disk to recover from a failed boot when you cannot solve the problem using the startup menu, or when you cannot boot from the hard drive. If you do not have a startup disk or if the one you have is corrupted with a virus, use a working computer to create a new one.

❑ Starting with Windows 9x, the Windows registry takes over the essential functions of .ini files. However, Windows 9x still supports System.ini and Win.ini for backward-compatibility with legacy hardware devices and legacy software applications.

❑ The registry is contained in two files, System.dat and User.dat. Windows 95 maintains backups of these files, called System.da0 and User.da0, that you can use when troubleshooting. Windows 98/Me keeps compressed backup files of the registry and system files in cabinet files named Ra000.cab, Ra001.cab and so forth.

❑ Changes in Control Panel, Device Manager, and other locations in Windows 9x can make changes to the registry automatically. The Regedit utility is used to edit the registry manually.

❑ User profiles allow the system to restore user preferences each time a user logs on to the system. User profiles include hardware and software settings as well as access permissions.

❑ Logon passwords and screen saver passwords help prevent unauthorized access to a computer.

❏ The Registry Checker (Scanreg.exe) backs up, verifies, and recovers the registry. It automatically backs up the registry every day and keeps the last five days of backups.

❏ The System Configuration Utility (Msconfig) allows you to temporarily modify the system configuration to help with troubleshooting. It reduces the startup process to its essentials.

❏ The Dr. Watson utility (Drwatson.exe) helps you troubleshoot applications by trapping errors in log files and taking a snapshot of the system.

❏ The System Configuration Editor (Sysedit.exe) is a text editor that is used to edit system files. When you run Sysedit, it automatically opens Protocol.ini, System.ini, Win.ini, Config.sys, and Autoexec.bat.

❏ The Ios.ini file contains the Windows 9x Safe Driver List. Windows 9x uses this file to determine whether it can safely substitute a protected mode driver for a real-mode one.

❏ System Monitor allows you to monitor how system resources are being used by applications.

❏ When troubleshooting hardware devices, try checking whether a problem device works with one application or not another or reversing changes made since the device last worked.

❏ Use the tools ScanDisk (which checks for physical errors on the drive) and Defrag (which reverses the effects of fragmentation and makes sure files are stored in contiguous clusters) to maintain and troubleshoot your hard drive.

❏ Clusters to which more than one file points in the FAT are called cross-linked clusters, and clusters to which no file points are called lost clusters. Both can be repaired with ScanDisk.

❏ Dr. Watson is a Windows utility that can record detailed information about the system, errors that occur, and the programs that caused them.

❏ Device Manager lists hardware devices installed on a system. For more information about a specific device in Device Manager, click the device and select Properties.

❏ Legacy devices demand specific resources and cannot have resources assigned by Plug and Play. Windows 9x sometimes has problems with the drivers, memory, and system resources needed for legacy devices.

❏ Some software problems can be solved by uninstalling and reinstalling the software. Before uninstalling software, save data and configuration files connected to the application. Be very careful when manually uninstalling software not to delete DLL files that are shared with other applications. Problems with DLL files can also be caused when new software is installed and conflicts with existing files.

❏ To improve performance, close applications you are not currently using and reduce the number of icons in the system tray.

18

KEY TERMS

chain	fragmentation	Protocol.ini
comment	group profile	Static VxD
cross-linked clusters	keys	Sysedit
defragment	lost allocation units	System.ini
DLL (dynamic-link library)	lost clusters	System Tray
Dr. Watson	memory leak	user profile
dynamic VxD	Plug and Play (PnP) BIOS	value data
		Win.ini

19

UNDERSTANDING AND SUPPORTING WINDOWS NT

> **In this chapter, you will learn:**
> ♦ About the new Windows architecture introduced with Windows NT
> ♦ How to install and customize Windows NT
> ♦ How to use and support Windows NT
> ♦ About the Windows NT boot process
> ♦ How to troubleshoot Windows NT

This chapter introduces you to Windows NT Workstation, including basic architecture, installation, maintenance, and troubleshooting. There are two versions of Windows NT: Windows NT Workstation and Windows NT Server. You can use Windows NT Workstation on a standalone PC or as the operating system on a workstation connected to a network. Windows NT Server, which is not covered in this book, can be used the same way and can also provide a domain environment on a network. There have been several upgrades of Windows NT; the last is version 4, which is the subject of this chapter.

A BREAK WITH THE PAST: A NEW WINDOWS ARCHITECTURE

Recall from Chapter 15 that Windows NT was designed with a different architecture than Windows 9x and provided the Windows OS family's first break with DOS. Windows 2000 and Windows XP, which you will learn about in the next chapters, also use the Windows NT architecture.

Windows NT was designed to be architecturally more like the Unix OS than like Windows 9x and is intended to port to several non-Intel-based platforms; to provide a high level of security, performance, and reliability; and to offer strong networking features. Windows NT also supports **POSIX (Portable Operating System Interface),** a set of standards based on Unix and adopted by the United States federal government to better ensure that operating systems and software can port more easily from one platform to another.

> To "port" a program or OS means to move it from one computer to another computer.

Windows NT was also designed with a strong emphasis on room for improvements and expandability, primarily accomplished by its modular approach to dealing with applications and hardware. We will begin this section by looking at that approach and then move to a discussion of user and kernel modes in Windows NT.

The Modular Concept of Windows NT

Here's an analogy to help you understand the modular concept of Windows NT. The idea is to isolate one process from another so that a change in one process has the least possible effect on the other processes. Consider the self-serve restaurant in Figure 19-1. In the process illustrated in Figure 19-1, customers arrive for breakfast, walk to the back of the restaurant, tell the cook what they want, wait for him to cook it, take it back to a table, and eat. Customers are responsible for getting their own drinks, silverware, and so forth. If someone in the kitchen moves the silverware or installs a new and different drink-dispensing machine, every customer must learn a new process so the system can continue to work. This process is nonmodular and clearly does not minimize the effect that a change in one part of the process has on other parts of the process.

Now consider Figure 19-2. A counter has been added, and customers are not allowed behind this counter. They come to the counter and tell others in the kitchen what they want to eat, and someone in the kitchen brings the food, drink, and silverware to them at the counter. Things work a little better now. When processes change in the kitchen, only employees who work in the kitchen must be retrained. However, there is still a flaw in the efficiency of this design. Every kitchen worker must know how to cook and make drinks and where the silverware is located. This model introduces some benefits of a modular design but still has flaws.

Figure 19-1   In a nonmodular restaurant model, every customer is responsible for many of the steps in the process

Figure 19-2   In a partially modular restaurant model, customers are isolated from some processes

19

Figure 19-3 further refines the process, and our restaurant is now a full-service, highly modular affair. Employees are divided into four groups, each with a different function. The first and second groups of employees, the hosts and hostesses, waiters, and waitresses, interact with the customers, greeting them at the door, showing them their seats, taking orders, and serving food. The second group (the waiters and waitresses) also serves as an interface between customers and counter workers. The third group (the counter workers) stands between the kitchen counter and the customer counter, where the drink machines and the silverware are located. The waiters and waitresses pass food requests to the counter workers, who pass the requests to the fourth group, the kitchen workers, who now only prepare the food. When the food is passed back to the counter workers, these workers gather up drinks, silverware, and food and pass them on to the waiters and waitresses, who serve the customers. This model uses a more modular arrangement that provides the benefits of separating processes from each other, even though the overhead (the additional resources needed to implement the new model) is higher than in the other models.

Figure 19-3   In a highly modular restaurant model, employees are grouped by function, and customers interact only with one group of employees; employee groups are analogous to different parts of the Windows NT operating system

In this model, if the drink machine is upgraded, only the counter workers must be retrained. If the oven or stove in the kitchen is replaced with an altogether new electronic unit, only the kitchen workers change their methods. The counter workers are unaffected. The waiters and waitresses don't need to know how to communicate with the cook, but can focus on customer service. The customer is isolated from the entire process. In comparing Figures 19-1 and 19-3, on first appearance it looks as though the process has been complicated. There are more workers, and customers now have to wait to be seated. In fact, a new layer of complexity has been added, and two counters are required. However, it turns out that the advantages of the new system outweigh its disadvantages and overhead. Not only can equipment be easily upgraded without having to retrain so many people or reorient customers to the new procedures, but the integrity of the operation is enhanced: because the processes have been separated from each other, they can now be more easily controlled. Standards and procedures can be more easily applied to each segment of the process because fewer people are involved at each step in the operation, which reduces confusion and improves the overall efficiency of the operation. In summary, the three main reasons to use the highly modular model rather than the nonmodular model are:

- To make upgrades of equipment easier (some employees and all customers are unaffected)

- To increase the overall efficiency of the operation (each part of the process involves fewer people than in the other models)

- To better ensure the integrity of processes (standards are more easily enforced)

The process of running the restaurant can be viewed as analogous to the way operating systems run a computer: the modular approach is analogous to the Windows NT OS, and the nonmodular approaches are analogous to earlier OSs. Customers can be viewed as a combination of users and applications software; employees can be viewed as the OS; the stove, drink machine, silverware stand, and so on, can be viewed as the hardware; and the cook can be viewed as those parts of the OS that relate directly to hardware, system BIOS, and device drivers. The process illustrated in Figure 19-1 is most analogous to DOS, in which applications were allowed "behind the counter" to interact directly with BIOS and device drivers, and even to perform some of their own operations with hardware, rather than necessarily turning to the OS to perform hardware operations. For example, in DOS, an application program written to address specific hardware configurations might depend on video BIOS always being found at certain memory addresses, and the program could access that BIOS directly.

The process illustrated in Figure 19-2 is most analogous to a model of the Windows 9x OS, because the customers (the applications) are isolated from some of the interaction with the equipment (hardware), but not all. Notice, for instance, that the silverware stand is still available for customer use; similarly, in Windows 9x, a 16-bit program can interact directly with video memory and other resources.

The process illustrated in Figure 19-3 is most analogous to the Windows NT OS, which includes an additional layer between the applications (customers) and hardware (the restaurant equipment); applications (customers) are almost completely isolated from interaction with hardware (restaurant equipment). The access that programs have to system resources is controlled through the two Windows NT modes: user mode and kernel mode.

19

Windows NT Modes

Windows NT operates in two modes, user mode and kernel mode, which each take advantage of different CPU functions and abilities (see Figure 19-4). **User mode** is a non-privileged processor mode in which programs have only limited access to system information and can access hardware only through other OS services. Several **subsystems** or OS modules (described in more detail below) use it. **Kernel mode** is a privileged processor mode in which programs have extensive access to system information and hardware. Kernel mode is used by two main components: the HAL (hardware abstraction layer), which was introduced in Chapter 15, and a group of components collectively called **executive services**, which interfaces between the subsystems in user mode and the HAL. Executive services components manage hardware resources by way of the HAL and device drivers. Applications in user mode have no access to hardware resources. In kernel mode, executive services have limited access to hardware resources, but the HAL primarily interacts with hardware.

Figure 19-4   User mode and kernel mode in Windows NT and how they relate to users, application software, and hardware

Memory management is an excellent example of how the user mode subsystems, executive services, and the HAL cooperate in Windows NT. Windows NT provides memory addresses to an application by way of the Win32 user mode subsystem. When an application requests this subsystem to write data to some of these assigned addresses, the subsystem turns to executive services. The component within executive services that manages memory, the virtual memory manager, is responsible for coordinating the interface between the user subsystem and the HAL. The virtual memory manager presents the request to the HAL, which is responsible for the actual writing of the data to memory and responds to the memory manager when finished. The memory manager then reports back to the user subsystem, which, in turn, reports back to the application. You will learn more about memory management under Windows NT later in this chapter.

Windows NT was designed to easily port to different hardware platforms. Because only the components operating in kernel mode actually interact with hardware, they are the only parts that need to be changed when Windows NT moves from one hardware platform to another. For instance, if a major piece of hardware changes, the HAL must change. Minor hardware changes might cause changes in one or more executive services components. When hardware changes are made, the subsystems in user mode require little or no change. When hardware improves, making new resources available to software, the software applications are not responsible for knowing how to interface with the hardware resources.

Limiting access to hardware mainly to the HAL increases OS integrity because more control is possible. With this isolation, an application cannot cause a system to hang by making illegal demands on hardware. Overall performance is increased because the HAL and executive services can operate independently of the slower, less efficient applications using them.

On the other hand, Windows NT requires much more robust hardware and can support more powerful applications than Windows 9x or DOS. The increased overhead of this OS only benefits you when hardware and applications software are hefty enough to take advantage of the more powerful OS.

User Mode

The purpose of the subsystems in user mode is to interface with the user and with applications; the tools you view when running Windows NT are primarily running in user mode. In Figure 19-4, note the Win32 subsystem, which is probably the most important user mode subsystem because it manages all 32-bit programs and provides an environment for these programs, including the user interface (such as the one for Explorer). (Remember from earlier chapters that 32-bit programs are programs written for protected mode using 32-bit code.) The Win32 security subsystem provides logon to the system and other security functions, including privileges for file access. Other subsystems might or might not be running while the Win32 subsystem and security subsystem are running.

All applications relate to Windows NT by way of the Win32 subsystem, either directly or indirectly. Figure 19-5 shows how various programs that run under Windows NT interact with subsystems. For instance, each DOS application resides in its own NTVDM. An **NTVDM (NT virtual DOS machine)** is a carefully controlled environment that Windows NT provides in which a DOS application can only interface with one subsystem and cannot relate to anything outside the system. All the 16-bit Windows 3.x applications reside in a **Win16 on Win32 (WOW)** environment. Within the WOW, these 16-bit applications can communicate with one another, and they can communicate with the WOW, but that's as far as their world goes. Figure 19-5 shows three 16-bit Windows 3.x applications residing in a WOW that resides in one NTVDM. Because each DOS application expects to run as the only application on a PC, each has its own NTVDM.

19

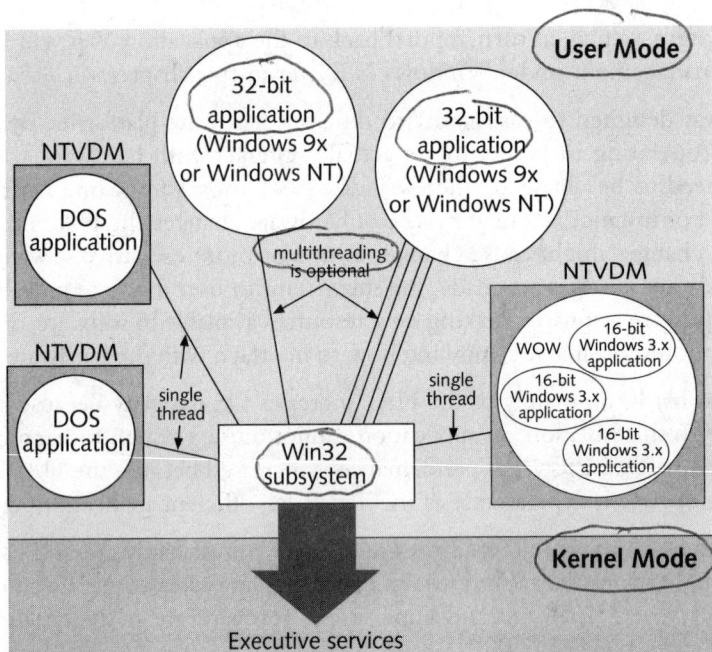

Figure 19-5 Environment subsystems in Windows NT user mode include NTVDMs for DOS and Windows 3.x applications and optional multithreading for 32-bit applications

You can see in Figure 19-5 that 32-bit applications do not require an NTVDM and can relate to the Win32 subsystem directly, because they are written to run in protected mode. The figure shows that 32-bit applications can also use a single line of communication (called single-threading) with the Win32 subsystem or can use multiple lines for interfacing (called **multithreading**) with the Win32 subsystem, depending upon what the process requests. A **thread** is a single task that the process requests from the kernel, such as the task of printing a file. A **process** is a program or group of programs that is running, together with the system resources assigned to it, such as memory addresses, environmental variables, and other resources. Sometimes a process is called an instance, such as when you say, "Open two instances of Internet Explorer." Technically, you are saying to open two Internet Explorer processes. An example of multithreading is Microsoft Word requesting that the subsystem read a large file from the hard drive while performing a print job at the same time. Single-threading happens when the application does not expect both processes to be performed at the same time but simply passes one request followed by another.

Kernel Mode

Remember that the kernel mode of Windows NT is the mode used by executive services and the HAL, which interface more directly with the hardware than do the subsystems operating in user mode. Figure 19-6 expands the information from Figure 19-4 to show several of executive services components operating in kernel mode. Most interaction with the hardware is done by executive services passing the request to the HAL. However, from the diagram, you see that executive services include device drivers, which have direct access to the hardware.

DEVICE DRIVER →

Figure 19-6 Components in the Windows NT kernel mode relate to subsystems in user mode and relate to hardware

Only kernel mode components can access hardware. However, in DOS, applications can access hardware resources directly, or they can use an API call to ask DOS to perform the task. In Windows NT, if a DOS application tried to directly access the printer port LPT1, Windows NT would shut down the DOS application. But if the DOS application tried to access the printer by passing a DOS API call to the Windows NT NTVDM, it would be allowed to proceed.

INSTALLING WINDOWS NT

Because Windows NT differs so fundamentally from Windows 9x, there is no automatic upgrade path from Windows 9x to Windows NT. When you change a PC from Windows 9x to Windows NT, you can install Windows NT in a different folder. No system settings in Windows 9x will be transferred to Windows NT. After Windows NT is installed, you must reinstall each application on the PC under Windows NT. Windows NT can be present as the only OS on a PC, or it can be installed on the same PC as Windows 9x. (How to set up this "dual boot" is coming up.)

19

The main reason that Windows 9x cannot be easily upgraded to Windows NT is that their registries are not compatible, which makes it difficult to transfer information from one to the other. (Remember that a registry is a database containing all configuration information for the OS. The Windows NT registry is not covered in detail in this chapter; you will learn more about it in Chapter 21.) Again, realize that Windows NT is not the next stepping stone beyond Windows 9x but is instead a new road altogether.

Before covering the installation process in detail, we'll look at two issues you need to consider before installing Windows NT: how to partition your hard drive and which file system to use.

Hard Drive Partitions

Windows NT assigns two different functions to hard drive partitions holding the OS (see Figure 19-7). The **system partition**, normally drive C, is the active partition of the hard drive. This is the partition that contains the OS boot record. Remember that the MBR looks to this OS boot record for the boot program as the first step in turning the PC over to an OS. The other partition, called the **boot partition**, is the partition where the Windows NT operating system is stored. The system partition and the boot partition can be the same partition, or they can be separate partitions. Windows NT is designed to use two partitions in this way so that the Windows system files do not have to be stored on the same partition that is used to boot the OS. Both partitions can be formatted with either FAT16 or NTFS. However, Windows 9x and DOS cannot read files formatted with NTFS. If you want these OSs to access this partition, you must use the FAT16 file system.

Figure 19-7   Two types of Windows NT/2000/XP hard drive partitions

 Don't be confused by the terminology here. It is really true that, according to Windows NT terminology, the Windows NT OS is on the boot partition, and the boot record is on the system partition, even though that might sound backward. The PC boots from the system partition and loads the Windows NT operating system from the boot partition.

Recall that Windows 9x, using Fdisk, can create two partitions, a primary partition and an extended partition. The primary partition contains drive C, and the extended partition can contain several volumes or logical drives. Also recall that each FAT16 volume can be no larger than 2 GB. Using Windows NT, you can have up to four partitions. The first partition must be a primary partition and, if it is the boot device, can have only a single drive C. There can be up to four primary partitions on the drive, each containing a single logical drive. However, one of the four partitions can be an extended partition, which means it can have several volumes or logical drives. Because of the way Windows NT uses the FAT, each FAT16 volume can be up to 4 GB.

A Choice of File Systems

Windows NT can work with two types of file systems: the FAT16 file system, which is used by Windows 9x and its predecessors, and the Windows NT file system (NTFS), which does not work with Windows 9x or DOS. Windows NT does not support FAT32. (Recall that FAT32 was introduced by Windows 95 OSR2 and uses 32 bits for each FAT entry.) Windows NT also does not support the High Performance File System (HPFS) used by OS/2. If a hard drive is using HPFS, use the Windows NT Convert.exe utility to convert an HPFS partition to an NTFS partition. This program can also convert a FAT16 partition to NTFS.

 Even though Windows NT 4.0 does not support FAT32, you can use third-party utility software packages, such as FAT32 for Windows NY 4.0 by Winternals (*www.winternals.com*) to manage the interface, making it possible for Windows NT to read from and write to FAT32.

The FAT16 file system uses three components to manage data on a logical drive: the FAT, directories, and data files. In contrast, the NTFS file system uses a database called the **master file table (MFT)** as its core component. The MFT tracks the contents of a logical drive using one or more rows in the table for each file or directory on the drive. As shown in Figure 19-8, the MFT contains in one record, or row, information about each file, including header information (abbreviated H in Microsoft documentation), standard information (SI) about the file (including date and time), filename (FN), security information about the file, called the security descriptor (SD), and data about the location of the file. Entries in the MFT are ordered alphabetically by filename to speed up a search for a file listed in the table. When a drive is formatted for NTFS, each cluster on the hard drive can range from 512 bytes on smaller disks to 4K on larger disks. Clusters are numbered sequentially by logical cluster numbers (LCN) from the beginning to the end of the disk.

Referring again to Figure 19-8, note that the data area in the MFT record is 2K for small hard drives but can be larger for larger hard drives. For small files, if the data can fit into the 2K area, the file, including its data, is fully contained within the MFT. For small files, all the cluster information for a file can fit into this one data area, including all the cluster numbers for the file. Each cluster number is stored in a 64-bit entry, compared to either 16 bits for FAT16 or 32 bits for FAT32.

If the file is moderately large and the data does not fit into the MFT, the data area in the MFT becomes an extended attribute (EA) of the file, which points to the location of the data. The data itself is moved outside the table to clusters called runs. The record in the MFT for this moderately large file contains pointers to these runs. Each data run, or cluster, assigned to the file is assigned a 64-bit virtual cluster number (VCN). The MFT maps the VCNs for the file onto the LCNs for the drive. This mapping is stored in the area of the MFT record that would have contained the data if the file had been small enough. If the file is so large that the pointers to all the VCNs cannot be contained in one MFT record, then additional MFT records are used. The first MFT record is called the base file record and holds the location of the other MFT records for this file.

19

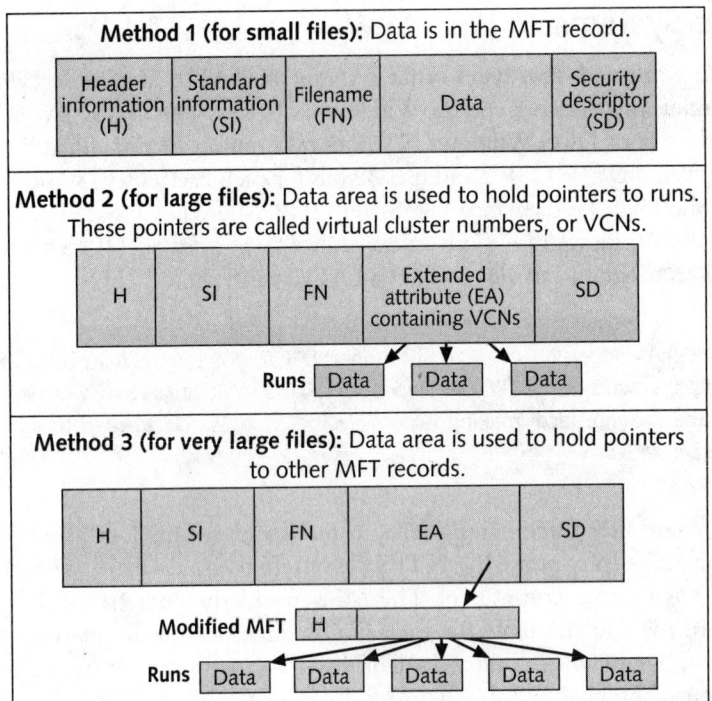

Figure 19-8   The Windows NT file system Master File Table uses three methods to store files, depending on the file size

Advantages of NTFS and FAT16

When choosing between the NTFS file system and the FAT16 file system, consider the advantages that NTFS offers over the FAT:

- NTFS is a recoverable file system. NTFS retains copies of its critical file system data and automatically recovers a failed file system, using this information the first time the disk is accessed after a file system failure.

- NTFS offers increased security over the FAT file system. Security is provided for each file, and auditing information about access to files is more complete.

- NTFS provides added security in the event you boot from floppy disks:
    - If the file system for the active partition of a PC is FAT, you can boot from a DOS or Windows 9x boot disk and bypass the Windows NT security logon. When you use NTFS, you can boot from a DOS or Windows 9x boot disk to an A:\> prompt, but you cannot access the hard drive. You can still boot the PC from Windows NT boot disks, but the Windows NT logon is required.
    - If you boot a PC using a DOS or Windows 9x boot disk, you will be able to access the hard drive of a Windows NT system that is using the FAT file system, but you cannot access an NTFS file system.

- If you boot a PC using the three Windows NT startup disks, you will only be able to access the NTFS file system if you provide an administrator account and password. Every Windows NT workstation has an **administrator account** by default. An administrator has rights and permissions to all computer software and hardware resources and is responsible for setting up other user accounts and assigning privileges to them.

- NTFS supports mirroring drives, meaning that two copies of data can be kept on two different drives to protect against permanent data loss in case of a hard drive crash. This feature makes the NTFS an important alternative for file servers.

- NTFS uses smaller cluster sizes than does FAT16, making more efficient use of hard drive space when small files are stored.

- NTFS supports large-volume drives. NTFS uses 64-bit cluster numbers, whereas FAT16 uses 16-bit cluster numbers. Because the number of bits assigned to hold each cluster number is so large, the cluster number itself can be a large number, and the table can accommodate very large drives with many clusters. Overall, NTFS is a more effective file system for drives over 1 GB and offers more robust drive compression, allowing compression of individual folders and files.

The advantages of the FAT file system over NTFS include:

- The FAT16 file system has less overhead than the NTFS file system and, therefore, works best for hard drives that are less than 500 MB.

- The FAT file system is compatible with Windows 9x and DOS operating systems. If you plan to use either DOS or Windows 9x on the same hard drive as Windows NT, use the FAT file system so that DOS and Windows 9x can access files used by Windows NT.

- In the event of a serious problem with Windows NT, if you are using FAT16 on the active partition of the drive, you can boot the PC from a DOS or Windows 9x startup disk, and gain access to the drive.

You can choose to have Windows NT use NTFS by directing it to convert the hard drive from FAT16 to NTFS or by having Windows NT partition a drive so that one partition of the drive uses the FAT format and the other uses the NTFS format. Windows NT allows you to format logical drives with either FAT16 or NTFS on the same extended partition.

Preparing to Install Windows NT

Before beginning the installation of Windows NT or upgrading from DOS or Windows 9x to Windows NT, you need to prepare for the installation. To determine if your hardware can support Windows NT, begin by searching the HCL. If a device on your system is not on the HCL, contact the manufacturer for a Windows NT driver. If no driver exists, you cannot use the device with Windows NT.

Be sure you have enough hard drive space. Windows NT requires about 120 MB of drive space to install itself, and more if the cluster size is large. In addition, a floppy drive and CD-ROM drive are required. For computers without a CD-ROM drive, Windows NT can be installed from a server over a network.

19

If you are using an Intel-based computer, you can use the **NT Hardware Qualifier (NTHQ)** program found on the Windows NT installation CD-ROM to determine if your system can handle Windows NT. To use Qualifier, boot from a disk onto which you have copied the program, and the utility will examine your system to determine if all hardware present qualifies for NT. Use the following directions to create and use the NT Hardware Qualifier:

Create the NTHQ bootable disk using any computer that has DOS or Windows 9x installed:

1. Insert a bootable disk in drive A.

2. To have Windows NT create the Hardware Qualifier disk, from a DOS prompt or from the Run dialog box of Windows 9x, enter this command substituting the drive letter of your CD-ROM drive:

   D:\Support\Hqtool\MakeDisk.bat

3. Using the computer that you want to install Windows NT, boot from the newly created disk. The following message will be displayed on your screen:

   ```
   Preparing NTHQ
   ```

   You can watch as NT tells you it is creating a RAM drive and copying files to it. Next a screen appears informing you that the log file the utility generates will take several minutes and will be written to the disk and saved as Nthq.txt.

4. Print the log file.

Figure 19-9 contains a portion of a sample report from the NTHQ. Note that the two devices listed at the top were not found in the NTHQ. To determine if these devices will work with Windows NT, check the latest HCL on the Microsoft Web site (*www.microsoft.com/hwtest*) or contact the manufacturer of each device.

```
Adapter Description: CIRRUS LOGIN PnP V34 MODEM
Adapter Device ID: CIR1000
Listed in Hardware Compatibility List: Not found-check the latest HCL

Adapter Description: OPL3-SAX Sound Board
Adapter Device ID: YMH0024
Listed in Hardware Compatibility List: Not found-check the latest HCL

Adapter Description: S3 Inc. 801/928/964
Listed in Hardware Compatibility List: Yes

Adapter Description: Adaptec AHA-1522
Listed in Hardware Compatibility List: Yes

Adapter Description: Sound Blaster Adapter or compatibles
Listed in Hardware Compatibility List: Yes

Adapter Description: Joystick/game port
Listed in Hardware Compatibility List: Yes
```

Figure 19-9   Sample log file from the NT Hardware Qualifier

The next sections give step-by-step instructions to install Windows NT as the only OS on a system, and as the second OS on a system that already has Windows 9x, creating a dual boot.

Installing Windows NT as the Only OS

Windows NT comes with three disks that contain a simplified version of Windows NT, enough to boot a PC. If the hard drive does not contain an OS, the installation begins by booting from these three disks. After Windows NT has loaded these three disks, it can access the CD-ROM drive, and installation continues from the CD. The program on the CD executed at that point is Winnt.exe, which is a 16-bit program. A faster version of Winnt.exe on the CD-ROM named Winnt32.exe, a 32-bit program, can, in certain situations, be used instead of Winnt.exe. Winnt32.exe can be run only after Windows NT has already been installed the first time; it is used to upgrade from an older version of NT to a new version or to reinstall a corrupted version and must be executed from within Windows.

The three startup disks can later be used to boot the PC if files on the hard drive become corrupted. You can also create a new set of bootable disks.

Follow these steps to install Windows NT as the only OS:

1. Insert the Windows NT CD in the CD-ROM drive, insert setup disk 1 into the floppy drive, and boot the PC. You will be asked to insert disk 2.

2. You see a *Welcome to Setup* message. You will be asked to insert disk 3. Press **Enter** to continue. Setup lists the mass storage devices it detected. Press **Enter** to continue.

3. The licensing agreement appears. Scroll to the bottom of the document and press **F8** to indicate your agreement and continue.

4. Setup lists hardware and software components it detected. Press **Enter** to continue.

5. Setup lists existing partitions and space available for creating new partitions. For example, if part of the drive has previously been formatted as drive C with 2047 MB of storage and the other part is still unpartitioned, the following information appears:

   ```
   2442 MB Disk 0 at Id 0 on bus 0 on atapi
   C: FAT 2047 MB
   Unpartitioned space 394 MB
   ```

   Setup is listing the spaces on the hard drive where it can install the OS, and asking you to make the choice. For this example, highlight **Unpartitioned Space**, and then press **C** to create a new partition.

6. Setup asks you for the size of the partition, creates it, informs you it will next format the partition, and prompts you to select a file system for the partition. It then lists the following file systems:

   ```
   Format the partition using the FAT file system
   Format the partition using the NTFS file system
   ```

   Select a file system and press **Enter**.

19

7. After the formatting is completed, Setup asks for this information:

```
Setup installs Windows NT files onto your hard disk.
Choose the location where you want those files to be
installed: \WINNT
```

The default choice is to install Windows NT in the \Winnt directory. Accept the default by pressing **Enter**.

8. Setup now asks for permission to examine the hard drive for corruption. You can either allow it by pressing **Enter** or skip this examination by pressing **Esc**.

9. Setup tells you that it is copying files to the hard drive. After the copying is complete, the following message appears:

```
Press ENTER to restart your computer.
```

When your computer restarts, Setup will continue.

10. Up to this point in the installation, all screens appeared to be DOS-like with little graphic user interface and no use of the mouse. When the PC reboots, you are using a true Windows GUI. The opening screen lists the three steps that Windows NT performs to complete the installation:

1) Gathering information about your computer

2) Installing Windows NT networking

3) Finishing Setup

The first item in the list is highlighted. Using the mouse, click **Next** to continue the installation.

11. Setup offers four options: Typical, Portable, Compact, and Custom. Select **Typical** and then click **Next** to continue.

12. Setup requests a name and the name of your organization. Provide them.

13. You are then asked to enter the CD key that identifies the copy of Windows NT being installed. Provide that.

14. Setup then requests a computer name. You are told that the name must be 15 characters or less and must be unique for your network. This computer name will later be used to identify this computer on a network. Enter the name, and then click **Next**.

15. Setup asks for the password for the administrator account. Administrators have full privileges on the workstation. Users have fewer privileges, depending on what the administrator assigns them. If other users who will not have administrator privileges will be using this workstation, or if you are concerned about security at this PC, enter a password, then enter it again to confirm it. If you are the sole user of this PC and security is not an issue, you do not need to enter a password. Just press **Enter**.

16. Setup gives you the option to create an Emergency Repair Disk (ERD, discussed later in this chapter). Select **Yes** to create the Emergency Repair Disk, and then click **Next** to continue.

17. Setup gives you the option to choose what components to install. Since you can later easily install components not installed during the installation, choose **Install the most common components**.

18. Setup returns to the opening Windows NT setup screen (see Step 11) and continues with Installing Windows NT networking. Click **Next** to continue.

19. The choices presented are:

    Do not connect this computer to a network at this time.
    This computer will participate on a network:
      Wired to the network:
        Your computer is connected to the network by an ISDN Adapter or Network Adapter.
      Remote access to the network:
        Your computer uses a modem to remotely connect to the network.

    For this example, choose **Do not connect the computer to a network at this time**, and then click **Next** to continue.

20. Setup returns to the opening screen (see Step 11). Click **Finish** to finish Setup. You are asked to select the date and time from the Date/Time Properties sheet. Click **Close**.

21. Setup automatically detects the correct display adapter. You can change any options on the Display Properties sheet and then click **OK**.

22. Setup requests that you insert a blank disk labeled Emergency Repair Disk. Insert a blank disk, and then click **OK**. Setup creates the repair disk.

23. You are instructed to remove the CD and disk from the drives and restart the PC. The installation is done.

 TIP   If you are having problems with Windows NT detecting your hard drive, the problem might be out-of-date system BIOS. Try flashing BIOS and then attempting the Windows NT installation again.

Installing Windows NT as the Second OS on the Hard Drive

Installing Windows NT on a hard drive to create a dual boot begins differently, but is otherwise the same as installing Windows NT as the only OS. The Windows NT installation files are stored in the \I386 directory on the CD-ROM drive. If hard drive space is plentiful, you can copy the contents of the \I386 directory and its subdirectories to the hard drive and perform the installation from there, which is faster because access to the hard drive is faster than access to the CD-ROM drive. If the computer is connected to a

19

network, the contents of the \I386 directory can be copied to a network server, and the Winnt.exe program can be executed from the server to install Windows NT on the PC, if certain conditions exist. (Installations from servers are not covered in this chapter.)

Remember that Windows NT can coexist on the same PC with either Windows 9x or DOS. The ability to boot from either Windows NT or another OS, such as Windows 9x or DOS, is called a **dual boot**. In a dual boot arrangement, the system partition must be FAT rather than NTFS, so that the non-NT OS (Windows 9x or DOS) can read it. When Windows 9x is used for a dual boot, the Windows 9x Msdos.sys file has the multiboot configuration entry, BootMulti=1. The main reason for having a dual boot is to accommodate legacy hardware or software that will not work under Windows NT.

> Remember that Windows NT cannot access a FAT32 drive without third-party software. If you are using Windows 98 with FAT32 and want to create a dual boot with Windows NT, first convert to FAT16 or use third-party software to manage the Windows NT and FAT32 interface. Otherwise, Windows NT will not be able to access data on the FAT32 volume. To convert from FAT32 to FAT16, use a third-party utility such as Partition Magic.

Windows NT resides on the boot partition, which can also be formatted for the FAT16 file system and can share the same partition with the other OS or reside on a second partition, such as drive D. You can format this second partition with either FAT or NTFS. If drive D is NTFS, Windows 9x cannot read any data stored on that drive. If drive D is a FAT16 partition, either OS can read data from either drive.

After both operating systems are installed, a **boot loader menu** appears, asking which OS to boot. The disadvantages of a dual boot are that application software cannot be shared between the two OSs; you must install applications in each OS. Also, you must reboot the PC to move from one OS to the other.

To install Windows NT with Windows 9x loaded, insert the Windows NT installation CD in the drive. If the PC autodetects the CD, you see the Windows NT opening screen. Click Windows NT Setup. If the PC does not autodetect the CD, click Start, Run and enter this command in the Run dialog box substituting the drive letter of your CD-ROM drive for D: D:\I386\Winnt.exe. If you want a dual boot, do not choose to store Windows NT in the C:\Windows folder because this will overwrite Windows 9x.

After the installation is complete, when the PC reboots, it detects two OSs, and shows a startup menu (called the boot loader menu), giving you the choice between Windows NT Workstation Version 4.0 and Microsoft Windows (Windows 95 or 98). Select Windows NT Workstation version 4.0, which then loads.

After a Windows NT installation is done, access the Internet and download and install any updates, service packs, and patches from the Microsoft Web site.

SUPPORTING WINDOWS NT

Recall that Windows NT manages devices, programs, and system resources more efficiently than Windows 9x in many cases and that Windows NT was designed to work with networks and to provide greater security. This section discusses supporting Windows NT, including information on its architecture, how to install hardware and software, and how to handle networking with Windows NT. You will also learn about supporting legacy applications and constructing user profiles for security.

Memory in Windows NT

As you learned in Chapter 16, managing memory under DOS and Windows 9x can be complicated because of having to deal with conventional, upper, and extended memory for backward-compatibility. Windows NT eliminates that complexity, because memory is simply memory; in other words, memory addresses are all used the same way. It also loses some backward-compatibility.

The Windows NT memory management model is illustrated in Figure 19-10, which shows the object-oriented approach to memory management. The application or device driver only says, "I want memory." It can not say to Windows NT which physical memory or which memory addresses it wants, or even the range of addresses that it wants to fall within. Windows NT uses its virtual memory manager to interface between the application or driver and the physical and virtual memory that it controls. Memory is allocated in 4K segments called **pages**. Applications and devices that are written for Windows NT only know how many pages they have. The virtual memory manager takes care of the rest. It is free to store these pages in RAM or on the hard drive in the swap file named **Pagefile.sys** (see Figure 19-10).

19

Figure 19-10   Windows NT memory management

Installing Hardware and Software

Hardware and software are installed using the Windows NT Control Panel (see Figure 19-11), which looks like, and works in a similar way to, that of Windows 9x (which you saw in earlier chapters). With both hardware and software installations, changes are made to the registry. We next look at examples of each, including how to manage legacy software.

Figure 19-11   The Windows NT Control Panel

 TIP Windows NT does not have a Device Manager. When installing and troubleshooting hardware, look for individual icons in the Control Panel to manage hardware devices. For a detailed report of the system configuration, use the WinMSD command. At a command prompt enter `WinMSD/a/f`. The command creates the report in the current directory.

Installing Hardware Devices

Windows NT builds its list of available hardware devices each time it is booted. This list is not permanently kept in the registry. However, when a new hardware device is installed, device driver information is kept in the registry. New hardware devices are installed from the Control Panel because Windows NT does not support Plug and Play and therefore does not have an Add New Hardware Wizard that automatically launches at startup as does Windows 9x. The steps below describe the installation of a sound card, because this installation is typical of many hardware devices.

1. To install a sound card, access the **Control Panel** and double-click the **Multimedia** icon. The Multimedia Properties dialog box is displayed.

2. Click the **Devices** tab to see a list of multimedia devices.

3. Select **Audio Devices**, and then click the **Add** button. The Add dialog box opens. You can either select a device driver from the list or click Unlisted or Updated Driver to install your own device driver from disk or CD-ROM.

4. If you choose to install your own driver, click **Unlisted or Updated Driver**, and then click **OK**. The Install Driver dialog box is displayed, asking for the location of the driver. As the example shown in Figure 19-12 shows, the vendor-provided driver is selected. Several versions of the driver (for each of the OSs supported) are located in directories on the CD-ROM that comes with the sound card.

Figure 19-12   When installing a device driver, you can use a driver provided by Windows NT or one from the device vendor

5. In the example CD, the location for the driver is E:\nt\. Enter the path, and then click **OK** to continue the installation. If Windows NT already has the driver you are installing, the OS gives you the choice to use the driver provided by the vendor or the Windows NT driver.

6. The driver is copied to the hard drive, then the hardware setup dialog box is displayed, as seen in Figure 19-13. The suggested I/O address, IRQ, and DMA channel are selected, but you can change these values if you are aware of a conflict. Otherwise, leave the values as suggested and click **OK** to complete the installation.

7. The Windows NT registry is then updated, and you are asked to restart the PC so the changes to the registry can take effect.

19

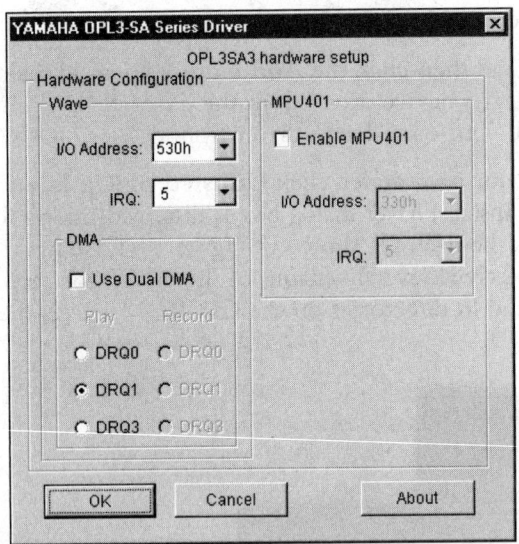

Figure 19-13 Windows NT suggests a hardware setup for the new device

8. Install the CD Player component of Windows NT to use the new sound card. As with many devices, software is necessary to use the sound card. The next step is to double-click the Add/Remove Programs icon of the Control Panel and install the CD Player component of Windows NT in order to use the sound card to play audio CDs. This installation window works just as with Windows 9x.

This example is typical of many hardware installations. The Control Panel was used to install the device driver, and you saw how Windows NT suggests the hardware setup resources to use. Next time the PC boots, the registry tells the **Ntldr (NT Loader)** program to load the sound card device driver. (The Ntldr file is the initially executed Windows NT OS file and is similar to Io.sys in DOS and Windows 9x.) As the driver loads, it looks to the registry for the list of resources that it will use.

The software to use the CD player is also installed from the Control Panel. This information is now kept in the registry to be used each time the OS loads. The OS uses this registry information to provide the CD Player option under Start, Accessories, Multimedia.

Installing Software

Software is installed from the Control Panel using the Add/Remove Programs icon. Installation works very much the same way as under Windows 9x. Access the Control Panel by clicking Start, pointing to Settings, and clicking Control Panel. From the Control Panel, double-click the Add/Remove Programs icon. The Add/Remove Programs Properties dialog box opens. Any software that installs with a Setup.exe or Install.exe program can be installed using this dialog box. Click Install, and the dialog box requests the location of the setup program.

To add new components to Windows NT that were not installed when Windows NT was originally installed, click the Windows NT Setup tab of the Add/Remove Programs Properties dialog box. You see a list of all of the Windows NT components. From this list, you can choose to install new components or to uninstall components that are already installed.

Even though it would be convenient if all software running under Windows NT were written in the newer 32-bit code used by Windows 9x and Windows NT, this doesn't always happen. As explained earlier, Windows NT makes provisions for running DOS applications by creating a separate NTVDM for each application, so that each program can run in its native environment. Windows 16-bit applications can run in individual NTVDMs, or several 16-bit Windows applications can run in the same NTVDM so they can share resources. How to do this is discussed next.

Windows NT Networking

One of the main reasons Windows NT is chosen as an OS is its strong networking features. Remember that there are two versions of Windows NT: Windows NT Workstation and Windows NT Server. In a general PC environment, a workstation is a desktop PC that both accesses a network and works as a standalone PC. In the most general sense, a server is a computer that contains data, software, and security validation files that are shared simultaneously by workstations on the network. A server on the network is generally not also a workstation. Even though it may have a keyboard and monitor connected to it, these are generally only used by a network administrator to administer and monitor the network; the server is solely dedicated to serving the network.

All the functionality offered by Windows NT Workstation is available with Windows NT Server. The primary difference between the two is that Windows NT Server offers the additional functionality of administering and monitoring the network from this centralized location. However, either OS can be configured to work as one node in a workgroup or as one node on a domain. A **workgroup** is a logical group of computers and users that share resources (Figure 19-14), where the control of administration, resources, and security is distributed throughout the network. A Windows NT **domain** is a group of networked computers that share a centralized directory database of user account information and security for the entire set of computers (Figure 19-15). A workgroup uses a peer-to-peer networking model, and a domain uses a client/server networking model.

When a group of computers is connected to share resources, you can configure these computers as a network using the workgroup model (the network is administered from individual PCs in a workgroup), or use the domain model (the network is administered from a centralized location in the domain). Resources including data, software, and printers can be shared using either model.

19

Figure 19-14   A Windows NT workgroup

Figure 19-15   A Windows NT domain

Also, as you learn about workgroups and domains, remember that in either case, the group of computers is a logical group, not a geographical group. A workgroup of computers can be in a single building, or it can include PCs in other cities. Distance makes no difference, as long as there is networked connectivity either over phone lines or by other means. PCs are grouped together to share resources. For example, a sales staff member might need to share a marketing database, and the accounting staff of a company might need to share a journals database. People in both groups are spread over several cities. Members of the sales staff make up the sales workgroup, and members of the accounting staff make up the accounting workgroup, so each user can access shared resources within the appropriate group.

When you implement Windows NT Workstation, it is often necessary to set users up in a workgroup with other PCs using Windows NT or Windows 9x and to configure the PCs to be members of a domain controlled by a Windows NT server. Understanding the concepts of workgroups and domains and how they are managed is the first step in learning how to support them.

Using Workgroups and Domains

In a workgroup, every computer has its own directory database of user accounts and security policies. Each computer in a workgroup manages the accounts on that computer for other users and computers that want to access information on it. If you are a member of a workgroup and want to allow another user on another PC to access files on your PC, you must establish an account for that user. The information about that account is kept only on your PC.

A workgroup can be made up of computers that use either Windows NT Workstation or Windows NT Server. However, PCs that have Windows NT Server installed must be configured as standalone units. A workgroup does not require a Windows NT server to be present. Workgroups have no centralized account management or security. Workgroups are generally used for a small group of workstations, and the PC support person usually manages each user account on each PC in the workgroup. A domain is used for a large number of workstations, and security for the domain shifts to a business-wide or enterprise function of a network administrator controlling security from a single console.

In a Windows NT domain, a network administrator manages access to the network through a centralized database. In Figure 19-15, you see the possible different components of a Windows NT domain. Every domain has a **primary domain controller (PDC)**, which stores and controls a database of (1) user accounts, (2) group accounts, and (3) computer accounts. This database is called the directory database or the **security accounts manager (SAM)** database.

An administrator logged on to any workstation or server on the domain can update the directory database by accessing the PDC, but the domain can have only one PDC. One or more read-only backup copies of the directory database can be kept on other computers. Each computer with a backup of the directory database is called a **backup domain controller (BDC)**. A system can be set up so that whenever the database on the PDC is updated, copies are written to each BDC; this is called replication or automated duplication. In Figure 19-15, there are two BDCs, each keeping a copy of the directory database. BDCs use their copy of the SAM database to authenticate users as they log on, thereby relieving the PDC of the burden of authentication functions. This sharing of functions improves performance in domains with many (more than 1000) workstations.

19

Workstations on the domain are in the lower part of Figure 19-15. A Windows NT network can contain these OSs functioning in these ways:

- Windows NT Server functioning as a PDC, a BDC, or as a standalone server (a server on the network that has no domain controller functions)

- Windows NT Workstation functioning as a workstation or as a standalone server

- Windows 9x, Windows 2000 Professional, or Windows XP Professional acting as clients on the network.

UNDERSTANDING THE WINDOWS NT BOOT PROCESS

Understanding the boot process and making changes to it are critical when supporting Windows NT. (Windows 2000 and Windows XP use this same boot process.) In this section you will learn what happens during the boot and in the next section you will learn how to solve boot problems.

The following is a look behind the scenes with a description of each step in the boot process. As you read, refer to Table 19-1 for an outline of the boot sequence for Intel-based computers.

1. *BIOS executes POST.* First, startup BIOS performs POST, which happens just as it would regardless of the OS present. After POST, BIOS turns to the hard drive to load an OS. Remember from earlier chapters that BIOS looks for the partition information at the beginning of the hard drive.

2. *BIOS executes the MBR program.* The first thing in the partition information that BIOS needs is the MBR (Master Boot Record) containing the master boot program. Remember from earlier chapters that the master boot program is the very first thing written in the first sector of a hard drive. The master boot program is followed by the partition table itself, and both are stored in the master boot sector. BIOS executes this master boot program, which examines the partition table, looking for the location of the active partition on the drive, and then turns to the first sector of the active partition to find and load the program in the boot sector of that active partition. So far in the boot process, nothing is different between Windows NT and other OSs.

Table 19-1 Steps in the Intel-based CPU boot process

Description	Step
POST (power-on self test) is executed.	1. Performed by startup BIOS
MBR (Master Boot Record) is loaded, and the master boot program within the MBR is run. (The master boot program is at the very beginning of the hard drive, as part of the partition table information. The program searches for and loads the OS boot record of the active partition.)	2. Performed by startup BIOS

Table 19-1   Steps in the Intel-based CPU boot process (continued)

Description	Step
The boot sector from active partition is loaded, and program in this boot sector is run.	3. Performed by MBR program
Ntldr (NT Loader) file is loaded and run.	4. Performed by boot sector program
The processor is changed from real mode to flat memory mode, in which 32-bit code can be executed.	5. Performed by Windows NT loader
Minifile system drivers (described below) are started so files can be read.	6. Performed by Windows NT loader
Read Boot.ini file and build the boot loader menu described in the file. (This menu is discussed later in this chapter.)	7. Performed by Windows NT loader
If the user chooses Windows NT, then run Ntdetect.com to detect hardware present; otherwise, run Bootsect.dos.	8. Performed by Windows NT loader
Ntldr reads information from the Registry about device drivers and loads them. Also loads the Hal.dll and Ntoskrml.exe.	9. Performed by Windows NT loader
Ntldr passes control to Ntoskrml.exe; load is complete.	10. Last step performed by the loader

3. *The MBR program executes the OS boot program.* Remember that when DOS or Windows 9x boots, the OS boot sector contains the name of the initial OS load program, Io.sys. When Windows NT is installed, it edits this boot sector of the active partition, instructing it to load the Windows NT program Ntldr at startup, instead of Io.sys. (It does this even when the PC is configured for a dual boot.)

4. *The boot program executes Ntldr.* With the execution of Ntldr, Windows NT then starts its boot sequence. This program is responsible for loading Windows NT and performing several chores to complete the loading process. It then passes off control to the OS.

5. *Ntldr changes the processor mode and loads a file system.* Up to this point, the CPU has been processing in real mode; every program had complete access to system resources. Windows NT does not process in real mode. Ntldr is a 32-bit program and begins by changing the CPU mode from real mode to a 32-bit mode called **32-bit flat memory mode**, in order to run its 32-bit code. Next a temporary, simplified file system called the **minifile system** is started so that Ntldr can read files from either a FAT or an NTFS file system.

6. *Ntldr reads and loads the boot loader menu.* Ntldr then is able to read the Boot.ini file, a hidden text file that contains information needed to build the boot loader menu discussed earlier. The menu is displayed, and the user can make a selection or, after the preset time expires, the default selection is used.

7. *Ntldr uses Ntdetect.com.* If Ntldr is to load Windows NT as the OS, Ntldr runs the program Ntdetect.com, which checks the hardware devices present and passes the information back to Ntldr. This information will later be used to update the Windows NT registry concerning the last-known good hardware profile used.

19

8. *Ntldr loads the OS and device drivers.* Ntldr then loads Ntoskrnl.exe, Hal.dll, and the System hive. The System hive is a portion of the Windows NT registry that includes hardware information that is now used to load the proper device drivers for the hardware present. You will learn more about this System hive in Chapter 21.

9. *Ntldr passes control to Ntoskrnl.exe.* Ntldr then passes control to Ntoskrnl.exe, and the boot sequence is complete.

10. *An operating system other than Windows NT is chosen.* If a selection was made from the boot loader menu to load an OS other than Windows NT, such as DOS or Windows 9x, Ntldr does not load Ntdetect.com or complete the remaining chores to load Windows NT. Instead, Ntldr loads and passes control to the program Bootsect.dos, which is responsible for loading the other OS.

 TIP When repairing a corrupted hard drive, a support person often copies files from one PC to another. However, the Bootsect.dos file contains information from the partition table for a particular hard drive and cannot be copied from another PC.

The files needed to successfully boot Windows NT are listed in Table 19-2. (In the table, references to \winnt_root follow Microsoft documentation conventions and mean the name of the directory where Windows NT is stored, which is \Winnt by default.)

Table 19-2 Files needed to successfully boot Windows NT

File	Location
Ntldr	Root directory of the system partition (usually C:\)
Boot.ini	Root directory of the system partition (usually C:\)
Bootsect.dos	Root directory of the system partition (usually C:\)
Ntdetect.com	Root directory of the system partition (usually C:\)
Ntbootdd.sys*	Root directory of the system partition (usually C:\)
Ntoskrnl.exe	\winnt_root\system32 directory of the boot partition
Hal.dll	\winnt_root\system32 directory of the boot partition
System	\winnt_root\system32\config of the boot partition
Device drivers	\winnt_root\system32\drivers of the boot partition

*Ntbootdd.sys is only used with a SCSI boot device.

TROUBLESHOOTING WINDOWS NT

In this section, you will learn about troubleshooting Windows NT, including the boot process and some diagnostic tools that you can use for maintenance and troubleshooting. Many of the general troubleshooting tips you learned in earlier chapters apply to Windows NT as well. Since you have just learned about the Windows NT boot process, we will begin this section with a discussion of troubleshooting that process.

Troubleshooting the Windows NT Boot Process

Listed below are the things you can do and the order in which you should do them to troubleshoot a failed Windows NT boot. You will learn more about these tools and processes in this section. Remember that Windows NT does not have a safe mode as does Windows 9x and several of the useful troubleshooting utilities of Windows 9x that you learned about in the last chapter are missing from Windows NT.

To recover from a failed Windows NT boot, do the following:

- If the Windows NT startup menu appears (it will if it thinks there is a problem you need to know about), use the Last Known Good configuration to return to the last registry values that allowed for a successful boot. Any configuration changes since the last good boot will be lost.

- If you cannot boot from the hard drive, boot using the three boot disks that came with the OS. If you don't have these three disks, you can create them on another PC that is working. Check for corrupted boot and system files that you can replace.

- Boot from the three disks and select the option "To repair a damaged Windows NT version 4.0 installation."

- Try reinstalling Windows NT into the same folder it currently uses. Tell the Setup program this is an upgrade.

- As a last resort, if you are using the NTFS file system and you must recover data on the hard drive, move the hard drive to another system that is running Windows NT and install the drive as a secondary drive. You might then be able to recover the data.

Last Known Good Configuration

Each time Windows NT boots and the first logon is made with no errors, the OS saves a copy of the hardware configuration from the registry, which is called the Last Known Good configuration. (All hardware configuration sets stored in the registry, including the Last Known Good are called control sets.) The next time the PC boots, if an error occurs, it can use the Last Known Good configuration.

The key in the registry that contains the Last Known Good configuration is:

```
HKEY_LOCAL_MACHINE\HARDWARE
```

If Windows NT detects the possibility of a problem, it adds the Last Known Good option to the Windows NT startup menu. You can select this Last Known Good option to revert back to the control set that was used for the last good boot. For example, if you install a new device driver, restart Windows NT, and find that the system hangs, you can use the Last Known Good option to revert back to the previous configuration.

19

Because the configuration information is not saved to the Last Known Good control set until after the logon, if you are having trouble with the boot, don't attempt to log on. Doing so will cause the Last Known Good to be replaced by the current control set, which might have errors.

For example, if you have installed a new video driver and you restart Windows, but the screen is very difficult to read, don't log on. Instead, press the reset button to reboot the PC. When given the choice, select Last Known Good from the startup menu.

To prevent hard drive corruption, if you are having problems booting Windows NT, wait for all disk activity to stop before pressing the reset button or turning off the PC, especially if you are using the FAT file system.

If you accidentally disable a critical device, Windows NT decides to revert to the Last Known Good for you. You are not provided with a menu choice.

Reverting to the Last Known Good causes the loss of any changes made to the hardware configuration since the Last Known Good was saved. Therefore, it is wise to make one change at a time to the hardware configuration and reboot after each change. That way, if problems during booting are encountered, only the most recent change is lost. When installing several hardware devices, install them one at a time, rebooting each time.

 TIP If you are having problems booting in Windows NT, don't log on, because if you do, you will overwrite your previous Last Known Good.

Windows NT Boot Disks

With Windows 9x and DOS, any single disk could be formatted as a boot disk or system disk. Windows NT is different. It requires three disks to hold enough of Windows NT to boot. However, formatting a single disk just to hold data or software can be done using Explorer.

When a disk is formatted by Windows NT, the boot sector is written to boot the Ntldr program instead of Io.sys as in DOS and Windows 9x. To format a disk, use Windows NT Explorer. Right-click the *3½ Floppy (A:)* line in Explorer and choose Format from the shortcut menu. Figure 19-16 is displayed.

The only file system available for a floppy disk is FAT. Note in the figure that there is no option to make the disk a system disk or boot disk. If you try to boot from a disk that has been formatted by Windows NT, this error message appears:

```
BOOT: Couldn't find NTLDR
Please insert another disk
```

Windows NT comes with a set of three disks that are initially used to boot the machine before the installation continues from the CD-ROM. After the OS is installed, you can use these disks in an emergency to boot the OS. These three disks come with Windows NT, but you can make extra sets. The set of boot disks is the same no matter what PC you are using. The disks contain no special information about your system.

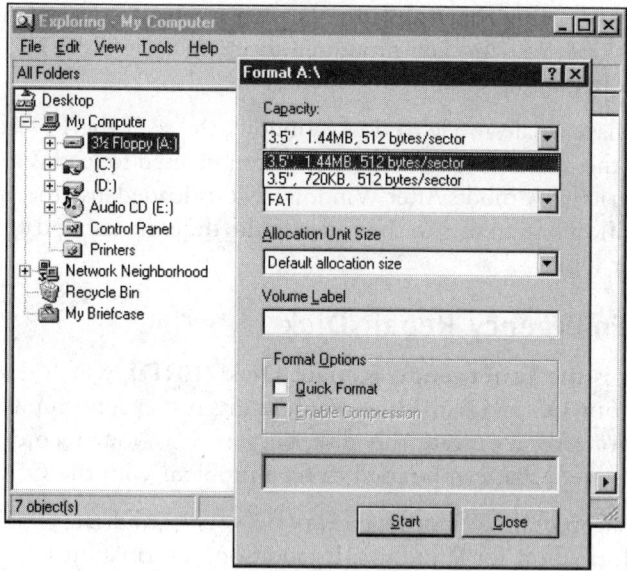

Figure 19-16   Windows NT dialog box used to format a disk

If the original three disks to boot Windows NT become corrupted or are lost, you can make extra copies using Winnt32.exe if you are running Windows NT, or using Winnt.exe if you are running another OS, such as DOS or Windows 9x. You do not have to be working on the PC where you intend to use the disks in order to make them, since the disks don't contain unique information for a specific PC.

Creating Windows NT Boot Disks   Proceed as follows to create boot disks using Windows NT:

1. Click **Start**, **Run** and then enter the path and name of the program with the /ox parameters. These parameters say to only create the set of three disks, without performing a complete installation. Note the E:\I386\winnt32.exe/ox entry in the Run dialog box of Figure 19-17. This is the command line from within Windows NT used to create the disks when drive E contains the Windows NT installation CD.

Figure 19-17   Using Winnt32.exe to create a set of boot disks

19

2. The program asks for the location of the installation files. In this example, you would enter E:\I386. You are then prompted to insert three disks. The program creates the disks beginning with disk 3, then 2, then 1.

Windows NT does not have a safe mode as does Windows 9x, so if the PC later cannot boot Windows NT from the hard drive, these three disks can be used to load Windows NT, which loads using a generic VGA mode. After Windows NT is loaded, use the Emergency Repair Disk to restore critical system files to their state at the time the last update was made to the Emergency Repair Disk.

The Windows NT Emergency Repair Disk

A fourth important disk is the **Emergency Repair Disk (ERD)**, which does contain information unique to your OS and hard drive. You are given the opportunity to create the disk during installation. Always create this disk, because it is your record of critical information about your system that can be used to fix a problem with the OS.

The ERD enables restoration of the Windows registry on your hard drive, which contains all the configuration information for Windows. In addition, information that is used to build a command window to run DOS-like commands is also included on the disk. The files on the ERD are listed in Table 19-3. Files stored on the ERD are also written to the hard drive during the installation process. Using Explorer, you can see the files listed in the \winnt_root\repair folder.

Table 19-3   Files on the Windows NT Emergency Repair Disk

File	Description
Setup.log	A read-only, hidden system file that is used to verify the files installed on a system
System._	A compressed file containing part of the registry
Sam._	A compressed file containing some of the security part of the registry
Security._	A compressed file containing some of the security part of the registry
Software._	A compressed file containing software information in the registry
Default._	A compressed file containing part of the registry
Config.nt	The Windows NT version of Config.sys used in creating a command window
Autoexec.nt	The Windows NT version of Autoexec.bat
Ntuser.da_	A compressed file containing information about authorized users of the system

After the installation, you can create a new ERD or update the current one by using the Rdisk.exe utility in the \winnt_root\system32 folder. You should update the disk any time you make any major changes to the system, for example, you install hardware or software. To use the Rdisk.exe utility, click Start, Run, and then either click Browse or enter the path to the utility. Add the /S option so that the utility also updates the registry.

If Windows NT is stored on drive D, the command line is:

D:\WINNT\System32\rdisk.exe /s

First, files are updated in the *winnt_root*\repair directory, then you are given the opportunity to create a new ERD.

Using the Boot Disks and the ERD to Recover from a Failed Boot

In the case of problems with the OS, there are several things you can do to attempt to load Windows NT from the hard drive, which are beyond the scope of this book. However, in the case of a hard drive failure, you can boot from the set of three boot disks that come with the Windows NT CD or that you made using either Winnt.exe or Winnt32.exe. The Windows NT programs on these disks may also request that you provide the ERD. Insert the first boot disk and reboot. You will be prompted to insert disk 2, followed by disk 3. The Setup menu in Figure 19-18 is then displayed. Select the option to repair a damaged installation by pressing R and follow directions on screen.

```
Windows NT Workstation Setup

Welcome to Setup.
The Setup program for the Microsoft(R) Windows NT(TM) OS version 4.0
prepares Windows NT to run on your computer.

     *To learn more about Windows NT Setup before continuing, press F1
     *To set up Windows NT now, press ENTER
     *To repair a damaged Windows NT version 4.0 installation, press R
     *To quit Setup without installing Windows NT, press F3
```

Figure 19-18   Windows NT Workstation Setup menu

CHAPTER SUMMARY

- Windows NT comes in two versions, Windows NT Workstation and Windows NT Server. Both versions can operate on standalone PCs or on a network, but Windows NT Server can also operate as a controller in a network domain.

- Windows NT can operate using two different file systems: FAT16 and NTFS. NTFS offers more security and power than does FAT16, but FAT16 is backward-compatible with older OSs.

- A PC can be configured to dual boot between Windows NT and another OS such as DOS or Windows 9x.

- Windows NT works on different platforms and with different software because of its modular approach to interfacing with both.

- The two architectural modes of Windows NT are user mode and kernel mode. Kernel mode is further divided into two components: executive services and the hardware abstraction layer (HAL).

- A process is a unique instance of a program running together with the program resources and other programs it may use.

- An NTVDM provides a DOS-like environment for DOS and Windows 3.x applications.

19

- Windows 3.x 16-bit applications run in a WOW.
- A workgroup is a group of computers and users sharing resources. Each computer maintains a list of users and their rights on that particular PC.
- A domain is a group of computers and users that is managed by a centralized controlling database on a computer called the primary domain controller (PDC).
- The NT Hardware Qualifier is on the Windows NT CD-ROM and can be used to survey the hardware devices on a PC to determine if they qualify to run under the Windows NT OS.
- Four disks are important in recovering from a failed Windows NT boot. Three disks are required to boot Windows NT, and an Emergency Repair Disk (ERD) can be prepared to recover critical system files on the hard drive.

KEY TERMS

32-bit flat memory mode
administrator account
backup domain controller (BDC)
boot loader menu
boot partition
domain
dual boot
Emergency Repair Disk (ERD)
executive services
kernel mode

master file table (MFT)
minifile system
multithreading
NTHQ (NT Hardware Qualifier)
Ntldr (NT Loader)
NTVDM (NT virtual DOS machine)
Pagefile.sys
pages
POSIX (Portable Operating System Interface)

primary domain controller (PDC)
process
security accounts manager (SAM)
subsystems
system partition
thread
user mode
VDD (virtual device driver)
workgroup
WOW (Win16 on Win32)

20

INSTALLING AND USING
WINDOWS 2000 PROFESSIONAL

> **In this chapter, you will learn:**
> ♦ About the architecture of Windows 2000
> ♦ How to install Windows 2000
> ♦ How to use Windows 2000
> ♦ How to install hardware and software under Windows 2000

Windows 2000 is the culmination of the evolution of Microsoft operating systems from the 16-bit DOS operating system to a true 32-bit, module-oriented operating system, complete with desktop functionality, user-friendly Plug and Play installations, and other easy-to-use features. Windows 2000 comes in several versions, some designed for the desktop and others designed for high-end servers. Windows 2000 Server, Advanced Server, and Datacenter Server are network server OSs, upgrades from Windows NT Server. Windows 2000 Professional is the next generation of Windows NT Workstation, and has become popular as a corporate desktop OS. This chapter focuses on Windows 2000 Professional. While taking advantage of the user-friendly features of Windows 98, Windows 2000 is founded on the technology of Windows NT and is committed to leaving behind the compromises that Windows 9x made with legacy hardware and application software. In addition, Windows 2000 introduces many new features, including a new approach to managing hard drive storage, called dynamic storage. In this chapter, you will learn about the architecture of Windows 2000, how to install the OS as well as hardware and applications with it, and how to use it.

WINDOWS 2000 ARCHITECTURE

In Chapter 19, you learned about the architecture of Windows NT, which Windows 2000 uses as well. You can also refer back to the survey of operating systems in Chapter 15, which described some of the differences between Windows NT and Windows 2000. This section looks at these differences in more detail.

As you learned in the last chapter, Windows NT does not support Plug and Play or the FAT32 file system and does not have a safe mode or Device Manager. Windows 2000 supports all of these.

New Features

A feature new to Windows 2000 is **Active Directory**, a directory database service that allows for a single point of administration for all shared resources on a network. Active Directory can track the location of files; peripheral devices, including printers, scanners, and other hardware; databases; Web sites; users; services; and so forth. It uses a locating method similar to that used by the Internet. Windows 2000 Server versions provide Active Directory, and Windows 2000 Professional acts as an Active Directory client, or user of the directory.

Recall from Chapter 19 that a Windows NT client/server network has one primary domain controller and may have one or more backup domain controllers. A Windows NT network can have no more than one primary domain controller, which maintains the only copy of the directory database that can be edited. When the directory database is changed, such as when a new user is added to the network, only the directory database on the primary domain controller is updated. The primary domain controller updates the directory databases on the backup domain controllers. With Windows 2000, a network can have any number of domain controllers, each keeping a copy of the directory that can be edited (see Figure 20-1). An administrator can update the directory on any one of these domain controllers, which will then communicate the change to the other domain controllers.

Figure 20-1   Windows 2000 allows for multiple domain controllers, each keeping a read/write copy of the domain database

When both Windows NT and Windows 2000 domain controllers are on the same network, conflicts can result because of the differences in the way the domain controllers work in each OS. For this reason, Windows 2000 runs in two modes: mixed mode and native mode. **Native mode** is used when no Windows NT domain controllers are present, and **mixed mode** is used when there is at least one Windows NT domain controller on the network. Mixed mode is necessary in a situation where a large network is being upgraded from Windows NT to Windows 2000 and some servers have received the upgrade but others have not. When installing Windows 2000 Server, the installer can choose mixed mode during the installation process and later migrate to native mode by using the Microsoft Management Console (MMC), which you will learn about in the next chapter. Once you have changed a domain to native mode, you cannot change it back to mixed mode.

Windows 2000 includes several new diagnostic and recovery tools, including Recovery Console, safe mode (similar to Windows 98 safe mode), and File Protection (which prevents system files from being corrupted or erased). For backups, Windows NT provides a backup utility to tape only, but Windows 2000 allows backups to tape, Zip drives, recordable CD-ROMs, and external hard drives. Windows 2000 supports the Internet Printing Protocol (IPP) so that users can print directly to a printer's URL anywhere on the Internet. In addition, several other features new to Windows 2000 are designed to support and improve Internet services for users.

20

Basic Disks and Dynamic Disks

Windows 2000 offers two ways to configure a hard drive: as a basic disk or a dynamic disk. A **basic disk** is the same as the configuration used with DOS, Windows 9x, and Windows NT. By default, Windows 2000 uses basic disk configuration. With basic disk, you generally create partitions of a set size and then do not change them. If you want to change the size of a partition, you either have to reinstall Windows (if Windows is installed on that partition) or use special third-party software that allows you to change the size of a partition without losing your data. Within partitions, you create logical drives (sometimes called basic volumes) of set size.

Dynamic disks, which are new to Windows 2000, don't use partitions or logical drives; instead, they use **dynamic volumes**, which are called dynamic because you can change the size. Data to configure the disk is stored in a disk management database that resides in the last 1 MB of storage space at the end of a hard drive. DOS, Windows 9x, and Windows NT cannot read dynamic disks. Dynamic disks are compatible only with Windows 2000 and Windows XP.

A dynamic volume is contained within a dynamic disk and is a logical volume similar to a logical drive in a basic disk. There are three types of dynamic volumes:

- A **simple volume** corresponds to a primary partition on a basic disk and consists of disk space located on a single physical disk.

- A **spanned volume** appears as a simple volume but can use space from two or more physical disks. It fills up the space allotted on one physical disk before moving onto the next. This increases the amount of disk space available for a volume. However, if one physical disk on which data that is part of a spanned volume fails, all the data in the volume is lost.

- A **striped volume** also can use space from two or more physical disks and increases the disk space available for a simple volume. The difference between a spanned volume and a striped volume is that a striped volume writes to the physical disks evenly rather than filling up allotted space on one and then moving on to the next. This increases disk performance as compared to access time with a spanned volume.

Figure 20-2 illustrates the difference between basic disk and dynamic disk organization. A basic disk or a dynamic disk can use any file system supported by Windows 2000 (FAT16, FAT32, and NTFS). Once Windows 2000 is installed, you can use the Windows 2000 Disk Management utility to switch from basic to dynamic or dynamic to basic and change the file system on either type disk.

Figure 20-2   Basic disks use partitions and logical drives to organize a hard drive, and dynamic disks use dynamic volumes to organize multiple hard drives

INSTALLING WINDOWS 2000 PROFESSIONAL

This section looks at installing Windows 2000 on a system with a newly installed hard drive, called a clean install, and also installing Windows 2000 as an upgrade from Windows 9x or Windows NT, called an upgrade installation. Just as with Windows NT, Windows 2000 can be installed to be dual-booted with another OS. Before any type of installation, verify that your system meets the minimum requirements for Windows 2000. You must have at least 650 MB of free space on your hard drive, at least 64 MB of RAM and a 133 MHz Pentium-compatible CPU or higher. As you read the following instructions, notice how the installation process is similar to that of Windows NT Workstation discussed in Chapter 19.

Plan the Installation

Windows 2000 has its roots in Windows NT. Just as with Windows NT, it does not use system BIOS to interface with hardware devices. For that reason, a hardware device must be designed to specifically interact with Windows 2000. Use the hardware compatibility list (HCL) to determine if all the hardware devices in your system qualify for Windows 2000. A version of the HCL is on the Windows 2000 CD in the \Support folder. However, to see the latest version of the list, check the Microsoft Web site at *www.microsoft.com/hcl*. Don't assume that because a device is compatible with Windows NT, it will work with Windows 2000. There are some instances in which this is not the case, so check the HCL for Windows 2000 to be sure.

20

TIP

Microsoft sometimes puts last-minute documentation in a Release Notes file in the root directory of an installation CD. Check the directory for Readme.htm and search it for information that might be important for the installation.

Software applications must also qualify for Windows 2000. To verify that all the applications you intend to use on the Windows 2000 PC are certified to work with Windows 2000, search the list of compatible software applications list at *www.microsoft.com/windows2000/ professional/howtobuy/upgrading/compat*. If an application is not on the list, it might still work with Windows 2000. You can verify that by checking with the application manufacturer's Web site or technical support, or you can just install the application under Windows 2000 and test it yourself.

Support for ACPI

The Advanced Configuration and Power Interface (ACPI) standards developed by Intel, Microsoft, and Toshiba apply to system BIOS, the OS, and certain hardware devices and software to control when a device goes into an inactive state in order to conserve power. To take full advantage of Windows 2000 power management abilities, your system BIOS must be ACPI-compliant. If you have a BIOS that is not ACPI-compliant and you install Windows, Windows will not install ACPI support and will install an older HAL that does not support ACPI. If you later flash your BIOS to make it ACPI-compliant, you will have to reinstall Windows to include ACPI support.

Some BIOS manufacturers offer a BIOS upgrade to make older systems compliant. Most system BIOSs made after January, 1999 are compliant. To learn if your BIOS is compliant, when you are upgrading from Windows 98 to Windows 2000, you can check for the ACPI feature under the Windows 98 Device Manager. Look for ACPI, Advanced Configuration and Power Management Interface in the Device Manager list of devices. Because Windows 95 and Windows NT do not support ACPI, it is not listed under these OS installations. You can also check the Web site of the BIOS manufacturer or the Microsoft Web site.

Microsoft calls a BIOS that is ACPI-compliant a "good BIOS" and puts it on the Good BIOS list. The Microsoft site allows you to search for ACPI-compatible computers. When you search by model and manufacturer, the Microsoft Web site tells you if the system is compatible with Windows 2000 and sometimes provides a link to the BIOS Web site where you can download an upgrade to the BIOS. If you are upgrading BIOS, do that before you begin the Windows 2000 installation. If the system is not ACPI-compliant, you can still install Windows 2000 but you cannot use some power management features.

TIP

For Microsoft links to hardware and software, and BIOS compatibility checks, see this URL: *www.microsoft.com/windows2000/professional/howtobuy/upgrading/compat/default.asp.*

Selecting a File System

When selecting a file system for an upgrade or replacing Windows 2000 with an existing OS, plan the installation by assuming that you have a basic disk. Later, after Windows 2000 is installed, you can switch to dynamic disk if you like. Plan which partition on the hard drive will hold Windows 2000 and what file system you will use on that partition. Windows 2000 supports the FAT16, FAT32, and NTFS file systems. For compatibility with Windows 98, use the FAT32 file system. For compatibility with DOS or Windows 95, use FAT16, and for the most security, use NTFS. If the hard drive is not yet partitioned or formatted, Windows 2000 does that for you during the installation. As an alternative, you can also use Fdisk to create a partition before you begin the installation. Create only a single partition, and then, after the installation, you can use Disk Management to create other partitions.

 TIP The NTFS file system supports encryption (encoding files so they can't be deciphered by others), compression (reducing the size of files and folders), and disk quotas (limiting the hard drive space available to a user). If you want to use any of these features, use NTFS because they are not supported by FAT file systems. (Windows 9x supports compression of an entire logical drive, but not of individual files or folders.)

Table 20-1 summarizes which file systems are supported by which operating systems. You will need this information when planning your Windows 2000 installation. Windows versions not discussed in this chapter are included for comparison.

Table 20-1   Operating system support for file systems

	DOS	Windows 95	Windows 98	Windows NT	Windows 2000	Windows XP
FAT16	X	X	X	X	X	X
FAT32		X (for OSR2)	X		X	X
NTFS				X	X	X

Installing Windows 2000 on Networked Computers

If you are installing Windows 2000 on a networked PC, consider where the Windows 2000 installation files are stored. You can install the OS from a CD in the computer's CD-ROM drive, or you can store the files on a file server on the network and perform the installation from the file server. If you will be doing multiple installations on the network, consider using a file server. Copy all the files from the \i386 folder on the Windows 2000 CD to a folder on the file server and then share that folder on the network. Later, during the installation, when you are ready for the CD, point the setup program to the file server folder instead.

Windows 2000 offers a number of options for installation that can be automated without requiring someone to sit at the computer responding to the questions that setup asks during the installation process. One method is called an **unattended installation** and is performed by storing the answers to installation questions in a text file or script that Windows 2000 calls

20

an **answer file**. A sample answer file is stored on the Windows 2000 CD. If you must perform many installations on computers that have the same Windows 2000 setup, it might be worth your time to develop an answer file to perform unattended installations. How to set up unattended installations is beyond the scope of this chapter. Another option is drive imaging. After the installation, use the sysprep.exe utility to remove configuration settings such as the computer name that uniquely identifies this PC. Then clone the entire hard drive to a new PC using third-party drive-imaging software.

 To learn how to create an unattended installation of Windows 2000, go to the Microsoft Support Web site (*support.microsoft.com*) and search on the Microsoft Knowledge Base article Q216258. You can also search the Web site for other articles on this subject.

When installing Windows 2000 on a network, just as with other operating systems, you need to know how to configure the computer to access the network. You should know these things before you begin the installation:

- The computer name and workgroup name for a peer-to-peer network
- The username, user password, computer name, and domain name for a domain network
- For TCP/IP networks, how the IP address is assigned, either dynamically (gets its IP address from a DHCP server when it first connects to the network) or statically (IP address is permanently assigned to the workstation). If the IP address is statically assigned, then have the IP address to assign the workstation.

Upgrade or Clean Install?

If you are installing Windows 2000 on a new hard drive, then you are doing a clean install, but if Windows 9x or Windows NT is already installed on the hard drive, then you have three choices:

- You can perform a clean install, overwriting the existing operating system and applications.
- You can perform an upgrade installation.
- You can install Windows 2000 in a second partition on the hard drive and create a dual-boot situation.

There are advantages and disadvantages to each of these options.

Clean Install, Erasing Existing Installations
If the hard drive does not have a lot of important data on it or if the data can be backed up, a clean install that overwrites the existing installation has some advantages. One advantage is that you get a fresh start. With an upgrade, problems with applications or the OS might follow you into the Windows 2000 load. If you erase everything (format the hard drive), then you are assured

that the registry as well as all applications are as clean as possible. The disadvantage is that, after Windows 2000 is installed, you must reinstall application software on the hard drive and restore the data from backups. If you do a clean install, you can choose to format the hard drive first, or simply do a clean install on top of the existing installation. If you don't format the drive, the data will still be on the drive, but the previous operating system settings and applications will be lost.

If you decide to do a clean install, verify that you have all the application software CDs or floppy disks and software documentation. Back up all the data and verify that the backups are good. Then, and only then, format the hard drive or begin the clean install without formatting the drive. If you don't format the hard drive, be sure to run a current version of antivirus software before you begin the installation.

Upgrade the Existing Operating System   All versions of Windows 9x and Windows NT Workstation 3.51 and higher can be upgraded to Windows 2000. The advantages of upgrading are that all applications and data are carried forward into the new Windows 2000 environment, most OS settings carry forward, and the installation is faster. If you perform an upgrade, you must begin the installation while you are in the current OS. If you are working from a remote location on the network, you cannot do an upgrade.

> You cannot upgrade a compressed Windows 9x drive. You must first uncompress it before you can upgrade to Windows 2000 Professional.

Create a Dual Boot   Don't create a dual boot unless you need two operating systems, such as when you need to verify that applications and hardware will work under Windows 2000 before you delete the old OS. Windows 2000 does not support a second operating system on the same partition, so you must have at least two partitions on the hard drive. All applications must be installed on each partition to be used by each OS.

> Recall that Windows NT/2000/XP can support up to four partitions on a hard drive. All four can be primary partitions (which can have only one logical drive) or one of the partitions can be an extended partition (which can have several logical drives). For the first primary partition, the active partition, that drive is drive C. For a dual boot with Windows 2000, one OS is installed in the active partition on drive C, and the other OS is installed on another partition's logical drive.

You must decide what file system to use for the Windows 2000 partition: FAT16, FAT32, or NTFS. If you choose to use a dual boot with DOS, use FAT16 for the Windows 2000 partition so that DOS can read the partition. For Windows 9x, use either the FAT16 or FAT32 file system, not NTFS, so that Windows 9x can read the Windows 2000 partition.

Windows 2000 uses the latest version of NTFS that was first introduced by Windows NT Server 4.0, NTFS Version 5.0 (NTFS5). NTFS4 is used by Windows NT Workstation 4.0.

20

The NTFS5 version includes numerous enhancements over previous versions, but cannot be read by Windows NT Workstation 4.0 unless Windows NT 4.0 Service Pack 4 is applied. For this reason, if you create a dual boot between Windows 2000 and Windows NT using NTFS for both operating systems, you can encounter the following problems:

- The file system data structures might not be the same.

- Disk utilities, such as Chkdsk under Windows NT, might not work on the drive.

- Windows NT will not be able to read encrypted files and folders.

- You cannot use Windows 2000 to repair a damaged Windows NT 4.0 NTFS partition. Windows NT 4.0 only allows access to an NTFS drive from within Windows NT 4.0 and not from any other OS.

For these reasons, using a dual boot between Windows 2000 and Windows NT is not recommended.

Features new to NTFS under Windows 2000 include file and folder encryption (protects from unauthorized access), disk quotas (controls user disk space), and mount points (adds a remote volume to a system without using a drive letter). These features were not included in Windows NT and might cause conflicts if you set up Windows 2000 and Windows NT as a dual boot.

Planning an Upgrade from Windows 9x to Windows 2000

So far in this chapter, you have learned that there are many similarities in structure between Windows 2000 and Windows NT. When you are upgrading from Windows 9x to Windows 2000, the Windows 2000 registry is not compatible with the Windows 9x registry; therefore, during an upgrade, Windows 2000 cannot easily import settings from the Windows 9x registry, even though it attempts to do so. Because of the difference in structure in the Windows 9x registry and the Windows 2000 registry, transfer of information from one to the other will not be as complete as with an upgrade from Windows NT. Until you have performed the upgrade, you will not know exactly what Windows 2000 was able to import from Windows 9x, though Setup might inform you or ask for additional help in some cases.

To test your system and be alerted to potential problems, it is a good idea to run the Check Upgrade Only mode of Windows 2000 Setup, which does not actually install Windows 2000 but instead just checks for compatibility and reports any upgrade issues with hardware or software. Run the utility to produce the report, Upgrade.txt, which is stored in the C:\Windows directory.

Hardware Compatibility   One issue to consider in upgrading from Windows 9x to Windows 2000 is that Windows 2000 does not import drivers from Windows 9x, because they are generally not compatible. As you learned earlier, a hardware device must be designed to be compatible with Windows 2000. If you want to install a device for which there is no device driver included in Windows 2000, you might have to download a driver from either the Microsoft site or the manufacturer's Web site. Check for compatibility and make sure you have all the required device drivers before you begin your Windows 9x-to-Windows 2000 upgrade. Windows 2000 attempts to carry over installed hardware devices that are compatible with Windows 2000, asking for new drivers where necessary; it ignores and does not install incompatible devices. If Setup cannot find a critical driver such as the driver to control a hard drive, it will cancel the upgrade.

Another thing you need to know is that Windows 2000 deletes all the Windows 9x system files and replaces them with Windows 2000 system files in the same directory.

Software Compatibility   Basically, the main advantage in performing an upgrade from Windows 9x to Windows 2000 rather than doing a clean install of Windows 2000 is that you do not have to reinstall software that is compatible with Windows 2000. If an application was written for Windows 9x, it might or might not be compatible with Windows 2000. Windows 9x applications store registry data differently from Windows 2000 applications and may rely on APIs specific to Windows 9x. If an application doesn't work after you upgrade to Windows 2000, try reinstalling it. If that doesn't work, check the software manufacturer's Web site for a patch or upgrade.

Planning an Upgrade from Windows NT to Windows 2000

Upgrading to Windows 2000 from Windows NT is much easier than upgrading from Windows 9x. However, here are some considerations you need to be aware of before performing the upgrade:

- You must install networking on Windows NT 3.51 machines before upgrading, or you will not be able to log on to Windows 2000.

- If you are upgrading from Windows NT using NTFS, Setup automatically upgrades to the Windows 2000 version of NTFS.

- If you are upgrading from Windows NT using FAT16 or Windows NT with third-party software installed that allows it to use FAT32, Setup will ask you whether you want to upgrade to NTFS.

Hardware Compatibility   Generally, most hardware devices and their corresponding drivers that worked under Windows NT will work under Windows 2000 as well, although some third-party drivers might need to be updated for Windows 2000. As always, it is a good idea to check the HCL on the Microsoft Web site or run the Check Upgrade Only mode of Windows 2000 Setup.

Software Compatibility   Nearly all applications that run with Windows NT Workstation 3.51 and later will run with Windows 2000 without modification. Here are some exceptions:

- Antivirus software and third-party network software, both of which must be removed before upgrading to Windows 2000

- Some disk management tools

- Custom tools for power management, which are replaced in Windows 2000 by ACPI. Windows 2000 also provides minimal support for APM (Advanced Power

20

Management) which also must be removed before the upgrade. Windows 2000 considers APM a legacy tool, uses it only on notebook computers, and uses only enough APM features to support the battery on a notebook computer. With ACPI-compliant BIOS, the BIOS senses information about the system and turns that information over to the OS to make decisions and manage the power management functions of the system.

- Custom solutions that are workarounds for Windows NT not supporting Plug and Play, which are unnecessary in Windows 2000 because it provides complete support for Plug and Play

- Software to monitor and control a UPS (uninterruptible power supply)

Now that you have learned about advantages and disadvantages to installing Windows 2000 as a clean install and as an upgrade, including issues to consider with specific upgrades, let's look at step-by-step procedures for how to do both.

 When installing Windows from across the network to a remote PC, you can only do a clean install. In this situation, run the Winnt.exe setup program. When working at the local computer, to perform a clean install, you can boot from the Windows CD or run Winnt32.exe from a command prompt. If you want to perform an upgrade, you must execute the Winnt32.exe program from within Windows. In any case, the program executed is called Setup in Windows documentation.

Clean Installation

The Windows 2000 package comes with documentation and a CD. For United States distributions, the package includes a floppy disk to provide 128-bit data encryption. (This disk is not included in distributions to other countries because of laws that prohibit 128-bit data encryption software from leaving the United States.)

If your PC is capable of booting from a CD, then insert the CD and turn on the PC. The Welcome to the Windows 2000 Setup Wizard screen appears. See Figure 20-3. Select Install a new copy of Windows 2000, and then click Next and proceed to Step 6 on the following page. However, if your PC does not boot from a CD and you have a clean, empty hard drive, first create a set of Windows 2000 setup disks to boot the PC and to begin the installation process. The remaining installation will be done from the CD.

To make the four setup disks, follow these directions:

1. Using a working PC, format four floppy disks.

2. Place the Windows 2000 CD in the CD-ROM drive and a formatted floppy disk in the floppy disk drive. For Windows 9x, click **Start**, **Run**, and enter this command in the Run dialog box: **D:\bootdisk\makeboot.exe A:** , substituting the drive letter of the CD-ROM drive for D: and the letter of the floppy drive for A:.

3. Insert new disks in the drive as requested. Label the disks Windows 2000 Setup Disks 1, 2, 3, and 4.

4. Now begin the Windows 2000 installation. Boot the PC from the first setup disk created in the previous steps. You will be asked to insert each of the four disks in turn and then asked to insert the Windows 2000 CD.

5. The Windows 2000 license agreement appears. Accept the agreement and the Welcome screen appears, as shown in Figure 20-3. The setup process is now identical to that of booting directly from the CD. Save the four setup floppy disks in case you have future problems with Windows 2000.

Figure 20-3   Using the Setup Wizard, you can do an upgrade, do a clean install, or create a dual boot

6. Windows 2000 searches the hard drive for partitions and asks which partition to use. If the partitions are not created, it creates them for you. You are asked to decide which file system to use. If the hard drive has already been formatted with the FAT16 or FAT32 file system, you are asked if you want to upgrade to the NTFS file system. Be aware that if you convert the file system to NTFS, you cannot revert to FAT16 or FAT32. You can also convert from FAT16 or FAT32 to NTFS after the installation is complete. If the hard drive is already partitioned and contains a partition larger than 2 GB and if you select the FAT file system, then Windows 2000 automatically formats the drive using the FAT32 file system. It puts the entire partition into one logical FAT32 drive.

7. During the installation, you are given the opportunity to change your keyboard settings for different languages, enter your name and company name, and enter the product key found on the CD case. You are also given the opportunity to enter date and time settings and an administrator password. Be sure to remember the password. It is required when you log on to the system later to set up new users and perform other administrative tasks. If you forget it and no one else has administrator privileges, you might have to reinstall Windows 2000.

20

8. If Setup recognizes that you are connected to a network, it provides the Networking Settings window to configure the computer to access the network. If you select Typical settings, then Setup automatically configures the OS for your network. After the installation, if the configuration is not correct, you can make changes.

9. At this point in the installation, you are asked to remove the Windows 2000 CD and click **Finish**. The computer then restarts. After Windows 2000 loads, it completes the process of connecting to the network. You are asked questions about the type of network (for example, does the network use a domain or workgroup?). When the configuration is complete, verify that you have access to the network if there is one.

Clean Install When the Hard Drive Has an Operating System Installed

Using Windows 9x, if your PC automatically detects a CD in the CD-ROM drive, follow these directions to do a clean install when another OS is already installed:

1. Using antivirus software, scan memory and your hard drive for viruses.

2. Insert the Windows 2000 CD in the CD-ROM drive. If your PC detects the CD, a window opens with the message "This CD-ROM contains a newer version of Windows than the one you are presently using. Would you like to upgrade to Windows 2000?" Answer **No**. The Install Windows 2000 window appears (see Figure 20-4).

Figure 20-4   Windows 2000 Setup window

3. Click **Install Windows 2000**. The Windows Setup Wizard opens, as in Figure 20-3. Select **Install a new copy of Windows 2000 (Clean Install)**. You will be asked to accept the license agreement, which is displayed; enter the product key from the

back of the CD case, and you will be given the opportunity to select special options. After a reboot, the installation process continues as described previously.

If your PC does not automatically recognize a CD, then insert the CD in the CD-ROM drive and do the following:

1. Click **Start**, **Run**. In the Run dialog box, enter the command: **D:\i386\ winnt32.exe**. Substitute the drive letter of the CD-ROM drive for D:.

2. The Windows 2000 Setup Wizard appears, as in Figure 20-3. Select **Install a new copy of Windows 2000 (Clean Install)**. The installation process continues as described previously.

Upgrade Installation

To upgrade your operating system from Windows 9x or Windows NT using the Windows 2000 CD, first prepare for the installation by doing the following:

1. Verify that all devices and applications are Windows 2000-compatible. Download and install any patches or upgrades from hardware or software manufacturers.

2. Using antivirus software, scan memory and your hard drive for viruses.

3. Back up all critical system files and data files. Back up the registry in case you need to backtrack to the current installation. If you have important data on your hard drive, back up the data.

4. Close all applications and disable any virus-scanning software. If the hard drive is compressed, decompress the drive.

You are now ready to perform the upgrade. Do the following:

1. Insert the Windows 2000 CD in the CD-ROM drive. If your system is set to automatically detect the CD, it runs the setup program and shows a message asking if you want to upgrade your computer to Windows 2000. Answer **Yes**, and the installation process begins. If Windows does not detect the CD, then click **Start**, **Run**, enter **D:\i386\winnt32.exe** in the Run dialog box, and then click **OK**. Substitute the drive letter of the CD-ROM drive for D:. On the Welcome to Windows 2000 Setup Wizard Screen, select **Upgrade to Windows 2000 (Recommended)**. Follow the directions on the screen.

2. Windows 2000 Setup performs the upgrade in two major stages: the Report phase and the Setup phase. During the Report phase, Windows 2000 Setup scans the hardware, device drivers, current operating system, and applications for compatibility. Also, in the Report phase, you are given the opportunity to provide third-party DLL files that make a device driver or application Windows 2000-compatible, if Setup recognizes that the device driver or application will not work without the fix. Next, Setup generates a report of its findings. If findings indicate that an unsuccessful installation is likely to happen, you can abandon the installation and perhaps check with hardware and software manufacturers for fixes. In the Report phase, Setup also creates an answer file that it will use during the Setup phase, installs the Windows 2000 boot loader, and copies Windows 2000 installation files to the hard drive.

20

3. The PC reboots and the Setup phase begins, which has two parts: the Text mode and the GUI mode. In the Text mode, Setup installs a Windows 2000 base in the same folder that the old OS is in, usually C:\Windows for Windows 9x and C:\WINNT for Windows NT. This target folder cannot be changed at this point. Setup then moves the Windows registry and profile information to %windir%\setup\temp, where %windir% is the path to the Windows folder, which most likely is C:\Windows\setup\temp.

4. The PC reboots again, and the GUI mode of Setup begins. Setup reads information that it saved about the old Windows system and makes appropriate changes to the Windows 2000 registry. It then migrates application DLLs to Windows 2000 and reboots for the last time. The upgrade is now done.

 During installation, Windows 2000 records information about the installation to a file called Setuplog.txt. This file is useful when troubleshooting any problems that occur during installation.

After the Installation: Backing Up the System State

After you have completed installing Windows 2000, do the following:

1. Access the Internet and download and install all OS service pack, updates and patches.

2. Verify that all hardware is working and install additional devices, such as printers, as needed.

3. Create user accounts for Windows 2000. (How to do this is covered later in this chapter.) You can also install any additional Windows components at this time.

4. Verify that the system is functioning properly and back up the system state. This backup of the system can later be used to help you recover the OS in the event of system failure. (You will learn more about recovering from system failure in Chapter 21.)

Windows 2000 calls the files critical to a successful operating system load the **system state data**. This includes all files necessary to boot the OS, the Windows 2000 registry, and all system files in the %SystemRoot% folder, the folder in which Windows 2000 is installed. For an upgrade, the folder will most likely be C:\Windows, the original Windows folder before the upgrade. For a clean install the default folder is C:\WINNT. When you perform a backup of the system state data, you cannot select which of these files you want to back up because Windows 2000 will always back up all of them. Here is the process:

1. Click **Start**, point to **Programs, Accessories, System Tools**, and then click **Backup**. The Backup dialog box opens. Click the **Backup** tab. See Figure 20-5.

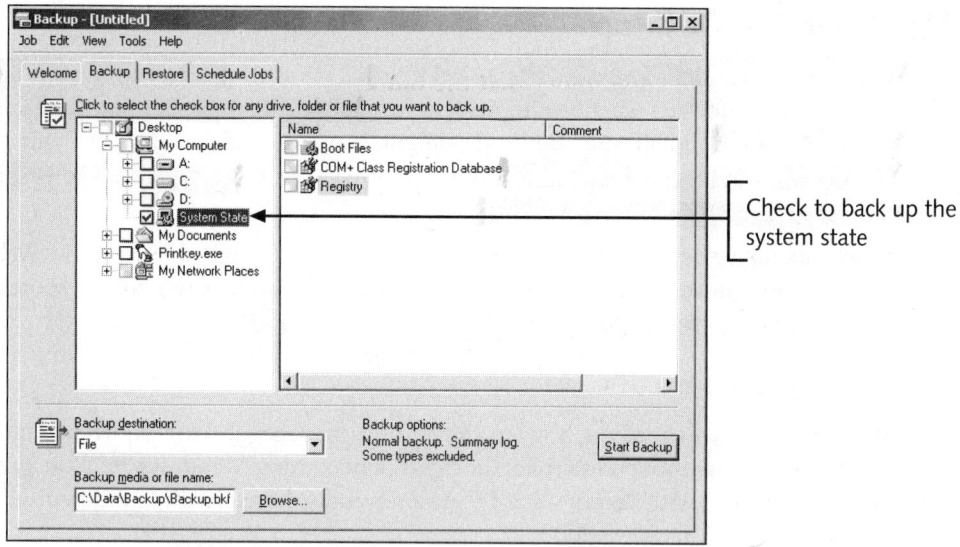

Check to back up the system state

Figure 20-5   Back up the Windows 2000 registry and all critical system files

2. Check the **System State** box in the list of items you can back up. Notice in Figure 20-5 that the system state includes the boot files and the registry. It also includes the COM+ (Component Object Model) Registration Database, which contains information about applications and includes files in the Windows folders.

3. Select the destination for the backup. You can back up to any media, including a folder on the hard drive, Zip drive, tape drive, or network drive. Click **Start Backup** to begin the process.

Later, if you have problems with a corrupted Windows 2000 installation, you can click the Restore tab in the Backup window illustrated in Figure 20-5 to restore the system to its state at the last backup.

 When you back up the system state, the registry is also backed up to the folder %SystemRoot%\repair\RegBack. If you later have a corrupted registry, you can copy files from this folder to the registry folder, which is %SystemRoot%\System32\Config.

USING WINDOWS 2000

In Chapter 17, you learned how keyboard shortcuts and Windows Explorer help you in using Windows 9x. Much of the information you learned about using Windows 9x applies to Windows 2000 as well. However, there are important differences and improvements that you need to know about, including how to manage the desktop and how to increase security of files and resources. As with any version of Windows, additional Windows components can be installed using the Add/Remove Programs applet in Control Panel.

20

Managing the Desktop

There are two basic ways to set up your desktop. One is the classic Windows style, used in Windows 95 and later versions, in which you single-click to select an item and double click to open it, and all your desktop content is offline and localized to your computer. The second is to use Active Desktop, which allows you to set your desktop to behave like a Web page and include Web content.

To activate Active desktop, right click anywhere on the desktop and select Show Web Content from the shortcut menu. Because Active Desktop uses considerable system resources, it is not recommended for most situations.

Managing Shortcuts

In Chapter 17 you learned how to create and manage desktop shortcuts and icons in Windows 9x and about keystroke shortcuts when using Windows 9x. You can use that same information with Windows 2000. As a reminder, here are three different ways to create a shortcut in Windows 2000:

- Select (single-click) the file, folder, or program in Explorer or in a My Computer window. From the File menu, select Create Shortcut.

- In Explorer, on the File menu, click New and then click Shortcut.

- Right-click on the file, folder, or program to which you want to create a shortcut and select Create Shortcut from the menu.

Once the shortcut is created in the same folder as the file it pertains to, drag the shortcut to the desktop.

Managing the Start Menu

As you know from earlier chapters and probably also from your own experience, the Start menu in Windows shows frequently used files and programs. This enables you to access these items quickly rather than having to search for them in Windows Explorer or with the Find command.

There are many ways you can customize the Start menu. For example, you can set the Program menu to only display recently used applications and show an arrow at the bottom by which you can expand the menu and access programs that were not initially shown. To make this change:

1. Click **Start**, **Settings**, and **Taskbar and Start Menu**.

2. The Taskbar and Start Menu Properties window opens. Click to place a check next to **Use Personalized Menus** (Figure 20-6).

3. Click **Apply** to execute the change, and then click **OK** to close the window.

4. Click **Start** and point to **Programs**. Only recently used programs are shown. (See Figure 20-7.)

Figure 20-6   Change Start menu and taskbar options

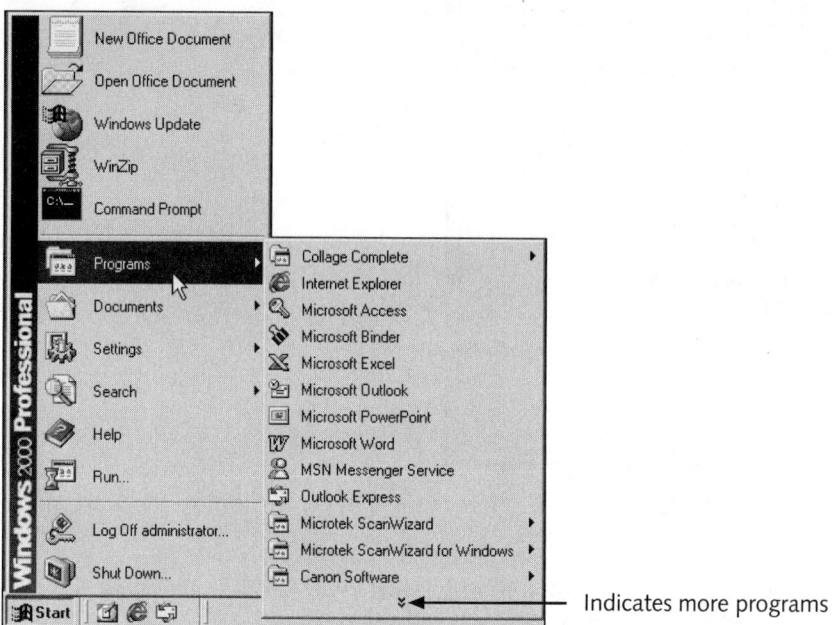

Indicates more programs

Figure 20-7   A personalized menu shows only recently accessed programs

20

5. Notice in Figure 20-7 that there is a small double arrow at the bottom of the personalized menu. To access programs not shown on the personalized menu, click the arrow. The complete menu appears with the programs that were not shown on the personalized menu shaded in a lighter color.

Notice in Figure 20-6 that you selected the personalized menus option from the General tab of the Taskbar and Start Menu Properties window. The Advanced tab offers additional options for customizing the Start menu (Figure 20-8). From this window, you can add, remove, and sort Start menu items as well as add commands or tools that are not usually shown on the Start menu. As an alternative to using personalized menus, you can even choose to display the Programs menu as a scrolling list. The scrolling list under Start Menu Settings offers a variety of options. To activate an option, scroll through the list and check the items that you want, and then click Apply and OK.

Managing the Taskbar

As with the Start menu, the taskbar in Windows 2000 offers more options for customization than were available with earlier versions of Windows. (One option that was available with Windows 9x, auto-hiding the taskbar, was covered in Chapter 17 and works the same way with Windows 2000.) The taskbar can show status information, provide quick links to common programs and files, and include an address bar in which to type paths and URLs to go to.

Figure 20-8   The Advanced tab offers many ways to customize the Start menu

The General tab of the Taskbar and Start Menu Properties window, which you saw in Figure 20-6, offers options to auto-hide the taskbar or to set it to be always on top of whatever windows are open. You can reach additional options for customizing the taskbar by right-clicking it and selecting options from the shortcut menu. For example, to add toolbars to the taskbar, right-click it, point to Toolbars, and then select the desired toolbar from the menu that appears (see Figure 20-9). Figure 20-10 shows the taskbar with toolbars added. Notice the system tray (systray) on the right side of the taskbar that contains icons indicating the status of several currently running services such as the sound controls.

Figure 20-9   Use this shortcut menu to add toolbars to the taskbar

Figure 20-10   Adding toolbars to the taskbar gives you quick access to common programs, tools, and locations

INSTALLING HARDWARE AND APPLICATIONS

This section discusses how to install hardware and software and includes special consider- ations for legacy hardware and software. As with Windows 98, Windows 2000 has an Add New Hardware wizard that automatically launched when new hardware is detected, and software is best installed from the Add/Remove Programs icon of Control Panel.

Installing Hardware

Windows 2000 can automatically detect and install Plug and Play devices, as long as you also have Plug and Play BIOS and drivers and devices that are Plug and Play compliant. If a device is Plug and Play, Windows 2000 automatically does the following:

- Identifies the device you are installing
- Determines what system resources the device needs and assigns them so that there are no conflicts with other devices
- Configures the device as necessary
- Loads any device drivers that are needed to run the device
- Informs the system of any changes in configuration

For PnP devices, the Add New Hardware Wizard automatically launches at startup. Any user can complete the installation if the following are true: installing the device drivers can be done without user input, all files necessary for a complete installation are present, the drivers have been digitally signed, and there are no errors during installation. If any of these conditions don't exist, the installation is abandoned until someone with administrator privileges logs on.

Most devices that are designed to work with Windows 2000 are Plug and Play compatible. If a device is not Plug and Play, you can use the Add/Remove Hardware applet in Control Panel to install the device if you are logged on with administrator privileges.

20

If you are using the Add/Remove Hardware Wizard, you will have to provide information such as where the driver for the device is located. Some devices that don't work with Windows 2000 may be completely incompatible and will not work at all. After a device is installed, if you have a problem with the device, you can attempt to update the device driver as follows:

1. In the Control Panel, double-click the **System** icon.

2. The System Properties window opens. Select the **Hardware** tab. See Figure 20-11.

3. Click the **Device Manager** button. The Device Manager opens, as shown in Figure 20-11. Expand the device class tree by clicking the plus sign, and locate the device for which you want to update a driver. For this example, we are using the floppy disk drive.

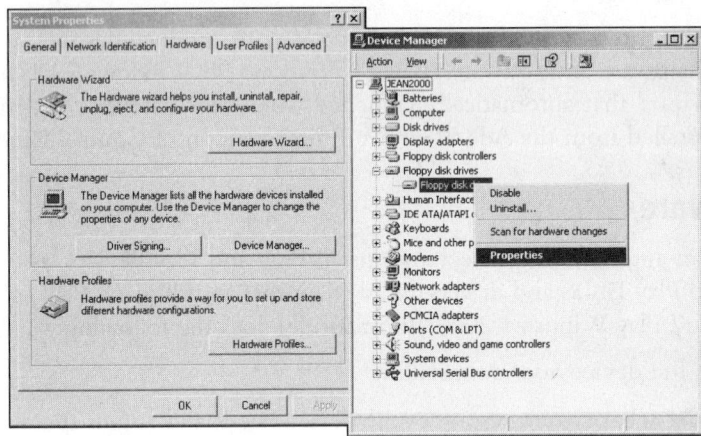

Figure 20-11   Use Device Manager to access a device's properties

4. Right-click the floppy drive and select **Properties** from the shortcut menu (Figure 20-11).

5. The Floppy disk drive Properties window opens (see Figure 20-12). On the **Driver** tab, click **Update Driver**. The Update Device Driver Wizard is displayed. Follow directions on screen to update the driver, if an update exists.

 You must be logged on with administrator privileges to make changes from the Device Manager.

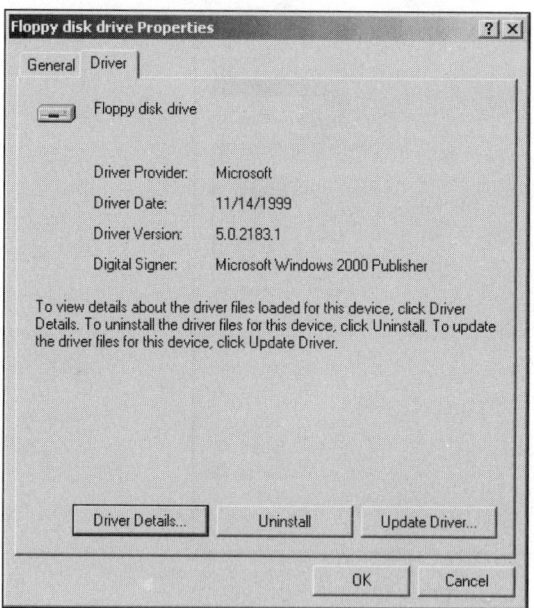

Figure 20-12   A device's Properties window provides a way to update its drivers

Installing Applications

The process of installing applications in Windows 2000 is not much different than in earlier versions of Windows. If you are familiar with the installation wizards and setup programs that were used with Windows 9x, you should recognize all but a few minor details of these same components in Windows 2000.

The Windows 2000 Add/Remove Programs utility looks significantly different than in Windows 9x, and it provides more options. From the Windows 2000 Add/Remove Programs window, you can change or remove presently installed programs (Figure 20-13); add new programs from a CD-ROM, a floppy disk, or from Microsoft over the Internet, and add or remove Windows components. Note that, in Figure 20-13, the drop-down menu in the upper-right corner is expanded for you, showing how you can sort the view of presently installed programs.

20

Figure 20-13   Making changes to currently installed programs

CHAPTER SUMMARY

- ❏ Windows 2000 makes use of ACPI-compliant system BIOS in order to fully enable power management features.
- ❏ If a system does not have ACPI BIOS, upgrade the BIOS before you do the installation, if the BIOS manufacturer offers the upgrade.
- ❏ Windows 2000 Active Directory is a new feature of Windows 2000 that provides a centralized point of administration for all shared resources on a network.
- ❏ Windows 2000 can have more than one domain controller, whereas Windows NT can have only a single primary domain controller.
- ❏ Windows 2000 allows for printing to a URL so that you can send a print job to anywhere on the Internet.
- ❏ Windows 2000 offers a clean install and an upgrade installation. A clean install overwrites all information from previous operating system installations on the hard drive.
- ❏ Both hardware and software must be compatible with Windows 2000. Check the HCL and the Compatible Software Applications list on the Microsoft Web site before beginning an installation.
- ❏ Windows 2000 supports the FAT16, FAT32, and NTFS file systems.
- ❏ Windows 2000 supports a dual boot, but each operating system must be installed in its own partition, and an application must be installed twice, once for each OS.
- ❏ A Windows 2000 upgrade installation is done in two phases, the Report phase and the Setup phase.

❐ Windows 2000 can run in native mode and mixed mode. Native mode is used when all domain servers are Windows 2000 servers. Mixed mode is used when a domain has both Windows 2000 and Windows NT servers controlling the domain.

❐ Windows 2000 supports basic disks and dynamic disks. Both types can use the FAT16, FAT32, and NTFS file systems. Dynamic disks are compatible only with Windows 2000 and Windows XP.

❐ Backing up the system state helps to ensure that you can recover from a failed OS, restoring the OS to its state at the time of the last backup.

❐ Windows 2000 Active Desktop allows you to view online content from the desktop.

❐ Windows 2000 supports Plug and Play and will automatically launch the Add New Hardware Wizard when it senses a new device has been installed on the system.

❐ Windows 2000 has a Device Manager to view, uninstall, and update devices.

❐ Applications can be installed using the Add/Remove Programs applet in Control Panel.

KEY TERMS

Active Directory	encryption	standard user
answer file	mixed mode	striped volume
basic disk	native mode	system state data
dynamic disk	simple volume	unattended installation
dynamic volume	spanned volume	

20

CHAPTER

21

MANAGING AND TROUBLESHOOTING WINDOWS 2000

In this chapter, you will learn:

♦ About the boot process for Windows 2000

♦ How to troubleshoot the Windows 2000 boot process

♦ How to use tools for maintenance, troubleshooting, and performance monitoring in Windows

In the last chapter, you learned how Windows 2000 is structured, how it is different from other versions of Windows, and how to install and work with it. This chapter covers managing, supporting, and troubleshooting Windows in more detail, including problems you might have with the boot process or with system errors and performance after the system is running. You will learn about many useful tools and sources of information to use when working with Windows 2000.

UNDERSTANDING THE BOOT PROCESS

The Windows 2000 boot process works just like the Windows NT process. You can review these steps in Chapter 19. In this section, we look at some of the troubleshooting tools provided by Windows 2000 to solve boot problems, but first let's turn our attention to customizing the boot process.

Customizing the Boot Process

The Boot.ini file contains information about how the Windows 2000 boot is configured and can be used to customize the boot process. As you learned in Chapter 19, Ntldr reads this file and uses it to see what operating systems are available and how to set up the boot. Figure 21-1 shows an example of a Boot.ini file.

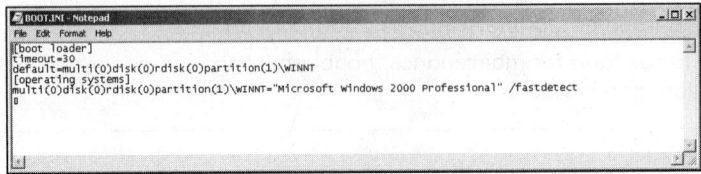

Figure 21-1   A sample Boot.ini file

There are two main sections in Boot.ini: the [boot loader] section and the [operating systems] section. The [boot loader] section contains the number of seconds the system gives the user to select an operating system before it loads the default operating system; this is called a timeout. In Figure 21-1, the timeout is set to 30 seconds. If the system is set for a dual boot, the path to the default operating system is also listed in the [boot loader] section.

The [operating systems] section of the Boot.ini file provides a list of operating systems that can be loaded, including the path to the boot partition of each operating system. Here is the meaning of each entry in Figure 21-1 that points to the location of the OS:

- *Multi (0)*. Use the first hard drive controller
- *Disk (0)*. Only used when booting from a SCSI hard drive
- *Rdisk (0)*. Use the first hard drive
- *Partition (1)*. Use the first partition on the drive

Recall from earlier chapters that you can use the Advanced Options menu when troubleshooting the boot process. You can set the OS to use many of the options found on the Advanced Options menu by adding certain switches to the end of entries in the [operating systems] section in the Boot.ini file. Some of those switches are shown in Table 21-1.

Table 21-1 Switches for entries in the Boot.ini [operating systems] section

Switch	Purpose
/basevideo	Boots using the standard VGA video driver. This switch is generally used when another video driver is malfunctioning.
/bootlog	Writes information about the boot to the file Ntbtlog.txt, which is located in the C:\WINNT folder.
/debug	Loads the kernel debugger and allows a host debugger to access the system.
/fastdetect=COM2	Specifies a COM port that you do not want the OS to inspect for the presence of a peripheral device.
/maxmem:*n*	Used when memory chips are suspected to be corrupted. The *n* is the amount of memory that the operating system is to use. It ignores the rest.
/noguiboot	Boots the operating system without displaying boot status graphically. This parameter does not affect whether the system boots to a command prompt or to the Windows GUI.
/safeboot:*parameter*	Starts the computer in safe mode, with these parameters: ■ *Minimal* boots the computer in safe mode with minimal drivers and without network support. ■ *Network* boots into Safe Mode with network support.
/sos	Used to determine whether a corrupted device driver is causing startup problems. This switch displays the names of device drivers as they are loaded.

In Figure 21-1, the only switch used in this Boot.ini file is /fastdetect with no COM port following, which means that peripherals connected to any COM port are not inspected at startup.

The recommended way to change Boot.ini settings, which is also easier and safer than manually editing the file, is through the System Properties window:

1. On the Start menu, point to **Settings**, and then click **Control Panel**.

2. Double-click the **System** icon.

3. The System Properties window opens. Click the **Advanced** tab (see Figure 21-2).

4. Click the **Startup and Recovery** button.

5. The Startup and Recovery window opens (see Figure 21-3). Change settings as desired, and then click **OK** to save them (or Cancel if you do not want to save them).

21

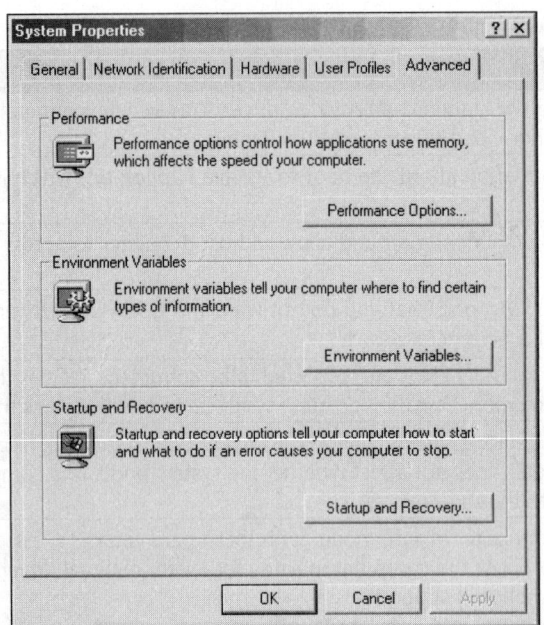

Figure 21-2   You can access startup and recovery options from the System Properties window

Figure 21-3   Changing the default operating system and timeout value in the Startup and Recovery window changes the Boot.ini settings

From the Startup and Recovery window, you can designate the default operating system and set the timeout value in the System startup pane. The default is 30 seconds, and you can change that value to reflect how long you want the system to wait before starting the default operating system. If you set the value to 0, the system will start the default operating system automatically and will not give the user a choice.

If you cannot get to the System Properties window, you can also edit the Boot.ini file using Notepad, as shown in Figure 21-1. The file is a hidden system file; therefore, in order to view it, you must first change the folder options to display these type files. In Windows Explorer, select the root directory, click Tools, Folder Options, and then select the View tab (see Figure 21-4). Uncheck the option to *Hide protected operating system files.*

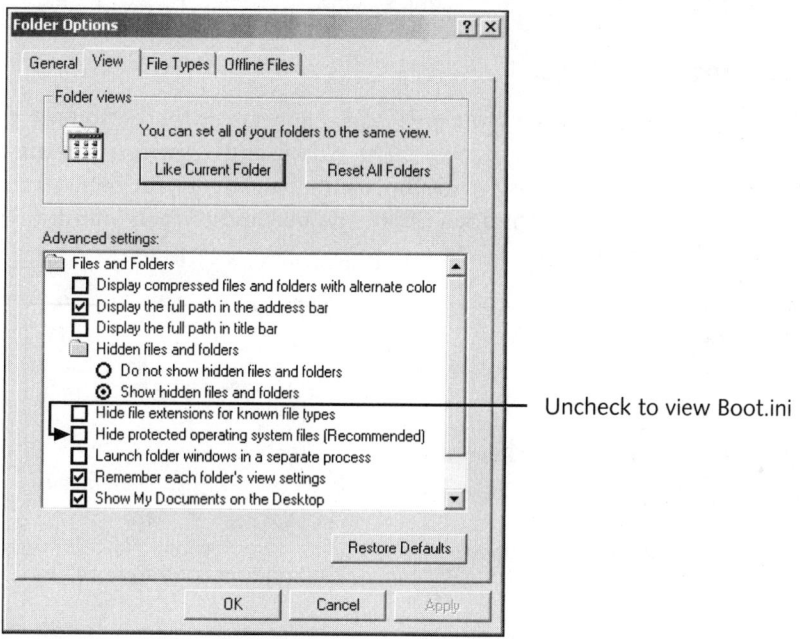

Uncheck to view Boot.ini

Figure 21-4   Change the folder options so that protected operating system files are not hidden

TIP   From a text editor such as Notepad, you can set the timeout value to –1, which will cause the system to wait for a selection indefinitely. You cannot set the timeout to –1 from the Startup and Recovery window.

TROUBLESHOOTING THE BOOT PROCESS

When problems arise with booting, as with all PC problems, try the simple things first. Turn off the power and restart the system. Check for loose cables, switches that are not on, stuck keys on the keyboard, a wall outlet switch turned off, and similar easy-to-solve problems. The

21

next step is to determine at what point in the boot process the system fails. Ask what has happened since the last successful boot. Has new hardware or software been installed? Has there been a power surge or electrical storm? Has a user tinkered with the system? If you cannot pinpoint the source of the problem, then you have several tools to help you troubleshoot the boot process. Windows 2000 offers an Advanced Options menu, which includes starting the computer in safe mode. Use this option to prevent many device drivers and system services that normally load during the boot process from loading. You can then fix or disable these devices or services once the OS loads. The second utility, called the Recovery Console, is new to Windows 2000. It provides a command-line interface that allows you to perform maintenance and repairs to the hard drive. Another tool is the emergency startup disk, which is used to recover from problems with corrupted or missing operating system files or a corrupted hard drive boot sector. These three tools are discussed next.

Advanced Options Menu

As a PC boots, when the message *Starting Windows* appears at the bottom of the screen, press the F8 key to display the Windows 2000 **Advanced Options menu**, shown in Figure 21-5. As with the Windows 9x startup menu, this menu can be used to diagnose and fix problems when booting Windows 2000. The purpose of each option on the menu is outlined in the following sections.

```
Windows 2000 Advanced Options Menu
Please select an option:

        Safe Mode
        Safe Mode with Networking
        Safe Mode with Command Prompt

        Enable Boot Logging
        Enable VGA Mode
        Last Known Good Configuration
        Directory Services Restore Mode (Windows 2000 domain controllers only)
        Debugging Mode

        Boot Normally

Use ↑ and ↓ to move the highlight to your choice.
Press Enter to choose.
```

Figure 21-5   Press the F8 key at startup to display the Windows 2000 Advanced Options menu

Safe Mode   Safe mode boots the OS with a minimum configuration and can be used to solve problems when a new hardware installation is causing problems or a user has made settings that are causing problems. Safe mode boots with the mouse, monitor with basic video, keyboard, and mass storage drivers loaded. It uses the default system services (it does not load any extra services) and does not provide access to a network. When you boot in safe mode, you see "Safe Mode" in all four corners of your screen. You have a GUI interface in safe mode. Once the OS loads in safe mode, you can disable the problem device, scan for viruses, run diagnostic software, or take other appropriate action to diagnose and solve problems. When you load Windows 2000 in safe mode, all files used for the load are recorded in the Ntbtlog.txt file.

Safe Mode with Networking   Use this option when you are solving a problem with booting and need access to the network to solve the problem. For example, if you have just attempted to install a printer, which is causing the OS to hang when it boots, and the printer drivers are downloaded from the network, boot into safe mode with networking. Uninstall the printer and then install it again from the network. Also use this mode when the Windows 2000 installation files are not loaded from CD, but from the network, and you need to access these files.

Safe Mode with Command Prompt   This safe mode option does not automatically load a GUI desktop. Use it to get a command prompt. If safe mode does not load the OS, then try this option.

Enable Boot Logging   When you boot with this option, Windows 2000 loads normally and you access the regular desktop as usual. However, all the files used during the load process are recorded in a file, Ntbtlog.txt. Use this option to see what did and did not load during the boot process. If you are having a problem getting a device to work, check Ntbtlog.txt for its driver files. Boot logging is much more effective if you have a copy of the file that was made when everything was working as it should, and then you can compare the good load to the bad load, looking for differences.

Enable VGA Mode   Use this option when the video setting is such that you can't see well enough to fix a bad setting. This can happen because of a corrupted video driver or when a user has created a desktop with black fonts on a black background, or something similar. Booting in this mode gives you a very plain VGA video. Go to the Display settings, correct the problem, and reboot normally.

Last Known Good Configuration   Just as with Windows NT, Windows 2000 keeps the Last Known Good configuration in the registry. Use this option if you suspect the system was configured incorrectly. Windows 2000 will be restored to the settings of the last successful boot and all system setting changes made after this last successful boot are lost.

 Each time the system boots completely and the user logs on, the Last Known Good is saved. If you have booted several times since a problem started, the Last Known Good will not help you recover from the problem, since all saved versions of the Last Known Good reflect the problem.

Directory Services Restore Mode (Windows 2000 Domain Controllers Only)   This option applies only to domain controllers and is used as one step in the process of recovering from a corrupted Active Directory. Recall that the Active Directory is the domain database managed by the domain controller that tracks users and resources on the domain. The details of how all this works are beyond the scope of this chapter.

21

Debugging Mode   This mode gives you the opportunity to move system boot logs from the failing computer to another computer for evaluation. Connect another computer to the failing computer by way of the serial port. In this mode, Windows 2000 sends all the boot information to the serial port. The details of how to do this can be found in the *Windows 2000 Professional Resource Kit* (Microsoft Press).

Recovery Console

The Advanced Options menu can be of help if the problem is a faulty device driver or system service. However, if the problem goes deeper than that, the next tool to use is the **Recovery Console**. Use it when the operating system does not start properly or hangs during the load. The Recovery Console does not use a GUI, and with it you can access the FAT16, FAT32, and NTFS file systems.

The purpose of the Recovery Console is to allow you to repair a damaged registry, system files, or file system on the hard drive. You must enter the Administrator password in order to use the Console and access an NTFS volume. If the registry is so corrupted that the Recovery Console cannot read the password in order to validate it, you are not asked for the password, but you are limited in what you can do at the Console. You are not allowed into all folders, and you cannot copy files from the hard drive to a floppy disk without setting certain parameters.

The Recovery Console software is located on the Windows 2000 CD and also on the four Windows 2000 setup disks. If you have not already created the setup disks, you can go to a working Windows 2000 PC and create the disks by following the directions given in Chapter 20. Follow these steps to load Windows 2000 from the disks and access the Recovery Console:

1. Insert the first of the four setup disks and restart the PC. You are directed to insert each of the four disks in turn, and then the Setup screen appears as shown in Figure 21-6.

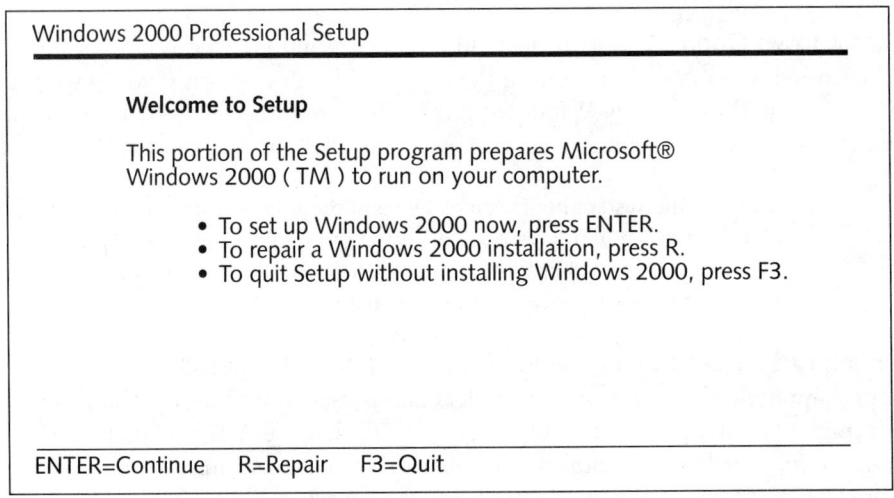

```
Windows 2000 Professional Setup
─────────────────────────────────────────────────

    Welcome to Setup

    This portion of the Setup program prepares Microsoft®
    Windows 2000 ( TM ) to run on your computer.

        • To set up Windows 2000 now, press ENTER.
        • To repair a Windows 2000 installation, press R.
        • To quit Setup without installing Windows 2000, press F3.




    ─────────────────────────────────────────────────
    ENTER=Continue    R=Repair    F3=Quit
```

Figure 21-6   Use this Windows Setup screen to access the Recovery Console

2. Type **R** to select the To repair a Windows 2000 installation option. The Windows 2000 Repair Options window opens. See Figure 21-7. Type **C** to select the Recovery Console.

3. The Windows 2000 Recovery Console window opens. See Figure 21-8. The Recovery Console looked at the hard drive and determined that there was only a single Windows 2000 installation on the drive installed in the C:\WINNT folder. (The WINNT folder might be on a different drive on your machine.) Press **1**, and then press **Enter** to select that installation.

```
Windows 2000 Professional Setup
_____

            Windows 2000 Repair Options:

                • To repair a Windows 2000 installation by using
                  the recovery console, press C.

                • To repair a Windows 2000 installation by using
                  the emergency repair process, press R.


            If the repair options do not successfully repair your system,
            run Windows 2000 Setup again.

_____

  C=Console    R=Repair    F3=Quit
```

Figure 21-7   Windows 2000 offers two repair options

```
  Microsoft Windows 2000 ( TM ) Recovery Console.

  The Recovery Console provides system repair and recovery functionality.

  Type EXIT to quit the Recovery Console and restart the computer.


  1:  C:\WINNT

  Which Windows 2000 installation would you like to log onto
  (To cancel, press ENTER)?  1
  Type the Administrator password:
  C:\WINNT>
```

Figure 21-8   The Windows 2000 Recovery Console command prompt

4. Enter the Administrator password and press **Enter**. If you don't know the password, you cannot use the console.

21

You now have a command prompt. You can use a limited group of DOS-like commands at this point to recover a failed system. These commands are listed and described in Table 21-2. To leave the Recovery Console and start Windows 2000, type **Exit** at the command prompt.

 At the command prompt, to retrieve the last command, press F3. To retrieve the command one character at a time, press the F1 key.

Table 21-2   Commands available from the Recovery Console

Command	Description
Attrib	Changes the attributes of a file or folder (works the same as the DOS version, as in the following example): `Attrib -r -h -s filename` This command removes the read, hidden, and system attributes from the file.
Batch	Carries out commands stored in a batch file: `Batch file1 file2` The commands stored in file1 are executed, and the results written to file2. If no file2 is specified, results are written to the screen.
Cd	Displays or changes the current directory.
Chkdsk	Checks a disk and repairs or recovers the data.
Cls	Clears the screen.
Copy	Copies a single uncompressed file, for example: `Copy A:\File1 C:\WINNT\File2` Copies the file on the floppy disk named File1 to the hard drive, WINNT folder, naming the file File2. Use the command to replace corrupted files. No wildcard characters are allowed.
Del	Deletes a file: `Del File1`
Dir	Lists files and folders.
Disable	Used when a service or driver starts and prevents the system from booting properly: `Disable servicename` This command disables a Windows 2000 system service or driver, restarts the computer without it, and helps you determine the problem.
Diskpart	Creates and deletes partitions on the hard drive. Enter the command with no arguments to display a user interface.
Enable	Enables a Windows 2000 system service or driver: `Enable servicename`
Exit	Quits the Recovery Console and restarts the computer.
Expand	Expands a compressed file and copies it from a floppy disk or a CD to the destination folder. For example: `Expand A:\File1 C:\WINNT` Expands the file on the floppy disk, copying it to the hard drive.

Table 21-2   Commands available from the Recovery Console (continued)

Command	Description
Fixboot	Rewrites the OS boot sector on the hard drive. If a drive letter is not specified, the system drive is assumed. `Fixboot C:` Use this command when the boot sector is damaged.
Fixmbr	Rewrites the Master Boot Record boot program. This command is the same as Fdisk/MBR. Use this command when the Master Boot Record is damaged.
Format	Formats a logical drive. If no file system is specified, NTFS is assumed: `Format C:/fs:FAT32` Uses FAT32 file system `Format C:/fs:FAT` Uses FAT16 file system
Help	Help utility appears for the given command:`Help Fixboot`
Listsvc	Lists all available services.
Logon	Allows you to log on to an installation with the Administrator password.
Map	Lists all drive letters and file system types.
Md or Mkdir	Creates a directory: `MD C:\TEMP`
More or Type	Displays a text file on screen: `TYPE filename.ext`
Rd or Rmdir	Deletes a directory: `RD C:\TEMP`
Rename or Ren	Renames a file: `Rename File1.txt File2.txt`
Set	Displays or sets Recovery Console environmental variables.
Systemroot	Sets the current directory to the directory where Windows 2000 is installed.
Type	Displays contents of a text file: `Type File1.txt`

Using the Recovery Console to Restore the Registry   If you suspect that the registry is damaged, you can use the Recovery Console commands to restore the registry from the last backup that you have created. The registry consists of five files, Default, Sam, Security, Software, and System, which are stored in the %SystemRoot%\System32\Config folder. A backup of the registry is stored in the %SystemRoot%\Repair\RegBack folder every time you back up the system state (see Figure 21-9).

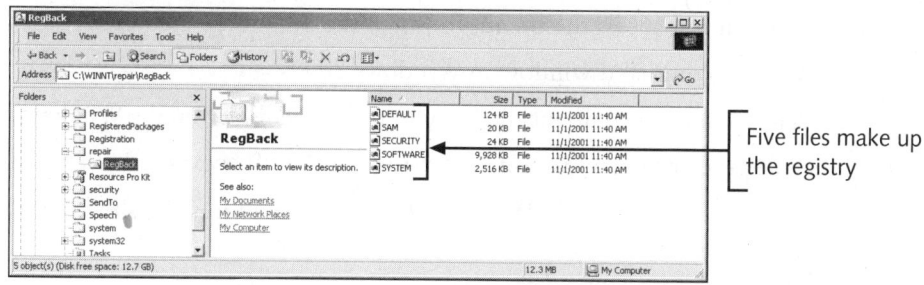

Figure 21-9   Windows puts a backup of the registry in the C:\WINNT\repair\RegBack folder

21

In Microsoft documentation, %SystemRoot% means the Windows 2000 folder on the boot partition. In most cases, that folder is C:\WINNT.

To restore the registry from this backup using the Recovery Console, first rename the registry files so that you can backtrack if necessary. From the Recovery Console command prompt, perform the steps outlined in Table 21-3. These actions will restore the registry to its state at the time of the last backup.

Table 21-3   Steps to restore the registry

Command	Description
1. Systemroot	Makes the Windows folder the current folder.
2. CD System32\Config	Makes the Windows registry folder the current folder.
3. Ren Default Default.save Ren Sam Sam.save Ren Security Security.save Ren Software Software.save Ren System System.save	Renames the five registry files.
4. Systemroot	Returns to the Windows folder.
5. CD repair\RegBack	Makes the registry backup folder the current folder.
6. Copy default C:\WINNT\system32\config Copy Sam C:\WINNT\system32\config Copy Security C:\WINNT\system32\config Copy Software C:\WINNT\system32\config Copy System C:\WINNT\system32\config	Copies the five registry files from the backup folder to the registry folder.

Installing the Recovery Console   Although the Recovery Console is often launched from the Windows CD to recover from system failure, you can also install it on your working system so it appears on the Start menu. Use it to address less drastic problems that occur, when you can access the menu. To install the Recovery Console:

1. Open a command window in Windows 2000.

2. Change from the current directory to the \I386 folder on the Windows 2000 CD.

3. Enter the command **winnt32 /cmdcons**. The Recovery Console is installed.

4. Restart your computer. Recovery Console should now be shown with the list of available operating systems on the Start menu.

Emergency Repair Process

If options on the Advanced Options menu fail to recover the system and the Recovery Console fails to do so, your next option is the **Emergency Repair Process**. Use this option only as a last resort because it restores the system to the state it was in immediately after the Windows 2000 installation. All changes since the installation will be lost. The process uses an Emergency Repair Disk (ERD), but the disk does not contain the same information as does the Windows NT ERD (Windows NT Emergency Repair Disk).

Recall that the Windows NT ERD contains a copy of the registry, and that you should update the disk any time you make significant changes to the registry. You can then use the disk to repair a corrupted registry, restoring it to its state when you last updated the ERD.

The Windows 2000 ERD contains information about your current installation, but does not contain a copy of the registry because it is too large to fit on a single floppy disk. The Windows 2000 ERD points to a folder on the hard drive where the registry was backed up when Windows 2000 was installed. This folder is %SystemRoot%\repair, which most likely is C:\WINNT\repair.

Using the Windows 2000 ERD to recover from a corrupted registry returns you to the installation version of the registry, and you lose all changes to the registry since that time. Because of the way the ERD works, you do not need to update the disk once you've created it. Before a problem occurs, follow these directions to create the disk:

1. Click **Start**, point to **Programs**, **Accessories**, and **System Tools**, and then click **Backup**. The Backup window appears with the Welcome tab selected. See Figure 21-10. Select **Emergency Repair Disk**.

2. The Backup tab and the Emergency Repair Diskette dialog box open. If you check the box shown in Figure 21-11, the system backs up your registry to a folder under the Repair folder, %SystemRoot%\repair\RegBack.

3. Click **OK** to create the disk. Label the disk Windows 2000 Emergency Repair Disk, and keep it in a safe place.

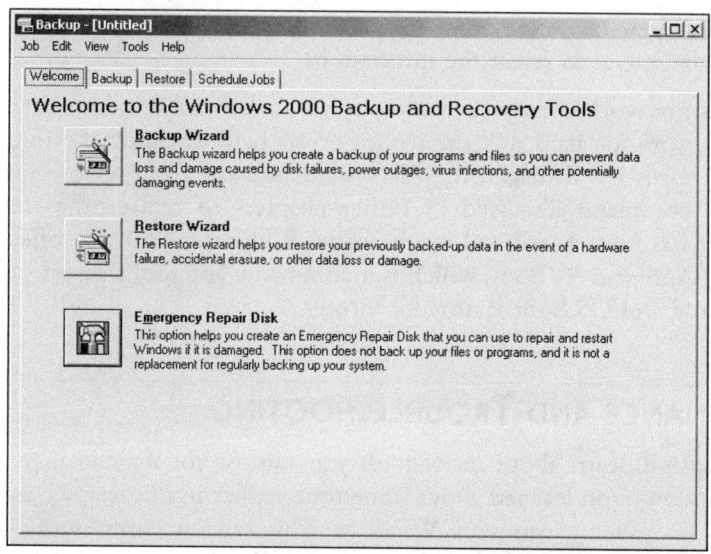

Figure 21-10   Use the Backup window to back up the registry and create an emergency repair disk

21

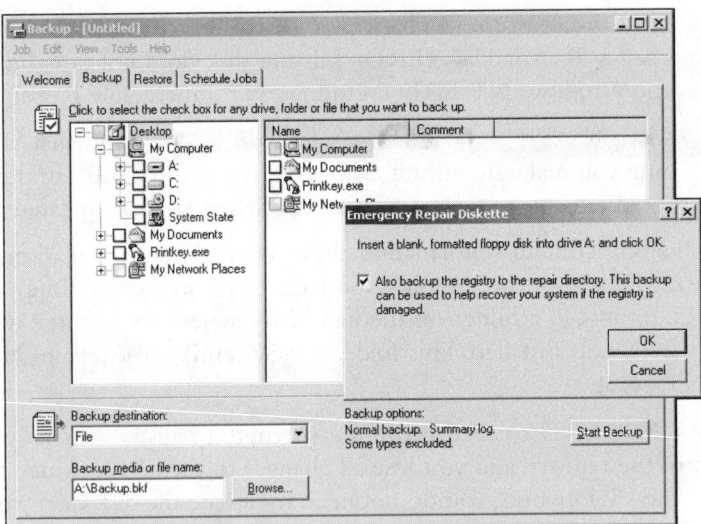

Figure 21-11   Create an ERD and back up the registry to the hard drive

If your hard drive fails, you can use the ERD to restore the system, including system files, boot files, and the registry, to its state at the end of the Windows 2000 installation. To do that follow these steps:

1. Boot the PC from the four Windows 2000 setup disks. The Setup menu appears (refer back to Figure 21-6). Select option **R**.

2. When the Windows 2000 Repair Options window opens (refer back to Figure 21-7), select option **R**.

3. You are instructed to insert the Emergency Repair Disk. Follow the instructions on the screen to repair the installation.

If this process does not work, then your next option is to reinstall Windows 2000. Be sure to use ScanDisk to scan the hard disk surface for errors before you do the installation. If you suspect that a virus has damaged the file system, also use the Fixmbr command or the Fdisk /MBR command discussed in earlier chapters to replace the master boot program in case it has been corrupted by the virus. Windows 2000 also offers a utility called InoculateIT Antivirus AVBoot, which is a command-line tool that can scan memory, the MBR sector, and OS boot sectors for viruses.

TOOLS FOR MAINTENANCE AND TROUBLESHOOTING

In this section, you will learn about many tools you can use for maintenance and troubleshooting in Windows. You learned about some tools earlier in this chapter, as well as in previous chapters on other versions of Windows. This section covers some additional tools. You will learn how use these tools to manage hard disks, applications, system processes, and other components of Windows.

Using the Backup Tool to Restore the System State

In Chapter 20, you learned how to back up the system state after installing Windows 2000 and verifying that the system is working. To use the backup (Ntbackup.exe) to restore the system state after a system failure or the registry becoming corrupted, begin the same way you did to make the backup by clicking Start, pointing to Programs, Accessories, and System Tools and then clicking Backup. The dialog box opens with the Backup tab showing. Click the Restore tab, which is shown in Figure 21-12.

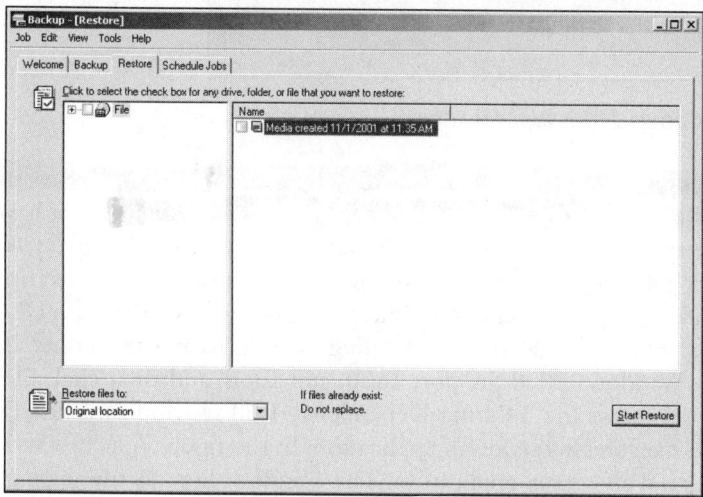

Figure 21-12   Restore the system state from the Restore tab of the Backup window

From the Restore tab, you select the backup you want to restore and, in the drop-down menu in the bottom-left corner, the location to which it is to be restored. Click the Start Restore button in the bottom-right corner to start the process. Remember that you can restore the system state as a way of restoring the registry.

Windows 2000 Support Tools

Windows 2000 offers several support tools that you can install. They are located in the \Support\Tools folder of the Windows 2000 CD. To install them, run the Setup program in that folder. Enter this command in the Run dialog box: D:\Support\Tools\Setup.exe. Substitute the drive letter of the CD-ROM drive for D in the command line. The list of tools installed is shown in Figure 21-13.

TIP   In addition to the support tools described here, third-party diagnostic software can be of help. For example, ConfigSafe by imagineLAN, Inc. (*www.imaginelan.com*) is a utility that tracks configuration changes to Windows 9x or Windows NT/2000/XP and can restore the system to a previously saved configuration.

21

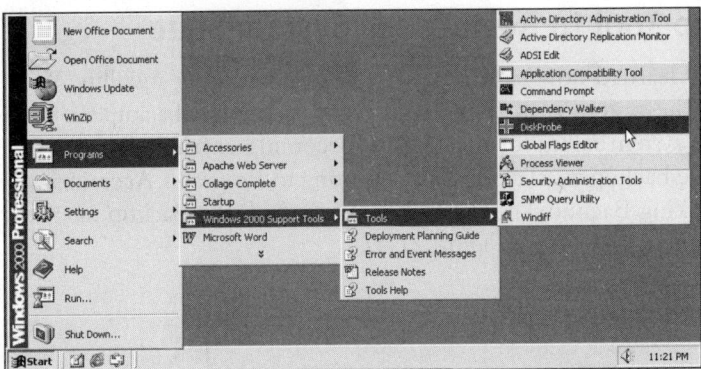

Figure 21-13 Windows 2000 support tools

One of these utilities is Dependency Walker, which lists all the files used by an application. It can be useful when troubleshooting a failed application installation if you have a report of files used by the application on a computer where the installation is good. Compare the reports, looking for DLL files that are missing on the bad installation or are not the correct size or are incorrectly date stamped. Software applications often use DLL files for added functionality and to relate to the operating system. To use the utility, click Start, point to Programs, Windows 2000 Support Tools, and Tools, and then click Dependency Walker. Figure 21-14 shows the resulting Dependency Walker window. Click File, Open, and select the main executable file for an application. In the figure, Apache.exe is selected. Apache is a popular Web server application. The window lists all supporting files that Apache.exe uses and how they are dependent on one another.

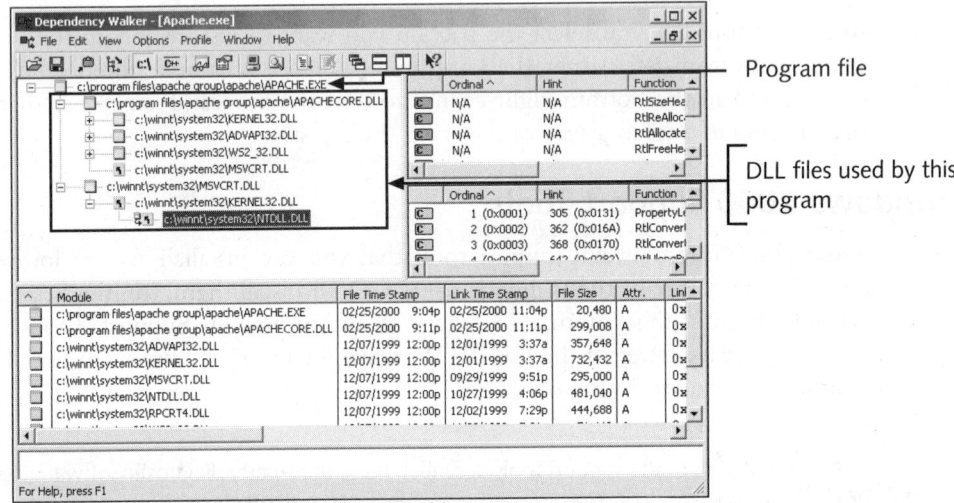

Figure 21-14 You can use Dependency Walker to solve problems with applications

Windows File Protection

Windows 2000 provides a feature called **WFP (Windows File Protection)** to protect system files such as .sys, .dll, or .exe files from modification. Earlier versions of Windows would sometimes allow these files to be overwritten by unsigned, non-Microsoft versions during program installations. Changes to shared system files can cause errors within a program, incompatibility between two or more programs, mismatches between file versions, or even system instability.

WFP prevents these problems and protects files from modification through two tools. One is a background process that notifies WFP when a protected file is modified. WFP then checks the file signature to see whether it is the correct Microsoft version of the file. If the file version is not correct, WFP looks in the Dllcache folder, which contains cached copies of system files, or asks for the Windows 2000 CD to be inserted so that it can find the file and restore it from there. Replacing incorrect system files with correct ones from the Windows 2000 CD requires administrative permissions. If a non-administrator user is logged on when WFP activates, WFP will not prompt that user for insertion of the Windows 2000 CD and will wait until an administrator logs on to request the CD and replace the file.

> **TIP** If a file has been modified, is correctly signed as a Microsoft-approved version, and is not present in the Dllcache folder, WFP adds it to that folder to be used as the correct version on future scans.

When WFP restores a file, it shows the following message by default, replacing *file_name* with the name of the system file it restored:

```
A file replacement was attempted on the protected system
file file_name. To maintain system stability, the file has
been restored to the correct Microsoft version. If
problems occur with your application, please contact the
application vendor for support.
```

If you see this message, carefully note what application was working at the time and what had just happened before the message. In addition to software installations, viruses, and software applications, errors can cause attempted modifications to system files, and it is important for you to have as much information as possible in order to figure out which applications might need to be scanned for viruses or replaced altogether.

The other tool that WFP provides is the **SFC (System File Checker)**. There are several situations in which the system or an administrator might use this tool. If the administrator set the system to perform an unattended installation, after Setup is completed, the SFC checks all protected system files to see whether they were modified by programs added during the installation, as well as the catalog files that contain the file signatures. If any incorrect modifications have been made or if any important system files are found to be

21

unsigned, WFP retrieves a copy of the file from the Dllcache folder or requests it from the Windows 2000 CD.

An administrator can also activate the SFC manually from a command prompt and use it to verify that the system is using correct versions of all protected system files, either as a preventative maintenance measure or when it is suspected that system files have become corrupted or deleted. To use System File Checker, from the command prompt, the administrator types *Sfc.exe* with one of the switches shown in Table 21-4. You can also access the Run dialog box from the Start menu and type *C:\WINNT\system32\sfc.exe /scannow* (or another switch).

Table 21-4   Switches for the Sfc.exe utility

Switch	Function
/cachesize=x	Sets, in megabytes, the size of the file cache.
/cancel	Discontinues scans of protected system files.
/enable	Enables normal operation of WFP.
/purgecache	Empties the file cache and immediately scans all protected system files, populating the Dllcache folder with confirmed correct versions of system files (may require insertion of the Windows 2000 CD as source for correct versions).
/quiet	Replaces incorrect versions of system files with correct ones without prompting the user.
/scanboot	Performs a scan of protected system files every time the system boots.
/scannow	Performs an immediate scan of protected system files.
/scanonce	Performs a scan of protected system files the next time the system boots.
/?	Displays a list of available switches for the sfc command.

Command Window

With Windows 2000, executing **CMD.exe** or Command.com from the Run dialog box opens a command interpreter window where you can use DOS-like commands at a command prompt. The Cmd.exe is the 32-bit version of the older 16-bit Command.com used with DOS. A command window is also available under Start, Programs, Accessories, Command Prompt. (In Windows 9x, it was listed as MS-DOS Prompt under Start, Programs.) Type Exit to close the window. You can also execute single commands from the Run dialog box without having to open the command window.

 To add a command prompt icon to your desktop for easy access, locate the icon in Windows Explorer under Start, Programs, Accessories, Command Prompt and, while holding down the Ctrl key, drag the icon to your desktop.

Disk Properties Window

The Disk Properties window provides a way for you to perform routine maintenance on a drive. It is not new to Windows 2000, but is included here to make the list of maintenance tools more complete. To access the window, using Windows Explorer, right-click the icon for the drive that you want to work with and select Properties from the shortcut menu. The Properties window for the selected drive opens, as shown in Figure 21-15. The General tab, which appears in front when you first open the window, provides information about the name, type, and file system of the selected drive, as well as the amount of free and used space.

Notice that the drive in Figure 21-15 is using the FAT32 file system. Compare this window for a FAT32 disk to the window shown in Figure 21-16 for an NTFS disk. One difference in the two windows is the Disk Properties window for an NTFS disk includes the option for drive compression at the bottom of the window. For an NTFS disk, check Compress drive to save disk space, and then click Apply to compress the volume. Later, if you decide to not use compression, clear the check box.

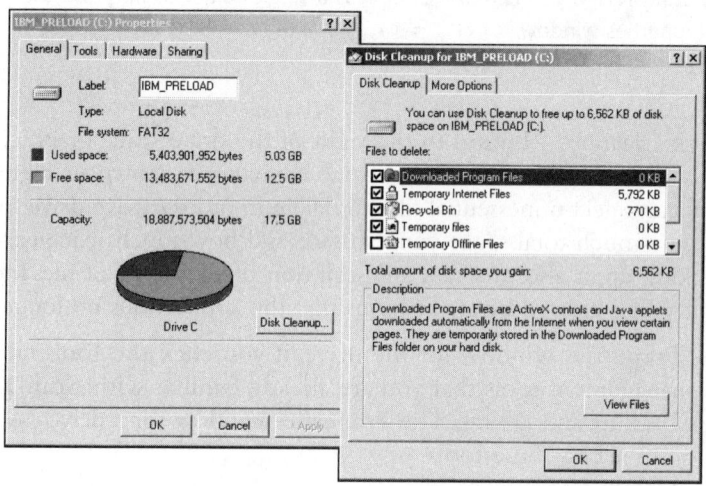

Figure 21-15   The Disk Properties window provides a shortcut to disk management tools

21

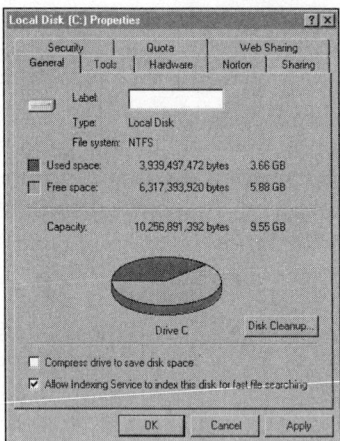

Figure 21-16   Disk Properties window for an NTFS disk

 TIP   If you are using NTFS, you can also compress a single folder or file from the General tab of its Properties window.

If you click the Disk Cleanup... button to the right of the drive space graphic, the Disk Cleanup window opens with the Disk Cleanup tab showing, as shown in Figure 21-15. From this view, you can select nonessential files to delete in order to save drive space. Disk Cleanup tells you how much total space you can save and how much space each type of removable file is taking up; it also provides a description of each type of file. Included in the list are temporary files created by applications that the applications no longer need.

Going back to the Properties window for the drive, if you click the Tools tab, you can access three drive management tools that you are already familiar with: ScanDisk (listed as Error checking), Backup, and Defrag. The Properties window for a drive just provides another way for you to access these tools.

Computer Management

Computer Management is a window that consolidates several tools that you can use to manage the local PC or other computers on the network. Computer Management combines several Windows 2000 administrative tools. To use most of these tools, you must be logged on as an administrator, although you can view certain settings and configurations in Computer Management if you are logged in with lesser privileges. To access Computer Management, from the Control Panel, open the Administrative Tools window and then double-click the Computer Management icon. The Computer Management window appears. See Figure 21-17. Some of the tasks you can perform from this window include monitoring problems with hardware, software, and security. You can share folders, view device configurations, add new device drivers, start and stop services, and manage server applications.

By default, the Administrative Tools group is located in the Control Panel. In addition, you can add the Administrative Tools group to the Start menu under Start, Programs, Administrative Tools. To do that, right-click the taskbar and select Properties. On the Taskbar and Start Menu Properties window, select the Advanced tab. Check Display Administrative Tools, and click OK.

Figure 21-17   Computer Management combines several administrative tools into a single easy-to-access window

Disk Management

The Computer Management console contains a tool called **Disk Management** that you can use to create partitions on basic disks or volumes on dynamic disks and to convert a basic disk to a dynamic disk. This graphical, user-friendly utility replaces the Fdisk utility of earlier Windows OSs. To access the utility, in the Computer Management console, select Disk Management.

When Disk Management first loads, it examines the drive configuration for the system and displays all drives laid out in a graphical format so you can see how each drive is allocated.

The Disk Management window shown in Figure 21-18 has three drives displayed: Disk 0 is a basic hard drive using the NTFS file system. Disk 1 is a dynamic hard drive that has not yet been allocated into volumes, and there is also a CD-ROM drive shown that has a CD in the drive.

After you install a new second hard drive in the system, when you first access Disk Management, it will ask you if you want to create a basic disk or dynamic disk using the new drive. (Basic and dynamic disks were discussed in Chapter 20.) Then Disk Management

21

displays the new disk with unallocated space, as shown in Figure 21-18. This second hard drive has been designated as a dynamic disk.

To create a volume on this dynamic disk, do the following:

1. Right-click on an unallocated area of the drive and select **Create Volume** from the shortcut menu (see Figure 21-18).

2. The Create Volume Wizard launches. Click **Next** to continue.

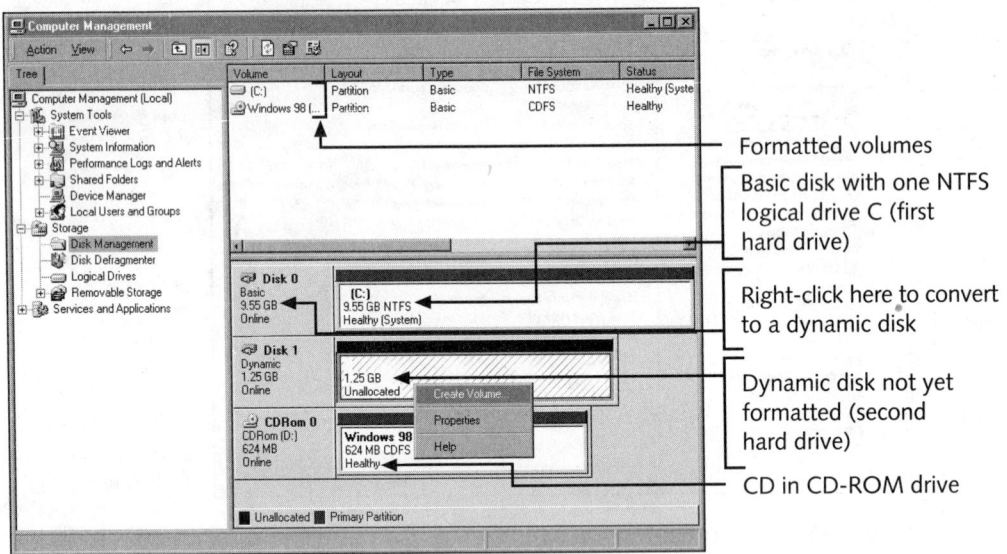

Figure 21-18   Create a volume on an unallocated dynamic disk

3. On the next screen (see Figure 21-19), you would select a volume type, either Simple volume, Spanned volume, or Striped volume. In our example, Simple volume is the only one available, because we are working with only one dynamic drive. You would have to have more than one dynamic drive to specify a volume as striped or spanned. Click **Next** to continue.

4. Follow the wizard through the process of specifying the volume size, a drive letter, file system (NTFS, FAT or FAT32), and allocation unit size (default is 512 bytes). The wizard then creates the dynamic volume.

The process for creating a partition on a basic disk is similar, with the main difference being that the wizard is called the Create Partition Wizard. Access it by right-clicking the unallocated portion of the basic disk, selecting Create Partition, and following the directions in the wizard.

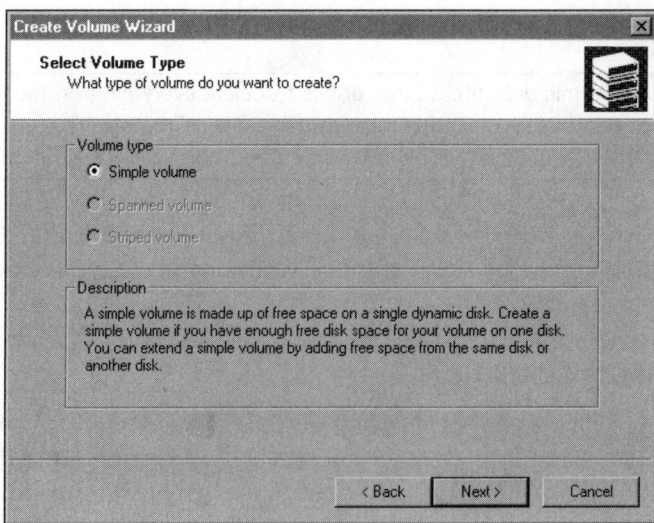

Figure 21-19   Disk Management provides the Create Volume Wizard to help you create volumes

Converting from a Basic Disk to a Dynamic Disk   When you are creating partitions on a basic disk, you should always leave at least 1 MB of space unallocated. If you later decide to convert this basic disk to a dynamic disk, the conversion will require 1 MB of free space to store a database of configuration information for all dynamic disks on the computer. The Disk Management tool can be used to accomplish this conversion by right-clicking on the small frame (see Figure 21-18) at the basic drive you want to upgrade and selecting Upgrade to Dynamic disk from the shortcut menu. This process also converts the partitions on the basic disk to volumes on the new dynamic disk. Table 21-5 shows how parts of a basic disk change when it is converted.

Table 21-5   Conversion of space from basic to dynamic

Type of basic disk space before upgrade	Type of dynamic disk space after upgrade
System partition	Simple volume
Boot partition	Simple volume
Primary partition	Simple volume
Extended partition	Simple volume
Logical drive	Simple volume
Free space	Unallocated space

21

CAUTION
The only way to make a dynamic disk into a basic disk is to delete everything on the dynamic disk, including all data and all volumes, and recreate a basic disk in the resulting unallocated space. Obviously, all the data on the disk will be lost, so be sure to first back up your data.

To change a dynamic disk to a basic disk, delete everything on the dynamic disk, open Disk Management, right-click the dynamic disk that you want to change back to a basic disk, and select Revert to Basic Disk.

Microsoft Management Console

When Windows combines several administrative tools into a single window, the window is called a **console**. Individual tools within the console are called **snap-ins**. An example of a console is Computer Management. Event Viewer and System Information are two snap-ins in that console. Another example of a console is Recovery Console, which was introduced earlier in the chapter. Windows offers a way for you to create your own customized consoles using the console-building utility **Microsoft Management Console (MMC)**. Table 21-6 lists some available snap-ins for MMC.

Table 21-6   Some available MMC snap-ins

Snap-in	Description
Active X Control	Enables you to add Active X controls to your system.
Certificates	Provides certificate management at the user, service, or computer level.
Component Services	Links to the Component Services management tool, which is located on the Control Panel.
Computer Management	Links to the Computer Management tools on the Control Panel.
Device Manager	Lets you see what hardware devices you have on your system and configure device properties.
Disk Defragmenter	Links to the Disk Defragmenter utility.
Disk Management	Links to the Disk Management tool.
Event Viewer	Links to the Event Viewer tool, which displays event logs for the system.
Fax Service Management	Enables you to manage fax settings and devices.
Folder	Enables you to add a folder to manage from MMC.
Group Policy	Provides a tool to manage group policy settings.
Indexing Service	Searches files and folders using specified parameters.
IP Security Policy Management	Manages Internet communication security.
Link to Web Address	Enables you to link to a specified Web site.

Table 21-6   Some available MMC snap-ins (continued)

Snap-in	Description
Local Users and Groups	Provides a tool to manage settings for local users and groups.
Performance Logs and Alerts	Gives you an interface from which to set up and manage logs of performance information and alerts about system performance.
Removable Storage Management	Enables you to manage settings and configuration information for removable storage devices such as Zip drives and tape backup drives.
Security Configuration and Analysis	Enables you to manage configuration of security settings for computers that use security template files.
Services	Provides a centralized interface for starting, stopping, and configuring system services.
Shared Folders	Provides information about shared folders, files that are open, and current sessions.
System Information	Contains information about the system that you can use when troubleshooting.

Creating a Customized Console

As with the Computer Management console, you must have administrative privileges to perform most tasks from the MMC. You can use MMC to create your own customized consoles. You can also save the console to a file, which is assigned a .msc file extension. Store the file in the C:\Documents and Settings*user*\Start Menu\Programs\Administrative Tools folder to make it appear as a program when you click Start, and point to Programs, Administrative Tools. In the path, substitute the name of the user. For example, for the Administrator, the path to the .msc file is C:\Documents and Settings\Administrator\ Start Menu\Programs\Administrative Tools.

  Once you create a console, you can copy the .msc file to any computer or place a short-cut to it on the desktop.

Follow these directions to open MMC and create a console that contains some popular utility tools:

    1. Click **Start**, **Run**, enter **MMC** in the Run dialog box, and then click **OK**. An empty console window appears, as shown in Figure 21-20.

21

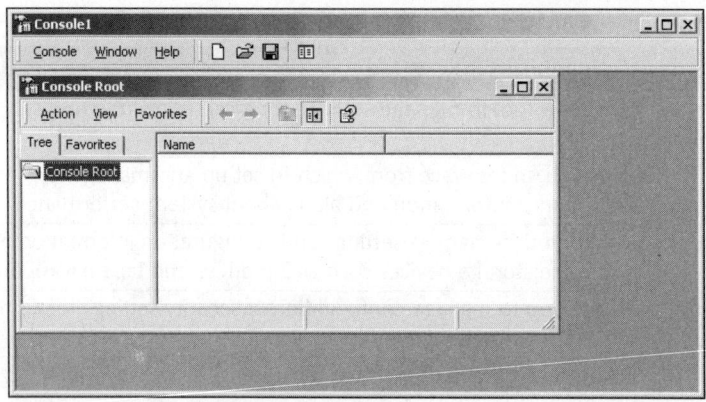

Figure 21-20   An empty console

2. Click **Console** on the menu bar, and then click **Add/Remove Snap-in**. The Add/Remove Snap-in window opens. The window illustrated in Figure 21-21 is empty because no snap-ins have been added to the console.

3. Click **Add**. You see a list of snap-ins that can be added to a console, as shown in Figure 21-21. Select a snap-in, and then click **Add**.

4. A dialog box opens that allows you to set the parameters for the snap-in. The dialog box offers different selections, depending on the snap-in being added. When you have made your selections, click **Finish**. The new snap-in appears in the Add/Remove Snap-in window.

5. Repeat Steps 3 and 4 until you have added all the snap-ins that you want to the console. When you are finished, from the Add Standalone Snap-in window illustrated in Figure 21-21, click **Close**, then click **OK**.

6. Figure 21-22 shows a console with four snap-ins added. To save the console, click **Console** on the menu bar, and then click **Save As**. The Save As dialog box opens.

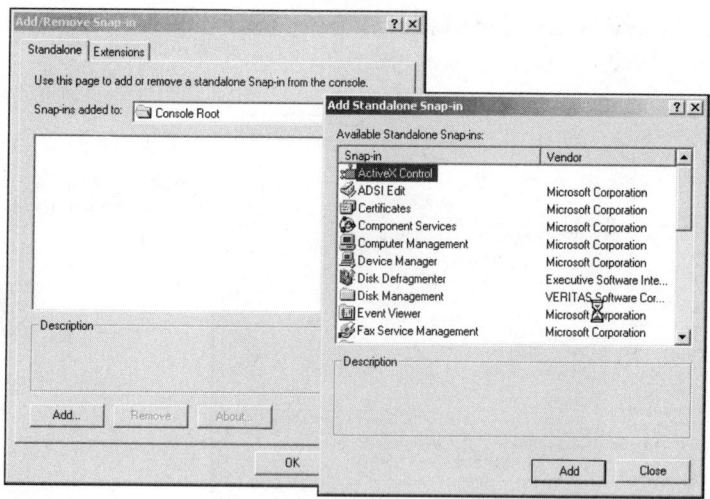

Figure 21-21   List of snap-ins available to be added to a console

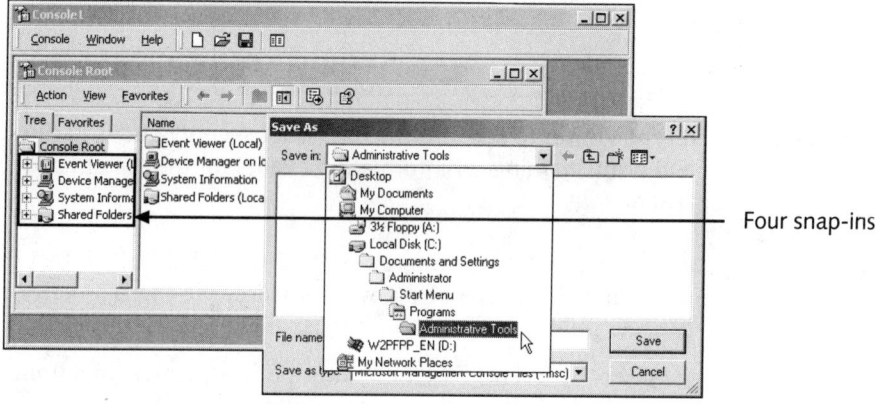

Four snap-ins

Figure 21-22   Saving a console with four snap-ins

7. The default location for the console file is shown in Figure 21-22—this is the location that ensures the console appears as an option under Administrative Tools on the Start menu. Select this location for the file, name the file, and click **Save**.

8. Close the console window by clicking **Console**, **Exit**.

To use the console, click Start, Programs, Administrative Tools, and select the console.

Event Viewer

In the list of MMC snap-ins, you saw that there is one that connects to the Event Viewer tool, which displays logs about significant system events that occur in Windows NT/2000/XP or in applications running under these OSs, such as a hardware or network failure, OS error

21

messages, or a device or service has failed to start. There are three different logs shown in Event Viewer, which are displayed in Figure 21-23:

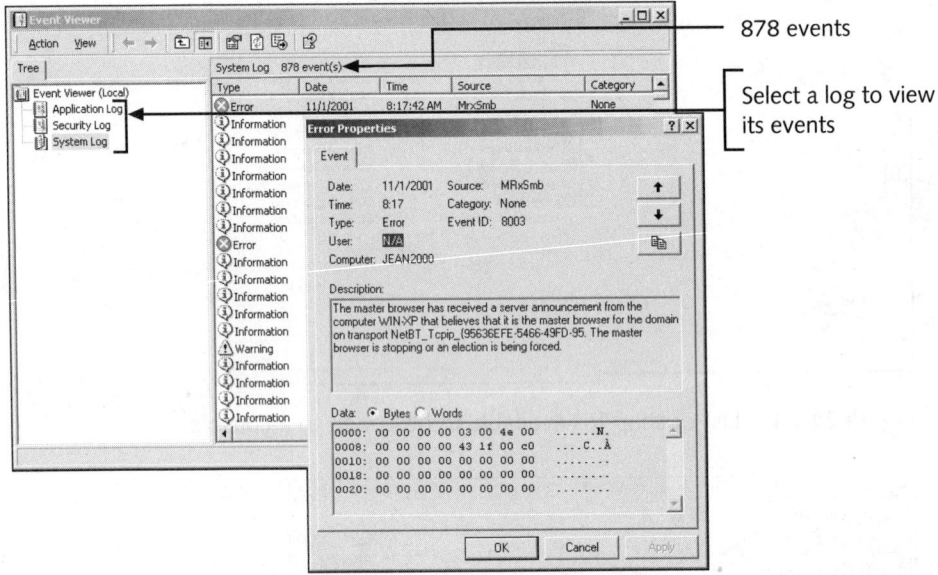

Figure 21-23 Use Event Viewer to see information about security audits in the security log and error, warning, or information events for the system and application logs

- *The application log* records application events that the developer of the program sets to trigger a log entry. One type of event recorded in this log is an error recorded by the Dr. Watson utility, which you will learn about later in this chapter.

- *The security log* records events based on audit policies, which an administrator sets to monitor user activity such as successful or unsuccessful attempts to access a file or log on to the system. Only an administrator can view this log.

- *The system log* records events triggered by components of Windows 2000, such as a device driver failing to load during the boot process. Windows 2000 sets which events are recorded in this log. All users can access this log file.

There are three types of events recorded in the system and application logs:

- *Information* events are recorded when a driver, service, or application functions successfully.

- *Warning* events are recorded when something happens that may indicate a future problem but does not necessarily indicate that something is presently wrong with the system. For example, low disk space might trigger a warning event.

- *Error* events are recorded when something goes wrong with the system, such as a necessary component failing to load, data getting lost or becoming corrupted, or a system or application function ceasing to operate.

You can open Event Viewer from the Computer Management Console, or you can locate it by double-clicking the Administrative Tools icon in the Control Panel. To view a log within Event Viewer, in the left pane click the log that you want to view. This will cause a summary of events to be shown in the right pane. Double-click a specific event to show details about it. (See Figure 21-23.)

Notice in the figure that 878 events are listed in the system log. You may only want to view certain events, without reading through the entire list to find what you're looking for. To filter events, right-click on a log in the left pane and select Filter from the shortcut menu. There are several criteria you can use to filter events, which are listed in Table 21-7.

Table 21-7   Log properties that can be used to filter events

Property	Description
Category	The category that the event falls under, such as an attempt to log on to the system or access a program.
Computer	The name of a computer on the system.
Event ID	A number that identifies the event, making it easier for support personnel to track events.
Event source	The application, driver, or service that triggered the event.
Event type	The type of event, such as information, error, or warning.
From: To:	The range of events that you want to view. You can view the events from first to last event, or you can view all events that occurred in a specific date and time range.
User	The logon name for a user.

Another way you can avoid a ballooning log file is to set a size limit and specify what is to happen when the log reaches this limit. If you right-click a log, select Properties from the shortcut menu, and click the General tab, you can set the maximum size of the log in megabytes (as well as view general information about the log). You can set it so that the log overwrites events as needed, overwrites events that are more than a specified number of days old, or does not overwrite events at all. Select this last option when system security is high and you do not want to lose any event information. If you select this option, the system will simply stop recording events when the log file reaches the maximum size. (See Figure 21-24.)

To allow the system to record events in the log after a log reaches maximum size, you will have to review the events and clear the log manually by clicking the Clear Log button from the Properties window or selecting Clear All Events from the Action menu. Before the log is cleared, Event Viewer will give you a chance to save it.

21

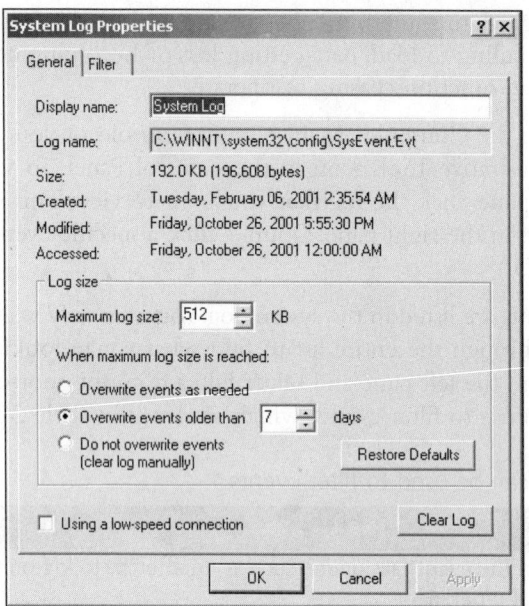

Figure 21-24   View information about a log, including maximum size of the log file, in the Log Properties window

Performance Monitoring and Optimization

Maintaining optimal performance, or addressing performance problems when they develop, involves a three-part process in which you analyze data provided by monitoring tools such as Task Manager and System Monitor, determine areas in which performance is below the baseline, and identify and take the steps necessary to correct this problem.

Principles for Optimizing Performance

Here are some principles to remember when trying to optimize performance on your system:

- One of the most important things you can do is establish a **baseline** of acceptable performance for your system, defining what you will consider normal performance under a typical workload. Figure out what resources the system uses when you are running all required programs and services, which will help you decide whether you need to add additional resources (such as more RAM) to the system. Heavily used Windows 2000 computers may benefit from having as much as 512 MB of RAM, whereas machines on which usage is more moderate may only need 128 MB of RAM.

- If you add RAM, remember that you will need to increase the size of the paging file. You might also increase paging file size if the peak usage of the paging file is too close to the limit.

- Replacing one component may not help that much if other components have not been upgraded. For example, if you install a faster CPU, you need to look at the amount of RAM and the size of the hard drive as well.

- Applications are assigned a priority level, which determines its position in the queue for CPU resources. This priority level can be changed for applications that are already loaded by using Task Manager. If an application is performing slowly, increase its priority. You should only do this with very important applications, because giving an application higher priority than certain background system processes can sometimes interfere with the operating system.

- In general, upgrading an existing PC is recommended as long as the cost of the upgrade stays below half the cost of buying a new machine. Even if you just keep the case, power supply, and an expansion card or two, buying a new motherboard and hard drive can be almost like having a whole new system at a lower cost.

The rest of this section discusses two tools that you can use to monitor system performance: Task Manager and System Monitor.

Task Manager

Task Manager (Taskman.exe) allows you to view applications and processes that are running on your computer as well as performance information for the processor and the memory. There are three ways that you can access Task Manager:

- Press the Ctrl, Alt, and Delete keys simultaneously. The Windows Security window will open. Click the Task Manager button.

- Right-click a blank area on the taskbar and select Task Manager from the shortcut menu.

- Press the Ctrl, Shift, and Esc keys simultaneously.

Task Manager has three tabs: Applications, Processes, and Performance. Under the Applications tab (see Figure 21-25), each application that is loaded can have one of two statuses: Running or Not Responding. If an application is listed as Not Responding, you can end it by selecting it and clicking the End Task button at the bottom of the window. You will lose any unsaved information in the application.

The Processes tab lists system services and other processes associated with applications together with how much CPU time and memory the process is using. This information can help you determine which applications are slowing your system down. The Performance tab, seen in Figure 21-26, shows more detail about how a program is using system resources. You can use these views to identify which applications and processes are using the most CPU time.

21

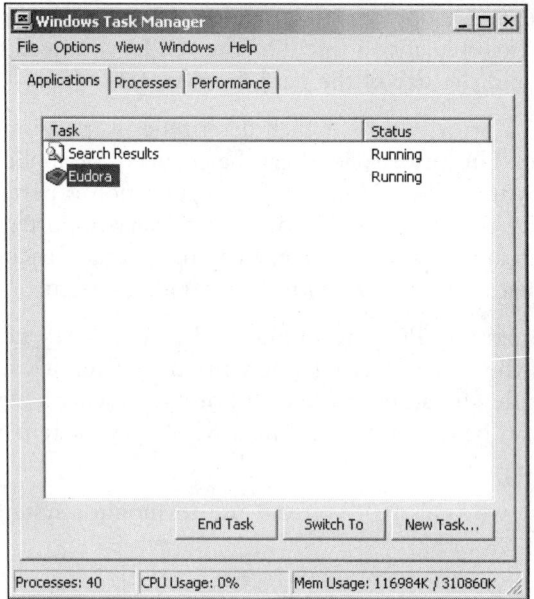

Figure 21-25 The Applications tab in Task Manager shows the status of active applications

Figure 21-26 The Performance tab shows more detail about how system resources are being used

On the Performance tab in Figure 21-26 note the four frames at the bottom of the window. These frames give the following information:

- The *Totals* frame indicates how much the system is currently being used by counting handles (indicates a device or file is being accessed), threads (unit of activity within a process), and processes (programs running). Use these entries to know how heavily the system is used.

- The *Physical Memory* frame lists Total (amount of RAM), Available (RAM not used), and System Cache (RAM in use). Use these entries to know if you must upgrade RAM.

- The *Commit Charge* frame lists Total (current size of virtual memory, also called the page file or swap file), Limit (how much of the page file can be allocated to applications before the size of the page file must be increased), and Peak (maximum amount of virtual memory used in this session). Use these entries to learn if you must increase the size of the page file.

- The *Kernel Memory* frame indicates how much RAM and virtual memory is used by the OS. This frame lists Total (sum of RAM and virtual memory), Paged (how much of the page file is used by the OS), and Nonpaged (how much RAM is used by the OS). Use this frame to how much memory the OS is using. If this is high, look for OS processes you can eliminate.

By reading the information in the frames in Figure 21-26, you can see that the OS is using about 28 MB of memory. The system contains about 130 MB of RAM, and the paging file maximum size is set to about 311 MB. How to change the maximum and initial size of the page file is covered later in the chapter.

System Monitor

In most cases, you can get what information you need from Task Manager to determine if the system is in need of performance tuning or upgrading. If this information is not detailed enough, use System Monitor, which provides more detail than Task Manager on system performance. There are three components of System Monitor: objects, instances, and counters. Objects are hardware or software system components, and instances are multiples of objects. For example, Microsoft Word is an object, but if you have Word open in two separate windows on the desktop, then there are two instances of this one object running. Counters show information on specific characteristics of an object and constantly gather the data and update the counter display. You can specify which counters to show for an object.

Important objects to monitor using System Monitor include Memory, Paging File, Processor, and Physical Disk (the hard drive). In the following example, we will access System Monitor and then add and view counters for the Memory object.

1. In the Control Panel, double-click the **Administrative Tools** icon.

2. From the Administrative Tools window, double-click the **Performance** icon.

3. The Performance window opens. See Figure 21-27. System Monitor is highlighted and the System Monitor details pane shows on the right. The pane is

blank because no objects are presently being monitored. Right-click in that
pane and select **Add Counters** from the shortcut menu (see Figure 21-27).

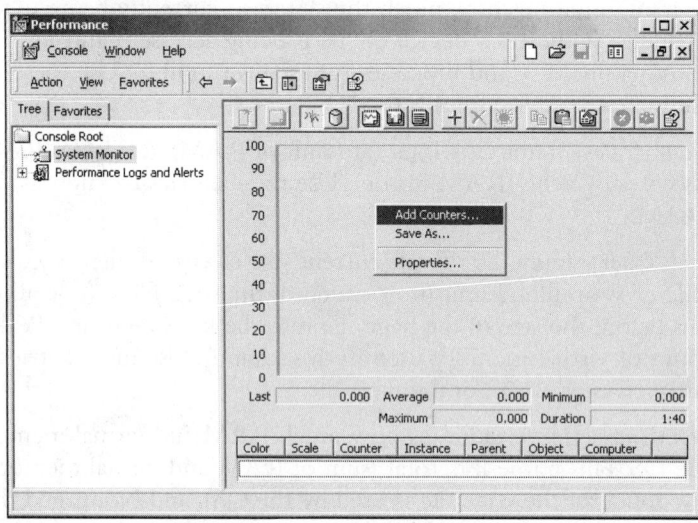

Figure 21-27 Access System Monitor through the Performance window

4. The Add Counters window opens (Figure 21-28). From the Performance
object drop-down list, select the **Memory** object.

5. You have the option to view all counters, but that makes for a messy display
that is hard to read. By default, the radio button is selected beside the option
Select counters from list. Locate and click the **Available Bytes** counter, which
will tell you how much physical memory remains. Click **Add**.

Figure 21-28 In the Add Counters window, select a performance object and counters
to monitor

6. Scroll down in the list until you see the **Page Faults/sec** counter. This will tell you how many pages were requested but were not immediately available in memory. Click **Add**.

7. Click **Close** to close the Add Counters window.

Figure 21-29 shows System Monitor in the process of monitoring the two counters you selected. The lines tracking the counters are color-coded to match the counters listed at the bottom of the graph. Look at the left side of the graph. The line representing Page Faults/sec begins at 0 and spikes when an application is opened. The line representing Available Bytes begins at 30 and dips lower, meaning fewer bytes are available, when applications are active. The vertical line on the right moves to the right as monitoring continues.

Figure 21-29   System Monitor shows how changes in system activity affect the selected object and counters

Managing Virtual Memory

Under Windows 2000, the default size of the paging file is set to 1.5 times the amount of RAM installed. You might need to make changes to the paging file in order to improve system performance. Here are some guidelines to remember in managing paging files:

- Set the initial and maximum sizes of the file to the same value. This will prevent disk fragmentation that might result from setting them to two different values. Windows 2000 does not normally need to change the size of the paging file during processing.

- To calculate the appropriate size of a paging file, multiply the counter Paging File object, % Usage Peak counter, which shows how much of the paging file the system is using, by the size of Pagefile.sys.

21

- Two situations in which you might want to change the size of the paging file are when 70% of the paging file is being used or when the Memory object, % Committed Bytes In Use counter, reaches 85%.

- When changing the size of a paging file, remember that you need to balance the size of the file with disk space usage and that Windows 2000 requires at least 5 MB of free space on a disk. In other words, don't make the file too large, especially when the disk it is stored on is active or has limited space. Test performance as you change paging file size, and make changes gradually.

- Moving the paging file to another volume besides the boot volume can help conserve disk space on the boot volume and optimize performance, especially when a system has multiple hard disks.

- In deciding where to put the paging file, know that memory dumps (covered in the next section) cannot be captured if the paging file is on a different physical disk from the operating system.

To change virtual memory settings and paging file size in Windows 2000, do the following:

1. Open the **Control Panel**.
2. Double-click the **System** icon.
3. The System Properties window opens. Click the **Advanced** tab.
4. Click the **Performance Options** button.
5. The Performance Options window opens. Click the **Change...** button.
6. The Virtual Memory window opens. In this window, you can change the size of the paging file and view information about the paging file and the registry. Figure 21-30 shows all three windows.

Figure 21-30 Use the System Properties window to change paging file settings

Dr. Watson and Memory Dumps

Two tools that can produce text output useful in diagnosing problems with the OS and applications are Dr. Watson and memory dumps. Recall from Chapter 18 that Dr. Watson is used to debug errors in applications by recording error events to a log file when illegal operations occur. It can help solve problems such as when an application fails to install or load, when the system locks up, or when error messages appear. In Windows 2000, these events are recorded in the Drwtsn32.log file. Dr. Watson automatically launches when an application error occurs or you can manually launch it by entering Drwtsn32.exe in the Run dialog box or at a command prompt. The log file is written to the\Documents and Settings*user*\Documents\ DrWatson folder.

Another tool that is helpful in understanding what happened when an error occurred is a **memory dump**, which saves the contents of memory at the time an error halted the system to a file called a **dump file**. The dump file is created in the event of a stop error. A **stop error** is an error severe enough that the operating system stops all processes. How to capture and interpret memory dumps is beyond the scope of this book.

Windows Update

In the process of maintaining and troubleshooting Windows 2000, remember that the Microsoft site offers patches, fixes, and updates for known problems and has an extensive knowledge base documenting known problems and their solutions. Recall that you learned how to download a critical update package in Chapter 17; the process is basically the same for Windows 2000 as it was for Windows 9x. You can access Windows Update by going to the Microsoft site and locating it from there, or you can click Windows Update on your Start Menu, which will take you directly to the site. If you think you might later want to uninstall a critical update or service pack, when given the opportunity, select the *Save uninstall information* option.

Later, to uninstall the fix, again execute the downloaded file. When given the option, select *Uninstall a previously installed service pack.*

In addition to critical updates and service packs that Microsoft creates to address known problems with Windows, the Windows Update tool will also use ActiveX controls to scan your system, find your device drivers and system files, and compare these files to the ones on the Windows Update server. If you do not already have Active Setup and the Active X controls installed on your computer, a prompt to install them will pop up when you access the site. Once Windows Update has scanned your system and located update packages and new versions of drivers and system files, it will offer you the option of selecting files for download.

 Because of the open access that ActiveX controls have to the Windows operating system, there is some risk of an ActiveX control causing damage to data or software on your computer. Some system administrators require that ActiveX controls be disabled when they are not specifically needed for tasks such as Windows Update downloads.

In addition to the information in this chapter, other important sources of information about Windows 2000 are the Microsoft Web site at *support.microsoft.com* and the *Windows 2000 Professional Resource Kit* by Microsoft Press. The *Resource Kit* includes a CD that contains additional Windows 2000 utilities. These resources can further help you understand Windows 2000 and solve problems with the OS. Also, remember that user manuals are an excellent source of information as well as the Web, training manuals, and product installation documentation.

21

CHAPTER SUMMARY

- The Windows 2000 boot process works like the Windows NT process.
- The boot process can be customized with entries in Boot.ini. The Boot.ini file can be edited with a text editor, but it is best to change the file using the System Properties window.
- Tools to use to troubleshoot problems loading Windows 2000 are the Advanced Options menu, the Recovery Console, and the Emergency Repair Process.
- Press F8 when starting Windows 2000 to access the Advanced Options menu.
- The Advanced Options menu includes safe mode, safe mode with networking, safe mode with command prompt, enable boot logging, enable VGA mode, Last Known Good configuration, directory services restore mode, and debugging mode.
- The Recovery Console is a command interface with a limited number of commands available to troubleshoot a failing Windows 2000 load. The console requires that you enter the Administrator password.
- Access the Recovery Console by first booting from the Windows 2000 CD or from the four setup disks, or the console can be installed under the startup menu and accessed from there.
- Using the Recovery Console, you can restore the registry to the state it was in at the time of the last backup of the registry.
- The Emergency Repair Process lets you restore the system to its state at the end of the Windows 2000 installation. Don't use it unless all other methods fail because you will lose all changes made to the system since the installation. It requires the emergency startup disk.
- Back up the Windows 2000 system state on a regular basis using the Backup utility. This backup includes system files, files to load the OS, and the registry. Back up the system state before editing the registry.
- Windows 2000 Support Tools can be installed from the Windows 2000 CD and include several utilities to support hardware and applications.
- Windows File Protection (WFP) protects the system files against an application, virus, or user changing or deleting them. System File Checker is part of the WFP system.
- A command window (called a DOS box in Windows 9x) is provided by Command.com or CMD.exe. The command prompt is sometimes called a DOS prompt.
- The Disk Properties window gives information about a disk and can be used to clean up a disk, defragment the disk, and check and repair errors on the disk using ScanDisk.
- Disk Management is a tool found in the Computer Management console. Disk Management replaces Fdisk in older Windows OSs and is used to partition and format a hard drive, and convert a basic disk to a dynamic disk.
- Microsoft Management Console (MMC) can be used to create customized consoles to manage the OS.
- Event Viewer is used to view system, application, and security events

- When monitoring performance, begin by establishing a baseline that helps determine what performance should be expected of a system.
- Task Manager is used to measure performance, giving information about the processor, memory, the hard drive, and virtual memory.
- System Monitor gives more detail than does Task Manager and can be used to monitor performance over time of objects and instances by using counters that you select for the monitoring.
- Virtual memory is managed from the System applet of Control Panel, Advanced tab.
- Information about application errors and stop errors can be recorded by Dr. Watson and memory dumps.
- Windows Update uses the Microsoft Web site to download patches and fixes to Microsoft OSs and applications.
- Sources of support for Windows 2000 include the Microsoft support Web site at *support.microsoft.com* and the *Windows 2000 Professional Resource Kit* by Microsoft.

KEY TERMS

Advanced Options menu	Emergency Repair Process	SFC (System File Checker)
baseline	hardware profile	snap-ins
Cmd.exe	memory dump	stop error
console	Microsoft Management Console (MMC)	WFP (Windows File Protection)
Disk Management	Recovery Console	
dump file		

21

22

INSTALLING AND USING
WINDOWS XP PROFESSIONAL

In this chapter, you will learn:

♦ About the features and architecture of Windows XP

♦ How to install Windows XP

♦ How to use Windows XP

♦ How to install hardware and applications with Windows XP

Windows XP is the latest generation of Microsoft operating systems. Windows XP currently comes as Windows XP Home Edition, Windows XP Professional, and Windows XP 64-bit Edition, although Windows .NET, an edition for the advanced server market, will likely be available by the time this book is published. This chapter focuses on Windows XP Professional, which is the upgrade from Windows 2000 Professional. Features of Windows XP that you already learned about in chapters on earlier versions of Windows are not covered in detail, where they have not changed in Windows XP; the discussion focuses on new features or changes to existing ones. This chapter builds the foundation you will need to manage and provide technical support for Windows XP, which is the focus of the next chapter.

FEATURES AND ARCHITECTURE OF WINDOWS XP

Windows XP integrates features of Windows 9x and 2000, while providing added support for multimedia and networking technologies. The look and feel of Windows XP is slightly different from its predecessors, and utilities and functions are organized differently under menus and windows. You'll see many of these differences in this chapter.

 Windows XP is replacing all previous versions of Windows in the home market and for the corporate desktop. If your hardware and applications qualify, select Windows XP Home Edition for a home PC over Windows 98/Me. For a corporate environment, use Windows XP Professional over Windows NT/2000. The only exception to this is compatibility issues with older hardware and software.

Windows XP Features

Windows XP Home and Windows XP Professional have these features, among others:

- A new user interface, shown in Figure 22-1. Notice how different it looks from the desktops for earlier Windows versions such as Windows 98 and Windows 2000.

Figure 22-1 The Windows XP desktop and Start menu

- The ability for two users to be logged on simultaneously. Each user has a separate profile, and Windows XP can switch between users, keeping a separate set of applications open for each user.

- Windows Media Player for Windows XP, a centralized application for working with digital media

- Windows Messenger for instant messaging, conferencing, and application sharing
- An expanded Help feature
- Advanced security features

In addition to these features of Windows XP Home edition, Windows XP Professional offers:

- A way for someone to remotely control your computer called Remote Desktop
- A way for an administrator to manage user profiles from a server (roaming profiles)
  - Additional security features
  - Multilingual capabilities
  - Support for new higher-performance processors

There is also Windows XP 64-bit Edition, designed to be used with a high-end 64-bit CPU such as the Intel Itanium. This version of Windows XP is designed mostly for servers or heavily technical workstations that need greater amounts of memory and higher performance than standard desktop PCs, such as for scientific and engineering applications. For example, an aircraft designer who uses software to simulate how various conditions affect aircraft materials might use Windows XP 64-bit Edition on a system that supports resource-intensive simulation and animation applications.

Windows Internet Explorer, Windows Media Player, a firewall, and other Microsoft products are tightly integrated with the Windows XP operating system. Some users see this as a disadvantage and others see it as an advantage. Tight integration allows applications to easily interact with other applications and the OS, but, on the other hand, makes it more difficult for third-party software to compete with Microsoft applications.

Windows XP provides several enhancements over Windows 2000 and other earlier versions. Table 22-1 summarizes the advantages and disadvantages of Windows XP.

Table 22-1   Advantages and disadvantages of Windows XP

Advantages	Disadvantages
Provides better integration of Windows 9x and NT than did Windows 2000.	Requires nearly a gigabyte of hard drive space for the operating system itself, and at least a 233 MHz processor with 64 MB of RAM.
Offers significant GUI enhancements over earlier versions of Windows.	Programs used with Windows XP may need more than the minimum system system specifications for the operating system.
Adds features but uses only slightly more total memory for the OS than does Windows 2000.	Nearly eliminates support for device drivers not approved by Microsoft.
Adds advanced file sorting options, such as sorting pictures by resolution or sound files by artist.	Security concerns with centralized storage of online information in Microsoft Passport, a repository of the user IDs and passwords you use on the Internet.

Table 22-1   Advantages and disadvantages of Windows XP (continued)

Advantages	Disadvantages
Includes built-in support for compressed files.	
Has improved troubleshooting tools and is generally more stable than previous Windows OSs.	

Windows XP Architecture

Windows XP uses the same kernel architecture as Windows NT and Windows 2000, with components operating in either user mode or kernel mode. Figure 22-2 shows how the different OS components relate. Notice in the figure that some low-level device drivers such as those that access the hard drive have direct access to hardware, just as they do with Windows NT and Windows 2000. All 16-bit and 32-bit applications relate to the kernel by way of the Win32 subsystem operating in user mode. As you will see in the next chapter, the boot process is also the same, and the files needed for a successful boot are the same as those for Windows NT/2000.

Figure 22-2   The Windows XP architecture uses the same basic structure and components as Windows NT and Windows 2000

22

Windows XP is generally more stable than Windows NT and Windows 2000. It was designed to avoid situations which caused drivers and applications to bring down the Windows NT/2000 systems. Installing Windows XP should also be easier than installing Windows NT or Windows 2000. In addition, Windows XP has increased security, including a built-in Internet firewall designed to protect a home PC connected directly to the Internet by way of an always-on connection such as cable modem or DSL.

INSTALLING WINDOWS XP

Installing Windows XP involves many of the same considerations and decisions that you learned about when installing Windows 2000. In this section, you learn how to install Windows XP as a clean install and as an upgrade, including how to set up a dual boot.

Planning the Installation

Before installing Windows XP, do the following:

- Verify that the system meets the minimum and recommended requirements shown in Table 22-2.
- Check the hardware compatibility list (HCL) to verify that all installed hardware components are compatible with Windows XP.
- Decide how you will partition your hard drive and what file system you will use.
- For a PC on a network, decide whether the PC will be configured as a workstation in a workgroup or as part of a domain. (Workgroups and domains were covered in Chapter 19.)
- Make a final checklist and verify that you have done all of the above and are ready to begin the installation.

Table 22-2   Minimum and recommended requirements for Windows XP Professional

Component or Device	Minimum Requirement	Recommended Requirement
One or two CPUs	Pentium II 233 MHz or better	Pentium II 300 MHz or better
RAM	64 MB	128 MB up to 4 GB
Hard drive partition	2 GB	2 GB or more
Free space on the hard drive partition	640 MB (bare bones)	2 GB or more
CD-ROM drive	12x	12x or faster
Accessories	Keyboard and mouse or other pointing device	Keyboard and mouse or other pointing device

Remember that the requirements of an OS will vary depending on which version you have installed and what applications and hardware you have installed with it.

Minimum Requirements and Hardware Compatibility

Recall from earlier chapters that you can use the My Computer icon on the Windows desktop to determine the current CPU and available RAM. To see how much hard drive space is available, using Windows Explorer, right-click on the drive letter and select Properties from the shortcut menu. Part of the installation process for an upgrade is to clean up the hard drive, which might free up some hard drive space. Even though Windows XP requires only 640 MB to install, you cannot achieve acceptable results unless you have at least 1.5 GB of free hard drive space on the volume that holds Windows XP.

There are several ways you can verify that software and hardware qualify for Windows XP. One way is to run the Readiness Analyzer. Use this command from the Windows XP CD, substituting the drive letter for your CD-ROM drive for D in the command line:

```
D:\I386\Winnt32 /checkupgradeonly
```

Depending on the release of Windows XP, your path might be different. The process takes about 10 minutes to run and displays a report that can be saved and later printed. The default name and path of the report is C:\Windows\compat.txt. The report is important if you have software you are not sure will work under Windows XP. If the analyzer reports that your software will not work under Windows XP, you might choose to upgrade the software or set up a dual boot with your old OS and Windows XP (dual-boot setup is covered later in this chapter).

Readiness Analyzer also checks hardware compatibility. Another way to verify your hardware is to go to the Microsoft Web site at *www.microsoft.com/hwdq/hcl*. Search on each hardware device by type (see Figure 22-3). There might be a copy of the Windows XP Professional HCL in the hcl.txt file on the Windows XP CD in the support folder. But for the most up-to-date information, use the Microsoft Web site.

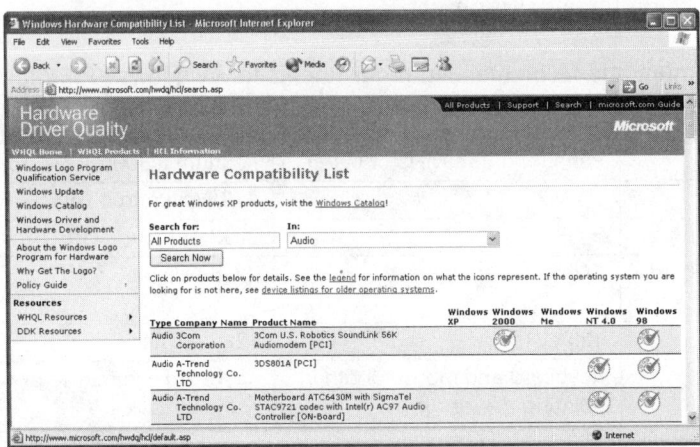

Figure 22-3   Search for each hardware component by type to determine if it qualifies for Windows XP

22

If your hardware does not qualify for Windows XP, check the hardware manufacturer's Web site for an upgrade and download the upgrade drivers before you begin the installation. If you plan to erase the hard drive as part of the installation, store these drivers on a floppy disk or on a network drive until you're ready to install them under Windows XP. If you can't find an upgrade, sometimes a device will work if you substitute a Windows driver written for a similar device. Check the documentation for your device, looking for information about other devices it will emulate. It is especially important to know that your network card or modem card qualifies for Windows XP before you install the OS because you will need the card to access the Internet to get upgrades. If you are not sure an important hardware component qualifies, then install Windows XP as a dual boot with your current OS. Later, when you get the component working under Windows XP, you can uninstall the other OS.

Hard Drive Partitions and File Systems

Windows XP needs at least a 2-GB partition for the installation and should have about 1.5 GB of free space on that partition. You can install Windows XP on the same partition as another OS, but Windows XP will overwrite the existing OS on that partition. If you do not have a free 2-GB partition for the installation, you must delete smaller partitions and repartition the drive. Deleting a partition erases all data on that partition, so be sure to create backups first. Follow these general directions to ensure that partitions on the hard drive are adequate to install Windows XP:

- For Windows 9x, use Fdisk at the command prompt, and, for Windows 2000, use Disk Management to determine what partitions are on the drive, how large they are, what logical drives are assigned to them, and how much free space is on the drive that is not yet partitioned.

- If existing partitions are too small, look at the free space on the drive. If there is enough free space that is not yet partitioned, use that free space to create a new partition that is at least 2 GB.

- If you cannot create a 2-GB or larger partition, back up your data, delete the smaller partitions, and create a 2-GB active partition on the drive.

- If you have free space on the drive for other partitions, don't partition them at this time. First, install Windows XP and then use Disk Management under Windows XP to partition the remaining free space on the drive.

The same concerns about selecting a file system for Windows 2000 apply to Windows XP. The file systems supported by Windows XP are the same as those supported by Windows 2000: FAT16, FAT32, and NTFS. Recall that the NTFS file system used by Windows 2000 was incompatible with the Windows NT NTFS file system, making for a potential problem when installing Windows 2000 and Windows NT on the same PC as a dual boot. Because the Windows XP NTFS file system is the same as that of the Windows 2000 NTFS file system, a dual boot between these two OSs should not be a problem. Here are the general directions for selecting a file system:

- Use the NTFS file system if you are interested in file and folder security, file compression, control over how much disk space a user is allowed, or file encryption.

- Use the FAT16 or FAT32 file system if you are setting up a dual boot with Windows 9x, and each OS must access all partitions.

- Use the FAT16 file system if you are setting up a dual boot with MS-DOS or Windows NT, and each OS must access all partitions.

Joining a Workgroup or a Domain

If you are installing Windows XP on a network, you must make decisions about how you will access the network. If you have less than 10 computers networked together, Microsoft recommends that you join these computers in a workgroup where each computer controls its own resources. In this case, each user account is set up on the local computer, independently from user accounts on other PCs. There is no centralized control of resources. For more than 10 computers, Microsoft recommends that you use a domain controller running a network operating system such as Windows 2000 Server to control resources on the network. (Windows XP Professional installed on a workstation can then be a client on this Windows network. Also, it is expected that Microsoft will soon release Windows .NET, a server OS.) You will also want to use a domain controller if you want to administer and secure the network from a centralized location or if there are several centralized resources on the network that are shared by many users.

Upgrade or Clean Install?

If you plan to set up a dual boot, then you will perform a clean install for Windows XP. If you already have an OS installed and you do not plan a dual boot, then you have a choice between an upgrade and a clean install. Things to consider when making this decision are:

- You can use the less expensive upgrade version of Windows XP Professional to upgrade from Windows 98, Windows Me, Windows NT 4.0, and Windows 2000 to Windows XP Professional.

- You can use the less expensive upgrade version of Windows XP Home Edition to upgrade from Windows 98 or Windows Me to Windows XP Home Edition.

- When using FAT16, so that the partition will be compatible with Windows 9x, make it no larger than 2 GB.

- If you currently have Windows 95 installed, you must do a clean install using the more expensive For a New PC version of Windows XP Professional or Windows XP Home Edition.

- Regardless of whether you have an OS currently installed, you can still choose to do a clean install if you want a fresh start. Unless you erase your hard drive, reformat it, or delete partitions before the upgrade, data on the hard drive is not erased even if you convert to a new file system during the installation. However, OS settings and installed software will not carry forward into the new installation.

Final Checklist

Before you begin the installation, complete the final checklist shown in Table 22-3 to verify that you are ready to begin.

Table 22-3   Checklist for use before installing Windows XP

Things to Do	Further Information
Does the PC meet the minimum or recommended hardware requirement?	CPU: RAM: Hard drive size: Free space on the hard drive:
Have you run the Readiness Analyzer or checked the Microsoft Web site to verify that all your hardware and software qualify?	List hardware and software that need to be upgraded:
Do you have the product key available?	Product key:
Have you decided how you will join a network?	Workgroup name: Domain name: Computer name:
Will you do an upgrade or clean install?	Current operating system: Does the old OS qualify for an upgrade?
Verify that your hard drive is ready.	Size of the hard drive partition: Free space on the partition: File system you plan to use:

For a clean install, will you set up a dual boot?	List reasons for a dual boot:
	For a dual boot
	    Size of the second partition:
	    Free space on the second partition:
	    File system you plan to use:

Have you backed up important data on your hard drive?	Location of backup:

Installation Process

Follow these general directions to perform a clean install of Windows XP on a PC that does not already have an OS installed:

1. Boot from the Windows XP CD, which displays the menu in Figure 22-4. Select the first option and press **Enter**. This menu might change slightly from

one Windows XP build to another. If your PC does not boot from a CD, go to a command prompt and enter the command D:\i386\Winnt.exe, substituting the drive letter for your CD-ROM drive for D. (The path might vary depending on the release of Windows XP.) The End-User License agreement appears. Accept the agreement.

```
Windows XP Professional Setup
======================= =

Welcome to Setup.

This portion of the Setup program prepares Microsoft ( R )
Windows ( R ) XP to run on your computer.

    •   To set up Windows XP now, press ENTER.

    •   To repair a Windows XP installation using Recovery Console,
        press R.

    •   To quit Setup without installing Windows XP, press F3.


ENTER=Continue  R=RepairF3=Quit
```

Figure 22-4   Windows XP Professional Setup opening menu

2. Setup lists all partitions that it finds on the hard drive, the file system of each partition, and the size of the partition. It also lists any free space on the drive that is not partitioned. From this screen, you can create and delete partitions and select the partition on which you want to install Windows XP. If you plan to have more than one partition on the drive, create only one partition at this time. The partition must be at least 2 GB in size and have 1.5 GB free. After the installation is done, you can use Disk Management to create the other partitions. Figure 22-5 shows an example of the list provided by Setup when the entire hard drive has not yet been partitioned.

3. If you created a new partition in Step 2, Setup asks you which file system you want to use to format the partition, NTFS or FAT. If the partition is at least 2 GB in size, the FAT file system will be FAT32. Select a file system for the partition. The Setup program formats the drive, completes the text-based portion of setup and loads the graphical interface for the rest of the installation. The PC then restarts.

4. Select your geographical location from the list provided. Windows XP will use it to decide how to display dates, times, numbers, and currency. Select your keyboard layout. Different keyboards can be used to accommodate special characters for other languages.

```
Windows XP Professional Setup
====================== =

    The following list shows the existing partitions and
    unpartitioned space on this computer.

    Use the UP and DOWN ARROW keys to select an item in the list.

        •    To set up Windows XP on the selected item, press ENTER.

        •    To create a partition in the unpartitioned space, press C.

        •    To delete the selected partition, press D.


    ┌──────────────────────────────────────────────────┐
    │  28663 MB Disk 0 at Id 0 on bus 0 on atapi [MBR]   │
    │                                                    │
    │     Unpartitioned space                28663 MB    │
    │                                                    │
    │                                                    │
    │                                                    │
    └──────────────────────────────────────────────────┘


    ENTER=Install      C=Create Partition      F3=Quit
```

Figure 22-5   During Setup, you can create and delete partitions and select a partition on which to install Windows XP

5. Enter your name, the name of your organization, and your product key.

6. Enter the computer name and the password for the Administrator account. This password is stored in the security database on this PC. If you are joining a domain, the computer name is the name assigned to this computer by the network administrator managing the domain controller.

 It is *very* important that you not forget the Administrator password. You will not be able to log onto the system without it.

7. Select the date, time, and time zone. The PC might reboot.

8. If you are connected to a network, you will be asked to choose how to configure your network settings, Typical or Custom. The Typical setting installs Client for Microsoft Networks, File and Printer Sharing, and TCP/IP using dynamically assigned IP addresses. The Custom setting allows you to configure the network differently. If you are not sure which to use, use the Typical settings. You can change them later.

9. Enter a workgroup or domain name. If you are joining a domain, the network administrator will have given you specific directions on how to configure user accounts on the domain.

For a clean install on a PC that already has an OS installed, follow these general directions:

1. Close any open applications. Close any boot management software or antivirus software that might be running in the background.

2. Insert the Windows XP CD in the CD-ROM drive. Autorun launches the opening window shown in Figure 22-6.

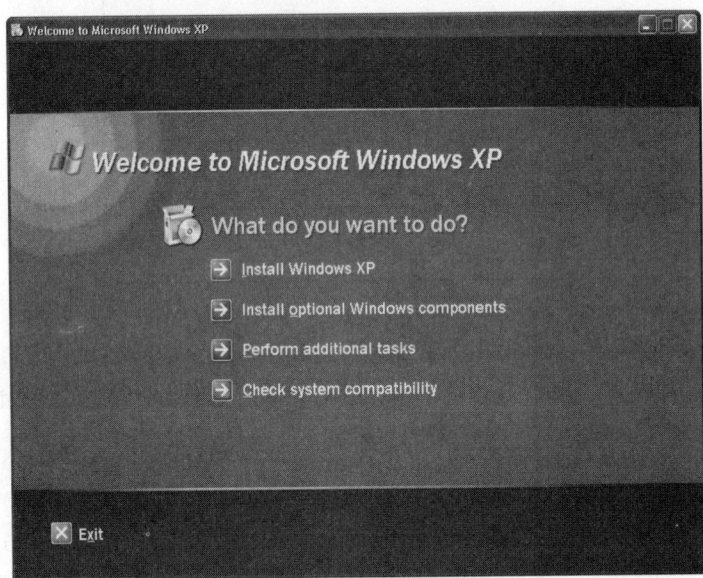

Figure 22-6 Windows XP Setup menu

3. Select the option to **Install Windows XP**. On the next screen, under Installation Type, select **New Installation**. Read and accept the licensing agreement. The installation process works the same as described above, picking up with Step 3.

When performing an upgrade to Windows XP, follow these general directions:

1. Before you begin the installation, do the following to prepare the system:

   ■ Clean up the hard drive: erase unneeded or temporary files, empty the Recycle Bin, run Disk Defragmenter, and do a ScanDisk of the drive.

22

- If you have determined that you must upgrade hardware or software and that these upgrades are compatible with your old OS, perform the upgrades and verify that the hardware or software is working.
- If you do not have the latest BIOS for your motherboard, flash your BIOS.
- Back up important files.
- Scan the hard drive for viruses using a current version of antivirus software.
- If you have a compressed hard drive, uncompress the drive. The only exception to this is that if you are using Windows NT file compression on an NTFS drive, you do not need to uncompress it.
- Uninstall any hardware or software that you know will not be compatible with Windows XP and for which you do not have an upgrade available.

2. Insert the Windows XP Upgrade CD in the CD-ROM drive. The Autorun feature should launch the Setup program, with the menu shown in Figure 22-6.

3. If the Setup menu does not appear, you can enter the Setup command in the Run dialog box. Select the option to **Install Windows XP**.

4. On the next screen, under Installation Type, select **Upgrade**. The following menu gives you two options:

- *Express Upgrade.* This upgrade uses existing Windows folders and uses all existing settings it can.
- *Custom Upgrade.* This upgrade allows you to change the installation folder and the language options. Using this option, you can also change the file system to NTFS.

5. Select the type of upgrade and accept the licensing agreement.

6. Select the partition on which to install Windows XP. If the drive is configured as FAT and you want to convert to NTFS, you specify that now. Note that Windows XP has an uninstall utility that allows you to revert back to Windows 98 if necessary. This uninstall tool will not work if you convert FAT to NTFS.

7. Setup performs an analysis of the system and reports any problems with compatibility. Stop the installation if the problems indicate that you will not be able to operate the system after the installation.

8. For an upgrade from Windows 98 or Windows Me to Windows XP, the Setup program converts whatever information in the registry it can to Windows XP. At the end of the installation process, you are given the opportunity to join a domain. For Windows NT and Windows 2000 upgrades, almost all registry entries are carried forward into the new OS, and the information about a domain is not requested because it is copied from the old OS into Windows XP.

Upgrading from Windows NT or Windows 2000 to Windows XP is the easiest type of upgrade because these operating systems all have similar registries and support applications and devices in the same way. Nearly all applications that run on Windows NT or Windows 2000 will run on Windows XP. When upgrading from Windows NT to Windows XP, the NTFS file system is automatically converted to the Windows XP version.

 Antivirus software designed to be used by the Windows NT NTFS file system might not run under the Windows XP NTFS file system because of the way some antivirus programs filter software as it accesses the file system. You might have to upgrade your antivirus software once Windows XP is installed.

Setting Up a Dual Boot

You can configure Windows XP to set up a dual boot with another operating system. Start the installation as you would for a clean install on a PC with another operating system already installed. When given the opportunity, choose to install Windows XP on a different partition than the other OS. Windows XP recognizes that another OS is installed and sets up the Startup menu to offer it as an option for booting. After the installation, when you boot with a dual boot, the Startup menu automatically appears, asking you to select an operating system, as shown in Figure 22-7.

```
Please select the operating system to start:


    Microsoft Windows XP Professional
    Microsoft Windows 98

Use the up and down arrow keys to move the highlight to your choice.
Seconds until highlighted choice will be starting automatically: xx
Press ENTER to choose.




For troubleshooting and advanced startup options for Windows, press F8.
```

Figure 22-7   Menu displayed for a dual boot

The first active partition (drive C) must be set up with a file system that both operating systems understand. For example, for a dual boot with Windows 98, use the FAT32 or FAT16 file system. For a dual boot with Windows 2000, use either the FAT or the NTFS file system. The other operating system should be installed first, and then you can install Windows XP in a different partition. When you install Windows XP on another active partition or an extended partition, it will place only the files necessary to boot in the first active partition, which it calls the system partition. This causes Windows XP to initiate the boot rather than the other OS. The rest of Windows XP is installed on a second partition, which Windows XP calls the boot partition. This is the same way that Windows NT and Windows 2000 manage a dual boot with an older OS.

 When setting up a dual boot, always install the older operating system first.

Earlier Windows operating systems were not aware of applications installed under the other OS in a dual boot, but Windows XP is. For example, if you set up a dual boot with Windows XP and Windows 98, an application installed under Windows 98 can be executed from Windows XP. This application might be listed under the Start menu of Windows XP. If it is not, you can use Windows XP Explorer to locate the program file. Double-click the application to run it from Windows XP. This makes it easier to implement a dual boot because you don't have to install an application under both OSs.

After the Installation

Immediately after you have installed Windows XP, there are several things to do to activate the OS, prepare the OS for use, and to back up the hard drive in preparation for a disaster. These steps are discussed in this section.

Product Activation

Product activation is a method used by Microsoft to prevent unlicensed use of its software, so you must purchase a Windows XP license for each installation of Windows XP. The method was introduced with Microsoft Office XP, and Microsoft has said it will continue using it for all future Microsoft products. The first time you log on to the system after the installation is complete, the Activate Windows dialog box appears giving these three options (see Figure 22-8):

- Yes, let's activate Windows over the Internet now

- Yes, I want to telephone a customer service representative to activate Windows

- No, remind me to activate Windows every few days

If you choose to activate Windows over the Internet and are connected to the Internet, the process is almost instant. Windows XP sends a numeric identifier to a Microsoft server, which sends a certificate activating the product on your PC. You have up to 60 days after installation to activate Windows XP, after which time the system will refuse to boot. If you install Windows XP from the same CD on a different computer and you attempt to activate Windows from the new PC, a dialog box appears telling you of the suspected violation of the license agreement. You can call a Microsoft operator and explain what caused the discrepancy. If your explanation is reasonable (for example, you uninstalled Windows XP from one PC and installed it on another), the operator can issue you a valid certificate. You can then type the certificate value into a dialog box to complete the boot process.

Now access the Internet and download any service packs, updates, or patches for the OS from the Microsoft Web site. You can also install any additional Windows components at this time.

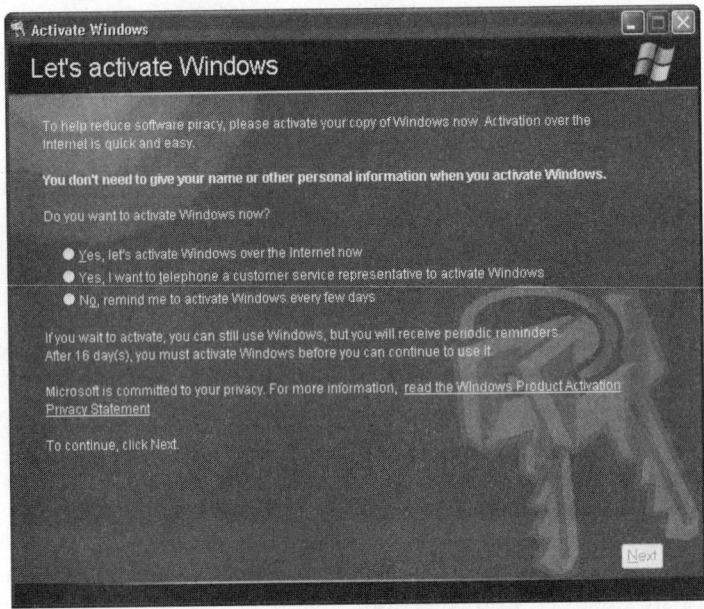

Figure 22-8   Product activation is a strategy used by Microsoft to prevent software piracy

Transferring User Files and Preferences to a New PC

Windows XP offers a utility that helps you transfer user files and preferences from one computer to another that has just had Windows XP installed. The **User State Migration Tool (USMT)** transfers user files and folders, display properties, taskbar options, and browser and e-mail settings from a Windows 9x or Windows NT/2000/XP computer. This utility can help make a smooth transition for a user moving from one PC to another; copying files and reconfiguring OS settings is not necessary. The process involves three steps:

1. Use a Windows XP computer to create a disk that contains the Files and Settings Transfer Wizard. This PC need not be the same PC that will later receive the transfer.

2. Use the disk on the source computer (the user's old computer) to run the Wizard and copy the user state to a server hard drive or removable media such as a Zip drive.

3. On the destination computer (the user's new computer), use the Wizard to transfer the user state to this computer.

To begin the process, use the Files and Settings Transfer Wizard to create the disk. To access the Wizard, click Start, All Programs, Accessories, System Tools, Files and Settings Transfer

Wizard. The Wizard launches and the Welcome to the Files and Settings Transfer Wizard window opens. Click Next and the Wizard asks you if this is the New computer or Old computer. Select New computer, and then click Next. Figure 22-9 shows the next screen, on which you can choose to create the disk or declare that you are ready to put the information on the new computer. On the screen, note that you can also use the Windows XP CD to launch the Wizard on the old computer rather than creating the disk.

Figure 22-9 The first step in using the Files and Settings Transfer Wizard is to create the Wizard Disk

After you have created the disk or chosen to use the Windows XP CD, go to the old computer, launch the Wizard, and retrieve the files and settings. Then, return to this screen on the new computer and choose to put the information on the new computer.

Instead of using the Wizard, you can also use two commands at the command prompt. Scanstate copies the information to a server or removable media, and Loadstate copies the information to the destination computer. These utilities can be included in batch files and executed automatically when implementing Windows XP over a large number of computers in an enterprise. For details on how to use the command lines in a batch file, see the *Windows XP Resource Kit* by Microsoft Press.

Preparing for Later Problems with the OS

Once the installation is completed, hardware and software are installed, and user preferences are set, it is a good idea to guard against later problems with the OS by creating a backup of the hard drive. Windows XP offers a utility called the **Automated System Recovery (ASR)** process that allows you to restore an entire hard drive volume or logical drive to its state at the time the backup of the volume was made. This process creates the backup and also creates an ASR floppy disk that allows you to use the backup to recover the system later. You will learn how to recover a failed system using a backup in the next chapter. In this section, you learn how to create the backup.

The backup file created will be just as large as the contents of the hard drive volume, so you will need a massive backup medium such as another partition on this or another local hard drive or file server, a tape drive, or a writeable CD-R or CD-RW drive.

| **CAUTION** | Do not back up the logical drive or volume to a folder on the same volume. The ASR backup process allows you to do this, but restoring later from this backup will not work. |

Follow these directions to create the backup and the ASR floppy disk:

1. Click **Start**, **All Programs**, **Accessories**, **System Tools**, **Backup**. The Backup and Restore window appears (see Figure 22-10).

Figure 22-10   Use the Backup or Restore Wizard to back up the hard drive partition once the Windows XP installation is completed

2. Click the **Advanced Mode** link. The Backup Utility window appears. Click **Automated System Recovery Wizard**. On the following screen, click **Next**.

3. The Backup Destination window appears. Select the location of the medium to receive the backup and insert a disk into the floppy disk drive. This disk will become the ASR disk. Click **Next**.

4. Click **Finish**. The backup process shows its progress as seen in Figure 22-11.

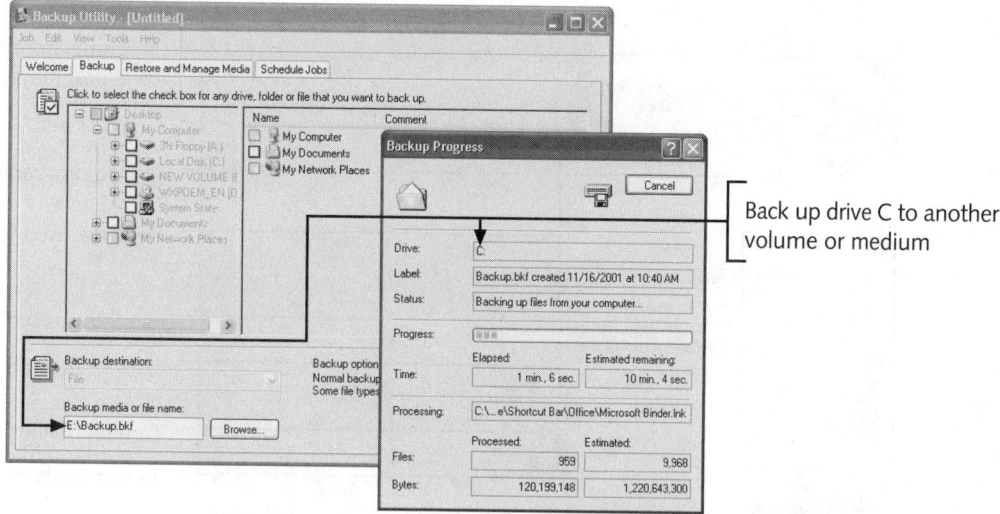

Back up drive C to another
volume or medium

Figure 22-11 The Backup utility can create a backup of drive C and an ASR disk to be
used later for the Automated System Recover Utility

5. When the backup is finished, label the ASR disk with the name of the disk, the
date it was created, and the computer's name, and put it in a safe place.

 Just as with Windows 2000, you can back up the system state as discussed in Chapter 20.
If you back up the system state when you complete an installation, and a failure occurs
in the future, you can restore the system state without overwriting user data on the
hard drive. This is less drastic than the Automated System Recovery process that
restores the entire volume.

USING WINDOWS XP

Now that you have learned how to successfully install Windows XP and guard the system
against a potential failure, let's take a closer look at how it works and what it can do. When
you use Windows XP for the first time, one difference you will note immediately is the
desktop, seen in Figure 22-12. When the OS is first installed, the Recycle Bin is the only
shortcut on the desktop. The Start menu also is organized with a more graphical look.
Notice in Figure 22-12 that the username for the person currently logged on shows at the
top of the Start menu. Applications at the top of the Start menu are said to be "pinned"
to the Start menu and are permanently listed there until you change them in a Start menu
setting. Applications that are used often are listed below the pinned applications and can
change from time to time. The programs in the white column of the Start menu on the left
side are user oriented, and the programs in the dark column on the right side of the menu
are OS oriented.

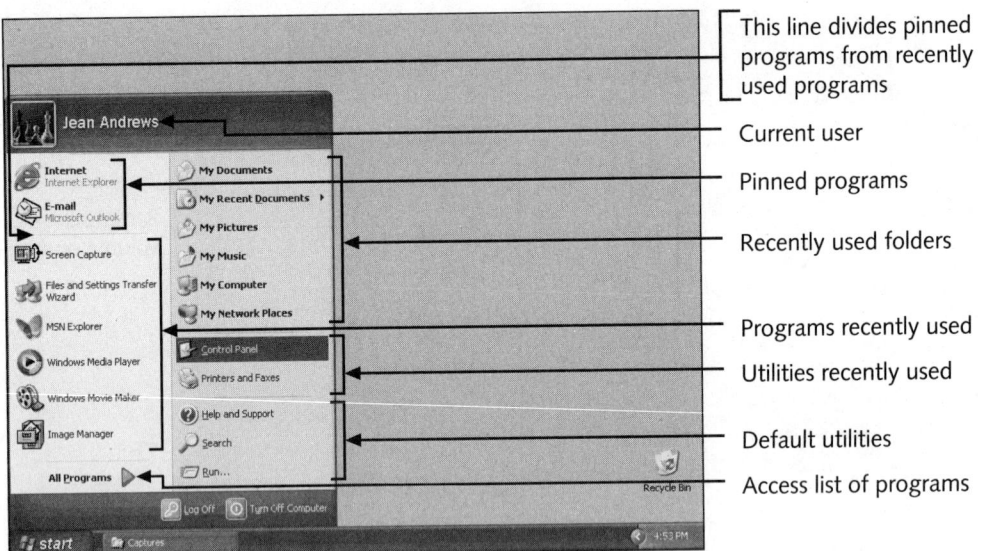

Figure 22-12   The Windows XP desktop and Start menu

When you click All Programs, the list of currently installed software appears. Figure 22-13 shows the default entries under Accessories, System Tools. You have already seen two of these, Backup and Files and Settings Transfer Wizard. Also, after Windows is installed, you can use the Activate Windows option on this menu to activate Windows XP. You will learn about some of the other options on this menu later in this chapter and in the next chapter.

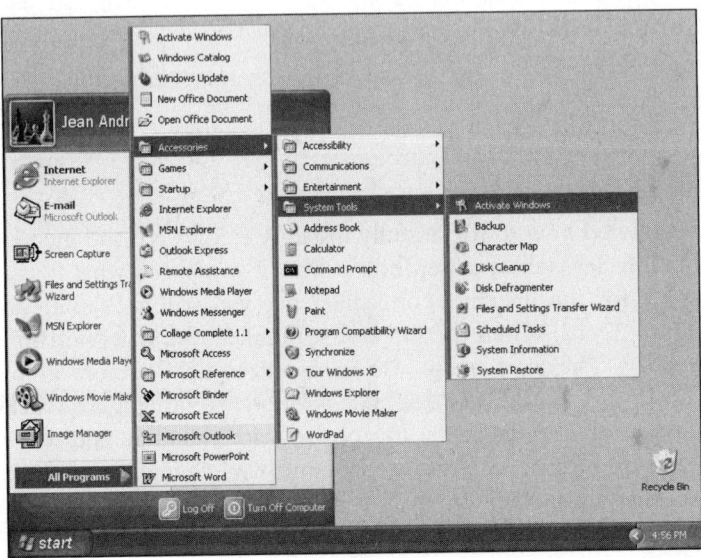

Figure 22-13   Click Start, All Programs to view the list of currently installed software

22

When you drill down to windows and menus on these windows, you will notice you have more control over how and where things are displayed. Overall, if you are familiar with earlier versions of Windows, learning to use Windows XP is easy and intuitive. One example of how you can change the way a window appears is through the Control Panel. To access the Control Panel, click Start, All Programs, and Control Panel. Figure 22-14 shows the Control Panel in Category View. Select a category in order to see the applets in that category, or click Switch to Classic View to see the applets when you first open the Control Panel as you did with earlier versions of Windows.

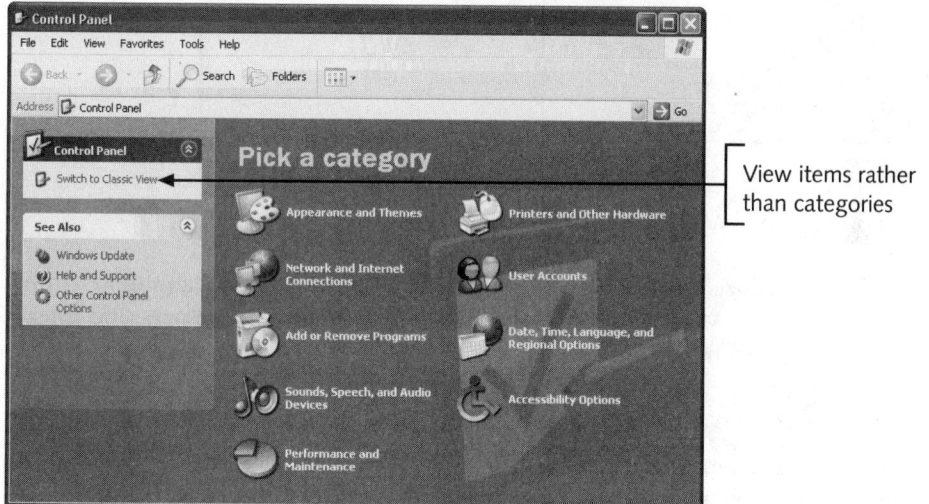

Figure 22-14   The Control Panel is organized by category, although you can easily switch to Classic View

Customizing the Windows XP Desktop

There are several things you can do to customize the Windows XP desktop. For example, you can change the background on the desktop (called the wallpaper), create shortcuts, and control what goes in the system tray. This section looks at each of these ways to make the desktop look and work the way you want it to.

 TIP   Each user account has a different desktop configuration, so if you want to create a customized desktop for a user, you must first log on to the system under that user account.

Managing Shortcuts

When you first install Windows XP, by default only the Recycle Bin shows on the desktop. To add other shortcuts that normally were on the Windows 2000 desktop, right-click anywhere on the desktop and select Properties from the shortcut menu. (You can also select the Display icon in Control Panel.) The Display Properties window appears (see Figure 22-15). Click the Desktop tab.

Figure 22-15   Managing the Windows XP desktop

Click Customize Desktop to display the Desktop Items window, also shown in Figure 22-15. You can check My Documents, My Computer, My Network Places, and Internet Explorer to add these icons to the desktop. Also notice on this window the option to have Windows clean up your desktop by moving any shortcuts that you have not used in the last 60 days to a separate folder.

You can add a program shortcut to the desktop by right-clicking a program name in the Start, All Programs list and then selecting Copy from the shortcut menu. Then right-click anywhere on the desktop and select Paste from the shortcut menu. A shortcut is created and placed on the desktop. You can also use Windows Explorer to create a shortcut. From Explorer, right-click a program filename or the filename of a document or data file, and then select Create Shortcut from the shortcut menu (see Figure 22-16). Then drag the created shortcut to the desktop.

Figure 22-16   Create a shortcut to a file using the file's shortcut menu in Explorer

Windows XP Taskbar and System Tray

22

The taskbar can be controlled from the Taskbar and Start Menu windows. Access these windows by using the Taskbar and Start menu icon in Control Panel or by right-clicking the taskbar and selecting Properties. Either way, the window in Figure 22-17 appears. From it you can add items to and remove items from the Start Menu, control how the taskbar manages items in the system tray, and specify how the taskbar is displayed.

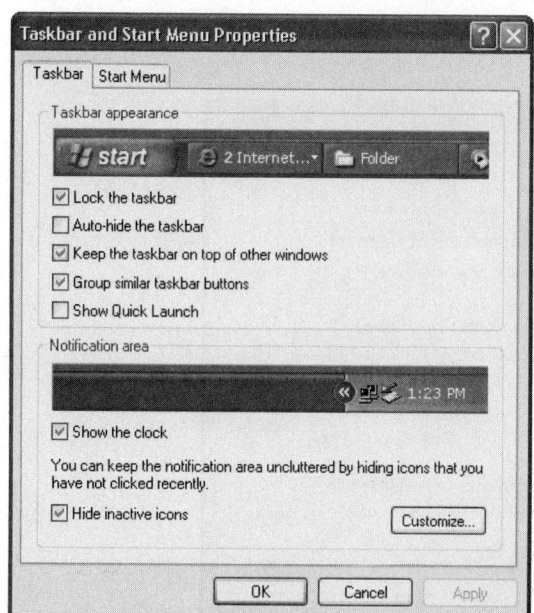

Figure 22-17   Use the Taskbar and Start Menu Properties window to control what is displayed in the Start menu and taskbar

You might want to display frequently used programs as icons in the taskbar. To do that, right-click the taskbar, select Toolbars, and then click Quick Launch. Also, the system tray sometimes gets cluttered with several icons for running services such as the volume control and network connectivity. Windows XP automatically hides these icons. When they are hidden, to unhide them, click the left arrow on the right side of the taskbar. In addition, by using the options available on the taskbar shortcut menu, you can add programs to the Quick Launch toolbar, customize the taskbar properties, and add new toolbars to the taskbar.

Windows Messenger

By default, when Windows XP first starts, it loads Windows Messenger, which takes up system resources even if you are not using it. To stop Windows Messenger from loading at startup, on the Windows Messenger menu, click Tools and then click Options. The Options window opens as shown in Figure 22-18. Click the Preferences tab and uncheck Run this program when Windows starts. Click OK.

Figure 22-18   Disable Windows Messenger at startup

Managing Audio and Video

Windows XP has several built-in features to manage audio and video, including support for inputting images from digital cameras and scanners, a Windows Movie Maker for editing video, and Windows Media Player, Version 8. (Windows Me has Media Player, Version 7.) With Media Player you can play DVDs, CDs, and Internet radio. There's a jukebox for organizing audio files, including MP3 files used on music CDs. You can also burn your own music CDs using Media Player with a CD-R or CD-RW drive. To access the Media Player, click Start, All Programs, Windows Media Player. Figure 22-19 shows the Media Player window.

Figure 22-19   Windows Media Player

Just as with older versions of Windows, you can record and manage sound from the Entertainment group of Windows and manage sounds for Windows events from the sounds applet in Control Panel. To record sound, if you have a microphone connected to a sound card, click Start, All Programs, Accessories, Entertainment, and Sound Recorder. The Sound Recorder appears, as shown in Figure 22-20. Click the Record button (red dot in lower-right corner) to record a sound, such as your own voice, into a sound file. There are several types of sound files, including MP3 files (with the .mp3 file extension), which can be used on audio CDs, and Wave files (with the .wav file extension). Windows uses .wav files to record sound. Later, you can substitute this .wav file for one of the Windows sounds that is played when you open or close applications, shut down Windows, or perform many other Windows activities that can be accompanied by sound. To change the sounds for various Windows events, from Control Panel, open the Sounds and Audio Devices applet, and select the Sounds tab.

Figure 22-20   Record sounds using Windows Sound Recorder

Media Player has its own volume control, but there is another way to adjust sound. From the Control Panel, open the Sounds and Audio Devices applet and select the Volume tab. If you check Place volume icon in the taskbar, you can easily adjust the sound from the taskbar.

Two ways to control sound volume are to use the Windows controls or use the manual controls on an amplifier or speaker.

Multiple Logins and Remote Assistance

Windows XP allows more than one user to be logged in at the same time. To switch from one account to another, click Start, Log Off. The Log Off Windows dialog box opens, giving you two choices: Switch User and Log Off. Click Switch User, and then select a new account from the list of user accounts. After you enter a password, the screen will go blank and then the desktop configured for the new user appears. Each user can have his or her own set of applications open at the same time. When users switch back and forth, Windows keeps separate instances of applications open for each user.

Windows XP also offers a new feature called **Remote Assistance**. Using this utility, a user sitting at the PC can give a support technician at a remote location full access to the desktop so the technician can use the desktop just as she would if sitting in front of the PC. This is useful when the user is inexperienced and is having trouble following the technician's directions as the technician is investigating and troubleshooting problems with Windows XP.

INSTALLING HARDWARE AND APPLICATIONS

In this section, you will learn how to install hardware and applications under Windows XP, and you will also learn several ways to solve problems with both. Later in this chapter and the next chapter, you will learn about more tools and procedures you can use to troubleshoot a failed system, program, or hardware device. We will first look at how to install hardware.

Installing Hardware

Since Windows XP is relatively new to the market, a device might not come with a Windows XP-compatible driver. To see if a hardware device has a driver that is known to be compatible with Windows XP, see the Microsoft Web site *www.microsoft.com/technet* and search on the driver or device. Download the latest driver from the Microsoft Web site or the Web site of the device manufacturer. Windows XP offers three processes that can help solve problems with devices:

- Verifying that the driver is certified by Microsoft
- Providing a way to automatically find an update for a driver
- Rolling back a driver in case an updated driver fails

Just as with earlier Windows operating systems, when Windows XP is first started, if it senses a new device is present, it automatically launches the Found New Hardware Wizard, which gives you two options:

- Install the software automatically (Recommended)

- Install from a list or specific location (Advanced)

Select the option to Install the Software automatically, and then click Next. During the installation process, you are given the opportunity to click Have Disk to provide a driver supplied by the manufacturer, rather than selecting the device from a list, which results in using a Windows driver. First, attempt to use the Windows XP driver. If it causes problems, search both the Microsoft Web site and the manufacturer's Web site for the latest updated driver. If the Wizard does not automatically launch when you start Windows, you can start it using the Add Hardware icon in Control Panel.

Using Device Manager

After a device is installed, you can use Device Manager to verify that Windows XP sees no problems with the device. There is more than one way to access Device Manager. One way is to click Start, right-click My Computer, and then select Manage from the shortcut menu. The Computer Management window appears (see Figure 22-21). This powerful tool offers several important utilities to support Windows XP, some of which you learned about in earlier chapters, that function the same as they did with Windows 2000 (such as Event Viewer), and some of which you will learn about in this chapter. Under System Tools, click Device Manager to view it. With Device Manager selected, use the View menu to control how you view devices and resources in Device Manager, similarly to previous versions of Windows. Another way to access Device Manager is to open the System applet in Control Panel, select the Hardware tab, and click Device Manager.

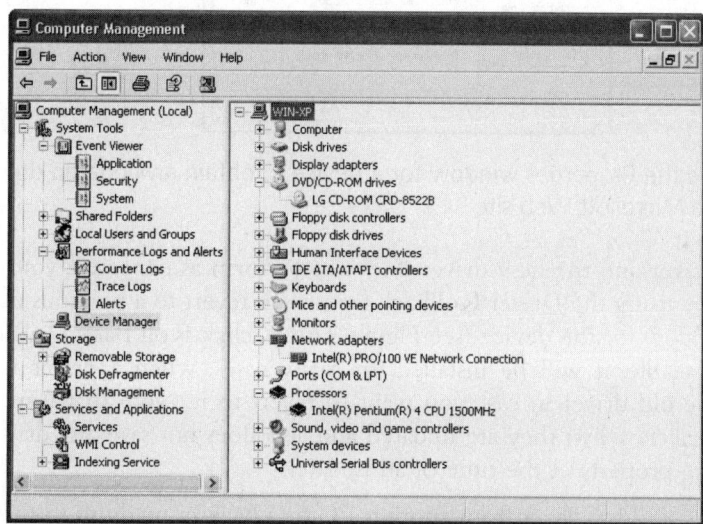

Figure 22-21   Device Manager is one tool available in the Computer Management window

Using Device Manager, you can verify that there are no resource conflicts with the device and that it is working properly as viewed by Windows XP. From Device Manager, Windows XP offers a way to update a driver using the Update Device Driver Wizard. Right-click a device and select Properties from the shortcut menu. The Properties window for that device appears (see Figure 22-22). Select the Driver tab and click Update Driver... to launch the Wizard and follow directions on the screen. The Wizard goes to the Microsoft Web site, searches for updates to the driver, informs you if there is an update, and asks permission to install the update. Windows XP will only suggest an update if the hardware ID of the device is an exact match to the hardware ID of the update. A hardware ID is a number assigned to a device by the manufacturer that uniquely identifies the product.

 TIP If you do not have an always-on connection to the Internet, connect to the Internet before you launch the Update Device Driver Wizard.

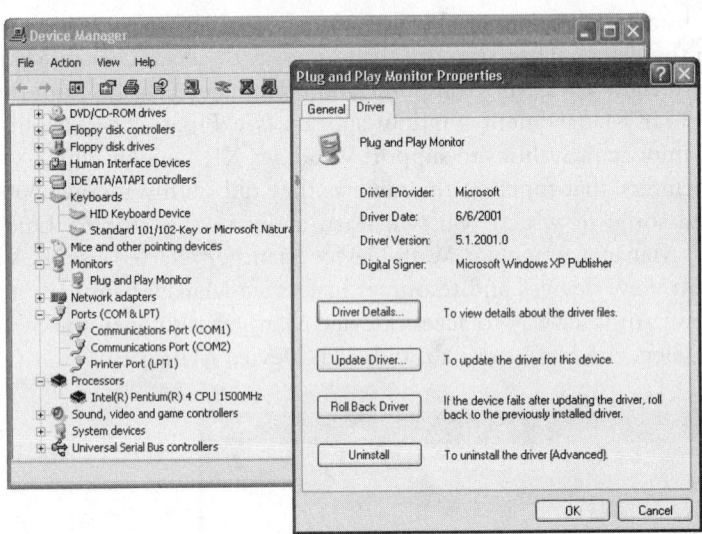

Figure 22-22 Use the Properties window for a device to obtain an updated driver from the Microsoft Web site

If you update a driver and the new driver does not perform as expected, you can revert to the old driver by using the Driver Rollback feature. To revert to a previous driver, from the Properties window for the device (see Figure 22-22), click Roll Back Driver. If a previous driver is available, it will be installed. In many cases, when a driver is updated, Windows saves the old driver in case you want to revert to it. Note that Windows does not save printer drivers when they are updated and also does not save any drivers if they are not functioning properly at the time of an update.

You can also copy an older driver from another PC or a backup medium to this PC for a rollback. Two files are needed: a .sys file and an .inf file. The .sys file is the actual driver, and the .inf file contains information about the driver. Put these files in the %systemroot%\ system32\reinstallbackups\ folder, and then perform the rollback.

> **TIP** By default, Device Manager does not show legacy devices that are not Plug and Play. To view legacy devices that are installed, on the View menu of Device Manager, check Show hidden devices (see Figure 22-23).

Figure 22-23   By default, Windows XP does not display legacy devices in Device Manager. Show these hidden devices by using the View menu.

Windows 2000 and Windows XP support the verification of digital signatures assigned to device drivers. If you suspect a problem with a driver, run **Sigverif.exe** to scan for drivers that are not digitally signed. To use the utility, enter the command in the Run dialog box. Also, during an installation, you can control how Windows handles a driver not digitally signed by using the Hardware tab of the System Properties window.

Installing Applications

Applications are installed under Windows XP as they are under other Windows OSs. You can use the Add or Remove Programs icon in Control Panel, or you can run the application's setup program from the Run dialog box. You can install software only if you have Administrator privileges. An installed program is normally made available to every user when they log on. If a program is not available to all users, try installing the program files in the Documents and Settings\All Users folder.

> **TIP** You can cause a program to automatically launch each time you start Windows by putting a shortcut to the program in the Startup menu folder for the user. For each user, this folder is Documents and Settings*Username*\Start Menu\Programs\Startup. If you want the software to automatically start up for all users, put the shortcut in this folder: Documents and Settings\All Users\Start Menu\Programs\Startup.

Software is uninstalled using the Add and Remove Programs applet in Control Panel. Open the applet and select the software to uninstall (see Figure 22-24). Then click the

Change/Remove icon. If other users are logged on to the system, the Warning message in Figure 22-24 appears. Log everyone off, and then uninstall the software.

Figure 22-24   To uninstall software using the Add or Remove Programs applet, only one user should be logged on to the system

Installing Legacy Software

DOS and Windows 9x applications that do not work under Windows NT and Windows 2000 are more likely to work under Windows XP. Some legacy applications that you should not attempt to run under Windows XP are older versions of antivirus software, and maintenance and cleanup utilities. In these cases, it is best to upgrade your software to versions that are designed to work under Windows XP.

If a legacy application does not start up and run successfully after you have installed it, try the following:

- Check the Microsoft Web site for updates to Windows XP or the Microsoft application (*windowsupdate.microsoft.com*). How to perform Windows XP updates is covered in the next chapter.

- Check the software manufacturer's Web site for updates or suggestions on how to run the software under Windows XP.

- Consider upgrading the software to a later version.

- Use the Windows XP Compatibility Mode utility.

The **Compatibility Mode utility** provides an application with the environment it expects from the operating system for which it was designed, including Windows 95, Windows 98, Windows Me, Windows NT, and Windows 2000. (Compatibility mode does not apply to DOS applications.) There is more than one way to use the utility, but the easiest way is to create a shortcut on the desktop to an installed application and then set the properties of the shortcut to use compatibility mode. After you have created the shortcut to the application, right-click it and select Properties from the shortcut menu. The Properties window is displayed (see Figure 22-25). Select the Compatibility tab. Check *Run this program in compatibility mode for*, and then select the operating system that you want Windows XP to emulate. Click Apply to apply the change. Run the software to find out whether the problem is solved.

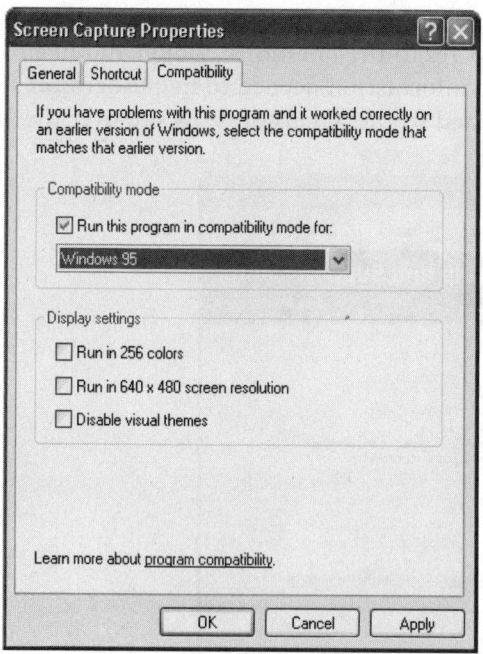

Figure 22-25   Setting Windows XP to run a legacy program in compatibility mode

If it is not solved, if you like, you can provide Microsoft with information that might help it fix the problem in some future Windows XP update. To provide the information, run the Program Compatibility Wizard. Click Start, All Programs, Accessories, Program Compatibility Wizard. Follow directions on the Wizard screen to locate the program file. After you locate the program file, you are asked to test the application and then respond to the questions show in Figure 22-26.

Figure 22-26   Using the Program Compatibility Wizard

If you answer, "No, I am finished trying compatibility settings," then the screen in Figure 22-27 appears. If you respond Yes to the question, "Would you like to send this information to Microsoft?", then the information needed to help Microsoft solve problems with the application is transmitted to the Microsoft Web site over the Internet.

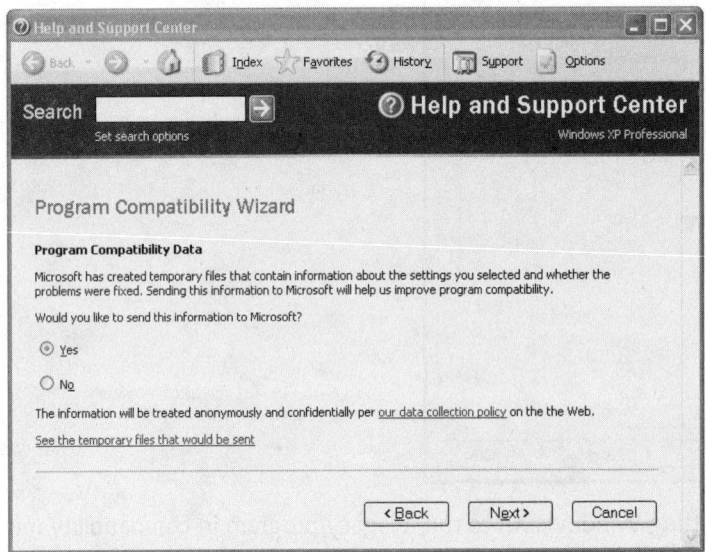

Figure 22-27 If running a legacy program in compatibility mode does not solve the problem, you can send helpful information to Microsoft

CHAPTER SUMMARY

- There are presently three versions of Windows XP: Windows XP Home Edition, Windows XP Professional, and Windows XP 64-bit Edition. Windows .NET is expected to be released soon.

- Windows XP integrates features of Windows 9x and 2000, while providing added support for multimedia and networking technologies.

- Though the Windows XP interface looks different from that of earlier versions of Windows and the OS organizes some utilities and functions differently, Windows XP is built on the same basic architecture as Windows NT and Windows 2000 and has the same basic kernel structure.

- Windows XP requires only 640 MB of free hard drive space for installation; however, acceptable performance cannot be achieved without 1.5 GB of free space on the Windows XP partition.

- Windows XP supports the same file systems as Windows 2000: FAT16, FAT32, and NTFS.

- You can install Windows XP as a dual boot with Windows 2000, because they both use the same version of NTFS. To dual boot Windows XP with Windows 9x or Windows NT, you must use FAT32. Always install the other OS first, and install Windows XP on a different partition than another OS.

22

- ❑ A clean install is required if you plan to dual boot Windows XP with another OS. Perform an upgrade if you have another version of Windows installed and you do not plan to dual boot.

- ❑ Before upgrading to Windows XP, clean up the hard drive by deleting unnecessary files and running Disk Defragmenter and ScanDisk, uncompress the drive, and delete known incompatible software.

- ❑ An Express Upgrade uses existing folders and settings as much as possible. A Custom Upgrade allows you to changes folders, language, and the file system.

- ❑ Unlike earlier versions of Windows, Windows XP is aware of applications installed under another OS when it is installed as a dual boot.

- ❑ Microsoft uses product activation to prevent the use of its software products, including Windows XP, on more than one computer.

- ❑ The User State Migration Tool (USMT) enables a user to make a smooth transition from one computer to another by transferring user files and settings. The Scanstate and Loadstate commands accomplish the same thing from the command prompt.

- ❑ Differences in the Windows XP desktop from earlier versions include the absence (by default) of any shortcuts other than the Recycle Bin and more graphical organization of the Start menu.

- ❑ In the Windows XP Control Panel, you can view applications in Category View or Classic View, which is the way it looked in earlier versions of Windows.

- ❑ Windows XP allows more than one user to be logged on at the same time, each with his own instances of open applications.

- ❑ Windows XP offers processes to help in finding updates for a driver, rolling back a driver if an update fails, and verifying that a driver is certified by Microsoft.

- ❑ The Computer Management, Disk Management, and Device Manager tools work much the same way in Windows XP as they did in Windows 2000.

- ❑ Windows XP Device Manager hides legacy devices (non-Plug and Play devices) by default.

- ❑ You can only install software in Windows XP if you have administrator privileges.

- ❑ DOS applications and older Windows applications that did not work under earlier versions of Windows are more likely to work under Windows XP.

- ❑ Compatibility mode in Windows XP provides an application written for Windows 9x or later with the environment for which it was designed.

KEY TERMS

Automated System Recovery (ASR)	product activation	User State Migration Tool (USMT)
Compatibility Mode utility	Remote Assistance	
	Sigverif.exe	

23

MANAGING AND SUPPORTING WINDOWS XP

In this chapter, you will learn:

♦ How to use Windows XP features to secure the PC and protect users and their data

♦ About the Windows NT/2000/XP registry

♦ About tools for troubleshooting and maintaining Windows XP

♦ How to troubleshoot the Windows XP boot process

You were introduced to Windows XP in the last chapter and learned how to install and use it. This chapter takes you further in learning to support this OS. You will learn about security features that protect the Windows XP system, its users, and their data. You'll also learn how the Windows NT/2000/XP registry is organized and how to edit it, and about many troubleshooting tools available under Windows XP. Finally, you will learn how to troubleshoot the Windows XP boot process. In later chapters, you will learn more about how Windows XP is used on networks and about additional security features it has when networked.

SECURITY USING WINDOWS NT/2000/XP

Security under Windows NT/2000/XP has two goals: to secure the system resources, including hardware and software, from improper use; and to secure users' data from improper access. In this section you will learn about some of the features of Windows NT/2000/XP that support these goals. At the heart of Windows NT/2000/XP security is the concept of user accounts.

User Accounts and Profiles

A **user account** defines a user to Windows and records information about the user, including the user name, password used to access the account, groups that the account belongs to, and the rights and permissions assigned to the account. There are three types of user accounts in Windows NT/2000/XP:

- **Global user accounts**, sometimes called domain user accounts, are used at the domain level, are created by an administrator, and stored in the SAM (security accounts manager) database on a domain controller. A user can log on to any computer on the networked domain using a global user account; the information about a global user account's rights and permissions apply to each workstation in the domain. The centralized SAM database is part of Active Directory, which is a repository of information used to manage a Windows network and is itself managed by Windows 2000 Server or soon-to-come Windows .NET.

- A **local user account** is created on a local computer and allows a user access to only that one computer. An administrator creates a local user account, assigns a user name and password to the account, and gives it rights and permissions. As a general rule, a user account should not be given more rights than necessary for a user to do his or her job. For example, an administrator who is responsible for setting up and maintaining user accounts in an office workgroup can set the permissions on a user account to deny the user the right to install a printer, install software, or do anything else that changes the PC software or hardware environment.

- **Built-in user accounts**. Every Windows XP workstation has two built-in user accounts that are set up when the OS is first installed: an administrator account and a guest account. An administrator has rights and permissions to all computer software, data, and hardware resources. Under Windows NT/2000/XP, the administrator has the ability to create other user accounts and assign corresponding rights and permissions to individual accounts, to groups of selected accounts, or to all accounts that use the computer. A guest account has very limited privileges and allows access to a computer by someone who does not have a user account. The guest account is useful in a business environment where many people use a computer for limited purposes, yet it is not practical for them to have a unique user account.

How user accounts are set up depends on whether the computer is a standalone workstation (not networked), belongs to a workgroup, or belongs to a domain. Recall from Chapter 19 that in a workgroup, each computer manages the security for its own resources. Each local user account is set up on the local computer independent of other accounts on other PCs, and there is no centralized control of resources. If a user on one computer needs access to resources on another computer in the workgroup, the other computer must have the same user account and password set up as is on the first computer. This chapter focuses on setting up security for standalone workstations and for workstations in a workgroup. Managing user accounts at the domain level is not covered.

After an administrator creates a local user account and the user logs on for the first time, the system creates a **user profile** for that user. When the user changes settings to customize his or her computer and then logs off, the user profile is updated so that settings can be restored the next time the user logs on.

If the computer is networked to other computers in a Windows workgroup, the administrator must create a user account on each computer in the workgroup that this user needs to access. When the user logs on to each computer in the workgroup, he or she would have to reestablish the user profile at each computer, and re-create desktop settings and application settings for each computer unless the administrator implements a feature called roaming user profiles. With **roaming user profiles**, settings established by a user at one computer are stored in a file on a file server on the network and shared with all computers in the workgroup. When a user moves from one computer to another computer in the workgroup, the roaming profile follows the user so that he or she does not have to redo settings at each computer.

Another type of profile used with workgroups is a **mandatory user profile**. This profile is a roaming user profile that applies to all users in a user group; individual users cannot change the profile. It is used in situations where users are limited to performing only specific job-related tasks. A profile that applies to a group of users is called a **group profile**. An administrator creates roaming and mandatory profiles using the Computer Management console under the Administrative Tools applet in the Control Panel.

You can view all the profiles stored on a Windows XP computer using the System Properties window. Click Start and right-click My Computer. Select Properties and then click the Advanced tab. Under User Profiles, click the Settings button (see Figure 23-1). Next, we turn our attention to how to create and manage local user accounts.

Figure 23-1   View all user profiles stored on this PC using the System Properties window

Administering Local User Accounts

When setting up accounts for users where security is a concern, here are a few guidelines about passwords for users and administrators:

- Usernames for Windows NT/2000/XP logon can consist of up to 15 characters.

- Passwords can be up to 127 characters.

- Do not use a password that is easy to guess, such as one consisting of real words, your telephone number, or the names of pets.

- The most secure type of password uses a combination of letters, numbers, and even non–alphanumeric characters.

- User accounts can be set up with or without passwords. Passwords provide greater security. Where security is a concern, always set a password for the Administrator account.

- Passwords can be controlled by the administrator but, generally, users should be allowed to change their own passwords.

An administrator can create a user account using the Computer Management console or the User Accounts applet in Control Panel. If the account is created in Computer Management it will have Limited privileges. If it is created using the Control Panel, it will have Administrator privileges. To create a local user account using Computer Management, follow these steps:

1. Log on to the computer as the administrator.

2. Click **Start** and right-click **My Computer**. Select **Manage** from the shortcut menu. The Computer Management console window opens. (Note that you can also access Computer Management by way of the Control Panel, Administrative Tools applet.)

3. Expand **Local Users and Groups** by clicking the plus sign to its left. Right-click **Users** and select **New User** from the shortcut menu. The New User window opens (see Figure 23-2). Enter the User name, enter the password twice, and check the boxes to decide how and when the password can be changed. You can also enter values for the Full name and Description to help identify the user. Click **Create**.

4. The account is created with the default type of Limited, which means the account cannot create, delete or change other accounts, make system-wide changes, or install software. If you want to give the account Administrative privileges, then open the **Control Panel** and double-click the **User Accounts** applet.

5. The User Accounts window opens, listing all accounts. To make changes to an account, click **Change an account**, and then click the account you want to change.

Figure 23-2   Create a user account using either Computer Management or the User Account applet in Control Panel

6. In the next window, you can choose to change the name of the account, change the password, remove a password, change the picture icon associated with the account, change the account type, or delete the account. Click **Change the account type**.

7. In the next window, select **Computer administrator** and click **Change Account Type**. Click **Back** twice on the menu bar to return to the opening window.

Sometimes a user forgets his or her password or the password is compromised. If this happens, and you have Administrator privileges, you can access the account by way of Control Panel or the Computer Management Console and provide the user with a new password from there. This action is called resetting the password. However, resetting a password under Windows XP causes the OS to lock out the user from using encrypted e-mail or files or using Internet passwords stored on the computer.

For this reason, all new users should create a **forgotten password floppy disk** that can be used if the user forgets their password. To create the disk, open the User Accounts applet in Control Panel, click your account, and select Prevent a forgotten password under Related Tasks in the left pane of this window. Follow the Wizard to create the disk. If a user enters a wrong password at logon, he or she is given the opportunity to use the forgotten password floppy disk to log on.

 The forgotten password floppy disk should be kept in a protected place so that others cannot use it to gain unauthorized access to the computer.

Controlling How a User Logs On

With Windows NT/2000, there was only one way to log on to the system: by pressing the Ctrl-Alt-Del keys to bring up the logon window. In a Windows XP workgroup, you have some log-on options:

- The default option is a Welcome screen that appears when the PC is first booted or comes back from a sleep state. All users are listed on the Welcome screen along with a picture (which can be the user's photograph); a user clicks his or her user name and enters the password.

- Instead of the Welcome screen, the user must press Ctrl-Alt-Del to get to a logon window similar to Windows NT/2000.

- Fast User Switching enables more than one user to be logged on to the system. If this option is disabled, only one user is logged on at a time. If the option is enabled, when a user clicks Start, Log Off, then the Log Off Windows dialog box offers three options: Switch User, Log Off, and Cancel. When Fast User Switching is disabled, the Switch User option is not displayed. Disable Fast User Switching when you want to conserve resources because performance suffers when several users leave applications open.

To change the way a user logs on, from Control Panel, open the User Accounts applet. Click Change the way users log on or off (see Figure 23-3). Make your selections and click Apply Options to close the dialog box.

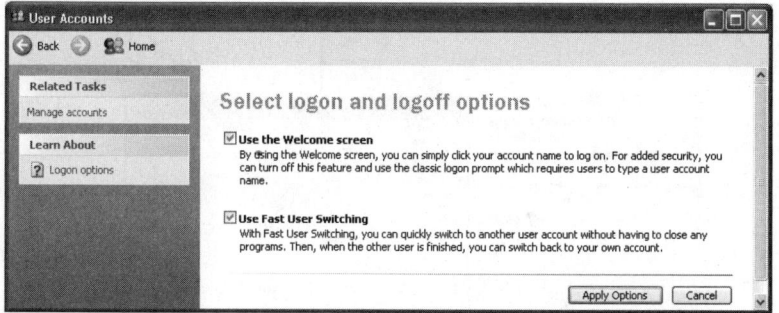

Figure 23-3   Options to change the way users log on or off

User Groups

User groups are an efficient way for an administrator to manage multiple user accounts that require the same privileges and similar profiles. When installed, Windows XP sets up several user groups including:

- **Administrators**, who have access to all parts of the system, can install or uninstall devices and applications, and perform all administrative tasks

- **Backup Operators** can back up and restore any files on the system regardless of their access privileges to these files.

- **Power Users** can read from and write to parts of the system other than their own local drive, install applications, and perform limited administrative tasks.

- **Limited Users** (known as Users in Windows NT/2000) have read-write access only on their own folders, read-only access to most system folders, and no access to other users' data. They cannot install applications or carry out any administrative responsibilities.

- **Guests** use a workstation once or only occasionally and have limited access to files and resources. A guest account has permission to shut down a computer.

Creating a New User Group

You can also create your own user group and customize the permissions and profiles for this group of users. To create a new group:

1. Click **Start**, right-click **My Computer** and select **Manage** from the menu.

2. The Computer Management console opens. Expand **Local Users and Groups** by clicking the plus sign.

3. To create a new group, right-click the **Groups** folder and select **New Group...** from the shortcut menu.

4. The New Group window opens, as shown in Figure 23-4. In this window, enter a name and description for the new group and click the **Add** button to find and select users to be added to this group. When finished, click **Create** to finish creating the group.

Figure 23-4   Create a new user group

You can also change the profile settings that are assigned users in a group. For example, to control what a user or a user group can do, including the ability to change the system date and time, go to the Control Panel and access the Administrative Tools applet. Double-click the Local Security Policy icon. The Local Security Settings window appears (see Figure 23-5). Under Local Policies, the User Rights Assignment group lists several activities, which can be managed by changing the user groups that have the right to do these activities. Right-click Change the system time, and then select Properties from the shortcut menu. The Change the system time Properties window appears, as shown in Figure 23-5. From this window you can add and remove the user groups that have the right to change the system time.

Figure 23-5   Local policies can be assigned to a user group, affecting all users in the group

23

Group Policy

Another way to control how the system can be used is by applying settings called a **Group Policy** to your computer. Group Policy is normally intended to be used on a domain, although you can use it on a standalone computer or a computer in a workgroup. Group Policy can be applied to your computer, regardless of the currently logged-on user (called Computer Configuration), or can be applied to each user who logs on (called User Configuration). The Group Policy console is a Microsoft Management Console (MMC) snap-in that can be accessed by typing gpedit.msc in the Run dialog box. From the console you can control things such as how Media Player, Internet Explorer, and NetMeeting work, as well as many Windows settings and components. For a standalone computer or a computer in a workgroup, use Computer Configuration instead of User Configuration to implement Group Policy settings.

Disk Quotas

An administrator can set **disk quotas**, which limit how much disk space a user has access to. This is important when two or more users are using a single computer and need to share its storage capacity. A disk quota does not specify where a user's files must be located; it just specifies how much total space the user can take up on a volume. The disk quota set applies to all users. You can set disk quotas only if you are using NTFS.

To set disk quotas:

1. Log on as an administrator and open **My Computer**.

2. Find the partition on which you want to set a disk quota. Right-click it and select **Properties** from the shortcut menu.

3. Click the **Quota** tab and the **Enable quota management** check box. See Figure 23-6.

Figure 23-6   Setting disk quotas

4. In this view, you can specify that users have unlimited access to disk space, you can specify the amount of space for users, and you can set a level of disk space used that will trigger a warning message to a user. For this example, all users are restricted to 500 MB of storage space and warned at 400 MB.

5. Click the **Limit disk space to** radio button, enter **500** in the box next to it, and select **MB** from the drop-down menu to the right of the box.

6. In the box next to Set warning level to, enter **400**, and select **MB** from the drop-down menu. This will warn users when they have used 400 MB of their allotted 500 MB of storage space.

7. Click **Deny disk space to users exceeding quota limit** so that no user can use more than the specified amount of disk space.

8. Click **OK**. You will be prompted to enable disk quotas. Click **OK** on the prompt. (See Figure 23-7.)

Figure 23-7   The prompt at the end of the quota-setting process gives you information about enabling quotas

EFS (Encrypted File System)

Another Windows 2000/XP security feature is the **Encrypted File System (EFS)**. EFS applies only to the Windows 2000/XP NTFS file system. In the past, it was possible to bypass an existing operating system's security measures by installing a new operating system or booting from a startup disk. In Windows 98, a password could be put on a file using a FAT file system, but you could boot from a startup disk, get to the file at a command prompt, copy it to a floppy disk, and access the file without using the password. That method does not work with EFS, which protects encrypted data even when someone who is not authorized to view those files or folders has full access to a computer's data storage. When an unauthorized user attempts to access an EFS-encrypted file, he or she receives the error "Access Denied."

Encryption is the process of putting readable data into code that must be translated before it can be accessed. This is usually done by using a **key** to encrypt the data and also provides a way to "unlock" the code and translate it back into readable data.

Do not confuse the term "key" as it is used in encryption with the term "registry key," which applies to information placed in the registry.

To ensure that a file can be accessed if a user is not available or has forgotten the password to log on to the system, an administrator for the OS can decrypt a file. In this case, the administrator is called a data recovery agent (DRA).

How to Use Encryption

A user does not have to go through a complex process of encryption to use EFS; from a user's perspective, it's just a matter of placing a file in a folder marked for encryption. Encryption can be implemented at either the folder or file level. At the folder level, if the folder is marked for encryption, every file created in the folder or copied to the folder will be encrypted. At the file level, each file must be encrypted individually. Encrypting with EFS at the folder level is encouraged and considered a "best practice strategy" because it provides greater security, since any file placed in an encrypted folder is automatically encrypted without the user having to remember to encrypt it. An encrypted file remains encrypted if you move it from an encrypted folder to an unencrypted folder on the same logical drive.

In the following example, you will encrypt the My Documents folder for an existing user named User2, create a file in that folder that will automatically become encrypted because the folder is encrypted, and decrypt the folder so that others can access it.

1. In Windows Explorer, locate the My Documents folder for User2. In this example, the correct path is C:\Documents and Settings\User2\My Documents.

2. Right-click the **My Documents** folder and choose **Properties** from the shortcut menu. The My Documents Properties window appears (see Figure 23-8).

Figure 23-8   Encrypt folder contents

3. If necessary, click the **General** tab. Click the **Advanced** button. The Advanced Attributes window appears.

4. Check the box labeled **Encrypt contents to secure data** and click **OK** (Figure 23-8).

5. Click **Apply**. This causes the Confirm Attribute Changes window to open if any files or folders exist in the selected folder (see Figure 23-9).

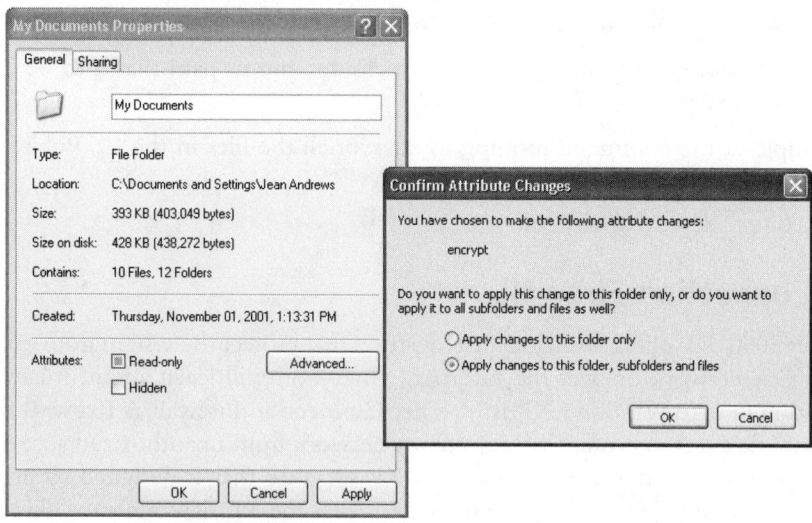

Figure 23-9 Apply changes to all folder contents

6. In this example, the subfolder My Pictures exists within the My Documents folder. If necessary click the radio button next to the option **Apply changes to this folder, subfolders, and files** to encrypt any existing objects in this folder and subfolders. (If you do not want to apply the changes to all subfolders and files, you select Apply changes to this folder only.) Click **OK**.

7. Open Microsoft Word, type some text into a file, and save the file to User2's **My Documents** folder. This file is automatically encrypted, because the My Documents folder is encrypted. If an unauthorized user attempts to access the encrypted document, they will receive an error message.

To allow others on the network to view this file, you would move or copy it to a folder that is not encrypted. Encryption is removed automatically when a file is sent over the network or moved off a logical drive where the folder is encrypted. If you move the file to another folder on the same logical drive or volume, you have to decrypt it manually. In this next example, to allow other users to view the file stored on your local hard drive, move the file to a folder that is not encrypted, share the folder, and decrypt the file.

To decrypt a file, from the file's Properties window, click the Advanced button. On the Advanced Attributes window, uncheck Encrypt contents to secure data, and then click OK.

The Cipher Command

If you are encrypting a large number of files or folders from a command prompt or using a batch file, you can use the Cipher command:

```
CIPHER [/E, /D] [/S:dir] [pathname[...]]
```

- /E encrypts the specified files or folders.
- /D decrypts the specified files or folders.
- /S:dir applies the action to the specified folder (directory) and all its subfolders.
- Pathname is the name of the file or folder and its path that is to be encrypted or decrypted.

For example, at the command prompt, to decrypt all the files in the C:\Public folder, use this command:

```
Cipher /D C:\Public\*.*
```

Internet Connection Firewall

Windows 2000/XP offers several security features that protect the system from unauthorized access over a network or over the Internet, which you will learn about in later chapters. One feature new to Windows XP is Internet Connection Firewall. A **firewall** is hardware or software that acts to protect a computer or network from unauthorized access. **Internet Connection Firewall (ICF)** is Windows XP software that is designed to protect a PC from unauthorized access from the Internet when the PC is connected directly to the Internet.

 You should not use ICF on a PC that gets its Internet access from a LAN (local area network) because it can prevent others on the LAN from accessing resources on the PC.

ICF works by examining every communication that comes to the PC to determine if the communication has been initiated by the PC or is being initiated by an outside device or computer. If the communication is initiated by some other source than the PC, it is refused. With ICF, you can browse the Web, but those on the Web cannot initiate a communication with your PC in order to gain unauthorized access to data stored there.

To enable ICF, open the Network Connections applet in Control Panel and right-click on the network connection icon that you use to connect to the Internet and select Properties from the shortcut menu. This might be a connection to the Internet by way of a dial-up modem, a cable modem, or a DSL connection. (All these type connections are covered in later chapters.) The connection Properties box opens as shown in Figure 23-10 for a modem connection. Click the Advanced tab and select Protect my computer and network by limiting or preventing access to this computer from the Internet. If you would like the firewall to record in a log file packets that it drops, click Log dropped packets. Click OK. Remember, don't do this for a regular network connection if you want others on the network to have access to resources on your PC.

We now turn our attention to several of the utilities that allow you to customize and troubleshoot Windows XP. We begin with looking at the Windows NT/2000/XP registry and how to edit it.

Figure 23-10   Enable Internet Connection Firewall and log dropped packets

THE WINDOWS NT/2000/XP REGISTRY

The Windows NT/2000/XP registry is a hierarchical database containing information about all the hardware, software, device drivers, network protocols, and user configuration needed by the OS and applications. Many components depend on this information, and the registry provides a secure and stable location for it. Table 23-1 lists ways in which some components use the registry.

In the next section, you will look at how the registry is organized, how to view the contents of the registry, how to back up and recover the registry, and how Windows makes changes to the registry.

How the Registry Is Organized

When studying how the registry is organized, keep in mind that there are two ways to look at this organization, the physical organization and the logical organization.

Logical Organization of the Registry

Logically, the organization of the registry looks like an upside-down tree with five branches, called keys or subtrees (see Figure 23-11), which are categories of information stored in the registry. Each key is made up of several subkeys that may also have subkeys under them, and subkeys hold, or contain, values. Each value has a name and data assigned to it. Data in the registry is always stored in values, the lowest level of the tree.

Table 23-1   Components that use the Windows NT/2000/XP registry

Component	Description
Setup programs for devices and applications	Setup programs can record configuration information in the registry and query the registry for information needed to install drivers and applications.
User profiles that are maintained and used by the OS	Windows maintains a profile for each user that determines the user's environment. User profiles are kept in files, but when a user logs on, the profile information is written to the registry, where changes are recorded and then later written back to the user profile file. The OS uses this profile to control user settings and other configuration information specific to this user.
Files active when Ntldr is loading the OS	During the boot process, NTDetect.com surveys the hardware devices present and records that information in the registry. Ntldr loads and initializes device drivers using information from the registry, including the order in which to load them.
Device drivers	Device drivers read and write configuration information from and to the registry each time they load. The drivers write hardware configuration information to the registry and read it to determine the proper way to load.
Hardware profiles	Windows can maintain more than one set of hardware configuration information (called a **hardware profile**) for one PC. The data is kept in the registry. An example of a computer that has more than one hardware profile is a notebook that has a docking station. Two hardware profiles describe the notebook, one docked and the other undocked. This information is kept in the registry.
Application programs	Many application programs read the registry for information about the location of files the program uses and various other parameters that were stored in .ini files under Windows 9x.

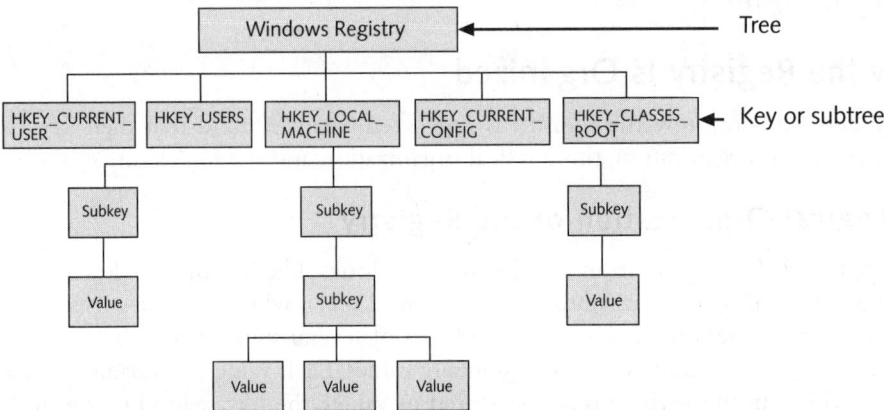

Figure 23-11   The Windows NT/2000/XP registry is logically organized in an upside-down tree structure of keys, subkeys, and values

23

Figure 23-12 shows the Windows Registry Editor, the window you see when you first open the editor: there are five high levels, one for each key or subtree. Notice in the figure that the HKEY_CURRENT_USER subtree has been opened to show subkeys under it, several of which have their own subkeys. If you click on a subkey that has a value assigned to it, that value appears in the right side of the window. Later in this section, you will see how to edit values in the registry.

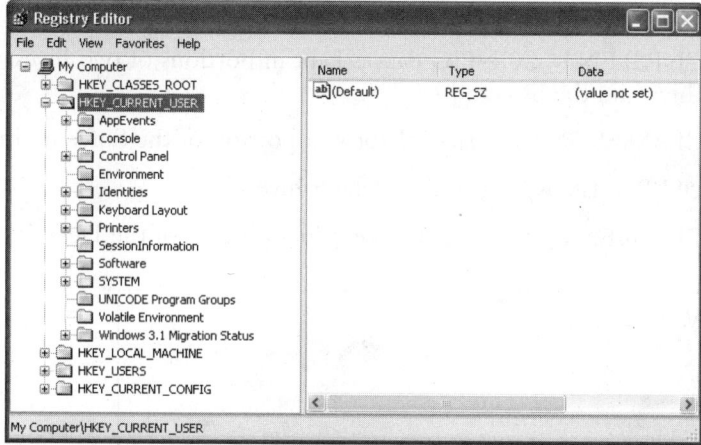

Figure 23-12   Windows Registry Editor shows the five high-level subtrees in the Windows NT/2000/XP registry

The five subtrees of the registry, displayed in Figure 23-12, are listed in Table 23-2 together with their primary functions. As you can notice from the table, the HKEY_LOCAL_MACHINE subtree is the mainstay key of the registry.

Table 23-2   The five subtrees of the Windows NT/2000/XP registry

Subtree (Main Keys)	Primary Function
HKEY_CURRENT_USER	Contains information about the currently logged-on user.
HKEY_CLASSES_ROOT	Contains information about software and the way software is configured. This key points to data stored in HKEY_LOCAL_MACHINE.
HKEY_CURRENT_CONFIG	Contains information about the active hardware configuration, which is extracted from the data stored in the HKEY_LOCAL_MACHINE subkeys called SOFTWARE and SYSTEM.
HKEY_USERS	Contains information used to build the logon screen and the ID of the currently logged-on user.
HKEY_LOCAL_MACHINE	This key contains all configuration data about the computer, including information about device drivers and devices used at startup. The information in this key does not change when different users are logged on.

Physical Organization of the Registry

The physical organization of the registry is quite different from the logical organization. Physically, the registry is stored in five files called **hives**. There is not a one-to-one relationship between the subtrees and these five files, even though there are five of each. Figure 23-13 shows the way the subtrees are stored in hives, as follows:

- HKEY_LOCAL_MACHINE consists of four hives, the SAM hive, the Security hive, the Software hive, and the System hive.

- HKEY_CURRENT_CONFIG data is kept in portions of two hives: the Software hive and the System hive.

- HKEY_CLASSES_ROOT data is kept in a portion of the Software hive.

- HKEY_USERS data is kept in the Default hive.

- HKEY_CURRENT_USER data is kept in a portion of the Default hive.

Figure 23-13   The relationship between registry subtrees (keys) and hives

From Figure 23-13, you can also see that some subtrees use data that is contained in other subtrees. For instance, the HKEY_CURRENT_USER data is a subset of the data in the HKEY_USERS subtree. HKEY_CURRENT_CONFIG and HKEY_CLASSES_ROOT subtrees use data that is contained in the HKEY_LOCAL_MACHINE subtree. However, don't let this physical relationship cloud your view of the logical relationship among these

23

subtrees. Even though data is shared among the different subtrees, logically speaking, none of the five subtrees is considered subordinate to any other.

The registry hives are stored in the \%SystemRoot%\system32\config folder as a group of files. In a physical sense, each hive is a file. Each hive is backed up with a log file and a backup file, which are also stored in the \%SystemRoot%\system32\config folder.

Editing the Registry

When you make a change in Control Panel, Device Manager, or many other places in Windows NT/2000/XP, the registry is modified automatically. For most users, this is the only way they will ever change the registry. However, there are rare occasions when you might need to edit the registry manually, such as when you are following the directions of Microsoft technical support staff to delete references in the registry to viruses or worms. Changes to the registry take effect immediately and are permanent.

Before you edit the registry, you should back it up so that you can restore it if something goes wrong. Backing up the system state, which you learned how to do in Chapter 20, is one way to back up the registry. In Chapter 20, you backed up the system state after a Windows 2000 installation, but you can also back up the system state at any time. When the system state is backed up, the Backup utility also puts a copy of the registry files in the %SystemRoot%\repair folder.

Windows NT/2000 offers two registry editors, each with a slightly different look and feel, although they both accomplish the same thing. They are:

- Regedt32.exe, located in the \%SystemRoot%\system32 folder, which shows each key in a separate window. Use it to edit the registry.

- Regedit.exe, located in the \%SystemRoot% folder, which shows all keys in the same window and has a look and feel similar to Explorer. Use it to search and view the registry.

To access a registry editor, type the program name in the Run dialog box. With Windows XP, if you type either Regedt32 or Regedit in the Run dialog box, the Regedit.exe program is launched.

In the following example, we use Regedit.exe under Windows XP to view the registry and take a look at registry values. To access Regedit.exe, double-click the filename in Explorer or enter the filename in the Run dialog box. Figure 23-14 shows a detailed view of the registry.

Nothing listed under Data indicates the default value is used

Figure 23-14   Editing a registry subkey value

Let's look at one example of editing the registry. Follow these directions to first back up the system state before editing the registry:

1. Click **Start**, **All Programs**, **Accessories**, **System Tools**, **Backup**. The Backup or Restore Wizard appears.

2. Click **Advanced Mode**. The Backup Utility window appears. Click the **Backup** tab.

3. Check the **System State** box and under **Backup media or file name:**, select the location to store the backup.

4. Click **Start Backup**. The Backup Job Information dialog box appears. Click **Start Backup**. After the backup is done, click **Close** to close the Backup utility.

To change the name of the Recycle Bin on the Windows XP desktop for the currently logged on user, do the following:

1. To open Registry Editor, click **Start**, **Run** and type **Regedit** in the Run dialog box. Click **OK**. The Registry Editor window appears.

2. Locate the following subkey, which is the name of the Recycle Bin on the Windows desktop, by double-clicking on the yellow folder icon of each subkey, moving down through the tree to the lowest subkey value. As you move down the tree, if the currently selected subkey has a value, that value displays in the right pane of the window.

   HKEY_CURRENT_USER\Software\Microsoft\Windows\CurrentVersion\ Explorer\CLSID\645FF040-5081-101B-9F08-00AA002F954E

3. Figure 23-14 shows the subkey displayed. The right pane shows nothing listed under Data, which results in the default value used, which is Recycle Bin. Position the window on the screen so that you can see the Recycle Bin icon.

4. Double-click the name of the value in the right pane. The Edit String dialog box appears. The Value data should be empty in the dialog box. If a value is present, you have selected the wrong value. Check your work and try again.

5. Enter a new name for the Recycle Bin. For example, in Figure 23-14, the new name is "Jean's Trash Can". Click **OK**.

6. To see your change, right-click somewhere on the desktop and select **Refresh** from the shortcut menu. The name of the Recycle Bin changes.

7. To restore the name to the default value, on the Registry Editor window, again double-click the name of the value. The Edit String dialog box appears. Delete your entry and click **OK**.

8. To verify the change is made, right-click on the screen and select **Refresh** from the shortcut menu. The Recycle Bin name should return to its default value.

From these directions, you can see that changes made to the registry take effect immediately. Therefore, take extra care when editing the registry. If you make a mistake and don't know how to correct a problem you have created, then you can restore the system state to recover.

OTHER MAINTENANCE AND TROUBLESHOOTING TOOLS

This section discusses other commonly used tools that Windows XP provides for maintenance and troubleshooting. Some tools are new or changed in Windows XP, and some operate the same way as they did under Windows 2000. Table 23-3 lists several tools and their functions. Some tools are executed from a command line (have an .exe file extension), others are Microsoft Management Console snap-ins (have a .msc file extension), and others are graphical tools built into Windows XP (such as Device Manager). MMC was discussed in Chapter 21. MMC snap-ins are executed from the Run dialog box or can sometimes be accessed using Windows menus. Some command-line programs can be executed from the Run dialog box and all of them can be executed from a command prompt window.

Several of the tools listed in the table are discussed later in the chapter. For more extensive information about any of these tools, search Help and Support on your Windows XP computer, search the Microsoft Knowledge Base at *support.microsoft.com*, or see the book, *Microsoft Windows XP Professional Resource Kit Documentation* by Microsoft Press. In addition, to get help about a command-line tool, from a command prompt, enter the tool name followed by /?. For example, to get help about Defrag, enter Defrag /?.

Table 23-3   Windows XP maintenance and troubleshooting tools

Tool	Description
Add or Remove Programs in Control Panel	Uninstall software that is causing a problem.
Automated System Recovery (ASR)	Drastically recovers a failed system. Only use this as a last resort, because the logical drive on which Windows is installed is formatted and restored from the most recent backup. All data and applications written to the drive since the last backup are lost.
Backup (Ntbackup.exe)	Backs up and restores data and software.
Boot logging	An option on the Advanced Options startup menu to log events to the Ntbtlog.txt file.
Bootcfg (Bootcfg.exe)	Views and edits the contents of the Boot.ini file used to hold startup settings.
Cacls.exe	Changes access control lists (ACL) assigned to a file or group of files to control what users have access to a file and the type of access they have (read, write, change, or full). For more information on CACLS, type Help Cacls at a command prompt.
Chkdsk (Chkdsk.exe)	Checks and repairs errors on a logical drive.
Cipher.exe	Displays and changes the encryptions applied to files and folders using the NTFS file system.
Compact.exe	Displays and changes the compressions applied to files and folders using the NTFS file system.
Computer Management (Compmgmt.msc)	Console provides access to several snap-ins used to manage and troubleshoot a system.
Convert.exe	Converts a FAT16 or a FAT32 logical drive to NTFS.

23

Table 23-3   Windows XP maintenance and troubleshooting tools (continued)

Tool	Description
Defrag.exe	A command-line tool to defragment a logical drive or floppy disk, it is similar to the graphic tool, Disk Defragmenter.
Dependency Walker (Depends.exe)	Provides a list of files needed for an application to load.
Device Driver Roll Back	Replaces a driver with the previous one that worked before the current driver was installed.
Device Manager	Displays and changes device drivers and other hardware settings.
DirectX Diagnostic Tool (Dxdiag.exe)(API)	Used to troubleshoot problems with the DirectX application programming interface used by Microsoft.
Disk Cleanup (Cleanmgr.exe) (Cleanmgr.exe)	Deletes unused files to make more disk space available.
Disk Defragmenter (Dfrg.msc)	Defragments a logical drive or floppy disk.
Disk Management (Diskmgmt.msc)	Displays and changes partitions on hard drives and formats drives.
DiskPart (Diskpart.exe)	A command-line tool to manage partitions and volumes of a hard drive similar to the graphic tool, Disk Management. Use DiskPart to write scripts to automate disk management tasks.
Dr. Watson (Drwtsn32.exe)	Records errors and information about those errors when applications fail. Errors are recorded in a log file named **Drwatson.log**. Note this is a different name than the log file in Windows 2000 which is Drwtsn32.log.
Driver Signing and Digital Signatures (Sigverifi.exe)	Verifies that drivers, software, and system files have been approved by Microsoft.
Error Reporting	Produces an error report and sends it to Microsoft when the error occurs and the PC is connected to the Internet.
Event Viewer (Eventvwr.msc)	Records and displays system problems.
Expand.exe	Extracts a file from a cabinet file or compressed file.
Fsutil (Fsutil.exe)	Displays information about drives and file systems and does advanced management tasks on those drives.
Group Policy (Gpedit.msc)	Displays and changes policies controlling users and the computer.
Help and Support	Provides helpful information, connects to Windows newsgroups, enables Remote Assistance, and steps you though many other troubleshooting tasks.
Last Known Good Configuration	A startup option used when normal or safe mode do not work. Using this tool, you can revert the system back to before a driver or application was installed that is giving problems.
Performance Monitor (Perfmon.msc)	Reports information about performance problems.
Program Compatibility Wizard	Looks at legacy software and attempts to resolve issues that prevent the software from working in Windows XP.

23

Table 23-3 Windows XP maintenance and troubleshooting tools (continued)

Tool	Description
Recovery Console	Provides a command line to perform troubleshooting tasks when the desktop will not load.
Registry Editor (Regedit.exe)	Displays and changes entries in the registry.
Remote Assistance	Allows a user to share his computer with a support technician at a remote location so that the technician can control the computer.
Remote Desktop	Allows a support technician to control a Windows XP computer remotely.
Runas.exe	Runs a program using different permissions than those assigned to the currently logged-on user.
Safe Mode	Loads the Windows desktop with a minimum configuration and then is used to troubleshoot problems with device drivers, display settings, and other startup options that are causing problems.
SC (Sc.exe)	Communicates commands to the Service Controller, which starts, stops, and manages programs that run in the background such as device drivers or Internet Connection Firewall.
Services (Services.msc)	Graphical version of SC.
System Configuration Utility (Msconfig.exe)	Controls settings used to troubleshoot a failing system.
System File Checker (Sfc.exe)	Verifies the version of all system files when Windows loads.
System Information (Msinfo32.exe)	Displays information about hardware, applications, and Windows that is useful when troubleshooting. Figure 23-15 shows a view of the System Information window.
System Information (Systeminfo.exe)	A version of System Information to be used from a command-prompt window. Information is listed onscreen as text only. To direct that information to a file, use the command Systeminfo.exe >Myfile.txt. Later the file can be printed and used to document information about the system.
System Restore	Used to restore the system to a previously working condition, it restores the registry, some system files, and some application files.
Task Killing Utility (Tskill.exe)	Stops a process or program currently running. Useful when managing background services such as an e-mail server or Web server.
Task Lister (Tasklist.exe)	Lists currently running processes similar to the list provided by Task Manager.
Task Manager (Taskman.exe)	Lists and stops currently running processes. Use Task Manager to stop an application that is locked up.
Uninstall Windows XP Professional	Used to uninstall Windows XP and revert back to a previously installed OS.
Windows File Protection	Protects system files and restores overwritten system files as needed.
Windows Update (Wupdmgr.exe)	Updates Windows by examining the system, comparing it to available updates on the Microsoft Web site, and recommending appropriate updates.

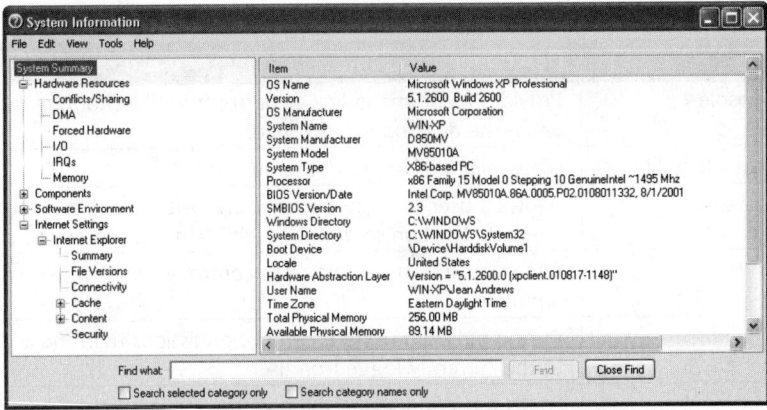

Figure 23-15   The System Information window displays important information about the system's hardware, software, and environment

Help on the Web

Microsoft offers help and updates on the Web. In earlier chapters, you learned to use the Microsoft Knowledge Base at *support.microsoft.com*. This section shows you how to access the Windows Update feature and Windows XP newsgroups.

Windows Update

Windows XP has an automated way to update the OS, applications, and device drivers made available on the Microsoft Web site. If no user interaction is required, anyone can perform the update, but if decisions must be made during the update, only someone with administrator privileges can perform the update. To do an update, including updating the OS, software and drivers, click Start, All Programs, and Windows Update. The Update Wizard takes you to the Microsoft Windows Update Web site (see Figure 23-16). Click Scan for updates and follow the directions onscreen. This update process includes updating drivers, a process that can also be started from Device Manager, as you learned in the last chapter.

Figure 23-16   The Windows Update utility manages the process of downloading updates from the Microsoft Web site

If there is an update available for your computer, a screen similar to that shown in Figure 23-17 appears. Note in the figure that the update process found one critical update, nine updates to Windows XP that are not considered critical, and no updates for drivers. To view information about these updates, click them. In this example, the Critical Update was designed to solve a problem with security, and the nine noncritical updates were about running Java applets, connecting to a UPS (uninterruptible power supply) service, using a CD burner, running legacy applications using compatibility mode, problems with the Files and Settings Transfer Wizard, problems using Remote Assistance across a firewall, and problems with Windows Messenger and Movie Maker. By default, only the critical update is selected for installation. To install noncritical updates, select the updates you want and then click Add. After you have selected what to update, click *Review and install updates* and follow the directions on the screen.

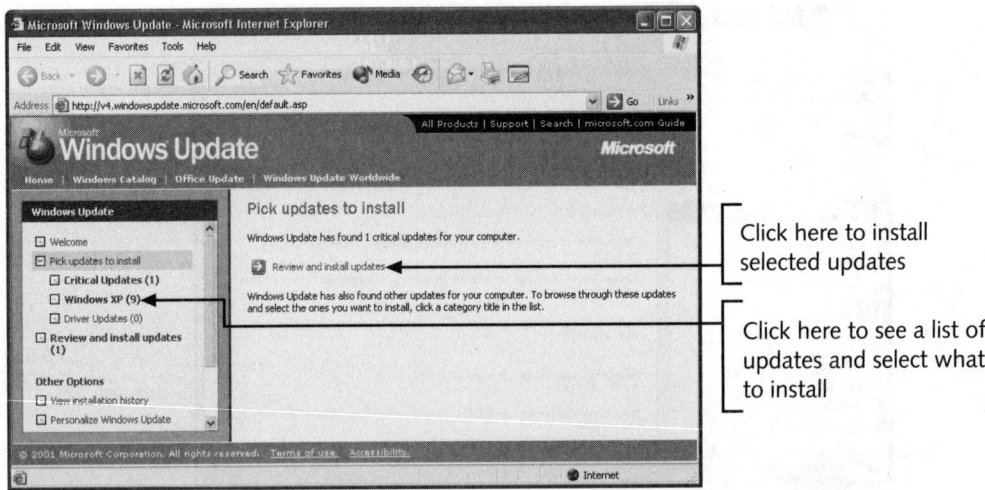

Figure 23-17 Windows Update process found updates appropriate to this computer

 TIP Windows XP does not ship with support for USB 2.0 (USB Hi-Speed). If you have a USB 2.0 port on your PC, the Update Wizard will recommend that you update the USB driver to support USB 2.0, unless you have already installed a third-party USB 2.0 driver. If you want to download the Microsoft USB 2.0 driver, first uninstall the third-party driver and then perform Windows Update.

Windows Newsgroups

If you have exhausted your sources of information and still have not resolved a problem, sometimes you can get help from a Windows newsgroup. To access a newsgroup, click Start, Help and Support. On the Help and Support window, click Get support, or find information in Windows XP newsgroups. Then click Go to a Windows Web site forum. Click Go to Windows Newsgroup. On the forum, you can post a question or read questions and answers posted by other users. Microsoft does not support this forum, so be careful about following the advice of users posting answers to questions on the forum.

In addition to newsgroups and the Microsoft Web site, many good Windows support Web sites exist. To get a very long list of these sites, go to a search engine on the Web such as *www.google.com* and enter Windows Help in the search box.

TROUBLESHOOTING THE BOOT PROCESS

The Windows XP boot process works the same way as the Windows NT and Windows 2000 boot process. Refer to Chapter 19 for a review of the process and the files that are required for a successful boot. Many of the tools you learned about in Chapter 21 to recover from a failed Windows 2000 boot also work under Windows XP. They are briefly mentioned in

23

this section to make the troubleshooting process complete. In addition, Windows XP has added two tools for solving problems with the boot process: System Restore and Automated System Recovery. The tools to use when troubleshooting a failed boot are listed below in the order you should use them. Each tool discussed is more drastic than the one before it, affecting more of the system, installed hardware and software, and user data.

- Last Known Good Configuration and, in certain situations, Driver Rollback
- Safe mode from the Advanced Options menu
- System Restore
- Recovery Console
- Automated System Recovery
- Reinstall Windows XP using the Windows XP CD

You learned how to use the Last Known Good Configuration in Chapter 19, under Windows NT and Windows 2000. In addition, you can use Driver Rollback discussed in Chapter 22 if you suspect that a single device driver is the source of the problem. The Windows XP Advanced Options menu, shown in Figure 23-18, is also similar to that of Windows 2000. Refer to Chapter 21 for a discussion of each of the options on the menu and how to use them. Try Safe Mode with Networking first. If that doesn't work, try Safe Mode.

 To access the Advanced Options menu, press F8 while Windows is loading.

```
Windows Advanced Options Menu
Please select an option:

    Safe Mode
    Safe Mode with Networking
    Safe Mode with Command Prompt

    Enable Boot Logging
    Enable VGA Mode
    Last Known Good Configuration (your most recent settings that worked)
    Directory Services Restore Mode (Windows domain controllers only)
    Debugging Mode

    Start Windows Normally
    Reboot
    Return to OS Choices Menu

Use the up and down arrow keys to move the highlight to your choice.
```

Figure 23-18 Windows XP Advanced Options menu

The next tool to use if these don't work is System Restore, a tool new to Windows XP, which is discussed next. If that doesn't work, then try the Recovery Console. Commands for the Recovery Console for Windows XP are the same as for Windows 2000 and were covered in Chapter 21. If the Recovery Console fails, then use the Automated System Recovery process to restore the hard drive to its state as of the last ASR backup. If you don't have an ASR backup, then your only recourse is to reinstall Windows XP following directions given earlier in the chapter. Be sure to scan for viruses before you reinstall.

System Restore

The **System Restore** utility is new to Windows XP. It is similar to ScanReg used on previous versions of Windows. ScanReg is not included in Windows XP. However, System Restore cannot be executed from a command prompt. If you can load Windows XP, then you can use System Restore to restore the system state to its condition at the time a snapshot was taken of the system settings and configuration. The restore process does not affect user data on the hard drive but can affect installed software and hardware, user settings, and OS configuration settings. The restoration is taken from a snapshot of the system state that was created earlier called a **restore point**. The system automatically creates a restore point before you install new software or hardware or make other changes to the system. You can also manually create a restore point at any time. To create a restore point, do the following:

1. Click **Start**, **All Programs**, **Accessories**, **System Tools**, and **System Restore**. The System Restore window appears.

2. The System Restore window gives you two choices: Restore my computer to an earlier time and Create a restore point. Select **Create a restore point** and then click **Next**.

3. Type a description of the restore point, such as "Just before I updated the video driver." The system automatically assigns the current date and time to the restore point.

4. Click **Create** and then **Close**. The restore point is saved.

Before using System Restore to undo a change, if the change was made to a hardware device, first try Driver Rollback so that as few changes as possible to the system are lost. If Driver Rollback does not work or is not appropriate, do the following to revert the system back to the restore point:

1. Click **Start**, **All Programs**, **Accessories**, **System Tools**, and **System Restore**.

2. If necessary, click **Restore my computer to an earlier time**, and then click **Next**. A window appears as shown in Figure 23-19. Notice in the figure that there are two restore points, one created by the system and one created manually.

3. Select the date and time and the specific restore point. Click **Next** twice.

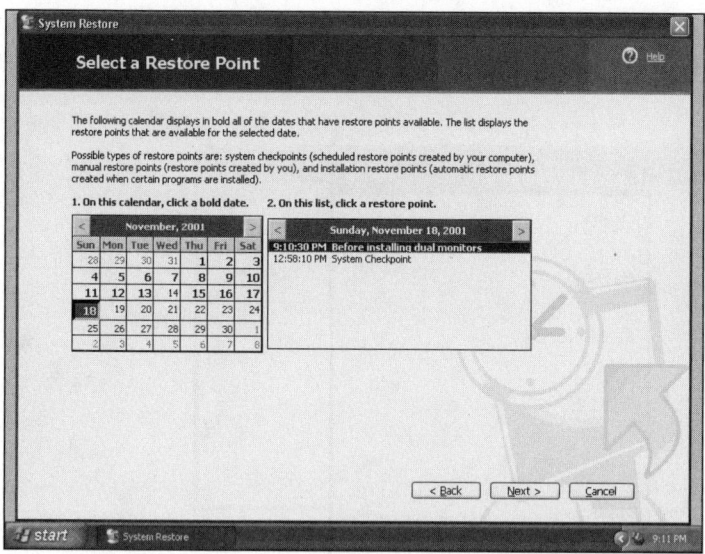

23

Figure 23-19 Restore points are automatically created daily and every time software or hardware is installed

Windows XP will reboot and restore the system state to the settings saved in the restore point. Changes to user data will not be affected but any installation or configuration changes made after the restore point are lost.

When selecting a restore point, select a point as close to the present as you can so that as few changes to the system as possible are lost. If System Restore does not work, try booting into safe mode and using it there. When you select Safe Mode from the Advanced Options menu, Windows XP asks if you want to go directly to System Restore rather than to safe mode. If safe mode does not work, then try going directly to System Restore.

 TIP The main difference between System Restore and Automated System Recovery is that System Restore does not affect user data on the hard drive, but Automated System Recovery does. In order to make it possible to recover a failed system without destroying data, make it a habit to always create a restore point every time you make a change to the system.

Windows XP Startup Disk

Using Windows Explorer, you can create an MS-DOS startup disk that can be used to boot into MS-DOS mode giving you an A prompt. If the hard drive is not using the NTFS file system, then you can access the drive and recover data files. You cannot launch Windows XP using the startup disk or use it to recover from a failed installation. To create a startup disk, using Windows Explorer, right-click on drive A and select Format from the shortcut menu. The Format window opens, as shown in Figure 23-20. Check Create an MS-DOS startup disk, and then click Start. The unhidden files put on the startup disk are shown in the Explorer window in Figure 23-21. In addition to these files, Autoexec.bat, Config.sys, and the Windows 98 versions of Io.sys and Msdos.sys are also placed on the disk as hidden files.

Figure 23-20   Windows XP gives you the ability to create an MS-DOS startup disk

Figure 23-21   Files on the MS-DOS startup disk created by Windows XP

Automated System Recovery

After you finished the Windows XP installation, if you created the Automated System Recovery disk set of the installation, you can use this or a later set of the recovery disks to restore the system partition to its state when the backup was made. You will lose any changes made to the volume or logical drive holding Windows XP since the backup. Everything on the volume since making the ASR backup and disk is lost, including software and device drivers installed, user data, and any changes to the system configuration. For this reason, it's a good idea to periodically make fresh copies of the ASR disk set. You learned how to make this backup and disk in the previous chapter.

If you use the Automated System Recovery process, be aware that you will lose all data stored on the Windows XP volume since the last backup was made.

To revert the hard drive to its state when the last ASR disk set was made, do the following:

1. Insert the Windows XP CD in the CD-ROM drive and hard boot the PC.

2. A message says "Press any key to boot from CD." Press any key.

3. A blue screen appears with the message, "Press F6 to load RAID or SCSI drivers." If your system uses RAID or SCSI, press **F6**.

4. At the bottom of the blue screen, a message says, "Press F2 to run the Automated System Recovery process." Press **F2**.

5. The screen shown in Figure 23-22 appears, instructing you to insert the ASR floppy disk. Insert the disk, and then press **Enter**.

```
Windows Setup
===========




        Please insert the disk labeled:

Windows Automated System Recovery Disk

         Into the floppy drive.



      Press any key when ready.
```

Figure 23-22   Automatic System Recovery process must have the ASR floppy disk

6. Windows XP Setup does the following:

   - Loads files it needs to run
   - Repartitions and reformats the drive
   - Installs Windows from the Windows XP CD
   - Launches the Automatic System Recovery Wizard to restore the Windows system state, applications, and data as they were when the last ASR backup was made

The ASR recovery process erases everything on the volume being restored. Figure 23-23 shows one of the above steps in the recovery process, in which you reformat the logical drive just before the Windows XP installation process begins.

```
Windows XP Professional Setup
==========================

·

        Please wait while Setup formats the partition

                \Device\Harddisk0\Partition1

   on  28663  MB  Disk  0  at  Id 0  on  bus  0  on  atapi  [MBR].


 ┌──────────────────────────────────────────────────────┐
 │  Setup is formatting...        45%                     │
 │  ┌──────────────────────────────────────────────────┐ │
 │  │                                                  │ │
 │  └──────────────────────────────────────────────────┘ │
 └──────────────────────────────────────────────────────┘
```

Figure 23-23   As part of the Automatic System Recovery process, Windows XP Setup repartitions and reformats the volume holding Windows XP

Error Messages and Their Meanings

Table 23-4 lists some Windows XP error messages and what they mean. Most of these errors occur when booting.

Table 23-4   Windows XP error messages and their meanings

Error Message	What It Means and What to Do About It
Invalid partition table Error loading operating system Missing operating system	These messages are displayed by the program in the MBR when it cannot find the active partition on the hard drive or the boot sector on that partition. Use Fdisk or Diskpart from a command prompt to check the hard drive partition table for errors. Sometimes Fdisk/mbr might solve the problem. Third-party recovery software such as PartitionMagic might help. If a setup program such as Data Lifeguard from Western Digital or MaxBlast from Maxtor came bundled with the hard drive, use the program to examine the drive. Check the hard drive manufacturer's Web site for other diagnostic software.
A disk read error occurred NTLDR is missing NTLDR is compressed	A disk is probably in the floppy disk drive. Remove the disk and reboot. When booting from the hard drive, these errors occur: if Ntldr has been moved, renamed, or deleted, or is corrupt, if the boot sector on the active partition is corrupt, or if you have just tried to install an older version of Windows, such as Windows 98, on the hard drive. First try replacing Ntldr. Then check Boot.ini settings.

Table 23-4 Windows XP error messages and their meanings (continued)

Error Message	What It Means and What to Do About It
An error is displayed in text against a blue screen and then the system halts. These Windows NT/2000/XP errors are called **stop errors** or **blue screens** (BSOD).	Stop errors are usually caused by viruses, errors in the file system, a corrupt hard drive, or a hardware problem.
Stop 0x00000024 or NTFS_File_System	The NTFS file system is corrupt. Immediately boot into the Recovery Console. Copy important data files that have not been backed up to other media before attempting to recover the system.
Stop 0x00000050 or Page_Fault_in_Nonpaged_Area	Most likely RAM is defective.
Stop 0x00000077 or Kernel_Stack_Inpage_Error	There are bad sectors on the hard drive, there is a hard drive hardware problem, or RAM is defective. Try running Chkdsk or Scandisk.
Stop 0x0000007A or Kernel_Data_Inpage_Error	There is a bad sector on the hard drive where the paging file is stored; there is a virus or defective RAM. Try running Chkdsk or Scandisk.
Stop 0x0000007B or Inaccessible_Boot_Device	There is a boot sector virus or failing hardware. Try Fdisk/mbr or fixmbr.

23

CHAPTER SUMMARY

- Windows NT/2000/XP requires a valid user account before you can use Windows. The user account identifies the user to Windows. Permissions assigned to a user account control what the user can and cannot do and access under Windows.

- Local user accounts apply to a single standalone computer or a single computer in a workgroup; global user accounts are managed from a domain controller and apply to every computer in the domain.

- When using Windows in a domain, global user account information is stored in the SAM, which is part of Active Directory in Windows 2000 Server and Windows .NET.

- When a user makes changes to the system, the changes are often recorded in the user profile so the next time the user logs on, these changes automatically take effect.

- Methods that administrators can use to manage and secure multiple computers and users include roaming user profiles, mandatory user profiles, and group profiles.

- Passwords on user accounts are needed to secure computers and their resources. Passwords should not be easy to guess and should be a combination of letters, numbers, and non–alphanumeric characters.

- An administrator can create a user account using the Computer Management console or the User Accounts applet in Control Panel.

- Resetting a password under Windows XP causes the OS to lock out the user from using encrypted e-mail or files or using Internet passwords stored on the computer. For that reason, it is a good idea for a user to create a Windows XP forgotten password floppy disk.

- Windows XP user groups include Administrators, Backup Operators, Power Users, Limited Users, and Guests. In this list, each group has fewer permissions and rights than the previous group.

- Using disk quotas, an administrator can limit the amount of hard drive space a user can use.

- File and folder encryption in Windows 2000/XP require using the NTFS file system.

- Internet Connection Firewall (ICF) prevents communication from the Internet to access the system if the communication has not been initiated by the local computer.

- The Windows NT/2000/XP registry is logically organized into five subtrees or keys and physically organized into five files called hives. There is no one-to-one correspondence between the subtrees and the hives.

- The registry is edited using a registry editor which is accessed by entering Regedit in the Run dialog box. Changes to the registry are immediate, so always make a backup of the system state before editing the registry.

- Windows XP offers many troubleshooting and maintenance tools. Some are available from the command line. Others are Microsoft Management Console (MMC) snap-ins and others are built into Windows XP.

- You can get help on the Web for Windows XP. Microsoft offers Windows Update and Microsoft Knowledge Base. There are also Windows newsgroups and other Web sites where you can get help.

- Two recovery tools new to Windows XP are Automated System Recovery and System Restore.

- The Automated System Recovery (ASR) process creates a backup and an ASR floppy disk that can be used to restore the backup of the volume or logical drive holding Windows XP.

- The Windows XP System Restore utility is similar to ScanReg in earlier versions of Windows but cannot be executed at a command prompt. System Restore restores the system state using restore points, which are snapshots of the system state.

KEY TERMS

administrator
Backup Operator
blue screen
built-in user account
disk quota
Drwatson.log
Encrypted File
    System (EFS)
encryption
firewall

forgotten password
    floppy disk
global user account
group policy
group profile
Guest user
hardware profile
hive
Internet Connection
    Firewall (ICF)
key

Limited user
local user account
mandatory user profile
Power User
restore point
roaming user profile
stop error
System Restore
user account
user profile

23

24

MANAGING AND TROUBLESHOOTING HARD DRIVES

In this chapter, you will learn:

♦ About supporting hard drives and making backups

♦ About troubleshooting hard drives

♦ About viruses and other computer infestations, and how to protect against them

In this chapter, you will learn about supporting hard drives, including how to protect against viruses. This chapter covers disk compression and caching for hard drives, as well as several ways to create hard drive backups. In addition, it discusses different types of viruses that can infect your hard drive as well as how to remove and prevent them.

Managing Hard Drives

Taking good care of your hard drive is not difficult, but it does require a little time. Here are some precautions you can take to protect your data and software as well as the drive itself.

- *Make backups and keep them current.* It's so important that it's worth saying again: keep **backups**, which are extra copies of files that you'll need if the originals get damaged or deleted. Never trust a computer; it'll let you down. Keep data files in directories separate from the software, to make backing up data easier. Back up the data as often as every four hours of data entry. Rotate the backup disks or tapes by keeping the last two or three most recent backups.

- *Run antivirus software regularly.* If you lose software or data on your hard drive, there's a good chance the source of the problem is a virus. Your best defense against data and software corruption is to install and run antivirus software. Keep the software current, because new viruses are constantly turned loose. You'll learn more about viruses, and the software you can use to combat them, later in this chapter.

- *Defragment files and scan the hard drive occasionally.* A fragmented hard drive increases access time, and reading and writing files wears out the drive. If you are trying to salvage a damaged file, it is much more difficult to recover a fragmented file than one stored in contiguous clusters. Regularly scan your hard drive for lost or cross-linked clusters.

- *Don't smoke around your hard drive.* To a read/write head, a particle of smoke on a hard drive platter is like a boulder with a 10-foot circumference on the highway. Hard drives are not airtight. One study showed that smoking near a computer reduced the average life span of a hard drive by 25 percent.

- *Don't leave the PC turned off for weeks or months at a time.* Once my daughter left her PC turned off for an entire summer. At the beginning of the new school term, the PC would not boot. We discovered that the Master Boot Record had become corrupted. PCs are like cars in this respect: long spans of inactivity can cause problems.

- *High humidity can be dangerous for hard drives.* High humidity is not good for hard drives. I once worked in a basement with PCs, and hard drives failed much too often. After we installed dehumidifiers, the hard drives became more reliable.

- *Be gentle with a hard drive.* Don't bump the PC or move it when the drive is spinning.

Making Backups

Losing data due to system failure, a virus, file corruption, or some other problem can really make you appreciate the importance of having backups. This section covers the hardware and software needed to make backups of data and software from a hard drive.

Windows 9x and Windows NT/2000/XP offer backup tools, which are also covered in this section.

 With data and software, here's a good rule of thumb: if you can't get along without it, back it up.

You can use sophisticated methods to create backups in which the backup process is selective, only backing up what's changed, what has not been recently backed up, and so forth. Traditionally, these methods all involve backing up to tapes, because a tape is most likely to be large enough to contain an entire backup of a hard drive. In the discussions below of specific backup methods, we use tapes as our medium. These backup methods are designed to reuse tapes and to make the backup process more efficient. On a network, often the backup media is a device such as another hard drive or a tape drive on a computer somewhere on the network. Full, incremental, and differential backup methods speed up the backup process, and scheduled backups minimize the inconvenience to users. Selective backups only back up data that changes often on the hard drive. By selecting only certain critical folders on the drive to back up, the backup routine goes much faster, and recovery of lost data is much easier.

The Child, Parent, Grandparent Method

Before you perform routine hard drive backups, devise a backup plan or procedure. One common plan, called the **child, parent, grandparent backup method**, makes it easy to reuse tapes. This method is explained in Table 24-1. Put the plan in writing and keep a log of backups performed.

Table 24-1 The child, parent, grandparent backup method

Name of Backup	How Often Performed	Storage Location	Description
Child backup	Daily	On-site	Keep four daily backup tapes and rotate them each week. Label the four tapes Monday, Tuesday, Wednesday, and Thursday. A Friday daily (child) backup is not made, because on Friday you'll make the parent backup.
Parent	Weekly	Off-site	Perform the weekly backup on Friday. Keep five backup weekly backup tapes, one for each Friday of the month, and rotate them each month. Label the tapes Friday 1, Friday 2, Friday 3, Friday 4, and Friday 5.
Grandparent backup	Monthly	Off-site, in a fireproof vault	Perform the monthly backup on the last Friday of the month. Keep 12 tapes, one for each month. Rotate them each year. Label the tapes January, February, and so on.

Full, Incremental, and Differential Backups

Some backup methods are more efficient because they do not always create a complete backup of all data. A **full backup** backs up all data from the hard drive or an area of the hard drive. An **incremental backup** backs up only files that have changed or that have been created since the last backup, whether that backup is itself an incremental or full backup. **Differential backups** back up files that have changed or been created since the last full backup.

Begin by performing a full backup. The next time you back up, choose the incremental method to back up only files that have changed or been created since the full backup. The second time you perform an incremental backup, you back up only the files that have changed or been created since the last incremental backup.

For example, using the child, parent, grandparent method, you can perform a full backup each Friday. Monday through Thursday, you perform incremental backups. The advantage of this method is that incremental backups are faster and require less tape space than full backups. The disadvantage is that, to recover data, you must begin with the last full backup and work your way forward through each incremental backup until the time that the data was lost. This process can be time-consuming. Plan to make a full backup after at least every sixth or seventh incremental backup. The Windows 9x and Windows NT/ 2000/XP backup utilities support incremental backups.

If you create differential backups with the child, parent, grandparent method, create a full backup on Fridays. On Monday, do a differential backup to back up all files that have changed since Friday. On Tuesday, a differential backup also backs up all files that have changed since Friday (the full backup). Differential backups don't consider whether other differential backups have been performed. Instead, they compare data only to the last full backup, which is how differential backups and incremental backups differ. Another difference is that incremental backups mark files as having been backed up, but differential backups do not. The advantage of differential backups over incremental ones is that if you need to recover data, you only need to recover from the last full backup and the last differential backup. Differential backups are not supported by Windows 95 but are supported by Windows 98 and Windows NT/2000/XP.

Scheduling Backups

Backups can be performed manually by a user sitting at the computer or can be scheduled to run automatically without user interaction. A scheduled backup is automatically performed by software when the computer is commonly not in use, such as during the middle of the night. Windows 98 and Windows NT/2000/XP support scheduling any program (including backup tasks) to execute at designated dates and times without user intervention.

24

Using Windows 98, do the following to create a program called Batch.bat to run a backup and schedule it to run at 11:59 p.m. every Monday night:

1. Using Notepad or WordPad, type this command line, where the tape drive is E and the /S parameter tells the OS to include subdirectories when copying (hidden files will not be copied, but data is not usually hidden):

```
Xcopy C:\Data\*.* E: /S
```

2. Save the file as **\Data\Batch.bat**, and exit the text editor.

3. Double-click **My Computer** on the desktop, and then double-click **Scheduled Tasks** to open the Scheduled Tasks window (see Figure 24-1).

Figure 24-1   Add a scheduled task under Windows 98

4. Double-click **Add Scheduled Task**. The Scheduled Task Wizard appears. Select the program to schedule: Click **Browse**, find and click the **Batch.bat** file in the \Data folder, and then click **Open**.

5. Enter a name for the scheduled task, select how often to perform the task, and then click **Next** (see Figure 24-2).

6. Enter the start time and select the day of the week for the task to execute. For example, enter **11:59 PM every Monday**. Click **Next**.

7. The wizard reports the scheduled task parameters. Click **Finish**.

8. To change the settings for a scheduled task, double-click **My Computer**, double-click **Scheduled Tasks**, and then right-click the task in the Scheduled Task window. Select **Properties** from the shortcut menu. The task Properties dialog box opens (see Figure 24-3).

Figure 24-2   Name the scheduled task and select how often it runs

9. Click the **Settings** tab to change the task settings. Notice at the bottom of the Settings sheet that you can direct the scheduler to wake the computer to perform the task. This feature requires a motherboard that supports the option for software to power up the PC. To learn if your motherboard supports the feature, see CMOS setup or the motherboard documentation. If not, then the PC must be turned on for the scheduler to work.

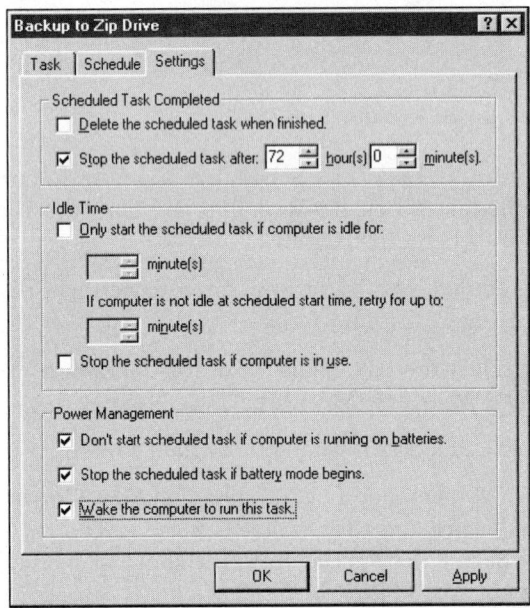

Figure 24-3   With some computers, the task scheduler can power up the computer to run the task

You have just learned how to use a batch file to execute a scheduled backup. Windows offers a more powerful and sophisticated utility called Windows Scripting Host (WSH), which uses Windows commands to execute scripts that programmers have written using a scripting language such as VBScript or JScript. This utility is good for making backups also. The script is stored in a file that can be placed as an icon on the desktop. To run the script, type *wscript.exe filename* in the Run dialog box, substituting filename with the name of the script file, or double-click on the desktop icon. You can also make a script file run as a scheduled task.

Backup Software

Most tape drives come with some backup software. You can also purchase third-party backup software or use Windows 9x or Windows NT/2000/XP for backing up your hard drive. Because the software only backs up files that are not currently in use, close all files before performing a backup.

Windows 9x Backup Utility

Windows 9x offers a backup utility that can back up to removable disks and tape drives. Windows 98 supports many popular backup devices that Windows 95 did not, including those using parallel ports, IDE/ATAPI devices, and SCSI devices. To use drives and tapes not supported by Windows 9x, use third-party backup software.

If the Windows 9x Backup component is not installed under Windows 9x, use the Control Panel, Add/Remove Programs applet to install it. You will need the Windows 9x CD or other access to the installation files. To use the Windows 98 Microsoft Backup utility (msbackup.exe), do the following:

1. Click **Start**, point to **Programs**, **Accessories**, **System Tools**, and then click **Backup**. The Backup Wizard first searches for backup devices such as Zip or tape drives. If it finds none, it asks if you want to install one. Otherwise, it displays a window asking if you want to create a new backup job or open an existing job. The Backup utility keeps information about backup jobs under a name that you give it, so you can use the same job many times. Select **Create a new backup job**, and then click **OK** to continue.

2. The Backup Wizard asks you questions about what type of backup you want (for example, back up all files or only those files that have changed since the last backup). Make your selections, and then click **Next**.

3. The Microsoft Backup utility opens the Backup window, as shown in Figure 24-4.

Figure 24-4   Windows 98 Microsoft Backup allows you to select files and folders to back up

4. To back up only certain folders, files, or logical drives, check the boxes to the left of their names. To display a list of all subfolders under a folder, click the box with the + sign in it. Backup indicates that only parts of a folder or drive are selected for backup by placing a gray check in the box.

5. In the **Where to back up** list box of the Backup window shown in Figure 24-4, select the medium and directory to use. In the figure, the medium is drive D, a Zip drive. The backup file will go into a folder named \Backup.

6. Click **Start** to begin the backup.

To recover files, folders, or the entire hard drive from backup using the Windows 98 Backup utility, follow these directions:

1. On the Backup utility window, shown in Figure 24-4, click the Restore tab. Select the backup job to use for the restore process. The Backup utility displays the folders and files that were backed up with this job. You can select the ones that you want to restore.

2. Click **Start** to restore the files.

Windows 2000/XP Backup Utility

To perform a backup for Windows 2000/XP (using Ntbackup.exe), follow these steps:

1. For Windows 2000, on the Start menu, click **Programs, Accessories, System Tools, Backup**. For Windows XP, click **Start**, point to **All Programs, Accessories, System Tools**, and click **Backup**. The Backup or Restore Wizard appears. Click **Advanced Mode**.

2. The Backup utility opens. Click the **Backup** tab (see Figure 24-5). If you want to perform a backup immediately, check the drive and subfolders to back up. Note the box labeled **Backup media or file name** in the lower-left corner, which says where to back up to. Click the **Start Backup** button in the lower-right corner to perform the backup.

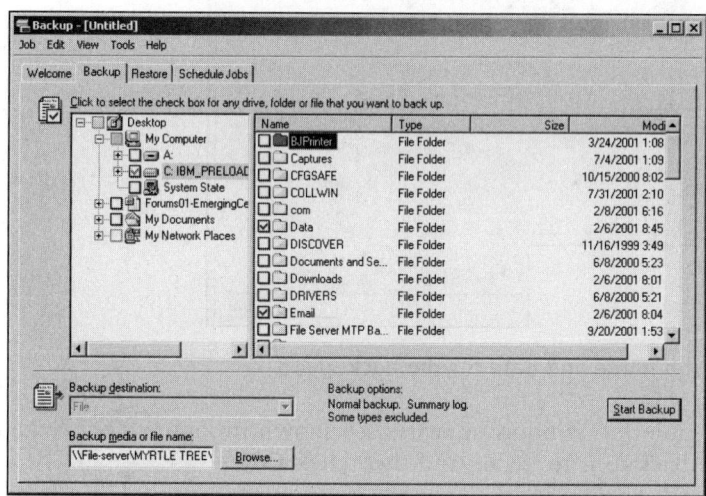

Figure 24-5 You can perform an immediate backup from the Backup tab

3. To perform a scheduled backup, begin by clicking the **Schedule Jobs** tab. Select a date on which you want to schedule a backup, and then click the **Add Job** button.

4. The Backup Wizard opens. On the first screen, click **Next**. Select **Backup selected files, drives, or network data** and click **Next**.

5. On the next screen, the Backup Wizard allows you to select what you want to back up. Select what you want to back up, and then click **Next**.

6. Follow the steps through the wizard to select the type of backup (Normal, Copy, Incremental, Differential, or Daily) and how to verify the data after the backup, control access to the backed-up data, and label the backed-up data. When asked if you want to perform the backup now or later, select **Later** and click **Next**.

7. The When to Back Up window appears (see Figure 24-6) for you to specify when to perform the backup and give it a name. Note that you can perform an immediate backup from the wizard instead of using the method you learned in step 1. After specifying a name and date for the job, click the **Set Schedule** button.

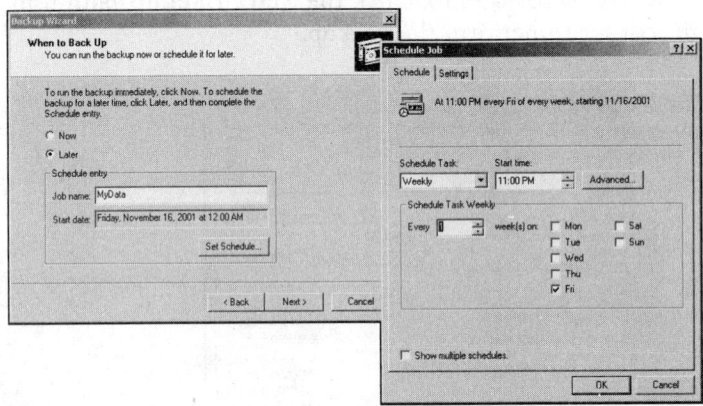

Figure 24-6   Select a name and date for the backup job

8. The Schedule Job window appears, also shown in Figure 24-6. Schedule how often the backup is to occur, and then click **OK**.

9. Click **Next** in the wizard and follow the remaining instructions to complete the backup. At the end of the process, the wizard gives you an on-screen report summarizing information about the backup.

Disk Cloning Software

For Windows 9x, you can back up a hard drive so that you can replicate the drive to a new computer or to another drive on the same computer, such as when you deploy a new operating system with application software on multiple computers in a corporate or educational lab. This process is called **disk cloning** or **disk imaging** and is best done with software designed for that purpose. Examples of disk imaging software are Drive Image by PowerQuest (*www.powerquest.com*), ImageCast by Innovative Software (*www.imagecast.com*), and Norton Ghost by Symantec Corp (*www.symantec.com*).

Planning for Disaster Recovery

The time to prepare for a disaster is before it occurs. If you have not prepared, the damage from a disaster will most likely be greater than if you had made and followed disaster plans. Suppose the hard drive on your PC stopped working and you lost all its data. What would be the impact? Are you prepared for this event? Backups are important, but you should also know how to use them to recover lost data. Also know when the backup was made and what to do to recover information entered since the last backup. Here's where careful recordkeeping can pay off.

When you perform a backup for the first time or set up a scheduled backup, verify that you can use the backup tape or disks to successfully recover the data. This is a very important step in preparing to recover lost data. After you have created a backup tape, erase a file on the hard drive, and use the recovery procedures to verify that you can recreate the file from the backup. This verifies that the tape or floppy disk works, that the recovery software is effective, and that you know how to use it. After you are convinced that the recovery works, document how to perform the recovery.

 Verify that your recovery plan will work by practicing it before a disaster occurs.

Always record your regular backups in a table with the following information:

- The folders or drives backed up
- The date of the backup
- The type of backup
- The name of the tape used

Refer to this table to recover data that was lost days or weeks before you discovered that it should be recovered. Keep the records in a notebook. You can also store the records in a log file (a file where events are logged or recorded) each time you back up.

Defrag and Windows Disk Defragmenter

The Defrag command detects and repairs fragmentation. **Fragmentation** is the undesirable placement of a single file in several cluster locations that are not right next to each other, so that data access time is increased. When a hard drive is new and freshly formatted, the OS writes files to the drive beginning with cluster 2, placing the data in consecutive clusters. Each new file begins with the next available cluster. Later, after a file has been deleted, the OS writes a new file to the drive, beginning with the first available cluster in the FAT. If the OS encounters used clusters as it is writing the file, it simply skips these clusters and uses the next available one. In this way, after many files have been deleted and added to the drive, files become fragmented.

Fragmentation occurs when files are written to a drive in more than one group of contiguous clusters. The clusters that make up a file are together called a **chain**. For a well-used hard drive, it is possible to have a file stored in clusters at 20, 30, 40, or more locations. Fragmentation is undesirable because (1) when the OS has to access many different locations on the drive to read a file, access time slows down, and (2) if the file should become corrupted, recovering a fragmented file is more complicated than recovering a file in one continuous chain.

For these reasons, one routine maintenance task is to periodically **defragment** the hard drive. Windows includes the Defrag command executed from a command prompt, and there is a utility available from the Windows desktop that has a graphical interface. With Windows NT, you must use third-party software, as Windows NT does not include the Defragmenter command. Regardless of the method used, you should defragment your hard drive every six months or so as part of a good maintenance plan.

To use Windows 9x or Windows 2000 Disk Defragmenter, choose Start, then Programs, then Accessories, and then System Tools. (For Windows XP, choose Start, All Programs, Accessories, and System Tools.) For Windows 98, the menu in Figure 24-7 is displayed. Click Disk Defragmenter and select the drive from the dialog box that is displayed. Click OK.

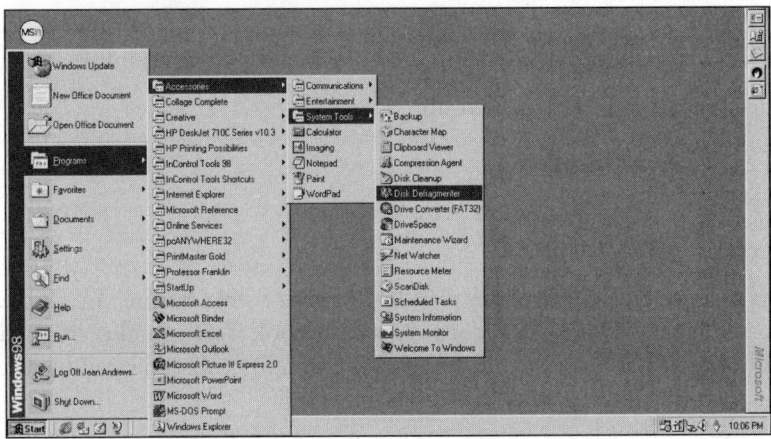

Figure 24-7   Windows 98 utilities

Defragmenting a large hard drive may take a long time, so plan for this before you begin. If you want to watch the progress as it moves through the FAT, click Show Details on the Disk Defragmenter dialog box.

24

Use ScanDisk to Correct Cross-Linked and Lost Clusters

As you learned in Chapter 6, a directory on either a floppy disk or hard drive is a table holding information about files in that directory or folder. The directory contains the number of the first cluster in the file. The FAT holds the map to all the other clusters in the file. Occasionally, the mapping in the FAT becomes corrupted, resulting either in lost clusters or in cross-linked clusters, as shown in Figure 24-8. Here, File 3 has lost direction and is pointing to a cluster chain that belongs to File 4. Clusters 29–31 are called **cross-linked clusters** because more than one file points to them, and clusters 15–17 and 28 are called **lost clusters** or **lost allocation units** because no file in the FAT points to them.

Figure 24-8 Lost and cross-linked clusters

Previously in this book, you learned that Chkdsk/F can be used to repair cross-linked and lost clusters. The ScanDisk utility is an improvement over Chkdsk and was designed to replace it. ScanDisk can repair cross-linked and lost clusters, check the FAT for other problems with long filenames and the directory tree, scan the disk for bad sectors, and repair problems with the structure of a hard drive that has been compressed using Windows DriveSpace or DoubleSpace. Using Windows 9x, ScanDisk can be used from a command prompt or from the Windows desktop. Windows NT/2000/XP do not support ScanDisk, but rather have an error-checking utility. To access the utility, using Windows Explorer, right-click on the drive and select Properties from the shortcut menu. Click the Tools tab.

ScanDisk from the Command Prompt

From the command prompt, the ScanDisk command takes this form:

```
SCANDISK Drive: /A /N /P
```

Use this command to only display information and not fix the drive:

```
SCANDISK C: /P
```

Use this command to display information and fix errors:

```
SCANDISK C:
```

For the above command, the screen in Figure 24-9 is displayed. When the program finishes scanning the disk, it returns you to a command prompt.

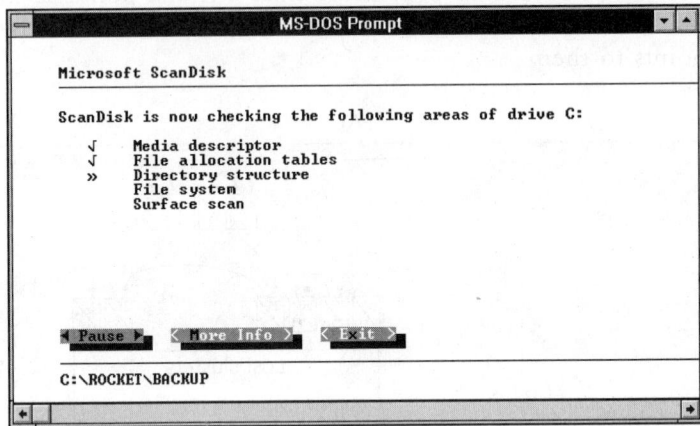

Figure 24-9 ScanDisk in MS-DOS mode

ScanDisk from the Desktop

From the Windows 98 desktop, click Start, then Programs, then Accessories, then System Tools, and then ScanDisk. The ScanDisk utility first asks which drive you want to scan and gives you the choice of a Standard or Thorough scan (see Figure 24-10). The Standard scan checks files and folders for errors. The Thorough scan does all that the standard scan does, and also checks the disk surface for bad sectors. Click Start to begin the scan.

Use ScanDisk for both troubleshooting and maintenance. Like Defrag, ScanDisk is a good tool to run occasionally to check the health of the drive and possibly avert future problems.

Figure 24-10   Use the Windows ScanDisk utility to check a hard drive and repair errors

Disk Compression

Disk compression software can help meet the ever-increasing demand for more space on hard drives to hold improved software. Software packages requiring 200 to 250 MB of hard drive space were unheard of three or four years ago but are now common. The sizes of hard drives have increased proportionately. Even so, we often seek ways to cram more onto nearly full hard drives.

Software to manage disk compression works by (1) storing data on your hard drive in one big file and managing the writing of data and programs to that file, and (2) rewriting data in files in a mathematically coded format that uses less space. Most disk compression programs combine these two methods. This section covers disk compression methods under several versions of Windows.

> Disk compression does save hard drive space, but you need to carefully consider the risks involved as well as performance issues such as longer disk access time. If you do choose to use disk compression, keep good backups of both the data and the software. If the data and software on your drive are especially valuable, you may want to invest in a larger hard drive instead of using compression.

Disk Compression in Windows 9x

A **compressed drive** is not a drive at all; it's a file. Figure 24-11 shows the two parts of a compressed drive. The **host drive**, in this case drive H, is not compressed and is usually a very small partition on the drive, generally under 2 MB. The host drive contains a special file called a **CVF (compressed volume file)**. The CVF holds everything on drive C, compressed into just one file.

Although there are several disk compression utilities on the market, Windows 9x offers its own, called **DriveSpace**. DriveSpace does the following things to compress a drive:

- Assigns a different drive letter to the hard drive, such as H

- Compresses the entire contents of the hard drive into a single file on drive H

- Sets up the drive so that Windows 9x and other applications view this compressed file as drive C

- Configures Windows 9x so that each time it boots, the DriveSpace driver will load and manage the compressed drive

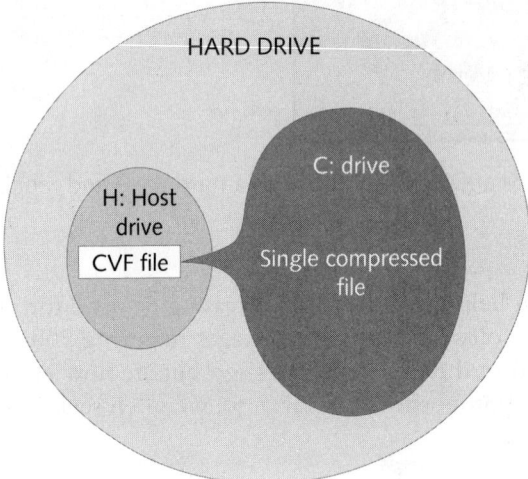

Figure 24-11   A compressed drive

 TIP   DriveSpace does not work with FAT32 under Windows 98.

Follow these steps to compress a drive in Windows 98 using DriveSpace:

1. Click **Start**, then **Programs**, then **Accessories**, then **System Tools**.

2. Click **DriveSpace** to display the dialog box in Figure 24-12. Drive A is used as the example here, but drive C gives similar results.

Figure 24-12   Selecting a drive using DriveSpace for Windows 98

3. Select drive A by clicking on it, and then choose **Compress** from the Drive menu. A dialog box is displayed, showing how much space would be created by compressing the drive. To get the most resources out of compression, begin with a relatively free hard drive.

4. Click **Options**, and the Compression Options box in Figure 24-13 appears. Note that you can allow extra space on drive H that will not be compressed. Click **OK**.

5. Click **Start** to begin compression. Dialog boxes appear, informing you that compressed drives will not be accessible to other OSs and suggesting that you make backups before compressing the drive.

 If a Windows 9x utility such as DriveSpace is missing from a menu list, the component might not have been installed when Windows was installed. To install a Windows component after Windows is installed, go to Control Panel, select Add/Remove Programs, and click the Windows Setup tab.

Figure 24-13   Drive compression options

Disk Compression Under Windows 2000 and Windows XP

In Chapter 21, you learned about file and folder compression under Windows 2000; this section covers compression of an entire volume. Disk and file compression work the same under Windows 2000 and Windows XP. Windows 2000 will be used in this section.

You can compress an entire volume under Windows 2000 as long as the volume is using NTFS. When you place a file or folder on a compressed volume, it will automatically be compressed. When you read a compressed file from a compressed volume, it will be decompressed automatically and will then be recompressed when it is saved back to the compressed volume.

To compress an NTFS volume:

1. Open Windows Explorer.

2. Locate and right-click the root folder for the volume you want to compress. You will find it in the left pane of Windows Explorer.

3. Select **Properties** from the shortcut menu. The Properties box appears.

4. If necessary, click the **General** tab (see Figure 24-14). Click the check box labeled **Compress drive to save disk space**. Click **OK**.

5. The Confirm Attribute Changes dialog box appears. Indicate whether you want to compress only the root folder or the entire volume, and then click **OK** to begin compression.

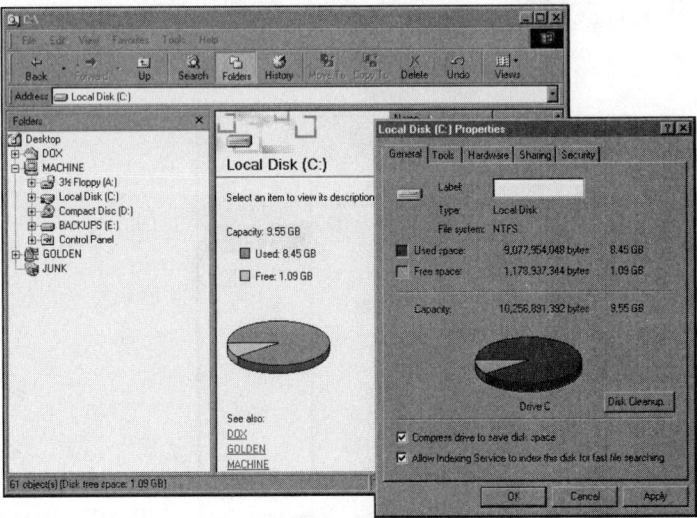

Figure 24-14   Compressing a NTFS volume

Disk Caching

A **disk cache** is a temporary storage area in RAM for data being read from or written to a hard drive, and is used to speed up access time to the drive. The process of disk caching works like this:

1. The CPU asks for data from a hard drive.

2. The hard drive controller sends instructions to the drive to read the data and then sends the data to the CPU.

3. The CPU requests more data, quite often data that immediately follows the previously read data on the hard drive.

4. The controller reads the requested data from the drive and sends it to the CPU. Without a cache, each CPU request requires that data be read from the hard drive, as indicated in the top part of Figure 24-15.

With a hard drive cache, the cache software handles the requests for data, as seen in the lower part of Figure 24-15. The cache program reads ahead of the CPU requests by guessing what data the CPU will request next. Since most data that the CPU requests is in consecutive areas on the drive, the cache program guesses correctly most of the time. The program stores the read-ahead data in memory (RAM). When the CPU requests the next set of data, if the cache program guessed right, the program can send that data to the CPU from memory without having to go back to the hard drive. Some cache software caches entire tracks at a time; other software caches groups of sectors.

Figure 24-15   A CPU asking a hard drive for data without cache (upper part) and with cache (lower part)

Hardware Cache or Software Cache

There are two kinds of hard drive caches: hardware and software. Some hard drive controllers have a **hardware cache** built right into the controller circuit board. The BIOS on the controller contains the cache program, and RAM chips on the controller hold the cache.

A **software cache** is a cache program that is stored on the hard drive like other software and is loaded into memory usually when a computer is booted. The software cache program uses system RAM to hold the cache.

There are advantages and disadvantages to both kinds of hard drive cache. A hardware cache does not use RAM on the system board, but a software cache uses RAM for both the cache program itself and the data being cached. Therefore, a disadvantage of a software cache is that RAM is used that might otherwise be used for applications software and its data.

On the other hand, a software cache is faster because of where the data is stored. Since data is stored in RAM, when the CPU is ready for the data, the data only needs to travel from RAM to the CPU on the system bus, the fastest bus on the motherboard. Since the hardware cache is on the controller board, when the CPU is ready for data stored in this cache, the data must travel from the controller board over one or more buses to the CPU.

Another disadvantage of a hardware cache is that it is a permanent part of the hard drive controller, and today's hard drives have the controller built into the drive housing. Exchanging hard drives to upgrade to a faster hardware cache is impractical, whereas upgrading to a faster software cache is a viable option.

 TIP When buying a new hard drive, check whether it includes hardware caches as an option. A controller with its own hardware cache is slightly more expensive than one without a cache.

How Disk Caching Methods Have Changed

As operating system technologies have changed, so have software disk caching methods. The following is a summary of how different OSs have accomplished disk caching.

- *DOS.* Before disk caching came along, DOS used buffers to speed up disk access. A **buffer** is an area in memory where data waiting to be read or written is temporarily stored. Disk caches do a better job of speeding up disk access than buffers, so the only reason to use buffers today is to satisfy the requirements of older software that uses them. Buffers are implemented by putting the Buffers=[*number*] command in Config.sys. This command specifies how many buffers DOS is to make available for use while data is being read.

- *DOS with Windows 3.x.* DOS with Windows 3.x used **SMARTDrive**, a 16-bit real mode software cache utility that came with DOS and Windows 3.x. SMARTDrive caches data both being read from and written to the hard drive and caches data being read from floppy disks.

- *Windows 9x.* Windows 9x has a built-in 32-bit, protected-mode software cache called **VCACHE**, which is automatically loaded by Windows 9x without entries in Config.sys or Autoexec.bat. VCACHE doesn't take up conventional memory or upper memory space the way SMARTDrive does, and it does a much better job of caching.

- *Windows NT/2000/XP.* Versions of Windows after 9x use automated disk caching as an inherited Windows component. When working with caching under these versions of Windows, remember that you can monitor physical disk performance using the counters discussed in Chapter 21.

24

RESOLVING COMMON HARD DRIVE PROBLEMS

If a hard drive is not functioning and data is not accessible, setting priorities helps focus your work. For most users, the data is the first priority unless they have a recent backup. The software can also be a priority if it is not backed up. Reloading software from the original installation disks or CD-ROM can be time-consuming, especially if the configuration is complex or you have written software macros or scripts that are not backed up.

If you have good backups of both the data and software, the hardware might be your priority. It could be expensive to replace, and downtime can be costly. The point is, when trouble arises, determine your main priority and start by focusing on that.

Be aware of what resources are available to help you resolve a problem:

- Documentation often lists error messages and their meanings.

- The Internet can also help you diagnose hardware and software problems. Go to the Web site of the manufacturer of the product and search for FAQs (frequently asked questions) list or bulletin board. It's likely that others have encountered the same problem and have posted the question and answer. If you search and can't find your answer, then you can post a new question.

- Technical support from the ROM BIOS, hardware, and software manufacturers can help you interpret an error message, or it can provide general support in diagnosing a problem. Most technical support is available during working hours by telephone. Check your documentation for telephone numbers. An experienced computer troubleshooter once said, "The people who solve computer problems do it by trying something and making phone calls, trying something else and making more phone calls, and so on, until the problem is solved." There is a lot of truth in that statement.

> **TIP** Remember one last thing. After making a reasonable and diligent effort to resolve a problem, getting the problem fixed could become more important than resolving it yourself. There comes a time when you might need to turn the problem over to a more experienced technician.

Once you've decided what your priorities are, you begin troubleshooting by interviewing the user experiencing the problem, being sure to ask the following questions:

- Can you describe the problem and show me how to reproduce it?
- Was the computer recently moved?
- Was any new hardware or software recently installed?
- Was any software recently reconfigured or upgraded?
- Does the computer have a history of similar problems?
- Did anyone else recently use the computer?

Let's now look at several common hard drive problems and what to do about them.

Problems When Installing Hard Drives

Sometimes trouble crops up during the installation process. Keeping a cool head, thinking things through carefully a second, third, and fourth time, and using all available resources will most likely get you out of any mess. Installing a hard drive is not difficult unless you have an unusually complex situation.

For example, your first hard drive installation should not involve installing a second SCSI drive into a system that has two SCSI host adapters (SCSI drives are covered in the next chapter). Nor should you install a second drive into a system that uses an IDE connection for one drive on the motherboard and an adapter card in an expansion slot for the other. If a complicated installation is necessary and you have never installed a hard drive, consider asking for expert help. Know your limitations. Start with the simple and build your way up. Using what you have learned in this chapter, you should be able to install a single IDE drive in a PC, or install a second slave IDE drive. After mastering that, tackle something more complicated.

Here are some errors that might occur during a hard drive installation, their causes, and what to do about them. This list has been compiled from experience. Everyone makes mistakes when learning something new, and you probably will, too. You can then add your own experiences to this list.

- We physically installed an IDE hard drive. We turned on the machine and accessed CMOS setup. The hard drive was not listed as an installed device. We checked and discovered that autodetection was not enabled. We enabled it and rebooted. Setup recognized the drive.

- When first turning on a previously working PC, we received the following error message: "Hard drive not found." We turned off the machine, checked all cables, and discovered that the data cable from the motherboard to the drive had become loose. We reseated the cable and rebooted. POST found the drive.

- We had physically installed a new hard drive, replaced the cover on the computer case, and booted the PC with a bootable floppy disk in the drive. POST beeped three times and stopped. Recall that diagnostics during POST are often communicated by beeps if the tests take place before POST has checked video and made it available to display the messages. Three beeps on most computers signal a memory error. We turned the computer off and checked the memory SIMMs on the motherboard. A SIMM positioned at the edge of the motherboard next to the cover had been bumped as we replaced the cover. We reseated the SIMM and booted from a floppy disk again, this time with the cover still off. The error disappeared.

- We physically installed a new hard drive and turned on the computer. We received the following error: "No boot device available." We forgot to insert a bootable disk. We put the disk in the drive and rebooted the machine successfully.

- We physically installed the hard drive, inserted a floppy disk in the disk drive, and rebooted. We received the following error message: "Configuration/ CMOS error. Run setup." This error message is normal for an older BIOS that does not support autodetection. POST found a hard drive it was not expecting. The next step is to run setup.

- We physically installed the card and drive and tried to reboot from a floppy disk. Error message 601 appeared on the screen. Any error message in the 600 range refers to the floppy disk. Because the case cover was still off, we looked at the connections and discovered that the power cord to the floppy disk drive was not connected. (It had been disconnected earlier to expose the hard drive bay underneath.) We turned off the machine and plugged the cable in. The error disappeared.

- The hard drive did not physically fit into the bay. The screw holes did not line up. We got a bay kit, but it just didn't seem to work. We took a break, went to lunch, and came back to make a fresh start. We asked others to help view the brackets, holes, and screws from a fresh perspective. It didn't take long to discover the correct position for the brackets in the bay.

- We set the jumpers on a hard drive and physically installed the drive. We booted and received the following error message: "Hard drive not present." We rechecked all physical connections and found everything was okay. After checking the jumper settings, we realized that we had set them as if this were the second drive of a two-drive system, when it was the only drive. We restored the jumpers to their original state. In this case, as in most cases, the jumpers were set at the factory to be correct when the drive is the only drive.

> **CAUTION**
>
> One last warning. When things are not going well, you can tense up and make mistakes more easily. *Be certain to turn off the machine before doing anything inside!* Not doing so can be a costly error. For example, a friend had been trying and retrying to boot for some time, and got frustrated and careless. He plugged the power cord into the drive without turning the PC off. Smoke went up and everything went dead. The next thing he learned was how to replace a power supply!

Computer Will Not Recognize a Newly Installed Hard Drive

If the computer will not recognize a newly installed hard drive, check the following:

- Does your system BIOS recognize large drives? Check CMOS setup.

- Does the manual state that you must first do a "low-level" format or run a Disk Manager? IDE drives are already low-level formatted. Older drives require the user to perform this routine.

- Has the Fdisk utility been successfully run? Choose "Display Partition Information" from the Fdisk menu to verify the status.

- Format C:/S is the last required "format" step. Has this been done?

- Has the CMOS setup been correctly configured?

- Are there any DIP switches or jumpers that must be set?

- Have the power cord and data cable been properly connected? Verify that the data cable stripes are connected to pin 1 on the edge connectors of both the motherboard and the drive.

- Check the Web site of the drive manufacturer for suggestions, if the above steps are not productive.

Hardware Problems

Hardware problems usually show up at POST, unless there is physical damage to an area of the hard drive that is not accessed during POST. Hardware problems often make the hard drive totally inaccessible.

Sometimes older drives refuse to spin at POST. Drives that are having trouble spinning often whine at startup for several months before they finally refuse to spin altogether. If your drive whines loudly when you first turn on the computer, never turn the computer off. One of the worst things you can do for a drive that is having difficulty starting up is to leave the computer turned off for an extended period of time. Some drives, just like old cars, refuse to start if they are left unused for a long time. Also, data on a hard drive sometimes "fades" off the hard drive over time.

Do not trust valuable data to a drive that is having this kind of trouble. Plan to replace the drive soon. In the meantime, make frequent backups and leave the power on.

The read/write heads at the ends of the read/write arms on a hard drive get extremely close to the platters but do not actually touch them. This minute clearance between the heads and platters makes hard drives susceptible to destruction. Should a computer be bumped or moved while the hard drive is in operation, a head can easily bump against the platter and scratch the surface. Such an accident causes a "hard drive crash," often making the hard drive unusable.

24

If the head mechanism is damaged, the drive and its data are probably a total loss. If the first tracks that contain the partition table, boot record, FAT, or root directory are damaged, the drive could be inaccessible, although the data might be unharmed.

Here's a trick that might work for a hard drive whose head mechanism is intact but whose first few tracks are damaged. Find a working hard drive that has the same partition table information as the bad drive. With the computer case off, place the good drive on top of the bad drive housing, and connect a spare power cord and the data cable from the adapter to the good drive. Leave a power cord connected to the bad drive. Boot from a disk. No error message should show at POST. Access the good drive by entering C: at the A prompt. The C prompt should show on the monitor screen.

Without turning off the power, gently remove the data cable from the good drive and place it on the bad drive. Do not disturb the power cords on either drive or touch chips on the drive logic boards. Immediately copy the data you need from the bad drive to floppy disks, using the Copy command. If the area of the drive where the data is stored, the FAT, and the directory are not damaged, this method should work.

Here's another trick for an older hard drive that is having trouble spinning when first turned on. Remove the drive from the case and, holding it firmly in both hands, give the drive a quick and sudden twist in such a way that the platters are forced to turn inside the drive housing. Reinstall the drive. It might take several tries to get the drive spinning. Once the drive is working, immediately make a backup and replace the drive soon.

Hard Drive Is Not Found

If your system BIOS cannot find your drive, giving an error message such as "Hard drive not found," the reason will most likely involve a loose cable or adapter card. Here are some things to do and check in this case:

- Confirm that both the monitor and computer switches are turned on.
- Sometimes startup BIOS displays numeric error codes during POST. Errors in the 1700s or 10400s generally mean fixed disk problems. Check the Web site of the BIOS manufacturer for explanations of these numeric codes.
- Check CMOS setup for errors in the hard drive configuration.
- Turn off the computer and monitor before you do anything inside the case.
- Remove and reattach all drive cables. Check for correct pin 1 orientation.
- If you're using an adapter card, remove and reseat it or place it in a different slot.

- Check the jumper or DIP switch settings on the drive.

- Inspect the drive for damage such as bent pins on the connection for the cable.

- To determine if the hard drive is spinning, listen to the hard drive or lightly touch the metal drive (with power on).

- Check the cable for frayed edges or other damage.

- Check the installation manual for things you might have overlooked. Look for a section about system setup and carefully follow all directions that apply.

- Be sure the power cable and disk data cable connections are good.

- If the drive still does not boot, exchange the three field-replaceable units—the data cable, the adapter card (optional), and the hard drive itself—for a hard drive subsystem. Perform the following procedures in order:

- Reconnect or swap the drive data cable.

- Reseat or exchange the drive adapter card, if one is present.

- Exchange the hard drive for a known good unit.

- If the hard drive refuses to work but the hard drive light stays on even after the system has fully booted, the problem might be a faulty controller on the hard drive or motherboard. Try replacing the hard drive and then the motherboard.

A bad power supply or a bad motherboard also might cause a disk boot failure. If the problem is solved by exchanging one of the above field-replaceable units, you still must reinstall the old unit to verify that the problem was not caused by a bad connection.

Invalid Drive or Drive Specification

If you get the error "Invalid drive or drive specification," the system BIOS cannot read the partition table information. When the partition table is damaged, BIOS will try to load the OS, first reading the master boot program at the beginning of the partition table information on the hard drive.

In this case, you should still be able to boot from a floppy disk. When you get to the A prompt and try to access the hard drive by entering C:, you will get the same error. To restore the boot program in the partition table (the MBR, or Master Boot Record), which is at the very beginning of the partition table information, for Windows 9x or Windows NT, use the Fdisk command to examine the table. If it is corrupted, which might be the result of a boot sector virus, try the Fdisk /MBR command to restore the master boot program. (For Windows 2000/XP, from the Recovery Console, use the command Fixmbr.)

If this does not work, you can repartition the drive, but you will lose all the data on the drive. If the data is important and is not backed up, try third-party data recovery software to recover the drive and its data before repartitioning.

24

> There is a danger in using the Fdisk/MBR command. Some viruses detect when the MBR is altered, or when an attempt is made to alter it, and do further damage at that time. Also, some third-party drive encryption software alters the MBR. If Fdisk/MBR overwrites the data encryption program in the MBR, the data encrypted on the hard drive might not be readable. If you have important data on the drive that is not backed up, try to recover the data before using Fdisk/MBR.

Restoring the partition table is impossible if the track is physically damaged. The partition table is written on the very first sector of the hard drive, and this sector must be accessible. After that, you can create a primary partition that covers the damaged area, which you will never use. Create an extended partition for the remainder of the drive. You will not be able to use this hard drive as your boot device, but it can be used as a secondary hard drive. Another thing you can do is to use third-party partition software that allows you to decide where on a hard drive you want to put a partition.

Don't perform a low-level format on an IDE drive unless the drive is otherwise unusable. Use the low-level format program recommended by the manufacturer, and follow its instructions. Call the drive manufacturer's technical support to find out how to get this program, or check the manufacturer's Web site for details.

Damaged Boot Record

If the boot record on a hard drive is damaged, you cannot boot from the hard drive. After you boot from a floppy disk and try to access the hard drive, you might get an error message such as "Invalid media type," "Non-DOS disk," or "Unable to read from Drive C." If the OS boot record is damaged, the best solution is to recover it from the backup copy you made when you first became responsible for the PC. Norton Utilities (*www.symantec.com*) can be used to make the backup. If you don't have a backup, try to repair it using Norton Disk Doctor, SpinRite by Gibson Research (*www.grc.com*), or GetDataBack by Runtime Software (*www.runtime.org*). If that doesn't work, reformat the volume.

Damaged FAT or Root Directory or Bad Sectors

The partition table and the boot record are easily backed up to disk; they will not change unless the drive is repartitioned or reformatted. Always back them up as soon as you can after you buy a new computer or become responsible for a working one. Unlike the partition table and the boot record, the FAT and the root directory change often and are more difficult to back up. The success of Windows or third-party utilities in repairing a damaged FAT or root directory depends on the degree of damage to the tables. If these tables are damaged, you may receive an error message that indicates a damaged FAT or root directory or bad sectors somewhere on the hard drive, such as "Sector not found reading drive C, Abort, Retry, Ignore, Fail?", "Bad Sector," and "Sector Not Found." Try ScanDisk to repair the damage, or try copying important files on the drive to another medium. If you encounter the error above, type *I* to ignore the bad sector and continue copying. If that doesn't work, try third-party recovery software, which might be able to recover the FAT or root directory. If these don't work, reformat the drive. If there is important data on the drive that is not backed up, before you format, try using the Copy command from a command prompt to copy these files to another medium.

Cannot Boot from the Hard Drive

Error messages that indicate the hard drive is not bootable are "Non-system disk or disk error...," "Invalid system disk...," and "Command file not found." First verify that the drive can be accessed from a floppy disk. Boot from a rescue disk and enter C: at the command prompt. If you can access the drive, the problem is missing or corrupted system files on drive C. Do these things:

- For Windows 9x, try the Sys C: command to copy Io.sys, Msdos.sys, and Command.com from the rescue disk to the hard drive.
- Use ScanDisk to scan the drive for errors.
- Run a current version of an antivirus program.

Drive Retrieves and Saves Data Slowly

If the drive retrieves and saves data slowly, run Defrag to rewrite fragmented files to contiguous sectors. Slow data retrieval might be caused by fragmented files that have been updated, modified, and spread over different portions of the disk.

Software Problems with Hard Drives

Problems with hard drives can be caused by either hardware or software. Data and program files can become corrupted for many reasons, ranging from power spikes to user error. Here are some general software causes of hard drive problems. The root cause of many of these causes is a virus:

- Corrupted OS files
- Corrupted partition table, boot record, or root directory, making all data on the hard drive inaccessible
- Corruption of the area of the FAT that points to the data, the data's directory table, or the sector markings where the data is located
- Corruption of the data itself

Data and Program File Corruption

To restore a data file that is not backed up, you have three options:

- Use operating system tools and commands to recover the file.
- Use third-party software such as Norton Utilities or SpinRite to recover the file.
- If neither of these approaches works, you can turn to a professional data recovery service. These services can be expensive, but, depending on how valuable the data is, the cost might be justified.

When a data file or program file is damaged, portions of the file may still be intact. The basic approach to recovering data in this situation is to create a new file on another disk or on the hard drive, containing all the sectors from the original file that can be read from the damaged disk or hard drive. Use the Copy command and when you get an error message, try to move on to the next sector. Some of the file might be copied to the new media. Then edit the newly created file to replace the missing data.

How successfully an OS recovers data depends on how badly damaged the file is. A few examples of how data commonly becomes damaged and what can be done to recover it are discussed below. If a file has been accidentally erased, or the disk or hard drive is otherwise damaged, remember these two things:

- Don't write anything to the disk or hard drive, because you might overwrite data that you could otherwise recover.

- If you are recovering data from a disk, use Diskcopy in DOS or, for Windows 9x, use Copy Disk in Explorer to make a copy of the disk before you do anything else. If Copy Disk or Diskcopy doesn't work, try copying the disk with a third-party program such as Norton Utilities.

Here are some problems you may experience with files and the file system:

- *Corrupted file header.* If an application cannot open or read one of its data files, the file header might be corrupted. Many applications place header information (called the file header) at the beginning of the file. This data follows a different format from the rest of the file. The application uses it to identify the file and its contents. If the file header is lost or corrupted and an application needs that header to read the file, you can sometimes recover the contents by treating the file as an ASCII text file.

TIP Most applications let you import a text file, and then convert it to the application's format. Read your application's documentation to learn how to import a text file.

- *Lost clusters.* A disk can develop lost clusters (also called lost allocation units) if a program cannot properly close a file it has opened. For example, if you boot your computer while an application is running (not a good thing to do for this very reason), the application will not have the opportunity to close a file and may lose clusters. Another way clusters can be lost is if you remove a floppy disk from a drive while the drive light is still on (also not a good thing to do). Some older applications, such as early versions of MS Access, might not complete writing a file to a floppy disk until the application is closed or another data file is opened. In this case, you must close the application or open a new file before it is safe to remove the floppy disk.

Lost clusters are clusters that are not incorporated into a file. The Chkdsk and Scandisk commands turn the clusters into a file with the name File0000.chk or a similar filename with a higher number, and store the file in the root directory. To use this utility at a command prompt to access lost clusters, use the command with the /F option, like this:

```
C:\> Chkdsk A:/F
```

Often the file created can be used by the application that it belongs to, although you might have to change the file extension so the application will recognize the file. You can also use the ScanDisk utility described in Chapter 5 to accomplish the same results.

If the drive is compressed, try booting to a command prompt and using ScanDisk to recover the compressed data. Include the name of the compressed volume file on the host drive, like this:

```
Scandisk drvspace.nnn
```

or

```
Scandisk dblspace.nnn
```

Substitute the file extension for the compressed volume file on the host drive (for example, Drvspace.001 or Dblspace.001).

- *Erased file.* If a file has been deleted, it can sometimes be recovered. First look for the file in the Recycle Bin. If it's not there, at a command prompt try the Unerase or Undelete command, which recovers some erased files.

TIP: Viruses cause many file system problems. When you have a problem with a corrupted system file, program file or data file, run a current version of antivirus software. The software will probably not help in recovering the file, but might prevent other files from becoming infected.

Troubleshooting Hard Drives with Third-Party Software

To troubleshoot hard drive problems, you might need to know how to use third-party utility software. Three popular utility software programs are Norton Utilities, SpinRite, and PartitionMagic. The following descriptions tell you what to expect from the software when you have a hard drive failure. Note that these are *not* complete listings of all the utility software functions, or of all available software packages. See specific software documentation for more detail.

- *Norton Utilities* (*www.symantec.com*) offers several easy-to-use tools to prevent damage to a hard drive, recover data from a damaged hard drive, and improve system performance. Many of the functions of these tools have been taken over and improved by utilities included with recent versions of Windows. The most commonly used Norton Utilities tools now are the recovery tools. Two examples are Norton Disk Doctor, which automatically repairs many hard

24

drive and floppy disk problems without your intervention, and UnErase Wizard, which allows you to retrieve files that you deleted accidentally. When using Norton Utilities, be certain you are using the version of the software for the operating system you have installed. Using Norton with the wrong OS can do damage.

- *PartitionMagic* by PowerQuest Corporation (*www.powerquest.com*) lets you manage partitions on a hard drive more quickly and easily than with Fdisk for Windows 9x or Disk Management for Windows NT/2000/XP. You can create new partitions, change the size of partitions, and move partitions without losing data or moving the data to another hard drive while you work. You can switch between FAT16 and FAT32 without disturbing your data, and you can hide and show partitions to secure your data.

- *SpinRite* by Gibson Research (*www.grc.com*) is hard drive utility software that has been around for years. Today, SpinRite is still a DOS application without a sophisticated GUI interface, but it has been updated to adjust to new drive technologies. It supports FAT32, SCSI, Zip drives, and Jaz drives. You can boot your PC from a floppy disk and run SpinRite from a floppy, which means that it doesn't require much system overhead. Because it is written in a language closer to the binary code that the computer understands, it is more likely to detect underlying hard drive problems than software that uses Windows, which can stand as a masking layer between the software and the hard drive. SpinRite analyzes the entire hard drive surface, performing data recovery of corrupted files and file system information. Sometimes, SpinRite can recover data from a failing hard drive when other software fails.

 TIP Always check compatibility between utility software and the operating system with which you plan to use it. One place you can check is the service and support section of the software manufacturer's Web site.

Getting Technical Support

Sometimes you may not be able to solve a hard drive problem on your own. The first step toward getting more help is to check the Web site of the hard drive manufacturer. Search for the hard drive and look for problems with solutions. If you still need more help, you might need to call technical support. To make calls to technical support more effective, have as much of the following information as you can available before you call:

- Drive model and description
- Manufacturer and model of your computer
- Exact wording of error message, if any
- Description of the problem
- Hardware and software configuration for your system

VIRUSES AND OTHER COMPUTER INFESTATIONS

A computer support person needs to know how to protect computers against computer infestations (including viruses), how to recognize them, and how to get rid of them. Understanding what infestations are, how they work, and where they hide helps technicians deal with them successfully. A computer **infestation** is any unwanted program that is transmitted to a computer without the knowledge of the user or owner, and is designed to do varying degrees of damage to data and software. Computer infestations do not damage PC hardware, although, when boot sector information is destroyed on a hard drive, it can appear as though the hard drive is physically damaged. What most people refer to as viruses really fall into four categories of computer infestations: viruses, Trojan horses, worms, and logic bombs. The four types of infestations differ in the way they spread, what damage they do, and how they hide.

Because viruses are by far the most common of the four kinds of computer infestations, one of the most important defenses against computer infestations is **antivirus (AV) software** that is designed to discover and remove a virus. This section looks at several AV programs and how to use them effectively.

Understanding Computer Infestations

A **virus** is a program that can replicate by attaching itself to other programs. The infected program must be executed for a virus to run. The virus might then simply replicate, or also do damage by immediately performing some harmful action. A virus might be programmed to perform a negative action in the future, such as on a particular date (for instance, Friday the 13th), or when some logic within the host program is activated.

A virus is different from a **worm**, a program that spreads copies of itself throughout a network without a host program. A worm is seldom seen except on a network, where it creates problems by overloading the network as it replicates. Worms do damage by their presence rather than by performing a specific damaging act, as a virus does. A worm overloads memory or hard drive space by replicating repeatedly.

A **Trojan horse** is a third type of computer infestation that, like a worm, does not need a host program to work; rather it substitutes itself for a legitimate program. Trojan horses cannot replicate themselves. (This last statement has some exceptions. One Trojan horse program was disguised as an automatic backup utility downloadable from the Internet. When used, it created backups and replicated itself to the backups. It was programmed to damage several systems on Friday the 13th. In this case, the Trojan horse program is also considered a virus because of its ability to replicate.) Because Trojan horse infestations cannot replicate and require human intervention to move from one location to another, they are not as common as viruses.

A **logic bomb** is dormant code added to software and is triggered by a predetermined time or event. For example, an employee might put code into a program to destroy important files if his or her name is ever removed from the payroll file. Also, viruses,

Trojan horses, logic bombs, and worms can occur in combination such as when a virus gains access to a network by way of a Trojan horse. The virus plants a logic bomb within application software on the network that sets off a worm when it executes.

Where Viruses Hide

A program is called a virus because (1) it has an incubation period (does not do damage immediately), (2) it is contagious (can replicate itself), and (3) it is destructive. There are several types of viruses and methods that viruses use to avoid detection by antivirus software.

Boot Sector Virus   A boot sector virus hides in a boot sector program. It can hide on a hard drive either in the program code of the Master Boot Record or in the boot record program that loads the OS on the active partition of the hard drive. On a floppy disk, a boot sector virus hides in the boot program of the boot sector. One of the most common ways a virus spreads is from a floppy disk used to boot a PC. When the boot program is loaded into memory, so is the virus, which can then spread to other programs.

Many CMOS setups have an option that prevents writing to the boot sector of the hard drive, which can protect against some boot sector viruses. This feature must be turned off before installing Windows 9x, or Windows NT/2000/XP, which must write to the boot sector during installation. Windows 9x does not tell you that you must turn the feature off and start the installation over until about halfway through the installation.

File Viruses   A **file virus** hides in an executable (.exe or .com) program or in a word-processing document that contains a macro. A **macro** is a small program contained in a document and can be automatically executed when the document is first loaded, or later by pressing a key combination. For example, a word-processing macro might automatically read the system date and copy it into a document when you open the document. Viruses that hide in macros of document files are called macro viruses. **Macro viruses** are the most common viruses spread by e-mail, hiding in macros of attached document files.

One well-known example of a macro virus is Melissa, first introduced on Friday, March 26, 1999, in a Word 97 macro. The virus immediately spread around the world within one working day. The e-mail that initially spread Melissa looked like this:

```
From: (name of infected user)
Subject: Important Message From (name of infected user)
To: (50 names from alias list)
Here is that document you asked for ... don't show anyone else ;-)
Attachment: LIST.DOC
```

When the recipient opened the document, a macro executed and immediately e-mailed the List.doc to 50 e-mail addresses listed in the user's address book. The virus infected other Word documents, which, when e-mailed, also spread the virus.

Melissa drops its payload, or activates, when a document is opened when the minutes of the hour match the day of the month (for example, at 09:18 on the 18th day of a month). It then inserts a phrase from the Simpsons TV show into the current document.

One type of file virus searches a hard drive for files with .exe file extensions and then creates another file with the same filename with a .com file extension, and stores itself there. When the user launches a program, the OS first looks for the program name with the .com file extension. It then finds and executes the virus. The virus is loaded into memory and loads the program with the .exe extension. The user appears to have launched the desired program. The virus is then free to do damage or spread itself to other programs.

Multipartite Viruses   A **multipartite virus** is a combination of a boot sector virus and a file virus. It can hide in either type of program.

Cloaking Techniques

A virus is programmed to attempt to hide from antivirus (AV) software. AV software can only detect viruses that are identical or similar to ones it has been programmed to search out and recognize. AV software detects a known virus by looking for distinguishing characteristics called the **virus signature**, which is why it is important to update your AV software.

TIP   Antivirus software cannot detect a virus it does not know to look for. Therefore, upgrade your AV software regularly, to keep your protection current as new viruses are discovered.

A virus attempts to hide from AV software in two ways: by changing its distinguishing characteristics (its signature) and by attempting to mask its presence. Three types of viruses that are categorized according to their cloaking techniques are polymorphic, encrypting, and stealth viruses, which are discussed next.

Polymorphic Viruses   A **polymorphic virus** changes its distinguishing characteristics as it replicates. Mutating in this way makes it more difficult for AV software to recognize the presence of the virus.

Encrypting Viruses   One key symptom AV software looks for is a program that can replicate itself. An **encrypting virus** can transform itself into a nonreplicating program to avoid detection. However, it must revert to a replicating program to spread or replicate and can then be detected by AV software.

Stealth Viruses   A **stealth virus** actively conceals itself, using one or more of the following techniques:

- Because AV software can detect a virus by noting the difference between a program's file size before the virus has infected it and after the virus is present, the virus alters OS information to mask the size of the file it is hiding in.

- The virus monitors when files are opened or closed. When it sees that the file it is hiding in is about to be opened, it temporarily removes itself or substitutes a copy of the file that does not include the virus. The virus keeps a copy of this uninfected file on the hard drive just for this purpose.

The Damage an Infestation Can Cause

Viruses, worms, and Trojan horses have not been known to physically damage a hard drive or other hardware device. The damage they do ranges from minor, such as displaying bugs crawling around on a screen, to major, such as erasing everything written on a hard drive. Infestation damage is called the payload and can be accomplished in a variety of ways. A virus can be programmed to drop its payload only in response to a triggering event such as a date, opening a certain file, or pressing a certain key. Figure 24-16 shows the results of a harmless virus that simply displays garbage on the screen.

How Infestations Spread

Understanding how infestations spread is essential to understanding how to protect your computer against them. Some computers are more vulnerable than others, depending on user habits. Below is a list of user activities that make a computer susceptible to infestations.

- Trading floppy disks containing program files

- Connecting the computer to an unprotected network

- Buying software from unreliable sources

- Downloading programs from the Internet

- Using floppy disks from unknown sources

- Using shared network programs

- Using used, preformatted floppy disks

- Reading e-mail that automatically executes a word processor to read attached files

- Executing attachments to e-mail messages without first scanning them for viruses

- Not write-protecting original program disks

Figure 24-16 The crash virus appears to be destructive, making the screen show only garbage, but does no damage to the hard drive data

How a Virus Replicates Once a program containing a virus is copied to your PC, the virus can spread only when the infected program is executed. The process is shown in Figure 24-17. Recall from earlier chapters that the first step in executing a program, whether it is stored in a program file or in a boot sector, is to load the program into memory. Viruses hidden in a program can then be executed from memory. A virus can either be a **memory-resident virus** and stay in memory, still working, even after the host program is terminated, or a **non-memory-resident virus**, which means that it is terminated when the host program is closed.

After a virus is loaded into memory, it looks for other programs that are loaded into memory. When it finds one, it copies itself there and into that same program file on disk. From Figure 24-17, you can see that a virus becomes more dangerous the longer it stays loaded into memory and the more programs that are opened while it is there. For this reason, if you want to use a computer that has been used by other people, such as in a computer lab, always reboot before you begin work to clear memory of programs. Use a hard boot, not just a soft boot, to erase all memory-resident programs (including a memory-resident virus) from memory.

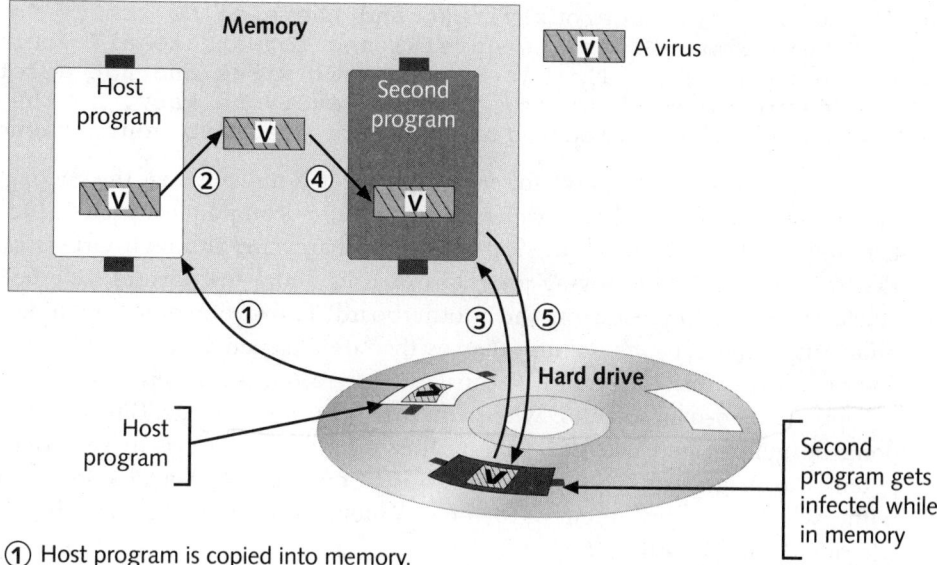

24

① Host program is copied into memory.
② The virus may or may not move itself to a new location in memory.
③ A second program is opened and copied into memory.
④ The virus copies itself to the second program in memory.
⑤ The newly infected second program is written back to the hard drive.

Figure 24-17   How a virus replicates

How a Trojan Horse Gets into Your Computer   A Trojan horse is an infestation
that masquerades as a legitimate program. One interesting example of a Trojan horse
is the AOL4FREE program. Originally this was an illegal program that could provide
unauthorized access to America Online. After the program's usefulness was blocked by
AOL, a new program emerged, also called AOL4FREE, which was not an online
access program, but a destructive Trojan horse. People passed the program around,
thinking that it would provide illegal access to AOL; however, if executed, it actually
erased files on their hard drives.

Virus Hoaxes

A virus hoax is a letter or e-mail warning about a nonexistent virus. The warning is itself
a pest because it overloads network traffic. Here's an example of a virus hoax e-mail message I received:

```
There is a new virus going around in the last couple of
days!! DO NOT open or even look at any mail that you get
that says: "Returned or Unable to Deliver." The virus will
erase your whole hard drive and attach itself to your
computer components and render them useless. Immediately
delete any mail items that say this. AOL has indicated this
```

```
is a very dangerous virus, and there is NO remedy for it at
this time. Please be careful and forward to all your online
friends ASAP. This is a new email virus and not a lot of
people know about it; just let everyone know, so they won't
be a victim. Please forward this email to your friends!!!
```

Viruses are getting more powerful every day, but it is unlikely that this message is accurate. It is unlikely that a virus can render computer components useless. No virus has been known to actually do physical damage to hardware, although viruses can cause a PC to be useless by destroying programs or data, and a few viruses have been able to attack system BIOS code on the motherboard. However, some can hide in word-processing documents containing macros that are attached to an e-mail message, and a few viruses are able to hide in Web pages that are transmitted as e-mail messages and interpreted by e-mail software when you first open the message. But most importantly, don't be gullible and take the bait by forwarding the message to someone else. The potential damage a hoax like this can do is to overload an e-mail system with useless traffic, which is the real intent of the hoax. When I received this e-mail, there were over a hundred names on the distribution list.

Before forwarding a virus warning, you can check the Web sites of virus software manufacturers such as the ones listed later in this section. In addition, here are some Web sites that specialize in debunking virus hoaxes:

- *hoaxbusters.ciac.org* by Computer Incident Advisory Capability
- *www.hoaxinfo.com* by Jeff Richards
- *www.hoaxkill.com* by Oxcart Software
- *www.viruslist.com* by Kaspersky Lab
- *www.vmyths.com* by Rhode Island Soft Systems, Inc

These are many sources for checking for virus hoaxes. Using a search engine, type "virus hoax," a similar phrase, or the name of the virus or virus warning, and you'll find a wealth of information. Always check before sending!

Protecting Against Computer Infestations

You can do a lot to protect your computer against viruses and other infestations. Your first line of defense is to regularly make backups and use antivirus software. After that, use wisdom when managing programs. Here are some general guidelines:

- Buy antivirus software and set your computer to automatically run the AV program at startup.
- Keep your AV software current by periodically downloading upgrades from the Internet. Many antivirus programs now offer an update feature that does this automatically.

- Set a virus scan program to automatically scan word-processing documents and other e-mail attachments as they are opened. Some Web-based e-mail clients, such as Yahoo! Mail, offer the option to scan attachments before downloading them.

- Establish and faithfully execute a plan to make scheduled backups of your hard drive to protect against potential infestation damage.

- Only buy software from reputable vendors.

- Don't trade program files on floppy disks.

- Don't use floppy disks from unknown sources, and always scan floppy disks for viruses, no matter where they came from.

- Download software from the Internet sparingly, and then always scan program files for viruses before executing them.

- Never use pirated software.

- Format floppy disks before first use.

- Write-protect original program floppy disks or use CDs to install programs.

- In a business environment, adopt strict company policies against using unauthorized software.

- Before using a running computer that others have already used, hard-boot the computer.

- Set your computer CMOS settings to boot from drive C, then drive A.

- Turn on antivirus protection for your MBR in the CMOS settings, if available.

Virus Symptoms

Here are some warnings that suggest a virus is at work:

- A message appears that a downloaded document contains macros, or an application asks whether it should run macros in a document. (It is best to disable macros if you cannot verify that they are from a trusted source and that they are free of viruses or worms.)

- A program takes longer than normal to load.

- The number and length of disk accesses seem excessive for simple tasks.

- Unusual error messages occur regularly.

- Less memory than usual is available.

- Files mysteriously disappear or appear.

- Strange graphics appear on your computer monitor, or the computer makes strange noises.

- There is a noticeable reduction in disk space.
- The system cannot recognize the hard drive when you have booted from a floppy disk.
- The system cannot recognize the CD-ROM drive, although it has worked earlier.
- Executable files have changed size.
- Executable files that once worked no longer work and give unexpected error messages.
- The access lights on the hard drive and floppy drive turn on when there should not be any activity on that device. (However, sometimes an OS will perform routine maintenance on the drive when the system has been inactive for a while.)
- Files constantly become corrupted.
- Strange or bizarre error messages appear.
- DOS or Windows error messages about the FAT or partition table are displayed.
- The hard drive boots but hangs up before getting a DOS prompt or Windows desktop.
- File extensions or file attributes change without reason.
- A message is displayed from the virus scanner software.
- The number of bad sectors on the hard drive continues to increase.
- The MEM command reveals unfamiliar TSRs loaded into memory.

What to Do When You Suspect a Virus Infestation

If you suspect a virus, run a virus scan program to detect and delete the virus. If the antivirus software is not already installed, you can still use it. Consult the documentation for instructions on how to proceed. In many cases, the installation process detects the virus and eliminates it before continuing the installation. However, if the AV software does not recognize the virus, or if the virus successfully hides, the AV program cannot detect the virus. If the AV software found nothing, but you still suspect a virus, get the latest upgrade of your AV software and try it or another AV program. Also download recent virus definitions; these are usually part of automatic AV software updates. If you know the name of the virus, check the Web site of the antivirus software for information about the virus and how to remove it.

Table 24-2 lists some popular antivirus software and Web sites that provide information about viruses.

Table 24-2   Antivirus software and information

Antivirus Software	Web Site
Norton AntiVirus by Symantec, Inc.	www.symantec.com
Dr. Solomon's Software	www.drsolomon.com
McAfee VirusScan by McAfee Associates, Inc.	www.mcafee.com
ESafe by Aladdin Knowledge Systems, Ltd.	www.esafe.com
F-Prot by Frisk Software International	www.f-prot.com
Command AntiVirus by Command Software	www.commandcom.com
PC-cillin by Trend Micro (for home use)	www.antivirus.com
NeaTSuite by Trend Micro (for networks)	www.antivirus.com

When selecting antivirus software, look for the ability to do the following:

- Download new software upgrades and virus definitions from the Internet so that your software knows about new viruses

- Automatically execute at startup

- Detect macros in a word-processing document as it is loaded by the word processor

- Automatically monitor files being downloaded from the Internet, including e-mail attachments and attachments sent during a chat session such as when using AOL Instant Messenger.

- The ability to both automatically and manually scan for viruses

Using Antivirus Software

Antivirus software can work at different times to scan your hard drive or a floppy disk for viruses. Most AV software can be configured to scan memory and the boot sector of your hard drive for viruses each time your PC is booted. Often it's not practical to have it scan the entire hard drive each time you boot, because that takes too much time. Consider scheduling the AV software to run at the same time every day, such as during the lunch hour.

Some AV software can run continuously in the background and scan all programs that are executed. However, the software can cause problems with other software, especially during installations. If you are having a problem installing a new application, try terminating your AV software first.

Make sure your AV software can scan files as they are downloaded from the Internet or a network, and that it can scan documents for macro viruses each time a document is opened by a word processor. Make sure the AV software can scan both files and boot sectors of hard drives and disks.

CHAPTER SUMMARY

- Disk compression works by storing data on a drive in one big file and managing how data and programs are written to that file, and by rewriting data files in a mathematically coded format that uses less space. Most compression software combines these two methods.

- Volumes can be compressed under Windows 2000 as long as they are using NTFS.

- Disk caching uses temporary storage to speed up access to hard drive data and can be controlled either by hardware or software.

- DOS used buffers rather than disk caching. Windows 3.x and 9x used built-in caching programs. Windows NT/2000/XP use automated caching.

- Three third-party utility software programs used to work with hard drives are Norton Utilities, SpinRite, and PartitionMagic.

- Hard drive problems can be caused by corruption in OS files, the partition table, the boot record, the root directory, the FAT, sector markings, or data itself.

- For DOS or Windows to be able to access a hard drive using the FAT file system, the following items must be intact, listed in the order in which they are accessed: the partition table, the boot record, the FAT, the root directory, the system files, and data and program files.

- The child, parent, grandparent backup method involves reusing tapes by making daily, weekly, and monthly backups.

- A full backup backs up all data from a hard drive. A differential backup backs up files that have changed or been created since the last full backup. An incremental backup backs up only files that have changed or been created since the last backup, whether or not it was a full backup.

- You can create backups using utilities included with tape drives or with Windows, or you can purchase third-party software.

- Disk cloning replicates a hard drive to a new computer.

- It is important to create and test a plan for disaster recovery, including keeping records of backups and recovery procedures.

- High humidity, smoking near the PC, and leaving the PC turned off for long periods can damage a hard drive.

- Sometimes the second copy of the FAT on a hard drive can be used when the first copy becomes corrupted.

- ScanDisk and Chkdsk can be used to recover lost allocation units caused when files are not properly closed by the application creating them.

- When data is lost on a hard drive, don't write anything to the drive if you intend to try to recover the data.

❏ Viruses, which replicate by attaching themselves to other programs, are the most common type of computer infestation. Other types include Trojan horses, worms, and logic bombs.

❏ Viruses can hide in the boot sector, files, macros within files, or in both the boot sector and a file.

❏ Types of viruses that attempt to hide from antivirus software are polymorphic viruses, encrypting viruses, and stealth viruses.

❏ Damage from viruses ranges from an altered monitor display to the erasure of files, or even an entire hard drive.

❏ Use antivirus software both to clean out known viruses and to scan regularly for undetected and unmanifested ones.

24

KEY TERMS

antivirus (AV) software

buffer

child, parent, grandparent backup method

compressed drive

CVF (compressed volume file)

differential backup

disk cache

disk cloning

disk compression

disk imaging

DriveSpace

encrypting virus

file virus

full backup

hardware cache

host drive

incremental backup

infestation

logic bomb

macro

macro virus

memory-resident virus

multipartite virus

non-memory-resident virus

polymorphic virus

RAID (redundant array of inexpensive disks or redundant array of independent disks)

SMARTDrive

software cache

stealth virus

Trojan horse

VCACHE

virus

virus signature

worm

25

SHARING RESOURCES ON A NETWORK

In this chapter, you will learn:

♦ How to connect to and share resources over a local area network

♦ How to control a computer remotely

If users on a LAN are working on a common project and need to share applications and files or need to share printers, then all these users must be assigned to the same workgroup or domain on the LAN. Recall that Windows 9x makes shared resources available by way of Network Neighborhood, and Windows 2000/XP uses My Network Places. Open either icon to see the names of all computers on the network. Figure 25-1 shows My Network Places. Drill down to see shared files, folders, and printers in your workgroup. Using Network Neighborhood or My Network Places, you can copy files from one computer to another, use shared applications installed on one computer from another computer, and share printers.

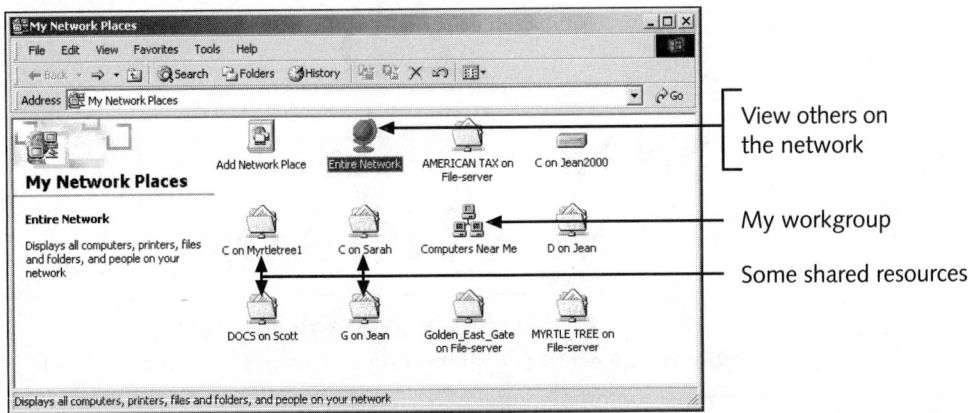

Figure 25-1   View and access shared resources on the network using My Network Places in Windows 2000

Workgroups can be effective when several people work on a common project. For example, if a group of people are building a Web site, sharing resources on the LAN can be an effective method of passing Web pages around as they are built. Or one computer on the LAN can be designated as the file server. The user of this computer makes a portion of hard drive space available for the Web site files. All users have access to this one resource, and the Web site files are neatly kept in a single location. When using workgroups, it is the responsibility of each user to protect the resources being shared by using password protection for read and write privileges to files and folders.

INSTALLING WINDOWS COMPONENTS NEEDED TO SHARE RESOURCES

To share resources over a peer-to-peer network, you must first install Client for Microsoft Networks and File and Printer Sharing. Client for Microsoft Networks is the Windows component that allows you to use resources on the network made available by other computers, and File and Printer Sharing allows you to share resources on your computer with others in your workgroup. After these components are installed, the last thing to do is to share the folders, files, or printers that you want others to be able to access. All these steps are covered in this section.

Installing Windows 98 Components Needed to Share Resources

For Windows 98, to install Client for Microsoft Networks and File and Printer Sharing:

1. Use the Control Panel to access the Network applet. In the Network window, click **Add**. The Select Network Component Type dialog box opens.

2. Select **Client**, and click then **Add**. The Select Network Client window opens. See Figure 25-2.

25

Figure 25-2   In Windows 98, install Client for Microsoft Networks so users on the LAN
can connect to other PCs to share files, folders, and printers

3. Select **Microsoft** on the left and **Client for Microsoft Networks** on the
   right. Click **OK** and insert the Windows 98 CD.

4. Install the service for sharing files and printers with others on the Microsoft
   network. In the Network window, click **Add**. The Select Network Component
   Type dialog box opens.

5. Click **Service**, and then click **Add**. The Select Network Service window
   opens. See Figure 25-3.

6. Select **File and printer sharing for Microsoft Networks**, and then click
   OK. Insert the Windows 98 CD.

7. The next step is to turn on file and printer sharing. In the Network window,
   click **File and Print Sharing**. The File and Print Sharing window opens. See
   Figure 25-4. Check both options to share both files and printers, and then
   click **OK**.

When they are installed, Client for Microsoft Networks and File and Printer Sharing
should automatically bind themselves to the TCP/IP protocol. You can verify this by
accessing the TCP/IP Properties window and clicking the Bindings tab. Verify that Client
for Microsoft Networks and File and Printer Sharing are checked.

Figure 25-3   Install Windows 98 file and printer sharing for Microsoft Networks to be used to share files and printers on a LAN

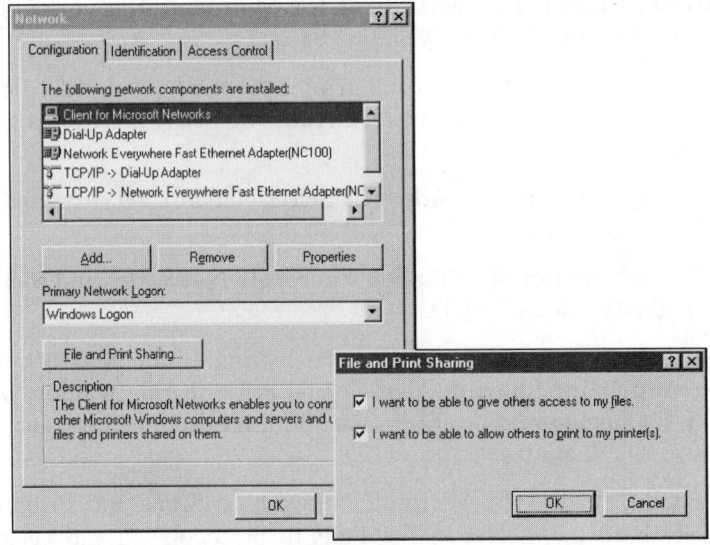

Figure 25-4   Turn on Windows 98 file and printer sharing so others on the LAN can access resources on this PC

Installing Windows 2000 Components Needed to Share Resources

Client for Microsoft Networks and File and Printer Sharing are installed by default during a Windows 2000 installation. However, if you are having a problem sharing resources on a LAN, you can try to uninstall and reinstall them.

1. Access the Control Panel and open the **Network and Dial-up Connections** applet.

2. Right-click the **Local Area Connection** icon and select **Properties** from the shortcut menu. The Local Area Connection Properties window opens (see Figure 25-5).

25

Figure 25-5   Use the Network and the Dial-up Connections applet in Control Panel to install a network protocol using Windows 2000

3. Click **Install**. The Select Network Component Type window appears, which is also shown in Figure 25-5.

4. Select **Client** and then click **Add**. (You will need the Windows 2000 CD or other access to the installation files to add the required components.)

Sharing Files and Folders with the Workgroup

After the computer has been configured for file and printer sharing, using Windows 98 or Windows 2000, follow these sample directions to make a folder on drive C named \data available to others on the LAN:

1. Using Windows Explorer, select the folder **C:\data**. Right-click the folder name. If the system is configured for file and printer sharing, the shortcut menu lists Sharing. Select **Sharing**. See Figure 25-6. The data Properties dialog box opens, as shown in Figure 25-7.

Figure 25-6   In Windows 98, use Windows Explorer to password protect a file or folder shared on a network

Figure 25-7   Using Windows 98, a user on a network can share a folder with others on the network

2. Click the **Shared As** option button and enter a name for the shared folder. In the figure, the name is JEAN'S DATA. This action makes the folder available to others on the network. They can see the folder when they open Network Neighborhood on their desktop.

3. In the section labeled Access Type, click the **Depends on Password** option button.

4. To allow others the right to make changes to the folder, enter a password under **Full Access Password**. For read-only access, enter a different password. Click **OK** to exit the window.

5. For added security when using Windows 2000, set up a user account and password for each user who will have access to shared resources. This added security requires that a user give a valid password before accessing shared files, folders, or printers on the Windows 2000 PC.

When using the option Depends on Password, be sure to enter a password in both fields. With this option, if a password field is empty, then no password is required to have that type of access to the folder. Distribute the two passwords to those people who need to access the folder. You control the access rights (permissions) by selecting which password(s) you give.

Applications can also be shared with others in the workgroup. If you share a folder that has a program file in it, a user on another PC can double-click the program file in Network Neighborhood and execute it remotely on their desktop. This is a handy way for several users to share an application that is installed on a single PC.

Setting Up a Direct Cable Connection

Windows 9x and Windows NT/2000/XP offer a direct cable connection service that allows you to connect two PCs, using either a null modem cable (a cable that connects two PCs using their serial ports) or a parallel cable. Each end of the parallel cable must have a PC connector, not a printer connector. Buy a parallel cable with two DB-25 male/male connections, or buy an adapter for a printer cable. Direct Cable Connection is a handy utility when all you need to do is have two PCs share files or printers, and a cable can reach between them, or you want to allow a guest computer to access shared network resources that a host computer can access.

To set up a direct cable connection, set up both computers to share their resources and install the Direct Cable Connection component under Windows. Then run Direct Cable Connection on both computers (click Start, Programs, Accessories, Communications, and Direct Cable Connection). A Direct Cable Connection dialog box appears asking if you want to be the host or guest PC. Make one PC the host and the other the guest. Next, select a port for the connection, either a serial or parallel port. The host computer will then wait for the guest computer to initiate communication. Use Windows Explorer on the guest computer to view the shared folders on the host computer.

Using Network Drive Maps

A **network drive map** is one of the most powerful and versatile methods of communicating over a network. By using network file service (NFS) client/server software, the network drive map makes one PC (the client) appear to have a new hard drive, such as drive E, that is really hard drive space on another host computer (the server). Even if the host computer is using a different OS, such as Unix, the drive map still functions. Using a network drive map, files and folders on a host computer are available even to network-unaware DOS applications. The path to a file simply uses the remote drive letter instead of a local drive such as drive A or drive C. To set up a network drive under Windows 98 or Windows 2000, follow these steps:

1. On the host computer, using directions given earlier in the chapter, share the drive or folder on a drive that you want to allow others to have access to.

2. On the remote computer that will use the network drive, while connected to the network, access **Windows Explorer**. Click the **Tools** menu shown in Figure 25-8. Select **Map Network Drive**.

Figure 25-8   Mapping a network drive to a host computer in Windows 98, using Windows Explorer

3. The Map Network Drive dialog box appears, as in Figure 25-9. Select a drive letter from the drop-down list.

4. Enter a path to the host computer. Use two backslashes, followed by the name of the host computer, followed by a backslash and the drive or folder to access on the host computer. For example, to access the folder Public on the computer named Scott, enter \\Scott\Public, and then click OK.

5. Figure 25-10 shows the results of the drive mapping. There is a new drive K displayed in Windows Explorer. Folders listed on the right side of the figure are on the host PC.

Figure 25-9   To map a network drive in Windows 98, enter a drive letter to use on your PC and the path to the host computer

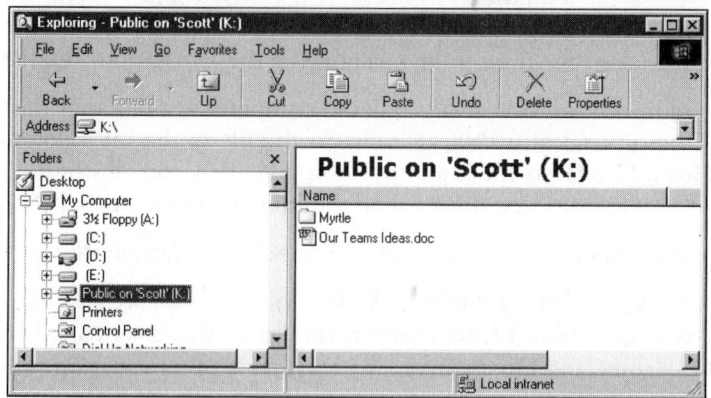

Figure 25-10   Content on the right side of Windows Explorer belongs to the host computer. This computer sees it as belonging to its drive K

 TIP   If a network drive does not work, go to Network Neighborhood or My Network Places and verify that the network connection is still good.

HOW COMPUTERS FIND EACH OTHER ON A LAN

When an application using NetBIOS or WinSock wants to communicate with another computer on the same TCP/IP LAN, the requesting computer knows the name of the remote computer. Before TCP/IP communication can happen between the two computers, the first computer must discover the IP address of the remote PC. For Windows 98 using NetBIOS names, the computer runs through the following checklist in order shown to discover the IP address. (A Windows 2000 computer that is using just TCP/IP and not NetBEUI uses DNS to resolve the name, not WINS, and begins at Step 5 below. If NetBEUI is running on this Windows 2000 computer, it tries DNS first, beginning at Step 5, and then turns to NetBEUI Steps 1 through 4 to resolve the name.)

1. The computer checks the NetBIOS name cache. This cache is information retained in memory from name resolutions made since the last reboot.

2. If the computer has the IP address of a WINS server, it queries the server. A WINS server is a Windows NT/2000 server on the network that maintains a database of NetBIOS names and IP addresses.

3. The computer sends a broadcast message to all computers on the LAN asking for the IP address of the computer with the broadcast NetBIOS name.

4. The computer checks a file named LMHosts, which is stored in the \Windows folder on the local computer. This file, called a **host table**, contains the NetBIOS names and associated IP addresses of computers on the LAN if someone has taken the time to manually make the entries into the file.

5. If the IP address is still not discovered, the computer assumes that the network is using DNS instead of WINS, so it checks the file in the \Windows folder named Hosts. The Hosts file is another host table that contains host names and associated IP addresses that is similar to the information kept by DNS servers.

6. If the computer has the IP address of a DNS server, it queries the DNS server.

Both the LMHosts and Hosts files are in the \Windows folder and are called **host tables**. **LMHosts** serves as a local table of information similar to that maintained by a WINS server for NetBIOS names, and **Hosts** serves as a local table of information similar to that kept by a DNS server.

If you look in the \Windows folder of a Windows 9x computer or the \Winnt\System32\drivers\etc folder of a Windows 2000/XP computer, you will see a sample of each file named LMHosts.SAM and Hosts.SAM, where the SAM stands for "sample." Open each file with Notepad to examine it. Entries in a host table file that begin with the # symbol are comments and are not read by the name resolution process. There are many commented lines in the sample files. You can add your entries to the bottom of the file without the # symbol. An example of a Hosts file is shown in Figure 25-11. It tells this computer what the IP address of the domain name apache.test.com is. Recall that a domain name is a name of a network. In the example, apache is the host name, and the domain name is test.com. The **fully qualified domain name (FQDN)** is apache.test.com, which is often loosely called the domain name.

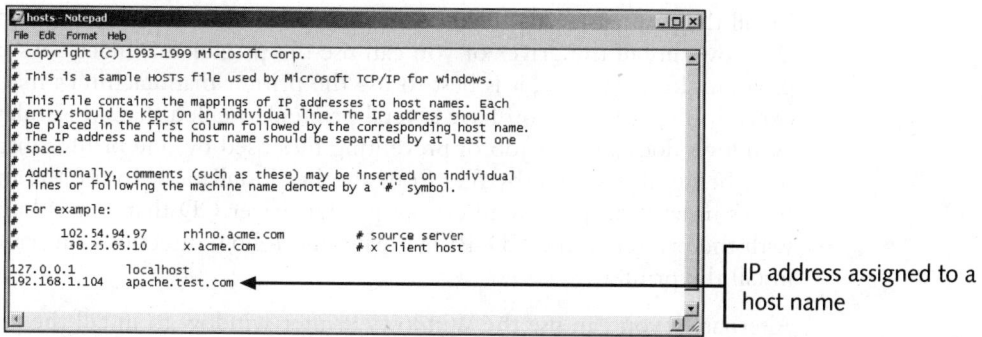

IP address assigned to a host name

Figure 25-11   An entry in your client Hosts file will tell the client the IP address of an intranet Web site when no DNS service is running in Windows 98

In this example, the computer named apache.test.com is used as a Web server for a private network. In order for those on the network to use this domain name, the hosts file on each PC must have the entry in Figure 25-11, and the Web server must have the same IP address at all times. One way to accomplish this is to assign a static IP address to the server. Alternately, if your DHCP server supports this feature, you can configure it to assign the same IP address to your Web server each time if you tell the DHCP server your Web server's MAC address.

INSTALLING AND SHARING A PRINTER

A printer can be connected to a port on a computer and then the computer can share the printer with others on the network. There are also network printers that have Ethernet ports that can be used to connect the printer directly to the network. Each computer on the network that uses the printer must have printer drivers installed so the OS on each computer can communicate with the printer and provide the interface between applications it supports and the printer. This section covers how to install a local printer, how to share that printer with others on the network and how a remote computer on the network can use a shared printer. A printer connected to a computer by way of a port on the computer is a **local printer**, and a printer that is accessed by way of a network is a **network printer**. A computer can have several printers installed. Windows designates one printer to be the **default printer**, which is the printer Windows prints to unless another is selected.

Install a Local Printer

Follow these basic steps to install a local printer:

1. Physically attach the printer to the computer by way of a parallel port, serial port, USB port, or wireless access point. For a parallel port connection, use an IEEE 1284–compliant printer cable.

2. Install the printer drivers. There are two approaches to do this. You can have Windows install the driver or you can use the printer manufacturer's installation program. In most cases, it is best to use the printer manufacturer's method. The exception to this is if you have several printers installed that are similar because Windows does a better job of preventing files used by one printer installation from being overwritten by files from another installation. To use the manufacturer's installation process, insert the printer driver CD that comes bundled with the printer in the CD-ROM drive and follow directions on screen to install the printer.

   Alternately, you can use the Windows Printer window to install the printer. For Windows 98 and Windows 2000 click Start, Settings, and Printer to open the Printer window. For Windows XP, to open the Printer window, click Start, Printers and Faxes. From the Printer window, click Add Printer and follow the Add Printer wizard to install the printer.

3. Once the printer drivers are installed, test the printer. To do this, open the Printer window and right click the printer. Select Properties from the shortcut menu. Click the General tab and then click the Print Test Page button.

From the Printer window you can also delete printers, change the Windows default printer, purge print jobs in order to troubleshoot failed printing, and perform other printer maintenance tasks. If a printer is giving problems or you want to upgrade the printer drivers in order to add new functionality, search the printer manufacturer's Web site for the latest drivers for your printer and operating system. Download the drivers to a folder on the hard drive such as C:\Downloads\Printer, and then double click on the driver file to extract files and launch the installation program to update the printer drivers.

Share a Printer with the Workgroup

To share a local printer with others in the workgroup connected to a Windows 9x or Windows 2000/XP computer, do the following:

1. Click **Start**, point to **Settings**, and then click **Printers**. The Printers window opens.

2. Right-click the printer you want to share. From the shortcut menu, select **Sharing**. (This Sharing option is grayed out if File and Printer Sharing is not installed.)

3. The Properties dialog box opens with the Sharing tab selected (see Figure 25-12).

4. Select **Shared As** and give the printer a **Share Name**. Click **OK** to exit.

5. The printer is listed in the Network Neighborhood group of other computers on the network.

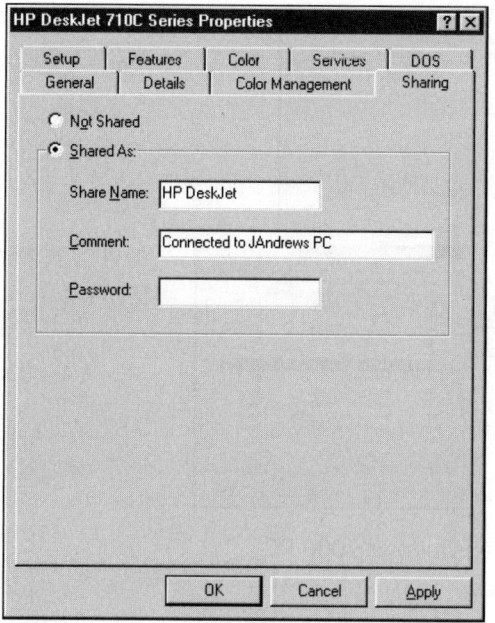

25

Figure 25-12   When using Windows 98, use the printer Properties window to share a connected printer with other computers on the network

To allow a remote PC to use a local printer connected to a Windows 2000 workstation, do the following:

1. On the Windows 2000/XP PC, allow print sharing: open the Printers window. Right-click the printer you want to share, and select **Sharing** from the shortcut menu. The printer's Properties dialog box opens, as seen in Figure 25-13 for Windows 2000, but Windows XP is similar. Select **Shared as** and enter a name for the printer.

2. If you want to make drivers for the printer available to remote users that are using an operating system other than Windows 2000/XP, then click **Additional Drivers**.

3. The Additional Drivers window appears, as also shown in Figure 25-13. Select the OS. In Figure 25-13, Windows 95 or 98 is selected so that those using these OSs will have the printer drivers they need. Click **OK** twice to close both windows. You might be asked for the Windows 2000/XP CD or other access to the installation files. A shared printer shows a hand icon under it in the Printer window.

Figure 25-13   Sharing a printer on a Windows 2000 PC

Using a Shared Printer

There are two approaches to installing a shared network printer on a remote PC. You can perform the installation using the printer drivers installed on the host PC or you can perform the installation using the drivers on CD (either the Windows CD or printer manufacturer's CD). The installations work about the same way for Windows 98 and Windows 2000/XP. The Windows 98 installation is shown here.

To use a printer on the network that is shared, using printer drivers from CD, do the following using Windows 98:

1. Add a new printer: click **Start**, point to **Settings**, and click **Printers**. Double-click **Add Printer**. The Add Printer Wizard window opens. Click **Next**.

2. In response to the question, "How is this printer attached to your computer?" select **Network printer**. Click **Next**. The wizard window in Figure 25-14 opens.

3. Enter the host computer name and printer name. Begin with two backslashes and separate the computer name from the printer name with a backslash. Or you can click **Browse** and search the list of shared printers on the network, selecting the printer to install. Click **Next**. (If your network is using static IP addressing and you know the IP address of the host PC, you can enter the IP address instead of the host name in this step.)

4. Select the printer manufacturer and then the printer model from the list of supported printers. Click **Next** when you are finished.

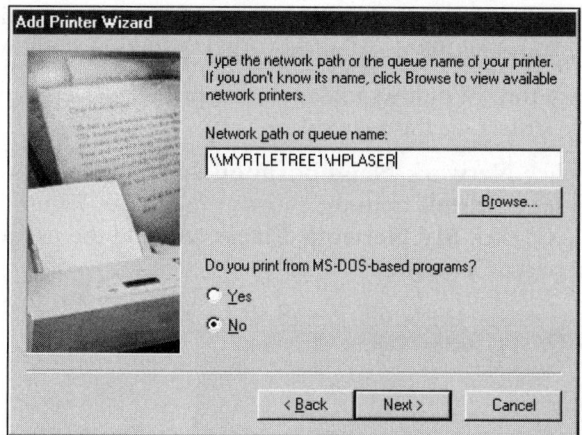

Figure 25-14   To use a network printer under Windows 98, enter the host computer name followed by the printer name

5. Enter a name for the printer. You might include the location of the printer, such as 3rd Floor Laser or John's Laser. In response to the question, "Do you print from MS-DOS based programs?" Answer **Yes** if you have any intention of ever doing that, and then click **Next**.

6. Sometimes a DOS-based program has problems printing to a network printer. You can choose to associate the network printer with a printer port such as LPT1 to satisfy the DOS application. To do that, click **Capture Printer Port**. The Capture Printer Port dialog box appears (see Figure 25-15). Select the port from the drop-down menu, and then click **OK**.

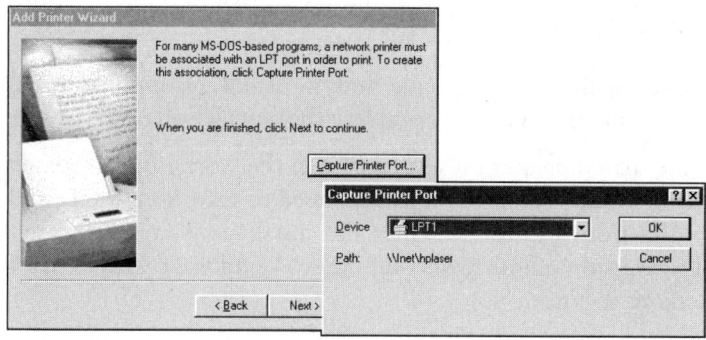

Figure 25-15   Associate a network printer with a printer port in order to help DOS applications in Windows 98

7. Click **Next** to continue.

8. Choose to print a test page, and then click **Finish**. The network printer is now available for use.

A quicker way to install a shared printer is to use the printer drivers already installed on the host PC. To do that using Windows 98 or Windows 2000/XP do the following:

1. On the host PC, share the \Windows folder so that printer drivers in this folder are available to others on the network.

2. On the remote PC, click **Network Neighborhood** and find the printer. Right-click the printer and select **Install** from the shortcut menu. See Figure 25-16. (For Windows 2000/XP, click **My Network Places** and find the printer. Right-click the printer and select **Connect**.)

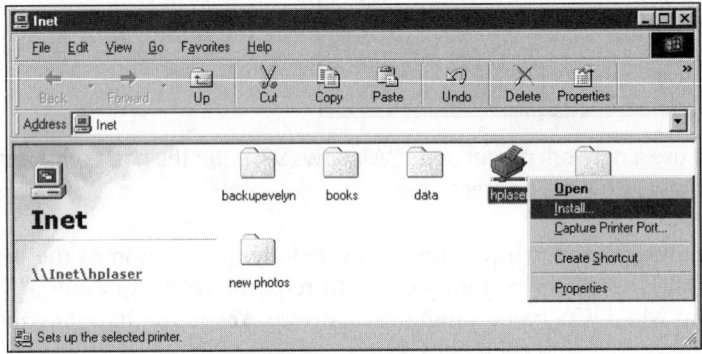

Figure 25-16   Install a shared printer in Windows 98 using drivers on the host computer

3. If the host computer is using the same OS as you are, or, in the case of a Windows NT/2000/XP host computer, if the additional drivers for your OS have been installed, you can use those drivers for the installation. If Windows cannot find the right drivers, it will give you an error message and give you the opportunity to install the drivers from your Windows CD or the printer manufacturer's CD.

4. Enter a name for the printer, decide how to handle printing from DOS applications, and print a test page to complete the installation.

If you must install the shared printer on several PCs in the workgroup, it's easier and faster to use the last method because each PC does not need to read from a CD, and you don't need to carry the CD from PC to PC. After the installations are complete, be sure to remove the shared permission on the host computer's \Windows folder so that this important folder will be more secure.

Other Methods of Sharing Printers over a Network

You have just seen how a printer can be installed as a local printer on one PC and then shared with others in a workgroup. There are three ways to make a printer available on a network, which are summarized here:

- A regular printer can be attached to a PC using the PC's parallel port, and then that PC can share the printer with the network (you just saw this method).

- A network printer with embedded logic to manage network communication can be connected directly to a network with its own NIC.

- A dedicated device or computer called a print server can control several printers connected to a network. For example, HP has software called HP JetDirect, designed to support HP printers in this manner. For more information, see the HP Web site at *www.hp.com*.

If printers are available on the network using one of the last two methods, follow the directions of the printer manufacturer to install the printer on each PC. If you don't have these directions, do the following: Download the printer drivers from the printer manufacturer's Web site and, if necessary, decompress the downloaded file. Open the Printers window and start the wizard to add a new printer. Select the option to install a local printer but do not ask Windows to automatically detect the printer. When given the opportunity, choose to create a new port rather than use an existing port (such as LPT1: or LPT2:). Choose to create a standard TCP/IP port. To create the port, you will need the IP address of the printer or the name of the printer on the network. When given the opportunity, click Have Disk so that you can point to and use the downloaded driver files that will then be used to complete the printer installation.

Troubleshooting Problems with Network Printers

Before we list the steps to take to troubleshoot problems with network printers, it is helpful to understand how Windows manages print jobs using one of three methods:

- For Windows applications using a non–PostScript printer, the print job data is converted to **Enhanced Metafile Format (EMF)**. This format embeds print commands in the data to help speed up printing.

- For Windows applications using a PostScript printer, the print job data is converted to the PostScript language. (A PostScript printer is a printer that uses a special language for data communication called PostScript, commonly used by the Mac OS.)

- Text data that contains no embedded control characters is sent to the printer as is. When DOS applications use this type printing, the data is called raw data and the print job is sent directly to the printer, bypassing the printer queue.

Normally, when Windows 9x receives a print job from an application, it places the job in a queue and prints from the queue, so that the application is released from the printing process as soon as possible. Several print jobs can accumulate in the queue, which you can view in the Printer window. This process of queue printing jobs is called **spooling**. (The word "spool" is an acronym for simultaneous peripheral operations on line.) Most printing from Windows 9x uses EMF spooling.

If the parallel port, printer cable, and printer all support bidirectional communication, the printer can communicate with Windows. For example, Windows 9x can ask the printer how much printer memory is available and what fonts are installed. The printer can send messages to the OS such as an out-of-paper or paper jam message.

Printing problems can be caused by the printer, the PC hardware or OS, the application using the printer, the printer cable, or, in the case of a printer installed on a network, the network. Follow the steps in Figure 25-17 to isolate the problem to one of the following areas:

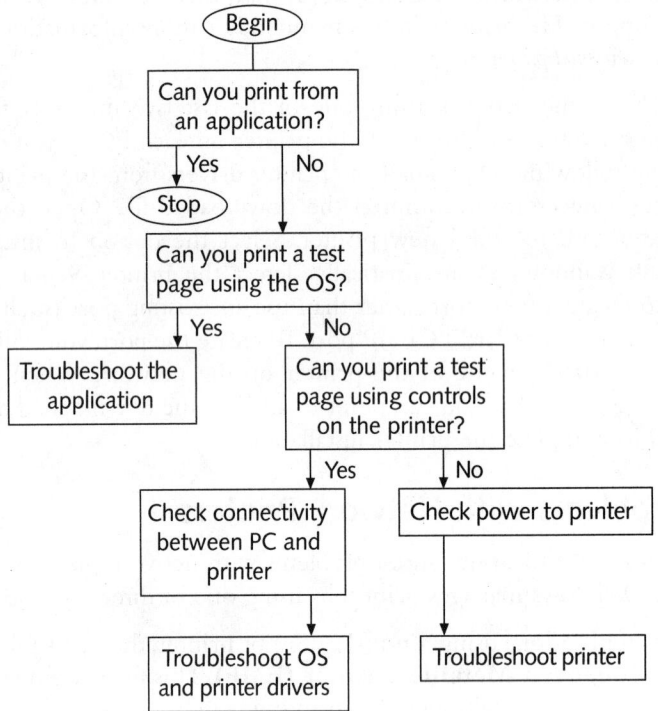

Figure 25-17   How to isolate a printer problem

- The application attempting to use the printer
- The OS and printer drivers
- Connectivity between the PC and the printer
- The printer

When troubleshooting problems with connectivity between a PC on the network and a network printer, try these things:

- First check that you can print from the computer that has the printer attached to it locally by printing a test page using the Printer window. Right-click the printer you want to test, and choose Properties from the shortcut menu. Click the Print Test Page button to send a test page to the printer. Verify the correct default printer is selected.

- The print spool might be stalled. Try deleting all print jobs in the printer's queue. Double-click the printer icon in the Printers window. Select Printer, Purge Print Documents. (Note that it may take a moment for the print jobs to disappear.)

- If you still cannot print, verify that you can print from the computer that has the printer attached locally. Try printing a test page, purging the print queue, and rebooting the PC. Try removing and reinstalling the printer driver. To uninstall the printer driver, right-click the printer icon in the Printers window, select Delete to remove the printer, and then reinstall the printer.

- Check the configuration of the USB, serial, or parallel port in CMOS setup that the printer is using.

- Try another printer driver. It may not print graphics correctly, but if another driver does work at all, then you can conclude that you have a faulty driver. For example, if you have an HP LaserJet 5L, try using the HP LaserJet III driver.

- In the printer's Properties dialog box, click Disable bidirectional support for this printer. The PC and printer might have a problem with bidirectional communication.

- Check the resources assigned to the printer port. Open Device Manager, select LPT1, and click Properties. Verify that the resources are assigned correctly for LPT1 (I/O addresses are 0378 to 037B) and that Device Manager reports "No conflicts."

- In the printer Properties dialog box, try disabling "Check Port State Before Printing."

- Verify printer properties. Try lowering the resolution.

- If you can print from DOS, but not from Windows, try disabling printer spooling. Go to the printer Properties dialog box and select Print Directly to the Printer. Spooling holds print jobs in a queue for printing, so if spooling is disabled, printing from an application can be slower.

- If you are having trouble printing from an application, it may be incompatible with Windows. One way to try to solve this problem is to click Start, Run, and type mkcompat.exe. This utility enables you to troubleshoot and solve problems that may make an application incompatible with a certain version of Windows.

- If you are having trouble printing from an application, you can also bypass spooling by selecting Print from the File menu in the application, selecting the option to print to a file, and then dragging that file to the icon representing your printer.

- Try the printer on another PC. Try another power cable and another printer cable.

- Once you know you can print from the local computer, return to the remote computer, and, using the Printers window, delete the printer, and then, using Windows 9x Network Neighborhood or Windows 2000/XP My Network Places, reconnect the printer.

25

GAINING REMOTE ACCESS TO A NETWORK

Sometimes users need to dial in to a company network while at home or on the road. A computer on the network can act as a server for the inbound calls. Once dialed in, users can access the network just like any other user connected directly to it, except that access is slower. Remote access is also valuable when a user or support technician wants to control a computer from a remote location just as though he or she were sitting at the host computer. Allowing inbound connections to the network and remote control of a host computer are covered in this section.

Allowing Inbound Connections

You can configure a Windows computer to allow inbound calls so that remote users can access resources on the network. The remote user must have been set up with a user ID and password, and drives and/or folders must be shared. In Windows 95, install the Microsoft Plus utility; in Windows 98, install the Dial-Up Server component. In Windows NT, install the **Remote Access Service (RAS)**. Windows 2000/XP has the ability to allow incoming calls by default.

To allow inbound calls to a Windows 2000 computer, open the Network and Dial-up Connections applet in Control Panel. Click Make New Connection. The Network Connection Wizard window appears (see Figure 25-18). Select Accept incoming connections, and then click Next. The wizard will step you though the process of selecting the modem, user, and protocol for the connection and giving the connection a name.

Figure 25-18 Use the Network and Dial-up Connections applet to allow incoming connections to your Windows 2000 PC

Remote Control

You have just seen how you can configure a Windows computer to allow a remote user to access the network through an inbound call. There is another use of a network called **remote control**. With remote control, you can be at one computer and control another host computer. If the remote control software is sophisticated enough, you can see the entire desktop of the host PC and every keystroke at your PC is directed to the other PC. Help-desk personnel find this kind of control very useful when supporting a user and PC at a remote location.

Using remote control, the remote PC sends commands to the host PC. The host PC uses these commands to execute software on the host PC and passes the results of the commands back to the remote PC. This method only passes commands from the remote PC to the host. The host PC cannot pass commands to the remote PC. To accomplish remote control over a network in Windows 9x and Windows 2000, use a third-party utility such as Symantec's pcANYWHERE (*www.symantec.com*). Figure 25-19 shows a remote PC desktop with the desktop of the host PC displayed by pcANYWHERE.

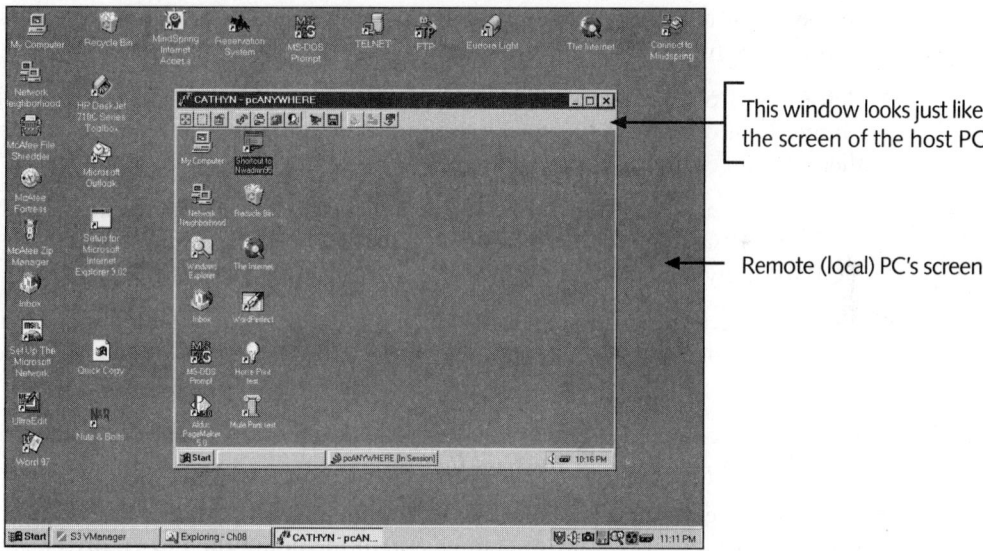

Figure 25-19   pcANYWHERE provides a window on the remote PC that replicates the screen on the host PC. From this window, the remote user can control the host PC

In Windows XP, you can accomplish remote control using a utility called Remote Assistance. This feature is designed to allow one user to send a request for help to another user, perhaps a technical support person, without the second person having physically to come to the first person's workstation.

There are three stages in using Remote Assistance in Windows XP:

1. The user on the host computer must send an invitation by clicking Start, Help and Support, Ask for Assistance, Invite a friend to connect to your computer with Remote Assistance, and Invite Someone to Help You.

2. The remote user (the helper) responds to the host user's request.

3. The host user accepts the remote user's assistance. When the remote user accepts the request for help, the Remote Assistance dialog box appears on the host computer, and the host user clicks **Yes** to enable the remote user to view the host computer screen and to send instant messages.

CHAPTER SUMMARY

❑ Using Network Neighborhood or My Network Places, you can copy files from one computer to another, use the applications installed on one computer from another computer, and share printers.

❑ In a workgroup, users on a LAN share control of resources, and in a domain, control of resources on the network is centralized.

❑ Before users on a network can view or access resources on a PC, Client for Microsoft Networks and File and Printer Sharing for Microsoft Networks must be installed, and these resources must be shared.

❑ Two files on a PC track IP addresses and related NetBIOS or host names. LMHosts tracks NetBIOS names on a NetBEUI network, and Hosts tracks host names on a TCP/IP network.

❑ Network drive mapping makes one PC appear to have a new hard drive when that hard drive space is actually on another host computer. Use Windows Explorer to map a network drive.

❑ Direct cable connection between two PCs using either a null modem cable or a parallel cable allows two PCs to share files or printers.

❑ When troubleshooting printers, first isolate the problem. Narrow the source to the printer, cable, PC hardware, operating system including the device driver, application software, or network.

❑ Windows can accept inbound dial-up connections so that users can dial into a network from home or on the road.

❑ Remote control of a computer can be used to obtain technical support by allowing a user on a remote computer to control your computer, called the host computer. Two utilities for remote control are Remote Assistance on Windows XP and pcANYWHERE by Symantec.

KEY TERMS

client

client/server

default gateway

default printer

DNS (domain name) service or domain name system)

DNS server

domain name

dynamic IP address

Enhanced Metafile Format (EMF)

fully qualified domain name (FQDN)

gateway

host

host name

Hosts

Intranet

IP address

LAN (local area network)

LMHosts

local printer

NetBIOS (Network Basic Input/Output System)

network drive map

network printer

peer-to-peer network

Remote Access Service (RAS)

spooling

WINS (Windows Internet Naming Service)

WinSock (Windows Sockets)

25

26

WINDOWS ON THE INTERNET

In this chapter, you will learn:

♦ How the OSI model applies to TCP/IP networks, such as the Internet

♦ How to connect to the Internet using a dial-up connection, cable modem or DSL

♦ About supporting some common Internet clients

In earlier chapters, you learned how different versions of Windows work on a single PC. This chapter takes the next logical step by discussing connections to the Internet using Windows. You will learn how the OSI model applies to TCP/IP (the Internet protocol suite), how to create and troubleshoot a dial-up connection to the Internet, and how to support some applications that use the Internet, such as Web browsers, e-mail clients, and FTP software.

THE OSI MODEL APPLIED TO A TCP/IP NETWORK

Recall that the OSI model is a universally accepted model describing the layers of communication over a network. You saw how this model applies to communication over a local network. You saw how the top five layers of the model work within the OS and the bottom two with the NIC. This section shows how the OSI model applies to a TCP/IP network such as the Internet or an **intranet** (a local network that uses TCP/IP as its networking protocol).

On a TCP/IP network, TCP/IP is managed by the operating system and covers the top five layers of the OSI model. Figure 26-1 shows the OSI model applied to TCP/IP, which is handling a request from a Web browser to a Web server. Recall that computers are identified by their IP addresses on a TCP/IP network. When a browser wants to access a Web server, it identifies the server by its IP address and uses the TCP/IP protocols of the OS to make the request.

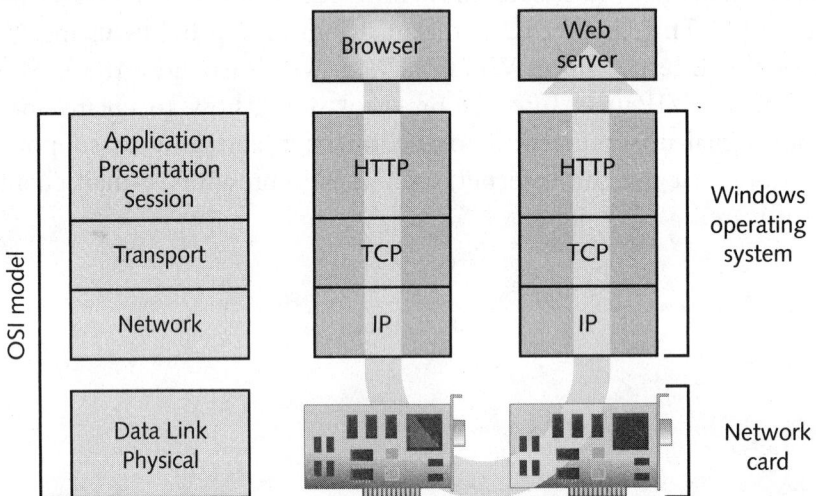

Figure 26-1   When a browser sends a request to a Web server, all layers of the OSI model are involved on both the client and the server

IP Address and Port Identifies a Service

A server on the Internet or an intranet might be running a Web server, an e-mail server, and an FTP server, all at the same time. (FTP is a quick and easy way to move files over a TCP/IP network.) Each service is an executable program running under the OS on that server. For example, one Web server is Apache.exe by the Apache Software Foundation (*www.apache.org*), and an e-mail server is Ntmail.exe by Gordano LTD (*www.ntmail.co.uk*). Both Apache.exe and Ntmail.exe can be running as background servers on a computer. How does a Web browser on a client PC say, "I want to speak with the Web server" and an e-mail program say "I want to speak with the e-mail server," each running on the same computer using the same IP address? The answer is by using an identifying number, called a **port**, **port address**, or **port number**, that has been assigned to each service when it is started. A service is said to be listening at a certain port. (Don't confuse these port addresses with I/O addresses assigned to hardware devices, which were discussed in previous chapters.) A Web server is normally assigned port 80, and an e-mail server receiving mail is normally assigned port 25. Another example of a port number assigned to a common service is the use of port 119 for **NNTP (Network News Transfer Protocol)**, the protocol used for newsgroups. If a Web server is assigned a different port number, it can be entered in the address box of the Web browser following the IP address of the server and separated from it by a colon, like this: 138.60.30.5:80. A port number enables the server to determine which server software gets the request, as shown in Figure 26-2.

26

Figure 26-2   Each server running on a computer is addressed by a unique port number

A network administrator can assign any port number to a server, but there are established port numbers for common services and protocols, as listed in Table 26-1. Unless the administrator has a good reason to do otherwise, he or she uses these common assignments. (One reason not to use the default port assignments is if there is concern about security. Some malicious software targets systems using default port assignments.) Using these default port assignments, on the server in our example, the Web server would communicate at 138.60.30.5:80, and the e-mail server would communicate at 138.60.30.5:25.

Table 26-1   Common TCP/IP port assignments for well-known services

Port	Protocol	Service	Description
20	FTP	FTP	File transfer data
21	FTP	FTP	File transfer control information
23	Telnet	Telnet	Telnet, an application used by Unix computers to control a computer remotely
25	SMTP	E-mail	Simple Mail Transfer Protocol; send e-mail used by client to send e-mail
80	HTTP or HTTPS	Web browser	World Wide Web protocol
109	POP2	E-mail	Post Office Protocol, version 2; used by client to receive e-mail
110	POP3	E-mail	Post Office Protocol, version 3; used by client to receive e-mail
119	NNTP	News server	News servers
143	IMAP	E-mail	Internet Message Access Protocol, the newer protocol used by clients to receive e-mail

The Web browser initiates a request using an IP address and port, but is unaware of all that happens in order for the request to reach the Web server. In this next section, you'll see a quick rundown of each layer and the protocols used at each layer.

TCP/IP Protocols at Each Layer

Recall that TCP/IP covers the top five layers of the OSI model and is included in an operating system as a group of utilities called a stack. Figure 26-3 shows the four major groupings of the OSI model as applied to TCP/IP networks. Within these layers, several protocols operate, and the more significant ones are introduced in this section, but you should know that the TCP/IP protocol suite covers more protocols than just these.

Protocols at the Application, Presentation, and Session Layers

The top three layers of the OSI model are handled by the protocol specific to the application using it and are best treated as a single group rather than unique layers. Four of the most common applications that use the Internet are Web browsers, e-mail, chat rooms, and FTP.

When one of these applications wants to send data to another counterpart application on another host, it makes an API call to the operating system, which handles the request. The API call causes the OS to generate a request. For Web browsers, the request will be an HTTP request. **HTTP (Hypertext Transfer Protocol)** is the protocol used for the World Wide Web, and is used by Web browsers and Web servers to communicate. HTTP works at the OSI Application, Presentation, and Session layers as illustrated in Figures 26-1 and 26-3. In other words, HTTP formats the request, and encrypts and compresses it as necessary. It adds an HTTP header to the beginning of the data that includes the HTTP version being used and how the data is compressed and encrypted, if that was done. Later, when the response is received from the server, it decrypts and decompresses it as necessary before passing it on to the browser.

Figure 26-3   How software, protocols, and technology on a TCP/IP network relate to the OSI model

The Session layer is something of a hybrid layer. **Sessions** (established communication links between two software programs), sometimes called **sockets**, can be managed by one of the high-level application protocols such as HTTP, but a limited type of session is created and managed by TCP at the Transport layer. For this reason, sometimes you'll see the Session layer assigned to the high-level application protocols and sometimes assigned to TCP. Note in Figure 26-3 that the Session layer slightly overlaps into the TCP and UDP area (refer to the section labeled 2 in Figure 26-3).

Protocols at the Transport Layer

A network has two protocols that work at the Transport layer; one protocol guarantees delivery and the other does not. With TCP/IP, the protocol that guarantees delivery is **TCP (Transmission Control Protocol)**, and the protocol that does not guarantee delivery is **UDP (User Datagram Protocol)**. Recall that TCP is used for client and server requests and responses. Because TCP establishes a connection, it is called a **connection–oriented protocol**. When a TCP packet reaches its destination, an acknowledgment is sent back to the source. If the source TCP does not receive the acknowledgment, it will resend the data or pass an error message back to the higher-level protocol. TCP is used by applications such as Web browsers and e-mail. In our example of a Web browser request, HTTP hands the request off to TCP to guarantee delivery to the server.

UDP is primarily used for broadcasting and other types of transmissions, such as streaming video or sound over the Web, where best effort delivery will do and fast transmission is important. UDP is a protocol that sends data without checking whether or not the data is received. It does not establish a connection first; thus it is called a **connectionless protocol** or a **best-effort protocol.**

Network Layer Protocols

TCP and UDP communicate with the Network layer, which is sometimes called the Internet layer, passing a request to **IP (Internet Protocol)**, the governing protocol at this layer, which is responsible for breaking up and reassembling data into packets and routing them to their destination. See Figure 26-4.

Figure 26-4   TCP turns to IP to prepare the data for networking

Up to this point, the data with its header information is one long stream of bytes, sometimes too much data for transmission over a network. IP looks at the size of the data and breaks it into individual packets, which can be up to 4K in size. IP adds its own IP header, which includes the IP address of its host (source IP address) and that of the server (destination IP address), and then passes the packet off to the hardware.

Other protocols that operate at the Network layer include the following:

- **ARP (Address Resolution Protocol)**, which is responsible for locating a host on a local network

- **RARP (Reverse Address Resolution Protocol)**, which is responsible for discovering the Internet address of a host on a local network

- **ICMP (Internet Control Message Protocol),** which is responsible for communicating problems with transmission (refer to the section labeled 3 in Figure 26-3). For example, if a packet has exceeded the number of routers (a device that routes packets over multiple networks) it can pass through on its way to its destination (called a hop count or a time to live), a router will kill the packet and return an ICMP message to the source, saying that the packet has been killed.

The Data Link and Physical Layer Protocols

When discussing communication over the Internet, the Data Link and Physical layers are generally treated as a single unit, because both of these layers are most often covered by the firmware on a single NIC or, for phone-line connections, by a modem and its drivers. The protocol used depends on the type of physical network that the data is traveling on. For example, for a regular phone line, the protocol is PPP (refer to the section labeled 4 in Figure 26-3) and the device managing that protocol is a modem. **PPP (Point-to-Point Protocol)** is used over phone lines, and allows a PC to connect to a network by using a modem. PPP is sometimes called a **line protocol** or, less commonly, a **bridging protocol**. An earlier version of a line protocol is **Serial Line Internet Protocol (SLIP),** which does not support encrypted passwords and is seldom used today. PPP is the most popular protocol for managing network transmission from one modem to another. As you learned in the last chapter, Ethernet is the most popular network technology used for LANs, and its protocol is Ethernet. The Ethernet protocol is sometimes called the hardware protocol or the network protocol. Token ring is also used for LANs. FDDI and ATM technologies are used mostly for high-speed fiber-optic networking.

What Happens at the Destination Computer

When a Web browser sends a request to a Web server, HTTP, TCP, IP, and the hardware protocols all are involved before the packet leaves the source computer and is placed on the network or phone line. At its destination, these same layers are used in reverse order to pass the packet from the hardware up through the OS and on to the application.

At the destination computer, if the computer is connected to a network, the network protocol, most likely Ethernet, receives the packet. If the computer is connected to a phone line, the line protocol, most likely PPP, receives the packet. PPP or Ethernet will pass the packet up to the IP layer. IP on the destination computer regroups the packets into one continuous stream of data with header information for the higher layers, removing the IP header. IP then passes the one data and header stream on to the Transport layer, which removes the TCP header information and sends an acknowledgment back to the Transport layer on the client (see Figure 26-5). The HTTP server is listening at port 80. It receives the data, removes HTTP header information, decompresses and decrypts the data as necessary and passes the data on to the Web server.

26

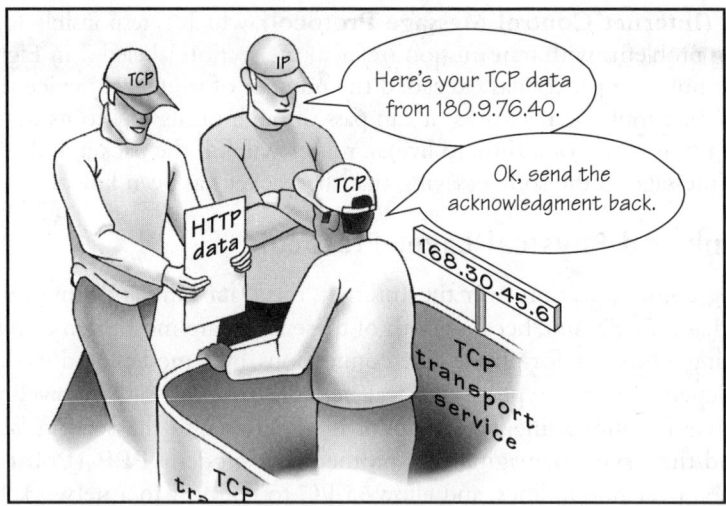

Figure 26-5   TCP guarantees delivery by requesting an acknowledgment

TCP/IP Utilities

When TCP/IP is installed as a Windows 98 or Windows 2000/XP component, a group of utility tools are also installed that can be used to troubleshoot problems with TCP/IP. The most commonly used TCP/IP utilities are Ping, Winipcfg, and Ipconfig, which you learned about in the last chapter. Table 26-2 lists these and other TCP/IP utilities and gives a purpose for each. The program files are found in the \Windows or \winnt folder.

Table 26-2   Utilities installed with TCP/IP on Windows

Command	Description
ARP (arp.exe)	Manages the IP-to-Ethernet address translation tables that are used to find the MAC address of a host on the network when the IP address is known.
Getmac (getmac.exe)	A windows XP utility that displays the NIC's MAC address.
Ipconfig (ipconfig.exe)	Displays the IP address of the host and other configuration information. (A command similar to Ipconfig used by Unix is Ifconfig.) Some parameters are: Ipconfig /all Displays all information about the connection Ipconfig /release Releases the current IP address Ipconfig /renew Requests a new IP address Ipconfig /? Displays information about Ipconfig
FTP (ftp.exe)	Transfers files over a network.
Nbtstat (nbtstat.exe)	Displays current information about TCP/IP and NetBIOS when both are being used on the same network.
Netstat (netstat.exe)	Displays information about current TCP/IP connections.
Ping (ping.exe)	Verifies that there is a connection on a network between two hosts.

Table 26-2   Utilities installed with TCP/IP on Windows (continued)

Command	Description
Route (route.exe)	Allows you to manually control network routing tables.
Telnet (telnet.exe)	Allows you to communicate with another computer on the network remotely, entering commands to control the remote computer.
Tracert (tracert.exe)	Traces and displays the route taken from the host to a remote destination; Tracert is one example of a trace routing utility.
Winipcfg (winipcfg.exe)	Displays IP address and other configuration information in a user-friendly window (not available under Windows 2000). On the Winipcfg window, use Release and Renew to cause the system to release the current IP address and request a new one, which can sometimes solve TCP/IP connectivity problems when using a DHCP server.

TIP When you have problems with connectivity, use Ping to test the connection. If Ping fails, use either Winipcfg (for Windows 9x) or Ipconfig (for Windows NT/2000/XP) to release and renew the IP address used by the PC. This can sometimes restore a connection.

Microsoft SNMP Agent

In addition to the utilities that are automatically installed with TCP/IP, another useful utility is Microsoft SNMP Agent. This utility can be installed after you install TCP/IP, and you can find it on the Windows 98 CD. **SNMP (Simple Network Management Protocol)** provides system management for networks. A system manager can monitor remote connections to computers running Windows clients with SNMP Agent. The manager will most likely use the utility sparingly because it can be a security risk. For more information about SNMP, see RFC 1156 (*www.rfc-editor.org*).

Using NSLookup

An interesting tool that lets you read information from the Internet name space is NSLookup, which requests information about domain name resolutions from the DNS server's zone data. Zone data is information about domain names and their corresponding IP addresses kept by a DNS server. The utility program is included in Windows 2000. For example, using Windows 2000, to retrieve what the DNS server knows about the domain name *www.microsoft.com*, follow these directions:

1. Open a command window: Click **Start**, **Programs**, **Accessories**, **Command Prompt**. A command window appears.

2. Enter the command: **Nslookup www.microsoft.com**. Figure 26-6 shows the results. Notice in the figure that the DNS server knows about three IP addresses that are assigned to *www.microsoft.com*. It also reports that this information is non-authoritative, meaning that it is not the authoritative, or final, name server for the *www.microsoft.com* name.

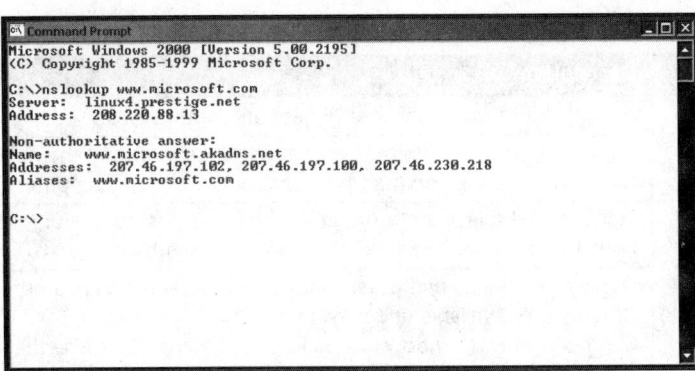

```
Command Prompt                                              _|□|×|
Microsoft Windows 2000 [Version 5.00.2195]
(C) Copyright 1985-1999 Microsoft Corp.

C:\>nslookup www.microsoft.com
Server:  linux4.prestige.net
Address:  208.220.88.13

Non-authoritative answer:
Name:    www.microsoft.akadns.net
Addresses:  207.46.197.102, 207.46.197.100, 207.46.230.218
Aliases:  www.microsoft.com


C:\>
```

Figure 26-6   The Nslookup command reports information about the Internet name space

CONNECTING TO THE INTERNET USING A DIAL-UP CONNECTION

This section covers how to connect to the Internet over a phone line using a dial-up connection. To make such a connection, you need to have a modem installed on your PC, as well as drivers to control the modem. (Installing modems is a hardware task that is not covered in this book.) In the last chapter, you learned how to install TCP/IP and bind it to your NIC; the same procedure is used for binding TCP/IP to a modem. This section assumes that TCP/IP is installed and bound to the modem and covers how to connect to the Internet, beginning with how to install and configure the Dial-up Networking feature in Windows and continuing with how to create and test the connection to your ISP.

When a Windows PC connects to a network using a modem and regular phone line, the process is called **dial-up networking**. In effect, the modem on the PC acts like a network card, providing the physical connection to the network and the firmware at the lowest level of communication. After the dial-up connection is made, the PC's application software relates to the network as though it were directly connected to the network using a network card, but a network card is not needed. The modems and phone lines in between are transparent to the user, although transmission speeds with direct network connections are much faster than those of dial-up connections.

This section covers how to use dial-up networking utilities in Windows 9x and Windows 2000/XP. Note that in Windows 9x, Dial-up Networking and Network Connections are two different applets and are located under My Computer. In Windows 2000, there is a single applet in the Control Panel called Network and Dial-up Connections that combines both functions, and in Windows XP, this single Control Panel applet is called Network Connections.

How Dial-up Networking Works

Dial-up networking works by using PPP to send packets of data over phone lines. The network protocol packages the data, making it ready for network traffic, and then PPP adds its own header and trailer to these packets. Figure 26-7a shows how this works. The data is presented to the network protocols, either TCP/IP, NetBEUI, or IPX/SPX, which add their header information. Then the packet is presented to the line protocol, PPP, which serves as the Data Link layer in the OSI model. A PPP header and trailer is added to the packet and then presented to the modem for delivery over phone lines to a modem on the receiving end.

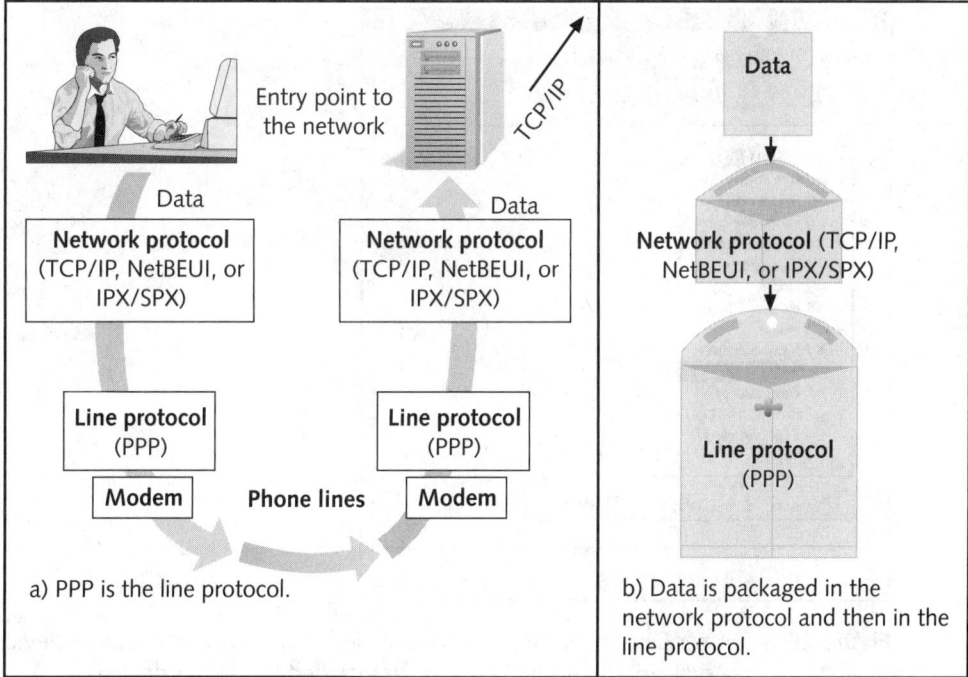

26

Figure 26-7   PPP allows a PC to connect to a network using a modem

The modem on the receiving end is connected to a PC or server. The receiving computer strips off the PPP header and trailer information and sends the packet on to the network still packaged in the TCP/IP protocols, or whatever other protocols the network is using. In Figure 26-7b, you can see how these two protocols act like envelopes. Data is put into a TCP/IP envelope for travel over the network. This envelope is put into a PPP envelope for travel over phone lines. When the phone line segment of the trip is completed, the PPP envelope is discarded.

Creating a Dial-up Connection in Windows 9x

To use Windows 9x or Windows NT to communicate with a network over phone lines, Dial-up Networking must be installed as an OS component on your PC using the Add/Remove Programs applet in Control Panel. (Network and Dial-up Connections in Windows 2000 and Network Connections in Windows XP are installed by default.)

When Windows 9x installs Dial-up Networking, it also "installs" a dial-up adapter. In terms of function, think of a dial-up adapter as a virtual network card. Remember that

TCP/IP is bound to a network interface card. A dial-up adapter is a modem playing the role of a network card for dial-up networking. After Dial-up Networking is installed, open the Device Manager to see your "new" dial-up adapter listed under Network adapters, as in Figure 26-8. You can also see it listed as an installed network component in the Network window of the Control Panel.

Figure 26-8   After Dial-up Networking is installed, a new virtual network device, a dial-up adapter, is listed as an installed hardware device

After installing Dial-up Networking, you create an icon in the Dial-up Networking group and then use the icon to make a connection. After you make the connection, you can use any Internet application, such as a Web browser or e-mail client, for which you have the software installed on your PC.

Make a New Connection

To create a new dial-up networking connection in Windows 98:

1. After Dial-up Networking is installed, click **Start**, point to **Programs**, **Accessories**, **Communications**, and then click **Dial-up Networking**. The Dial-up Networking dialog box appears, as in Figure 26-9.

2. Double-click **Make New Connection**. The Make New Connection Wizard appears, also shown in Figure 26-9. Click **Next** to move past the first screen.

3. Enter a name for the connection. When you are connecting to the Internet, you can use the name of your ISP and the city in which the server is located. An example would be Earthlink Boston. If your modem is already installed, it appears in the modem list.

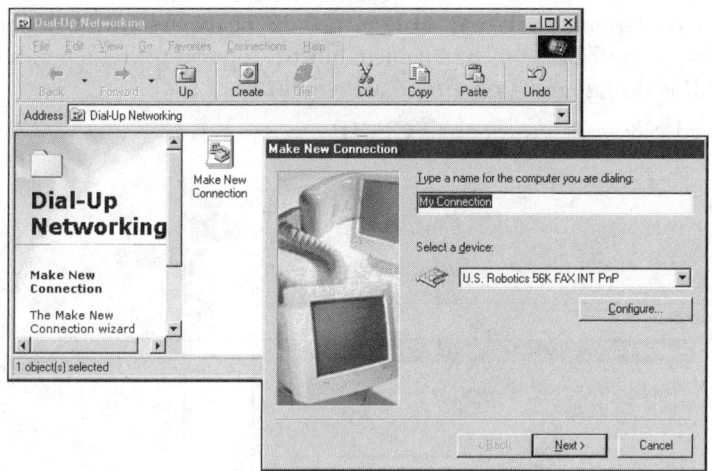

Figure 26-9   Creating a Windows 98 Dial-up Networking Connection icon

4. In the next dialog box, type the phone number to dial, and then click **Next** to continue.

5. Click **Finish** to build the icon. The icon is displayed in the Dial-up Networking window.

Set up a Connection to Your ISP

In order for your PC to connect to your ISP and use the Internet, you need answers to the following questions:

- What is the phone number of the ISP?

- What is your user ID and password for the ISP?

- Will DNS servers be assigned at connection? If not, what is the IP address of one or two DNS servers?

- How will your IP address be assigned (most likely dynamic)?

To set up an ISP connection, do the following:

1. Right-click the icon you created for the connection and select **Properties** from the drop-down menu.

2. Click the **General** tab. Verify that the correct phone number for your ISP is entered.

3. Click **Server Types**. Figure 26-10 shows the resulting dialog box. Verify that these selections are made:

  - Type of Dial-up Server: **PPP Internet, Windows NT Server, Windows 98**

- Advanced Options: Select **Enable software compression** (software compression is most likely to be enabled, but this option really depends on what
  the ISP is doing) and **Log on to network**.
- Allowed Network Protocols: **TCP/IP**

Figure 26-10   Configuring the server type for a connection to the Internet in Windows 9x

4. Click **TCP/IP Settings** to open the TCP/IP Settings dialog box, as shown in
   Figure 26-11. Verify that these settings (or other settings as specified by your ISP)
   are chosen:
   - **Server assigned IP address**
   - **Specify name server addresses**
   - **Use IP header compression**
   - **Use default gateway on remote network**
5. Enter the IP addresses of the primary and secondary DNS servers. (This information is provided by your ISP. If it is not provided, then select Server assigned
   name server addresses.)
6. Click **OK** two times to complete building the Dial-up Networking connection.

Figure 26-11   TCP/IP settings for a connection to the Internet in Windows 9x

7. To connect to your ISP, double-click the icon you created for it, which is now correctly configured. The first time you use the icon, you enter the user ID and password to connect to your ISP. Check the option to remember the user name and password if you don't want to have to enter it every time, but remember that this might not be wise if others who cannot be trusted have access to your PC.

8. Click **Connect**. You should now hear the modem making the connection.

Creating a Dial-up Connection in Windows 2000

Windows 2000 adds more wizards to make the configuration process easier than it was with Windows 9x. To create a new dial-up connection to the Internet in Windows 2000:

1. From the Start menu, click **Programs**, **Accessories**, **Communications**, and **Network and Dial-up Connections.**

2. The Network and Dial-up Connections window opens, as shown in Figure 26-12. Double-click the **Make New Connection** icon. If the Location Information screen opens, click **Next** to continue on to the Network Connection Wizard.

3. The Network Connection Wizard opens. Click **Next** to skip the welcome screen. On the next screen, select the second option, **Dial-up to the Internet**, and then click **Next**.

4. The Internet Connection Wizard opens. Select the option to configure an Internet connection manually, and then click **Next**.

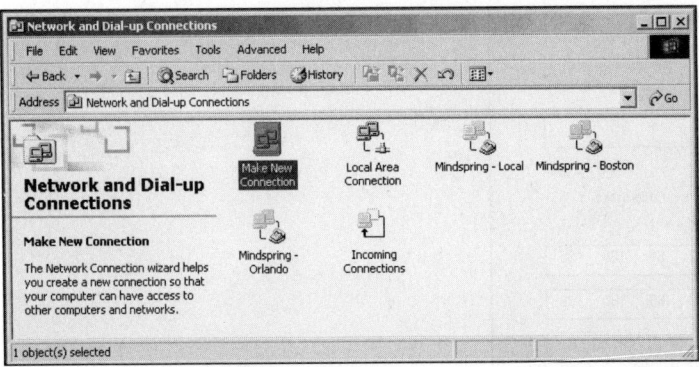

Figure 26-12   Network Dial-up connections applet in Windows 2000

5. Choose how you connect to the Internet. For this example, select the option **I connect through a phone line and a modem,** and then click **Next** (see Figure 26-13). Notice in Figure 26-13 that you can also choose to connect through a LAN at this point. (This option was not available through a wizard in Windows 9x.)

6. Follow the directions in the remainder of the wizard to enter the phone number to dial to connect to your ISP, your username and password, a name for the connection, and whether to set up a new e-mail account. (For this example, assume that you already have an e-mail account, and choose not to set up a new one.)

7. On the final screen of the wizard, which informs you that you have created the connection successfully and can access it through your browser, click **Finish** to close the wizard. Your new connection is shown in the Network and Dial-up Connections window.

8. If you want to create a shortcut to the dial-up connection on the desktop, right-click the icon in the Network and Dial-up Connections window and select **Create Shortcut** on the shortcut menu.

9. A message appears saying, "Windows cannot create a shortcut here. Do you want the shortcut to be placed on the desktop instead?" Click **Yes** to create a shortcut on the desktop.

The procedure for creating a dial-up networking connection from Windows XP is similar to the procedure in Windows 2000. Double-click the Network Connections icon from the Windows XP Control Panel, and in the resulting window, click the option to create a new dial-up connection, then follow the wizard's instructions.

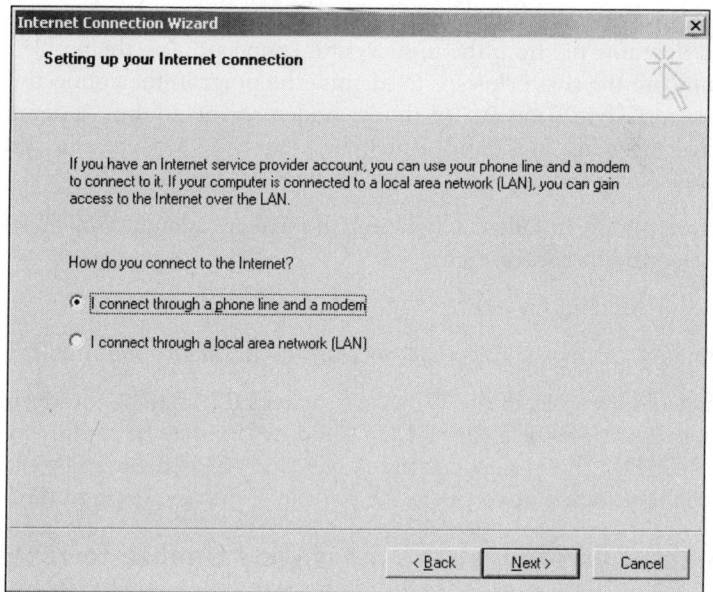

Figure 26-13   Using the Windows 2000 Internet Connection Wizard

Dial-up Networking Problems

In this section, you will learn about some of the most common problems and errors that you may encounter with dial-up networking and what to do about them. As always, check the simple things first before trying more difficult solutions.

You cannot make a connection

If you have a problem connecting to the Internet using a dial up connection, first find out what works and what doesn't work. Try the following:

- Find out the answers to these questions: At what point does the connecting process fail? Do you hear the modem hissing? If so, the problem is probably with the user ID and password. If not, then the problem might be the phone number, phone line, or modem. Is the phone line plugged in? Does the phone line work? Can you hear a dial tone?

- Check the Dial-up Networking connection icon for errors. Is the phone number correct? Does the number need to include a 9 to get an outside line? Has a 1 been added in front of the number by mistake?

- Try dialing the number manually from a phone. Do you hear beeps on the other end?

- Try another phone number.

- Does the modem work? Check Device Manager for reported errors about the modem.

- Print out the Modemlog.txt file from a successful connection on another computer and the same file from the unsuccessful connection on the problem computer. Compare the two printouts to identify the point in the connection at which an error occurs. (For Windows 9x, to log modem events to the Modemlog.txt file, double-click Modems in Control Panel, then select the modem, click Properties, Connection, Advanced, and turn on Recording to a log file.)

- Are all components installed? Check for the dial-up adapter and TCP/IP, and check the configuration of each.

- Reboot your PC and try again.

- Try removing and reinstalling each network component. Begin with TCP/IP.

- Sometimes older copies of the Windows socket DLL may be interfering with the current Windows 9x socket DLL. (Windows 9x may be finding and executing the older DLL before it finds the newer one.) Search for and rename any files named Winsock.dll except the one in the \Windows\System directory.

You can connect, but you get the message "Unable to resolve hostname..."

This error message means that TCP/IP is not able to determine how to route a request to a host. Right-click the Dial-up Networking connection icon, select Properties, and check for these things:

- Under Server Type, try making TCP/IP the only network protocol allowed.

- Under TCP/IP settings, check the IP addresses of the DNS servers.

- Make sure *Using the default gateway* is selected.

- Try *not* selecting IP header compression.

After connecting, you get the error message "Unable to establish a compatible set of network protocols"

This error is most likely to be caused by a problem with the installation and configuration of Dial-up Networking or TCP/IP. Try these things:

- Verify that the dial-up adapter and TCP/IP are installed and configured correctly.

- Remove and reinstall TCP/IP. Be sure to reboot after the installation.

- For Windows 9x, try putting the PC in a different workgroup.

- Windows 9x can write the events that occur when PPP processes a call to a log file. Create the Ppplog.txt file on a PC that makes a successful connection, and compare it to the log file of your bad connection to see exactly when the problem began. To turn on the logging of events to the file, double-click the Network icon in Control Panel. Click Dial-up Adapter, click Properties, select the Advanced tab, and then select Record a log file. On the Value list, click Yes, then click OK. Reboot the PC. The file Ppplog.txt is created in the Windows folder as the connection is made and used.

When you double-click the Web browser, the modem does not dial automatically

When this occurs, right-click the browser icon and select Properties from the drop-down menu. Under the Connection tab, check Connect to the Internet as needed.

DSL AND CABLE MODEM CONNECTIONS

26

When using cable modem, DSL, ISDN, wireless, LAN, or satellite, if you are connecting a single PC to the Internet using an ISP, then the TCP/IP settings are no different from those used by a modem-to-phone line connection. Cable modem, DSL and a LAN all use a network card in the PC for the physical connection. The network card provides a network port for a network cable. For cable modem service to the Internet, the other end of the network cable connects to a cable modem. For DSL, the other end of the cable connects to a DSL box and, for a satellite, the other end connects to a satellite converter box. For a LAN, the other end of the network cable connects to a network hub. The connection between the NIC and the broadband device most likely uses the **PPPoE (Point-to-Point Protocol over Ethernet)** protocol, a protocol specifically designed to support broadband connections and is included in Windows XP.

For each of these types of Internet connections, generally the installation goes like this:

1. Install the network card and the drivers to control the card.

2. Use a network cable to connect the PC to a cable modem, DSL box or network hub. For wireless, position the PC within range of a wireless access point.

3. Install TCP/IP and bind TCP/IP to the card.

4. Configure TCP/IP to connect to the Internet or LAN.

5. Install the applications software (for example, a browser) to use the connection.

In the following section, you'll learn about the different ways to connect to the Internet using these faster-than-phone line connections and the details of installing these services.

Cable Modem

The cable modem uses a regular TV cable cord to connect to a TV cable wall outlet. Figure 26-14 illustrates what the arrangement looks like. The cable modem also has an electrical connection to provide power to the box. A cable modem connects to your PC by way of a network port or a USB port using either a network cable or a USB cable from the modem to the PC. Your cable modem company will provide you with the TCP/IP settings to use to configure TCP/IP. For a home installation, some cable modem companies will do the entire installation for you. You might need to purchase the cable modem and NIC or they might be included in the installation fee. A service technician will come to your home, install the network card, and configure your PC to use the service.

Rear of PC

Network cable

Cable modem

TV cable
Wall outlet

Regular TV cable

Network card installed
in PC provides network port

Transformer   Power outlet

Figure 26-14   Cable modem connects to a PC through a network card installed on the PC

If you don't have on-site service from the cable modem company, follow these instructions to install cable modem when using a network card:

1. Install the network card and drivers. The cable modem company records the MAC address of the cable modem or the NIC in your PC into an online list of valid addresses that identifies your system as a subscriber to the cable modem service. The MAC address of the cable modem is written somewhere on the modem. If the cable company wants the MAC address of the NIC, use WinIPcfg or Ipconfig to obtain the address. Call the cable company help desk and give the technician the address. Also find out how to configure TCP/IP to use their service. Most likely an IP address, subnet mask, IP address of the default gateway and IP address of a domain name server are all dynamically assigned when the PC connects to the service.

2. Configure TCP/IP to use the network card, using the TCP/IP configuration information provided by the cable modem company.

3. Shut down the PC and connect one end of the network cable to the network port on the back of the PC. Connect the other end of the cable to the cable modem. Be sure the cable modem is plugged in and turned on. There is usually a switch on the back of the box. Connect the TV cable from the TV cable outlet to the cable modem. (Refer back to Figure 26-14.) Turn on the PC.

4. When the PC starts up, you should immediately be connected to the Internet. Test the connection using your web browser or e-mail client. If you are not connected, try the following:

   ■ For Windows 9x, use WinIPcfg or, for Windows 2000/XP, use Ipconfig to release the IP address and renew it. Check for Internet connectivity again.

   ■ If the above did not work, turn off the PC and the cable modem. Wait a full five minutes until all connections have timed out at the cable modem company.

Turn on the cable modem and then turn on the PC. After the PC boots up, again check for connectivity.

- If this doesn't work, call the cable modem help desk. The technician there can release and restore the connection at that end, which should restore service.

DSL

DSL is provided by the local telephone company. The telephone company's responsibility for the phone system ends at your house. Inside your house, you are responsible for your home phone network. A DSL connection uses a DSL converter box that is sometimes combined with a router as a single device so that more than one PC can use the DSL line. The device connects to the PC by way of a network cable and card.

As with cable modem, a technician from the phone company most likely will do an ISDN or DSL installation for you. The installation process on the PC works the same as that of cable modem.

Sharing Internet Connections

There are several ways that computers on a LAN can share an Internet connection. Here are a few options:

- If one computer on the LAN has a direct connection to the Internet by way of a phone line, cable modem or DSL, it can serve as a host computer for others on the LAN. Windows 98 and Windows XP Internet Connection Sharing (ICS) is designed to mange this type of connection. Using ICS, the host computer uses NAT and acts as the proxy server for the LAN. Windows XP ICS also includes a firewall.

- For broadband connections (cable modem and DSL), the broadband converter box can connect to a network device such as a router that manages the connection for the entire network. The router has a network connection to the converter box and one or more network ports for devices on the network. In this situation, the router is likely to also have firewall software embedded in it and is controlled by way of a Web browser. A user on any computer on the network can enter the IP address of the router in a Web browser window and bring up the software on the router to configure the router. The router can serve as a DHCP server, a NAT proxy server and a firewall.

- The router can also serve as a wireless access point for computers to connect wirelessly to the Internet. An example of a router that is also a wireless access point is the AirPlus D1-714P+ by D-Link (*www.d-link.com*) showing in Figure 26-15. It has one port for the converter box, four ports for computers on the network and a parallel printer port designed to manage a network printer. The router can also support several computers with wireless adapters.

26

Figure 26-15   This D-Link router allows computers on a LAN to share a broadband Internet connection and also is an access point for computers with wireless adapters

Windows Internet Connection Sharing

Windows XP and Windows 98 offers Internet Connection Sharing that allows others on a small office or home LAN to share an Internet connection with a host computer. To use Internet Connection Sharing, the computer that has a direct connection to the Internet by way of a phone line, cable modem or DSL is the host computer. Follow these general directions to configure the LAN for Internet Connection Sharing using Windows XP:

1. Following directions earlier in the chapter, install and configure the hardware (modem, cable modem or DSL) to connect to the Internet and verify the connection is working.

2. Open the Network Connections window in the Windows XP Control Panel and click on the link to **Set up a home or small office network**. The Network Setup Wizard opens. Click **Next**.

3. Select the connection method for your host computer, which is **This computer connects directly to the Internet. The other computers on my network connect to the Internet through this computer.** Click **Next**.

4. The wizard will look at your hardware connections (NIC or modem) and select the one that it sees as a "live" connection. Verify it selected correctly and then follow the wizard to enter a description for your computer, your computer name and workgroup name.

5. The next screen of the wizard offers you the option of creating a Network Setup Disk that you can use to quickly configure every other computer on the LAN that is to use the Internet connection (see Figure 26-16). Select the option to **Create a Network Setup Disk**, insert a blank floppy disk in the drive and click **Next**.

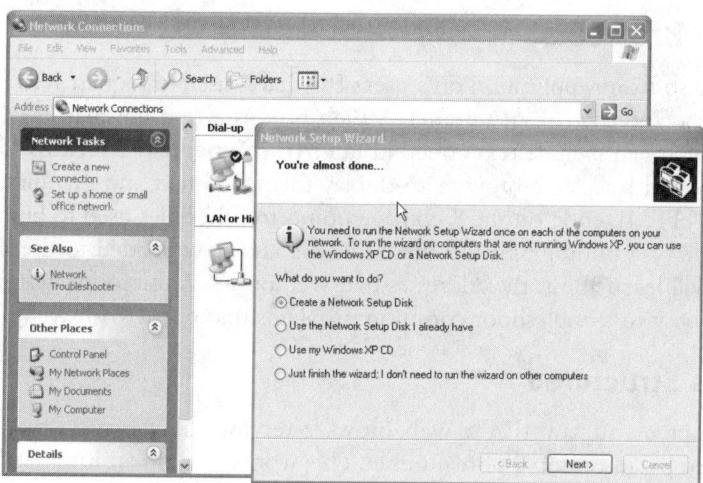

Figure 26-16   Create a Network Setup Disk to configure other computers on the LAN

6. The next screen gives you the option to format the disk. If it needs formatting, click **Format Disk**. Otherwise, click **Next**.

7. The wizard tells you that to use the disk, insert it into the next computer on the network and run the program on the disk named Netsetup.exe. Click **Next** and then click **Finish**.

8. Recall from Chapter 23 that you can enable Internet Connection Firewall to protect the connection to your ISP against unsolicited activity from the Internet. On the host computer only, to enable Internet Connection Firewall, in the Network Connections widows, right click on the network connection and select **Properties** form the shortcut menu. On the Properties box, click the **Advanced** tab and select **Protect my computer and network by limiting or preventing access to this computer from the Internet**.

9. Use the Network Setup Disk on each computer on the LAN that is to use the shared connection.

SUPPORTING INTERNET CLIENTS

Now that you've learned how to connect to the Internet and how to troubleshoot connections with it, let's look at some ways of using it. Earlier in the chapter in Table 26-1, you saw a list of applications that use the Internet. These applications are also called Internet clients. In this section, you will learn how to support some of the most common: Web browsers, e-mail, and FTP.

Supporting Web Browsers

A Web browser is a software application on a user's PC that is used to request Web pages from a Web server on the Internet or an intranet. A Web page is a text file that has an .htm or .html file extension. It can include text coded in **HTML (Hypertext Markup Language)** that can be interpreted by a Web browser to display formatted text and graphics, as well as play sounds. If the HTML code on the Web page points to other files used to build the page such as a sound file or a photograph file, these files are also downloaded to the browser. In this section, you will learn about the addresses that Web browsers use to locate resources on a Web server and how to troubleshoot common problems that occur with Web browsers.

How a URL Is Structured

Earlier in the chapter you saw that a Web browser requests a Web page by sending an IP address followed by an optional port number. This works well on an intranet, but on the Internet, a more user-friendly URL is preferred. A **URL (Uniform Resource Locator)** is an address for a Web page file or other resource on the Internet. Figure 26-17 shows the structure of a URL.

Figure 26-17 A URL contains the protocol used, the host name of the Web server, the network name, and the path and filename of the requested file

The first part of the URL shown in Figure 26-17 indicates the protocol, which in this case is HTTP. If secure HTTP were used to encrypt the data being transmitted, the protocol shown would be **HTTPS (HTTP secure)** and the secure protocol being used is SSL (secure socket layer). The protocol part of the URL specifies the rules, or protocol, the Web server should use when transmitting the page to the browser. Recall that rules of communication are called protocols and that although the browser can use several different protocols, HTTP is the one used for Web pages. A Web server is sometimes called an HTTP server.

Recall that a host name identifies a server or another computer within a network. In this example, the host name is *www* (a Web server), and *course.com* is the name of the Course Technology network, sometimes called the domain name. A name that contains not only the network name (in this case, course.com) but also the host on that network is, as you learned in the last chapter, called a fully qualified domain name (FQDN) (in this case, *www.course.com*). The Web page requested is located in the folder *myfolder* on the www server, and the file within that folder is named *myfile.html*. The FQDN must be resolved to an IP address before the request can happen.

The last segment, or suffix, of a domain name is called the **top-level domain** (.com in our example) and tells you something about the organization or individual that owns the name. Some domain names in the United States end in the suffixes listed in Table 26-3. There are other endings as well, including codes for countries, such as .uk for the United Kingdom. With the growth of the Internet, there has been a shortage of available domain names; because of this shortage, additional suffixes are being created.

Table 26-3   Suffixes used to identify top-level domain names

Domain Suffix	Description
.air	Aviation industry
.biz	Businesses
.com	Commercial institution
.coop	Business cooperatives
.edu	Educational institution
.gov	Government institution
.info	General use
.int	Organizations established by international treaties between governments
.mil	U.S. military
.museum	Museums
.name	Individuals
.net	Internet provider or network
.org	Nonprofit organization
.pro	Professionals

Domain names stand for IP addresses and provide an easy way to remember them, but domain names and IP addresses are not necessarily permanently related. A host computer can have a certain domain name and can be connected to one network and assigned a certain IP address, and then be moved to another network and assigned a different IP address. The domain name can stay with the host while it connects to either network. It is up to a name resolution service, such as DNS or WINS, to track the relationship between a domain name and the current IP address of the host computer. Using Internet Explorer, you can control support options such as how scripts are handled by clicking Tools, Internet Options. The Internet Options window opens. Click the Advanced tab.

Solving Browser Performance Problems

If you notice poor browser performance, use the tools you have seen in earlier chapters, such as Defrag, ScanDisk, and System Information, to make sure that you have enough free hard drive space, that the hard drive is clean, and that the virtual memory settings are optimized. If you perform these tasks and the browser is still slow, try the procedures given below using the most popular browser, Internet Explorer.

Internet Explorer If Internet Explorer (IE) is slow even after you have taken steps to optimize your system, do the following:

1. Right-click the **Internet Explorer** icon on the desktop and then click **Properties** on the shortcut menu. The Internet Properties window opens, as shown in Figure 26-18. (If the icon is not on the desktop, double-click on the **Internet** icon in Control Panel.)

Figure 26-18 Use the Internet Properties dialog box to control the Internet Explorer environment

2. Click **Delete Files** under the Temporary Internet files heading to clean out the IE cache. The Delete Files dialog box appears asking you to confirm the deletion. Click **OK**. IE must search the entire cache each time it accesses a Web page. If the cache is too big, performance is affected.

3. Click **Clear History** under the History heading to clean out the shortcuts cache. The Internet Options dialog box appears asking you to confirm the deletions. Click **OK**. If this cache gets too big, performance can be slowed down. Also, if you reduce the days that Internet Explorer keeps pages in the history folder, performance might improve because there will be less material for Internet Explorer to search. For example, change the days to keep pages in history from the default value of 20 to 7.

4. Click **OK** to close the window.

Suppress the Downloading of Images Slow browser performance can be caused by a slow Internet connection. In this case, one thing you can do is to suppress the downloading of images. Image files can be large and account for most of the downloaded data from Web sites. For Internet Explorer 5.x, you can download and install Web Accessories for Internet Explorer 5.x, which can be used to suppress the downloading of images from Web sites. If the Microsoft site has been updated since the writing of this book, you may need to search for the Web Accessories for Internet Explorer. Follow these directions:

1. Go to this Microsoft Web site: *www.microsoft.com/windows/ie/downloads/archive/default.asp*

2. Scroll down and click the heading **Web Accessories from Microsoft**, and then scroll down click the **Download it now** link.

3. Another page opens, with more information about the Internet Explorer 5.x Web Accessories. On the right side of the page, in a box labeled Download, click the link to the file **ie5wa.exe.**

4. Click **OK** to save the file to disk. When the download window opens, choose to download it to a location on your hard drive, and then click **Save**. Remember where you have saved the file.

5. After you have downloaded the file ie5wa.exe, double-click it, then click **Yes** to install accessories.

6. Close the IE browser window and reopen it.

7. To use the IE Web Accessories to suppress downloading images, right-click the IE menu bar. If Favorites is already checked and is already on your menu bar, you can move on to Step 8. If it is not, click **Links** on the shortcut menu. This action adds the Links menu to the menu bar items.

8. Click **Favorites** on the menu bar, then click **Links**, and then click **Toggle Images**. Web pages should now download without their images. You may have to click the **Refresh** button on your toolbar for the changes to take effect on an open page.

9. To reset the browser to download images, click **Favorites**, then **Links**, and then click **Toggle Images** again.

IE version 6 includes the option to suppress images, sound, animation, and video. Use the following procedure:

1. Open the **Tools** menu, and then click **Internet Options**.

2. The Internet Options window opens. Click the **Advanced** tab.

3. Scroll down to the multimedia section of the check box list and clear the check box or boxes for the feature or features that you do not wish to display (**Show pictures**, **Play animations**, **Play videos**, or **Play sounds**).

 To display an individual video or picture when you have cleared the related check boxes, right-click the icon with which it has been replaced on the Web page.

26

Browser Updates and Patches

Browser manufacturers are continually improving their products, and generally speaking, you should be using the most current version of the browser on your PC to take advantage of the latest features and fixes to known problems. However, if you have an older computer or operating system, you might not want to update a browser that requires a lot of system resources, because your older PC might not be able to support it. In this case, it's better to keep an older version on your PC unless you are having problems with the version.

If you are using Internet Explorer, check the Windows support Web site at *support.microsoft.com* for specific problems with Internet Explorer. Search on the product and the error message for articles that describe the problem and possible solutions. Also check the Windows update Web site at *windowsupdate.microsoft.com* for updates or patches for known Internet Explorer problems. Download the patch and install it following the same general instructions you have seen in earlier chapters.

If you are not using the latest version of Internet Explorer, try downloading the latest version. If you use your browser for banking on the Internet, be sure to download the version of Internet Explorer for 128-bit encryption in order to get better security features. If the new version creates problems on your system, you can revert to your original version by uninstalling the new version.

Supporting E-Mail

E-mail is a client/server application that is used to send text messages to individuals and groups of individuals. When you send an e-mail message, it travels from your computer to your e-mail server. Your e-mail server sends the message to the recipient's e-mail server. The recipient's e-mail server sends it to the recipient's PC, but not until the recipient asks that it be sent by logging in and downloading e-mail. Different parts of the process are controlled by different protocols.

Figure 26-19 shows the journey made by an e-mail message as well as the protocols that control the different parts of the journey. The sender's PC and e-mail server both use **SMTP (Simple Mail Transfer Protocol)** to send an e-mail message to its destination. Once the message arrives at the destination e-mail server, it remains there until the recipient requests delivery. The recipient's e-mail server uses one of two protocols to deliver the message: either **POP (Post Office Protocol)** or **IMAP4 (Internet Message Access Protocol, version 4)**, a newer e-mail protocol. The current version of POP is version 3, often abbreviated as POP3.

Figure 26-19   The SMTP protocol is used to send e-mail to a recipient's mail server, and the POP3 or IMAP4 protocol is used to download e-mail to the client

> **TIP**   SMTP is defined in RFC821 and RFC822. When e-mail experts speak of error messages created during e-mail transactions, they sometimes call these messages 822 messages.

E-mail client software communicates with an e-mail server when it sends and receives e-mail. Two of the most common e-mail clients are Eudora and Microsoft Outlook Express. Figure 26-19 shows a user with one e-mail server. In fact, it's possible to have two e-mail servers, one for sending e-mail and the other for receiving e-mail. Figure 26-20 shows this arrangement.

The e-mail server that takes care of sending e-mail messages (using the SMTP protocol) is often referred to as the SMTP server. The e-mail server from which you collect messages that were sent to you is often referred to as the POP server, because it uses the POP protocol.

When you configure your e-mail client software for the first time, you need to enter the addresses of your e-mail servers. If you are connecting to e-mail via an Internet service provider, the ISP can tell you these addresses. For example, if your ISP is MyISP.net, you might have an outgoing mail server address of *smtp.myISP.net,* and an incoming mail server address of *pop3.myISP.net.*

In most e-mail client software, you enter the addresses of your POP server and your SMTP server in a dialog box when setting up the program. Look for menus or icons labeled Options, Preferences, Configuration, Setup, or similar names. After you have entered the addresses, the software saves this and other configuration information in an initialization file, the Windows registry, or some other location.

Figure 26-20   An e-mail client can use one server to send e-mail and another to receive e-mail

Supporting FTP

A common task of communications software is file transfer, the passing of files from one computer to another. For file transfer to work, the software on both ends must be using the same protocol. The most popular way to transfer files over the Internet is with the **File Transfer Protocol (FTP)**, which is used to transfer files between two computers using the same or different operating systems. A popular use of the Internet for companies is to provide files for customers to download to their PCs, for example, when new upgrades for software become available. This service is commonly provided by Windows NT, 2000, or Unix servers that offer access to files using FTP and are called FTP servers or FTP sites. These commercial FTP sites only provide the ability to download a file to your PC. However, FTP offers more power than just that. A user who has first logged on to a remote computer can use FTP utility software to copy, delete, and rename files, make directories, remove directories, and view details about files and directories.

Most communications applications provide an FTP utility that has a unique look and feel, but the basics of file transfer are the same from one utility to another. If you don't have graphical FTP software installed on your PC, you can use FTP commands from a command prompt.

File Transfer from a Command Prompt

FTP can be initiated at a DOS, Windows 9x, or Windows NT/2000/XP command prompt, if a connection is established to a network or the Internet. The FTP commands work like the dialog in Table 26-4.

Table 26-4   A sample FTP session from a command prompt

Command Entered at the Command Prompt	Description
FTP	Execute the FTP program, ftp.exe.
OPEN 110.87.170.34	Open a session with a remote computer having the given IP address.
LOGIN: XXXXXX	The host computer provides a prompt to enter a user ID for the computer being accessed.
PASSWORD: XXXXXX	The host computer requests the password for that ID. Logon is then completed by the host computer.
CD /DATA	Change directory to the /DATA directory.
GET YOURFILE.DAT	Copy the file YOURFILE.DAT (or whatever file you want) from the remote computer to my computer.
PUT MYFILE.DAT	Copy the file MYFILE.DAT (or whatever file you want) from your computer to the remote computer.
BYE	Disconnect the FTP session.

File Transfer Using FTP Software

FTP client software can be downloaded from the Internet or directly from your ISP. This example looks at how to execute FTP using such software:

1. Start the FTP utility software. In this example we are using WS_FTP Pro by Ipswitch (*www.ipswitch.com*). The FTP utility screen appears similar to the one in Figure 26-21.

Figure 26-21   A typical FTP utility provided by an Internet service provider

2. Click **Connect** to log on to an FTP site. A Session Profile dialog box appears, similar to the one in Figure 26-21.

3. Enter the Host Name, for example *ftp.course.com*. Enter the User ID and Password for this host computer, and then click **OK**.

4. The connection is made, and your ID and password are passed to the host. After you have been authenticated by the host computer, a screen similar to that in Figure 26-22 is displayed.

5. The files on the left belong to you, and the files on the right belong to the remote host computer. You can drag and drop files either to or from the other computer, or you can use the commands at the bottom of the window. Notice in Figure 26-22 the choices toward the bottom of the window: ASCII, Binary, or Auto. These choices refer to the format that is to be used to transfer the files. Use ASCII only for text files, and use Binary for all others. If you are not sure which to use, choose **Auto**.

Figure 26-22   An FTP utility screen showing local and remote files

6. When the transfer of files is complete, click **Exit** to leave the utility.

Many Web pages provide a link on the page offering to you the ability to download a file. Click on the link to download the file. It is likely that this file is not being downloaded from the Web server but rather is downloaded from an FTP server. When you click the filename on the Web page, the program controlling the page executes FTP commands to the FTP server to download the file to you. If you receive an error, you can sometimes solve the problem by going directly to the company's FTP server and using an FTP utility (such as the one used above) to download the file or even see a list of other files that you might also like to download.

A Web browser can also serve as an FTP client. Enter the URL of the FTP server in the address box (for example, *ftp.course.com*). The browser changes menu options to become an FTP client. For Internet Explorer, to log onto the FTP server, on the menu bar, click File, and then click Login As. The Log On As dialog box appears for you to enter a user ID and password. Files and folders on the FTP server then display in the browser window.

CHAPTER SUMMARY

26

- ❏ Ports are used to address particular software or services, such as protocols, running on a computer. Common port assignments are port 80 for HTTP, port 25 for SMTP, port 110 for POP3, and port 20 for FTP.

- ❏ Generally, an API call is a way for an application to ask an operating system to do something. A browser uses an API call to access a Web server and make its request for information.

- ❏ HTTP works at the Application, Presentation, and Session OSI layers.

- ❏ TCP guarantees that a packet reaches its destination and so is called a connection-oriented protocol. UDP does not guarantee delivery and so is called a connectionless or best-effort protocol. Both operate at the Transport layer.

- ❏ IP is responsible for breaking data into packets and passing it from TCP or UDP to the hardware. It is the governing protocol at the Network layer.

- ❏ When data is sent, each layer adds header information, and the Data Link layer adds a trailer. On the receiving side, each layer removes its header and trailer information and passes the data to the layer above it.

- ❏ PPP is used in dial-up networking to send packets of data over phone lines. It operates at the Data Link and Physical layers and manages network transmission from one modem to another.

- ❏ Before you can create a dial-up connection to the Internet, you need to have a modem installed along with the drivers to run it as well as TCP/IP installed and bound to the modem.

- ❏ The Windows Dial-up Networking utility is used to connect to a network using a modem and a phone line. When a dial-up connection is made, a PC's application software relates to the network as though the computer were directly connected to the network using a network card.

- ❏ You can create a new dial-up networking connection in Windows 9x and Windows NT through the Dial-up Networking applet in My Computer, through the Network and Dial-up Connections applet in the Control Panel of Windows 2000, and through the Network Connections applet in the Control Panel of Windows XP.

- ❏ When experiencing problems with dial-up networking, make sure the modem is working, all necessary components are installed, and the phone number to dial and other settings are configured correctly.

- Winipcfg and Ipconfig both report configuration information about the current TCP/IP connection for a device and can release and restore the IP address. Winipcfg is not supported in Windows NT/2000/XP.

- Other TCP/IP utilities useful in solving networking problems are Tracert, Ping, and Nbtstat.

- DSL and cable modem are broadband Internet connections that use a converter box that connects to a PC by way of a network USB Port. The connection can use the PPPoE protocol.

- Computers can share an Internet connection. Windows 98 and Windows XP uses Internet Connection Sharing (ICS) to manage the connection on the host computer, or you can use a router that stands between the converter box and the network.

- Use a firewall on the host computer or router to protect the network from unsolicited activity from the Internet.

- A URL consists of a protocol, a host name, a network or domain name, and a top-level domain extension. Common top-level domains include .com for commercial institutions, .gov for divisions of government, and .org for nonprofit organizations.

- When you experience poor browser performance, try cleaning up your hard drive and making sure your system settings are optimized. If that doesn't work, try clearing your browser cache, clearing the Web page history, suppressing image downloads, or downloading updates.

- E-mail uses SMTP to send messages and POP to receive messages. POP is being replaced by IMAP. Your ISP will provide you with the server types and addresses that it uses to send and receive e-mail.

- FTP is used to transfer files from one computer to another, whether or not the computers are using the same operating system. Both computers must have FTP installed. It can be executed from user-friendly GUI software or from a command prompt.

KEY TERMS

ARP (Address Resolution Protocol)

best-effort protocol

bridging protocol

connectionless protocol

connection-oriented protocol

dial-up networking

FTP (File Transfer Protocol)

HTML (HyperText Markup Language)

HTTP (HyperText Transfer Protocol)

HTTPS (HTTP secure)

ICMP (Internet Control Message Protocol)

IMAP4 (Internet Message Access Protocol version 4)

intranet

IP (Internet Protocol)

line protocol

NNTP (Network News Transfer Protocol)

POP (Post Office Protocol)

port

port address

port number

PPP (Point-to-Point Protocol)

PPPoE (Point-to-Point Protocol over Ethernet)

RARP (Reverse Address Resolution Protocol)

session

SLIP (Serial Line Internet Protocol)

SMTP (Simple Mail Transfer Protocol)

SNMP (Simple Network Management Protocol)

socket

TCP (Transmission Control Protocol)

top-level domain

UDP (User Datagram Protocol)

URL (Uniform Resource Locator)

26

27

LINUX, MACS, AND NOTEBOOKS

In this chapter, you will learn:

♦ About starting up, using, and supporting hardware in the Mac OS

♦ About the file structure of the Linux OS and how to use some Linux commands

♦ How to support notebooks

So far in this book we have focused on Microsoft operating systems, because they are the most popular OSs for the desktop. However, as a software technician, you will need to be familiar with a variety of operating systems, including the Mac OS and Linux. In addition, this chapter covers the specific concerns of supporting operating systems installed on notebook computers.

INTRODUCING THE MAC OS

Recall from Chapter 15 that Mac OS X is the latest version of the proprietary OS for Apple Macintosh computers. This section covers the basic file and folder organization and startup process for the Mac OS. It is not intended to qualify you to support Macs but rather to give you a passing familiarity with them so that you will recognize some of the main features of the OS and know where to go for more information.

Starting Up a Mac

When the Mac starts up, you see a graphical illustration of some of the events occurring in the startup process, such as the loading of the desktop and system applets, including the **Finder window** (which is used to explore the Mac system). Most of the startup process, however, is hidden from the user. Here are the main steps in the process:

1. Self-test controlled from ROM

2. PRAM (parameter RAM) settings retrieved

3. System folder located

4. Mac OS ROM file loaded

5. Smiling Mac icon and welcome screen displayed

6. Enablers loaded

7. Disk First Aid runs if the Mac was not shut down properly

8. Other System folder contents located

9. Mac desktop displayed

10. Finder and startup programs located

Each of these steps is described in more detail below, and major differences between Mac OS X and Mac OS 9 are noted.

1. *Self-test is controlled from ROM.* When you press the power button on a Mac and power is sent to the motherboard, the ROM signals the Mac to perform a self-test. Components tested include the hard drive, the processor, ports, controllers, and expansion cards. The self-test ensures that they are operating correctly. Once this is confirmed, the Mac tests its RAM and halts the startup process if major damage or incorrect installations of RAM modules are detected. Minor damage to RAM may not be detected during the startup test of RAM and may manifest itself in system malfunctions later.

2. *PRAM settings are retrieved.* In the Mac, **PRAM**, or **parameter RAM**, stores configuration information for the Mac OS. After tests of components and RAM are completed, the Mac looks at the PRAM for settings that tell the system which drive is presently designated as the bootable drive (the startup disk). If it looks in that drive and does not find the Mac OS, it keeps looking in drives

until it finds a bootable drive. If it cannot find one, the system displays a flashing question mark and pauses the startup process.

3. *The System folder is located.* After the Mac locates a bootable disk, it looks for an active **System folder**, which is the folder that the system designates as the one from which the Mac OS is to be loaded. A System folder is required for a disk to be bootable. In Mac OS 9, the System folder is named System Folder, and in Mac OS X, the System folder is named System. See Figure 27-1.

Figure 27-1   Mac OS 9 is stored in the System Folder, but Mac OS X uses System

4. *The Mac OS ROM file is loaded.* The first item that the Mac loads into memory from the System folder is the **Mac OS ROM file**, which contains commands required for interaction with hardware and the lower levels of the Mac OS. Before the iMac, these commands were stored in ROM on the motherboard in the Mac.

5. *The smiling Mac icon and welcome screen are displayed.* When the smiling Mac icon is displayed, the system is loading the OS into RAM, beginning with the **System file** containing the libraries and commands that make up the core of the OS.

6. *The system loads enablers for hardware components.* If Mac hardware is put on the market before the instructions to control it are included with the OS, an **enabler file** will be included with it that will enable it to function with the version of Mac OS being used on the computer. The enabler files are loaded after the System file. Generally, each revision of the Mac OS incorporates information included in enabler files that were necessary with the previous version.

7. *Disk First Aid runs if the system was not shut down properly.* If the system is not shut down properly, the next time the computer starts up the system will run **Disk First Aid**, a free Mac disk utility, to search for and repair any problems that it finds with the hard drive. Disk First Aid runs after the System file and any enabler files are loaded.

8. *Other contents of the System folder are loaded.* In Mac OS 9, in addition to the System file and enabler files, the System folder also contains the Control Panels and Extensions folders (see Figure 27-2). The **Control Panels folder** controls system settings such as time and date, speaker volume, and the configuration of the Finder window and the desktop. The **Extensions folder** contains add-ons to provide new features to a Mac, as well as shared libraries and icons. These no longer exist in Mac OS X; their functions are incorporated into a single **Library** folder, which is shown in Figure 27-3.

Figure 27-2   In OS 9, the Control Panel and Extensions folders are used to contain OS and applications utilities

Figure 27-3   In OS X, the Library folder replaces the Control Panel and Extensions folders of OS 9

9. *The Mac desktop is displayed.* The Mac desktop is displayed after the necessary contents of the System folder have been loaded. All the required components of the Mac OS have been loaded at this point.

10. *The Finder window and startup programs are loaded.* After the Mac OS is completely loaded, the Finder window launches so that the user can access programs and files. The Finder itself is an application that is loaded automatically during the startup process, not a part of the OS. When the Finder window has been loaded, the system loads items in the Startup Items folder, which contains items that the user wants to open immediately upon startup. In Mac OS 9, it also opens the Launcher, which provides easy access to commonly used folders, programs, and files, if the Launcher control panel has been installed.

27

Using the Mac

Now that you've had an overview of the Mac OS startup process, let's look at some major features of the Mac interface and learn some important procedures and hints for using the Mac. In this section, you'll learn about the Finder window, the Apple menu, and procedures to help you work with files and applications in a Mac environment.

The Mac Desktop

The Mac OS X desktop, with its major components labeled, is shown in Figure 27-4. The Finder application is open and active. Because it is the currently active application, the menu bar for the Finder window is displayed at the top of the screen. The menu bar provides pull-down menus that contain options for working with applications, files, and the interface. A new feature in the Mac OS X user interface is the **dock** that appears at the bottom of the desktop. It contains icons that provide access to frequently used applications. When you click the minus button to minimize a window, an icon representing that window appears in the dock. To open an application from its icon in the dock, just click it once. The icons in the dock that represent open applications have a small triangle underneath them. The Mac OS X desktop also includes shortcut icons that are usually located on the right side of the screen and provide quick access to files, folders, and programs.

The Mac OS X interface has been redesigned, and it does not use its own interface to run applications that were written for OS 9. Instead, it stores the Mac OS 9 applications in a separate folder and launches the OS 9 interface, which it calls the classic interface, whenever a user wants to use one of those applications. In this way, a user can still use older Mac applications with the newer Mac interface. In Figure 27-4 you can see the icon on the right side of the screen to launch the Desktop (Mac OS 9) classic interface.

Using the Finder

The Mac's Finder window functions something like Explorer or My Computer in Windows, enabling the user to navigate and access the Mac's files and applications. The Finder window at the computer level, which is the top level of the Mac OS X's hierarchical file structure,

Figure 27-4   The Mac OS X desktop with a Finder window showing

shows an icon for the computer's hard drive as well as a Network icon to provide access to any other workstations that the computer is connected to. The Finder window and other windows contain a toolbar that appears at the top of the window and contains buttons that function much like the buttons in a Web browser, such as Back, Home, and Favorites. The Home button on the Mac OS X window toolbar takes the user back to the computer level.

> **TIP**   If you use a folder frequently, such as the Documents folder, you can keep it open all the time without having it in your way. In Mac OS 9, drag it down to the bottom of the screen until it becomes a tab on the title bar. In Mac OS X, drag it down to the dock, and it will become an icon on the dock.

Besides allowing you to access programs, files, and folders, the Finder window provides you with a way to organize and manage them. For instance, to create a new folder, locate the folder in which you want to create the new folder using the Finder. When you've reached the desired folder, go to the File menu and click New Folder. The new folder will appear with its name highlighted. Type its new name and press the Return key to rename the folder.

It is easier to locate a file or folder in the Finder window if you know exactly where it is, especially if there are several levels of folders inside each other. If you don't know the location of the file or folder you want to find, use the Sherlock utility to search for it. By default, the dock in Mac OS X contains an icon for Sherlock; it looks like a hat and a magnifying glass. The search screen for Sherlock is shown in Figure 27-5. Type the name of the file, folder, or text you want to find, click the check box next to the location you want to search, and then click the green magnifying glass button to begin the search. In the figure, you are searching the hard drive for a file that is named Myfile.

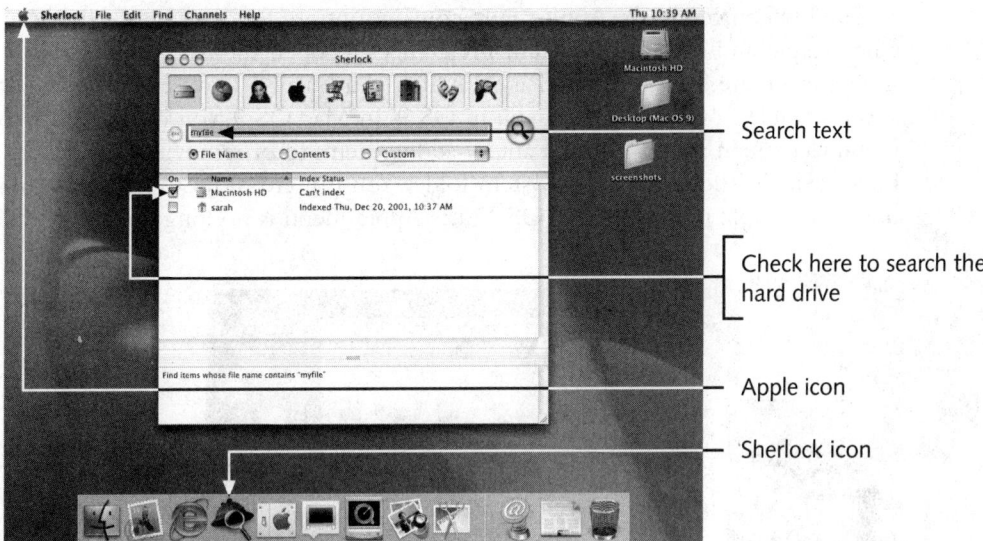

Figure 27-5   Use Sherlock to search for files and folders

When you don't need a file or folder any more, just drag its icon to the Trash Can until the Trash Can is highlighted, and release the mouse button. Note that this is the only way you can delete icons from the Finder window. When an item is moved to the Trash Can, you can still recover it by double-clicking the Trash Can and locating the item. Items are not actually removed from the system until you chose File, Empty Trash from the menu.

Using the Apple Menu

The menu at the top of the Mac OS screen changes with each application that is active except for the Apple icon, which is always shown at the far left of the menu bar. The **Apple menu**, which opens when you click the Apple icon, and is similar to the Microsoft Windows Start menu, is present and is constantly accessible no matter what folder, window, or application you are using. It contains accessories to help you manage system tasks as well as programs such as media players, a calculator, search programs, and word-processing programs. The Mac OS X Apple menu is shown in Figure 27-6.

Figure 27-6   The Apple menu is always available no matter what application is active

System Preferences on the Apple menu contains options for customizing the Mac interface. Click Apple and then click System Preferences to open the System Preferences window, shown in Figure 27-7. Control Panels, which you learned about earlier in the chapter, are also accessible from the Apple menu in OS 9. In Mac OS 9, you can customize the Apple menu to contain anything you want by adding items to or removing items from the Apple folder, which is located in the System folder. You can create up to five levels of submenus under the Apple menu. In Mac OS X, the Apple menu is no longer customizable.

Figure 27-7   The System Preferences window is used to customize the Mac interface

In Mac OS 9, there are three submenus on the Apple menu, called Recent Applications, Recent Documents, and Recent Servers. To customize these submenus, from the Apple menu, select Control Panels, Apple Menu Options. From this control panel, you can select whether or not to use recent menus and how many items to include on them. In Mac OS X, the Recent Items submenu on the Apple menu (shown in Figure 27-8) gives you access to recently accessed documents and applications.

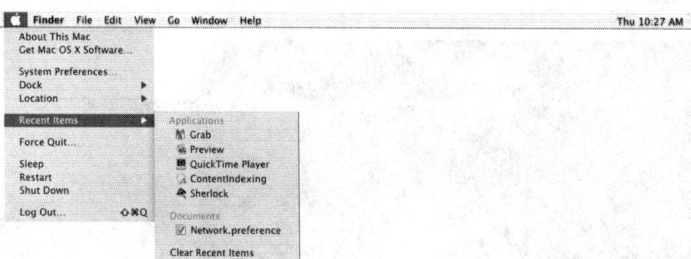

Figure 27-8   Using Mac OS X, the Recent Items menu under the Apple menu lists recently accessed documents and applications

Launching an Application

There are four ways to access applications on the Mac:

- Double-click the icon for the application from the Finder window or another window or from the desktop.

- Choose the application from the Recent Applications submenu on the Apple menu.

- Double-click the icon of a file associated with that application, such as a text file saved from the Notepad application.

- Drag to the application's icon the icon of a document that you want to open with it.

27

The first two methods have already been discussed. The last option works well if you want to open a document with an application other than the one in which it was originally saved.

As you work with applications on the Mac, you may find that you want to have more than one open at a time. In Mac OS 9, the Applications menu, which you can access from the upper right-hand corner of your screen, allows you to switch between open applications easily. The menu will show the icon and name of the currently active application. To access other open applications, click the menu and choose the name of the application you want to access. Recall that in Mac OS X, open applications are shown as icons in the dock with a small triangle under them.

Supporting Hardware

In addition to working with files and applications, you will also need to know how to support hardware in a Mac system, such as monitors and hard drives, and including changing settings for video, understanding the file system used on the hard drive, and using system maintenance tools. Again, this section will not give you all you need to know to work with Mac hardware; it is simply intended to show you some important tools for working with the system. For more information specific to working with Mac hardware, study books devoted specifically to the Mac, documentation and manuals that come with your system or with specific components, and the Apple Computer, Inc. Web site (*www.apple.com*).

Adjusting Display Settings

To change display settings such as color depth and resolution, double-click the Display icon under System Preferences. The Displays window appears, as seen in Figure 27-9. You can change the following settings in the Displays window:

- *Resolution.* The **resolution** of a display affects how many **pixels** are shown on-screen. A resolution of 1,024 × 768 means that there are 1,024 columns of pixels and 768 rows of pixels. When you change the resolution of your monitor, remember that the size of the items on the screen will change; the more pixels there are, the smaller items will be. This can be good if you want to see more items and space on your screen at one time, but it can be a drawback if you have vision problems. Two advantages to an 800 × 600 resolution are that it will produce a view close to what you will actually see in a printed document and that many Web pages are designed to be viewed at this resolution. A Web page optimized at 800 × 600 will look cramped at a lower resolution such as 640 × 480.

Figure 27-9   The Displays icon in System Preferences window is used to adjust the display settings

- *Contrast and brightness.* The sliders on the bottom of the Display tab of the Displays window enable you to control how much contrast there is between colors on your screen and how bright the overall display is. It is not a good idea to set a monitor to the highest brightness setting, because this can burn out the monitor prematurely.

- *Color depth.* Click the Color tab on the Displays window to view and change the settings for depth of color. The Color Depth box allows you to change how many colors can be shown on the screen: either 256, thousands, or millions. More colors mean a more realistic and more detailed picture. Sometimes a picture will have been created using a certain setting and will not be displayed correctly in a different setting. If a picture appears blurred or too gray, change the color depth until it appears correctly.

- *Display geometry.* Click the Geometry tab in the Displays window to reach options for changing the shape of the display on the screen. On most monitors, the display area is actually slightly smaller than the screen size, and you may see some black space around the display area. Use the Geometry settings to change the height, width, position, and shape of the display area.

Supporting the Hard Drive

As with other OSs, the Mac OS supports IDE and SCSI drive technologies and, for hard drives, there is a choice of file systems to use.

Drive Technologies: IDE and SCSI   Recall from earlier chapters that IDE drives follow an interface standard that allows for up to four IDE drives in a system. SCSI drives are faster than IDE drives, and there can be up to 15 SCSI devices on a system. It is possible to mix IDE and SCSI devices on a system.

> The terms IDE and SCSI refer not only to hard drives but also to other devices such as CD-ROM drives, Zip drives, and DVD drives.

In the mid-1990s, IDE became the main technology for connecting internal devices in a Mac, partially because it is less expensive than SCSI and is more widely used in the computer industry. However, because it is faster and can support more devices, SCSI can be a better choice for complex multimedia and graphics work. If you have a Mac that uses IDE technology and want to convert to SCSI, you can purchase a SCSI host adapter for that purpose. Choose a drive technology according to your needs, your budget, and what technology your system supports.

File Systems on the Mac   A file system is the overall structure that an OS uses to name, store, and organize files on a disk. The two main choices for a file system on a Mac hard drive are **HFS (Hierarchical File System)**, also called **Mac OS Standard Format**, and **HFS+**, also called the **Mac OS Extended Format**. HFS was the format used for Mac disks before 1998, when drives larger than 1 GB started to become more common. HFS limited the number of allocation units on a disk to 65,536; how big each allocation unit was depended on the total size of the drive. These allocation units are called **allocation blocks** or simply **blocks**, and are similar to the Microsoft Windows file system's clusters; they are sets of hard drive sectors where the Mac's file system stores files. Files smaller than the size of a block still take up an entire block, which can cause a significant amount of space to be wasted; this wasted space is called slack.

In 1998, with the release of Mac OS 8.1, HFS was updated to HFS+, which allows for smaller blocks and can format drives up to 2,048 GB. Any drive larger than 1GB should be formatted with HFS+. Hard drives or removable media disks (such as floppy disks) smaller than 1 GB should be formatted with HFS, as should any hard drive that you plan to use with a Mac running Mac OS 8.1 or earlier.

> In Mac OS 9, the File Exchange control panel is a component that can be installed to allow the Mac to use Microsoft Windows FAT16 and FAT32 partitions. Macs can read some NTFS or Linux/Unix file systems using utilities specially designed for that purpose. Mac OS X includes the ability to mount FAT drives but does not include a utility to format them as Mac OS 9 did.

The formatting of a hard drive with a file system creates blocks. It also creates a **directory structure** that allows the OS to access the drive. Some important elements of the directory structure are listed below.

- **Boot blocks** are the first two allocation blocks on the hard drive. They are initially empty, but once a System folder is installed on a computer, the boot blocks contain the location of the System folder so that the system can find and load the OS. You can correct damage to the boot blocks or replace erased boot blocks by installing a new System folder.

- Right after the boot blocks comes the **volume information block**, which holds information about the drive, including its format, name, number of files and folders, and allocation block size. This information must be present for a Mac to be able to access a drive. Because of the importance of the volume information block, a copy of it is stored in the next to last allocation block on the drive.

- A map of the allocation blocks on a hard drive is contained in the **volume bit map**, which uses a 1 to indicate that a block is storing files and a 0 to indicate that it is empty and is available for use. Damage to or corruption of the volume bit map does not prevent the Mac from being able to access the drive. However, when the Mac cannot determine from the volume bit map which allocation blocks are used, it might write new information to blocks that are full, overwriting the existing information. Regular disk maintenance (including use of the tools described in the next section) can help guard against this problem.

- The **catalog tree** is a database of the folders and files on a Mac hard drive, including information such as filenames and extensions, the application used to open a file, the creator of the file or folder, and the date the file or folder was created.

- The **extents tree** contains information about where the allocation blocks are located for files that take up more than one allocation block. When a file is larger than one allocation block, it is broken up into pieces called **extents**. One extent is stored in one allocation block. If a large proportion of the space on a hard drive is being used, the extents that make up a file might not be stored next to each other. The catalog tree and the extents tree work together and are both necessary for the Mac to be able to access data stored on the hard drive. They are the closest thing in the Mac to the FAT and the root directory in Windows.

Drive Maintenance Tools

Now that you've learned about some of the components and structures created when a Mac hard drive is formatted, let's look at some utilities you can use to format, maintain, and repair hard drives on a Mac. This is not an exhaustive list but rather points you to a few common tools used for typical hard drive tasks.

In Mac OS 9, disk maintenance tools were accessed as separate applications. In Mac OS X, the Utilities folder (shown in Figure 27-10) contains various system tools, including Disk Utility (shown in Figure 27-11), which combines the functions of the Mac OS 9 tools Drive Setup and Disk First Aid.

Figure 27-10   The Mac OS X Utilities folder contains several utilities, including those to manage a hard drive

Figure 27-11   The Mac OS X Disk Utility is in the Utilities folder and can be used to set up and repair a hard drive

Drive Setup   The **Drive Setup** function can be used to format a hard drive when it is initially installed or to reformat a damaged hard drive. Remember that reformatting a drive erases all data and programs on it because the format process creates new allocation blocks and directory structures. When you format a drive, you can choose whether or not to create partitions on it. Partitioning a drive is not required, but can be done to divide the drive into one or more logical drives. Drive Setup can format most IDE and SCSI drives. To use Drive Setup, on the Disk Utility window, click Drive Setup, select the disk you want to partition, and then click Partition. When you repartition a drive, all data on the current partitions is erased, and you cannot partition a drive that is currently used as the startup drive.

Defragmentation Utilities Third-party software, such as Norton Utilities (*www.symantec.com*) or TechTool Pro, which is specifically designed for use with Macs, (*www.micromat.com*) can be used to defragment your hard drive. These utilities copy the extents that make up a file into RAM on the Mac, reassemble the file, and save the complete file back onto the hard drive. One danger with these tools is that if a power failure occurs while they are running, any extents stored in the Mac's RAM will be lost. An alternate method, which is safer but much more time-consuming and cumbersome, is to back up the hard drive, reformat it, and then copy the files back onto the drive. You should always have a backup of your hard drive in case of any type of system failure.

Disk First Aid As you learned earlier in the chapter, Disk First Aid is a disk repair tool that checks for errors on the hard drive and runs automatically on reboot when a Mac is not shut down properly. You can also run this tool manually as a preventive maintenance measure or as an attempt to address poor hard drive performance. Disk First Aid is part of the free Apple utility Disk Utility and is less powerful than third-party disk repair utilities such as Norton Disk Doctor, which is part of Norton Utilities, or Alsoft's Disk Warrior (*www.alsoft.com*). There are some problems that these utilities can repair that Disk First Aid can only detect.

INTRODUCING LINUX

Generally, the Mac OS is very user-friendly and is ideal for many desktop computer uses. Linux is more often used as a file server, Web server, or e-mail server than as a desktop OS; therefore, our approach to it will be different. This introduction to Linux is designed to give you a behind-the-scenes look at what a system administrator must know in order to manage the Linux OS in a corporate setting. In this section, you will learn about root and user accounts, file structure, some common commands, and how to use the vi editor.

Recall from Chapter 15 that there are several different distributions of Linux. There are different versions within each distribution as well. The material in this section is meant as a general introduction to the OS. The organization of files and folders, the desktop's appearance, and the way each command works might be slightly different with the distribution and version of Linux you are using.

Root Account and User Accounts

Recall that an operating system is composed of a kernel, which interacts with the hardware and other software, and a shell, which interacts with the user and the kernel. Linux is a Unix-like operating system, and, just as with other versions of Unix, can use more than one shell. The default shell for Linux is the Bash shell. The name stands for "Bourne Again Shell" and takes the best features from two previous shells, the Bourne and the Korn shells.

For a Linux or Unix server, the system administrator is the person who installs updates to the OS (called patches), manages backup processes, supports the installation of software and hardware, sets up user accounts, resets passwords, and generally supports users. The system administrator has **root privileges**, which means that he or she can access all the functions of the OS and the principal user account called the **root account**. The administrator protects the password to the root account because this password gives full access to the system. When the administrator is logged on, he or she is logged on as the user root. You can use the *who* command to show a list of all users currently logged on to the system. In the example shown below, typing *who* shows that three users are currently logged on: the root, james, and susan.

27

```
who
root      tty1    Oct 12 07:56
james     tty1    Oct 12 08:35
susan     tty1    Oct 12 10:05
```

 TIP The Linux command prompt for the root is different from the command prompt for ordinary users. The root command prompt is #, and other users have the $ command prompt.

Directory and File Layout

The main directory in Unix and Linux is the **root directory** and is indicated with a forward slash. (In Unix and Linux, directories in a path are separated with forward slashes, in contrast to the backward slashes used by DOS and Windows.) Use the *ls* command, which is similar to the DOS Dir command, to list the contents of the root directory. The command (*ls -l /*) and its results are shown in Figure 27-12. Notice that the *-l* parameter is added to the command, which displays the results using the long format, and that there are spaces included before and after the parameter of the command. Also notice in the figure the format used to display the directory contents. The *d* at the beginning of each entry indicates that the entry is a directory, not a file. The other letters in this first column have to do with the read and write privileges assigned to the directory and the right to execute programs in the directory. The name of the directory is in the last column. The rights assigned the directory can apply to the owner of the directory, to other users, or to an entire group of users.

Table 27-1 lists directories that are created in the root directory during a typical Linux installation. The actual list of directories for a Linux computer that you work with may be a little different, because the directories created in the root directory depend on what programs have been installed.

Figure 27-12   A directory listing using the Is command

Table 27-1   Directories in a typical Linux root directory

Directory	Description
/bin	Contains programs and commands necessary to boot the system and perform other system tasks not reserved for the administrator, such as shutdown and reboot.
/boot	Consists of components needed for the boot process, such as boot loaders.
/dev	Holds device names, which consist of the type of device and a number identifying the device. Actual device drivers are located in the /lib/modules /[kernel version]/ directory.
/etc	Contains system configuration data, including configuration files and settings and their subdirectories. These files are used for tasks such as configuring a user account, changing system settings, and configuring a domain name resolution service.
/home	Contains user data. Every user on the system has a directory in the /home directory, such as /home/jean or /home/scott, and when a user logs on, that directory becomes the current working directory.
/lib	Stores common libraries used by applications so that more than one application can use the same library at one time. An example is the library of C programming code, without which only the kernel of the Linux system could run.
/lost+found	Stores data that is lost when files are truncated or when an attempt to fix system errors is unsuccessful.
/opt	Contains installations of third-party applications such as Web browsers that do not come with the Linux OS distribution.
/root	The home directory for the root user; contains only files specific to the root user. Do not confuse this directory with the root directory, which contains all the directories listed in this table.

Table 27-1   Directories in a typical Linux root directory (continued)

Directory	Description
/sbin	Stores commands required for system administration.
/tmp	Stores temporary files, such as the ones that applications use during installation and operation.
/usr	Constitutes the major section of the Linux file system and contains read-only data.
/var	Holds variable data such as e-mail, news, print spools, and administrative files.

Linux Commands

This section describes some basic Linux and Unix commands, together with simple examples of how some are used. As you read along, be aware that all commands entered in Linux or Unix are case sensitive, meaning that uppercase and lowercase matter. Table 27-2 shows some common commands for Linux and Unix. This is not meant to be a comprehensive list of commands but simply to list some that might be useful to you in working with files, directories, network connections, and system configuration. In the rest of the section, you will learn how to use a few common commands. For all of these procedures, assume that you are in your home directory (which would be /home/<*yourname*>/).

Table 27-2   Some common Linux and Unix commands

Command	Description
cat	Lets you view the contents of a file. Many Linux commands can use the redirection symbol > to redirect the output of the command. For example, use the redirection symbol with the cat command to copy a file: `cat /etc/shells > newfile` The contents of the shells file are written to newfile.
cd	Change directory. For example, `cd /etc` changes the directory to /etc.
chmod	This command changes the attributes assigned to a file and is similar to the DOS Attrib command. For example, to grant read permission to the file myfile: `Chmod +r myfile`
clear	Clears the screen. This command is useful when the screen has become cluttered with commands and data that you no longer need to view.
cp	Used to copy a file: `cp <source> <destination>`
date	Entered alone, this command displays the current system date setting. Entered in the format `date <mmddhhmmyy>`, this command sets the system date. For example, to set the date to Dec 25, 2002 at 11:59 in the evening: `Date 1225235902`
echo	Displays information on the screen. For example, to display which shell is currently being used, enter this command: `echo $SHELL`
fdisk	Creates or makes changes to a hard drive partition table: `fdisk <hard drive>`
grep	Searches for a specific pattern in a file or in multiple files: `grep <pattern> <file>`

Table 27-2 Some common Linux and Unix commands (continued)

Command	Description
hostname	Displays a server's FQDN: `hostname`
ifconfig	Used to troubleshoot problems with network connections under TCP/IP. This command can disable and enable network cards and release and renew the IP addresses assigned to these cards. For example, to show all configuration information: `ifconfig -a` To release the given IP address for a TCP/IP connection named en0 (the first Ethernet connection of the system): `ifconfig en0 -168.92.1.1`
kill	Kills a process instead of waiting for the process to terminate: `kill <process ID>`
ls	The ls command is similar to the DOS Dir command, which displays a list of directories and files. For example, to list all files in the /etc directory, using the long parameter for a complete listing use: `ls -l /etc`
man	Displays the online help manual called the man pages. For example, to get information about the echo command: `man echo` The manual program displays information about the command. To exit the manual program, type `q`.
mkdir	This command makes a new directory: `mkdir <directory>`
|more	Appended to a command to display the results of the command on the screen one page at a time. For example, to page the ls command: `ls |more`
mv	Moves a file or renames it, if the source and destination are the same directory: `mv <source> <destination>`
netstat	Shows statistics and status information for network connections and routing tables: `netstat`
nslookup	Queries domain name servers to look up domain names: `nslookup`
ping	Used to test network connections by sending a request packet to a host. If a connection is successful, the host will return a response packet. `ping <host>`
ps	Displays the process table so that you can identify process IDs for currently running processes (Once you know the process ID, you can use the kill command to terminate a process): `ps`
pwd	Shows the name of the present working directory: `pwd`
reboot	Reboots the system: `reboot`
rm	Removes the file or files that are specified: `rm <file>`
rmdir	This command removes a directory: `rmdir <directory>`
route	Entered alone, this command shows the current configuration of the IP routing table. Entered in the format `route [options]`, it configures the IP routing table.
traceroute	Shows the route of IP packets; used for debugging connections on a network: `traceroute <host>`
useradd	Adds a user to a system: `useradd [option] <user>`
userdel	Removes a user from a system: `userdel <user>`

Table 27-2   Some common Linux and Unix commands (continued)

Command	Description
vi	Launches a full-screen editor that can be used to enter text and commands: `vi <file>`
whatis	Displays a brief overview of a command. For example, to get quick information about the echo command: `whatis echo`
who	Displays a list of users currently logged in: `who`

Editing Commands

When you add options and file or directory names to a command, it can get quite long, and if you make a mistake while typing the command, you will want to edit it. Also, once the command has been entered, you can retrieve it, edit it, and press Enter to reissue the command. Some shells allow you to use the arrow, Backspace, Insert, and Delete keys to edit command lines, and other shells do not allow you to use these keys. Instead, use the following keystrokes to edit a command line:

- Alt+D   Delete a word
- Ctrl+K   Delete from the current position to the end of the line
- Ctrl+A   Move the cursor to the beginning of the command line
- Alt+B   Move the cursor left one word
- Alt+F   Move the cursor right one word

For example, follow these steps to edit a command line:

1. Type **who is this** but DO NOT press Enter.
2. To move one word to the left, press **Alt+B** so that your cursor is positioned on the word "is."
3. To delete the word "is," press **Alt+D**.
4. To delete the portion of the command line that follows the current cursor position, press **Ctrl+K**.
5. To move the cursor to the beginning of the command line, press **Ctrl+A**.

Viewing the Shells File

The shells file in the /etc directory contains a list of available shells to use on a Linux system. Each shell incorporates slightly different support for programming and scripting languages. Additionally, different Linux shells may use keystrokes other than the ones you just learned in supporting command line editing; the keystrokes in the procedure in the last section work in Bash, the default Linux shell. To determine whether you are using the Bash shell, type `echo $shell` and press Enter. If you see the output /bin/bash, you are using the Bash shell. If you are not using the Bash shell, type `bash` and press Enter to change to the Bash shell.

To view a list of available shells:

1. Type **cat /etc/shells**, and then press **Enter**.

2. A list of available shells appears. This list may include the entries /bin/bash, /bin/bsh, /bin/csh, /bin/sh, /bin/tcsh, and /bin/zsh. Notice that all these shells are stored in the /bin directory. Type **clear**, and then press **Enter** to clear the screen.

3. Type **cat –n /etc/shells**, and then press **Enter**. Notice that this time, the same list of shells is displayed with a number before each line because you used the –n option. (See Figure 27-13.) Notice in the figure that the current user is root.

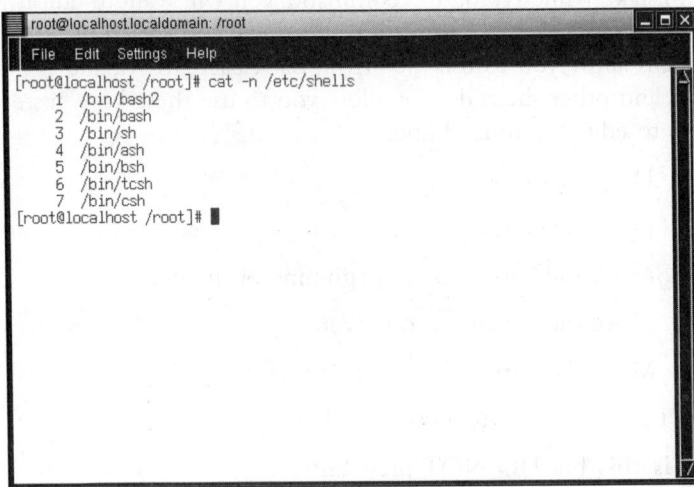

Figure 27-13   Use the Cat command to display a list of shells

Redirecting Output

Recall the list of available shells that you created using the `cat` command. When you entered the command `cat /etc/shells`, the list, which is the output of that command, was sent to the screen. What if you wanted to save that list? You would use the **redirection symbol**, which is the greater-than (>) sign, to direct the output to a file, perhaps with the name available_shells. Use these steps:

1. Go to the root directory by typing **cd /** and pressing **Enter**.

2. Type **cat /etc/shells > available_shells**, and then press **Enter**.

3. Notice that no command output appears on the screen, because the output has been saved to the new file available_shells (the file is created when the command is entered). To view the contents of the file, type **cat available_shells**, and then press **Enter**.

The file was created in the current directory which is the root directory.

Creating a Directory

It is not a good idea to store data files in the root directory, so let's create a new directory to which to move the new file available_shells:

1. Type **mkdir myfiles**, and then press **Enter**. This creates a new directory named myfiles under the current directory, which is root.

2. Type **cd myfiles** to change from the current directory to the new directory.

3. Type **mv /available_shells .** and then press **Enter** (don't overlook the period at the end of the command line; type it, too). This copies the file from the root directory to the current directory, which is /myfiles. The source directory is the root and the destination directory is /myfiles. The period in a command line means the current directory.

4. Type **ls** to see the contents of the myfiles directory. The available_shells file is listed. (See Figure 27-14.)

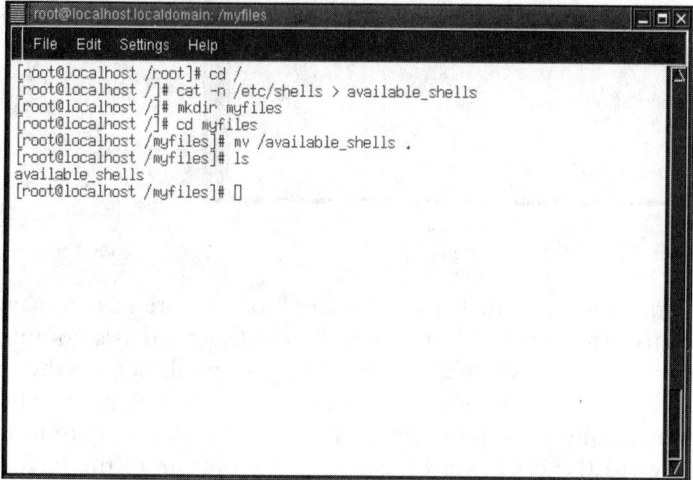

Figure 27-14 Creating and moving files to a directory

Using the vi Editor

Recall that you were introduced to the vi command in Table 27-2 earlier in the chapter. This command launches the **vi editor**, which got its name because it is a visual editor that was, at one time, the most popular Unix text editor. It is still used with shells that don't allow the use of the arrow, Delete, or Backspace keys. The editor can be used in **insert mode**, in which you can enter text, or **command mode**, which allows you to enter commands to perform editing tasks to move through the file. In this section, you will learn how to create and use commands on a text file in the vi editor. All of these commands are case sensitive.

Let's create and work with a file called mymemo.

1. To open the vi editor and create a file at the same time, type the command followed by the file name, as follows: **vi mymemo**

2. The vi editor screen is shown in Figure 27-15. Notice that the filename is shown at the bottom of the screen and that the cursor is at the top of the screen.

Figure 27-15 The vi text editor

3. At this point, when you first open the vi editor, you are in command mode, which means that anything you type will be interpreted as a command by the vi editor. Type **i** to switch to insert mode. You will not see the command on the screen, and you do not need to press Enter to execute it. The command automatically switches you to insert mode. When you are in insert mode, the word INSERT will be shown at the bottom of the screen.

4. Type the first two sentences of Step 3 as the text for your memo. If your shell supports it, practice using the arrow keys to move the cursor through the text, up, down, left, and right, one character at a time. You will see the keystrokes used to perform the same movements in Table 27-3; they can be used if the arrow keys are not supported.

5. To switch back to command mode, press the **Esc** key. Now you are ready to enter commands to manipulate your text. Type **H** to move the cursor to the upper-left corner of the screen. You must use an uppercase H, because all these commands are case sensitive.

6. Type **w** repeatedly until you reach the beginning of the word "first."

7. Type **dw** to delete the word "first." To delete one character at a time, you would use x; to delete an entire line, you would use dd.

8. To save the file and exit the vi editor, type **:x** and press **Enter**. This will save the file and close the editor.

Table 27-3 lists the vi editor commands to move the cursor. There are many more commands to manipulate text, set options, cancel, or temporarily leave a vi editor session. For a more complete list of vi editor commands, see a reference dedicated to Linux.

Table 27-3   vi editor commands

Command	Alternate	Description
Ctrl+B	Pg up	Back one screen
Ctrl+F	Pg down	Forward one screen
Ctrl+U	--	Up half a screen
Ctrl+D	--	Down half a screen
k	Up arrow	Up one line
j	Down arrow	Down one line
h	Left arrow	Left one character
l	Right arrow	Right one character
W	--	Forward one word
B	--	Back one word
0 (zero)	--	Beginning of the current line
$	--	End of current line
NG	--	Line specified by number n
H	--	Upper left corner of screen
L	--	Last line on the screen

27

Window Managers

Because many users prefer a Windows desktop, several applications have been written to provide a GUI for Unix and Linux. These GUIs are called window managers. You saw a typical window manager screen for Linux in Chapter 15. One popular desktop environment software is GNU Network Object Model Environment (GNOME). GNOME (pronounced "guh-nome") provides a desktop that looks and feels like Windows 98, and is free software designed to use a Linux kernel. The major components of a GNOME window are shown in Figure 27-16. For more information about GNOME, see the organization's Web site at *www.gnu.org*.

Figure 27-16   GNOME is popular desktop environment software used on Linux systems

SUPPORTING NOTEBOOKS

Supporting notebook computers is another essential task of a PC technician. This section discusses the special requirements for supporting notebooks, including changing power management options, understanding and supporting PC Cards, and using special Windows components available for supporting notebooks. Notebooks use the same technology as PCs do but with modifications so as to use less power, take up less space, and work when on the move.

A **notebook** or **laptop computer** is a computer designed for portability (see Figure 27-17). Notebooks use thin LCD panels instead of CRT monitors for display, compact hard drives that can withstand movement even during operation, and small memory modules and CPUs that require less power than regular components. Notebook LCD panels use one of two technologies. Active matrix (sometimes called thin film transistor or TFT) technology generally provides better quality than does passive matrix (sometimes called dual-scan twisted nematic, or DSTN) technology.

Notebooks cost more than PCs with similar features, because components are designed to be more compact and to endure movement when in use. The types and features of notebooks vary widely as they do for PCs. However, notebooks are generally purchased as a whole unit, including both hardware and software, and you are not as likely to upgrade a notebook's hardware and OS as you might be with a PC. In fact, some notebook manufacturers no longer support a notebook that has had the OS upgraded or new hardware components added. In contrast, recall that PCs are highly modular, letting you easily interchange, upgrade, and enhance components. In fact, PCs are often assembled from components purchased from various vendors and manufacturers. Notebook computers, on the other hand, are designed

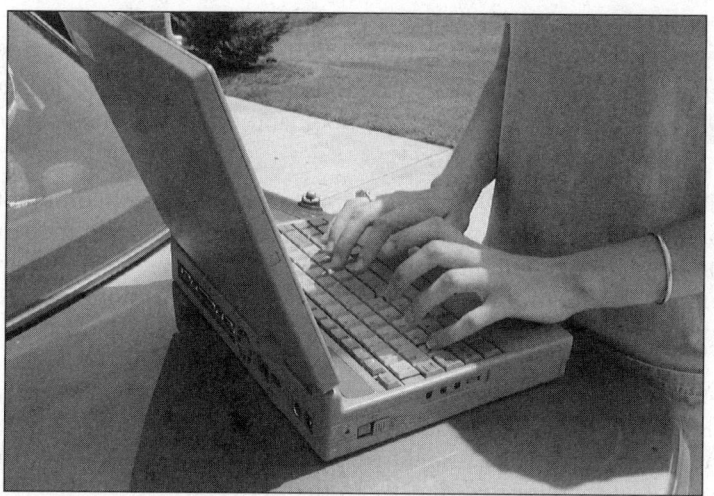

Figure 27-17   A notebook is a computer designed for travel

with a different goal in mind and can be very proprietary in design, which means that the skills needed to support them are brand specific. In this chapter, we'll look at some universal support issues, but remember that procedures can vary from one notebook brand to another.

 The LCD panels on notebooks are fragile and can be damaged. Take precautions against damaging the notebook's LCD panel through rough use.

When supporting any notebook, pay careful attention to the stipulations on the warranty that accompanies it. Some warranties are voided if you open the notebook case or install memory, batteries, or a hard drive that was not made by, or at least authorized by, the notebook's manufacturer. Almost all operating system installations on notebooks are customized by the manufacturer, and a floppy disk comes with the notebook that contains data and utilities specific to the configuration. Read the supporting documentation for the notebook before you consider upgrading or reinstalling the OS.

Windows 98 Notebook Features

The Windows 98 features designed to support notebooks include:

- Multilink Channel Aggregation, a feature that allows you to use two modem connections at the same time to speed up data throughput when connected over phone lines. It works on both regular analog phone lines and ISDN. To use the feature, you must have two phone lines and two modem cards that are physically designed to connect two phone lines at the same time.

- ACPI (Advanced Configuration and Power Interface) developed by Intel, Microsoft, and Toshiba to control power on a notebook and other devices. ACPI allows a device to turn on a notebook or allows a notebook to turn on a device. For example, if you connect an external CD-ROM drive to the notebook, it can turn on the notebook, or the notebook can cycle up and turn on an external CD-ROM drive. The BIOS of the notebook and the device must support ACPI for it to work.

- Several improvements over Windows 95 for managing power consumption for notebooks. Windows 98 automatically powers down a PC Card modem when its not in use, supports multiple battery packs, and lets you create individual power profiles. Power profiles are described in the next section.

- Improved support for PC Cards, adding several new drivers.

- Microsoft Exchange lets a user select what e-mail to download when traveling with a notebook. Downloading large e-mail messages with attachments takes a long time over a modem. You might prefer to leave this e-mail to download when you are later connected directly to the network.

 TIP   When returning from a trip with a notebook, you might want to update your desktop PC with all e-mail documents and other files created or updated during the trip. To do this, use Windows 9x **Briefcase**, a system folder used to synchronize files between two computers. Briefcase automatically updates files on the original computer to the most recent version. You can use a null modem cable, disk, or network for the file transfer.

Windows 2000 Notebook Features

Windows 2000 Professional has several features designed to support notebooks. When choosing between Windows 98 and Windows 2000 Professional for a notebook OS, use Windows 98 for low-end notebooks and Windows 2000 for high-end notebooks that are used in a business environment in which security is important. Windows 2000 has stronger power management and security features. The features new to Windows 2000 include:

- Offline Files, which replaces Briefcase, stores shared network files and folders in a cache on the notebook hard drive so you can use them offline. When you reconnect to the network, Offline Files synchronizes the files in the cache with those on the network.

- Hibernate mode, support for ACPI and APM (Advanced Power Management) have been improved.

- Improved battery support includes the ability to use two batteries and to monitor battery performance with greater control.

- Hot swapping of IDE devices and floppy disk external drives is a new feature.

- Folder redirection lets you point to an alternate location on a network for a folder. This feature can make the location of a folder transparent to the user.

Windows XP Notebook Features

Windows XP includes several features to make mobile computing easier, including power management features that build on similar capabilities in earlier versions of Windows. It also includes the ability to create **hardware profiles**, which specify which devices are to be loaded on startup for a particular user or set of circumstances. For example, you might set two different hardware profiles for a notebook computer, one for when it is connected to a port replicator and one for when it is not. A **port replicator** provides a means to connect a notebook to a power outlet and to the same external peripherals as are available to a desktop PC. A **docking station** does that and also provides additional secondary storage.

To create a hardware profile for a mobile user, follow these steps:

1. From the Start menu, open the **Control Panel**.

2. Double-click the **System** icon.

3. The System Properties dialog box opens. Click the **Hardware** tab.

4. Click the **Hardware Profiles** button at the bottom of the Hardware tab.

5. The Hardware Profiles dialog box opens (Figure 27-18). Click **Profile1 (Current)**, and then click the **Copy** button.

Figure 27-18   Windows XP allows you to set a hardware profile for each user

6. Type a new name for the profile, and then click **OK**.

7. Under When Windows starts, select either the option for Windows XP to wait for you to select a hardware profile or the option for Windows XP to start with the first profile listed if you don't select one in the specified number of seconds.

8. Restart the computer and, when prompted, select the new hardware profile.

9. Open the System Properties window. Click the **Hardware** tab, click **Device Manager**, and then double-click the icon for a device that you want to be enabled or disabled in the new profile.

10. Click the **General** tab in the Properties window for the device and in the area for device usage, select the option to enable the device, disable it for the current profile, or disable it for all hardware profiles.

Power Management

A notebook can be powered by a battery pack or an AC adapter connected to a power source. The length of time that a battery pack can power the notebook before being recharged varies according to the quality of the battery, the power consumption as determined by the devices being used, and how power is being managed.

Windows 98 and Windows 2000/XP have features to help manage power consumption. The goal is to minimize power consumption to increase the time before a battery pack needs recharging. Using Windows 98, to access the power management window, click Start, point to Settings, click Control Panel, and double-click the Power Management icon. Figure 27-19 shows the Power Management Properties dialog box for one notebook. (Other brands of notebooks may have different tabs in their Properties dialog box.) Use this dialog box to create, delete, and modify multiple power management schemes to customize how Windows 98 manages power consumption.

Figure 27-19   The Power Management Properties box of Windows 98 allows you to create and manage multiple power schemes

For example, one power-saving feature of Windows 98 puts a notebook into hibernation. When a computer hibernates, it stores whatever is currently in memory and then shuts down. When it returns from hibernating, it restores everything to the way it was before the shutdown. When hibernating, the notebook is using only a very small amount of power. When you step away from the notebook for a few minutes, direct the notebook to hibernate in order to save power. Before you direct a notebook to hibernate, make sure you know which keystrokes or buttons are required to restore the system to an active state without turning the computer off.

If the notebook supports hibernating, to configure Windows 98 to cause the notebook to hibernate when you close the lid of the notebook, do the following:

1. In the Power Management Properties dialog box, click the **Hibernate** tab (see Figure 27-20) and verify that hibernate support is enabled.

27

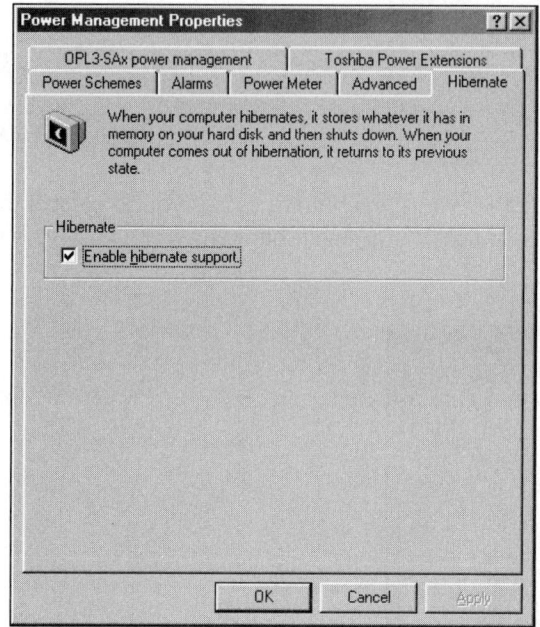

Figure 27-20   Verify that hibernate support is enabled

2. Click the **Advanced** tab. Figure 27-21 shows the Advanced page, which you use to control what happens when you press the shutdown button or close the lid of the notebook.

3. Click the list arrow for "When I close the lid of my portable computer" and select **Hibernate**. See Figure 27-22.

4. Click **Apply** and **OK** to close the Properties dialog box, saving your changes.

Figure 27-21   The Advanced tab of Power Management allows you to control the behavior of the power button and what happens when you close the lid of your notebook

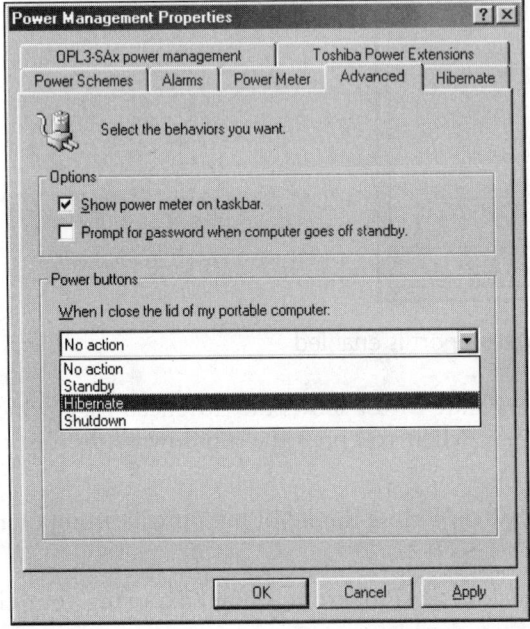

Figure 27-22   Choices of action when you close the lid of your notebook

If you need to use the notebook for extended periods away from an electrical outlet, you can use extra battery packs. When the notebook signals that power is low, remove the old battery and replace it with a charged one. See the notebook's user guide for directions. Here is an example of directions for exchanging the battery pack for one notebook:

1. Save your work and turn off the notebook.

2. Remove all cables connected to the notebook.

3. Set the notebook on its back, (as in Figure 27-23).

4. Slide the battery release panel to the left to expose the battery.

5. Lift the battery out of the computer.

6. Before placing a new battery in the slot, clean the edge connectors of the battery with a clean cloth.

27

Figure 27-23 Slide the battery release panel to the left to expose the battery pack

To extend the life of your battery, don't leave the battery in the notebook while the notebook is turned on and it's connected to an electrical outlet. When using the notebook while it is connected to an electrical outlet, remove the battery from the case. To recharge the battery, leave the notebook turned off while it is connected to an electrical outlet with the battery inserted. Some older battery types required that to keep the battery operating at optimum performance, you allowed the battery to almost completely discharge before recharging it and then completely recharge it before using it again. Some newer battery types do not require this. Check the documentation for your particular notebook and battery, and never use a battery charger on a battery type other than the one for which it was designed.

Windows 2000 improves the power management features of Windows 98, including, as you have learned, adding ACPI and APM. In Windows 2000, you can monitor and manage batteries on notebooks that are ACPI- and APM-enabled. You can access the battery meter directly by adding the battery status icon to the taskbar (see Figure 27-24). Follow these steps:

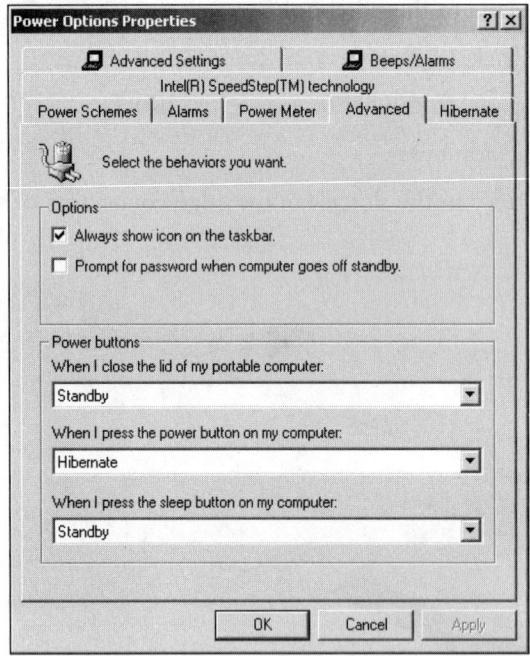

Figure 27-24   Use the Power Options Properties window to tell the Notebook what to do when you close the lid, press the power button, or press the sleep button

1. On the Start menu, click **Settings**, **Control Panel**.

2. Double-click **Power Options** to open the Power Options Properties dialog box.

3. Click the **Advanced** tab.

4. Click the check box labeled **Always show icon on the taskbar**.

Note that the Power Options box also offers tabs on which you can create power profiles and set alarms to alert you when battery power is low or critical.

Windows XP also includes power management features for notebooks, including support for ACPI and ACM. You can access these features from the Power Options icon in Control Panel. In the Power Options window, click the Power Schemes tab to select a **power scheme**, which is a collection of settings for a particular set of circumstances, such as for home/office desk use or portable/laptop use.

Online Resources for Notebooks

Except for the differences discussed in this section, notebooks work identically to desktop PCs, and the troubleshooting guidelines in previous chapters also apply to notebooks. When troubleshooting notebooks, be especially conscious of warranty issues; know what you can do within the guidelines of the warranty. The documentation that comes with a notebook is much more comprehensive than what comes with a PC and most often contains troubleshooting guidelines for the notebook. Remember that the loaded OS and the hardware configuration are specific to the notebook, so you can rely on the notebook's manufacturer for support more than you can for a desktop PC. Sometimes a notebook is designed so that the hard drive can be replaced or upgraded without violating warranties. See the notebook documentation for details. For questions about supporting a notebook that are not answered in the documentation, see the Web site of the notebook manufacturer. Some popular manufacturers of notebooks and their Web sites are listed in Table 27-4.

27

Table 27-4   Notebook manufacturers

Manufacturer	Web site
Acer America	global.acer.com
ARM Computer	www.armcomputer.com
Compaq Computer	www.hp.com
Dell Computer	www.dell.com
Gateway	www.gateway.com
Hewlett-Packard	www.hp.com
IBM	www.ibm.com
Micron PC	www.micronpc.com
PC Notebook	www.pcnotebook.com
Sony	www.sonystyle.com/vaio
Toshiba America	www.csd.toshiba.com
WinBook	www.winbook.com

CHAPTER SUMMARY

- The Finder Window in the Mac OS functions somewhat like Explorer or My Computer in Microsoft Windows. It allows you to navigate through the Mac's hierarchical file structure.

- The Mac OS boot process begins with ROM-initiated self-test of hardware components and ends with the loading of the interface after necessary components, including the Mac OS ROM file, enablers, and System folder contents, are loaded.

- The dock at the bottom of the Mac desktop is new to Mac OS X. It provides access to frequently used applications.

❑ The Apple menu contains options that are accessible no matter what application you are in. It is customizable in Mac OS 9 but not in Mac OS X.

❑ There are four ways to launch an application on the Mac: double-click its icon, choose it from Recent Applications under Recent Items on the Apple menu, double-click the icon of a file associated with it, and drag a document icon to the application icon.

❑ Use the Display window, accessible from the System Preferences window, to change and monitor settings such as resolution, contrast, brightness, and geometry. Other system settings can also be accessed from System Preferences.

❑ The Drive Setup and Disk First Aid utilities, which are separate in Mac OS 9, have been combined into the Disk Utility in Mac OS X. This utility and other system tools are accessible in the Utilities folder, which is located under Applications.

❑ Macs can recognize, format, and support most IDE (Integrated Device Electronics) and SCSI (Small Computer System Interface) hard drives.

❑ The main file systems available for Mac are HFS and HFS+, but you can also mount FAT16, FAT32, and NTFS volumes on a Mac.

❑ Linux is based on Unix and uses many of the same commands.

❑ The default shell for Linux is the Bash shell.

❑ The system administrator for a Linux computer has root privileges and can access all the functions of the OS, support installations, manage backups, and make changes to system configuration.

❑ The root directory is the top level in the Linux file structure. The directory for each user is their /home directory, and unless a user has the root account, he or she is automatically in his or her home directory after logging on to the system.

❑ All commands in Linux and Unix are case sensitive. For example, in some of the text-editing commands, the same letter in lowercase and in uppercase can mean two different things.

❑ The vi editor is a text editor in Linux that runs in insert mode and command mode, allowing you to enter text and enter commands to manipulate that text.

❑ GUI interfaces for Linux are called window managers. One popular Linux window manager is GNOME.

❑ Notebook computers are designed for travel. They use the same technology as PCs, with modifications for space, portability, and power conservation. A notebook will generally cost more than a PC with the same specifications.

❑ When supporting notebooks, pay careful attention to what the warranty allows you to change on the computer.

❑ Windows 98 notebook computer features include Multilink Channel Aggregation, ACPI and APM, improved support for and management of PC cards, and the Briefcase.

❑ Windows 2000 notebook features support high-end notebooks better than Windows 9x and include offline files, improved battery support, hot-swapping, and folder redirection.

❑ A notebook can be powered by its battery pack or by an AC adapter connected to a power source.

❐ Windows XP notebook support includes the ability to create hardware profiles and power schemes that manage the computer's attached devices and its power settings differently depending on whether the computer is connected to a port replicator or not.

❐ Notebook settings and procedures vary more widely from model to model than with desktop computers. Check the manufacturer's documentation and Web site for information specific to your notebook model.

KEY TERMS

allocation blocks
Apple menu
block
boot blocks
Briefcase
catalog tree
command mode
Control Panels folder
directory structure
Disk First Aid .
Disk Utility
dock
docking station
Drive Setup
enabler file
Extensions folder
extents

extents tree
Finder window
hardware profiles
HFS (Hierarchical File System)
HFS+
insert mode
laptop computer
Library
loopback device
Mac OS Extended Format
Mac OS ROM file
Mac OS Standard Format
notebook
pixel

port replicator
power scheme
PRAM (parameter RAM)
redirection symbol
resolution
root account
root directory
root privileges
System file
System folder
vi editor
volume bit map
volume information block
window manager

27

APPENDIX

A

ERROR MESSAGES AND THEIR MEANINGS

The following table of error messages and their meanings can help when you are diagnosing computer problems. For other error messages, consult your motherboard or computer documentation.

Error Message	Meaning of the Error Message and What to Do
Bad sector writing or reading to drive	Sector markings on the disk may be fading. Try ScanDisk or reformat the disk.
Bad command or file not found	The OS command just executed cannot be interpreted, or the OS cannot find the program file specified in the command line. Check the spelling of the filename and, for DOS or when working from a Windows startup disk, check that the path to the program file has been given to the OS.
Beeps during POST	Before the video is checked, during POST, the ROM BIOS communicates error messages with a series of beeps. Each BIOS manufacturer has its own beep codes, but the following are examples of some BIOS codes. For specific beep codes for your motherboard, see the Web site of the motherboard or BIOS manufacturer.
One single beep followed by three, four, or five beeps	Motherboard problems, possibly with DMA, CMOS setup chip, timer, or system bus.
Two beeps	The POST numeric code is displayed on the monitor.
Two beeps followed by three, four, or five beeps	First 64K of RAM has errors.
Three beeps followed by three, four, or five beeps	Keyboard controller failed or video controller failed.
Four beeps followed by two, three, or four beeps	Problem with serial or parallel ports, system timer, or time of day.
Continuous beeps	Problem with power supply.
Configuration/CMOS error	Setup information does not agree with the actual hardware the computer found during boot. May be caused by a bad or weak battery or by changing hardware without changing setup. Check setup for errors.

Error Message	Meaning of the Error Message and What to Do
Insufficient memory	This error happens under Windows when too many applications are open. Close some applications. A reboot may help.
Hard drive not found	The OS cannot locate the hard drive, or the controller card is not responding.
Fixed disk error	The PC cannot find the hard drive that setup told it to expect. Check cables, connections, power supply, and setup information.
Incorrect DOS version	When you execute a DOS external command, the OS looks for a program file with the same name as the command. It finds that this file belongs to a different version of the OS than the one that is now running. Use the Setver command in Autoexec.bat.
Invalid drive setup tells specification	The PC is unable to find a hard drive or a floppy drive that setup told it to expect. Look for errors in setup, or for a corrupted partition table on the hard drive.
Invalid or missing the disk Command.com	This may be caused by a nonbooting disk in drive A. Remove and boot from drive C. Command.com on drive C may have been erased, or the path could not be found.
No boot device available	The hard drive is not formatted, or the format is corrupted, and there is no disk in drive A. Boot from a floppy and examine your hard drive for corruption.
Non-system disk or disk error	Command.com or one of two OS hidden files is missing from the disk in drive A or the hard drive. Remove the disk in drive A and boot from the hard drive. Use the SYS command to restore system files.
Not ready reading drive A: Abort, Retry, Fail?	The disk in drive A is missing, is not formatted, or is corrupted. Try another disk
Numeric codes during POST	Sometimes numeric codes are used to communicate errors at POST. Some examples for IBM XT/AT error codes include:
Code in the 100 range	Motherboard errors
Code in the 200 range	RAM errors
Code in the 300 range	Keyboard errors
Code in the 500 range	Video controller errors
Code in the 600 range	Floppy drive errors
Code in the 700 range	Coprocessor errors
Code in the 900 range	Parallel port errors
Code in the 1100–1200 range	Async (communications adapter) errors
Code in the 1300 range	Game controller or joystick errors
Code in the 1700 range	Hard drive errors
Code in the 6000 range	SCSI device or network card errors
Code in the 7300 range	Floppy drive errors

Error Message	Meaning of the Error Message and What to Do
Track 0 bad, disk not usable	This usually occurs when you attempt to format a floppy disk using the wrong format type. Check the disk type and compare to the type specified in the format command.
Write-protect error writing drive A:	Let the computer write to the disk by setting the switch on a 3½-inch disk or removing the tape from a 5½-inch disk.
Missing operating system, error loading operating system	The MBR is unable to locate or read the OS boot sector on the active partition, or there is a translation problem on large drives. Boot from a floppy and examine the hard drive file system for corruption.
Unknown error at POST	See the Web site of the system BIOS manufacturer: • AMI BIOS: *www.ami.com* • Award BIOS and Phoenix BIOS: *www.phoenix.com* • Compaq: *www.compaq.com* • Dell: *www.dell.com* • IBM: *www.ibm.com*
Error in Config.sys line xx	There is a problem loading a device driver or with the syntax of a command line. Check the command line for errors. Verify that the driver files are in the right directory. Reinstall the driver files.
Himem.sys not loaded, missing or corrupt Himem.sys	Himem.sys is corrupted, not in the right directory, or not the right version for the currently loading OS. Verify Himem.sys.

APPENDIX

B

INTERRUPT VECTORS

Most microcomputer activity is interrupt-driven. This means that the CPU performs a task in response to an interrupt. Hardware, software, or the CPU itself can initiate an interrupt. An interrupt initiated by the CPU is called an "exception," and most often is the result of a problem or error, such as when the CPU is instructed to divide by zero.

Hardware interrupts begin when the BIOS controlling the hardware device raises its IRQ line. The interrupt controller receives the IRQ and signals the CPU that a hardware interrupt has occurred. The CPU responds by signaling to the interrupt controller that it will process the interrupt. The interrupt controller or the hardware BIOS then sends an interrupt value to the CPU. This interrupt value is used by the CPU to point to a row in the interrupt vector table. This row contains the memory location of the request handler that will service the hardware device. Software can also initiate an interrupt, but does not need or use the IRQ lines to do so, because the software is already running when the interrupt is issued, and so already has the attention of the CPU.

The memory locations listed in the interrupt vector table and the BIOS and device drivers assigned to these memory locations are determined during booting, but can be changed later. Software can make changes to the interrupt vector table to create its own user software interrupts, which it can later use to gain access to hardware devices. This ability of software to alter the interrupt vector table is sometimes used by a virus to replicate itself. Whether the CPU, hardware, or software initiates the interrupt, the same interrupt values are used, which are listed in the following table. These functions for the interrupt values are not universal; there are some variations.

Interrupt Value	Function
0	Divide by zero (exception interrupt)
1	Single step
2	Nonmaskable interrupt
3	Breakpoint instruction
4	Overflow
5	Print screen
6	Invalid opcode
7	Math coprocessor not present
8	System timer interrupt (IRQ 0)
9	Keyboard data ready (IRQ 1)
A	Reserved (IRQ 2) cascade from slave interrupt controller
B, C	Hardware interrupt for serial communication
D	Parallel port hardware interrupt (IRQ 5, LPT 2)
E	Floppy controller hardware interrupt (IRQ 6)
F	Printer hardware interrupt (IRQ 7, LPT 1)
10	Software interrupt to use video
11	Equipment check call
12	Memory check call
13	Software interrupt to use hard drive
14	Software interrupt to use serial port
15	Not used
16	Keyboard software interrupt
17	Software interrupt to use printer
18	ROM basic entry call
19	Bootstrap loader
1A	Time of day call
1B	Get control on keyboard break
1C	Get control on timer interrupt
1D	Pointer to video initialization table
1E	Pointer to floppy disk parameter table
1F	Pointer to graphics character generator
20–3F	Used by DOS
40	Reserved
41	Fixed disk parameter table
46	Fixed disk parameter table
47–5F	Reserved
60–67	Reserved for user software interrupts

Interrupt Value	Function
68–6F	Not used
70	Real-time clock hardware interrupt
72	Reserved (IRQ 10)
73	Reserved (IRQ 11)
74	Reserved (IRQ 12)
76	Fixed disk controller (IRQ 14)
77	Reserved (IRQ 15)
80–F0	Used by BASIC programs and interpreter
F1–FF	Not used

B

C

THE PROFESSIONAL PC TECHNICIAN

As a professional PC technician, you can manage your career by staying abreast of new technology and striving for top professional certifications. In addition, you should maintain excellent customer relationships, behave with professionalism, and seek opportunities for joining professional organizations. As you know, PC technicians provide service to customers over the phone, in person on-site, and sometimes in a shop where they have little customer contact. While each setting poses specific challenges, almost all of the recommendations made in this appendix apply across the board.

WHAT CUSTOMERS WANT: BEYOND TECHNICAL KNOW-HOW

Probably the most significant indication that a PC technician is doing a good job is that his or her customers are consistently satisfied. You should provide excellent service and treat customers as you would want to be treated in a similar situation. One of the most important ways to achieve customer satisfaction is to do your best by being prepared, both technically and nontechnically. Being prepared includes knowing what customers want, what they don't like, and what they expect from a PC technician.

Your customers can be "internal" (you both work for the same company) or "external" (your customers come to you or your company for service). Customers can be highly technical or technically naive, represent a large company or simply own a home PC, be prompt or slow at paying their bills, want only the best (and be willing to pay for it) or be searching for bargain service, be friendly and easy to work with or demanding and condescending. In each situation, the key to success is always the same: don't allow circumstances or personalities to affect your personal commitment to excellence.

Listed in this section are some traits that distinguish one competent technician from another in the eyes of the customer.

- *Have a positive and helpful attitude.* A positive and helpful attitude helps to establish good customer relationships.

- *Be dependable.* Customers appreciate those who do as they say. If you promise to be back at 10:00 the next morning, be back at 10:00 the next morning. If you cannot keep your appointment, never ignore your promise. Call, apologize, let the customer know what happened, and reschedule your appointment.

- *Be customer-focused.* When you're working with or talking to a customer, focus on him or her. Make it your job to satisfy this person, not just your organization, your boss, your bank account, or the customer's boss.

- *Be credible.* Convey confidence to your customers. Being credible means being technically competent and knowing how to do your job well, but a credible technician also knows when the job is beyond his or her level of expertise and when to ask for help.

- *Maintain integrity and honesty.* Don't try to hide your mistakes, not with your customer or with your boss. Everyone makes mistakes, but don't compound them with a lack of integrity. Accept responsibility and do what you can to correct the error.

- *Know the law with respect to your work.* For instance, observe the laws concerning the use of software. Don't use or install pirated software.

- *Act professionally.* Customers want a technician to look and behave professionally. Dress appropriately for the environment. Consider yourself a guest at the customer site.

- *Perform your work in a professional manner.* If a customer is angry, allow the customer to vent, keeping your own professional distance. (You do, however, have the right to expect a customer not to talk to you in an abusive way.)

SUPPORT CALLS: PROVIDING GOOD SERVICE

Customers want good service. Even though each customer is different and might expect different results, the following characteristics consistently constitute good service in the eyes of most customers.

- The technician responds and completes the work within a reasonable time.

- For on-site visits, the technician is prepared for the service call.

- The work is done right the first time.

- The price for the work is reasonable and competitive.

- The technician exhibits good interpersonal skills.

- If the work extends beyond a brief on-site visit or phone call, the technician keeps the customer informed about the progress of the work.

C

Planning for Good Service

Whether you support PCs on the phone, on-site, or in a shop, you need a plan to follow when you approach a service call. This section surveys the entire service situation, from the first contact with the customer to closing the call. Follow these general guidelines when supporting computers and their users:

- Almost every support project starts with a phone call. Follow company policies to obtain the specific information you should take when answering an initial call.

- Don't assume that an on-site visit is necessary until you have asked questions to identify the problem and asked the caller to check and try some simple things while on the phone with you. For example, the customer can check cable connections, power, and monitor settings, and can look for POST error messages.

- Be familiar with your company's customer service policies. You might need to refer questions about warranties, licenses, documentation, or procedures to other support personnel or customer relations personnel. Your organization might not want you to answer some questions, such as questions about upcoming releases of software or new products, or questions about your personal or company experience with supporting particular hardware or software.

- After reviewing your company's service policies, begin troubleshooting. Take notes, and then interview the customer about the problem so you understand it thoroughly. Have the customer reproduce the problem, and carefully note each step taken and its results. This process gives you clues about the problem and about the technical proficiency of the customer, which helps you know how to communicate with the customer.

- Search for answers. If the answers to specific questions or problems are not evident, become a researcher. Learn to use online documentation, expert systems, and other resources that your company provides.

- Use your troubleshooting skills. Isolate the problem. Check for user errors. What works and what doesn't work? What has changed since the system last worked? Reduce the system to its essentials. Check the simple things first. Use the troubleshooting guidelines throughout this book to help you think of approaches to test and try.

- If you have given the problem your best, but still haven't solved it, ask for help. You learn when to ask for help from experience. Once you have made a reasonable effort to help, and it seems clear that you are unlikely to be successful, don't waste a customer's time.

- After a call, create a written record to build your own knowledge base. Record the initial symptoms of the problem, the source of the problem you actually discovered, how you made that discovery, and how the problem was finally solved. File your documentation according to symptoms or according to solutions.

Making an On-site Service Call

When a technician makes an on-site service call, customers expect him or her to have both technical and interpersonal skills. Prepare for a service call by reviewing information given you by whoever took the call. Know the problem you are going to address; what computer, software, and hardware need servicing, and the urgency of the situation. Arrive with a complete set of equipment appropriate to the visit, which might include a tool kit, flashlight, multimeter, grounding strap and mat, and bootable disks that have been scanned for viruses.

Set a realistic time for the appointment (one that you can expect to keep) and arrive on time. When you arrive at the customer's site, greet the customer in a friendly manner. Use Mr. or Ms. and last names rather than first names when addressing the customer, unless you are certain that the customer expects you to use first names. The first thing you should do is listen; save the paperwork for later.

As you work, be as unobtrusive as possible. Don't make a big mess. Keep your tools and papers out of the customer's way. Don't use the phone or sit in the customer's desk chair without permission. If the customer needs to attend to his or her own work while you are present, do whatever is necessary to accommodate that.

Keep the customer informed. Once you have collected enough information, explain to the customer what the problem is and what you must do to fix it, giving as many details as the customer wants. When a customer must make a choice, state the customer's options in a way that does not unfairly favor the solution that makes the most money for you as the technician or for your company.

After you have solved the problem:

- Allow the customer time to be fully satisfied that all is working before you close the call. Does the printer work? Print a test page. Does the network connection work? Can the customer log on to the network and access data on it?

- If you changed anything on the PC after you booted it, reboot one more time to make sure that you have not caused a problem with the boot.

- Review the service call with the customer. Summarize the instructions and explanations you have given during the call. This is an appropriate time to fill out your paperwork and explain to the customer what you have written.

- Explain preventive maintenance to the customer (such as deleting temporary files from the hard drive or cleaning the mouse). Most customers don't have preventive maintenance contracts for their PCs and appreciate the time you take to show them how they can take better care of their computers.

Phone Support

When someone calls asking for support, you must control the call, especially at the beginning. Follow these steps at the beginning of a service call:

- Identify yourself and your organization. (Follow the guidelines of your employer as to what to say.)

- Ask for and write down the name and phone number of the caller. Ask for spelling if necessary. If your help desk supports businesses, get the name of the business that the caller represents.

- Your company might require that you obtain a licensing or warranty number to determine if the customer is entitled to receive your support free of charge, or that you obtain a credit card number, if the customer is paying by the call. Get whatever information you need at this point to determine that you should be the one to provide service, before you start to address the problem.

- Open up the conversation for the caller to describe his or her problem.

Providing phone support requires more interaction with customers than any other type of PC support. To give clear instructions, you must be able to visualize what the customer is seeing at his or her PC. Patience is required if the customer must be told each key to press or command button to click. Help-desk support requires excellent communication skills, good phone manners, and lots of patience. As your help-desk skills improve, you will learn to think through the process as though you were sitting in front of the PC yourself. Drawing diagrams and taking notes as you talk can be very helpful.

If you spend many hours on the phone at a help desk, use a headset instead of a regular phone to reduce strain on your ears and neck. If you are accidentally disconnected, call back immediately. Don't eat or drink while on the phone. If you must put callers on hold, tell them how long it will be before you get back to them. Don't complain about your job, your company, or other companies or products to your customers. A little small talk is okay and is sometimes beneficial in easing a tense situation, but keep it upbeat and positive. As with on-site service calls, let the user make sure that all is working before you close the phone call. If you end the call too soon and the problem is not completely resolved, the customer can be frustrated, especially if it is difficult to contact you again.

When the Customer Is Not Knowledgeable

A help-desk call is the most difficult situation to handle when a customer is not knowledgeable about how to use a computer. When on-site, you can put a PC in good repair without depending on a customer to help you, but when you are trying to solve a problem over the phone, with a customer as your only eyes, ears, and hands, a computer-illiterate user can present a very challenging situation. Here are some tips for handling this situation:

- Don't use computer jargon while talking. For example, instead of saying, "Open Windows Explorer," say, "Using your mouse, right-click on the Start button and select Explore from the menu."

- Don't ask the customer to do something that might destroy settings or files without first having him or her back them up carefully. If you think the customer can't handle what you need done, then ask for some on-site help.

- Frequently ask the customer what he or she sees on the screen to help you track the keystrokes and action.

- Follow along at your own PC. It's easier to direct the customer, keystroke by keystroke, if you are doing the same things.

- Give the customer plenty of opportunity to ask questions.

- Compliment the customer whenever you can, to help the customer gain confidence.

- If you determine that the customer cannot help you solve the problem without a lot of coaching, you may need to tactfully request that the caller have someone with more experience call you.

 TIP When solving computer problems in an organization other than your own, check with technical support instead of working only with the PC user. The user may not be aware of policies that have been set on the PC to prevent changes to the OS, hardware, or applications software.

When the Customer Is Overly Confident

Sometimes a customer is proud of what he or she knows about computers. This type of customer may want to give advice, take charge of a call, withhold information that he or she thinks you don't need to know, or execute commands at the computer without letting you know, so that you don't have enough information to follow along. A situation like this must be handled with tact and respect for the customer. Here are a few tips:

- When you can, compliment the customer concerning his or her knowledge, experience, or insight.

- Ask the customer's advice. Say something like, "What do you think the problem is?" (However, don't ask this question of customers who are not confident, because they most likely don't have the answer and might lose confidence in you.)

- Slow the conversation down. You can say, "Please slow down. You're moving too fast for me to follow. Help me understand."

- Don't back off from using problem-solving skills. You must still have the customer check the simple things, but direct the conversation with tact. For example, you can say, "I know you've probably already gone over these simple things, but could we just do them again together?"

- Be careful not to accuse the customer of making a mistake.

- Use technical language in a way that conveys that you expect the customer to understand you.

C

When the Customer Complains

When you are on-site or on the phone, a customer might complain to you about your organization, products, or service, or the service and product of another company. Consider the complaint to be helpful feedback that can lead to a better product or service and better customer relationships. Here are a few suggestions on how to handle complaints and customer anger:

- Be an active listener, and let the customer know that he or she is not being ignored. Look for the underlying problem. Don't take the complaint or the anger personally.

- Give the customer a little time to vent, and apologize when you can. Then start the conversation from the beginning, asking questions, taking notes, and solving problems. If this helps, don't spend a lot of time finding out exactly whom the customer dealt with and what exactly happened to upset him or her.

- Don't be defensive. It's better to leave the customer with the impression that you and your company are listening and willing to admit mistakes.

- If the customer is complaining about a product or service that is not from your company, don't start off by saying, "That's not our problem." Instead, listen to the customer complain. Don't appear as though you don't care.

- If the complaint is against you or your product, identify the underlying problem if you can. Ask questions and take notes. Then pass these notes on to whoever in your organization needs to know.

- Sometimes simply making progress or reducing the problem to a manageable state for the customer reduces his or her anxiety. As you are talking to a customer, summarize what you have both agreed on or observed so far in the conversation.

- Point out ways that you think communication could be improved. For example, you might say, "I'm sorry, but I'm having trouble understanding what you want. Could you please slow down, and let's take this one step at a time."

When the Customer Does Not Want to End a Phone Call

Some customers like to talk and don't want to end a phone call. In this situation, when you have finished the work and are ready to hang up, you can ease the caller into the end of the call. Ask if there is anything that needs more explanation. Briefly summarize the main points of the call, and then say something like, "That about does it. Call if you need more help." Be silent about new issues. Answer only with "yes" or "no." Don't take the bait by engaging in a new topic. Don't get frustrated. As a last resort, you can say, "I'm sorry, but I must go now."

When You Can't Solve the Problem

You are not going to solve every computer problem you encounter. Knowing how to escalate a problem to those higher in the support chain is one of the first things you should learn on a new job. When escalation involves the customer, generally follow these guidelines:

- Before you escalate, first ask knowledgeable coworkers for suggestions for solving the problem, which might save you and your customer the time and effort it takes to escalate it.

- Know your company's policy as to how to escalate. What documents do you fill out? Who gets them? Do you remain the responsible "support" party, or does the person now addressing the problem become the new contact? Are you expected to still keep in touch with the customer and the problem, or are you totally out of the picture?

- Document the escalation. It's very important to include the detailed steps necessary to reproduce the problem, which can save the next support person lots of time.

- Pass the problem on according to the proper channels of your organization. This might mean a phone call, an online entry in a database, or an e-mail message.

- Tell the customer that you are passing the problem on to someone who is more experienced and has access to more extensive resources. In most cases, the person who receives the escalation will immediately contact the customer and assume responsibility for the problem. However, you should follow through, at least to the point where you know that the new person and the customer have made contact.

- If you check back with the customer only to find out that the other support person has not called or followed through to the customer's satisfaction, don't lay blame or point fingers. Just do whatever you can to help, within your company guidelines. Your call to the customer will go a long way toward helping in the situation.

RECORDKEEPING AND INFORMATION TOOLS

If you work for a service organization, it will probably have most of the tools you will need to do your job, including forms, online recordkeeping, procedures, and manuals. In some cases, help-desk support personnel may have software to help them do their jobs, such as programs that support the remote control of customers' PCs (one example is pcAnywhere), an online help utility, or a problem-solving tool developed specifically for their help desk.

There are several types of resources, records, and information tools that can help you with your work supporting PCs, such as the following:

- Specific software or hardware that you support must be available to you to test, observe, and study, and to use to re-create a customer's problem whenever possible.

- You should have a copy of—and be familiar with—the same documentation that the user sees.

- Hardware and software products generally have more technical documentation than just a user manual. This technical documentation should be made available to you by a company when you support its product.

- Online help targeted specifically to field technicians and help-desk technicians is often available for a product. This online help will probably include a search engine that works by topics, words, error messages, and the like.

- Expert systems software is designed and written to help solve problems. It uses databases of known facts and rules to simulate human experts' reasoning and decision-making processes. Expert systems for PC technicians work by posing questions about a problem, to be answered either by the technician or by the customer. The response to each question will trigger another question from the software, until the expert system arrives at a possible solution or solutions. Many expert systems are "intelligent," meaning that the system will record your input and use it in subsequent sessions to select more questions to ask and approaches to try.

- Call tracking can be done online or on paper. Most organizations will have a call-tracking system that tracks (1) the date, time, and length of help-desk or on-site calls, (2) causes of and solutions to problems already addressed, (3) who did what, and when, and (4) how each call was officially resolved. Call-tracking software or documents can also be vehicles used to escalate calls when necessary and to track the escalation.

PROFESSIONAL ORGANIZATIONS AND CERTIFICATIONS

The work done by PC technicians has been viewed as a profession only within the past few years. The one most significant certifying organization for PC technicians is the Computing Technology Industry Association (CompTIA, pronounced "comp-TEE-a"). CompTIA sponsors the A+ Certification Program and manages the A+ Service Technician Certification Examination, which measures the knowledge of job tasks and behavior expected of entry-level technicians. To become certified, you must pass two test modules: the A+ Core Hardware exam and the A+ Operating System Technologies exam. A+ Certification is gaining increasing industry recognition, so it should be your first choice for certification as a PC technician. As evidence of this industry recognition, these companies now include A+ Certification in their requirements for employment:

- Compaq Computer Corporation requires that all work done under its warranty agreements be done by A+ Certified personnel.

- Digital Equipment Corporation requires A+ Certification for all international and domestic warranty work.

- ENTEX Information Services requires that all service employees have A+ Certification.

- GE Capital Services requires that all service employees have A+ Certification one year after hire.

- Okidata requires that all field service technicians have A+ Certification.

- Packard Bell requires all employees to be A+ certified within 90 days of hire.

Some other organizations where A+ Certification is mandatory are Aetna U.S. Healthcare; BancTec, Inc.; Computer Data, Inc.; Computer Sciences Corp.; Delta Airlines; Dow Jones & Company; the FBI, the U.S. Department of Justice; Gateway 2000; New Horizons; Tandy Corporation; TSS IBM; US Airways; and Wang.

CompTIA has over 6,000 members, which include every major company that manufactures, distributes, or publishes computer-related products and services. For more information about CompTIA and A+ Certification, see the CompTIA Web site at *www.comptia.org*.

Other certifications are more vendor-specific. For example, Microsoft, Novell, and Cisco offer certifications to use and support their products. These are excellent choices for additional certifications when your career plan is to focus on these products.

Why Certification?

Many people work as PC technicians without any formal classroom training or certification. However, by having certification or an advanced technical degree, you prove to yourself, your customers, and your employers that you are prepared to do the work and are committed to being educated in your chosen profession. Certification and advanced degrees serve as recognized proof of competence and achievement, improve your job opportunities, create a higher level of customer confidence, and often qualify you for other training and/or degrees.

In addition to becoming certified and seeking advanced degrees, the professional PC technician should also stay abreast of new technology. Helpful resources include on-the-job training, books, magazines, the Internet, trade shows, interaction with colleagues, seminars, and workshops. Probably the best-known trade show is COMDEX and Windows World, where you can view the latest technology, hear industry leaders speak, and network with vast numbers of organizations and people. For more information about COMDEX and Windows World, see the Web site *www.comdex.com*.

PROTECTING SOFTWARE COPYRIGHTS

As a computer support technician, you will be faced with the legal issues and practices surrounding the distribution of software. When someone purchases software from a software vendor, that person has only purchased a license for the software, which is the right to use the software, and does not legally *own* the software; he or she therefore does not have the right to distribute the software. The right to copy the work, called a copyright, belongs to the creator of the work or others to whom he or she has transferred this right.

As a PC technician you will be called upon to install, upgrade, and customize software. You need to know where your responsibility lies in upholding the law, especially as it applies to software copyrights. Copyrights are intended to legally protect the intellectual property rights of organizations or individuals to creative works, whether they be books, images, or, in the case of this discussion, software. While the originator of a creative work is the original owner of a copyright; the copyright can be transferred from one entity to another.

The Federal Copyright Act of 1976 was designed in part to protect software copyrights by requiring that only legally obtained copies of software be used; the law also allows for one backup copy of software to be made. Making unauthorized copies of original software violates the Federal Copyright Act of 1976, and is called software piracy, or, more officially, software copyright infringement. Making a copy of software and then selling it or giving it away is a violation of the law. Because it is so easy to do this, and because so many people do it, many people don't realize that it's illegal. Normally only the person who violated the copyright law is liable for infringement; however, in some cases, an employer or supervisor is also held responsible, even when the copies were made without the employer's knowledge. The Business Software Alliance (a membership organization of software manufacturers and vendors) has estimated that 26 percent of the business software in the United States is obtained illegally.

Site licensing, whereby a company can purchase the right to use multiple copies of software, is a popular way for companies to provide software to employees. With this type of license, companies can distribute software to PCs from network servers or execute software directly off the server. Read the licensing agreement of any software to determine the terms of distribution.

One of two associations committed to the prevention of software piracy is the Software & Information Industry Association, a nonprofit organization that educates the public and enforces copyright laws. Their Web address is *www.siia.net*, and their antipiracy hotline is 1-800-388-7478. Another organization is the Business Software Alliance, which manages the BSA Anti-Piracy Hotline at 1-888-NOPIRACY. The BSA can also be reached at their e-mail address: software@bsa.org. Their Web site is *www.bsa.org*. These associations are made up of hundreds of software manufacturers and publishers in North and Latin America, Europe, and Asia. They promote software raids on large and small companies, and, in the U.S., they receive the cooperation of the United States government to prosecute offenders.

What Does the Law Say?

The Federal Copyright Act of 1976 protects the exclusive rights of copyright holders. It gives legal users of software the right to make one backup copy. Other rights are based on what the copyright holder allows. In 1990, the United States Congress passed the Software Rental Amendment Act, which prevents the renting, leasing, lending, or sharing of software without the expressed written permission of the copyright holder. In 1992, Congress instituted criminal penalties for software copyright infringement, which include imprisonment for up to five years and/or fines of up to $250,000 for the unlawful reproduction or distribution of 10 or more copies of software.

What Are Your Responsibilities under the Law?

Your first responsibility as an individual user is to use only software that has been purchased or licensed for your use. As an employee of a company that has a site license to use multiple copies of the software, your responsibility is to comply with the license agreement. It is also your responsibility to purchase only legitimate software. Purchasers of counterfeit or copied software face the risk of corrupted files, virus-infected disks, inadequate documentation, and lack of technical support and upgrades, as well as the legal penalties for using pirated software.

D

ASCII CHARACTER SET AND ANSI.SYS

ASCII (American Standard Code for Information Interchange) is a coding system that is used by personal computers to store character data, such as letters of the alphabet, numerals, some symbols, and certain control characters. There are 128 characters defined by the standard ASCII character set. Each ASCII character is assigned an 8-bit code that converts to a decimal number from 0 to 127, although in the standard set, the first bit is always 0. The first 31 values, which are nonprintable codes, are used for control characters and can be used to send commands to printers or other peripheral devices. Files that store data as ASCII characters are sometimes called ASCII files, ASCII text files, or simply text files. ASCII can be read by most editors and word processors and is considered the universal file format for personal computers. Autoexec.bat is one example of an ASCII file.

In addition to the standard ASCII character set, some manufacturers use an extended ASCII character set that is specific to their equipment and is not necessarily compatible with other computers. The extended ASCII character sets use the codes 128 through 255.

The American National Standards Institute (ANSI), an organization responsible for many computer standards, developed an extended character set using codes 128 through 255 that includes special characters such as letters in an international alphabet and accents, currency symbols, and fractions. ANSI has also defined a series of control codes that can be used to control monitors. For example, a sequence of control codes can clear a monitor, cause characters to be displayed upside down, or put color on a DOS screen. Ansi.sys is a device driver that, when loaded in a DOS environment, provides these monitor and keyboard functions. Ansi.sys is loaded from the Config.sys file with this command:

```
Device=C:\DOS\Ansi.sys
```

Some DOS programs need Ansi.sys loaded in order to interpret the extended character set entered from the keyboard, display these characters on the screen, and control the monitor in other ways.

Table D-1 lists the standard ASCII character set. Note that items 2 through 32, the control characters, and the extended ASCII character set are not included.

Table D-1 Standard ASCII character set

Item Number	Symbol	Meaning	ASCII in Decimal Representation	ASCII in Binary Representation	ASCII in Hex Representation
1	.	Null	0	0000 0000	0
33	b/	Space	32	0010 0000	20
34	!	Exclamation point	33	0010 0001	21
35	"	Quotation mark	34	0010 0010	22
36	#	Number sign	35	0010 0011	23
37	$	Dollar sign	36	0010 0100	24
38	%	Percent sign	37	0010 0101	25
39	&	Ampersand	38	0010 0110	26
40	'	Apostrophe, prime sign	39	0010 0111	27
41	(	Opening parenthesis	40	0010 1000	28
42	)	Closing parenthesis	41	0010 1001	29
43	*	Asterisk	42	0010 1010	2A
44	+	Plus sign	43	0010 1011	2B
45	,	Comma	44	0010 1100	2C
46	-	Hyphen, minus sign	45	0010 1101	2D
47	.	Period, decimal point	46	0010 1110	2E
48	/	Slant	47	0010 1111	2F
49	0		48	0011 0000	30
50	1		49	0011 0001	31
51	2		50	0011 0010	32
52	3		51	0011 0011	33
53	4		52	0011 0100	34
54	5		53	0011 0101	35
55	6		54	0011 0110	36
56	7		55	0011 0111	37
57	8		56	0011 1000	38
58	9		57	0011 1001	39
59	:	Colon	58	0011 1010	3A
60	;	Semicolon	59	0011 1011	3B

Table D-1   Standard ASCII character set (continued)

Item Number	Symbol	Meaning	ASCII in Decimal Representation	ASCII in Binary Representation	ASCII in Hex Representation
61	<	Less than sign	60	0011 1100	3C
62	=	Equals sign	61	0011 1101	3D
63	>	Greater than sign	62	0011 1110	3E
64	?	Question mark	63	0011 1111	3F
65	@	Commercial at sign	64	0100 0000	40
66	A		65	0100 0001	41
67	B		66	0100 0010	42
68	C		67	0100 0011	43
69	D		68	0100 0100	44
70	E		69	0100 0101	45
71	F		70	0100 0110	46
72	G		71	0100 0111	47
73	H		72	0100 1000	48
74	I		73	0100 1001	49
75	J		74	0100 1010	4A
76	K		75	0100 1011	4B
77	L		76	0100 1100	4C
78	M		77	0100 1101	4D
79	N		78	0100 1110	4E
80	O		79	0100 1111	4F
81	P		80	0101 0000	50
82	Q		81	0101 0001	51
83	R		82	0101 0010	52
84	S		83	0101 0011	53
85	T		84	0101 0100	54
86	U		85	0101 0101	55
87	V		86	0101 0110	56
88	W		87	0101 0111	57
89	X		88	0101 1000	58
90	Y		89	0101 1001	59
91	Z		90	0101 1010	5A
92	[	Opening bracket	91	0101 1011	5B
93	\	Reverse slant	92	0101 1100	5C
94	]	Closing bracket	93	0101 1101	5D

D

Table D-1   Standard ASCII character set (continued)

Item Number	Symbol	Meaning	ASCII in Decimal Representation	ASCII in Binary Representation	ASCII in Hex Representation
95	^	Caret	94	0101 1110	5E
96	_	Underscore	95	0101 1111	5F
97	`	Acute accent	96	0110 0000	60
98	a		97	0110 0001	61
99	b		98	0110 0010	62
100	c		99	0110 0011	63
101	d		100	0110 0100	64
102	e		101	0110 0101	65
103	f		102	0110 0110	66
104	g		103	0110 0111	67
105	h		104	0110 1000	68
106	i		105	0110 1001	69
107	j		106	0110 1010	6A
108	k		107	0110 1011	6B
109	l		108	0110 1100	6C
110	m		109	0110 1101	6D
111	n		110	0110 1110	6E
112	o		111	0110 1111	6F
113	p		112	0111 0000	70
114	q		113	0111 0001	71
115	r		114	0111 0010	72
116	s		115	0111 0011	73
117	t		116	0111 0100	74
118	u		117	0111 0101	75
119	v		118	0111 0110	76
120	w		119	0111 0111	77
121	x		120	0111 1000	78
122	y		121	0111 1001	79
123	z		122	0111 1010	7A
124	{	Opening brace	123	0111 1011	7B
125	I	Split vertical bar	124	0111 1100	7C
126	}	Closing brace	125	0111 1101	7D
127	~	Tilde	126	0111 1110	7E
128	Δ	Small triangle	127	0111 1111	7F

E

THE HEXADECIMAL NUMBER SYSTEM AND MEMORY ADDRESSING

Fundamental to understanding how computers work is understanding the number system and the coding system that computers use to store data and communicate with each other. Early attempts to invent an electronic computing device met with disappointing results as long as inventors tried to use our own decimal number system, with the digits 0–9. Then John Atanasoff proposed using a coding system that expressed everything in terms of different sequences of only two numerals: one represented by the presence of a charge and one represented by the absence of a charge. The numbering system that can be supported by the expression of only two numerals is the base 2, sometimes called binary, numbering system, invented by Ada Lovelace many years before, using the two numerals 0 and 1. Under Atanasoff's design, all numbers and other characters would be converted to this binary number system, and all storage, comparisons, and arithmetic would be done using it. Even today, this is one of the basic principles of computers. Every character or number entered into a computer is first converted into a series of 0s and 1s. Many coding schemes and techniques have been invented to manipulate these 0s and 1s, called **bits** for **bi**nary dig**its**.

The most widespread binary coding scheme for microcomputers, which is recognized as the microcomputer standard, is called the ASCII (American Standard Code for Information Interchange) coding system. (Appendix D lists the binary code for the basic 127-character set.) In ASCII, each character is assigned an 8-bit code called a **byte**. Table E-1 lists the terms used in the discussion of how numbers are stored in computers. The byte has become the universal single unit of storage for data in computers everywhere.

Table E-1   Computer terminology

Term	Definition
Bit	A numeral in the binary number system: a 0 or a 1
Byte	8 bits
Kilobyte	1,024 bytes, which is 2^{10}, often rounded to 1,000 bytes
Megabyte	Either 1,024 kilobytes or 1,000 kilobytes, depending on what has come to be standard practice in different situations. For example, when calculating floppy disk capacities, 1 megabyte = 1,000 kilobytes; when calculating hard drive capacity, traditionally, 1 megabyte = 1,024 bytes.
Gigabyte	1,000 megabytes or 1,024 megabytes, depending on what has come to be standard practice in different situations
ASCII	American Standard Code for Information Interchange coding scheme used for microcomputers, which assigns a 7- or 8-bit code to all characters and symbols. See Appendix D for more information.
Hex	Short for hexadecimal. A number system based on 16 values (called base 16), which is explained in detail below. Uses the sixteen numerals 0, 1, 2, 3, 4, 5, 6, 7, 8, 9, A, B, C, D, E, and F. Hex numbers are often followed by a lowercase h to indicate they are in hex (example: 78h).

Computers convert binary data into the hexadecimal number system (shortened to hex system) because it is much less complex for computers to convert binary numbers into hex numbers than into decimal numbers, and it is much easier for human beings to read hex numbers than to read binary numbers. This way, even though the actual processing and inner workings of computers use the binary system, they often display information using the hex system.

Learning to "Think Hex"

One skill a knowledgeable computer support person must have is the ability to read hex numbers and convert hex to decimal and decimal to hex. Once you understand one numbering system (decimal), you can understand any numbering system (including binary and hexadecimal), because they all operate on the same basic principle: place value. So we begin there.

Place Value

A key to understanding place value is to think of a number system as a method of grouping multiple small units together until there are enough of them to be packed into a single larger group, then grouping multiple larger groups together until there are enough of them to form an even larger group, and so on. In our (decimal) number system, once there are 10 units of any group, that group becomes a single unit of the next larger group. So, groups of 10 units are packed into groups of tens; groups of ten tens are packed into groups of hundreds; groups of 10 hundreds are packed into groups of thousands, and so forth.

E

An easy way to understand number systems is to think of the numbers as being packaged for shipping, into boxes, cartons, crates, truckloads, and so on. For the decimal numbering system, consider packing widgets (units) into boxes (tens) which are packed into cartons (100s) which are packed into crates (1000s), and so forth. The same analogy works for binary, decimal, and all other number systems.

Our friend Joe, in Figure E-1, is a widget packer in the shipping department of the ACE Widget Co. Joe can ship single widgets, or he can pack them in boxes, cartons, crates, and truckloads. He can fit three, and only three, widgets to a box; three, and only three, boxes into one carton ($3 \times 3 = 9$ widgets); three, and only three, cartons into one crate ($3 \times 9 = 27$ widgets); and three, and only three, crates into one truck ($3 \times 27 = 81$ widgets). He is not allowed to pack more widgets into boxes, cartons, crates, or truckloads than those specified. Neither is he allowed to send out a box, carton, crate, or truckload that is not completely filled.

1 truckload	1 crate	1 carton	1 box	single
holds 3 crates	holds 3 cartons	holds 3 boxes	holds 3	widgets
(81 widgets)	(27 widgets)	(9 widgets)	widgets	

Figure E-1   Joe in the shipping department groups widgets in singles, boxes, cartons, crates, and truckloads—all in groups of three

Joe receives an order to ship out 197 widgets. How does he ship them? The answer is shown in Figure E-2. Joe sends out 197 widgets grouped into 2 truckloads ($2 \times 81 = 162$ widgets), 1 crate (27 widgets), no cartons, 2 boxes ($2 \times 3 = 6$ widgets), and 2 single widgets. We can write this grouping of widgets as 21022, where the "place values" from left to right are truckloads, crates, cartons, boxes, and units, which in this case are (in decimal) 81 widgets, 27 widgets, 9 widgets, 3 widgets, and single widgets. Notice that each "place value" in our widget-packing system is a multiple of 3, because the widgets are grouped into three before they are packed into boxes; the boxes are grouped into three before they are packed into cartons, and so on. By grouping the widgets into groups of 3s in this manner, we converted the decimal number (base 10) 197 into the ternary number (base 3) 21022. Joe's widget-packing method is a base three, or ternary, system. The numerals in the ternary number system are 0, 1, and 2. When you get to the next value after 2, instead of counting on up to 3, you move one place value to the left and begin again with 1 in that position, which represents 3. So, counting in base 3 goes like this: 0, 1, 2, 10, 11, 12, 20, 21, 22, 100, 101 and so on. This is the same as Joe's never shipping out 3 of any one group unless they are packed together into one larger group. For example, Joe wouldn't ship 3 individual boxes, he would ship one carton.

2 trucks	1 crate	0 cartons	2 boxes	2 singles

Figure E-2   Joe's shipment of 197 widgets: 2 trucks, 1 crate, 0 cartons, 2 boxes, and a group of 2 singles

You can easily apply the widget-packing analogy to another base. If Joe used 10 instead of three, he would be using base ten (decimal) rules. So, numbering systems differ by the different numbers of units they group together. In the hex number system, we group by 16. So, if Joe were shipping in groups of 16, as in Figure E-3, single widgets could be shipped out up to 15, but 16 widgets would make one box. Sixteen boxes would make one carton, which would contain 16×16, or 256, widgets. Sixteen cartons would make one crate, which would contain 16×256, or 4,096, widgets.

Suppose Joe receives an order for 197 widgets to be packed in groups of 16. He will not be able to fill a carton (256 widgets), so he ships out 12 boxes (16 widgets each) and 5 single widgets:

$12 \times 16 = 192$, and $192 + 5 = 197$

1 truckload holds 16 crates (65,536 widgets)	1 crate holds 16 cartons (4,096 widgets)	1 carton holds 16 boxes (256 widgets)	1 box holds 16 widgets	single widgets

Figure E-3   Widgets displayed in truck loads, crates, cartons, boxes, and singles grouped in 16s

You approach an obstacle if you attempt to write the number in hex. How are you going to express 12 boxes and 5 singles? In hex, you need single numerals in hex to represent the numbers 10, 11, 12, 13, 14, and 15 in decimal. Hex uses letters for these numerals. A, B, C, D, E, and F are used for the numbers 10 through 15. Table E-2 shows values expressed in the decimal, hex, and binary numbering systems. In the second column in Table E-2, you are counting in the hex number system. For example, 12 is represented with a C. So you say that Joe packs C boxes and 5 singles. The hex number for decimal 197 is C5 (see Figure E-4).

Table E-2   Decimal, hex, and binary values

Decimal	Hex	Binary	Decimal	Hex	Binary	Decimal	Hex	Binary
0	0	0	14	E	1110	28	1C	11100
1	1	1	15	F	1111	29	1D	11101
2	2	10	16	10	10000	30	1E	11110
3	3	11	17	11	10001	31	1F	11111
4	4	100	18	12	10010	32	20	100000
5	5	101	19	13	10011	33	21	100001
6	6	110	20	14	10100	34	22	100010
7	7	111	21	15	10101	35	23	100011
8	8	1000	22	16	10110	36	24	100100
9	9	1001	23	17	10111	37	25	100101
10	A	1010	24	18	11000	38	26	100110
11	B	1011	25	19	11001	39	27	100111
12	C	1100	26	1A	11010	40	28	101000
13	D	1101	27	1B	11011			

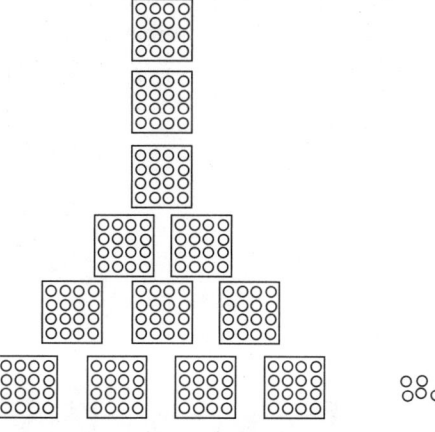

Figure E-4   Hex C5 represented as C boxes and 5 singles = 197 decimal

For a little practice, calculate the hex values of the decimal values 14, 259, 75, and 1,024 and the decimal values of FFh and A11h.

How Exponents Are Used to Express Place Value

If you are comfortable with using exponents, you know that writing numbers raised to a power is the same thing as multiplying that number times itself the power number of times. For example, $3^4 = 3 \times 3 \times 3 \times 3 = 81$. Using exponents in expressing numbers can also help us easily see place value, because the place value for each place is really the base number multiplied by itself a number of times, based on the place value position . For instance, look back at Figure E-1. A truckload is really $3 \times 3 \times 3 \times 3$, or 81, units, which can be written as 3^4. A crate is really $3 \times 3 \times 3$, or 27, units. The numbers in Figure E-1 can therefore be written like this:

Truckload = 3^4 Crate = 3^3 Carton = 3^2 · Box = 3^1 Single = 3^0

(Any number raised to the 0 power equals 1.) Therefore, we can express the numbers in Figure E-2 as multiples of truckloads, crates, cartons, boxes, and singles like this:

	Truckloads	Crates	Cartons	Boxes	Singles
21022 (base 3)	2×3^4	1×3^3	0×3^2	2×3^1	2×3^0
Decimal equivalent	162	27	0	6	2

When we sum up the numbers in the last row above, we get 197. We just converted a base 3 number (21022) to a base 10 number (197).

Binary Number System

It was stated earlier that it is easier for computers to convert from binary to hex or from hex to binary than to convert between binary and decimal. Let's see just how easy. Recall that the binary number system only has two numerals, or bits: 0 and 1. If our friend Joe in shipping operated a "binary" shipping system, he would pack like this: 2 widgets in a box, 2 boxes in one carton (4 widgets), two cartons in one crate (8 widgets), and two crates in one truckload (16 widgets). In Figure E-5, Joe is asked to pack 13 widgets. He packs 1 crate (8 widgets), 1 carton (4 widgets), no boxes, and 1 single. The number 13 in binary is 1101:

$$(1 \times 2^3)+(1 \times 2^2)+(0 \times 2^1)+(1 \times 2^0)= 8 + 4 + 0 + 1 = 13$$

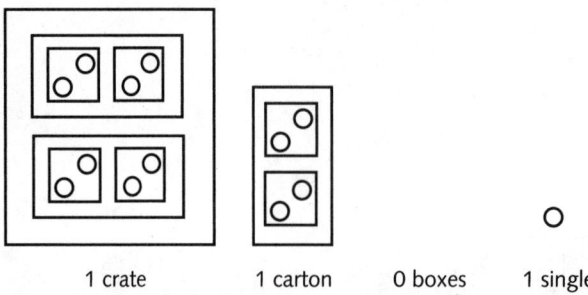

1 crate   1 carton   0 boxes   1 single

Figure E-5 Binary 1101 = 13 displayed as crates, cartons, boxes, and singles

Now let's see how to convert binary to hex and back again. The largest 4-bit number in binary is 1111. This number in decimal and hex is:

```
binary 1111 = 1 group of 8 = 8
              1 group of 4 = 4
              1 group of 2 = 2
                1 single = 1

              TOTAL = 15 (decimal)
Therefore, 1111 (binary) = 15 (decimal) = F (hex)
```

This last calculation is very important when working with computers: F is the largest numeral in the hex number system and it only takes 4 bits to write this largest hex numeral: F (hex) = 1111 (binary). So, every hex numeral (0, 1, 2, 3, 4, 5, 6, 7, 8, 9, A, B, C, D, E, and F) can be converted into a 4-bit binary number. Look back at the first 16 entries in Table E-2 for these binary values. Add leading zeroes to the binary numbers as necessary.

When converting from hex to binary, take each hex numeral and convert it to a 4-bit binary number and string all the 4-bit groups together. Fortunately, when working with computers, you will almost never be working with more than 2 hex numerals at a time. Here are some examples:

1. To convert hex F8 to binary, do the following: F = 1111, and 8 = 1000. Therefore, F8 = 11111000 (usually written 1111 1000).

2. To convert hex 9A to binary, do the following: 9 = 1001, and A = 1010. Therefore, 9A = 1001 1010.

Now try converting from binary to hex:

1. To convert binary 101110 to hex, first group the bits in groups of 4, starting at the right and moving left, adding leading zeros as necessary: 0010 1110.

2. Then convert each group of 4 bits in binary to a single hex numeral: 0010 = 2, and 1110 = E. The hex number is 2E.

Writing Conventions

Sometimes when you are dealing with hex, binary, and decimal numbers, it is not always clear which number system is being used. If you see a letter in the number, you know the number is a hex number. Binary numbers are usually written in groups of four bits. This book follows the convention of placing a lowercase h after a hex number, like this: 2Eh.

Memory Addressing

Computers often display memory addresses in the hex number system. You must either "think in hex" or convert to decimal. It's really easier, with a little practice, to think in hex. Here's the way it works:

Memory addresses are displayed as two hex numbers. An example is C800:5

The part to the left of the colon (C800) is called the *segment address*, and the part to the right of the colon (5) is called the *offset*. The offset value can have as many as four hex digits. The actual memory address is calculated by adding a zero to the right of the segment address and adding the offset value, like this: `C800:5 = C8000 + 5 = C8005`

The first 640K of memory is called conventional memory. Look at how that memory is addressed, first in decimal and then in hex (assuming 1 kilobyte = 1,024 bytes):

$640K = 640 \times 1,024 = 655,360$

There are 655,360 memory addresses in conventional memory, where each memory address can hold 1 byte, or 8 bits, of either data or program instructions. The decimal value 655,360 converted to hex is A0000 (10×16^4). So, conventional memory addresses begin with 00000h and end with A0000h minus 1h or 9FFFFh. Written in segment-and-offset form, conventional memory addresses range from 0000:0 to 9FFF:F.

Recall that upper memory is defined as the memory addresses from 640K to 1,024K. The next address after 9FFF:F is the first address of upper memory, which is A0000, and the last address is FFFFF. Written in segment-and-offset terms, upper memory addresses range from A000:0 to FFFF:F.

Here is one way to organize the conversion of a large hex value such as FFFFF to decimal (remember F in hex equals 15 in decimal).

FFFFF converted to decimal:

```
15 × 16⁰ = 15 × 1     =             15
15 × 16¹ = 15 × 16    =            240
15 × 16² = 15 × 256   =          3,840
15 × 16³ = 15 × 4096  =         61,440
15 × 16⁴ = 15 × 65,536 =       983,040

            TOTAL =          1,048,575
```

Remember that FFFFF is the last memory address in upper memory. The very next memory address is the first address of extended memory, which is defined as memory above 1 MB. If you add 1 to the number above, you get 1,048,576, which is equal to 1024×1024, which is the definition of 1 megabyte.

Displaying Memory with DOS DEBUG

In Figure E-6 you see the results of the beginning of upper memory displayed. The DOS DEBUG command displays the contents of memory. Memory addresses are displayed in hex segment-and-offset values. To enter DEBUG, type the following command at the C prompt and press Enter:

`C:\> DEBUG`

Type the following dump command to display the beginning of upper memory (the hyphen in the command is the DEBUG command prompt) and press Enter:

`-d A000:0`

Memory is displayed showing 16 bytes on each line. The A area of memory (the beginning of upper memory) is not used unless the computer is using a monochrome monitor or this area is being used as an upper memory block. In Figure E-6, the area contains nothing but continuous 1s in binary or Fs in hex. The ASCII interpretation is on the right side. To view the next group of memory addresses, you can type *d* at the hyphen and press Enter. DEBUG displays the next 128 addresses.

Figure E-6   Memory dump: –d A000:0

The A and B ranges of upper memory addresses (upper memory addresses that begin with A or B when written in hex) are used for monochrome monitors. The C range contains the video BIOS for a color monitor. Figure E-7 shows the dump of the beginning of the C range.

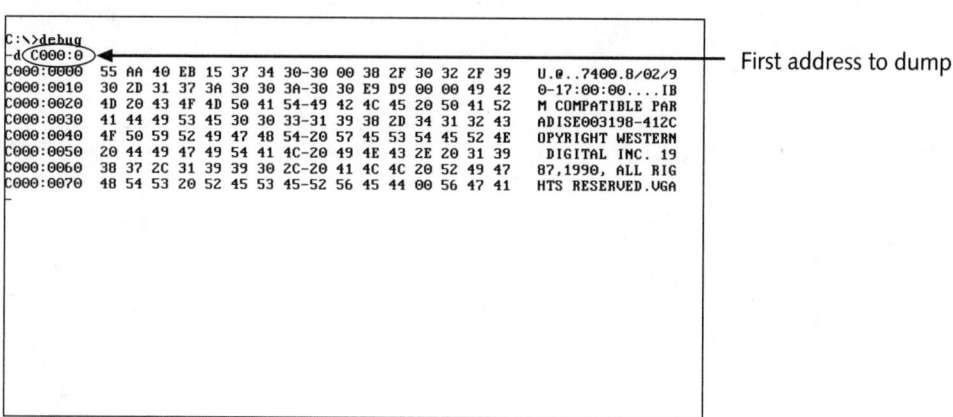

Figure E-7   Memory dump: –d C000:0

There is more than one way—in fact there are many ways—to identify the same segment-and-offset value. Try these commands to display the same upper memory addresses:

```
-d C000:0
-d BFF1:00F0
-d BFFF:0010
-d BEEE:1120
```

In summary, reading and understanding binary and hex numbers are essential skills for managing computers. All data is stored in binary in a computer and is often displayed in hex. Memory addresses are often displayed in hex segment-and-offset terms. An address in memory can be written in a variety of segment-and-offset values. The actual memory address is calculated by placing one zero to the right side of the segment address and adding the resulting value to the offset value. To exit DEBUG, type *q* for quit at the hyphen prompt.

GLOSSARY

100BaseFX — A variation of 100BaseT that supports fiber optic cable.

100BaseT — An Ethernet standard that operates at 100 Mbps and uses STP cabling. Also called Fast Ethernet. Variations of 100BaseT are 100BaseTX and 100BaseFX.

10Base2 — An Ethernet standard that operates at 10 Mbps and uses small coaxial cable up to 200 meters long. Also called ThinNet.

10Base5 — An Ethernet standard that operates at 10 Mbps and uses thick coaxial cable up to 500 meters long. Also called ThickNet.

1394.3 — A new standard, developed by the 1394 Trade Association, that is designed for peer-to-peer data transmission and allows imaging devices to send images and photos directly to printers without involving a computer.

16-bit mode — *See* real mode.

3-D RAM — Special video RAM designed to improve 3-D graphics simulation.

32-bit flat memory mode — A protected processing mode used by Windows NT/2000/XP to process programs written in 32-bit code early in the boot process.

32-bit mode — *See* protected mode.

80 conductor IDE cable — An IDE cable that has 40 pins but uses 80 wires, 40 of which are ground wires designed to reduce crosstalk on the cable. The cable is used by ATA/66, ATA/100, and ATA/133 IDE drives.

822 messages — Error messages that occur during e-mail transactions. 822 messages are named after RFC 822, which is the RFC that defines them.

Accelerated Graphics Port (AGP) — A slot on a motherboard for a video card that transfers video data from the CPU and runs at a frequency synchronized with the system bus.

ACPI (Advanced Configuration and Power Interface) — Specification developed by Intel, Compaq, Phoenix, Microsoft, and Toshiba to control power on notebooks and other devices. Windows 98 and Windows 2000/XP support ACPI.

active backplane — A type of backplane system in which there is some circuitry, including bus connectors, buffers, and driver circuits, on the backplane.

Active Directory — A Windows 2000 and Windows .NET directory database service that allows for a single point of administration for all shared resources on a network, including files, peripheral devices, databases, Web sites, users, and services.

active matrix — A type of video display that amplifies the signal at every intersection in the grid of electrodes, which enhances the pixel quality over that of a dual-scan passive matrix display.

active partition — The primary partition on the hard drive that boots the OS. Windows NT/2000/XP calls the active partition the system partition.

active terminator — A type of terminator for single-ended SCSI cables that includes voltage regulators in addition to the simple resistors used with passive termination.

adapter address — *See* MAC address.

adapter card — A small circuit board inserted in an expansion slot and used to communicate between the system bus and a peripheral device. Also called an interface card.

address bus — Lines on the system bus used by the CPU to communicate memory addresses and I/O addresses to the memory controller and I/O devices.

administrator account — In Windows NT/2000/XP, an account that grants to the administrator(s) rights and permissions to all hardware and software resources, such as the right to add, delete, and change accounts and to change hardware configurations.

Advanced Options menu — A Windows 2000/XP menu that appears when you press F8 when Windows starts. The menu can be used to troubleshoot problems when loading Windows 2000/XP.

Advanced Transfer Cache (ATC) — A type of L2 cache contained within the Pentium processor housing that is embedded on the same core processor die as the CPU itself.

AGP (Accelerated Graphics Port) bus — A bus or slot on the motherboard used for a single video card.

allocation blocks — Sets of hard drive sectors used by a Macintosh computer where the Mac's file system stores files.

alternating current (AC) — Current that cycles back and forth rather than traveling in only one direction. In the U.S., the AC voltage from a standard wall outlet is normally between 110 and 115 V AC. In Europe, the standard AC voltage from a wall outlet is 220 V AC.

ammeter — A meter that measures electrical current in amps.

ampere or **amp (A)** — A unit of measurement for electrical current. One volt across a resistance of one ohm will produce a flow of one amp.

amplifier repeater — A repeater that does not distinguish between noise and signal; it amplifies both.

ANSI (American National Standards Institute) — A nonprofit organization dedicated to creating trade and communications standards.

answer file — A text file that contains information that Windows NT/2000/XP requires in order to do an unattended installation.

antivirus (AV) software — Utility programs that prevent infection or scan a system to detect and remove viruses. McAfee Associates' VirusScan and Norton AntiVirus are two popular AV packages.

API (Application Program Interface) — A method used by an application program to call another program or the OS to perform a utility task.

Apple menu — The Mac OS menu accessed by an apple icon in the upper-right corner of the desktop. The Apple menu contains options that are always available no matter what application you are in.

Application layer — The OSI layer responsible for interfacing with the application using the network.

application program interface (API) call — A request from software to the OS to access hardware or other software using a previously defined procedure that both the software and the OS understand.

ARP (Address Resolution Protocol) — A protocol that TCP/IP uses to translate IP addresses into physical network addresses (MAC addresses).

ASCII (American Standard Code for Information Interchange) — A popular standard for writing letters and other characters in binary code. Originally, ASCII characters were 7 bits, so there were 127 possible values. ASCII has been expanded to an 8-bit version, allowing 128 additional values.

ASPI (Advanced SCSI Programming Interface) — A popular device driver that enables operating systems to communicate with a SCSI host adapter. The "A" originally stood for Adaptec before that company licensed the technology to others.

asynchronous SRAM — Static RAM that does not work in step with the CPU clock and is, therefore, slower than synchronous SRAM.

AT — A form factor, generally no longer produced, in which the motherboard requires a full-size case. Because of their dimensions and configuration, AT systems are difficult to install, service, and upgrade. Also called full AT.

AT command set — A set of commands that a PC uses to control a modem and that a user can enter to troubleshoot the modem.

ATAPI (Advanced Technology Attachment Packet Interface) — An interface standard—part of the IDE/ATA standards—that allows tape drives, CD-ROM drives, and other drives to be treated like an IDE hard drive by the system.

attenuation — Signal degeneration over distance. The problem caused by attenuation is solved on a network by adding repeaters to the network.

ATX — The most common form factor for PC systems presently in use, originally introduced by Intel in 1995. ATX motherboards and cases make better use of space and resources than did the AT form factor.

audio/modem riser (AMR) — A specification for a small slot on a motherboard to accommodate an audio or modem riser card. A controller on the motherboard contains some of the logic for the audio or modem functionality.

autodetection — A feature on newer system BIOS and hard drives that automatically identifies and configures a new drive in the CMOS setup.

Autoexec.bat — A startup text file that was once used by DOS and is used by Windows 9x to provide backward compatibility. It tells the computer what commands or programs to execute automatically during boot and is used to create a 16-bit environment.

Automated System Recovery (ASR) — The Windows XP process that allows you to restore an entire hard drive volume or logical drive to its state at the time the backup of the volume was made.

autorange meter — A multimeter that senses the quantity of input and sets the range accordingly.

Baby AT — An improved and more flexible version of the AT form factor. Baby AT was the industry standard from approximately 1993 to 1997 and can fit into some ATX cases.

back side bus — The bus between the CPU and the L2 cache inside the CPU housing.

backplane system — A form factor in which there is no true motherboard. Instead, motherboard components are included on an adapter card plugged into a slot on a board called the backplane.

backup — An extra copy of a file, used in the event that the original becomes damaged or destroyed.

backup domain controller (BDC) — In Windows NT, a computer on a network that holds a read-only copy of the SAM (security accounts manager) database.

Backup Operator — A Windows 2000/XP user account that can back up and restore any files on the system regardless of its having access to these files.

backward-compatible — Refers to new hardware and software that is able to support older, existing technologies. This is a common choice of hardware and software manufacturers.

bandwidth — In relation to analog communication, the range of frequencies that a communications channel or cable can carry. In general use, the term refers to the volume of data that can travel on a bus or over a cable stated in bits per second (bps), kilobits per second (Kbps), or megabits per second (Mbps). Also called data throughput or line speed.

bank — An area on the motherboard that contains slots for memory modules (typically labeled bank 0, 1, 2, and 3).

baseline — The level of performance expected from a system, which can be compared to current measurements to determine what needs upgrading or tuning.

basic disk — A way to partition a hard drive, used by DOS and all versions of Windows, that stores information about the drive in a partition table at the beginning of the drive. Compare to dynamic disk.

batch file — A text file containing a series of OS commands. Autoexec.bat is a batch file.

baud rate — A measure of line speed between two devices such as a computer and a printer or a modem. This speed is measured in the number of times a signal changes in one second. *See also* bits per second (bps).

beam detect mirror — Detects the initial presence of a laser printer's laser beam by reflecting the beam to an optical fiber.

best-effort protocol —*See* connectionless protocol.

binary number system — The number system used by computers; it has only two numbers, 0 and 1, called binary digits, or bits.

binding — (1) Associating an OSI layer to a layer above it or below it, such as when an IP address (Network layer) is associated with a network card and its MAC address (Data Link layer). (2) The process by which a protocol is associated with a network card or a modem card.

BIOS (basic input/output system) — Firmware that can control much of a computer's input/output functions, such as communication with the floppy drive and the monitor. Also called ROM BIOS.

bit (binary digit) — A 0 or 1 used by the binary number system.

bits per second (bps) — A measure of data transmission speed. For example, a common modem speed is 56,000 bps, or 56 Kbps.

block — *See* allocation blocks

block mode — A method of data transfer between hard drive and memory that allows multiple data transfers on a single software interrupt.

blue screen — A Windows NT/2000/XP error that displays against a blue screen and causes the system to halt. Also called a stop error.

Bluetooth — A standard for wireless communication and data synchronization between devices, developed by a group of electronics manufacturers and overseen by the Bluetooth Special Interest Group.

BNC connector — A connector used with thin coaxial cable. Some BNC connectors are T-shaped and called T-connectors. One end of the T connects to the NIC, and the two other ends can connect to cables or end a bus formation with a terminator.

boot blocks — The first two allocation blocks on a Macintosh computer's hard drive. They are initially empty, but once a System folder is installed on a computer, the boot blocks contain the location of the System folder so that the system can find and load the OS.

boot loader menu — A startup menu that gives the user the choice of which operating system to load such as Windows 98 or Windows 2000 which are both installed on the same system creating a dual boot.

boot partition — The hard drive partition where the Windows NT/2000/XP OS is stored. The system partition and the boot partition may be different partitions.

boot record — The first sector of a floppy disk or logical drive in a partition; it contains information about the disk or logical drive. On a hard drive, if the boot record is in the active partition, then it is used to boot the OS. Also called boot sector.

boot sector — *See* boot record.

boot sector virus — An infectious program that can replace the boot program with a modified, infected version of the boot command utilities, often causing boot and data retrieval problems.

bootable disk — For DOS and Windows, a floppy disk that can upload the OS files necessary for computer startup. For DOS or Windows 9x, it must contain the files Io.sys, Msdos.sys and Command.com.

booting — The process that a computer goes through when it is first turned on, preparing the computer to receive commands.

bootstrap loader — A small program at the end of the boot record that can be used to boot an OS from the disk or logical drive.

break code — A code produced when a key on a computer keyboard is released.

bridge — A device used to connect two or more network segments. It can make decisions about allowing a packet to pass based on the packet's destination MAC address.

bridging protocol — *See* line protocol.

Briefcase — A system folder in Windows 9x that is used to synchronize files between two computers.

broadband — A transmission technique that carries more than one type of transmission on the same medium, such as cable modem or DSL.

broadcast — Process by which a message is sent from a single host to all hosts on the network, without regard to the kind of data being sent or the destination of the data.

brouter — A device that functions as both a bridge and a router. A brouter acts as a router when handling packets using routable protocols such as TCP/IP and IPX/SPX. It acts as a bridge when handling packets using nonroutable protocols such as NetBEUI.

brownouts — Temporary reductions in voltage, which can sometimes cause data loss.

buffer — A temporary memory area where data is kept before being written to a hard drive or sent to a printer, thus reducing the number of writes to the devices.

built-in user account — An administrator account and a guest account that are set up when Windows NT/2000/XP is first installed.

burst EDO (BEDO) — A refined version of EDO memory that significantly improved access time over EDO. BEDO was not widely used because Intel chose not to support it. BEDO memory is stored on 168-pin DIMM modules.

burst SRAM — Memory that is more expensive and slightly faster than pipelined burst SRAM. Data is sent in a two-step process; the data address is sent, and then the data itself is sent without interruption.

bus — (1) The paths, or lines, on the motherboard on which data, instructions, and electrical power move from component to component. (2) Wires or printed circuits used to transmit electronic signals or voltage on the motherboard to other devices.

bus enumerator — A component of Windows Plug and Play that locates all devices on a particular bus and inventories the resource requirements for these devices.

bus mastering — A device other than the CPU controlling a bus on the motherboard in order to access memory or another device.

bus mouse — A mouse that plugs into a bus adapter card and has a round, 9-pin mini-DIN connector.

bus riser — *See* riser card.

bus speed — The speed, or frequency, at which the data on the motherboard is moving.

bus topology — A LAN architecture in which all the devices are connected to a bus, or one communication line. Bus topology does not have a central connection point.

byte — A collection of eight bits that is equivalent to a single character. When referring to system memory, an additional error-checking bit might be added, making the total nine bits.

C-RIMM (Continuity RIMM) — A placeholder RIMM module that provides continuity so that every RIMM slot is filled.

cabinet file — A file with a .cab extension that contains one or more compressed files and is often used to distribute software on disk. The Extract command is used to extract files from the cabinet file.

cable modem — A technology that uses cable TV lines for data transmission requiring a modem at each end. From the modem, a network cable connects to a NIC in the user's PC.

cache — A location in memory or some other place used to store frequently used data.

cache memory — A kind of fast RAM that is used to speed up memory access because it does not need to be continuously refreshed.

CAM (Common Access Method) — A standard adapter driver used by SCSI.

capacitor — An electronic device that can maintain an electrical charge for a period of time and is used to smooth out the flow of electrical current. Capacitors are often found in computer power supplies.

CardBus — The latest PCMCIA specification. It improves I/O speed, increases the bus width to 32 bits, and supports lower-voltage PC Cards, while maintaining backward compatibility with earlier standards.

cards — Adapter boards or interface cards placed into expansion slots to expand the functions of a computer, allowing it to communicate with external devices such as monitors or speakers.

carrier — A signal used to activate a phone line to confirm a continuous frequency; used to indicate that two computers are ready to receive or transmit data via modems.

CAS Latency (CL) — A feature of memory that reflects the number of clock cycles that pass while data is written to memory.

catalog tree — A database of the folders and files on a Macintosh computer's hard drive, including information such as filenames and extensions, the application used to open a file, the creator of the file or folder, and the date the file or folder was created. Works with the extents tree to allow the Mac to access hard drive data.

CAU (Controlled-Access Unit) — *See* MAU.

CCITT (Comité Consultatif International Télégraphique et Téléphonique) — An international organization that was responsible for developing standards for international communications. This organization has been incorporated into the ITU. *See also* ITU.

CD (change directory) command — A command given at the command prompt that changes the default directory, for example CD \Windows.

CD-R (CD-recordable) — A CD drive that can record or write data to a CD. The drive may or may not be multisession, but the data cannot be erased once it is written.

CD-RW (CD-rewritable) — A CD drive that can record or write data to a CD. The data can be erased and overwritten. The drive may or may not be multisession.

CDFS (Compact Disc File System) — The 32-bit file system for CD discs and some CD-R and CD-RW discs that replaced the older 16-bit mscdex file system used by DOS. *See also* UDF.

central processing unit (CPU) — Also called a microprocessor or processor. The heart and brain of the computer, which receives data input, processes information, and executes instructions.

chain — A group of clusters used to hold a single file.

checksum — A method of error checking transmitted data, whereby the digits are added up and their sum compared to an expected sum.

child directory — *See* subdirectory.

child, parent, grandparent backup method — A plan for backing up and reusing tapes or removable disks by rotating them each day (child), week (parent), and month (grandparent).

chip creep — A condition in which chips loosen because of thermal changes.

chip set — A group of chips on the motherboard that controls the timing and flow of data and instructions to and from the CPU.

CHS (cylinder, head, sector) mode — The traditional method by which BIOS reads from and writes to hard drives by addressing the correct cylinder, head, and sector. Also called normal mode.

circuit board — A computer component, such as the main motherboard or an adapter board, that has electronic circuits and chips.

CISC (complex instruction set computing) — A type of instruction set used by CPUs that has a large number of instructions.

clamping voltage — The maximum voltage allowed through a surge suppressor, such as 175 or 330 volts.

clean install — Installing an OS on a new hard drive or on a hard drive that has a previous OS installed, but without carrying forward any settings kept by the old OS including information about hardware, software, or user preferences. A fresh installation.

client — A software program or computer that requests information from another software program on another computer.

client/server — A computer concept whereby one computer (the client) requests information from another computer (the server).

clock speed — The speed, or frequency, expressed in MHz, that controls activity on the motherboard and is generated by a crystal or oscillator located somewhere on the motherboard.

clone — A computer that is a no-name Intel- and Microsoft-compatible PC.

cluster — One or more sectors that constitute the smallest unit of space on a disk for storing data (also referred to as a file allocation unit). Files are written to a disk as groups of whole clusters.

cluster chain — A series of clusters used to hold a single file.

Cmd.exe — The 32-bit program that provides a command window.

CMOS (complementary metal-oxide semiconductor) — One of two types of technologies used to manufacture microchips (the other type is TTL, or transistor-transistor logic chips). CMOS chips require less electricity, hold data longer after the electricity is turned off, are slower, and produce less heat than TTL chips. The configuration, or setup, chip is a CMOS chip.

CMOS configuration chip — A chip on the motherboard that contains a very small amount of memory, or RAM—enough to hold configuration, or setup, information about the computer. *See also* CMOS setup chip.

CMOS RAM chip — *See* CMOS setup chip.

CMOS setup — (1) The chip on the motherboard that holds configuration information about the system, such as date and time, and which CPU, hard drives, or floppy drives are installed. Also called CMOS or CMOS RAM. The chip is powered by a battery when the PC is turned off. (2) The program in system BIOS that can change the values in CMOS RAM.

CMOS setup chip — A microchip on the motherboard that contains a small amount of RAM, enough to hold the configuration information for a motherboard. Also called CMOS configuration chip, CMOS RAM chip.

COAST (cache on a stick) — Memory modules that hold memory used as a memory cache. *See* cache memory.

coaxial cable — Networking cable used with 10-Mbps Ethernet ThinNet or ThickNet.

cold boot — *See* hard boot.

collision — Conflict that occurs when two computers send a signal on the same channel at the same time.

color depth — The number of possible colors used by a monitor. Determines the number of bits used to compose one pixel and affects the amount of data sent to the video card to build one screen.

combo card — An Ethernet card that contains more than one transceiver, each with a different port on the back of the card, in order to accommodate different cabling media.

command mode — The Linux vi editor mode in which you can type commands to manipulate text or to change the status of the editor.

Command.com — Along with Msdos.sys and Io.sys, one of the three files that are the core components of the real-mode portion of Windows 9x. Command.com provides a command prompt and interprets commands.

comment — A line or part of a line in a program that is intended as a remark or comment and is ignored when the program runs. A semicolon or an REM is often used to mark a line as a comment.

communication and networking riser (CNR) — A specification for a small expansion slot on a motherboard that accommodates a small audio, modem, or network riser card.

compact case — A type of case used in low-end desktop systems. Compact cases, also called low-profile or slimline cases, follow either the NLX, LPX, or Mini LPX form factor. They are likely to have fewer drive bays, but they generally still provide for some expansion.

Compatibility mode — A Windows XP utility that provides an application with the older Microsoft OS environment it was designed to operate in.

compressed drive — A drive whose format has been reorganized in order to store more data. A compressed drive is really not a drive at all; it's actually a type of file, typically with a host drive called H.

Config.sys — A text file used by DOS and supported by Windows 9x that lists device drivers to be loaded at startup. It can also set system variables to be used by DOS and Windows.

Configuration Manager — A component of Windows Plug and Play that controls the configuration process of all devices and communicates these configurations to the devices.

connection-oriented protocol — In networking, a protocol that confirms that a good connection has been made before transmitting data to the other end. An example of a connection-oriented protocol is TCP.

connectionless protocol — A protocol such as UDP that does not require a connection before sending a packet and does not guarantee delivery. An example of a UDP transmission is streaming video over the Web. Also called a best-effort protocol.

console — A centralized location from which to execute commonly used tools.

constant angular velocity (CAV) — A technology used by hard drives and newer CD-ROM drives whereby the disk rotates at a constant speed.

constant linear velocity (CLV) — A CD-ROM format in which the spacing of data is consistent on the CD, but the speed of the disc varies depending on whether the data being read near the center or the edge of the disc.

contention-based — A network system in which each computer on the system must compete for the opportunity to transmit a signal on the network.

continuity — A continuous, unbroken path for the flow of electricity. A continuity test can determine whether or not internal wiring is still intact, or whether a fuse is good or bad.

control blade — A laser printer component that prevents too much toner from sticking to the cylinder surface.

control bus — The lines on the system bus used to send control signals to manage communication on the motherboard.

Control Panels folder — In Mac OS 9, a folder that contains control panels for system settings such as time and date, speaker volume, and the configuration of the Finder window and the desktop. In Mac OS X, control panels no longer exist; their functions are incorporated into the Library folder.

conventional memory — Memory addresses between 0 and 640K. Also called base memory.

cooperative multitasking — A type of pseudo-multitasking whereby the OS switches back and forth between programs loaded at the same time. One program sits in the background waiting for the other to relinquish control. Also called task switching.

CPU — *See* central processing unit.

CRC (cyclical redundancy check) — A process in which calculations are performed on bytes of data before and after they are transmitted to check for corruption during transmission.

credit card memory — A type of memory used on older notebooks that could upgrade existing memory by way of a specialized memory slot.

cross-linked clusters — Errors caused when more than one file points to a cluster, and the files appear to share the same disk space, according to the file allocation table.

crossover cable — A cable used to connect two PCs into the simplest network possible. Also used to connect two hubs.

CSMA/CA (Carrier Sense Multiple Access with Collision Avoidance) — A method to control collisions on a network, whereby each computer signals its intent to send data before sending it. This method is used on wireless LANs.

CSMA/CD (Carrier Sense Multiple Access with Collision Detection) — A method that Ethernet networks use to monitor the network to determine if the line is free before sending a transmission.

CVF (compressed volume file) — The file on the host drive of a compressed drive that holds all compressed data.

data bus — The lines on the system bus that the CPU uses to send and receive data. *See also* data path.

data cartridge — A type of tape medium typically used for backups. Full-sized data cartridges are 4 × 6 × ⅝ inches in size. A minicartridge is only 3¼ × 2½ × ⅝ inches in size.

data line protector — A surge protector designed to work with the telephone line to a modem.

Data Link layer — The OSI layer that disassembles packets and reassembles data into packets, preparing the packets to be passed on to the physical media.

data packet — *See* packet.

data path — That portion of a bus that carries data. A data bus is usually 32 or 64 bits wide. Also called a data bus.

data path size — The number of lines on a bus that can hold data, for example, 8, 16, 32, and 64 lines, which can accommodate 8, 16, 32, and 64 bits at a time.

data throughput — *See* bandwidth.

datagram — *See* packet.

DC controller — A card inside a notebook that converts voltage to CPU voltage. Some notebook manufacturers consider the card to be a FRU.

DCE (Data Communications Equipment) — The hardware, usually a dial-up modem, that provides the connection between a data terminal and a communications line.

de facto standard — A standard that does not have official backing but is considered a standard because of widespread use and acceptance by the industry.

default gateway —The gateway a computer on a network will use to access another network unless it knows to specifically use another gateway for quicker access to that network.

default printer — The printer Windows prints to unless another printer is selected.

defragment — To "optimize" or rewrite a file to a disk in one contiguous chain of clusters, thus speeding up data retrieval.

demodulation — The process by which digital data that has been converted to analog data is converted back to digital data. *See* modulation.

desktop — The initial screen that is displayed when an OS has a GUI interface loaded.

device driver — A small program stored on the hard drive that tells the computer how to communicate with an input/output device such as a printer or modem.

DHCP (Dynamic Host Configuration Protocol) server — A service that assigns dynamic IP addresses to computers on a network when they first access the network.

diagnostic cards — Adapter cards designed to discover and report computer errors and conflicts at POST time (before the computer boots up), often by displaying a number on the card.

diagnostic software — Utility programs that help troubleshoot computer systems. Some DOS diagnostic utilities are CHKDSK and SCANDISK. PC-Technician is an example of a third-party diagnostic program.

dial-up networking — A Windows 9x and Windows NT/2000/XP utility that uses a modem and telephone line to connect to a network.

differential — A signaling method for SCSI cables in which a signal is carried on two wires, each carrying voltage, and the signal is the difference between the two. Differential signaling provides for error checking and greater data integrity. Compare to single-ended.

differential backup — Backup method that backs up only files that have changed or have been created since the last full backup. When recovering data, only two backups are needed: the full backup and the last differential backup.

digital certificate — *See* digital signature.

digital diagnostic disk (DDD) — A floppy disk that has data written on it that is precisely aligned. Used to test the alignment of a floppy disk drive.

digital signature — Digital codes used to identify and authenticate the source of a file or document.

DIMM (dual inline memory module) — A miniature circuit board used in newer computers to hold memory. DIMMs can hold up to 2 GB of RAM on a single module.

diode — An electronic device that allows electricity to flow in only one direction. Used in a rectifier circuit.

DIP (dual inline package) switch — A switch on a circuit board or other device that can be set on or off to hold configuration or setup information.

direct current (DC) — Current that travels in only one direction (the type of electricity provided by batteries). Computer power supplies transform AC to low DC.

Direct Rambus DRAM — A memory technology by Rambus and Intel that uses a narrow, very fast network-type system bus. Memory is stored on a RIMM module. Also called RDRAM or Direct RDRAM.

Direct RDRAM — *See* Direct Rambus DRAM.

directory structure — Files created during formatting that allow a Macintosh computer to access its hard drive. Important directory structures include the boot blocks, the volume information block, the volume bit map, the catalog tree, and the extents tree.

directory table — An OS table that contains file information such as the name, size, time and date of last modification, and cluster number of the file's beginning location.

discrete L2 cache — A type of L2 cache contained within the Pentium processor housing, but on a different die, with a cache bus between the processor and the cache.

disk cache — A method whereby recently retrieved data and adjacent data are read into memory in advance, anticipating the next CPU request.

disk cloning — Making an exact image of a hard drive, including partition information, boot sectors, operating system installation, and application software to replicate the hard drive on another system or recover from a hard drive crash. Also called disk imaging.

disk compression — Compressing data on a hard drive to allow more data to be written to the drive.

Disk First Aid — A free Mac OS disk repair utility included with Mac OS 9. In Mac OS X, Disk First Aid and Drive Setup are combined into the single Disk Utility.

disk imaging — *See* disk cloning.

Disk Management — A Windows 2000/XP utility used to display and create and format partitions on basic disks and volumes on dynamic disks.

disk mirroring — A strategy whereby the same data is written to two hard drives in a computer to safeguard against hard drive failure. Disk mirroring uses only a single controller for two drives.

disk quota — A limit placed on the amount of disk space that is available to users. Requires a Windows 2000/XP NTFS volume.

disk striping — Treating multiple hard drives as a single volume. Data is written across the multiple drives in small segments, in order to increase performance and logical disk volume. When parity is used, disk striping also provides logical fault tolerance. RAID 5 is disk striping with parity information distributed over all drives in the array.

disk thrashing — A condition that results when the hard drive is excessively used for virtual memory because RAM is full. It dramatically slows down processing and can cause premature hard drive failure.

Disk Utility — A Mac OS X utility that can be used to set up a drive, reformat a damaged drive, or detect and repair problems on it. It combines the functions of the Mac OS 9 tools Disk First Aid and Drive Setup.

Display Power Management Signaling (DPMS) — Energy Star standard specifications that allow for the video card and monitor to go into sleep mode simultaneously. *See also* Energy Star systems.

distributions — Different versions of an OS by different vendors.

DLL (dynamic-link library) — A file with a .dll file extension that contains a library of programming routines used by programs to perform common tasks.

DMA (direct memory access) channel — A number identifying a channel whereby the I/O device can pass data to memory without involving the CPU. Think of a DMA channel as a shortcut for data moving to/from the device and memory.

DNS (domain name service or **domain name system)** — A distributed pool of information (called the name space) that keeps track of assigned domain names and their corresponding IP addresses, and the system that allows a host to locate information in the pool. Compare to WINS.

DNS server — A computer that can find an IP address for another computer when only the domain name is known.

dock — A new feature of the Mac OS X interface that consists of icons representing frequently used and currently open applications on a bar at the bottom of the desktop.

docking station — A device that receives a notebook computer and provides additional secondary storage and easy connection to peripheral devices.

domain — In Windows NT/2000/XP, a logical group of networked computers, such as those on a college campus, that share a centralized directory database of user account information and security for the entire domain.

domain name — A unique, text-based name that identifies a network.

domain user account — An account for a user that has permission to access resources, folders, and files on a domain. A domain user can log on to a domain and access the network.

DOS box — A command window.

Dosstart.bat — A type of Autoexec.bat file that is executed by Windows 9x in two situations: when you select Restart the computer in MS-DOS mode from the shutdown menu or you run a program in MS-DOS mode.

dot pitch — The distance between the dots that the electronic beam hits on a monitor screen.

Double Data Rate SDRAM (DDR SDRAM) — A type of memory technology used on DIMMs that runs at twice the speed of the system clock.

doze time — The time before an Energy Star or "Green" system will reduce 80 percent of its activity.

Dr. Watson — A Windows utility that can record detailed information about the system, errors that occur, and the programs that caused them in a log file. Windows 9x names the log file \Windows\ Drwatson\WatsonXX.wlg, where XX is an incrementing number. Windows 2000 names the file \Documents and Settings\user\Documents\ DrWatson\Drwtsn32.log.

Drive Setup — A Mac OS 9 tool that can be used to format a hard drive when it is initially installed or to reformat a damaged hard drive. In Mac OS X, Drive Setup and Disk First Aid are combined into the Disk Utility.

DriveSpace — A utility that compresses files so that they take up less space on a disk drive, creating a single large file on the disk to hold all the compressed files.

drop height — The height from which a manufacturer states that its drive can be dropped without making the drive unusable.

Drwatson.log — The log file for the Dr. Watson utility in Windows XP.

DSL (Digital Subscriber Line) — A telephone line that carries digital data from end to end, and can be leased from the telephone company for individual use. DSL lines are rated at 5 Mbps, about 50 times faster than regular telephone lines.

DTE (Data Terminal Equipment) — Both the computer and a remote terminal or other computer to which it is attached.

dual boot — The ability to boot using either of two different OSs, such as Windows 98 and Windows 2000.

dual porting — Allows the video chip set (input) and the RAM DAC (output) to access video memory at the same time. A special kind of video RAM is required.

dual-scan passive matrix — A type of video display that is less expensive than an active-matrix display and does not provide as high-quality an image. With dual-scan display, two columns of electrodes are activated at the same time.

dual-voltage CPU — A CPU that requires two different voltages, one for internal processing and the other for I/O processing.

dump file — A file that contains information captured from memory at the time a stop error occurred.

duplexing — An improvement of disk mirroring in which each hard drive had its own adapter card.

DVD (digital video disc or **digital versatile disk)** — A faster, larger CD-ROM format that can read older CDs, store over 8 GB of data, and hold full-length motion picture videos.

dynamic disk — A way to partition one or more hard drives, introduced with Windows 2000, in which information about the drive is stored in a database at the end of the drive. Compare to basic disk.

dynamic IP address — An assigned IP address that is used for the current session only. When the session is terminated, the IP address is returned to the list of available addresses.

dynamic RAM (DRAM) — The most common type of system memory, it requires refreshing every few milliseconds.

dynamic volume — A volume type used with dynamic disks for which you can change the size of the volume after you have created it.

dynamic VxD — A VxD that is loaded and unloaded from memory as needed.

ECC (error-correcting code) — A chip set feature on a system board that checks the integrity of data stored on DIMMs or RIMMs and can correct single-bit errors in a byte. More advanced ECC schemas can detect, but not correct, double-bit errors in a byte.

ECHS (extended CHS) mode — *See* large mode.

ECP (Extended Capabilities Port) — A bidirectional parallel port mode that uses a DMA channel to speed up data flow.

EDO (extended data out) — A type of RAM that may be 10-20 percent faster than conventional RAM because it eliminates the delay before it issues the next memory address.

EEPROM (electrically erasable programmable ROM) — A type of chip in which higher voltage may be applied to one of the pins to erase its previous memory before a new instruction set is electronically written.

EFS (Encrypted File System) — A way to use a key to encode a file or folder to protect sensitive data. Because it is an integrated system service, EFS is transparent to users and applications and is difficult to attack.

EIDE (Enhanced Integrated Drive Electronics) — A standard for managing the interface between secondary storage devices and a computer system. A system can support up to four IDE devices such as hard drives, CD-ROM drives, and Zip drives.

EISA (Extended ISA) bus — A 32-bit bus that can transfer 4 bytes at a time at a speed of about 20 MHz.

Emergency Repair Disk (ERD) — A Windows NT record of critical information about your system that can be used to fix a problem with the OS. The ERD enables restoration of the Windows NT registry on your hard drive.

Emergency Repair Process — A Windows 2000 process that restores the OS to its state at the completion of a successful installation.

emergency startup disk (ESD) — *See* rescue disk.

EMI (electromagnetic interference) — A magnetic field produced as a side effect from the flow of electricity. EMI can cause corrupted data in data lines that are not properly shielded.

Emm386.exe — A DOS and Windows 9x utility that provides access to upper memory for 16-bit device drivers and other software.

enabler file — A file included with Macintosh hardware that is released before the instructions to control it are incorporated into the Mac OS. Enabler files allow a device to function with the version of Mac OS being used on the computer.

encrypting virus — A type of virus that transforms itself into a nonreplicating program in order to avoid detection. It transforms itself back into a replicating program in order to spread.

encryption — The process of putting readable data into an encoded form that can only be decoded (or decrypted) through use of a key.

Energy Star systems — "Green" systems that satisfy the EPA requirements to decrease the overall consumption of electricity. *See also* Green Standards.

enhanced BIOS — A system BIOS that has been written to accommodate large-capacity drives (over 504 MB, usually in the gigabyte range).

Enhanced IDE (EIDE) — A drive standard that allows systems to recognize drives larger than 504 MB and to handle up to four devices on the same controller.

enhanced metafile format (EMF) — A format used to print a document that contains embedded print commands. When printing in Windows 9x, EMF information is generated by the GDI portion of the Windows kernel.

environment — As related to OSs, the overall support that an OS provides to applications software.

EPIC (explicitly parallel instruction computing) — The CPU architecture used by the Intel Itanium that bundles programming instructions with instructions as to how to use multiprocessing abilities to do two instructions in parallel.

EPP (Enhanced Parallel Port) — A parallel port that allows data to flow in both directions (bidirectional port) and is faster than original parallel ports on PCs that only allowed communication in one direction.

EPROM (erasable programmable ROM) — A type of chip with a special window that allows the current memory contents to be erased with special ultraviolet light so that the chip can be reprogrammed. Many BIOS chips are EPROMs.

error correction — The ability of a modem to identify transmission errors and then automatically request another transmission.

ESD (electrostatic discharge) — Another name for static electricity, which can damage chips and destroy motherboards, even though it might not be felt or seen with the naked eye.

Ethernet — A LAN architecture that uses a bus or star topology, uses CSMA/CD when two computers are trying to gain access to the network at the same time, and is the most popular network architecture in use today.

Execution Trace Cache — A type of Level 1 Cache used by some CPUs to hold decoded operations waiting to be executed.

executive services — In Windows NT/2000/XP, a group of components running in kernel mode that interfaces between the subsystems in user mode and the HAL.

expansion bus — A bus that does not run in sync with the system clock.

expansion card — A circuit board inserted into a slot on the motherboard to enhance the capability of the computer.

expansion slot — A narrow slot on the motherboard where an expansion card can be inserted. Expansion slots connect to a bus on the motherboard.

extended memory — Memory above 1024K used in a DOS or Windows 9x system.

extended partition — The only partition on a hard drive that can contain more than one logical drive.

Extensions folder — A Mac OS 9 folder that contains add-ons to provide new features to a Mac, as well as shared libraries and icons. Extensions no longer exist in Mac OS X; their functions are incorporated into the Library folder.

extents — On a Mac, the pieces into which a file is broken when it is larger than one allocation block.

extents tree — A Mac directory structure that contains information about where the allocation blocks are located for files that take up more than one allocation block.

external bus — *See* system bus.

external cache — Static cache memory, stored on the motherboard or inside CPU housing, that is not part of the CPU (also called L2 or L3 cache).

external command — Commands that have their own program files.

faceplate — A metal plate that comes with the motherboard and fits over the ports to create a well-fitted enclosure around them.

Fast Ethernet — *See* 100BaseT.

FAT (file allocation table) — A table on a hard drive or floppy disk that tracks the clusters used to contain a file.

FAT12 — The 12-bit wide, one-column file allocation table for a floppy disk, containing information about how each cluster or file allocation unit on the disk is currently used.

fatal system error — An error that prevents Windows from loading. An example is a damaged registry.

fault tolerance — The degree to which a system can tolerate failures. Adding redundant components, such as disk mirroring or disk duplexing, is a way to build in fault tolerance.

FDDI (Fiber Distributed Data Interface) — A ring-based network that does not require a centralized hub and can transfer data at a rate of 100 Mbps.

field replaceable unit (FRU) — A component in a computer or device that can be replaced with a new component without sending the computer or device back to the manufacturer. Examples: power supply, DIMM, motherboard, floppy disk drive.

file allocation table (FAT) — A table on a disk that tracks the clusters used to contain a file.

file allocation unit — *See* cluster.

file extension — A three-character portion of the name of a file that is used to identify the file type. In command lines, the file extension follows the filename and is separated from it by a period. For example, Msd.exe, where exe is the file extension.

file system — The overall structure that an OS uses to name, store, and organize files on a disk. Examples of file systems are FAT16 and FAT32.

file virus — A virus that inserts virus code into an executable program and can spread wherever that program is accessed.

filename — The first part of the name assigned to a file. In DOS, the filename can be no more than eight characters long and is followed by the file extension. In Windows, a filename can be up to 255 characters.

Finder window — A type of Mac window that allows a user to navigate the Mac OS hierarchical file structure. It functions something like My Computer or Explorer in Windows and includes buttons similar to those on a Web browser.

FireWire — An expansion bus that can also be configured to work as a local bus. It is expected to replace the SCSI bus, providing an easy method to install and configure fast I/O devices. Also called IEEE 1394 and i.Link.

firmware — Software programs permanently embedded on a microchip. The BIOS on a motherboard is an example of firmware.

flash memory — A type of RAM that can electronically hold memory even when the power is off.

flash ROM — ROM that can be reprogrammed or changed without replacing chips.

flat panel monitor — A desktop monitor that uses an LCD panel.

FlexATX — A version of the ATX form factor that allows for maximum flexibility in the size and shape of cases and motherboards. FlexATX is ideal for custom systems.

flow control — When using modems, a method of controlling the flow of data to adjust for problems with data transmission. Xon/Xoff is an example of a flow control protocol.

folder — *See* subdirectory.

forced perfect terminator (FPT) — A type of SCSI active terminator that includes a mechanism to force signal termination to the correct voltage, eliminating most signal echoes and interference.

forgotten password floppy disk — A Windows XP disk created to be used in the event the user forgets the user account password to the system.

form factor — A set of specifications on the size, shape, and configuration of a computer hardware component such as a case, power supply, or motherboard.

formatting — Preparing a new floppy disk for use by placing tracks and sectors on its surface to store information (for example, FORMAT A:). Old disks can be reformatted, but all data on them will be lost.

FPM (fast page mode) — A memory mode used before the introduction of EDO memory. FPM improved on earlier memory types by sending the row address just once for many accesses to memory near that row.

fragmentation — On a hard drive, the distribution of data files such that they are stored in noncontiguous clusters.

fragmented file — A file that has been written to different portions of the disk so that it is not in contiguous clusters.

frame — The header and trailer information added to data to form a data packet to be sent over a network.

front side bus — The bus between the CPU and the memory outside the CPU housing. Also called the system bus.

FTP (File Transfer Protocol) — The protocol used to transfer files over a TCP/IP network such that the file does not need to be converted to ASCII format before transferring.

full AT — *See* AT.

full backup — A complete backup, whereby all of the files on the hard drive are backed up each time the backup procedure is performed. It is the safest backup method, but it takes the most time.

full-duplex — Communication that happens in two directions at the same time.

fully qualified domain name (FQDN) — A host name and a domain name such as jsmith.amazon.com. Sometimes loosely referred to as a domain name.

gateway — A computer or other device that connects networks.

GDI (Graphics Device Interface) — A Windows 9x component that controls screens, graphics, and printing.

General Protection Fault (GPF) — A Windows error that occurs when a program attempts to access a memory address that is not available or is no longer assigned to it.

Gigabit Ethernet — The newest version of Ethernet. Gigabit Ethernet supports rates of data transfer up to 1 gigabit per second but is not yet widely used.

gigahertz (GHz) — One thousand MHz, or one billion cycles per second.

global user account — Sometimes called a domain user account, the account is used at the domain level, created by an administrator, and stored in the SAM (security accounts manager) database on a domain controller.

graphics accelerator — A type of video card that has an on-board processor that can substantially increase speed and boost graphical and video performance.

Green Standards — A computer or device that conforms to these standards can go into sleep or doze mode when not in use, thus saving energy and helping the environment. Devices that carry the Green Star or Energy Star comply with these standards.

ground bracelet — A strap you wear around your wrist that is attached to the computer case, ground mat, or another ground so that ESD is discharged from your body before you touch sensitive components inside a computer. Also called static strap, ground strap, ESD bracelet.

group files — Windows 3.x files with the .grp file extension that contain information about a program group of Program Manager.

group profile — A group of user profiles. All profiles in the group can be changed by changing the group profile.

guard tone — A tone that an answering modem sends when it first answers the phone, to tell the calling modem that a modem is on the other end of the line.

Guest user — A user who has limited permissions on a system and cannot make changes to it. Guest user accounts are intended for one-time or infrequent users of a workstation.

GUI (graphical user interface) — A user interface, such as the Windows interface, that uses graphics or icons on the screen for running programs and entering information.

HAL (hardware abstraction layer) — The low-level part of Windows NT/2000/XP, written specifically for each CPU technology, so that only the HAL must change when platform components change.

half-duplex — Communication between two devices whereby transmission takes place in only one direction at a time.

half-life — The time it takes for a medium storing data to weaken to half of its strength. Magnetic media, including traditional hard drives and floppy disks, have a half-life of five to seven years.

handshaking — When two modems begin to communicate, the initial agreement made as to how to send and receive data.

hard boot — Restarting the computer by turning off the power or by pressing the Reset button. Also called a cold boot.

hard copy — Output from a printer to paper.

hard-disk loading — The illegal practice of installing unauthorized software on computers for sale. Hard-disk loading can typically be identified by the absence of original disks in the original system's shipment.

hard drive — The main secondary storage device of a PC, a small case that contains magnetic coated platters that rotate at high speed.

hard drive controller — The firmware that controls access to a hard drive contained on a circuit board mounted on or inside the hard drive housing. Older hard drives used firmware on a controller card that connected to the drive by way of two cables, one for data and one for control.

hard drive standby time — The amount of time before a hard drive will shut down to conserve energy.

hardware — The physical components that constitute the computer system, such as the monitor, the keyboard, the motherboard, and the printer.

hardware address — *See* MAC address.

hardware cache — A disk cache that is contained in RAM chips built right on the disk controller.

hardware interrupt — An event caused by a hardware device signaling the CPU that it requires service.

hardware profile — A set of hardware configuration information that Windows keeps in the registry. Windows can maintain more than one hardware profile for the same PC.

hardware tree — A database built each time Windows 9x starts up that contains a list of installed components and the resources they use.

HCL (hardware compatibility list) — The list of all computers and peripheral devices that have been tested and are officially supported by Windows NT/2000/XP. (See *www.microsoft.com/hcl*)

head — The top or bottom surface of one platter on a hard drive. Each platter has two heads.

heat sink — A piece of metal, with cooling fins, that can be attached to or mounted on an integrated chip (such as the CPU) to dissipate heat.

hertz (Hz) — Unit of measurement for frequency, calculated in terms of vibrations, or cycles per second. For example, for 16-bit stereo sound, a frequency of 44,000 Hz is used. *See also* megahertz.

hexadecimal notation — A numbering system that uses sixteen digits, the numerals 0–9 and the letters A–F. Hexadecimal notation is often used to display memory addresses.

HFS (Hierarchical File System) — The file system used for Macintosh computer disks before 1998, when drives larger than 1 GB started to become more common. HFS limited the number of allocation units on a disk to 65,536. Also known as Mac OS standard format.

HFS+ — The file system used for Mac disks since the release of Mac OS 8.1 in 1998. HFS+ is an update of HFS, and can format drives up to 2,048 GB. Also called Mac OS extended format.

hidden file — A file that is not displayed in a directory list. Whether to hide or display a file is indicated by one of the file's attributes kept by the OS.

high-level formatting — Formatting performed by means of the DOS or Windows Format program (for example, FORMAT C:/S creates the boot record, FAT, and root directory on drive C and makes the drive bootable). Also called OS formatting.

Himem.sys — The DOS and Windows 9x memory manager extension that allowed access to memory addresses above 1 MB.

hive — Physical segments of the Windows NT/2000/XP registry that is stored in a file.

HMA (high memory area) — The first 64K of extended memory.

host — Any computer or other device on a network that has been assigned an IP address. *See also* node.

host adapter — The circuit board that controls a SCSI bus supporting as many as seven or fifteen separate devices. The host adapter controls communication between the SCSI bus and the PC.

host bus — *See* memory bus or system bus.

host drive — Typically drive H on a compressed drive. *See* compressed drive.

host name — A name that identifies a computer, printer, or other device on a network.

Hosts — A text file located in the Windows folder that contains host names and their associated IP addresses. This file is used for name resolution for a TCP/IP network using DNS.

hot-pluggable — *See* hot-swappable.

hot-swappable — A device that can be plugged into a computer while it is turned on and the computer will sense the device and configure it without rebooting, or the device can be removed without an OS error. Also called hot-pluggable.

HTML (HyperText Markup Language) — A markup language used for hypertext documents on the World Wide Web. This language uses tags to format the document, create hyperlinks, and mark locations for graphics.

HTTP (HyperText Transfer Protocol) — The protocol used by the World Wide Web.

HTTPS (HTTP secure) — A version of the HTTP protocol that includes data encryption for security.

hub — A network device or box that provides a central location to connect cables.

HVD (High Voltage Differential) — A type of SCSI differential signaling requiring more expensive hardware to handle the higher voltage. HVD became obsolete with the introduction of SCSI-3.

hypertext — Text that contains links to remote points in the document or to other files, documents, or graphics. Hypertext is created using HTML and is commonly distributed from Web sites.

i.Link — *See* FireWire.

I/O addresses — Numbers that are used by devices and the CPU to manage communication between them. Also called ports or port addresses.

I/O controller card — An older card that can contain serial, parallel, and game ports and floppy drive and IDE connectors.

IBM-compatible PC — A computer that uses an Intel (or compatible) processor and can run DOS and Windows.

ICMP (Internet Control Message Protocol) — Part of the IP layer that is used to transmit error messages and other control messages to hosts and routers.

IDE (Integrated Drive Electronics) — A standard governing hard drive technology and how secondary storage devices, such as hard drives, CD-ROM drives and Zip drives, relate to a system.

IEEE (Institute of Electrical and Electronics Engineers) — A nonprofit organization that develops standards for the computer and electronics industries.

IEEE 802.11b — An IEEE specification for wireless communication and data synchronization that competes with Bluetooth. Also known as Wi-Fi. Apple Computer's version of 802.11b is called AirPort.

IEEE 1284 — A standard for parallel ports and cables developed by the Institute for Electrical and Electronics Engineers and supported by many hardware manufacturers.

IEEE 1394 — *See* FireWire.

IMAP4 (Internet Message Access Protocol version 4) — Version 4 of the IMAP protocol, which is an e-mail protocol that has more functionality than its predecessor, POP. IMAP can archive messages in folders on the e-mail server and can allow the user to choose not to download attachments to messages.

in-band signaling — In modem communication, the name of the signaling used by software flow control, which pauses transmission by sending a special control character in the same channel (or band) that data is sent in.

incremental backup — A time-saving backup method that only backs up files changed or newly created since the last full or incremental backup. Multiple incremental backups might be required when recovering lost data.

infestation — Any unwanted program that is transmitted to a computer without the user's knowledge and that is designed to do varying degrees of damage to data and software. There are a number of different types of infestations, including viruses, Trojan horses, worms, and logic bombs.

information (.inf) file — Text file with an .inf file extension, such as Msbatch.inf, that contains information about a hardware or software installation.

initialization files — Configuration information files for Windows. System.ini is one of the most important Windows initialization files.

insert mode — A Linux vi editor mode in which you can type text into the editor.

Installable File System (IFS) — A Windows 9x Plug and Play component that is responsible for all disk access.

instruction set — The set of instructions, on the CPU chip, that the computer can perform directly (such as ADD and MOVE).

Integrated Device Electronics or **Integrated Drive Electronics (IDE)** — A hard drive whose disk controller is integrated into the drive, eliminating the need for a controller cable and thus increasing speed, as well as reducing price.

intelligent UPS — A UPS connected to a computer by way of a serial cable so that software on the computer can monitor and control the UPS.

interlaced — A type of display in which the electronic beam of a monitor draws every other line with each pass, which lessens the overall effect of a lower refresh rate.

internal bus — The bus inside the CPU that is used for communication between the CPU's internal components.

internal cache — Memory cache that is faster than external cache, and is contained inside 80486 and Pentium chips (also referred to as primary, Level 1, or L1 cache).

internal command — Commands that are embedded in the Command.com file.

Internet Connection Firewall (ICF) — Windows XP software designed to protect a PC from unauthorized access from the Internet.

interrupt handler — A program (either BIOS or a device driver), that is used by the CPU to process a hardware interrupt. Also called request handler.

interrupt vector table — A table that stores the memory addresses assigned to interrupt handlers so the CPU can find one when needed. Also called a vector table.

intranet — A private network that uses the TCP/IP protocols.

Io.sys — Along with Msdos.sys and Command.com, one of the three files that are the core components of the real mode portion of Windows 9x. It is the first program file of the OS.

IP (Internet Protocol) — The rules of communication in the TCP/IP stack that control segmenting data into packets, routing those packets across networks, and then reassembling the packets once they reach their destination.

IP address (Internet Protocol address) — A 32-bit address consisting of four numbers separated by periods, used to uniquely identify a device on a network that uses TCP/IP protocols. The first numbers identify the network; the last numbers identify the host, or the device. An example of an IP address is 206.96.103.114.

IPX/SPX (Internetwork Packet Exchange/Sequenced Packet Exchange) — A networking protocol first used by Novell NetWare, which corresponds to the TCP/IP protocols.

IRQ (interrupt request) line — A line on a bus that is assigned to a device and is used to signal the CPU for servicing. These lines are assigned a reference number (for example, the normal IRQ for a printer is IRQ 7).

ISA (Industry Standard Architecture) — An 8-bit or 16-bit slot first used in the 1980s on motherboards and sometimes still used today.

ISA bus — An 8-bit industry standard architecture bus used on the original 8088 PC. Sixteen-bit ISA buses were designed for the 286 AT, and are still used in some Pentium motherboards for devices such as modems.

ISA slot — An older slot on the motherboard used for slower I/O devices, which can support an 8-bit or a 16-bit data path. ISA slots are mostly replaced by PCI slots.

ISDN (Integrated Services Digital Network) — A digital telephone line that can carry data at about five times the speed of regular telephone lines. Two channels (telephone numbers) share a single pair of wires.

ISO (International Organization for Standardization) — A standards organization composed of standards bodies from several countries. The ISO developed the OSI model.

isochronous data transfer — A method used by IEEE 1394 to transfer data continuously without breaks.

ISP (Internet service provider) — A commercial group that provides Internet access for a monthly fee. AOL, Earthlink, and CompuServe are large ISPs.

ITU (International Telecommunications Union) — The international organization responsible for developing international standards of communication. Formerly CCITT.

JPEG (Joint Photographic Experts Group) — A graphical compression scheme that allows the user to control the amount of data that is averaged and sacrificed as file size is reduced. It is a common Internet file format. Most JPEG files have a .jpg extension.

jumper — Two wires that stick up side by side on the motherboard that are used to hold configuration information. The jumper is considered closed if a cover is over the wires, and open if the cover is missing.

kernel — The portion of an OS that is responsible for interacting with the hardware.

kernel mode — A Windows NT/2000/XP "privileged" processing mode that has access to hardware components.

key — (1) In encryption, a secret number or code used to encode and decode data. (2) In Windows, a section name of the Windows registry.

keyboard — A common input device through which data and instructions may be typed into computer memory.

LAN (local area network) — A computer network that covers only a small area, usually within one building.

lands — Microscopic flat areas on the surface of a CD or DVD that separate pits. Lands and pits are used to represent data on the disk.

laptop computer — *See* notebook.

large-capacity drive — A hard drive larger than 504 MB.

large mode — A mode of addressing information on hard drives that range from 504 MB to 8.4 GB, addressing information on a hard drive by translating cylinder, head, and sector information in order to break the 528-MB hard drive barrier. Also called ECHS mode.

LBA (logical block addressing) mode — A mode of addressing information on hard drives in which the BIOS and operating system view the drive as one long linear list of LBAs or addressable sectors, permitting drives to be larger than 8.4 GB (LBA 0 is cylinder 0, head 0, and sector 1).

legacy — A term used to refer to older computer devices or software that does not use the most current technologies.

Level 1 (L1) cache — *See* internal cache.

Level 2 (L2) cache — *See* external cache.

Level 3 (L3) cache — *See* external cache.

Library — The Mac OS X folder that takes over the functions of the Mac OS 9 control panels and extensions, which do not exist in Mac OS X. System settings and add-ons are controlled from the Library folder.

Limited user — Windows XP user accounts known as Users in Windows NT/2000, which have limited access to other users' data.

line conditioner — A device that regulates, or conditions, power, providing continuous voltage during brownouts and spikes.

line-interactive UPS — A variation of a standby UPS that shortens switching time by always keeping the inverter that converts AC to DC working, so that there is no charge-up time for the inverter.

line protocol — A protocol used to send data packets destined for a network over telephone lines. PPP and SLIP are examples of line protocols.

line speed — *See* bandwidth.

LMHosts — A text file located in the Windows folder that contains NetBIOS names and their associated IP addresses. This file is used for name resolution for a NetBEUI network.

local bus — A bus that operates at a speed synchronized with the CPU frequency and the system bus. The system bus is a local bus.

local I/O bus — A local bus that provides I/O devices with fast access to the CPU.

local printer — A printer connected to a computer by way of a port on the computer.

local profile — User profile that is stored on a local computer and cannot be accessed from another computer on the network.

local user account — A user account that applies only to a local computer and cannot be used to access resources from other computers on the network.

logic bomb — Dormant code added to software that is triggered by a predetermined time or event.

logical drive — A portion or all of a hard drive partition that is treated by the operating system as though it were a physical drive. Each logical drive is assigned a drive letter, such as drive C, and contains a file system. Also called a volume.

logical geometry — The number of heads, tracks, and sectors that the BIOS on the hard drive controller presents to the system BIOS and the OS. The logical geometry does not consist of the same values as the physical geometry, although calculations of drive capacity yield the same results.

loopback device — A virtual device, which consists of the local system and has the IP address 127.x.x.x. It is used to test the TCP/IP configuration on a computer.

lost allocation units — *See* lost clusters.

lost clusters — File fragments that, according to the file allocation table, contain data that does not belong to any file. The command CHKDSK/F can free these fragments. Also called lost allocation units.

low insertion force (LIF) socket — A socket that requires the installer to manually apply an even force over the microchip when inserting the chip into the socket.

low-level formatting — A process (usually performed at the factory) that electronically creates the hard drive tracks and sectors and tests for bad spots on the disk surface.

low-profile case — *See* compact case.

LPX — A form factor in which expansion cards are mounted on a riser card that plugs into a motherboard. The expansion cards in LPX systems are mounted parallel to the motherboard, rather than perpendicular to it as in AT and ATX systems.

LUN (Logical Unit Number) — A number assigned to a logical device (such as a tray in a CD changer) that is part of a physical SCSI device, which is assigned a SCSI ID.

LVD (Low Voltage Differential) — A type of differential signaling that uses lower voltage than does HVD, is less expensive, and can be compatible with single-ended signaling on the same SCSI bus.

MAC (Media Access Control) address — A 6-byte hexadecimal hardware address unique to each NIC card and assigned by the manufacturer. The address is often printed on the adapter. An example is 00 00 0C 08 2F 35. Also called a physical address, an adapter address, or a hardware address.

Mac OS extended format — *See* HFS+.

Mac OS ROM file — The first item that the Mac loads into memory from the System folder during the startup process. This file contains commands required for interaction with hardware and the lower levels of the Mac OS.

Mac OS standard format — *See* HFS.

macro — A small sequence of commands, contained within a document, that can be automatically executed when the document is loaded, or executed later by using a predetermined keystroke.

macro virus — A virus that can hide in the macros of a document file. Typically, viruses do not reside in data or document files.

main board — *See* motherboard.

make code — A code produced by pressing a key on a computer keyboard.

mandatory user profile — A roaming user profile that applies to all users in a group, and individual users cannot change that profile.

Master Boot Record (MBR) — The first sector on a hard drive, which contains the partition table and other information needed by BIOS to access the drive.

master file table (MFT) — The database used by the NTFS file system to track the contents of a logical drive.

material safety data sheet (MSDS) — A document that explains how to properly handle substances such as chemical solvents; it includes information such as physical data, toxicity, health effects, first aid, storage, disposal, and spill procedures.

MAU (Multistation Access Unit) — A centralized hub used in token ring networks to connect stations. Also called CAU or MSAU.

MBR (Master Boot Record) — The first sector on a hard drive, which contains the partition table and a program the BIOS uses to boot an OS from the drive.

MDRAM (multibank DRAM) — A special kind of RAM used on video cards that is able to use a full 128-bit bus path without requiring the full 4 MB of RAM.

megahertz (MHz) — One million Hz, or one million cycles per second. *See* hertz (Hz).

memory — Physical microchips that can hold data and programming, located on the motherboard or expansion cards.

memory address — A number assigned to each byte in memory. The CPU can use memory addresses to track where information is stored in RAM. Memory addresses are usually displayed as hexadecimal numbers in segment/ offset form.

memory bus — *See* system bus.

memory cache — A small amount of faster RAM that stores recently retrieved data, in anticipation of what the CPU will request next, thus speeding up access. *See also* system bus.

memory dump — The contents of memory saved to a file at the time an event halted the system. Support technicians can analyze the dump file to help understand the source of the problem.

memory extender — For DOS and Windows 9x, a device driver named Himem.sys that manages RAM giving access to memory addresses above 1 MB.

memory leak — Occurs when software unloads from memory but does not release the memory addresses that it was using for its data back to the OS.

memory paging — In Windows, swapping blocks of RAM memory to an area of the hard drive to serve as virtual memory when RAM is low.

memory-resident virus — A virus that can stay lurking in memory even after its host program is terminated.

Micro Channel Architecture (MCA) bus — A proprietary IBM PS/2 bus, seldom seen today, with a width of 16 or 32 bits and multiple master control, which allowed for multitasking.

microATX — A recent version of the ATX form factor. MicroATX addresses some new technologies that have been developed since the original introduction of ATX.

microprocessor — *See* central processing unit (CPU).

Microsoft Management Console (MMC) — A utility to build customized consoles. These consoles can be saved to a file with a .msc file extension.

Mini-ATX — A smaller ATX board that can be used with regular ATX cases and power supplies.

Mini-LPX — A smaller version of the LPX motherboard.

minicartridge — A tape drive cartridge that is only 3¼ × 2½ × ⅜ inches. It is small enough to allow two drives to fit into a standard 5½-inch drive bay of a PC case.

minifile system — In Windows NT/2000/XP, a simplified file system that is started so that Ntldr (NT Loader) can read files from any file system the OS supports.

mixed mode — A Windows 2000 mode for domain controllers used when there is at least one Windows NT domain controller on the network.

MMX (Multimedia Extensions) — Multimedia instructions built into Intel processors to add functionality such as better processing of multimedia, SIMD support, and increased cache.

modem — From MOdulate/DEModulate. A device that modulates digital data from a computer to an analog format that can be sent over telephone lines, then demodulates it back into digital form.

modem eliminator — *See* null modem cable.

modem riser card — A small modem card that uses an AMR or CNR slot. Part of the modem logic is contained in a controller on the motherboard.

modem speed — The speed at which a modem can transmit data along a phone line, measured in bits per second (bps). Also called line speed.

modulation — Converting binary or digital data into an analog signal that can be sent over standard telephone lines.

monitor — The most commonly used output device for displaying text and graphics on a computer.

motherboard — The largest and main circuit board inside the computer; it holds the CPU, slots, connections, and ports for other devices and wires for communication called a bus. The CPU, ROM chips, SIMMs, DIMMs, RIMMs, and interface cards are plugged into the motherboard. Also called system board.

motherboard bus — *See* system bus.

motherboard mouse — *See* PS/2-compatible mouse.

mouse — A pointing and input device that allows the user to move a cursor around a screen and select programs with the click of a button.

MP3 — A method to compress audio files that uses MPEG level 3. It can reduce sound files as low as a 1:24 ratio without losing much sound quality.

MPEG (Moving Pictures Experts Group) — A processing-intensive standard for data compression for motion pictures that tracks movement from one frame to the next and only stores the data that has changed.

MSAU — *See* MAU.

Msdos.sys — In Windows 9x, a text file that contains settings used by Io.sys during booting. In DOS, the Msdos.sys file was a program file that contained part of the DOS core.

multicasting — A process in which a message is sent by one host to multiple hosts, such as when a video conference is broadcasted to several hosts on the Internet.

multimedia — A type of computer presentation that combines text, graphics, animation, photos, sound, and/or full-motion video.

multimeter — A device used to measure the various components of an electrical circuit. The most common measurements are voltage, current, and resistance.

multipartite virus — A combination of a boot sector virus and a file virus. It can hide in either type of program.

multiplier — The factor by which the bus speed or frequency is multiplied to get the CPU clock speed.

multiprocessing — Having two or more CPUs in a system.

multiscan monitor — A monitor that can work within a range of frequencies and thus can work with different standards and video cards. It offers a variety of refresh rates.

multisession — A feature that allows data to be read from or written to a CD during more than one session. This is important if the disk was only partially filled during the first write.

multitasking — Doing more than one thing at a time. A true multitasking system requires two or more CPUs, each processing a different thread at the same time. Compare to cooperative multitasking and preemptive multitasking.

multithreading — The ability to pass more than one function (thread) to the OS kernel at the same time, such as when one thread is performing a print job while another reads a file.

name resolution — The process of associating a NetBIOS name or host name to an IP address.

narrow SCSI — One of the two main SCSI specifications. Narrow SCSI has an 8-bit data bus. The word "narrow" is not usually included in the names of narrow SCSI devices.

NAT (Network Address Translation) — A process that converts private IP addresses on a LAN to the proxy server's IP address before a data packet is sent over the Internet.

native mode — A Windows 2000 mode used by domain controllers when there are no Windows NT domain controllers present on the network.

NetBEUI (NetBIOS Extended User Interface) — A fast, proprietary Microsoft networking protocol used only by Windows-based systems, and limited to LANs because it does not support routing.

NetBIOS (Network Basic Input/Output System) — An API protocol used by some applications to communicate over a NetBEUI network. NetBIOS has largely been replaced by Windows Sockets over a TCP/IP network.

network adapter — *See* network interface card.

network drive map — Mounting a drive to a computer, such as drive E, that is actually hard drive space on another host computer on the network.

network interface card (NIC) — An expansion card that plugs into a computer's motherboard and provides a port on the back of the card to connect a PC to a network. Also called a network adapter.

Network layer — The OSI layer responsible for routing packets.

network printer — A printer that is available to users on a network.

NIC — *See* network interface card.

NLX — A low-end form factor that is similar to LPX but provides greater support for current and emerging processor technologies. NLX was designed for flexibility and efficiency of space.

NNTP (Network News Transfer Protocol) — The protocol used by newsgroup servers and client software.

node — Any computer, workstation, or device on a network.

noise — An extraneous, unwanted signal, often over an analog phone line, that can cause communication interference or transmission errors. Possible sources are fluorescent lighting, radios, TVs, lightning, or bad wiring.

noninterlaced — A type of display in which the electronic beam of a monitor draws every line on the screen with each pass.

non-memory-resident virus — A virus that is terminated when the host program is closed. Compare to memory-resident virus.

nonparity memory — Eight-bit memory without error checking. A SIMM part number with a 32 in it (4 × 8 bits) is nonparity.

nonvolatile — Refers to a kind of RAM that is stable and can hold data as long as electricity is powering the memory.

normal mode — *See* CHS mode.

North Bridge — That portion of the chip set hub that connects faster I/O buses (for example, AGP bus) to the system bus. Compare to South Bridge.

NOS (network operating system) — An operating system that resides on the controlling computer in the network. The NOS controls what software, data, and devices a user on the network can access.

notebook — A portable computer that is designed for travel and mobility. Notebooks use the same technology as desktop PCs, with modifications for conserving voltage, taking up less space, and operating while on the move. Also called a laptop computer.

NTFS (NT file system) — The file system for the Windows NT/2000/XP operating systems. NTFS cannot be accessed by other operating systems such as DOS. It provides increased reliability and security in comparison to other methods of organizing and accessing files. There are several versions of NTFS that might or might not be compatible.

NTHQ (NT Hardware Qualifier) — A utility found on the Windows NT installation CD-ROM that examines your system to determine if all hardware present qualifies for NT.

Ntldr (NT Loader) — In Windows NT/2000/XP, the OS loader used on Intel systems.

NTVDM (NT virtual DOS machine) — An emulated environment in which a 16-bit DOS application resides within Windows NT/2000/XP with its own memory space or WOW (Win16 on Win32).

null modem cable — A cable that allows two data terminal equipment (DTE) devices to communicate in which the transmit and receive wires are cross-connected and no modems are necessary.

octet — Term for each of the four 8-bit numbers that make up an IP address. For example, the IP address 206.96.103.114 has four octets.

ohm (Ω) — The standard unit of measurement for electrical resistance. Resistors are rated in ohms.

on-board ports — Ports that are directly on the motherboard, such as a built-in keyboard port or on-board serial port.

operating system (OS) — Software that controls a computer. An OS controls how system resources are used and provides a user interface, a way of managing hardware and software, and ways to work with files.

operating system (OS) formatting — *See* high-level formatting.

OSI (Open Systems Interconnect) reference model — A network communication model that provides a universally accepted reference that illustrates how data is transmitted on a network or between two or more networked devices. This model separates communication into seven layers.

overclocking — Running a motherboard at a frequency that is not recommended or guaranteed by CPU or chip set manufacturers.

P1 connector — Power connection on an ATX motherboard.

P8 connector — One of two power connectors on an AT motherboard.

P9 connector — One of two power connectors on an AT motherboard.

packet — Segment of network data that also include header, destination address, and trailer information that is sent as a unit. Also called data packet or datagram.

page fault — An OS interrupt that occurs when the OS is forced to access the hard drive to satisfy the demands for virtual memory.

page file — *See* swap file.

page-in — The process in which the memory manager goes to the hard drive to return the data from a swap file to RAM.

page-out — The process in which, when RAM is full, the memory manager takes a page and moves it to the swap file.

Pagefile.sys — The Windows NT/2000/XP swap file.

pages — 4K segments in which Windows NT/2000/XP allocates memory.

parallel port — A 25-pin female port on a computer that can transmit data in parallel, 8 bits at a time, and is usually used by a printer. The port is sometimes configured as LPT1 or LPT2.

parity — An error-checking scheme in which a ninth, or "parity," bit is added. The value of the parity bit is set to either 0 or 1 to provide an even number of ones for even parity and an odd number of ones for odd parity.

parity error — An error that occurs when the number of ones in the byte is not in agreement with the expected number.

parity memory — Nine-bit memory in which the ninth bit is used for error checking. A SIMM part number with a 36 in it (4 × 9 bits) is parity. Older PCs almost always use parity chips.

partition — A division of a hard drive that can be used to hold logical drives.

partition table — A table at the beginning of the hard drive that contains information about each partition on the drive. The partition table is contained in the Master Boot Record.

passive backplane — A type of backplane system in which the backplane contains no circuitry at all. Passive backplanes locate all circuitry on a mothercard plugged into a backplane.

passive terminator — A type of terminator for single-ended SCSI cables. Simple resistors are used to provide termination of a signal. Passive termination is not reliable over long distances and should only be used with narrow SCSI.

patch — An update to software that corrects an error, adds a feature, or addresses security issues. Also called an update or service pack.

patch cable — A network cable that is used to connect a PC to a hub.

path — (1) A drive and list of directories pointing to a file such as C:\Windows\command. (2) The OS command to provide a list of paths to the system for finding program files to execute.

PC Card — A credit-card-sized adapter card that can be slid into a slot in the side of many notebook computers and is used for connecting to modems, networks, and CD-ROM drives. Also called PCMCIA Card.

PC Card slot — An expansion slot on a notebook computer, into which a PC Card is inserted. Also called a PCMCIA Card slot.

PCI (Peripheral Component Interconnect) bus — A bus common on Pentium computers that runs at speeds of up to 33 MHz or 66 MHz, with a 32-bit-wide or 64-bit-wide data path. PCI-X, released in September 1999, enables PCI to run at 133 MHz. For some chip sets, it serves as the middle layer between the memory bus and expansion buses.

PCI bus IRQ steering — A feature that makes it possible for PCI devices to share an IRQ. System BIOS and the OS must both support this feature.

PCMCIA (Personal Computer Memory Card International Association) Card — *See* PC Card.

PCMCIA Card slot — *See* PC Card slot.

PDA (Personal Digital Assistant) — A small, handheld computer that has its own operating system and applications.

peer-to-peer network — A network of computers that are all equals, or peers. Each computer has the same amount of authority, and each can act as a server to the other computers.

peripheral devices — Devices that communicate with the CPU but are not located directly on the motherboard, such as the monitor, floppy drive, printer, and mouse.

physical address — *See* MAC address.

physical geometry — The actual layout of heads, tracks, and sectors on a hard drive. Refer also to logical geometry.

Physical layer — The OSI layer responsible for interfacing with the network media (cabling).

PIF (program information file) — A file used by Windows to describe the environment for a DOS program to use.

pin array cartridge (PAC) — The cartridge that houses the Intel Itanium processor.

pin grid array (PGA) — A feature of a CPU socket whereby the pins are aligned in uniform rows around the socket.

Ping (Packet Internet Groper) — (1) A program that allows one computer to send a packet to another computer and then receive a reply. Used as a method of testing connectivity. (2) A Windows and Unix command used to trouble-shoot network connections. It verifies that the host can communicate with another host on the network.

pinout — A description of how each pin on a bus, connection, plug, slot, or socket is used.

pipelined burst SRAM — A less expensive SRAM that uses more clock cycles per transfer than nonpipelined burst but does not significantly slowdown the process.

pits — Recessed areas on the surface of a CD or DVD, separating lands, or flat areas. Lands and pits are used to represent data on a disc.

pixel — A small spot on a fine horizontal scan line. Pixels are illuminated to create an image on the monitor.

Plug and Play (PnP) — A standard designed to make the installation of new hardware devices easier by automatically configuring devices to eliminate system resource conflicts (such as IRQ or I/O address conflicts). PnP is supported by Windows 9x, Windows 2000 and Windows XP.

Plug and Play (PnP) BIOS — System BIOS that supports the Plug and Play standards and is designed to automatically recognize new devices when they are installed.

polling — A process by which the CPU checks the status of connected devices to determine if they are ready to send or receive data.

polymorphic virus — A type of virus that changes its distinguishing characteristics as it replicates itself. Mutating in this way makes it more difficult for AV software to recognize the presence of the virus.

POP (Post Office Protocol) — The protocol that an e-mail server and client use when the client requests the downloading of e-mail messages. The most recent version is POP3. POP is slowly being replaced by IMAP.

port — (1) As applied to services running on a computer, a number assigned to a process on a computer so that the process can be found by TCP/IP. Also called a port address or port number. (2) Another name for an I/O address. *See also* I/O address. (3) A physical connector, usually at the back of a computer, that allows a cable from a peripheral device, such as a printer, mouse, or modem, to be attached.

port address — *See* I/O address.

port number — *See* port.

port replicator — A device designed to connect to a notebook computer in order to make it easy to connect the notebook to peripheral devices.

port settings — The configuration parameters of communications devices such as COM1, COM2, or COM3, including IRQ settings.

port speed — The communication speed between a DTE (computer) and a DCE (modem). As a general rule, the port speed should be at least four times as fast as the modem speed.

POSIX (Portable Operating System Interface) — A set of standards for Unix and similar operating systems used to create applications to comply with standards used by federal agencies for their software.

POST (power-on self test) — A self-diagnostic program used to perform a simple test of the CPU, RAM, and various I/O devices. The POST is performed by startup BIOS when the computer is first turned on and is stored in ROM-BIOS.

power conditioner — A line conditioner that regulates, or conditions, power, providing continuous voltage during brownouts.

power on password — A password that a computer uses to control access during the boot process.

power-on self test — See POST.

power scheme — A feature of Windows XP support for notebooks that allows the user to create groups of power settings for specific sets of conditions.

power supply — A box inside the computer case that supplies power to the motherboard and other installed devices. Power supplies provide 3.3, 5, and 12 volts DC.

Power User — See standard user.

PPP (Point-to-Point Protocol) — A protocol that governs the methods for communicating via modems and dial-up telephone lines. The Windows Dial-up Networking utility uses PPP.

PRAM (parameter RAM) — A small amount of RAM on a Mac that contains configuration information for the Mac.

preemptive multitasking — A type of pseudo-multitasking whereby the CPU allows an application a specified period of time and then preempts the processing to give time to another application.

Presentation layer — The OSI layer that compresses and decompresses data and interfaces with the Application layer and the Session layer.

primary cache — See internal cache.

primary domain controller (PDC) — In a Windows NT network, the computer that controls the directory database of user accounts, group accounts, and computer accounts on a domain. Also see backup domain controller.

primary partition — A hard disk partition that can contain only one logical drive.

primary storage — Temporary storage on the motherboard used by the CPU to process data and instructions. Memory is considered primary storage.

printer — A peripheral output device that produces printed output to paper. Different types include dot matrix, ink-jet, and laser printers.

printer maintenance kit — A kit purchased from a printer manufacturer that contains parts, tools, and instructions needed to perform routine printer maintenance.

private IP address — An IP address that is used on a private TCP/IP network that is isolated from the Internet.

process — An executing instance of a program together with the program resources. There can be more than one process running for a program at the same time. One process for a program happens each time the program is loaded into memory or executed.

processor — See central processing unit (CPU).

processor speed — The speed, or frequency, at which the CPU operates. Usually expressed in GHz.

product activation — The process that Microsoft uses to prevent software piracy. For example, once Windows XP is activated for a particular computer, it cannot be installed on another computer.

program — A set of step-by-step instructions to a computer. Some are burned directly into chips, while others are stored as program files. Programs are written in languages such as BASIC and C++.

program file — A file that contains instructions designed to be executed by the CPU.

protected mode — An operating mode that supports preemptive multitasking, the OS manages memory and other hardware devices, and programs can use a 32-bit data path. Also called 32-bit mode.

protocol — A set of rules and standards that two entities use for communication.

Protocol.ini — A Windows initialization file that contains network configuration information.

proxy server — A server that acts as an intermediary between another computer and the Internet. The proxy server substitutes its own IP address for the IP address of the computer on the network making a request, so that all traffic over the Internet appears to be coming from only the IP address of the proxy server.

PS/2-compatible mouse — A mouse that plugs into a round mouse PS/2 port on the motherboard. Sometimes called a motherboard mouse.

public IP address — An IP address available to the Internet.

Quarter-Inch Committee or **quarter-inch cartridge (QIC)** — A name of a standardized method used to write data to tape. These backup files have a .qic extension.

RAID (redundant array of inexpensive disks or **redundant array of independent disks)** — Several methods of configuring multiple hard drives to store data to increase logical volume size and improve performance, and to ensure that if one hard drive fails, the data is still available from another hard drive.

RAM (random access memory) — Memory modules on the motherboard containing microchips (such as SIMMs) used to temporarily hold data and programs while the CPU processes both. Information in RAM is lost when the PC is turned off.

RAM drive — An area of memory that is treated as though it were a hard drive, but that works much faster than a hard drive. The Windows 98 startup disk uses a RAM drive. Compare to virtual memory.

random access memory — *See* RAM.

RARP (Reverse Address Resolution Protocol) — A protocol used to translate the unique hardware NIC addresses (MAC addresses) into IP addresses (the reverse of ARP).

RDRAM — *See* Direct Rambus DRAM.

read/write head — A sealed, magnetic coil device that moves across the surface of a disk either reading data from or writing data to the disk.

real mode — A single-tasking operating mode whereby a program has 1024K of memory addresses, has direct access to RAM, and uses a 16-bit data path. Using a memory extender (Himem.sys) a program in real mode can access memory above 1024K. Also called 16-bit mode.

Recovery Console — A Windows 2000/XP command interface utility and OS that can be used to solve problems when Windows cannot load from the hard drive.

rectifier — An electrical device that converts AC to DC. A PC power supply contains a rectifier.

redirection symbol — The greater than (>) symbol used in OS commands to redirect output to a file or printer instead of to a screen.

refresh — The process of periodically rewriting data, such as on dynamic RAM.

refresh rate — As applied to monitors, the number of times in one second an electronic beam can fill the screen with lines from top to bottom. Also called vertical scan rate.

registry — A database that Windows uses to store hardware and software configuration information, user preferences, and setup information.

re-marked chips — Chips that have been used and returned to the factory, marked again, and resold. The surface of the chips may be dull or scratched.

Remote Access Service (RAS) — The Windows NT service used to configure a computer to allow inbound calls.

Remote Assistance — A Windows XP feature that allows a support technician at a remote location to have full access to the Windows XP desktop.

repeater — A device that amplifies signals on a network so they can be transmitted further down the line.

request handler — *See* interrupt handler.

rescue disk — A floppy disk that can be used to start up a computer when the hard drive fails to boot. Also called ESD or startup disk.

resistance — The degree to which a device opposes or resists the flow of electricity. As the electrical resistance increases, the current decreases. *See* ohm and resistor.

resistor — An electronic device that resists or opposes the flow of electricity. A resistor can be used to reduce the amount of electricity being supplied to an electronic component.

resolution — The number of pixels on a monitor screen that are addressable by software (example: 1024 × 768 pixels).

resource arbitrator — A Plug and Play component that decides which resources are assigned to which devices.

resource management — The process of allocating resources to devices at startup.

restore point — A snapshot of the Windows Me/XP system state, usually made before installation of new hardware or applications.

restricted user — *See* user.

REt (Resolution Enhancement technology) — The term used by Hewlett-Packard to describe the way a laser printer varies the size of the dots used to create an image. This technology partly accounts for the sharp, clear image created by a laser printer.

RFC (Request for Comments) — A document that proposes a change in standards or protocols for the communications industry. An RFC can be presented by different organizations but is managed under the general guidance of the Internet Architecture Board (IAB).

RIMM — A type of memory module used on newer motherboards, produced by Rambus, Inc.

ring topology — A network topology in which the nodes in a network form a ring. Each node is connected only to two other nodes, and a centralized hub is not required.

RISC (Reduced Instruction Set Computing) chips — Chips that incorporate only the most frequently used instructions, so that the computer operates faster (for example, the PowerPC uses RISC chips).

riser card — A card that plugs into a motherboard and allows for expansion cards to be mounted parallel to the motherboard. Expansion cards are plugged into slots on the riser card.

RJ-11 — A phone line connection found on modems, telephones, and house phone outlets.

RJ-45 connector — A connector used with twisted-pair cable that connects the cable to the NIC.

roaming user profile — A user profile for a roaming user. Roaming user profiles are stored on a server so that the user can access the profile from anywhere on the network.

roaming users — Users who can move from PC to PC within a network, with their profiles following them.

ROM (read-only memory) — Chips that contain programming code and cannot be erased.

ROM BIOS — *See* BIOS.

root account — The principal user account in Linux, accessible by the system administrator. Only the owner of the root account has the ability to make certain alterations to the system and perform certain system tasks.

root directory — The main directory created when a hard drive or disk is first formatted. In Linux, indicated by a forward slash. In DOS and Windows, indicated by a backward slash.

root privileges — The privileges that the system administrator has on a Linux system, which allow the system administrator full access to the system.

routable protocol — A protocol that can be routed to interconnected networks on the basis of a network address. TCP/IP is a routable protocol, but NetBEUI is not.

router — A device that connects networks and makes decisions as to the best routes to use when forwarding packets.

run-time configuration — An ongoing Plug and Play process that monitors changes in system devices, such as the removal of a PC card on a notebook computer or the docking of a notebook computer to a docking station.

sampling rate — The rate of samples taken of an analog signal over a period of time, usually expressed as samples per second, or hertz.

scanning mirror — A component of a laser printer consisting of an octagonal mirror that can be directed in a sweeping motion to cover the entire length of a laser printer drum.

SCSI (Small Computer System Interface) — A fast interface between a host adapter and the CPU that can daisy chain as many as 7 or 15 devices on a single bus.

SCSI ID — A number from 0 to 15 assigned to each SCSI device attached to the daisy chain.

SDRAM II — *See* Double Data Rate SDRAM (DDR SDRAM).

secondary storage — Storage that is remote to the CPU and permanently holds data, even when the PC is turned off, such as a hard drive.

sector — On a disk surface, one segment of a track, which almost always contains 512 bytes of data.

security accounts manager (SAM) — A portion of the Windows NT/2000/XP registry that manages the account database that contains accounts, policies, and other pertinent information about local accounts.

sequential access — A method of data access used by tape drives, whereby data is written or read sequentially from the beginning to the end of the tape or until the desired data is found.

serial mouse — A mouse that uses a serial port and has a female 9-pin DB-9 connector.

serial port — A male 9-pin or 25-pin port on a computer system used by slower I/O devices such as a mouse or modem. Data travels serially, one bit at a time, through the port. Serial ports are sometimes configured as COM1, COM2, COM3, or COM4.

server — (1) A software program that interacts with client software in a client/server environment. (2) A computer that runs server software and responds to requests for information from client computers.

service pack — *See* patch.

session — An established communication link between two software programs. On the Internet, a session is created by TCP.

Session layer — The OSI layer that makes and manages an extended connection between two hosts on a network.

SFC (System File Checker) — A Windows tool that checks to make sure Windows is using the correct versions of system files.

SGRAM (synchronous graphics RAM) — Memory designed especially for video card processing that can synchronize itself with the CPU bus clock.

shadow RAM or **shadowing ROM** — ROM programming code copied into RAM to speed up the system operation, because of the faster access speed of RAM.

shell — The portion of an OS that relates to the user and to applications.

shielded twisted-pair (STP) cable — A cable that is made of one or more twisted pairs of wires and is surrounded by a metal shield.

shortcut — An icon on the desktop that points to a program that can be executed or to a file or folder.

signal-regenerating repeater — A repeater that is able to distinguish between noise and signal. It reads the signal and retransmits it without the accompanying noise.

Sigverif.exe — A Windows 2000/XP utility that allows you to search for digital signatures.

SIMD (single instruction, multiple data) — A process that allows the CPU to execute a single instruction simultaneously on multiple pieces of data, rather than by repetitive looping.

SIMM (single inline memory module) — A miniature circuit board used in older computers to hold RAM. SIMMs hold 8, 16, 32, or 64 MB on a single module.

simple volume — A type of dynamic volume used on a single hard drive that corresponds to a primary partition on a basic disk.

single-ended (SE) — A type of SCSI signaling in which two wires are used to carry a signal, one of which carries the signal itself and the other is a ground for the signal.

single-tasking — When only one program is running at a time.

single-voltage CPU — A CPU that requires one voltage for both internal and I/O operations.

slack — Wasted space on a hard drive caused by not using all available space at the end of clusters.

sleep mode — A mode used in many "Green" systems that allows them to be configured through CMOS to suspend the monitor or even the drive, if the keyboard and/or CPU have been inactive for a set number of minutes. *See also* Green Standards.

slimline case — *See* compact case.

SLIP (Serial Line Internet Protocol) — A line protocol used by regular telephone lines that has largely been replaced by PPP.

SMARTDrive — A hard drive cache program that came with Windows 3.x and DOS and can be executed as a TSR from the Autoexec.bat file (for example, Device=Smartdrv.sys 2048).

SMAU (Smart Multistation Access Unit) — *See* MAU.

SMTP (Simple Mail Transfer Protocol) — The protocol used by e-mail clients and servers to send e-mail messages over the Internet. *See* POP and IMAP.

snap-ins — Components added to a console using the Microsoft Management Console.

SNMP (Simple Network Management Protocol) — A protocol used to monitor and manage network traffic on a workstation. SNMP works with TCP/IP and IPX/SPX networks.

SO-DIMM (small outline DIMM) — A type of memory module used in notebook computers that uses DIMM technology and can have either 72 pins or 144 pins.

SO-RIMM (small outline RIMM) — A 160-pin memory module used in notebooks that uses Rambus technology.

socket — *See* session.

soft boot — To restart a PC without turning off the power, for example, by pressing three keys at the same time (Ctrl, Alt, and Del). Also called warm boot.

soft power — *See* soft switch.

soft switch — A feature on an ATX system that allows an OS to power down the system and allows for activity such as a keystroke or network activity to power up the system. Also called soft power.

software — Computer programs, or instructions to perform a specific task. Software may be BIOS, OSs, or applications software such as a word-processing or spreadsheet program.

software cache — Cache controlled by software whereby the cache is stored in RAM.

software interrupt — An event caused by a program currently being executed by the CPU signaling the CPU that it requires the use of a hardware device.

South Bridge — That portion of the chip set hub that connects slower I/O buses (for example, ISA bus) to the system bus. Compare to North Bridge.

spacers – *See* standoffs.

spanned volume — A type of dynamic volume used on two or more hard drives that fills up the space allotted on one physical disk before moving to the next.

SPI (SCSI Parallel Interface) — The part of the SCSI-3 standard that specifies how SCSI devices are connected.

spikes — Temporary surges in voltage, which can damage electrical components.

spooling — Placing print jobs in a print queue so that an application can be released from the printing process before printing is completed. Spooling is an acronym for simultaneous peripheral operations online.

SSE (Streaming SIMD Extension) — A technology used by the Intel Pentium III and later CPUs designed to improve performance of multimedia software.

staggered pin grid array (SPGA) — A feature of a CPU socket whereby the pins are staggered over the socket in order to squeeze more pins into a small space.

standard user — Also called power user. Standard users can read from and write to parts of the system other than their own local drive, install applications, and perform limited administrative tasks.

standby time — The time before a "Green" system will reduce 92 percent of its activity. *See also* Green Standards.

standoffs — Round plastic or metal pegs that separate the motherboard from the case, so that components on the back of the motherboard do not touch the case.

star bus topology — A LAN that uses a logical bus design, but with all devices connected to a central hub, making a physical star.

star ring topology — A topology that is physically arranged in a star formation but is logically a ring because of the way information travels on it. Token ring is the primary example.

star topology — A LAN in which all the devices are connected to a central hub.

startup BIOS — Part of system BIOS that is responsible for controlling the PC when it is first turned on. Startup BIOS gives control over to the OS once it is loaded.

startup disk — *See* rescue disk.

startup password — *See* power on password.

stateless — Term for a device or process that manages data or some activity without regard to all the details of the data or activity.

static electricity — *See* ESD.

static IP address — An IP address permanently assigned to a workstation.

static RAM (SRAM) — RAM chips that retain information without the need for refreshing, as long as the computer's power is on. They are more expensive than traditional DRAM.

Static VxD — A VxD that is loaded into memory at startup and remains there for the entire OS session.

stealth virus — A virus that actively conceals itself by temporarily removing itself from an infected file that is about to be examined, and then hiding a copy of itself elsewhere on the drive.

stop error — An error severe enough to cause the operating system to stop all processes.

streaming audio — Downloading audio data from the Internet in a continuous stream of data without first downloading an entire audio file.

striped volume — A type of dynamic volume used for two or more hard drives that writes to the disks evenly rather than filling up allotted space on one and then moving on to the next. Compare to spanned volume.

subdirectory — A directory or folder contained in another directory or folder. Also called a child directory or folder.

subnet mask — A subnet mask is a group of four numbers (dotted decimal numbers) that tell TCP/IP if a remote computer is on the same or a different network.

subsystems — The different modules into which the Windows NT/2000/XP user mode is divided.

surge suppressor or **surge protector** — A device or power strip designed to protect electronic equipment from power surges and spikes.

suspend time — The time before a green system will reduce 99 percent of its activity. After this time, the system needs a warmup time so that the CPU, monitor, and hard drive can reach full activity.

swap file — A file on the hard drive that is used by the OS for virtual memory. Also called page file.

switch — A device used to segment a network. It can decide which network segment is to receive a packet, on the basis of the packet's destination MAC address.

synchronization — The process by which files and programs are transferred between PDAs and PCs.

synchronous DRAM (SDRAM) — A type of memory stored on DIMMs that runs in sync with the system clock, running at the same speed as the motherboard.

synchronous SRAM — SRAM that is faster and more expensive than asynchronous SRAM. It requires a clock signal to validate its control signals, enabling the cache to run in step with the CPU.

SyncLink DRAM (SLDRAM) — A type of DRAM developed by a consortium of 12 DRAM manufactures. It improved on regular SDRAM but is now obsolete.

Sysedit — The Windows System Configuration Editor, which is a text editor generally used to edit system files.

system BIOS — BIOS located on the motherboard.

system board — *See* motherboard.

system bus — The bus between the CPU and memory on the motherboard. The bus frequency in documentation is called the system speed such as 200 MHz. Also called the memory bus, front-side bus, local bus, external bus, or host bus.

system clock — A line on a bus that is dedicated to timing the activities of components connected to it. The system clock provides a continuous pulse that other devices use to time themselves.

system disk — Windows terminology for a bootable disk.

System file — The Mac OS file that contains the libraries and commands that make up the core of the OS.

System File Protection — A Windows Me feature that prevents system files from being deleted.

System folder — The folder that a Mac system designates as the one from which the OS is to be loaded.

System.ini — A text configuration file used by Windows 3.x and supported by Windows 9x for backward-compatibility.

system partition — The active partition of the hard drive containing the boot record and the specific files required to load Windows NT/2000/XP.

system resource — A channel, line, or address on the motherboard that can be used by the CPU or a device for communication. The four system resources are IRQ, I/O address, DMA channel, and memory address.

System Restore — A Windows Me/XP utility, similar to the ScanReg tool in earlier versions of Windows, that is used to restore the system to a restore point. Unlike ScanReg, System Restore cannot be executed from a command prompt.

system state data — In Windows 2000/XP, files that are necessary for a successful load of the operating system.

System Tray — An area to the right of the taskbar that holds the icons of small applets launched at startup.

TAPI (Telephony Application Programming Interface) — A standard developed by Intel and Microsoft that can be used by 32-bit Windows 9x communications programs for communicating over phone lines.

task switching — *See* cooperative multitasking.

TCP (Transmission Control Protocol) — Part of the TCP/IP protocol suite. TCP guarantees delivery of data for application protocols and establishes a session before it begins transmitting data.

TCP/IP (Transmission Control Protocol/Internet Protocol) — The suite of protocols that supports communication on the Internet. TCP is responsible for error checking, and IP is responsible for routing.

telephony — A term describing the technology of converting sound to signals that can travel over telephone lines.

Terminate-and-stay-resident (TSR) — A program that is loaded into memory and remains dormant until called on, such as a screen saver or a memory-resident antivirus program.

terminating resistor — The resistor added at the end of a SCSI chain to dampen the voltage at the end of the chain.

termination — A process necessary to prevent an echo effect of power at the end of a SCSI chain, resulting in interference with the data transmission.

ThickNet — *See* 10Base5.

ThinNet — *See* 10Base2.

thread — Each process that the CPU is aware of; a single task that is part of a longer task or program.

throughput performance — Also called data throughput. Throughput performance is a measure of the actual data transmitted by the bus, not including error-checking bits or redundant data.

token — A small packet used on token ring networks to send data from one station to the next.

top-level domain — The highest level of domain names, indicated by a suffix that tells something about the host. For example, .com is for commercial use and .edu is for educational institutions.

tower case — The largest type of personal computer case. Tower cases stand vertically upright and can be as much as two feet tall. They have more drive bays and are a good choice for computer users who anticipate making significant upgrades.

trace — A wire on a circuit board that connects two components or devices.

tracks — The concentric circles into which the surface of a disk is divided.

training — *See* handshaking.

transceiver — The component on a NIC that is responsible for signal conversion. Combines the words transmitter and receiver.

transformer — A device that changes the ratio of current to voltage. A computer power supply is basically a transformer and a rectifier.

transistor — An electronic device that can regulate electricity and act as a logical gate or switch for an electrical signal.

translation — A technique used by system BIOS and hard drive controller BIOS to break the 504-MB hard drive barrier, whereby a different set of drive parameters are communicated to the OS and other software than that used by the hard drive controller BIOS.

Transport layer — The OSI layer that verifies data and requests a resend when the data is corrupted.

Trojan horse — A type of infestation that hides or disguises itself as a useful program, yet is designed to cause damage at a later time.

TSR (terminate-and-stay-resident) — A program that is loaded into memory but is not immediately executed, such as a screen saver or a memory-resident antivirus program.

UART (universal asynchronous receiver-transmitter) chip — A chip that controls serial ports. It sets protocol and converts parallel data bits received from the system bus into serial bits.

UDF (Universal Disk Format) — A file system for optical media used by all DVD discs and some CD-R and CD-RW discs.

UDP (User Datagram Protocol) — A connectionless protocol that does not require a connection to send a packet and does not guarantee that the packet arrives at its destination. UDP works at the Transport layer and is faster than TCP because TCP takes the time to make a connection and guarantee delivery.

UMB (upper memory block) — In DOS and Windows 9x, a group of consecutive memory addresses in RAM from 640K to 1MB that can be used by 16-bit device drivers and TSRs.

unattended installation — A Windows NT/2000/XP installation that is done by storing the answers to installation questions in a text file or script that Windows NT/2000/XP calls an answer file so that the answers do not have to be typed in during the installation.

unshielded twisted-pair (UTP) cable — A cable that is made of one or more twisted pairs of wires and is not surrounded by a metal shield.

upgrade install — The installation of an OS on a hard drive that already has an OS installed in such a way that settings kept by the old OS are carried forward into the upgrade, including information about hardware, software, and user preferences.

upper memory — In DOS and Windows 9x, the memory addresses from 640K up to 1024K, originally reserved for BIOS, device drivers, and TSRs.

UPS (uninterruptible power supply) — A device designed to provide a backup power supply during a power failure. Basically, a UPS is a battery backup system with an ultrafast sensing device.

URL (Uniform Resource Locator) — An address for a resource on the Internet. A URL can contain the protocol used by the resource, the name of the computer and its network, and the path and name of a file on the computer.

USB (universal serial bus) — A bus that is expected to eventually replace serial and parallel ports. USB is designed to make installation and configuration of I/O devices easy, providing room for as many as 127 devices daisy-chained together. The USB uses only a single set of resources for all devices on the bus.

USB host controller — Manages the USB bus. For the 400 series Intel chip set, the USB host controller is included in the PCI controller chip.

USB port — A type of port designed to make installation and configuration of I/O devices easy, providing room for as many as 127 devices daisy-chained together.

user — In reference to Windows NT/2000/XP permissions, a restricted user who has read-write access only on his or her own folders, read-only access to most system folders, and no access to other users' data.

user account — The information, stored in the SAM database, that defines a Windows NT/2000/XP user, including username, password, memberships, and rights.

user component — A Windows 9x component that controls the mouse, keyboard, ports and desktop.

user mode — In Windows NT/2000/XP, a mode that provides an interface between an application and the OS, and only has access to hardware resources through the code running in kernel mode.

user profile — A personal profile about a user that enables the user's desktop settings and other operating parameters to be retained from one session to another.

User State Migration Tool (USMT) — A Windows XP utility that helps you migrate user files and preferences from one computer to another in order to help a user makes a smooth transition from one computer to another.

V.90 — A standard for data transmission over phone lines that can attain a speed of 56 Kbps. It replaces K56flex and x2 standards.

value data — In Windows, the name and value of a setting in the registry.

VCACHE — A built-in Windows 9x 32-bit software cache that doesn't take up conventional memory space or upper memory space as SMARTDrive did.

VDM — *See* virtual DOS machine.

vector table — *See* interrupt vector table.

vertical scan rate — *See* refresh rate.

VESA (Video Electronics Standards Association) VL bus — An outdated local bus used on 80486 computers for connecting 32-bit adapters directly to the local processor bus.

VFAT — *See* virtual file allocation table (VFAT).

vi editor — A text editor in Linux that operates in two modes: insert mode, in which you can type text into the editor, and command mode, in which you can enter commands to work with the text or change the status of the editor.

video card — An interface card installed in the computer to control visual output on a monitor. Also called display adapter.

virtual device driver (VxD or VDD) — A Windows device driver that may or may not have direct access to a device. It might depend on a Windows component to communicate with the device itself.

virtual DOS machine (VDM) — Environment in which Windows runs a 16-bit DOS application. In a VDM, the application "thinks" it is running in real mode, but the OS is managing hardware resources using 32-bit drivers and providing virtual memory to the application.

virtual file allocation table (VFAT) — A variation of the original DOS 16-bit FAT that allows for long filenames and 32-bit disk access.

virtual machine — One or more logical machines created within one physical machine by Windows, allowing applications to make serious errors within one logical machine without disturbing other programs and parts of the system.

Virtual Machine Manager (VMM) — A Windows 9x program that controls virtual machines and the resources they use including memory. The VMM manages the page table used to access memory.

virtual memory — A method whereby the OS uses the hard drive as though it were RAM. Compare to RAM drive.

virtual real mode — An operating mode that works similarly to real mode provided by a 32-bit OS for a 16-bit program to work.

virus — A program that often has an incubation period, is infectious, and is intended to cause damage. A virus program might destroy data and programs or damage a disk drive's boot sector.

virus signature — A set of distinguishing characteristics of a virus used by antivirus software to identify the virus.

volatile — Refers to a kind of RAM that is temporary, cannot hold data very long, and must be frequently refreshed.

volt (V) — A measure of potential difference in an electrical circuit. A computer ATX power supply usually provides five separate voltages: +12V, −12V, +5V, −5V, and +3.3V.

voltage — Electrical differential that causes current to flow, measured in volts. *See* volt.

voltmeter — A device for measuring electrical AC or DC voltage.

volume — *See* logical drive.

volume bit map — On a Macintosh computer, a map of the allocation blocks on a hard drive. It uses a 1 to indicate that a block is storing files and a 0 to indicate that it is empty and is available for use.

volume information block — On a Macintosh computer, the directory structure that comes right after the boot blocks on a hard drive. It holds information about the drive, including its format, name, number of files and folders, and allocation block size.

VRAM (video RAM) — RAM on video cards that holds the data that is being passed from the computer to the monitor and can be accessed by two devices simultaneously. Higher resolutions often require more video memory.

VxD — *See* virtual device driver.

wait state — A clock tick in which nothing happens, used to ensure that the microprocessor isn't getting ahead of slower components. A 0-wait state is preferable to a 1-wait state. Too many wait states can slow a system down.

warm boot — *See* soft boot.

watt (W) — The unit used to measure power. A typical computer may use a power supply that provides 200W.

wattage — Electrical power measured in watts.

WDM (Win32 Driver Model) — The only Windows 9x Plug and Play component that is found in Windows 98 but not Windows 95. WDM is the component responsible for managing device drivers that work under a driver model new to Windows 98.

WFP (Windows File Protection) — A Windows 2000/XP tool that protects system files from modification.

wide SCSI — One of the two main SCSI specifications. Wide SCSI has a 16-bit data bus.

Win386.swp — The name of the Windows 9x swap file. Its default location is C:\Windows.

window manager — A graphical user interface for a Linux computer. A popular window manager is GNOME.

Win.ini — The Windows initialization file that contains program configuration information needed for running the Windows operating environment. Its functions were replaced by the registry beginning with Windows 9x, which still supports it for backward compatibility with Windows 3.x.

WINS (Windows Internet Naming Service) — A Microsoft resolution service with a distributed database that tracks relationships between NetBIOS names and IP addresses. Compare to DNS.

WinSock (Windows Sockets) — A part of the TCP/IP utility software that manages API calls from applications to other computers on a TCP/IP network.

wireless LAN (WLAN) — A type of LAN that does not use wires or cables to create connections, but instead transmits data over radio or infrared waves.

WIS (Windows Installer Service) — A feature new to Windows 2000 that standardizes the installation process for applications.

workgroup — In Windows, a logical group of computers and users in which administration, resources, and security are distributed throughout the network, without centralized management or security.

worm — An infestation designed to copy itself repeatedly to memory, on drive space or on a network, until little memory or disk space remains.

WOW (Win16 on Win32) — A group of programs provided by Windows NT/2000/XP to create a virtual DOS environment that emulates a 16-bit Windows environment, protecting the rest of the OS from 16-bit applications.

WRAM (window RAM) — Dual-ported video RAM that is faster and less expensive than VRAM. It has its own internal bus on the chip, with a data path that is 256 bits wide.

zero insertion force (ZIF) socket — A socket that uses a small lever to apply even force when you install the microchip into the socket.

zone bit recording — A method of storing data on a hard drive whereby the drive can have more sectors per track near the outside of the platter.

INDEX

& (ampersand), 443

* (asterisk), 684

\ (backslash), 88

/ (forward slash), 684

. (period), 21

? (question mark), 684

~ (tilde character), 685

A

AC (alternating current) voltage, 32–34, 103–104, 113, 124. *See also* electrical system

Accelerated Graphics Port expansion slot. *See* AGP (Accelerated Graphics Port) expansion slot

accounts, 934–941, 1086–1087

ACPI (Advanced Configuration and Power Interface)

  BIOS and, 36

  described, 36, 141

  notebook computers and, 1097, 1098, 1104

  Windows 2000 and, 629–630, 838, 844

active backplanes, 121

Active Directory, 834

active partitions, 333, 681. *See also* partitions

active-matrix monitors, 255. *See also* monitors

adapter cards, 323

address bus, 41–42. *See also* buses

administrator accounts, 811

Administrators group, 939

Advanced Configuration and Power Interface. *See* ACPI (Advanced Configuration and Power Interface)

Advanced Options menu, 864–866

Advanced Power Management. *See* APM (Advanced Power Management)

Advanced SCSI Programming Interface. *See* ASPI (Advanced SCSI Programming Interface)

Advanced Technology Attachment Packet Interface. *See* ATAPI (Advanced Technology Attachment Packet Interface)

Advanced Transfer Cache. *See* ATC (Advanced Transfer Cache)

AGP (Accelerated Graphics Port) expansion slot, 28, 172

AirPort, 477–478

alternating current. *See* AC (alternating current) voltage

ALUs (arithmetic logic units), 39–40

AMD, 15, 163–164, 169, 171

American National Standards Institute. *See* ANSI (American National Standards Institute)

American Standard Code for Information Interchange. *See* ASCII (American Standard Code for Information Interchange)

ammeter, 101

ampersand (&), 443

amps, 99, 100–101

AMR (audio/modem riser), 429

ANSI (American National Standards Institute), 318, 319, 1129

answer files, 840

APIs (application program interfaces)

  AT command set and, 443

  virtual machines and, 701

  Windows 9x and, 701

APM (Advanced Power Management), 141

Apple Computer, 15, 477–478, 1081. *See also* Macintosh

Apple menu, 1079–1080

AppleTalk, 458, 502

application(s)

  16-bit Windows, 78–79, 612

  32-bit Windows, 78–79, 612

  caches, 988

  compatibility, 843–844

  copying, into memory, 91

  described, 4–6, 34

  file corruption, 996–998

  hardware and, relationship of, 4–6, 51–64

  initializing, 86–88

  installing, 738–744, 818–824, 855–856, 927–930

  interrupts, 63–64

  launching, 85–86, 88–91

  loading, 92–93, 760

  operating systems and, relationship of, 75–85

  selecting, 572

  troubleshooting, 739–740, 792–795

  uninstalling, 794–795